Maximizing Windows 98

About the Author...

Lenny Bailes is a journalist, consultant, and teacher who has been writing about computers since 1987. Known to product managers and tech support staffs from Redmond to Boca Raton, his columns and reviews have appeared in *Windows Magazine*, *Computer Shopper*, *InfoWorld*, *Computer World*, *Boardwatch*, *PC Magazine*, and *Maximize*. He also co-authored *BYTE's Guide to Optimizing Windows 95* and the *BYTE's DOS Programmer's Cookbook*. He resides in the Bay Area in a house filled with cats and computers.

Maximizing Windows 98

Lenny Bailes

Osborne/**McGraw-Hill**
Berkeley New York St. Louis San Francisco
Auckland Bogotá Hamburg London Madrid
Mexico City Milan Montreal New Delhi Panama City
Paris São Paulo Singapore Sydney
Tokyo Toronto

Osborne/**McGraw-Hill**
2600 Tenth Street
Berkeley, California 94710
U.S.A.

For information on translations or book distributors outside the U.S.A., or to arrange bulk-purchase discounts for sales promotions, premiums, or fund raisers, please contact Osborne/**McGraw-Hill** at the above address.

Maximizing Windows 98

1234567890 AGM AGM 90198765432109

ISBN 0-07-882539-3

Publisher
Brandon A. Nordin

Editor-in-Chief
Scott Rogers

Acquisitions Editor
Megg Bonar

Project Editor
Jody McKenzie

Editorial Assistant
Stephane Thomas

Technical Editor
Patrick Marshall

Copy Editor
Judy Ziajka

Proofreaders
Karen Mead
Laurie Stewart

Indexer
Richard Shrout

Computer Designer
Jean Butterfield
Jani Beckwith

Illustrator
Brian Wells

Series Design
Peter Hancik

Cover Design
Regan Honda

This book is dedicated to my family: my father, Murray Bailes (who sat with me and explained algebra when school teachers thought only of mastering times tables); my brother Kenny (who was programming Atari and T-I computers before I bought my first IBM PC Jr.); and my brother Mitchell (who has a warm smile and can still solve differential equations in his head when he feels like doing so). We're a bunch of stubborn puzzle-solvers. (Also, in memory of Mom, who had to constantly kick us all out of the house to remind us to get some sunshine.)

Contents at a Glance

Contents

Acknowledgments

Thanks to all of the people and companies whose cooperation made this book possible. Special thanks to Osborne editor Megg Bonar, whose patience made it possible for me to produce the kind of book I wanted to write, and to Jody McKenzie, the project editor. Thanks also to John M. Ross, who constructed the initial drafts of Chapters 4, 11, and 12 of this book and contributed to Chapter 13.

Kudos to the Windows 98 beta-testing team: programmers, gurus, tech support engineers, and rank-and-file testers who lent me invaluable moral support.

Thanks to the hardware and software companies that assisted me during this project: Gateway 2000 Computers for their trusty Solo 9100 notebook; Sony Computers for the use of their powerful VAIO PCV-E205 multimedia desktop machine; Asus, a precision motherboard vendor; DecaView, Nokia, and Compaq for their crisp, well-designed monitors; Kodak and Xirlink for their reliable USB cameras; Creative Labs for their flexible Encore DVD drive; and ATI Technologies for their wondrous video adapter/TV tuner.

And finally, kind words for the counter brigade/"music directors" at Muddy Waters Coffee House in San Francisco, who provided a pleasant environment for me to work in and produce most of this book.

"I'm a working man in my prime—cleaning windows."

—Van Morrison

Introduction

Why This Book Is for You

This book contains late-breaking information on Windows 98 Multimedia upgrade components and other Windows 98 system patches. See Appendix B for details.

You may be surprised when you open the Windows 98 box to discover that this complex and powerful operating system ships with a slim, under-100-page welcome booklet instead of an operating manual. From word-of-mouth descriptions and magazines, you may know that Windows 98 includes built-in peer-to-peer networking support, Internet connectivity, and a new desktop that integrates the functionality of Windows 95 with the capabilities of the Internet Explorer Web browser. Surely these features can't possibly be documented in such a small book.

Although all these features can't possibly be explained in the slim welcome booklet, you may optimistically assume that the Windows 98 online Help system will give you all the instructions you need. It is conceivable that you might teach yourself basic competency in Windows 98 by successively pointing and clicking on various entries in Microsoft's online Help system. This is how the authors of all the Windows 98 guidebooks at your local bookstore learned how to use it. However, many of these people began their exploration of Windows 98 more than two years ago as participants in Microsoft's beta program.

There are, of course, some simple, intuitive aspects of Windows 98 that you should expect to pick up simply by using the operating system. This was Microsoft's intent in its design philosophy. For instance, you should easily be able to find and run programs, save your work, and gain simple access to the file structure of your hard disk.

But how do you install Windows 98 and keep a backup copy of Windows 3.1 or Windows 95, just in case? What installation choices should you make to avoid having to add and change things later on? How do you know your computer is powerful enough for Windows 98? Where's the hardware compatibility list? What about your network and your old system utilities? What do you need to know to install and run Windows 98 on a notebook computer?

How do you create an efficient, project-oriented desktop? Can you have more than one desktop? Can you send a fax cover page to another computer? How do you make your e-mail manager automatically collect your messages every *x* hours or *y* days? What if you want to collect Internet messages from more than one account? How do you set up an Internet connection, anyway? Suppose you want to view, copy, or rename only the documents with a .DOC file extension? How can you make Microsoft's Backup applet (which lacks command-line support) perform automated, unattended backups? How do you capture audio or video from a CD-ROM or DVD to your hard disk or attach sound and video files to your documents? How do you set up your applications to use Adobe PostScript fonts or print a file to disk? Can you still use third-party Win 3.1 font management utilities? How do you optimize the Win98 swap file and CD-ROM cache or change the IRQ assigned to your modem?

This book is designed for people who want to bend Windows 98 to their will with the least possible effort. You'll find answers here to all of the questions posed in the preceding two paragraphs—and a great deal more. This book attempts to cover all aspects of Windows 98 for people who want to cut to the chase and get their work done. You'll find in-depth treatments of partially documented and undocumented features, plus sidebars, tips, and easy-to-follow numbered procedures for setting up and using the best of Win98's productivity utilities. You'll also find answers to these questions:

- How do I make it run faster?
- How can I do things in fewer steps?
- What are the pitfalls and "gotchas" I should avoid?
- Where are the hidden shortcuts?

Guide to What's Inside

This book is actually several books within a book.

The first four chapters are a tutorial to help you set up your hardware, install the operating system, and exploit the features of the new Windows 98 desktop. You'll learn that despite Microsoft's design policy, which tells you that you must overwrite older versions of Windows and DOS or lose all your old program settings, you can actually have your cake and eat it, too. Windows 98 can easily be set up to coexist on the same hard disk with older versions of Windows and other operating systems, including OS/2 Warp and Windows NT. You can also transfer either the floppy disk or CD-ROM installation files for Windows 98 to a local hard disk. This allows you to install and update the operating system on notebook computers and other machines with no permanent access to a CD-ROM drive.

Chapter 4 shows you all of the desktop features and shortcuts that you won't find in Microsoft's Discover Windows 98 Tour. You'll find the kinds of tips, shortcuts, and time-saving procedures here that are typically the bread and butter of Windows magazines.

Chapters 5 and 6 are a short course in the bundled Microsoft applications and utilities included in the Windows 98 Accessories folder. Chapter 5 provides productivity tips for Imaging for Windows, Dial-Up Networking, Direct Cable Connection, HyperTerminal, Phone Dialer, Paint, WordPad, and all of the other Win98 mini-apps, plus a mini-manual on installing and using the "extra" Microsoft Fax program. Chapter 6 focuses on using the System Tools: Backup, ScanDisk, Disk Defragmenter, System Monitor, and the new diagnostic features included in the System Information utility.

Chapter 7 provides a guide to Windows 98 system architecture. You'll learn about the new 32-bit enhancements to the operating system and see how to take advantage of Win98's hidden Boot Menu and Startup options. This chapter documents the new commands that have been added to "DOS 7.1" through MSDOS.SYS and CONFIG.SYS and shows you how to replace real-mode device drivers with their protected-mode counterparts. You'll find productivity guides for optimizing the DOS aspect of Windows 98 with MemMaker and DriveSpace.

Chapter 8 is devoted to preventive maintenance. It addresses compatibility issues related to older DOS and Windows 3.1 applications and contains practical tips on getting the most from the Windows 98 Maintenance Wizard. This chapter also contains a tutorial on the Microsoft Backup utility and consumer advice on selecting and deploying third-party backup and antivirus packages. The chapter includes sections on maintaining the Windows 98 system registry and working with the RegEdit registry tool.

Chapter 9 is a complete guide to the Windows 98 Control Panel and all of its hidden features.

Chapter 10 tells you what you need to know about managing printers and fonts. You'll find a description of the basic Win98 font features and see how to integrate TrueType and PostScript fonts into your productivity environment. You'll also find information about plug-and-play printer features, bidirectional printing, network printing, and enhanced spooler features that improve the performance of the Windows 98 printing system.

Chapters 11 through 13 are your Win98 Connectivity and Internet guide. You'll find easy-to-follow, step-by-step tutorials on setting up modems and Dial-Up Networking (your dial-up connection to remote LANs and the Internet) followed by tips on using all of Windows 98's Internet applications and pointers to popular and useful online resources.

Chapter 11 provides diagnostic and troubleshooting information for configuring modems, serial ports, and Internet connections, plus a section on configuring the "extra" Windows Messaging feature (still useful for faxing and for LAN-based Microsoft Mail).

Chapter 12 is your ABCs of World Wide Web surfing. It starts with an introduction to how the Internet works with information on configuring accounts through Online Services or independent Internet service providers (ISPs). This section is followed by a tutorial on using Microsoft's Internet Explorer and Netscape's Navigator/ Communicator Web browsers. The section "The World Wide Web as a Way of Life" is your guide to Internet resources. It contains tips on using popular Internet search engines plus pointers to specialized search tools, Win98 technical support resources, and news, financial, and recreational Web sites. This chapter also tells you what you need to know about configuring and exploiting Windows 98's Active Desktop.

Chapter 13 is your guide to the rest of the Internet. You'll find some Internet history and practical information on working with e-mail clients, Usenet newsreaders, Telnet, and FTP applications. The section "Still More Things You Can Do Through the Internet" discusses resources that complement the World Wide Web: text-based information sites, online communities, and real-time Internet chat. This chapter also contains a troubleshooting/Internet diagnostics section and pointers to shareware sites where you can download useful Internet applications.

Chapter 14 is your manual for dedicated peer-to-peer networking with Windows 98. It contains step-by-step instructions for installing and configuring network hardware and software, working with Win98's Network Neighborhood, and sharing file and printer resources with other members of a workgroup. You'll also find tips on establishing remote-access connections to a network through dedicated phone lines or over the Internet. You don't need a Windows NT or Novell server to exploit these features, although this chapter also contains information on using Windows 98 in these client-server topologies.

Chapter 15 is devoted to multimedia. It provides tips on choosing and setting up a multimedia PC and tutorials on all of Win98's multimedia applications. You'll learn about playing and recording audio and video and gain information about the new video standards and compression protocols built into Windows 98. This chapter also contains information about working with MPEG-2/DVD and WebTV/WaveTop and integrating third-party multimedia utilities into Windows 98. You'll find sections on setting up multiple display monitors, configuring and working with Universal Serial Bus (USB) peripherals, plus troubleshooting tips and a brief survey of hot, must-have multimedia games, movies, and music products.

Chapter 16 is a collection of power-user tips, designed to help you customize the Windows 98 desktop, manipulate the Windows registry, and troubleshoot performance problems.

Appendix A discusses mobile computing with Windows 98 and how to move an existing Win98 configuration from computer to computer. Appendix B has the latest information on Microsoft upgrades and patches for Windows 98 and pointers to the most useful and popular Windows 98–related Web sites.

How to Use the Book

You can use this book as a guided tour of various Windows 98 features, or browse the table of contents for specific references to the information you need. You can also just cruise through for tips, tricks, and nuggets of information. Watch for the Note, Tip, and Caution icons.

This book uses several conventions designed to make it easier for you to follow. You'll find basic how-to configuration information in numbered procedures throughout all of the chapters. Since Windows 98 lets you configure your desktop to open programs with either a single- or double-click mouse command, in general, this book uses the words "open" or "launch" instead of "double-click" to describe the procedure for opening an application.

Bold type is used for text that you are to type from the keyboard, such as "Type **CD \WINDOWS** at the C prompt." *Italic type* is used for variables that you may need to replace with a value specific to your situation and to call attention to important terms in the text.

SMALL CAPITAL LETTERS are used for keys on the keyboard such as ENTER and SHIFT. Multiple keys to be pressed together are presented like this: "Press CTRL-C."

I hope that your experience with Windows 98 turns out to be pleasant and productive. And once you get your Internet connection set up, be sure to visit http://www.osborne.com for information on *Maximizing Windows 98*.

Lenny Bailes, August 1998

Chapter 1

Welcome to Windows 98

Chapter Highlights

The advantages of Windows 98

How easy is it to upgrade?

Important Win98 user features: a quick tour of the interface

Who's buying? Who should buy?

Questions to ask yourself to see if you really *need* to upgrade

"Windows 95 is just software," Microsoft executive Brad Silverberg said several times before its release. "It's not a cure for cancer. It doesn't grow hair. It's not a dessert topping, and it's not a floor wax. It's only software."

The same can be said for Windows 98. But this declaration notwithstanding, each new version of Windows boosts your computer's IQ. Windows 98 is just "a little bit better" than the 95 flavor in most ways that count. It's easier to install, easier to use to find and manage files, easier to use with the Internet, and easier to maintain on your hard disk.

Some industry pundits have criticized Microsoft for not offering a major paradigm shift or revolutionary "killer app" in this latest version of Windows—but they've overlooked the steady flow of incremental improvements that make Windows 98 more reliable and more convenient than its predecessors.

The jump from Windows 3.x to Windows 95 was a big one. Win95's seamless desktop, 32-bit application engine, plug-and-play support, and built-in networking were major improvements, establishing Windows 95 as the dominant operating system on computers throughout the world. The changes that appear in Windows 98 are less sensational. They are evolutionary rather than revolutionary.

As Windows 98 reaches the shelves of stores, you may be asking yourself some questions: Why should I upgrade? Does Windows 98 have something I need? Is it worth the price? How much trouble is it to install? Will it run smoothly on the computer I own now?

The information you'll find in this introductory chapter will help you answer these questions.

The Advantages of Windows 98

In a nutshell, Windows 98 offers these improvements over Windows 95:

- Greater ease of use through a more flexible desktop
- Simplified software and hardware setup
- Improved performance and reliability
- Easier Internet access and better Internet tools
- New multimedia and entertainment support
- Better system maintenance tools
- Support for new PC hardware standards

For former Windows 3.x users, Windows 98 offers a wholesale revision of the interface that integrates a Macintosh-like desktop, better multitasking capabilities, dedicated and dial-up networking support, and a host of other features.

Windows 98 can make Internet search tools an extension of your desktop and let you browse file folders, Web pages, network resources, and system configuration utilities from a single, integrated Explorer. (Users who prefer the Windows 95 way of doing things can continue to use classic interface features while exploiting Win98's better Help system, better dial-up and dedicated networking, and more automatic hardware recognition.) Windows 98 simplifies the process of setting up an Internet account and takes the drudgery out of installing new monitors, printers, scanners, and cameras.

Some of Win98's enhancements are features that gradually trickled into service releases of Windows 95. The Internet Explorer (IE) 4 Web browser and its Active Desktop, Universal Serial Bus (USB) support, Dial-Up Networking 1.2, and FAT32 (support for large hard disks) are features that were previously available only on new computers preloaded with OEM service releases of Windows 95. Windows 98 gathers all of these incremental improvements and installs them automatically.

A number of other Win98 features are brand new. The Help system, revised and translated to HTML (World Wide Web document) format, complements textual information with full-color graphics, new "smart" troubleshooters, indexed cross-references, and hyperlinks to Internet resources. Windows 98 also delivers better performance by supporting a variety of new hardware standards. Lightweight USB scanners, cameras, speakers, and other devices install themselves automatically simply by being plugged into the computer. The new CD-ROM and digital video disk (DVD) file systems support a streaming device driver model, which allows audio and video playback to begin before an entire file is downloaded onto your system.

"Streaming" playback can significantly improve the efficiency of your multimedia peripherals. Playback and recording of digital audio and video, video conferencing, and interactive 3-D games are all better than ever.

Windows 98 is also a smarter Windows. It takes care of you by taking better care of itself. New system optimization and diagnostic tools and other self-correcting features reduce the time you previously had to spend on system troubleshooting.

Easy Upgrading

Almost every popular DOS and Windows application works under Windows 98. (Chapter 7 contains information about the few incompatibilities that you may find in some application and utility software.) If you upgrade to Windows 98 on an older computer running DOS or a previous version of Windows, the software environment is updated automatically. You can continue to use your old productivity programs or switch to newer, faster, and more flexible versions.

An upgrade from either a "pure" DOS or Windows 95 computer to Windows 98 is fairly automatic. Upgrades from Windows 3.x or Windows for Workgroups are also generally seamless, *provided your computer meets the minimum hardware requirements for the new operating system*. This caveat assumes more significance for Windows 3.x upgrades because the older operating system is more likely to be running on an older computer.

Your computer's central processing unit (CPU) must be 486 DX2 66 or better to permit a Windows 98 installation to proceed. Microsoft states that you'll need 16MB of memory, 150 to 350MB of available hard disk space, a VGA video system, and a standard mouse pointing device. To install the version of Windows 98 sold in stores, the computer also needs a CD-ROM drive. (Floppy disk versions are available by special order.) To take advantage of Win98's Internet features, the computer must have a direct cable connection or a standard modem with a minimum speed of 14.4 Kbps.

In actuality, for your Windows 98 experience to be pleasant, Microsoft's hardware requirements should be upgraded slightly. Chapter 2 of this book lists some practical hardware requirements for a comfortable Windows 98 business computer. Chapter 15 discusses the requirements for a multimedia or home-entertainment PC.

Simplified Configuration

The most striking feature of Windows 98—the one that new users will notice right away—is the coordination of setup and productivity features. You don't have to hunt for obscure configuration menus or scavenge up third-party driver diskettes to set up the operating system. (Those menus are still there, but context-sensitive installation wizards pop up to help you install new hardware and enter configuration information.) Video cards, disk controllers, PC Card peripherals, modems, and sound cards are usually detected and set up automatically. Where the operating system does require you to enter personalized information, the wizards provide step-by-step guidance.

The Windows 98 online Help system is linked directly to system configuration utilities. For example, if you open the Help index and enter **modem**, the entry "modems, installing" appears. The explanatory text includes a Click Here option to open the New Modem Installation Wizard (see Figure 1-1). Other Windows 98 setup wizards can also be invoked through Help entries. These wizards walk you step-by-step through the process of adding new printers, modems, sound cards, and network components; sending a fax; or changing your video display. If you enter **wizards** in the Help Index field, you'll see a list of available configuration assistants.

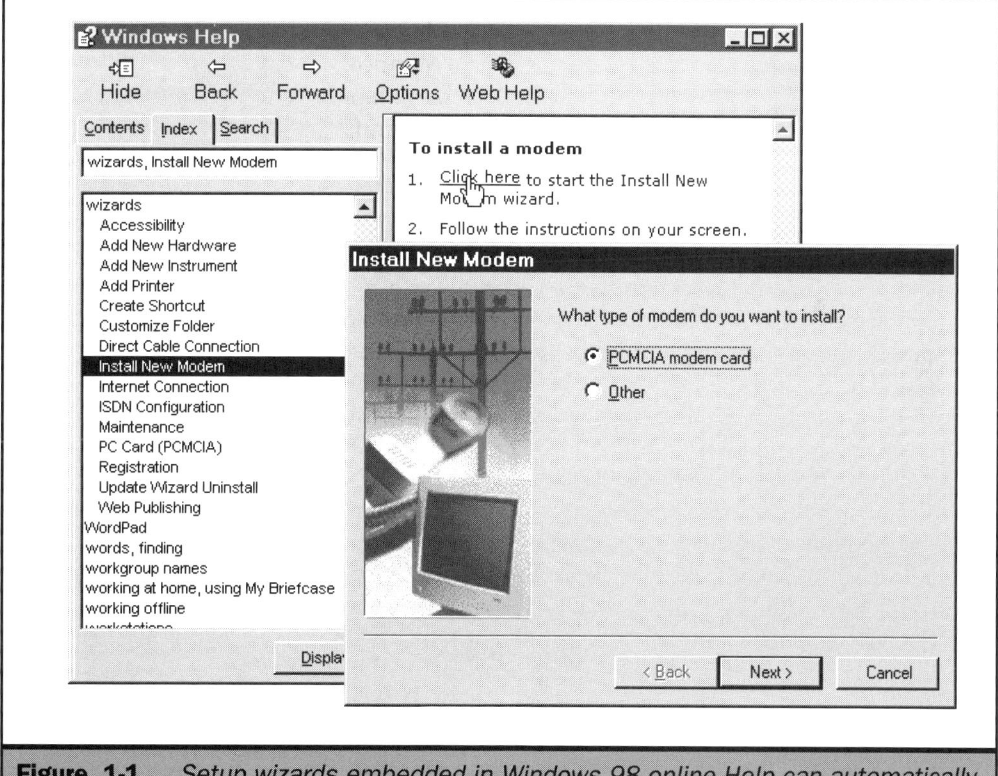

Figure 1-1. *Setup wizards embedded in Windows 98 online Help can automatically start and configure operating system features*

Another obvious new feature of Windows 98 is its more flexible desktop. New Windows users won't need to master the Program Manager and File Manager as separate interfaces to start applications and access hard disk files. (Windows 95 users will already be familiar with this ease of use.) Tools for running programs, managing the hard disk, and (optionally) surfing the Internet are integrated into a more intuitive, unified desktop.

Before you start customizing the Windows 98 desktop, it has a simple, obvious structure: a Start button for running programs, a My Computer icon for accessing files, a Recycle Bin for discarding unwanted files, and other icons for optional features you select during the setup process. The strict Windows 3.x restrictions on where icons can be placed on the desktop are gone. Programs, data files, and system control icons can now be dragged out of their original locations and positioned anywhere you like for easy access.

Does Away with DOS?

You've probably heard this more than once from Microsoft: this version of Windows does away with DOS. However, if this is true, why are there Windows 98 files called COMMAND.COM and MSDOS.SYS in the root directory of your boot drive? And why does the system execute DOS CONFIG.SYS and AUTOEXEC.BAT files before loading the graphic interface? The answer is that Microsoft has streamlined the link between the Windows 98 graphic interface and the text-based DOS operating system that boots it onto the screen, but the link still exists.

Windows 98 doesn't have to use the separate CONFIG.SYS or AUTOEXEC.BAT files required by DOS and Windows 3.x. They are now optional control features. Windows 98 automatically determines the required drivers and settings for your computer and loads them during its boot process without DOS configuration files. However, if your system hardware configuration isn't directly supported, CONFIG.SYS can still be used to load legacy DOS drivers supplied by third-party manufacturers.

You can start Windows 98 without a CONFIG.SYS or AUTOEXEC.BAT file, but many users retain these files for the useful tweaks they can enable you to perform. (You'll find all the details in the section "Startup Strategies" in Chapter 7.) Windows 98 bootstraps itself from the real-mode DOS operating kernel. The WIN.COM file in your \WINDOWS directory still loads the graphic interface, but it does so automatically. You don't have to type **WIN** at the C: prompt.

Windows 98 gives you the option, for running eccentric or ill-behaved DOS programs, of pressing the CTRL key at startup to boot into a real-mode DOS session.

Important User Features

The following summaries describe other important features you'll find in Windows 98. You'll find detailed discussions on how to use these features in subsequent chapters of this book.

A Modified GUI

The Windows 98 desktop is less cluttered than the one in Windows 3.x and more versatile than the one in Windows 95. Anyone who has seen Warp OS/2 or the Macintosh Finder will notice a resemblance, although Windows 95 and Windows 98 add their own spin. The screen is wide open, with icons arranged to the user's convenience. Certain options are required—My Computer, Recycle Bin, Network Neighborhood—but most of the rest is your own choice.

Windows 98 integrates the three major Windows 3.x interface components—the Program Manager, the File Manager, and the Task Manager—into a more cohesive whole. The desktop can mimic the Windows 95 format exactly, or it can take the shape of a local Web page. If you choose the Active Desktop feature, you can literally create your own interface with embedded HTML, Java, and ActiveX links to any objects you want.

The taskbar in Windows 95 and Windows 98 takes the place of the Windows 3.x feature that minimized open windows at the bottom of the desktop. Located at the bottom of the screen by default, the taskbar keeps track of your minimized open windows. It also contains the Start button and the System Tray, providing quick access to internal system controls. Users upgrading from Windows 95 will appreciate the new Quick Launch and Address toolbars that add functionality to the Win98 taskbar. You can use these features to immediately open your favorite programs or jump to a Web site with a single mouse-click.

By default, the desktop focuses on the Start button, positioned on the taskbar at the lower-left corner of the screen. This configurable program menu brings the most needed Win98 features up front, replacing the Program Manager's cumbersome groups. When you click the Start button, a cascading set of pop-up menus appears (see Figure 1-2). These menus provide quick access to all of your installed programs, the Printers folder and Control Panel (under Settings), and the Windows 98 online Help system. The Documents list tracks the most recently opened documents, allowing you to quickly reopen frequently accessed files. The Find feature lets you search for files on your computer by name, type, date, size, or internal text strings.

The Win98 Start menu also provides new flexibility. For example, the new, enhanced Find command allows you to search for personal addresses and other information on the Internet. You can right-click its program groups at any level to add, remove, or edit icon entries.

Windows 98 contains a wide variety of convenient mouse options. In many cases, a single click will suffice where a double click was once required—or you can let the mouse point and hover while the menus pop open by themselves. Like Warp OS/2, Windows 98 makes good use of the right mouse button. Highlight any desktop object or taskbar item, right-click it, and a context menu appears, full of utility features and configuration options (see Figure 1-3). These commands can be basic, such as Move or Delete, or specific to the application. Consistent mouse controls are a valuable improvement. Knowing that a right click always pops up a list of menu options gives people more assurance in working with the operating system.

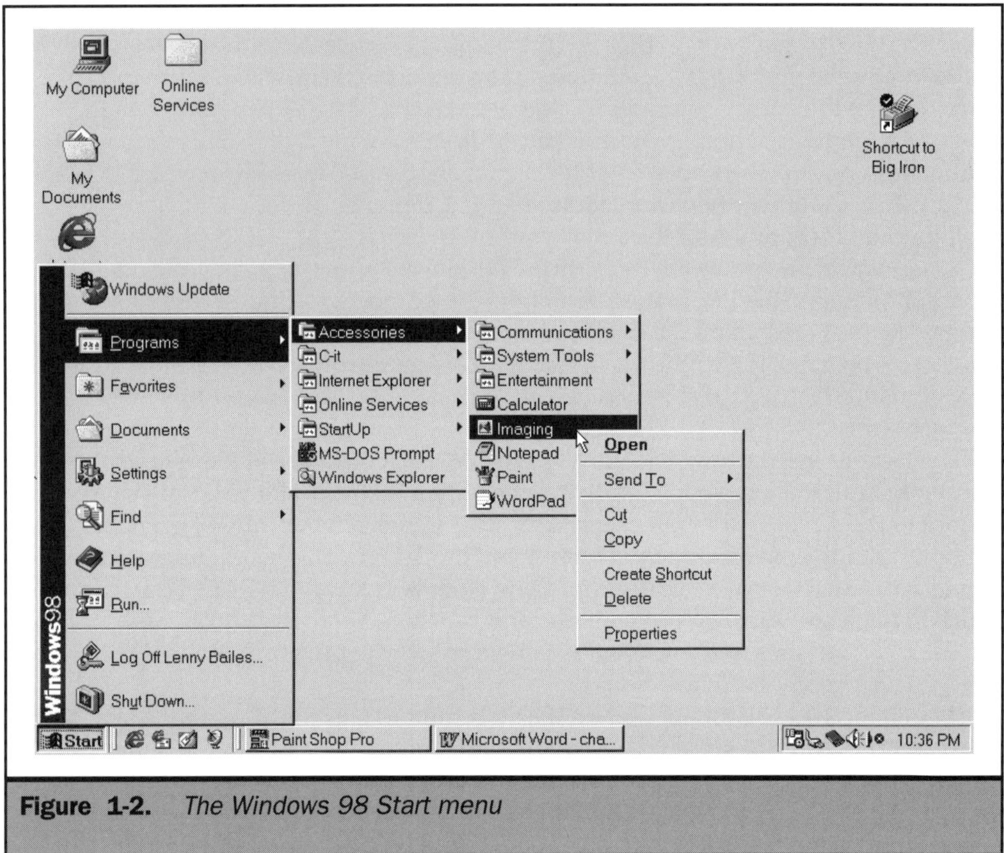

Figure 1-2. *The Windows 98 Start menu*

Windows 98 also emulates Warp OS/2's use of desktop shortcuts. In Windows 3.x, the icons in Program Manager groups were a kind of limited desktop shortcut. In Windows 95/98, any file or resource in the operating system can be represented by an icon link placed anywhere on the desktop or in another folder.

The basic Windows 95/98 shell makes a lot more sense than its Windows 3.x predecessor. Windows 98 makes it easy to create nested menus, put related applications and files into their own folders, and so on. The Recycle Bin, where you can drag files to purge them from the desktop, imitates the familiar Macintosh trashcan and saves a lot of aggravation.

Windows 98 permits you to browse documents in a number of formats even if you don't own the application that created the file. The bundled Inso Quick View feature allows you to inspect files in more than 30 different formats without opening them in their source applications. You can open a Quattro Pro spreadsheet without owning a copy of Quattro Pro or browse a WordPerfect document without owning WordPerfect.

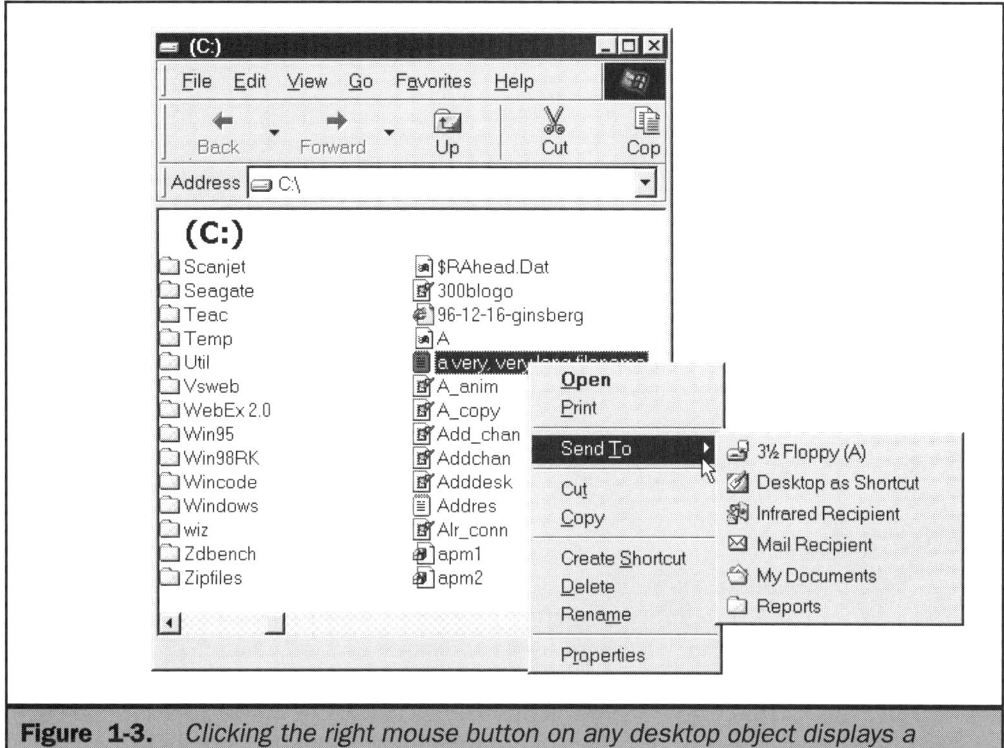

Figure 1-3. *Clicking the right mouse button on any desktop object displays a context-sensitive menu of system options*

You can right-click files, folders, and applications in Windows 98 to pop up their Properties options. This replaces the settings in the Windows 3.x Program Manager, File Manager, and DOS PIF editor. Pop-up Properties options also replace some Windows 3.x Control Panel features. In Windows 98, you can directly access application settings, screen display properties, and other internal system functions simply by right-clicking strategic desktop objects. Windows 98 also maintains a Control Panel that consolidates many functions formerly scattered throughout the operating system.

Quick File Management and System Access

When you open the My Computer/Windows Explorer object on the desktop, you gain quick access to all of the drives and directories on your computer. (My Computer and Windows Explorer are really just alternative display views for the same file browsing application. By default, you can double-click an object to open a My Computer view or hold down the SHIFT key and double-click to open an Explorer view.) The My Computer/Windows Explorer window can display hierarchical file folders, the Printers and Dial-Up Networking folders, Scheduled Tasks, or the Control Panel. In

Windows 98, the Explorer display window contains new toolbar and pull-down menu options to improve usability.

Unlike the Windows 3.x File Manager, My Computer is an integrated part of the desktop. You can freely open drives and folders, drag their contents to the desktop, and start applications from a My Computer window. Windows Explorer is a two-pane file management window. In addition to using SHIFT-double-click as described earlier, you can open Windows Explorer by right-clicking the My Computer icon and choosing Explore. The Explorer view of your computer includes the All Folders tree-list pane, which makes it easy to move and copy multiple files.

Tip *To gain faster access to Windows Explorer, you can create a shortcut for it in the Quick Launch toolbar on the taskbar. Click the Start button, open Programs, and right-click the Windows Explorer icon while you drag it with the mouse to the Quick Launch section of the taskbar. This will create a new one-click Explorer shortcut on the taskbar without disturbing the original one in the Programs group.*

Long Filenames

The ability to break out of the 8.3-character file naming system is one of the most noticeable Windows 95/98 improvements over DOS and Windows 3.x. Having the freedom to be explicit in the naming of files is a tremendous convenience. This may not be an overriding reason to switch operating systems, but it is one of the first things you notice after you do. Windows 98 supports filenames of up to 256 characters for all files, folders, and other desktop objects. Files with these long filenames also retain a conventional 8.3 DOS filename that can be accessed under DOS or on non-Windows 98 computers. Several third-party utility vendors now provide software that can extend Win98's long filename recognition to ordinary Windows 3.x applications (see Chapter 8 for details).

Enhanced Communication Features

Windows 98 contains useful telecommunications enhancements. The HyperTerminal application bundled with the operating system can double as a direct terminal program or a network Telnet client. Unlike Windows 3.x, Windows 98 includes internal support for high-speed telecommunications, allowing you to manipulate the serial port's internal data buffer. Telecommunication programs specifically written for Windows automatically know which serial port and modem configuration to use. Your modem is detected and configured automatically from a list that contains hundreds of different manufacturers and models.

The Dial-Up Networking component of Windows 98 can seamlessly replace third-party Windows 3.x Internet dialers. Internet accounts are easier to set up than they were under Windows 95. Microsoft supplements the Internet Explorer World Wide Web browser in Windows 98 with other useful Internet tools, including a full-featured electronic mail client and Internet news browser. Dial-Up Networking under Windows 98 allows you to increase the bandwidth of an Internet connection by multilinking two modems simultaneously to boost the connection speed. For instance, two 33.6K modems connected simultaneously can be combined to achieve a connection speed of 67.2K. (For this feature to work, it must be supported by your Internet service provider or remote network server.)

Better Networking Support

Peer-to-peer networking in Windows 98 improves upon the support offered in Windows for Workgroups 3.11 and Windows 95. Workstation addresses for a small TCP/IP local area network are now configured automatically. Windows 98 and Windows 95 computers can connect to each other on a peer-to-peer network with a minimum of configuration effort. In addition, Windows 98 includes clients for Windows NT, Novell, and NFS networks. Machines running Windows 98 can be integrated seamlessly into a Windows NT, Windows for Workgroups, or Novell/NetBIOS-compatible network. The Share option (built into the right-click context menu for all folder and printer objects) makes it easy to provide shared network access to selected folders, disk drives, and printers.

The Windows 98 Dial-Up Adapter allows you to connect to a dedicated network via a modem, establish an Internet connection, or turn your local computer into a dial-up server. The Virtual Private Networking feature allows a Windows 98 computer to establish a reasonably secure connection to a local area network through a dial-up Internet account.

Direct Cable Connection allows you to set up a peer-to-peer network connection between two computers through a serial or parallel cable.

Better Multimedia Support

Windows 98 can automatically play audio CDs and DVDs or start programs on data CDs and DVDs as they are inserted into the drive. Multimedia support is an area where Windows 98 leapfrogs Windows 95 and its serious business brother, Windows NT 4. DVDs can hold about 10 times as much information as ordinary CDs. Windows 98 exploits the added DVD storage capacity and speed with a new streaming file system and bundled DVD player. You can view a two-hour motion picture under Windows 98 at better-than-laser-disc, 30-frames-per-second, true-color resolution.

The Media Player and Active Movie programs can handle larger video and audio files without generating out-of-memory errors. A series of compression technologies are built into the operating system to reduce the storage space overhead for multimedia presentations. A series of sound schemes includes a variety of 10-minute classical MIDI compositions and sound effects for all occasions. Improvements in the video handling system provide better performance for 3-D games and presentation graphics.

Support for DOS Programs

Windows 98 lets you run each of your DOS applications or command sessions in separate, independent sections of memory. These CPU "virtual machines" have more crash protection than DOS sessions under Windows 3.x. They can be preemptively multitasked just like 32-bit Windows applications. Preemptive multitasking is the intelligent management by the operating system of the CPU time allocated to each concurrently running program. Each DOS session can run in a desktop window with a toolbar that permits you to easily cut and paste, change the display font, and access DOS session properties.

For the few ill-behaved DOS programs that won't run under the Windows 98 interface, the operating system permits you to boot to a full-fledged DOS 7.1 command prompt. You can also invoke these programs from the Windows 98 desktop, and a special feature will shut down the Windows interface, opening an exclusive MS-DOS-mode session. Custom CONFIG.SYS and AUTOEXEC.BAT startup files can be created for MS-DOS-mode sessions that require the loading of specific real-mode drivers at boot time.

Preemptive Multitasking and Multithreading

Preemptive multitasking and multithreading enables more intelligent multitasking of applications written for the Windows 95 and Windows 98 application interface. This feature also improves the performance of the printing subsystem and DOS sessions. Multithreading enables the intelligent management of independent functions of a single program. When an application wants to print, for example, Windows 98 allocates more CPU time to the print module. Multithreaded communications packages allow file downloads without slowing down message composition or online browsing.

Under Win98's preemptive multitasking, applications are less likely to become memory hogs, eating up idle CPU time and slowing down performance. The operating system itself determines when access to the CPU is granted to programs that request it.

Note *Sixteen-bit applications written for the Windows 3.x environment are not preemptively multitasked. These programs are still multitasked cooperatively, determining their own priority through internal programming functions (see Chapter 7 for more information).*

Easier System Maintenance

Windows 98 includes new tools to optimize hard disk performance, provide system diagnostic information, automatically back up your system configuration, and troubleshoot system problems. The Windows 98 Disk Defragmenter is designed to rearrange the order of files on your hard disk so that the time required to open your favorite applications can be cut in half.

New Hardware Technologies

In addition to its new interface, user options, and utilities, Windows 98 includes a series of new and adapted technologies designed to make it run more efficiently.

Plug-and-Play

The plug-and-play feature enables automatic recognition and configuration of your system hardware. As the Microsoft/Intel plug-and-play standard becomes fully supported by hardware and peripheral vendors, users can install new monitors, modems, printers, scanners, network cards, and other internal system components without having to do any work to reconfigure the computer, its physical hardware components, or the operating system.

Plug-and-play operation works through a combination of hardware and software. Windows 98 has many plug-and-play features that work even if you don't have plug-and-play hardware. Even with non-plug-and-play peripherals (now referred to as legacy technology), Windows 98 can still save you lots of time and trouble. If you have legacy peripherals, Windows 98 may not identify them exactly, but it will make its best guess at what you have. Your components will often be identified by manufacturer, if not by specific model number, and easy-to-read component lists allow you to fill in missing information. If your system includes PCI bus peripherals or uses PC Card peripherals, Windows 98 will probably identify these components and correctly assign interrupts and port addresses. (In various feature-specific sections of this book, you'll find information about manual hardware configuration procedures for the few instances when Windows 98 fails.)

Universal Serial Bus, IEEE-1394, and Accelerated Graphics Port

The Universal Serial Bus (USB), IEEE-1394, and Accelerated Graphics Port (AGP) technologies are a subset of Win98's plug-and-play feature. USB and IEEE-1394 (nicknamed firewire) are input/output standards for new, faster hardware ports on your computer. Windows 98's support for USB is far superior to the "Detroit" module that was patched into some versions of Windows 95. A single USB port can accommodate up to 127 separate hardware accessories (such as cameras, scanners, keyboards, mice, modems, and printers), allocating only one port address and system interrupt (IRQ) to manage them all. This frees up scarce system resources on your computer. The maximum 1.5 Mbps data throughput on the USB bus allows better performance than a serial or parallel port interface.

IEEE-1394 is a super fast input/output standard with a data throughput of up to 400 Mbps. Currently, IEEE-1394 is used primarily as a vehicle for high-end video production, but manufacturers are constantly talking about developing firewire disk peripherals that will far exceed the speeds permitted by SCSI and Ultra-DMA IDE.

Configuration of USB and firewire devices is generally automatic. Plug the component into the port, and Windows 98 sets it up with minimal user intervention.

AGP video can process raw pixel data at a much higher bandwidth than even the 128-bit PCI video adapters commonly used to support Windows 95. This feature benefits graphic designers, who will no longer be able to drink a cup of coffee during complicated Photoshop operations.

Advanced Power Management

Microsoft's new Advanced Power Management standard can conserve battery time on older notebook computers and provide complete power management on newer Advanced Configuration and Power Interface (ACPI)–compliant machines. On Now technology permits newer machines to remain permanently switched on in a low-power state, coming to life instantly when you press a key.

FAT32: Large Disk Support

FAT32 technology was integrated into some service releases of Windows 95 shipped with computers sold in 1997, but until Windows 98, the only way to get FAT32 was to purchase a brand-new computer or hard disk.

FAT32 is a tweaked version of the traditional MS-DOS file system that existed beneath the surface of previous versions of Windows. This improved disk-management scheme supports individual disk partitions up to 2,000 gigabytes (GB) in size. The old FAT16 system imposed a maximum partition size of 2GB (or 2,048 megabytes). Most hard disks included with currently shipping computers exceed the old FAT16 limit.

FAT32 allows you to place Windows 98 and all your personal files on one large C drive rather than requiring you to split a large disk into C, D, and E partitions. The new file system is also more economical with disks of any size greater than 512MB, grabbing less overhead space to store boot information and directory tables. Whereas the old system typically used 16 or 32 kilobytes (K) of disk space to manage clusters containing only 1 byte of actual data, FAT32 uses a cluster size of 8K for partitions containing up to 8GB.

Windows 98's Disk Defragmenter also uses the FAT32 system to speed up the load time for files stored on your hard disk. For more information, see Chapter 8.

Multiple Display Support

Under Windows 98 you can install and use up to nine monitors and graphic adapter cards. Each monitor can be configured to display a separate portion of the desktop. You can configure your "virtual desktop" so that icons or windows can be dragged left, right, up, or down to move them to another display screen. Applications can be moved seamlessly from one monitor to another, or the second display can be used to duplicate data on the first. For example, you can simultaneously edit and proofread a presentation. (You'll find information on installing and using multiple display support under "Using Multiple Displays" in Chapter 15.)

Who's Buying? Who Should Buy?

With all the improvements and advantages described so far, you might think that people would be upgrading to Windows 98 in droves.

The truth takes a slightly different turn. The people who upgraded immediately are those who love to tinker with their PCs and try out the "latest and greatest" technology to see what it can do. Windows 95 was in many ways a complete makeover of the older Windows operating system. Windows 98 has been greeted by some members of the computer press with the response that "it just looks like a maintenance upgrade for the previous version."

These pundits have their vision fixed upon the future of large-scale, corporate computing. In that arena, Microsoft's announced Windows NT 5.0 operating system will introduce major structural changes and paradigm shifts. Industry mavens concerned with enterprise computing see Windows 98 as essentially a series of patches and small feature upgrades to an operating system that remains Windows 95 at its core.

This point of view is reasonable as far as it goes. However, it overlooks the fact that the incremental tuning and feature enhancements in Windows 98 make it more flexible and also more reliable than Windows 95.

Windows 98 doesn't have revolutionary changes; it's just a better operating system.

For home-computer users, Internet-related businesses, and mobile road warriors, Windows 98 is a winner. Its superior hardware support ensures that Windows 98 will be the default operating system bundled with most new computers sold in 1998 and 1999.

Before you buy Windows 98, you'll want to determine whether your current computer is compatible with Windows 98 or can be made compatible with just a few strategic peripheral upgrades. You'll find more specific information about Windows 98 hardware requirements in Chapter 2.

Windows 3.x and Windows 95 users who may want to upgrade their current computers should weigh the issues described in the following paragraphs before buying Windows 98.

Plug-and-Play Compatibility

One of Windows 98's most compelling features is its ability to run legacy applications, Windows 3.x and DOS programs that you already own, while simultaneously providing access to state-of-the-art new productivity applications.

Plug-and-play—the technology that means you can just plug in a peripheral and it will work—is exciting to anyone who has ever cracked a system case or been irked by an IRQ. There are, however, levels of plug-and-play support, and you should assess your computer to determine the degree to which it is plug-and-play compatible with Windows 98.

Dynamic plug-and-play ease of use depends on how many of the three main components—the operating system, system BIOS, and hardware devices—support plug-and-play standards.

At the lowest level, none of your components support plug-and-play. In this case, you'll need to set card jumpers and switches manually and load drivers from floppies.

At the next level, your operating system supports plug-and-play, but your computer does not contain a plug-and-play BIOS. The computer may have a PCI bus, which helps Windows 98 recognize components, but you may also have non-plug-and-play (legacy) peripherals. This level of support is typical of many older computers. With these systems, user intervention is reduced but not completely eliminated. To help you set up your hardware, Windows 98 provides tools such as the setup wizards, the Device Manager, and system troubleshooters, which can install and configure devices semiautomatically.

At the highest level, your operating system, system BIOS, and hardware devices all provide plug-and-play support. In this case, adding new devices is as easy as plugging them in and turning on the power. Just plug a new printer into a parallel cable or switch video cards, and Windows 98 detects the change automatically, installing appropriate system drivers. If the computer has a Microsoft/Intel-compatible plug-and-play BIOS, then the system supports full dynamic operation, including hot docking, advanced power management, automatic configuration of boot devices, and programming of motherboard devices.

The good news is that your system may already be partially plug-and-play compliant even before you install Windows 98. Many manufacturers have been shipping systems with a plug-and-play BIOS for some time now. A complete plug-and-play system provides substantial benefits to its users. With Windows 98 it's easy to turn a compliant desktop computer into a multimedia tool or home entertainment system.

Windows 98 on a plug-and-play notebook computer also offers great user convenience and mobility. For example, hot-docking stations that support the plug-and-play standard allow you to remove or plug in a portable notebook computer while it is running. The computer automatically senses its annexation or removal from the docking station, reconfiguring itself to work with the new display and adjusting for the new presence or absence of network cards, CD-ROM drives, and other I/O peripherals. On Now Power Management, still in its final development stage at the time of this writing, allows computers to be left on continuously in a very low power state. When you want to use the computer, all you need to do is press a key, and the computer instantly wakes up.

Less Documentation, More Help

One thing that you may notice about Windows 98 is the lack of printed documentation included in the package. Instead of a fat book, you get a 130-page manual and a few loose pieces of paper. However, once you install the operating system, you gain access to a sophisticated set of cross-indexed Help files on your hard disk. Much of the information that was formerly available in printed manuals can now be accessed online.

For users who need complete documentation of technical procedures and features, there are several options: Microsoft has placed the complete text of the *Windows 98 Resource Kit* on the installation CD. This database (in Help file format) can be opened easily from the Run menu, accessed with the Start button.

In addition, the book you're currently reading is designed to help you gain mastery over Windows 98. This book lists procedures and documents features that increase Windows 98 functionality—in ways not spelled out in Microsoft's online documentation.

Integrated Internet Support

The integrated Internet support offered by Windows 98 is its most talked-about feature. If working with Internet resources is an important part of your personal computing agenda, you should consider whether Windows 98 may afford you more convenience. You'll find extensive information about exploring and exploiting the Internet with Windows 98 in Chapters 12 and 13.

Microsoft's Internet Explorer 4 includes a number of new features that help users organize and manage Web sites they've visited for offline viewing:

- The History feature saves a copy of every site you visit in Internet Explorer, including background graphics. You can specify how long to keep these files and then redisplay them offline through a convenient chronological site list.
- The Favorites feature in Internet Explorer 4 is more sophisticated than in Internet Explorer 3. In addition to being able to bookmark your favorite sites and organize them into folders, you can subscribe to a site, specifying that updates be downloaded automatically to your computer at scheduled intervals. Individual URLs can be monitored through up to three levels of onsite links, and you can choose whether to collect inline images, sound and video, and ActiveX applications. However, sophisticated Windows users should be aware that Internet Explorer's subscription support is not competitive with professional third-party Web tracking software. Some third-party packages can run under Windows 95 or Windows 98, tracking and downloading onsite and offsite links up to 100 levels deep. These programs also include more powerful indexing features, allowing you to perform intricate information searches through all the pages of downloaded Web sites.
- Microsoft's Active Channels are another way to track your favorite Web sites. The Windows 98 Channel bar allows you to automatically subscribe to participating sites, which are updated and sent to your computer according to the publisher's schedule. The content of a subscribed channel can be sent to your computer in a variety of formats. In addition to straight HTML pages, it can appear as an Active Desktop screensaver, stock ticker report, or as flashing

news bulletins. True Webcasting allows an event (such as a sports competition or corporate board meeting) to be broadcast to your computer in real time. Webcasting can also be used to send regularly scheduled bulletins to users on a local area network.

The future of Microsoft's Active Channel technology is currently uncertain. This feature may be discontinued in the next generation of Internet Explorer (version 5). However, the discontinuation of push subscription features from a prearranged group of Web sites will not interfere with Internet Explorer's ability to pull site updates from the Internet when the user manually tells it to do so.

Security Zones

Recognizing all the traffic that can now travel between the Internet and your computer, Microsoft has implemented a series of security zones in Internet Explorer 4. These security zones provide encryption for online transactions and protect you from unwanted invasive activity. You can configure access rights for the sites you visit in High, Low, Medium, and Custom zones, allowing or disallowing the downloading of ActiveX and Java components to your computer and toggling on or off the automatic launching of specified applications on your local disk.

Why Not Just Install IE 4 Under Windows 95?

Microsoft has made the entire Internet Explorer version 4 interface available from its Web site as a free download for users of Windows 95. Users willing to invest time and energy in retrieving and installing this module can add the new Internet Explorer browser, taskbar toolbars, and Active Desktop to a Windows 95 computer without purchasing and upgrading to Windows 98. However:

- The IE 4 upgrade procedure for Windows 95 can require from 4 to 10 hours, depending on your modem speed.
- IE 4 under Windows 95 runs slower than it does under Windows 98.
- Adding the free IE 4 upgrade to Windows 95 does not provide Win98's file system enhancements, new help system, hardware and multimedia support, or added system maintenance utilities. You don't gain the performance benefits built into Windows 98 with the free Windows 95 update, only the desktop interface.

Support for Existing Utilities

Running Windows 98 will probably require you to update the arsenal of utility software you accumulated for DOS, Windows 3.x, and Windows 95. Backup, antivirus, and disk recovery utilities that worked in previous versions of Windows and DOS retain partial functionality at best under Windows 98. The good news about backup is that Windows 98 includes a new backup program that supports most current tape drives.

You'll find information about working with older Windows and DOS utility software in Chapter 8 of this book.

Windows 98 Versus Windows NT

At the time of this writing, Windows NT 5.0 is still in early beta testing and at least 18 months away from consumer availability. The current Windows NT version 4.0 is a dependable, useful tool for network-centered business enterprises, and it is particularly useful where sophisticated control over user access rights is an issue. However, Windows NT 4.0 lacks widespread compatibility with current computers and peripherals. It has no automatic plug-and-play configuration support and is much less compatible with DOS and older Windows applications.

Managers of large businesses where Windows 3.x is the current operating system for data entry and accounting may rightly prefer to take the long-term view: wait for Windows NT 5.0 before initiating global system upgrades.

In enterprises that have already upgraded to Windows 95, managers are apprehensive about training and technical support costs for large-scale upgrades to Windows 98. They ask what benefits the new operating system will provide to users whose primary tasks center around word processing and spreadsheets, with occasional exchange of e-mail and Internet use.

Windows 98 does offer a nontrivial upgrade advantage to a Windows 95 office. If productivity software is updated on a regular basis, the Windows 98 system maintenance features can significantly reduce the time and money spent on troubleshooting and administration. The System File Checker built into Windows 98 provides a much sought-after version control feature. System File Checker can track and record the file dates and version numbers of every file on the hard disk—in particular, the program files, system dynamic link libraries (DLLs), and other support files written in the \WINDOWS, \WINDOWS\SYSTEM, and other system subdirectories. Periodic use of this maintenance tool can guard against the kinds of system crashes and erratic behavior that occur in Windows 95 as a result of frequent installation and updating of productivity applications. The Windows Update feature of Windows 98 also reduces the burden of obtaining and installing patches and incremental maintenance upgrades on a large number of computers.

The bottom line is that Windows 98 is easier to use, and if you have the hardware to support it, it will crash less and be more useful than Windows 3.x or Windows 95. Many people in the second wave of Windows 98 upgrades are finding this out even without having explored the nooks and crannies that can make them Windows 98 power users. It is for this group of users that this book was largely written.

Take This Test

If you depend on your computer for your livelihood, upgrading to Windows 98 is not something you should do on the spur of the moment. The following is a short list of questions that you can use to determine whether a Windows 98 upgrade will probably be advantageous to you.

If you answer yes to the following questions, you should upgrade:

- Do you feel restricted by your current computing environment? Are you looking for a more flexible operating system to assist you in conveniently getting your work done?
- Are features that facilitate working with the Internet important to accomplish daily tasks?
- Do you have access to high-end, multimedia-capable hardware? Are you looking to enjoy the latest benefits of state-of-the-art Windows technology?
- Do you need access to the most current Windows technology for personal or business purposes?

If you answer yes to these questions, you should probably stay put:

- Is your computer functional and useful, able to accomplish all of the tasks you assign to it?
- Are you are satisfied with your current Internet service connections? Is your current Internet browsing software adequate to satisfy your online needs?
- Is your existing hardware functional but not state of the art? Would a system upgrade be too costly or inconvenient?
- For MIS managers and administrators: Do you lack the time and money necessary to retrain staff and support new operating system features? Would the expenditure of time and money outweigh the benefits of Windows 98 outlined in this chapter?

If Windows 98 still sounds like a good bet for you, read on. This introductory chapter has provided just an overview of the new wrinkles and benefits of Windows 98. The next chapter shows you what computer preparations you'll need to make before you make the jump to the new operating system.

Chapter 2

Before You Make the Jump

Chapter Highlights

Is your computer powerful enough?

Taking a system inventory

What hardware can you add later on?

What to expect from old productivity applications and utilities

Finding pre-installation help on the Win98 CD

Migrating Windows 3.1, Windows for Workgroups, and Windows 95 networks

Pre-installation preparation: getting your hard disk ready for Windows 98

Windows 98 and other operating systems

Installation strategies: dual-boot tricks

As you prepare for your jump to Windows 98 from DOS, Windows 3.x, or Windows 95, you may have a lot of questions on your mind. Ideally, upgrading an operating system should be as easy as flash-upgrading a computer or modem. Microsoft designed Windows 98 to accommodate this attitude. But if you're a conservative user or an MIS professional, you'll appreciate the pre-installation roadmap that this chapter provides.

If you're the kind of user who likes to look before you leap, you may be asking yourself some of these questions:

- Is my computer powerful enough to run Windows 98 comfortably?
- Will my old software applications and utilities still work under Windows 98?
- How will my network be affected?
- What will happen with my old DOS and Windows maintenance utilities and antivirus programs? Can I still use them?
- What kind of configuration and disk maintenance preparations should I make before installing Windows 98?
- Should I install Windows 98 over my existing Windows operating system or into a new directory? Can I keep more than one copy of Windows on my system?

This chapter answers these questions, helping you to prepare for your Windows 98 installation. The first few sections provide basic information about what you can do to ensure a smooth transition to Windows 98 from your current operating system. The "What About Your Network" section contains strategic details about upgrading an existing Windows 3.x or Windows 95 network to Windows 98.

Finally, the "Planning the Installation" and "Have Your Cake and Eat It, Too!" sections are designed for advanced users and professionals. They show how to extract the most convenient access to Windows 98, allowing it to coexist with other operating systems on the same computer.

The actual Windows 98 setup process is discussed in option-by-option detail in the next chapter.

Is Your System Powerful Enough: Taking a System Inventory

Is your computer ready for Windows 98? The bare requirements, as stated by Microsoft, call for a 486 DX2/66 CPU, 16MB of RAM, VGA graphics, a mouse, and 125MB to 350MB of hard-disk space (depending on the options selected). Although such a minimal system may be physically capable of running the operating system, it's bound to deliver disappointing performance. Most users will want to know what they can expect from more powerful systems that handled the last version of Windows well but were not specifically designed to run Windows 98: Are the individual hardware peripherals compatible? Will Windows 98 provide the necessary drivers and support files for video cards, disk drives, printers, and modems?

Chapter 15 discusses Windows 98 requirements for a fully loaded, multimedia PC. If you don't plan to watch movies, play 3-D games, record music, or capture television output on your computer, the following hardware minimums should be comfortable:

- You should have a Pentium 133 CPU with 16MB of RAM (32MB of RAM for heavier Internet browsing, 64MB of RAM plus Pentium 166 MMX CPU for heavier multimedia playback or graphic editing).
- Motherboard should support PCI Bus video and onboard IDE disk controller, to avoid sluggish screen display and program response. Universal Serial Bus (USB) ports are desirable to accommodate new scanners, cameras, and other hardware accessories.
- Your computer should have a 2GB hard disk for a system that will handle multiple applications, office suites, graphic editing, preserve Web browsing history, etc. Disk should be at least Enhanced IDE speed (12ms access time, PIO 3, 10MB/sec transfer rate.)
- Video card should support 800×600 pixel display. 2MB of RAM and High Color (16-bit) color depth desirable.

- Modem should support minimum 28.8 Kbps speed for light Internet browsing; 33.6 Kbps or 56 Kbps recommended.
- CD-ROM drive should be 8x or faster for use as playback device.
- Notebook computers should support the Microsoft APM 1.1 power management standard. You may also need BIOS updates or supplementary configuration files from the vendor to make some notebooks Windows 98–compatible.

Table 2-1 shows the disk space requirements for Windows 98 that Microsoft lists in its *Windows 98 Resource Kit*. Table 2-2 lists Microsoft's optional hardware requirements.

Installation method	Required disk space	Typical disk space
Windows 95 upgrade	120–295MB	195MB
Windows 3.1x or Windows for Workgroups 3.1x upgrade	120–295MB	195MB
New installation (FAT32 file system)	140–255MB	175MB
New installation (FAT16 file system)	165–355MB	225MB
Installation over the network:	165–355MB	225MB
On the server	170MB	170MB
On the client	175–225MB	175–225MB

Table 2-1. *Disk Space Requirements for Windows 98*

Optional component	Minimum requirement	Recommended[1]
Mouse	Windows 98–compatible pointing device	Microsoft Mouse or Microsoft pointing device
Modem	14.4 baud modem for Microsoft Network (MSN™), Messaging, and Internet access	28.8 baud modem or higher
CD-ROM drive (if installing from compact disc)	1x speed or faster. You need to have the correct driver for your CD-ROM. Refer to the documentation for your CD-ROM drive.	8x speed or faster
Network adapter (if installing from the network)	NDIS 2.0 or MAC driver support	NDIS 4.0 or 5.0 with OnNow power management support
Audio card and speakers	Sound Blaster–compatible	Full-duplex sound card or external digital audio using Universal Serial Bus (USB) or IEEE-1394
DVD-ROM and decoder card (if you want to view full-size motion pictures)	Supports industry standards	Supports DVD-video and MPEG-2 playback
Scanner or digital camera (if you want to scan/import digital images or pictures)	Plug and Play–compatible	Use IEEE-1394 port connections
Second monitor and video card (if you want to use the multimonitor feature)	Optional	PCI, AGP, or other non-1SA bus

Table 2-2. *Optional Hardware Requirements*

IEEE-1394 bus (firewire) (if you want high-speed digital sound and video transfer)	Optional	Device and controller support IEEE-1394 standards, Plug and Play, and OnNow power management
USB bus and HID hardware	Optional	Hardware complies with Universal Bus specifications and supports On Now Power Management
ATI All-in-Wonder-Card	Optional	Required for watching television using WebTV for Windows

[1]Microsoft strongly recommends that you choose hardware components that carry the "Designed for Microsoft Windows" logo because these products have been stringently tested to ensure that the hardware and its driver provide the optimal user experience when used with Microsoft Windows operating systems.

Table 2-2. *Optional Hardware Requirements (continued)*

If you have questions concerning your system's suitability as a Windows 98 hardware or software platform, do some reading and preparation before you install the operating system. (In a subsequent section of this chapter, you will see how to extract some useful technical documents from the Win95 CD before running Setup.) You may want to undertake one or more of the following pre-installation projects:

- Take an inventory of your system's components. Rate your system's performance with commercial or shareware benchmark packages.

- Examine the various README text files on hardware and software compatibility that Microsoft includes in the basic Windows 98 package. (You can extract and access these files before installing the new operating system.)
- Consult your computer's manufacturer to determine whether there are known compatibility issues with Windows 98 (older computers may require a BIOS update or vendor-specific hardware patches).
- Perform hardware or software upgrades based on the information you obtain from your reading and your system inventory.

Several common freeware and shareware utilities can help you inventory your system. Diagnostic programs can help you assess hardware compatibility, and benchmark results can give you a rough idea of what to expect in the way of performance efficiency. This information is particularly useful when you can compare it to diagnostic results for other widely used systems and hardware components.

What Hardware Can You Add Later?

Windows 98 includes software support for very large hard disks, 3D graphics accelerators, multiple monitors and video cards, DAT storage devices, ISDN modems, digital video disks, wireless infrared devices, Universal Serial Bus and firewire peripherals (cameras, scanners, modems, keyboards, remote control devices), plus desktop television reception. You don't have to have all of these bells and whistles to begin using Windows 98 and take advantage of its benefits, however. Many of these hardware devices can be added to an existing computer piece by piece as you need them.

The tips in the next section, "Evaluating System Performance," can help you decide whether your current computer is up to the basic task of running the Windows 98 operating system. If your system evaluation suggests that hardware upgrades are desirable, you'll want to buy wisely to avoid having to replace components a second or third time. Sometimes it's better to buy a brand new computer if vital components must be upgraded. Other times you can tweak your current machine one part at a time. Some parts of a computer are linked: if you upgrade one facet, you need to make sure your computer still supports other facets.

Here are some rough guidelines:

- If you determine that you need a hard-disk upgrade, confirm that your current system BIOS includes support for large disk partitions. Also consider whether your current system supports fast Ultra-DMA IDE drives. If the answers to these questions are no, consider a motherboard upgrade or new disk controller as well as a new hard disk.
- If you determine that you need a CPU or memory upgrade, consider whether your current system motherboard supports fast Pentium II processors and fast SDRAM memory. If not, consider a motherboard upgrade or a new computer instead of a CPU or memory upgrade. You may be able to patch a current system up to a 266MHz Pentium CPU with 128MB of EDO RAM, but today's computers offer faster memory and CPUs, fast AGP graphics support, Ultra-DMA disk support, wireless infrared connections, and Universal Serial Bus support.

Some hardware upgrades can be added as you need them to either a new or an older computer. Peripherals that fall into this category are tape drives; better monitors, sound cards, and printers; scanners and cameras; fast modems; faster CD-ROM drives and DVD players; and good speakers.

If you want to add a DVD player, portable scanner, or camera in the near future, consider upgrading to a computer that includes Universal Serial Bus support. USB versions of scanners and cameras are cheap and abundant. Good USB speakers support six-channel, streaming Dolby sound and work well with a DVD player.

Evaluating System Performance

Several shareware and public-domain benchmark utilities can help you obtain a statistical rating of your system's performance. You can then compare the numerical rating achieved by your computer or peripherals with ratings using the same benchmark for other systems. If you're looking for benchmarks to provide you with a quick rating, download a copy of WINDSOCK, a simple, integrated utility written for Windows 3.1. (This file is currently available at http://www.winsite.com/win3/util as WSK320.ZIP.)

Other freeware and shareware benchmarks are useful in testing performance aspects of individual system components. You may want to look for CORETEST.EXE, a venerable but reliable disk benchmark; SPEEDY, a video benchmark; and WINTACH, another integrated Windows benchmark. TORQUE, a video benchmark developed by Steve Gibson of SpinRite fame, is especially useful in evaluating high-performance video cards that operate in 64K and 16M color resolutions. These utilities are widely available on the World Wide Web, CompuServe, GEnie, America Online, and public bulletin board systems. You may find some of them at http://www.irtech.com/treehous/files/T3.htm.

To test the performance of a computer that's already running Windows 95, you can take advantage of Wintune 97/98 and Winstone\WinBench, free testing utilities distributed by commercial computer magazines.

Wintune 97/98

Wintune is a quick and convenient performance test suite compiled by the staff of CMP Media's *Windows Magazine*. Wintune 97 can be downloaded from the magazine's Web site at http://www.winmag.com. Wintune 98 is currently available as a set of online benchmarks that must be run through Internet Explorer 3.02 or higher.

In addition to running raw CPU, video, memory, and hard disk tests, Wintune runs a set of simulated 32-bit application tests. You can compare or graph the results generated by your computer with a database of other tested machines ranging from a 486 DX2 66 to a Pentium 200MHz machine with a variety of memory and video configurations (as shown here).

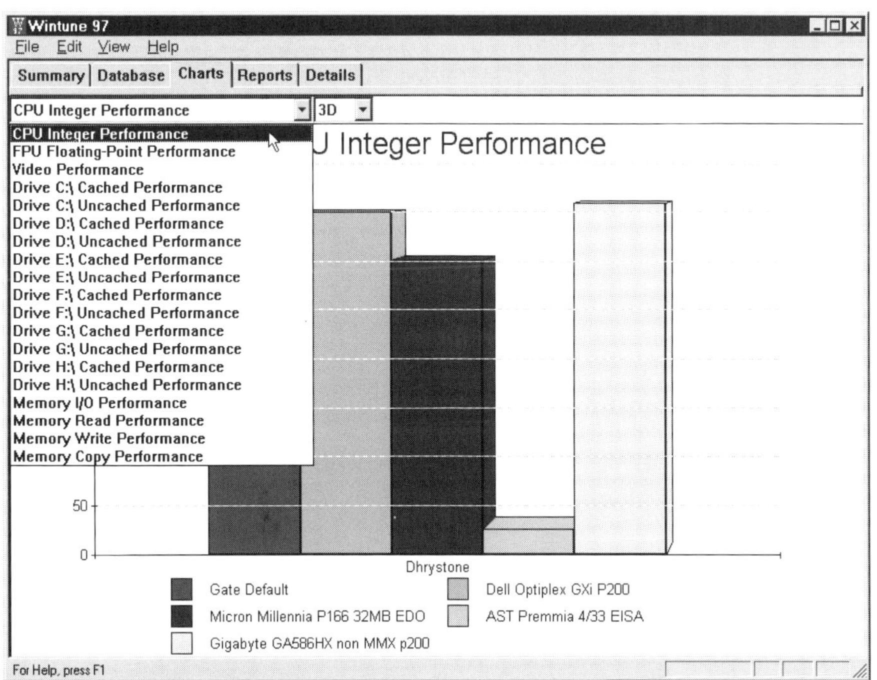

Wintune 98 performs more sophisticated tests, including the measurement of 3D OpenGL and Direct Draw graphics performance. It must be run through Internet

Explorer 3.02 or higher while you are connected to http://winweb.winmag.com/wintune98/default.htm over the Internet. (Since the benchmarks employ Microsoft ActiveX controls, they cannot be run through Netscape Navigator.) The speed of your modem or Internet connection does not influence the test results.

Winstone\WinBench

One of the most exhaustive and widely used benchmarks in the computer industry is the Winstone\WinBench evaluation suite. This set of utilities is distributed on a CD-ROM available from Ziff-Davis for a nominal shipping charge. Installing and running this suite takes a little time and effort, and sometimes its execution is not trouble free. However, once you complete the tests, you'll be able to compare the results for your computer to the ratings for systems and hardware peripherals frequently reviewed in computer magazines. You'll find information about obtaining those benchmark suites at http://www.zdnet.com/zdbop/winstone.html.

Extracting README Files from the Windows 98 CD

The Windows 98 CD includes a number of useful documents concerning Win98 performance and compatibility. However, you won't find them, because Microsoft decided to compress these files into the Windows cabinet (.CAB) archives rather than allowing easy access to them up front. Once you've installed Windows 98, you'll find that DISPLAY.TXT, EXCHANGE.TXT, EXTRA.TXT, FAQ.TXT, GENERAL.TXT, HARDWARE.TXT, PRINTERS.TXT, PROGRAMS.TXT, and other files are available for browsing in your \WINDOWS directory.

If you want to read these documents *before* installing Windows 98, there is a way. These files are all contained within the cabinet file called WIN98_47.CAB. The EXTRACT.EXE utility located in the root directory of the Win98 CD or on the first installation diskette can be used to unpack all of the README files for inspection before you install Windows 98. The easiest way to do this is to create a directory called READMES on your hard drive. If you are installing from the WIN98 CD, log onto the CD-ROM drive and change to the WIN98 directory where EXTRACT.EXE is located. Then use the EXTRACT command with the following syntax:

EXTRACT /L *C:\READMES* *d*:\WIN98\WIN98_47.CAB *.TXT

where *d*: represents your Windows 98 source drive and the "/L *C:\READMES*" switch specifies a target directory for the text files you're unpacking. (You can use this parameter to specify any drive and directory.)

If you are installing from floppy diskettes, place the first one in drive A. Then use the EXTRACT command with the following syntax:

A:\> EXTRACT /L C:*READMES* WIN98_47.CAB *.TXT

Note *There are additional text files for Windows 98 scattered around in other cabinet archives. If you want to search the rest of the .CAB text files, you can modify the EXTRACT command described here by adding the /A parameter to the command line. The command EXTRACT /A /L* d:\PATH *BASE4.CAB *.TXT will search all the .CAB files in the \WIN98 directory, unpacking all files with the .TXT extension to the specified path on your hard drive.*

What About Your Old Applications and Utilities?

The good news is that most of your DOS and Windows 3.x productivity applications will work under Windows 98 with no significant problems or performance degradation. The PROGRAMS.TXT file, which you learned how to extract in the preceding section, can help you identify application problems that you may encounter.

The bad news is that a lot of the utility software you've amassed for DOS, Windows 3.x, and Windows 95 will become nonfunctional as soon as the new operating system is installed. Various DOS and Windows 3.x backup utilities retain partial functionality, but you won't be able to use them to make reliable system backups that include the new Windows 98 long filenames and system registry information. (For a workaround to this problem, see "Working with Older DOS Backup Programs" in Chapter 8.) Chances are good, however, that you'll be able to use Win98's new backup utility with your current tape drive, since it supports a wide number of devices. You'll find a list of compatible tape drives on Seagate's website at http://apps.smg.seagatesoftware.onwardtech.com/win98/.

File managers and system recovery utilities developed for DOS and Windows 3.x will also have to be replaced. Windows 95 file managers may be somewhat more compatible. You may be able to get along provisionally without bells and whistles, such as emergency disk recovery and complete unerase protection, but you will probably want to restore these features eventually by purchasing a Windows 98–specific utility package.

Windows 98 includes an improved disk optimizer (the descendant of the MS-DOS Defrag program). The Win98 Disk Defragmenter is completely compatible with the DoubleSpace/DriveSpace compression features offered in previous versions of DOS. The Win98 ScanDisk disk repair utility is not much different from previous versions, but it includes support for the new FAT32 file system.

ScanDisk has a bare-bones capacity to repair file and directory errors, but it is not nearly as powerful as the Windows 98 versions of Norton Disk Doctor or Nuts & Bolts Disk Minder. None of the pre-Win95 disk repair utilities can be depended upon to reliably repair problems arising under the new operating system. In a pinch,

About FAT32

FAT32 is a new disk format developed by Microsoft that permits Windows 98 to run on a large disk partition of more than 2GB. The older, traditional file system created by MS-DOS or the original Windows 95 is referred to as FAT16. FAT32 partitions cannot be used to boot MS-DOS versions 3 to 6, Windows 3.x, or other operating systems such as Windows NT or OS/2. Windows 98 can run on disk partitions formatted for either FAT16 or FAT32.

If you are upgrading a computer from MS-DOS or Windows 3.x to Windows 98, the FAT16 file system on the hard disk will be preserved. Later, when Windows 98 is active, you have the option of converting the disk partition to the FAT32 format.

Recent versions of Windows 95 may be installed over the FAT32 file system. If you have a Windows 95 computer, you can determine whether this is the case by right-clicking drive C in the Windows Explorer and selecting Properties, as shown here:

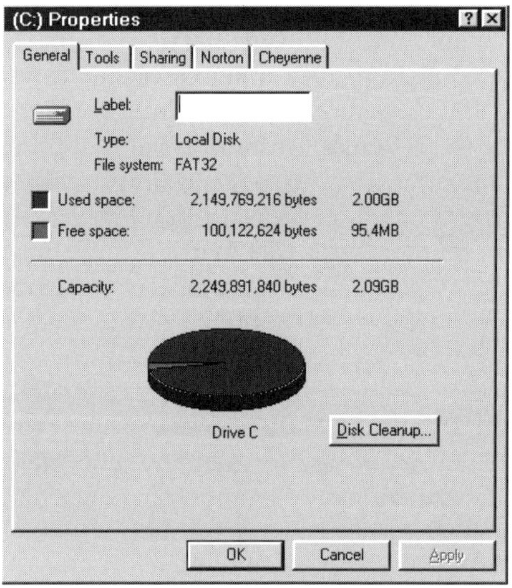

If you upgrade Windows 95 to Windows 98 on a FAT32 partition, the FAT32 format is retained by the new operating system.

If you plan to format a hard disk from scratch and install Windows 98 on it, you can create either FAT16 or FAT32 disk partitions. The FDISK utility included with Windows 98 allows any hard disk larger than 256MB to be formatted for either FAT16 or FAT32. (You'll find more information about the FAT32 file system in the section "FAT32" in Chapter 7.)

third-party Windows 95 utilities may be able to rescue data on non-FAT32 disk partitions without inflicting further damage.

Windows 3.x program launchers and file management shells retain partial functionality, at best, under Windows 98. Some of them may not work at all or may cause system compatibility problems. Users who previously enjoyed Norton Desktop for Windows 3.0 and PC Tools for Windows 2.0 may want to upgrade to shareware packages such as Canyon Software's Drag and File Gold or Pacific Gold Coast's TurboBrowser 98. (See Chapter 4 for more information about third-party file managers that are Win98 compatible.)

Windows 3.x and Windows 95 uninstallers (older versions of MicroHelp, Remove-It, Symantec's Norton Uninstaller, Quarterdeck's Clean-Sweep, and so on) will probably not work reliably under Windows 98. Check the Symantec and Quarterdeck Web sites for Win98-compatible upgrades to older products.

Fax programs, telecommunication packages, and Internet utilities developed for DOS and Windows 3.x will generally retain their functionality under Windows 98. This is an area where upgrading to newer Windows 95 or Windows 98 versions will deliver feature enhancements and performance improvements, but no functionality will be lost. Telecommunications-related programs written for Windows 95 should work transparently under Windows 98. If you are a power-user who has installed a substitute Internet dialer TCP/IP package, such as NetManage Chameleon or FTP's OnNet32, you'll probably want to switch to Windows 98's built-in Dial-Up Networking, at least until a Win98-specific upgrade appears for your third-party dialer. (Windows 98 includes built-in upgrades for some national online services: America Online, CompuServe, Prodigy, AT&T Worldnet, and the Microsoft Network.)

Multimedia applications and CDs written for DOS and Windows 3.x will generally continue to work under Windows 98. Packages that specifically add Windows 3.x performance enhancements (such as the Monty Python Complete Waste of Time CD) will lose functionality. Windows 3.x screensavers and some Windows 3.x and DOS games may be incompatible with Windows 98. See the Windows 98 PROGRAMS.TXT file for more compatibility information.

Many real-mode DOS drivers for SCSI peripherals, CD-ROM drives, PCMCIA cards, and sound cards operate transparently under Windows 98 when they are loaded in CONFIG.SYS and AUTOEXEC.BAT. Check vendor Web sites for more information. Many of these drivers can be replaced by Win98's protected-mode support after installation is complete. See Chapter 7 for details. DOS memory managers and software drivers for Enhanced IDE tend to be more problematic.

For more information about working with DOS and Windows 3.x software under Windows 98, see Chapter 4.

What About Your Network?

Users who depend on the peer-to-peer network connection bundled with Windows for Workgroups or connections to a Windows NT server should experience no difficulty in migrating to Windows 98's Client for Microsoft Networks. Sites that use combined Microsoft-Novell network configurations should make sure that Novell Bindery Services are enabled to use Windows 98's built-in Client for Novell NetWare.

If you want to network a group of computers for the first time, upgrade them to Windows 98 before attempting to install and configure the network hardware. Win98's plug-and-play features will greatly reduce the amount of work you have to do. (See Chapter 14 for detailed information about configuring and using a Windows 98 peer-to-peer network.)

Upgrading a Windows for Workgroups Network

The information in this section applies to a direct network upgrade from Windows for Workgroups to Windows 98. For information about upgrading from a Windows 95 to a Windows 98 network, see the next section, "Upgrading a Windows 95 Network."

If your office workstations are already part of a Windows for Workgroups network, the Windows 98 upgrade should detect and configure their existing network hardware. Note that while remote network connections are migrated to Windows 98, shared local resources (such as shared folders, drives, and printers) are not. If a Windows for Workgroups machine on the network is active as a file or print server, you'll need to record a list of its shared resources. After the server has been upgraded to Windows 98, you can manually reestablish its shared resources.

Note

Unlike Windows 95, Windows 98 does not install Microsoft Mail post office support or offer built-in fax capability.

If you have installed Microsoft Mail post office, groupware, or network e-mail packages under Windows for Workgroups, you can continue to use your Windows for Workgroups post office with MS Mail and Schedule + under Windows 98. Even though this 16-bit mail system operates under Windows 98, it lacks the features and performance speed of Microsoft's separate, enhanced Exchange server-client package or of the Windows Messaging Services feature that was part of Windows 95. The Windows for Workgroups At Work Fax feature is automatically disabled when you upgrade to Windows 98.

Tip

If you want to continue using the older MS Mail and Schedule + programs under Windows 98, you can also reenable the Windows for Workgroups At Work Fax feature. (You might want to do this if you've migrated some, but not all, workstations from Windows 3.x to Windows 98 and you want to retain your network's Windows for Workgroups post office.) You can reenable At Work Fax by adding the following lines to the WIN.INI configuration file located in your \WINDOWS directory:

```
[Windows]
Device= Microsoft At Work Fax,EFAXDRV,FAX:
[PrinterPorts]
Microsoft At Work Fax=EFAXDRV,FAX:,15,45
[Devices]
Microsoft At Work Fax=EFAXDRV,FAX:
```

Once you add these lines and reboot the system, the At Work Fax printer will reappear in the Win98 PRINTERS folder. You can use this feature just as you did under Windows for Workgroups, until you upgrade to a 32-bit Windows 98–aware mail and fax system.

Alternative Solutions

As an alternative mail-and-fax stopgap solution, Microsoft has included the Workgroup Postoffice, Messaging Services, and Fax support that was once part of Windows 95 in the \TOOLS\OLDWIN95\MESSAGE\US directory on the Windows 98 CD. (There's also a subdirectory for International versions.) These Windows 95 programs are not technically a part of Windows 98. You won't find menu options in the new Control Panel to install them. However, you can add this support to Windows 98 *after* the operating system upgrade has been completed.

If you add Win95's Workgroup Postoffice, Windows Messaging, and Fax support after installing Windows 98, these utilities will function just as they did under Windows 95:

- The Win95 Messaging Services (Inbox) can replace the Windows for Workgroups MS Mail as your network e-mail client. Messages stored in the older .MMF mail format can be migrated to the newer Messaging Services/Exchange format.
- The Win95 Microsoft Fax utility can replace the older Windows for Workgroups At Work Fax applet.
- The Win95 Workgroup Postoffice can replace the older Windows for Workgroups post office. If you upgrade your network to use a Windows 95 post office, you must also upgrade the older Windows for Workgroups MS Mail, At Work Fax, and Schedule + clients to the newer Win95 Messaging Services or to Microsoft Outlook 97/98.

Upgrading a Windows 95 Network

As stated in the previous section, Windows 98 does not directly install a Microsoft Mail post office, a network mail client, or a fax utility. However, if these components were installed under Windows 95, they will be migrated and preserved during a Windows 98 upgrade.

- If your current Windows 95 network already uses a Win95 Workgroup post office, the post office will remain operational under Windows 98.
- If Win95's Messaging Services/Inbox client has already been installed on a computer, it will be migrated automatically to Windows 98 and remain operational.
- If Win95's Microsoft Fax applet has already been installed on a computer, it will be migrated automatically to Windows 98 and remain operational.

If these Microsoft Mail and Fax components are not currently installed on a Windows 95 computer, they will not appear as Control Panel options under Windows 98.

Note that the Outlook Express applet included in Windows 98 does not support Microsoft Mail or fax management. The Outlook 97 applet bundled with Microsoft Office 97 supports Microsoft Mail and fax management as long as the Windows 95 messaging components are also installed on the computer.

Microsoft's new Outlook 98 mail client supports Microsoft Mail, Internet mail, and fax management independent of older Windows 95 components.

Pre-installation Preparation

Before you take the plunge and run the Windows 98 Setup program, you may want to optimize your hard disk, make some system configuration preparations, and develop an installation strategy.

Some utility packages can fine-tune your system to make it more receptive to Win98 installation. These programs can optimize your hard disk and help you back up, compress, or delete unnecessary files. Quarterdeck's CleanSweep Deluxe and Tune-Up products can help you clean your hard disk before you perform a Windows 98 upgrade.

Windows 98 Setup automatically runs a new version of ScanDisk to check the integrity of your hard disk. Before beginning an upgrade, you may also want to run a disk optimizer, such as Microsoft's Defrag, Norton Utilities SpeedDisk, or Nuts&Bolts Disk Tune to organize your hard disk and speed the installation process.

Antivirus Scan

Before installing Windows 98, you would be well advised to scan your hard disk with a recently updated antivirus utility, particularly if you plan to use floppy disk media to install the new operating system. If there are any boot sector viruses lurking on your hard disk, they can infect and corrupt your Windows 98 floppy disk installation. After you confirm that your hard disk is virus free, you should turn off your virus checker before beginning the Windows 98 upgrade. If you install Windows 98 from floppy disks, enable the write-protect option on each disk before beginning the upgrade.

Preserving Useful DOS and Windows 3.x Accessories

If you install Windows 98 by upgrading to a Windows 3.x directory, several useful Windows 3.x productivity applets are overwritten, and others may be deleted. Some of the applets bundled with Windows 3.1 contain features that are not implemented in their Windows 98 replacements. Although Windows 98 leaves program stubs in the upgraded directory for Write and Paintbrush, they launch copies of the new WordPad and Paint applets instead of the original Win 3.1 programs. Windows Calendar, Terminal, Recorder, and Cardfile are also missing from Windows 98. Microsoft regards these applets as relics of an obsolete operating system, overlooking the fact that some people find them useful.

If you want to preserve some of these utilities for use in Windows 98, create a \TEMP directory on your hard disk before you begin the Windows 98 installation. Copy both the .EXE and .HLP files for each application you want to preserve into the \TEMP directory. After Windows 98 is installed, you can run these programs from the \TEMP directory or recopy them back to your \WINDOWS directory. (See Chapter 5 for more information on differences between Windows 3.x and Windows 95 accessories.)

If Windows 98 is installed over an existing Windows 3.x directory, the Setup program will also remove most of the contents of any DOS directories on your hard disk. Some of the deletions that Setup performs make good sense: current versions of DriveSpace, ScanDisk, Defrag, Fdisk, Format, Xcopy, and so on replace older versions that would not work under Windows 98. (You'll find a complete list of all the DOS utilities that Windows 98 replaces in the sidebar "What Happens to DOS?" in Chapter 3.)

Windows 98 also erases a few DOS utilities without replacing them: Append, Assign, MemMaker, Interlink, Replace, Backup, Restore, Graphics, and Undelete. MemMaker may be useful if you want to optimize DOS conventional memory. Interlink is a networking utility that can establish a parallel or serial cable connection between two computers running MS-DOS on FAT16 partitions. Interlinked computers can share files or applications.

The older DOS Backup and Restore utilities are necessary if you want to work with file archives created by DOS backup. The Undelete utility allows you to reclaim files deleted in DOS sessions that can't be reclaimed through the Windows 98 Recycle Bin.

If you think you might want to use these programs after Windows 98 is installed, make copies of them in another directory before beginning your Windows 98 installation.

Preserving Useful Windows 95 Accessories

As mentioned earlier in this chapter, Windows 98 does not install the Inbox e-mail client, Microsoft Fax, or Microsoft Workgroup post office. If you want to use these features under Windows 98, the simplest way to make them available is to add them to your Windows 95 configuration before performing the upgrade. Also, the Windows 95 version of Microsoft Paint has features absent in the Win98 version. To preserve it, copy MSPAINT.EXE from the \PROGRAM FILES\ACCESSORIES folder to your \TEMP directory.

The Windows 95 Installation CD also contains a few features and utilities that aren't present on the Windows 98 CD, including a set of multimedia music videos and an emergency recovery utility. To preserve these utilities, all you need to do is keep your old Windows 95 CD.

Creating an Emergency Boot Disk

It's a good idea to make an emergency boot disk under your current operating system before installing Windows 98. This will allow you to restore dual-boot options on a FAT16 disk partition if the Win98 installation process aborts prematurely. More important, it will guarantee that you can access your CD-ROM drive or other device-driven peripherals if Windows 98 Setup fails and corrupts your hard disk. It's actually pretty unlikely that this will occur, but it's better to be safe than sorry.

The Windows 98 CD includes a utility that will create an emergency boot disk with the new, Win98 version of DOS. This boot disk will also permit you to completely reformat your hard disk to install the FAT32 file system.

To create a FAT32 EBD under Windows 95:

1. Open the \TOOLS\MTSUTIL\FAT32EBD folder in Windows Explorer.
2. Insert a 1.44MB disk in drive A and double-click the FAT32EBD program in Windows Explorer.

To create a FAT32 EBD under Windows 3.x or MS-DOS

1. If Windows 3.x is running, exit to a DOS command prompt. Make sure your DOS CD-ROM drivers are loaded in CONFIG.SYS and AUTOEXEC.BAT so that you can access your CD-ROM drive.
2. Log onto your CD-ROM drive and go to the FAT32EBD directory by issuing the command CD\TOOLS\OLDWIN95\FAT32EBD.
3. Insert a 1.44MB disk in drive A, enter FAT32EBD at the DOS command prompt and press ENTER.

Windows 98 will copy some generic SCSI and IDE drivers to the boot disk. If there's room, you may want to include files and drivers specific to your computer:

- Backups of your current AUTOEXEC.BAT and CONFIG.SYS files
- Important system drivers for disk compression, SCSI controller, CD-ROM drive, sound card, and other I/O peripherals
- An antivirus utility such as McAfee's shareware SCAN and VSHIELD

Windows 98 will also prompt you to create an emergency boot disk early in the installation process. If you've already done this before starting the installation, you can skip making the additional disk.

Backing Up Your System

It's not strictly necessary to back up your hard disk before installing Windows 98, but it never hurts to have a recent system backup available on tape. You may also want to back up your Windows 3.x or Windows 95 configuration files to guard against the unlikely, but possible, event that they become lost or corrupted. (Windows 98 offers the option of backing up your entire old operating system during installation. The procedure below is useful primarily to save disk space by backing up only the configuration files.)

Tip

To perform a quick backup of your Windows 3.x configuration files, create a subdirectory under your \WINDOWS directory called \INIS. Go to the DOS command prompt, open the \WINDOWS directory, and execute the following commands:

```
COPY *.INI INIS
COPY *.GRP INIS
```

To back up Windows 95 configuration files, create a subdirectory under your \WINDOWS directory called \INIS (or choose your own name). Go to the DOS command prompt, open the \WINDOWS directory, and execute the following commands:

```
COPY *.INI INIS
ATTRIB *.DAT -R -H -S
COPY *.DAT INIS
CD \WINDOWS\INF
COPY*.INF \WINDOWS\INIS
```

Making System Configuration Changes

Question: Should I modify my system configuration before installing Windows 98?
Answer: Making certain configuration preparations will ease the Win98 Setup process.

Modifying CONFIG.SYS and AUTOEXEC.BAT to Disable TSRs and Extra Memory Managers

The Win98 Setup program will take care of SmartDrive, MSCDEX, Setver, and other Microsoft utilities, but you should take the additional step of disabling third-party disk caches, pop-up utilities, video and hard-disk speed-up utilities, and third-party memory managers

Don't remove commands in your AUTOEXEC.BAT file that adjust the scan rate frequency for your monitor. These adjustments can be used by the Windows 98 setup routine to select the proper graphics adapter and monitor configuration.

Cleaning Up the Windows 3.x or Windows 95 System Configuration

Open your Windows 3.x or Windows 95 Startup folder and remove shortcuts to any system utility applications. (You can copy the icons to a temporary program group or folder if you want to restore them after you complete the upgrade.) From Windows 3.x, if you are running Norton Desktop for Windows or PC Tools for Windows as your default desktop shell, disable them and restore Program Manager. There's generally no need to disable high-resolution video drivers. They won't interfere with Windows 98's hardware detection routines.

You may be wondering what to do with all of the DLLs and virtual drivers that have been placed in your old Windows directory by third-party applications. In general, you needn't worry about these DLLs. They probably won't interfere with the Windows 98 setup. If you have an Uninstall utility such as Quarterdeck CleanSweep, CyberMedia FirstAid, or Norton Uninstaller, you can use it to purge extraneous orphan files from your hard disk.

What About Disk Compression?

You should have no trouble installing Windows 98 on a system that has been compressed with Microsoft's DriveSpace/DoubleSpace. Any third-party compression utility such as Stac Electronics' Stacker should be uninstalled before you begin Windows 98 setup.

Microsoft's FAT32 file system cannot be installed on a disk partition that contains DriveSpace-compressed volumes. If you want to take advantage of FAT32, you must first uncompress any DriveSpace volumes installed on your boot partition. If your computer has multiple hard disks or multiple partitions on a single disk, you can install Windows 98, convert your boot partition to FAT32, and use DriveSpace on secondary FAT16 partitions.

Planning the Installation Strategy

During Windows 98 installation, you'll be prompted to choose among four installation types: Typical, Portable, Compact, and Custom. These options are designed to fit your productivity needs and available disk resources. Most users will want to select the Typical installation. In the section "Selecting Setup Options" in Chapter 3, you'll find an overview of Windows 98 features that are installed automatically and suggestions for adding supplementary features.

Windows 98 and Windows 3.x

Before you actually start the Setup program, you should decide whether to install Windows 98 into a clean directory or to upgrade over your current version of Windows. The theoretical advantage of a clean install is that it allows you to retain your previous versions of DOS and Windows 3.x on the same hard disk. This option may be desirable for programmers, software testers, computer training centers, and technical support agents. If you perform a clean install of Windows 98, you can select an operating system at boot time and work in the environment of your choice.

Note *With respect to backward Windows 3.x compatibility, Windows 98 is more limited than Windows 95. You cannot run Windows 3.x from a Windows 98 disk partition by booting to a real-mode DOS prompt and typing* **WIN** *at the command line. (Some versions of Windows 95 allowed this option.) To run Windows 3.x from a hard disk that also contains Windows 98 you must boot from a traditional FAT16 disk partition while pressing the* CTRL *key and then choose the Previous Version of DOS option from the Windows 98 Startup menu. (This option appears when you upgrade a computer by installing Windows 98 into a new directory. The Previous Version of DOS option does not appear if you upgrade over a current Windows 3.x directory, but you will see how to get this option back in the section "Have Your Cake and Eat It, Too!" later in this chapter.)*

Drawbacks of Dual-Boot Installation

The disadvantage for most users of a clean dual-boot installation is that existing Windows 3.x program groups and application settings don't migrate to Windows 98.

To run your Windows 3.x programs under both operating systems, you'll need to reinstall them under Windows 98. Furthermore, you may have to install multiple copies of some programs in separate directories to get them to work properly under both Windows 98 and Windows 3.1. This is time consuming, and it's also a waste of disk space.

The recommended way to upgrade a computer to Windows 98 from Windows 3.x is to install the new operating system over the existing version of Windows. You'll be able to run most of your older programs in the new environment, and your program groups and application settings are migrated automatically.

What you lose in a standard upgrade is the ability to switch back and forth to your previous versions of DOS and Windows. Unless you're a computer journalist, software tester, or tech support agent, you probably won't miss this option. Windows 98 includes an Uninstall feature for users who discover that they really want to pull the plug. You can wipe out the new operating system and bring back the old one with 99 percent internal integrity. (If you select the Uninstall option during Windows 98 setup, you will need approximately 50MB of additional disk storage space.)

Windows 98 and Windows 95

In general, you won't want to install Windows 98 into a clean directory on a computer that's already running Windows 95. While it is possible to have Windows 95 and Windows 98 coexist on the same hard disk, Microsoft doesn't recommend it: The new operating system is meant to replace the old one. (If you're a software tester, computer trainer, or tech support agent who really wants both systems on a single hard disk, see "Have Your Cake and Eat It, Too!" to learn how to achieve this.)

Windows 98 and Windows NT

You can install Windows 98 on a computer that's already running Windows NT 3.51 or 4.0 (or on a computer that currently dual-boots Windows NT with DOS, Windows 3.x, or Windows 95). System administrators with limited hardware resources may want to dual-boot Windows 98 and Windows NT to let a single computer pinch-hit as a server, workstation, or training tool. Programmers and technical support agencies may want to set up a dual-boot environment for product-compatibility testing.

The easiest way to make Windows 98 and Windows NT coexist on a single computer is to create two FAT16 disk partitions under DOS. Install Windows 98 on the first partition. After Windows 98 has been installed, hold down the CTRL key and boot to a real DOS prompt. Then install Windows NT on the second partition with the Boot to DOS option enabled. When you reboot the computer, the Windows NT boot manager appears. If you select the Boot to DOS option, the system will start under Windows 98.

If you install Windows 98 on a computer *after* Windows NT is installed, you'll need to reenable Windows NT's Boot Sector manager to toggle between operating systems. See Appendix A for details.

Windows 98 and Warp OS/2

To make Windows 98 coexist with Warp OS/2, it's generally best to have the two operating systems reside on separate disk partitions. This prevents conflicts that can arise from the systems' different approaches to storing long filenames. If you have OS/2 on your computer and attempt to install Windows 98, you'll see some warning messages from Win98 Setup. The messages warn that your OS/2 functionality may be lost. *Provided you install Windows 98 into a separate disk partition,* it's safe to ignore these messages.

Installing Windows 98 deactivates the OS/2 Boot Manager partition. Instead, the system will boot directly into Windows 98 from your primary drive C partition. To restore the OS/2 Boot Manager, run FDISK (located in the \WINDOWS\COMMAND directory) from within Windows 98. You'll see Boot Manager listed on the FDISK screen as a non-DOS partition. To restore Boot Manager (and regain the ability to start OS/2), change the active partition from drive C to the Boot Manager partition.

Have Your Cake and Eat It, Too!

This section is for those programmers, computer trainers, and tech support agents mentioned earlier. It describes some additional tricks and installation options for Windows 98 that Microsoft doesn't publicize:

- You can duplicate an existing Windows 3.x directory on another drive or directory on your hard disk and then upgrade to Windows 98 in the clone directory. A simple trick, described in the next section, lets you preserve the Previous Version Of DOS option. This lets you run existing Windows 3.x applications from both operating systems and also retains your old copy of DOS.
- You can switch between Windows 98 and Windows 95 on a single computer by placing the two operating systems on two primary partitions. (They can be FAT16 or FAT32 partitions.) This is accomplished by using a third-party utility such as PowerQuest's Partition Magic or Quarterdeck's Partition-It to create an additional primary partition on your hard disk. (Microsoft's FDISK does not support this option.)

Quarterdeck's Remove-It 98: The Easy Way to Clone Windows 3.x

Quarterdeck's Remove-It 98 utility includes a Windows 95/98 version and a Windows 3.x version in the same box. In addition to functioning as a program uninstaller and application migration tool, Remove-It includes an Upgrade Assistant utility that transfers an existing Windows 3.x configuration to a clean copy of Windows 98 in a separate directory (see Figure 2-1). Upgrade Assistant runs under Windows 3.x, taking a snapshot of your .INI files, program groups, system registry, and application settings. Once this snapshot has been taken, you can use it at any time to migrate Windows 3.1 configuration information to a "plain vanilla" installation of Windows 98.

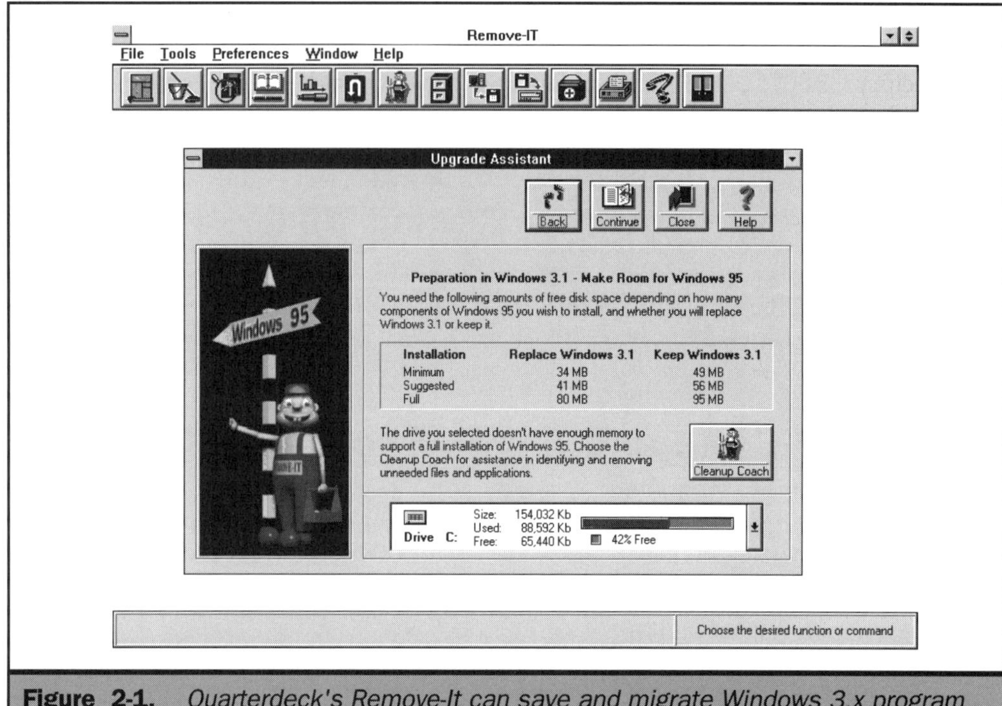

Figure 2-1. *Quarterdeck's Remove-It can save and migrate Windows 3.x program settings to a clean Windows 98 configuration*

Here's how you can use this utility in the Win98 installation process:

1. Install and run Remove-It under Windows 3.x. The Clean-Up Coach feature can be used to archive or remove any unnecessary applications or extra files on your hard disk to free up storage space. The Upgrade Assistant component of Remove-It takes a snapshot of your Windows 3.1 system configuration.
2. After you've taken a configuration snapshot, exit to DOS and run the Windows 98 Setup program. When you're prompted for an installation directory, specify a directory other than the current \WINDOWS directory. A clean copy of Windows 98 will be installed in the directory you specify. Your Windows 3.x program groups and application settings are not migrated at this point.
3. After your computer has restarted in Windows 98, open My Computer or Explorer and run the Upgrade Assistant utility again. (Open the REMOVEIT directory that was installed under Windows 3.x and double-click RTUPGR.EXE.)
4. Follow the on-screen instructions to migrate your Win 3.x program configuration to Windows 98.

To run your old copy of Windows 3.1, hold down the CTRL key at boot time and choose Previous Version Of DOS from the Windows 98 Startup menu. Then change to the directory that contains your old version of Windows and enter **WIN** at the command prompt. To run Windows 98, just restart the computer and let it boot straight through to the Windows 98 desktop.

The Do-It-Yourself Method for Cloning Windows 3.x

You don't have to buy a third-party application to keep a working copy of Windows 3.x and migrate concurrently to Windows 98. It's possible to clone Windows 3.x and upgrade the original directory to Windows 95 without using third-party tools. This procedure is a bit tedious, but it can come in handy for maintaining a dual-compatibility work environment. Here's how to do it:

1. Before installing Windows 98, exit Windows 3.x to a DOS command prompt. Use the DOS XCOPY command to duplicate your current Windows directory on another partition or in another directory on the same partition. Here's an example:

   ```
   XCOPY C:\WINDOWS\*.* D:\WIN98\*.* /E /V
   ```

   Be sure to append the /E and /V switches to include all subdirectories.

Note *You can clone your Windows 3.1 directory by "XCOPYing" it to a new directory on the same partition, but if you have two partitions defined on your system, it will simplify things to have one version of Windows that corresponds to each drive letter.*

2. Back up your current DOS directory. The Windows 98 installation program is going to think this is an Upgrade installation and eliminate most of its contents. So you'll want to restore the files later on. Here's an example of how to do it:

   ```
   MD C:\DOSBAK
   XCOPY C:\DOS\*.* C:\DOSBAK\*.* /E /V
   ```

3. Back up your AUTOEXEC.BAT and CONFIG.SYS files. For example:

   ```
   COPY C:\CONFIG.SYS CONFIG.W31
   COPY C:\AUTOEXEC.BAT C:\AUTOEXEC.W31
   ```

   You'll need these original versions later when you want to dual-boot to your pre-Win98 configuration.

4. Edit your AUTOEXEC.BAT and CONFIG.SYS files to change all references to your current \WINDOWS directory to the directory name that will be used by Windows 98, such as \WIN98. This will ensure that the Windows 98 installation routine locates and updates the proper files. Here are some examples:

- Change DEVICE=C:\WINDOWS\IFSHLP.SYS to DEVICE=D:\WIN98\IFSHLP.SYS.
- Change PATH=C:\DOS;C:\WINDOWS to PATH=D:\WIN98.

5. Edit all files with the .INI extension in the newly cloned \WIN98 directory. Change all references from your old \WINDOWS directory to the drive and directory that will contain Windows 98. This is, perhaps, the trickiest step in this procedure. It is necessary so that your application settings and program groups will migrate correctly. The following command issued from the DOS prompt or in a batch file will successively open each .INI file in the DOS text editor, allowing you to globally substitute the name of your new \WIN98 directory for your old \WINDOWS directory:

   ```
   FOR %A IN (D:\WIN98\*.INI) DO EDIT %A
   ```

   In this example, D:\WIN98 is the name chosen for the directory that will contain Windows 98. You may substitute the drive and directory you've chosen. The DOS editor will open to the first .INI file in the directory.
6. Use the Replace function on the Search menu to enter the name of your original Windows directory on the Find What line and the name of your proposed Windows 98 directory on the Replace With line. For example:

   Find What: **C:\WINDOWS**

   Replace With: **D:\WIN98**
7. After the global replacement has been made, save the file and exit the DOS editor. It will automatically restart with the next .INI file loaded. Repeat the global replace procedure until all of the .INI files have been updated.
8. Reboot your PC so that CONFIG.SYS and AUTOEXEC.BAT now point to the cloned Windows directory. Start the cloned version of Windows that now resides in the \WIN98 directory. You should be able to do this simply by changing to the \WIN98 directory and entering **WIN** at the command prompt.
9. Inspect and edit your Program Manager icons. This step is optional. Generally, most of the applets in your Accessories folder will have Properties settings that simply list the program name with no path or directory specified. However, if you have other applications residing in the \WINDOWS directory identified by drive and path, you may need to edit the properties for their icons to change the reference to your new \WIN98 directory. Select the icon and click Properties on the Program Manager File menu. Change references in the Command Line and Working Directory boxes as necessary. Look for any icons that you know represent Windows applications but which now show an MS-DOS icon (there may not be any). You can also perform this step after Windows 98 has been installed if you're in a hurry.

10. Edit the Windows system registry to update directory references. This step is necessary so that OLE servers and clients will function properly for the various Windows 3.1 applications that will be migrated to the new operating environment. Open REGEDIT in verbose mode by entering **REGEDIT.EXE /V** in the Program Manager File | Run screen. You will have to scroll through the database manually, searching for references to your original Windows directory. When you find one, click it and change the reference to your new Windows directory. (When you click a key, it will appear in the Value window toward the top of the screen. You can click the text in this window and edit it.) When you've replaced all instances of C:\WINDOWS with D:\WIN98 (or the drive and directory names that apply to your system), exit REGEDIT.
11. You're now ready to run the Windows 98 Setup program from the Program Manager File | Run menu to install Windows 98. When you are prompted for an installation directory, make sure Setup is pointed to the cloned directory you've created. (See Chapter 3 for detailed information about the installation process.)
12. After Windows 98 is installed, you will need to perform a few mop-up maneuvers to make sure that the dual-boot option works properly. (This is because the installation program now thinks that you've upgraded your only copy of Windows. It is unaware of the original copy that still resides on your hard disk.) To start, restore your original DOS directory from the backup you made in step 2.
13. Copy the pre-Win98 backups of AUTOEXEC.BAT and CONFIG.SYS that you made to the filenames that Windows 98 uses for its dual boot option:

```
COPY C:\CONFIG.W31 C:\CONFIG.DOS
COPY C:\AUTOEXEC.W31 C:\AUTOEXEC.DOS
```

14. Enable the Dual Boot option in MSDOS.SYS. From Windows 98, open a DOS command prompt and issue the command ATTRIB -R -H C:\MSDOS.SYS. Next, open MSDOS.SYS in a text editor (such as Notepad or the MS-DOS Editor) and add the following command under the [Options] section of the file:

```
BOOTMULTI=1
```

These steps should make your migrated Windows 3.1 applications 99.5 percent compatible with the new Windows 98 operating environment. To obtain 100 percent compatibility for some applications, you may need to modify the registration information the application stores in its default directory. For instance, Microsoft Word for Windows version 6 refers to a file called SETUP.STF located in the WINWORD directory (or in the MSOFFICE\SETUP directory, if you're using the complete MS Office suite).

You can open SETUP.STF in the DOS Editor and perform a global search-and-replace operation to substitute the name of your Windows 98 directory for the name of your previous Windows 3.x directory. If you do this, you may experience some minor problems with the OLE Server function when you run your Office applications from your original Windows 3.x configuration. This is usually no worse than having to open an application manually or specify path information if an OLE error message pops up when you attempt to automatically launch an application by double-clicking an embedded OLE object.

Dual-Booting Windows 98 and Windows 95

The best way to install a dual-boot configuration for Windows 98 and Windows 95 is to split your hard disk into two primary partitions. You can't do this with the FDISK utility supplied with DOS or Windows 98, but you can do it with a third-party partitioning utility such as PowerQuest's Partition Magic, V-Communications' System Commander, or Quarterdeck's Partition-It.

Once you've created a second primary partition on your hard disk, you can copy your existing Windows 95 configuration onto it. Upgrade one partition to Windows 98, and leave the other partition alone. This lets you toggle the active boot partition between the two operating systems and set up a bulletproof dual-boot configuration:

1. If Windows 95 is installed on drive C, use your partitioning utility to create an additional primary partition. You can do this with either FAT16 or FAT32 disk partitions. (Leave drive C as the active boot partition.)
2. Boot to the Windows 95 desktop. Because of the way Windows 95 works, the second partition should appear as drive D.
3. Clone your existing Windows 95 partition from drive C to drive D. Open a DOS command prompt within Windows 95 and issue this command:

   ```
   XCOPY /E /H /R /C C:\*.* D:
   ```

4. Now upgrade your original partition to Windows 98.

After Windows 98 is active on the computer, you can return to Windows 95 by holding down the CTRL key to boot to MS-DOS. Then run your partitioning utility (or DOS FDISK) and set the second partition as the active boot partition. To return to Windows 98, reset the first partition as the active boot partition (as shown in Figure 2-2).

Installing Windows 98 from Scratch

If you've purchased the full version of Windows 98, you can install it on a new hard disk that contains no other operating system. You might want to do this if you've just purchased a new hard disk or if you're a power user who's assembled a new computer. Here's a quick outline of how to proceed:

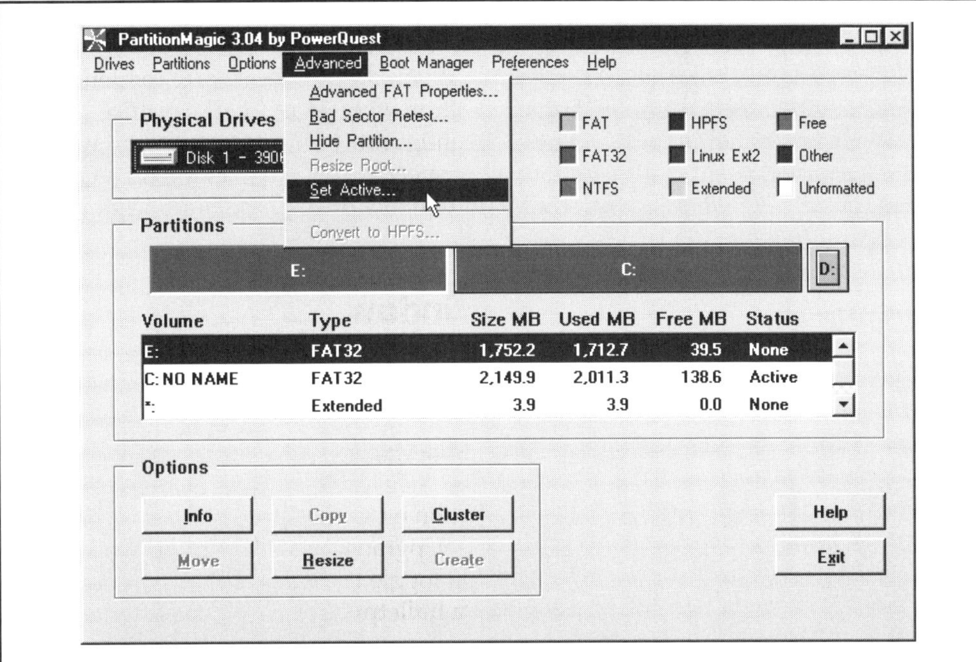

Figure 2-2. *PowerQuest's Partition Magic can toggle the active boot partition to switch between Windows 98 and Windows 95*

1. Boot the computer with a Windows 98 Emergency Boot Disk. (See the section "Creating an Emergency Boot Disk" earlier in this chapter. Partition and format the hard disk with the FDISK and FORMAT utilities. For help with these commands, refer to your MS-DOS, Windows 95, or Windows 98 documentation.
2. Install the necessary drivers to log onto a network or recognize the CD-ROM drive on the hard disk.
3. Copy the Windows 98 installation files to the hard disk over a network or insert the CD in your CD-ROM drive.
4. Run Setup and perform the installation.

Now You're Ready to Run Setup

This chapter has given you the information you need to prepare your computer for the jump to Windows 98. Chapter 3 provides a step-by-step overview of the Windows 98 installation process. It shows you how to run Win98 SETUP from different media (or over a network), provides a pre-installation checklist, and takes you through all of the setup option prompts with strategic recommendations. Chapters 4, 5, 6, and 8 provide supplementary information to help you make a smooth transition to Windows 98 from your current software and hardware configuration. Chapter 4 is an introduction to using the Win98 desktop interface. Chapters 5 and 6 provide a guide to Windows 98 productivity accessories and system utilities. Chapter 8 contains detailed information about system maintenance: optimizing and backing up your hard disk, virus prevention, working with the Windows 98 Registry, and emergency recovery procedures.

Chapter 3

Installing Windows 98

Chapter Highlights

Before you begin:

- What's new since Win95
- A pre-installation checklist
- Installing from different media
- New upgrade (from DOS) versus upgrading from Windows 3.x or Windows 95

The installation:

- Preparing to run Windows 98 Setup
  - Setup command-line options
- Collecting information about your computer
  - Installation types and selecting components
- Copying Windows 98 files to your computer
- Windows 98 directories
- Restarting your computer
- Setting up hardware and finalizing settings

Post-installation checklist

Here's a welcome fact about Windows 98: The operating system may have become more complex, but the installation process has become easier. Chances are good that Windows 98 will automatically find and configure your computer's CD-ROM drive, high-res video card, network adapter, or SCSI card. If you start your installation from a network drive, Windows 98 will probably maintain your connections. The need to run third-party software and studiously insert driver disks has been largely eliminated.

This chapter walks you through the Windows 98 setup procedure. You'll find out about the different media on which Win98 is distributed: how to install from floppies, from a CD-ROM, from your hard disk, or even across a network. This chapter presents step-by-step documentation of the installation process, with discussions of the various screen options that pop up along the way. You'll learn how to respond to various prompts that request information or offer instructions for your individual computer. You'll also find information about how to resolve problems and coax the setup process to continue if it prematurely aborts.

If your computer was pre-shipped with Windows 98 already installed, you may want to skip the bulk of this chapter, but check out the "Welcome to Windows!" section near the end. This section contains post-Setup tips for testing installed components and configuring useful system features. Sophisticated users who've already encountered system hang problems after Setup's first reboot may want to flip immediately to the section "Phase 5: Setting Up Hardware and Finalizing Settings" in this chapter for troubleshooting tips.

The good news is that Windows 98 setup is less likely to fail than its predecessors. The section "Getting Ready for Setup: A Pre-installation Checklist" in this chapter offers some tips that will help ensure a smooth Windows 98 upgrade process.

Before You Begin

If you're upgrading your computer from Windows 3.x, Windows for Workgroups, or Windows 95 and want to perform the "perfect" installation, I suggest reading (or at least skimming) Chapter 2 of this book before proceeding. Chapter 2 answers the question: Do I need to do anything to my computer before installing Windows 98? It contains a set of sensible tips designed to make your Win98 upgrade more bulletproof (for instance, it recommends disabling third-party memory managers, removing system maintenance TSRs from your Windows startup group, and shutting down open applications). Chapter 2 also provides information for people who want to preserve useful applications and system features that Windows 98 might otherwise wash away.

The good news is that Microsoft designed Windows 98 to upgrade a DOS, Windows 3.x, or Windows 95 system and retain most of the critical system settings. Win98 Setup will migrate your old DOS and Windows applications, preserve existing network connections and Microsoft Mail accounts, and recognize system hardware. Generally, it will also upgrade the drivers for previously installed peripherals.

If you're in a hurry, you may get away with just popping in the Win98 CD, starting Setup, and following the prompts. The next few sections in this chapter are designed for readers who want to know a little bit more about Windows 98 Setup before beginning an upgrade. A screen-by-screen description of the actual setup process begins in the section "Performing the Installation."

If you're a cautious user, read the SETUP.TXT file in the WIN98 directory on the Windows 98 installation CD before beginning a system upgrade. It contains instructions for finding and fixing hard disk problems, information about installing Windows 98 over other operating systems, and notes about the Win98 compatibility of hardware peripherals, complete computer systems, and older Windows utility software.

What's New in Windows 98 Setup?

Microsoft has done its best to make the Windows 98 installation easy and automatic. Windows 3.x Setup had inherent potential for chaos: The process might fail halfway through, leaving you with a computer unable to run either the old or the new operating system. This problem was addressed in Windows 95 by including a Safe Recovery feature. The new Safe Recovery feature saves your old configuration until the new one is in place. Furthermore, upgrades from earlier versions of Windows to Windows 98 are multitasking. If the need arises, you can open maintenance applications during the installation process or escape to DOS to format a floppy disk.

Users upgrading from Windows 3.x will find a number of new features in Windows 98 Setup: It will check your hard disk, detect your hardware peripherals, and prompt you to select an installation type. Windows 98 includes a number of new accessories and system components. By choosing an installation type, you can tell Setup to install the most common features, or you can select an installation tailored to a portable or minimal configuration. (More details on Win98 installation types are provided later in this chapter.)

If you're upgrading from Windows 95, you'll find that Windows 98 Setup is similar to its predecessor. These are the most significant changes in Setup from Windows 95 to Windows 98:

- Windows 98 postpones hardware detection until after the first reboot. Plug-and-play configuration doesn't start until after all basic system files have been copied to the hard disk and the system reboots to Windows 98. Legacy (non-plug-and-play) hardware is detected last, after all plug-and-play devices on the system have been found.
- A Windows 95 to Windows 98 upgrade is fairly transparent. Minimal user input is required to migrate system settings.
- Windows 98 handles file version conflicts differently than Windows 95. Instead of asking the user to make decisions about overwriting old files, Windows 98 automatically uses newer versions and backs up older versions elsewhere on the hard disk. (After Windows 98 is fully installed, the user is prompted when a newer file version tries to overwrite an older one.)

Getting Ready for Setup: A Pre-installation Checklist

The Windows 98 setup process can detect a wide number of hardware and software variations in computer systems. You'll be warned about potential conflicts in most cases, and the setup process will automatically correct itself. To facilitate a smooth installation and reduce the possibility of setup failure, study the following checklist before you begin:

1. Make sure your computer's hardware components meet the minimum requirements for running Windows 98. (Microsoft's SETUP.TXT and Chapter 2 of this book supply the information you need to know.)
2. Back up your critical data, third-party device drivers, and Internet and mail account information before attempting to install Windows 98.
3. If your computer is a network workstation or server, verify that the network software is running properly before beginning the installation. Windows 98 uses the existing network configuration to set up the new configuration.
4. Determine whether your installation will be an upgrade of Windows 3.1 or Windows for Workgroups, an upgrade of Windows 95, or a "clean installation" (copying Windows 98 into a brand new directory). See Chapter 2 for information about application and settings migration for each upgrade type. Chapter 2 also contains information about maintaining dual-boot options with other operating systems.
5. Check and defragment the partition that will contain the Windows 98 operating system.
6. Have a blank, formatted floppy disk at hand to insert when Windows 98 asks you to create an emergency boot disk.
7. Locate the driver disks supplied with network cards, hard drive controllers, video adapters, scanners, CD-ROM drives, and so on. These may not be needed, but it's a good idea to have them near at hand.
8. Before beginning the Win98 installation, remove all third-party memory managers, such as QEMM, NETROOM, or 386MAX. The best way to do this from within Windows 3.x is to load SYSEDIT and disable all references to these programs in CONFIG.SYS and AUTOEXEC.BAT with REM commands. (Restore the Microsoft DEVICE=HIMEM.SYS statement to CONFIG.SYS if you disable a third-party memory manager.)
9. Disable third-party disk cache programs and resident system utilities (optimizers, antivirus utilities, pop-up TSRs, and so on) that load under DOS.

10. Under Windows 3.x, inspect LOAD= and RUN= statements in WIN.INI and comment out pop-up utilities, screen savers, and so on. You may also want to turn 32-bit Disk Access off through the Control Panel's 386 applet—particularly if Windows is running on a large (greater than 512MB) disk partition.
11. Under Windows 3.x and Windows 95, clear the Startup group of disk maintenance, antivirus, Windows optimizer, system enhancer, watchdog, and troubleshooting utilities (Quarterdeck MagnaRAM, Connectix Agent 95/97, Helix Hurricane, CyberMedia First Aid, Vertisoft Name-It, and so on). Some—but not all—of these may be returned to the Startup group after the Windows 98 desktop appears.
12. If you have new peripherals to install (such as a modem or printer), it's best to plug them into your computer before issuing the Setup command and turn them on. Let Windows 98 do the configuration work!

Installing Windows 98 from Different Media

Most users who upgrade to Windows 98 will use an installation CD (compact disk) included in the operating system package. To upgrade a computer to Win98 through the installation CD, the computer's current operating system must recognize your CD-ROM drive.

Windows 98 is also distributed on 3.5-inch floppy disks. However, if possible, you should buy the CD version for convenience and faster installation. The CD version of the operating system also contains additional software such as the *Windows 98 Resource Kit*, extra driver support, video animations, and tutorials.

If you have a computer without a CD-ROM drive, you can install Windows 98 from floppy disks or use one of the following workarounds:

- Copy the Windows 98 installation files from the CD to your computer's hard disk through a network or cable connection. Then run Setup from the hard disk.
- Perform the Windows 98 installation through a mapped drive over a network.

Copying CD Installation Files to Your Computer's Hard Disk

To copy the Windows 98 setup files from the CD, create a directory called WIN98 on the hard disk. You'll need approximately 165MB of disk space to store the installation files for a complete Windows 98 setup. You can shrink this to 101MB by omitting Online Service, Web Channels, and Windows 98 Tour support.

To transfer all of the installation files from the CD under Windows, select the WIN98 folder on the CD (use the Windows 3.x File Manager or Windows 95 Explorer) and drag it to the hard disk as shown next.

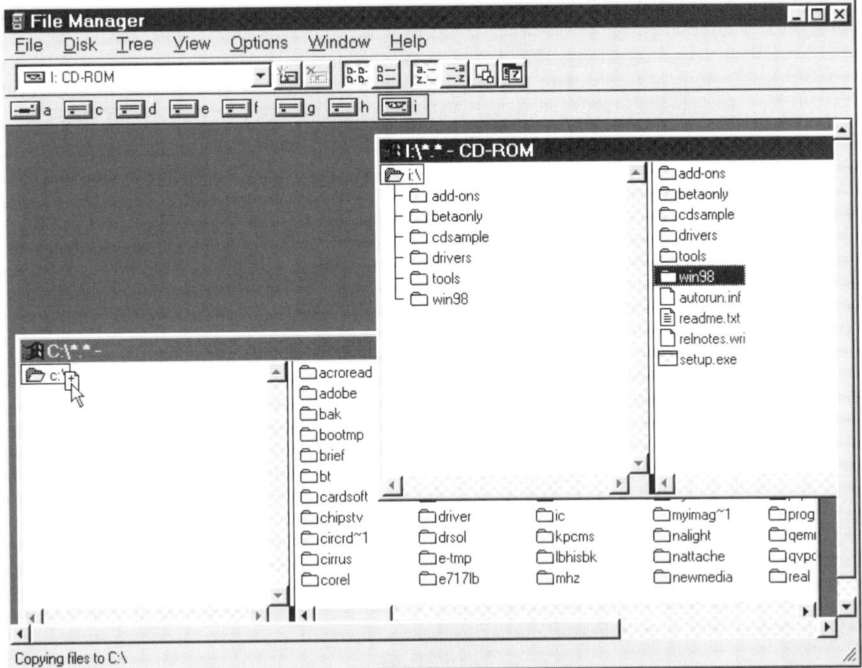

To transfer all of the installation files from the CD under DOS, enter the DOS XCOPY command **XCOPY *d*:\WIN98*.* *c*:\WIN98 /s**, where *d*: is the CD-ROM drive and *c*: is a local disk partition. (If you have more than one disk partition, you can transfer the files to any drive letter.) To perform a basic installation (without Online Services, Subscription Channels, and Windows 98 Tour), you can omit copying the Channels, Content, OLS, and Tour subdirectories from the CD.

Copying Floppy Disk Installation Files to Your Computer's Hard Disk

To copy the Windows 98 installation files from a set of 3.5-inch floppy disks to a hard disk directory, insert each of the disks in turn into the floppy drive and COPY *.* to a WIN98 directory on your hard drive. Once the installation files have been copied, you can run SETUP.EXE under DOS, Windows 3.x, or Windows 95 from the local hard disk directory.

Note *If you have difficulty copying the disks with the DOS COPY command, then copy the EXTRACT command (found on disk 1) to your hard drive and run it on each of the other installation diskettes with the following syntax:*
EXTRACT /C A:.* d:\WIN98*

Copying CD Installation Files to a Computer Without a CD-ROM Drive

To copy the CD installation files to a computer that doesn't have a CD-ROM drive, you need to give the target computer access to a computer with a CD-ROM drive through a Microsoft or Novell network or through a cable connection. Then copy the WIN98 installation directory from the CD to the target machine's hard disk (as described in the previous section). After copying the installation files, you can run Windows 98 Setup from your hard disk under DOS, Windows 3.x, or Windows 95.

Installing Windows 98 over a Network

You can perform the Windows 98 installation over a mapped network drive on a Microsoft or Novell network. The easiest way to do this is to share a CD-ROM drive on an available server and then insert the Win98 installation CD in that computer and map its CD-ROM drive to a local drive letter on the target computer.

Note *When installing from a local hard disk directory or a mapped network drive, you should run Windows 98 Setup from a directory named WIN98.*

Performing the Installation

If you're upgrading to Windows 98 from a previous version of Windows, close all applications other than Windows 3.x Program Manager or Windows 95 Explorer before running Setup. Should you discover that you need to create space on your hard disk or format a floppy disk after the installation has begun, Setup lets you launch applications or open a DOS session to make last-minute system modifications.

When Setup begins, the opening screen informs you that the process will take from 30 to 60 minutes, depending on the number and types of selected options. This estimate may not be completely reliable! A long, drawn-out installation could be a warning that Windows 98 will deliver poor performance on outdated hardware.

The Windows 98 setup procedure is divided into five phases:

1. Preparing to run Windows 98 Setup
2. Collecting information about your computer
3. Copying Windows 98 files to your computer
4. Restarting your computer
5. Setting up hardware and finalizing settings

This chapter describes each of these phases in detail.

Windows 98 reboots your computer at least two times before the desktop appears to complete the installation. Some computers may reboot an additional one or two times as plug-and-play peripherals are detected and video or disk drivers are updated.

To begin a Windows 98 installation, you need to locate and run the SETUP.EXE file on your CD-ROM, local server or network, or floppy disk drive. Setup can be executed from an MS-DOS prompt, from an existing copy of Windows 3.x, or from Windows 95.

Locating and Launching Setup

Here are some follow-the-dots instructions for locating and launching the Setup program for each upgrade scenario. If you already know how to do this, you can skip this section and proceed to the section "Phase 1: Preparing to Run Windows 98 Setup."

Starting Windows 98 Setup from Windows 95

Here's how to start Windows 98 Setup from Windows 95:

1. Start your computer in the usual way and run Windows 95.
2. Disable TSRs and close all applications (as outlined in the section "Getting Ready for Setup: A Pre-installation Checklist").
3. Do one of the following:
    - If you're installing from the CD, insert the Windows 98 CD in your CD-ROM drive. If auto-insert notification is turned on, you'll be prompted to start the Windows 98 installation. Otherwise, open the CD in My Computer or Windows Explorer and launch SETUP.EXE.
    - If you've copied the installation files to your hard disk, choose Start | Run and enter ***d*:\WIN98\SETUP.EXE**.
    - If you are installing Windows 98 from a set of disks, insert disk 1 in drive A, choose Start | Run and enter **A:\SETUP.EXE**.

Starting Windows 98 Setup from Windows 3.1 or Windows for Workgroups

If you're starting Windows 98 Setup from Windows 3.1 or Windows for Workgroups, follow these steps:

1. Start your computer in the usual way and run Windows.
2. Disable TSRs and close all applications (as outlined in the section "Getting Ready for Setup: A Pre-installation Checklist").

3. Do one of the following:

   - If you're installing from the CD, insert the Windows 98 CD in your CD-ROM drive. Open the CD in File Manager and launch SETUP.EXE.
   - If you've copied the installation files to your hard disk, choose File | Run in the Program Manager or File Manager and enter ***d*:\WIN98\SETUP.EXE**.
   - If you are installing Windows 98 from floppy disks, insert disk 1 in drive A, choose File | Run in the Program Manager or File Manager and enter **A:\SETUP.EXE**.

Starting Windows 98 Setup from MS-DOS

Start Windows 98 Setup from MS-DOS as follows:

1. Start your computer in the usual way.
2. Disable TSRs (as outlined in the section "Getting Ready for Setup: A Pre-installation Checklist").
3. Do one of the following:

   - If you're installing from the CD, insert the Windows 98 CD in your CD-ROM drive. On the DOS command line, enter ***d*:\SETUP.EXE**, where *d*: is the CD-ROM drive letter.
   - If you've copied the installation files to your hard disk, enter ***d*:\WIN98\SETUP.EXE** on the DOS command line.
   - If you are installing Windows 98 from floppy disks, insert disk 1 in drive A and enter **A:\SETUP>EXE** on the DOS command line.

Starting Windows 98 Setup from a Mapped Network Drive

If you're starting Windows 98 Setup from a mapped network drive, follow these steps:

1. Start your computer in the usual way. Log on to your network. Make sure the target computer has read access to the mapped network drive that contains the Win98 installation files. (For example, with Microsoft Networking under DOS, you might enter the command **NET USE D: \\SERVER\\WIN98**.)
2. Disable TSRs (as outlined in the section "Getting Ready for Setup: A Pre-installation Checklist").
3. If you are installing Windows 98 from CD, put the compact disc in the shared CD-ROM drive on the network server.
4. Use Windows Explorer (Windows 95) or File Manager (Windows 3.x) to locate and run SETUP.EXE from the mapped network drive. Under DOS, enter ***d*:\SETUP.EXE** on the command line, where *d*: is the mapped network drive.

Starting Windows 98 Setup from a Network Computer Using a Setup Script

If you want to install identical Windows 98 configurations on multiple network clients, you can construct a script file that automates the procedure by filling in responses at all user prompts. The Batch 98 utility (shown here) located in the \TOOLS\ADMIN\BATCH directory on the Windows 98 CD can assist you in creating setup scripts.

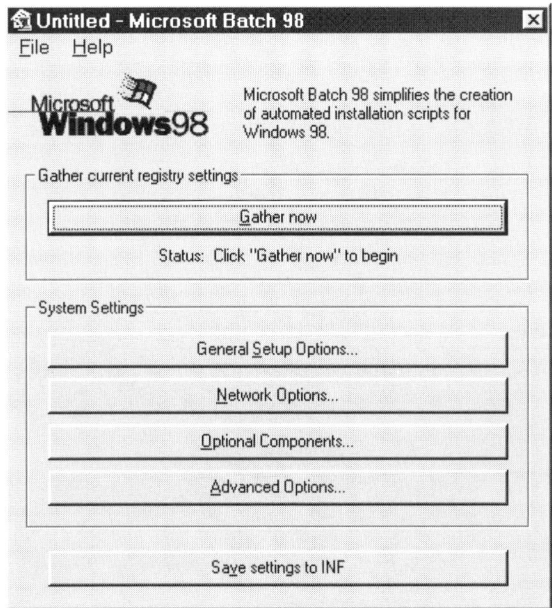

Once a script has been completed, you implement it as follows:

1. Log on to the network running the existing network client.
2. Connect to the server that contains the Windows 98 distribution files.
3. At the DOS command prompt, run Windows 98 Setup by specifying the batch file that contains the setup script. Use this syntax:

   SETUP *MSBATCH*.INF

For example, type **SETUP \\SERVER1\WIN98\SCRIPT1.INF** to run Setup using a script named Script1.inf, stored in the WIN98 directory on a server named Server1.

Phase 1: Preparing to Run Windows 98 Setup

The first phase of Windows 98 setup checks the integrity of your hard disk, asks for your assent to the license agreement, and allows you to specify where the operating system will be installed.

System Integrity (Disk) Check

The first Setup screen you may see is a warning if any conflicting processes have been detected that might interfere with Setup. If all is well, the Welcome screen shown in Figure 3-1 appears. (If you run Setup from DOS, ScanDisk performs a disk check and searches for an existing copy of Windows before the Welcome screen appears.)

The left side of the Welcome screen lists the five stages of the setup routine and a time estimate for the duration of the installation process. Click the Continue button in the Windows 98 Setup box to proceed.

If you are upgrading from within Windows, ScanDisk performs its disk integrity check at this point. It will flag and correct obvious disk errors before continuing the installation. If your hard disk passes the integrity check, Setup will scan your

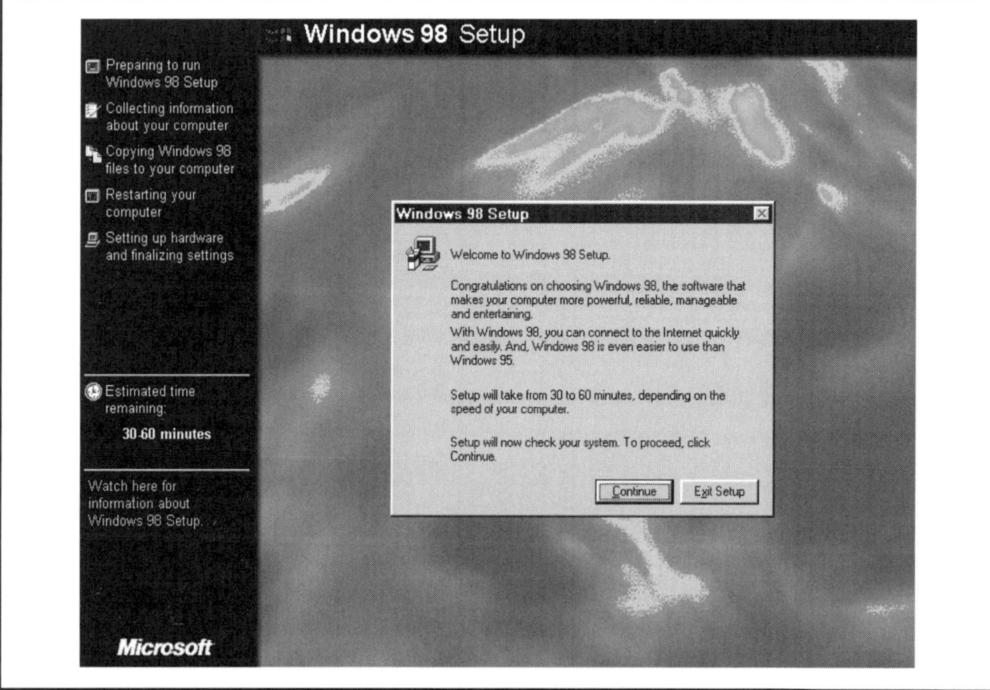

Figure 3-1. *Welcome to Windows 98 Setup*

computer for an existing WINDOWS directory and check the integrity of any existing Windows registry.

PROBLEMS WITH SYSTEM INTEGRITY (DISK) CHECK If your computer's hard disk passes a ScanDisk check under DOS but fails under the Windows interface, you can bypass the Windows disk check by running Setup with the /IS parameter (SETUP /IS).

The Win98 Setup program permits the use of command-line switches to troubleshoot various installation problems. These include the following:

/?	Provide help on the syntax and use of Setup command-line switches
/c	Instruct Windows 98 Setup not to load the SmartDrive disk cache
/d	Instruct Windows 98 Setup not to use the existing version of Windows for the early phases of Setup. Use this switch if, when starting Setup, you have problems that may be due to missing or damaged supporting files for Windows
/DOMAIN: *domain name*	Set the Windows NT domain used for logon validation by Client for Microsoft Networks
/f	Bypass the local cache when looking for filenames (slightly slower, saves some memory)
/ia	Turn off the "after providers" listed in the [AfterProvider] section of the SETUPC.INF file
/ib	Turn off the "before providers" listed in the [BeforeProvider] section of the SETUPC.INF file
/ic	Does a clean boot. If this option is set and KeepRMDrivers=1 is not in the registry, drivers are commented out in the CONFIG.SYS and AUTOEXEC.BAT
/id	Instruct Windows 98 Setup not to check for the minimum disk space required to install Windows 95
/ie	Skip the screen that prompts users to make a Startup disk
/if	Fast setup; skip check for filenames in cache
/ih	Run ScanDisk in the foreground so that users can see the results. Use this switch if the system stalls during the ScanDisk check or if an error results

/iL	Load the Logitech mouse driver. Use this option if you have a Logitech Series C mouse
/im	Bypass check for low conventional memory
/in	Bypass detection/configuration of network
/iq	Instruct Windows 98 Setup not to perform the ScanDisk quick check when running Setup from MS-DOS
/ir	Don't update the master boot record
/is	Bypass running ScanDisk
/nostart	Instruct Windows 98 Setup to copy a minimal installation of the required Windows 3.x DLLs used by Windows 98 Setup and then to exit to MS-DOS without installing Windows 98
/NA#	Don't notify user when other applications are running: #1 don't display warning message; #2 don't display error message for running MS-DOS; #3 don't display either message
/NF	Don't prompt to remove floppy disk at the end of Setup phase 3
/NH	Don't run HWINFO.EXE when installing from Win98 user interface
/NR	Skip registry check
/PI	Keep forced hardware configuration (present in some BIOS settings)
Script_file	Instruct Windows 98 Setup to use settings in the specified script to automatically install Windows 95. Use this option, for example, when MSBATCH.INF is used
/SRCDIR	Specify source directory where Win98 installation files are located
/S *filename*	Use specific SETUP.INF file during installation
/T:tempdir	Set a specific temporary directory for installation (must already exist on disk, all current files in it will be overwritten)

/U: *UPI*	Specify UPI
/IV	Bypass display of billboards
/IW	Bypass display of license screen
/IX	Skip character set check
/IY	Ignore language mismatches

Safe Recovery

If Windows 98 setup finds problems or terminates abnormally in the early stages, you can reboot your machine, run Setup again, and select the Safe Recovery option, shown here. Safe Recovery may allow Setup to continue and compensate for the problems encountered in the earlier attempt.

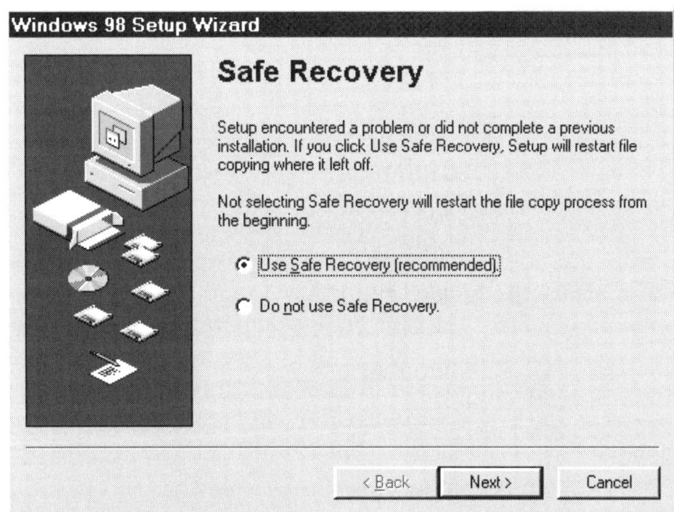

Phase 2: Collecting Information About Your Computer

In phase 2, Setup asks you to review the Windows 98 user license, enter identification information for the computer, and create an emergency startup disk. If this is a new installation or a Windows 3.x upgrade, you'll be prompted to select a directory for Windows 98 and choose which optional components you want activated.

Accepting the License Agreement

The next Setup screen you see displays the Windows 98 license agreement, as shown next. Most people just click the I Accept The Agreement button and then click Next to proceed. If you're curious as to exactly what you're agreeing to, you can scroll through the agreement.

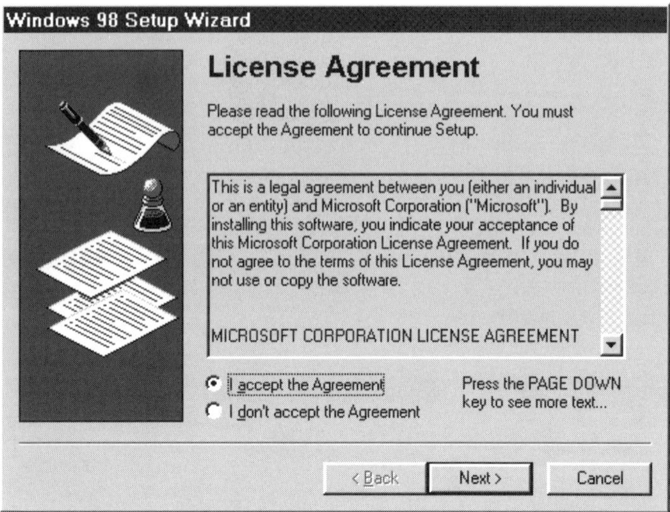

The multilingual license agreement forbids the illegal copying of software. Windows 98 is not copy protected. You will, however, be prompted to enter your product identification number, located on the label pasted to the CD case or on the OEM seal affixed to the user manual. The full version of Windows 98 can be installed on any machine running some version of the DOS operating system. The upgrade version must see files from a previously installed copy of Windows 3.x or Windows 95.

The Windows 98 license differs from the licenses that typically govern Microsoft's application software. If you buy a copy of Microsoft Word, for instance, you are within your rights to install it on every machine that you use. However, two people are *not* allowed to use the programs simultaneously.

The license agreement for Windows 98 specifies that the operating system be installed only on a single machine. So if you wish to upgrade both your laptop and your desktop machine to Windows 98, you are required to purchase two copies of the upgrade package.

To continue with the installation, you must click the I Accept The Agreement button and then click Next.

Entering the Product Identification Number

The Windows 98 Setup Product Identification screen, shown next, pops up next, asking you to enter a 25-digit serial number. You will find this number pasted onto the case for your CD-ROM, on the cover of your Windows 98 user manual, or enclosed with the floppy disk set.

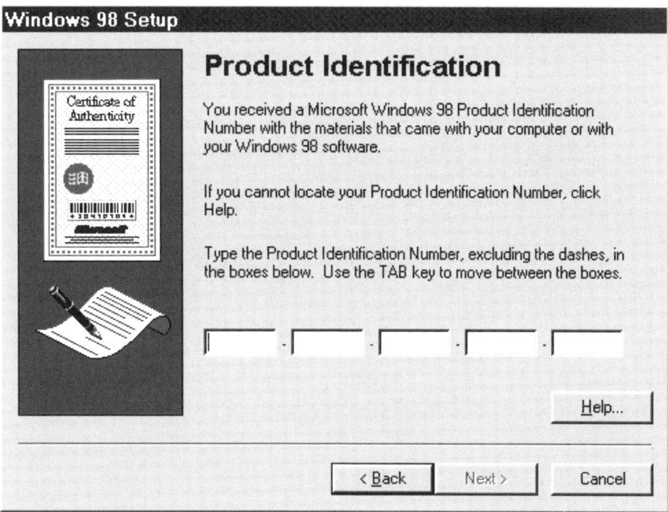

Selecting a Directory (Clean Installation and Windows 3.x Upgrade)

If you are upgrading from Windows 3.x or from the DOS command prompt, Setup presents the Select Directory screen shown here. The default specification will point to an existing Windows directory on the disk (or to C:\WINDOWS, if no Windows directory was found). If you are upgrading to Windows 98 from within Windows 95, this screen will not appear.

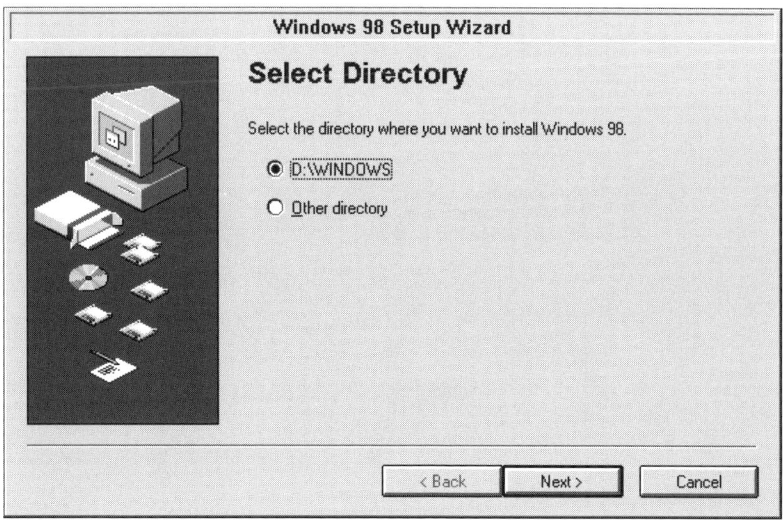

You can use the Other Directory option on this screen to specify an alternative location for Windows 98. You might want to do this to preserve an existing Windows 3.1 or Windows for Workgroups 3.11 configuration. (Preserving a separate Windows 95 directory on the same partition as Windows 98 is not recommended.)

To keep your Windows 3.x configuration, specify a Windows 98 directory on another partition or install to C:\WIN98 instead of to C:\WINDOWS.

If you place Windows 98 in a brand new directory, a dual-boot environment will be set up with your previous version of DOS and Windows 3.x. The disadvantage is that your current Windows 3.x applications and settings will not be migrated to Windows 98 (see Figure 3-2).

If you select a directory that contains a previous version of Windows, an upgrade installation will be performed. Your current Windows program groups and application settings will be migrated to Windows 98, and the old versions of Windows and DOS will be overwritten.

Checking Your System

Setup next checks the WINDOWS directory (if present) for installed components and determines whether there is enough space on your hard disk to continue the installation.

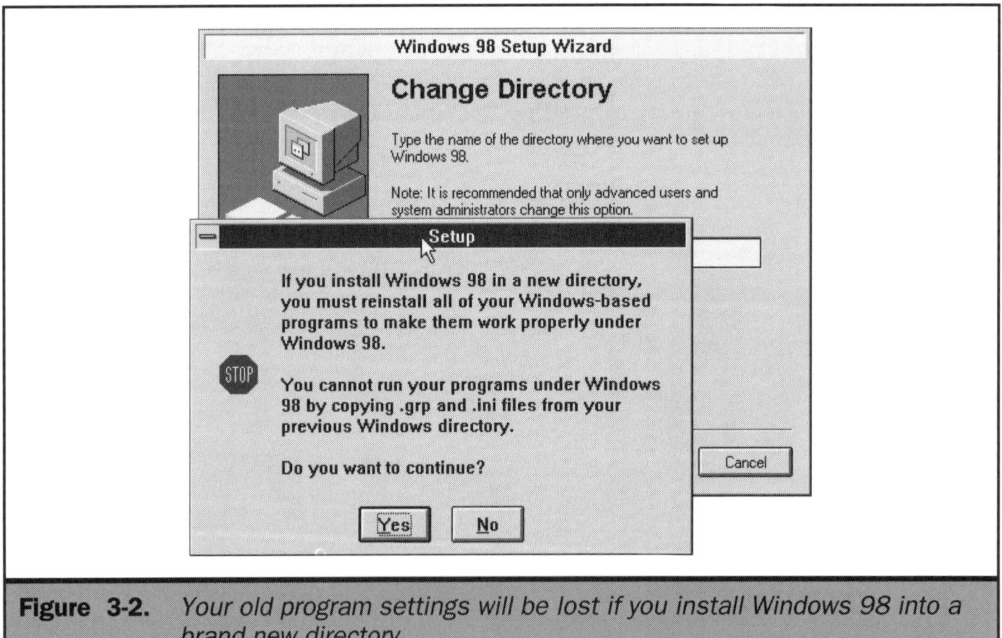

Figure 3-2. *Your old program settings will be lost if you install Windows 98 into a brand new directory*

What Happens to DOS?

Whether you decide to perform a new or an upgrade installation, Windows 98 will copy a few MS-DOS utilities into a new \WINDOWS\COMMAND directory on your hard disk. These utilities have been enhanced to work with the DOS command kernel that underlies Windows 98.

If you're upgrading Windows 3.x, the following MS-DOS utility files will be deleted from your old DOS directory:

DEFRAG.HLP
MWUNDEL.EXE
MWUNDEL.HLP
METWORKS.TXT
OS2.TXT

These MS-DOS utility files will be deleted from your old DOS directory with substitutes placed in the new \WINDOWS\COMMAND directory:

ANSI.SYS	EGA.CPI	MSCDEX.EXE
ATTRIB.EXE	EMM386.EXE	NLSFUNC.EXE
CHKDSK.EXE	FC.EXE	RAMDRIVE.SYS
CHOICE.COM	FDISK.EXE	README.TXT
COUNTRY.SYS	FIND.EXE	SCANDISK.EXE
DEBUG.EXE	FORMAT.COM	SCANDISK.INI
DEFRAG.EXE	KEYB.COM	SETVER.EXE
DELTREE.EXE	KEYBOARD.SYS	SHARE.EXE
DISKCOPY.COM	LABEL.EXE	SMARTDRV.EXE
DISPLAY.SYS	MEM.EXE	SORT.EXE
DOSKEY.COM	MODE.COM	SUBST.EXE
DRVSPACE.EXE	MORE.COM	SYS.COM
EDIT.COM	MOVE.EXE	XCOPY.EXE

If Setup determines that there is sufficient disk space available, it will present the next options screen (Save System Files, if you are upgrading a previous version of Windows, or Setup Options if this is a clean installation).

You must have approximately 125MB available on your boot drive (drive C) to contain the Win98 installation files. If there's not enough room, Setup will inform you. You will need to quit the installation, free up additional space on drive C, and begin again.

Additionally, there must be enough free disk space on the partition that will contain the Windows 98 operating system. If Setup thinks insufficient space is available, you'll see a message like the one shown here:

If this message appears, you will either need to free up space on the partition selected for Windows 98 or place Windows 98 in a new directory on a different drive. Miraculously, if you started Setup from within Windows, you can escape to DOS or bring up your previous Windows File Manager to delete files and create additional disk space.

Note *If you think you have enough disk space to install Windows 98, you can override the Not Enough Disk Space complaint by rerunning Setup with the following command-line switch:* ***SETUP /id****. You may want to do this if your current Windows 3.x or Windows 95 configuration occupies a large amount of disk space and you believe that Windows 98 will replace it without filling the entire disk.*

Responding to Messages About Other Operating Systems

If Windows 98 detects the presence of other operating systems on your hard disk, it may display a series of warning messages such as the ones shown here. If you have been using OS/2's Boot Manager, you can safely disregard warning messages SU-0010 and SU 0016 and click OK. After Windows 98 is installed, the OS/2 Boot Manager will be temporarily disabled, but you can easily reactivate it with the DOS FDISK utility. (For information on installing Windows 98 on a computer running Windows NT 3.5 or 4.0, see Chapter 2 and Appendix A.)

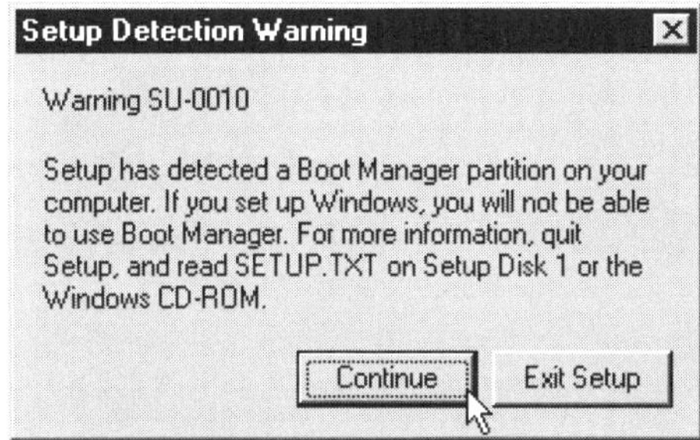

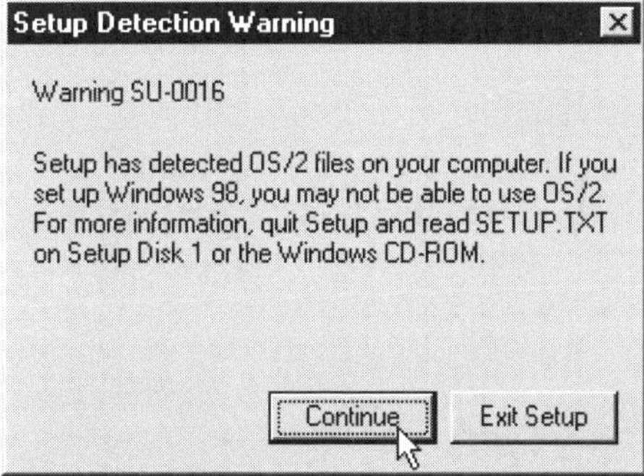

Saving System Files (Windows 3.x or Windows 95 Upgrade)

If you are installing Windows 98 over an existing copy of Windows 3.x (including Windows for Workgroups) or Windows 95, Setup will ask whether you want to save system files, as shown next. If you answer Yes, your existing Windows configuration will be archived and stored on disk. If you later decide that you want to uninstall

Windows 98, you will be able to restore the previous version of Windows. Typically, this option requires about 50MB of additional disk storage space.

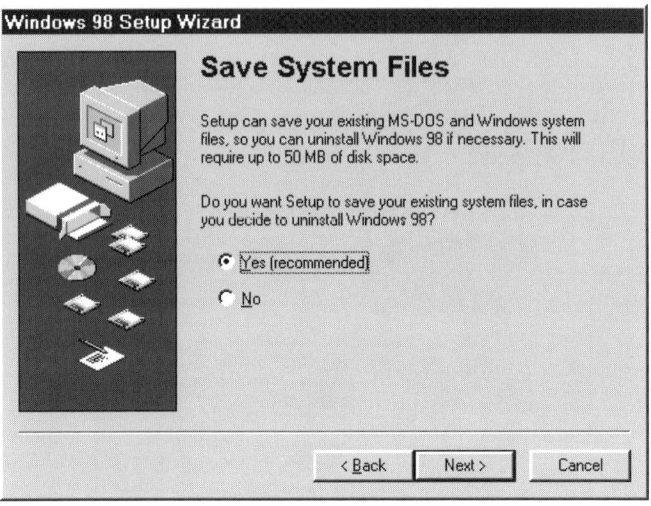

Note *If you started Setup from within Windows 3.x, but have chosen to install Windows 98 in a new directory, this option will not appear.*

Selecting Setup Options

If you are performing a clean installation of Windows 98 or upgrading from Windows 3.x, the Setup Options screen, shown here, will appear. You can select from four installation types: Typical, Portable, Compact, and Custom.

If you are performing a clean installation of Windows 98, a User Information screen pops up after you select the installation type. You can enter your user and company names on this screen for the purpose of registering your copy of Windows 98. If you are upgrading an older version of Windows, this screen does not appear.

When you select a Typical, Portable, or Compact installation, the Windows Components screen pops up next. Select Install the Most Common Components to continue Setup with a preconfigured selection list for each installation type. Selecting Show Me The List Of Components So I Can Choose displays the preconfigured selection for your installation type, permitting you to sort through it and add or remove individual items. (If you choose the Custom installation, the complete component list appears automatically.) I recommend choosing the Show Me The List option no matter which installation type you select. Even if you scan the list quickly without changing anything, you'll get a better idea of what's going to be installed and how much disk space will be used. In all cases, you can select the Details button on the Select Components screen, shown here, to learn more about a particular component and its importance to the system.

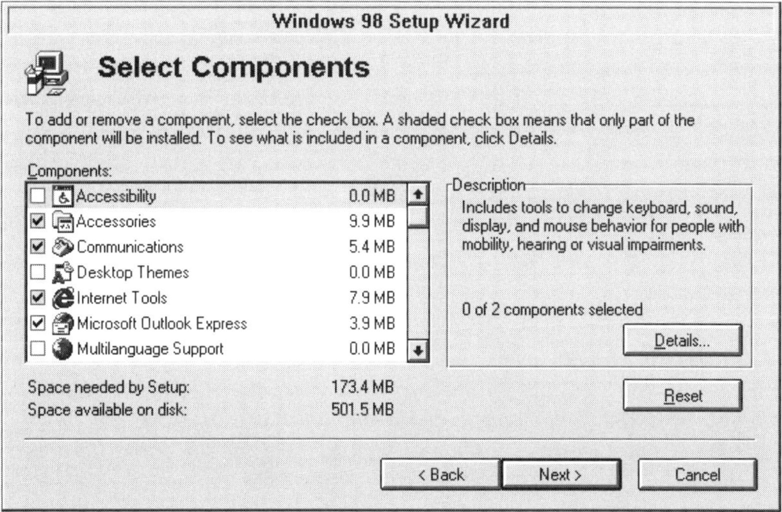

If you are unsure about the importance or usefulness of any component, you can easily reverse the decision to install or omit a feature by clicking the Back button at the bottom of each screen.

TYPICAL INSTALLATION The default installation type is Typical. This selection installs the basic Windows 98 operating system and the most frequently used optional components. When you choose Typical and click Next, Windows 98 asks whether you want to install the most common components or display a complete component list so you can choose the features you want. If you select the Install The Most Common

Components option, you should be aware that the following useful features are not installed:

- **QuickView File Filters** These filters allow you to view documents in several popular formats without loading them into their source applications.
- **Win98 Backup** This utility can archive files to most SCSI, IDE, and floppy-controller tape drives as well as to removable hard disk media and floppy disks.
- **Win98 Clipboard Viewer** This option allows you to inspect the contents of the Windows clipboard and save to disk.
- **HyperTerminal** You can use this communications program to establish modem-to-modem terminal connections, or direct connections through cable, or it can serve as a Telnet client over a TCP/IP network.
- **Direct Cable Connection** This option establishes a miniature peer-to-peer connection between two computers through serial or parallel port cables.

You can select these features in a Typical installation Install by choosing the Show Me The List option and placing check marks next to the ones you want. The Components list contains eleven categories or features. When you select a category with the mouse, the Details button becomes active if there are additional subcomponents. You can view the subcomponents in a category by clicking the Details button or double-clicking the category in the Components list. The Description box to the right of the Components list describes the function of the currently selected component and shows how many subcomponents have been selected. Categories that are only partially selected will display a check mark in a gray box. You can open these categories individually and place check marks next to the additional components you want.

Tip

To select an entire category with the fewest possible mouse clicks, deselect an existing check mark next to a gray box and reinsert the check mark again after it becomes blank. When you deselect a gray box, a message may warn you that key components will not be installed. Since you are going to immediately reselect the category, this doesn't matter.

PORTABLE INSTALLATION A Portable installation activates Win98 options specially designed for use with portable computers. This choice skips a number of desktop features, including the wallpaper, backup program, document templates, games, network tools, and applets like Calculator, Windows Imaging, and Paint. You do get the Briefcase utility, used to synchronize directories and files with another computer and the Direct Cable Connection feature. If you want to add more desktop components to the default Portable configuration, choose the Show Me The List option

COMPACT INSTALLATION Choosing Compact installs only the files necessary to run the basic Windows 98 operating system. This option should be used in instances when hard disk space is limited. The only auxiliary tools that are copied are disk utilities (Defrag, DriveSpace, the FAT32 converter, and ScanDisk). This is the absolute bare bones of Windows 98. It provides only what you need to run your programs with no frills whatsoever.

CUSTOM INSTALLATION If you select the Custom option, Setup goes directly to the itemized component list, allowing you to select any and all components. (The options checked by default are the same ones as in the Typical installation.) Custom is the best installation choice for power users and for those who want diagnostic information about the internal workings of Windows 98.

If Setup reports that there isn't enough room for the installation type you selected, you have two options:

- Select a different installation (Laptop or Compact).
- If you started the upgrade from within a previous version of Windows, press ALT-TAB go to the Program Manager or CTRL-ESC to go to the Start menu and run the File Manager or Windows Explorer, where you can then delete nonessential files from the hard disk. If you started the upgrade from DOS, you will have to quit Setup, delete nonessential files under DOS, and then restart Setup.

SHOW ME THE LIST OR CUSTOM INSTALLATIONS If you've selected the Show Me the List or Custom installation option, the Select Components screen appears, displaying the amount of disk space required for each component and the total disk space required for the Windows 98 installation. Note that even in a Custom installation, all of the features available under Windows 95 are not automatically selected. Table 3-1 summarizes the components in the various categories and the amount of memory each requires.

Entering Identification Information

On the Identification screen, shown here, Windows 98 asks you to enter a computer name, workgroup, and (optionally) workgroup description. This information will be

Component	Memory Required
Accessibility Options	4.7MB
Accessories	16.1MB
Calculator	0.2MB
Desktop Wallpaper	0.7MB
Document Templates	0.4MB
Games	0.6MB
Imaging	4.4MB
Mouse Pointers	0.5MB
Paint	2.5MB
QuickView	3.2MB
Screen Savers	1.3MB
Windows Scripting Host	1.2MB
WordPad	1.7MB
Communications	12.2MB
Dial-Up Networking	1.2MB
Dial-Up Server	0.1MB
Direct Cable Connection	0.5MB
HyperTerminal	0.8MB
Microsoft Chat 2.1	4.8MB
Microsoft NetMeeting	4.9MB
Phone Dialer	0.2MB
Virtual Private Networking	0.1MB
Desktop Themes	30.8MB
Internet Tools	12.6MB
Microsoft Frontpage Express	4.4MB
Microsoft VRML 2.0 Viewer	3.7MB
Microsoft Wallet	0.9MB
Personal Web Server	0.2MB
Real Audio Player	1.1MB
Web Publishing Wizard	1.1MB

Table 3-1. *Windows 98 Components and Memory Requirements*

Component	Memory Required
Web-Based Enterprise Management	1.3MB
Microsoft Outlook Express	5.3MB
Multilanguage Support	12.1MB
Multimedia	14.2MB
Audio Compression	0.2MB
CD Player	0.2MB
DVD Player	0.3MB
Macromedia Shockwave Director	1.7MB
Macromedia Shockwave Flash	0.2MB
Media Player	0.3MB
Microsoft Netshow Player 2.0	4.1MB
Multimedia Sound Schemes	6.1MB
Sample Sounds	0.6MB
Sound Recorder	0.2MB
Video Compression	0.5MB
Volume Control	0.2MB
Online Services	1.2MB
America Online	0.2MB
AT&T Worldnet Service	0.2MB
Compuserve	0.1MB
Prodigy Internet	0.8MB
The Microsoft Network	0.1MB
System Tools	6.1MB
Backup	5.2MB
Character Map	0.1MB
Clipboard Viewer	0.1MB
Drive Converter (FAT32)	0.4MB
Group Policies	0.0MB
Net Watcher	0.2MB

Table 3-1. *Windows 98 Components and Memory Requirements* (continued)

Component	Memory Required
System Monitor	0.2MB
System Resource Meter	0.1MB
WinPopup	0.1MB
WebTV for Windows	42.0MB
Broadcast Data Services	0.8MB
WaveTop Data Broadcasting	10.8MB
WebTV for Windows	30.4MB

Table 3-1. *Windows 98 Components and Memory Requirements* (continued)

used when you connect to the Internet or establish local network connections. (You can leave the Workgroup field at its default Workgroup setting.)

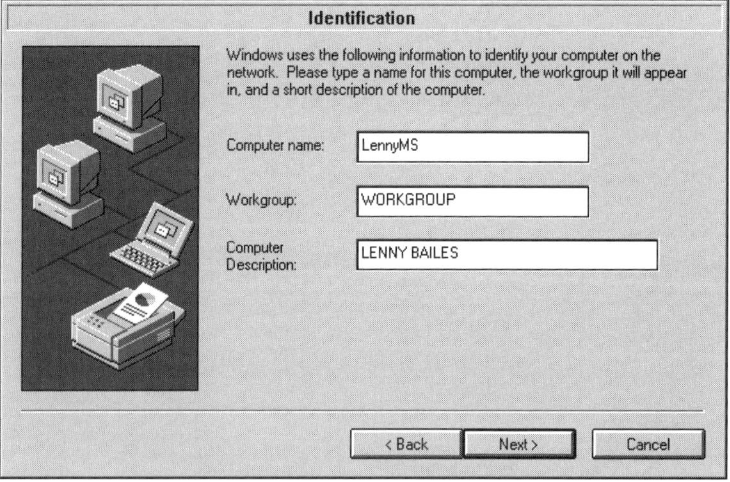

Selecting Internet Channels

Windows 98's channel subscription feature lets you gather region-specific news and information through the World Wide Web. On the Internet Channels screen, shown next, you can select the default local country or region to search.

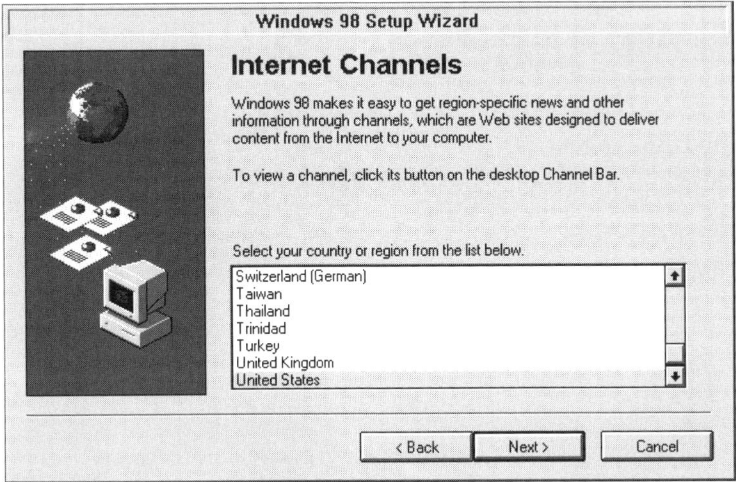

Creating a Startup Disk

The next screen prompts you to create a Windows 98 startup disk. You should always have a clean startup disk for your system. Later, if you experience problems loading Windows 98 from your hard disk, the emergency startup disk will allow you to boot from drive A and diagnose system problems. In Windows 98, the startup disk is prepared with DOS CD-ROM and SCSI drivers (if they can be found). It also contains ScanDisk and other diagnostic utilities in an archived format. When you boot from this diskette, it unpacks these files and provide a series of tools to let you correct system problems.

Windows 98 won't format a disk that it thinks contains Win95 installation files, so if you want to recycle an old beta disk, you will need to erase or reformat it prior to its reassignment as a startup disk.

If you've already created a Win98 startup disk for this computer, or if you want to skip this step for some other reason, click Next on the first Startup Disk screen and then click the Cancel button when the Insert Disk prompt appears, as shown here:

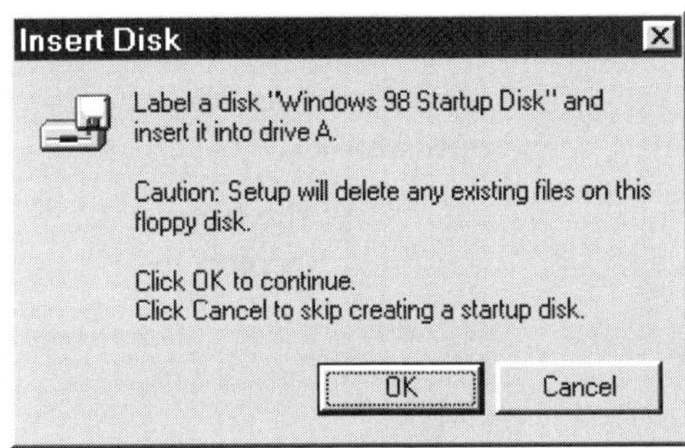

Phase 3: Copying Windows 98 Files to Your Computer

Phase 3 is the longest part of the installation. As soon as you click Next on the Start Copying Files screen, shown next, Windows 98 creates appropriate directories and copies operating system files to your hard disk. Depending on the installation type you chose (or the components that were active under Windows 95), the files for each Win98 module are installed. (Files for components you didn't select are not copied; see Chapter 9 for information on how to add these components later by choosing Control Panel | Add/Remove Programs.)

The Windows 98 Directories

Windows 98 creates the subdirectories listed here within the \WINDOWS directory on your hard disk. (Note that the terms "directories" and "folders" are used here interchangeably.)

Windows Directory/Folder	Default Contents
All Users	Contains information about Windows 98 user accounts created on this computer.
Application Data	Stores information for some Windows 98 applications.
CatRoot	Stores information about drivers for detected hardware devices.
Command	Stores MS-DOS commands for executing standard file functions.

Windows Directory/Folder	Default Contents
Config	Stores multimedia configuration information.
Cursors	Stores custom cursor programs with the suffix .ANI.
Desktop	Stores link (.LNK) files that control desktop shortcuts.
Downloaded Program Files	Hidden directory for temporary storage of downloaded Internet files.
DrWatson	Contains the Doctor Watson system diagnostic program.
Favorites	Stores Internet Explorer bookmarked Web sites.
Fonts	Stores all files for fonts installed on the system.
Help	Stores Help files for the operating system and installed programs.
History	Stores pointers to Web sites visited with Internet Explorer.
Inf	Stores information files used by Windows 98 to automatically configure hardware and plug-and-play devices.
Java	Stores Windows 98 Java support files.
Media	Stores multimedia sound and video files.
NetHood	Stores shortcuts created for Network Neighborhood.
Pif	Stores program information files used to run MS-DOS applications under Windows.
Recent	Stores links (.LNK) to the most recently used files across the system.
Samples	Stores files for sample Microsoft applications.
SendTo	Stores links used for sending files to various locations on the system (floppy drivers, networks, and the Briefcase).
Shellnew	Stores Windows 98 document templates.

Windows Directory/Folder	Default Contents
Spool	Stores temporary print files generated for installed output devices.
Start Menu	Stores links to all of the programs listed on the Start menu. Links are organized in directory and subdirectory style.
Sysbckup	Stores backup versions of all .DRV and .DLL files that are installed on the system.
Subscriptions	Stores information about Web sites subscribed to through Internet Explorer.
System	Stores drivers, viewers, and I/O subsystem files.
Temp	Stores temporary files created by Windows 98, many of which are automatically deleted when you quit the related application or shut down the operating system.
Temporary Internet Files	Temporarily caches Web sites visited with Internet Explorer.
Web	Stores Internet Explorer channel information.

Windows 98 creates a separate set of subdirectories under the Program Files folder. At the minimum, this hierarchy will contain support for installed Accessories and Internet Explorer features. Other contents will vary, depending upon the optional components you've installed.

Tip *If you decide that you want to change any configuration settings before starting the file copy phase of the installation, click the Back button.*

During the file copy phase, Windows 98 replaces the previous version of Windows (if it's located in the selected installation directory) and overwrites MS-DOS system files.

While File Copy Is In Progress

Generally, after the file copy sequence begins, you can leave your computer and do something else for at least 20 minutes. If you hang around to watch the screen, you'll be treated to a list of new Windows 98 features and other Microsoft wit and wisdom. This presentation is designed to whet your appetite for the new operating system.

Coincidentally, it may also alert you to the presence of some features that you didn't know about.

You can cancel the installation process at any time by pressing the on-screen Cancel button or the F3 function key. However, if you wait till the file copy phase to do this, your previous version of Windows will be unstartable. (If you selected the option to back up your previous Windows configuration, you can boot from a floppy disk and uninstall Windows 98 to revert to your previous operating system.)

Phase 4: Restarting Your Computer

When the file copy phase is complete, you will be prompted to reboot your computer. You may do this by clicking the Restart Now button or waiting for the system to reboot automatically.

If the restart process hangs at this point, you can press your computer's hardware reset button or turn the power off and on to force a system reboot.

Phase 5: Setting Up Hardware and Finalizing Settings

When your computer restarts, the Windows 98 hardware detection phase begins. If Setup is successfully restarted, it initializes the Windows 98 driver database and searches for plug-and-play hardware devices. This query process is more efficient and accurate if your PC has a plug-and-play BIOS, since all plug-and-play devices are registered and identified through a central registry.

In this first hardware detection phase, Windows detects and installs basic input/output peripherals: disk controllers, video adapters, and (if present) the PCI bus, PCI-to-ISA bridge, USB controller, and other system board extensions. Higher-function PNP peripherals such as modems, printers, scanners, and external USB hubs may not be configured until the second reboot.

Installing 32-Bit I/O Devices

If your computer has built-in support for PC cards, the PCMCIA Setup Wizard will appear to replace older, real-mode drivers with 32-bit Windows 98 equivalents. If Setup detects a network card or SCSI controller, it will ask whether Windows 98 is being installed over a network or from a CD-ROM drive connected to a SCSI controller. If you answer Yes, the Add New Hardware Wizard appears at this point. You can use Add New Hardware to install 32-bit Win98 drivers for PCMCIA, SCSI, USB, and IEEE 1394 controllers and network adapters. This allows Setup to continue without relying on older DOS or Windows 3.x drivers that were previously active.

You can find detailed information in Chapter 9 about selecting and installing component drivers with Add New Hardware.

If Win98 Setup Fails to Resume

Windows Setup will sometimes fail to resume after the first system reboot. All of the basic operating system files have been copied to the hard disk, but device drivers left over from the previous operating system may be causing conflicts.

Problems with Old Device Drivers and VXDs

If your computer hangs after Setup reboots the machine, try booting to a real-mode DOS prompt to inspect the contents of the CONFIG.SYS, AUTOEXEC.BAT, and WIN.INI system files. Here's how:

1. Press your computer's hardware reset button or toggle the power switch. Hold down the CTRL key as soon as the "Starting Windows 98" message appears on the screen and select Command Prompt Only from the Windows 98 Startup menu.
2. Open CONFIG.SYS in a text editor. (You can use the MS-DOS Edit program located in the \WINDOWS\COMMAND directory.) Remove any unnecessary driver statements such as those for third-party memory managers and disk cache utilities. If there are real-mode drivers loaded in CONFIG.SYS for PCMCIA services or for peripherals (such as a pointing device, scanner, digital camera, sound card, or network card), try deactivating these statements by prefixing them with REM statements.
3. Open AUTOEXEC.BAT in a text editor and comment out any unnecessary commands, such as statements that load DOS terminate-and-stay-resident (TSR) utilities.
4. Open SYSTEM.INI (located in the \WINDOWS directory) in a text editor. Inspect the [386enh] section for statements that load third-party Windows .VXD or .386 files and comment them out. Generally, these statements in SYSTEM.INI take the form DEVICE=*d:\path*xxxxx.VXD or DEVICE=*d:\path*xxxxx.386. In particular, look for statements in SYSTEM.INI that load third-party block drivers (disk I/O drivers). Typically, in an upgrade from Windows 3.x, these drivers may be present if you have a hard disk larger than 504MB (1,024 cylinders) or a SCSI hard drive. Some examples are WIN8XX.386 and WINEIDE.386.
5. After removing these entries in system files, try rebooting your computer and see whether Windows 98 Setup will now resume properly. If the computer still hangs, try booting to a DOS command prompt and temporarily renaming CONFIG.SYS and AUTOEXEC.BAT so that Setup loads without them. If you are installing Windows 98 from a CD-ROM or a network drive, you may need to copy the WIN98 installation directory to your local hard disk before taking this step.

Problems with Old Network Drivers

If you're upgrading to Windows 98 from a Windows 3.x machine on an active network, you may see startup messages telling you that Windows can't find device drivers specified in SYSTEM.INI or in the Windows registry. Typically, the system may complain that it can't find VNETBIOS.VXD, VWC.VXD, VNETSUP.VXD, VREDIR.VXD, or VSERVER.VXD. These are internal network drivers used by Windows 3.x that are eventually replaced with Windows 98 equivalents. You can temporarily bypass complaints about these missing drivers by pressing any key to continue the setup process after each error message is displayed.

To make Windows 98 stop displaying error messages about these drivers, you can modify the SYSTEM.INI file once the setup process has been completed. Open SYSTEM.INI in a text editor and then search for and comment out a statement that reads Network=*Vnetbios,*vwc,*vnetsup,*vredir,*vserver.

Problems with New Hardware Detection

If you've followed the preceding suggestions and Setup continues to hang your computer, there may be a conflict with the hardware that Windows 98 is currently detecting. Check the SETUP.TXT file in your Win98 installation directory and the HARDWARE.TXT file in the WINDOWS directory for information about problems with specific computers and peripherals.

Setup problems can be resolved by booting Windows 98 in Safe mode. Hold down the CTRL key when you see the "Starting Windows 98" message at boot time and select Safe Mode from the Windows 98 Startup menu. If the Windows 98 desktop will load in Safe mode, you can open the Windows 98 Device Manager (choose Start | Settings | Control Panel | System | Device Manager) and inspect the list of currently installed hardware components. If you see yellow exclamation points next to some components, try removing them and rebooting the computer.

Detecting Non-Plug-and-Play Devices

Next, Windows 98 searches your computer for non-plug-and-play hardware devices. These generally include peripheral cards, controllers, and ports not installed on a PCI bus. This portion of Setup is analogous to the Detect New Hardware process that was used in Windows 95. Microsoft warns that this is the most likely place for your system to stall or become inoperable. If you see no disk or screen activity for a long period of time, you should reboot your computer, and Setup will resume. Generally, it will autocorrect the problems that caused the system to hang.

If Windows 98 contains no built-in support for a detected hardware component, you may be prompted to insert a third-party driver disk in drive A.

Configuring and Finalizing System Settings

After the detection of non-plug-and-play hardware, Windows 98 configures system settings. If you are upgrading from a previous version of Windows, its configuration is migrated to the Windows 98 environment.

The Time Zone prompt asks you to confirm that the proper time zone for your geographic location has been selected. You can click a different location on the map or select a different time zone from the drop-down list above the map. If you want Windows 98 to automatically adjust for Daylight Savings Time changes, make sure the check box below the map is selected as shown here:

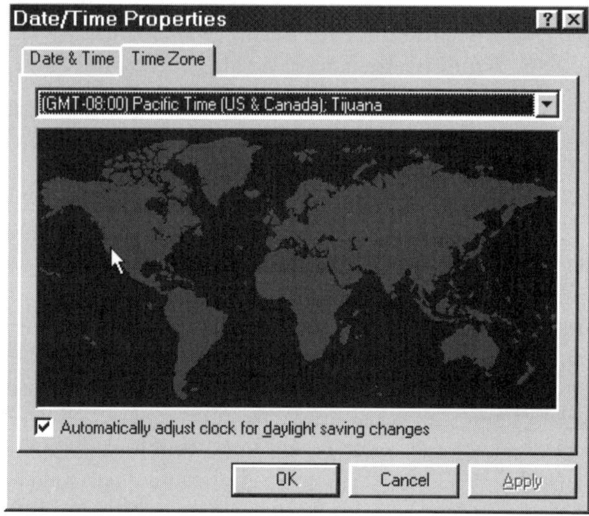

The Control Panel is installed next. Then old Program Manager or Windows 95 program groups are migrated to the Windows 98 Start menu. The online Help system is installed, MS-DOS program settings are configured, and Setup performs a special tuneup of Windows 98 system and program files.

The application tuneup is a new feature of Windows 98. This is a special program code optimization feature. Windows 98 examines the structure of system files stored on your hard disk and physically pads them out. Dummy code is added to executables and .DLL files so they will load evenly into 4K memory pages. This process makes Windows 98 more robust by decreasing the time required to transfer code from disk to memory. The WinAlign tuneup process operates only on new files listed in Microsoft's Win98 database. Third-party applications and drivers written prior to Windows 98 are not affected.

Note that the WinAlign tuneup is *not* equivalent to the Tune Up Your Computer Maintenance Wizard that you can run after Windows 98 is installed. The optimization performed during setup is an automatic, once-only process. The tuneups that you can perform after installing Windows do not alter the physical code structure of any program modules. Instead, they improve performance by optimizing the storage order of files on your hard disk. (See Chapter 6 for more information about Windows 98 disk optimization with the Disk Defragmenter and Maintenance Wizard.)

When these steps are completed, you will see a Restart button. Clicking it will reboot the system once again to set up Internet Explorer features and configure the Windows 98 desktop.

Final Reboot

For the final Setup reboot, Windows 98 will ask you to enter a username and password. If you upgraded the computer over a network, a network login box should appear. After you log in to Windows or your network, additional Windows components (such as the monitor, advanced power management, printers, and modems) may be detected and configured.

Windows 98 customizes Internet Explorer for the current user and loads the desktop. Then the Welcome to Windows 98 applet appears.

Welcome to Windows!

Welcome to Windows contains a series of options to assist new users with their Windows 98 experience. From this applet, you can register your copy of Windows 98, take an online tour of the Windows 98 operating system, set up an Internet connection, and perform a computer hard disk tuneup.

Registering Windows 98

You can register your copy of Windows 98 with Microsoft if you have a modem connected to your computer. Registering entitles you to additional technical support options and lets you receive product update information from Microsoft. To start the Registration Wizard, choose the Register Now option on the Welcome to Windows 98 Contents menu.

You'll be prompted to fill in your name, street address, e-mail address, and other personal contact information. You can answer Yes or No to prompts asking whether you want to receive Microsoft product literature and then send Microsoft a system inventory of the hardware and software components on your computer. If Windows 98 doesn't recognize a currently installed modem, clicking the Register button on the last screen will automatically open the Modem Installation Wizard. If your computer has a modem, you can follow the prompts to let Windows 98 detect and configure it. (See Chapter 9 for more details on using the Modems applet.)

Discover Windows 98

You can select the Discover Windows 98 option on the Welcome menu to open an interactive tour of the Windows operating system. The Discover tour contains a Computer Essentials module for new users, an Overview module for users migrating from Windows 3.x, and a What's New module for users migrating from Windows 95.

The More Windows 98 Resources option opens a step-by-step multimedia tutorial for Windows 98.

Connect to the Internet

Selecting this option opens the Windows 98 Internet Connection Wizard. You'll find detailed information about using this Wizard to configure an Internet connection under "Setting Up Your Internet Connection" in Chapter 12.

Maintain Your Computer

Selecting the Maintain Your Computer option on the Welcome menu opens the Windows 98 Maintenance Wizard, which will optimize your hard disk and allow you to schedule periodic Windows 98 maintenance sessions. (See Chapter 6 for more information about using the Maintenance Wizard.)

The CD-ROM Advantage

After installation, the Windows 98 CD-ROM continues to be of use, allowing you access to a number of useful features. Under Windows 98, a CD-ROM menu screen pops up automatically as soon as you insert the disk in the drive. CD-ROM features, not included in the floppy disk kit, include the following:

- **Interactive CD Sampler** Microsoft includes a number of free and trial applications on the CD. See Chapter 5 for detailed information.
- **Cool Video Clips** In Windows 98, these are promotional advertisements for software products; there are no rock-and-roll videos. Nevertheless, these AVI and MPEG video presentations may still be useful for testing Windows 98 multimedia performance on your computer.
- **Supplemental Drivers and Tools** The Windows 98 CD contains an extensive driver library for third-party peripherals and a series of system maintenance tools. It also contains the *Windows 98 Resource Kit*, a supplementary group of Windows applications, including network administration tools and the Windows 98 PowerToys.

Note *Owners of the floppy diskette version of Windows 98 can download most of the extra components present on the CD through the Microsoft Bulletin Board Download Service or Microsoft's Internet sites.*

Post-installation Checklist

Windows 98 Setup is better than its predecessors at putting the operating system on your computer in a "ready-to-run" state. However, you may still find it useful to conduct a post-installation inventory. Setup is not perfect. This section highlights some configuration settings that you may want to check or edit.

Configuring Your Monitor and Display Adapter

Open the Display applet (choose Start | Settings | Control Panel | Display) and select the Settings tab. If Windows 98 doesn't automatically recognize your monitor, it will assign a generic or Unknown value under Display: You may be missing out on some available screen resolution and power management options. You can choose a display type that corresponds to your actual monitor by clicking the Advanced button, selecting the Monitor tab, and clicking the Change button, as shown in Figure 3-3. (Chapter 9 provides more details on this process if you need them.) If you know your monitor includes power-saving features, you can check mark the Monitor Is Energy Start Compliant option on the Monitor tab if Windows 98 doesn't do this for you. Energy saving features for your monitor are located on the Screen Saver tab of the Display applet.

Generally, Windows 98 will find your video display adapter (its name follows the monitor type on the first Settings tab). If you think the wrong display adapter has been

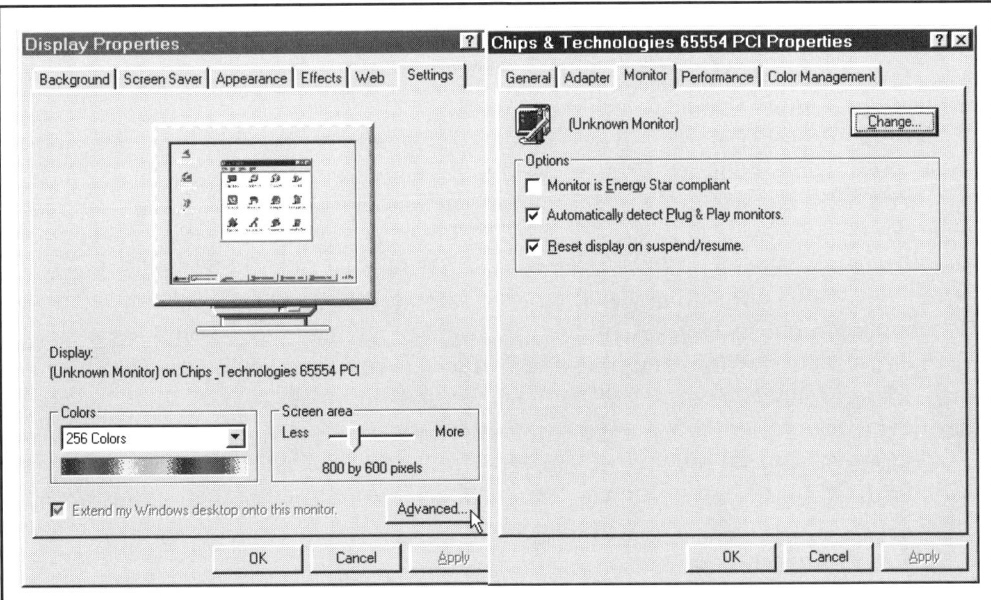

Figure 3-3. *Click the Change button to select a new Monitor profile*

selected, you can override this choice by selecting the Adapter tab and clicking the Change button.

Sometimes Windows 98 will identify your hardware but set a vanilla 640 by 480 screen resolution at 16 or 256 colors. You can adjust this using the Colors and Screen Area options on the Settings tab.

Tip *To quickly switch between screen resolutions on the fly, open the Display applet and select the Settings tab, click the Advanced button, and place a check mark next to Show Settings Icon On Taskbar on the General tab. Click OK to exit. A QuickRes display icon will appear in the System Tray area of the taskbar. You can click this icon with the mouse to pop up a list of available display resolutions and color depths. (The QuickRes icon does not show 16 color modes. To set the display to 16 colors, you'll need to use the pull-down Color option on the Settings tab of the Display applet.)*

Enabling Volume Control and Other System Tray Utilities

If your computer has a supported sound card, you should see a speaker icon in the System Tray area of the taskbar. This icon is your volume control. If you don't see it, open the Multimedia applet (choose Start | Settings | Control Panel | Multimedia) and verify that a sound card has been selected. Place a check mark next to Show Volume Control On The Taskbar at the bottom of the screen. If this option is dimmed, there may be problems with your sound card. See section below on resolving Device Manager problems. You may also want to open the Windows 98 Media Player (choose Programs from the Start menu and then choose Accessories | Entertainment | Media Player) and attempt to play one of the MIDI files in the Media folder to determine whether your sound system is working properly.

For convenience, Windows 98 provides access to other system utilities through the System Tray. If your computer has an inserted PC Card you should see a PC Card controller icon in the System Tray. If you don't see it, open the Control Panel | PC Card applet and place a check mark next to Show Control On Taskbar. If this option is grayed out, there may be problems with your computer's PC Card Controller. See the section "Resolving Device Manager Problems" later in this chapter.

If your computer supports Advanced Power Management, you should see a power icon in the System Tray (either a plug or a battery). If you don't see it, choose Control Panel | Power Management, select the Advanced tab and place a check mark next to Show Power Meter On Taskbar.

If you prefer, you can remove any of these icons from the System Tray by opening the appropriate applet in the Control Panel and removing the check mark that toggles its display.

Testing Printers and Scanners

Windows 98 Setup allows you to install a printer and print a test page to see whether it is working. If you didn't test your printer during Setup, you can open the Printers folder (choose Start | Settings | Printers), right-click an installed printer, choose the Properties option, and click the Print Test Page button on the General tab. If you didn't install a printer during setup, you can do so now by double-clicking the Add Printer icon.

If your computer has a TWAIN-compliant scanner, you can test it by opening the Imaging for Windows application (choose Start | Programs | Accessories | Imaging), choosing File | Select Scanner, selecting the Scanner, and then choosing File | Scan New. If your scanner doesn't appear in the Select Scanner list, there may be a hardware problem, or you may need to run a third-party utility to make Windows 98 recognize it. See Chapter 15 for more information.

You can also open the Control Panel and Printers folders by opening the My Computer icon (double- or single-click, depending on your desktop settings) and selecting them from there.

Testing Your Modem

To see if Windows 98 has recognized your computer's modem, open the Modems applet on the Control Panel (choose Start | Settings | Control Panel | Modems.) If you don't see your modem displayed on the General tab, you can click the Add button to start the Modem Installation Wizard.

To test an installed modem, click the Diagnostics tab, select the port the modem is configured for, and click the More Info button.

Checking Network Connectivity

If your computer is connected to other machines through a network adapter, you should see a Network Neighborhood icon on the desktop. Open Network Neighborhood to see a list of available network connections. If servers or printers were available before you installed Windows 98 and you don't see them now (or if the Network Neighborhood icon doesn't appear on the desktop), there may be a problem with your network setup. Open the Control Panel Network applet (choose Start | Settings | Control Panel | Network) and verify that the network adapter and appropriate network clients have been installed and properly configured. (You'll find information on how to do this in Chapter 14.) To perform a quick check of your network adapter's functionality, see the section "Resolving Device Manager Problems" later in this chapter.

Checking Pointing Device Settings

Windows 98 may choose a generic driver for your mouse or other pointing device. For instance, a Glidepath touchpad may be identified as a PS/2 mouse. You can check the settings for your pointing device by opening the Device Manager (choose Start | Settings | Control Panel | System and select the Device Manager tab). Double-click the Mouse component to see what kind of pointing device Win98 thinks you are using. If you think the setting is wrong, click the specific device listing, click the Properties button near the bottom of the window, and select the Driver tab. Click the Update Driver button to select a different driver for your pointing device, as shown here. (If you're unfamiliar with this process, see "When to Install Hardware Manually" in the section "Add New Hardware Applet" in Chapter 9. It provides details on choosing a compatible device, displaying all hardware choices, and installing a third-party driver from disk.)

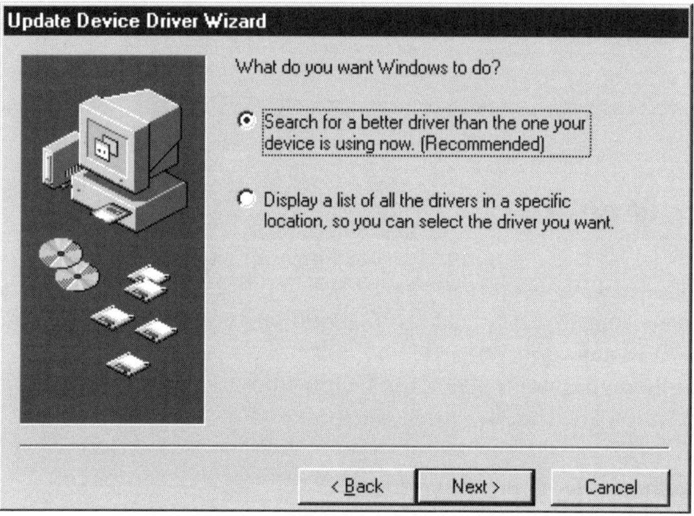

Note *Users of Microsoft's Intellimouse should choose one of Win98's built-in drivers rather than installing support from an older disk.*

Resolving Device Manager Problems

In addition to verifying that the proper driver is installed for your pointing device as discussed earlier, the Windows 98 Device Manager can show you whether there are problems with any of your other hardware components. Choose Control Panel | System, select the Device Manager tab, and inspect the Component list.

If you see devices marked "Unknown" or in an "Unknown Component Group," Windows 98 has not completely identified those devices. You can try completing the installation by selecting the device name, clicking the Properties button at the bottom of the Device Manager screen, selecting the Driver tab, and clicking the Update Driver button. When Windows 98 prompts you to search for a better driver, enter the path to an OEM driver disk or driver directory in the Specify a Location box as shown next. (This procedure is described in more detail in the section "Add New Hardware Applet" in Chapter 9.)

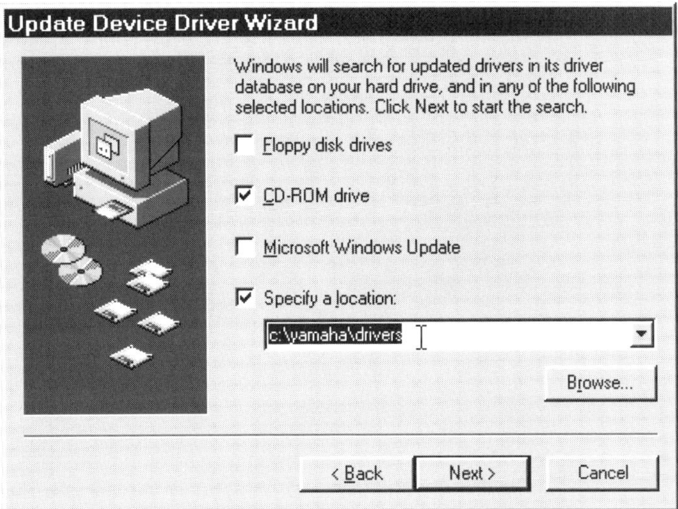

If you see a device marked with a yellow exclamation point (in any component group), Windows is experiencing a conflict with it. If you select the device in the Component list and look at its properties (as just described), you may find some diagnostic information on the General tab. Depending on the problem Windows 98 reports, you may try reinstalling the driver or changing the system resources allocated to the device. (Details on how to do this are provided in the section "Device Manager Tab" in Chapter 9 and in the section "Troubleshooting" in Chapter 16.)

Congratulations!

If you've made it this far in the chapter, you probably now have a functional copy of Windows 98 installed on your computer, ready to do your bidding. The next chapter will help you familiarize yourself with the Windows 98 desktop and interface features.

Chapter 4

Introduction to the Interface

Chapter Highlights

What's new in Windows 98:

- **Enhanced taskbar**
- **Enhanced Start menu**
- **Integrated Explorer**

Desktop ins and outs:

- **Controlling window display defaults**
- **Folder options**

Working with files and folders

Exploiting the Help system

Desktop strategies and secrets

Working with the Start menu

Customizing the taskbar

Customizing the interface

Creating project folders

Running DOS applications under Windows 98

If you've been using Windows 95 for a while, much of the Windows 98 interface will be familiar to you. Floating desktop icons, the hierarchical pop-up program menu, and easy-to-follow wizards for installing and configuring your software in Windows 98 are all similar or identical to the same features in Windows 95. However, there are also several optional new enhancements to the interface, most of them designed to give you fast access to information from the Internet and the World Wide Web.

In this chapter, you'll take a brief tour of the Windows 98 interface. You'll learn about the most important elements of the desktop and the critical user issues related to each element. This chapter is not a point-by-point tutorial on using Windows Explorer or the taskbar, because you probably know most of the basics already. This chapter does, however, discuss the internal logic of the interface and provide thumbnail sketches of the most important features. These sketches include the how-to-do-it and configuration information that you can't always get from the Windows 98 Help system.

Later in the chapter, you'll find some labor-saving tips for making the most of Explorer, the taskbar, and the Active Desktop—and you'll find useful productivity shortcuts and configuration strategies for your desktop. You'll also learn some tips and tricks that will help you avoid some ugly Windows 98 pitfalls.

What's New in Windows 98

If you upgrade from Windows 95 to Windows 98, your first impression of the new operating system may be that it is very similar to the old one. Like Windows 95, Windows 98 supports long file names and displays convenient, context-sensitive shortcuts when the right mouse button is clicked. On the other hand, if you're jumping directly from Windows 3.1 to Windows 98, you will see a new and quite different desktop layout on your screen. The Windows 98 interface depends on the mouse a lot more than the older Windows 3.1 desktop did. Windows 98 is a lot more difficult to navigate with the keyboard alone.

Tip *If you're a Macintosh user who has been dragged kicking and screaming to a Windows computer, you can ease some of the pain by moving the Windows taskbar from the bottom to the top of your desktop and moving the Recycle Bin icon to the lower-right corner. These sound like trivial changes, but you'll be amazed how much more comfortable you'll feel when the taskbar and Start menu are up on top and the "trashcan" is down at the bottom "where they belong."*

The Windows 98 interface also includes new features for users who upgrade from Windows 95. Some of these updates are part and parcel of Microsoft's Internet Explorer 4 Web browser, which can run under Windows 95 as well as under Windows 98. Other improvements are unique to the new operating environment. Windows 98 takes the enhanced taskbar, new Windows Explorer, and Active Desktop of Internet Explorer and integrates them with a new My Documents folder, Task Scheduler, and better HTML-based Help system. (HTML, or Hypertext Markup Language, is the format used to display pages on the World Wide Web.)

The following paragraphs summarize the most obvious changes from Windows 95 "Classic."

Enhanced Taskbar

You'll see a new set of small icons on the taskbar near the Start button. These icons demonstrate the convenience of Win98's new toolbar feature. Point the mouse at one of them, and a bubble-help caption will appear to identify the icon's function. This is the Win98 Quick Launch toolbar: click an icon shortcut in this part of the taskbar, and an associated application, document, or folder will open. By default, the Quick Launch toolbar contains shortcuts to launch the Internet Explorer and Outlook Express applications, minimize and restore open windows on the desktop, and open World Wide Web subscription channels. To try this toolbar, open My Computer or another desktop window and then click the broom (Show Desktop) icon. You'll see that this action minimizes all open windows to display a clear view of the desktop. Click the Show Desktop icon again, and your open application and file windows reappear in their original positions.

You're not limited to the default icons that Microsoft places on the Quick Launch toolbar. You can install your own shortcuts by dragging and dropping them over this region of the taskbar. For instance, you can select My Computer, Recycle Bin, or another desktop icon and drag it to the Quick Launch toolbar. To remove an item, right-click it and choose Delete from the pop-up menu.

In addition to the Quick Launch toolbar, Windows 98 lets you create several other toolbars on the taskbar. Right-click an empty area of the taskbar, and you'll find a Toolbars option that controls this feature. Optional toolbars can mirror all the shortcuts on your desktop, open Internet Explorer Links, or display shortcuts for any custom set of folders and programs. The Address toolbar lets you type or select a World Wide Web universal resource locator (URL) to load into your default Web browser. (For more information on working with these toolbars, see "Customizing the Taskbar" later in this chapter.)

Like Windows 95, Windows 98 normally displays the taskbar at the bottom of your screen. It displays a Minimized Task button for each active program and a System Tray (on the right) for operating system utilities.

Enhanced Start Menu

The Start button looks like the one in Windows 95, but the menu that appears when you click has undergone a few changes: The shortcut links on the Start menu are now movable and editable. You can move submenus, program groups, and individual shortcuts up and down by clicking and dragging. The core settings icons below the bar on the first level (Programs, Favorites, Documents, and so on) are still fixed, but you can rearrange items above this bar or within program groups. For instance, try pointing to the Programs group. When the menu opens, drag the Internet Explorer subgroup above the Accessories subgroup. You'll see the Internet Explorer folder reappear at the top of the menu. You can then drag it back to its original location.

Unlike Windows 95, Windows 98 permits you to add, remove, and edit Start menu items directly. Try selecting the Outlook Express shortcut on the desktop and dragging it over the Start button. The Start menu opens. You can continue to drag, pointing to the Programs group or any subgroup within Programs. Release the mouse button when the shortcut is positioned in the group you want, as shown next.

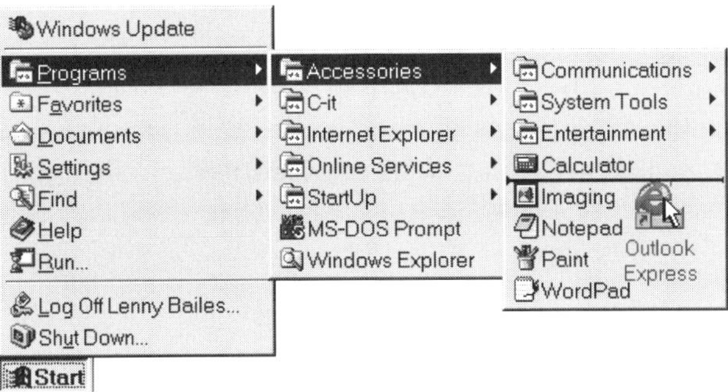

If you right-click any Start menu entry (above the bar or within a submenu), a pop-up options menu appears, as shown here:

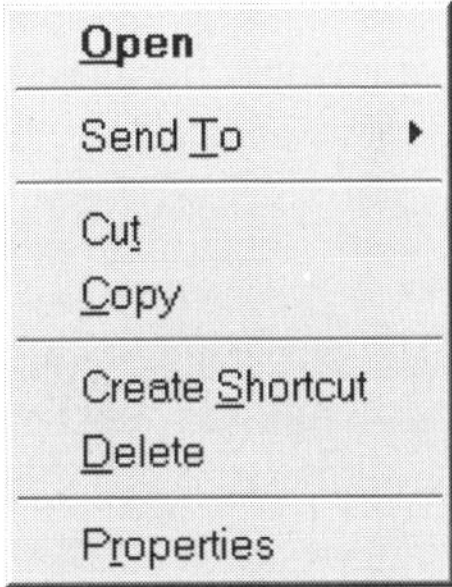

The Windows 98 Start menu also contains commands that permit you to load Web pages from Internet Explorer's Favorites and Links lists, as well as new options in the Settings and Find menus. Any item in the Favorites and Programs submenus can be dragged directly to the desktop or to the Recycle Bin.

There is one other change in the Start menu: Under Windows 95, if you had too many program groups to fit in a single screen column, the Start menu would fan open to show them all. In Windows 98, if there's insufficient screen height to display all the groups, two elevator buttons will appear at the top and bottom of the Start menu. To see the off-screen groups, you must click the up or down elevator button to scroll the display. Many Windows 98 beta testers preferred the old system and protested this change—but according to Microsoft, this change was necessary to add the new drag-and-drop editing options.

My Documents

The My Documents folder on the Windows 98 desktop is a special "smart folder." In addition to being a shortcut to the C:\MY DOCUMENTS folder on your hard disk, it is the default storage location for most Microsoft applications, including the

Notepad, WordPad, and Paint accessories and the programs in Microsoft's Office 97 productivity suite.

You can reconfigure the My Documents icon on the desktop to point to any specified folder on your hard disk. Right-click the My Documents desktop icon and choose Properties. Then specify the path to any folder on your hard disk in the Target Folder Location field.

The Integrated Explorer

The integrated Windows Explorer allows you to handle folders, files, and programs on your own computer or local network and Web pages, files, and other Internet resources from a single, consistent set of windows. If you want, you can open the Windows Explorer or My Computer once and use it to move among local files, shared network resources, scheduled tasks, Web sites, the Recycle Bin, Dial-Up Networking, Printers, and the Windows Control Panel. You no longer need to shift mental gears between two different programs that use different commands and display formats. For example, you can easily switch Windows Explorer from a folder and file view to install a new printer by choosing the Printers icon in the All Folders pane, as shown here:

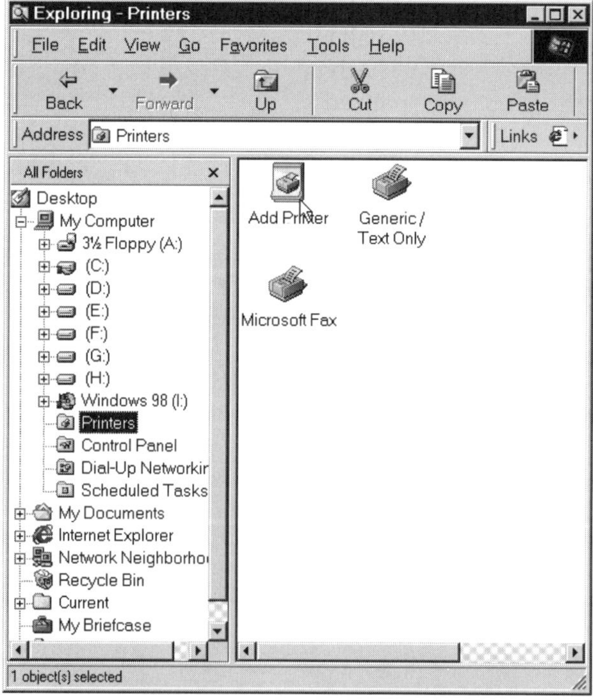

New Folder Display Options

Windows Explorer has a new set of display options, accessible from the pull-down View menu.

In addition to the Standard Buttons toolbar, the Address bar lets you switch quickly among the file and folder view, network resources, system utilities, and a URL (a World Wide Web address). Click the arrow to the right of the Address bar, and you can select a different view from the drop-down list. The Quick Links toolbar allows you to set up links to your favorite Web sites; it can also contain shortcuts to applications, documents, and folders.

The All Folders Explorer pane on the left can be replaced with a pane that displays Internet search tools, URL Favorites bookmarks, Web subscription channels, or your Web browsing History list. To switch panes, choose View | Explorer Bars and select the pane you want. (You'll find more information about working with the Web-related panes under "Web Browsers: Internet Explorer vs. Netscape Communicator" in Chapter 12.)

The View As Web Page option permits you to display the contents of any folder or group of folders as an HTML (Web) page on your local hard disk. The default HTML template that Microsoft uses for View As Web Page shows the names of open folders against a white background with a light blue sky at the upper left. When an individual file is selected, its statistical information appears under the folder name. Some file types can be set up to display a small bitmap image that previews the contents of the first page, as shown in Figure 4-1. Advanced users can edit the View As Web Page HTML template to create personalized file and folder views. (See "Desktop Ins and Outs" and "Customize This Folder" later in this chapter for details.)

Windows 98 also permits you to open files, folders, and shortcuts on the desktop or in My Computer and Explorer with a single mouse click, as though they were Web links. This option may be particularly useful for novices who have difficulty learning to double-click the mouse button. The Forward and Back buttons that you know from your Web browser are now available in all types of Explorer views. If you switch from Explorer to browse Printers or the Control Panel, you can click the Back button to return to the folder listing. For more information about customizing and working with Windows Explorer, see "Working with Files and Folders" later in this chapter.

Active Desktop

One of the most important new features of the Windows 98 desktop is the optional Active Desktop. Active Desktop permits you to open links to World Wide Web pages and other Web objects without launching a separate Web browser. You can place an image, an entire Web page, a scrolling Java ticker tape application, or even a live video stream in a window on your desktop. Or you can use one of these objects as your desktop wallpaper. Some computer vendors have taken advantage of Active Desktop

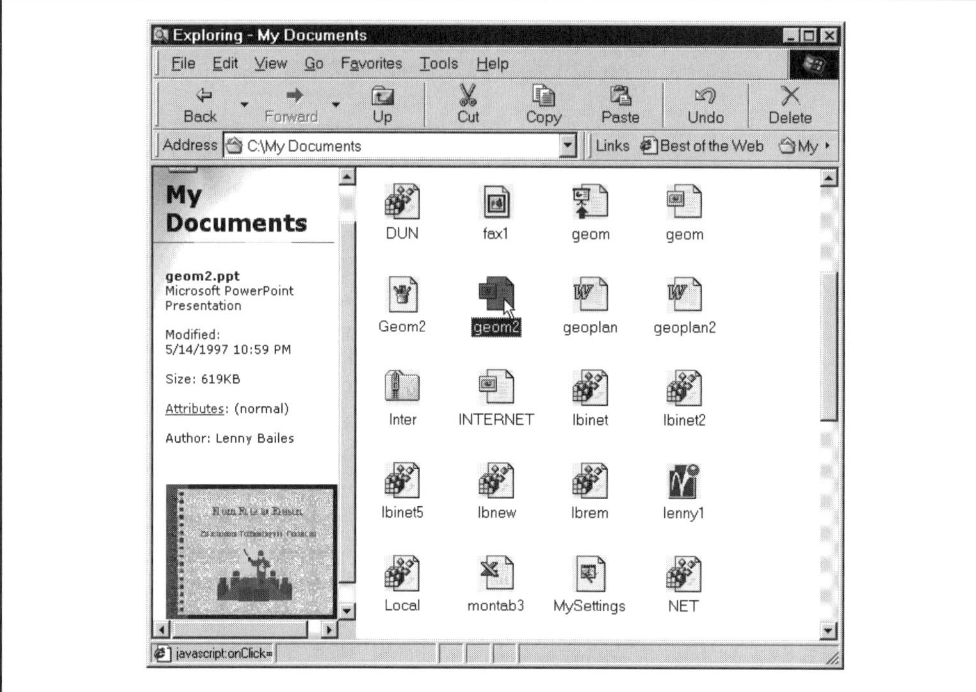

Figure 4-1. *When folders are viewed as Web pages, bitmap previews are available for some file types*

to embed HTML help links directly into the default Windows 98 wallpaper, as shown in Figure 4-2.

If you install or upgrade to Windows 98 yourself, the Active Desktop is turned off by default. If Windows 98 has been preinstalled on your computer by an OEM vendor, Active Desktop may be turned on initially to let you take advantage of additional, vendor-supplied help links.

Not Everything Has Changed

Windows 98 also retains many of the interface features from Windows 95.

Free-Floating Icons

Icons for shortcuts to programs, folders (directories), data objects, and system control options are still free floating; you can place them anywhere on the desktop. Unlike

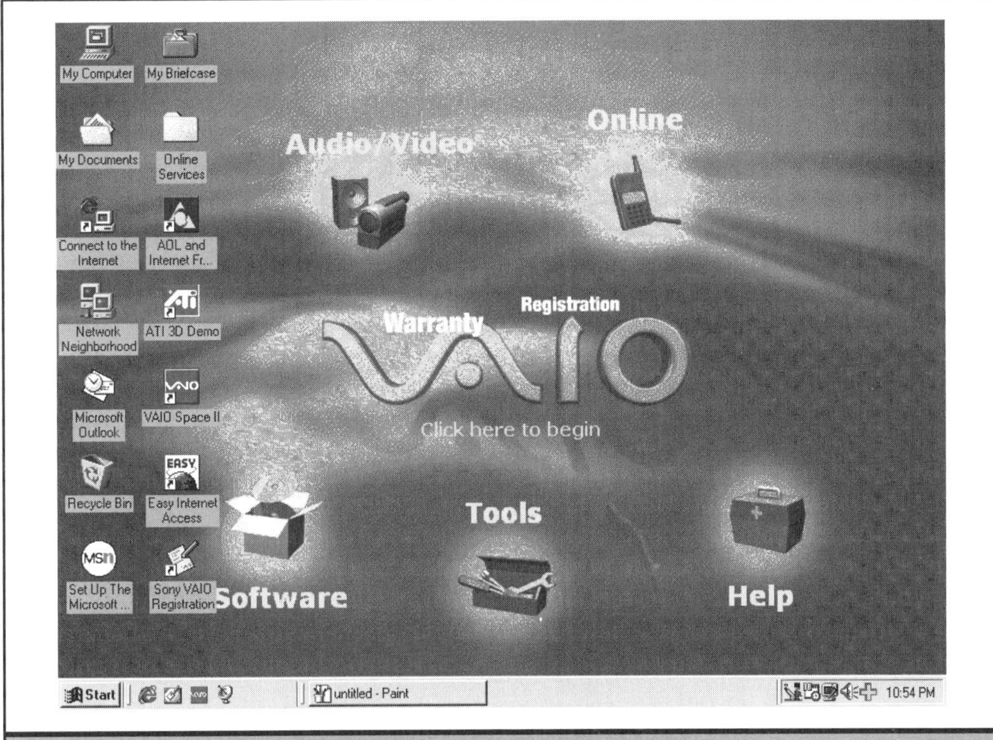

Figure 4-2. *The Active Desktop with HTML links embedded in the default wallpaper*

in Windows 3.1, you're not restricted by the separate Program Manager and File Manager windows.

Start Menu

The Windows 98 Start menu still pops up to give you a bird's eye view of all your installed applications and utilities, as shown in Figure 4-3. You can also start programs and manage files from desktop folder windows or shortcut icons. If you want, you can create custom project folders with shortcut links to programs and data files and place these folders on the desktop or in the Start menu.

Mouse-Click Convenience

Many parts of the Windows 98 interface include convenient, context-sensitive right-click mouse options. This is a very useful feature that Microsoft has lifted

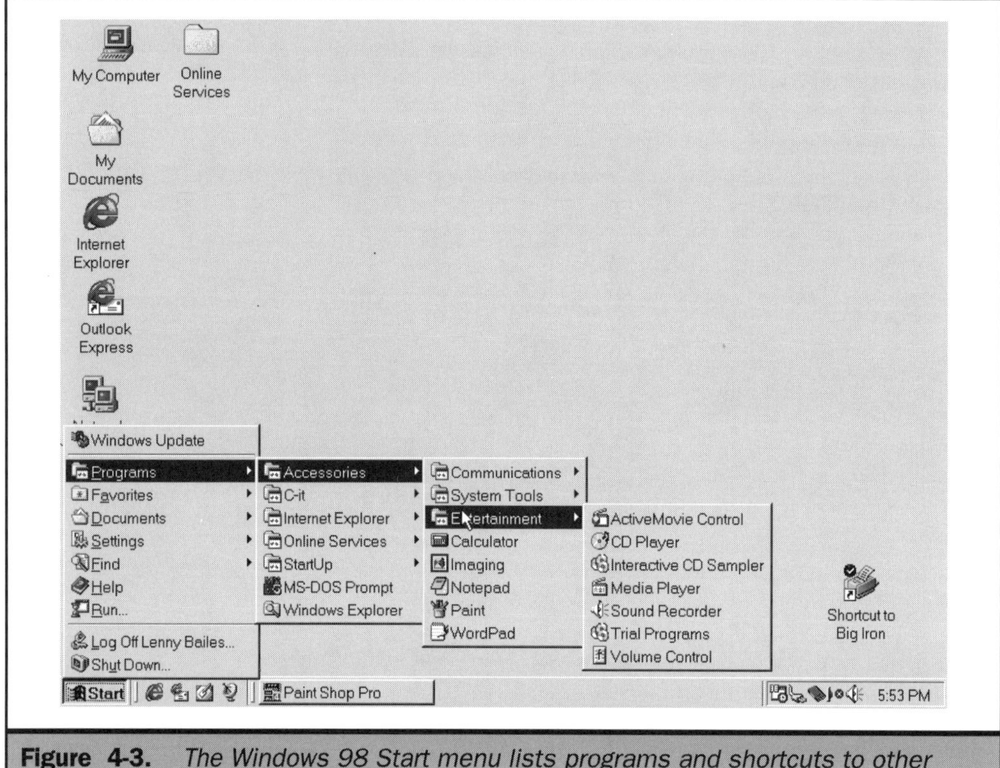

Figure 4-3. *The Windows 98 Start menu lists programs and shortcuts to other resources in nested menus and submenus*

from IBM's Warp OS/2. You can add toolbars to your taskbar, customize icon objects on the desktop and Start menu, and even change the appearance of the desktop itself simply by selecting an item from a right-click menu. You can even add your own selection of context-sensitive commands to right-click menus.

Streamlined Dialog Boxes

Windows 98 continues the trend that began in Windows 95 away from searching through pull-down menus for hidden configuration options. Shortcuts to most configuration functions are grouped together in the Control Panel.

Windows Explorer

Windows 98 gives you two ways to view the contents of your drives and folders: you can use the My Computer window or choose Windows Explorer. Windows Explorer is shown in Figure 4-4.

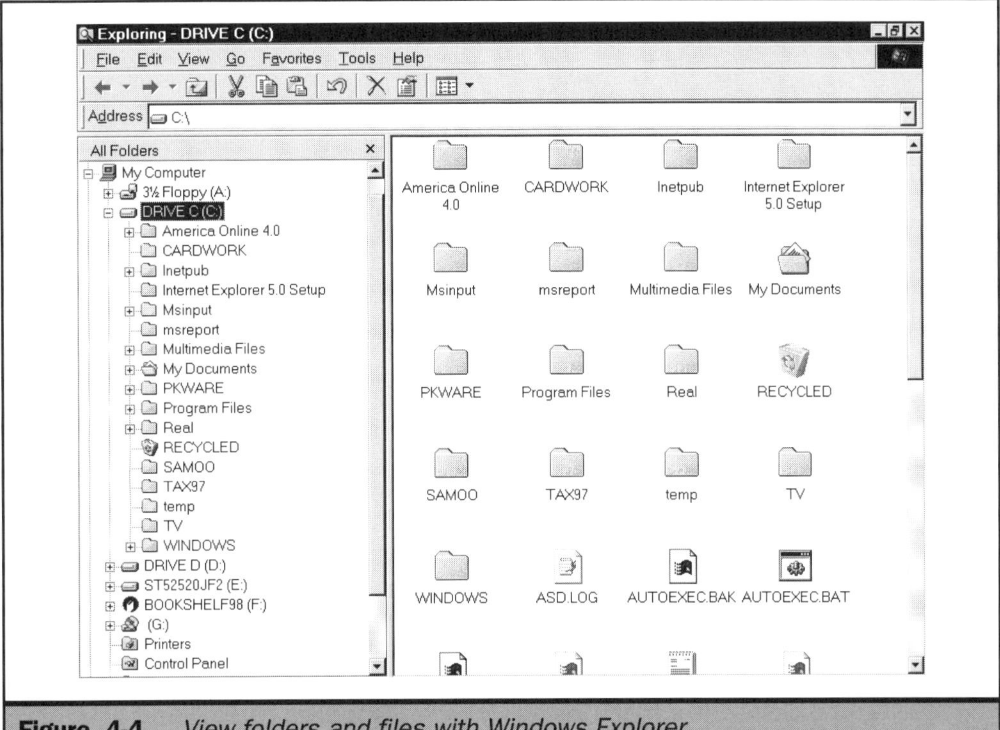

Figure 4-4. *View folders and files with Windows Explorer*

Moving Around Your Computer

The most important difference between My Computer and Windows Explorer is that the Explorer includes an optional All Folders bar that contains a tree-like display of drive and directory contents. Because you can drag a file or folder between panes in Windows Explorer (relocating it to a different folder or drive), Explorer offers more flexibility than My Computer, which normally displays just one folder at a time.

You can choose several ways to display the contents of a different folder:

- Double-click a folder object or shortcut to open that folder. (You can also set the desktop to single-click open as described in "Folder Options" later in this chapter.)
- Click the Up One Level icon on the toolbar or choose Go | Up One Level from the pull-down menu to move to the parent of the current folder.
- Click the Forward and Back arrows on the toolbar or use these commands in the Go menu to move to a folder you have recently visited.
- Use the drop-down Address list to jump directly to a different drive, network resource, or system folder.

- In the Address field, type the file path of the folder, the network workgroup, or the URL of a Web site you want to open.
- In Windows Explorer, click the name of the folder or other object you want to open in the All Folders list.

Tip *You can also go back to the last folder level you viewed in My Computer or Windows Explorer by pressing* BACKSPACE *in the current view.*

Entering Commands

Windows Explorer offers several ways to access commands: you can right-click any directory or file icon to open a context-sensitive menu; you can click the icon buttons on the toolbar; you can choose the commands in the menus across the top of the Explorer window; or you can use keyboard shortcuts. When you move from a local file or folder to a Web site or other Internet resource, some of the commands in the toolbar and menus change. (See "Customizing the Interface" later in this chapter for a useful list of keyboard command shortcuts.)

Viewing Icon Objects

The default view format in both My Computer and Windows Explorer shows each object in a listing as a large icon, but if you prefer, you can display file objects as small icons or as an item list. Item lists can be displayed with or without details. If you select the Details view from the toolbar or pull-down View menu, the content of the display window changes to provide useful statistical information about objects in the current folder.

Automatically Resizing and Re-sorting Details View Display Columns

When you open a My Computer or Windows Explorer file list in the Details view, each of the display columns (Name, Size, Type, and Modified) can be manually expanded or compressed by double-clicking a column border and dragging to the right or left.

You can also automatically resize columns to accommodate the largest filename or folder name in a list. If any of the Details display columns are too narrow or too wide, place the mouse at the column border until the cursor changes into a double-arrow cross. Double-click, without dragging in either direction, and the display will resize itself to fit the data in the column list. This trick is particularly useful in a Find File results box when you want to view all of the columns in the file list.

You can sort the Details view display by any column (name, size, type, date, and so on) by clicking the column header. To reverse a column's sort order, click the header again.

Working with the Start Menu

The Start button (normally in the lower-left corner of the screen) opens the Start menu—a hierarchical, pop-up listing of Windows and DOS applications and utilities. The list of programs and shortcuts fans out into submenus.

The Start menu also includes choices that let you reopen documents that you have recently used, jump to Web pages in your Internet Explorer Favorites list, open the Windows 98 Control Panel and other internal system tools, search for files and folders on your own computer and other computers on your local network, and search for Web pages or e-mail addresses through the Internet. (By default, access to the Control Panel is hidden within the Settings submenu. To move it to the top level of the Start menu, see "Making Printers, Dial-Up Networking, Control Panel, and Other System Folders More Accessible" later in this chapter.)

The Start menu can also be used as a container for shortcuts to applications or individual data files. To add or remove items from the Start menu, drag and drop icons in and out of the menu. (You can't easily remove items from Settings, Find, Help, or Run in the top-level menu, but you can easily add new menus or individual items to the top-level menu or any level within Programs.)

If you want more precise control of the Start menu, right-click the Start button and select Open or Explore. Or you can select Taskbar and Start Menu from the Settings menu, choose the Start Menu Programs tab, and then click the Advanced button. These commands open the Start menu in Windows Explorer, showing a subfolder for each submenu instead of a collapsible list. You can add, remove, or edit Start menu items in this view as though they were ordinary files and folders. (See "Desktop Strategies and Secrets" later in this chapter for more details.)

Long File Names

Like OS/2 Warp and Windows NT, Windows 98 can assign and display long names for files and folders, both on the desktop and at a command prompt. A Windows filename can contain up to 255 characters, including spaces and punctuation marks. If you try to copy a file with a long filename to a computer that uses MS-DOS or Windows 3.x, the name will be truncated to the traditional 8.3 format.

Note *Because Windows 98 uses file extensions to associate data files with application programs, it's still often necessary to assign a three-letter extension when you create a new file. Many applications apply the correct file extension automatically when you save the file, but others require you to enter it manually. By default, Windows 98 hides the file extension for many common file types on the desktop and in My Computer and Windows Explorer. You can unhide these extensions if you wish. See "Working with Files and Folders" later in this chapter for details.*

The System Tray

The System Tray, located at the right edge of the taskbar, contains icons that show you when programs are running in the background, such as the clock, the Task Scheduler, or an antivirus program. The System Tray also displays icons for controlling hardware features such as Advanced Power Management, PC cards, and a sound control, if your PC has these devices installed. Move your mouse cursor over one of these icons, and you will usually see a pop-up caption that describes the icon's function. If you left-click, right-click, or double-click (the procedure varies from one program to another), an options list or configuration window for that program will open. To open a menu of frequently used commands for a program in the System Tray, right-click the icon.

For example, if you click the digital clock, a calendar and an analog clock appear; if you pause the mouse cursor over the digital clock, you will see the day of the week and the date. When there's a sound card in your computer, you will see a speaker icon in the System Tray. Clicking the speaker icon opens a multimedia volume control.

The System Tray can also act as a status display for Windows 98 system events. For example, when you use Dial-Up Networking, a flashing pair of linked computers appears. When you print, a busy printer icon appears.

DOS Details

Windows 98 offers flexible support for DOS applications and utilities. DOS applications appear in a window that includes a toolbar. The toolbar lets you conveniently cut and paste objects to the Windows clipboard. You can also use the toolbar to toggle execution of a program in the background or set the display font for the window. Performance parameters for DOS applications running under Windows 98 are set through a pop-up Properties dialog box associated with each program. (You'll find detailed information in "Running DOS Applications Under Windows 98" later in this chapter.)

Features That Make Computing Easier

Windows 98 includes a number of features designed to make computing easier and more accessible for users with physical disabilities. You can turn on a StickyKeys feature to help you execute multiple-key commands; create visual equivalents of system sound events; and adjust the screen for a large-font high-contrast display. The MouseKeys feature allows you to duplicate mouse movements and operations with your keyboard. An Accessibility Wizard and the Accessibility Options icon in the Control Panel both provide easy control of most of the accessibility features in Windows 98.

Desktop Objects

The Recycle Bin, Network Neighborhood, My Briefcase, Connect to the Internet, Outlook Express, Online Services folder, and other icon controls are Windows 98 features that appear on the desktop. None of these features is absolutely essential, but you'll want to know what they do before you remove them in haste.

The Recycle Bin is Microsoft's answer to the Macintosh trashcan and a replacement for the old DOS Undelete program. When you remove an item from the desktop or from Windows Explorer or My Computer, the object moves to the Recycle Bin. The object stays there unless you drag it out to another location or permanently delete it. It's important to know that the Recycle Bin doesn't store files deleted by DOS applications or in DOS command sessions. (See "Outwitting the Recycle Bin" later in this chapter to learn how you can get around this limitation.)

Network Neighborhood appears on the desktop (and in Windows Explorer) if you've installed network support files. An open Network Neighborhood window lists any shared network computers, folders, or printers available for local use. It does not generally display Internet resources. You can use the Network Neighborhood to map drive letters to shared folders, or you can double-click an object within a network drive or folder listing to automatically reestablish a connection. When Network Neighborhood is active, the name of the My Computer window suddenly makes a lot more sense. (See Chapter 14 for detailed information about Windows 98 networking.)

My Briefcase is installed if you selected the Portable setup option or if you add it in a custom setup. You can also add My Briefcase to the desktop after installation through Add/Remove Programs in the Windows 98 Control Panel. My Briefcase lets you synchronize changes made to files located on a remote server or connected workstation. It can also synchronize files between a desktop computer and a laptop system. If you drag and drop items into My Briefcase, you can copy new or edited versions back to their source locations with just a few mouse clicks.

Online Services is a folder with links to setup programs for several online information services and Internet service providers (ISPs), including the Microsoft Network, America Online, Prodigy, CompuServe, and AT&T. (The Online Services folder contains a different set of services in other parts of the world.) If you already have an account with one of these services, or if you want to establish a new account, click that service's icon. Remember, however, that there are literally thousands of other ISPs out there, some of which may be better choices for your particular needs. See Chapter 12 for more information about choosing an ISP. After you have set up your account with an ISP or online service, or if you choose not to connect this computer to any service, you can delete the Online Services icon from your desktop.

The Internet Explorer icon on the desktop is a shortcut to Microsoft's own Web browser, Internet Explorer. You can use it to open the browser and view your default home page by double-clicking the icon.

Note

The dialog box that appears when you right-click the Internet Explorer icon and open its Properties screen includes settings that affect all of your Internet connections. Specifically, the Connections tab shows the Dial-Up Networking profile or direct network connection that your system will use when you start any Internet application, and the Programs tab identifies the default mail, news, conferencing, and personal information programs. (See "Setting Up Your Internet Connection" in Chapter 12 for more information.)

Outlook Express is the e-mail and Internet news client program included with Windows 98. Chapter 13 describes Outlook Express in detail. If you use Eudora, Netscape Communicator, or other mail and news clients, you can remove the Outlook Express icon from the desktop.

Tip

If you don't use the programs or utilities associated with a desktop icon, that icon just contributes to the overall clutter on your desktop. Therefore, if you want, you can delete any icons that you don't expect to use. The best way to remove an icon from the desktop without deleting the actual program is to install the Tweak UI program (found in the \TOOLS\RESKIT\POWERTOY folder on the Windows 98 CD-ROM) and use the options on its Desktop tab. (For more information on working with Tweak UI, see "Working with Registered Templates" in this chapter and "Tweak UI Applet" in Chapter 9.)

Desktop Ins and Outs

This section shows you how to gain control of the Windows 98 desktop interface. Microsoft designed the desktop to be more or less intuitive, but some of its features are well-camouflaged. There are many more options hidden beneath the surface. This section provides information about working with desktop windows—Windows Explorer, My Computer, and the File Manager, along with some third-party alternatives.

The Windows 98 desktop is extremely flexible. You can launch applications from the Start menu in several ways and also place program objects, work folders, or shortcuts to these resources in strategic locations on the desktop. Notice that some of the default objects on the Windows 98 desktop are ordinary programs, some launch system utilities, and others open a hierarchical file and folder display. Like desktop shortcuts, folders can have different purposes—some system objects are disguised to look like folders.

The distinction between a system object and a "real file" folder is not always obvious. A system object (such as the Recycle Bin) may actually point to a hidden directory on the hard disk that contains a set of shortcut file links. Some of these system objects use directories as storage areas for file and program templates. Later in this chapter you'll see how to use Win98 templates to create a project-oriented object desktop.

In Windows 98, system and ordinary folder windows include at least four pull- down menus: File, Edit, View, and Help. The menu options let you manage the appearance of the window, and they also control the properties of objects contained within.

My Computer

The My Computer object on your desktop opens to display all of your available disk drives. You can open any of the available drive letters to drill down to any folder, subfolder, or file listing. My Computer also contains a set of special system objects:

- The **Printers folder** allows you to configure settings for existing printers and install new ones. (You'll find detailed information about printers in Chapter 10.)
- The **Control Panel** contains a series of applets that allow you to customize the Windows 98 desktop and adjust internal performance settings. (You'll find detailed information on using the Control Panel in Chapter 9.)
- **Dial-Up Networking** (DUN) is another special folder that contains profiles for each network host and online service that connects through a modem and telephone line using the TCP/IP protocol. Note that America Online uses its own proprietary protocols, so you won't find an AOL profile in the DUN folder. (You'll find detailed information about Dial-Up Networking in Chapters 11 and 12.)
- **Scheduled Tasks** is a list of applications and utilities that Windows automatically runs at a predetermined time or date. When you install Windows, the only task scheduled is the Tune-up application, which runs once a month. (You'll find detailed information on using Scheduled Tasks in "Scheduled Tasks" in Chapter 6 and in "Scheduling Custom Maintenance Tasks" in Chapter 8.)
- **Infrared Recipient** is a file transfer utility that works through an Infrared port on your computer. (You'll find information on using Infrared Recipient in "Infrared File Transfer" in Chapter 5.)

Folder windows opened under My Computer include five pull-down menus: File, Edit, View, Go, and Help. The commands in these menus let you manage the appearance of the window, control the properties of the objects in the window, and move from the current window to other local windows, network resources, or a remote Web page. The My Computer window, in Detail view with the Icon toolbar visible, is shown in Figure 4-5.

Note *Many of the commands on My Computer's pull-down menus are also available when you right-click the mouse in a strategic area of the window. These commands are also available on the Standard Buttons toolbar, which can be turned on or off from the View | Toolbars menu.*

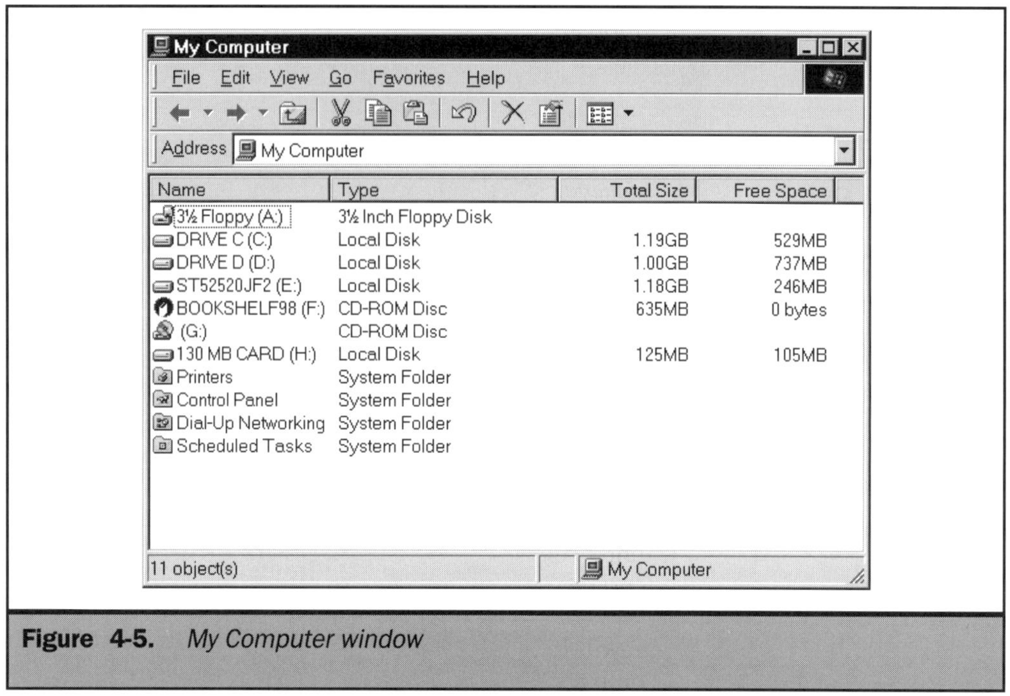

Figure 4-5. *My Computer window*

My Computer Versus Windows Explorer

When you open My Computer, you are actually launching a special version of Windows Explorer with internally defined startup attributes. By default, the drives and directories listed in My Computer windows appear in Large Icon view, but you can easily change the display option from the View menu or by clicking icons on the toolbar.

A Windows Explorer folder contains exactly the same objects as a My Computer view of the same folder, but it also includes an optional All Folders pane that displays your computer's entire file structure in a tree diagram. Windows Explorer offers several advantages over My Computer.

Windows Explorer makes it much easier to browse for files and subfolders nested deep within your hard disk's directory structure. (With the exceptions discussed earlier, a folder in the All Folders hierarchy is identical to a DOS file directory. For example, the Media folder located within your Windows folder is also the *d:*\WINDOWS\MEDIA subdirectory from a DOS prompt.)

Windows Explorer is also a better tool to use for the strategic copying or moving of files: You can drag an object from the currently open folder to any other folder on your system, jumping directly to the new folder by selecting it in the All Folders list.

You'll find more specific information about Windows Explorer as a file management tool, keyboard shortcuts, and strategic tips in "Working with Files and Folders" later in this chapter.

Any folder can be opened in Explorer view from My Computer by right-clicking its icon and selecting the Explore command.

Moving from Local Files and Folders to Web Pages

The Integrated Explorer feature in Windows 98 enables you to view local files, folders, and system objects (or Web pages, FTP file directories, and other Internet resources) in the same window. To open a Web page from My Computer or Windows Explorer, you can type the URL of the site you want to view directly in the Address field. Alternatively, you can click one of the shortcuts in the Links toolbar or select an option on the Go menu. You can also use the View | Explorer Bar command to display a list of Internet search engines, URL Favorites and Bookmarks, Internet subscription channels, or your Internet browsing History list in the left Explorer pane. (To use the search engine list, you must be concurrently connected to the Internet. You'll find extensive information about using search engines and navigating the Internet in Chapter 12 of this book.)

Windows 98 lets you create new folders on your hard drive with shortcuts to both Web sites and local files. To log onto a Web site from a folder, just open it the same way you would open a local file or folder.

Controlling Window Display Defaults

The information in this section about controlling window display defaults applies to both My Computer and Windows Explorer.

The View menu controls both the appearance and behavior of a window. Some of the display settings on the View menu are automatically passed down to child windows. Other settings are preserved only for the specific window that you customize. Still other options are passed globally to all folder windows when you change them in a single window.

This section describes the most important commands in the View menu.

Toolbars

The Toolbars submenu displays or hides three toolbars: the Standard Buttons toolbar contains icon buttons that duplicate important pull-down menu commands. The Address bar shows the path of the current window and lets you to jump to another folder, system object, or Web page by typing an entry or using the drop-down menu of drives and objects The Links toolbar contains shortcuts to individual Web pages and local files and folders. The Text Labels command hides or displays the names of the commands in the Standard Buttons toolbar.

Explorer Bar

The Explorer bar is a separate pane of the My Computer or Windows Explorer window. It contains links to Internet search tools and to your lists of Favorite sites and recently visited Web pages. (In Windows Explorer, the Explorer menu also lets you choose the All Folders hierarchical structure.)

View As Web Page

The View As Web Page command converts the folder window to an HTML page like the one in Figure 4-6. When you select an item in a View As Web Page window, the text section of the page displays information about that item. When you select a drive, the window shows a pie chart of drive use. When you select a graphic image (such as a bitmap or HTML file), the Web page shows a thumbnail view of the selected item.

Customize This Folder

The Customize This Folder option appears when View As Web Page is enabled and a disk drive or file folder is displayed. This option offers even more control over the

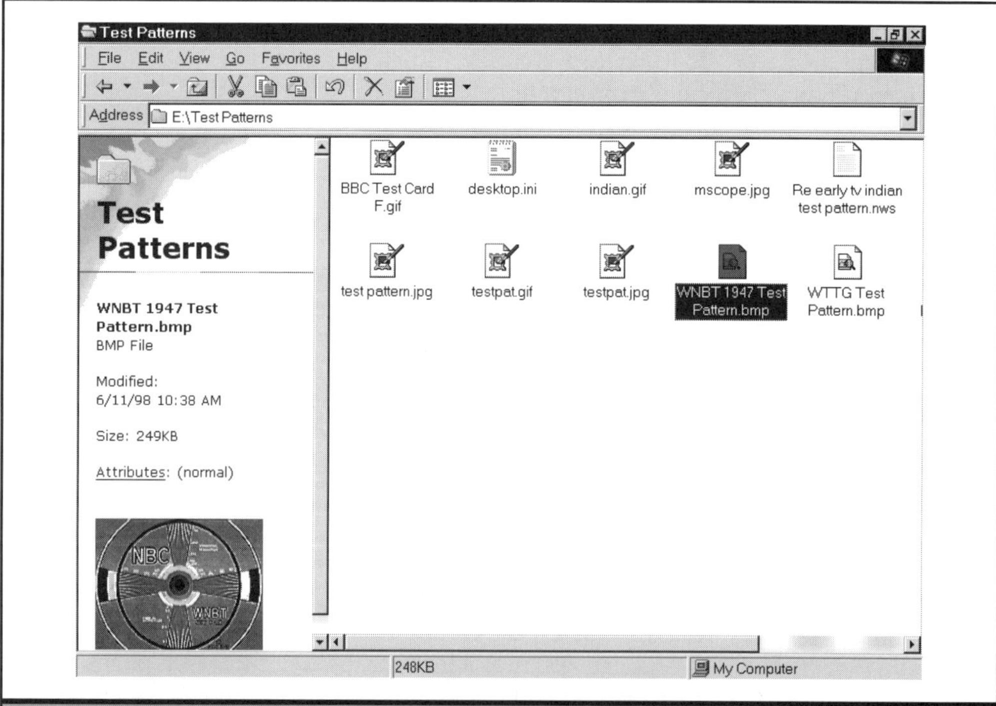

Figure 4-6. *The View As Web Page option adds a description and sometimes a thumbnail view to My Computer and Windows Explorer windows*

appearance of the current folder window. Customizing This Window opens a wizard with three options: Create or Edit an HTML Document; Choose a Background Picture; and Remove Customization. The HTML Document option changes or replaces the text on the right side of the window when View As Web Page is active. This allows you to add objects: pictures (or maybe a corporate logo), links to Web pages, existing text, or any other text of your own choosing. You can use the FrontPage Express program included with Windows 98 to create an HTML document for the folder display.

The Choose A Background Picture option places a tiled image underneath the icons in the main body of the window. The Remove Customization option cancels whatever document or picture you may have added to the window.

Note *These options can easily take you past the optimizing stage and well along toward "advanced messing around." You can spend many otherwise-productive hours finding and tweaking the appearance of your windows, but this probably won't contribute much to your ability to actually perform useful work on your computer.*

Arrange Icons

You can use the Auto Arrange option in the Arrange Icons submenu to customize the appearance of a window. When Arrange Icons is not active and the View is set to either Large or Small Icons, you can drag any icon to any location within a window to organize the contents of a folder (or even an entire drive) into logical groups or interesting geometric groupings. When Arrange Icons is active, the icons automatically snap into neat rows.

Line Up Icons

The Line Up Icons command lines up the icons in a window on a once-only basis.

Refresh

The Refresh command updates the display of the current window. If you've changed the contents of a folder (for instance, by creating a new document), choosing Refresh will update the file and folder listing.

Folder Options

The Folder Options for My Computer and Windows Explorer are important enough to have a section of their own. This command on the pull-down View menu opens a multitabbed Properties screen that controls the appearance of all your My Computer and Windows Explorer windows.

The General Tab

The Folder Options | General tab, shown in Figure 4-7, offers three options: Web Style, Classic Style, and Custom.

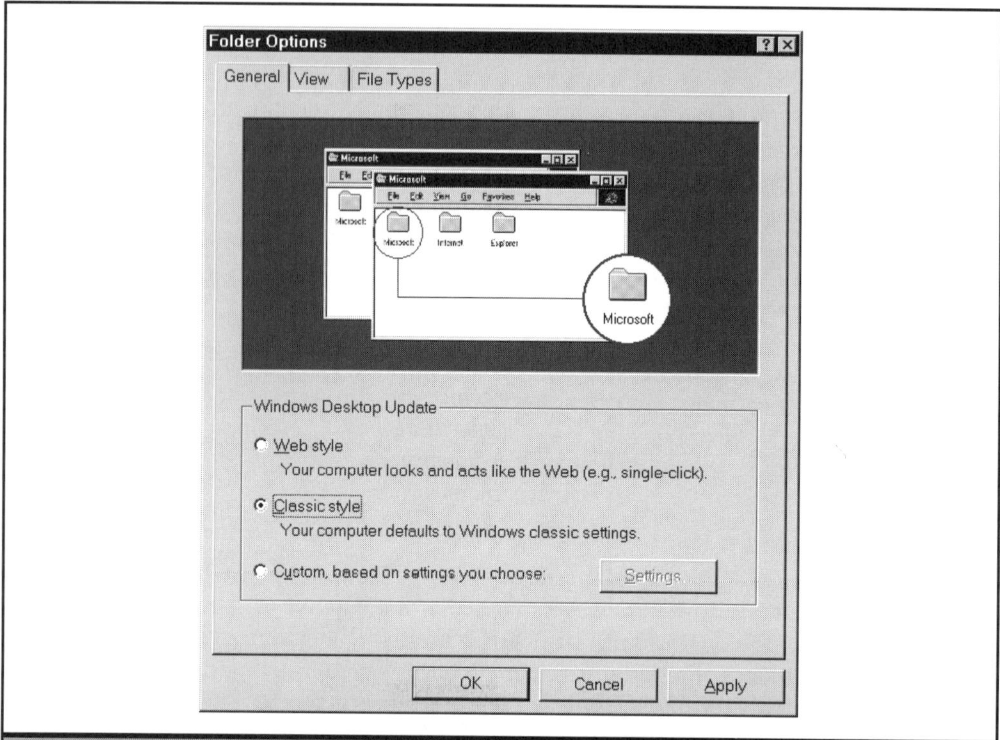

Figure 4-7. *Use the General tab in the Folder Options dialog box to change the appearance of your Windows Explorer windows*

WEB STYLE Web Style windows behave like pages viewed in Internet Explorer. Links to files, folders, and other objects are underlined and require a single mouse click to open. When you open a folder or object window, it replaces the current window.

CLASSIC STYLE Classic Style windows follow the traditional Windows conventions. Icon titles are not underlined, and they require a double-click to open. When you open a folder or object window, the new item appears in a separate window while the original window remains open.

CUSTOM The Custom option allows you to configure each setting separately so you can use custom settings to combine elements of both Web Style and Classic Style. For example, if you want Classic Style windows that open new folders in the same window, choose the appropriate custom settings.

To customize HTML (Web view) related settings for individual folders, choose the Custom, Based On The Settings You Choose option on the General tab and then click the Settings button. A new Custom Settings screen appears with four sets of display choices (see Figure 4-8).

You can use the Active Desktop section on the Custom Settings screen to toggle global settings between the Use Windows Classic Desktop and Enable All Web-Related Content On My Desktop settings. If you choose Enable All Web-Related Content On My Desktop, you can click the Customize button to install HTML objects through the Web tab of the Display Settings Control Panel applet. (You'll find more information about working with the Web tab in the "Web Tab" section in Chapter 9.)

The Browse Folders As Follows section lets you choose whether to have My Computer open a new file window or replace the existing window when you open a new folder.

Tip

Have your cake and eat it, too! No matter which way you choose to browse desktop windows, you can temporarily force the opposite display option. Hold down the CTRL *key when you open a new folder to reverse the new window and replace window browsing behavior. For instance, with Windows 98 set to Open Each Folder In Its Own Window, you can hold down the* CTRL *key to make a new folder replace the current folder in the* same *window.*

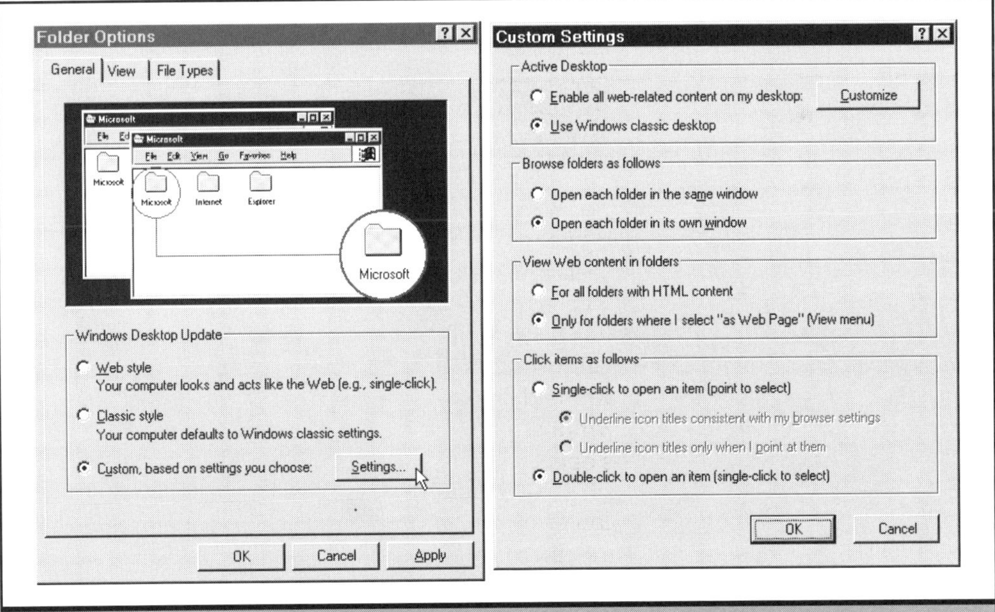

Figure 4-8. *The Custom Settings screen contains four sets of window display options*

The View Web Content In Folders section lets you apply the View As Web Page folder display option globally or only to folders that you specify individually.

The Click Items As Follows section lets you shift the desktop, My Computer, and Windows Explorer mouse defaults between single-click and double-click to open an item. You can also toggle underline options to make the desktop simulate links in your Web browser.

The View Tab

Still more file and folder display controls are available under Folder Options on the View tab. The settings you'll find here correspond roughly to the old Windows 95 display controls.

The View tab has two sections, as shown in Figure 4-9. The Folder Views section allows you to apply the current settings for this folder globally to all of the folders on your computer. Alternatively, you can also choose Reset All Folders to restore Windows 98 to its original display defaults.

The Advanced Settings section has more than a dozen options that control the appearance of My Computer and Windows Explorer windows and of individual files and folder icons.

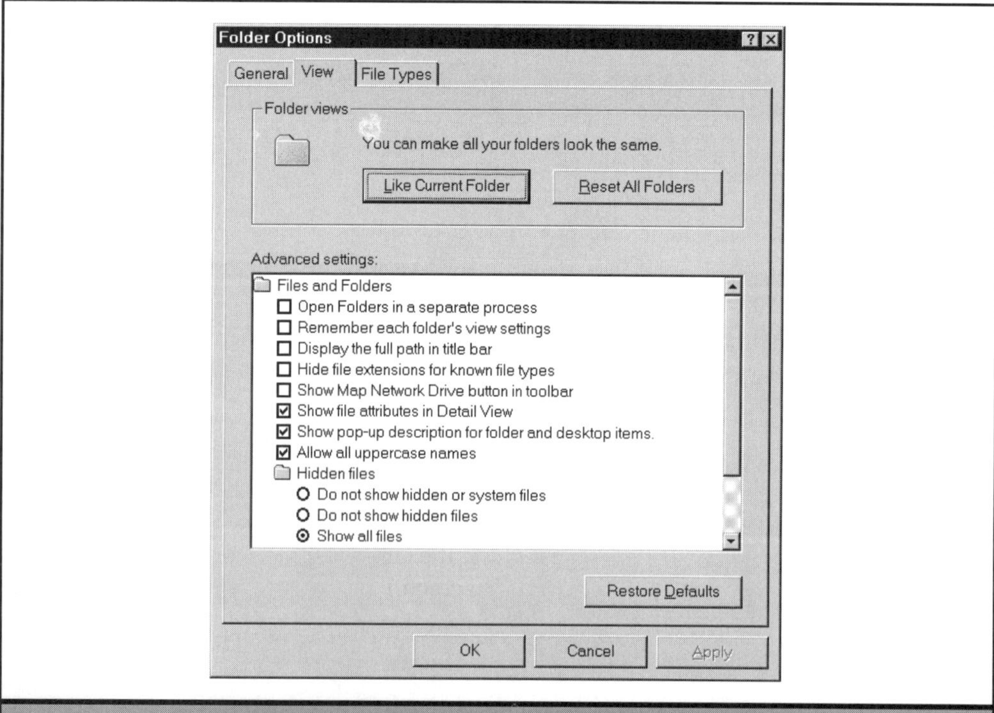

Figure 4-9. *The Folder Options View tab controls additional options that affect the appearance of your folder windows*

One default setting that you might want to change is Hide File Extensions For Known File Types. Turning off this setting enables you to easily distinguish among files with names like MYFILE.TXT, MYFILE.DOC, and MYFILE.RTF. (See "Turning on DOS File Extensions" later in this chapter for further discussion of this point.)

If you're a programmer or developer who needs to work with system files, you may want to select Show All Files in the Hidden Files options.

If you enable the Win98 Active Desktop feature, you may want to select Hide Icons When Desktop Is Viewed As A Web Page in the Visual Settings options. (For more information about using Active Desktop, see "What Does the Active Desktop Mean to You?" in Chapter 12.)

The File Types Tab

The File Types tab controls associations between application programs and filename extensions. When a file type has been assigned to a program, Windows automatically uses that program to open and display (or run) a data file with the registered filename extension. For example, when you open a file with the .TXT extension from Windows Explorer, the file automatically appears in Notepad. Similarly, files with the .RTF extension open into WordPad. In most cases, the file associations are assigned when you install your application programs. However, you can use the File Types screen to change current file associations or create new ones manually. See "Using File Associations" later in this chapter for more detailed information.

Desktop Navigation: What the Windows 98 Tour Doesn't Tell You

The Windows 98 CD-ROM includes a multimedia Discover Windows 98 tour that provides information about navigating the Windows 98 desktop. This section shows you some shortcuts, tricks, and secret desktop options that the tour does not mention.

Starting Programs

In addition to the commands in the Start menu, you can also use one of these techniques to start a program:

- Single- or double-click an associated document, or a shortcut to an associated document, in My Computer or Windows Explorer or on the desktop. (Whether you single- or double-click depends on the Click Items As Follows setting on the General tab of the Folder Options screen.)
- Single-click a command button in the Links, Desktop, or Quick Launch toolbar in the Windows taskbar at the bottom of your screen.
- Right-click any object on the desktop or in a folder and select the Open command from the pop-up menu.

- Open the Run window from the Start menu and type the path and name of a DOS or Windows application, a Help file, or a data file associated with an application program.
- Type the path and file name of any application from a DOS command prompt.

The Find Utility

The Windows 98 tour describes the basic search options that allow you to locate files on your hard disk. It doesn't tell you that the Date and Advanced tabs in the Find dialog box let you add sophisticated search filters. In addition, you can make the Find utility search all of the drives and directories on your computer with a single command. Normally, to search for files in a particular directory, you must click the Start menu, select Find | Files or Folders, and enter the directory name in the Look In box located on the Name And Location tab. However, you can also search for files in a particular folder by selecting the folder in a Windows Explorer window and pressing F3.

To perform a global search, select My Computer instead of an individual drive letter. To limit the search to your hard drives (while omitting floppy disks, CD-ROMs, and removable drives), select Local Hard Drives. You can also specify more than one search string or file extension in the Named field (separated with commas) to locate several file types in a single search.

Tip

Bring the power of the AltaVista search tool to your local hard disk. The AltaVista search engine (at www.altavista.digital.com) is a well-known tool that indexes nearly every word of every page published on the World Wide Web. AltaVista Personal Search 97 is a free tool that brings the internal indexing mechanism of its Internet big brother to your local hard disk. Upon installation, it scours your directories for downloaded HTML pages, Eudora and Microsoft Exchange mail stores, and documents from 100 common PC applications. The AltaVista indexing features are broad enough so that you can create a comprehensive picture of your local disk. Your Web browser interacts with this local copy of AltaVista just the way it does with the online version. Menu options are added to the standard interface, allowing you to perform keyword searches of all indexed files on your computer or look only in specific areas, such as personal mail stores. You can download a copy of AltaVista Personal Search 97 at http://www.altavista.digital.com/av/content/searchpx.htm.

Switching Between Windows

The Windows 98 tour tells you that you can switch between open windows on the desktop by clicking them with your mouse or by selecting their minimized representations on the taskbar. You can also move to a different window by holding down the ALT key and pressing the TAB key. This opens a quicklist, as shown next, in the center of the screen. Each time you press TAB, you select one of the icons in the quicklist. To switch to a particular program or open file window, release the TAB key when the focus is on its icon.

To move to a different window without opening the quicklist, press ALT-ESC. To open the Start menu, press the Windows logo key or CTRL-ESC.

Working with Files and Folders

The My Computer and Windows Explorer interface works well for simple file-management chores. However, Microsoft left out a number of useful options that used to be available in the Windows 3.1 File Manager. The File Manager is still there as a backup for global file maintenance, but it works properly only when long filenames are not involved. If you prefer the classic File Manager look and feel, you'll probably want to get a third-party file management utility with long filename support. (See "Windows Explorer Versus Other File Managers" later in this section for more information.)

Microsoft's strategy behind the Windows Explorer and My Computer tools is to get users to accept a new document-centered desktop metaphor. In other words, Microsoft wants to wean users away from the DOS-conditioned approach of organizing computers into directories with large, bloated file listings. Microsoft also wants users to avoid shuffling large groups of data files from place to place on the hard disk. Instead, Microsoft wants users to rely on shortcut links to create an *object-oriented desktop*.

Microsoft's programming style guides recommend that the file extension be dropped whenever a file name appears in an application's title bar. Even better, the title bar should display the document name before the application name. The reason for this recommendation can be seen when you minimize several open windows in the taskbar. If you open several instances of Notepad with different documents loaded, you will see the document title first so you can distinguish among the documents.

Despite Microsoft's attempts to prod users to share its vision of the future, many people will continue to work with the habits learned under DOS and earlier versions of Windows. Some users may find it necessary or useful to prune and graft directories, move subdirectories between drives, and occasionally inspect the contents of their hard drives underneath the pretty Windows 98 desktop.

Windows Explorer and My Computer are not ideal tools for performing these functions. Users who depended on file management shells such as XTree, Norton Desktop, or Central Point's PC Tools for Windows may sometimes miss the quick access to file browsers, unzip utilities, DOS command-line options, system information, and flexible file display options. Toward the end of this section, you'll find pointers to some current file management solutions offered by third-party utility vendors. For now, though, you may want to know what you can do with the tools available in Windows 98.

The following tips show you how to get the most out of Windows Explorer and My Computer as file management tools.

Turning on DOS File Extensions

By default, when you view a file list in a My Computer or Windows Explorer window, the three-letter DOS file extensions for registered file types are suppressed. Microsoft has configured Windows 98 in this way to encourage new users to think about "registered file types" rather than "DOS file extensions."

But this behavior can sometimes be annoying. For instance, you may see three files in the same directory all listed as PROGRAM. One may be PROGRAM.EXE, an application; another might be PROGRAM.INF, a configuration file; and the third could be PROGRAM.DOC, a document—but without the extensions, they all bear the same filename.

You can switch on the display of DOS file extensions in My Computer or Windows Explorer by selecting View | Folder Options | View and deselecting the Hide File Extensions For Known File Types check box.

If you prefer to keep the DOS file extensions hidden in My Computer and Windows Explorer, here's a quick way to see them if you find multiple files with the same name: Select the file and drag it to the Start | Run box. The file's DOS file extension will be revealed.

Using Drag-and-Drop Copy and Move

To drag and drop files or directory folders from one drive to a specific location on another drive, you must either have two My Computer windows open at the same time or use the All Folders folder bar in Windows Explorer.

The rules for drag-and-drop file transfers are not entirely consistent:

- If you click an object and drag it to a folder on the same drive, the object is moved, not copied.
- If you click an object and drag it to a folder (or root) on a different drive, the object is copied. The original file remains in the source directory.
- Program files with .EXE and .COM file extensions are exceptions. If you click and drag a program file to a new location, Windows 98 creates a shortcut link in the target folder rather than moving or copying the file.
- To force a copy operation, hold down the CTRL key while you click and drag the object. This will produce a copy in the target folder, no matter what kind of file you're dragging or where you drop it.
- To force a move operation, hold down the SHIFT key while you click and drag the object. This will move the file no matter what its extension or where you drop it.
- To create a shortcut, hold down both the CTRL and SHIFT keys while you left-click and drag the object or right-click and drag the object. When you

release the object in the target folder, select Create Shortcut(s) Here from the pop-up menu.

Moving an object to the desktop works just like moving it to any other folder. Clicking and dragging a file from a folder to the desktop will *move* the file if the desktop is on the same drive, *copy* the file if the desktop is on a different drive, or *create a shortcut* if the file has an .EXE or .COM extension. If you right-click and drag the file, the pop-up Options menu will appear. If you right-click and drag an HTML document (with an .HTM extension), the pop-up menu will include a Create Active Desktop Item(s) Here option along with the Copy, Move, and Create Shortcut commands.

To avoid becoming confused by Win98's various left-click file operations, you can remind yourself to right-click when you drag objects to a new location. If you right-click and drag, Windows 98 always displays a pop-up menu that lets you choose what to do.

Performing Multiple File Operations: The SHIFT-click Follies

You can copy or move multiple files between folders by selecting and dragging the files with your mouse or by using the Windows clipboard. If you click a file or folder while holding down the SHIFT key, you will highlight a *range* of objects from the one you first selected to the last one you clicked. (If you haven't clicked any other icons yet, the selected range will extend from the current icon to the first file in the listing. Or it may extend to the top or upper-left corner of the window. This depends upon the window's current display default: Large Icons, Small Icons, List, or Details view.)

This variable selection range is often annoying. You may want to force My Computer, or a single folder on the desktop, to open in Explorer view with the All Folders pane enabled. The keyboard and mouse shortcut for this trick is SHIFT-double-click (no matter whether your desktop opens with a single- or a double-click). However, if you try to open an Explorer view of a folder from within My Computer by using the SHIFT-double-click keyboard shortcut, you will probably end up opening a whole group of desktop objects instead of just the one you want. This happens because sometime previously in your work session, you selected those other objects on the desktop. Now you decide you want to SHIFT-double-click a single object. Windows remembers those other objects you clicked and crowds your desktop with lots of other open windows. Microsoft thought it was adding a feature by allowing SHIFT-double-click to automatically select a range of objects, but this shortcut can also be a big headache.

The bottom line: To avoid this desktop behavior and use the force Explorer-View option, click a folder before you SHIFT-double-click on it.

Note

If you configure the desktop for single-click file launching, you can select a range of files by pointing to the first one, holding down the SHIFT key, and pointing to the last file you want to include.

Using the Send To Command

If you often copy files to specific destinations (such as a floppy disk, a particular folder on a hard drive, or a utility program that opens or processes files), the right-click Send To command may be the easiest way to perform the copy operation. When you install Windows 98, the list of Send To destinations includes your floppy disk drive(s), the Windows desktop, the My Documents folder, Outlook Express, and My Briefcase (if installed) as targets for shortcuts. Some programs automatically add themselves to the list when you install them. You can add other destinations, including folders, applications, and printers, by dragging shortcuts to the target into the SendTo folder. For instance, to create a shortcut to a folder on your hard disk called Reports, follow these steps:

1. Open the SendTo folder by choosing Start | Run, typing **SendTo**, and clicking OK.
2. Open My Computer or Windows Explorer to the Reports folder (for instance, C:\REPORTS).
3. Drag a shortcut to the Reports folder out of My Computer or Windows Explorer and drop it into the open SendTo folder. (Right-click, drag, and select Create Shortcut from the pop-up menu.)

From now on, you can right-click any file or folder, choose Send To from the pop-up menu, and point to the new shortcut location you've created, as shown next. This trick may be particularly useful for putting away documents you've temporarily placed on the desktop in a specific folder.

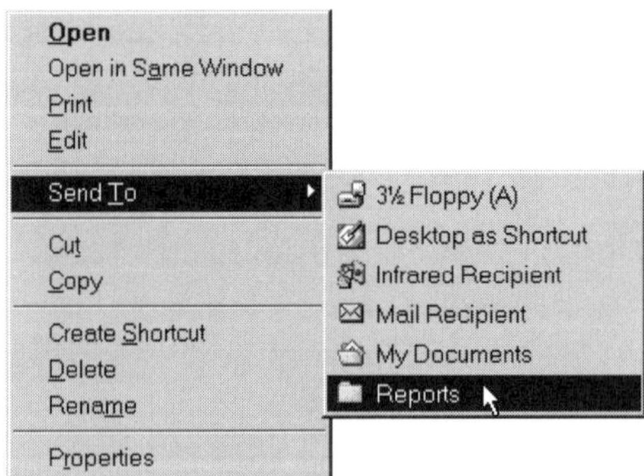

The Send To feature is extremely flexible. You'll find a number of Send To tips like the preceding one and the one in the following sidebar scattered throughout various chapters in this book.

Make WordPad Your My Computer or Windows Explorer File Browser via the SendTo Folder

One feature that Windows Explorer lacks is a quick and convenient file viewer. It's true that you can right-click any registered file type in an Explorer window and open the file in the application that created it, but this approach is sometimes less than convenient.

First, it may be overkill to open a short Word document in Microsoft Office. Second, you may want to view a document that consists primarily of text but doesn't bear a registered file extension (.BAT, .BK, .INF, .CFG, .NOT, .ASC, .#, READ.ME, or any custom extension you may assign to an ASCII text file). These documents have no default ASCII text viewer, but the Win98 SendTo folder makes it easy to create one.

1. Right-click the Start menu, select Explore, and open Programs | Accessories. Select WordPad, right-click, and choose Create Shortcut.
2. Open the Win98 SendTo folder. Choose Start | Run, enter **SendTo** in the Run box, and click OK.
3. Paste a WordPad shortcut in the SendTo folder. (Right-click anywhere inside the SendTo folder and choose Paste Shortcut.)

From now on, you can view the contents of a variety of files by right-clicking them on the desktop or in Windows Explorer and choosing Send To | WordPad.

Working with Multiple Windows in Explorer

One of the places where My Computer and Windows Explorer are a step backward from the old Windows File Manager is in the procedures used to move objects from one folder to another. There are several ways to accomplish this, but none is really satisfactory:

- You can open one instance of My Computer that contains the source drive or folder and then a second instance to the target folder. Drag from one to the other.
- You can select the object you want to move or copy in My Computer and use the Edit | Cut or the Edit | Copy command. Then use the Back, Forward, or Up One Level Command to move to the target folder, or type the target folder's path in the Address field. Then use the Paste command to place the object in the new folder.
- In Windows Explorer, you can open the All Folders bar to display the drive that contains the target folder in tree format; then drag the object to the target folder.

Here's a shortcut that lets you open two file windows quickly from a single instance of Windows Explorer:

1. Open Windows Explorer, or right-click a desktop folder and select Explore, to open the first view.
2. Right-click any drive or folder in the All Folders pane and select Open to produce a My Computer view of the file or folder contents.
3. Copy or move from one window to the other, or right-click the folder icon in the upper-left corner of the My Computer view and choose Explore to open another Explorer view.

Using Windows Explorer Command-Line Options

With command-line switches, you can open Windows Explorer in a number of different views into a specified drive and directory. If you just enter the command **Explorer** on the command line, the window opens to the drive and folder where Windows 98 is installed (the default display view).

As mentioned earlier, the My Computer desktop object is actually a special instance of Windows Explorer. You can open My Computer folder windows from the command line by entering **Explorer /root, *d*:\path, /n** at any DOS command prompt. The /root and /n parameters allow you to open multiple instances of the same folder. They can be omitted to open just one folder instance: for example, **Explorer C:\WINDOWS**; in the Start | Run box, you can enter just the path and name of the folder to open it.

Explorer accepts the following command-line parameters:

Explorer [/n][/e][,/root,object,][[,/select],subobject]

Table 4-1 describes the Explorer command-line options.

Windows Explorer Examples

Remember that each Explorer command switch is followed by a comma. You've already seen the syntax to launch Explorer in Open View and simulate My Computer. Here are additional statements for opening and viewing windows:

Explorer *d:\path*	Opens a My Computer window on a specific drive or folder
Explorer *d:\path*, /n	Opens a second My Computer window on the same drive or folder
Explorer /e, *d:\path*	Displays a window in Explorer view
Explorer /e, *d:\path*, /n	Opens a second Explorer window on the same drive and path

Explorer /e, /root,c:\,c:\windows	Opens an Explorer window that begins at the C drive and focuses on the C:\WINDOWS folder
Explorer /select,*d:\path\filename*	Opens a window in the My Computer view with the focus on a particular file

If you're connected to a network, you can open Explorer to display a view of the server and nothing else with the following syntax:

Explorer /e, /root, *Servername*

Windows Explorer Versus Other File Managers

Windows Explorer has some definite shortcomings as a file management tool compared to the old Windows File Manager and other third-party offerings.

- **Tiling file windows horizontally and vertically** Windows Explorer displays only one file listing, unless you specifically open more instances of it.
- **Customizing confirmation preferences for Copy, Move, Delete, and so on** Windows Explorer has fixed confirmation preferences. You can't suppress the confirmation prompt when you replace a file, and you can't add a prompt for

Parameter	Description
/n	Always opens a new window (even if the specified folder is already open).
/e	Uses the Windows Explorer view. The default is Open (My Computer) view.
/root,object	Specifies the object in the normal name space (the folder display hierarchy) that will be used as the root of this Windows Explorer folder. The default is to just use the normal name space called root (the desktop).
Subobject	Specifies the folder that will receive the initial focus, unless the /select parameter is used. The default is the root object.
/select	Specifies that the parent folder is opened and the specified object is selected.

Table 4-1. *Explorer Command-Line Options*

More Windows Explorer Esoterica

Here a some additional tips on using Windows Explorer:

- To use the Clipboard for global file copy operations, select a range of files (select the first file in the range and then SHIFT-click the last file in the range or use your mouse to drag a box around all the files you want to select). Then press CTRL-C or CTRL-X (or use the Cut or Copy commands on the Edit menu) to copy or transfer the selected files to the clipboard. Finally, open the target directory and either press CTRL-V or use the Paste command.
- To quickly open the Properties window for any file object, hold down the ALT key and double-click the object.
- To quickly close a child window and all parent windows connected with it, hold down the SHIFT key and select File | Close.
- To quickly open any drive or folder, choose the Run command on the Start menu, type the drive and path name, and click OK.
- To change the My Computer default display to Window Explorer, select View | Folder Options | File Types. Scroll down to the Folder file type and click the Edit button. Click Explore in the Actions field and then click Set Default and OK.
- Windows Explorer has lost the Windows 3.1 option of sorting a list of files in a directory by their three-letter file extensions. Instead, the Arrange Icons by Type option sorts files by type name in the registration database. This type name may or may not correspond to the file extension. See "Using File Associations" later in this chapter for details.
- To select a group of files by file name or extension string in Windows Explorer, use the Find command on the Tools menu. Type the file name or *\.extension* in the Named field and use the Browse button to specify the folder. Since Windows Explorer doesn't have a direct menu option to filter the file display in a directory, you must work with the results in the Find window instead. For more information, see "Building Work Folders with Find" later in this chapter.

other operations, such as Move or Copy. (The confirmation prompt that appears when you delete files can be suppressed by simultaneously holding down the SHIFT key when you press the DEL key.)

- **Globally renaming, copying, or moving a selected range of files** Windows Explorer does not permit files to be selected by specifying a wildcard. It has no global function key shortcuts for Move, Copy, Run, or Rename. You can't use Explorer to globally apply a DOS command or batch file to a range of files.

- **Controlling file information details displayed in directory windows** Windows Explorer does not permit you to filter the file display. For instance, you can't hide or display files by specifying an extension, modification date, or file attribute. The View | All File Details command turns all of this information on or off as a global unit.

The Windows 3.x File Manager (WINFILE.EXE) included in Windows 98 supports all the features listed here, but it does not display or support long filenames, and it does not show accurate free drive space on FAT32 drives that are more than 2GB

The best way to work around these potential problems and the limitations of Windows Explorer may be to use a third-party file management program designed for Windows 95 and Windows 98. Several developers offer shareware programs that provide better control of your system than either Windows Explorer or File Manager:

Drag and File Gold	http://www.canyonsw.com/dnf.htm
TurboBrowser 98	http://www.TurboBrowser.com
PowerDesk 98	http://www.mijenix.com/powerdesk98.htm

These packages all support features that Windows Explorer lacks, and they also contain additional bells and whistles. Drag and File Gold includes multiple display windows, a ZIP file manager, an FTP client, optional floating toolbars, the ability to edit and reassign file associations, and a file synchronization feature that can bidirectionally match up the contents of any two folders.

TurboBrowser 98 is the package to choose if you need to view and manipulate lots of word processing, spreadsheet, or graphics data. It lacks the ability to show simultaneous multiple drive displays, but it includes a viewing pane for multiple file formats, a bitmap file converter, and a smart print queue that overcomes the limitations of Windows 98's built-in print spooler.

PowerDesk 98 supports two simultaneous file listings and includes customizable user toolbars, bidirectional folder synchronization, a ZIP file manager, and a file viewer that can display 80 individual file formats. It also includes Size Manager, a nicely written hard disk cleanup utility.

You may also want to check out the following freeware file managers:

File Maven	http://www.briggsoft.com
Nico's Commander	http://www.geocities.com/SiliconValley/Way/2686
Servant Salamander	http://vorvan.sh.cvut.cz/salamander

Exploiting the Help System

The Help system in Windows 98 has undergone a major overhaul. It is now based on the same Hypertext Markup Language (HTML) that's used for Web pages. This means that a Help page can include ActiveX controls, animations, and links to the very latest information available from Microsoft and other software developers. Windows 98 Help is more interactive than the Windows 95 version. It is sprinkled with links to diagnostic aids, troubleshooting wizards, and online information resources. However, the new Help system lacks Win95's ability to create strategic bookmarks and annotations to sections you may want to revisit.

The new Help window (which you can open by choosing Start | Help or pressing F1) contains two panes: a topic pane that lets you search for information in three different ways and a viewer pane that displays the information you requested in the topic pane (see Figure 4-10).

If you select the Contents tab in the Topic pane, Windows Help displays a series of book icons, each representing a chapter entry. If you click a chapter topic, the book opens to reveal additional topics, until eventually individual entries (represented by

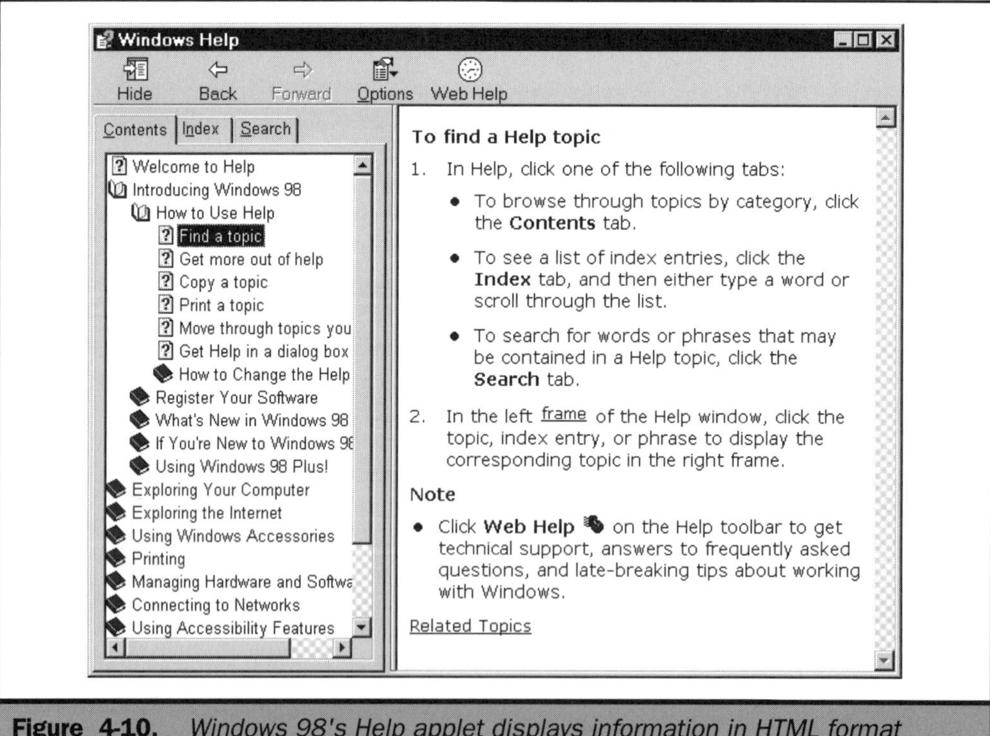

Figure 4-10. *Windows 98's Help applet displays information in HTML format*

question marks) appear. When you click a question mark entry, its content is displayed in the viewer pane on the right. The help text may contain hyperlinks that open other help entries, launch Windows 98 system utilities and troubleshooters, or open Internet Explorer to seek information on the World Wide Web.

If you select the Index tab on the Contents pane, Windows Help displays an alphabetical index of key words. You can browse the index with the scrollbar on the right or enter a search term in the blank field at the top. The index searches, alphabetically, for the words or phrases you enter. To display the content, either double-click the keyword entry in the Topic list or select the entry and click the Display button at the bottom of the window.

If you select the Search tab in the Contents pane, Windows Help creates an indexed database of all the words contained in the Help files. To search for information from this tab, type a keyword or keywords and click the List Topics button. Entries that contain at least one of the keywords will appear in the Topic list. To search for a phrase instead of occurrences of individual words, place quotation marks around the words you enter in the Type In The Keyword field.

Several housekeeping functions are available from the drop-down Options menu in Help. You can also right-click the mouse button in the display pane to open a pop-up options menu. Options on this menu let you move back or forward, select the entire current text, view and edit the current text as HTML source code, print the current text, and view a Properties sheet for the current Help screen. To jump from the Help files on your own hard drive to Microsoft's Technical Support Web site, click Web Help at the top of the Help window.

Tip

Although Win98 Help has lost its bookmarking feature, you can copy strategic information into another application that permits bookmarking or supports refined text searches. With the viewer pane selected, press CTRL-A to select the entire window contents and CTRL-C to copy it to the clipboard. Then open WordPad (Start | Programs | Accessories | WordPad) and use the Edit menu or press CTRL-V to paste in the help content. Once the help content appears in WordPad, you can search for additional keywords with the Edit | Find command, or flag relevant portions of the file and drag them to the desktop as Scrap shortcuts. If you have Microsoft Word 7 or 8, those applications will do a slightly better job than WordPad at preserving internal formatting features in help content. (See "WordPad" in Chapter 5 for more information about using its Scrap drag-and-drop feature.)

Help for older Windows 95 and Windows 3.1 programs still uses the help formats that were introduced with those versions of Windows.

Context-sensitive help is also available from within many dialog boxes. If you see a What's This? question mark icon in the upper-left corner of a Help window or program dialog box, you can click it once to change your cursor to a question mark. Move the question mark to any item in the window. Click again to open a brief explanation of that item. In many dialog boxes you can also open an item description by right-clicking the item and then clicking the What's This? button.

You can save information from a pop-up window by selecting the text you want with your mouse and pressing CTRL-C to copy it to the clipboard. (Don't try to drag the text out of the window—use the keyboard!) You can then paste the text from the clipboard into an application, save it in a file, or print it. If you right-click within a pop-up box, another menu pops up that allows you to copy the entire contents to the clipboard or to a printer.

Using the Windows 98 Resource Kit Book

The *Windows 98 Resource Kit* book is a thick, richly detailed volume that contains useful information about every aspect of the Windows 98 operating system. An online version of this help resource is included on the Windows 98 CD, but it's not installed automatically.

You can access the online *Resource Kit* book in several ways:

- Open it quickly by inserting the Windows 98 CD and entering ***d:*\TOOLS\RESKIT\HELP\RK98BOOK.CHM** (where ***d:*** is the letter of your CD-ROM drive).
- Create a desktop shortcut to this file on the CD by opening Windows Explorer to the *d*:\TOOLS\RESKIT\HELP folder and dragging a copy of the Rk98book icon to the desktop.
- Install the *Windows 98 Resource Kit* on your hard drive by inserting the Windows 98 CD, opening the \TOOLS\RESKIT folder, and running the Setup program.

Once open on your desktop, the *Windows 98 Resource Kit* online book has an interface very similar to that of standard Windows 98 Help. The Topic pane contains only Content and Search tabs. To retrieve relevant information on the Search tab, enter your keywords (enclosing phrases in quotation marks) and click the Start Search button. Two check marks at the bottom of the pane give you additional options: You can search for matching words similar to the keywords you enter, and you can limit the search to *Resource Kit* book chapter titles, omitting the main text.

The results of your search are displayed in a three-column window (see Figure 4-11). You can sort the results by title, location, or rank (the default) by clicking the appropriate column header. To get a clearer view of the retrieved topic title, you can position the mouse at the right-column border and drag right. The Search In drop-down box permits you to refine your search results by entering a new keyword or phrase and repeating the search only within the previously retrieved results. To display the results of a search, double-click the entry in the Select Topic list or highlight the entry and click the Display Topic button.

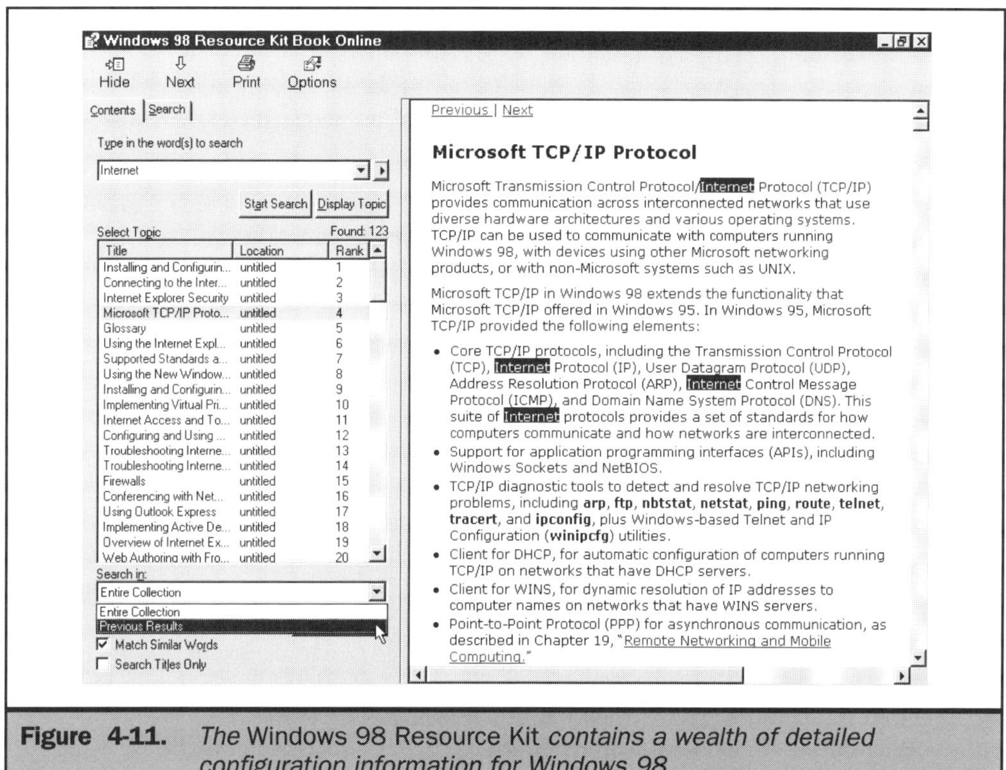

Figure 4-11. *The* Windows 98 Resource Kit *contains a wealth of detailed configuration information for Windows 98*

Desktop Strategies and Secrets

This part of the chapter explains how to solve problems related to launching programs, managing files, and managing the desktop. It includes information about creating convenient desktop shortcuts, customizing the Start menu, and configuring the desktop options, plus a liberal assortment of productivity tips and tricks.

Working with the Start Menu

Although it appears on your screen as a single package, the Start menu actually has three parts: a set of fixed items that you can't easily change, including the Settings, Find, Help, Run, and Shut Down commands; a pair of file lists that you can remove with Tweak UI; and a variable collection of shortcuts to programs, data files, Web pages, and other objects. If you can find or create an item in a My Computer or

Windows Explorer window or place a shortcut on your desktop, you can add a shortcut to that item on the Start menu.

Microsoft has made it easy for you to customize the Start menu to include the programs and data files you actually use. You can add new programs, folders, shortcuts, and data files to the Start menu in a variety of ways:

- To add a shortcut to the top-level Start menu, click the target object in My Computer or Windows Explorer and drag it to the Start button.
- To add a shortcut to the Programs menu or to a submenu within Programs, drag the target object to the Start button but don't release the mouse button yet. When the Start menu opens, drag your mouse to the location within the menu structure where you want the shortcut to appear.
- To add several shortcuts to the Start menu or a submenu, click the Start button and click either Open or Explore. This will open the editable part of the Start menu as a folder. You can add, delete, or move folders and shortcuts to programs and data files (or shortcuts to Web pages) just as with any other folder in My Computer or Windows Explorer.
- You can also add programs to the Start menu by opening the Start button and selecting Settings | Taskbar & Start Menu, then clicking the Start Menu Programs tab. Click the Add button to open the Create Shortcut Wizard, where you can either type the path and file name of the object you want to add to the Start menu or use the Browse button to find the object in a file browser. To open the Start menu in an Explorer window, click the Advanced button.
- To change the order in which items appear in the Start menu or to move an item to or from a submenu, click the item you want to move and drag it to the new location.
- To remove an item from the Start menu, either drag and drop the item in the Recycle Bin or right-click the item and select Delete from the pop-up menu.

Using the Start Menu as a Surrogate Program Manager

The Start menu is a flexible tool that you can use in several different ways. You're already familiar with its standard configuration as a pop-up program launcher. You can also use the Start menu to display programs and groups on the desktop. Some people are used to this look and feel and may prefer it to the nested menus displayed by the Start button.

To configure a desktop that looks like the old Windows 3.x Program Manager, right-click the Start button and select the Open command. The Start menu window that you see on your desktop corresponds to the variable portion of the Start menu—it includes the Programs submenu and any additional items you've added to the menu, but not the Settings, Favorites, Help, Find, or other fixed sections. These folders and shortcut links that you see are physically located in the Start menu directory (\WINDOWS\START MENU). You can drag a shortcut to the Programs folder onto your desktop or open the Programs folder and drag out shortcuts to any of your favorite program groups.

If you open and size one or more Start menu windows on your desktop, those windows will remain open the next time you start Windows 98. The advantage of emulating the Program Manager with group folder windows is that it's super easy to create new subfolders and applications or move them in and out of a group window.

Jumping to Favorite Web Sites

The Favorites item on the Start menu contains shortcuts to all of the items in the Internet Explorer Favorites list. This list is most commonly used to store shortcuts to Web sites, but you can also add shortcuts to local files, folders, programs, and other objects. You can open the same list from the Favorites menu in My Computer and Windows Explorer.

Returning to a Document

The Documents menu is a list of shortcuts to the 15 documents that you have viewed, created, edited, or otherwise worked on most recently (provided that you used a program created for Windows 95 or Windows 98 or opened the file from My Computer or Windows Explorer). When you select an item from the Documents menu, Windows automatically opens the document in the program that created it. So, for example, if you created an Excel spreadsheet, you can reopen that spreadsheet in Excel by selecting it in the Document menu. The Documents menu can provide a quick and easy way to return to a work-in-progress after a break.

The Documents menu also contains a shortcut to your My Documents folder, which is the default location for saving data files in many applications.

To remove individual items in the Documents menu, open the hidden \WINDOWS\RECENT folder in Windows Explorer and delete the items you don't want to see. (You may need to turn on the display of hidden and system files through Explorer's View | Folder Options | View menu, as described in "Turning On DOS File Extensions" earlier in this chapter.) To remove everything (except the link to My Documents) from the Documents menu, open the Start menu and select Settings | Taskbar & Start Menu. Choose the Start Menu Programs tab and click the Clear button in the Documents Menu section.

Removing Favorites and Documents from the Start Menu

If you don't ever use the Favorites and Documents lists on the Start menu, you can remove them from the menu with the Tweak UI program included in the *Windows Resource Kit* section of the Windows 98 CD-ROM (see "Tweak UI Applet" in Chapter 9 for installation details). After you install Tweak UI, open it from the Control Panel, choose the IE4 tab, and scroll down to the Show Documents On Start Menu and Show Favorites On Start Menu options. Turn off these options to remove the corresponding items from the Start menu, as shown here:

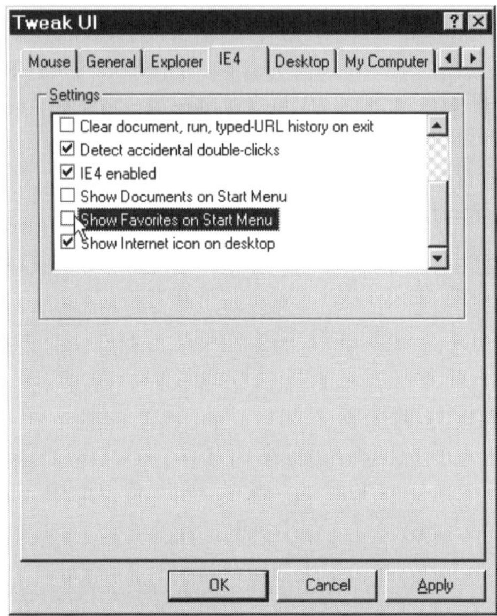

Housekeeping Options: The Settings Menu

The Start | Settings menu is a catch-all for shortcuts to folders and objects that control the way various parts of Windows 98 operate. Almost everything in this menu is also accessible from some other location, but the Start menu provides a convenient place to start searching for most configuration options.

CONTROL PANEL The Control Panel is a folder that contains configuration applets. Chapter 9 describes each of the items in the Control Panel.

PRINTERS The Printers folder contains a profile for each of the printers and printer emulators installed on your computer. Chapter 10 explains how to create and use printer profiles.

TASKBAR & START MENU The Taskbar Properties dialog box controls the configuration of the Windows taskbar and the contents of the Start menu. You can find instructions for using the Start menu options earlier in this section and information about the taskbar options in the next part of this chapter.

FOLDER OPTIONS The Folder Options command on the Start menu is identical to the command on the My Computer and Windows Explorer menus, described earlier in this chapter.

ACTIVE DESKTOP The Active Desktop options enable you to hide or display your desktop as a Web viewer, open the Display Properties applet (where you can change the appearance and behavior of most of the elements of your desktop), and choose an Update command that retrieves the most recent versions of the HTML objects on your desktop from their Web servers. See "What Does the Active Desktop Mean to You?" in Chapter 12 for more information.

WINDOWS UPDATE Microsoft offers a free update service for Windows 98 and other products. The Windows Update program opens Internet Explorer and connects you to the Microsoft Windows Update Web site, which will search your computer for out-of-date components and show you a list of new features and device drivers that are not installed on your system. If you select one or more of the items, the server will download them to your computer and automatically install them.

Making Printers, Dial-Up Networking, Control Panel, and Other System Folders More Accessible

The Win98 Printers and Control Panel folders are normally two layers down on the Start menu. Dial-Up Networking is reached by selecting Start | Programs | Accessories | Communication in a long foldout chain. And once you open one of these folders, you still have to click the individual icon that you want to open.

You can save some time and mouse clicks by moving these and other system objects (such as Fonts or Network Neighborhood) to the top level of the Start menu. When you point at your new Start menu shortcuts, they will cascade open, allowing you to select the application, printer, or file you want to access in one fluid motion. The procedure for adding a special Control Panel folder to the Start menu is described in detail in the sidebar "Express Shortcut on the Start Menu" in Chapter 9. The same procedure can be used to create the other special folders.

For instance, here's how to create a cascading Printers shortcut:

1. Right-click the Start button and select Open to open the Start menu in a window.
2. Create a new folder in the Start menu window by selecting New | Folder from the File menu.
3. Rename the folder from the default name New Folder to the following:

   Printers.{2227A280-3AEA-1069-A2DE-08002B30309D}

Use this exact string. Remember to include the period (.) character and the right and left curly brackets.

This long string instructs the Win98 registration database to convert the folder to a new Printers folder. The next time you open the Start menu by using the Start button, you will see a Printers item in the top-level menu. When you select this item, you will open a submenu that lists all of the output devices in the Printers folder, as shown here:

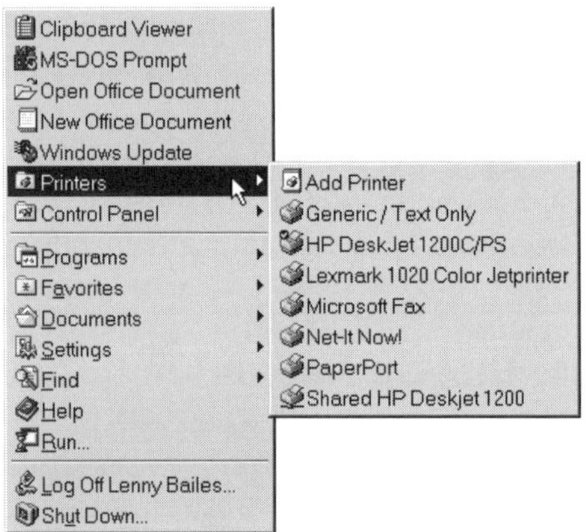

This trick works because the long serial number in the folder name tells the registration database to create a special object. You can also create special folders in the Start menu window for Fonts, the Recycle Bin, and the Windows desktop. The names for these folders are listed here:

Dial-Up Networking	Dial Up Networking.{992CFFA0-F557-101A-88EC- 00DD010CCC48}
Control Panel	Control Panel.{21EC2020-3AEA-1069-A2DD-08002B30309D}
Briefcase	Briefcase.{85BBD920-42A0-1069-A2E4-08002B30309D}
Desktop	Desktop.{00021400-0000-0000-C000-000000000046}
Fonts	Fonts.{BD84B380-8CA2-1069-AB1D-08000948F534}

Network Neighborhood	Network Neighborhood.{208D2C60-3AEA-1069-A2D7-08002B30309D}
Recycle Bin	Recycle Bin.{645FF040-5081-101B-9F08-00AA002F954E}
Inbox (if Windows Messaging is installed)	Inbox.{00020D75-0000-0000-C000-000000000046}

There are no similar registration serial numbers for other commonly used features, such as the clipboard or the MS-DOS prompt. However, you can place these features anywhere on the Start menu by selecting the original object, dragging it to the location you want, and choosing Create Shortcut from the pop-up menu.

Searching for Resources: The Find Menu

The Find utility in Windows 98 provides a quick way to move directly to a program, file, folder, or other object without having to inspect the contents of dozens of separate folders. When you know the name of the file or other object you want, you can type that name on the Find menu's Name & Location tab. You can also search for a text string (such as a name) by typing the target words in the Containing Text field. The Date tab allows you to search for files created within a specified date and time range. The Advanced tab allows you to limit a search to files of a particular type or to files larger or smaller than a specific size.

Once the results of a search appear in the Find window, you can open any file in the list and copy, move, print, rename, or delete a file just as in a My Computer or Windows Explorer file list.

You can save the results of a file search on the desktop by selecting Options | Save Results from the Find window's pull-down menu. At any time, you can open the desktop shortcut that's created in this way to review the results of this particular search.

The Find | Computer command extends your search to other computers connected to yours through a network. When the Find utility identifies one or more computers whose name matches the computer name you request, it displays a list of shared resources on that computer.

Find | On the Internet opens Internet Explorer and connects you to an Internet search engine.

Find | People opens the Find People dialog box in Outlook Express. This window provides a direct link to your own address book and to at least eight different Internet directory services that may help you locate an e-mail address, and possibly a voice telephone number or postal address, for the name you specify.

Entering Commands Manually: Using the Run Dialog Box

The Run command on the Start menu opens a dialog box that provides command-line access to Windows and DOS programs. It accepts several different kinds of commands:

- To run a program located in the \WINDOWS or \WINDOWS\COMMAND folder or in a folder listed on the path= line of your AUTOEXEC.BAT file, simply type the name of the program in the Run box and click OK or press ENTER.
- To run a program located anywhere else on your system, type the full path to the program file or click the Browse button to open the Browse window. Select the program you want to run, click Open, and then click OK or press ENTER.
- To open a My Computer folder window, enter the name and path of the folder and then click OK or press ENTER.
- To load a data file into a program, type the name (and path, if necessary) to the program followed by the path and file name to the data file, such as **"C:\WINDOWS\NOTEPAD.EXE C:\DOCUMENTS\MYFILENAME.TXT"**. (If the path includes long filenames, you must enclose it in quotation marks.) Then click OK or press ENTER. To use the Browse window to list all files instead of only program files, change the selection in the Browse window's Files Of Type field from Programs to All Files.
- To quickly open a shared network resource, enter the Universal Naming Convention (UNC) path to the resource in the Run box: for example, **\\WORKHORSE\\BIGIRON**. Then click OK or press ENTER.
- To load a Web page into Internet Explorer, type the URL of the page you want to open.
- To send an e-mail message, type **mailto:*address***, using the recipient's e-mail address in place of *address*.

Ending a Windows Session: Log Off and Shut Down

When you have finished using your computer, it's important to allow all of the active programs (including internal utilities running in the background) to close down in an orderly manner. If you simply turn off the computer, you run the risk of losing configuration information or even damaging your hard drive—it's not likely, but it is possible.

Therefore, you should use the Shut Down command on the Start menu before you hit that power switch. (It takes a certain kind of perverse mind to place the command that stops the computer in the *Start* menu, but there it is.) When the computer has closed down everything, it will display a message that says "It's now safe to turn off your computer." Some computers configured with advanced power management will turn themselves off automatically at this point.

If you share your computer with other users who have their own user profiles, you can close down your session without turning off the power by selecting the Log Off command. The other users will have to enter their names and passwords to load their own user profiles.

The Shut Down command also offers three other options:

- **Standby** This option appears if your computer supports Microsoft's Advanced Power Management standard. Selecting it will shut down the computer's monitor and hard disk, putting it into a suspended, low-power state. When you press the Power On button for your computer, the system will reload the Windows session that was previously active instead of rebooting the machine from scratch. (See "Power Management Applet" in Chapter 9 for more information on this feature.)
- **Restart** Choose Restart to shut down the computer and immediately start it up again. This feature is useful when a program mysteriously freezes, or if you have just installed a new program or changed one or more configuration settings. If you hold down the SHIFT key when you click the OK button, the computer will generally skip its power-on self-test diagnostic routine and restart without reprocessing your CONFIG.SYS and AUTOEXEC.BAT files.
- **Restart in MS-DOS Mode** Choose this option to shut down Windows and restart the computer in a real-mode MS-DOS session. (See "Running DOS Applications Under Windows 98" later in this chapter for more information.)

Other Start Menu Tricks

Normally, when you create a new folder on the Start menu, the folder bears a program group icon. When you open the Start menu, you'll see that each program group icon has a right-pointing triangle. If you move the mouse over an icon that has one of these triangles, it opens to display nested files and subfolders in a pop-up list. Earlier in this section, you learned how to create a few special system folders on the Start menu. You can also drag existing folders from My Computer or Windows Explorer to the Start button, or right-click the Start menu, select Open, and use the File | New | Folder command to create a blank folder. You can subsequently populate this new folder with custom shortcut links.

In addition to making cascading folders, the Start menu permits you to create folder shortcuts. A shortcut to a folder is not the same thing as a physical folder on the hard disk. If you drag a folder shortcut onto the Start menu, it will not open up with a triangular pointer. Instead, it will be represented by a standard yellow folder icon, and a standard My Computer file listing will open when you select it. The HyperTerminal folder shortcut on the Programs | Accessories | Communications menu is a preconfigured example of this type of shortcut.

To place a new folder shortcut on the Start menu (that opens a file window instead of a pop-up list), open My Computer or Windows Explorer and select an existing folder or create a new one. Next, right-click and drag the folder to the Start button or to an open Start menu window. Choose Create Shortcut from the pop-up context menu (not Move or Copy).

Customizing the Taskbar

The taskbar in Windows 98 has a several new features. To add one of the preconfigured toolbar options to your taskbar, move your mouse cursor within the taskbar and right-click. Choose Toolbars from the pop-up menu and select the specific toolbar you want from the submenu.

You can add several kinds of toolbars to the taskbar.

Address Toolbar

The Address toolbar contains a field where you can enter a local command or file path or type the address of a Web page, Internet news group, e-mail destination, or other Internet resource. The arrow button on the right side of the Address field opens a menu of recently visited sites and local objects.

Links Toolbar

The Links toolbar on the taskbar is identical to the same toolbar in Internet Explorer. To add the current page open in Internet Explorer to the Links toolbar, drag the icon in the Address bar to the word "Links" in the Links bar. To remove icons from the Links toolbar, start Internet Explorer, open the Favorites menu, and select Organize Favorites. Choose the Links folder, select the icon you want to remove, and click the Delete button.

Desktop Toolbar

The Desktop toolbar contains the same set of shortcuts that appears on your desktop. Clicking an icon on the toolbar does exactly the same thing as double-clicking a desktop icon (or single-clicking if you have configured the desktop to work like a Web page).

If you view a Web page directly on the Active Desktop, you may want to hide the desktop icons and use the Desktop toolbar (the Hide Icons option is on the Effects tab of the Display Properties dialog box) to keep the icons out of the way of text or images in the Web page.

Tip *If you don't want a full-time Desktop toolbar on your taskbar, you can create one on demand with this command: Choose Start | Run, enter a period (.) in the Run box, and click OK. A window will open on the screen that displays all the icons on your desktop.*

Quick Launch Toolbar

The Quick Launch toolbar contains one more set of shortcuts. Windows 98 and some of its application programs automatically load shortcuts onto the Quick Launch toolbar.

You can easily add additional shortcuts to programs, data files, folders, and Internet URLs by dragging them onto this toolbar. To remove existing shortcuts, right-click the icon of the shortcut you want to delete.

Adding a New Toolbar

You can create an entirely new, custom toolbar, which may contain any other folder on your hard disk (or shortcuts to Web pages or other Internet resources). To create a new toolbar, select New Toolbar from the pop-up menu and either select a folder from the list or type a Web address or other URL in the Destination field. In most cases, you will want to use My Computer or Windows Explorer to create a new folder and place shortcuts to the items you want to use in the toolbar. This is a better idea than trying to use an existing folder that probably contains items you really don't want in the toolbar.

If Active Desktop is turned on and you've added a live, scrolling Internet window, you can convert this window into a new toolbar. For example, you might want to move an Active Desktop object that displays the NASDAQ stock ticker to a toolbar, as shown here:

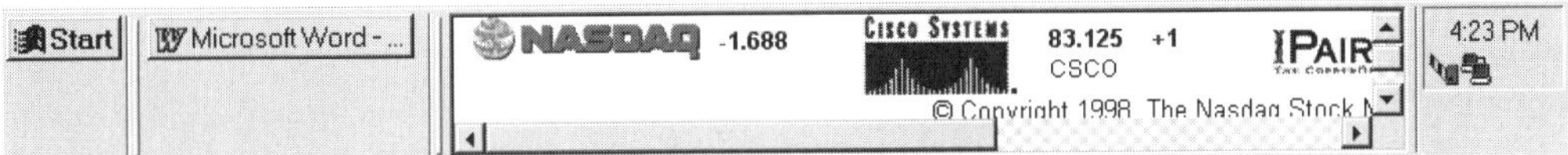

To place a scrolling Web window in a toolbar, follow these steps:

1. Enter **Desktop** in the Address or URL field of your Web browser to open a display of all the desktop objects.
2. Right-click the scrolling text and select Properties from the pop-up menu.
3. On the General tab, find and highlight the address of this window.
4. Right-click the selected text and choose Copy from the pop-up menu.
5. Close the Properties window.
6. Right-click the taskbar and select Toolbars | New Toolbar from the menu.
7. In the New Toolbar dialog box, right-click the address field and select Paste from the pop-up menu.
8. Click OK.

Creating Free-Floating Toolbars

By default, the toolbars you create are located within the taskbar, but you don't have to keep them there. To move a toolbar onto your desktop, move your cursor over an empty space in the toolbar you want to move and hold down the right mouse button.

When the cursor changes to a four-way arrow, drag the toolbar to the approximate location where you want to place it. To change the size or proportions of a floating toolbar, drag one or more of the edges or corners.

To restore a floating toolbar to the taskbar, click the toolbar's title bar and drag the toolbar back to the taskbar.

Tip *After you've created a few toolbars, you may find that you're running out of taskbar space. Luckily, all of the custom toolbars you create for the Internet Explorer 4 taskbar can be dragged out and docked on the desktop. Click the mouse on the double-stripe handle for the toolbar and drag it to the right, left, or upper edge of the screen. This will dock the toolbar and clear display space on your original taskbar. (You can also drag toolbars to the center of the desktop to create free-floating tool palettes.) You can save even more space by making a docked toolbar self-hiding: right-click the toolbar, open its Properties screen, and place check marks next to Always On Top and AutoHide. This will make your docked toolbar disappear until you move the mouse over the edge of the screen where you've placed it.*

Removing Toolbars from the Taskbar

To remove any preconfigured or custom toolbar from the taskbar, right-click an empty area of the taskbar, choose Toolbars from the menu, and remove the check mark next to the toolbar's name.

Changing the Appearance of the Taskbar

If you have more than one active toolbar on the taskbar, or if you want to make more room for the buttons that appear on the taskbar when you run a program, you have a couple of choices: you can increase the size of the entire taskbar by dragging the edge up onto the desktop, or you can slide individual toolbars out of sight by clicking and dragging the double line at the left edge of each toolbar. When there isn't enough space to display all the items on a toolbar, you will see a tiny pair of left and right arrows (like this: <- ->) on either side of the toolbar. When you click either arrow, the remaining shortcuts on the toolbar will appear as the list rotates right or left.

You can also save some space by hiding the title of each toolbar or even hiding the caption that appears next to each icon. Both of the options are on the right-click menu.

If you right-click the taskbar and select Properties, you'll see a number of other customization options. By default, the taskbar always floats on top of other applications on the desktop. By changing the Taskbar Options, you can disable this feature, hide the digital clock in the System Tray, or condense the Start menu display to show small icons. You can also select the Auto Hide option to reduce the taskbar to a thin line at the bottom of your screen. If you choose this option and you want the taskbar to be available when you run full-screen programs, you should select both the Always On Top and Auto Hide options.

Tip

You can customize the color, icon size, and fonts on the taskbar by using the Control Panel's Display options. Either open Display from the Control Panel or right-click the desktop and select Properties. Choose the Appearance tab and select Inactive Title Bar to change the size and font of text on the taskbar. Select 3D Objects to change the background color and text color.

Working with the System Tray

The System Tray, on the far right end of the taskbar, can contain a number of resident system controls and status indicators. To use any of these tools, click or right-click the tool to open its available options.

- The digital Windows clock is installed automatically on the taskbar. Other taskbar utilities, such as Scheduled Tasks, QuickView Display Properties, Infrared Monitor, Power Management, PC Card support, and Volume Control, are installed if your hardware supports them. Additionally, a small status area to the left of the digital clock is used to display messages from Windows 98 applications. When you use a fax, printer, modem, or other Win98-aware utility, a pop-up status box appears in this message area.
- The Scheduled Tasks icon appears by default and contains a scheduled Windows Tuneup event.
- The QuickView Display switcher appears in the System Tray if you select this option in the Control Panel | Display applet. (See Chapter 9 for more information.)
- The Volume Control, installed if you have a sound card, can be started in two views. A single click on the Speaker icon brings up a simple slider; a double-click brings up a more complete set of sound options.
- The Battery Meter is installed on laptop computers and other systems that support Advanced Power Management. It is represented by a plug icon, when the machine is plugged into an external source, and a battery icon, when the machine is running on battery power.
- The PC Card control icon appears on the taskbar if you have a computer that supports PCMCIA peripherals.

Note

Some third-party applications allow you to add your own custom events to the System Tray. Microsoft includes one called QuikTray as part of the Windows 98 Resource Kit *on the Win98 CD.*

Customizing the Interface

Windows 98 includes a number of power-user desktop options. Some of these options are not well-documented in the online Help system, but they are well worth knowing about and using. In this section you'll find some tips and tricks for improving your productivity.

Using Keyboard Shortcuts

If you don't want to use a mouse for all your operations, you'll find that you can perform many desktop functions by entering keyboard shortcuts. Many of these keyboard shortcuts are obscure, and you won't find all of them listed in online Help. Some tasks (such as switching between objects on the desktop or selecting minimized programs on the taskbar) require a ridiculous number of keystrokes.

Tables 4-2 through 4-9 list a wealth of Windows 98 keyboard shortcuts for the desktop, My Computer and Windows Explorer, the Explorer tree, Property sheets, and the Open, Save, and File Browser dialog boxes, as well as keyboard plus mouse shortcuts, shortcuts using special Windows keys, and accessibility shortcuts.

Key or Combination	Action
F1	Activates Help
F2	Renames the currently selected object
F3	Opens Find Files or Folders
F5	Refreshes the desktop
CTRL-A	Selects all objects on the desktop
CTRL-ESC	Opens the Start menu and sets the focus on the Start menu
CTRL-ESC, ESC	Opens and closes the Start menu and sets the focus on the Start button
CTRL-ESC, ESC, TAB	Accepts left and right arrow keystrokes to switch between buttons on the taskbar
CTRL-ESC, ESC, TAB, TAB	Accepts left, right, up, and down arrow keystrokes to move between objects on the desktop
SHIFT-F10	When the focus is on the desktop, opens the context-sensitive (right-click) menu

Table 4-2. *Keyboard Shortcuts for the Desktop*

Key or Combination	Action
ESC	Closes an open menu
ALT-TAB	Switches between open windows and applications
ENTER	Opens the currently selected object
ALT-ENTER	Displays the currently selected object's properties
DELETE	Moves the currently selected object to the Recycle Bin
SHIFT-DELETE	Deletes the currently selected object
ALT-F4	Shuts down the currently active program, or if no program is active, shuts down Windows
Arrow keys	Moves between objects on the desktop or items in a menu
PRINTSCRN	Copies an image of the desktop or the currently active window to the clipboard

Table 4-2. *Keyboard Shortcuts for the Desktop* (continued)

Key or Combination	Action
F1	Opens Help
F3 or CTRL-F	Opens the Find window
F4	Opens or closes the drop-down Address menu
F5 or CTRL-R	Refreshes the current window
F6 or TAB	Moves forward between toolbars and panes
SHIFT-F6 or SHIFT-TAB	Moves backward between toolbars and panes
F10 or ALT	Opens a menu on the menu bar
ALT-spacebar	Opens the System menu
ESC	Closes an open menu

Table 4-3. *Keyboard Shortcuts for My Computer and Windows Explorer*

Key or Combination	Action
SHIFT-F10	Opens the context-sensitive (right-click) menu
Arrow keys	Moves between items in a menu, toolbar, or folder view
ALT-F4 or CTRL-W	Closes the Windows Explorer or My Computer window
ALT-left arrow	Moves back to the previous folder view
ALT-right arrow	Moves forward to the next folder view
BACKSPACE	Moves up one level in the directory tree structure
CTRL-A	Selects all the objects in the current folder
CTRL-B	Organizes the Favorites list
CTRL-C	Copies the currently selected object
CTRL-X	Cuts the currently selected object
CTRL-V	Pastes the selected object on the clipboard
CTRL-Z	Undoes the last command
ENTER	Opens the currently selected item
DELETE	Moves the currently selected object to the Recycle Bin
SHIFT-DELETE	Deletes the currently selected object

Table 4-3. *Keyboard Shortcuts for My Computer and Windows Explorer* (continued)

Key or Combination	Action
Right arrow	Expands the current item or goes to the first child folder
Left arrow	Collapses the current item or goes to the parent item

Table 4-4. *Keyboard Shortcuts for the Explorer Tree*

Key or Combination	Action
TAB	Moves forward between options
SHIFT-TAB	Moves backward between options
CTRL-TAB	Moves between pages
F1	Displays help for the currently selected option
ENTER	Performs the currently selected option
ALT-F4 or ESC	Closes the dialog box

Table 4-5. *Keyboard Shortcuts for Property Sheets*

Key or Combination	Action
F1	Displays Help
F4 or arrow keys	Opens or closes the currently selected drop-down menu
F5	Refreshes the current view
TAB	Moves forward between options
SHIFT-TAB	Moves backward between options
Arrow keys	Moves within the currently selected option
ENTER	Runs or opens the currently selected option
BACKSPACE	Moves up one level

Table 4-6. *Keyboard Shortcuts for Open, Save, and File Browser Dialog Boxes*

Key or Combination	Action
ALT-double-click on an icon	Opens the Property sheet
SHIFT-double-click in My Computer	Opens the object in Windows Explorer
Hold down CTRL while dragging to a folder	Copies the object to the folder
Hold down CTRL-SHIFT while dragging to a folder or the desktop	Creates a shortcut to the dragged object
Hold down SHIFT while clicking Close	Closes this folder and all parent folders

Table 4-7. *Keyboard plus Mouse Shortcuts*

Key or Combination	Action
WIN	Opens the Start menu
WIN-R	Opens the Run dialog box
WIN-M	Minimizes all open windows
SHIFT-WIN-M	Undoes the Minimize All command
WIN-F1	Opens Help
WIN-E	Opens Windows Explorer
WIN-F	Opens the Find window
CTRL-WIN-F	Opens the Find Computer window
WIN-TAB	Moves to the next taskbar button
WIN-BREAK	Opens the System Properties dialog box
APP	Opens the context-sensitive (right-click) menu

Table 4-8. *Keyboard Shortcuts Using Special Windows Keys*

Key or Combination	Action
Press SHIFT five times	Turns StickyKeys on or off
Hold down the right SHIFT key for eight seconds	Turns FilterKeys on or off
Hold down NUM LOCK for five seconds	Turns ToggleKeys on or off
Press left ALT-left SHIFT-NUM LOCK	Turns MouseKeys on or off
Press left ALT-left SHIFT-PRINT SCRN	Turns High Contrast on or off

Table 4-9. *Accessibility Shortcuts*

Creating Your Own Shortcut Keys

In addition to using the preassigned keyboard shortcuts, you can also assign a shortcut key to launch any DOS or windows application or to open any document or data file present on the desktop or in the Start menu. To create or change a shortcut key, follow these steps:

1. Right-click the object on the desktop or in the Start menu.
2. Select Properties from the pop-up menu and click the Shortcut tab (for Windows applications) or the Program tab (for DOS applications and batch files).
3. In the Shortcut Key field (shown in Figure 4-12), type the names of the keys you want to use for the keyboard shortcut to this program or file. Keyboard shortcuts for Windows applications may use CTRL-ALT plus a letter, number, or function key. Shortcuts for DOS applications may use CTRL plus a letter, number, or function key; ALT plus a letter, number, or function key; and so on. If you want to use CTRL-ALT-S as a shortcut, you can simply type **S**, and the other keys will be filled in.
4. To make your startup shortcuts take effect, restart your system.

No other program can use a particular shortcut key combination once you assign it to a desktop shortcut. If the assigned hot key conflicts with an access key in a Windows program, the access key in the program will not work. To cancel a shortcut key assignment, open the Properties dialog box, select the shortcut key, and press the spacebar.

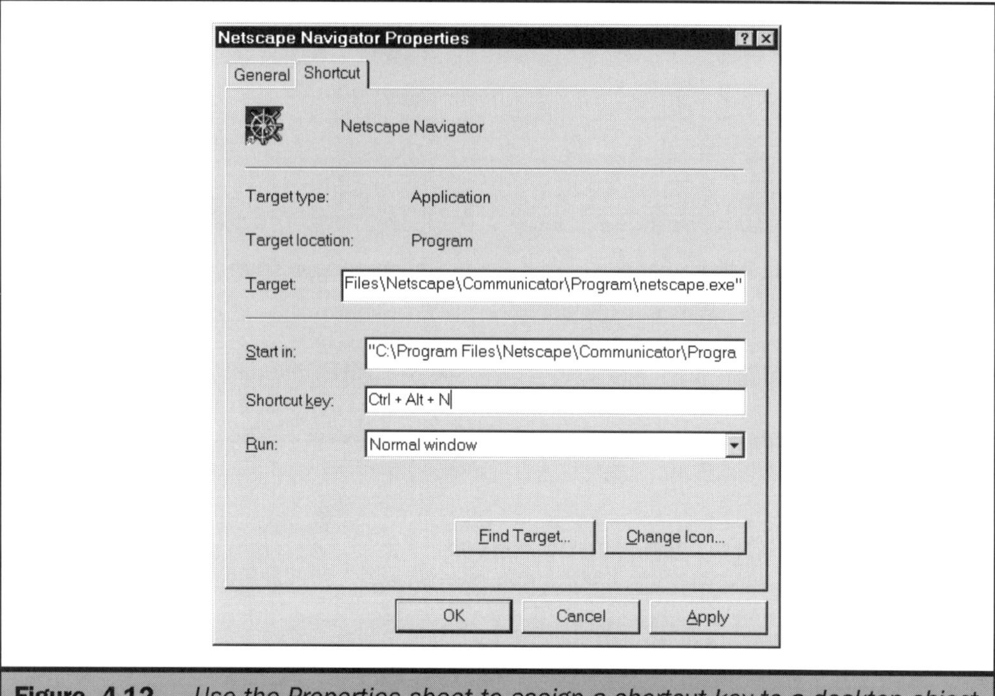

Figure 4-12. *Use the Properties sheet to assign a shortcut key to a desktop object*

You can also assign a shortcut key to open a folder if there's a shortcut link to that folder on the desktop or Start menu.

Using Quick View

Windows 98 includes a utility called Quick View that allows you to preview certain types of documents and graphic images. If you install this option during installation (or later using Add/Remove Programs in the Control Panel), filters for supported file types are added to the desktop.

If Quick View supports a file type, you will see a Quick View command on the My Computer or Windows Explorer File menu and on the menu that appears when you right-click the file in My Computer or Windows Explorer or on the desktop.

Quick View allows you to view files created in several popular formats, including the most widely used word processors and spreadsheets, but it does not recognize many other file types. For example, if you right-click an icon for a .INI or .BAT file, you won't see a Quick View command on the menu, even though both of these file types are just ASCII text.

There are several things you can do to improve Quick View's flexibility:

- Add Quick View to the Send To menu by dragging a shortcut to QUIKVIEW.EXE from the \WINDOWS\SYSTEM\VIEWERS folder to \WINDOWS\SENDTO.
- Enable Quick View for additional file types by opening the View | Folder Options | File Types dialog box, selecting a file type, and clicking the Edit button to open the dialog box shown in Figure 4-13. The Enable Quick View option is near the bottom of the dialog box.
- Install Quick View Plus, which can recognize more than 200 Windows, DOS, Macintosh, and Internet file types. You can download a free 30-day trial version of Quick View Plus from http://www.inso.com/qvp or order a copy (with a 30-day money-back guarantee) by telephone at (800) 333-1395. This application is also bundled free with some productivity suites, such as Corel WordPerfect Office.

Once you've installed Quick View in the SendTo folder, you can try it out on a file with any extension. (Right-click, choose Send To, and point to **QUIKVIEW.EXE**.) When you try to use Quick View on a file type that hasn't been enabled, you may see a message that says, "There are no viewers registered for this type of file. Would you like to try the Default Viewers?" Go ahead and answer yes. If the file is in a supported format, Quick View will load and display it.

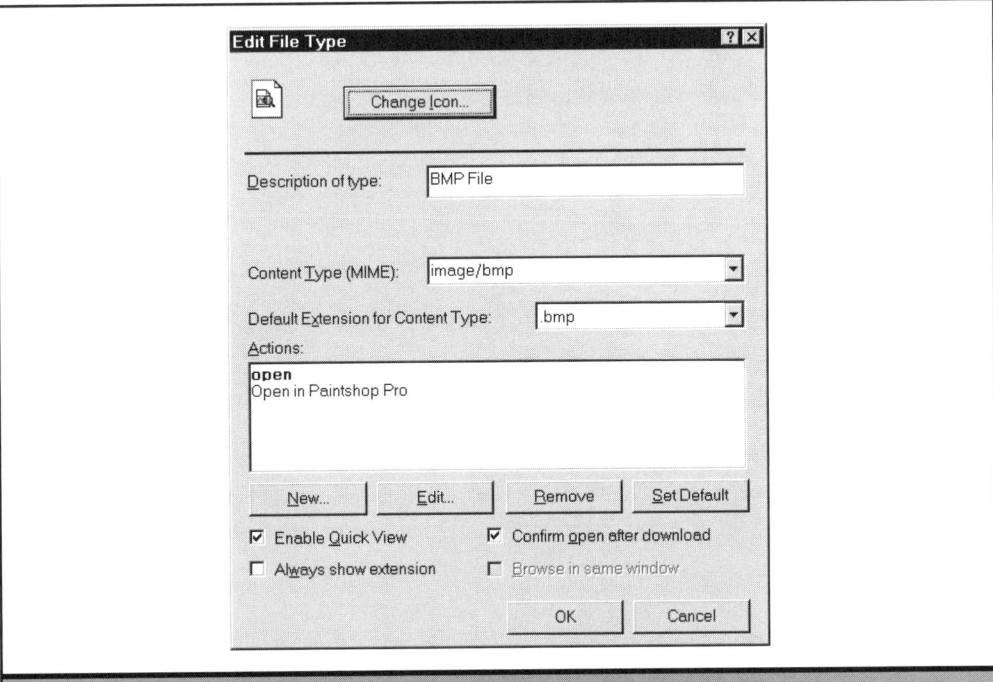

Figure 4-13. *Add a check mark to the Enable Quick View option box to include Quick View in the right-click menu for the current file type*

Assigning Additional Icons for DOS and Windows Programs

Are you looking for a larger assortment of icons to dress up your Windows desktop? If you don't like the default selections that Windows offers, you will find a wider choice of icons embedded in various Windows 98 system files.

To change the icon for a shortcut on the Start menu or desktop, right-click the shortcut, select Properties, go to the Shortcut tab, and click the Change Icon button. (For DOS programs, the Change Icon button is located on the Program tab.)

When you click the Change Icon button, a dialog box displays a File Name box and a Current Icon field. The Current Icon field shows all of the available icons embedded in the default icon file. The File Name box points to the binary file that contains the icons.

By default, icons for a Windows application may be embedded in the program itself. (The icon for Microsoft Word is contained in WINWORD.EXE, and so on.) Icons for DOS applications are chosen from special system files in the Windows directories. (The default icon file for most DOS applications is PIFMGR.DLL in the \WINDOWS\SYSTEM directory.)

In actuality, you can assign any icon to any file object by selecting the file that contains the icon in the File Name field in the Change Icon dialog box.

To browse for new icons for your programs and documents, follow these steps:

1. Change the display defaults for My Computer or Windows Explorer to display all files on your hard disk. (Open My Computer; choose View | Folder Options, select the View tab, and click the Show All Files button.
2. Right-click the icon you want to change, select Properties, and click the Change Icon button. (See the preceding discussion to find the Change Icon button for a Windows or DOS application.)
3. Scroll through the available icons in the Current Icon field.
4. If you want to see some additional icons, choose a different file in the File Name field; click the Browse button, and click a new file in the File List window. If the file contains embedded icons, they will appear in the Current Icon field.

Where do you find additional icons? Here are some places to look:

- In the \WINDOWS directory, PROGMAN.EXE contains lots of traditional Windows 3.1 icons.
- The \WINDOWS\MORICONS.DLL file contains a set of icons for long-forgotten DOS applications that might have other uses.
- Each Windows applet contains a few icons to choose from.
- In the \WINDOWS\SYSTEM directory, PIFMGR.DLL and SHELL32.DLL contain a wide selection of icons.
- ICONLIB.DLL contains a number of paper and document icons.

- MAILNEWS.DLL (installed by Internet Explorer 3) contains a number of mail and telecommunication icons.
- If you've installed Microsoft Plus!, check out \WINDOWS\SYSTEM\COOL.DLL for a number of 3-D icons.
- In the Program Files directory, IEXPLORE.EXE is an icon storehouse.
- Icon libraries that contains thousands of additional Windows icons are available from many online software archives, including ZDnet's Software Library (http://www.hotfiles.com), Download.com (http://www.download.com), Jumbo! (http://www.jumbo.com), and FilePile (http://filepile.com). Each of these sites has a search engine where you can look for the keyword "icons."

Creating Multiple Desktops

When two or more people share a computer, or if a single user uses the same computer for different purposes, it may be convenient to create a different desktop configuration for each user or each type of activity. Each individual desktop can have its own screen colors, wallpaper, Start menu, desktop shortcuts, and other features.

To set up multiple desktops, follow these steps:

1. From the Control Panel, select Users.
2. Follow the prompts of the Enable Multi-User Settings Wizard. Enter a name for the new user, and (optionally) a password.
3. On the Personalized Items Settings screen, place check marks next to the items you want to individualize on the new user's desktop, as shown next. You can choose to share a common Start menu or common desktop icons among all of your desktops, or you can set up each desktop to use an independent configuration.

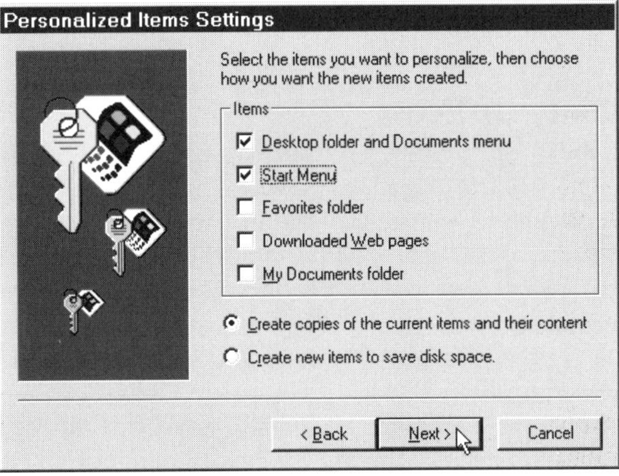

4. The next time you start the computer, it will ask for a user name and a password (if you entered one). Type the new user's name and password (if any). Windows will create and save a new user profile folder for the name you assigned. (See "Passwords Applet" and "Users Applet" in Chapter 9 for more detailed information about creating additional user accounts.)

This feature is not limited to creating new accounts and desktops for other people. You can create new accounts with names such as "Desktop Publishing" or "Games" to load alternative desktops and Start menus for a variety of productivity situations for your own work.

You can add, remove, or change any of the elements of your new desktop—wallpaper, desktop shortcuts, the Start menu, fonts, Active Desktop windows, and toolbars in the taskbar—without affecting your original configuration. For example, if you're setting up a special Desktop Publishing desktop, you might want to remove all the extraneous program groups and objects (don't worry; they're still there on your original desktop). You can add a special work folder on the desktop with shortcuts to PageMaker or Quark Xpress templates and supplement these objects with shortcuts to the Printers control panel, the Font folder, or an image cataloging utility. If you have a folder dedicated to DTP utilities, you might want to put a shortcut to it on your desktop or create a new toolbar that contains links to the objects in that folder.

When you have set up the new desktop the way you want, you can shut down the system. The next time you turn it on, this new desktop will appear if you log onto Desktop Publishing. If you use your original user name, Windows will load the original desktop.

To remove a user profile or to add or change the password for a profile, open the Control Panel and select Users. In the User Settings dialog box, select the profile you want to remove and click the Delete button.

If you have only one desktop profile and you don't use a password, you can bypass the login screen when you start your computer. Open the Control Panel, select Passwords, and click the User Profiles tab. Then select the All Users Use The Same Profile option.

Using Accessibility Options

Windows 98's Accessibility options are primarily designed to allow users with special needs to take advantage of features such as StickyKeys keyboard combinations, pop-up visual versions of sound events, a large-font high-contrast screen display, and a screen magnifier. However, some of the accessibility options may also be of interest to general users. For instance, the ToggleKeys option produces a sound whenever you press the CAPS LOCK, NUM LOCK, or SCROLL LOCK keys. This feature is particularly useful for people who accidentally press the CAPS LOCK key and then become irritated because their data entry is messed up.

Another Accessibility option allows you to use a keyboard mouse simulator. If you prefer to use the keyboard instead of the mouse, this is an invaluable feature. Some

Windows functions can't be accessed through the keyboard at all, and others require a cumbersome number of keystrokes. The MouseKeys feature cures this problem.

Using File Associations

By associating file types with programs, Windows 98 can automatically open a text file, formatted word processing document, database, or spreadsheet when you double-click a file icon. Double-clocking file icons also permits you to display pictures, connect to a Web page, or download files through the Internet. By default, the registration database contains more than 40 individual file types, and many application programs automatically add even more.

Open Windows Explorer or any folder on the desktop and select View | Folder Options | File Types. You'll see a list of all the file types registered on your system. This list also displays the file extensions and icon associated with each file type and the application program (if any) that has been assigned to open it. If you select a file type and click the Edit button, you'll see that a number of actions can be preconfigured, as shown here:

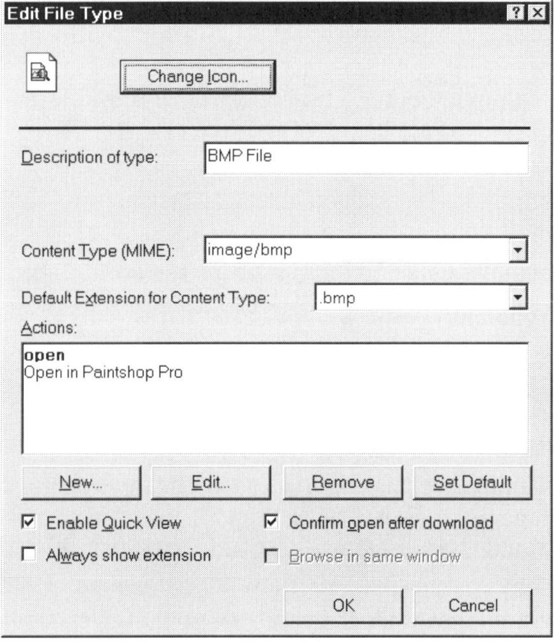

Each of the actions on the Edit File Type screen also appears on the right-click context-sensitive menu for all files of this type. Only one action (highlighted in bold type) can be the default action for a file type. In most cases, the default action is simply opening a file of this type in a specified application when you double-click it.

The registration database also identifies the Multipurpose Internet Mail Extensions (MIME) type assigned to each file type. Internet Explorer, Netscape Navigator, and many other Internet client programs use the MIME type to decide how to handle downloaded files. For example, when Internet Explorer receives a file with an .HTM or .HTML file extension, it knows that it can display it in the browser. However, when it receives a .RAM file, it must load that file into a RealAudio player.

Associating Files with Your Favorite Browsing and Editing Utilities

Windows 98 and many application programs automatically associate file types with specific applications. This is supposed to be a convenience, but in many cases, it's really more of an annoyance because every new program that works with a particular file type assumes that you want to make that program the default for all the file types it handles. So, for example, if you load a new bitmap image editor, it associates itself with bitmap (.BMP) files whether you want this to be the default or not. The next time you double-click the icon for a bitmap image file, the file will open in the new viewer program.

Fortunately, you don't have to keep the file associations your applications create if you prefer to open certain file types with other programs. You can use the Folder Options | File Types dialog box to associate any file type with any DOS or Windows application program.

To change the default viewer for a file type, follow these steps:

1. Select the file type from the alphabetical list of registered file types in the File Types dialog box.
2. Click the Edit button.
3. Choose Open in the list of actions and click the Edit button.
4. Type the file path and name of the program you want to use to open this file in the Application Used To Perform Action field, or click the Browse button to select the program from a file browser. If the program you specify supports Dynamic Data Exchange, you can select the Use DDE check box and enter the DDE commands that you want the program to perform.
5. Click the OK and Close buttons to close all the open dialog boxes.

Adding Options to the Right-Click Context Menu

In many cases, you may want to perform more than one kind of action on the same file type. For example, you may want to configure bitmap images to open in Kodak Imaging Preview when you double-click an icon, but sometimes you may want to use another image editor, such as Paintshop Pro or Corel PHOTO-PAINT, to modify the picture, or you may want to send the image as part of an e-mail message or just send it directly to your printer.

Some file types have preconfigured options, such as Print or Explore, and many others lend themselves to such options. These options are listed in the context-sensitive menu that appears when you right-click on a file. Any additional options in the Actions list can also be edited, or you can create new ones. To create an additional action for an existing file association, follow these steps:

1. Open the View | Folder Options dialog box in My Computer or Windows Explorer and click the File Types tab.
2. Select the file type you want to work with from the alphabetical Registered File Types list and click the Edit button.
3. In the Edit File Types dialog box, click the New button.
4. In the Action field in the New Action dialog box, type a short description of the action you want to perform (this text will appear in the right-click menu).
5. In the Application Used To Perform Action field, type a DOS or Windows command or the name of the program you want to run with this file type, or use the Browse button to select a program.
6. Click the OK and Close buttons to save your new settings.
7. Test your new command by right-clicking an icon of the specified file type and choosing the new command from the pop-up menu.

Make sure you specify a command or program that will actually work on the type of file you selected. For example, if you create a new action for a text file (.TXT), don't try to load it into a graphic image viewer.

Tip *If you want to use the context menu to perform the same action (such as printing or adding the file to a compressed archive) for many different file types, the easiest approach is to place the target program or object in the SendTo folder. For example, if you add a shortcut to your printer in the SendTo folder, Windows will use the default program for each file type to print the file. (See "Extending Drag-and-Drop Printing with the Send To Option" in Chapter 10 for more information.)*

Adding New File Types

You can also add your own new file types to the registration database. In the Folder Options | File Types dialog box, click the New Type button. Then enter the appropriate information for the new file type in the Add New File Type dialog box (see Figure 4-14).

For example, suppose you want to create an association for PSD image files created in Adobe Photoshop. Follow these steps to create a new file type in the system registry and associate it with Paintshop Pro (a shareware image editor):

1. Open the Folder Options | File Types dialog box.
2. Click the New Type button.

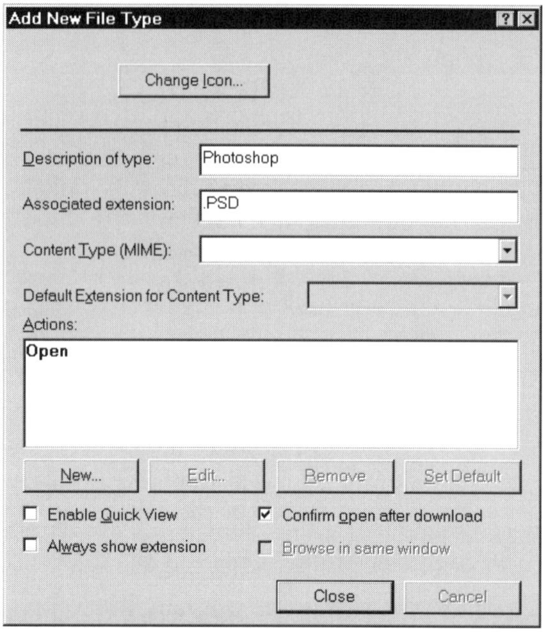

Figure 4-14. *Use the Add New File Type dialog box to create a new file association*

3. In the Description of Type field, type **Adobe Photoshop**.
4. In the Associated Extension field, type **.PSD**.
5. If you know that this file type has a MIME type, select the MIME type from the drop-down Content Type (MIME) menu. Otherwise, leave this field empty.
6. Under Actions, click the New button.
7. In the New Action dialog box, type **Open** in the Action field.
8. Click the Browse button and use the file browser to find the program you want to use to open this file type.
9. Click OK to close the New Action window.
10. If Quick View supports this file type, place a check mark in the Enable Quick View option box.
11. Click the OK button.
12. Confirm that the new file type is in the Registered File Types list and close the Folder Options window.

Whenever you double-click an object with a .PSD extension, that file will automatically open in Paintshop Pro.

Creating Multiple Right-Click Open Options

It's not necessary to replace the default Open action for a file type. To create an additional right-click action, follow the procedure outlined in the preceding section, but assign a different name to the action in step 7. For instance, if you want to retain the default application association for Adobe PSD image files to Paintshop Pro, you can define an *additional* right-click action for Adobe Photoshop, Corel PHOTO-PAINT, or another heavy-hitting image editor. Follow the procedure described earlier in "Adding Options to the Right-Click Context Menu."

Changing File Extensions in Associations

Once Windows 98 associates a given file extension with an application in My Computer and Windows Explorer, you will not be able to edit the association to assign the file extension to a different file type. This is another of Microsoft's attempts to wean users away from the habit of thinking about the file extension as the primary identifier of a file.

This can be very annoying if you have assigned several file extensions to the same file type but later want to change the default program that handles just one of those extensions, or if you install a new program that grabs control of several file extensions even though you really want to continue to open some of those file types in a different program. It's easy to change the default program for all the file extensions in a file type, but it's more difficult to modify only some of the extensions.

There are several workarounds for this problem. First, you can delete the existing file type and replace it with two or more new ones: one for each group of file extensions. This can be tedious if you have several complex actions assigned to an existing file type.

Second, you can add a new action to the context-sensitive menu. However, this assigns the new action to all the file extensions associated with this file type, not just the one you want.

Fortunately, there's another, better way to deal with this problem: you can split up multiple file associations assigned to a single program and reassign them individually with the Win98 File Manager. File Manager is a utility left over from Windows 3.1, but it's still available in Windows 98. Here's what you need to do:

1. From the Start menu, select Run and type **WINFILE**.
2. Open the File menu and choose the Associate command. The Associate dialog box appears.
3. In the Files with Extension field, enter the file extension you want to remove from an existing file type. For instance, if Microsoft Word has usurped the .RTF extension from Win98's WordPad, you may want to restore it. Enter **RTF** in the

Files With Extension field. The current file type assigned to this extension appears in the Associate With field, and the application name appears in the scrolling menu.

4. To reassign .RTF to WordPad, click the Browse button and locate WORDPAD.EXE, as shown next. (Since File Manager doesn't support long filenames, you may have to search through PROGRA~1, PROGRA~2, and PROGRA~3 to find the file that corresponds to the \PROGRAM FILES\ACCESSORIES folder.

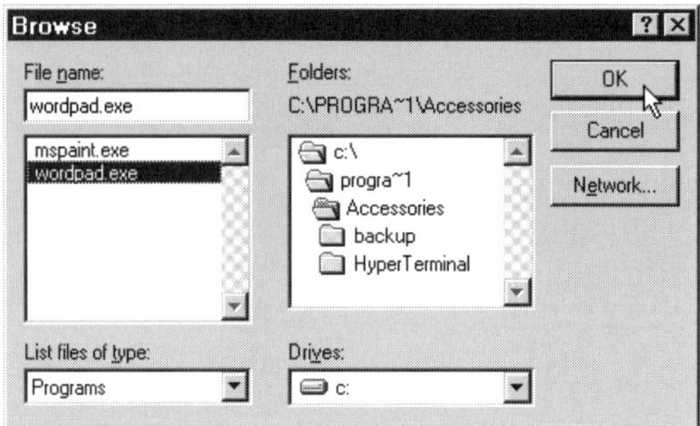

5. To move this file extension to a different existing file type, select the target file type in the scrolling menu.
6. Click the OK button to save your changes and close the dialog box.
7. Close the File Manager.

Building Work Folders with Find

As an alternative to using the Start menu or desktop program icons to run your applications, you can build an object-oriented desktop. Instead of cluttering your desktop with shortcuts to applications or open program folders, you can create a set of work folders that contain shortcuts to the reports, spreadsheets, and other documents you use most frequently.

For instance, you may have spreadsheets scattered over your hard disk in many disk partitions and subdirectories. Instead of opening Excel and searching for your work, it's easy to gather your spreadsheets into project folders that you can place on your desktop.

Here's how to construct a work folder for your spreadsheets:

1. Run the Find utility from the Start menu or by pressing the F3 key from your desktop.
2. In the Named field, type ***.XLS *.XLM** (the extensions for Excel spreadsheets and macros).

3. Select Local Hard Drives in the Look In field. Make sure the Include Subfolders option is checked.
4. Click the Find Now button. The Find utility will locate all of the Excel spreadsheets and macros on your entire system. The results of your search will be listed in the lower portion of the Find window. Notice that you can limit the date range of your search by using the options on the Date tab.
5. Create a new desktop work folder. Right-click the desktop and select New | Folder from the pop-up menu. Then assign any name you want to the folder.
6. Return to the list of retrieved .XLS and .XLM files. Hold down the right mouse button and drag each of the files you want to place in the work folder to the folder icon on the desktop. Choose Create Shortcut(s) Here from the pop-up menu.

You now have a work folder that contains shortcuts to all of your frequently used spreadsheets. You can double-click any worksheet in this folder to quickly load it into Excel.

Obviously, this process is not limited to Excel spreadsheets. You can use the same technique to create a work folder that contains any kind of data file organized by project, date, category, or any other method that seems logical to you.

Working with Registered Templates

Windows 98 includes a convenient option that automatically creates new, empty file and folder templates on the desktop. Double-clicking a file template automatically opens a new or preformatted file in the template's associated application. You can see a list of current templates by right-clicking an empty area of the desktop, or inside a folder, and choosing the New option (see Figure 4-15).

By default, Windows 98 usually includes a small handful of templates. These are created by Microsoft applications and by third-party programs that exploit the registration database. To add or remove document templates in this list, use the Tweak UI program on the Windows 98 CD-ROM (see Chapter 9 for installation information). If you don't have the CD-ROM, you can download a copy of Tweak UI from Microsoft's Web site.

Once you have installed Tweak UI, open it from the Control Panel and select the New tab, shown in Figure 4-16. To add a new template type, drag it from the desktop or Windows Explorer into the list of templates. To remove a template type from the pop-up menu, remove the check mark next to its name. To permanently remove a template type from the list, right-click the item in the Tweak UI list and select Remove.

Creating Project-Oriented Folders

You can combine the New Folder and New Template features of the Windows 98 desktop to plan a work project in advance. For example, you may know that a project

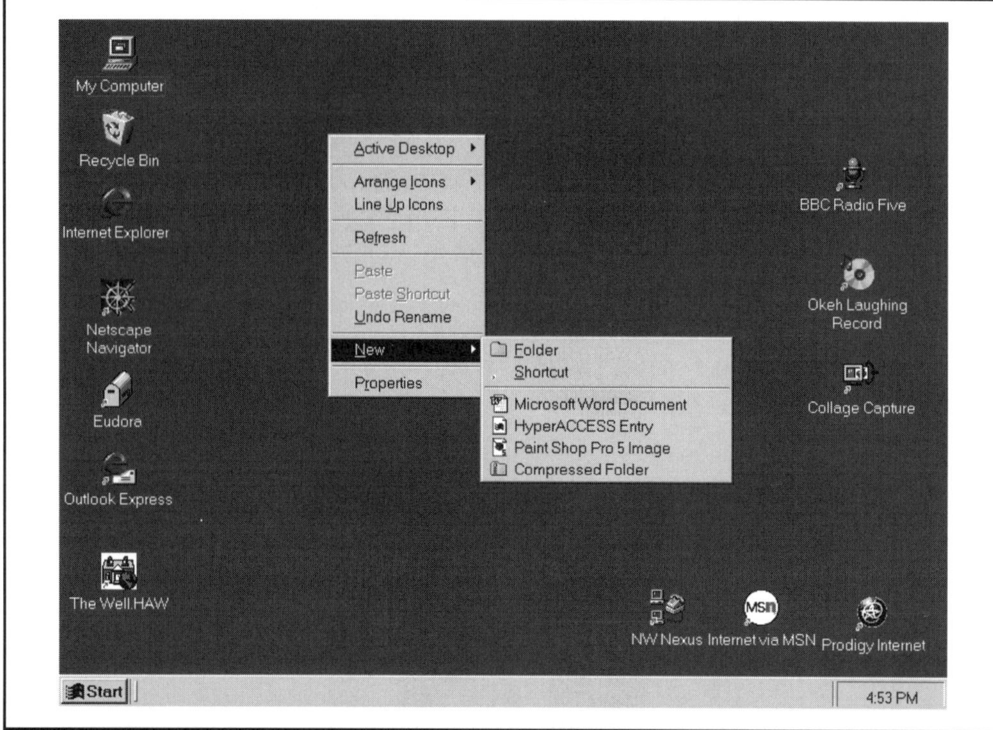

Figure 4-15. *Use the right-click menu to create a new document or other file*

for a client is going to require a report, a slide presentation, and several memos. If you have Microsoft Office installed on your system, there will be template options for a Word document, a Powerpoint presentation, and an Excel spreadsheet. For novice users, this feature makes it easy to create named documents and automatically load them in the proper application. You don't have to know how to use the Start menu, and you don't need to know anything about DOS or hard disk directories. Just right-click the desktop and move the mouse over the New option to specify a new spreadsheet or text document.

Running DOS Applications Under Windows 98

When you replace Windows 3.1 with Windows 98, your DOS Program Information Files (PIFs) are upgraded to the Windows 98 format. All existing settings should be preserved, but you may want to verify that they have been. When you double-click a program for the first time in a folder or in Windows Explorer or My Computer,

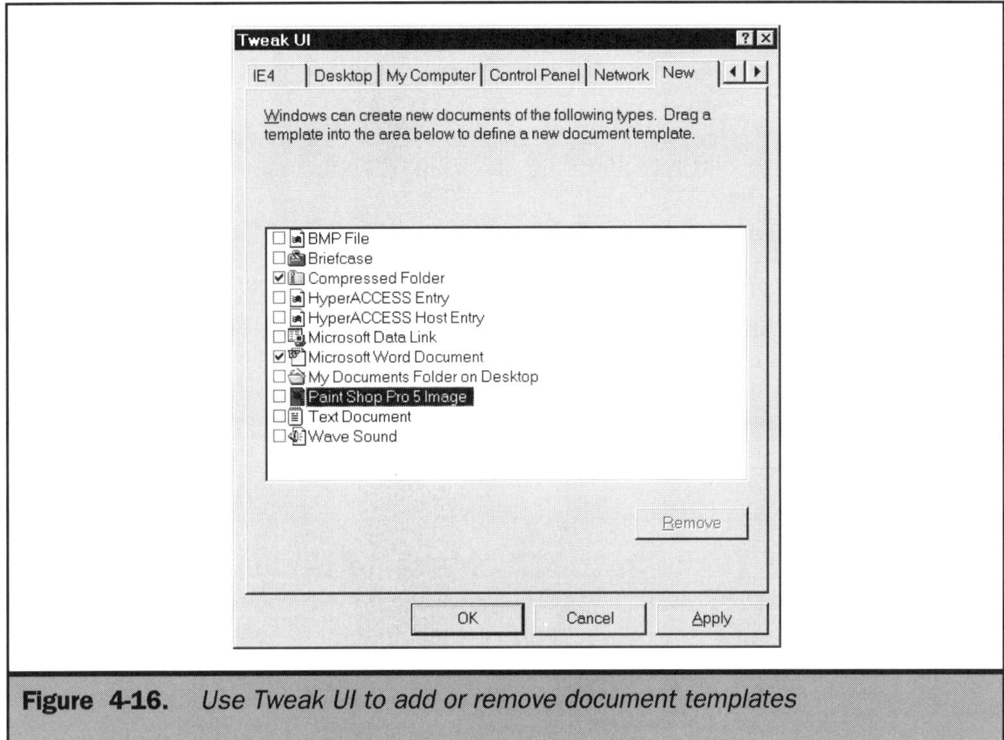

Figure 4-16. *Use Tweak UI to add or remove document templates*

Windows 98 automatically creates a shortcut for the program if there wasn't one before. Windows 98 searches first for a PIF in the directory that contains the executable file you are starting. If Windows 98 can't find a PIF there, it searches the Windows PIF directory. If there is no PIF in the Windows PIF directory, Windows 98 searches the path specified in the AUTOEXEC.BAT file. If no PIF is found, Windows 98 searches a special migration database listing of DOS applications for a match.

Windows 98 maintains a database of commonly used DOS applications. The file is called APPS.INF and is located in the \WINDOWS\INF directory. When you add a DOS application through the Start menu or File | New option in My Computer and no PIF file is found, Windows 98 searches the APPS.INF database. If a listing is found there, then relevant program information is copied automatically to the shortcut created for the application. A program title, an icon, and specific memory configuration parameters are read from the APPS.INF file and incorporated into the shortcut.

If Windows 98 does not find an entry for an application in the APPS.INF file, it uses default settings for the application. When you replace Windows 3.1 with Windows 98, a _DEFAULT.PIF file remains in the directory. In this case, Windows 98 uses information in the _DEFAULT.PIF file to create a PIF for the application.

If you don't have a _DEFAULT.PIF file and want to create one, you can do so by copying the DOSPRMPT.PIF file to _DEFAULT.PIF.

DOS Properties and Configuration Settings

Performance options for DOS sessions are now controlled through the Properties menu, accessed by right-clicking any program or shortcut icon and selecting Properties. This system replaces the PIF Editor that was used in Windows 3.1.

When you open the Properties menu of a DOS program or shortcut, you'll find six tabbed configuration screens that allow you to modify the program name and location, assign hot key shortcuts, and customize various screen and memory options. You probably won't need to access these screens very often since most DOS applications will configure themselves and run automatically.

Running DOS Tasks in the Background Under Windows 98

If you'd like to add some of the background command-line convenience offered by UNIX and OS/2 to Windows 98, you can do so with a simple batch file.

1. Create a batch file (you can choose any name) in your \WINDOWS directory that contains the following commands:

```
(BGR.BAT>

START /M COMMAND /C %1 %2 %3 %4 %5 %6 %7 %8 %9
```

2. Open Explorer to your \WINDOWS directory, right-click BGR.BAT (or select the file with the name you've chosen), and choose Properties.
3. On the Program tab, place a check mark in the Close On Exit box. In the Run field, select Minimized.

You now have a convenient way to execute any DOS command-line process quietly in the background. Open the Start | Run box and type **BGR** followed by the command or process that you want to run.

Here are some examples:

```
BGR COPY C:\MYFILES\*.* C:\BACKUPS

BGR PKUNZIP C:\ZIPS\MYZIP.ZIP C:\MYFILES
```

These operations will run transparently without disturbing the system's focus on your desktop window or application.

This section summarizes the features you will most frequently want to access. To get information on any of the Properties options from Windows 98 itself, click the question mark (?) icon at the top of the Properties box and then move the mouse over the option you want explained and click. An explanation of the option appears on the screen, as shown here on this MS-DOS Properties screen.

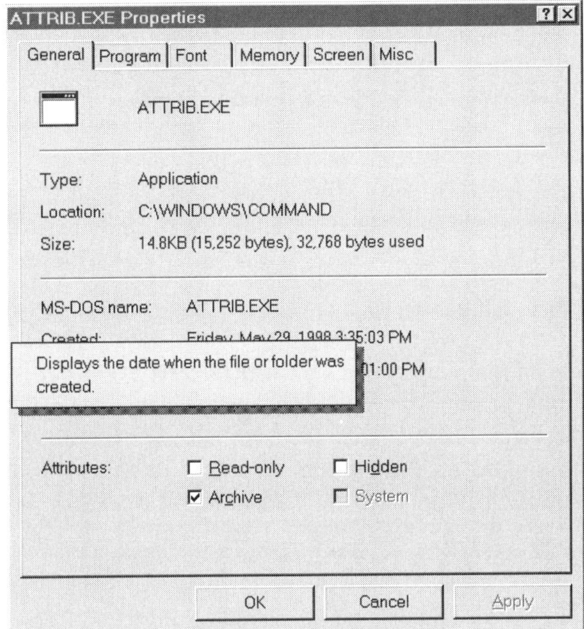

The General Tab

The General tab on the Properties screen displays the name of the program or its desktop shortcut, allowing you to change the file attribute. You can raise or lower the archive byte and make the file read-only or hidden.

The Program Tab

The Program tab on the Properties screen specifies the program title, the directory location of the file, and any parameters you may want to add to the startup command line. You can also assign a keyboard shortcut on the Program tab to automatically open the program without using the mouse. Finally, this screen lets you specify whether the program should appear in a minimized, normal, or maximized window on the desktop.

If you want to add command-line parameters to the program (for instance, to tell it to open a specific file), you add them after the path and filename in the Cmd Line box. The Working box lets you specify a working folder or directory for an application. This directory may contain support files or the data files that the program will access.

Here's an example. Entering the following information will cause WordPerfect 5.1 to open and automatically load a file called TEMPLATE.W51, located in a folder on drive D called \TEMPLATES.

```
CMD LINE: D:\WP51\WP.EXE TEMPLATE.W51
WORKING: D:\TEMPLATES
```

You can also use the Cmd Line box to open an application from a batch file, setting DOS environment information the application may need. For instance, to open ProComm Plus for DOS, you might create a batch file called PP.BAT containing this information:

```
SET PCPLUS=D:\PCPLUS
PCPLUS.EXE
```

You would then enter **PP.BAT** in the Cmd Line box.

If the Working box is left blank, the program opens to the working directory where the physical shortcut or program file is located.

The Batch File box allows you to run an additional DOS batch file before running the program or batch file entered in the Cmd Line box. You probably won't need to use this feature, but it allows you to get fancy without having to create complicated, nested batch files for the command line. For example, you might want to create a backup directory for your data files before starting a specified application. The Batch File box allows you to do this as follows:

```
BACKUP.BAT
COPY D:\WP51\*.W51 D:\BACKUPS
REN D:\BACKUPS\*.W51 *.BAK
```

To start WordPerfect for DOS and simultaneously perform the backup, you could enter **D:\WP51\WP.EXE** in the Cmd Line box, **D:\WP51** in the Working box, and **BACKUP.BAT** in the Batch File box.

Note *If you run a shortcut or program from the Run box on the Start menu, any parameters you specify in the Run box will override the default parameters specified in the shortcut's Cmd Line box.*

For an assigned shortcut key to work, the shortcut or associated program file you're configuring must be located on the desktop or on the Windows 98 Start menu.

The Close On Exit button is not selected by default when you create a new shortcut. If you want an application window on the desktop to shut down when you exit the program, place a check mark in this box.

Advanced Program Options in MS DOS Mode

The Advanced Options button on the Properties Program tab allows you run a DOS program in exclusive MS-DOS mode. When you do this, your Windows 98 desktop and all open applications shut down, and a full-screen, real-mode DOS session is opened. By default, Windows 98 is programmed to detect when certain DOS applications require this treatment. When you try to run these programs, you'll see a warning message on the screen before the desktop shuts down. Click the Advanced button on the Program tab for options that let you place further controls and restrictions on this feature.

For example, suppose you have a DOS program that you think should be able to run on the Win98 desktop. You can place a check mark in the Prevent MS-DOS-Based Programs From Detecting Windows box. This option should be used with caution since it will disable any automatic interception of the program, forcing it to open under the Win98 desktop. Note that if you place a check mark in this box for a DOS command-prompt session, Windows 98 will no longer be able to launch Windows applications from the DOS command prompt in that session.

Suggest MS-DOS Mode As Necessary is the default setting for most DOS applications. The programs will be opened under the Win98 desktop unless specific incompatibilities are detected (in which case, you'll see a dialog box suggesting that you run the application in MS-DOS mode).

Placing a check mark in the MS-DOS mode box on the Advanced Program Settings screen forces any DOS program to shut down the Windows 98 desktop and open in a full-screen, real-mode MS-DOS mode session. When this box is checked, three other options become available that apply only to programs running in MS-DOS mode:

- If you want to proceed directly to the application and skip the warning dialog box, you can remove the check mark in the Warn Before Entering The MS-DOS Mode box.
- If you want to retain the real-mode settings included in your main Windows 98 startup files, select the Use Current MS-DOS Configuration option. This will pass on the real-mode device drivers, path, and environment parameters incorporated in your main CONFIG.SYS and AUTOEXEC.BAT files. Note that if your system is using Win 98's protected-mode drivers for your CD-ROM drive or SCSI adapter, these peripherals won't be available in MS-DOS mode sessions. See "Working with MS-DOS Mode" for tips on how to reactivate them.
- If you want to load custom CONFIG.SYS and AUTOEXEC.BAT files for your MS-DOS mode program, select the Specify A New MS-DOS Configuration option. This will allow you to import or type in a new set of startup files that will be loaded for your application. This option is particularly useful for loading special device drivers or settings for DOS games and multimedia programs.

Working with MS-DOS Mode

If you've opened an MS-DOS mode session with the Use Current MS-DOS Configuration option, your CD-ROM drive may not be available even if your original CONFIG.SYS file retains real-mode drivers for it. This is because Windows 98 automatically comments out the MSCDEX command in your AUTOEXEC.BAT file. If your real-mode CD-ROM and SCSI drivers are still present in your main CONFIG.SYS file, you can restore access to your CD-ROM drive for MS-DOS mode without creating a custom CONFIG.SYS file.

By default, when an MS-DOS mode session begins, Windows 98 runs a special startup batch file called DOSSTART.BAT, located in the \WINDOWS directory on your hard drive. Open this file in an ASCII text editor and determine whether the MSCDEX command has been placed there. If it has not, then copy the line to the DOSSTART.BAT file from your original AUTOEXEC.BAT file, removing the REM statement. You can also place other commands in DOSSTART.BAT, such as additional path and environment statements or a command-line mouse driver.

If the necessary real-mode drivers were removed from your main startup files, you can create custom CONFIG.SYS and AUTOEXEC.BAT files for an MS-DOS mode session by selecting the Specify A New MS-DOS Configuration option, as shown in Figure 4-17. You can enter CONFIG.SYS commands directly into the dialog boxes provided or paste them in through the Windows clipboard. (Use CTRL-V to paste from the clipboard.) You can also let Windows 98 choose command settings by clicking the Configuration button.

Some MS-DOS mode options can be set automatically from the Configuration Wizard shown here (invoked by clicking the Configuration button):

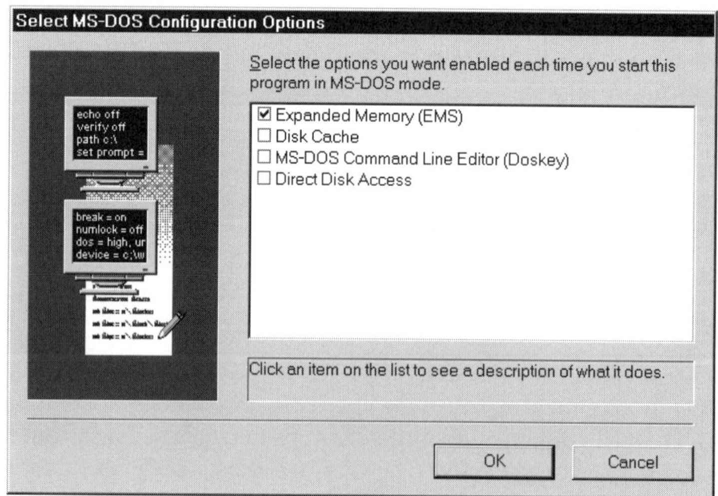

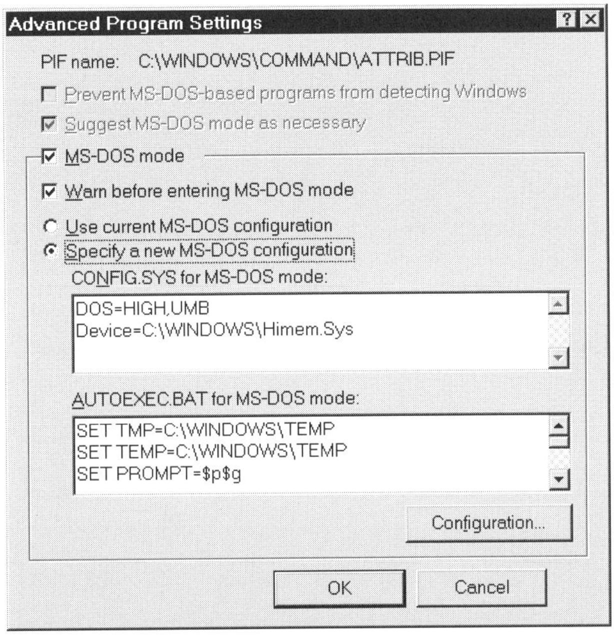

Figure 4-17. *Setting up a custom CONFIG.SYS file for an MS-DOS mode session*

When you're satisfied with the custom CONFIG.SYS and AUTOEXEC.BAT files shown in the dialog boxes, click OK and close the Program Settings screen. Now when you open this program, it will shut down the Windows 98 desktop and start a real-mode DOS session using the specified custom startup files.

Outwitting the Recycle Bin

As you're probably aware, the Recycle Bin on the Windows 98 desktop can recover only files or icon objects that have been deleted through the desktop interface. No record is kept of files that are erased at the DOS command prompt. However, you can recover files deleted from DOS with the aid of a third-party undelete tool such as DELETE97 (available from http://www.easytools.com/pages/freebies.html). Download and install this utility, and when you delete files at the DOS prompt, they will be transferred automatically to the Recycle Bin, just as when you delete files in Windows Explorer or from the desktop.

The Font Tab

The Font tab sets the default display font for windowed DOS applications. Either the TrueType or the bitmapped display fonts can be removed from the menu. This option works the same way as the Font option on the toolbar that appears in the session window.

The Memory Tab

The Memory tab, shown next, allows you to control the amount of conventional, expanded (EMS), extended (XMS), and DOS protected-mode (DPMI) memory allocated to a DOS session.

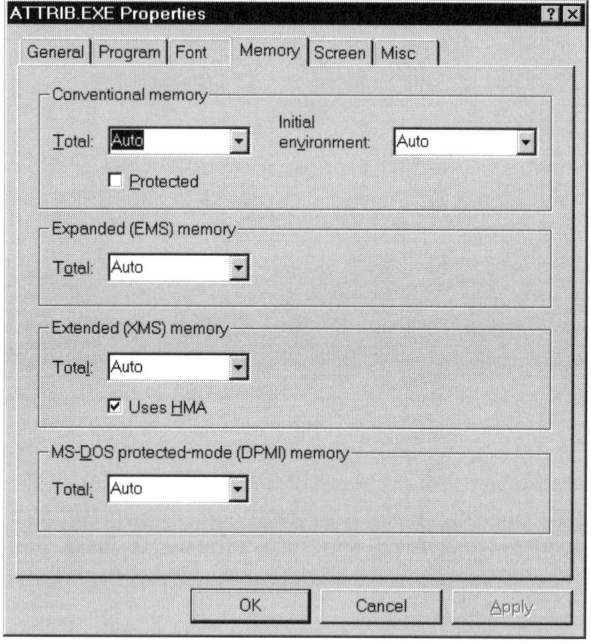

These options used to be available on the Advanced Settings screen in the Windows 3.1 PIF editor. By default, these settings are determined by the values in preexisting PIF files or information contained in the APPS.INF migration database. Experience has shown that the settings specified in the migration database are not transferred to the shortcut 100 percent of the time, so you may want to examine them and make appropriate alterations. Generally, the settings can be left in the default configuration, or you can choose Auto to let Windows 98 decide how much of each type of memory to allocate.

The Initial Environment list in the Conventional Memory box on the Memory tab sets the number of bytes allocated to contain DOS environment strings. If Auto is specified, the amount is determined by the Shell= setting in your CONFIG.SYS file or is set to 256 bytes if there is no Shell= statement.

Checking the Protected box in the Conventional Memory box may slow down application performance somewhat, but this feature provides additional shielding for the Win98 system to protect it from ill-behaved DOS programs.

The Uses HMA check box in the Extended (EMS) Memory box makes the first 64K of extended memory available to individual DOS applications if there is no DOS=HIGH statement in your Win98 CONFIG.SYS file. Since very few DOS programs can actually use this memory, it's to your advantage to load the DOS command kernel high at boot time and ignore this check box.

Note *If the Expanded (EMS) Memory settings on your system are dimmed, check your CONFIG.SYS file for the presence of the following statement:*
DEVICE=D:\WINDOWS\EMM386.EXE NOEMS
If you find such a statement, substitute the RAM parameter for the NOEMS parameter or remove the entire line from CONFIG.SYS.

The Screen Tab

The Screen tab establishes the settings for the display of your DOS application on the Windows desktop. The Screen tab shown here sets MS-DOS prompt properties.

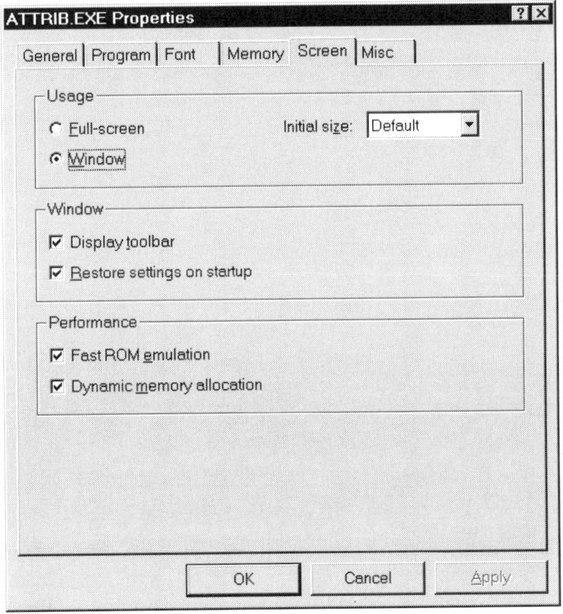

You can configure DOS sessions or programs to start in either full-screen or windowed environments, preserve the size and position of the display window on the desktop, and optimize performance parameters by enabling fast ROM emulation or dynamic memory allocation.

Fast ROM emulation tells the display driver to shadow video functions from read-only memory (ROM) to faster RAM. If you check this option, screen writes should be slightly accelerated. If you experience problems with text writing to the screen, clear this check box.

Dynamic memory allocation retrieves dormant memory assigned to an idle application and saves it for allocation to other programs. If your DOS application uses any high-resolution graphic modes, you should probably deselect this option, so that the screen will be refreshed properly.

Tip *You can open a DOS command prompt to a 43- or 50-line screen display by changing the Initial Size setting in the Usage box to 43 lines or 50 lines. When the default settings are retained, an application uses its own internal configuration to determine the number of lines it will display. If the program is set internally to display 43 or 50 lines, this setting may also override a Properties setting for 25-line display.*

The Misc Tab

The Misc tab contains a number of useful, miscellaneous options, as shown here:

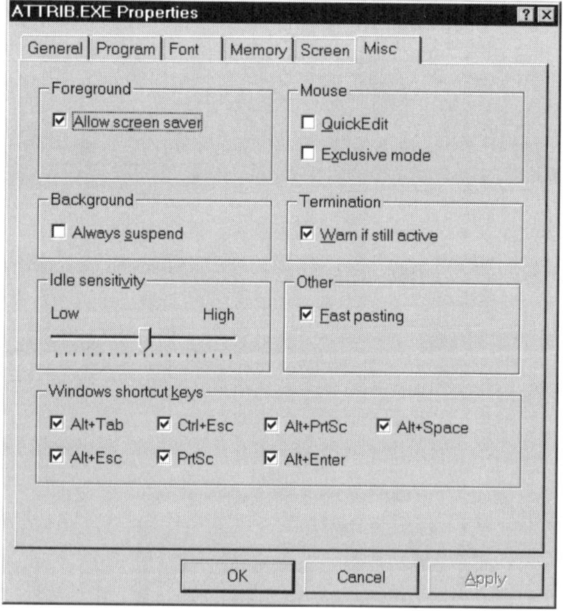

If your application is a word processor or other application that tends to remain idle in the background, the Always Suspend check box in the Background box should be checked. (Don't check this option if your program has an internal print spooler and you want to print large documents in the background.) A telecommunications program should not have the Always Suspend option selected since this can cause online connections or file transfers to be terminated if you switch to a different desktop window.

The Warn If Still Active check box, if selected, causes a pop-up dialog box to warn you if you attempt to close a program window while an application is still running in it.

The Idle Sensitivity slider allows you to control the extent to which Windows 98 monitors a dormant application and steals back unused CPU processor time. Low idle sensitivity lets a program run longer before the CPU resources allotted to it are reduced. High idle sensitivity reduces the CPU resources allotted to the program sooner. Newer DOS applications are programmed to detect whether they are running within Windows. They automatically send a suspend message when they are just waiting for a keystroke. This saves Windows from having to allocate processor time to a session when the CPU time is not needed.

If a program running in the background is not getting enough CPU resources, move the Idle Sensitivity slider toward Low. If the application is an older DOS application that doesn't appear to be doing anything in the background, move the slider toward High. If the application is a newer DOS application, you may want to experiment with moving the slider toward Low.

The QuickEdit option in the Mouse box on this screen restores the single-click cut-and-paste functionality that used to be available under Windows 3.0. If an application does not use the mouse internally, enabling QuickEdit allows you to select text by simply clicking the mouse button. (This eliminates the need to first click the Mark option on the toolbar or Control Menu.) The Exclusive Mode check box disables the mouse as a standard Windows 98 pointer. You should check Exclusive Mode if, for some reason, you see two mouse pointers on the screen when you're working in a mouse-aware DOS application.

Passing Command-Line Parameters to DOS Programs On the Fly

Would you like to click an icon for a text editor or other DOS application and be able to enter a filename or other startup parameters on the fly? This capability is useful when you need to launch the same program frequently with different startup variables, such as the MS-DOS editor or PKZIP and PKUNZIP. Here's how:

1. Create a shortcut to your MS-DOS application or click an existing shortcut. For example, create a desktop shortcut to the MS-DOS Editor, C:\WINDOWS\COMMAND\EDIT.COM.
2. Right-click the shortcut and select Properties. Go to the Program tab and enter **?** (the question mark character) after the program's name in the Cmd Line field.

From now on, when you open the shortcut from the desktop, a dialog box will pop up that permits you to enter additional parameters. For example, if you click the MS-DOS Editor shortcut, you can enter the name of a file to open.

Note that you can use this trick to create shortcuts within the Start menu as well as on the Desktop.

Getting to Work

This chapter described the desktop features in Windows 98 and offered some tips for using Windows Explorer and the Start menu, and it revealed some of the hidden power that lurks beneath the surface of the desktop

Next up is a discussion of the mini-applications that you'll find in Windows 98's Accessories folder.

Chapter 5

Accessories I: Productivity and Communication Tools

Chapter Highlights

What's new in Windows 98:

- **A new Hyperterminal with Telnet support**
- **New multimedia applets (ActiveMovie, DVD Player)**
- **New dial-up networking: Quick setup of Internet connections**
- **Imaging for Windows, rubber stamps, and scanner support**
- **Interactive CD sampler**
- **Windows 98 Resource Kit**

Working with MS Fax

Paint and WordPad

—and more

In this chapter and the next, you'll find profiles of all the Windows 98 accessories. Where appropriate, I've included "need-to-know" installation and configuration tips and step-by-step procedures for exploiting useful productivity features. For some of the applets in the Accessories folder, the interface and functionality are self-evident. Other applets have hidden features not covered in Windows 98's Online Help. This chapter provides more extensive information on these programs. The object is to spare you from time-consuming trial and error and reduce your need for technical support calls.

Chapter 5 covers the Windows 98 productivity accessories: the Accessibility, Communications, Entertainment, Fax, and Games groups, and the other contents of the Accessories folder—excepting System Tools. The System Tools group, which contains all the Windows 98 maintenance and diagnostic applications, is now important enough to deserves its own chapter. You'll find it covered in Chapter 6.

What's New in Windows 98

Windows 98 includes most of the accessories provided in Windows 95 (though Win95 veterans will find that a few applets have been shuffled into different program groups). New productivity accessories carry forward some incremental improvements that Microsoft made in service upgrades to Windows 95, including the following:

- Better multimedia control in the new ActiveMovie application
- Better fax viewer and editor that can also become a scanner tool or document manager in the enhanced Imaging for Windows application
- A new, more sophisticated Dial-Up Networking application—which power users will recognize as DUN Service Pack 1.2
- A new DVD player
- Enhanced Accessibility options

Improved disk maintenance and optimization tools, diagnostic aids, and some system utilities round out the list of new goodies that can be installed into the Windows 98 Accessories folder. (You'll find information about these System Tools in Chapter 6.)

You will also find the Accessory applet staples from Windows 95: Calculator, Direct Cable Connection, HyperTerminal, Notepad, Phone Dialer, Paint, WordPad, Media Player, Sound Recorder, and so on. However, if your Windows 98 is a fresh installation rather than a Win95 upgrade, you won't find the Microsoft Fax utilities; see the section "Fax" later in this chapter to learn how to get them back. Your Accessories folder may also be missing the Windows Clipboard Viewer or some of the other applets and utilities, depending on which Win98 installation option you selected or which applets were present before you upgraded to Win98.

To view or install new Windows 98 accessories, choose Settings from the Start menu and then choose Control Panel | Add/Remove Programs | Windows Setup. You'll find good stuff in the Communications, Disk Tools, Internet Tools, and Multimedia groups, as well as in the Accessories group.

In addition, some useful undocumented accessories and utilities are dumped into your \WINDOWS directory during installation, though they don't appear in the Accessories folder. These include Doctor Watson, File Transfer and Infrared File Transfer, Group Converter, OLE Object Packager, and Task Manager.

A complement of Internet Tools (NetMeeting, NetShow Player, MS Chat, and Outlook Express) are actually part of the Internet Explorer suite. You'll find information about these applications in Chapter 13.

Figure 5-1 shows the contents of the Windows 98 Accessories folder.

If you've upgraded your system from Windows 3.1 or Windows 95, you may want to keep some of the older applets from these operating systems. Windows 98 does not include the Calendar program. Furthermore, the old Windows Write and Paintbrush programs contain features you won't find in WordPad and Paint. Microsoft Fax from Windows 95 can provide all the functionality you need for occasional fax document transmittal and receipt.

The remainder of this chapter discusses the programs in the Accessibility, Communications, Entertainment, Fax, and Games groups and other applets in the main Accessories folder.

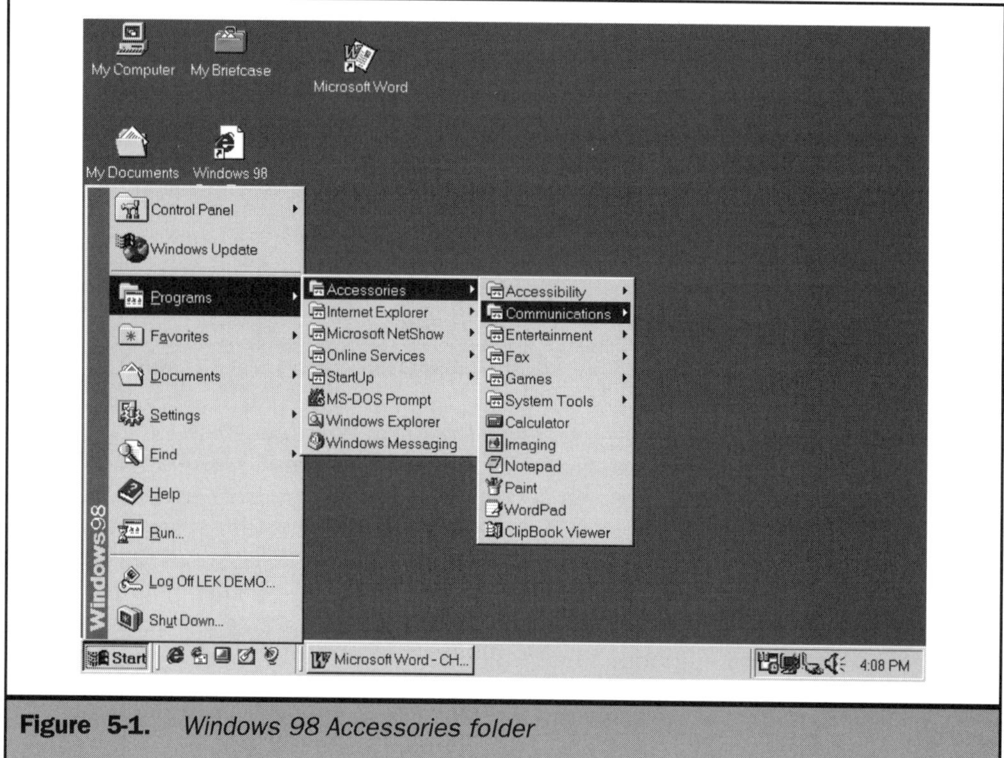

Figure 5-1. *Windows 98 Accessories folder*

Accessibility

In Windows 98, the Accessibility options that were available on the Control Panel in Windows 95 can be accessed through a new Accessibility Wizard. This Wizard allows you to systematically choose a number of Desktop display options that maximize ease of use for visually, aurally, or tactilely challenged users. The Accessibility options are shown here.

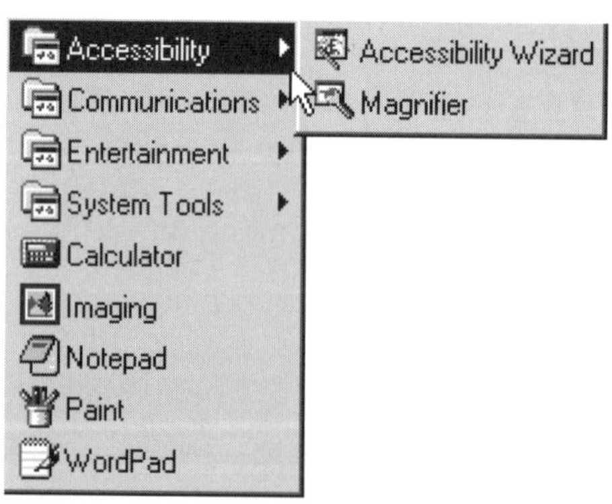

Here's what you can do with the Accessibility options:

- Replace the mouse or keyboard with other input devices
- Set up special accessibility shortcut keys
- Adjust keyboard repeat rates
- Use the keyboard for standard mouse functions
- Set up a special high-contrast screen display
- Adjust the sizes of screen fonts and mouse cursors
- Enable visual captions for system warnings and sound events
- Magnify selected portions of the screen display

Here's what you can't do with the Accessibility wizard:

- Automatically change the size of the Taskbar
- Selectively customize fonts and colors for portions of the desktop
- Use voice-activated commands to run programs or configure the operating system
- Customize the button functions of a mouse

Some of these options can also be configured through the Control Panel, but the Accessibility Wizard lets you set up viewing, sound, and screen manipulation options with one integrated configuration tool. The Wizard, shown in Figure 5-2, asks a series of questions, offering to set up a large-font screen display, present visual captions and warnings for system sound events, enable sticky-key control combinations, disable keystroke repetition, substitute keyboard combinations for mouse movements, and display extra button tooltips and other instructions for additional keyboard help.

If you want to save a customized set of display, sound, and keyboard defaults, check the I Want To Set Administrative Options box on the Set Wizard Options screen. This will allow you to click a Save Settings button before exiting the Accessibility Wizard. You can then load your saved settings whenever you want or transfer them to another computer.

Windows 98 provides a significant increase in the number of display options that a user can customize for increased accessibility. You can specially configure scrollbar and window border size, desktop icons, and screen colors. You can also use the new Microsoft Magnifier tool to increase the size of selected portions of the screen. This tool can be set to follow the mouse cursor, keyboard focus, or text editing cursor. For more information about Windows tools for users with disabilities, see the Microsoft Accessibilities and Disabilities Group Web page (currently located at http://www.microsoft.com/enable).

Figure 5-2 shows one of the Accessibility Wizard screens and the Microsoft Magnifier.

Communications

Windows 98 bundles the Dial-Up Networking, Direct Cable Connection, HyperTerminal and Phone Dialer applets into a new Communications group, shown here. This group also includes a new ISDN Configuration wizard to accommodate internal Integrated Services Digital Network (ISDN) devices that don't emulate standard modems. ISDN is a digital telephony standard that allows you to achieve an Internet connection that is up to five times faster and more efficient than a typical 28.8 Kbps modem connection.

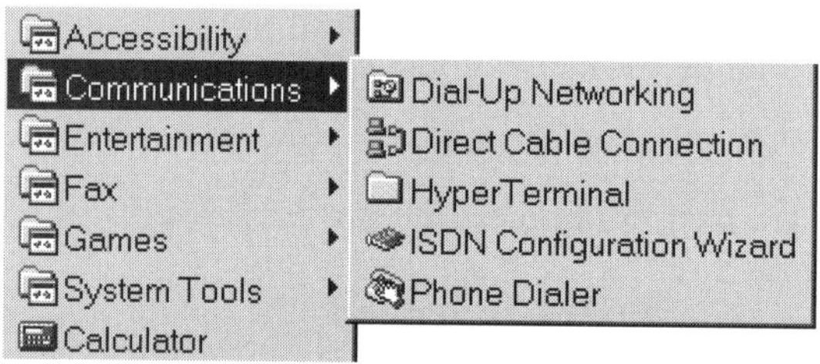

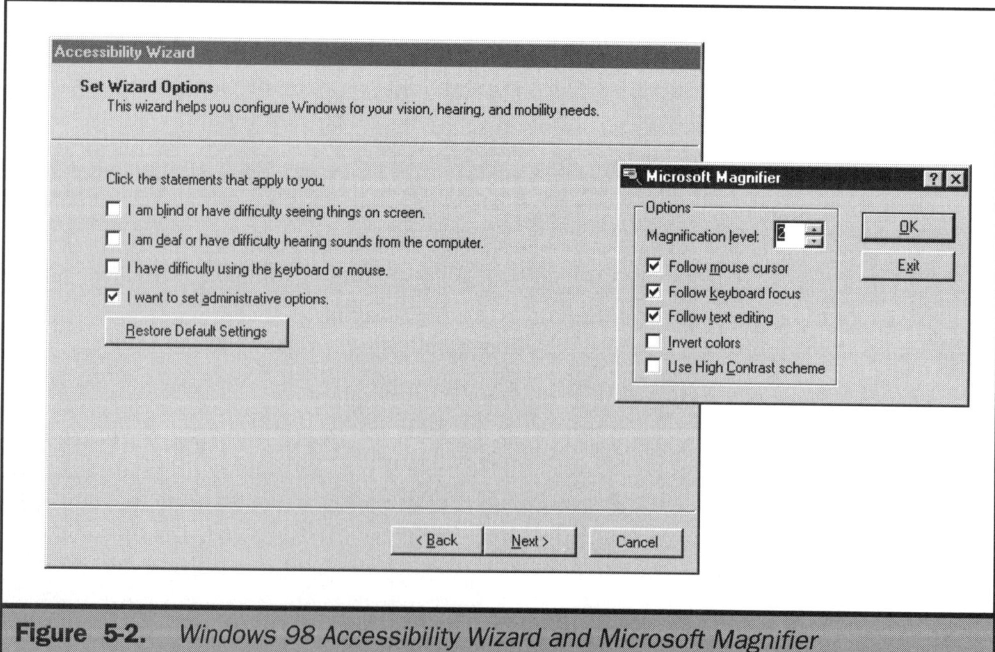

Figure 5-2. *Windows 98 Accessibility Wizard and Microsoft Magnifier*

The Dial-Up Networking and Direct Cable Connection features are linked to each other through the installation of a common network protocol. All of these features can be installed from the Control Panel by choosing Control Panel | Add/Remove Programs and clicking the Communications tab. You may already find them in the Accessories folder. Dial-Up Server and Virtual Private Networking are subcomponents of the Dial-Up Networking feature. The Infrared component permits the transfer of file data between two computers through infrared communication ports (if these devices are present). Microsoft Chat and Microsoft NetMeeting are conferencing tools; you'll find detailed information on them in Chapter 13.

Dial-Up Networking

Dial-Up Networking (DUN) in Windows 98 is more powerful than it was in Windows 95. It supports dial-up Internet connections through a single modem or high-bandwidth Multilink connections through multiple modems. The new Dial-Up Networking application also permits secure logons to a dedicated local area network (LAN) over the Internet.

Here's what you can do with Dial-Up Networking:

- Connect to an Internet service provider through your modem(s) with a Serial Line Internet Protocol (SLIP) or Point-to-Point Protocol (PPP) account.
- Connect to your local area network through a dial-up Internet service provider (ISP) account.
- Connect directly to another Windows 95 machine through your modem.
- Connect directly to a Microsoft, Novell, or TCP/IP-based network through your modem.
- Configure your computer as a dial-up server to which other Windows 95 computers can connect by modem.
- Make multiple, simultaneous network connections.

Here's what you can't do with Dial-Up Networking:

- Allow direct PPP TCP/IP connections through a parallel or serial port.
- Use a Windows 98 machine as a network router (without third-party software).
- Configure a Windows 98 machine as a DHCP (Dynamic Host Configuration Protocol) or WINS (Windows Internet Naming Service) server. These options facilitate network setup by allowing automatic assignment of Internet addresses and rapid lookup of other machines on the network.

This convenient utility allows you to connect to any Windows 98-supported network through a modem. Most people use DUN primarily as an Internet dialer. If you have an account with an ISP, Dial-Up Networking links you to the Internet, allowing your World Wide Web browser and other utilities to seamlessly receive and transmit Internet data. SLIP and PPP are data transmission protocols that enable the Internet to appear as an extension of your local computer's desktop.

If you don't already have a Dial-Up Internet account, Windows 98 provides several tools to help you find a service provider. The Internet Connection wizard (activated by choosing Programs | Internet Explorer from the Start menu) leads you through a series of screens that will install your modem, configure an existing Internet account, or call the Microsoft Internet Referral Service. The Internet Referral Service downloads a list of Internet service providers available in your area. (See Chapter 11 for more information on setting up Dial-Up Networking connection profiles once you've chosen an ISP.)

Installing Dial-Up Networking

Dial-Up Networking is not always added to the Start Menu as a standard Windows 98 option (although perhaps it should be). To connect to the Internet, you may need to install DUN along with your modem and the TCP/IP transport protocol.

If your modem wasn't set up in the Windows 98 installation, do that first by running the Modems applet in the Control Panel. You can also use the Internet Connection Wizard, mentioned earlier. (For more detailed information about modem installation, refer to Chapters 9 and 11.)

If Dial-Up Networking has not yet been installed on your computer, you can place it in the Accessories | Communications folder as follows:

1. Open the Add/Remove Programs applet by choosing Settings | Control Panel | Add/Remove Programs from the Start menu.
2. Click the Windows Setup tab and then double-click Communications (the Telephone icon) in the Components list.
3. Click to place a check mark next to Dial-Up Networking in the Communications dialog box and then click OK. (If there's already a check mark in that box, Dial-Up Networking is already installed on your system, and you can just close this dialog box.)
4. After Dial-Up Networking is installed for the first time, let Windows reboot and activate the new system components.

Note *To make Dial-Up Networking connect to the Internet, you'll also need to install the TCP/IP network protocol. Double-click the Network icon in the Control Panel. You'll see Dial-Up Adapter displayed in the network components list, along with several network protocols. (If you don't see Dial-Up Adapter after the machine reboots, something is wrong. You may need to return to Add/Remove Programs and then remove and reinstall Dial-Up Networking.)*

5. After the system reboots, right-click the Network object on the desktop and select Properties. If you don't see a listing for TCP/IP, you'll need to add it manually: on the Network Configuration tab, click the Add button under the components list.

6. Double-click Protocol on the Select Network Component Type screen. Then select Microsoft in the Manufacturer's pane on the screen that follows, and select TCP/IP in the Network Protocols pane, as shown in Figure 5-3.

Tip *After Dial-Up Networking is installed, you can quickly set up an Internet Connection. For assistance in setting up an existing Internet account or obtaining a new one, open the Internet Connection Wizard (located in the Internet Explorer program group). It will guide you through the steps of setting up a Dial-Up Networking connection profile (see Chapter 11 for more information on DUN connection profiles). To connect to the Internet, open the Dial-Up Networking folder and double-click the connection profile you just created.*

Changes from Windows 95

If you're an experienced Win95 user, you will note these differences between the old version of Dial-Up Networking and the new one in Windows 98:

- The configuration options for a Dial-Up Networking profile (accessed by right-clicking the profile icon and then selecting Properties) are now displayed on four tabs.
- The General tab allows you to edit the telephone number for the connection, the geographic dialing location, and the modem used to establish the connection.
- The Server Types tab corresponds to the button that you clicked in Windows 95 Classic (the original version). It allows you to enter login and protocol information for the connection profile. (See Chapter 11 for details.)

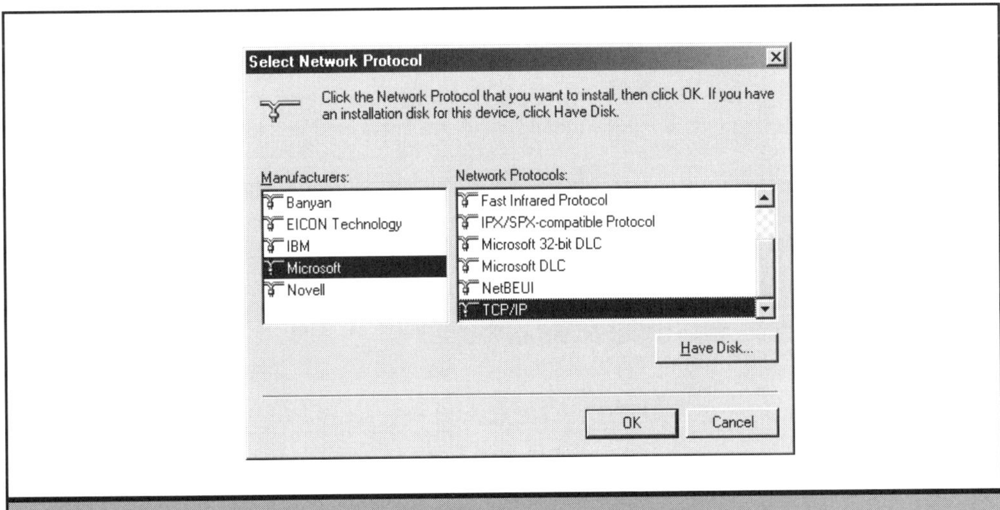

Figure 5-3. *Adding Microsoft TCP/IP for dial-up networking*

- The Scripting tab allows you to configure a Dial-Up Networking login script for a network or ISP. The Windows 98 scripting language is more complex than the original Windows 95 scripting language, but you can continue to use login scripts composed for Windows 95.

Windows 98 provides a few sample scripts in the Program Files | Accessories folder to demonstrate the use of the Dial-Up Networking scripting language . Among these files (which have an .SCP file extension) you'll find a login script for Compuserve and one for a system that uses the SLIP protocol. Fuller documentation of the DUN scripting language is contained in SCRIPT.DOC, located in the \WINDOWS directory.

- The Multilink tab is a new DUN feature borrowed from Windows NT.

If your ISP or network server supports multilink Internet connections, you can dial into it from several modems simultaneously. This has the effect of increasing the bandwidth of your connection. For instance, if you make a multilink connection to an ISP with a 56-Kbps modem on COM1 and a 56-Kbps modem on COM2, you can achieve a basic data transfer rate of 112 Kbps. To test this feature on your machine, select the Multilink tab on a DUN connection profile, click the Use Additional Devices button, and then click the Add button to dial into the connection with a second modem and telephone number, as shown here. (For more information on multilink connections, see Chapter 11.)

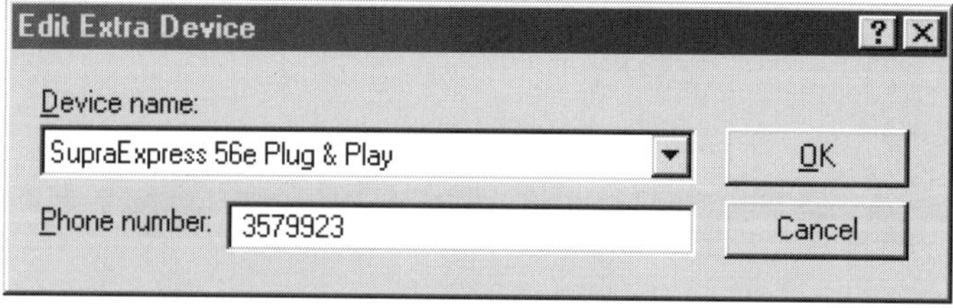

Note

Not all ISPs support multilink connections.

Making the Most of Dial-Up Networking

This section provides some tips for making the most of the Dial-Up Networking application.

LOGGING ONTO YOUR ISP AUTOMATICALLY You can set Internet Explorer (or another default Web browser, mail, or FTP client) to automatically log onto your ISP when you open the browser application.

1. Choose Control Panel | Internet and select the Connection tab.

2. Click the Settings button and select your ISP connection profile in the Use the Following Dial-Up Networking Connection field. (For details on how to make an application the default web browser, mail, or FTP client, see Chapter 12.)

CHANGING DIAL-UP NETWORKING SETTINGS You can modify the way Dial-Up Networking displays the connection status, the number of keystrokes required to initiate a connection, and the number of retries after a busy signal.

1. Choose Dial-Up Networking | Connections | Settings.
2. Modify the options you want to change and then click OK. (For more information on these options, see Chapter 12.)

TURNING YOUR WINDOWS 98 SYSTEM INTO A SERVER Dial-Up Networking allows you to turn your Win98 computer into a server that can be accessed remotely by other machines.

1. If necessary, install the Dial-Up Server component by choosing Control Panel | Add/Remove Programs, clicking the Windows Setup tab, and selecting the Communications group. Place a check mark next to Dial-Up Server. Then click OK twice to exit the dialog box and install the application.
2. Open the Dial-Up Networking folder and choose Dial-Up Server from the pull-down Connections menu. (See Chapter 11 for more details.)

MAKING A SECURE CONNECTION TO A LAN Dial-Up Networking allows you to make a secure connection to an office LAN through an ISP if the LAN is also wired to the Internet.

1. Enable the Virtual Private Networking feature by choosing Control Panel | Add/Remove Programs from the Start menu, clicking the Windows Setup tab, and selecting the Communications group. Place a check mark next to Virtual Private Networking in the Components group. Then click OK twice to exit the dialog box and install the program. VPN will be enabled as soon as you reboot the machine.
2. Open the Dial-Up Networking folder. In addition to the connection for your ISP, you'll need to create a new connection profile for your office LAN. Click the Make New Connection icon.
3. In the Select a Device field on the next screen, select Microsoft VPN Adapter.
4. Enter the appropriate Host name or IP address information for your Office LAN. (If you don't know how to do this, see Chapter 14 for detailed information.)
5. Click Next and then click Finish.

6. To log onto your office LAN, connect to the Internet through your ISP profile. Once you've established your ISP connection, double-click the profile you've created for your Office LAN and enter your name and password to log on.

DIALING INTO A NOVELL NETWARE SERVER Dial-Up Networking can be used to dial into a Novell NetWare server.

To access the Microsoft client for NetWare, NetWare file, and printer services, or IPX/SPX-compatible protocols, install them through the Network object in the Control Panel. For any NetWare connection, specify NetWare Connect as the server type in the associated property sheet. Right-click the profile icon in the DUN folder, choose Properties, select the Server Types tab, and select NRN: Netware Connect Version 1.0 and 1.1 as the type of Dial-Up server.

If you use Dial-Up Networking to access NetWare resources, you can access data remotely, but you can't control another computer remotely. For that, you need Novell's NetWare Connect client software.

If you use Dial-Up Networking to access remote drives over any network, you can automatically reestablish a connection whenever you click a network drive: Choose Dial-Up Networking | Connections | Settings and select Don't Prompt To Use Dial-Up Networking.

Direct Cable Connection

Direct Cable Connection is the Windows 98 replacement for the MS-DOS 6.x Interlink/Interserver utility. It's a handy tool for connecting two computers that are both running Windows 95 or Windows 98.

Here's what you can do with Direct Cable Connection:

- Establish a quick serial or parallel port connection between two computers running Windows 98
- Mount remote drives (including CD-ROM drives) as local drives
- Share printers
- Run DOS and Windows programs from remote drives
- Set user access levels on shared resources

Here's what you can't do with Direct Cable Connection:

- Establish a connection to a non-Windows 95 or Windows 98 computer
- Maintain simultaneous cable connections while using a Dial-Up Networking connection through a modem

You can use Direct Cable Connection to transfer files quickly between a laptop and an office computer running Win95 or Win98 or between any two Win98 machines. The connection is established through a serial or parallel cable. A laptop can simulate a network connection with the host computer: you can run remote programs and share a printer and/or CD-ROM drive attached to the host. Direct Cable Connection is a very nifty utility, although it can't be used on machines that aren't running Windows 95 or Windows 98.

Tip *You can use the DOS 6 Interlink utility to establish a connection between a Win98 machine and a computer running DOS, Windows 3.1, Windows for Workgroups, or OS/2 Warp. Add the DEVICE=INTERLNK.EXE command to CONFIG.SYS on the client machine, just as you would under DOS 6.x. Run a parallel or serial cable between the host and client machines and run the Intersvr utility in AUTOEXEC.BAT on the server. This works reliably only on FAT16 partitions. (OS/2 machines can be configured only as clients, not as servers, by loading INTERLNK.EXE in a DOS image session launched from the OS/2 desktop.)*

File transfers and remote program access work faster through parallel ports than serial ports, so use a parallel connection if you can. Any straight-through 4-bit parallel cable should work. Both ends of the cable should have 25-pin connectors (usually male), instead of the Centronics interface. Direct Cable Connection also supports extended capabilities port (ECP) and universal connection module (UCM) cables attached to an ECP-enabled port. These connections enable even faster file access.

If Direct Cable Connection doesn't appear in your Accessories | Communication group, here's how to install it:

1. Open the Add/Remove Programs object in the Control Panel and select the Windows Setup tab.
2. Double-click Communications in the Components list.
3. In the dialog box that appears, place a check mark in the box next to Direct Cable Connection. (This will also select the Dial-Up Networking files and appropriate network protocols Direct Cable Connection requires.)

Tip *When Win98 tells you the system must be rebooted for changes to take effect, you can save time by declining the option to immediately restart the system. Instead, save your work in any open programs and select Start | Shut Down | Restart. Hold down the SHIFT key as you click OK or press ENTER. The system will quickly restart itself. (This trick won't work on some systems, where real-mode drivers in CONFIG.SYS or AUTOEXEC.BAT cause the system to reboot instead of simply reloading the Win98 interface.)*

Using Direct Cable Connection

When you open Direct Cable Connection, one computer must be the host and the other must be the guest. (See the discussion of Direct Cable Connection in Chapter 14 for a trick that allows you to set up a two-way peer-to-peer connection.)

You need to assign the two computers different names. (If you performed the default Windows 98 installation on both machines, the machines may have the same computer name until you change one.) To change the name of the host or the guest, open the Network object in the Control Panel (or right-click Network Neighborhood on the desktop and then select Properties). Select the Identification tab and enter a new name in the Computer name field.

Drives, directories, files, or printers must be designated as shared resources on the host system before the guest computer can access them. To share resources, Microsoft File and Print Sharing must be installed on the host system. To do so, right-click Network Neighborhood, select Properties, and then click the File and Print Sharing button on the Configuration tab. Check the options you want to use, as shown here, and click OK. Then let the system reboot after the appropriate files have been copied.

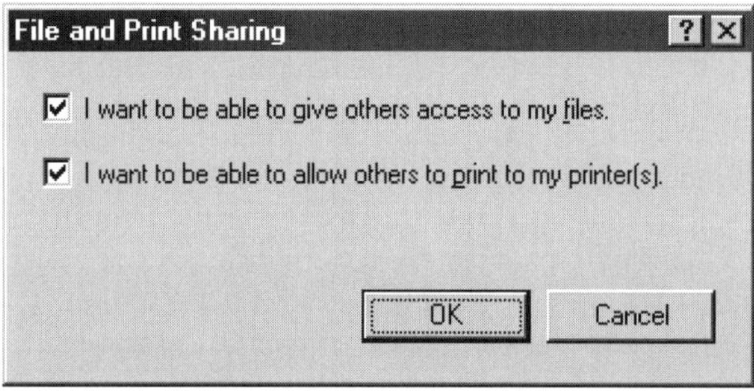

Tip

The simplest way to share drives, directories, and files is to open My Computer on the host desktop, right-click the resource to be shared, and select the Sharing option from the pop-up menu. The type of access (read only, full, or password protected) can be specified in the Properties menu.

The first time you run Direct Cable Connection, a dialog box pops up on the guest system asking for the host's name. Enter the name of the host computer without any preceding \ character for the network path.

Mapping Shared Resources Locally

Once you make a direct cable connection from a guest machine, a window will open on the desktop, displaying the shared resources that have been made available on the host machine. You can map individual drives and directories on the local computer individually or all at once. To map individually, just right-click the drive or directory. To map everything at once, hold down the CTRL key and click each disk item. Then select Map Network Drive from the File menu in the Shared Resource window. You will be able to assign a drive letter to each disk item in turn.

To use a shared printer, right-click the printer in the Shared Resource window and choose Install.

If you will frequently be connecting to a host computer via Direct Cable Connection, you may want to drag a shortcut for the Direct Cable Connection object into the Win98 StartUp folder.

Troubleshooting

Here are a few tips to help you troubleshoot any problems with Direct Cable Connection:

- The Microsoft NetBEUI protocol should be installed on both the host and guest computers for Direct Cable Connection to work properly. File and Print Sharing must be installed on the host. NETBEUI should be installed automatically along with Direct Cable Connection, but sometimes it isn't. If you're having trouble establishing a connection, right-click Network Neighborhood and verify that NETBEUI is listed in the components list on the Configuration tab. (For information on installing File and Print sharing, refer to the previous section.)
- If you encounter difficulty in setting up a parallel port Direct Cable Connection, the problem may be resolved by changing the Printer Port configuration of one or both machines. Reboot, open the CMOS settings for one or both computers and configure the port as a standard parallel port rather than an ECP or EPP. Reboot the system(s) again and let Windows 98 change the plug-and-play configuration. (As a last resort, you can try setting up a serial connection instead of using the printer ports.)

Accessing the Internet and Direct Cable Connection Simultaneously

The way Microsoft has designed the Dial-Up Networking and Direct Cable Connection utilities prevents them from being used simultaneously. But what if you want to remain connected by cable to another computer while you log onto the Internet to collect e-mail or surf the World Wide Web? To do this with Win98's Dial-Up Networking, you must shut down the Direct Cable Connection before you log onto your ISP.

However, you can have your cake and eat it too by falling back on a third-party TCP/IP dialer such as Trumpet Winsock or Chameleon Netmanage. To make a third-party TCP/IP dialer work, you may need to temporarily rename the instance of WINSOCK.DLL that Win98 places in the Windows directory. That done, you should be able to maintain your direct cable connection and dial into the Internet simultaneously.

HyperTerminal

Although not a full-featured telecommunication program, HyperTerminal in Windows 98 is more flexible and powerful than it was in Windows 95 and is an immense improvement over the old Windows 3.1 Terminal. The difference is that HyperTerminal is user-friendly enough for novices to perform basic telecommunication chores. The iconized toolbar and easily accessible Service Profiles should encourage beginners to log on and off of various services and even download a file or two.

In Windows 98, HyperTerminal v.1.2 includes Zmodem crash recovery for file transfers, the ability to redial busy numbers, better terminal emulation, and the ability to serve as an Internet Telnet client.

Here's what you can do with HyperTerminal:

- Connect to a bulletin board or commercial service.
- Capture the text of a communications session.
- Upload and download files with six standard protocols.
- Support six terminal emulations. (VT100 is improved in this version.)
- Telnet to an Internet site via Windows 98's built-in Dial-Up Networking feature.
- Establish a direct connection to another computer via a serial port.

Here's what you can't do with HyperTerminal:

- Execute automated scripts (not even to log on and enter your password).
- Support a terminal-to-terminal host mode connection.
- Support a user chat screen.
- Support keyboard mapping, macros, access to a shared network modem, and other features found in more sophisticated telecommunications packages.

Although HyperTerminal's feature set will seem pretty feeble to an experienced modem user, the program should serve the purpose for which it was written. It can demystify telecommunications and make getting online a transparent process. As soon as you open HyperTerminal, it systematically guides you through the construction of a dial-up service profile. Once you've established a terminal connection, every basic telecommunications function is accessible through icons on the toolbar.

The big news in Windows 98 is HyperTerminal's ability to function as an Internet Telnet client. With several built-in terminal emulations, HyperTerminal makes a much better Telnet client than the TELNET.EXE applet that Microsoft surreptitiously tosses into the \WINDOWS directory.

Tip *To Telnet to an Internet location, choose Start | Run and enter **telnet:*** **location***. To Telnet into the National Library of Medicine through the Internet, for example, you would enter **telnet: medlars.nlm.nih**. HyperTerminal will automatically establish a connection to the Internet address you enter.*

HyperTerminal supports six standard terminal emulations, including ANSI, VT52, and VT100. The addition of fast file transfer protocols (Zmodem, Ymodem, Ymodem-G, and Kermit) actually makes it possible to use the program to do something other than read e-mail.

Tip

By default, HyperTerminal autodetects the terminal emulation used by the host system. If you want to change this setting when creating a new profile, click the Modify button when you get to the Connect screen. Then, in the Properties dialog box, select the Settings tab and the Emulation scrollbox. The ASCII button in the Properties box lets you further customize your terminal emulation to echo or not echo typed characters on the screen and toggle line feeds and carriage returns on and off.

This version of HyperTerminal also contains a new menu option that automatically switches the program to Auto Answer mode (choose Call | Wait for a Call on the pull-down menu.) This is the equivalent of entering a Hayes ATA command in the terminal window. Once a personal computer-to-computer connection is established, users must still enter commands interactively on both the host and calling computers. HyperTerminal does not offer a dedicated host mode feature.

ISDN Configuration Wizard

The ISDN Configuration Wizard is used to install internal ISDN adapters in Windows 98. An internal ISDN adapter is a telecommunications device that does not emulate a standard modem.

Here's what you can do with the ISDN Configuration Wizard:

- Detect internal ISDN devices installed in ISA or PCI slots on your computer
- Step through the configuration of an ISDN device to make it ready for a dial-up connection

Here's what you can't do with the ISDN Configuration Wizard:

- Detect or configure an external ISDN modem (such as a U.S. Robotics Courier I-Modem)

After you install an internal ISDN terminal adapter in a computer slot, the ISDN Configuration Wizard detects it and installs Windows 98 drivers for it. The Configuration Wizard then prompts you for appropriate information to get the ISDN device online, such as the type of digital switch used by your local telephone company and SPID (Service Profile Identifier) telephone numbers for your digital account.

The ISDN Configuration Wizard cannot be used to enable a terminal adapter that contains its own serial port: UART, or an external ISDN device that connects through a standard serial or parallel port or an Ethernet hub. (See Chapter 11 for more information on setting up ISDN devices.)

More information about ISDN and Windows 98 is available at http://www.microsoft.com/windows/getisdn/about.htm.

Phone Dialer

The Phone Dialer is a cute pop-up utility that lets you configure up to eight common phone numbers which you can dial at the click of a mouse. You can also paste in telephone numbers from the clipboard or point and click a number through touch-tone dial buttons. This little applet does quite a lot of things right, and it does what you need without being overcomplicated.

Here's what you can do with Phone Dialer:

- Digitally dial telephone numbers through the numeric keypad or a speed-dial list
- Maintain an editable log of dialed telephone numbers that can be redialed
- Select multiple telephone devices or modems
- Recognize the difference between local and long distance calls
- Flexibly format phone numbers
- Pick a number off the screen and paste it directly into the dialer for action
- Log both incoming and outgoing calls

Here's what you can't do with Phone Dialer:

- Link entries in a call log to a more complete contact management database

If you make your living calling other people, you'll probably need a full-blown contact management program, but if you just call a few people regularly—or if you make a lot of calls to numbers you pluck off the screen while doing various tasks—this applet could be all you need.

The Phone Dialer adds the letter "Z" to the 9 key on the screen and the letter "Q" to the 7 key. These are typically not used and are omitted on all real telephones.

Phone Dialer Tips

Keep these handy Phone Dialer tips in mind:

- You can switch to an alternative phone line by selecting the Connect Using option from the Tools menu.
- If eight speed dialer buttons aren't enough for your most frequently called numbers, you can use Phone Dialer's Call Log feature. Every time you type a number to dial and connect, the connection information is saved as an entry in

your call log. To redial a number, all you have to do is double-click it in the call log.

- For repeated calls to just a few numbers, you can use the history list that pops up in the Number to Dial scrollbox. It remembers the name last associated with the number and enters it into the call log for you.
- If you frequently pluck numbers off the screen and paste them into your dialer, it's easy to forget what the last number was that you copied from the screen. If you keep the clipboard open in one corner of the screen just big enough to show the first part of one line of text, you will be able to see at a glance what number the clipboard contains.
- When you paste a number copied from somewhere other than the log file, the dialer by default lists Unknown as the name of the person called. To enter the actual name once you're connected, click Talk. Then you can adjust the log entries until you finally click Hangup.

Note *As with other Win98 telephony applications, you can change the default location (origin) for a call, automatically charge calls to a calling card, and control various long-distance dialing options. (See Chapter 11 for more information on these options.)*

Entertainment

The Win98 Entertainment group, shown here, includes a number of significant upgrades over the Win95 Multimedia group and the Windows 3.1 version.

The most immediately noticeable new features for Windows 3.1 upgraders are the stand-alone CD Player and Volume Control options. Although the Media Player doesn't look outwardly different from the Windows 3.1 version, it has been enhanced to handle long videos in Microsoft's AVI format that formerly wouldn't play. In Win98, the volume control is built in, so if you have a supported sound card, you can access the volume control directly from all of the Entertainment group applets, as well as from the speaker icon on the taskbar. For more information about all of the Entertainment applications, see Chapter 15.

If any of the applet icons shown here are missing from your Entertainment folder, choose Control Panel | Add/Remove Programs, click the Windows Setup tab, and select the Entertainment group in the Components list. Place check marks next to any missing components that you want to install and click OK twice to exit to the desktop.

ActiveMovie Control

In Windows 98, ActiveMovie replaces Media Player as the principal display tool for multimedia files. With built-in support for MPEG movie display and cross-platform sound formats, ActiveMovie can display multimedia more quickly than other viewing tools. It can begin playback while a file is being downloaded from the Internet or a LAN server.

Here's what you can do with ActiveMovie:

- Play back movies and sound clips encoded in a wide variety of file formats
- Display movies in various, automatically configured screen sizes (including full-screen size)
- Display real-time information about frames or playback time or filters embedded in a multimedia file
- Select and save portions of a movie or sound clip to a new file (in the same format as the original)

Here's what you can't do with ActiveMovie:

- Display single bitmap images
- Conveniently copy selections within a file to the clipboard or paste them into other programs

ActiveMovie is the default multimedia viewer that appears when you double-click movies and sound clips in these formats:

- **Video** Video for Windows (.AVI), MPEG1 and 2 (.M1V, .MPA, .MPE, and .MPG), and QuickTime (.QT and .MOV)
- **Sound** MIDI (.RMI, and .MID), Macintosh (AU, .AIF, and .SND), and Windows (.WAV)

Using ActiveMovie

In addition to appearing when you double-click a multimedia file, ActiveMovie can be started by launching it from the Start menu and choosing Accessories | Entertainment. If you double-click a file, playback begins automatically. If you open ActiveMovie from the Start menu shortcut, a dialog box permits you to browse files in supported formats. When you load a file into ActiveMovie through this menu, the file won't begin playing until you click the start arrow control in the display window.

The eight button controls for ActiveMovie playback can be toggled on and off by right-clicking the display window and placing a check mark next to Controls, as shown here. (You can select the Run option to begin playback without displaying the button controls.)

ActiveMovie's right-click menu does not contain an Open option, but you can load a new file into ActiveMovie while it's on the desktop by using the following trick: Right-click the display window and choose the Save As option. This opens a standard Windows 98 file window, which you can focus on any target folder and file list. Browse to the folder that contains the file you want to open, point to the file with the mouse, and right-click. Now you can choose Open or Play from the pop-up menu to load this file into another ActiveMovie window.

For more information on working with ActiveMovie, see Chapter 15.

CD Player

CD Player performs all of the standard functions typically included in third-party CD applications. Since most CD-ROM drives in computers don't have the hardware controls of a dedicated CD player, Windows 98 emulates them in software. When used in conjunction with the Win98 Sound Recorder and a supported CD-ROM drive, CD Player also lets you save CD musical selections to disk in digitized waveform format. A feature called AutoPlay lets a CD start automatically as soon as you insert it in the drive.

Here's what you can do with CD Player:

- Play CD musical tracks in sequence, in user-selected order, or play samples of each track

Here's what you can't do with CD Player:

- Mark a specific section of a CD track for replay

Windows 98 can detect when a user inserts a disc into a CD-ROM drive. The operating system can tell the difference between most data and music CDs. If you want to insert a music CD without activating CD Player, hold down the SHIFT key after you place the CD in the drive.

You can customize Windows 98 to launch CD Player upon insertion of a disk without beginning to play it. You can also permanently disable the auto-launch feature. To do this, you must edit the properties associated with the music CD file type. To do this, you must edit the properties associated with the music CD file type. Select the CD Audio file type in the View | Folder Options | File Types list, click the Edit button and modify the Play action. Select Play, click the Edit button on this screen, and remove the play parameter from the command line in the Editing action dialog box. See Chapter 4 for more information on editing file type properties. For information on working with CD Player to create customized play lists and on saving a CD selection to disk, see Chapter 14.

The Windows 98 PowerToys include FlexiCD, a replacement for CD Player that adds CD startup and selection options to the System Tray.

DVD Player

DVD Player is a new utility that takes advantage of the DVD-ROM storage format, which can hold a complete digital movie on a single disk.

Here's what you can do with DVD Player:

- Play full-length digital video disc (DVD) movies on your monitor or route the output to an NTSC (National Television System Committee) or PAL (Phase Alternation by Line) display device
- Password protect access to the DVD Player or selected disks. You can assign password- and rating-related access rights to multiple users on the computer
- Toggle various DVD play options: subtitles, language display, camera angles, and screen format

What you can't do with DVD Player:

- Play Laser videodiscs in older formats

See Chapter 15 for more information on installing and using the DVD Player applet.

Interactive CD Sampler

The Interactive CD Sampler is an impressive bit of Microsoft propaganda that displays a series of full-screen multimedia ads from the Windows 98 installation CD for a variety of software and hardware products. When you first click the icon, you're asked whether you want to install 700K of the presentation on your hard drive or run the entire thing from the CD. You'll probably avoid some stuttering and clipping if you allow the help files to be installed on your hard disk.

This presentation is also a good test of your system's CD-ROM performance. If you discover that the voice-over narrative and music are clipping, you may want to try the following adjustment to your CD-ROM settings:

1. Choose Control Panel | System and click the Device Manager tab.
2. Click the + sign in front of the CD-ROM listing, select CD-ROM drive, and click Properties.
3. Click the Settings tab in the CD-ROM Properties dialog box. Place a check mark next to the box marked Sync Data Transfer. You may also want to put a check mark next to the DMA box. A warning, shown in Figure 5-4, will inform you that enabling DMA data transfer may have adverse effects on some systems. If CD-ROM performance degrades or the system becomes unstable, you can return to this screen and uncheck the box.

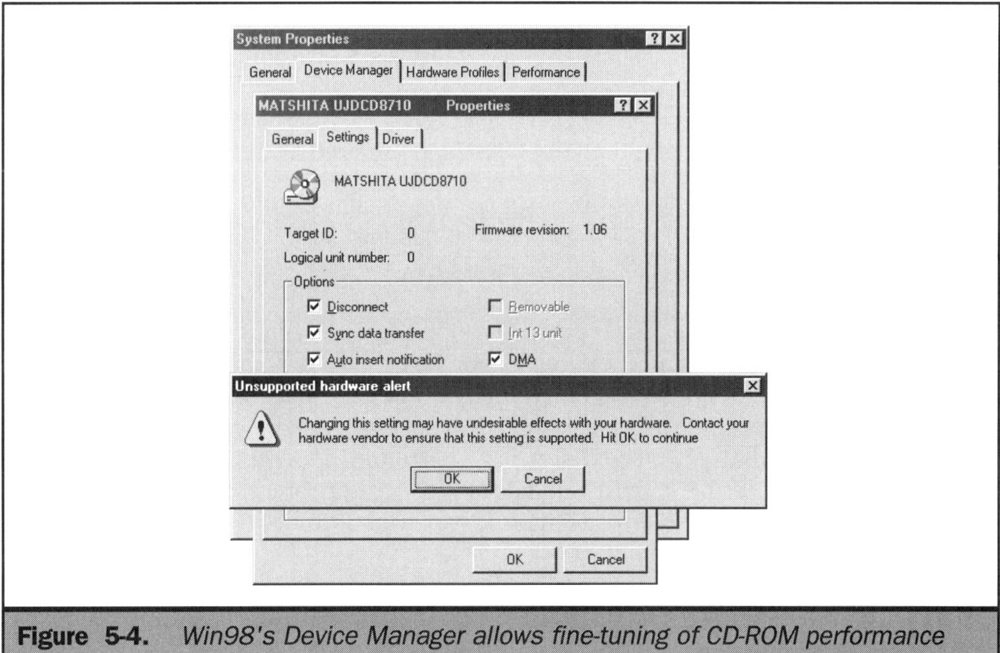

Figure 5-4. *Win98's Device Manager allows fine-tuning of CD-ROM performance*

You can click the various onscreen options in the CD Sampler presentation to see advertisements for the different product categories. The Accessories button on the main screen allows you to set playback defaults for the presentation and obtain licensing and purchase information.

Demo versions of several advertised products are included on the CD. To see a list and pick trial versions to install, click the Install Software icon on the main presentation menu. (You can also go directly to the list of available programs by clicking the Trial Programs icon on the menu for the Accessories Entertainment group. See the Trial Programs section later in this chapter for more details.)

Media Player

The Win98 Media Player resembles the Windows 3.1 version on the surface, but it includes a number of enhancements. The Win98 version will play most full-length .AVI-format motion pictures without generating out-of-memory messages. Media Player is no longer the default multimedia viewer in Windows 98, but it has one valuable feature that ActiveMovie lacks: You can use Media Player to conveniently cut and paste multimedia selections into Sound Recorder or another multimedia editing program.

Here's what you can do with Media Player:

- Load and play digitized analog sound files (.WAV), digital MIDI files (.MID), CD audio files, and video for Windows (.AVI) files
- Automatically resize the screen display of video for Windows (.AVI) clips
- Play third-party QuickTime (.MOV), Autodesk Animation (.FLI//FLC), and MPEG video files

Here's what you can't do with Media Player:

- Play third-party digital and digitized analog sound formats (.VOC, .CMF, .MOD, and so on)
- Queue and mix multiple video or sound files

Like ActiveMovie, Media Player permits you to adjust playback options directly from its display window. You can adjust volume and channel balance for sound playback (by choosing Device | Volume Control) and directly control the driver and instruments used in MIDI playback. (When a MIDI file is loaded, a Properties option appears on the Device menu). AVI video files can be played back in adjustable window sizes or in full-screen mode. However, full-screen playback degrades video quality and sound sequencing unless you have a newer graphics card with advanced multimedia features.

Note *Unlike Windows 3.1, Windows 98 does not permit you to add support for third-party video formats through the Control Panel. If you install third-party viewing software for QuickTime or Autodesk animation, support may not be added automatically for Win98's Media Player. If you have installed third-party drivers for these formats and Media Player doesn't recognize them, you can manually modify SYSTEM.INI to add them to the list of supported multimedia devices. MPEG support is now built into Windows 98. (See Chapter 15 for more information about Win98 and third-party multimedia software.)*

Sound Recorder

The Windows 98 Sound Recorder resembles the Windows 3.1 version on the surface, but it includes a number of enhancements.

Here's what you can do with Sound Recorder:

- Load and play back digitized sound files in Windows .WAV format
- Record and save waveform sounds from a microphone, a CD, or line input to a sound card
- Add simple effects to sounds (for example, you can add an echo and slow down or speed up sound files)
- Provide rudimentary mixing through volume control
- Save files at several different quality and compression levels
- Merge and mix .WAV and MIDI input from multiple files

Here's what you can't do with Sound Recorder:

- Perform sophisticated manipulation of sound files: cut and paste segments, alter sound through graphic representation, and add advanced special effects
- Save files in third-party formats

Attaching Sounds to Documents or System Events

Windows 98 support for sound compression makes attaching sounds to documents a more attractive option. It's easy to use a microphone to record a verbal description of a document, instructions for a user, or other spoken material. The recorded message can be embedded in a spreadsheet, word processing document, graphic report, or memo to play back with a click of the mouse.

To attach a sound to a document, open Sound Recorder, click the Record button (the red dot) in the Sound Recorder window, pick up your microphone and begin speaking. When you're done, click the Stop button (the black rectangle) in Sound Recorder. Then choose File | Save As. Once you've saved the file, you can drag it from My Computer/Windows Explorer directly into documents produced by OLE-aware applications such as Microsoft Office. Some of these programs let you start Sound Recorder directly from a Wave Sound menu option: choose Insert | Object | Wave Sound.

When you save a file in Sound Recorder, the Format option at the bottom of the dialog box allows you to set the audio quality and degree of compression in the .WAV file. For simple vocal recordings, you may want to choose a high-compression monaural format to conserve disk space. For a high-fidelity message (including music), choose a stereophonic format with a higher sampling rate.

You can also assign your own recorded messages or prerecorded sounds in .WAV format to Win98 events such as the opening and closing of programs, critical stop, and so forth. See the discussion of Control Panel options in Chapter 9 for details.

See Chapter 15 for more information on working with Sound Recorder.

Trial Programs

The Trial Versions icon complements the Interactive CD Sampler presentation. If you open it, you will see a list of trial applications that you can install on your hard disk and evaluate, as shown in Figure 5-5. (Dilbert's Desktop Games takes only 1MB of disk

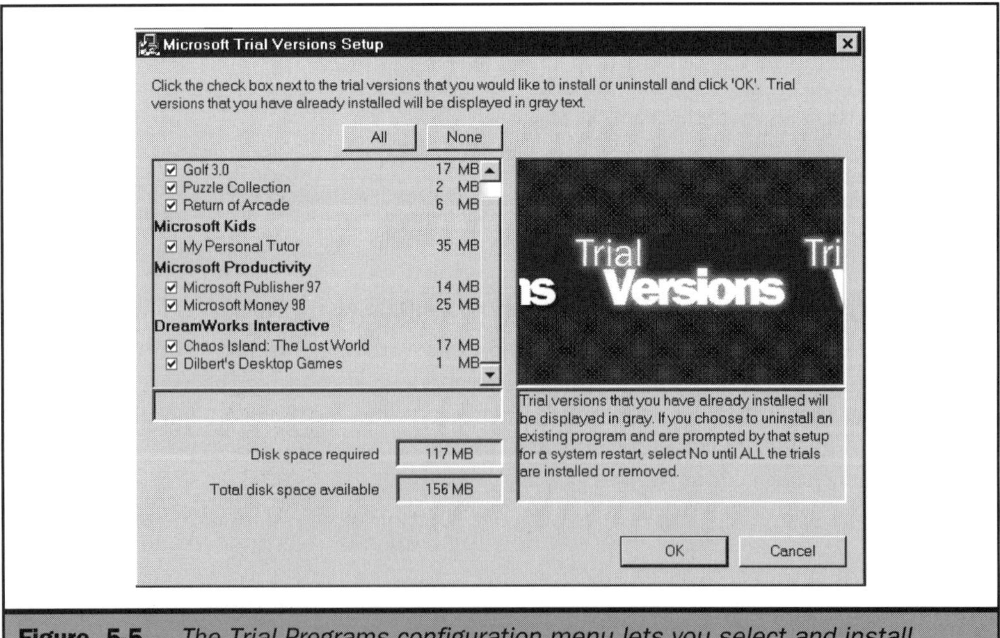

Figure 5-5. *The Trial Programs configuration menu lets you select and install sample applications from the Win98 CD*

space.) Select or deselect the programs you want to evaluate or ignore and click the OK button to install the ones you've chosen.

Volume Control

The Windows 98 Volume Control allows you to adjust the playback and record volume for multimedia events on your system. It will appear in the System Tray on the taskbar (click the speaker icon to the left of the clock). Some low-grade, 8-bit cards, such as the original Creative Labs Soundblaster, don't support the Win98 Volume Control. With such a card, you must rely on OEM tools bundled with the card to adjust playback defaults.

For most sound cards, a single click on the volume control in the System Tray opens the Master Volume Control Balance screen. A double-click opens slider controls for all your multimedia devices.

Here's what you can do with Volume Control:

- Adjust the volume and the right-left channel balance for multiple sound sources, both during playback and during recording
- Mute output from individual sources (such as a microphone or CD player) during playback
- Select input from specific sources (excluding others) during recording
- Filter display of slider controls to include or exclude settings for selected devices
- Fine-tune sound playback with advanced sound cards (controlling treble and bass, 3D effects, WaveTable balance, and so on)

Here's what you can't do with Volume Control:

- Show metered (into the red) distortion problems
- Equalize playback frequencies in individual ranges

If you don't see the volume control in the System Tray and the system doesn't play the Windows startup sound, your sound card may be improperly configured.

If you hear a startup sound but the volume control isn't displayed on the taskbar, choose Control Panel and open the Multimedia applet. At the bottom of the Audio tab, place a check mark next to Show Volume Control on Taskbar. (If this option is dimmed but the system plays sounds, you may have an unsupported, 8-bit sound card or a more advanced card using Windows 3.x drivers. See Chapter 15 for troubleshooting tips that may make the volume control appear.)

When you double-click the volume control on the taskbar, you should see a series of mixing sliders that adjust playback volume and channel balance for each multimedia source.

If your system supports sound sources missing from the Volume Control mixer, select Properties from the Options menu and place a check mark next to any additional type of sound source you want to display in the Volume Control mixer.

The full-featured Volume Control option can also be opened from the Multimedia folder by choosing Start | Programs | Accessories | Multimedia or from the Device menu in Media Player.

Fax

It's not as full featured as Delrina's Winfax Pro, but Microsoft's Fax group, shown here, supports the basic fax features that casual users commonly need.

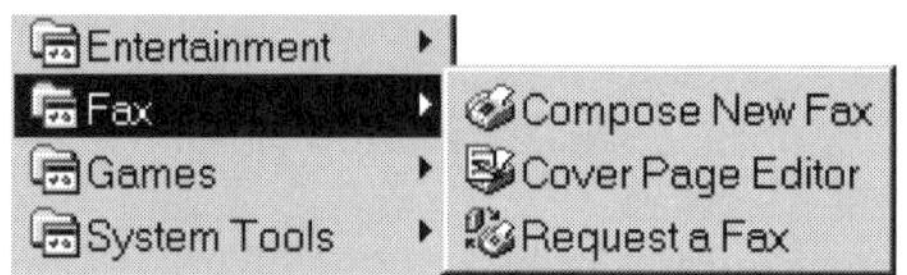

Here's what you can do with the Fax options:

- Compose and send brief ASCII text memos with attached text or binary documents
- Choose recipients on the fly or from an address book
- Request fax documents automatically from a remote server
- Send multiple documents in a single fax transmission
- Fax documents from within any Windows application
- Share a fax/modem over a network
- Receive faxes in the background while other telecommunication programs are open on the desktop

Here's what you can't do with the Fax options:

- Send or receive color fax documents
- Send faxes from DOS applications
- Scan or convert bitmapped faxes to editable text
- Sign or otherwise edit a bitmapped fax
- Read or view faxes in bitmapped formats produced by most third-party fax software

This section discusses how to prepare and send faxes using the tools on the Start menu (Compose New Fax, Cover Page Editor, and Request a Fax) and how to fax from Windows applications. For information about sending and receiving faxes through Inbox or Outlook 97/98, see Chapters 11 and 13.

Installing and Configuring Microsoft Fax

In Windows 98, Microsoft has removed Windows 95's Windows Messaging Client (Inbox), replacing it with the new Outlook Express mail client. One side effect of this change is that the useful Microsoft Fax utility has also disappeared.

If you performed a clean installation of Windows 98 on your computer or upgraded from Windows 3.x, there will be no Inbox icon on the desktop, and no Microsoft Fax support. (In a minute, I'll tell you how to get these services back.) If Microsoft Fax migrated successfully to your computer during a Windows 95 to Windows 98 upgrade, you can skip this section.

You can see whether your system currently supports Microsoft Fax by looking for an Inbox icon on your desktop, right-clicking it, and selecting Properties. If you see an entry for Microsoft Fax in the Services list, then this feature has been migrated to Windows 98 and is operational. If you don't see a listing for Microsoft Fax, this service was not active at the time you upgraded from Win95 to Win98. If there is no Inbox icon on the desktop, then Windows Messaging Service has not been migrated from Windows 95.

If you have Microsoft Outlook 97 or 98 on your computer, open this mail client, choose Tools | Services, and see whether a Microsoft Fax option appears in the Service tab list. (If you don't see it, click the Add button and look for Microsoft Fax in the Available Information Services list. If you don't see this option, you will need to install Microsoft Fax support files from the Windows 98 CD.

The pressure of feedback from testers during the Windows 98 beta cycle was sufficient to convince Microsoft not to entirely do away with Windows Messaging Service and Microsoft Fax. Support files for these features can be found in the \TOOLS \OLDWIN95\MESSAGE directory on your Windows 98 CD.

If your desktop contains an Inbox icon but no Microsoft Fax service, you can install Microsoft Fax support by running the AWFAX.EXE file in the CD's \TOOLS \OLDWIN95\MESSAGE directory. (Choose the INTL directory for foreign-language versions of Windows 98.)

If your desktop contains no Inbox icon, you can install the Windows Messaging Service by running the WMS.EXE file in the CD's \TOOLS\OLDWIN95\MESSAGE directory. After the Inbox appears on your desktop, you can then install Microsoft Fax support by running the AWFAX.EXE file.

If either Outlook 97 or 98 (from the Microsoft Office application suite) is active on your computer, you can add Microsoft Fax support by running the AWFAX.EXE file without running WMS.EXE. It's not necessary to reinstall Windows Messaging Services if you use the Outlook 97 or 98 mail client.

To configure a fax profile after you've installed the necessary support files, follow these steps:

1. If Inbox is your default mail client, right-click the Inbox icon, choose Properties, and click the Add button on the General tab (or click Add on the Services tab if you've already created a Windows profile). Make sure the Microsoft Fax service is checked in the Inbox Setup Wizard or the Add Service To Profile window that appears. (See Figure 5-6.) You can deselect the other services if you don't want them.
2. Click the Next button in the Inbox Setup Wizard. You'll be prompted to select a modem, configure auto-answer options, and enter your name and telephone number. The Setup Wizard also prompts you to create a Personal Address Book and a Personal Folder for storing your fax documents.
3. If Outlook 97 or 98 is your default mail client, open it, choose Services from the Tools menu, and click the Add button. Check the Microsoft Fax service and follow the prompts to choose a modem and enter your fax telephone number.

Working with Microsoft Fax

Once you've installed Microsoft Fax, you can send or receive faxes in a variety of ways:

- You can open the Inbox (or Outlook 97 or 98), with the Compose New Fax option by selecting Programs | Accessories | Fax from the Start Menu.
- You can print to the fax driver from individual Windows applications. (You can't use Microsoft Fax to send a fax from a DOS application.)
- You can drag and drop a document onto a Microsoft Fax Printer icon on the desktop.

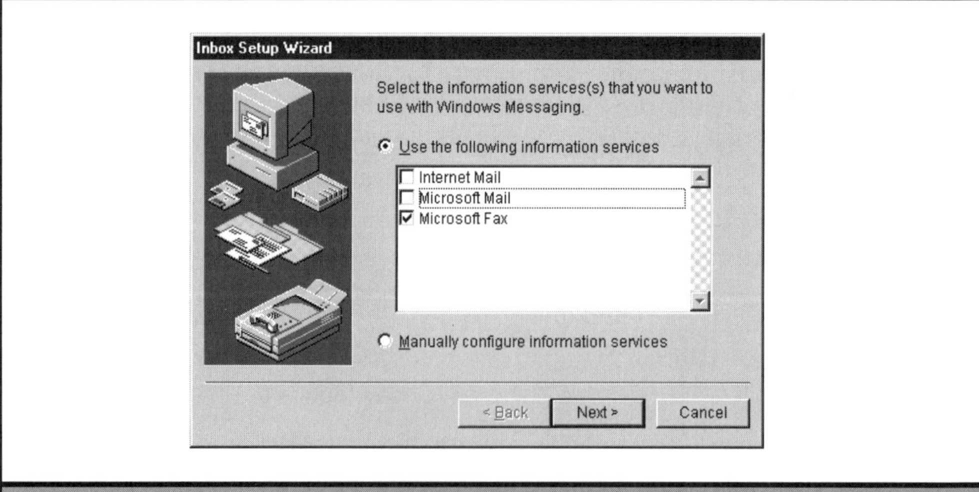

Figure 5-6. *Add Microsoft Fax from the Inbox Setup Wizard (shown here) or from the Add Service To Profile dialog box*

To create a Microsoft Fax printer shortcut on the desktop, open the Printers folder (Start | Settings | Printers). Right-click the Microsoft Fax printer icon and select Create Shortcut. Answer Yes to the prompt that asks you to place the shortcut on the desktop.

The Microsoft Fax driver has an intricate and confusing set of configuration options best left at their default settings. On the Details tab of the Properties menu, the chosen port should be FAX: (Unknown Local Port), and the chosen driver should be Microsoft Fax Driver. Change these settings at your own risk. The Capture Printer Port button is provided to specify an alternative path to a shared network printer.

Faxing with the Accessories Fax Tools

The Fax group on the Start menu includes a Compose New Fax option (choose Start | Programs | Accessories | Fax). You can use this option to type a subject and enter text for a one-page memo. The Fax Wizard will also let you attach a document to your fax as a binary file.

Attached documents can be received only by Class I or Class II fax/modems on a recipient computer (attachments cannot be sent to a dedicated fax machine).

For convenience, you can create a shortcut for the Compose New Fax icon and drag it to the root level of the Start menu or the main Programs group.

Faxing from Windows Applications

You can send a formatted document directly to a dedicated fax machine or to a fax/modem by printing from a Windows application. To fax from an application, use the Print command and select Microsoft Fax as the printer. When you click OK in the Print dialog box, a Microsoft Exchange screen may appear asking you to select a user profile, or the profile may be loaded automatically (depending on the way Microsoft Exchange is configured on your system).

You can toggle the option to automatically open a user profile or to pause and select a profile. From the Inbox, choose Tools | Options and select When Starting Windows Messaging. From Outlook 97 or 98, choose Tools | Options | General and select Startup Settings.

If Microsoft Fax has been installed properly, there should be at least one preconfigured user profile. If you don't find this profile the first time you try to print a fax, you can create it by clicking the New button in the Choose Profile dialog box and following the Fax Setup Wizard.

After your application's Print command dispatches a document to the print spooler, the Microsoft Fax Wizard appears on the screen. It offers the same set of choices as when you select Compose Fax from the Start menu. If you want, you can disable the first screen, which specifies the originating location for the transmission. However, if you fax frequently from a portable computer, you will probably want this screen to appear, since you'll be dialing from different geographic locations.

The Fax Wizard then lets you select a recipient or type a phone number. You can click the Address Book button to open a list of addresses and phone numbers that you create and store for repeated use. On the next Wizard screen you can choose a cover page to send, if you want, or you can use the Subject and Note boxes on the next screen, shown here, as substitutes for a cover page. You can use these fields to enter a subject heading or the recipient's name and a quick message.

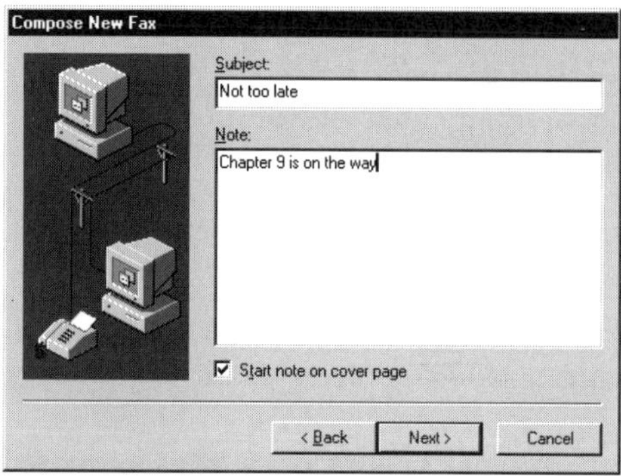

When you print a fax from an application, the first page transmitted is the cover page (if selected). The second page transmitted is the text you enter in the Subject and Note fields. The document you've printed is the third page received at the other end of the connection. If you check the Start Note on Cover Page box, the printed document becomes the second page.

If you're sending a fax to another fax/modem instead of to a dedicated fax machine, then the cover page isn't transmitted at all. You can send a cover page to a Class I fax/modem as a separate binary file. (See "Cover Page Editor" later in this chapter for details.)

Receiving Faxes in the Background

Microsoft Fax can automatically answer the telephone and receive faxes in the background. If you didn't choose this option during the initial installation, it's a bit hard to find. Here's how to toggle automatic fax answering on and off:

1. Open Inbox or Outlook 97 or 98 with a user profile that includes Microsoft Fax. Choose Tools | Microsoft Fax Tools | Options from the pull-down menus.
2. Select the Modem tab in the Microsoft Fax Properties window, choose the modem you want to answer the telephone, and click the Properties button, as shown in Figure 5-7.
3. In the Answer Mode section on the next screen, specify how you want the modem to answer the phone. You can specify a number of rings to wait before the modem answers the telephone, or you can choose Manual. If you choose Manual, Microsoft Fax displays a dialog box when a call comes in, asking if you

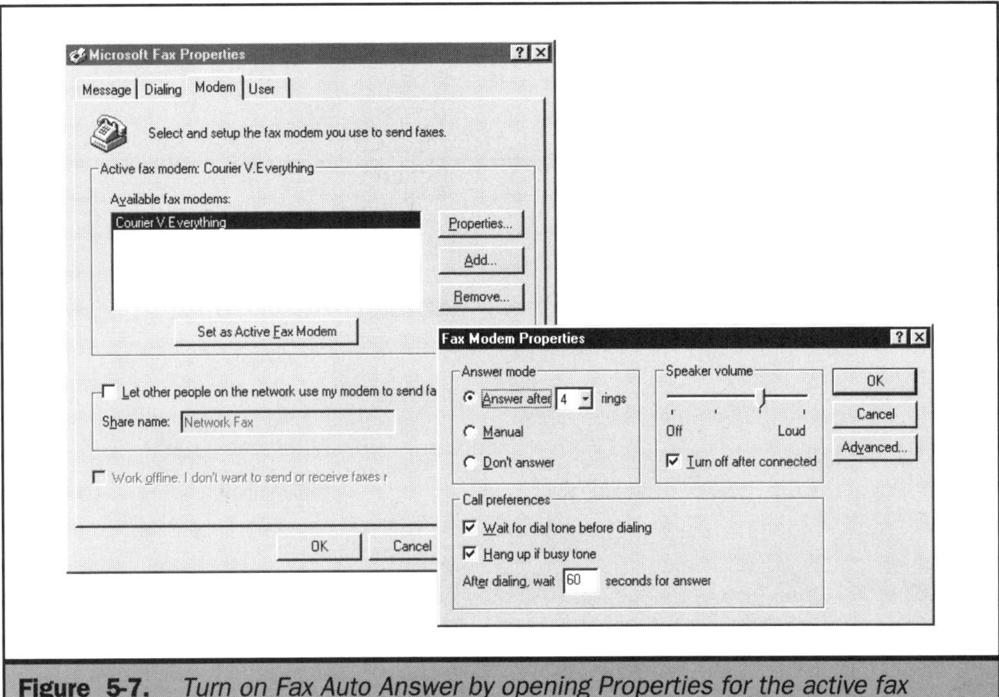

Figure 5-7. *Turn on Fax Auto Answer by opening Properties for the active fax modem on the Modem tab in Microsoft Fax Properties*

want to receive the fax or ignore it. If you choose not to answer, you can pick up the telephone receiver or let the call pass through to an answering machine.

To receive faxes in the background, you must first open Inbox or Outlook 97 or 98. You can then minimize the mail client (click the Minimize button on its title bar), and it will remain dormant while you work. If Inbox or Outlook 97 or 98 is already running, this will decrease the amount of time before the Fax Wizard appears.

If an open DOS program is using your modem, you'll see a message prompting you to assign the modem port to either Windows or DOS. If you choose a DOS session, Windows 98 will refuse communication port access to your fax program until you close the DOS program.

Compatibility

Microsoft Fax supports the following international standards for fax communications:

- International Telecommunications Union (ITU, formerly the CCITT) T.30 standard for Group 3 fax
- ITU V.17, V.29, and V.27 standards for high-speed fax communications (up to 14.4 Kbps)

Currently there is no support for Intel CAS modems, such as the older SatisFAXion. The fax/modem combinations shown in Table 5-1 are also not supported by Microsoft Fax (although they may work with third-party Windows fax software).

Manufacturer	Model	Country
AT&T® Paradyne	Keep in Touch Card 3761	U.S.
Best Communications, Inc.	14496EC	U.S.
BIT	MX-6, XM124S	Italy
Cardinal	14400 V.32bis, MB2296SR	U.S.
CPV Datensysteme	F-1114HV, StarLine	Germany
CTK-Systeme	CTK V.32	Germany
Datatronics	Discovery 2496CX	U.S.
DIGICOM	SNM28, SNM41PC	U.S.
Digicom Systems, Inc.	Scout Plus	U.S.
E-Tech Research	E1414MX	U.S.
EEH GmbH	Elink 301	Germany
ELSA	MicroLink, MicroLine	Germany
Gateway	Telepath PM144	U.S.
Hidem	14400 Fax	Japan
Kortex	KX PRO 2400	Germany
LCE	MiniModem 23	
Macronix, Inc.	Maxfax 9624s, VOMAX 2000	U.S.
Megahertz	P22 Pocket Fax/Modem	U.S.
MultiTech Systems	MT932ba	U.S.
National Semiconductor	TyIN 2000	Japan
Neuhaus Mikroelektronik	Fury 2400	Germany
PNB	TT9624	France

Table 5-1. *Incompatible Fax/Modems*

Manufacturer	Model	Country
Practical Peripherals	PM2400 FX96SA, V.32 Pocket	U.S.
QuickComm	SprintII V.32 Fax	
Sysnet	SMF44 Fax	U.S.
TeleJet	TeleJet 14400	
U.S. Robotics	Sportster 28.8 V.FC, Sportster 9600	U.S.
Woerlein GmbH	M288 Fax	Germany
Zoom Telephonics	FC 96/24, VFX 28.8	U.S.

Table 5-1. *Incompatible Fax/Modems* (continued)

Fax "Gotchas"

Here are some "gotchas" to watch out for when using Microsoft Fax:

- Inside the Fax Wizard, the F1 Help key is as dead as a doornail. If you need to consult the Win98 Help system about fax options, open Inbox or Outlook 97 or 98 and choose Microsoft Fax from the Help menu. If you want to know what some fax option means (for instance, Editable If Possible versus Not Editable), the F1 Help option *is* active if you access the Fax Wizard from Inbox or Outlook 97 or 98.
- By default, Microsoft Fax dials the intended recipient only once. If you don't get through, the faxing dialog box closes and deposits the message in your Outbox folder. If you open the message in the Outbox, you'll see that the Send option is dimmed. The way to resend is to look for a System Administrator note deposited in your Inbox folder. This note reports the failure to complete transmission of a listed fax message and includes a Send Again button that you can click. Alternatively, you can right-click the original fax message in the Outbox folder and then click Forward.
- You can change the number of redial attempts on a fax transmission through another obscure dialog box. From Exchange or Outlook 97 or 98, choose Tools | Microsoft Fax Tools | Options and select the Dialing tab. This screen has a Retries section, shown next, where you can specify the number of times to redial a number and the interval between each retry attempt. (You can also

display the Retries screen from the Compose New Fax Wizard by clicking the Options button on the Do You Want A Cover Page? screen.)

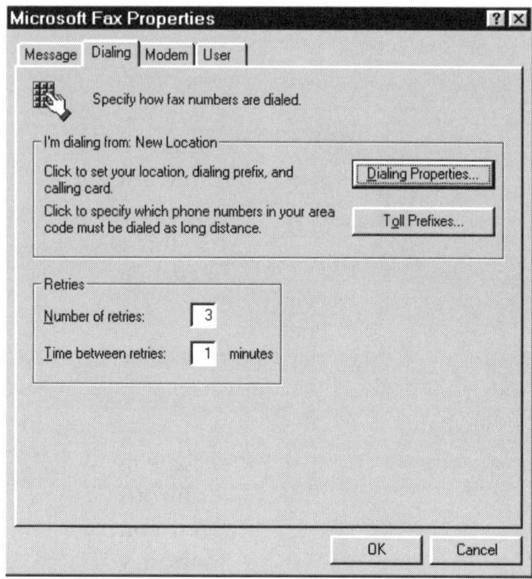

Other Microsoft Fax Bells and Whistles

Here are a few other features of Microsoft Fax:

- If your system has a Class I fax/modem, you can attach text or binary files to your fax messages. The attachments can be received by any other Class I fax/modem.
- You can schedule faxes to be sent at specific times of the day. From the Compose New Fax Wizard, click Options. (The button appears on the page that follows the Address and Phone Number options.) The Time To End dialog box has three options: As Soon as Possible, Discount Rates, and Specific Time. If you select Discount Rates, the Set button pops up a dialog box that lets you specify a starting and ending time for discount rates in your local phone area. This setting will be preserved for subsequent use. If you select Specific Time, the Set button lets you enter a specific time to schedule the fax.
- You can automatically call a Fax-Back service to request faxed information, using the Fax options in the Microsoft Exchange Inbox.
- You can protect your faxes with a password. If you send a fax through the Exchange Inbox, you can also invoke the additional protection of encryption.

Sending a Cover Page as an Embedded Document

You can use the cover page embedding features as an alternative way to attach a file to a fax transmission. For example, you can embed a spreadsheet, video for Windows, or other object directly into a cover page. When the resulting cover page is attached to a fax, the embedded objects are printed at the receiving end.

Better yet, you can embed objects in a cover page, save it, and send the resulting Cover Page Editor (CPE) file as a binary attachment: If the recipient has Win95, he or she can load the received CPE file into the Cover Page Editor—and the embedded objects are automatically linked to corresponding programs on the receiving computer. Pretty slick! You can use this trick to exchange and update Excel spreadsheets quickly, to cite one example. Or use it to collaborate on a graphic drawing project.

Cover Page Editor

Microsoft Fax offers various predefined cover page templates that you can automatically attach to a fax. These are not humorous or particularly striking, but you can use the Cover Page Editor to enhance them if you want to add some variety. The templates include sender and recipient information, which is useful if your recipient doesn't already know you pretty well.

The Cover Page Editor works like a drawing program, allowing different elements on the Cover Page template to be relocated and resized on the page. The Cover Page Editor also includes drawing tools for rectangles, ovals, polygons, lines, and other shapes. A wide variety of objects (Excel spreadsheets, CorelDRAW documents, PowerPoint slides, .WAV and MIDI files, and so on) can be inserted or attached to a cover page. Remember that, by default, cover pages are transmitted only to a dedicated fax machine, not to a Class I or Class II fax/modem.

The Cover Page Editor can spice up fax transmissions with a wide range of added frills. If you're so inclined, you can use it as a mini-vector drawing program. You can't paste the designs you create into other applications, but you can save and print them. You can even add a series of Recipient and Sender fields to a cover page to create a mini-database that can be easily transmitted along with the body of your fax. If you don't want to bother with a full-featured database application, this is a quick way to send an address list.

Tip *When you start the Cover Page Editor, you can turn on a Wizard that automatically displays a new tip about its use. If you cycle through all of the tips, you'll eventually find a list of all the Cover Page Editor* CTRL-*key shortcuts.*

Fax Viewer Versus Imaging for Windows

The Fax Viewer included in Windows 95 has been replaced in Windows 98 by the new Imaging for Windows application. When you double-click a fax attachment in an Inbox or Outlook 97 or 98 message window, it appears in an Imaging for Windows preview screen. Imaging for Windows is a much more sophisticated viewing tool than the old Fax Viewer was. From the preview screen, you can resize or rotate the document without affecting the original copy. A fax document is really a bitmap image.

In an Imaging for Windows preview screen, you can switch documents and open up other bitmaps in a variety of formats.

To actually edit the content of a fax or other image, select Open Image for Editing from the File menu. (A dialog box appears asking whether you want images to open in the editor by default. You can answer Yes or No.)

The Imaging for Windows editor provides a variety of options for manipulating and saving fax documents and other bitmapped images. When your computer sends or receives a fax, it is not saved as a separate disk item, although it appears that way in an Inbox or Outlook 97 or 98 message list. The fax is actually stored in a cumulative information store, usually located in the \WINDOWS or \EXCHANGE folder. The default name for this cumulative storage file is MAILBOX.PST. Once you've loaded a fax into the Imaging for Windows editor, you can then save it to disk as a separate file. Microsoft's proprietary format for faxes has an .AWD (for "at work document") file extension.

Tip *If you want to make copies of any of your fax documents, load them into the Imaging for Windows editor (double-click the fax attachment icon in the message window and choose File | Open Image for Editing in the Imaging for Windows preview applet.) To save a copy of the fax to disk, choose File | Save As in the Imaging for Windows editor. Once you've saved a fax to disk as an .AWD file, you can load it into Imaging for Windows by double-clicking its icon or launching Imaging for Windows from the Start menu (choose Programs | Accessories | Imaging).*

The Microsoft .AWD format is not compatible with more widely used fax formats like Intel's or Delrina's, but if you have leftover fax files in Intel's .DCX format, you can load them into the Imaging for Windows editor.

Games

The Games group, shown next, includes two new games: Freecell and Hearts, which complement the Solitaire and Minesweeper games that have long been distributed with Windows. You can play Hearts against the computer on a local workstation or over a network. Freecell is a card game that lets you choose from over 32,000 canned hands. According to the Microsoft documentation, "It is believed (although not proven) that every game is winnable."

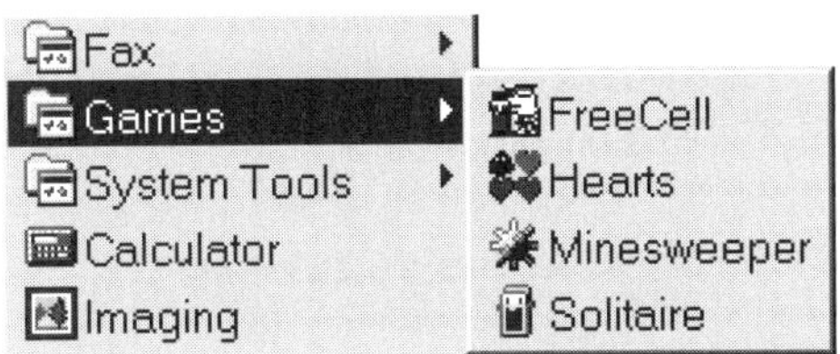

If you haven't explored the mysteries of Solitaire in Windows, keep an eye on the pattern designs on the back of some of the decks as you play. If you watch the magician's arm, you'll see an occasional ace come out of his sleeve. In the Palm Tree deck, once in awhile the sun comes up wearing dark glasses and sticks out its tongue.

In Minesweeper, you'll find that the version included in Win98 has a scantier Help file than the Windows 3.1 version. If you've saved the WINMINE.HLP file from Windows 3.1, you can run the old Help file under Win98 by choosing Run from the Start menu and typing the path to WINMINE.HLP.

Solitaire has a hidden "cheat key "for the impatient. If you start a "Draw Three" game and decide that you want to win against all odds, hold down the CTRL-ALT-SHIFT *keys at the same time and click the deck with the mouse. As long as you hold down these keys, you can riffle through the deck one card at a time.*

Calculator

The infamous Calculator bug in Windows 3.1 has been fixed in Windows 98 (and in Windows 95). You can now subtract 3.10 from 3.11 and get the correct answer, .01, instead of 0. (This flaw made Microsoft the butt of a series of jokes along the lines of "The difference between Windows 3.11 and 3.1 is … nothing. Just perform the calculation and see for yourself!")

Here's what you can do with Calculator:

- Perform both standard and scientific calculator functions, including square root, percentage and reciprocal conversions in standard view, and a variety of trigonometric and logarithmic calculations in scientific view
- Perform numerical conversions between decimal, hexadecimal, octadecimal, and binary numbers

Here's what you can't do with Calculator:

- Perform calculations with natural logarithms, compound interest, and more complex algebraic formulas

Windows 98 Calculator is pretty much identical to the Win95 version (some of the button names are spelled out instead of abbreviated).

To learn some interesting tricks you can do with Calculator, open the Help file and read the sections on scientific calculations and converting values to other number systems. The Tips and Tricks entry will also tell you how to transfer numbers between the scientific and standard calculators.

Imaging

Imaging for Windows is probably the most powerful productivity application in the Accessories folder. It can serve triple-duty as a fax viewer/editor, scanner client, and bitmap image editor. This application was developed by Wang Systems for Microsoft to include in Windows 95 service release 2. Eastman Kodak acquired it and enhanced it for Windows 98.

Here's what you can do with Imaging for Windows:

- View or edit faxes (including annotating faxes with text and graphics, inserting from a file, attaching Post-it-type notes (sticky notes), and adding rubber stamp marks)
- View, import, and edit bitmap images, choosing from a wide variety of formats, including TIFF, PCX, GIF, and JPEG as well as Microsoft Fax (.AWD) and Intel Fax (.DCX)
- Zoom in and out to any custom magnification
- View faxes, scanned pages, and bitmap images as thumbnails
- Scan and edit output from TWAIN-compliant scanning devices
- Create new image documents in TIFF, Microsoft Fax, or .BMP format

Here's what you can't do with Imaging for Windows:

- Perform optical character reader conversion of faxes and scanned images to text
- Scale or resize scanned or imported images
- Manage images through indexing and cataloging

Imaging for Windows is installed as the default viewing application for Windows Messaging or Outlook Express. When you first click a fax document (in a Windows Messaging or Outlook 97/98 window), it opens in Preview mode. You can zoom or rotate views of the document, but the editing options are disabled. To load the document into the full application, you choose File | Open Image for Editing. The first time you do this, you will see a message asking whether you want to make loading documents into the full editing application the default setting. Imaging for Windows Preview mode is also available by default when you right-click images in the .PCX (PC Paintbrush) file format and choose Open or Preview.

Tip *To toggle the Open option between Preview and Full Edit modes, choose Tools | General Options in Edit Mode and choose the default setting you want.*

Preview mode is actually a separate Imaging for Windows applet (KODAKPRV .EXE). The filename for the Full Edit mode application is KODAKIMG.EXE. This information may be useful to savvy users who want to set up Preview and Open options for other supported file types in Imaging for Windows. By default, .GIF and .JPG bitmaps are set to open in the Internet Explorer browser and have no right-click Preview option. A little knowledge of registered Windows file types allows you to set .GIF and .JPG images to open in Imaging for Windows, where you can edit them. You can also add a right-click Preview option for any file type that Imaging for Windows supports. See Chapter 4 for more information about working with Windows file types.

Working with Imaging for Windows

Imaging for Windows can be opened in Edit mode by choosing Programs from the Start menu and then choosing Accessories | Imaging. If you don't see the Imaging icon, add it by choosing Control Panel | Add/Remove Programs | Windows Setup | Accessories. Imaging Help (opened by choosing Help | Imaging Help from the Imaging for Windows pull-down menu) provides a basic tutorial on how to use the application.

The following sections provide a few quick pointers to useful features.

SHOWING OR HIDING ANNOTATIONS If you've added provisional text, sticky notes, or graphic elements to a document, you can toggle their display on and off by adding or removing the check mark next to Show Annotations on the Annotations pull-down menu. (This works only if your original document is a TIFF file.)

ROTATING ALL PAGES If you received an upside-down or sideways fax, you can choose Page | Rotate All Pages to turn the whole document right-side up.

USING THE PAGE AND THUMBNAIL OPTION FOR EASY DOCUMENT VIEWING To conveniently browse through a multipage document, choose View | Page and Thumbnails.

SCANNING A DOCUMENT INTO IMAGING FOR WINDOWS Choose File | Select Scanner to choose a scanning device installed on your system. (See Chapter 9 for information on installing scanners.) Once you've selected a scanner, choose File | Scan New to scan a document into the Imaging for Windows editor. Choose Tools | Scan Options to fine-tune scanner performance. (Your scanner interface may also offer calibration tools when you choose File | Scan New Document.) Figure 5-8 shows the screen for scanning a document with the Storm Technology PageScan USB device.

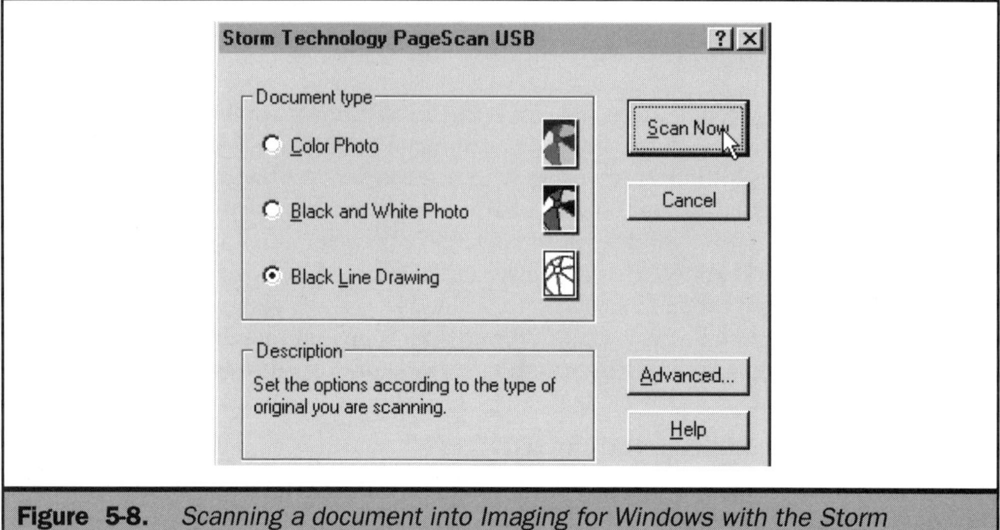

Figure 5-8. *Scanning a document into Imaging for Windows with the Storm Technology PageScan USB device*

Once you've scanned a document into Imaging for Windows, you can do the following:

- Send it as a fax by choosing File | Print and selecting Microsoft Fax or another active fax printer
- Send it as an e-mail attachment by choosing File | Send
- Save it to disk by choosing File | Save.Resizing an Imaging for Windows Document

RESIZING AN IMAGING FOR WINDOWS DOCUMENT Imaging for Windows does not scale or resize images, but Microsoft Paint can. To resize an Imaging for Windows document, follow these steps:

1. Select Edit | Copy Page.
2. Open Microsoft Paint by choosing Start | Programs | Accessories | Paint.
3. Paste the image into Paint from the clipboard.
4. Use Paint's scaling tools (choose Image | Stretch/Skew) to resize the image.
5. Use Paint's Edit | Copy To option to save the modified image to a .BMP file on disk.

If you want to convert the .BMP image to another format, open it in Imaging for Windows and resave it.

APPENDING IMAGES OR TEXT TO AN EXISTING FAX OR TIFF DOCUMENT

Imaging for Windows allows you to append bitmap images or text as new pages to an existing fax or TIFF document. Choose Page | Append.

If you want to append to a document in .BMP format, first convert the document to the fax (.AWD) or TIFF format:

1. Choose Edit | Select Image. Select the entire page and copy it to the clipboard with the Copy command.
2. Choose File | New and create a new TIFF or .AWD document.
3. Paste the contents of the clipboard into the new document.

You can now insert new text or graphics with the Page | Append command.

SIGNING AND RETURNING A FAX WITH IMAGING FOR WINDOWS Here's a trick to let you receive, sign, and fax back a document (such as a contract or rental agreement) without printing it.

1. Double-click the received fax in an Inbox or Outlook 97/98 message window. If you haven't configured the Imaging for Windows (IFW) editor as the default fax viewer, choose File | Open Image for Editing from the Preview applet.
2. Scroll down to the place in the document where you want to place your signature. Choose Annotation | Freehand Line from the Imaging for Windows pull-down menu.
3. Sign your name with the mouse, as shown in Figure 5-9. (It may take some practice to learn how to draw a legible signature. You can increase the thickness of the freehand line by right-clicking the Freehand tool at the bottom of the editing window.) You can also enter character-based text into the fax by choosing Annotation | Typed Text.
4. Save a copy of the modified fax document.
5. Fax the signed document back to the sender by choosing File | Print and selecting Microsoft Fax Driver as the output device.

If you expect to sign a lot of documents, you can paste the signature you've created with the mouse into another document, save it, and turn it into an Imaging for Windows stamp, as described next.

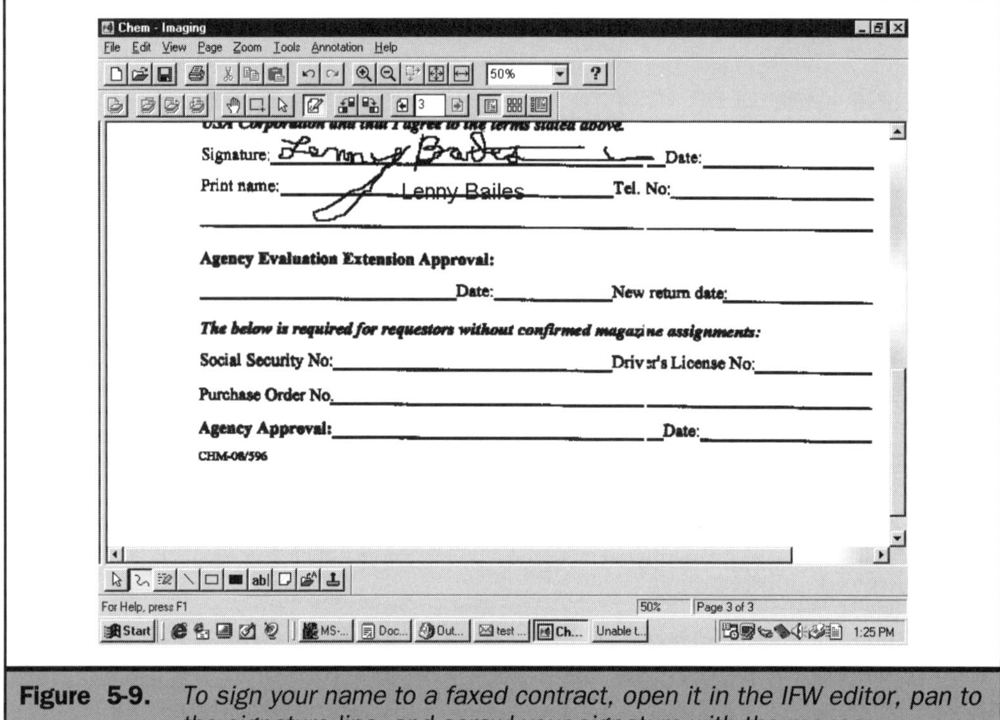

Figure 5-9. *To sign your name to a faxed contract, open it in the IFW editor, pan to the signature line, and scrawl your signature with the mouse*

CREATING AN IMAGING FOR WINDOWS RUBBER STAMP If you expect to be signing a lot of documents, you can save the signature you created in the last section in Microsoft Paint. Then you can convert it into a convenient Imaging for Windows rubber stamp. Here's how:

1. Draw your signature with the mouse. (You can do this in an Imaging for Windows document or directly in Microsoft Paint.)
2. If you draw the signature in Imaging for Windows, copy it to the clipboard and paste it into a new document in Microsoft Paint.
3. When you have the signature in Microsoft Paint, select Attributes from the pull-down Image menu and reduce the size of the file to 320 by 200 pixels (or some other value that will contain the signature without cutting it off or adding too much white space). Once you've used this tool, you can click the lower-right corner of the document to further adjust the pixel size.
4. Save the signature as a monochrome .BMP file (for instance, SIG.BMP).

5. Open (or switch to) the Imaging for Windows application and open a new document.
6. Choose Annotation | Rubber Stamps from the pull-down menu. Enter a name for the stamp and the path and filename for the signature file you saved.

Figure 5-10 shows a completed rubber stamp.

Notepad

The Windows 98 version of Notepad is identical to the Windows 3.1 and Windows 95 versions. By default, Win98 makes an association between Notepad and all files with the .TXT file extension. If the file is too long to be opened in Notepad, a dialog box pops up asking if you want to load the file into WordPad.

Here's what you can do with Notepad:

- Read and write small text files in ASCII format, with or without automatic word wrapping

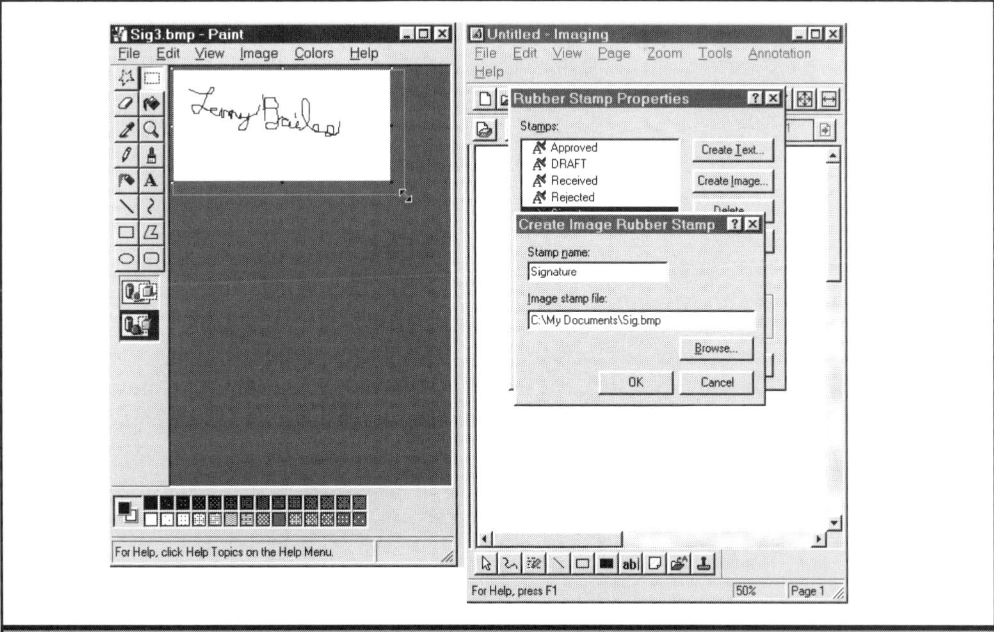

Figure 5-10. *Creating an Imaging for Windows rubber stamp signature*

Here's what you can't do with Notepad:

- Perform word processing functions other than simple text entry
- Manage graphic elements or OLE-linked files from other applications

If you would like to change the automatic association of .TXT files from Notepad to another text browser or word processing program, follow these steps:

1. Open Windows Explorer or My Computer and choose Folder Options from the View menu.
2. Select the File Types tab and scroll down to Text Document.

You can also associate other file extensions with Notepad by clicking the New Type button. (See Chapter 4 for more information on file associations.)

Notepad's WordWrap feature can be a bit deceptive if you're working with a text file that contains really long lines. When you toggle WordWrap on (by choosing Edit | WordWrap), the text appears neatly organized on the screen—but this option does not automatically reformat the document. If you save the file with WordWrap turned on, the text will still stretch over long lines when viewed in another editor. To truly truncate long lines in a document, you need to turn WordWrap off and manually press ENTER where you want the lines to wrap.

An unsung Notebook feature allows you to create headers of footers that contain the filename, date, time, or document page numbering. Here's how:

1. Choose File | Page Setup from Notepad's pull-down menu.
2. Use the following codes to insert information into a header or footer field:
   &f Prints the filename
   Page &p Prints the word "Page" followed by the current page number.
   &d Prints the current date
   &t Prints the current time

The filename and page number codes should already be entered by default.

For a complete list of Notepad header and footer codes, right-click the question mark in the upper-right corner of the window and drag it to the header or footer field.

Paint and WordPad

Paint and WordPad manage to step forward and backward at the same time in the transition from Windows 3.x. Both programs include new and useful options, but the Microsoft programming team also let some valuable Win 3.x and Windows 95 features disappear. If you've already read Chapter 2 on making the jump from Windows 3.x, you know that you can squirrel away copies of the old Windows 3.x Paintbrush and Write (or the Windows 95 Microsoft Paint). If you depend on Microsoft's bundled word processor and graphics program to handle real productivity chores, you may appreciate having the old versions around when you hit a blank spot in their Win98 replacements. (Of course, there are a large number of commercial and shareware utilities that can fill these holes even better.)

Paint

Win98 Paint has changed in many ways from Windows 3.1 Paintbrush. Although the two applications have many features in common, there are enough differences between them to justify keeping both programs around on your hard disk. Windows 98 Paint has also lost a few features that were available in the Windows 95 version.

Here's what you can do with Paint:

- Construct or edit simple bitmapped graphic images with rudimentary geometric shapes, bezier curves, solid color fills, airbrushing, integrated text, scaled and skewed images, and simple 90-degree image rotation.
- Read bitmaps in Microsoft's BMP format.
- Save images in Windows .BMP format.

Here's what you can't do with Paint:

- Read or save images in popular third-party formats such as .PCX, .TIF, JPG, and .GIF. (.JPG and .GIF support are added if Microsoft Office 97 is installed.)
- Draw freehand curves.
- Globally replace colors or create multicolor fills or other advanced image effects.
- Edit Win98 icons.
- Save and retrieve user-defined color palettes.

Win Some

Here are the improvements of Paint over Win 3.1 Paintbrush:

- Win98 Paint can handle 16-bit and 24-bit color images, even when running with a lower-depth display driver.
- The pallet of a color-rich bitmap is not destroyed when you save it under 16-color or 256-color screen resolution.
- Unlike Windows 3.1 Paintbrush, Paint doesn't truncate larger images when they're pasted in from the Windows clipboard. If a clipboard image is larger than the current file size, Paint automatically resizes its display window to

accommodate the new image. You can also resize the drawing area manually, by selecting and dragging one of the eight handles on the outer border of the display window.

- Paint allows you to go back and undo your last three image manipulations
- The spray can now creates more watercolor-like special effects, and the Win 3.1 paintbrush roller has been replaced by a more Macintosh-like bucket.
- The toolbox pallet floats; so you can click it with the left mouse button depressed and drag it around to different positions in the editing screen.
- You can now use the selection tools to copy a selected portion of a drawing with an opaque or transparent background. (The area underneath the regular toolbox icons changes with each selected drawing tool. Solid and transparent masking icons appear when you click either selection tool: the square marquee or the cookie-cutter.)
- New menu features in Paint allow you to automatically send a drawing as a fax or select the image as Win98 wallpaper. The Print Preview option on the File menu replaces the old Paintbrush Zoom Out option located on the View menu.

Lose Some

Now, here's what's lost in Win98 Paint:

- The solid shape drawing tools are gone, replaced by an eyedropper color selection tool and a redundant magnifying glass (which offers four alternative views to the five you can get with the Zoom option on the View menu).
- The Color Eraser in the old Windows 3.1 Paintbrush program allowed you to globally replace all instances of one color in a picture with another. In Paint, the regular and color erasers have been combined into one tool that no longer offers this feature. The Paint eyedropper does allow you to pick up a color from one part of a drawing and copy it elsewhere, but you have to make your color changes in a tedious, piecemeal manner.

Tip

The Windows 3.1 Shrink-and-Grow tool has been replaced by a two-step Stretch/Skew feature on Paint's Image menu. To scale a drawing with the new menu options, you must type a horizontal increment, press ENTER, *and then select the Stretch/Skew option again to type a vertical adjustment. Instead of going through all of this, you can rescale objects with the mouse by clicking one of the selection tools and dragging over the screen area you want to resize. A marquee box with eight handles appears around the selected area. As you move the mouse over any of the handles, the cursor changes into a double arrow. You can then click the mouse button and drag the mouse to shrink or expand the selected portion of the image.*

- In the transition from Windows 95 to Windows 98, Paint has lost the ability to open files in the .PCX (PC Paintbrush) file format. However, you can now open these files in the Imaging for Windows application. If you need to edit a .PCX image in Paint, you can load it into Imaging for Windows and then copy and transfer it to Paint through the Windows clipboard.
- Another lost feature in Win98 Paint is the ability to save and retrieve custom color palettes. If you saved the Win95 Paint program before upgrading, you can run it under Win98 in place of the new version to regain this feature (but not the ability to automatically load .PCX files).

WordPad

WordPad is another example of the Microsoft forward-and-back shuffle, at least in terms of productivity features. WordPad's design makes it a tease for Microsoft's full-featured Office 97 suite. But WordPad is missing several useful tools that were available in Write for Windows 3.1.

Here's what you can do with WordPad:

- Perform basic word processing tasks
- Format documents with ruler, toolbar, and simple paragraph styles
- Read Word 97 and below (.DOC), Rich Text Format (.RTF), Windows Write (.WRI), and ASCII, MS-DOS, and Unicode (.TXT) documents
- Save files in Word for Windows version 6 format, in Rich Text Format, or as Text-, MS-DOS Text-, or Unicode-compliant text
- Insert or link bitmap or vector graphics, spreadsheets, and other OLE objects
- Preview full-page graphics

Here's what you can't do with WordPad:

- Edit two files concurrently
- Import or export text and graphic selections to and from existing files
- Check spelling
- Create headers and footers
- Insert page numbers or hard page breaks or adjust leading (the space between lines of text)

Like Word for Windows, WordPad has an icon toolbar, a format bar, and a ruler. You can easily change fonts; justify text right, left, or center; add bold or italic formatting; and so on. The style settings on the Format menu are equivalent to the options that were available on the Windows Write Paragraph menu.

The addition of automatic bullet characters in WordPad is balanced by the loss of Windows Write's single-, double-, and 1.5-line leading option. WordPad's ruler lets you set left and right margins, paragraph indents, and simple tab stops. The Windows Write decimal tab option has disappeared.

The big improvement in WordPad is its ability to read and write Microsoft Word and Rich Text Format documents. The old Windows Write and WordPad share the ability to link and embed OLE objects through the Windows clipboard, but WordPad can also create OLE objects from files on a specified directory path. As in Microsoft's other Win98-aware applets, a Send option on the File menu lets you include the document as a Windows Messaging, Outlook 97/98, or Outlook Express e-mail attachment.

In the transition from Windows 95, WordPad has gained the ability to read and write text with embedded Unicode characters. Unicode is a standard used to represent a variety of foreign-language characters (using 2 bytes per character). WordPad now retains these special characters when you choose the Unicode Open or Save As option.

Missing WordPad Features Available in Windows Write

Windows Write has the ability to insert decimal tabs into documents and create leading options, as already mentioned. Write also has several other features that are missing from WordPad. Windows Write can do the following:

- Create headers and footers in a document
- Generate page numbers in a document
- Insert hard page breaks in the middle of a page

Drag and Drop Selected Text Directly to the Desktop

WordPad's Scrap Pad option lets you select any amount of text in a document and drag it to the desktop to automatically create a new file. Just highlight the text you want to copy and drag the selection to the desktop or to an open folder. This creates a Scrap Memo icon wherever you drop the text.

You can subsequently drag and drop this object back in an open document window in WordPad or Word for Windows. When you drop a Scrap Memo object into a WordPad window, it immediately reappears as a text block. If you drop the Scrap object into Word 6, it reappears as a bitmapped graphic of the original text. In other Windows 3.1 OLE-aware applications, the Scrap Memo may appear as an iconized, embedded object or be rejected as an unknown file format.

Still, the ability to park selected text temporarily as a visible object on the desktop is very handy. Eventually, Microsoft and other vendors will upgrade all of their applications to reconvert Scrap objects automatically to formatted text. Can you say "Object-oriented Desktop"? IBM can, with OS/2 Warp, which is why you'll see more of this feature in Windows as well.

One good use for WordPad is as a browsing utility for various README and other documents composed primarily of text. See Chapter 4 to learn how to automatically load any text file into WordPad from a My Computer or Explorer window.

Extras

In addition to the applications installed into the Accessories folder, Windows 98 contains a number of other useful utilities. Some of these are quietly dumped into your \WINDOWS directory and others are stored on the Windows 98 installation CD. Windows 3.1 also included a few good tools that disappeared when Windows 95 was invented. Here's some information about Windows Extras.

The Same Old C's (Calendar, Cardfile, Clock)

The Cardfile, Calendar, and Clock were axed from Windows 95. (Maybe "C" just wasn't Bill Gates' favorite letter of the alphabet.) To learn how to preserve some of these during an upgrade from Windows 3.x, see Chapter 2.

Document Templates

The Document Templates Accessories option on the Windows Setup tab of the Add/Remove Programs screen prepares Windows 98 to produce document templates for a series of third-party applications. When you activate it, templates for existing applications are added. Templates for some third-party applications (Microsoft Office, Lotus 1-2-3, Ami Pro, Quattro Pro, and so on) are also copied to the \WINDOWS \SHELLNEW directory. If these applications are subsequently installed, the templates are activated. To see which document templates are current available, right-click an empty area of the desktop and select New as shown here:

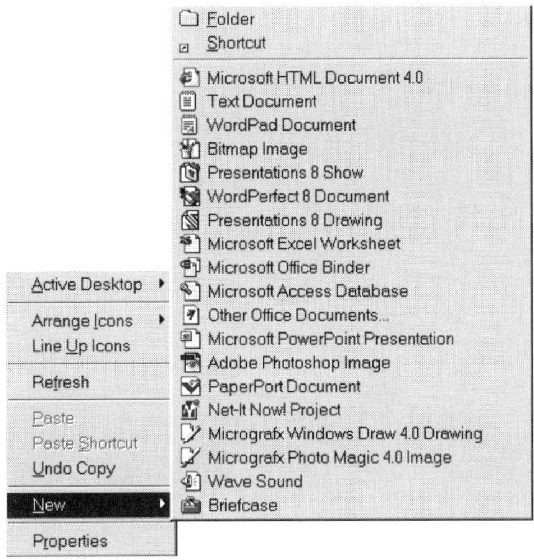

Infrared File Transfer

This utility allows you to quickly transfer files between two computers equipped with infrared serial ports. For it to work, Windows 98's infrared serial support must be active, and the two computers must be placed within several feet of one another, with the infrared ports on each computer in the line of sight. (See Chapter 9 for information on activating infrared serial support.)

To use Infrared File Transfer, open the Infrared applet in My Computer or Explorer. To send files, select a device in the Infrared Transfer window, click the Send Files button, and choose the files you want to send to the other computer. To view files that have been received on this computer, click the Received Files button. Figure 5-11 shows the Infrared Transfer screens.

File Transfers by Modem

In Windows 95, a companion applet called FILEXFER.EXE allowed you to quickly send and receive files through a modem-to-modem terminal connection between two computers. This utility has been removed from Windows 98, but if you upgraded from Windows 95, you should find FILEXFER.EXE in your \WINDOWS directory and its Help file, FILEXFER.HLP, in the \WINDOWS\HELP directory. The FileXFER interface works just like the Infrared File Transfer interface. To use it, you must first establish a dial-up terminal-to-terminal connection between two computers. (For details on how to do this with HyperTerminal or another communication program, see Chapter 11.)

FileXFER requires a Voice-View enabled modem.

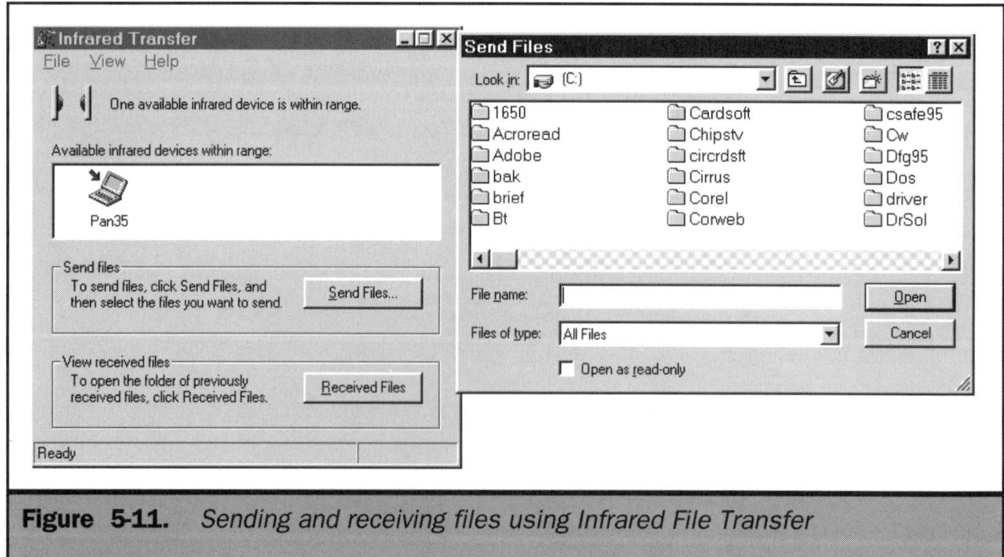

Figure 5-11. *Sending and receiving files using Infrared File Transfer*

OLE Object Packager

Many newer Windows applications contain direct support for Microsoft's OLE (Object Linking and Embedding) protocol, which permits animations, sound files, graphics, spreadsheets, and other data objects to be copied and embedded into a document. The application that creates and saves the data object is called the OLE Server. The application that accepts the object as an insertion into a document is called the OLE Client.

Object Packager lets you insert objects created with non-OLE applications into an OLE client application. In effect, any old DOS or Windows program can become an OLE Server. For example, here's how to embed a database created with Windows 3.1 Cardfile (a non-OLE Server) into a WordPad document:

1. Make sure that the Cardfile database (.CRD file) is associated with the CARDFILE.EXE application. (If you have Cardfile on your hard disk, you can do this by double-clicking a .CRD file from within Windows Explorer. If Cardfile doesn't open the database, you may choose it from the Open With dialog box that pops up for unassociated file types.)
2. Open the Object Packager application (choose Start | Run, enter PACKAGER.EXE in the Open field and click OK).
3. Choose Import from the Object Packager File menu and select the Cardfile database (for example: MYCARDS.CRD). An icon for the package appears in the left Object Packager Pane, and the name of its file contents appears in the right window.
4. Choose Copy Package from Object Packager's Edit menu. This places a copy of the package on the Windows clipboard.
5. Open a Wordpad document (or create a new one). Choose Paste from Wordpad's Edit menu. An icon for the Cardfile database should appear within the Wordpad document. If you double-click this icon, the database will automatically open in the Cardfile program.

QuickView

This option, found in the Add/Remove Programs | Windows Setup Tab | Accessories group, allows you to view the contents of some files by right-clicking them in a My Computer/Explorer window. See Chapter 4 for information on installing and using QuickView.

Windows Scripting Host

This option, found in the Add/Remove Programs | Windows Setup Tab | Accessories group allows Windows 98 to execute Active-X and Microsoft VBA scripts that can automate some desktop and system procedures. You'll find information about working with WSH in the Help files for the Windows 98 Resource Kit.

CD Extras

In addition to the extra features available through Add/Remove Programs and the Interactive CD Sampler (described in the "Entertainment" section of this chapter), the Windows 98 CD includes utilities and software evaluation packages in the \ADD-ONS and \TOOLS folders.

Personal Web Server 4.0

Personal Web Server allows your Windows 98 computer to publish and administer Web documents over the Internet or a local area network. It includes support for Front Page 98 Server extensions. To install Personal Web Server, open your Windows 98 CD to the \ADD-ONS\PWS folder and run SETUP.EXE.

For more information about using Personal Web Server, see Chapter 12.

Remote Data Services 1.5

The Remote Data Services 1.5 Microsoft utility is a data publishing framework for custom applications hosted within Internet Explorer. Through data-aware Active-X controls, individual database records can be distributed from a Windows NT Server, sorted and filtered in an Internet Explorer 4 client window.

For more information on this application, open the \ADD-ONS\PWS\ADCRLNTS .HTM file in Internet Explorer.

Windows 98 Policy Editor

The Windows 98 Policy Editor (located in the \TOOLS\ADMIN\POLEDIT folder of the Win98 CD) allows you to set administrative restrictions on the features available to various users who log onto this Windows 98 computer. It also supports remote administration of other Windows 98 computers through a network. Extensive information on using the Policy Editor is available in the *Windows 98 Resource Kit*. (Also see Chapter 15 of this book.)

Windows 98 Resource Kit

The *Windows 98 Resource Kit* utility suite will be of interest mostly to system administrators and technical support personnel. As shown here, it provides a variety of diagnostic tools to track software and hardware conflicts.

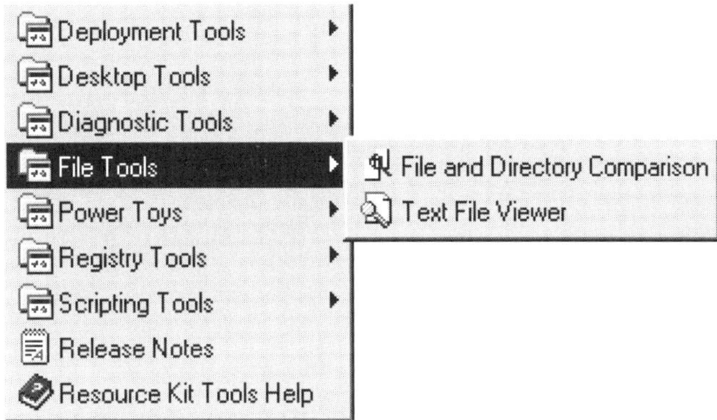

The suite also contains a few end-user desktop applications. Before you rush to install the desktop goodies listed here, you should know that there are far more functional shareware and freeware equivalents for all except the Time Zone Editor. You'll find lots of shareware and freeware enhancements to Windows 98 at http://www.wwfiles.com.

- *ClipTray* lets you create boilerplate text entries for rapid insertion into documents.
- *QuickTray* allows you to add a launch icon for any DOS or Windows application to the System Tray area of the taskbar.
- *File and Directory Comparison* compares the contents of two folders or files, showing the differences in a desktop window.
- *TextFile Viewer* displays an Explorer-like file tree combined with a contents window that allows you to select any ASCII file and view its contents.
- *Time Zone Editor* lets you edit the particulars of any time zone entry that appears in the Windows 98 Date/Time properties or to create new entries.

For information on using the administrative and diagnostic tools in the *Windows 98 Resource Kit*, consult the Resource Kit Tools Help file.

Note that the \TOOLS\RESKIT folder on the Win98 CD contains a series of network administration tools that are copied to your hard disk when you install the *Windows 98 Resource Kit*. Within the RESKIT\NETADMIN folder you'll find subfolders for the Windows 98 Policy Editor, Network Monitor, and Remote Registry Administrator.

To install these tools, open the folder that contains the files, right-click the file in the folder with the .INF file extension, and choose the Install option on the pop-up menu. (To see the three-letter extensions for files shown in Windows Explorer, you may need to toggle this display option on: From any Explorer window, choose View | Folder Options and click the View tab. Then remove the check mark next to Hide File Extensions for Known Filetypes.)

For instance, to install the Network Monitor, open the \TOOLS\RESKIT\NETADMIN\NETMON folder on the CD, right-click NETMON.INF, and choose the Install option from the pop-up menu.

Chapter 6

Accessories II: System Utilities and Maintenance Tools

Chapter Highlights

New System Tools in Windows 98

Applet-by-applet descriptions:

- **Backup and disk maintenance**
- **Scheduling tasks**
- **System information and diagnostics**

Extra utilities

The big news in the Accessories department is in the System Tools folder, which includes a variety of new system maintenance and troubleshooting tools, shown here. These additional utilities bring the operating system a step closer to Microsoft's goal of "zero administration" problem diagnosis and resolution.

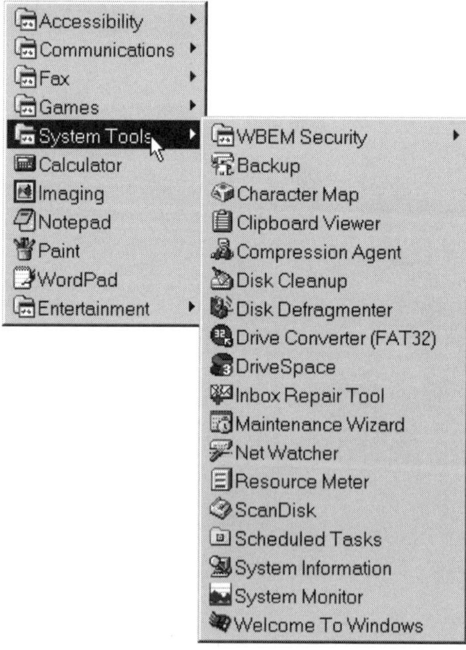

The truth is that this happy ideal has not yet been achieved. Windows 98 builds upon its predecessors, providing support and controls for new hardware and software standards—the operating system is more complex than Windows 95. The new system tools address this complexity, but they don't automatically resolve all system problems.

The good news is that some of the new utilities, such as the Maintenance Wizard, offer new watchdog features. A knowledgeable user can find out what's going on when problems occur and experiment with different configuration settings. And Windows 98 does include wizards that automate a few system maintenance tasks.

New System Tools in Windows 98

The System Tools folder contains an assortment of system monitoring and maintenance utilities. In Windows 98, you'll find utilities that offer the following improvements over Windows 95:

- More user control over startup options and the loading of system service components
- Version control for Windows 98's numerous system files
- Detailed diagnostic information about installed peripherals
- Management of the FAT32 file system
- System registry maintenance
- Automated performance tuning.
- System watchdog and diagnostic tools

In addition, some traditional Windows 95 accessories (Character Map and Clipboard Viewer) have been transferred to this group from the main Accessories folder.

Better Disk Tools

Windows 98 offers new, improved disk maintenance utilities that build on those in MS-DOS 6.x, Windows 3.x, and Windows 95: ScanDisk, Disk Defragmenter, and DriveSpace cooperate fully within the 32-bit Windows environment.

The enhanced version of DriveSpace, formerly distributed in the Microsoft Plus! package, can create its compressed partitions only in the "classic" FAT16 environment. (See Chapters 2 and 7 for more information about FAT16 and FAT32 file systems.)

The Microsoft Disk Defragmenter now includes a special optimization tool that can speed up disk performance by rearranging your most frequently used programs. A new Disk Cleanup option lets you free up space on a drive by removing unnecessary temporary files or unused applications.

To apply Disk Cleanup, ScanDisk, Defragmenter, or Backup to a specific drive, open My Computer, right-click the icon for the desired drive, and open its Properties. You can run Disk Cleanup from the General tab. The Tools tab (shown here) allows you to run ScanDisk (click Check Now), Backup, or Defragmenter. One nice touch: The Tools tab also shows when you last performed each maintenance operation.

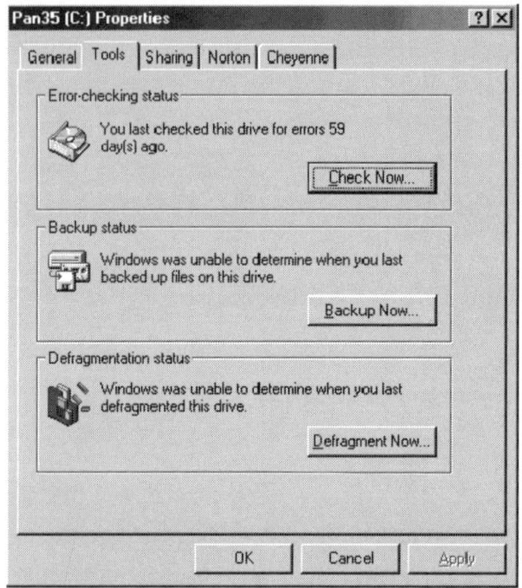

The Maintenance Wizard can assist you in the process of cleaning, checking, and optimizing your hard drive by automatically scheduling these tasks at regular intervals. See the Maintenance Wizard section later in this chapter for details.

Better Diagnostics

Windows 98 offers improved diagnostic tools to help you monitor and protect your system:

- The System File Checker can protect the integrity of Windows 98 by inspecting your system and program directories for changed and missing operating system files. (Missing files can be extracted from the Win98 installation CD.)
- The System Information tool displays an inventory of system resources allocated to installed hardware and software components. The System Information Tools menu contains a variety of diagnostic programs that can help you resolve startup problems and system conflicts.
- The Net Watcher Resource Meter and System Monitor tools allow you to view real-time statistics about network use and system performance.

System Tools

Discussions of the individual applets contained in the System Tools folder are presented in the remainder of this chapter in alphabetical order. If your System Tools group is missing any of the icons shown in the illustration at the beginning of this chapter, you can add them by choosing Control Panel | Add/Remove Program, selecting the Windows Setup tab and then choosing the System Tools group. The Inbox Repair Tool will appear in the folder only if you've upgraded to Windows 98 from Windows 95 or manually installed the Windows Messaging Service (see the section "Fax" in Chapter 5 for more information).

Backup

The Backup application has changed radically in the transition from Windows 95 to Windows 98. The new Microsoft Backup supports a wide range of tape devices, allowing you to archive your system on state-of-the-art hardware. Win98 Backup can't read and restore backup sets created with the Windows 3.x Backup tool, but it can read backups made with the Windows 95 version.

Despite its usefulness, Backup is not installed in Windows 98 by default. To add it to the System Tools group, follow these steps:

1. Choose Control Panel | Add/Remove Programs and select the Windows Setup tab.
2. Scroll down to and open the System Tools group.
3. Place a check mark next to Backup in the Components list.
4. Click OK twice to exit.

The Win98 Backup utility was designed for Microsoft by Seagate Software, and it has many of the features of Seagate's stand-alone backup product. However, Win98 Backup lacks a scheduler and the ability to create emergency recovery diskettes.

Here's what Backup can do:

- Create full system backups to floppy disks, hard disks, and most standard tape devices and tape media, including the QIC 40/80, 150, 510, 1000, 2000, 3010/3020/3080/3095, floppy controller, parallel port, Travan, SCSI, and DAT 4mm/8mm
- Create incremental or differential backups based on the standard DOS Archive file attribute
- Use two types of file compression in backups (to save time or save space)
- Compare and verify backup sets
- Back up and restore Windows 98 systems remotely, over a network

- Restore backup sets created with Windows 95 Backup and Seagate Backup 1.1 to 2.0

Here's what Backup can't do:

- Run scheduled, unattended backups automatically
- Save temporary catalogs that you reconstruct from a tape
- Sort backup and restore display by filename or file type
- Create emergency recovery Windows diskettes for file restore operations under DOS

In Win98, Microsoft finally provides a backup utility that works with most tape drives. If you have a Seagate, HP, Iomega, or Exabyte QIC Wide, Travan, SCSI, or DAT drive, the odds are good that Win98 Backup supports it. Figure 6-1 shows some of the devices Backup supports. A full list of supported tape drives and tape media is available from Seagate in Adobe Acrobat PDF format at http://apps.smg.seagatesoftware.onwardtech.com/win98/.

If you don't have a tape drive or don't want to bother with one, you can use Win98 Backup to archive and restore files on floppy disks, a local hard disk, removable media

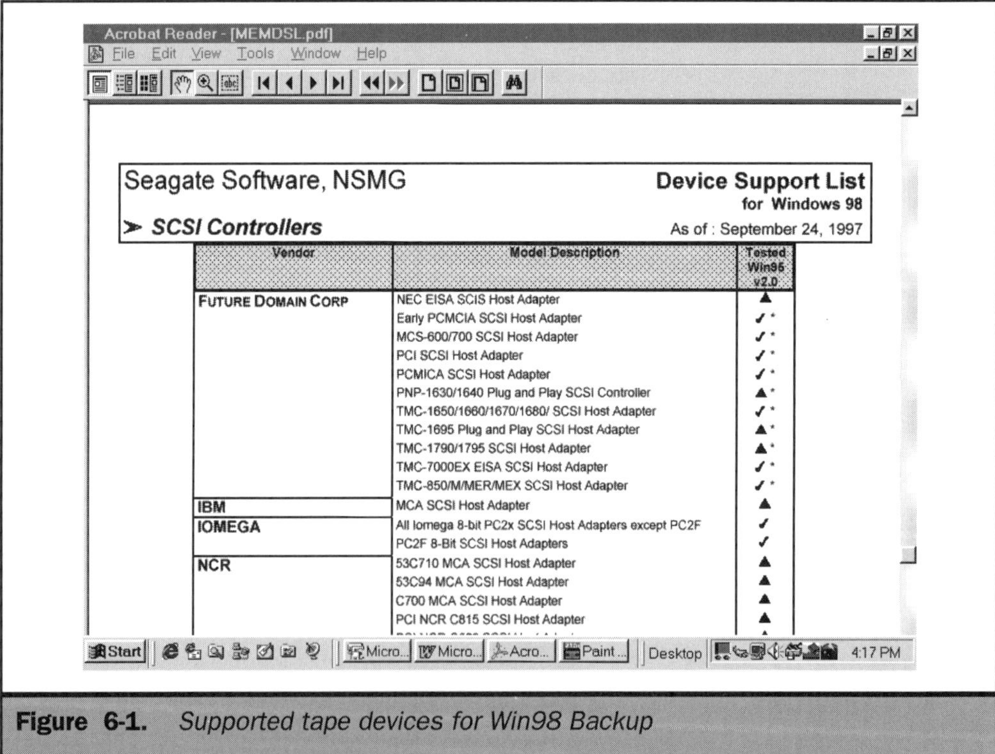

Seagate Software, NSMG

Device Support List for Windows 98

➤ SCSI Controllers

As of : September 24, 1997

Vendor	Model Description	Tested Win95 v2.0
FUTURE DOMAIN CORP	NEC EISA SCIS Host Adapter	▲
	Early PCMCIA SCSI Host Adapter	✓ *
	MCS-600/700 SCSI Host Adapter	✓ *
	PCI SCSI Host Adapter	✓ *
	PCMICA SCSI Host Adapter	✓ *
	PNP-1630/1640 Plug and Play SCSI Controller	▲ *
	TMC-1650/1660/1670/1680/ SCSI Host Adapter	✓ *
	TMC-1695 Plug and Play SCSI Host Adapter	▲ *
	TMC-1790/1795 SCSI Host Adapter	▲ *
	TMC-7000EX EISA SCSI Host Adapter	✓ *
	TMC-850/M/MER/MEX SCSI Host Adapter	✓ *
IBM	MCA SCSI Host Adapter	▲
IOMEGA	All Iomega 8-bit PC2x SCSI Host Adapters except PC2F	✓
	PC2F 8-Bit SCSI Host Adapters	✓
NCR	53C710 MCA SCSI Host Adapter	▲
	53C94 MCA SCSI Host Adapter	▲
	C700 MCA SCSI Host Adapter	▲
	PCI NCR C815 SCSI Host Adapter	▲

Figure 6-1. *Supported tape devices for Win98 Backup*

(such as a Jaz Zip drive), or a network directory. This can be a useful approach for backing up incremental copies of your daily work. Here's what to do:

1. Choose Start | Accessories | System Tools and launch the Backup applet.
2. By default, the Backup Wizard appears and asks you what to back up. If you just want to archive your daily work, click the Back Up Selected Files button. Then click Next to display the file selection screen.
3. Select the folders and files you want to back up. (A check mark in the box next to a folder selects every file in the folder. Click the folder name instead of the check box to open a folder without selecting everything.) Click Next to continue.
4. The What To Back Up screen allows you to select between differential (all selected files) and incremental (only new and changed files) backup types. For this example, choose All Selected Files and click Next to continue. (For a detailed discussion of differential versus incremental backup strategies, see Chapter 8.)
5. Select the backup destination and name the archive file. If you're not using a tape drive, select File. A Browse button appears to let you choose a local or network location. Choose a destination (for example, A:\ or C:\MY BACKUPS) and assign an archive name. (You can keep the default name if you wish). If necessary, you can create a new folder while you're browsing the Where To Back Up file list. To do so, click the Create New folder icon, shown here.

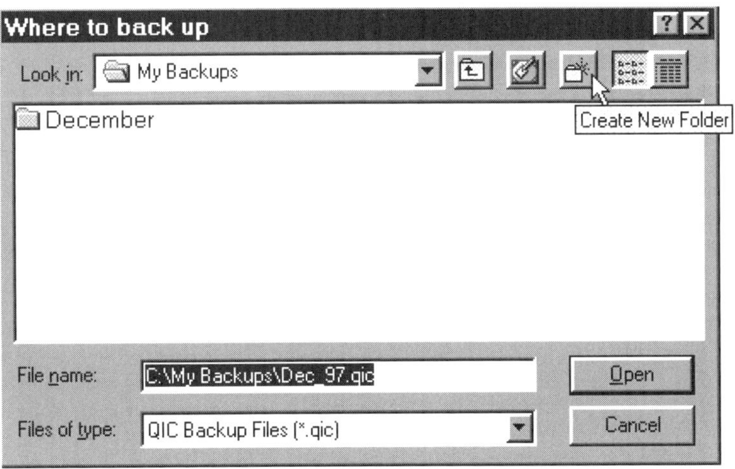

6. The How To Back Up screen lets you toggle data verification and backup compression on and off. Select the options you want and click Next to continue.
7. Choose a name to identify the backup job and click the Start button to perform the backup. A status window displays the results of the backup operation.

Repeating a Backup Operation

After you've completed the backup procedure described in the preceding steps, the specifications of your backup job are saved. When the time comes for tomorrow's backup, the procedure is very simple:

1. Choose Open An Existing Backup Job from the initial menu. Select the job you created to archive your daily work and click the Open button.
2. The Backup screen appears. Your daily job should be listed in the Backup job window. Click the Start button to begin the backup.
3. A dialog box will ask whether you want to overwrite yesterday's backup with the same name. Since you specified a backup of "all selected files" in your work folders, you can select Yes to overwrite the previous backup with today's work.

Tip *After you get used to the way Microsoft Backup works, you can disable the display of the Backup Wizard. Choose Tools | Preferences from Backup's pull-down menu and remove the check mark next to Show Startup Dialog When Microsoft Backup Is Started. This will allow you to go directly to the Backup tab, select a saved job specification, and click the Start button to archive your work.*

Restoring a Backup Archive

If you need to restore archived files, here's what to do:

1. Select Restore Backed Up Files on the opening Backup Wizard screen. (If you've disabled the wizard, you can go directly to the Restore tab or invoke the Restore Wizard by choosing Tools | Restore Wizard.)
2. Choose the device you want to restore from. (If you select File, specify the path to the stored QIC backup archive. Backup stores its archives in the QIC tape format whether or not your computer has a physical tape device.)
3. Select the backup set you want to restore from the archive.
4. Choose the files in the backup set that you want to restore.
5. Select the target drive and folder where the files will be restored.
6. Specify how to replace existing files.
7. Click the Start button. Confirm that the proper QIC archive is selected in the Media Required box and click OK.

Note *If you are backing up and restoring to a tape device, don't erase the local copies of your job catalogs from your hard disk! (Backup can rebuild a catalog from the contents of a tape, but on large tapes this process can take hours.)*

Backup Odds 'n Ends

Here are some points to keep in mind when using Backup:

- Win98 Backup lets you exclude specific file types. Click the Options button at the bottom of the Backup screen, select the Exclude tab, and click the Add button to exclude a specific file type.
- Backup does not support date filters.
- You should not use Win98 Backup to archive the physical container file for DriveSpace compressed volume. Instead, you should mount the compressed volume and back up the files and directories on the drive directly, as you would with an uncompressed drive.

For a more detailed discussion of Windows 98 backup strategies, Microsoft Backup, and third-party products, see Chapter 8. You'll learn how to create emergency recovery disks, back up and restore your system from DOS, and a few other things worth knowing.

Character Map

The Win98 version of Character Map is slightly skimpier than the Windows 3.1 version, but you're not really missing anything critical.

Here's what Character Map can do:

- Display the character sets and numerical ASCII assignments for any installed Windows font
- Copy selected characters into any Windows application through the clipboard (useful for creating special effects in documents and for handling foreign-language characters)

Here's what Character Map can't do:

- Generate print samples of font
- Remap the keyboard assignments for specific characters

The best use for Character Map is to examine the upper ASCII characters of various Windows fonts. The program lets you determine quickly whether a font contains foreign-language characters, box-drawing characters, or other symbols that you might need in a word processing document.

For example, suppose you're working in WordPad using Times New Roman, and you want to draw a box around a paragraph.

If you open Character Map and select Times New Roman in the Font window, you won't find the ASCII box-drawing characters there. However, as illustrated in Figure 6-2, you can switch the Character Map window to Terminal Font, which *does* contain box-drawing characters. This makes it easy to draw your box.

Clipboard Viewer

The Windows 98 Clipboard Viewer is not much changed from the Windows 3.1 and Windows 95 versions, but Microsoft did give the Display menu some extra options. You can render a clipboard object in several formats in the Viewer: Depending on the source of the object, you can view it as text or a picture, and you can display information about the source of OLE-linked objects.

These operations don't change the nature of the clipboard contents. If the source was text, you can't change the clipboard contents into a picture (to paste into a graphics program, for instance).

Here's what Clipboard Viewer can do:

- View or transfer text, graphics, and specially formatted objects between Windows applications or between Windows and DOS applications
- Show a color palette of graphic images
- Save and reload clipboard contents to disk in a proprietary (.CLP) format

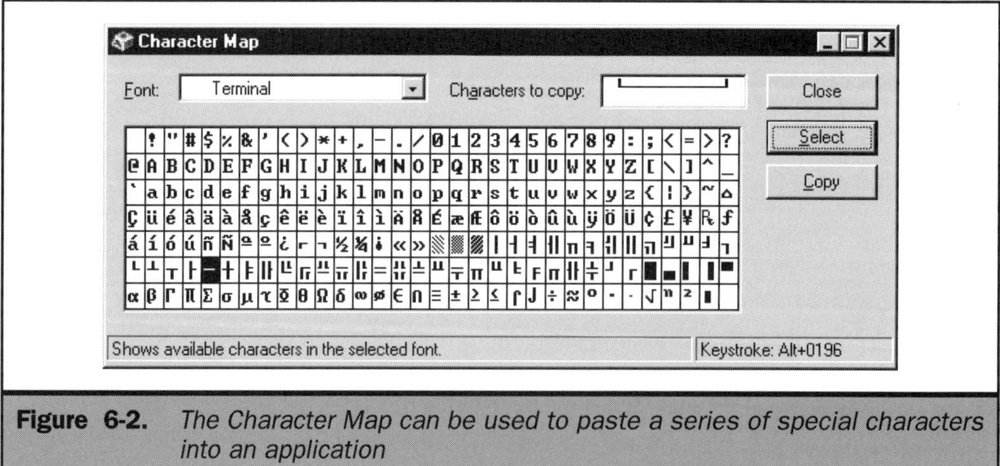

Figure 6-2. *The Character Map can be used to paste a series of special characters into an application*

Here's what Clipboard Viewer can't do:

- Save clipboard contents in formats that applications can import
- Transfer specially formatted objects between DOS and Windows applications

If you installed Windows 98 over a previous version of Windows, the old Clipboard Viewer is left in the directory, and the new one won't be installed. If you don't see the Clipboard Viewer in the System Tools folder, you can add it by choosing Control Panel | Add/Remove Programs, selecting the Windows Setup tab, and placing a check mark next to Clipboard Viewer in the System Tools group. If the check mark is already present, you can deselect it, click OK twice to close Add/Remove Programs, and then reopen this applet and reinstall it. (Another way to restore the Clipboard Viewer is to check the \WINDOWS directory for the file CLIPBRD.EXE. If you find it, you can re-create the Clipboard Viewer by creating a program shortcut to CLIPBRD.EXE.)

Users who upgraded from Windows for Workgroups or Windows 95 will probably want to keep their old clipboard utilities. These versions of Windows contain a more powerful network Clipbook as well as the standard Clipboard Viewer. The Clipbook feature allows you to view, cut, and paste contents from applications to multiple clipboards. These clipboard files can be shared with other users across a network.

If you upgraded from Windows for Workgroups, Clipbook will still be present in your \WINDOWS directory, waiting for you to install it. (Just create an Accessories shortcut to *d*:\WINDOWS\CLIPBRD.EXE.)

If you still have your old Windows 95 CD, you'll also find the more powerful Clipbook utility there. (Microsoft has omitted it on the Windows 98 CD!) If you performed a clean installation of Windows 98, you'll probably want to install the Windows 95 Clipbook instead of using the default Clipboard Viewer. Here's how:

1. Choose Control Panel | Add/Remove Programs and select the Windows Setup tab.
2. Click the Have Disk button, point the wizard to the \OTHER\CLIPBOOK folder on your Windows 95 installation CD, and click OK.
3. Place a check mark next to Clipbook Viewer in the Components list and click the Install button.

The Win95 Clipbook viewer will be added to your Accessories group.

To share a file over a network with Clipbook, copy it to the clipboard in the usual way, using the Edit | Copy command or CTRL-C. Then open the Clipbook Viewer. Select Edit | Paste from the Clipbook pull-down menu. Assign a page name and place a check mark next to Share Item Now. Click OK and another dialog box will appear, as shown here, allowing you to assign access rights and to password-protect the shared clipboard file.

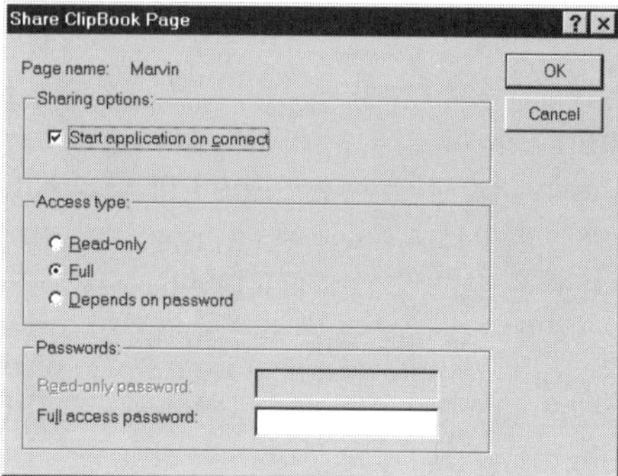

In Windows 98 the Clipboard Viewer's Display menu allows you to view the color palette used by imported graphics. Since Windows 98 typically reserves some colors for internal use, this feature may be useful in studying the composition of a graphic. The color palette can show you whether all colors in the graphic will be accurately transferred to another application.

Compression Agent

See "DriveSpace" later in this chapter for a discussion of this utility.

Disk Cleanup

The Disk Cleanup utility allows you to free up space on your hard drive by deleting temporary files. When you run Disk Cleanup, it presents a list of "unnecessary" files in four categories, as shown here:

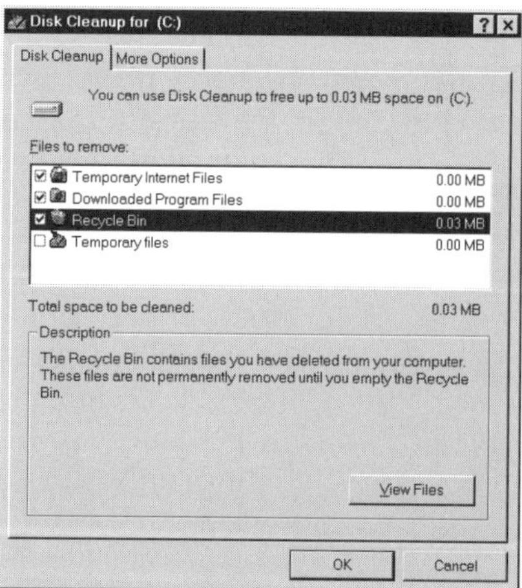

- Temporary Internet Files are the Web pages stored on disk by Internet Explorer for quick reviewing. (Deleting these files does not affect your personalized subscription settings for Web sites.)
- Downloaded Program Files are Java and Active-X applets downloaded from the Internet to enhance the display of some Web pages.
- The Recycle Bin contains files that you've deleted from your computer either from the Desktop or by using My Computer or Windows Explorer.
- Temporary Files are data caches written to the TEMP folder by Windows applications. Some applications don't delete these files when they close, although the files no longer serve any purpose.

The Disk Cleanup tab displays the amount of storage space occupied by files in each of these four categories. You can place a check mark next to any category you want to remove and click OK to purge those files from your disk. To inspect and save individual files in any category, click the View Files button. If you see something you want to keep, you can drag it out of its TEMP folder window to another location.

The More Options tab of the Disk Cleanup window provides quick access to some other space-saving options:

- Click the Clean Up button under Windows Setup to open the list of installed Windows 98 components and accessories. (This is the same list you see when you select the Windows Setup tab after choosing Control Panel | Add/Remove Programs.) You can deselect any unnecessary components to remove them from the system.
- Click the Clean Up button under Installed Programs to bring up a list of the third-party applications you've installed in Windows 98. You can select any programs you no longer want and click the Add/Remove button to uninstall them.
- If your disk is still using the FAT16 partitioning system, you can click the Convert button under Drive Conversion to change the file system to FAT32. On disks larger than 500MB, this will probably free up some space by reducing the individual cluster size allocated to the files stored on the disk. (See "Drive Converter (FAT32)" later in this chapter and Chapter 7 for more information about the FAT32 file system.)

Disk Defragmenter

Disk Defragmenter is more efficient in Windows 98 than either the DOS 6.x Defrag utility or the Windows 95 version. In Windows 98, Disk Defragmenter has been given a simplified interface. It can't be controlled to the same degree as the Speed Disk or Disk Minder optimizers in Symantic's Norton Utilities or Network Associates' Nuts & Bolts, but it does have a built-in feature that optimizes the loading of your most frequently used programs.

Here's what Disk Defragmenter can do:

- Optimize FAT16 and FAT32 partitions
- Check drives for errors
- Optimize the order of your favorite programs, for faster performance
- Optimize DriveSpace partitions

Here's what Disk Defragmenter can't do:

- Perform quick Unfragment Only optimization
- Sort or reorder disk file structure to user specification
- Display drive fragmentation statistics
- Defragment stacker-compressed volumes

Disk Defragmenter has changed, somewhat, in concept for Windows 98. The Windows 95 version had a series of options that allowed users to customize its performance. You could run a quick Unfragment Only operation on the disk or a complete optimization that consolidated all free space at the end of the drive.

In Windows 98, Disk Defragmenter optimizes the disk automatically. The default setting rearranges your program files for faster performance. Previous to Windows 98, disk optimizers did this by arranging each file on your hard disk in sequential order. In Windows 98, every time you boot into the interface or open a new program, this activity is recorded in a special log file. (These log files are stored in the \WINDOWS\APPLOG directory.) When the Rearrange option is active during optimization, Disk Defragmenter examines your usage logs and tries to rearrange bits and pieces of files in optimum loading order. For instance, if Windows 98 determines that 2MB of a WINWORD.EXE file are usually loaded into memory followed by a 3MB MS097.DLL file and then the remainder of WINWORD, the files are arranged on disk in that fragmented order because they load faster that way.

Running the defragmenter Rearrange Program Files option is more time consuming than a straight file-by-file reordering of the disk. If you're in a hurry, you can deselect this option. Then Disk Defragmenter will simply consolidate free space at the end of the disk.

Note *If you optimize a disk with Disk Defragmenter's Rearrange Program Files option turned on, don't reoptimize the disk with Norton Utilities 3.0, Nuts & Bolts 1.03, or earlier versions of these packages. They will just undo the special ordering that Disk Defragmenter has created. Symantic has a patch for Norton Utilities 3.0 that can be downloaded and installed through "live update" to make the package completely compatible with Windows 98.*

To turn off Disk Defragmenter's Rearrange Program Files and Check Drive For Errors options, click the Settings button on the opening Select Drive screen.

Disk Defragmenter's Rearrange Program Files option will be most effective on FAT32 disk partitions. If you're running Windows 98 on a FAT16 partition, you may want to turn this feature off.

Using the Check Drive for Errors Option

When the Check Drive For Errors setting is checked (the default), Disk Defragmenter will scan the files and directories on the disk for errors before the optimization process starts. This option is highly recommended—if you defragment a drive that harbors disk errors, your problems can multiply drastically.

OPTIMIZING IN THE FOREGROUND Microsoft tells you that you can repair or optimize a disk in the background. In reality, this feature does not work as well as you might hope. Running programs and saving files in the foreground with a disk maintenance tool active in the background can cause constant restart interruptions. For fastest results, I suggest closing active applications and running Disk Defragmenter by itself.

For more information on disk optimization, see "More About Hard Disk Tuning" in Chapter 8.

Note

There is no DOS command-line version of Disk Defragmenter. Microsoft recommends that you not use the Defrag utility that came with earlier versions of DOS.

Drive Converter (FAT32)

Drive Converter is Microsoft's utility for performing a one-way conversion from the FAT16 partition format to the new FAT32 file format.

The primary advantage of converting to FAT32 is that FAT32 permits you to use a single disk partition (drive C) larger than 2048MB.

A secondary advantage of FAT32 is that it offers a smaller file cluster size for large partitions. This is usually less wasteful of disk storage space on large partitions than is the case with FAT16. (See Chapter 7 for more details.)

Nevertheless, there are several disadvantages of converting to FAT32:

- You must boot Windows 98 or use a Windows 98 startup diskette to see a FAT32 partition. (If you boot your computer from another operating system or from a DOS or Windows 95 startup diskette, the partition will be invisible.)
- If you convert an existing Windows 98 system to FAT32, you cannot uninstall Windows 98 to return to your previous operating system.
- Hardware suspend-to-disk or hibernate features on most computers will not work with FAT32 partitions. (Standby and suspend-to-RAM features do work.)

- Some older antivirus and disk maintenance utilities do not work on FAT32 partitions. You'll have to remove or upgrade these programs before you convert your drive.
- If you convert your Win98 boot drive to FAT32, your computer will lose the ability to dual boot other operating systems (such as Windows NT or OS/2).

Here's what Drive Converter can do:

- Convert partitions of 512MB or larger from FAT16 to FAT32 file format on IDE and SCSI drives
- Warn you about operating features that you may lose with the FAT32 format, as shown here:

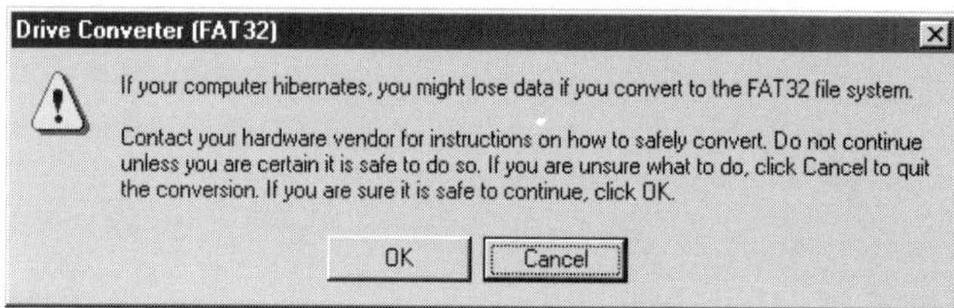

- Check your disk for older antivirus and disk utilities that don't work properly under FAT32
- Allow you to back up your hard disk before converting to the new format

Here's what Driver Converter can't do:

- Convert partitions smaller than 512MB to FAT32
- Convert a partition back to FAT16

If you decide to convert your boot drive (or another partition) to FAT32, the Drive Converter Wizard guides you through the necessary steps. If you don't see Driver Converter in the System Tools group, you can add it by choosing Control Panel | Add/Remove Programs.

The first wizard screen allows you to click a Details button to display more information about FAT32 partitions.

The next screen displays a list of partitions eligible for conversion. (You must convert them one at a time.)

The next screen checks your partition for antivirus and disk utilities that are incompatible with FAT32. (Some productivity applications and uninstallers have minor incompatibilities with FAT32. They may report the amount of available disk space inaccurately, but remain otherwise functional. These marginal programs will not be detected by Drive Converter. You may want to consult program documentation or the program vendor if you suspect an application may have problems with FAT32.)

Next, you'll be given an opportunity to create a backup of the partition before starting the conversion process. Click the Create Backup button to launch Microsoft Backup.

The final screen warns you that the computer will reboot in MS-DOS mode to complete the conversion, which may take several hours.

DriveSpace

The version of DriveSpace included with Windows 98 is the same DriveSpace 3 compression utility that was formerly bundled with Microsoft Plus! and Windows 95 OEM Service Release 2. The basic DriveSpace 2 program in Windows 95 offered compression ratios no greater than 2 to 1 and was limited to disk sizes of 512MB or less.

DriveSpace 3 in Windows 98 can manage volumes of up to 2GB. It can also achieve better compression ratios. The HiPack and UltraPack settings available in the Compression Agent allow ratios of better than 3 to 1.

With large hard disks as cheap as they are today, the principal use you may have for DriveSpace is to compress a partition on a notebook computer. (Large notebook drives are typically 50 percent more expensive than their desktop counterparts.)

Here's what DriveSpace can do:

- Create and mount compressed volumes in the foreground or background
- Mount or dismount volumes without rebooting the computer
- Provide full 32-bit file access to compressed volumes
- Store the Windows 98 swap file on a compressed volume
- Compress the contents of floppy diskettes (even on FAT32 systems)

Here's what DriveSpace can't do:

- Compress volumes on a FAT32 host drive
- Coexist with Stacker 3.1 or 4.0 compressed volumes
- Create compressed floppies readable on systems that don't have DriveSpace or DoubleSpace installed

DriveSpace 3 automatically recognizes compressed volumes created by previous versions of DoubleSpace or DriveSpace. These volumes will coexist with any new compressed volumes that you create within Windows 98. You can even use a

DriveSpace-compressed volume on a FAT16 partition to store the Windows 98 swap file.

If you're upgrading from DOS or Windows 3.1, here's how DriveSpace works: Upon installation, Windows 98 automatically replaces real-mode drivers in CONFIG.SYS with 32-bit protected mode drivers. For example, the real-mode DBLSPACE.BIN driver from DOS 6.x is replaced by the protected-mode driver DRVSPACE.VXD. The protected-mode driver allows faster access to the files on your compressed volumes.

To determine whether a particular disk drive is running in real mode or in 32-bit protected mode, check the Performance tab of the System applet in the Control Panel.

Compressing a Partition

To compress a partition with DriveSpace, follow these steps:

1. Start the DriveSpace application from the System Tools group. (If the icon isn't displayed, add DriveSpace by choosing Control Panel | Add/Remove Programs.) Highlight the drive you want to compress.
2. Select Drive | Compress from the pull-down menu. If the drive is eligible for compression, the Compress A Drive window shows the used and free space ratios for the current contents and the projected size of the drive after compression. (A floppy disk must contain at least 512K of free space to be eligible for compression.)
3. Click the Start button on the Compress A Drive screen. If you want to back up the files on the disk before compressing them, click the Back Up Files button. When you're ready to begin compressing, click the Compress Now button, shown here:

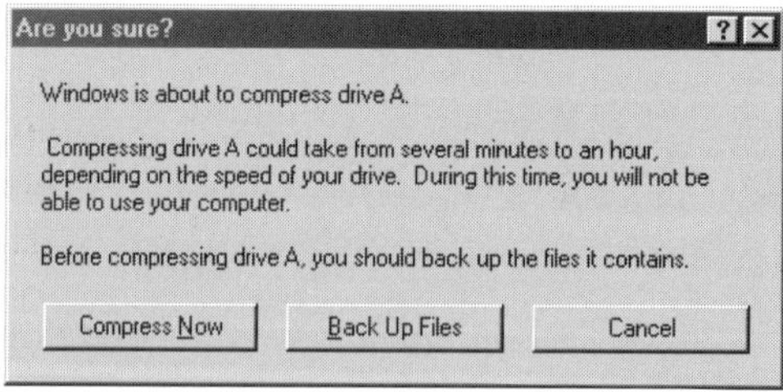

On-the-Fly Options

DriveSpace lets you perform a number of compression-related operations as you work:

- DriveSpace can mount, unmount, and create new compressed volumes in the background, allowing you to continue working in another application. You can create and mount new drives in a single session, with no need to reboot the computer.

- To mount or unmount a compressed partition, select Advanced | Mount or Advanced | Unmount from the DriveSpace menu.
- If you want to change the default ratio between compressed and uncompressed space on a physical partition, select Drive | Adjust Free Space.
- To upgrade a compressed partition from DriveSpace 2 to the DriveSpace 3 format, select Drive | Upgrade. If you created your DriveSpace partition under DOS or Windows 95, you'll need to upgrade it to the DriveSpace 3 format to gain more storage space with the Compression Agent.

Compression Agent

The Compression Agent is also a part of DriveSpace. It allows you to fine-tune DriveSpace compression options. To access the Compression Agent, choose Advanced | Settings from the DriveSpace pulldown menu or launch the Compression Agent icon in the System Tools folder. You can select from three compression types: Standard, HiPack, and UltraPack. (For more information on these compression types, click the Overview button on the first Compression Agent screen.

To change the compression settings for a DriveSpace partition, click the Settings button on the first Compression Agent screen to display the screen shown here. The higher the compression ratio you set, the slower the access for files stored on the DriveSpace partition. (In actuality, with a Pentium-class machine, the slowdown from using UltraPack compression is negligible. With a 486 CPU, you may notice a significant difference in file access times.)

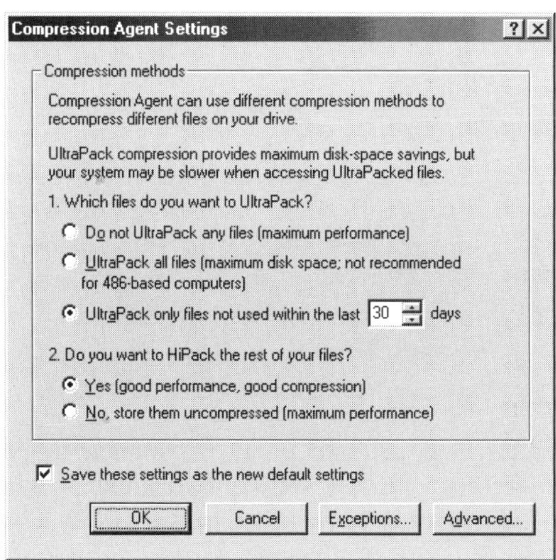

Once you've configured the HiPack and UltraPack settings to your liking, click OK. Click the Start button on the first Compression Agent screen to recompress the drive with the new defaults.

You can further customize Compression Agent to exclude specific folders or files from high compression. To do so, click the Exceptions button on the Compression Agent Settings screen. You can click the Advanced button to set a free-space threshold that prevents compression reduction. (By default, DriveSpace automatically attempts to improve performance by reducing the compression of files that you've recently opened.)

Reserving Drive Letters for Removable Media

You can reserve specific drive letters for removable media. That way, if you build a new compressed volume, the drive letter assignment won't conflict with drive letters you've already reserved for specific removable disks. Here's how to do it:

1. Choose the System object in the Control Panel and click the Device Manager tab.
2. Double-click the option in the hardware tree that represents the removable device.
3. Click the Settings tab, shown here:

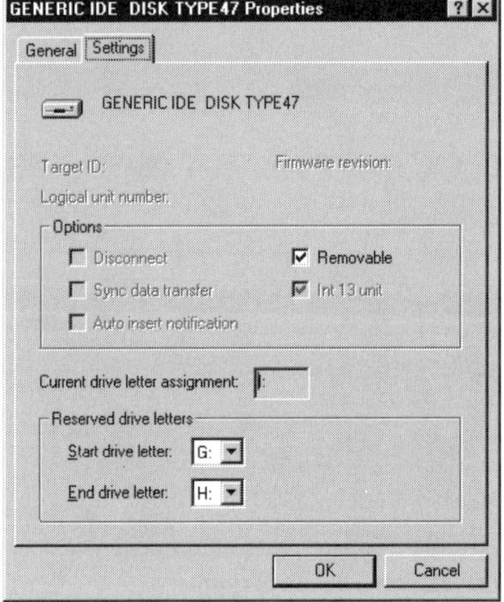

4. In the Reserved Drive Letters box, select a letter in the Start Drive Letter list to define the first drive to be assigned to this device. In the End Drive Letter list, select the last drive to be assigned to this device. (These options will be active for removable drives such as the Iomega Zip and Jaz drives.)
5. Click OK and close the System Properties sheet. Then shut down and restart the computer to make the changes take effect.

Inbox Repair Tool

If your Windows 98 is a brand-new installation, you won't find Inbox Repair Tool, which is a maintenance applet for Windows Messaging Services. If you use Outlook Express as your default mail client, Windows Messaging is bypassed.

The Inbox Repair Tool performs maintenance operations on the mailbox file used by Windows Messaging (the Inbox icon) to store your mail and fax messages and folders. (Windows Messaging mail files have a .PST file extension and are usually located in the \EXCHANGE directory on your Windows host drive.) Occasionally, a Windows Messaging mailbox file may grow to huge proportions after sending or receiving complicated fax documents. Simply deleting the documents from the Inbox won't reshrink the file back to its normal size, but the Inbox Repair Tool will do the job.

Maintenance Wizard

The Maintenance Wizard applet is an important one. It allows you to automate a series of disk maintenance tasks that will keep your system running at optimal speed.

Here's what Maintenance Wizard can do:

- Display screens that help you schedule Disk Cleanup, Disk Defragmenter, and ScanDisk applications at regular intervals
- Allow you to enable or disable the launching of programs in your Startup group

Here's what Maintenance Wizard can't do:

- Schedule Microsoft Backup jobs
- Schedule execution of third-party disk utilities

You can start Maintenance Wizard from within the Welcome To Windows applet or select it by choosing Start | Accessories | System Tools. The opening screen asks what type of tune-up schedule you want: Express or Custom. If you choose Express, you'll be asked to choose convenient times for running the three Windows 98 disk maintenance utilities:

- Disk Defragmenter will optimize your hard disk, rearranging the postion of application files to make your most frequently used programs run faster.
- ScanDisk will check the integrity of your hard disk(s).
- Disk Cleanup will delete unnecessary temporary files from the disk to free up space.

When you click the Finish button on the last screen, the operations you define are entered into the Task Scheduler and will run at the times you've selected. You can also select an option to immediately tune up your system.

If you select the Custom option, the wizard walks you through a more complete set of scheduling options for each of the three maintenance tools. Each process can be individually enabled or disabled. You can click the Settings button to customize the way each disk tool works, as shown here. (For information about modifying settings for Disk Cleanup, Disk Defragmenter, and ScanDisk, see the individual sections for each utility in this chapter.)

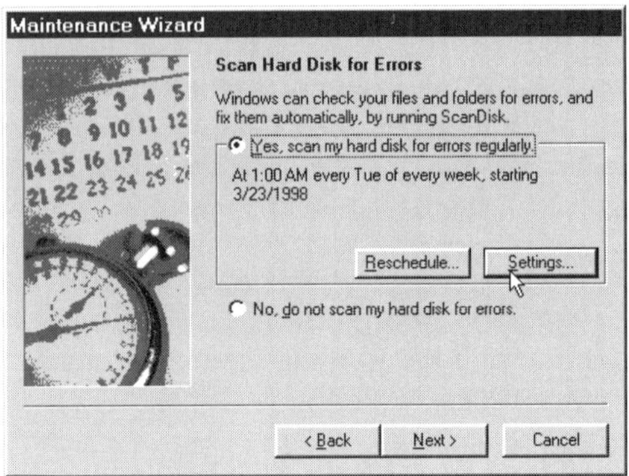

Net Watcher

Net Watcher is a network administration tool. In Windows 98, Net Watcher includes more watchdog options than the tools that were supplied with Windows for Workgroups. You can use Net Watcher to monitor network users and shared resources on multiple servers.

Here's what Net Watcher can do:

- Add a shared network resource or stop using a network resource
- Show all shared resources, connected users, and open files
- Close files that have been opened and disconnect a user

Here's what Net Watcher can't do:

- Automatically establish a server connection

Net Watcher is not installed by default. You can add it to the System Tools group by choosing Control Panel | Add/Remove Programs | Windows Setup | System Tools.

When you open Net Watcher, the Connections To This Server window shows a list of users currently logged onto this computer. You can monitor other servers on the network by choosing Select Server from the Administer menu. The options on the View menu allow you to display usage by shared drives and folders or files that are currently open on any selected server.

Using Net Watcher, an administrator can remotely monitor connections to any resource on any workstation. (For remote administration, permission must be enabled

Sharing a Resource Remotely Using Net Watcher

Here's how to share a resource remotely using the Net Watcher utility:

1. After connecting to the remote computer in Net Watcher, click the Show Shared Folders icon. (See Figure 6-3.)
2. Click the Add Share icon (this icon is dimmed until you click the Show Shared Folders icon).
3. In the Enter Path dialog box, type the drive and the complete path to the resource that you want to share and then click OK.
4. Complete the property screen, also shown in Figure 6-3, and then click OK.

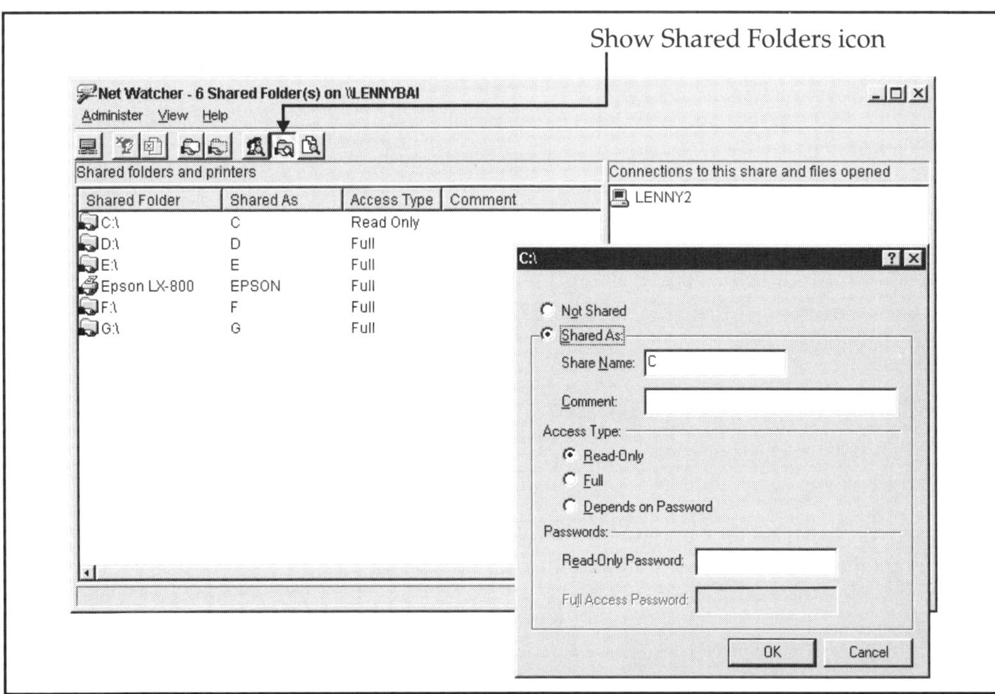

Figure 6-3. *Net Watcher screen for monitoring shared resources on your network and resetting access rights*

on monitored computers.) The network administrator can disconnect users, change access rights, and administer the file system for users on a particular computer.

Resource Meter

Resource Meter is a simple TSR program that allows you to view the available Windows 98 system resources, user resources, and GDI resources without opening the System object in the Control Panel. If any of these settings fall below 25 percent, you should probably close some applications and save your work to avoid a system crash.

ScanDisk

ScanDisk is supplied in both DOS and Windows flavors. In Windows 98, ScanDisk has been updated to accommodate FAT32 disk partitions. Other than that, it is very similar to the Windows 95 version. (ScanDisk was upgraded in Windows 95 to handle long filenames and to repair DriveSpace-compressed volumes.)

Here's what ScanDisk can do:

- Check the disk for FAT and directory errors
- Repair cross-linked files
- Report invalid long filenames and invalid date and time signatures
- Scan for media defects, mark bad sectors, and relocate good file clusters
- Repair compression errors on Microsoft DoubleSpace and DriveSpace volumes

Here's what ScanDisk can't do:

- Repair serious FAT or directory structure problems
- Restore corrupted partition information

When you run ScanDisk , a dialog box pops up on the desktop allowing you to set a number of default options. You can enable or disable automatic media scanning, specify which portions of the disk will be examined, enable or disable report logging, and change the way ScanDisk makes repairs.

Preserving Lost Data Clusters

To preserve lost data clusters in damaged files, change the default ScanDisk settings as follows:

1. Open ScanDisk by choosing Start | Accessories | System Tools. Click the Advanced button near the bottom of the window.

2. In the Cross-Linked Files section, select Make Copies.
3. In the Lost File Fragments section, select Convert To Files.

Figure 6-4 shows advanced options you can change according to your personal preferences. You can also change ScanDisk's surface scan options.

Note *If you change any ScanDisk settings, the changes won't be preserved unless you actually run a scan on at least one drive before closing the dialog box.*

Although ScanDisk will run in the background, it runs much faster if you close your other applications first. Sometimes, even if you've closed all windows and applications on the desktop, ScanDisk continues to restart and repeatedly perform the same operations. If you notice this behavior, try this trick to speed up ScanDisk: Press CTRL-ALT-DELETE *from the desktop and inspect the Close Program list. You should see entries for Explorer, Systray, and ScanDisk itself. If you see other entries in the list, try removing them by highlighting the items and clicking the End Task button. In particular, remove listings for Osa and FindFast. These Microsoft Office processes, loaded at boot time, are a principal cause of ScanDisk hesitation.*

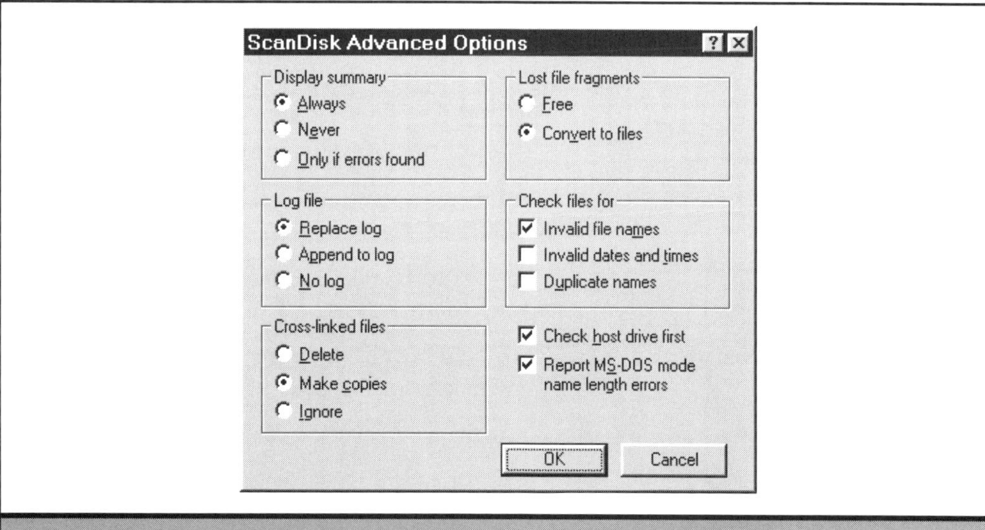

Figure 6-4. *The Advanced button on the ScanDisk menu provides a number of additional options*

If you run ScanDisk in MS DOS mode, there are a number of command-line options that you can tack on. These options are summarized in Table 6-1.

If you run ScanDisk with the custom parameter, you have complete control over the repair, logging, and surface scanning options. By editing parameters in the SCANDISK.INI file, located in the same directory on your hard disk as SCANDISK.EXE, you can specify any series of default operations to be run with the custom switch.

Scheduled Tasks

Scheduled Tasks will be a familiar applet to Windows 95 users who also purchased the Microsoft Plus! package. In Windows 98, this applet is integrated directly into the Explorer interface. The Maintenance Wizard uses it to schedule ScanDisk and Disk Defragmenter disk maintenance tasks. If you used the Plus! System Agent to schedule tasks in Windows 95, they are automatically migrated to Win98's Scheduled Tasks when you upgrade.

Here's what Scheduled Tasks can do:

Command	Function
Scandisk /all	Automatically checks and repairs all drives
Scandisk /autofix	Makes repairs without prompting for user input
Scandisk /checkonly	Scans a drive without making repairs
Scandisk /custom	Configures and runs ScanDisk according to SCANDISK.INI settings
Scandisk /nosave	With /autofix, deletes lost clusters rather than saving them as files
Scandisk /nosummary	With /checkonly or /autofix, prevents ScanDisk from stopping at summary screens
Scandisk /surface	Performs a surface scan after other checks
Scandisk /mono	Configures ScanDisk for use with a monochrome display
Scandisk /undo *drive*:	Undoes previously made repairs on the specified drive

Table 6-1. *ScanDisk Command Options*

- Schedule any DOS or Windows application to run at any specified time (at startup, hourly, daily, weekly, monthly, or whenever the system is idle)
- Pass command-line options to scheduled tasks
- Automatically reschedule a task if it doesn't run at the scheduled time
- Set a maximum time duration for a task to run
- View scheduled tasks on a remote computer
- Customize task schedules to accommodate system power management

Here's what Scheduled Tasks can't do:

- Pop up custom on-screen reminders at specified times
- Script macro events that shut down the system or boot to MS-DOS

To view a list of previously scheduled tasks or create a new one, choose Start | Accessories | System Tools | Scheduled Tasks. You can also access Scheduled Tasks directly from the Explorer window. Click the drop-down Address list and choose Scheduled Tasks.

To view or edit the properties for a scheduled task, right-click the task in the list and select Properties. To create a new task, click the Add Scheduled Task icon. (You can also schedule tasks by dragging a file or program icon directly into the Task List. If you have a lot of installed Windows 98 programs, this is likely to be a faster method.)

If you're using the Scheduled Tasks Wizard, select an application from the list or click the Browse button to find one. The next several screens will help you assign dates and times to run your task.

Tip *If you want to fine-tune a task created with the Scheduled Tasks Wizard, place a check mark next to Open Advanced Properties For This Task When I Click Finish on the last screen.*

If you create a task by simply dragging an icon into the Task List window, it will be assigned a default boilerplate schedule. To modify and fine-tune this schedule, right-click the task and select Properties.

To view tasks scheduled on a remote computer, choose Network Neighborhood. Then select the computer that you want to view and open its Scheduled Tasks folder. For convenience, the remote machine should make the following a shared resource: *d*:\WINDOWS\START\PROGRAMS\ACCESSORIES\SYSTEM TOOLS.

Tip *Make sure the system date and time for your computer are set accurately if you want your tasks to run at the times you choose for them.*

Scheduled Tasks was not designed to manage your Internet Explorer Web subscriptions. Internet Explorer has a separate feature (Manage Subscriptions) to handle that chore. See Chapter 12 for details.

Scheduled Tasks can be used to automate Internet connections to collect e-mail or to schedule other non-IE4 online tasks. (IE4 has separate internal support for automated Web browsing.) With the addition of a small freeware utility, Scheduled Tasks can also gain the capability of passing startup macros to applications. See Chapter 8 for some productive task scheduling strategies, including an undocumented pop-up reminder trick.

To get more help with Scheduled Tasks, choose Help | Using Windows Accessories | System Tools | Scheduled Tasks. Click the shortcut arrow at the bottom of the Using Scheduled Tasks entry in the right Help pane.

System Information

System Information is a Swiss Army knife set of inventory and diagnostic troubleshooting tools. It provides comprehensive information about installed hardware peripherals, the allocation of system resources, and all installed software drivers. Additionally, its Tool menu contains a set of diagnostic and configuration tools.

Here's what System Information can do:

- Display Win98 system resource information, such as interrupt assignments and potential conflicts, DMA channel assignment, I/O ports, and reserved memory addresses
- Display an inventory of installed hardware components, such as multimedia, display, infrared, and input devices; modems; network components; ports; and system components such as the BIOS, APM, motherboard resources, storage devices, and USB
- Display a list of installed software components (16- and 32-bit drivers), currently active tasks, startup programs, and OLE registration information
- Launch the System File Checker (which checks system file integrity and reports file changes in specified directories)
- Launch the Registry Checker (which parses, backs up, and repairs the system registry)
- Launch the Automatic Skip Driver Agent (which disables and enables problem hardware devices)
- Launch Dr. Watson (a system snapshot tool that can identify low-level driver conflicts)

- Launch the System Configuration Utility (which can filter and control Windows 98 startup and shutdown options)
- Launch the ScanDisk disk maintenance utility
- Launch the Version Conflict Manager (which can restore backed-up versions of system files)

Here's what System Information can't do:

- Run diagnostic tests on hardware peripherals
- Automatically detect interrupt and port address conflicts
- Display detailed information on system and application memory use

The System Information tool is designed primarily to help Windows support technicians troubleshoot problems, but that shouldn't stop you from exploiting some of the useful options it offers.

If you're familiar with the principles and mechanics of PC hardware, System Information can help you troubleshoot problems. It provides concise lists of IRQ assignments, port and memory addresses, installed peripherals, and corresponding entries in the Windows system registry. As shown in Figure 6-5, a three-button display allows you to toggle basic information, advanced information, and a driver installation history for each hardware device.

Even if you're a not a programming guru, you should be aware of the options available on System Information's pull-down Tools menu.

System File Checker

The System File Checker utility verifies the integrity of the system files in your \WINDOWS and \PROGRAM FILES directories, allowing you to replace corrupt or outdated drivers. It can provide help with the most problematic Windows annoyances: system crashes, general protection faults, and application failure caused by incorrect or missing system files.

System File Checker has the following useful features:

- It examines the contents of your \WINDOWS and \PROGRAM FILES directories and detects changed, corrupt, or incorrect system files (such as .DLL, .DRV, .VXD, and .386 files).
- It permits customization to check user-specified directories and file extensions.
- It allows automatic back up and replacement of existing system files.
- It allows extraction of specified system files from the Windows 98 CD.
- It creates logs reporting system file detection, backup, and replacement activity.

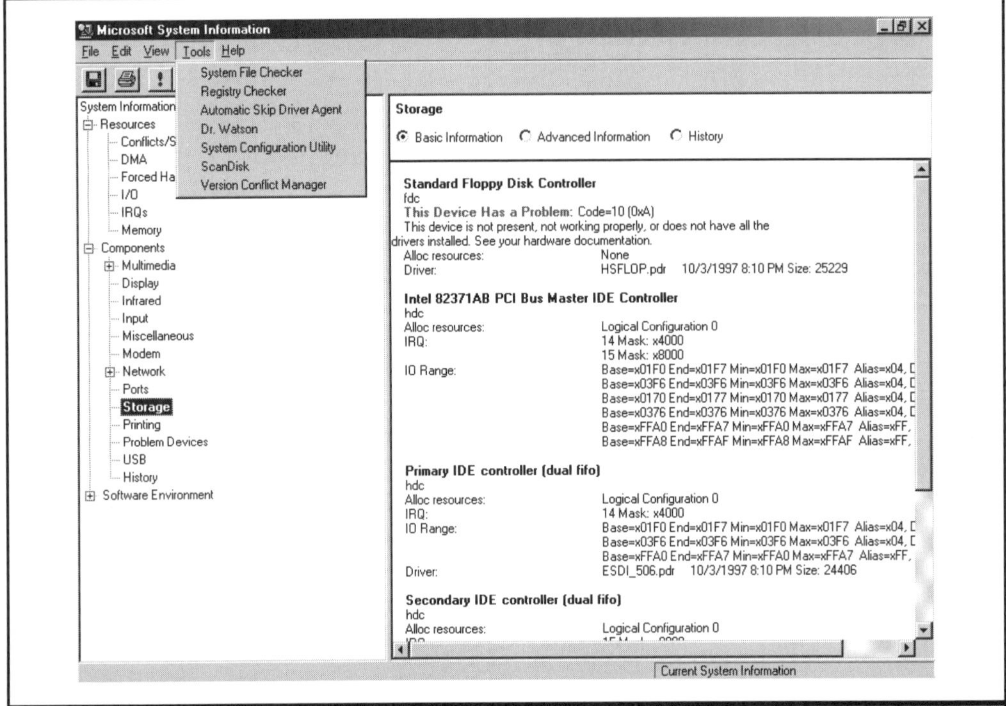

Figure 6-5. *The System Information Tool displays configuration information and launches a series of troubleshooting agents*

Microsoft placed this applet in Windows 98 to assist technical support agents who must help users resolve system conflicts—but you can use it, too. Mismatched Dynamic Link Libraries (DLL files) and other mismatched system files are a common cause of Windows operating problems. In the past, third-party applications have freely written to the \WINDOWS and \WINDOWS\SYSTEM directories, replacing Windows 98 system files with earlier or incompatible versions.

By default, Windows 98 performs a routine file inspection every time you boot the machine, but the automatic safety check is limited to critical files that affect the core operating system. Running System File Checker extends Win98's safety inspection to track the status of system files stored in common disk locations.

You can add new file locations and file types to scan by clicking the Settings button on the first screen and selecting the Search Criteria tab, but this probably won't be necessary. Microsoft's verification database knows about files in the default directories, but it may not deliver accurate analysis of files in user-added locations. The Microsoft verification database can be updated or switched by using options located on the Advanced tab.

To inspect your disk for system file incompatibilities, launch System File Checker by choosing Accessories | System Tools, click the Scan Files For Errors button, and click Start.

When a questionable file is spotted, the file checker opens a dialog box that prompts you for action:

- If the file has been changed, the date, time, size, and version number of both the original and current instances are displayed, as shown here. You can update verification information if you believe the current setting is correct.

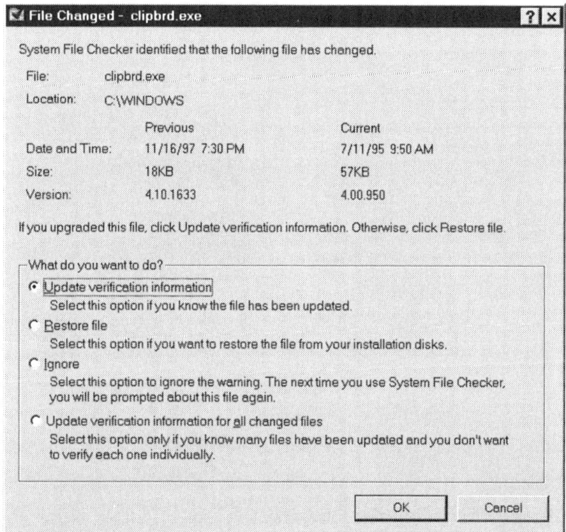

In this illustration, an earlier version of the Windows Clipboard Viewer has been detected, because the default application was overwritten with the more powerful Windows 95 network version (see "Clipboard Viewer" earlier in this chapter for details). To record this information, select Update Verification Information and click OK. (If you wanted to restore the Win98 version, you would select Restore File.)

- Some system files update themselves each time Windows boots. If a changed file is reported with the same size and version number but a different file date, it's probably OK. If you encounter a large number of messages of this type, you can click the fourth screen option, Update Verification Information For All Changed Files. System File Checker will continue to parse for corruption, but will stop reporting changed file dates. If System File Checker reports that a file may be corrupted, as shown next, the date and version number are not displayed. If you select the Restore File option, you'll be prompted for the location of your Windows 98 CD (or the installation directory), and the file will be replaced. (At this point, when prompted, you may also want to make a back up of the suspect file.)

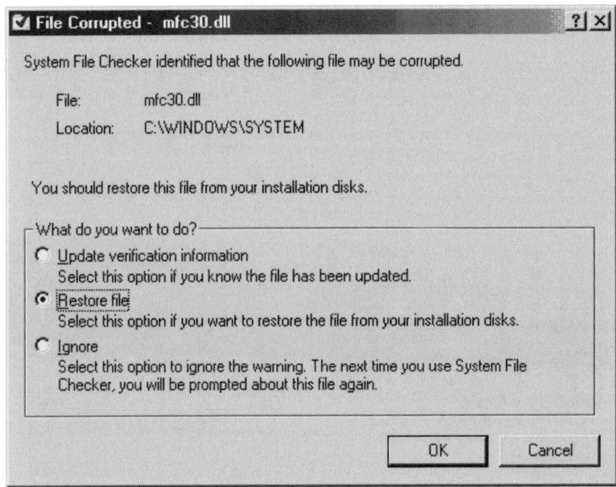

Note

Windows 98 includes a Windows Update feature that can search Microsoft's Internet site for new drivers and software patches. If Windows 98 driver conflicts aren't resolved by System File Checker, you can use Windows Update to retrieve new patch modules. Windows Update is an extension of Internet Explorer. You can start it by choosing Start | Settings | Windows Update. (See "Updating Windows" in Chapter 8 for more information on Windows Update.)

More File Checking and Replacement Options

Once you've run System File Checker, an activity log is created. For a quick view of your system's status, you can click the View Log button on the Settings tab. Recorded information about system files is also used by a short-form diagnostic tool called Version Conflict Manager. (See "Version Conflict Manager" later in this chapter for more information.)

If you become confused by the status of replaced system files, click the Restore Defaults button on the System File Checker Advanced tab. This will make System File Checker prompt you again about any files that have changed since you installed Windows 98.

Registry Checker

Sometimes referred to as ScanReg, the Registry Checker utility checks the integrity of the entries in your Windows 98 system registry. The system registry is the brain of the Windows 98 operating system. It performs the functions that were handled by WIN.INI and SYSTEM.INI in Windows 3.x. The registry contains information on installed hardware and software, user account and network information, system and program settings, and user preferences.

If the Registry Checker finds errors, you're given an option to restore the system registry from a set of previous backups. You may also use Registry Checker to create a new backup. The Registry Checker can run under MS-DOS and under the Windows 98 interface. It verifies the registry structure every time you restart your computer. Under the Windows 98 interface, Registry Checker doesn't replace the registry unless it confirms a problem in the current version.

The DOS version of Registry Checker lets you revert to any previous registry backup. This can be a useful option if you've installed a program or a piece of hardware that's causing problems. The Windows 98 version of the Registry Checker may not report any errors, but you may want to run the Registry Editor under DOS to return to a previous Windows configuration.

To install a previous registry backup as the current registry, follow these steps:

1. Restart Windows 98 in MS-DOS mode (choose Start | Shutdown | Restart In MS-DOS Mode) or boot the computer in MS-DOS mode by holding down the CTRL key during startup and selecting Command Prompt from the Boot menu.
2. Run SCANREG at the C:\ prompt. Click the Scan button on the first screen.
3. On the next screen, click the View Backups button.
4. Select a dated backup file from the list on the next screen, as shown here, and click Restore.

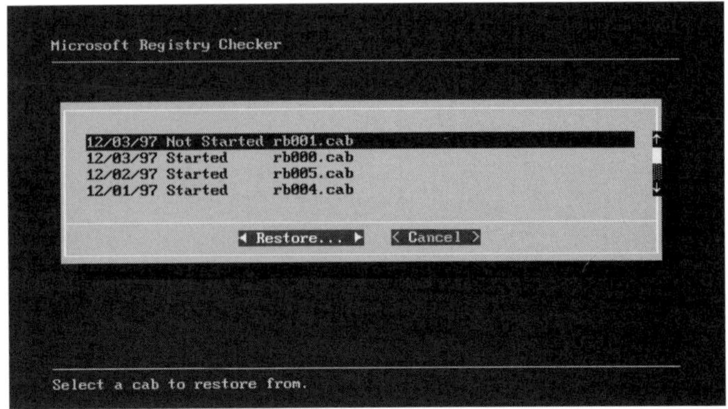

Automatic Skip Driver Agent

For some internal Windows 98 services and hardware drivers, the Automatic Skip Driver Agent will appear after repeated system failures. For instance, if repeated attempts to put your computer into APM Suspend mode result in crashes, the Automatic Skip Driver Agent will display a dialog box indicating that system failures have been detected. Windows 98 will then ask whether you want to permanently disable the function that caused the system crash.

When you open Automatic Skip Driver Agent from the System Information Tools menu, it displays a list of all processes that have been disabled. You can reenable any device in this list, and Windows 98 will attempt to load it at the next startup.

Dr. Watson

Dr. Watson is an improved version of the Windows 3.x diagnostic utility that disappeared in Windows 95. When Dr. Watson is resident in the background, it quietly monitors system events. If you experience a Win98 operating mishap while Dr. Watson is running, a snapshot of the current system status is taken automatically. Dr. Watson displays a message window, like the one shown here, that offers more extensive diagnostic information than a standard Windows 98 error message. The technical content of some of these messages may be too obscure for you (or, confidentially, me), but saved Dr. Watson logs can help a support technician or programmer resolve pernicious application problems.

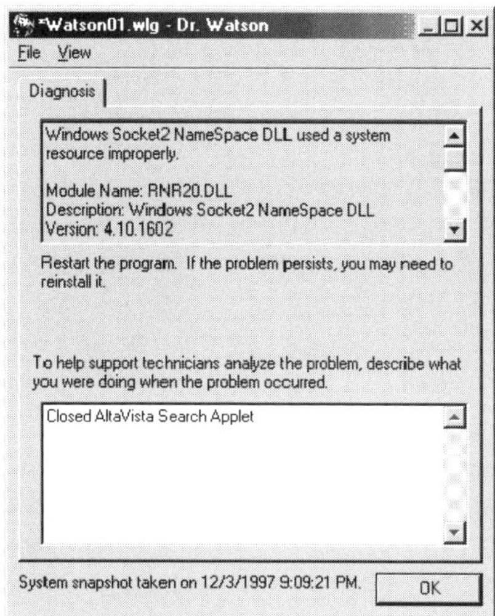

Windows 98 does not load Dr. Watson by default. You can take advantage of the doctor's diagnostic skills in all of your Win98 sessions by creating a Startup group shortcut to d:\WINDOWS\DRWATSON.EXE. *(For more information on creating and using application shortcuts, see Chapter 4.)*

System Configuration Utility

The System Configuration utility, shown next, gives you extensive control over Windows 98 startup options.

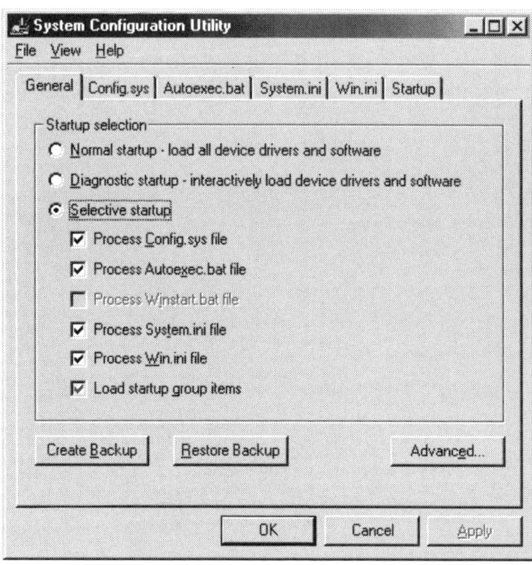

The System Configuration utility has six tabs full of options.

GENERAL TAB The General tab can be used to specify a selective Win98 startup process. You can make the boot process skip CONFIG.SYS, AUTOEXEC.BAT, or SYSTEM.INI. (The Create Backup and Restore Backup buttons allow you to back up or restore previous versions of these files.). You can also disable the loading of Win98 Startup group items or set up a step-by-step diagnostic boot process.

Tip *If Windows 98 repeatedly hangs during shutdown, click the Advanced button on the General tab and place a check mark next to Disable Fast Shutdown.*

CONFIG.SYS, AUTOEXEC.BAT, AND SYSTEM.INI TABS These tabs allow you to enable or disable the processing of individual drivers, programs, and commands loaded in each boot file. For example, if CONFIG.SYS contains a line that reads DEVICE=EMM386.EXE, you can select the Config.sys tab and remove the check mark next to this statement.

For WIN.INI and SYSTEM.INI, the statements are organized into sections. You can disable an entire section by removing its check mark, or you can expand the section listing and then remove check marks in front of individual statements.

STARTUP TAB The Startup tab, shown next, lets you enable or disable Windows 98 startup services, third-party drivers that normally load before the desktop and the applications in your Startup group. To disable a specific item, deselect the check mark next to it in the listing.

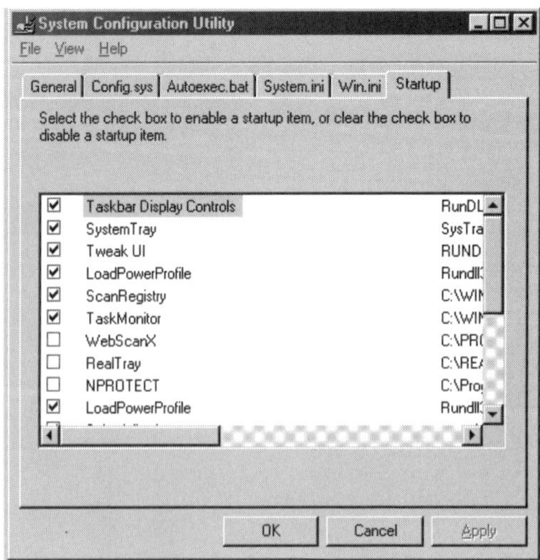

ScanDisk

The ScanDisk utility checks your hard disk and repairs hard disk errors. (See "ScanDisk" earlier in this chapter for a detailed description of this utility.)

Version Conflict Manager

The Version Conflict Manager can be used to restore backed-up versions of Windows system files that were archived with the System File Checker. When you open Version Conflict Manager, it displays a list of backed-up and currently installed system files (.CPL, .DLL, .DRV, .VXD, and so on). The list shows the version numbers of backed-up system files and compares them with the numbers of currently active versions.

If the list shows any current system files with earlier version numbers than the backups, you will probably want to restore the backed-up versions. Follow these steps to restore the backups:

1. Highlight the files you want to restore (you can hold down the CTRL key to select more than one file in the list).
2. Click the Restore Selected Files button.

If system files installed by third-party vendors on your hard disk have dates or version numbers later than the ones on the Windows 98 CD, they are overwritten and backed up during a Windows 98 upgrade. If you experience system problems after an upgrade, Version Conflict Manager can also restore these original OEM files.

If there's a wide discrepancy between the version numbers of backed-up and active files, keep the current files unless you experience performance problems. Microsoft sometimes resequences the version number of a system file to 1.xx from a higher number, if the file has been significantly rewritten.

System Monitor

If you suspect that some aspect of system performance is slow or inefficient, you can use System Monitor as a diagnostic tool to track the problem. System Monitor reports real-time performance statistics for a wide variety of processes.

Here's what System Monitor can do:

- Clock the speed of local and network disk access, chart CPU use, measure Dial-Up Networking modem speed, and graph system memory use
- Display performance statistics in line chart, bar chart, and simple numeric formats

Here's what System Monitor can't do:

- Perform detailed system benchmark analysis
- Measure Direct Cable Connection performance

After you launch System Monitor, you can leave it open on the screen to display real-time graphs of your system's performance. If you think your modem is too slow or your network is congested, you can select appropriate sensors (choose Edit | Add Item) to clock performance. System Monitor's statistics are organized into eight basic categories, which you can access by choosing Edit | Add:

- **Dial-Up Adapter** Measures dial-up modem performance.
- **Disk Cache** Shows minimum and maximum cache pages, hits and misses, and so on.
- **File System** Shows bytes read and written per second on your hard disk.
- **IPX/SPX Protocol** Measures network packet speed through this protocol.
- **Kernel** Shows CPU use, the number of threads, and the number of open virtual machines.
- **Memory Manager** Shows a variety of system memory and cache statistics.
- **Microsoft Network Client** Shows bytes read and written as a NETBEUI client.
- **Microsoft Network Server** Shows bytes read and written as a NETBEUI server.

System Monitor can be resized—for example, to fit in a corner of your screen. The real-time graphs will be resized to fit the new window, but you'll lose some information from captions if you reduce the size too much.

The various options on the toolbar allow you to display performance statistics in several different graphic formats.

To measure the performance of network drives, select the Connect option from the File menu and type the name of the server to which you want to connect.

WBEM: Web-Based Enterprise Management

Web-Based Enterprise Management (WBEM) is an application standard established to let programmers create publishing tools for a wide variety of database objects. The goal of a WBEM application is to correlate data and events from multiple sources for distribution on an enterprise network. This is an open Windows standard that Microsoft hopes third-party vendors will adopt. For more information visit the WBEM Web site at http://wbem.freerange.com.

Welcome To Windows

Welcome To Windows is the first application you see after Windows 98 has been installed. It allows you to go online to register your copy of Windows 98, set up an Internet connection, open an introductory tutorial, and also has an option that launches the Maintenance Wizard (discussed earlier in this chapter).

In order to take advantage of Win98's live Internet "Windows Update" feature, you must register your copy of Windows 98. Selecting Register Now on the Welcome screen opens a Registration Wizard that prompts you to fill in your name, address, and other optional contact information. The System Inventory screen gives you the option of including information about your computer's configuration with the completed registration form. Microsoft states that this information may help you get more efficient product support for Windows 98. The inventory does not include personal information about the contents of your hard disk or the third-party software that's installed on the computer.

To complete the online registration, you must have a modem installed on your computer.

You'll find more information about the Internet Connection Wizard in the section "Using the Internet Connection Wizard" in Chapter 12. For more information about the Discover Windows tutorial, see "Discover Windows 98"in Chapter 3. The Maintain Your Computer (Maintenance Wizard) option is discussed under the "Maintenance Wizard" section earlier in this chapter.

Extra Utilities

A number of useful system utilities are not installed in the System Tools folder. Instead, they are surreptitiously dropped into the WINDOWS or \WINDOWS \SYSTEM directories. These include the Group Converter, MkCOMPAT, Registry Editor, System Editor, and Telephony Location Manager utilities.

Group Converter

The Windows 98 Start menu uses its own special folders and shortcuts to applications to duplicate the functions of the Windows 3.x Program Manager. During Win98 installation, a utility called GRPCONV.EXE runs automatically to change Windows 3.1 Program Manager groups into Startup menu folders. This program searches for all .GRP files listed in the old PROGMAN.INI file, creating shortcuts for those entries in the Start menu folder. GRPCONV also searches the SETUP.INI file, creating shortcuts in the Program Files folder for the Windows 98 components you select during installation.

Updating Additional Program Groups from Windows 3.x

In a standard installation of Windows 98, no additional Win 3.1 .GRP files are created after setup. If you install new Windows applications under the new interface, Win98 places their shortcuts directly in the Start menu folder.

If you have any Windows 3.x program groups that were not transferred to the Start menu, you can run Group Converter after installation to update your desktop. To update the Start menu with a previously unrecognized Win 3.xprogram group, choose Start | Run and run the GRPCONV utility with the following syntax: **GRPCONV *FILENAME*.GRP**.

Windows 98 will create a new folder and shortcut link to this group in the Programs folder. The correct folder title, program title, filename, and path will be transferred from the Windows 3.1 .GRP file.

Converting Groups of Files

If you want to convert or update a series of .GRP files, then enter the following command in the Run box on the Start menu: **GRPCONV /m**.

This will open a Group Converter dialog box on the desktop. Scroll through the file list and successively double-click each .GRP file that you want to convert. You can also use GRPCONV to re-create the default folders and links established during a Windows 98 installation. Use the following syntax: **GRPCONV /s**.

MkCOMPAT

The undocumented MkCOMPAT utility, located in the \WINDOWS\SYSTEM directory, can resolve some problems with older Windows 3.1 applications that may be unable to successfully print, open, or save files under Windows 98.

MkCOMPAT can intercept system calls to Windows 3.x programs, removing incompatibilities with the Windows 98 interface. You can open MkCOMPAT through the Run box on the Start menu and then specify the Windows 3.x application to be modified on the command line; for example, you can enter **MKCOMPAT C:\WP\WPWIN.EXE**. Alternatively, you can specify an application by selecting it from the Choose A Program dialog box displayed from MkCOMPAT's File menu.

MkCOMPAT has five basic filters corresponding to the Windows version number, print spooler, and internal memory space. Some filters may not appear if they don't apply to your program. You can display advanced filter options by selecting Advanced Options on the pull-down File menu. The advanced filters can check a program's print, font, save, and screen display functions, as well as other internal functions.

Registry Editor: RegEdit

The Windows 98 version of RegEdit is much more powerful than the version included in Windows 3.1. In fact, it's so powerful that Microsoft doesn't really want you to use it. There's nothing about it in the Windows 98 Help files, even though Win98 stores a good deal more information about applications in the registration database than Windows 3.1 did.

Here's what RegEdit can do:

- Save and export all or part of the Windows 98 system registry to a text file
- Modify registry information that affects registered file types, the desktop, system and application settings, and installed hardware configuration
- Merge two system registries into a single registry (DOS only)

Here's what RegEdit can't do:

- Find and replace individual or global registry entries
- Compare the current registry with a backed-up version
- Conveniently cut and paste information from one registry section to another

The RegEdit utility is included primarily so you can copy specific vendor instructions from documentation to fix problems. Although no information about RegEdit is provided in Win95's Help files, Microsoft's *Windows 98 Resource Kit* does point out one useful RegEdit function: The entire registry can be saved or backed up using the Export Registry feature in the Registry Editor. This saves information on either a specific branch or the entire registry in a text-format file. Later, you can restore the registry using the Import Registry feature. This rebuilds a branch or the entire registry from a saved, exported registry file.

If the registry is corrupted or the system no longer starts at all, you can run the Registry Editor in real mode to diagnose and correct the problem. The registry can be exported, imported, or created using Registry Editor, as shown in the following command examples:

Command	Description
regedit /e export.reg	Exports the entire registry to the file EXPORT.REG
regedit /I export.reg	Imports the registry file EXPORT.REG
regedit /c export.reg	Replaces the registry with the contents of EXPORT.REG

Microsoft advises caution: Use the REGEDIT /C option with extreme care, and only when you are sure that the .REG file specified contains a complete image of the registry. The REGEDIT /C option completely replaces the entire contents of the registry. That's dangerous if you use a partial export file as your source.

Backing Up the Registry

Because the system registry contains many important settings that are difficult to duplicate if it becomes corrupt, you should always make a backup copy before manually tweaking and customizing individual settings. See "Backup" and "Registry Checker" earlier in this chapter for instructions on registry backup.

You'll find a detailed study of the Windows 98 registry in Chapter 8, along with a tutorial on the interactive use of RegEdit to recover a corrupt registry and tweak performance settings. You'll also find some RegEdit tips for customizing your desktop in Chapter 16.

System Editor: SysEdit

SysEdit is a convenient text editor that automatically opens most of the ASCII-based Windows configuration files. You can use it to modify settings in AUTOEXEC.BAT, CONFIG.SYS, WIN.INI, SYSTEM.INI, MSMAIL.INI, and PROTOCOL.INI.

Telephony Location Manager: TLOCMGR.EXE

The Telephone Location Manager (TLOCMGR.EXE) lets you quickly switch the computer's default dial-up location and modify existing telephony location settings or create new ones. These options can also be accessed through the Control Panel, but if you open TLOCMGR.EXE through the Start menu's Run box, the Telephony Location Manager is installed as a pop-up utility on the System Tray for faster access.

Chapter 7

System Architecture and Memory Management

Chapter Highlights

- **Windows 98 system architecture:**
  - **Multithreading and preemptive multitasking**
  - **Win32 Driver Model borrowed from WinNT**
  - **Optimization of program loading with WinAlign**
  - **16-bit versus 32-bit virtual machines**
  - **Memory-management features**
- **Startup strategies:**
  - **Working with CONFIG.SYS**
  - **Hidden boot options in MSDOS.SYS**
  - **Restore or enable dual-boot feature**
  - **Optimizing conventional memory with EMM386.EXE**
- **Third-party DOS memory managers:**
  - **Do you need them?**
  - **Third-party Windows 98 memory utilities**
- **More system configuration secrets:**
  - **Replacing real-mode drivers with protected-mode VXDs**
  - **Regaining 32-bit file access and 32-bit virtual memory**

This chapter serves as a nuts-and-bolts tutorial on what's going on beneath Win98's desktop interface. If you need to juggle DOS, Windows 3.1, and Windows 95 and 98 applications in complicated single-user or network configurations, read on. You'll find both conceptual and practical material on how Windows 98 manages memory. This information will also be of service to power users and system administrators who want to tweak hardware performance and reduce the risk of application crashes.

The first part of the chapter describes the Windows 98 system architecture. You'll get the information you need to understand how 16-bit (Windows 3.1), 32-bit (Windows 95 and 98), and DOS applications are coordinated under the new operating system. This section is provided for more technically minded (or curious) readers. It outlines how the limits of Windows 3.1 have been redefined and stretched for Windows 98, and where they still pertain.

If you're a pragmatic user, just interested in collecting your e-mail and producing your documents, you don't need to understand all of the concepts in the first section. You can move quickly to the second part of the chapter, which is a tutorial on Windows 98 startup strategies. It assumes that you've already installed Windows 98 and want to bend it to your will. You'll learn how to boot directly to a DOS prompt, how to control the loading of startup devices, and how to troubleshoot the boot process.

The next section in this chapter is devoted to DOS and Windows memory management. This section shows you how to migrate the MS-DOS 6.22 MemMaker to Windows 98. It also provides strategies for obtaining more conventional memory for DOS applications. This section includes a discussion of the advantages and disadvantages of using third-party add-ons such as McAfee's Hurricane and Symantec's CrashGuard Deluxe to tweak Windows 98 performance.

Finally, this chapter concludes with a brief section on the memory management options for Windows 98 that you can easily fine-tune through accessible desktop settings.

Windows 98 System Architecture

The system architecture of Windows 98 is not much different from that of Windows 95, but it is significantly changed from the model used in Windows 3.x.

For typical, single-user workstations, Windows 95 eliminated the need for third-party memory managers, disk cache programs, and DOS peripheral device drivers. A new series of protected-mode virtual device drivers (VXDs) was built into Windows 95. These VXDs are loaded automatically at boot time to replace real-mode drivers such as DBLSPACE.BIN, MOUSE.SYS, MSCDEX.EXE, and SMARTDRV.EXE.

Protected mode is an instruction set built into all Intel CPUs after the original 8088. Newer Intel processors can recognize and exploit more than the original 640K of memory that was used by MS-DOS. Running Windows 95 and 98 in protected-mode results in smoother overall operating system performance. With faster access to more memory, applications can have more features, and they can be linked to one another through services provided by the operating system: the Windows clipboard, object linking and embedding (OLE), and smart monitoring of system events. Since Windows 95 and 98 load most device drivers in protected mode, they can also provide more conventional memory for DOS sessions than Windows 3.1 allowed.

DOS Independent?

Many people believe that Windows 98 (and its Windows 95 predecessor) are DOS-independent operating systems. It's true that in Windows 95 and 98, the graphic interface can start without the CONFIG.SYS and AUTOEXEC.BAT files required by DOS to recognize peripherals and configure the computer. But despite its many enhancements, the protected-mode Win95 and Win98 operating systems, like Windows 3.1, sit atop of a kernel of real-mode code. (See "Startup Strategies" later in this chapter for details.)

To maintain compatibility with older DOS and Windows 3.1 applications, Windows 98 loads critical input/output services in the first 640K of memory. Windows 98 loads more of these services automatically than does DOS, selecting proper drivers and accommodating itself to hardware without user intervention. Windows 98 offers more protection for Windows 3.x and DOS applications than its predecessors, but the memory protection scheme is not bulletproof. Users will still occasionally encounter general protection faults and, even worse, system faults and exception errors. "Blue screen" errors can bring down not just one application, but the entire system. Even 32-bit Win95 and Win98 applications are not wholly shielded from one another.

Integrated 32-Bit, Protected-Mode Operating System

Windows 98 largely eliminates the need for a separate copy of MS-DOS. In addition to running 32-bit Windows applications, the operating system multitasks 16-bit DOS and Windows applications. Here's a rough summary of the way this works:

- **DOS sessions** Each DOS session is executed in a separate, 16-bit virtual machine, using the virtual 8086 mode built into all Intel CPU models 80386 and higher. Each DOS session runs in a separate address space. This means that, generally, a program code defect in one session will not corrupt a program running in a second session. However, all DOS sessions share common access to certain strategic real-mode drivers loaded in the first 640K of system memory. Because DOS applications can write to this memory area, they can bring down the entire system by overwriting pointers established by other Win98 system functions. The probability of an individual DOS session or program doing this is small, unless you construct a DEBUG script specifically designed to corrupt the system. (Several Win95 beta testers delighted in creating such scripts.) For the most part, DOS session functions are isolated in protected virtual machines. Additionally, Microsoft has sealed off the first 64K of conventional memory, which is where vulnerable system pointers are most likely to reside.
- **Windows 3.1 (16-bit Windows) applications** Windows 3.1 applications all run in a common 16-bit virtual machine. This virtual machine is controlled by the same Krnl386 module that managed applications in Windows 3.x. Windows 3.x applications share a common memory address space, so malfunctioning

code in one program can adversely affect other currently active applications. If a program malfunctions while accessing instructions shared by the operating system (video display and disk I/O are good examples), the program can bring down all of Windows 98.

- **Windows 95 and 98 (32-bit Windows) programs** Windows 95 and 98 programs include the printing subsystem and various applets and utilities as well as full-featured applications written for Microsoft's 32-bit application programming interface (API). These modules are loaded, almost entirely, into separate protected-mode address spaces and managed by Win98's 32-bit system kernel. Theoretically, 32-bit applications are insulated from each other and from the operating system. However, several Win95 beta testers offered a convincing refutation of this claim early in the operating system testing cycle. They produced examples of 32-bit applications that make calls to the Krnl386.exe module that manages 16-bit Windows applications. If this can happen, then a poorly programmed 32-bit application can disrupt the 16-bit Windows 3.1 virtual machine—and consequently disrupt other 32-bit programs and the overall operating system. Microsoft maintains that the statistical probability of this occurring with real 32-bit applications (instead of specially constructed test cases) is extremely low.

Aristocrats in the Low-Rent District

What's the bottom line on Windows 98 memory protection? Well, in simple terms, Windows 98 programs are theoretically each living in private 32-bit mansions on the right side of town. The DOS programs dwell across the tracks in separate, 16-bit bungalows. The Windows 3.1 applications are all lumped together in an upscale boarding house with a common dining room. The implication of what theWin95 beta testers found is that the aristocratic 32-bit applications sometimes secretly go slumming to the Win16 boarding house to get their work done—and when the aristocrats venture into the 16-bit neighborhood, they may get mugged by disgruntled Windows 3.x gangsters.

Each 32-bit application running under Windows 98 requires a special pointer, called a program segment prefix (PSP). Application PSPs are stored in real-mode conventional memory.

Note *You should know that it's possible to gain memory protection in Windows 98 above and beyond the support Microsoft built into the operating system. Third-party application vendors (Symantec, CyberMedia, and Network Associates/McAfee) market "watchdog" utilities that can write-protect segments of Windows memory to strengthen the integrity of the operating system. You'll find information on these programs in "Third-Party DOS and Windows Memory Utilities" later in this chapter.*

Preemptive Multitasking and Multithreading Support

DOS sessions under Windows 3.1, were multitasked by allocating each session a fixed, cyclical share of CPU time. This round-robin scheme (originally developed by

Quarterdeck Office Systems for DESQview) simply shifted control of the CPU back and forth between the Windows virtual machine and individual DOS sessions according to a specified numerical ratio. Users could adjust this ratio through the Control Panel and PIF settings, but the system had no dynamic response to programs. If one application was configured to consume 70 percent of the available CPU time, it would do so, whether it was running idle or performing a complex calculation. There was no chance for a program allocated 30 percent of the CPU time to pipe up and say, "Hey, I'm overworked here, and you're doing nothing! How about sending over a little processor time?"

Under Windows 98, the situation is different. DOS programs can be preemptively multitasked. This means that Win98's Virtual Machine Manager monitors the activity of each individual DOS session. If WordPerfect for DOS is sitting idle while Lotus 1-2-3 for DOS is chewing on a spreadsheet, the system can dynamically take time away from the WordPerfect session and shunt it over to the Lotus virtual machine. If you switch to WordPerfect and start a big print job, the system registers this and transfers some processor time back to WordPerfect to help with the printing task

Windows 3.1 (16-bit) programs running under Windows 98 behave the same way as they did under previous versions of Windows; the situation is more or less a cooperative anarchy. The operating system makes no attempt to budget CPU time between competing applications. Instead, the internal structure of each program determines how much CPU time it grabs. If Microsoft Word 6 has code that says, "I'm heavy and bad; give me all of your CPU time," then a less aggressively programmed application, such as Excel 5.0, just hands it over— slowing concurrent spreadsheet recalculations to a crawl.

Windows 95 and 98 (32-bit) applications in their separate address spaces are preemptively multitasked in the same way as DOS sessions. If you are running the Windows 95 or Windows NT versions of Word and Excel, the system monitors their individual demands on the CPU, dynamically transferring processor time from one application to the other. You'll find that two 32-bit Windows applications running concurrently can accomplish more work than two 16-bit Windows applications running concurrently. The system deals out processor time intelligently so that you can print, perform background recalculations, or run a search and replace macro without one task monopolizing the CPU.

Additionally, Windows 98 can manage multiple processes executing concurrently within an individual 32-bit application. This feature, called multithreading, allows an application to accept keyboard input, accept or transmit data through an external port, or perform other background tasks simultaneously without causing deterioration in the performance of other applications.

New Wrinkles in Win98 Memory Management

Although Windows 98 has the same basic system architecture as Windows 95, it does incorporate several new technologies that affect memory management and system performance.

Win32 Driver Model

In Windows 98, Microsoft complements Windows 95's VXD system with the Win32 Driver Model (WDM). This is a new standard for writing device drivers that is unified under both Windows 98 and Windows NT. With this new, common programming interface, peripheral manufacturers can provide device drivers that allow their products to work transparently under either operating system.

WDM operates by grafting a set of Windows NT services to Windows 98 through a driver called NTKERN.VXD. When Windows 98 loads this driver, WDM drivers may call upon the Windows NT kernel services that it provides. These services include extensions that support plug and play, device power management, and low-latency streaming I/O. The WDM Stream class driver optimizes data flow through the operating system. New streaming audio and streaming video drivers bundled in Windows 98 illustrate the performance improvements that are possible with WDM.

The Win32 Driver Model enables new classes of devices and new hardware busses:

- Human Interface Device (HID) compliant peripherals (keyboards, pointing devices, and game controllers)
- Digital audio, DVD player, still image, and video-capture devices
- Universal Serial Bus (USB)
- IEEE 1394 (firewire) bus

Driver modules can cooperate dynamically to support a specific hardware device. For instance, a digital camera can have commands defined by the Imaging class, and delivered by the Function Control Protocol (FCP) to the USB or IEEE 1394 bus class. All WDM class drivers and minidrivers execute as privileged threads at the lowest level of the operating system. Deferred procedure calls (DPCs) can enhance system response to interrupts by reducing the time during which interrupts are disabled.

Universal Serial Bus and IEEE-1394 are high-speed hardware interfaces that allow peripherals such as digital cameras, modems, and scanners to operate more efficiently than they can through legacy serial and parallel port connections. See Chapter 15 for more information on working with USB and IEEE.

The Human Interface Device specification is a firmware standard that allows keyboards, mouse devices, and so on to work transparently in Windows 98 through the USB and IEEE 1394 interfaces. Users can install multiple keyboards and multiple pointing devices without confusing the operating system.

You can find extensive information on WDM busses and classes supported in Windows 98 at Microsoft's Web site at http://www.microsoft.com/hwtest.

New System Registry Controls

Microsoft claims that Windows 98's registry handling code has been rewritten to execute faster and improve the robustness of the operating system. Since changes in the registry structure are not exposed through APIs or within Regedit, it's difficult to verify the difference.

Windows 98 does include a new system for backing up and restoring the system registry to safeguard against corruption. The ScanReg application (see Chapter 6) checks the integrity of the registry each time Windows 98 starts and is capable of performing some compaction to eliminate superfluous binary code.

Cache Management and Virtual Memory

In Windows 95, the system wasted memory by duplicating the physical code for an active application in program memory and within the disk cache. In Windows 98, only one copy of an active application is maintained in RAM. Pointers map the code simultaneously to the program and disk cache address ranges.

The efficiency of the Windows 98 swap file has been improved. On the average, swap file size when running multiple applications will be smaller. The smaller swap file can produce better system response and induce a greater percentage of disk cache hits. (When program code requests are filled from cache memory instead of being reread from the hard disk, application performance is more robust.)

WinAlign Code Optimization

WinAlign is a transparent fine-tuning feature of Windows 98. It runs automatically when you install the operating system or add WinAlign-aware applications later on. When the operating system and program code are copied to the hard disk, WinAlign examines the internal structure of the component files, rearranging code into even 4K clusters so that programs will load faster. Third-party vendors have the option of invoking WinAlign when their programs are installed.

WinAlign decreases the time required to load programs (and the Windows 98 operating system) from disk, primarily on disk partitions formatted with the FAT32 file system and 4K file clusters. Because Windows memory is organized into 4K pages, the operating system can process and execute code faster when files are stretched to align code segments exactly into 4K page boundaries. This process involves physically altering program code, inserting dummy padding to align code into even clusters. The process is performed automatically and *only on files that Microsoft has certified to be WinAlign compatible.* Older third-party programs and support files remain untouched.

On disk partitions with a cluster size other than 4K, WinAlign has little effect on system and program performance.

WinAlign technology should not be confused with Win98's new Defrag option for tuning the hard disk.

The disk defragmenter can rearrange the position of files (and chunks of files) on the disk, but it does not alter the internal code structure of programs and system files. The Defrag Rearrange Program Files option is a user feature that can be invoked or disabled. WinAlign is an internal Windows 98 process that executes without user intervention.

Java "Virtual Machine"

Calling Win98's built-in Java support a virtual machine is a bit of a misnomer. What the Java "virtual machine" actually consists of is a multithreaded, 32-bit application space that can read and execute Java class objects. It is *not* a virtual machine in the same sense as the virtual 8086 mode memory segments that run DOS applications or the common virtual machine for 16-bit Windows 3.x programs.

The Java virtual machine is actually an application that can run a number of Java class objects. It supports JDK1.1 objects, including Serialization, Reflection, and Inner classes, ActiveX controls, and Java Beans.

32-Bit Installable File Systems

The 32-bit file systems in Windows 98, VFAT and FAT32 for fixed-disk media, CDFS for CD-ROM drives, DVD-UDF for DVD-ROM drives, and the internal network redirector, include support for long file names and better performance. FAT32, first implemented in Windows 95 OEM Service Release 2 and included in Windows 98 is a fixed-disk file system that greatly reduces the overhead required to track and index directory and file locations.

FAT32

The FAT32 file system is designed to make large hard drives more manageable, but it also introduces a new set of compatibility issues. For users with new machines and large (4GB and larger) hard drives, FAT32 is an apparent blessing. If you run Windows 98 on older hardware (with a smaller hard disk), the benefits may not be as obvious.

WHAT IS FAT32? FAT32 is an updated version of Microsoft's file allocation system. In addition to supporting very large disk partitions, FAT32 banishes the cumbersome, cluster-consuming behavior of the older FAT16 file system. On new, large drives, FAT32 permits Windows 98 to run from a single 2GB partition—busting the traditional limitations of the FAT file system.

With the constantly increasing disk overhead required to operate Windows and its programs, the size of hard disks installed in new computers is doubling or tripling every year. The FAT16 file system is largely unable to handle the storage capacity of the large disks that new computers offer.

IS FAT32 INSTALLED ON MY COMPUTER? FAT32 began shipping in October 1996 with OEM Service Release 2 (OSR2) of Windows 95. Many computer systems sold with large disk drives within the past 18 months have been shipped with the OSR2 version of Windows 95. If you upgraded to Windows 98 on one of these machines (or if you purchased a computer with Windows 98 preinstalled), then the chances are good that its hard disk is formatted with FAT32.

To verify the file system of a disk partition under Windows 98, select the drive icon from My Computer or Windows Explorer and right-click Properties. You'll see either FAT or FAT32 listed in the file system description (see Figure 7-1).

WHY SHOULD I WANT FAT32? FAT32 lets Windows 98 and its applications all reside on a single large partition of up to 2 terabytes (2,000 gigabytes)—no more worrying about carving a large disk into subsidiary partitions. Better yet, you eliminate the typical cluster space waste that large partitions produce under the FAT16 file system.

Note *By default, the FDISK utility included with Windows 98 (located in the \WINDOWS\COMMAND directory) will not create a FAT32 disk partition smaller than 512MB. This limitation can be overridden with an undocumented command switch. If you enter* ***FDISK/FPRMT*** *at a DOS command prompt (inside or outside of Windows), the minimum size for FAT32 partitions is reduced to 260MB.*

The following cluster sizes are the defaults for FAT32 drives:

Partition Size	Cluster Size
Less than 260MB	512 bytes
260MB to 8GB	4K
8GB to 16GB	8K
16GB to 32GB	16K
More than 32GB	32K

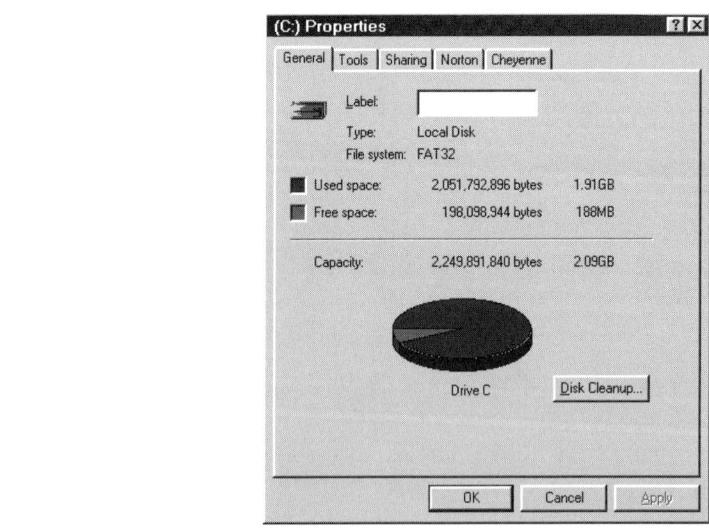

Figure 7-1. *The File System used by a disk partition is displayed on the General properties tab*

For partitions of up to 8GB, the default file cluster size under FAT32 is 4K. (A cluster is a basic unit used by the file system to mark and index portions of stored disk files.) Under the older FAT16 file system, disk partitions of 512MB and larger require a file cluster size of 16K to 32K. This wastes disk space, since a simple 1,000-byte document is automatically allocated a minimum of 32,000 bytes on the hard drive. Files that exceed 32K multiples by fractional amounts must also fill up the balance of their last 32K cluster. Besides wasting disk space, this tends to create a series of holes in the file structure, placing added wear and tear on hard disk heads as they scurry back and forth over the drive.

FAT32 solves this problem for most common partition sizes and also includes other improvements in its architecture. The root directory on a FAT32 drive is now an ordinary cluster chain, so it can be located anywhere on the drive. For this reason, the previous limitation on the number of root directory entries (typically 512) no longer exists. In addition, according to Microsoft: "The boot record on FAT32 drives has been expanded to allow a backup of critical data structures. This means that FAT32 drives are less susceptible to a single point of failure than existing FAT volumes."

Additionally, Windows 98's new WinAlign (discussed earlier in this chapter) and Tuneup (see Chapter 6) work with FAT32 partitions to speed up the loading and execution of Windows program code. Microsoft claims that applications open up to 50 percent faster on a FAT32 disk.

ARE THERE DRAWBACKS TO USING FAT32? Running Windows 98 from a FAT32-formatted drive may create some problems for users who want to rely on legacy hardware and software. Here are some typical problems and some possible solutions:

- *FAT32 partitions are invisible to operating systems that don't have FAT32 support built in.* If you boot your computer to DOS, UNIX, Windows NT, or Windows 95 Classic, these operating systems won't see any of the files on a FAT32 partition. (Windows 3.1 won't run from a FAT32 partition, even if you boot to a real-mode command prompt first.) If Windows 98 refuses to start, you can't repair a FAT32 partition unless you boot from a Windows 98 emergency diskette.
- *It's difficult to dual boot Windows 98 and another operating system from a FAT32 host drive.* Most people will tell you that it's impossible to do this! Windows 98 includes no built-in tools to facilitate dual booting. However, with the help of a third-party tool like PowerQuest's Partition Magic or V-Communications' System Commander, you can create a cumbersome dual-boot workaround by creating and switching between multiple primary partitions that contain different operating systems.
- *Microsoft's DriveSpace disk compression does not work on FAT32 partitions.* If you're frugally trying to keep an older notebook computer (with a small hard disk) in service, you may want to stick to running Windows 98 from a FAT16 partition that supports disk compression.

- *To use FAT32, you must upgrade all of your third-party disk utilities and antivirus software to new, compatible versions.* This may not be a significant deterrent to FAT32, since an upgrade from Windows 95 to Windows 98 mandates a general utility upgrade in any event.
- *Some older application packages, including Microsoft Office 95 and Microsoft Office 4.3, may not install properly under FAT32.*

See Chapter 8 for information on how to work around program installation difficulties.

Microsoft's Drive Converter utility (located in the Programs | Accessories | System Tools group) allows you to convert an existing FAT16 partition to the FAT32 format, preserving files and the current Windows 98 configuration. Drive Converter does not permit you to change your mind afterward, but several third-party tools allow reverse conversions from FAT32 to FAT16. (See Chapter 8 for details.)

32-bit Kernel

Windows 98 has a single virtual machine (VM) called the system VM, in which all system processes run. All Win32- and Win16-based applications also run in this VM. Each DOS-based application runs in its own VM. Figure 7-2 shows this architecture.

The Virtual Machine Manager, which replaces WIN386.EXE used in Windows 3.1, provides each application with the system resources it needs. The Virtual Machine Manager is responsible for three key areas of services:

- Process scheduling
- Memory paging
- MS-DOS mode support for DOS-based applications that must have exclusive access to system resources

Resources allocated for each Win32-based application tracked on a per-thread basis are automatically freed when the application ends. If an application stops responding, you can press CTRL-ALT-DELETE to display the Close Application dialog box and then close the unresponsive application without affecting other running tasks. Figure 7-3 illustrates this process.

To support a 16-bit operating environment including Windows 3.1 and DOS, the Intel processor architecture uses a mechanism called segment addressing. Segments reference physical memory by using a 16-bit segment address and a 16-bit offset address within the segment. A segment is 64K, and applications and the operating system both suffer a performance penalty for accessing information across segments.

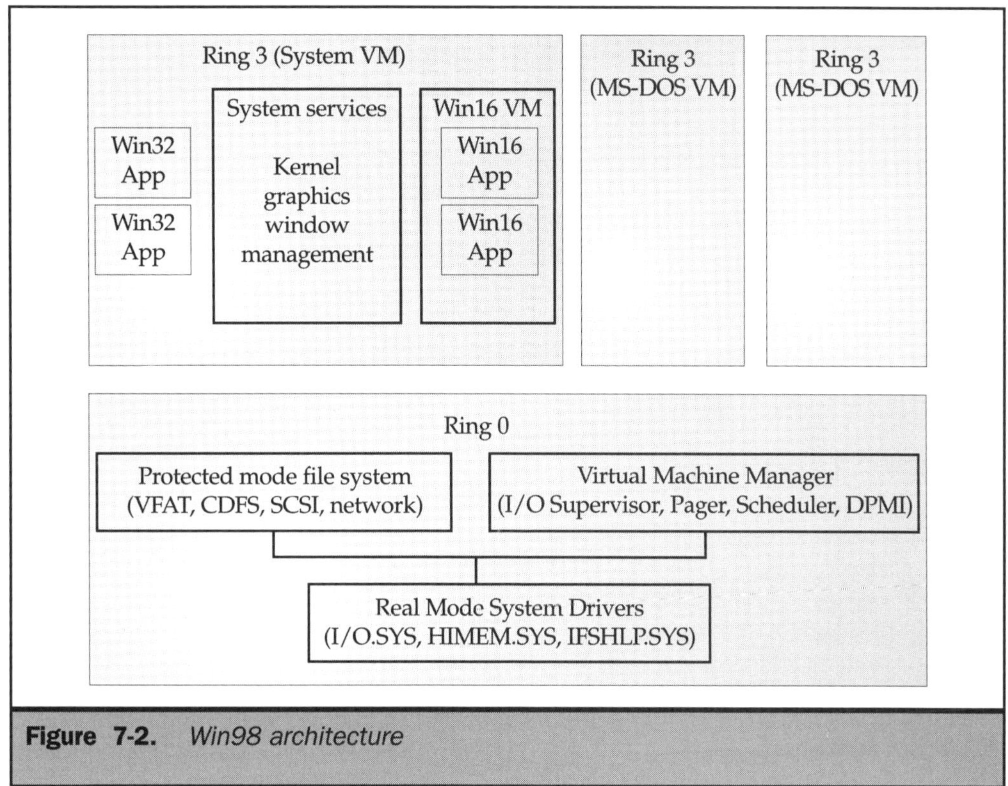

Figure 7-2. *Win98 architecture*

Windows 98 addresses this issue by supporting a flat, linear memory model for 32-bit operating system functionality and Win32-based applications. A linear addressing model makes it easier to write applications and removes the performance limitations inherent in the segmented memory architecture. Microsoft's George Moore, the product manager and spiritual godfather for Windows 95 and 98, had this to say about Win32 applications, memory protection, and memory paging in a message to beta testers:

> When you run a 32-bit application, the entire EXE is divided into "pages" of information of 4K each. When you first load the application, Windows will load the first 4K page into memory and then start executing the application's code. Pretty soon the application will execute all of the initial code in that 4K page and will attempt to make reference to another page of the program which isn't currently in memory. When this happens, it is

known as a "pagefault" because the page isn't present in physical memory. This is a hardware interrupt that the 386 and higher processors support.

The page fault causes the virtual memory manager (VMM) to look at the required address and then calculate the offset into the executable file for the requested page. Windows then seeks into the file and loads the correct page. The app starts executing again on the new page. Eventually it will need another 4K page, and the process repeats.

The beauty of this method is that the operating system only needs to load the bare minimum number of pages in order to satisfy the requests of the application. This is known as the application's "working set." Unused (nonexecuted) pages are never loaded into memory. By running automated tools, developers can reshuffle their application's subroutines so that the most heavily used routines are on physically contiguous pages at the beginning of the file. In doing so, they can reduce the working set of their application so that it uses less memory under most conditions. Less memory equals faster execution because of less page faults that occur.

Windows 95 itself is page-tuned in this method. For example, the 32-bit Explorer is page-tuned for the most common case of running two applications and using the taskbar to switch between the apps. Therefore, a portion of the taskbar's pages are usually in memory all the time, but (for example) the shell code to deal with network browsing is located on less-used pages.

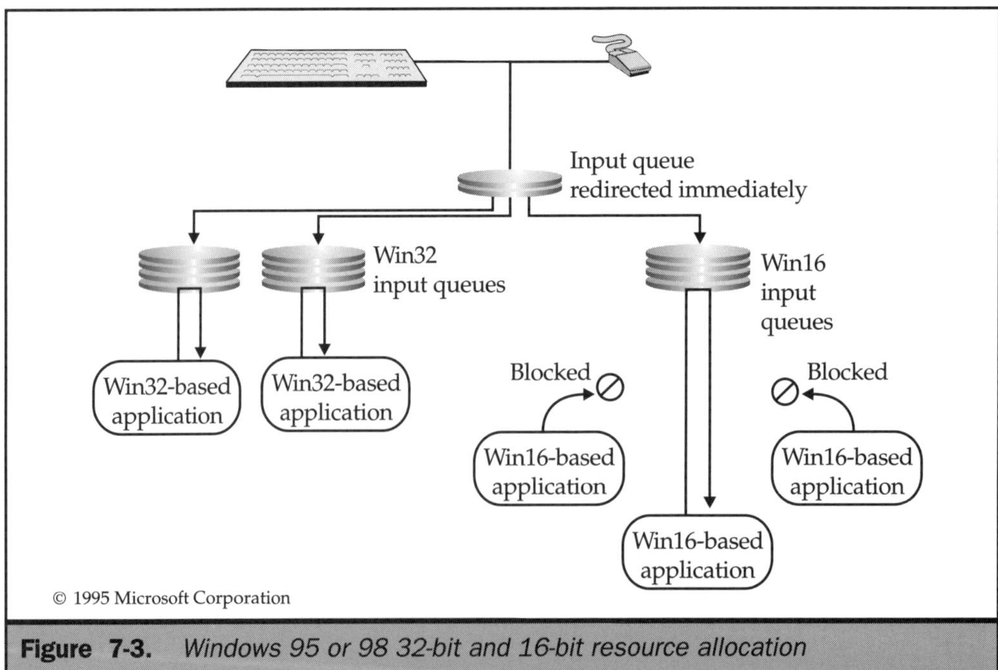

Figure 7-3. *Windows 95 or 98 32-bit and 16-bit resource allocation*

Windows 98 allows full use of the 4GB of addressable memory space for all 32-bit operating system components and applications. Each 32-bit application can access up to 2GB of addressable memory space.

Improved System Capacity

Windows 3.1 required that all protected-mode applications access a series of special resource heaps in conventional memory that were inherently limited to a maximum size of 64K. In Windows 98, system resources that were previously stored in these 16-bit heaps are stored in 32-bit heaps. This provides more storage space for data elements created by individual applications.

Table 7-1, adapted from the *Microsoft Windows 95 Resource Kit*, shows the improvements that have been made. (Windows 98 has the same configuration.)

Windows Memory Management at a Glance

Windows memory is divided into three logical control areas: physical memory, virtual memory, and linear memory. Here is a quick overview of memory management for each area:

- **Physical memory** Windows recognizes and addresses the physical RAM chips installed in your computer. An Intel 486 or higher CPU can provide address space for up to 4GB of physical RAM.
- **Virtual memory** In addition to reading and writing instruction code in physical RAM, Windows borrows space on your hard disk to create virtual memory. This allows the operating system to run and store more program and data code than can fit into all of your physical memory. Windows 98 manages virtual memory by paging information in and out of the Windows swap file.
- **Linear memory** Linear memory is an address space (usually about four times the amount of physical RAM in your computer). Windows 98 creates this address space at startup to provide greater flexibility for organizing and storing system and program code. (This default multiplier can be manually overwritten by adding a PageOverCommit=xx statement to the [386Enh] section of SYSTEM.INI.) Since the address space that Windows creates is almost always larger than physical memory, linear memory includes virtual memory (the swap file) as a subset. Each time a program asks Windows 98 for storage space, a portion of the linear memory address range is assigned.

16-bit application code is still read and processed from linear memory in 64K segments. However, 32-bit applications are processed with the flat memory model described in the previous section (which means fewer pauses to write and grab another chunk). This allows 32-bit programs to load and run faster, requiring less system overhead to manage memory pointers.

More about Linear Memory

Linear memory is divided into three regions: the system region, private region, and shared region.

Resource	Windows 3.1[1]	Windows 95/98[2]
Windows menu handles	~299	32K
Timers	32	Unlimited
COM and LPT ports	4 per type	Unlimited
Items per list box	8K	32K
Data per list box	64K	Unlimited
Data per edit control	64K	Unlimited
Regions	All in 64K segment	Unlimited
Physical pens and brushes	All in 64K segment	Unlimited
Logical pens and brushes	All in 64K segment	All in 64K segment
Logical fonts	All in 64K segment	750 to 800
Installed fonts	250 to 300 (best case)	1,000
Device contexts	200 (best case)	16K

[1]Limits for GDI objects in Windows 3.1 are not exact because all regions, physical objects, logical objects, device contexts (DCs), and installed fonts had to fit in a single 64K segment. Because many of these have been moved to the 32-bit heap, Windows 98 provides much more room for those remaining items, such as logical pens, brushes, and so on. The remaining items in the Windows 98 local heap are all less than 10 to 20 bytes each.

[2]System-wide resources, unless noted otherwise

Table 7-1. *Windows 95/98 System Limits*

The *system region* corresponds to what was called the entire linear memory region in Windows 3.1. Typically, the system region now stores the code for low-level control functions: VXDs, the VCACHE disk cache, and the operating system shell.

The *private region* is the address space reserved for 32-bit applications written for the 32-bit Windows 95 or 98 API. MS Office 95, 97, and 98 applications, Windows Explorer, resident system tray utilities, and the Win98 print spooler are examples of code modules stored in this area.

The *shared region* is a sequential address space reserved for programs and data files that may be accessed by a number of different system processes. The Win98 clipboard and its contents, antivirus filters, watchdog utilities such as Norton System Doctor, and Nuts & Bolts BombShelter all place code in this area. The Nuts & Bolts Discover utility, shown below, can display a graphic chart of Windows 98 memory usage.

Note *Remember that linear memory is address space. It doesn't correspond one to one with the physical memory in your computer.*

How Much Memory Do I Have?

The memory distinctions outlined in the preceding sections are primarily of interest to programmers. Microsoft does not provide any diagnostic utilities that break down your Windows memory inventory that finely (though third-party vendors do, as shown below).

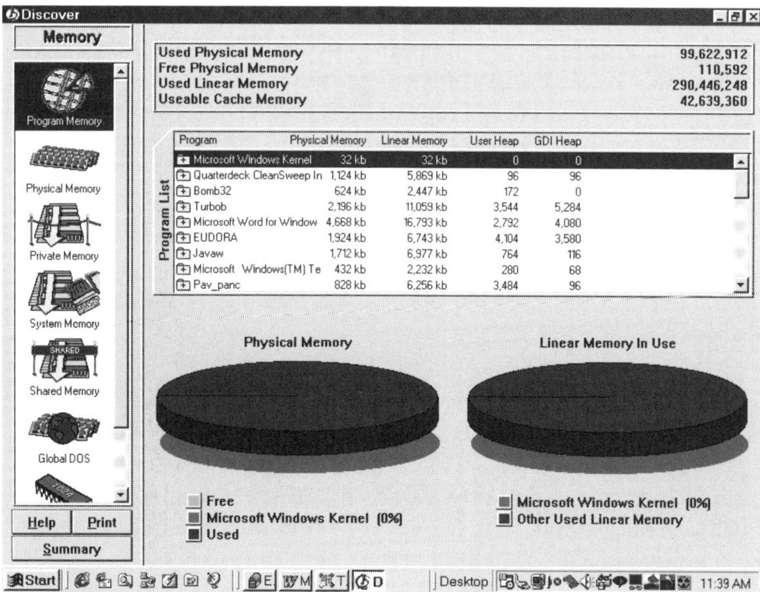

If you right-click My Computer and choose Properties, you'll see a number at the bottom of the General tab that corresponds to the total amount of physical RAM that is under the control of Windows 98. You can play games in AUTOEXEC.BAT and CONFIG.SYS, preloading applications that claim huge amounts of physical RAM before Windows 98 starts. If you do that, the My Computer memory listing may be significantly less than the computer's total RAM. Generally, though, this number is roughly equivalent to the computer's physical RAM.

Tip

If you see a discrepancy between the amount of RAM installed in the computer and the number on the My Computer Properties screen, something may be preventing Windows from claiming all the memory that it should. Check your CONFIG.SYS and AUTOEXEC.BAT files. You may also want to reboot your computer and examine its CMOS settings to determine whether the motherboard is properly configured. Some systems attempt to use part of the installed RAM as a huge disk cache unless otherwise instructed.

What About System Resources?

If you open My Computer properties to the Performance tab, you'll see a figure that reports the percentage of free System Resources. Windows resources are specific chunks of linear memory that are reserved for administrative processes of the operating system. These resources are sometimes called Windows heaps. The window management (User) and graphic display (GDI) modules of Windows 98 use six heaps to track information on window sizes, on drop-down menus, and on fonts, pen colors, and other information related to graphics display.

The system resources percentage reported on the Performance tab is the lowest free percentage of all the resource heaps. The percentage is derived by dividing the available address space in the smallest heap by 64K.

Note

The significant thing to remember about the free system resources percentage is that if it drops below 30 percent, your system is in danger of becoming unstable. If you see the number drop this low, you should immediately start saving files and closing applications.

The Win98 System Resource Meter (located in the System Tools group on the Accessories menu, if installed) allows you to display a real-time resource monitor on the System Tray portion of the taskbar. Run the System Monitor if you think some of your applications may be huge memory hogs that might bring the system to its knees.

For more information about how to manage Windows resources and gain additional memory protection, see "Win98-Aware Utilities May Help" later in this chapter.

Startup Strategies

This is the hands-on, system-tweaking portion of the chapter.

Windows 98 is installed on your hard disk, and you're looking at the desktop. You may now have questions such as the following about what to do with your CONFIG.SYS file, DOS, and Windows memory managers, and TSR utilities:

- Do I need CONFIG.SYS and AUTOEXEC.BAT files? If I do, what device drivers and utilities should I load? Are my CD-ROM drive and SCSI devices being recognized?
- Do I have enough conventional memory for DOS sessions? What about expanded memory for DOS applications: Can I use a third-party product like QEMM?
- What if I want to dual boot back to DOS 6.x? Will this capability be installed automatically for me? What about dual booting to Windows NT or to a copy of Windows 95?
- How is the DOS 7 part of Windows 98 different from Windows 95 or DOS 6.x? Are there new commands and switches for CONFIG.SYS and AUTOEXEC.BAT?

The next sections provide some answers to these questions.

Is CONFIG.SYS Necessary?

One of the bases for Microsoft's claim that Windows 98 "does away with DOS" is that the system can start the Windows interface automatically without either a CONFIG.SYS or AUTOEXEC.BAT file present in the root directory of your boot drive. How does this work? Like DOS, Windows 98 bootstraps and loads itself off two kernel files called IO.SYS and MSDOS.SYS. The difference is that the low-level machine instructions in Win98's IO.SYS are more sophisticated than in the older DOS equivalent. The system is instructed to automatically load a series of real-mode device drivers from your hard disk without reading a CONFIG.SYS file. The following drivers are loaded at boot time by IO.SYS if they can be located on your hard drive:

- HIMEM.SYS
- IFSHLP.SYS
- SETVER.EXE
- DBLSPACE.BIN or DRVSPACE.BIN

Additionally, most of the standard settings and command switches for DOS that you used to place in CONFIG.SYS are also loaded automatically by IO.SYS.

Table 7-2 (adapted from the *Microsoft Windows 95 Resource Kit*) lists the common entries in CONFIG.SYS that are now loaded and configured automatically in Windows 98.

Setting	Description
DOS=HIGH	Specifies that DOS should be loaded in the high memory area (HMA). Also, the UMB value is included if EMM386 is loaded from CONFIG.SYS. (IO.SYS does not load EMM386.)
HIMEM.SYS	Enables access to the HMA. This line loads and runs the real-mode Memory Manager. HIMEM.SYS is loaded by default in Windows 98.
IFSHLP.SYS	Installable File System Helper, which loads device drivers. This allows the system to make file system calls. Until this is loaded, only the minimal file system from IO.SYS is used. After this point, the full file system is available.
SETVER.EXE	Optional TSR-type device. It is included for compatibility reasons. Some DOS–based applications require a specific version of DOS to be running. This file responds to applications that query for the version number and sets the version number required.
FILES=	Specifies the number of file handle buffers to create. This is specifically for files opened using DOS calls and is not required by Windows 95. It is included for compatibility with older applications. The default value is 60.
LASTDRIVE=	Specifies the last drive letter available for assignment. This is not required for Windows 98 but is included for compatibility with older applications. If Windows 98 Setup finds this entry, the entry is moved to the registry. The default value is z.
BUFFERS=	Specifies the number of file buffers to create. This is specifically for applications using IO.SYS calls and is not required by Windows 98. The default value is 30.

Table 7-2. *CONFIG.SYS Settings Incorporated in Windows 95 IO.SYS*

Setting	Description
STACKS=	Specifies the number and size of stack frames. This is not required for Windows 95 but is included for compatibility with older applications. The default value is 9,256.
SHELL= COMMAND.COM	Indicates what command processor to use. By default, the /p switch is included to indicate that the command process is permanent and should not be unloaded. If the /p switch is not specified, AUTOEXEC.BAT is not processed, and the command process can be unloaded when quitting the operating system.
FCBS=	Specifies the number of file control blocks that can be open at the same time. You should use an FCBS= line in CONFIG.SYS only if you have an older program that requires such a setting. The default value is 4.

Table 7-2. *CONFIG.SYS Settings Incorporated in Windows 95 IO.SYS* (continued)

Note *EMM386.EXE is not loaded by default. To take advantage of upper-memory program loading or to provide expanded memory for DOS applications, you must construct a CONFIG.SYS file that contains a DEVICE=[d:]\WINDOWS\EMM386.EXE statement.*

IO.SYS

Windows 98 performance settings, preset in IO.SYS, allow you to successfully boot the Win98 interface without a CONFIG.SYS startup file. If you want to customize the startup settings, then you will need a traditional CONFIG.SYS file in the root directory of your boot drive.

For example, you may want to add new directories to the DOS PATH statement, add an environment parameter to the Shell statement, increase or decrease the allocation of files and buffers, or load additional DOS device drivers before launching the Win98 interface.

The Windows 98 IO.SYS file is automatically renamed JO.SYS if you boot your computer to MS DOS 6.x from a FAT16 disk partition. (You can do this by pressing F4 at startup after the "Starting Windows 98" message appears on the screen.)

MSDOS.SYS

MSDOS.SYS is the second file that Windows 98 reads at boot time. In Windows 98, this file consists of ASCII text instructions instead of binary code. Like IO.SYS,

MSDOS.SYS is a hidden, read-only system file in the root of the computer's boot drive. This file contains path information used to locate other Windows files, including the registry and device drivers loaded automatically by IO.SYS. MSDOS.SYS also supports an [Options] section that is used to customize the startup process.

A typical instance of MSDOS.SYS contains the following default values:

```
[PATHS]
WINDIR=C:\WINDOWS
WINBOOTDIR=C:\WINDOWS
HOSTWINBOOTDRV=C
UNINSTALLDIR=C:\
[OPTIONS]
BOOTGUI=1
```

The configuration instructions in MSDOS.SYS are followed by a series of dummy comment lines (;xxxxxxxxxxx) to round out the file size to 1,024 bytes. Most values in the [Options] section are Boolean: a value of 1 enables the option, and a value of 0 disables it. The critical values in MSDOS.SYS are the ones just described. They can be modified if you want to boot Windows 98 from another host partition or force the system to boot to a DOS command prompt. Other settings in MSDOS.SYS are used to enable or disable the loading of the DBLSPACE.BIN compression driver and to control the behavior of Windows 98's pop-up Startup menu.

Table 7-3 lists all of the entries in MSDOS.SYS with their typical default values. (For bi-valued commands, 1 enables and 0 disables.)

Here are uses for some of these MSDOS.SYS parameters:

- Make the Win98 Startup menu appear automatically at boot time. The default setting of BootMenu=0 causes the system to start directly in the graphic interface unless you press the CTRL key. A setting of BootMenu=1 will display the Startup menu on the screen automatically at boot time.
- Change the default location of the Win95 or Win 98 operating system. If you performed a clean rather than an upgrade installation of Windows 98, you may have Windows 95 in one directory or on one disk partition, and Windows 98 installed in another. You can manipulate the WinDir and WinBootDir settings in MSDOS.SYS to boot the computer to different operating systems from different directories. For example, set WinDir and WinBootDir=D:\WIN95 to run Windows 95, where Windows 95 resides on drive D. Set WinDir and WinBootDir=C:\WIN98 to run Windows 98 from drive C
- Boot to an MS-DOS command prompt instead of loading the Windows interface. By default the setting BootGUI=1 is assumed in MSDOS.SYS. This setting automatically loads Windows 98 if it is present in the directory designated by WinBootDir. If you specify BootGUI=0, the computer will open to a real-mode MS-DOS prompt (the version contained in Windows 98) instead of loading the graphic interface.

Entry	Description
[Paths] section:	
HostWinBootDrv=	Defines the location of the boot drive root directory (default is C)
WinBootDir=	Defines the location of the necessary startup files. The default is the directory specified during setup; for example, C:\WINDOWS
WinDir=	Defines the location of the Windows 98 directory as specified during setup
UninstallDir=	Defines the location of the directory used for uninstall data, to return the computer to a previous operating system
[Options] section:	
Autoscan=	Controls the automatic launching of ScanDisk after a bad Windows 98 shutdown. AutoScan=0 disables the running of ScanDisk; AutoScan=1, the default, causes the system to prompt you to run ScanDisk after a bad shutdown; AutoScan=2 bypasses system prompts and runs ScanDisk automatically
BootDelay=*n*	Sets the initial startup delay to *n* seconds. The default is 2. BootKeys=0 disables the delay. The only purpose of the delay is to give the user sufficient time to press F8 after the "Starting Windows" message appears
BootFailSafe=	Enables Safe mode for system startup. The default is 0. (This setting is sometimes enabled by equipment manufacturers for installation purposes)
BootGUI=	Enables automatic graphical startup in Windows 95. The default is 1
BootKeys=	Enables the startup option keys (that is, CTRL, F5, F6, and F8). The default is 1. Setting this value to 0 overrides the value of BootDelay=*n* and prevents any startup keys from functioning. This setting allows system administrators to configure more secure systems
BootMenu=	Enables automatic display of the Windows 98 Startup menu, so that the user must press F8 to see the menu. The default is 0. Setting this value to 1 eliminates the need to press F8 to see the menu

Table 7-3. *CONFIG.SYS Settings Incorporated in Windows 95 IO.SYS*

Entry	Description
BootMenuDefault=#	Sets the default menu item on the Windows Startup menu. The default is 3 for a computer with no networking components, and it is 4 for a networked computer
BootMenuDelay=#	Sets the number of seconds to display the Windows Startup menu before running the default menu item. The default is 30.
BootMulti=	Enables dual-boot capabilities. The default is 0. Setting this value to 1 enables you to start DOS by pressing F4 or by pressing F8 to use the Windows Startup menu.
BootWarn=	Enables the Safe mode startup warning. The default is 1.
BootWin=	Enables Windows 95 as the default operating system. Setting this value to 0 disables Windows 95 as the default; this is useful only with DOS version 5 or 6.x on the computer. The default is 1.
DblSpace=	Enables automatic loading of DBLSPACE.BIN. The default is 1.
DoubleBuffer=	Enables loading of a double-buffering driver for a SCSI controller. The default is 0. Setting this value to 1 enables double-buffering, if required by the SCSI controller.
DrvSpace=	Enables automatic loading of DRVSPACE.BIN. The default is 1.
LoadTop=	Enables loading of COMMAND.COM or DRVSPACE.BIN at the top of 640K memory. The default is 1. Set this value to 0 with Novell® NetWare® or any software that makes assumptions about what is used in specific memory areas.
Logo=	Enables display of the animated logo. The default is 1.
Network=	Enables Safe Mode with Networking as a menu option. The default is 1 for computers with networking installed. This value should be 0 if network software components are not installed.
Winver=	Designates the version and build number of the Windows operating system installed on the host drive.

Table 7-3. *CONFIG.SYS Settings Incorporated in Windows 95 IO.SYS* (continued)

Recovering the Dual-Boot (F4) Option to Run a Previous Version of DOS

If your computer was originally running MS-DOS and you installed Windows 98 in a new directory on a FAT16 partition, the earlier version of DOS on the hard disk is preserved. However, if you installed Windows 98 over Windows 3.x, the Boot to Previous Version of DOS option will not appear on the Win98 Startup menu. If you want to restore this option, you can add a command to the MSDOS.SYS control file. MSDOS.SYS is located in the root directory of your boot drive. To open this file in Notepad, you must turn on the Windows Explorer display option that unhides system files in folder lists. (See Chapter 4 for details.)

Open MSDOS.SYS in Notepad and enter the statement **BootMulti=1** under the [Options] section. This will allow you to start the earlier version of DOS by pressing F4 when the "Starting Windows 98" message appears on the screen.

If you choose to start a previous version of DOS, Windows 98 makes the following system adjustments at boot time:

- The current versions of IO.SYS, MSDOS.SYS, and COMMAND.COM are renamed JO.SYS, MSDOS.W40, and COMMAND.W40, respectively.
- Windows 98 searches for kernel files from your previous version of DOS in the root directory of your boot drive. IO.DOS, MSDOS.DOS, and COMMAND.DOS are renamed IO.SYS, MSDOS.SYS, and COMMAND.COM. If any of these files can't be found, then your previous version of DOS will not be booted. Instead, Windows 98 ignores your dualboot request and loads its own system kernel.
- If the old version of DOS boots successfully, the Windows 98 CONFIG.SYS and AUTOEXEC.BAT files are renamed CONFIG.W40 and AUTOEXEC.W40.
- The system looks for two files named CONFIG.DOS and AUTOEXEC.DOS in the root directory of your boot drive. If these files are found, they are renamed CONFIG.SYS and AUTOEXEC.BAT and then processed.

If, for some reason, your Windows 98 installation fails during the first pass, restoring the dual-boot option is a little trickier, because when you make your second installation attempt, Windows 98 has already renamed the DOS 6.x system files. Running Win98 Setup a second time completely overwrites the DOS 6.x system files. If this happens to you, you'll find that selecting the Previous DOS boot option loads a Windows 98 (MS DOS 7.1) command prompt.

You can replace the missing system files from your previous operating system to restore the dual-boot option. *This will work only on a FAT16 partition, not FAT32!* You need a floppy boot diskette formatted with your previous version of DOS. Under the Windows 98 interface, insert the boot disk from your previous operating system into drive A. Open a DOS command prompt within Windows 98 and perform the following operations:

1. Enter **XCOPY A:\IO.SYS C:\IO.DOS /H**. If XCOPY asks you whether the target is a file or a directory, answer File.
2. Enter **XCOPY A:\MSDOS.SYS C:\MSDOS.DOS /H**. If XCOPY asks you whether the target is a file or a directory, answer File.
3. Enter **copy A:\COMMAND.COM C:\COMMAND.DOS**.

Be sure to copy these files to a .DOS file extension in the target directory, or you will overwrite the Windows 98 system files, which you don't want to do!

4. If you have backups of the CONFIG.SYS and AUTOEXEC.BAT files from your previous version of DOS, copy them to the root directory of drive C as CONFIG.DOS and AUTOEXEC.DOS. If necessary, you can re-create these files from scratch or modify the Windows 98 versions, but be sure to save them in the root directory with the .DOS file extension.
5. From inside Windows 98, open the current MSDOS.SYS file in Notepad, as described earlier, and make sure MSDOS.SYS contains the command Bootmulti=1 in the [Options] section.

Working with CONFIG.SYS and AUTOEXEC.BAT

If you decide to have CONFIG.SYS and AUTOEXEC.BAT files with Windows 98, here are some things to bear in mind:

- You can retain a CONFIG.SYS but eliminate AUTOEXEC.BAT. This can speed the startup process incrementally.
- If you need to retain DOS environment variables in Windows 98, you can enter SET statements directly in CONFIG.SYS. For instance, a SET PATH= entry can be substituted for the AUTOEXEC.BAT PATH statement. If you need to run MSCDEX.EXE for CD ROM drives, it can be loaded in CONFIG.SYS by specifying **DEVICE=MSCDEX.EXE**. For most newer computers, this step should not be necessary; since Windows 98 will substitute protected-mode VXDs for real-mode CD-ROM drivers.
- Certain other commands normally entered in AUTOEXEC.BAT can be loaded in CONFIG.SYS by using INSTALL= statements.

Tip

Sometimes, real-mode device drivers for SCSI controllers, CD-ROM drives, sound cards, notebook PCMCIA cards, and power management are migrated into the CONFIG.SYS file for Windows 98, even though they may not be necessary. Windows 98 autodetects most of your hardware automatically, but it does not automatically substitute protected-mode drivers for statements present in CONFIG.SYS. If you open the Add New Hardware component in the Control Panel and specify No for the Autodetect option, you will see a list of all the devices and drivers that the operating system supports. If your particular hardware is supported, you can tell Windows 98 to install its protected-mode drivers and remove corresponding real-mode drivers from CONFIG.SYS and AUTOEXEC.BAT. (See Chapter 9 for more information on how to use Add New Hardware.)

For detailed information about all of the DOS commands that you can use in CONFIG.SYS and AUTOEXEC.BAT, refer to the MSDOSDRV.TXT file in your WINDOWS directory.

New CONFIG.SYS Commands

The following list (adapted from the *Microsoft Windows 95 Resource Kit*) describes new optional command switches for CONFIG.SYS that have been added to the version of DOS that underlies Windows 95 and 98.

BUFFERSHIGH	Allocates memory for a specified number of disk buffers when the computer starts. The BUFFERSHIGH form causes reserved memory to be taken out of the upper memory address (UMB). You can use this command only in CONFIG.SYS.
FCBSHIGH	Specifies the number of file control blocks (FCBs) that the operating system can have open at the same time. The FCBSHIGH form causes reserved memory to be taken out of the UMB. You can use this command only in CONFIG.SYS.
FILESHIGH	Specifies the number of files that the operating system can access at one time. The FILESHIGH form causes reserved memory to be taken out of the UMB. You can use this command only in CONFIG.SYS.
INCLUDE	Includes the contents of one configuration block within another. You can use this command only in CONFIG.SYS.
LASTDRIVEHIGH	Specifies the maximum number of drives you can access. The LASTDRIVEHIGH form causes reserved memory to be taken out of the UMB. You can use this command only in CONFIG.SYS.

MENUCOLOR	Sets the text and background colors for the Startup menu. You can use this command only within a menu block in CONFIG.SYS.
MENUDEFAULT	Specifies the default menu item on the Startup menu and sets a time-out value, if desired. You can use this command only within a menu block in CONFIG.SYS.
MENUITEM	Defines up to nine items on the Startup menu. You can use this command only within a menu block in CONFIG.SYS.
NUMLOCK	Specifies whether the NUMLOCK setting on the numeric keypad is set to ON or OFF. You can use this command only within a menu block in CONFIG.SYS.
SUBMENU	Defines an item on the Startup menu that, when selected, displays another set of choices. You can use this command only within a menu block in CONFIG.SYS.

EMM386—Do You Need It?

EMM386.EXE is the DOS component that allows you to load TSR utilities and drivers into upper memory blocks (UMBs). In Windows 98, EMM386.EXE must also be loaded if you want to provide expanded memory for DOS applications. Thus, there are two reasons for placing a DEVICE=EMM386.EXE statement in a new or preexisting CONFIG.SYS file:

- You want to gain more conventional memory for DOS sessions by loading some drivers into upper memory blocks.
- You want to provide expanded memory for DOS applications such as WordPerfect for DOS.

EMM386.EXE under Windows 98 functions in exactly the same way as it did under DOS 6.x and Windows 95. You have a choice between two key command-line parameters:

- **DEVICE=EMM386.EXE RAM** enables both expanded memory and UMB device loading.
- **DEVICE=EMM386.EXE NOEMS** enables UMB device loading only (and the NOEMS parameter gains you a potential extra 64K of UMB space, since it disables the use of an EMS pageframe).

MORE CONVENTIONAL MEMORY FOR DOS PROGRAMS As in DOS 6.x, individual drivers and executable TSRs are loaded into upper memory by substituting DEVICEHIGH= for DEVICE= in CONFIG.SYS or by placing LOADHIGH (or LH) in front of the program name in AUTOEXEC.BAT. You can do this manually by editing your startup files. You may want to optimize conventional memory if you have a DOS application that won't run comfortably under Windows 98 with the default memory allocation or if your computer requires that you load real-mode disk devices, or PCMCIA or network drivers (which consume large amounts of conventional memory before Windows 98 opens).

In DOS 6.x and in the original version of Windows 95, Microsoft provided a memory optimization tool called MemMaker. MemMaker examined your computer and automatically rewrote CONFIG.SYS and AUTOEXEC.BAT to load programs and drivers in upper memory. Microsoft removed MemMaker from the Win95 CD in OEM System Release 2 and has not restored it in Windows 98.

Notwithstanding Microsoft's decision to discontinue it, MemMaker is a useful tool for optimizing DOS conventional memory. If you can find a copy, MemMaker will still work under Windows 98. If you upgraded to Windows 98 from Windows 95 Classic, you may find a copy of MemMaker in your \WINDOWS directory. MemMaker is also present on the Windows 95 Classic CD in the \TOOLS\OLDMSDOS folder. Finally, you can obtain a working copy of MemMaker from Microsoft's Web site at http://support.microsoft.com/support/downloads.

If you run MemMaker from within the Windows 98 interface, you may see an error message stating that Windows can't find the working directory for the program. Generally you can click Yes to ignore this message and then click Yes again to launch it in MS-DOS mode. You can also exit to MS-DOS mode first (from the Start menu, choose Shut Down | Restart Computer in MS-DOS Mode) and run MemMaker from the DOS command line. A series of prompts will guide you through several system reboots as MemMaker parses your CONFIG.SYS and AUTOEXEC.BAT files and attempts to free up more conventional memory. (See "Working with MemMaker" later in this chapter for more information.)

STRATEGIES FOR "ROLL-YOUR-OWN" MEMORY OPTIMIZATION The same strategies that applied to optimizing EMM386.EXE under DOS also apply to its use in Windows 98. The bottom line is that you may be able to get the conventional memory you need for DOS sessions under Windows 98 without extensive system tweaking. You may gain enough conventional memory simply by replacing real-mode DOS drivers with protected-mode Win98 VXDs. (See the tip in the previous section.) Yet situations may arise where you need even more conventional memory for DOS and don't have it, for example:

- You may be running a network that doesn't include 32-bit Windows 98 driver support.
- You may have a series of peripherals that insist on loading real-mode drivers under DOS.
- You may want to run a DOS-based game or multimedia program that requires a large amount of conventional memory.

If you boot your computer to a real-mode DOS command prompt, you may find that the amount of available conventional memory is drastically reduced. For instance, if your computer has DriveSpace-compressed volumes, you'll see that the real-mode compression driver consumes more than 100K. When you boot to a command prompt instead of the Windows 98 interface, none of the protected-mode VXDs can load. Instead, DriveSpace volumes, SCSI drives, CD-ROMs, network cards, and so on must all be recognized through DOS device drivers.

Here are some common ways to increase the amount of upper memory block (UMB) space available for loading programs high:

- Add the HIGHSCAN parameter. The statement DEVICE=EMM386.EXE RAM HIGHSCAN aggressively scans the reserved memory area between 640K and 1MB for areas that can be mapped for an EMS pageframe or for upper memory blocks. On some systems, adding HIGHSCAN may cause the computer to hang or reboot constantly. If this happens to you, you'll need to remove this parameter and determine through trial and error which upper memory addresses are safe to add. For instance, append the parameter INCLUDE=F000-F7FF to the EMM386 command line and see whether the system remains stable. If it doesn't, decrease the range to F400 to F7FF, and so on.
- Substitute NOEMS for RAM on the DEVICE=EMM386.EXE line. If you don't require expanded memory, this will provide an additional 64K for use as upper memory blocks.
- Experiment with the location of the EMS pageframe to obtain larger contiguous upper memory blocks. On many systems EMM386.EXE defines an EMS pageframe at address D000h, creating one UMB block from C800 to CFFFh, and sometimes a second block from E000 to EFFFh. One optimization strategy that often works is to place the parameter FRAME=C800 on the DEVICE= EMM386.EXE line. This rearranges the UMB allocation, typically allowing a contiguous block to be created from D800h to EFFFh. This larger UMB block can contain larger DOS device drivers and TSRs that will not fit into two smaller blocks. If the entire range from D800h to EFFFh is not recognized by EMM386, you can sometimes force recognition through INCLUDE statements. Here's an example:

```
DEVICE=EMM386.EXE FRAME=C800 RAM INCLUDE=D800-EFFF
```

- On some notebook computers, the upper memory area reserved for video ROM sometimes begins at address E000 instead of C000. You can see if your notebook follows this pattern by opening the System Information tool (choose Programs | Accessories | System Tools) and looking under System Information | Resources | Memory. If your computer follows this pattern, you may want to try the following EMM386 statement:

```
DEVICE=EMM386.EXE FRAME=C000 RAM INCLUDE=D000-DFFF
```

- Sometimes you can increase the amount of available upper memory by including the range reserved for monochrome video adapters, as follows:

```
DEVICE=EMM386.EXE FRAME=C800 RAM INCLUDE=B000-B7FF INCLUDE=D800-EFFF
```

Note *On some systems where network cards, disk controllers, or SCSI devices map upper memory for adapter ROM, the tricks described here may not work. If the system won't start, or if you experience performance anomalies, you should always remove additional INCLUDE, FRAME, and HIGHSCAN parameters from the DEVICE=EMM386.EXE line in CONFIG.SYS.*

- Use BUFFERSHIGH, FCBSHIGH, FILESHIGH, LASTDRIVEHIGH, and STACKSHIGH to ensure that memory for these system resources is allocated from the upper memory area.
- Run MemMaker, shown here. (See the beginning of this section for information on where to find it.) MemMaker may help you gain additional upper memory, it but will probably not optimize your system as thoroughly as manually tweaking the CONFIG.SYS and AUTOEXEC.BAT files. For instance, MemMaker does not automatically substitute the new BUFFERSHIGH and FILESHIGH statements in CONFIG.SYS for the older commands that load resources into conventional memory.

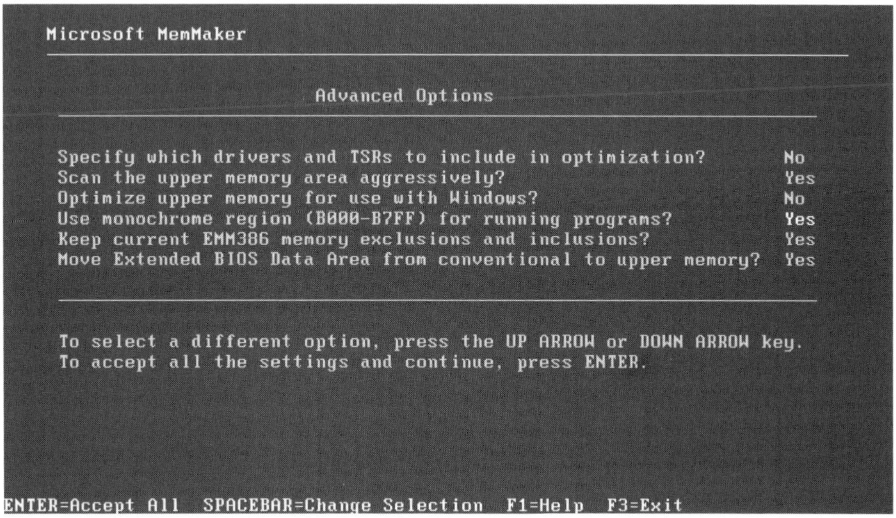

```
Microsoft MemMaker

                          Advanced Options

Specify which drivers and TSRs to include in optimization?      No
Scan the upper memory area aggressively?                        Yes
Optimize upper memory for use with Windows?                     No
Use monochrome region (B000-B7FF) for running programs?         Yes
Keep current EMM386 memory exclusions and inclusions?           Yes
Move Extended BIOS Data Area from conventional to upper memory? Yes

To select a different option, press the UP ARROW or DOWN ARROW key.
To accept all the settings and continue, press ENTER.

ENTER=Accept All  SPACEBAR=Change Selection  F1=Help  F3=Exit
```

Tip *For best results, you may want to try optimizing CONFIG.SYS manually with the tips described here. Then run MemMaker to see if it can create additional improvements.*

Working with MemMaker

To run MemMaker, first boot to a DOS command prompt by holding down the Ctrl key and selecting Command Prompt Only from the Windows 98 Startup menu. After you start MemMaker and select Continue on the first screen, you can choose between Express and Custom setups. If you choose Custom Setup, you have a chance to extract a greater amount of upper memory. If you answer No to the question about programs needing expanded memory, you will gain an additional 64K to load drivers and TSRs above 640K. In the advanced options, try choosing Scan Upper Memory Area Aggressively and Use Monochrome Region For Running Programs. If these options cause problems on your system, MemMaker will subsequently offer to reoptimize using conservative settings.

After you confirm the drive and path where Windows 98 is installed, MemMaker reboots the system several times and attempts to optimize conventional memory by establishing an EMS pageframe (if you answered Yes to the EMS question) and loading device drivers and TSRs above 640K. If you answered No to the EMS question, no pageframe is configured. You don't have to hold down the Ctrl key to boot again. MemMaker will automatically reboot the system to a DOS prompt several times until memory optimization is completed.

Third-Party DOS and Windows Memory Utilities

This section tells you what you need to know about third-party add-ons designed to increase available memory or improve system performance with Windows 98. The bottom line is that almost all memory and performance enhancement utilities designed for earlier versions of DOS and Windows are incompatible with Windows 98. The good news is that a small cottage industry has grown up around new, Windows 98-aware, tools that can actually provide some help.

DOS Memory Managers Are Obsolete

Third-party DOS memory managers once played a significant role in maximizing the amount of conventional memory available to your computer. However, the development of Windows 98 and new hardware management techniques makes most of them obsolete. None of the older DOS memory-management packages is completely compatible with Windows 98, and only Quarterdeck's QEMM97 is partially compatible. You shouldn't even think about trying to boot Windows 98 with 386MAX or Netroom installed.

QEMM

Even QEMM97, the last version of Quarterdeck's memory management package, may be more trouble to run than it's worth. Changes in the ways new computers stuff firmware code into upper memory reduce the possibility that QEMM will free up more conventional memory than Microsoft's MemMaker. Some rough tests that I did with QEMM 97's built-in Turboload and MagnaRAM optimization modules failed to yield any significant performance benefits for the Windows 98 interface. Additionally, I found that QEMM interfered with Windows 98 Advanced Power Management on some systems.

For a quick-and-dirty way to get more memory in a real mode MS-DOS session, hold down the CTRL key when the computer boots and select Step-By-Step Configuration from the Windows 98 Startup Menu. When you're prompted to load the Doublespace driver, press the ESC key to bypass it. This will add approximately 100K to the conventional memory available in a dedicated MS-DOS session.

Win98-Aware Utilities May Help

Most older utility packages that purport to speed up Windows performance and increase system memory are ineffective or incompatible with Windows 98. However, Helix/Network Associates' Hurricane is a standout utility that can significantly speed up operating system performance. Other new utility suites from Helix/Network Associates, Symantec, and Quarterdeck offer preventive system diagnosis and application crash protection not built into the basic Windows 98 operating system.

Hurricane 98 (Version 3.0)

If you're looking for a Windows performance optimizer that isn't pure snake oil, you may want to check out Hurricane 98. It won't substitute for a CPU upgrade, but it does actually improve system performance incrementally on both new and old hardware, across the Windows 3.x, 95, and 98 family.

Hurricane 98 contains all of the features that were available in previous versions: a print spooler, intelligent RAM disk, and memory compression algorithms that boost Win98 performance on overloaded hardware configurations.

New in this version are Boot Rocket and Launch Rocket, modules that optimize the speed of Windows 98 bootup and decrease application launch times. Boot Rocket can cut Windows 98 startup times by 10 to 40 percent. (I found a consistent 15 percent improvement on several tested systems, with both 32MB and 64MB RAM configurations.) Launch Rocket, shown next, is more impressive, consistently cutting launch time in half for applications like Microsoft Word, Netscape Communicator, and Internet Explorer.

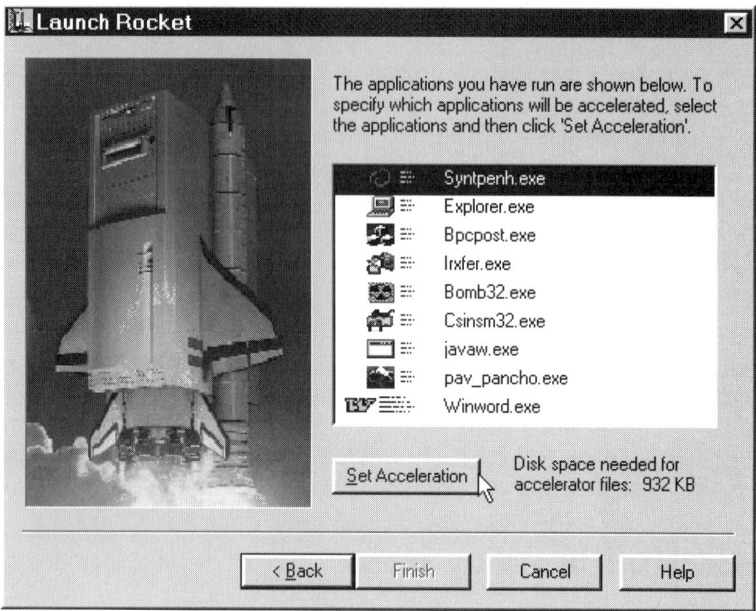

Hurricane 98 also contains a Top Down CD-ROM cache (which improves choppy playback of multimedia files on low-end systems) and a Reverse Cache feature. Reverse Cache allows large applications to restart quickly if you open and close them several times in a session. Hurricane's cache optimization is not very noticeable in situations where you open one program, close it, and then open another one. The cache benefits come into play when you have a loaded desktop: many applications open at the same time. Without Hurricane, a loaded desktop typically slows down Windows performance by forcing heavy swap file access. Programs opened early in a session are forced out of the regular Windows disk cache. Hurricane, however, continues to track these processes, allowing you to close an application like Pagemaker or Microsoft Access and reopen it quickly with minimal disk access.

Hurricane's WinGauge functions as both a performance meter and an application launch bar. Discover is a system inventory program that displays more extensive information than Win98's bundled System Information utility. As shown in Figure 7-4, Discover also contains a full suite of benchmark tests.

Third-Party Crash Protection

As mentioned at the beginning of this chapter, Windows 98 offers a number of enhancements to Windows 3.1's memory management techniques. However, there's still room for improvement. Microsoft did not provide rock-steady memory protection for 16-bit applications, and even 32-bit applications are not completely shielded from the operating system and from each other.

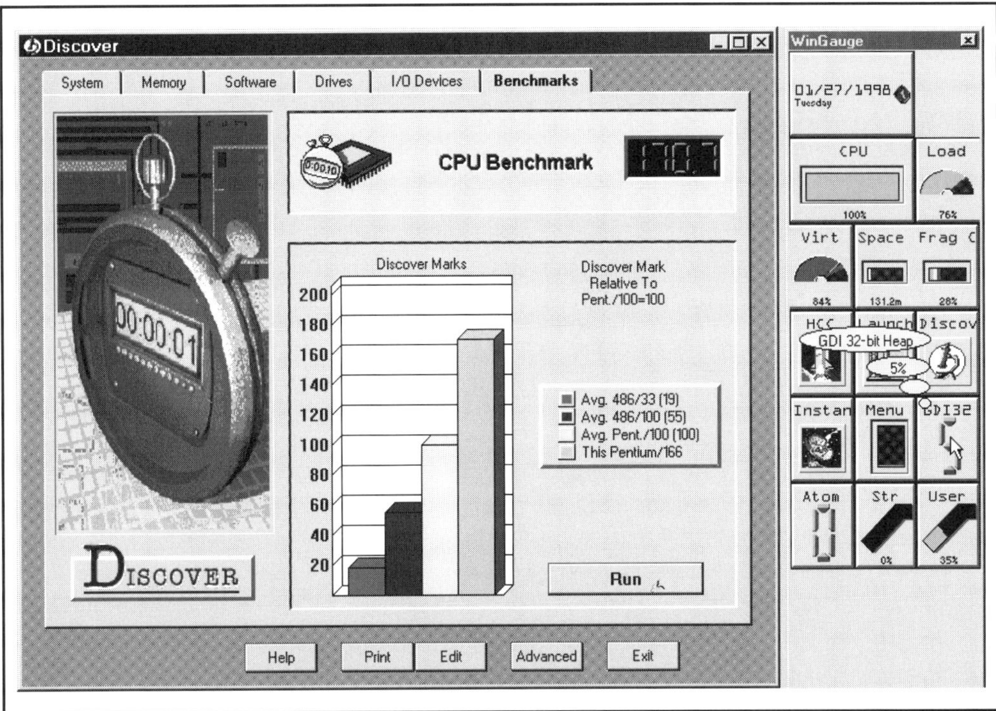

Figure 7-4. *Nuts and bolts Discover contains a full Benchmark suite*

Helix Software (now a division of the larger Network Associates), Quarterdeck, Symantec, and CyberMedia all offer Windows 98 enhancements that provide additional memory protection. These crash protection modules are bundled with larger utility suites that diagnose and correct a wide number of system problems:

- Bomb Shelter (bundled with Network Associates Nuts & Bolts)
- CrashGuard 3.0 (bundled with Symantec Norton Utilities 3.0 and CrashGuard Deluxe)
- Crash Protector (bundled with CyberMedia First Aid 98)
- Crash Defender (bundled with Quarterdeck Real Help)

These utilities prevent data loss by loading filters into Win98 memory that can intercept a number of common program malfunctions. Before an application has a chance to terminate irrevocably, the crash protection filters can restore enough functionality to allow you to save your work and close the application properly.

In a few informal tests, I found that Network Associates BombShelter and Norton CrashGuard 3.0 (shown here) were about equally effective and had a slight edge over current versions of Quarterdeck's Crash Defender and CyberMedia's Crash Protector. All of them are useful. Running a protection TSR may mean the difference between losing a valuable document or preserving it when Microsoft Office throws a temper tantrum.

You'll find more comprehensive discussions of preventive maintenance utilities for Windows 98 in Chapter 8.

Fine-Tuning Performance from the Windows 98 Desktop

Having completed our survey of Windows 98 internal system architecture and issues related to DOS and Windows memory management, let's return to the Windows 98 desktop for a few final notes about tuning and tweaking system performance.

The Win98 Swap File

The best way to ensure high swap file performance is to make sure that the disk containing the swap file has ample free space so that the swap file size can shrink and grow as needed. Under Windows 98, the swap file can reside on a compressed DriveSpace drive, although this will slow down performance. Win98 marks the swap file as uncompressible and places it as the last file in the sector heap. (This allows room for the swap file to grow.)

The Windows 98 swap file (WIN386.SWP) is not a permanent file. By default, it will dynamically shrink and grow in response to system requests for virtual memory. Windows 98 can also use a fixed-size swap file. This may help you to eliminate disk thrashing on systems that habitually keep adjusting the swap file when you'd rather give the CPU time to applications.

Although Microsoft advises you to use the system defaults for the swap file, you can adjust the parameters used to define the swap file, and you can override its default location and size. A good strategy is to place the swap file on the drive or partition with the fastest performance (unless that disk is overused).

Microsoft warns that completely disabling virtual memory might cause the computer to stop operating properly.

To adjust the virtual memory swap file, follow these steps:

1. Choose Control Panel | System and click the Performance tab.
2. Click the Virtual Memory button to display the dialog box shown here:

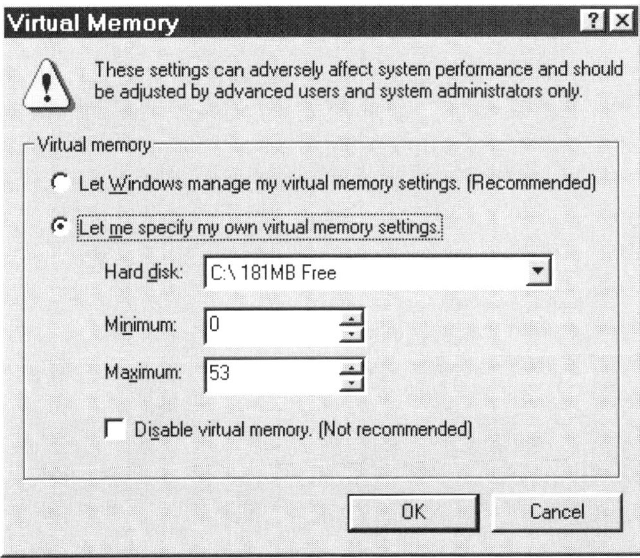

3. To specify a different partition, click Let Me Specify My Own Virtual Memory Settings. Then specify the new drive letter in the Hard Disk box or type values (in kilobytes) in the Minimum or Maximum box. Then click OK.

If the maximum swap file size in the Virtual Memory dialog box is set to correspond to the total amount of free space available on a drive, Windows 98 may expand the swap file beyond that size if more free disk space becomes available. If you want to set a fixed limit on the swap file size, make sure that the limit you specify is less than the current maximum.

Banishing the MS-DOS Compatibility Mode and Regaining 32-Bit File Access and Virtual Memory

Real-mode drivers in CONFIG.SYS that are unrecognized by Windows 98 sometimes force the system to switch from 32-bit file access and virtual memory to 16-bit MS-DOS compatibility mode. MS-DOS compatibility mode uses slower, more generic procedures for disk and file access. It is invoked by Windows 98 as a safety measure against corrupted data and system crashes. You can find out whether any components of your Windows configuration have been forced into this slower performance mode by opening the System applet in the Control Panel and inspecting the Performance tab, as shown next.

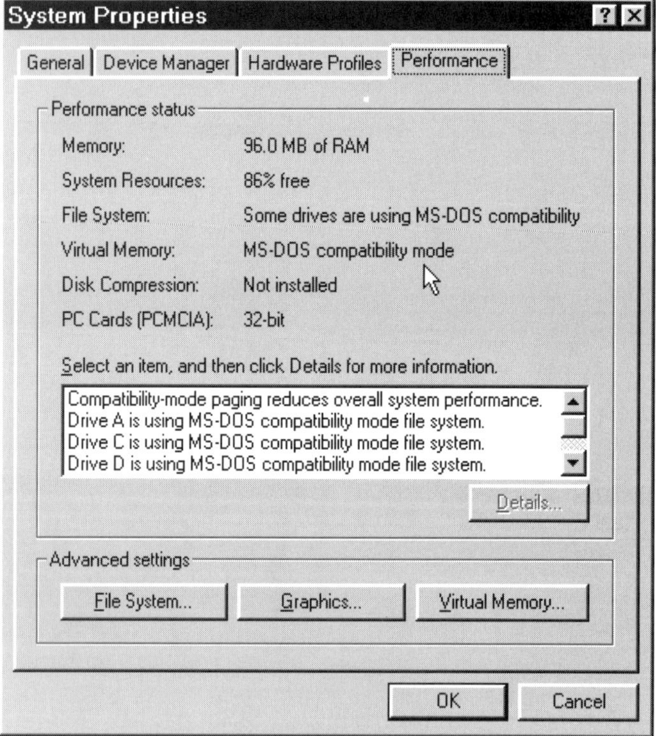

Sometimes a real-mode driver loaded in CONFIG.SYS can cause an unnecessary switch to MS-DOS compatibility mode. Windows 98 maintains a list of so-called safe drivers that will not interfere with its 32-bit operations. Examples of device drivers that may inadvertently force Windows 98 into compatibility mode are unsupported SCSI or CD-ROM drivers, real-mode PCMCIA drivers, DOS power-management utilities, network utilities, and fax drivers.

Tip *Your computer may also be forced into MS-DOS compatibility mode if Win98's file system troubleshooting properties have been toggled on. Check this by opening the Control Panel System applet, choosing the Performance Tab, clicking the File System button, and selecting the Troubleshooting tab. If there's a check mark next to Disable All 32-bit Protected-Mode Disk Drivers, try removing the check mark, clicking OK twice, and rebooting the system.*

You can find a list of known safe and unsafe real-mode device drivers in the file IOS.INI. This is an ASCII text file, located in your \WINDOWS directory.

If you discover that your computer has been forced into MS-DOS compatibility mode, consider examining your CONFIG.SYS file for driver load statements that fall into one of the categories described above. If you find a device driver loaded in CONFIG.SYS that is not included in IOS.INI, you can experiment by adding the driver to the IOS.INI "safe list." (Don't try this with disk compression drivers, VESA and PCI disk controller drivers, or DOS disk cache utilities; CD-ROM, network, and SCSI drivers are good candidates.) After you add your drivers to the safe list, Windows 98 will attempt to run them in the faster, 32-bit access mode. If the drivers are compatible, Windows 98 will shift back into its default 32-bit operating mode. If you experience unusual system quirks or problems in doing this, then remove your real-mode drivers from the IOS.INI safe list and drop back to MS-DOS compatibility mode.

Another way to attack the problem is to contact the manufacturers of hardware that forces Windows 98 into MS-DOS compatibility mode and request 32-bit drivers from them. Theoretically, they should comply. Talk to a Windows NT user sometime if you want to check out how well this really works.

MS-DOS Mode Versus Virtual DOS Sessions

Most DOS applications should be able to run under the Windows 98 interface in virtual DOS sessions. However, some ill-behaved DOS programs and games may have problems. For these applications, Windows 98 allows you to shut down the graphic interface and launch a true MS-DOS session from the desktop.

Any DOS application or shortcut to an application can be set to run in MS-DOS mode. Here is how to do it:

1. Open the application's right-click Properties menu.
2. Select the Programs tab on the Properties screen and click the Advanced button. If you place a check mark in the MS-DOS Mode option box, three additional memory options appear.

By default, when an application opens in MS-DOS mode, it uses the settings and drivers that were loaded in the original Windows 98 CONFIG.SYS file. If your application requires a unique set of device drivers or TSRs, you can create new CONFIG.SYS and AUTOEXEC.BAT files for it. When an application is set to run in MS-DOS mode, all existing Windows utilities, applications, and desktop windows are closed. The computer switches to a real-mode MS-DOS session and runs your application. If you have information stored on a RAM disk, the RAM disk is preserved.

Fine-Tuning MS-DOS Mode Startup

If you open an MS-DOS mode application with Use Current Configuration checked, a special AUTOEXEC-like batch file is run before the command prompt opens. If you have a CD-ROM drive on your system, DOSSTART.BAT (located in the WINDOWS directory), will usually attempt to load MSCDEX.EXE to activate your CD-ROM drive under DOS. This command will succeed only if a real-mode CD-ROM driver was loaded in the CONFIG.SYS file that originally started Windows 98.

If your computer does not load real-mode CD-ROM drivers in CONFIG.SYS, you'll need to follow one of the following procedures to access CDs in MS-DOS mode:

1. Reinsert real-mode SCSI, proprietary, or IDE CD-ROM drivers in the CONFIG.SYS file that usually starts Windows 98. When you configure an MS-DOS mode shortcut, check Use Current DOS Configuration.
2. Check the Specify a New MS-DOS Configuration box under Advanced Program Settings and create new CONFIG.SYS and AUTOEXEC.BAT files that load your real-mode CD-ROM drivers (see Figure 7-5).

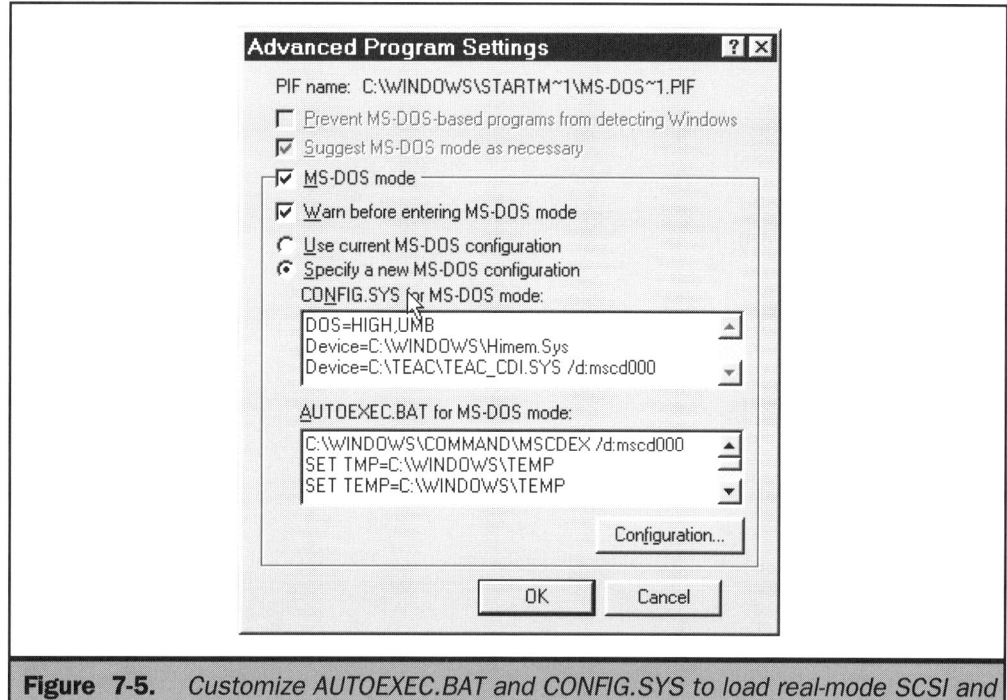

Figure 7-5. *Customize AUTOEXEC.BAT and CONFIG.SYS to load real-mode SCSI and CD-ROM drivers in an MS-DOS mode session*

If you decide to select Use Current MS-DOS Configuration, you can edit DOSSTART.BAT with a text editor to add commands (such as a new PATH statement) or delete extraneous commands.

For details on configuring and running MS-DOS applications under the Windows 98 interface, see "Running DOS Applications Under Windows 98" in Chapter 4.

Chapter 8

Migration and Maintenance

Chapter Highlights

Application compatibility

Routine maintenance strategies

Virus-prevention strategies

Backup strategies

Automating Win98 Backup

Backing up and restoring the system registry

Working with RegEdit

Backing up and migrating modular registry settings

Emergency recovery tips

The best defense is a good offense! This chapter will show you how to keep Windows 98 from failing just when you need it most.

The secret, known to all Windows professionals, is to practice preventive maintenance strategies that stop trouble before it can start. In this chapter you'll learn the most convenient ways to optimize and back up your hard disk, to preserve and restore the Windows 98 registry, and to "quick fix" modular Windows 98 component settings. You'll also find tips on removing hard-disk clutter and migrating older programs to Windows 98 as well as a strategic virus protection guide. Have you ever wanted to migrate your Win98 Dial-Up Network settings or Internet History list from one computer to another? You won't find these tricks in Microsoft's online help, but the secrets are revealed here.

Microsoft gave Windows 98 the ability to run some important preventive maintenance tasks automatically—but you should know that the operating system may not run forever for you on autopilot. The state of the art in Windows 98 doesn't permit all system conflicts to fix themselves by magic (although its wizards are more powerful than the old Windows 95 soothsayers). If something goes wrong in Windows 98, intelligent user input may be required to put things back exactly the way you want them.

Application Compatibility

Will your Windows 95, Windows 3.1, and DOS applications run better under Windows 98, suffer performance problems, or not run at all? The quick answer is that most of your productivity applications should run under Windows 98 with little or no difficulty. If Windows 98 has enough memory and hard-disk space, you should see no performance degradation. Utility programs will be more problematic.

Some applications, tweaked for performance under Windows 3.1, may show minor display glitches in menus under Windows 98. Others may produce general protection faults when you invoke certain features. A small number of Windows 3.1 productivity applications are completely incompatible with Windows 98.

Tip *You can find some basic information about migrating and using older programs under Windows 98 in a file called PROGRAM.TXT, located in your \WINDOWS directory.*

Microsoft also maintains a software compatibility report for more than 2,000 Windows 3.x and DOS applications (see Figure 8-1). The list is part of the Microsoft Support Assistant package for Windows 95. You can download it from CompuServe or from the World Wide Web at http://support/microsoft.com/download/support/mslfiles/assist.exe. Running ASSIST.EXE unpacks and installs the WIN95APP.HLP file that contains the application compatibility database.

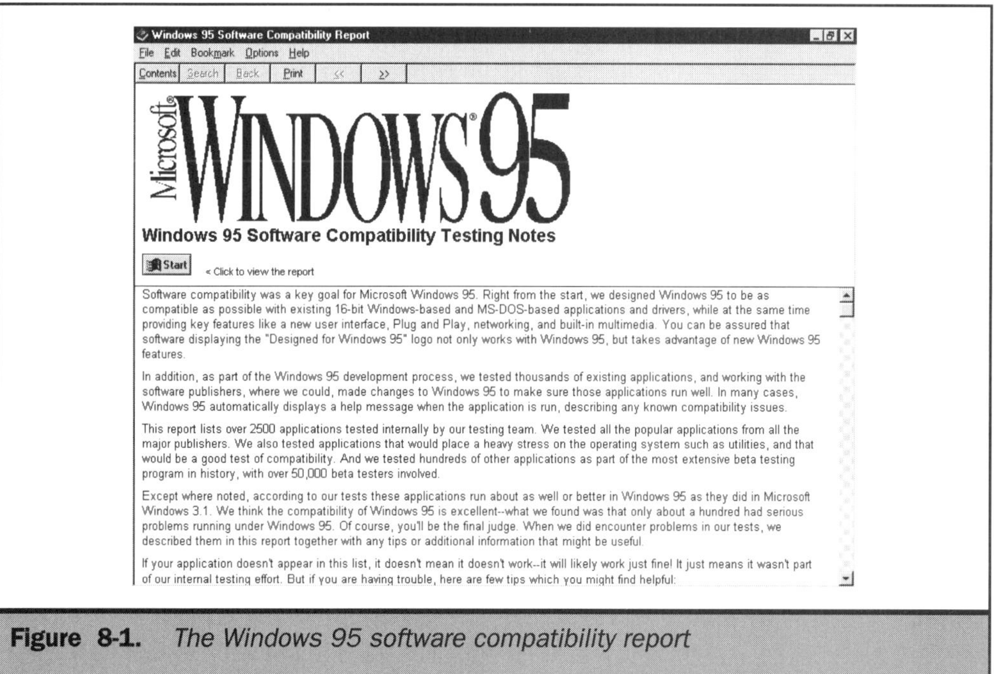

Figure 8-1. *The Windows 95 software compatibility report*

Although this database was prepared for Windows 95, it is also useful for determining Windows 98 compatibility with DOS and Windows 3.1 programs. The list is compiled in the standard Windows Help format. To inspect the database under Windows 95 or Windows 98, click the Start button and open the WIN95APP.HLP file on the Run menu by entering its name and clicking OK. (If you browse for the file from the Run box, set the Browse option to display all files.) Some of the entries in this compatibility database contain notes on how to fix specific application problems.

The good news is that you probably won't have to worry about most older programs. In fact, you may find that Windows 98 enhances their appearance or productivity features. If you've installed Windows Messaging Services, other applications from Microsoft gain two new options on the File menu: Send and Routing Slip. These options are equivalent to what you would see under Windows 3.1 or Windows for Workgroups if you installed Microsoft Mail.

General Migration Strategies

Perhaps the most visible difference between Windows 3.x and Windows 95/98 applications is support for long filenames. Older applications not written for the 32-bit API do not recognize these long filenames. Instead, they identify files by their conventional 8.3 letter DOS filenames. If you don't need to save data files with long filenames, this isn't a critical limitation. However, long filenames may occasionally cause problems when they are linked to automated procedures. When a data file reaches your hard disk, it may be pre-associated with a Windows 3.x program as a file viewer. For instance, Microsoft Excel 5 or Word 6.0 may attempt to automatically load a file you've downloaded from the Internet, but the long filename isn't recognized. As a result, the load process is aborted with an error message.

If you have an older version of Microsoft Office, one way to get around this problem is to change the default association for files with the .RTF or .DOC extension from Word 6.0 to WordPad. (See Chapter 4 for details on how to do this.) Another solution is to use a third-party utility that adds the capability to recognize long filenames to Windows 3.x programs. (One such shareware program, File Ex, is available at http://www.cottonwoodsw.com.) Ultimately, the best solution is to upgrade to Windows 98 versions of programs that you use frequently to display and manipulate common data formats.

If you installed Windows 98 as an upgrade over a previous version of Windows, your existing applications were automatically migrated to the new operating system. Setting the issue of long filenames aside, most problems you're likely to encounter will stem from the individual idiosyncrasies of a small group of programs.

Tips for Resolving Common Conflicts

If you experience problems with Win 3.x applications after an upgrade installation, read the various .TXT files placed in your Windows directory (especially PROGRAM.TXT). Open these files in Notepad or WordPad and try performing a text search for your problem application's name (or use the Find | Files or Folders command on the Start menu and enter ***.TXT** in the Named box, **C:\WINDOWS** in the Look In box, and the name of your application in the Containing Text box).

MAKING WINDOWS 3.X APPLICATIONS MORE COMPATIBLE WITH MKCOMPAT If you're having problems opening Windows 3.x applications under Windows 98 or printing and saving files, an undocumented utility called MKCOMPAT may provide some relief. Located in the \WINDOWS\SYSTEM directory, this applet can intercept system calls to Windows 3.x programs, removing incompatibilities with the Windows 98 operating system.

To open MKCOMPAT, enter its name in the Run box on the Start menu. You can modify the performance of a Windows 3.x program by selecting it in the MKCOMPAT File | Choose a Program dialog box. (You can also specify the Windows 3.x application to be modified on the command line when you open MKCOMPAT. For example, you might enter **Run MKCOMPAT C:\WP\WPWIN.EXE**.)

This utility provides five basic settings: filters that modify the reported Windows version number, menu controls, print spooling, and internal memory allocation. If your Windows 3.x program crashes unexpectedly, develops display problems, or refuses to print, these filters may cure the problem. (Filter options that don't apply to your program may not appear.)

MKCOMPAT also offers a set of Advanced Options filters. You can display them by choosing File | Advanced Options from the MKCOMPAT pull-down menu, as shown in Figure 8-2. The advanced filters can watchdog a program's printing, font

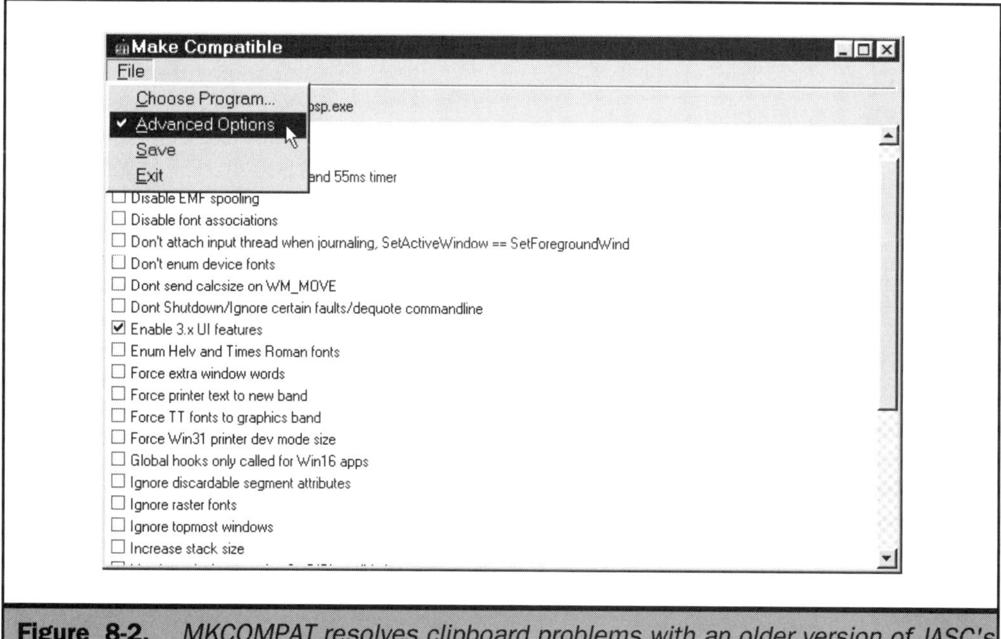

Figure 8-2. *MKCOMPAT resolves clipboard problems with an older version of JASC's Paintshop Pro*

handling, save options, screen display, and other internal functions to normalize performance under Windows 98. To activate program changes, check the options you want and choose File | Save to write them to the system registry.

MORE TIPS FOR RESOLVING PROGRAM COMPATIBILITY PROBLEMS If you can't identify or resolve your application's problem, you may want to try one of the following strategies:

- Back up your data files and make backups of Win98's WIN.INI and SYSTEM.INI files. Delete the problem application from your hard disk and remove references to it from the Start menu. Reinstall the program from your original source disks. Note that your program may attempt to replace some Windows 98 drivers and dynamic link libraries (DLLs) with older versions. In general, don't allow this to happen—if you're offered a choice, keep your existing Win98 drivers. Windows 98 has the ability to detect driver substitution and restore files from the SYSBACKUP directory. (These files can be restored with the System File Checker and Version Conflict Manager utilities, which are part of the Win98 System Information tools. See the "System Information" section in Chapter 6 for details.)
- If your problem application is vital to you and reinstalling it doesn't cure performance problems, consider reinstalling the entire Windows 98 operating system in a clean directory. An upgrade over Windows 3.1 can carry over many virtual driver extensions (VXDs), configuration settings, and DLLs from third-party vendors. These may conflict with one another, causing general protection faults (GPFs) and system crashes. If you experience apparently unrelated performance problems with Windows 98, a clean installation may be your best option. If you decide to take this course, you will have to reinstall all of your third-party applications from their source media or use a special third-party package such as Quarterdeck's Clean Sweep Deluxe. Clean Sweep Deluxe can take snapshots of an existing Windows configuration and transfer application information to a new, clean installation. (See Chapter 2 for more details on migrating Windows 3.1 or Windows 95 system configurations to Windows 98.)

A small number of Windows 3.x programs will not install properly under Windows 98, but they can be migrated from an existing Windows 3.x configuration. The Microsoft WIN95APP.HLP database flags some programs that have this problem.

Resolving DOS Application Problems

If a DOS program doesn't work properly under Windows 98, try creating a shortcut for it instead of launching it from a command prompt. Choose File | New in My Computer or open the Start menu, choose Settings | Taskbar, and click the Add button on the Start Menu tab. (See Chapter 4 for more information on adding new programs and creating shortcuts.) Windows 98 contains a special migration database of DOS applications and program settings. If the filename for your application is recognized, a shortcut may be created that resolves the performance problem.

Some DOS programs (mostly disk utilities, multimedia applications, and games) will not run in ordinary Win98 DOS sessions. For these programs, you may have to restart the system in MS-DOS mode or create custom CONFIG.SYS and AUTOEXEC.BAT files. See "DOS Properties and Configuration Settings" in Chapter 4 for detailed information on how to do this and for other tips on DOS program configuration.

Working with Windows 3.x Applications

Windows 98 migration issues are most likely to involve utility software: disk utilities, antivirus packages, backup programs, and Windows command shells. Before discussing these, here are a few quick notes concerning older versions of some popular productivity programs.

Note *The easiest cure for problems such as the ones described here is to upgrade to a current version of the application. This "Ace bandage" may help when an application upgrade is not an immediately viable option.*

Older Versions of Microsoft Office

You may encounter difficulty installing the 16-bit Microsoft Office 4.3 suite or the original Microsoft Office 95, Standard Edition, package under Windows 98.

The Office 4.3 installation program may complain that it can't find SHARE.EXE, a DOS utility that managed file sharing under Windows 3.x. If you see this message, you can resolve the problem by choosing another small DOS utility, such as DOSEDIT.EXE, temporarily renaming it as **SHARE.EXE**, and inserting a command to load the "new" SHARE.EXE in your AUTOEXEC.BAT file. Reboot the computer and try the Office 4.3 installation again. Once the installation has been completed, you can remove the dummy SHARE.EXE from AUTOEXEC.BAT.

If you own the original version of Microsoft Office 95, Standard Edition, it may refuse to install on a FAT32 disk partition under Windows 98. To resolve this problem, you can obtain a patch at Microsoft's Web site or upgrade to the Microsoft Office 95 Professional Edition or Office 97.

WordPerfect and WordPerfect Presentations

If you use WordPerfect 6.0 or 6.0a for Windows, you may have difficulty pasting in text or graphics from 32-bit Win98 applications (including MS Paint and WordPad). The quick fix for this is to perform an interim copy-and-paste operation from the 32-bit application to a compatible 16-bit program that can accept the object (possibly

Windows Write from Windows 3.x). Then paste from there into WordPerfect. The WordPerfect 6.0 tutorial also stalls under Windows 98. In WordPerfect 6.1, the Introductory Tutorial (Coach) may not work correctly.

WordPerfect Presentations 2.0 for Windows will not install correctly under Windows 98. However, it can be migrated from an existing Windows 3.1 configuration.

Lotus Ami Pro and Notes

Ami Pro 3.01, a Windows word processor, has a tutorial that does not run correctly under Windows 98. The problem can be corrected by setting the Windows 98 taskbar to AutoHide. (Right-click the taskbar and select Properties. Then place a check mark in the AutoHide box.)

Older versions of Lotus Notes cannot be installed from a network computer unless a drive letter is mapped as follows:

1. Click the Start button, select Programs, and open Windows Explorer.
2. On the Tools menu, choose Map Network Drive.
3. In the Path box, type the path to the network server and click OK.
4. Select the drive you just mapped and find the Notes setup program.

When you run Lotus Notes Windows Client 3.2, workstations running the NetBIOS interface over IPX and NetBEUI protocol stacks must configure the port for NetBIOS using the unit number that corresponds to the correct protocol. The default number for the first NetBIOS protocol is set to zero. Any additional NetBIOS interface will start at port 7 through 1. It's likely that NetBIOS will be unit number 7 or 6 if NetBEUI is using zero. To make changes in the Notes Windows client, choose Tools | Setup and select Ports.

Aldus PageMaker

Aldus PageMaker 5.0 or 6.0 may refuse to start under Windows 98 if you've installed Novell network support and are not currently logged onto the network. This is a copy-protection problem inherent in this version of PageMaker. To make the "Unable to access network" error message go away, on an unconnected workstation, either log onto the network or open the Control Panel | Network applet to remove the IPX protocol from the component list. (This problem apparently does not surface in Microsoft Network configurations using TCP/IP or NetBEUI protocols.)

Quark Xpress

Quark Xpress 3.31 has the same network problem that PageMaker has. Quark Xpress versions 3.30 and earlier are totally incompatible with Windows 98. A patch can be obtained from Quark to update version 3.30 to version 3.31, which will run under Windows 98.

Other Applications

Some Windows 3.x games and multimedia programs may have problems installing under Windows 98. If you can't get a new version, some of these packages can be migrated from an existing Windows 3.x configuration. Before upgrading to Windows 98, you may want to consult the application vendor or refer to the Microsoft software compatibility report referred to earlier in this chapter.

Telecommunications applications written for DOS and Windows 3.x maintain modem and communication profiles independent of the modem settings in the Windows 98 Control Panel.

Working with Windows 3.x Utility Software

The best solution for working with Windows 3.x or Windows 95 file managers, backup programs, and antivirus utilities is to upgrade to versions specifically written for Windows 98. The most obvious problem in working with Windows 3.x file management and backup programs is their lack of support for long filenames. Using these older utilities can wipe out any long filenames you've created under Windows 98.

Even if you don't like Win98's built-in Windows Explorer, it makes little sense to continue using a Windows 3.x file manager. There are many freeware and shareware file management shells available for Windows 98. (You can find quite a few at http://www.winfiles.com in the Shareware/File Managers section.) For a discussion of stopgap fixes for DOS and Windows 3.x backup programs, see "Backup Strategies" later in this chapter.

The case for using older disk-maintenance and antivirus utilities is very weak. In general, you should remove these applications from your computer, *especially if your hard disk uses the new FAT32 file system*. The next section discusses system and disk maintenance strategies for Windows 98. You'll find a section later in this chapter devoted to virus-prevention strategies.

Routine Maintenance Strategies

The best way to avoid Windows 98 trouble is to use the preventive maintenance options built into the operating system. Some of these options must be initiated by the user, but Windows 98 also does some housekeeping without your lifting a finger. Out of the box, it performs periodic system registry backups, scans the hard disk on shutdown failure, and issues low-disk-space warnings. It's easy to add other routine maintenance tasks to the list: regularly scheduled disk integrity checks, disk optimization, and purging of temporary files.

The Windows 98 Maintenance Wizard (from the Start menu, choose Accessories | System Tools | Maintenance Wizard) allows you to schedule these additional chores at any convenient time. The Maintenance Wizard performs its magic by invoking the ScanDisk, Defrag, and CleanMgr applets through the Windows 98 Task Scheduler.

Task Scheduler is a useful system applet for automating user-defined maintenance tasks. For instance, you can make Task Scheduler pop up personal reminder notes and use it to schedule additional system registry backups, run third-party virus checkers, or (with a little ingenuity) schedule full system or incremental disk backups. You'll find more information about working with Task Manager to schedule these chores throughout this chapter.

After you open the Maintenance Wizard and schedule the first tuneup, a dialog box appears asking whether you want to perform maintenance now or change settings. To edit an existing maintenance schedule, choose Change My Maintenance Settings and click OK to open the Express/Custom options screen.

More About Hard Disk Tuning

It's generally a good idea to perform ScanDisk integrity checks and defragment your hard disk at least once a week. To maximize the benefits of disk optimization, you should select the Defrag Rearrange Program Files option. This option is selected by default when you run the Maintenance Wizard. To confirm it, select Custom on the What Do You Want to Do? Maintenance Wizard screen; click Next until you get to the Speed Up Programs screen, and then click the Settings button.

When Disk Defragmenter optimizes the program order on your hard disk, it takes considerable time to finish. The tuneup may take 4 to 6 hours the first time you rearrange a loaded 2GB disk partition. Subsequent disk tuneups will run much faster if you schedule them at regular intervals.

The benefit of Defrag's Rearrange Program Files option is most noticeable when Windows 98 is installed on a FAT32 disk partition of 260MB to 8GB. The program optimization exploits the 4K file cluster size on these partitions to significantly speed the loading of your most frequently accessed applications. You may find that programs such as Microsoft Word or Excel pop up twice as fast on an optimized disk. Your Start menu and Windows Explorer will also pop up faster.

Getting the Most from Disk Defragmenter

The newest third-party disk optimizers (Norton Utilities 3.0 Speed Disk and Nuts & Bolts 1.5 Disk Tune) can duplicate the Defrag Rearrange Program Files option. These utilities read the Microsoft logs stored in the \WINDOWS\APPLOG directory to achieve the most advantageous file placement on your disk. (Only the most recently updated versions of these utility suites offer this feature.) Some earlier third-party disk optimizers are compatible with Windows 98, but if you use them, they will undo all the benefits of the Rearrange Program Files option.

Some third-party disk optimizers have tuning options that Windows 98 Defrag lacks. These programs can defragment the Windows 98 swap file and let you specify certain file directories or programs to place at the beginning or end of the hard disk.

Depending on the structure of your hard disk (FAT16 versus FAT32) and on your ordinary computing habits, these third-party disk optimizers may be more effective than Win98's built-in Maintenance Wizard.

SWAP FILE FRAGMENTATION If you use your computer over a long period of time without regular disk optimization, the Windows 98 swap file becomes fragmented: broken into little pieces throughout the partition. A fragmented swap file can slow down system performance just as much as poorly placed program and system files. You can determine whether the swap file on your hard disk is clustered consecutively or fragmented by starting Win98 Disk Defragmenter (from the Start menu, choose Programs | Accessories | System Tools | Disk Defragmenter). Select your Windows 98 boot drive (usually drive C) and click OK. Click the Show Details button in the Defrag window and then click the Legend button on the Details (Defragmenting Drive) screen. Wait until the Details screen reports that 10 percent of the disk has been optimized (see the bottom of the window) or the first few squares of the Details screen have been filled in blue (see Figure 8-3); then click the Pause button.

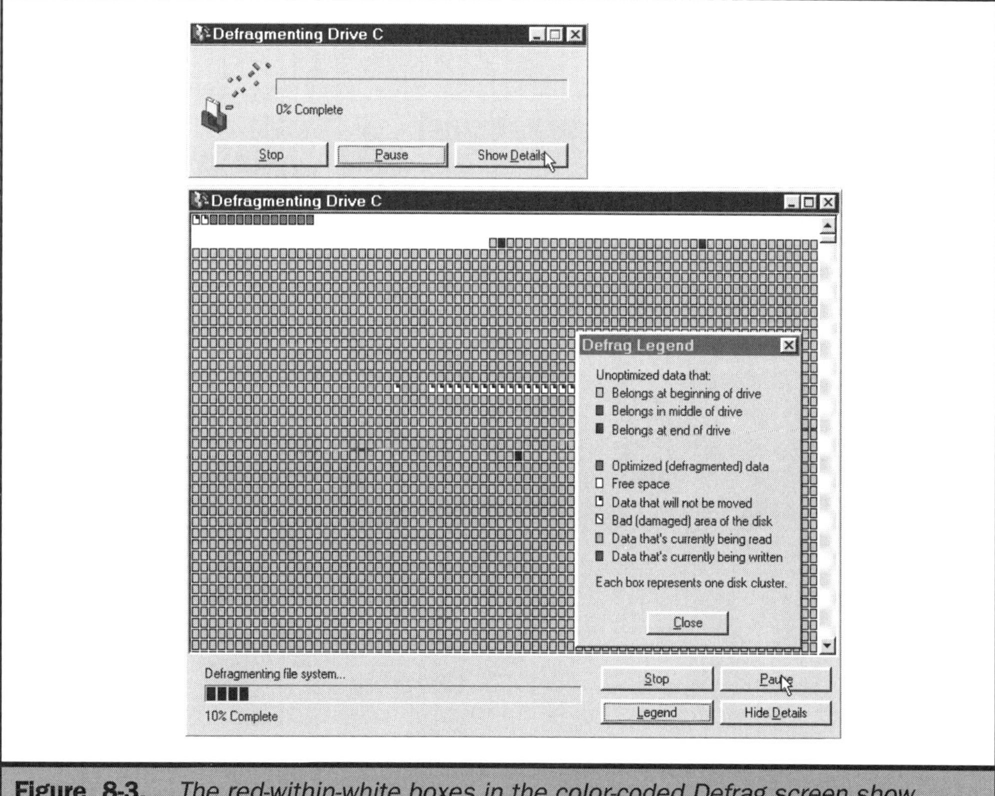

Figure 8-3. *The red-within-white boxes in the color-coded Defrag screen show the location and fragmentation of Windows system files, including the swap file*

You should also see a few red markers within white squares near the upper-left corner of your screen. If you don't see any markers, click the Resume button and let the optimization process run a little longer; then click Pause again when you see some red-in-white squares. The Defrag Legend window reports these as data that will not be moved.

You should see a few "data that will not be moved" squares near the beginning of the disk; these represent operating system kernel files. The Windows 98 swap file is also indicated with this symbol. Page through the paused Details screen (you can use the PAGEUP and PAGEDOWN keys) and look for clusters of "data that will not be moved." The largest clusters of these squares represent the Windows 98 swap file.

- If you see one big cluster of red-in-white squares near the end of the drive, your swap file is relatively unfragmented (see Figure 8-4).
- If you see a series of red-in-white clusters (each more than two rows), your swap file is fragmented throughout the partition.

The Defrag Legend can also provide a rough sketch of how much optimizing must be done to complete the Rearrange Program Files ordering. Light green squares represent files that will load best at the beginning of the disk, darker green squares

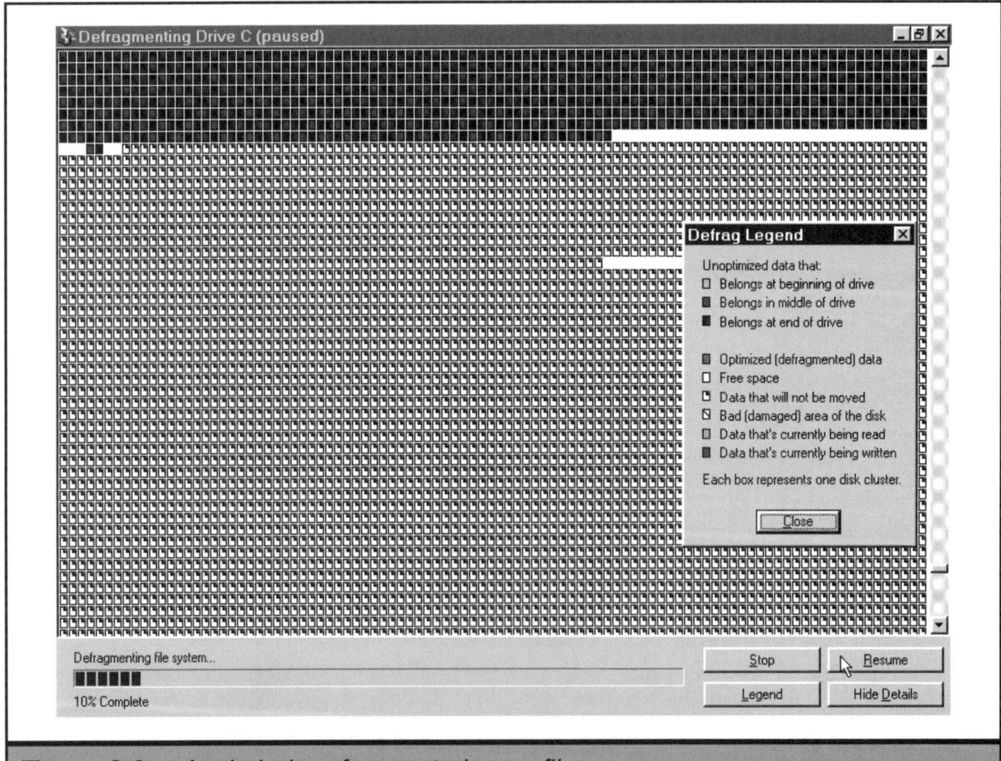

Figure 8-4. *A relatively unfragmented swap file*

show files that belong in the middle of the disk, and green-black squares represent files that belong near the end of the disk.

MANUALLY DEFRAGGING THE SWAP FILE Win 98's Maintenance Wizard leaves a fragmented swap file in place, working around it to rearrange other system files and programs. Over the long run this can be detrimental to system performance. If you have more than one disk partition, here's how you can defragment the swap file:

1. Open the Control Panel | System applet, choose the Performance tab, and click the Virtual Memory button.
2. Choose Let Me Specify My Own Virtual Memory Settings in the Virtual Memory window and select a different disk partition to contain the swap file. (If you own an on-the-fly partitioning utility such as PowerQuest's Partition Magic, you can create a temporary new partition without reformatting your hard disk.) Click OK twice to close the dialog box and allow your computer to reboot.
3. With the swap file resident on the alternate disk partition, run the Maintenance Wizard (or start Disk Defragmenter directly) and optimize your Windows 98 boot drive.

After the Windows 98 boot drive has been optimized, you can run the Control Panel | System applet again to restore the swap file to its original location.

Some users prefer to leave the Windows 98 swap file in a separate, dedicated partition. This permanently eliminates the possibility that it will subsequently become fragmented. Best results are achieved when the swap file partition is located near the front of a second physical drive, but you can also create a dedicated partition at the end of a single disk.

To adjust the way Windows 98 runs the ScanDisk integrity check, select the Custom option in the Maintenance Wizard and click the Settings button on the Scan Hard Disk for Errors screen (shown here).

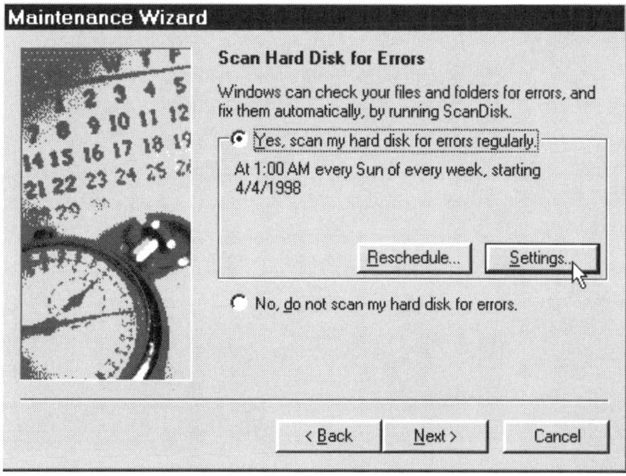

You can then click the Options or the Advanced button on the Scheduled Settings for ScanDisk screen to change the way your disk is examined. For instance, you can specify whether lost file fragments are deleted or converted to files, as shown here. (For more information about Advanced ScanDisk options, see the "ScanDisk" section in Chapter 6.)

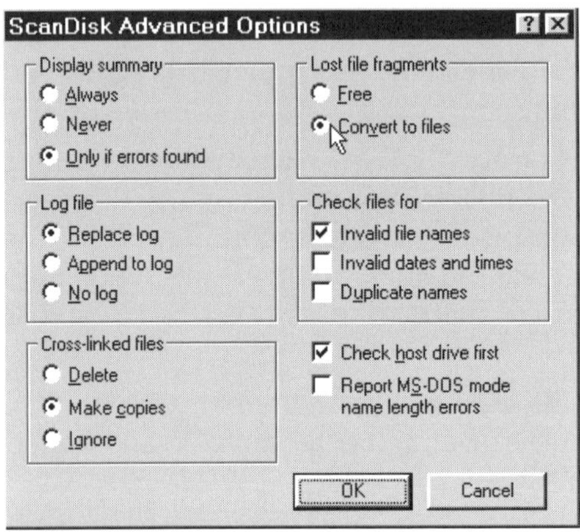

Using ScanDisk and Disk Cleanup

Your schedule for disk cleanup should depend on your personal computing style. Some users may want to retain an accumulated browser history of Internet sites or maintain \TEMP directories to hold files for later disposition.

To adjust the way that Disk Cleanup removes files from your hard disk, choose the Custom option in the Maintenance Wizard. Select Speed Up Programs and Scan Hard Disk for Errors and then click the Settings button on the Delete Unnecessary Files screen (shown here).

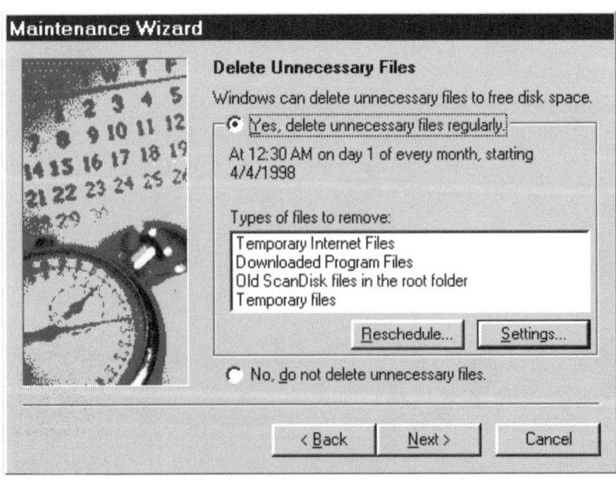

On the next screen, you can select or deselect purge file categories. For instance, you might decide to remove temporary setup files and clean the Recycle Bin but retain downloaded program files and temporary Internet files.

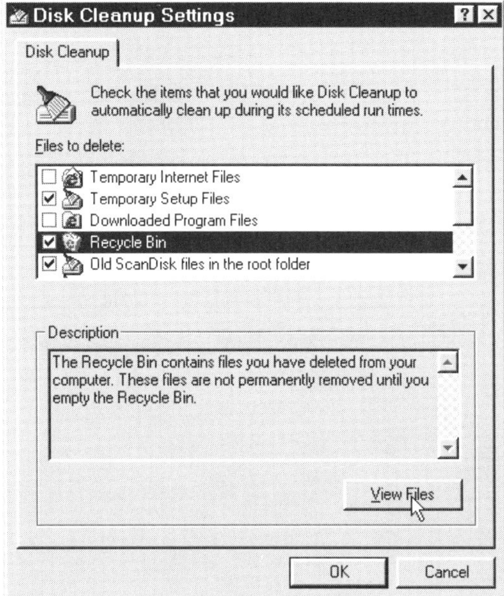

Using Microsoft Plus! 98 Extensions

If you have purchased and installed Microsoft's Plus! 98 supplement for Windows 98, three additional options are added to the Maintenance Wizard menu: you can schedule virus scans with the bundled McAfee VirusScan applet, purge nonworking shortcuts from the Start menu, and extend the functionality of the Disk Cleanup Wizard.

The added Plus! 98 Clean Up Your Start Menu screen allows the Maintenance Wizard to automatically remove broken program shortcuts and empty folders from the Start menu.

The added Plus! 98 Scan for Viruses screen allows you to schedule regular virus scans of your hard disk. You can customize the partitions or directories that will be scanned through the VirusScan Configuration utility, located by choosing Programs from the Start menu and then choosing Microsoft Plus! 98 | McAfee VirusScan. (Other third-party antivirus programs are not automatically integrated into the Maintenance Wizard like Plus! 98, but under certain conditions they can be manually added to a list of Task Manager maintenance chores. See "Scheduling Custom Maintenance Tasks," later in this chapter, for details.)

The Plus! 98 Delete Non-Critical Files option extends the Win98 Maintenance Wizard's ability to remove unwanted hard disk files. This module, licensed from CyberMedia's First Aid 98 suite, can be accessed by clicking the Settings button on the

Maintenance Wizard's Delete Unnecessary Files screen and then selecting Non-Critical Files on the Disk Cleanup tab. Unlike the other Disk Cleanup modules, this one does not automatically remove files from your hard disk. Instead, when the Maintenance Wizard runs the tuneup, the Cybermedia File Cleaner appears on the desktop. You can use it to select and delete, copy, or move files in any of the various "unnecessary" categories (see Figure 8-5).

IS PLUS! 98 USEFUL? The Plus! 98 antivirus and file removal features described in the preceding paragraphs are similar to those available in many other third-party packages, but they are less full-featured than modules included in other utility suites. If you buy Plus! 98 to take advantage of its entertainment features (an assortment of multimedia games), the system maintenance utilities are an added bonus. If you're

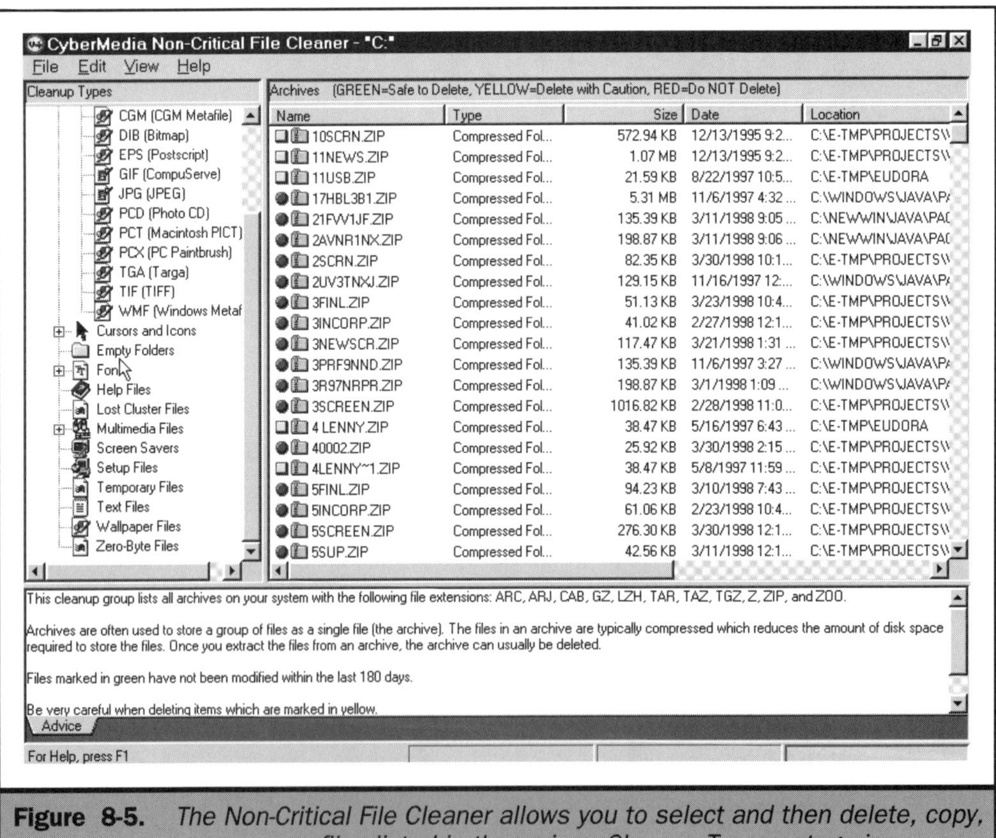

Figure 8-5. *The Non-Critical File Cleaner allows you to select and then delete, copy, or move any files listed in the various Cleanup Types categories*

looking specifically for an antivirus program or an uninstall utility, you'll get more functionality for your dollar by purchasing a dedicated package.

Scheduling Custom Maintenance Tasks

The Windows 98 Task Manager can help you perform a variety of system maintenance chores in addition to those performed by the preconfigured options available in the Maintenance Wizard. For instance, you may want to complement the occasional backups and integrity checks that Windows 98 runs on the system registry. This precaution can protect your Internet Explorer Web browsing history. It also preserves the latest system configuration if you frequently add and remove applications. Step through the following procedure to learn how to work with the Task Manager. When you're finished, you can remove the task from the Scheduled Tasks folder if you decide you don't want additional registry checks.

Here's how to schedule periodic registry checks and backups:

1. Open the Scheduled Tasks folder (you can access it through My Computer or by choosing Programs from the Start menu and then choosing Accessories | System Tools | Scheduled Tasks). Click the Add Scheduled Tasks button and then click Next to continue.
2. Click the Browse button on the next screen of the Scheduled Task Wizard and select SCANREGW.EXE in the \WINDOWS directory.
3. Enter a name for this task (for instance, **Registry Backup**). Then indicate when you want the task to run (for example, select Daily to perform a registry integrity check once a day).
4. On the next screen, set any additional scheduling options as shown here:

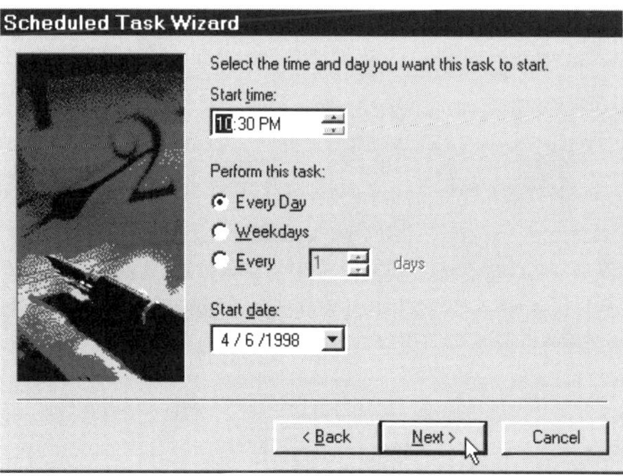

5. If the schedule you've configured suits your needs, click the Finish button to add this task to the Scheduled Tasks folder.

You can fine-tune the task by selecting Open Advanced Properties For This Task When I Click Finish. A three-tabbed window appears when you click the Finish button. If your scheduled application supports command-line options, you can add them in the Run field on the Task tab. Advanced time options are available on the Schedule tab. You can click the Advanced button to specify a start date and end date for the task or to repeat the task at regularly scheduled intervals as long as your computer is on. The Settings tab allows you to set a stop time for the task or make it conditional on the state of your computer.

To test the ScanReg task you've created, right-click it in the Scheduled Tasks folder and choose the Run option. The Windows Registry Checker parses the system registry for errors and offers to create an additional backup. Note that this task requires user input: you need to answer yes or no to the Backup prompt to complete the task.

Scheduling Backups Without User Intervention

Maintenance applications that run without requesting keyboard input can be automated more completely. Some programs support command-line options to bypass user prompts. One example is the Image disk recovery utility included in Symantec's Norton Utilities versions 2 and 3. This utility preserves the FAT and directory table information of a disk partition to repair corruption and make it easier to reclaim erased files.

If you own Norton Utilities, you can use the Task Manager to schedule regular Image backups without user intervention. (This may be particularly useful if you leave your computer on for prolonged periods of time and other people have access to it.)

1. Open the Scheduled Tasks folder and choose Add Scheduled Task.
2. Click Next and select Image in the Scheduled Task application list.
3. Specify when you want to perform the task. (If you select the Daily option, you can also specify the time of day on the next configuration screen.)
4. Select the Open Advanced Properties box and then click the Finish button.
5. Add the following parameters to the command line in the Run field on the Task tab: **IMAGE32 *d:* /q**, where *d:* is the drive you want to record a snapshot of, as shown next. Then click OK to complete the task. (More than one drive can be imaged; for instance, both drives C and D.)

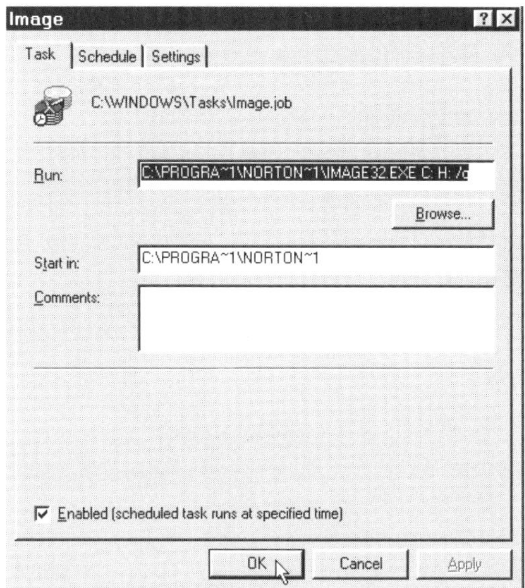

Scheduling a Pop-Up Reminder

Although the Task Manager has no direct support for pop-up screen alerts, you can use Notepad to simulate that feature.

1. Open Notepad and compose the reminder note you want to display (for example, enter **Remember, the report folders have to be backed up today!**).
2. Save the reminder to a Memos folder and close Notepad.
3. Open the Scheduled Tasks folder.
4. Open Windows Explorer to the Memos folder that contains your reminders. Drag the appropriate text file out of the Memos folder and create a shortcut in the Scheduled Tasks folder.
5. To schedule your pop-up reminder, right-click the Text Memo task in the Scheduled Tasks folder and select Properties. Go to the Schedule tab to set the date and time when the message will appear.

Scheduling a DOS Batch File Task

In addition to running programs or opening documents, the Task Manager can execute DOS batch files. This feature can come in handy for very basic data backups. For instance, you can create a procedure to periodically copy the contents of the My

Documents folder to a shared network drive. Here's how to periodically archive the contents My Documents to a personal directory on a Network server:

1. Assume that a network resource called \\SERVER\MYFILES is mapped at login to drive E on your local computer. Open a text editor (such as Notepad) and create a DOS batch file similar to the following:

   ```
   QUIKBAK.BAT
   XCOPY"C:\My Documents\*.*" E: /M
   ```

   Appending the /M parameter to the XCOPY command incrementally copies new or changed files and ignores previously copied files that haven't been touched.

2. Drag a- copy of QUIKBAK.BAT into the Scheduled Tasks folder. After the task shortcut appears in the folder, right-click and choose Properties to set a schedule.

Automating Third-Party Applications with Macros

If you're a sophisticated user, you may have noticed an inherent limitation in the Windows 98 Task Manager: it can't transmit startup instructions to complex applications. The Win98 Maintenance Wizard and Plus! 98, discussed earlier, can open and run a few built-in Win98 utilities—but what if you want to use a virus checker or backup program that the Maintenance Wizard doesn't support? Can the Task Manager do more than open such a program to its initial screen?

The answer is yes if you use a helper applet that passes startup macros to applications. A number of commercial and shareware programs can do this, some replacing Task Manager with a more sophisticated set of scheduling options. MacroMagic and Automate, available from Unisyn, Inc. (http://www.unisyn.com), are two fine shareware programs that provide industrial-strength automation.

But you don't need to spend any money if you have DOS batch-level programming skills. Script is a simple freeware applet authored by Gary Rumble that you can use to create startup macros for most Windows applications. You can download Script at http://ourworld.compuserve.com/homepages/grumble/windows.htm (or select from a wide variety of other Windows scripting utilities at http://www.winfiles.com/apps/98/auto.html).

Script uses commands embedded in an ASCII text file to open any application and transmit appropriate startup instructions. Here's a practical example that can be used in conjunction with the Win98 Task Manager and Dr. Solomon's Antivirus 7.71, a good virus checker that does not include a dedicated scheduling utility:

1. Open Notepad (or another text editor) and create the following ASCII script file in the same folder that contains the SCRIPT.EXE macro utility:

   SOL.SCR

```
start,c:\\drsol\\wtool95.exedelay, 100
while,FindVirus
wait,Dr Solomon's Anti-Virus,
send,Dr Solomon's Anti-Virus,\n
wait,FindVirus Exit
send,FindVirus Exit,\n
delay, 100
send,FindVirus,\n
send,Dr Solomon's Anti-Virus,%f \n
:exit
```

2. Open the Win98 Scheduled Tasks Folder and click the Add Scheduled Task button. Click Next and then click the Browse button. Go to the folder that contains SCRIPT.EXE and select it as your scheduled task.
3. Specify a name and schedule for the task, select Open Advanced Properties for This Task, and then click Finish.
4. Add the ASCII script you've created to the command line in the Run field of the Task tab. For example, enter **C:\SCRIPT\SCRIPT.EXE SOL.SCR**.
5. Click OK to add the job to the Scheduled Tasks window.

The Dr. Solomon Antivirus scanner will now run at the time you've specified and check for viruses on drive C. If no viruses are found, the program will exit upon completion. If viruses are detected, the script will pause, and you'll see a screen prompting you to take action.

Some virus checkers support additional preset options. They can be opened to scan designated folders or drives or to automatically clean infected files. The SCRIPT.EXE macro language permits you to choose more options by manipulating the cursor and sending specific commands to any open screen window.

Virus-Prevention Strategies

A PC virus is a bit of rogue program code designed to copy itself into memory and onto your hard disk. Once active in memory, virus code may interfere with your operating system, corrupt your program and data files, or simply post intrusive messages on the screen. Virus code usually enters your system in one of two ways: it may be read by your operating system at boot time, or it may load itself into memory along with a commonly run system file, application, or document.

As people find new ways to spread computer viruses, antivirus software packages must evolve to meet the challenge. Word and Excel macro viruses can now embed themselves in documents and spreadsheets. When infected documents are sent as e-mail attachments, viruses proliferate over the Internet. You may need to scan your hard disk more than occasionally to avert virus disasters. Mopping up infected documents—locking the hen house after the fox has already gotten in—can be a time-consuming, frustrating exercise. A good antivirus product for Windows 98 needs real-time intercept features as well as the capacity to run basic disk scans. The watchdog utilities in current antivirus packages can nail a virus before it has a chance to find a home on your hard disk.

How Do Computer Viruses Spread? How Do I Know I Have One?

Your computer can catch a virus when you boot from an infected floppy disk, execute an infected program, or open an infected document. Viruses spread when users share infected files and diskettes or transmit infected documents as e-mail attachments (over company LANs and the Internet). "Rent-a-computer" copy shops are notorious carriers of all kinds of viruses. Although the better shops may install antivirus protection to deal with the problem, the sheer traffic of users still makes these places hotbeds of potential infection.

Many viruses found "in the wild" are not deliberately programmed to erase files on your hard disk or to corrupt file directories, but they can be unintentionally destructive. For instance, the author of the Stoned virus intended only that it would make a PC display the messages "Your PC is Stoned" and "Legalize Marijuana" every eighth time the system booted. This author anticipated that his code would be distributed only on 360K low-density diskettes. When the Stoned virus found its way to higher-capacity floppies, it destroyed their boot sectors, ruining all files on the diskette.

When a file virus is loaded into computer memory, it searches the hard disk for other program files to infect. Some viruses try to go for broke, infecting as many files as they can in a short time. Other viruses are slow infectors; by contaminating files only at regulated intervals over a longer period of time, they hope to escape immediate detection. Slow infectors try to attach themselves to system files that would also be modified in the ordinary use of your computer. (Some applications update themselves automatically to include new configuration information.) Slow infectors attach themselves to self-updating programs hoping to fool antivirus utilities that track file-creation dates and file sizes.

Signs of Infection

The time to suspect that your PC has a virus is when it starts exhibiting unusual behavior. Here are some typical symptoms:

- The computer won't boot properly.
- A familiar program refuses to start.
- You're unable to save a document.
- You see unfamiliar messages on the screen.
- The hard disk becomes sluggish, with the disk light constantly on.
- The computer keeps trying to access a floppy drive.

Although these behaviors are sometimes not the results of viral infection, finding them may be an ominous signal. If you don't already own an antivirus package, symptoms like these should prompt you to get one as soon as possible.

If you are a more experienced PC user, you may know that certain programs on your hard disk have specific date signatures and file sizes. If you notice that COMMAND.COM or WIN.COM has a strange date or unusual file size, you should immediately be suspicious.

What Is a Macro Virus?

Macro viruses attach themselves to Microsoft Word and Excel documents. Their annoying (and sometimes devastating) effects are possible because of the flexibility of Microsoft's Word Basic and VBA programming languages. One way to eliminate the threat of unexpected document infection is to use a different word processor or spreadsheet, such as the applications included in the Corel WordPerfect Office suite. This solution may not be practical if you use or depend upon documents created with Microsoft Office, which dominates the Windows marketplace.

A macro virus conceals itself as a bit of automated script code in a document. If you double-click an infected document in a folder (or load it through Word's File | Open command), the macro virus can execute any instructions supported by the macro language. If you're lucky, the virus will just be annoying, like the message and graphic shown here:

However, macro viruses can be devastating. The virus can make it impossible to save the document, insert random data into the document, corrupt document templates—and worse. Access to Microsoft's WordBasic and VBA languages lets macro viruses do more than just ruin documents. Through calls to system DLLs, they can delete system files or execute DDE commands that destroy the file system on your hard disk. Some recent strains can even wipe out the settings in a computers's BIOS.

How Can I Combat Viruses?

An ounce of prevention is worth a pound of cure. Regular backups of critical data files coupled with a good virus-detection package will pay off many times over in the amount of money and time they save you.

Shopping for a Workstation Antivirus Product

A good antivirus package should offer the features described here.

EFFECTIVE PREVENTION Good antivirus products designed for personal workstations include real-time sensors that monitor each new file copied to or created on your hard disk. This feature can effectively prevent the spread of viruses through e-mail attachments or files shared over a network. A good workstation antivirus package should also include real-time shields against macro infections and boot sector viruses. Upon system shutdown, it should check for a contaminated diskette left in the

A drive. If any rogue code is introduced into your system, the antivirus program should report it to you immediately.

HEURISTIC SCANNING In addition to scanning byte patterns on your hard disk, the antivirus monitor should track suspicious program behavior. Attempts to change boot records, perform extraneous read and write operations, or alter system files should be intercepted. Heuristic scanning deters damage by stealth and polymorphic viruses that don't exhibit identifiable signatures.

RELIABILITY Choose an antivirus package that is good at scanning your hard disk and detecting and cleaning infected files. Your antivirus agent should be able to clean most infected files, restoring program or document integrity. Avoid antivirus packages that solve problems by simply deleting infected files from the hard disk.

FLEXIBILITY Ask these questions when choosing antivirus software: How easy is the package to use? Can it automate virus checking with a built-in scheduler? What options do you have for performing disk scans? Can you perform interactive scans and customize scans for different scenarios? Can you scan network drives? Can you create an emergency rescue disk that boots from DOS?

SUPPORT Your antivirus package should have good documentation, including an online help file or printed manual that assists with virus detection and removal. The documentation should clearly identify various virus types and describe their characteristic behavior. The package should also include at least one year of technical support and free virus pattern updates. You'll want to consider how easy it is to obtain update modules. Some newer packages allow you to retrieve and install updates automatically over the Internet.

BELLS AND WHISTLES Some antivirus programs offer additional options for handling a virus that is found. For instance, some let you isolate infected files to a quarantine directory as an alternative to automatically attempting to clean up the files. Some programs also provide protection for your Internet browsers and e-mail programs. Add bonus points for packages that create emergency recovery boot disks, allow selective scanning of network drives, and update themselves automatically over the Internet.

How to Become a Local Office Hero

If a virus enters a computer in your office, your colleagues will treat you like Superman if you take these steps:

1. Prepare emergency floppy boot diskettes that include backups of each workstation's AUTOEXEC.BAT, CONFIG.SYS, WIN.INI, and SYSTEM.INI files. (You can do this withWin98's Add/Remove Programs | Startup Disk option.) If possible, try to include a DOS antiviral scanning utility on the diskette. Then *write protect it* and store it in a safe place.
2. Back up your Microsoft Word document templates. Copy all of the .DOT files you normally use to a backup directory. Then temporarily rename the backups as .DT or some other file extension that will elude questing macro viruses. If you suspect that a Word macro virus may be present in your office, then change the file attributes on the original .DOT files to read-only. This prevents the creation of new macros and also protects these templates from infection.
3. Back up each workstation's system configuration with the ScanReg utility described earlier in this chapter.
4. Periodically inspect mail repository files created by mail clients such as Microsoft Windows Messaging, Outlook 97/98, Outlook Express, and Netscape Navigator. These storage repositories may contain infected e-mail attachments that were transmitted and archived before a virus-detection package was installed.

What You Should Know About Word Macro Viruses

Several years ago, when the first Prank macro virus appeared, Microsoft posted a cure for it in the Word support section of the Microsoft World Wide Web site. This antiviral template (named SCANPROT.DOT) *is not effective against current Word macro viruses!* In fact, Microsoft's Scanprot template may actually interfere with newer, more sophisticated third-party antivirus programs, making document disinfection more difficult. If you installed this template several years ago, you should replace it with a newer, third-party antivirus product. Microsoft posts a list of vendors at http://www.microsoft.com/kb/articles/q49/5/00.htm. Note that the latest version of Microsoft Word displays a warning dialog box when some suspicious macros are activated, but it does not automatically remove or clean them.

In a pinch, you can temporarily control some macro virus infections by opening your Word style templates (.DOT files), opening the Macro menu, and manually inspecting and deleting suspicious AutoOpen and AutoClose macros (choose Tools | Macro and then Edit or Delete). However, this technique doesn't work reliably on all of the virus variations that have recently materialized.

Tip *If you suspect that your system is infected with a Word macro virus but don't have any antiviral software installed, the best course of action is to avoid saving or opening any additional Word documents on the infected system. If you're concerned with preserving the integrity of the current document after damaging changes appear, it's probably better to close Word with* CTRL-ALT-DELETE *than to resave the file. Microsoft has some instructions for manually removing Word macro viruses posted at http://www.microsoft.com/mswordsupport/content/usage/macrovirus/default.htm.*

Backup Strategies

All computer professionals will tell you that regular backups of your hard disk are necessary to avoid computer heartbreaks and disasters. No matter how good your hardware or conservative your computer use, a day may come when something fails. You may accidentally overwrite a precious document, critical files may become lost or scrambled, or worse yet, the entire hard disk may become unreadable.

At the very least, you should develop a backup strategy that preserves your irreplaceable documents. Some people reason that Windows 98 and its applications can always be reinstalled from manufacturers' disks. However, this can be an inconvenient and time-consuming process. There are several viable strategies for creating backup archives that will adequately protect the Windows 98 operating system and all of your work:

- Perform a full backup of your hard disk to tape, to a network server, or to removable media (such as an Iomega Jaz cartridge). Then perform periodic incremental backups of your document files.
- Install two hard drives in your computer. Use the second hard drive to store a duplicate image of the first hard drive and perform periodic updates. If problems arise or one drive fails, you can quickly resume operations and restore files from the second drive.
- Install duplicate Windows 98 configurations on two separate computers. Use a file management utility to regularly synchronize file contents over a network or cable connection.

- Use a third-party utility to create a binary image of your hard disk's contents. Then upload the disk image to a network server.

There are advantages and disadvantages to each of these backup strategies. Tape drives provide plenty of bulk storage space, but they are slower and more awkward to work with than straight file copies from disk to disk. Removable media, such as Iomega's Zip and Jaz cartridges, offer flexibility not provided by streaming tape drives. A Jaz removable cartridge (with an uncompressed capacity of 1GB or 2GB) is approximately twice as expensive as a Travan TR4 tape cartridge (with an uncompressed capacity of 4MB)—but oh, the difference in speed and flexibility! A standard Jaz cartridge is the equivalent of a 1GB hard disk. Backed up files can be stored on a Jaz drive in a standard DOS/Win98 format that permits retrieval in seconds.

Only the tape backup solution requires a dedicated backup applet such as Windows 98 Backup. The two-hard-drives solution can be implemented with nothing more complicated than the DOS XCOPY command. The duplicate Win98 solution requires two computers and an inexpensive third-party utility such as Canyon Software's Drag and File (available at http://www.canyonsw.com). The binary image solution requires access to a network server and a disk imaging utility such as Ghost Software's Ghost (available at http://www.ghostsoft.com) or PowerQuest's DriveImage (available at http://www.powerquest.com).

People who have the resources to support network file storage or hard-disk cloning generally find these strategies to be very convenient. Tape-drive backup is the least expensive and most commonly selected option.

Working with Windows 98 Backup

The Backup program included with Windows supports a wide variety of tape devices and is also compatible with backup sets produced by Windows 95 Backup and Seagate Backup 1.1 to 2.0. This isn't surprising, since Windows 98 Backup is licensed by Microsoft from Seagate Software. Unlike some OEM backup packages bundled with tape drives, Win98 Backup can read and archive files to floppy disks and to local and network disk directories—a useful feature. You'll find some basic instructions for installing and running this applet in the "Backup" section in Chapter 6.

Although Windows 98 Backup is much more full-featured than the Windows 95 version, it falls short of being an industrial-strength, professional package:

- Windows 98 Backup includes no support for automated, unattended sessions. Unlike Seagate Backup 2.0, its third-party big brother, Windows 98 Backup can't accept scheduling command-line parameters. Thus, it does not work out of the box with the Windows 98 Task Scheduler. (In the next section of this chapter, "Automating Win98 Backup with Task Scheduler and SCRIPT.EXE," you'll find a workaround that overcomes this limitation.)

- Windows 98 Backup can't save content catalogs rebuilt from tape. If the original catalog created at the time of the backup is lost, the file contents must be rebuilt from the tape every time you want to restore a file. For 2GB to 8GB tapes that contain multiple backup sets, this process can literally take hours.
- Windows 98 Backup lacks sophisticated options for selective backups. It can't filter and re-sort the file display, and it has no date filters.

Notwithstanding these limitations, Windows 98 Backup is an adequate tool for creating and restoring basic file archives. It supports full-system backups and selective backups in both incremental and differential formats.

Backup Types

A full-featured backup program can perform several common types of backup. These options let you create a complete archive of your hard disk files and track subsequent changes. All files created under Windows 98 include an archive bit that can be either turned off after the file is backed up or left in the raised position.

FULL BACKUP A full backup duplicates all files on the selected partition to the backup media (floppy disk, local fixed disk, removable drive, network directory, or tape drive). When the backup is executed, the current state of the archive bits on your files is ignored. At the conclusion of the backup, files with raised archive bits have their flags lowered. This prevents the files from being copied on subsequent incremental backup passes. If you open and resave a file, its archive bit is automatically reset to the unbacked-up position. To create a full backup with Win98 Backup, select Back Up My Computer from the Backup Wizard or place a check mark next to the letter of the drive you want to back up in the left pane on the Backup tab. Make sure All Selected Files is selected. (To back up Windows 98 registry settings, select Tools | Preferences and confirm that the Back Up or Restore the Registry option is selected.)

INCREMENTAL BACKUP An incremental backup makes copies only of files with archive flags in the raised state. Other files are ignored. At the conclusion of the backup, the archive flag for each copied file is lowered. To create an incremental backup with Win98 Backup, select the drives, folders, and files you want to archive in the left and right panes on the Backup tab. Make sure New and Changed Files is selected. Click the Options button, choose the Type tab, and select Incremental Backup Type, as shown next.

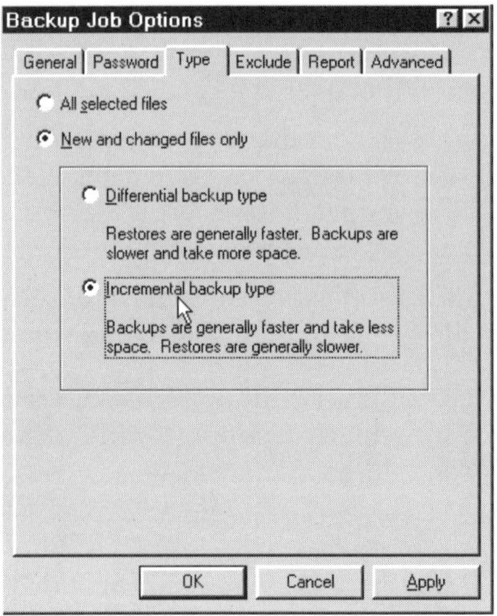

Incremental backups are useful when you want to maintain a series of backup sets that contain the files that have been modified since the last full or incremental backup. This is the most economical way of preserving all of your data without wasting storage space with duplicate files.

DIFFERENTIAL BACKUP A differential backup makes copies of files with archive flags in the raised state, like an incremental backup. The difference is that the archive flags for copied files are not changed at the conclusion of the backup. To create a differential backup with Win98 Backup, select the drives, folders, and files you want to archive in the left and right panes on the Backup tab. Make sure New and Changed Files is selected. Click the Options button, choose the Type tab, and select Differential Backup Type.

Differential backups are useful when you want to preserve a sequence of progressively edited versions of the same file in a single backup set. Each time you restore a differential backup set, you restore not just the latest version of a file, but also a progressive sequence of versions modified since the last full backup. You might be writing a novel or struggling with a difficult report. This technique gives you access to successive drafts.

Automating Win98 Backup with Task Scheduler and SCRIPT.EXE

You can use the SCRIPT.EXE freeware utility described earlier in this chapter to automate Windows 98 Backup just as you can use it to schedule virus scans. To make this trick work, you must first open Backup by choosing Programs | Accessories |

System Tools and disable the Startup Wizard. (Choose Tools | Preferences and deselect the Show Startup Dialog option.)

Next, you must define the custom backup job that you want to automate: For instance, you might choose to back up new and changed files on drive C to a network directory called \\SERVER\BACKUPS. You'll need to open the Backup Options settings and select Overwrite The Media With This Backup. (If you chose a tape drive as your target, you could also select Append This Backup To My Media.)

Assign a name to the job by selecting Job | Save As. This will cause Win98 Backup to select this job as the default whenever you open it.

Next, open a text editor such as Notepad and compose an ASCII script file for the SCRIPT.EXE macro utility. The following is a simple example that will launch Win98 Backup, open the default backup job, run it, and exit the program when the job is complete:

BACK.SCR

```
start,c:\\progra~1\\Access~1\\backup\\msbackup.exe
delay, 100
wait,Microsoft B*,
send,Microsoft B*,\n
delay, 100
wait,Microsoft Backup,
send,Microsoft Backup,\n
delay, 50
send, Backup Progress*,\n
delay, 50
send,Microsoft Backup*,%Jx
:exit
```

By using Task Scheduler to run this script, you can create an automated backup routine. (As mentioned earlier in this chapter, you can download Script, a simple freeware applet that passes keystrokes to Windows applications, from http://ourworld.compuserve.com/homepages/grumble/windows.htm.)

1. Open the Win98 Scheduled Tasks Folder and select Add Scheduled Task. Click Next and then click the Browse button. Go to the folder that contains SCRIPT.EXE and select it as your scheduled task.
2. Specify a name and schedule for the task and select Open Advanced Properties For This Task. Then click Finish.
3. Right-click the task and open its Properties to add the ASCII script you've created to the command line in the Run field of the Task tab. For example, enter **C:\SCRIPT\SCRIPT.EXE BACK.SCR**.

4. Enter the path to Win98 Backup's system files in the Start In field on the Task tab. (The program won't run without this.) For example, enter

   C:\PROGRA~1\ACCESS~1\BACKUP\SYSTEM

   as shown here:

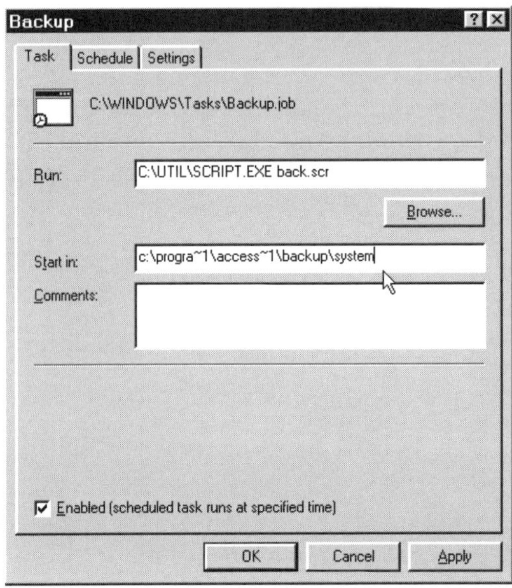

5. Click OK to add the job to the Scheduled Tasks window.

To test the script, right-click the backup job you just created and choose the Run option. Since the SCRIPT.EXE language supports a variety of keyboard commands, you can also construct more complex variations that load alternative backup jobs at designated times.

Emergency System Recovery with PCRESTOR

Windows 98 Backup supports a cumbersome procedure for recovering your hard disk in the event that a crash completely disables the operating system. The procedure involves using an emergency boot disk to run a batch file on the Win98 installation CD. PCRESTOR.BAT, located in the \TOOLS\SYSREC directory on the CD, launches a complete reinstallation of the operating system on your hard disk. It then runs a System Recovery Wizard that invokes Win98 Backup to restore a previous full-system backup you've made. To use this procedure, you must first do the following:

1. Create a full-system backup with Win98 Backup on an external drive or tape device.

2. Create an emergency startup disk by choosing Control Panel | Add/Remove Programs | Startup Disk and selecting Create New Disk.
3. Verify that the emergency startup disk properly loads DOS drivers that permit you to access your CD-ROM drive from a real-mode DOS command prompt.

When you boot the emergency disk, a message prompts you to load CD-ROM support. Microsoft includes generic IDE ATAPI and SCSI drivers in Windows 98. If your computer can use these, the CD-ROM drive will become accessible from a DOS command prompt. If you test and discover that this doesn't work, you can manually add other driver statements to the CONFIG.SYS file on the emergency boot disk.

EXAMPLES If you have a Teac IDE CD-ROM drive, you can copy the Teac device driver to the emergency boot disk and edit the CONFIG.SYS file on the disk to add the following statement to the [CD] section of the file:

```
DEVICE=TEAC_CDI.SYS /D:mscd001
```

If you have a SCSI CD-ROM drive and NCR/Symbios 4.0 SCSI adapter, you can copy the Symbios drivers to the emergency boot disk and edit the CONFIG.SYS file on the disk to add the following statements to the [CD] section of the file:

```
DEVICE=ASPI8xx.SYS
DEVICE=SYMCD.SYS /D:mscd001
```

To use the emergency recovery disk, all you need to do is insert it in drive A and start the computer. When the command prompt appears, change to the drive letter for the CD-ROM drive, issue the command **CD TOOLS\SYSREC**, type **PCRESTOR**, and press ENTER. This will initiate the entire process of reinstalling Windows 98 on the hard disk and will subsequently run the Win98 Backup utility to restore your full-system backup.

Working with Third-Party Backup Programs

If you don't want to wrestle with Windows 98 Backup and write macro scripts, a number of third-party products offer built-in schedulers and better emergency recovery. From multiple streaming device support to fine-tuned file-selection options, these packages offer mission-critical features for creating automated backup routines.

NovaStor's NovaBack and Cheyenne's Backup for Windows 95/98 are two multipurpose backup suites sold independent of any manufacturer's tape drive. Both of these products support a wide number of tape devices and share the following useful features:

- Fine control of file selection by all four DOS file attributes

- Numerous selectable include and exclude filters on file lists
- Support for sequential arrayed tape devices
- Built-in virus scanners
- Complete logging of operations
- Unfettered access to the Windows registry on remote machines
- Tape diagnostic tools

The NovaBack programmers should win a special award for reintroducing the ability to sort a file list by name, size, and date in ascending or descending order. (This feature was absent from Windows 95 backup programs for many years and is only now beginning to reappear.) The included Doctor Tape diagnostic utility is another potentially useful cookie. Doctor Tape can perform a sector-by-sector ASCII or hex data dump of the contents of almost any tape cartridge regardless of format. NovaBack would be just about ideal as a backup solution if only it allowed users to store archives on floppy diskettes or fixed and removable hard disks, but it is for tape drives only. NovaStor does make a companion product called NovaDisk that supports backups to floppies, fixed and removable media, and network drives. The two products can be purchased together in a package called Nova Backup. (See http://www.novastor.com for more product information.)

Cheyenne Backup is the backup utility with the largest set of biceps. Its interface includes a multiplicity of statistical screens and interface windows. Each window contains a separate fascinating display of hardware configuration information, file statistics, or customizable performance options. For instance, users can select from four types of shared file access to capture open files during background backups. Cheyenne Backup also includes a built-in virus scanner that can rename or delete infected files. (See http://www.cheyenne.com for more product information.)

Seagate Backup Exec 2.0 is a slightly less powerful backup package that is bundled with Seagate's ubiquitous tape drives. Sporting an interface very similar to that of the Windows 98 Backup applet, it contains a built-in scheduler and an emergency recovery feature that doesn't require reinstallation of the entire operating system. However, Seagate Backup Exec lacks a virus checker or sophisticated file selection filters. A companion product, Seagate Direct Tape Access, can work in conjunction with Backup 2.0 to mount a tape device as a virtual disk drive on the Windows 98 desktop. This allows you to view, select, cut, and paste archive contents from Windows Explorer just as if the backup archive were another disk drive. Although this feature is more convenient than opening a backup program every time you want to restore a file, the process is limited by the speed of your streaming tape device. You can quickly select the files you want to copy, but the tape drive must page sequentially through the backup cartridge before the files are actually retrieved. (See http://www.seagate.com for more product information.)

Working with Older DOS Backup Programs

Believe it or not, there are advantages to performing system backups from a real-mode DOS command prompt with older DOS backup software—but you have to know how to do it! The main problem with using DOS or Windows 3.x software on a Windows 98 computer is that these older programs have no support for Win98's VFAT long filenames. If you attempt to back up or restore a disk from DOS, you get all of the physical files and directories, but when you boot to Windows 98, your desktop is a mess. All files are treated as if they have standard DOS 8.3 filenames, with tilde (~) symbols inserted if a name contains excess characters.

But suppose, for a minute, that you had a way to record and restore Win98's long filenames in a real-mode DOS session. Here are some of the advantages you might gain:

- If you already own a reliable, older DOS backup program that works with your tape drive; one that works automatically without fighting for interrupts and port addresses under the Windows 98 interface, you will be able to continue to use it.
- The DOS backup program (running under a simpler operating system) seldom times out with mysterious error messages in the middle of a backup or restore job.
- Emergency recovery procedures are greatly simplified. You can effortlessly back up and restore hard-disk partitions by booting to a DOS command prompt. There's no need to start an operational version of Windows 98 to access Windows 98 software.
- If your hard disk fails or becomes scrambled, all you need to do is boot from a floppy disk, format the hard disk, install the DOS Backup program, and restore the Windows 98 operating system exactly the way it was at the time of your last backup.

Accurately backing up or restoring a Windows 98 partition from a real-mode DOS prompt depends upon having a way to back up and restore Windows 98 long filenames. Microsoft bundles a limited utility called LFNBK in the \TOOLS\RESKIT\FILES\LFNBACK folder on the Windows 98 CD. LFNBK can record and restore long filenames to your hard disk—but only if you run it from within the Windows 98 interface. This makes LFNBK useless for emergency system backups and restore operations from a real DOS command prompt.

Enter the Windows hacker community to the rescue! D. J. Murdoch's DOSLFNBK is a better version of Microsoft's utility. It has no difficulty recording and restoring long filename attributes from a true MS-DOS command prompt. DOSLFNBK is a $10 shareware program that can be downloaded from http://www8.pair.com/dmurdoch/programs/doslfnbk.htm or from CompuServe's file library. (Make sure you get the latest version, 2.2 or higher, that supports FAT32 disk partitions.)

Creating a DOS File Backup and Emergency Disk with DOSLFNBK

With DOSLFNBK, the construction of a Win98 file backup under MS-DOS and an emergency recovery diskette becomes a simple matter:

1. Run DOSLFNBK at a command prompt inside or outside of Windows 98 to record your long filename information in the root directory of each partition. The syntax is

   DOSLFNBK *drive:\directory*

   Perform this operation for each individual disk partition. This default also parses all subdirectories below the one specified on the command line. Long filename information is saved to a file in the root directory called BACKUP.LFN.
2. Run your DOS, Windows 3.1, or Windows 98 backup software on the partition you want to archive. Make sure that the BACKUP.LFN file in the root directory of each partition is included in the backup. Perform a full backup that archives all files on the disk, including the USER.DAT and SYSTEM.DAT files in the \WINDOWS directory. (These two files contain the Windows 98 system registry.)
3. Create a standard Windows 98 emergency startup disk with the usual information, including real-mode CD-ROM or SCSI drivers, if necessary.

Restoring Windows 98 with DOSLFNBK

Once you have created an emergency disk and a file backup with DOSLFNBK information, restoring your Windows 98 system is easy:

1. If your Windows 98 system becomes corrupted, boot to a real-mode DOS command prompt with your Windows 98 startup disk. Then perform whatever disk maintenance is necessary on the hard drive. The emergency startup disk creates a special RAM drive that allows you to run the DOS version of ScanDisk on your hard drive. If necessary, you can even completely reformat the partition and create a blank disk.
2. Install or copy your DOS backup software to the repaired hard disk partition.
3. To restore your Windows 98 backup, run your DOS backup software and restore the full system backup that you previously created.
4. Exit to a real-mode DOS prompt and run DOSLFNBK from the root directory of each partition to restore the partition's long filename information. The syntax is DOSLFNBK /R.

That's it. It works! Reboot the computer, and Windows 98 will appear in the same configuration that you backed up.

File Mirroring Strategies

Mirroring the file structure of your disk to a second local drive, removable disk, or network directory is an alternative to the conventional backup procedures discussed in the preceding sections. The advantage of this protection strategy is that individual files and folders can be accessed and retrieved very quickly. If one hard disk fails, you can remove it and boot from the other one. If you've created a file backup on a removable disk, you can insert the cartridge and use XCOPY to copy the contents back to your hard disk.

Note *To restore long filenames and system files from a real-mode DOS session, you must also use a utility such as DOSLFNBK to back up and restore long filename information. This is not necessary if you boot to the Windows 98 operating system and use your removable drive to restore application and data file directories.*

To create a mirror backup with two physical hard drives or with a network directory, simply select the contents of the source drive in the Windows Explorer and paste the contents into the target drive.

The Iomega Jaz Drive

Iomega's Jaz drive is one of the more significant bits of PC wizardry developed within the last few years. It consists of either an internal or external SCSI unit that can contain portable cartridges with 540MB, 1GB, or 2GB of uncompressed capacity. The Jaz drive installs effortlessly; you simply plug it into a SCSI adapter and install the Windows 95/98 Guest software. Once present on your system, the Jaz drive can be configured as either a removable or a nonremovable disk volume. (Some users have expressed unhappiness at the way it changes assigned drive letters when they add and remove devices from the PC. But with a little ingenuity, this limitation can be overcome.)

One-megabyte Jaz cartridges are rated with a burst transfer rate of 10 MB/second and an access time of 12 milliseconds. The Jaz drive is noticeably faster and more responsive than its little brother, the Zip drive, or a conventional tape device.

The Jaz Drive Tool Kit includes some useful utility software. Right-clicking its icon in My Computer or Explorer brings up a series of context menu options. Copy Machine allows you to quickly duplicate a Jaz volume on another cartridge or to transfer the entire contents of a regular fixed disk to the Jaz drive. Users have a choice between creating a sector-by-sector physical image of a drive or a file-by-file copy. The Jaz drive's ability to masquerade as an ordinary fixed disk permits it to be a storage repository for many third-party backup programs, including the Backup applet bundled with Windows 98. A sector-by-sector physical image backup allows you to restore the entire Windows 98 operating system (including long filenames) from a real-mode DOS session. See the following section, "Binary Image (Sector-by-Sector) Backups," for more information on image backups.

The Jaz drive can be a minor annoyance to someone who wants to boot a real-mode DOS session, because the drive letter is assigned differently under DOS than under Windows 98. One way to match the drive letter assignments under DOS and Windows 98 is to keep the cartridge out of the drive during startup. If you boot to a real-mode command prompt and *then* insert the cartridge, the drive letter under DOS will match the Windows 98 drive letter. The drawback to this trick is that it makes your system stall for 2 to 3 minutes at startup while the empty Jaz drive is recognized.

A similar situation occurs if you boot directly to Windows 98. If you start without a cartridge in the Jaz drive, the system stalls for 2 to 3 minutes while the drive is detected—so you always have to remember to put in a cartridge unless you like twiddling your thumbs.

Tip *You can avoid the delay in booting a computer with an attached Jaz drive and automatically resolve the DOS–Windows 98 drive letter mismatch issue. By default, the Iomega software configures a primary FAT partition on each cartridge. This is what confuses DOS. To avoid the problem, you can boot to Windows 98 and repartition a Jaz cartridge with FDISK. After copying any data that you want to save to another location, delete the existing primary partition on the Jaz cartridge and use FDISK to define an extended partition. Format the extended partition, and all the annoyances disappear. You can leave the cartridge in the drive to make the system boot quickly, and it will have the same drive letter under both DOS and Windows 98.*

Binary Image (Sector-by-Sector) Backups

No computer chore wastes time like having to rebuild an entire hard disk from scratch. Disk imaging utilities can provide relief to individual users and system administrators who need to transfer single partitions or multiple-partition disk images from one physical location to another. The advantage of a disk image backup is that it's an exact replica of the current contents of your hard disk. You don't need to worry about long filenames, file attributes, times, dates, hidden files, empty directories, and so on. You can copy and restore disk images from the source to the target under MS-DOS without losing any information.

If you want to create a binary image backup of your hard disk, you are not limited to the Iomega software (bundled with the Jaz drive and discussed in the previous section). Innovation Software's Ghost (see http://www.ghostsoft.com) and PowerQuest's Drive Image Professional (see http://www.powerquest.com) are two packages designed to back up and transfer partitions or complete disk images from one physical drive to another. Both applications can dump the physical structure of a disk to a binary file and store it on a local machine or on a network server. The compressible binary image files may occupy much less storage space than the original partitions. Image backups can then be transferred to a freshly partitioned drive in a new machine or used to restore a damaged file structure on the original disk. In addition to this two-step procedure, both products allow real-time copying of multiple partitions in a single step (only Ghost permits real-time copying across a network).

Currently, Ghost and Drive Image Professional have limitations relating to their dependence on the DOS operating system to physically copy partition information. In Drive Image Professional, replication across a network is accomplished by logging onto a server under DOS, dumping an image file to a server directory, and then subsequently retrieving it from a shared Network drive. Ghost can clone disks in this way, but it also offers real-time partition copying across a network in a DOS-to-DOS or DOS-to-Windows environment. Both packages support command-line scripting commands that permit automated backup and transfer through batch files.

To take advantage of real-time replication across a network, you must install DOS network drivers on the target system. (The creators of Ghost are currently hard at work developing a real-time Windows version.) Installing DOS network drivers isn't difficult on desktop workstations, but it may be problematic for disk duplication on notebook computers. Both Innovation Software and PowerQuest provide instructions for creating a DOS network boot disk. Ghost has the advantage of offering parallel cable connection support. You can link two computers, each running the Ghost client, and avoid fussing with DOS network settings. Ghost can also dynamically resize a partition, condensing free space to transfer from a larger to a smaller physical drive.

Drive Image Professional includes the latest version of PowerQuest's Partition Magic, a useful utility that can resize disk partitions on the fly and convert between Microsoft's FAT16 and FAT32 file formats. DriveMapper, another useful included utility, can globally remap the drive letter assigned to system files in the Windows registry and .INI files (a partition that was drive C on one computer can become drive D on another).

In addition to backing up and protecting partitions on a single computer, disk imaging utilities can help you clone an entire Windows 98 configuration from one computer to another. You'll find step-by-step instructions in the section "Mobile Computing" in Appendix A.

Maintaining the Windows Registry

The Windows 98 registry is the underlying genetic code that glues everything in the operating system together, but for most users, it is also an arcane mystery. The only time most users think about the registry is when something goes wrong with it. In this section you'll find a guide to safeguarding Windows 98 from registry corruption. You'll learn how to augment Microsoft's automatic registry backups and also how to protect smaller registry components. (If you're having a problem with your modem, dial-up network settings, or Internet browsing history, you don't necessarily want to restore the entire system registry to cure the problem. Your last full registry backup may be missing application settings or other recent changes in the Windows 98 operating state.)

All of the secret inner workings of Windows 98 are controlled through the Windows registry. This unified binary database largely replaces the WIN.INI and

SYSTEM.INI control files that governed the performance of Windows 3.x. (These two ASCII control files are still maintained in the \WINDOWS directory, but they exist only for compatibility with older Windows 3.x applications that expect to find them.) In Windows 3.x, the registry played a minor role. It was used mainly to record file paths for OLE-enabled applications.

In Windows 95, Microsoft moved almost all of the system configuration options out of WIN.INI and SYSTEM.INI and into the registry. This configuration database is created during the installation of Windows 95 or Windows 98. All hardware defaults, display options, font information, file associations, 32-bit device listings, and internal information about program defaults are contained within two binary files, SYSTEM.DAT and USER.DAT, which reside in the \WINDOWS directory. When you install new programs or make changes to Windows through the Control Panel, the information is written directly to the registry instead of to WIN.INI or SYSTEM.INI.

System Protection: Backing Up and Restoring the Registry

Windows 98 has a better method of tracking and backing up the registry than Windows 95 had. Instead of creating a copy of the registry that's overwritten every time the computer starts, Windows 98 periodically archives and compresses the current registry. If you start Windows 98 every day, the system will make one registry backup each day. Successive copies of the registry (plus WIN.INI and SYSTEM.INI) are stored in the \WINDOWS\SYSBCKUP directory in Microsoft's compressed cabinet (CAB) format. Typically, these copies might be named RB000.CAB, RB001.CAB, RB002.CAB, and so on. The highest number represents the most recent backup. By default, five backups are stored. Subsequent backups replace the oldest ones sequentially.

When the familiar Windows desktop refuses to load, suddenly the registry becomes an all-important concern. Sinister error messages may announce that the registry is corrupt and must be restored. If you're lucky, a recent backup is available to bring back most of your program and desktop settings. However, if you've spent the day browsing the Internet and installing new programs, a registry error can wipe out all of your work.

Sometimes the situation can be less serious but no less annoying. For example, icons may be displayed incorrectly or disappear, the Windows 98 desktop may appear and issue a series of complaints about missing system files, or a series of invisible start-up programs may try to load, forcing the computer into a state of paralysis.

The "Registry Checker" section of Chapter 6 contains information about using ScanReg to manually create a new registry backup or restore an existing copy. By default, the Windows 98 Registry Checker verifies the integrity of the Windows registry every time you boot the computer to Windows 98. If the startup check turns up a specific problem that Microsoft programmers have identified (and if a backup exists), you'll see a system message informing you that the registry is corrupt and will be replaced. If no backup exists, the Registry Checker will attempt to repair the existing version of the registry.

If you've recently made changes to Windows 98 or visited a series of Web sites that you want to view again offline, you may want to create a manual backup of the registry. You can do this entering ***SCANREGW.EXE*** *in the Start menu Run box.*

Editing ScanReg Defaults

The default behavior of ScanReg can be controlled through settings listed in SCANREG.INI, a file located in the \WINDOWS directory.

- You can increase or decrease the number of saved registry backups. (The default is five.)
- You can change the location where registry backups are stored.
- You can specify additional files (such as CONFIG.SYS and AUTOEXEC.BAT) to be saved with each registry backup.
- You can disable automatic registry backups and automatic registry optimization.

The syntax for settings in SCANREG.INI is shown in Table 8-1.

The directory codes for the Files= setting in SCANREG.INI are as follows:

10: Windows directory (example: C:\WINDOWS)

11: System directory (example: C:\WINDOWS\SYSTEM)

Command	Action	Default
Backup=	Runs ScanReg at system startup to back up the registry	1 enables, 0 disables
Optimize=	Automatically optimizes the registry at Win98 startup	1 enables, 0 disables

Table 8-1. *Customized settings for the Windows 98 Registry Checker (SCANREG.EXE)*

Command	Action	Default
MaxBackupCopies=	Preserves the specified number of registry backups in the backup folder	5 (five copies)
BackupDirectory=	Specifies the backup directory where .CAB files are stored (must be full-path backups)	C:\WINDOWS\ SYSBCKUP
Files=*dir code*,file1,file2	Specifies additional system files to back up into the .CAB file	None

Table 8-1. *Customized settings for the Windows 98 Registry Checker (SCANREG.EXE) (continued)*

30: Boot directory (example: C:\)

31: Boot host directory (example: C:\)

EXAMPLES To make ScanReg automatically include AUTOEXEC.BAT and CONFIG.SYS with its registry backups, you would enter the following statement in SCANREG.INI:

```
Files=30,AUTOEXEC.BAT,CONFIG.SYS
```

By default, ScanReg does not back up user profile information. If multiple Windows 98 user profiles are enabled on your computer, you can preserve them by entering the following statement in SCANREG.INI:

```
Files=10, PROFILES\<USERNAME1>\USER.DAT,PROFILES\<USERNAME2>
\USER.DAT,
```

where <USERNAMEX> is the logon name for the user.

Fixing a Corrupted Registry

When ScanReg replaces a corrupted registry with an older backup, you may lose your most recent program settings and Internet browsing history. If you're not comfortable with this idea, you can force ScanReg to attempt to repair the corrupted registry.

ScanReg is actually capable of repairing a number of internal problems in a bad registry, but that's not its default behavior.

Before restoring the last backup copy of the registry, ScanReg also archives the corrupted version. If you discover that Windows 98 is missing too many recent configuration changes after a registry replacement, you can attempt to repair and reinstall the corrupted version. To do this you'll need to retrieve the corrupted versions of WIN.INI, SYSTEM.INI, SYSTEM.DAT, and USER.DAT from a file called RBBAD.CAB. (ScanReg writes this file in the \SYSBCKUP directory when it restores the "good" registry.)

1. From within Windows 98, create a temporary directory (for instance C:\TEMP). Then right-click RBBAD.CAB in Windows Explorer and select View to display its contents.
2. Select all the files in the RBBAD.CAB window. Right-click and choose the Extract option from the pop-up menu. Extract the contents of RBBAD.CAB to the temporary folder you've created, as shown in Figure 8-6.
3. Exit Windows 98 to MS-DOS mode. Go to the \WINDOWS directory and issue the DOS command **ATTRIB -R -H -S *.DAT**.
4. Copy the corrupted versions of WIN.INI, SYSTEM.INI, SYSTEM.DAT. and USER.DAT from the temporary directory to the \WINDOWS directory. (For

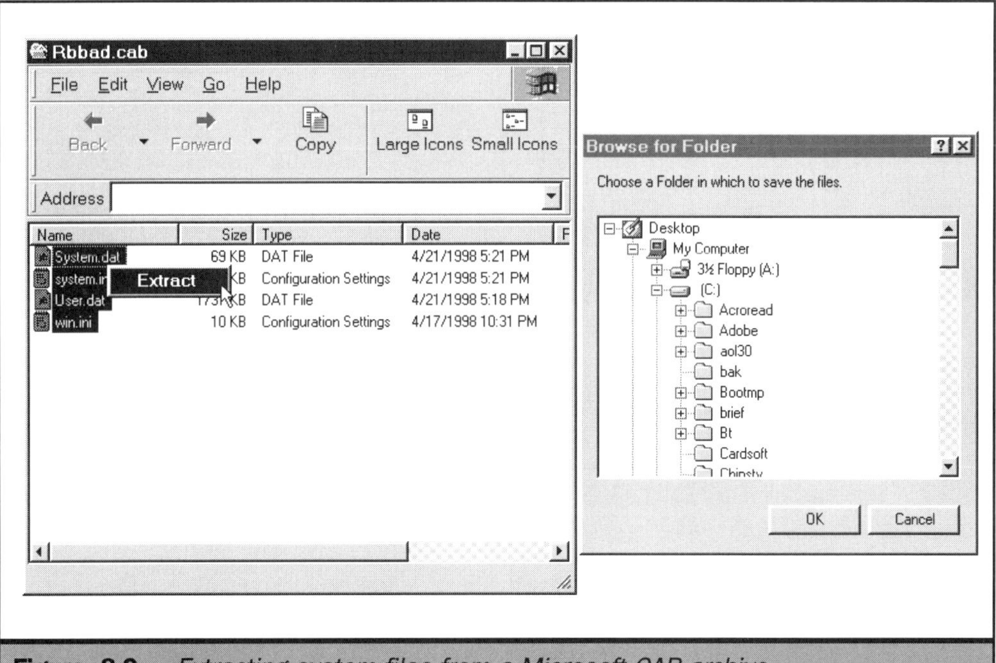

Figure 8-6. *Extracting system files from a Microsoft CAB archive*

example, enter **COPY C:\TEMP*.* \WINDOWS**.) You don't have to worry about losing the "good" registry. It will still be archived, and if the repair attempt fails, ScanReg can unpack and restore it again.

5. Enter **SCANREG /FIX** on the DOS command line. ScanReg will examine the corrupted SYSTEM.DAT and USER.DAT files you've placed in the \WINDOWS directory and attempt to repair them.

After ScanReg completes its work, reboot the computer. If the repair attempt was successful, Windows 98 will return with your most recent program settings and Internet browsing history. If the attempt was unsuccessful, ScanReg will run again and repeat the installation of the older version of the registry.

Note *The registry contents of RBBAD.CAB can also be unpacked in a real-mode DOS session with the EXTRACT.EXE utility that Microsoft places in the \WIN98 directory on the installation CD. Copy EXTRACT.EXE to your hard disk and use the following syntax at a real-mode DOS prompt:* ***EXTRACT /E C:\WINDOWS\SYSBCKUP\ RBBAD.CAB /L C:\TEMP****. Don't unpack the corrupted registry to the \WINDOWS directory while the Windows 98 interface is running, since this will only make things worse! Use a temporary directory.*

Other Ways to Back Up and Restore the Registry

One quick and dirty way to back up the Windows 98 registry is to open a DOS command prompt to the \WINDOWS directory (while Windows 98 is running) and issue the following commands:

```
ATTRIB -R -H -S *.DAT
COPY SYSTEM.DAT SYSTEM.BK
COPY USER.DAT USER.BK
```

You might want to do this if you intend to perform some temporary experiment on Windows 98 and you want the ability to quickly return to the current state of the operating system. To restore this kind of temporary registry backup, restart the computer, hold down the CTRL key, and boot to a real-mode DOS prompt. Then go to the \WINDOWS directory and issue the following DOS commands:

```
ATTRIB -R -H -S *.DAT
COPY SYSTEM.BK SYSTEM.DAT
COPY USER.BK USER.DAT
```

Restart the computer, and Windows 98 will revert to the state it was in when you performed the quick registry backup.

The section "Registry Editor: RegEdit" in Chapter 6 shows you yet another way to back up and restore the Windows 98 registry. The Registry Editor, REGEDIT.EXE, is placed in your \WINDOWS directory during installation, but it is not added to the Start menu. You can use RegEdit to export registry contents to an ASCII .REG file or reimport registry settings while Windows 98 is running.

You can open REGEDIT.EXE from the Start menu Run box, or you can create a program shortcut to it on the Start menu or the desktop.

When RegEdit is opened, it translates the binary data contained in the SYSTEM.DAT and USER.DAT files into an organized ASCII format. The registry is displayed in six hierarchical folder trees, called *keys* in the RegEdit display.

The six root keys displayed in RegEdit represent six categories of Windows 98 system information. Three of the six groups duplicate selected portions of the other three. The HKEY_CLASSES_ROOT, HKEY_CURRENT_USER, and HKEY_CURRENT_CONFIG keys provide a convenient way to access specific cross-sections of the larger HKEY_LOCAL_MACHINE, HKEY_USER, and HKEY_DYN_DATA keys.

The Import Registry File and Export Registry File commands on RegEdit's Registry menu allow you to save current registry contents or reintegrate a previously exported version. In addition to enabling you to export the entire registry, RegEdit allows you to select and export individual sections, as shown in Figure 8-7.

Third-Party Registry Trackers

If you're a program developer or product tester, you can gain even more control over the Windows registry with a third-party tracking utility. Cybermedia's First Aid 98 and Symantec's Norton Utilities 3.0 both offer this service, but Imagine Lan's ConfigSafe is a better and more comprehensive tool.

ConfigSafe lets you save as many different versions of the registry as your hard disk can hold. Furthermore, it allows you to save only specific portions of the registry or to complement registry backups with any additional files that you choose. ConfigSafe monitors all incremental changes made to the registry as you work in Windows 98. If you change desktop settings, add new hardware, or install or delete programs, ConfigSafe tracks your work. The File Changes window highlights all the "before" and "after" settings entered in the system registry, Windows .INI files, AUTOEXEC.BAT file, and CONFIG.SYS file over any specified set of snapshots. Furthermore, ConfigSafe can monitor file changes in any directory on your hard disk. Most important, it can monitor the \WINDOWS and \WINDOWS\SYSTEM directories, revealing which files have been added, replaced, or deleted since the last system snapshot.

More information about ConfigSafe is available at http:\\www.imagine-lan.com.

If you look at the contents of an exported .REG file in a text editor (such as WordPad), you'll see that the file is simply an ASCII listing of Windows 98 configuration settings similar to what used to be stored in the SYSTEM.INI file. You can import a previously saved .REG file back into the registry by selecting Registry | Import Registry from RegEdit's pull-down menu, shown here:

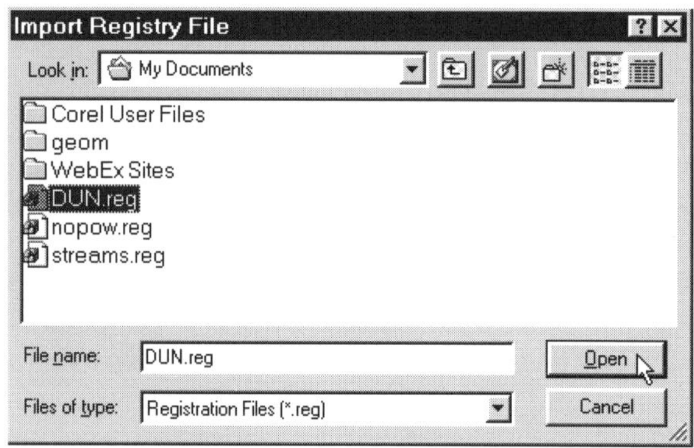

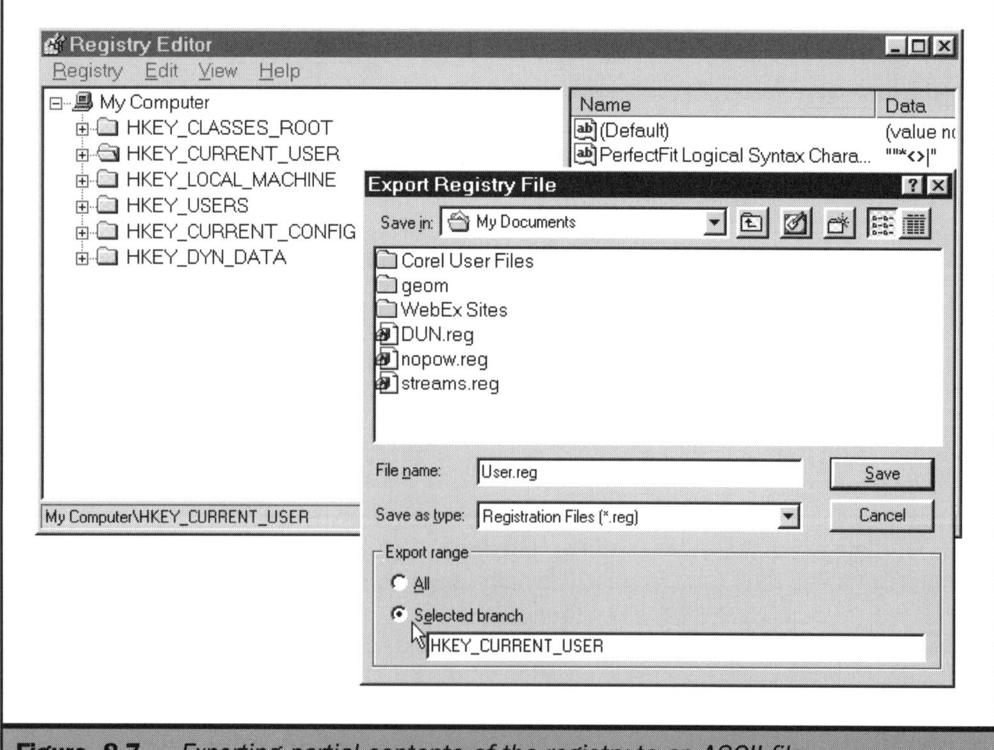

Figure 8-7. *Exporting partial contents of the registry to an ASCII file*

While you can use this feature to import or export a complete Windows 98 registry, its best application is in preserving and restoring individual registry components. For instance, if you back up your Dial-Up Networking settings, modem profiles, or program and file associations, you can use Registry | Import Registry File to undo adverse changes and restore your saved configurations that work, and you can do this without replacing the entire registry. You'll see how in the section "Preserving System Settings with RegEdit" later in this chapter.

Rebuilding the Registry from Real-Mode DOS

Here's one more global registry recovery technique that may prove useful.

What if Windows 98 won't start? You get system messages that the registry is corrupt, but there's no available backup file. As you've seen, sometimes the corrupt registry can be repaired by issuing the **SCANREG /fix** command from a real-mode DOS prompt. However, this won't always work.

Sometimes startup problems are caused by temporarily skewed hardware settings. The symptoms of this type of problem are a computer that simply hangs at boot time instead of reporting that the registry is corrupt. You may be able to resolve this kind of registry problem by force-booting to Windows 98 Safe mode (hold down the CTRL key during bootup and select Safe Mode from the Win98 Startup menu). If the computer will run Windows 98 in Safe mode, you may be able to adjust Device Manager settings to remove hardware conflicts. (See "Device Manager Tab" in Chapter 9 for step-by-step troubleshooting procedures.)

Sometimes neither ScanReg nor a Device Manager change will allow Windows 98 to load normally. What then?

If you haven't been overzealous about purging files from your computer, you'll find that there is a hidden file in the root directory of your boot drive called SYSTEM.1ST. This file is created during the Windows 98 installation and contains all of the preliminary default registry information for the first startup of the operating system. RegEdit makes it possible to extract part or all of the information from this file and merge it into a corrupted registry. You can do this from a real-mode DOS prompt if the Windows 98 interface won't start. If your computer develops registry problems and you have no "good" backup copy to restore, you can try the following jump-start procedure before giving up and completely reinstalling Windows 98:

1. Boot to the real DOS prompt. Use RegEdit to extract the entire contents of SYSTEM.1ST to an ASCII .REG file. From the DOS prompt in the root directory of drive C, issue the following command:

   REGEDIT /L:SYSTEM.1st /E MY.REG.

2. Merge the .REG file you created in step 1 with your existing system registry by entering this command:

   REGEDIT MY.REG.

This command merges the preinstallation ASCII registry you've exported into the current corrupt registry in the \WINDOWS directory.

This operation has the effect of refreshing all of the default Windows 98 registry information while retaining application configuration information you've accumulated in the corrupted registry.

When you next boot to Windows 98, the operating system will behave as though you had just performed a refresh installation, redetecting your hardware and initializing the desktop, but the program settings that were integrated into the previous registry will be preserved. This trick will work a fair percentage of the time to restore Windows 98 to working order. It can fail if your problems are caused by a corrupt system file on the hard disk or by a destructive set of third-party program settings. If that turns out to be the case, you may have to reinstall Windows 98 from the CD.

First try reinstalling Windows 98 over the existing registry. If that doesn't resolve your problems, you can obliterate the corrupt registry entirely by deleting it from the \WINDOWS directory. Then reinstall Windows 98 again. If you take this last course, you'll need to reinstall all of your applications since their registry information will be gone.

Preserving System Settings with RegEdit

You don't have to have a complete backup of the Windows registry to restore certain important user information; it doesn't make sense to swat flies with an elephant gun. If your Dial-Up Networking won't dial or you lose your IE4 History files, you don't need to restore the registry or reinstall the operating system to regain functionality. A working knowledge of RegEdit will let you create small ASCII backups of Dial-Up Networking and Internet Explorer settings, modem profiles, and program and file associations.

After you start RegEdit, you'll see an editing screen divided into two panes. The left portion of the screen displays an expandable tree view of all the keys in the registry. You can open or collapse the subkey listings by clicking on the + or – sign next to each main key. The right portion of the screen displays the active value name and value data for the key highlighted on the left.

The Registry, Edit, and View pull-down menus allow you to manipulate the registry contents. The Registry menu has options to import or export portions of the registry in ASCII format. The Edit menu lets you create new registry keys, modify the contents of existing keys, copy key information to the clipboard, or search the registry for particular keys, value names, and value data. The View menu lets you adjust the size of the two RegEdit display windows.

RegEdit organizes the registry database of Windows 98 software and hardware settings as follows:

- **HKEY_CLASSES_ROOT key** Contains settings that govern Windows 98 object linking and embedding (OLE) information, file associations, and file type information. This key is a database for all of your installed applications, duplicating information that is also stored in the HKEY_LOCAL_MACHINE\SOFTWARE\CLASSES subkey.
- **HKEY_CURRENT_USER key** Stores information for the current user logged onto Windows 98. It contains individual desktop settings, network connections, passwords, and program defaults that users can customize. (You may recall that Win98's User Profiles feature permits different user defaults to be assigned to each individual logon ID.) This key duplicates a subsection of the more general HKEY_USERS key group.
- **HKEY_LOCAL_MACHINE key** The master database for the computer itself. This contains individual program settings, device driver configuration, and hardware information (video display settings, installed devices, interrupt assignments, and plug-and-play information).
- **HKEY_USERS key** Contains system information for all users of Windows 98. If the computer isn't set up for multiple user profiles, only the Default subkey will exist. The .Default subkey contains the preferences and desktop information for the default user ID. When the computer is set up for multiple users, each user ID has a corresponding set of subkeys to store individual preferences and system defaults.
- **HKEY_CURRENT_CONFIG key** Contains information about the current hardware configuration. (Windows 98's Device Manager allows you to set up multiple hardware profiles if your computer will be used with different monitors, SCSI devices, or network configurations.) This key duplicates the currently active portion of the HKEY_LOCAL_MACHINE\CONFIG key.
- **HKEY_DYN_DATA key** Stores real-time information about Windows 98 system performance. You may be familiar with the Tweak UI component of Windows 98 Power Toys, which allows you to speed up or slow down several desktop display options. Those defaults are stored in this key. Additionally, this key stores the statistical performance information that you can display with the System Monitor utility (disk cache size, memory use, network throughput, and so on). See the section "System Monitor" in Chapter 6 for more information.

Now, let's put this information to work. (Before you make any changes to the registry, be sure to make a backup copy using one of the techniques discussed earlier.)

PRESERVING DIAL-UP NETWORKING SETTINGS You may sometimes find it necessary to remove and reinstall Dial-Up Networking to resolve a configuration problem. (Microsoft recommends this action when the password box gets stuck or a missing driver prevents a PPP login.) Occasionally, uninstalling and reinstalling Dial-Up Networking will wipe out all of your ISP profiles and TCP/IP address information. This is not supposed to happen, but you can safeguard your Dial-Up Networking settings by exporting this registry component with RegEdit. The .REG backup of your ISP profiles will contain all of the IP addresses and login settings. It can easily be reintegrated into the registry if Dial-Up Networking information is wiped out or misplaced. You can also use this trick to migrate Dial-Up Networking settings to another computer, eliminating the task of cloning ISP connection profiles from scratch.

Windows 98 stores Dial-Up Networking information in the HKEY_CURRENT _USER key group in a subkey called RemoteAccess. Here's how to back up your Dial-Up Networking profiles:

1. Open RegEdit to the HKEY_CURRENT_USER\RemoteAccess subkey and select this key in the left pane.
2. From the Registry menu, select Export Registry File. Enter a filename such as **MY DUN** in the Export Registry File dialog box. The Selected Branch option at the bottom of the dialog box should be active and should point to HKEY_CURRENT_USER\RemoteAccess.
3. Click Save, and a copy of your Dial-Up Networking settings will be saved to the My Documents folder with a default extension of .REG, as shown next.

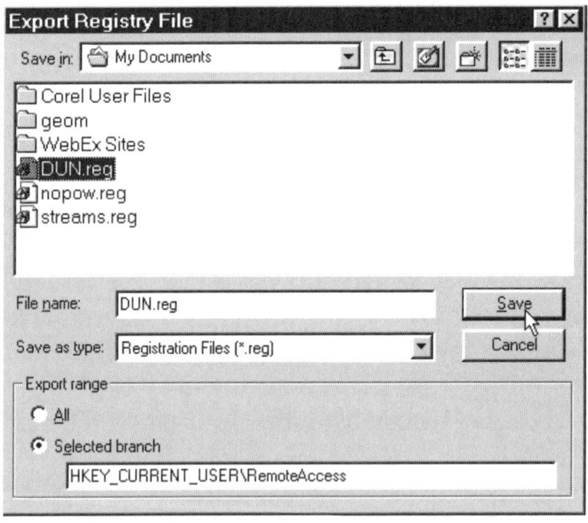

If your Dial-Up Networking profiles become corrupted, you can simply import this file back into the registry. Open RegEdit, select Import Registry File from the Registry menu, and double-click MY DUN.REG. All of your connection profiles will reappear in the Dial-Up Networking folder with all of the original information except for the login passwords. (To save those, you need to back up a series of password files in the \WINDOWS directory by entering **COPY *.PWL *.PBK**. If the password files become corrupted, delete them and issue the command **COPY *.PBK *.PWL**.)

Note *Note, if you have Windows 98 or Windows 95 installed on another computer, you can use this trick to transfer your Dial-Up Networking profiles to the second machine. Just copy MY DUN.REG to a diskette, run RegEdit on the second machine, and import this file into the second computer's registry.*

Restoring Internet Explorer Favorites and History List

For some people, loss of Internet Explorer's browsing history can be a disaster equivalent to deleting an entire folder full of reports or spreadsheets. If a system problem forces you to restore an old registry backup or reinstall Windows 98, you can lose all of the URL references in the History list and the pages that you've downloaded for offline viewing. Some users have also reported that Internet Explorer occasionally deletes pages from the cache at random. If Internet Explorer's Favorites and History list are critical for you, read this section to learn how to protect yourself against data loss.

The Internet Explorer Favorites folder works just like an ordinary folder. You can preserve your Favorites bookmarks simply by copying the contents of the \WINDOWS \FAVORITES directory to another location. (If your computer is configured for multiple user profiles, you'll want to back up the \WINDOWS\PROFILES \USERNAME\FAVORITES folder to preserve individual user settings.) You can archive your Favorites folder with a Windows 98 backup program or copy the contents through Windows Explorer.

The Internet Explorer History list (shown in Figure 8-8) works a little differently. The History folder is a virtual folder. Its contents are a combination of physical disk files and cross-references in the system registry. To back up your Internet Explorer History list, you must export a registry key and also back up the contents of the \WINDOWS\HISTORY folder from a DOS prompt. You can't copy the History folder from the Windows 98 desktop with Explorer. Its contents must be copied from a DOS session within Windows 98.

Here's how to back up the History list:

1. Open a DOS session within Windows 98 and create a backup directory for your URL History list. For example, enter **MD C:\HISTBAK**.
2. Log onto your backup directory (enter **CD \HISTBAK**) and issue the following command:

XCOPY C:\WINDOWS\HISTORY*.* /E /H /V.

(If your computer is configured for multiple user profiles, enter :

XCOPY C:\WINDOWS\PROFILES\USERNAME\HISTORY*.* /E /H /V.)

3. Open RegEdit and export a copy of the following registry key: HKEY_USERS\.Default\Software\Microsoft\Windows\CurrentVersion\Internet Settings. For instance, you might export this key to a file called MYHIST.REG in the My Documents folder. (If your computer is configured for multiple user profiles, you'll need to export each HKEY_USERS\USERNAME\Software\Microsoft\Windows\CurrentVersion\InternetSettings key instead of the .Default key.)

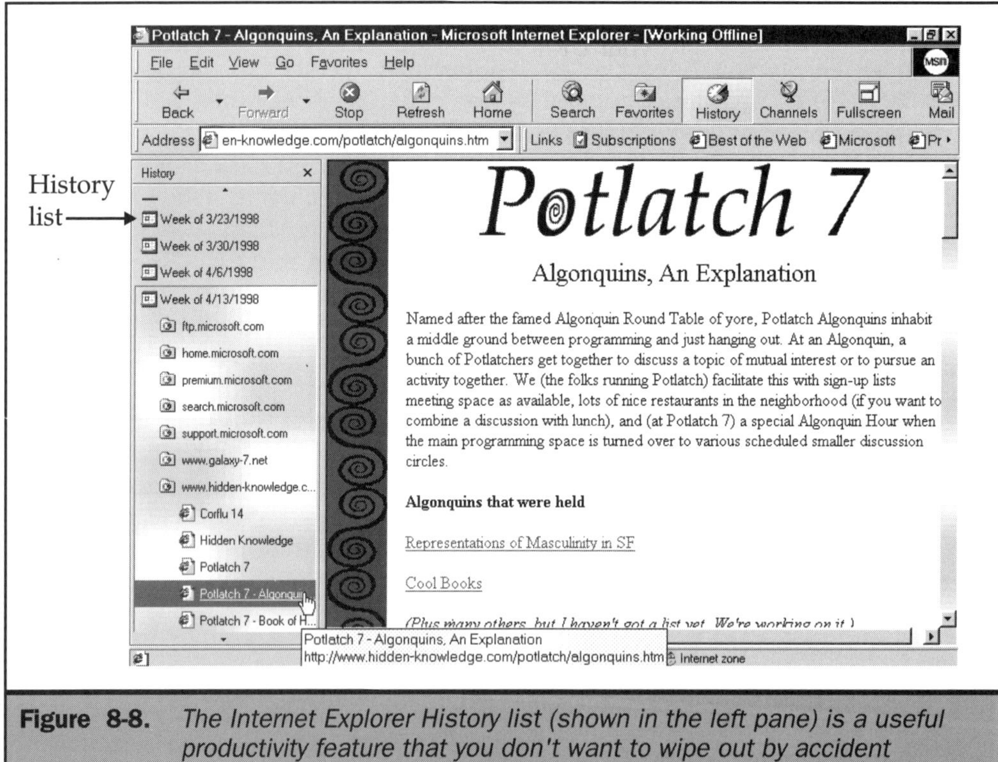

Figure 8-8. *The Internet Explorer History list (shown in the left pane) is a useful productivity feature that you don't want to wipe out by accident*

Restoring the History List

If a system crash corrupts your History folder, you can now restore it. After performing disk and registry maintenance to recover from the crash, open a DOS session within Windows 98.

1. At the DOS prompt, enter **CD WINDOWS\HISTORY**.
2. Use XCOPY to restore the file backup you that you previously created. For instance, if you backed up to C:\HISTBK, enter **C:\WINDOWS\HISTORY> XCOPY C:\HISTBK*.* /E /H /V**. (If multiple user profiles are enabled, restore the History files to the \PROFILES\USERNAME\HISTORY directory for each user.)
3. Open RegEdit and reimport the MYHIST.REG file that contains recent Internet Explorer settings. (For multiple user profiles, reimport each .REG file that you previously exported.)
4. Reboot the computer. The next time you launch Internet Explorer and open the History window, all of your URL bookmarks (listed by week and site) should be intact.

This procedure preserves URL links to the Web sites you've visited. If the content of the Temporary Internet Files folder in the \WINDOWS directory hasn't been disturbed, then you should also be able to continue browsing the sites that you've downloaded offline. If data in the Temporary Internet Files folder has been lost, you can go online and revisit the URLs in the History list to reload the pages in the cache.

To avoid losing data downloaded to the Temporary Internet Files cache, increase Internet Explorer's Days To Keep Pages In History setting. You'll find this option by choosing Control Panel | Internet and selecting the General tab (shown in Figure 8-9).

If the History or Temporary Internet Files folders still don't properly display your Internet browsing history, you can repair them with the Tweak UI utility included on the Windows 98 CD (this will usually do the trick). See "Repairing Desktop Problems with Tweak UI" later in this chapter for details.

Note *An extension of the procedure described here lets you migrate the complete Internet Explorer History list and all downloaded Web resources to a second Windows 98 computer. See "Replicating the Internet Explorer History List" in Chapter 12 for step-by-step instructions.*

Removing Stubborn Applications (and Error Messages)

If you attempt to uninstall a program by deleting its files from the hard disk and removing it from the Start menu, Windows 98 may display complaining messages about missing DLLs and other drivers that it can't find. The best way to avoid this problem is to use the Uninstall utility supplied with the application. Most Windows 95/98 programs have uninstallers that can be invoked through the Control Panel | Add/Remove Programs applet. (Select the program from the listing on the Install/Uninstall tab and click the Add/Remove button.)

Uninstalling programs with this procedure is generally reliable, but it's not 100 percent bulletproof. Sometimes the application vendor misses entries in the system registry. If your budget permits, third-party utilities such as Quarterdeck CleanSweep Deluxe (see http://www.quarterdeck.com) or Norton Uninstaller (see http://www.symantec.com) can automate the process of removing recalcitrant programs and their system files, saving you some time. But here's how to do it yourself.

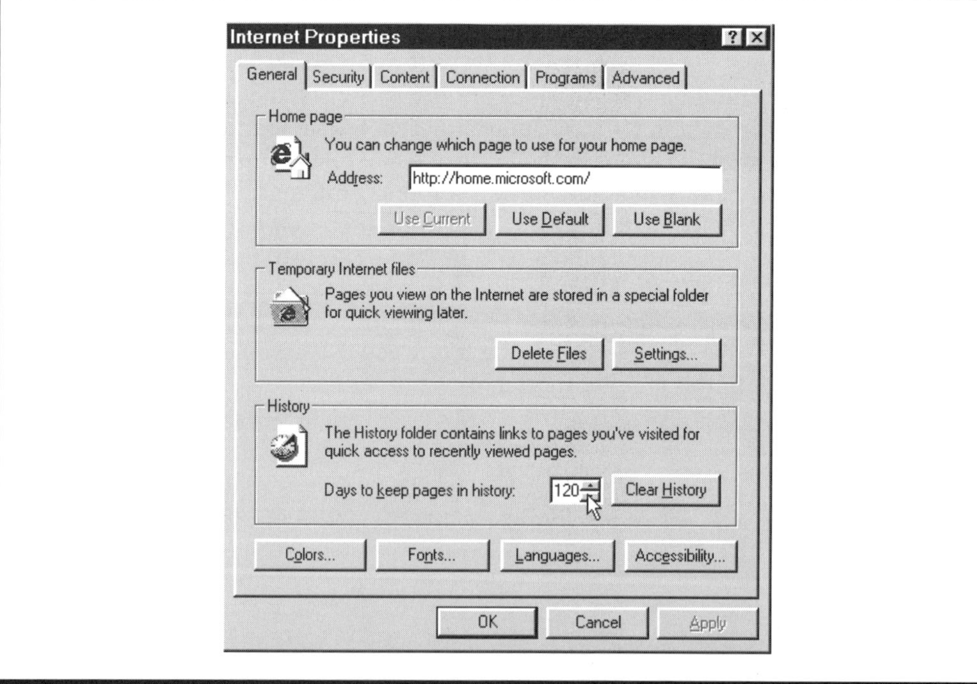

Figure 8-9. *Increasing the Clear History value on the Internet Properties screen extends the time before your browsing history is reset*

In Windows 3.1, you could eliminate complaining system messages about missing .DLL and .VXD files by opening and inspecting SYSTEM.INI to remove statements that loaded these drivers. In Windows 98 the statements that load these files are all embedded in the Windows registry.

Suppose, for instance, that you've uninstalled MYPROGRAM, but the system keeps telling you that it can't load MYPROGRAM.DLL. An entry for this file was embedded in the registry, and the uninstall program didn't remove it. Usually you can just click OK and continue when this happens. However, if you don't want to see this message every time you boot your computer (and you probably don't), here's how to permanently banish it:

1. Open RegEdit. Move the mouse to the top of the left RegEdit pane and select My Computer. Press CTRL-F or select Find from the Edit menu.
2. Type **MYPROGRAM.DLL** in the Find What field. Then click the Find Next button.
3. Eventually RegEdit will find and highlight MYPROGRAM.DLL in the Name column or the Data column in the right pane. To remove the entry, press the DELETE key.
4. Press F3 to continue the search and delete all subsequent references you find to MYPROGRAM.DLL.

If you remove references to missing files as just described, and Windows 98 still complains, you can try searching for the file path to a recently uninstalled program. For instance, if you just removed C:\TURKEYS\MYPROGRAM from your hard disk, open RegEdit, press CTRL-F, and enter **C:\TURKEYS\MYPROGRAM** in the Find What box. If references to system files show up in the registry with this file path, you can purge them.

You might ask yourself, "What if some other program wants to use these files? Is it safe to delete them?" The registry has a special key, HKEY_LOCAL_MACHINE\SOFTWARE\Microsoft\Windows\CurrentVersion\SharedDLLs, that contains references to all of the system files shared by one or more applications. If you open this key in RegEdit, you'll find an entry for each shared file in the Name column in the right RegEdit pane and a parenthetical value in the Data column, as shown in Figure 8-10. The number in parentheses represents the number of currently installed programs that have established links to this file. Thus, if you find MYPROGRAM.DLL in the Shared DLL list followed by (1), it's probably safe to delete all references to this file and to others marked (1) in the same directory. You can save a backup of this version of the registry until you confirm that the system remains stable after you make changes.

Emergency Recovery Tips: Before You Restore a Full-System Backup

If you notice Windows 98 behaving oddly, or if you can't boot to the desktop, there are several repair strategies that you may want to try before restoring a full-system backup or reinstalling the entire operating system.

To review what's been discussed in this chapter, your general strategy for preventing or correcting erratic Windows 98 behavior should include the following procedures:

- Review README files in the \WINDOWS directory to determine whether any hardware or software component in your computer may be a potential problem source.
- Create a Windows 98 emergency startup disk at your earliest convenience.

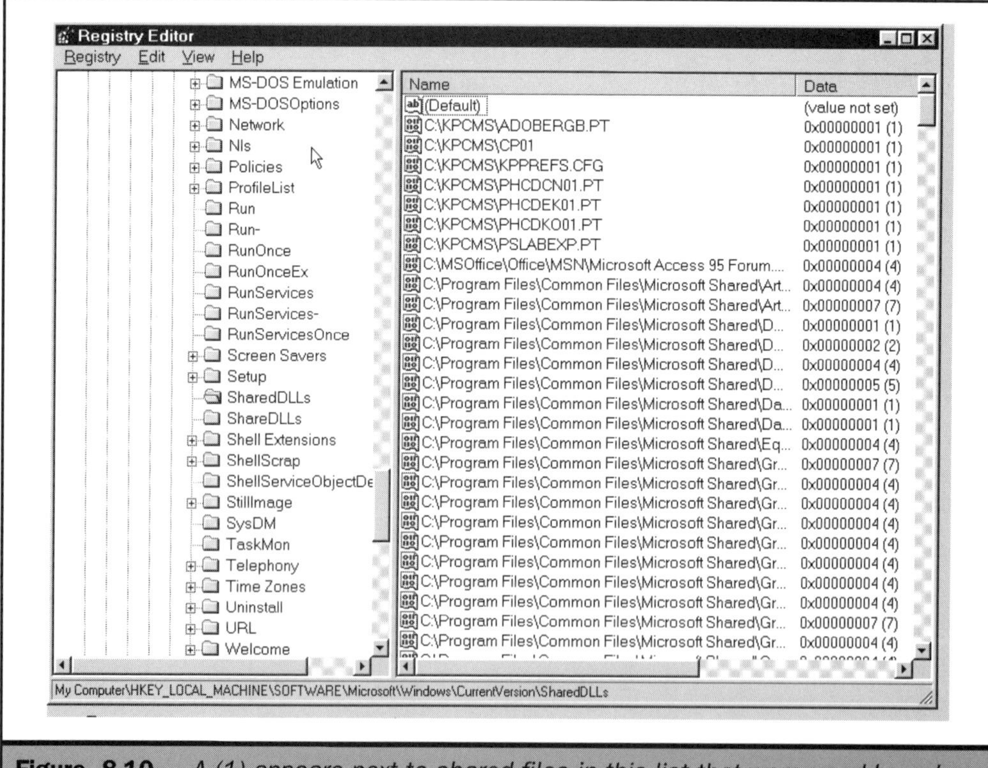

Figure 8-10. *A (1) appears next to shared files in this list that were used by only one application*

- Run ScanDisk regularly to eliminate a bad hard disk or file system errors as the problem source.
- Optimize (tune) your hard disk at regular intervals. Install a virus checker and perform regular virus scans.
- Back up your Windows 98 boot partition, applications, and data files so they can be restored in the event of hard disk failure.
- Make sure you have a recent backup of the Windows 98 registry that can be restored if the current version is reported as corrupt. Optionally, you may want to export separate, small ASCII backups of individual registry components.

Additional Quick Fixes

As you've seen in the previous sections, some, but not all, system problems may be related to a corrupt registry. Other problems can be caused by improper configuration of hardware peripherals and missing or incorrect versions of system files.

You'll find information about using the Windows 98 Device Manager to troubleshoot hardware configuration problems under "Resolving Device Manager Problems" in Chapter 3, "Device Manager Tab" in Chapter 9, and "Resolving Startup Error Messages" in Chapter 14.

System file incompatibilities may occur when third-party applications overwrite the .DLL files in the \WINDOWS\SYSTEM directory with older, vendor-supplied versions. The System File Checker and Version Conflict Manager tools, available within the System Information utility, can help you track down system file conflicts. The two tools complement each other. The System File Checker systematically examines the contents of \WINDOWS and its subdirectories to verify that the latest versions of Windows 98 operating files are present. If older files are detected, you can update them from the Windows 98 installation CD, verify that you want to keep the older versions, or postpone action until a future time.

The Version Conflict Manager monitors files with a more recent version number or file date than your current version of Windows 98. During installation, if Windows 98 replaces any of these files, they are backed up in the \WINDOWS\SYSBCKUP directory. The Version Conflict Manager displays a table that shows which files were replaced, allowing you to reinstall them.

In particular, problems with automatic Windows 98 shutdown and advanced power management features are often related to incorrect system files. It's a good idea to run System File Checker and Version Conflict Manager occasionally to check the integrity of the operating system. (Open the System Information applet in the Accessories | System Tools folder and choose the Tools menu.) For more detailed information about using these utilities, see "System Information" in Chapter 6.

Updating Windows

Microsoft has established a maintenance center for Windows 98 on the World Wide Web. Enhancements to Windows 98, patches, new drivers, and service packs can be downloaded over the Internet and installed in the operating system automatically through the Windows Update tool.

If Windows 98 is configured to connect to the Internet when you launch the Internet Explorer browser, you can access the Update Center by clicking the Windows Update icon on the Start menu. (You'll also find a copy under Start menu | Settings.) Otherwise, connect to the Internet first through Dial-Up Networking and then open the Windows Update tool.

Windows Update automatically launches an Internet Explorer window at Microsoft's Update Center Web site. After contact with the Web site is established, an ActiveX script compares your Windows 98 configuration with the newest available drivers and service patches. The Available Updates list displays new Windows 98 components and fixes that your system can use. The Description column contains date, size, and download time information about each update module.

To download and install a new Windows 98 component or driver fix, select it in the Available Updates column and click the Install button in the Update Wizard window. After the file is downloaded to your hard disk, the Confirm Install dialog box pops up, prompting you to unpack and install the update module, as shown in Figure 8-11. Click OK to continue. You can also click the Cancel button to postpone insulation of the update.

You can make the Update Wizard repeat the scan for other new components by clicking the Rescan button.

Note *Additional drivers for Windows 98 may be available from the Microsoft Download Library at http://support.microsoft.com/support/downloads/default.asp. You can also connect directly by modem through HyperTerminal at (425) 936-6735 in the United States or (905) 507-3022 in Canada. (See Chapters 5 and 11 for more information on using HyperTerminal and your modem.) If you don't have a modem, you can request driver updates on disk from Microsoft Technical Support.*

Repairing Desktop Problems with Tweak UI

The Windows 98 CD includes an all-purpose utility applet called Tweak UI. In addition to providing desktop and system controls, Tweak UI includes a Repair tab that can resolve a number of desktop problems: It can correct the display of desktop icons and repair application and file associations. It can also restore internal information necessary for the Font, URL History, and Temporary Internet Files folders to work properly.

To install Tweak UI, open the \TOOLS\RESKIT\POWERTOY folder on the Windows 98 Installation CD in Windows Explorer. Right-click the file called

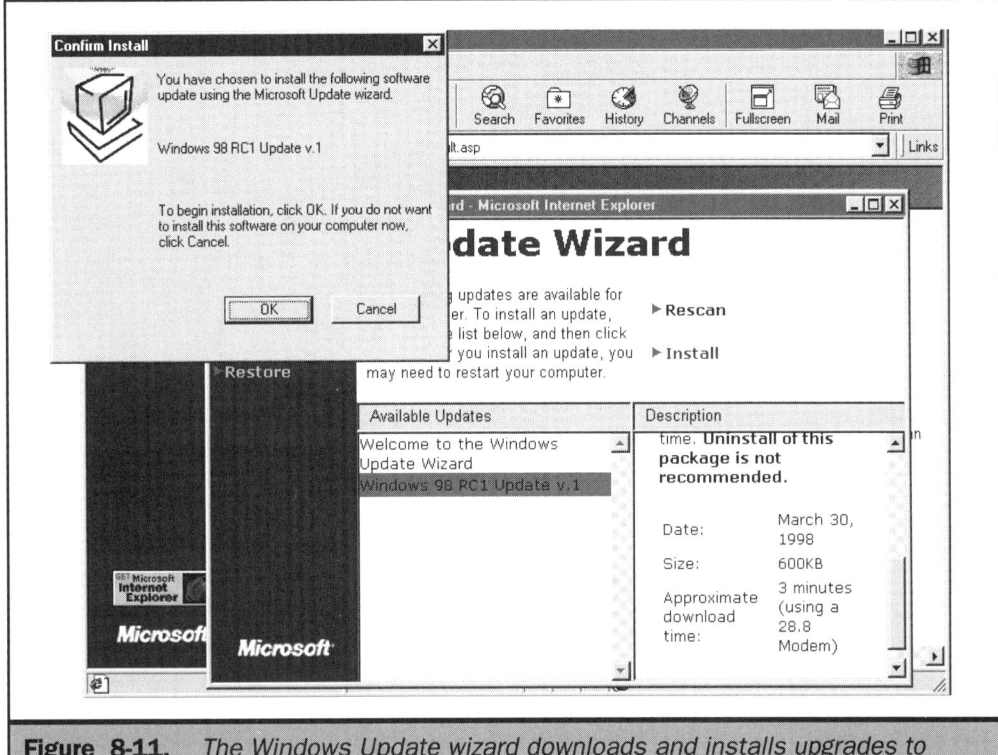

Figure 8-11. *The Windows Update wizard downloads and installs upgrades to Windows 98 in one step through the Internet*

TWEAKUI.INF and choose the Install option from the pop-up menu. After Tweak UI is installed, it appears as an applet in the Control Panel folder.

To take advantage of Tweak UI's desktop repair features, open the applet (from the Start menu, choose Settings | Control Panel | Tweak UI). Click the right scroll arrow at the top of the Tweak UI window until the Repair tab comes into view; then select it. Open the drop-down list on the Repair tab to select the fix you want to apply (see Figure 8-12). Then click the Repair Now button.

A description of each Tweak UI repair option appears in the description field when the option is selected in the drop-down list. As discussed earlier, the Repair Temporary Internet Files and Repair URL History commands can restore the special display features for these folders. Rebuild Desktop Icons refreshes the Windows 98 shell cache, ensuring that Start menu, taskbar, and desktop shortcuts display the correct icon bitmaps. Repair Associations returns icons to their factory settings and also restores installation defaults for Win98 file associations. (For instance, if the .BMP extension has

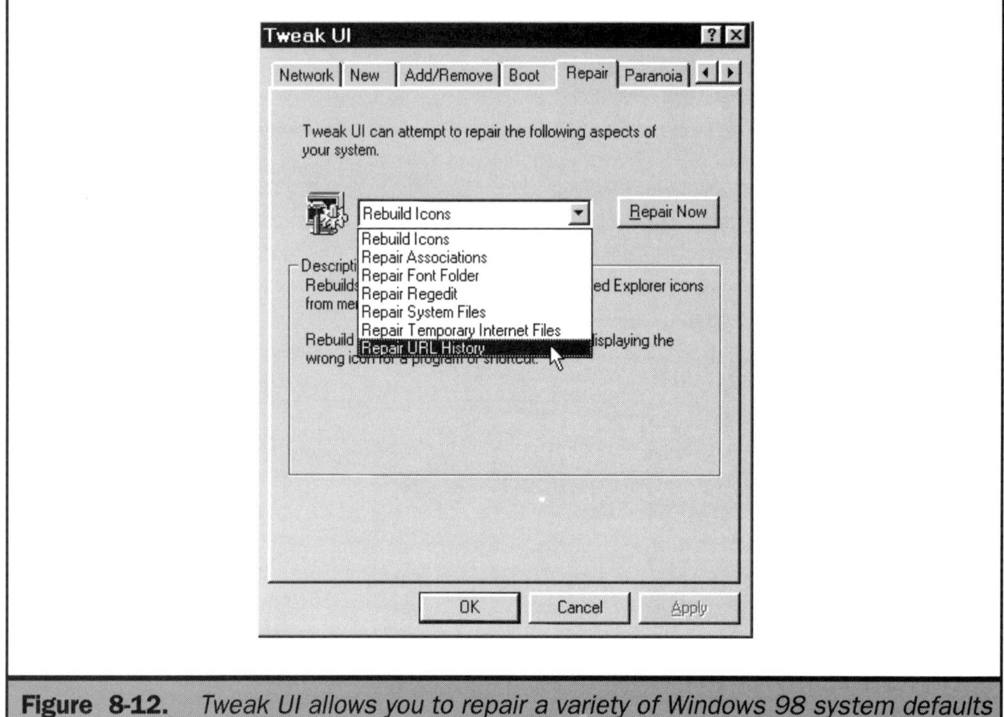

Figure 8-12. *Tweak UI allows you to repair a variety of Windows 98 system defaults*

been associated with a third-party application, this command relinks it with Microsoft Paint.)

Tweak UI includes a wide variety of other system configuration options not directly related to desktop maintenance. You'll find more information about working with this useful tool (and the other Win98 Control Panel applets) in the next chapter.

Chapter 9

Tweaking the System: The Windows Control Panel

Chapter Highlights

What's new in Windows 98

Fast access to Control Panel features

Working with the Control Panel:

> **Using Display, Add New Hardware, Add/Remove Programs, System, Modems, Network, Printers, and the rest of the applets**

Adding components overlooked by Windows Setup

Fine-tuning Win98 performance settings: the optional Tweak UI applet

Staying in control: A review of strategic adjustments that most users will want to make right away

---

This chapter is your guided tour through the Windows 98 Control Panel. You'll see how to get fast access to the most common setup and customization features. You'll also find detailed explanations of more obscure features, including pertinent tips on fine-tuning the interface and obtaining diagnostic information. The Control Panel in Windows 98 lets you manage most of your system's performance settings from one centrally located folder. Approximately 25 applets in the Control Panel govern various aspects of the Win98 operating environment. (Third-party applications can install additional modules).

Through these applets, you can adjust almost every physical, visual, and operational detail of your computer. Though the defaults assigned by Windows 98 will let many users get to work immediately, a knowledge of what you can do in Control Panel can still be useful. The various applets allow you to delve into system internals: change display values, install or remove Active Desktop components, adjust multimedia defaults, add or remove programs and hardware, and so on.

Here are some of the important operations you'll learn in this chapter:

- How to adjust and customize your desktop display
- How to add Web resources to Win98's Active Desktop
- How to add valuable accessories that may have been skipped during setup
- How to activate a network
- How to set up multiple user accounts

- How to use Windows 98 Advanced Power Management
- How to tweak Windows 98 settings for added system flexibility and better performance

The first section, "What's New in Windows 98," is intended for experienced Windows 95 users. It provides a capsule summary of new and changed Control Panel features.

The next section, "Accessing the Control Panel," shows how to create quick access shortcuts to the Control Panel and its most commonly used individual applets.

Following the quick-access tips, the section "Working with Control Panel Applets" contains an overview and an applet-by-applet guided tour. This part of the chapter can be used as either a reference guide or as a tutorial on customizing Windows 98. The individual applets are treated in the order of their probable strategic importance. The early entries show how to make cosmetic changes to the Windows 98 desktop. The middle portion discusses the applets that add and remove Windows accessories and hardware components. The final part of this section describes the applets that configure and change internal system settings.

Users seeking a quick-card guide for strategic Control Panel adjustments may want to skip to the section "Stay in Control" at the end of the chapter. This last section is a review of the top twelve convenience changes you'll want to make as soon as Windows 98 appears on your hard disk.

What's New in Windows 98

For experienced users of Windows 95, here's a brief rundown of new features and changes in the Windows 98 Control Panel:

- The Add New Hardware Wizard now has a plug-and-play detection module that allows certain devices to be quickly re-enabled or installed before your computer is searched for non-PNP peripherals.
- Add/Remove Programs has new component groups that list features specific to Windows 98: Desktop Themes, Internet Tools, Microsoft Outlook Express, Online Services, and TV Viewer. The applets in the System Tools accessories folder are now added and removed through the System Tools group.
- The Display applet has two new tabs: Effects and Web. The Web tab adds and configures Win98 Active Desktop components. (You'll find more information about Active Desktop in Chapter 4, Chapter 12, and in the section "Display Applet" later in this chapter.) The Effects tab allows changes in default desktop icons and controls desktop animation settings. The Background tab now has enhanced Wallpaper options. It permits HTML documents as well as bitmap images to be used as Windows wallpaper.
- The Joystick applet is now called Game Controllers.

- The Internet applet now sets defaults for Internet Explorer version 4.
- The Keyboard applet no longer has a General tab. Defaults are set on the Speed and Language tabs.
- In the Multimedia applet the Advanced tab is now called Devices. Advanced playback and recording settings are now buttons on the Audio tab. The CD tab now supports digital sound playback.
- The Power Management applet now implements Microsoft's Advanced Power Management (APM) 1.2 and/or Advanced Control Power Interface (ACPI) standards on compliant computers. The software Suspend button has been removed from the Start menu and replaced by a Standby option on the Shutdown menu.
- A Scanners and Cameras applet now lists and configures these peripherals at a system level.
- A new Telephony applet has been added to allow quick configuration of dial-up properties from remote locations.
- The Tweak UI applet, offered in Windows 95 as part of the Windows 95 PowerToys is available in Windows 98 as an optional component installed from the \TOOLS\RESKIT\POWERTOY folder on the Win98 CD.
- A new Users applet has been added to allow quick configuration of multiple user profiles to permit alternative logins to a single computer.

Accessing the Control Panel

By default, the Control Panel appears in two obvious places: You can get to it by clicking the Start button and selecting Settings, or you can open the Control Panel icon that appears on the first level of My Computer. When you open it in either location, Control Panel displays a desktop window with a series of icons as shown in Figure 9-1. Each icon in the Control Panel folder opens configuration settings for a component of the Windows 98 interface.

Windows 98 determines the options that will appear in the Control Panel during installation. These depend partly on the individual contents of your system. If your computer has PC Card slots, a game port, or an infrared port, corresponding options will appear. Microsoft Mail and Mail and Fax appear if you installed these options under Windows 95 before upgrading to Windows 98.

The Control Panel looks like an ordinary Win98 folder, but it is a fixed object. You can't drag new shortcuts into it or delete the existing applets. (You can hide selected

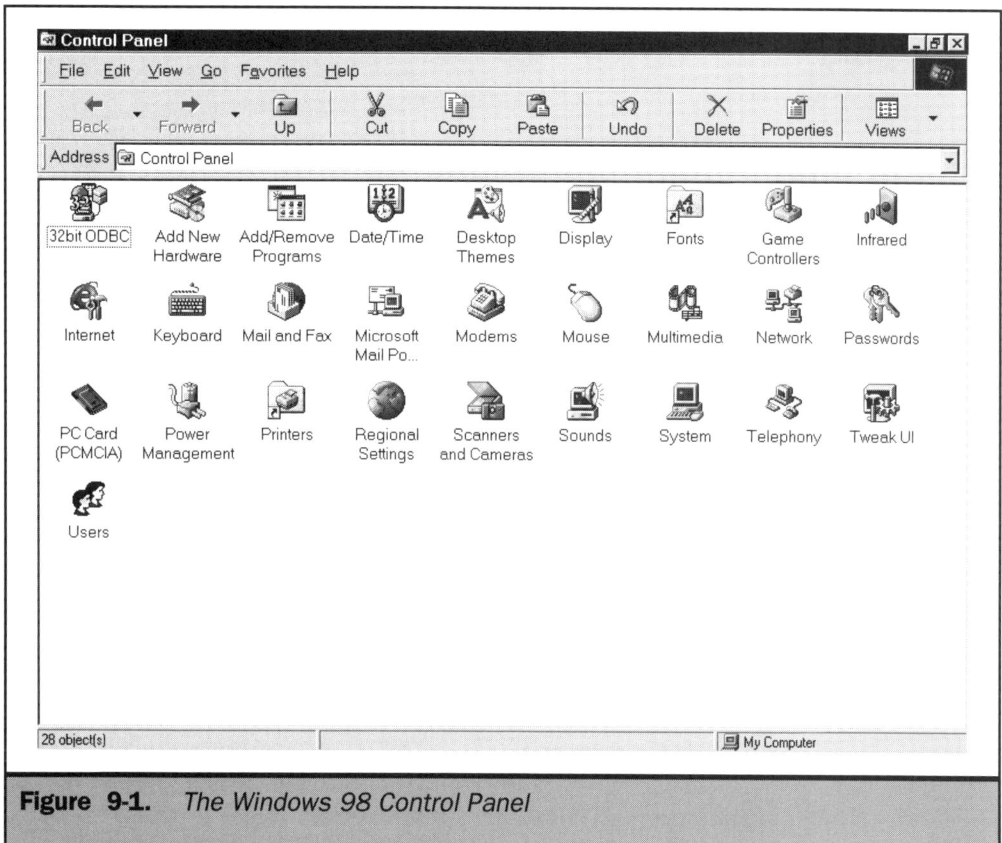

Figure 9-1. *The Windows 98 Control Panel*

Control Panel applets from view with the Tweak UI Powertool included on the Windows 98 CD. You'll find information later on in this chapter on how to use and install this utility.) When you add or remove new hardware and software on your computer, some Control Panel features may disappear, and additional objects may be installed. The important point to remember is that you can't drag programs or shortcuts *into* the Control Panel from the desktop, but you can drag shortcuts for individual components *out of* the Control Panel to the desktop. You can create shortcuts to Control Panel items directly on the desktop or in any Start menu program group. You may find this feature convenient for creating custom shortcuts for the Control Panel applets you use most frequently.

Express Shortcut on the Start Menu

If you want quick access to Control Panel applets from the first level of the Start menu, try this trick:

1. Right-click the Start button and choose Open from the pop-up menu.
2. Right-click inside a white area of the Start menu folder and choose New | Folder. A folder icon bearing the name New Folder will appear.
3. Rename the new folder. (If you haven't clicked the mouse again, you can type the new name directly. Otherwise, right-click New Folder and select Rename). Enter the following string for the folder's new name:

   Control Panel.{21EC2020-3AEA-1069-A2DD-08002B30309D}

   Copy this string exactly, including the right and left curly brackets.

You'll find that this procedure creates a cascading Control Panel shortcut at the top of the Start menu. You can point to it with the mouse, and it will open up to display all of the currently active Control Panel applets. This trick works because the Control Panel is a special folder that is defined internally by a Windows 98 class ID. Assigning this class ID as a folder name re-creates the Control Panel folder in a more convenient location. Microsoft documented this shortcut in Windows 95, but chose to omit it from the Windows 98 version of TIPS.TXT (located in the \WINDOWS directory) because a few Control Panel applets added by third-party vendors may cause this shortcut to crash when you try to open it. If you encounter this (not common) difficulty, you can simply delete the class ID shortcut from the Start menu folder and create a different kind of Control Panel shortcut. (See the section "Customizing Control Panel Access" for details.)

Customizing Control Panel Access

You may use some Control Panel utilities frequently, and ignore others completely. For example, when Windows 3.x was released, some users spent hours fine-tuning color schemes but never touched the mouse module. It worked well enough, so why bother?

The Windows 98 Control Panel is more complex than its Win 3.x and Windows 95 predecessors—but you can still modify settings that are important to you and leave the rest alone.

The most obvious way to get quick Control Panel access is to drag shortcuts to one or more of the internal applets directly onto the desktop. For instance, if you use the multimedia settings a lot, open the Control Panel folder, right-click and drag the Multimedia icon onto the desktop, and then choose Create Shortcut Here. (You can also left-click and drag a Control Panel shortcut to the desktop if you click past the annoying message: "You cannot move or copy this item to this location." Click Yes to create a desktop shortcut, instead of moving the original.) Once the shortcut appears on the desktop, you can change its name from "Shortcut to Multimedia" to plain old "Multimedia." Dragging Control Panel shortcuts to the desktop is probably best as a temporary solution: At first, you may use the shortcut repeatedly to fine-tune an aspect of system performance. When you're satisfied, you can delete the shortcut from the desktop.

Another way to gain quick access to a Control Panel component is to drop it onto the first level of the Start menu. Perhaps you want convenient access to the Printers folder. You can open Control Panel, select the Printers folder, and then drag and drop it on the Start button (as shown here).

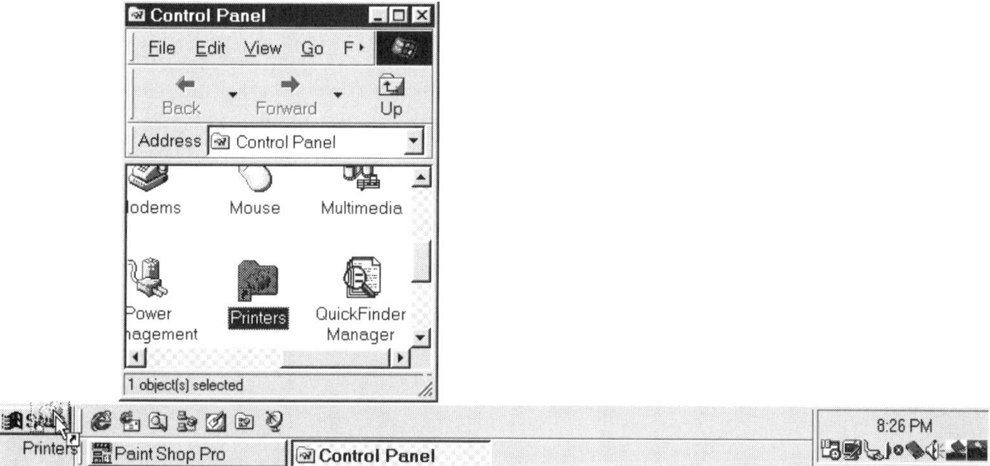

What if you want quick access to a related group of Control Panel objects, but not the entire list? For instance, you might want Display, Printers, Fonts, and Multimedia available on the desktop, but have no need for Keyboard, Mouse, PC Cards, and other components. You can do the following to create a shortcut for just a selected group of components:

1. Open the Control Panel folder on the desktop.
2. Right-click the Start button and choose Open.
3. Create a new folder in the Start menu window (choose File | New | Folder). Enter a name (such as Control) for the new folder.
4. Select and drag the desired Control Panel components into the new folder. (Right-click and drag to avoid the "can't copy or move" message).
5. You may rename the shortcuts you've just created if you want to eliminate the words "Shortcut to."

This procedure creates an abbreviated Control Panel at the top of the Start menu for quick access. Unlike the class ID shortcut presented earlier, this technique is crash-proof under Windows 98. Place the mouse cursor over your new, abbreviated Control Panel, and a menu will fan open to show the shortcuts you've dragged in.

If you keep creating shortcuts by dragging file objects out of an Explorer window and systematically remove the words "Shortcut to," Windows 98 eventually stops adding these words to the filename. If you want Win98 to immediately stop prefixing your shortcuts with these words, you can set this default with the Tweak UI applet available on the Win98 CD. See "Installing Tweak UI" later in this chapter for details.

Another strategy you can use is to create a series of Control Panel subfolders grouping utilities into function-related categories. To do this, you can create folders within folders in the Start menu window, as shown in Figure 9-2. For instance, a Hardware group might contain shortcuts to Add New Hardware, Mouse, Joystick,

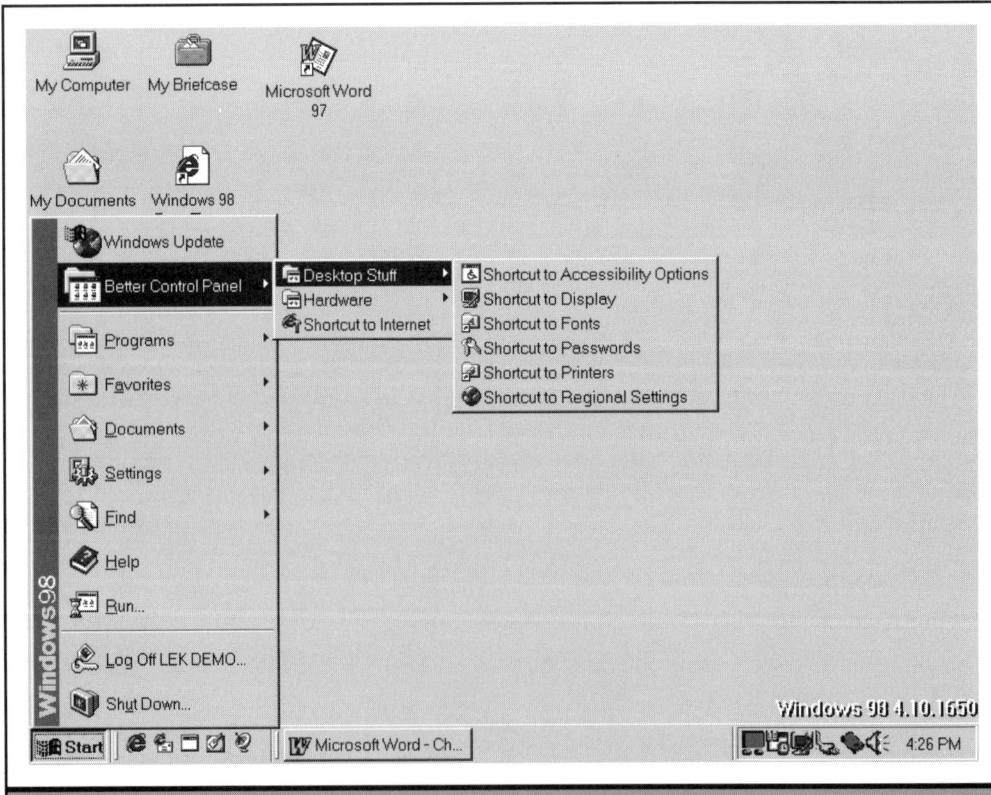

Figure 9-2. *A smart way to build an organized Control Panel*

Keyboard, and Modems. A Desktop group might contain Accessibility, Display, Fonts, Passwords, and Regional Settings. Both subfolders can be placed in a folder called Better Control Panel on the first level of the Start menu. This strategy may be more efficient than always opening the entire collection of Control Panel applets.

Working with Control Panel Applets

The Windows 98 Control Panel carries on a Windows tradition: It can regulate a potpourri of display and performance defaults. Like other parts of Windows 98, the Control Panel can be approached by users with a wide range of technical sophistication. You may want to configure a Microsoft Mail post office or just add some wallpaper. You don't have to know what every applet in the Control Panel does to accomplish your purpose. No matter what your level of Windows 98 expertise, there will probably be utilities in the Control Panel that you never use; at the same time, you don't have to be a Win98 guru to exploit a remarkable range of useful system controls.

The balance of this chapter provides thumbnail sketches of each Control Panel applet, plus some guidelines to help you customize Windows 98 to your liking. The applet information is presented in strategic order (rather than in alphabetical order):

Desktop Themes Applet
Display Applet
Accessibility Options Applet
Date/Time Applet
Regional Settings Applet
Add/Remove Programs Applet
Add New Hardware Applet
System Applet
Game Controllers Applet
Infrared Applet
Keyboard Applet
Mouse Applet
Internet Applet
Modems Applet
Mail and Fax Applet
Microsoft Mail Postoffice Applet
Network Applet
Telephony Applet
Passwords Applet
Users Applet
Sounds Applet
Multimedia Applet

32-Bit ODBC Applet
Fonts Applet
Printers Applet
PC Card (PCMCIA) Applet
Power Management Applet
Tweak UI Applet

To look up an applet alphabetically, see the index at the back of the book.

To access Microsoft's online descriptions of the Control Panel applets, open Help from the Start menu, select the Index tab, and type **Control** in the Search field. You can click the Display button to see topics under any Help entry, as shown here:

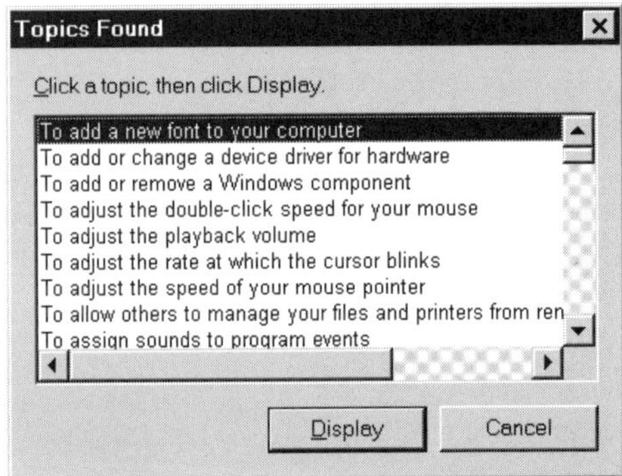

Desktop Themes Applet

The popular Desktop Themes applet has been transferred to Windows 98 from the Microsoft Plus supplement for Windows 95. Desktop Themes includes supplemental Windows wallpaper, screen savers, mouse pointers, icons, screen colors, fonts, and system sounds that completely make over the appearance of the Windows 98 desktop. This feature is designed to appeal to the escapist or interior decorator that lurks in the heart of some Windows users. You'll find themes that are either beautiful or garish, with titles like The '60s, Nature, Science, and Sports. The animated cursors and hi-res wallpaper can be fun to look at, but loading these options may noticeably slow down system performance.

Desktop Themes is not installed in a standard Windows 98 setup. To activate it, choose Control Panel | Add/Remove Programs, select the Windows Setup tab, and place a check mark next to Desktop Themes in the Components list. Note that the complete list of themes consumes about 16MB of disk space. You may want to highlight Desktop Themes in the Components list, click the Details button, and select just a few samples rather than adding the whole works.

After it has been added to the Control Panel, you can open the Desktop Themes applet to browse through the available desktops (click the Themes drop-down list) as shown in Figure 9-3. You can preview the screen saver or click the Pointers, Sounds, Etc. button to preview those elements.

Tip *Individual elements of a Desktop Theme can be enabled or disabled by toggling the check mark to the right of each component in the Settings list.*

Display Applet

Windows is praised by many users for the flexibility of its appearance. The ability to create a personalized desktop can help users relate to the operating system, so the Display component might be considered one of the most important Control Panel applets. You will probably want to gain some familiarity with it to fine-tune the Win98 desktop to provide your own custom look and feel.

Display properties are important enough that Microsoft provides both front- and back-door access to them. In addition to reaching the Display window by opening it in

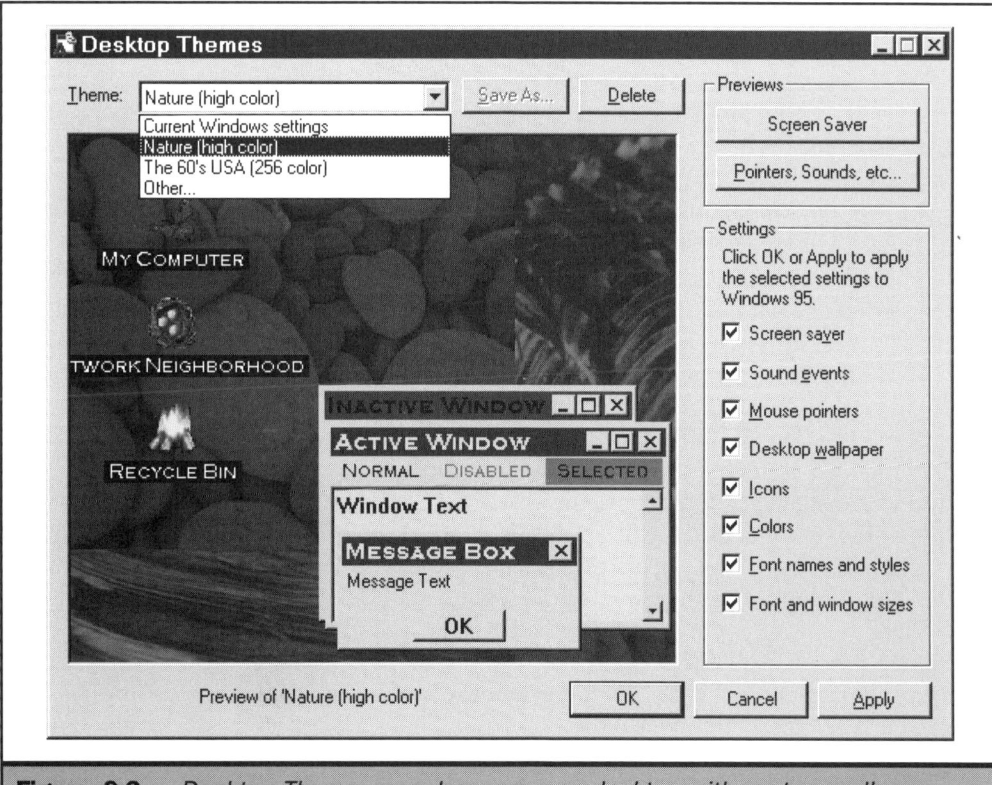

Figure 9-3. *Desktop Themes can dress up your desktop with custom wallpaper, mouse pointers, and sound events*

the Control Panel, you can get to it by right-clicking an empty area of the desktop and selecting Properties from the pop-up menu. If you're specifically interested in customizing Win98's Active Desktop controls, you can right-click an empty area of the desktop and choose Active Desktop | Customize My Desktop from the pop-up menu.

If you're a hard-case geek like I am, the first thing you'll want to do after Windows 98 appears on your computer is to get rid of any Setup wallpaper placed by OEM computer vendors. Open the Display applet, select the Background tab, scroll up in the Wallpaper list, and select None. I also suggest changing the default electric blue or green background of the desktop to a lighter, more sedate color. Select the Appearance tab in the Display applet, click the Color box, and select a white or light gray background to create an uncluttered, Macintosh-like look. (Some people really prefer psychedelic colors and wallpaper. The choice is up to you!)

Those who know the old Windows 3.x Control Panel will notice that the Windows 98 version combines two related Windows 3.x utilities: Color and Desktop. Windows 98 lets you select color schemes, choose wallpaper and screensavers, and adjust other desktop defaults from the six-tabbed Display Properties window. (There are six default tabs. OEM vendors of video drivers and other screen utilities may add more.)

Background Tab

The Background tab lets you add desktop wallpaper and patterns to fill out empty space around centered wallpaper. In Windows 98, you can create wallpaper from bitmap images in several formats: GIF and JPG as well as Microsoft BMP. You can select one of the preconfigured images (identified with a paintbrush icon) in the Wallpaper list or click the Browse button to load your own image from disk. If you select the Center option in the Display field, you can also click the Pattern button to add a textural pattern around the image.

If you turn on Win98's Active Desktop, you can also create wallpaper from a World Wide Web page (HTML document). You may want to take advantage of this feature if you like the idea of having direct links to Internet resources embedded in your desktop. For instance, if you choose the WALLPAPR.HTM file at the end of the default Wallpaper list, you can quickly jump to Microsoft's World Wide Web site by clicking the Windows 98 logo. You can also design customized Web wallpaper with embedded links to sites of your own choosing (search engines, FTP resources, and so on). Note that adding Web wallpaper is not exactly the same as adding an HTML, Java, or ActiveX control (such as the Windows 98 Channel bar) to the desktop, although the end result is similar. See "Web Tab" later in this chapter for information on adding individual Web objects to the desktop.

You can add bitmap wallpaper to the classic Windows 98 desktop and then switch to the Active Desktop to superimpose a Web page background. This creates two different wallpaper settings. The bitmap wallpaper will reappear when you switch from Active Desktop to the classic desktop. The current wallpaper selection on the

Display background tab will switch back and forth when you toggle between the classic desktop and Active Desktop. If you change the selected wallpaper in either view, the wallpaper in the other view will also be changed. (See Chapter 4 for more information on working with HTML objects using the Active Desktop.)

You can add a new bitmap image or Web page to the Wallpaper list by dragging its file icon from My Computer or Windows Explorer and dropping it on the list.

Screen Saver Tab

Like the Background, Appearance, and Web tabs, the Screen Saver tab, shown in Figure 9-4, displays a preview of changed settings before they're actually implemented. The drop-down Screen Saver list lets you sample the thirteen available patterns. If you install new, third-party screen savers in Windows 98, they will also appear in this

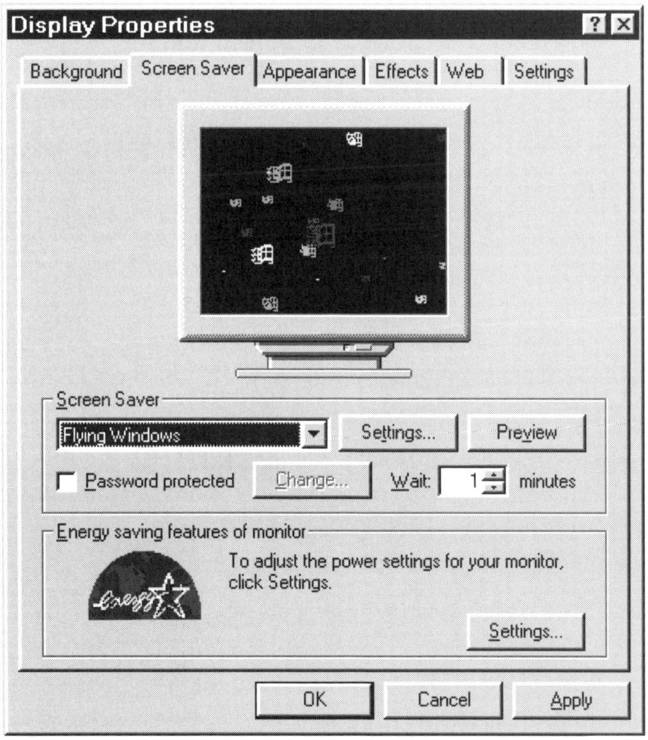

Figure 9-4. *Windows 98 built-in screen savers*

drop-down list. To sample a screen saver in full-screen mode, click the Preview button to the right of the Screen Saver list.

Settings are specific to each screen saver and allow you to adjust the number and speed of the various flying objects. For some screen savers, you can also customize the text that appears and the texture of the colors.

What's the use of screen savers? They offer another way for you to personalize your computer. Back when most people were using monochrome display monitors, screen savers prevented high-contrast text from being permanently burned into the CRT display. With VGA monitors, it's highly unlikely that any image will be burned in, even if you leave it on your screen for weeks.

If you're looking for an intrinsic value for screen savers, you can use them for privacy by placing a check mark in the Password Protected box; you'll then need to enter your password to restore your screen after the screen saver kicks in. What if you forget your screen saver password and lock yourself out of your own computer? Not really a big deal. See Chapter 16 to learn what to do.

The screen saver that may make the most sense is Blank Screen, which switches off all display elements and makes the monitor appear to be off. Touch the keyboard or the mouse, and it comes back to life. This module is unexciting, but it works—and with no drain on memory, resources, or hard disk space.

Creating a Screen Saver Shortcut on the Desktop

Ordinarily, the screen saver switches on after a specified number of minutes. However, you can make your screen saver kick in immediately instead of waiting for it to appear. Just create a shortcut icon on your desktop that will automatically activate any screen saver. Here's how:

1. Retrieve a list of all the Windows 98 screen savers available on your system: Choose Start | Find | Files or Folders and search for *.SCR in the \WINDOWS\SYSTEM folder.

2. Choose the screen saver you want from the list that appears in the Find window, right-click it, and choose Create Shortcut from the pop-up menu. Answer Yes when prompted to place the shortcut on the desktop.

3. To configure the screen saver, right-click the new desktop shortcut you created and choose Install from the pop-up menu. This allows you to password-protect the screen saver and adjust its other properties.

4. If you wait for the specified number of minutes, your screen saver will open automatically. If you want to leave your desktop and activate it immediately, just open the desktop shortcut. You can also create a keyboard shortcut to activate the screen saver. Right-click the shortcut, choose Properties, and go to the Shortcut tab. Click the Shortcut Key field and enter the keystrokes you want to use to launch the screen saver.

Appearance Tab

The Appearance tab, shown in Figure 9-5, allows you to customize the screen colors, fonts, and icons that are used to display the desktop. These elements can be modified individually or all at once. To change the appearance of the entire desktop, you can browse through the various choices shown in the Schemes list. The preview window shows you what the new desktop scheme will look like before you implement it. Desktop features such as window colors, fonts, and icon defaults can be changed individually by selecting the appropriate category in the Item list.

SCHEME LIST The Scheme box contains a variety of preconfigured desktop color and font schemes. Windows 98 gives you 33 of these out of the box. By default, the Scheme box is empty. Before you start experimenting with new schemes, I recommend saving your current desktop settings. (Click the Save As button to the

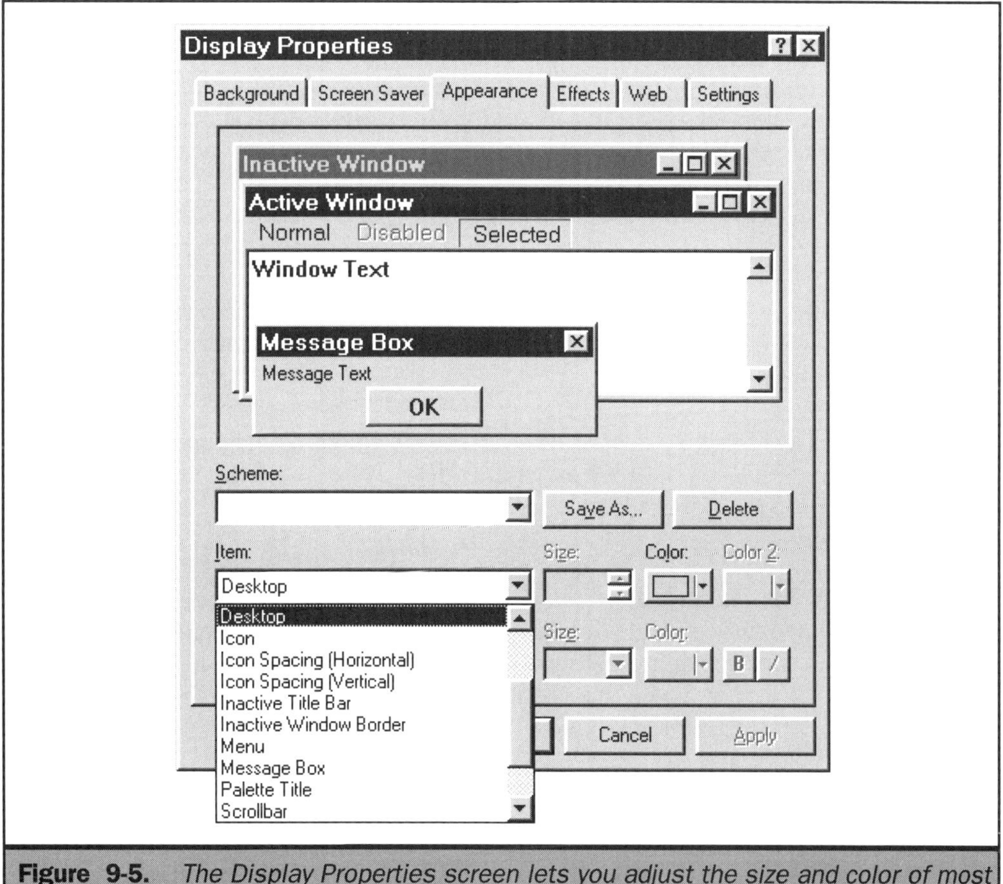

Figure 9-5. *The Display Properties screen lets you adjust the size and color of most desktop components*

right of the Scheme list and enter a name.) You can then feel free to try out some of Microsoft's alternatives.

The Wheat scheme, for instance, adds an odd light yellow tinge to the desktop; and Lilac provides displays in shades of blue and purple. These schemes range from innocuous to obnoxious. Their best use is as starting points for developing your own custom color schemes. Two convenient schemes—Large and Extra Large—automatically increase font size for all icons, desktop windows, and the taskbar for easier reading.

Don't confuse the Scheme feature of Display Properties with Desktop Themes, a separate Control Panel applet. Desktop Themes provides much more than just the color and font changes of a scheme. (See "Desktop Themes Applet" earlier in this chapter for more information.)

ITEM LIST The Item drop-down list, shown in Figure 9-5, lets you individually edit 18 attributes of the desktop's appearance. Each attribute in the list has different properties. Icon Spacing (Vertical), for instance, provides a variable point size for the space between rows of desktop icons (the default is 43 points).

When you highlight an attribute, you can then modify applicable font and color settings. For the Desktop item, for instance, you can modify only the color. For the Menu item, you can change the background color as well as font style, font size, and the foreground color. This option gives you serious personalization capabilities, even allowing you to use a bold italic symbol font for your menu titles, if that's what you want.

Tip *As an alternative to selecting attributes from the Item drop-down list, you can simply click an object in the Appearance preview window (such as Active Window, Window Text, Message Box, and so on).*

FONT LIST Font is the third drop-down list. Font becomes active only when the desktop component selected in the Item list uses text. The Size, Color, Bold, and Italics buttons to the right of the Font list allow you to further modify the font's display attributes.

SAVING CHANGES When you change any display attribute on the Appearance tab, the change is immediately reflected in the preview display at the top of the Properties window. You can cancel changes that you don't like by clicking the Cancel button at the bottom of the window. To implement your changes to the desktop, you can either click Apply (to keep the Display Properties window open) or click OK (to close the Display Properties window).

One element of the display interface that you can't change with the Display Properties Appearance tab is the Window Text font (the font used for the text that appears when you enter data into an application). The display font used for text in an application window is usually determined by the application running in the window.

Effects Tab

The Effects tab lets you customize the appearance of Windows 98's internal desktop icons. You can click any component in the Desktop Icons field and change its appearance. (See Chapter 4 for more information about assigning customized icons to desktop objects.) The check boxes under Visual Effects let you change the way icons are displayed on the desktop For more information about each check box function, right-click the question mark icon in the upper-right corner of the Display Properties window and drag it to a check box.

Web Tab

The Web tab allows you to customize the appearance of the Windows 98 Active Desktop. The View My Active Desktop as a Web Page check box is equivalent to the View as Web Page option that appears when you right-click on the desktop. (Another way to open the Effects tab is to right-click the desktop and choose Active Desktop | Customize My Desktop.

The box on the lower half of the Effects tab displays all of the currently selected HTML, ActiveX, and Java objects that will appear when the View as a Web Page display option is toggled on. By default, one object should be listed: the Internet Explorer channel bar. The display of individual objects on the Active Desktop can be toggled on or off by selecting or deselecting the check mark next to the object's name.

To add new objects to the Active Desktop, click the New button. You can connect to the Active Desktop gallery at the Microsoft Web site (see Chapters 5 and 11 for more information on configuring Internet connections) or load an Active Desktop object from disk. To go online to retrieve an Active Desktop element, click Yes in the New Active Desktop Item dialog box. To add an Active Desktop element from a file on your local disk, click No. Select the file you want to embed in the Browse window and click Open, followed by OK to add it to the Active Desktop web list.

By default, Active Desktop objects can include Web pages with the .HTM, .HTML, or Microsoft .ASP file extension and favorite Web links with the .URL extension, in addition to Internet Explorer channels (.CDF files) and bitmapped images (.BMP, .GIF, and .JPG files).

Tip

*Although they're not directly supported in the New Active Desktop Item dialog box, you can embed and run Internet Common Gateway Interface (.CGI) scripts and Netscape Javascript (.SHTML) objects. To do this, click the New button on the Web tab, choose No at the prompt to browse Microsoft's Active Desktop gallery, and click the Browse button in the New Active Desktop Item screen. When the Browse window opens, you can enter custom extensions in the File name field: for instance, *.CGI to display all the .CGI files in a folder, *.SHTML to display the Javascript files, or *.* to display all files. Choose the file you want to embed, as described above.*

USEFUL ITEMS YOU CAN ADD TO THE ACTIVE DESKTOP If you're comfortable with the idea of allocating screen space for Active Desktop bells and whistles, Active Desktop permits you to add a number of useful desktop elements.

In addition to Internet Explorer URL favorites and Microsoft channel subscriptions, you can capture and embed your favorite Internet search page or other information resource on the desktop. Figure 9-6 shows a few applications of this trick. Here, the Altavista Private Extensions search engine and an all-purpose Web reference guide have been added to the desktop. (See Chapter 12 for more information on capturing Web resources to disk for this purpose.)

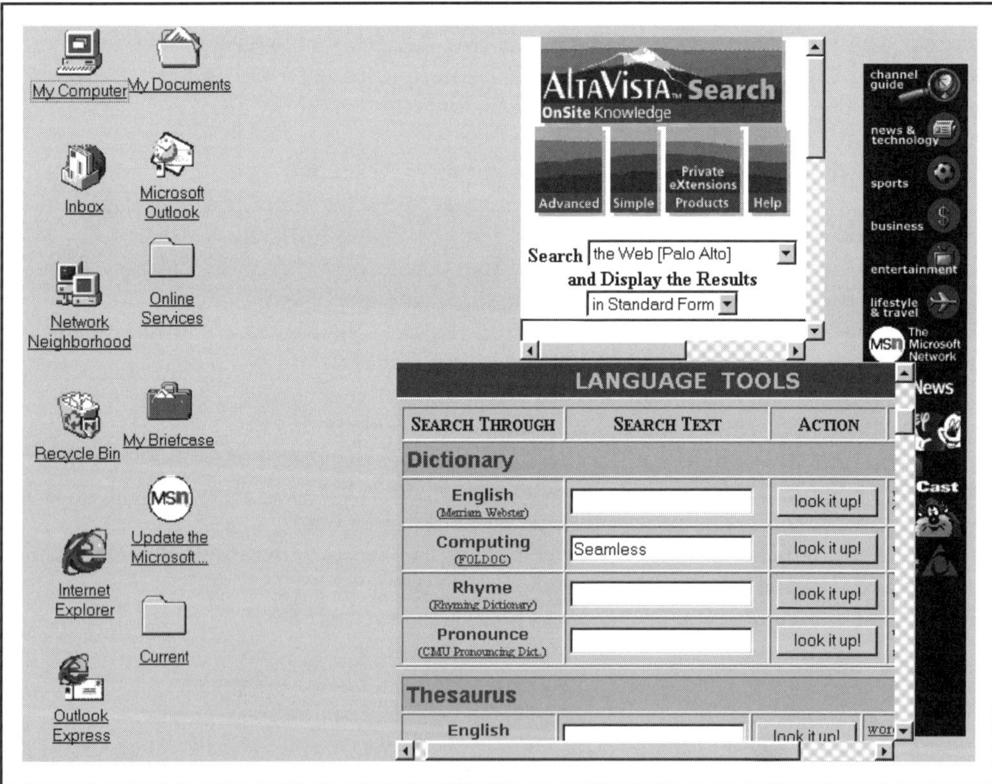

Figure 9-6. *Useful resources embedded in the Active Desktop*

Tip *Once you've embedded an object in the Active Desktop, you can adjust its display size. Point to the right, left, top, or bottom edge of the object, or point to the lower-right corner, and drag to resize, just as you would with an ordinary desktop window. To move an embedded object, place the mouse within it until you see the "selection" and "close" (triangle and x) options appear on the top border. Position the pointer in the top border between the triangle and the x to click and drag.*

Settings Tab

The Setting tab lets you change Windows 98 screen resolution and color depth. The options you see depend on your computer's monitor(s) and graphic adapter(s). (Windows 98 permits the use of more than one monitor-adapter combination.) The Advanced button lets you change your monitor and display adapter type and adjust hardware settings.

CUSTOMIZING THE DISPLAY TO SUIT YOUR WORK To change color-depth or screen resolution on the Settings tab, use the drop-down Colors box or Screen Area slider.

The settings you choose should suit your preferences and the kind of work you do with Windows 98. For business use (word processing, spreadsheets, and so on), many users find a screen resolution of 800 by 600 pixels and a color-depth of 256 to be suitable. For page layout and design work, you'll probably want a higher screen resolution. Higher screen resolutions generally create a larger desktop (more visible window space) with smaller icons and fonts. You can sample different resolutions by moving the Screen Area slider with the mouse and clicking the Apply button. If you don't like what you see, you can answer No to the "Do you want to keep this setting?" prompt.

If you work with graphic images or want to see images displayed properly on the Internet, you'll want to increase the color depth to High Color (16-bit) or True Color (24-bit). If you change the color depth shown in the Colors list and click the Apply button, Windows 98 displays a Compatibility Warning dialog box. This dialog box offers you the choice of making the change on the fly or rebooting the computer first. Rebooting the computer is the default setting. If you prefer, you can change the default to automatically choose the other option. (See the following section, "Other Advanced Display Settings," for details.)

To switch back to the original color depth, reselect it in the Colors list and click the Apply button again.

If the screen resolution or color depth you want doesn't appear as an option, this may be due to the limitations of your hardware or to an improperly configured system. Commonly, limited options are caused by an incorrectly selected monitor type. You can change the monitor configuration by clicking the Advanced button and choosing the Monitor tab in the Display Adapter Properties window. When you click the Change button, a list of manufacturers and models appears, as shown next.

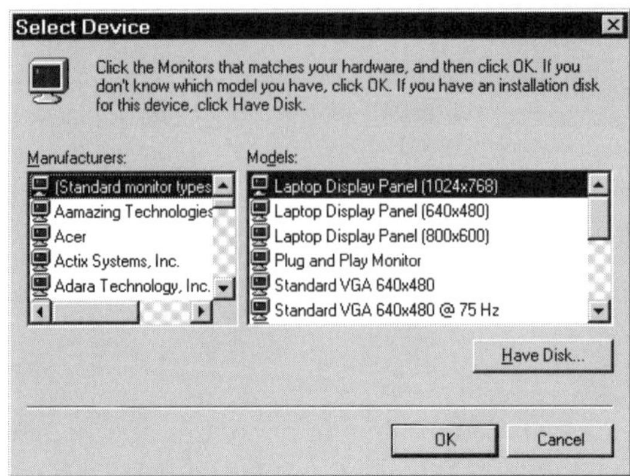

If you don't see your monitor in the list, you can click the Have Disk button, insert an OEM disk in drive A and click OK. (If you've downloaded a new monitor profile to your hard disk, enter the path to the file in the Copy Manufacturer's Files From field.

OTHER ADVANCED DISPLAY SETTINGS The Advanced Display Properties settings also permit you to change display adapters (on the Adapter tab), fine-tune display performance (on the Performance tab), and change the proportional display font size for your monitor (on the General tab). These advanced options began to appear in Windows 95 OEM Service Release 2, so they may already be familiar to you.

You can add a QuickRes icon to the System Tray that provides convenient access to screen resolution and color depth settings. Click the Advanced button on the Display Properties Settings tab and place a check mark next to the Show Settings Icon On Taskbar box on the General tab in Display Properties.

The General tab in Advanced Display Properties settings allows you to change the default Compatibility option for switching color depth. You can select Apply The New Color Settings Without Restarting to avoid a dialog box when you switch, or you can choose Restart The Computer Before Applying The New Color Settings to cleanly reboot the machine before making the switch.

To avoid a dialog box when you switch colors, select Apply The New Color Settings Without Restarting. To cleanly reboot the machine before making the switch, choose Restart The Computer Before Applying The New Color Settings.

The FontSize field on the General tab provides an alternative method for increasing the size of display fonts for icon titles and the taskbar. You can toggle between Small Fonts (96 dots per inch) and Large Fonts (120 dots per inch) without affecting the proportional display of documents in application windows. The Other option brings up a Custom Font Size box that lets you manually set the system font size.

Note *If you personalize the display font size with the Other option, line wrap and page preview displays in some applications may be distorted.*

COLOR MANAGEMENT TAB The Advanced | Color Management tab is a new feature in Windows 98. You can use this tab to adjust your computer's monitor and printer to synchronize the colors of the images you scan or display with printer output. With scanned documents, the screen image should closely match the colors of the original source. Individual applications such as PageMaker, Quark Express, and Adobe Photoshop have long included color management features to assist users in calibrating their monitors and printers. For most everyday purposes, the small differences in image hue, saturation, and intensity among various output devices are hard to distinguish. Color Management is an advanced feature primarily of interest to people involved in the creation of production graphics.

Windows 98 provides a number of color management profiles for specific monitor and printer types. You can activate a display management profile by clicking the Add button on the Color Management tab. In some cases, if your monitor type has been automatically detected, a management profile will be preinstalled. If your monitor is not automatically detected and matched, how can you tell which profile is which? The only way I can suggest is to click the Add button and then right-click each profile (.ICM file) in the \WINDOWS\SYSTEM\COLOR folder and open its properties. The Profile Information tab reveals the manufacturer and intended device for the profile.

Tip *You can find out more about Windows 98 color management by opening Help and typing **Color Management** in the Search field on the Index tab. Windows 98–aware applications will cooperate with the color management feature by adding a File | Color Management option on the pull-down menu. Interested professionals should read the Rendering Intent discussion in Help for more detailed information. (Even more information is contained in the* Windows 98 Resource Kit *book on the Win98 CD in the Printing, Imaging, and Fonts | Imaging Support in Windows 98 section.)*

Multiple Monitors

Windows 98 includes support for displaying the desktop across multiple monitors attached to multiple video adapters in your computer. For information on configuring and working with multiple displays, see "Multiple Displays" in Chapter 15.

Accessibility Options Applet

The Accessibility Options applet is designed to meet the special needs of Windows users who have some sort of physical disability. For some users, these options may make the difference between PC use and PC uselessness. The Accessibility options also offer benefits to all users. They allow one to speed up or slow down the keystroke repeat rate, transpose audio and visual system messages, and use the keyboard as a mouse.

The Windows 98 Accessibility Properties dialog box, shown next, includes five tabs.

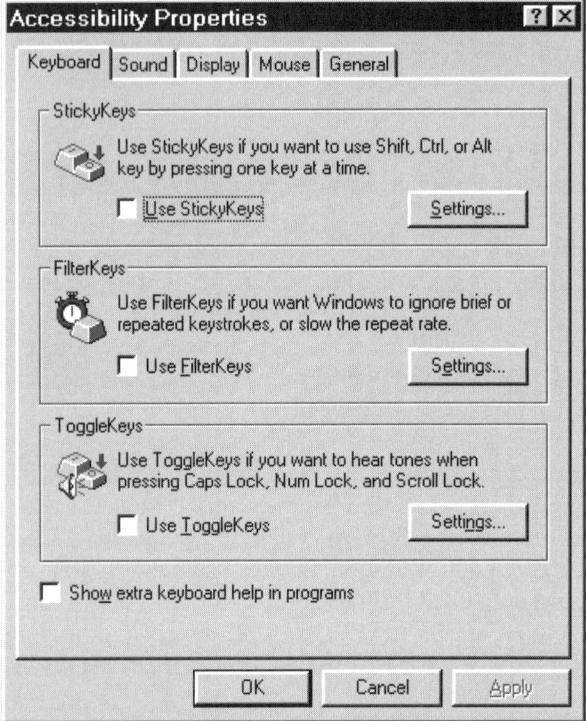

Keyboard Tab

The Keyboard tab enables the use of StickyKeys, FilterKeys, and ToggleKeys.

StickyKeys sensitizes the CTRL, ALT, and SHIFT keys and keeps them active until you press a key other than one of those keys. This feature is provided to help people who have trouble pressing two keys simultaneously to execute multiple key commands used by some applications. It can also help "lazy" typists, or those who feel that multiple key commands are confusing or require too-complicated hand configurations.

FilterKeys disables repeated keystrokes. For instance, an unsure typist might hold down the "s" key too long and end up typing "sssss." This feature also lets you adjust the keyboard repeat rate, which can help prevent such mistakes by less skilled typists.

ToggleKeys provides audio cues for the CAPSLOCK, NUMLOCK, and SCROLLLOCK keys, beeping when they are toggled on or off to help you know when these features are active or disabled (though the SCROLLLOCK key doesn't have many real uses). This feature raises the interactivity level of the PC just a notch.

Sound Tab

The Sound tab lets you complement system alerts with visual cues, to help the hearing impaired or those who prefer visual event messages.

SoundSentry lets you configure display window components to flash on and off instead of using sounds and beeps to announce system warnings. You can apply SoundSentry to three categories of programs: Windows programs, full-screen text programs, and full-screen graphics programs. For instance, you can set the title bar of the active window to flash when system error messages appear.

ShowSounds works like closed captioning, common in television. When it is enabled, programs display screen captions corresponding to their system event sounds. (These options must be added to an application by the developer.)

Display Tab

The Display tab provides options for making the screen easier to see. The Use High Contrast box, when checked, enables a high-contrast, large-font display that makes the screen easier to read.

This screen mode flattens out graphics, raises the contrast, and enlarges fonts and icons as shown in Figure 9-7. The Settings button next to the Use High Contrast check box opens an additional options screen where you can choose a white-on-black, black-on-white, or custom color scheme.

To switch quickly between a high-contrast and conventional desktop, place a check in the Use Shortcut check box on the Settings For High Contrast screen. This allows you to toggle the display through a keyboard shortcut (LEFTALT-LEFTSHIFT-PRINTSCREEN).

Mouse Tab

The Mouse tab activates Win98's Mousekeys feature, which allows your keyboard's numeric keypad to control the desktop pointing device. The keypad arrows move the mouse in all four directions, the 5 key executes a left click, the + sign executes a double-click, and the - sign followed by the 5 key executes a right-click. For complete information on Mousekeys, open Windows Help, go to the Index tab, and type **Mousekeys** in the Search field.

When Mousekeys is enabled, a mouse symbol appears in the System Tray on the taskbar. When this feature is installed but toggled off, the System Tray icon is covered by a standard circle-with-a-slash symbol. Mousekeys can be set to toggle on and off with the NUMLOCK key set in either the on or off position.

If you use Mousekeys, you'll probably want to increase the pointer speed (click the Settings button on the Mouse tab) to at least the second-to-the-highest notch or the pointer will be unbearably slow.

General Tab

The General settings control user notification when Accessibility options are turned on. The Automatic Reset field can turn Accessibility features off after a specified idle

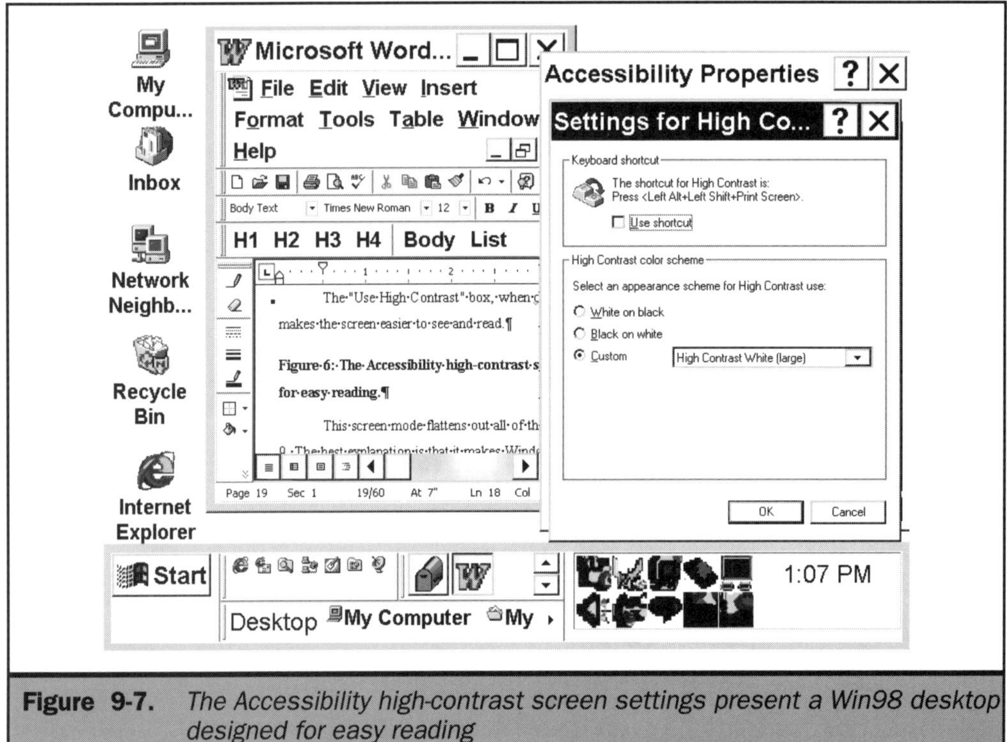

Figure 9-7. *The Accessibility high-contrast screen settings present a Win98 desktop designed for easy reading*

period. The Serialkey Device option supports auxiliary input devices attached to a serial port.

Date/Time Applet

The Date/Time and Regional Settings applets allow you to configure system display options that depend upon your geographic location.

Windows 98 configures the computer's date and time settings during setup, asking you to select an appropriate time zone. The Date/Time Properties dialog box, shown in Figure 9-8, lets you manually choose a month, year, and day from the calendar on the Date & Time tab. Avoid the temptation to use this tab as a pop-up personal calendar. If you pull down a different month or year, the system will switch to that setting immediately, before you click the OK button. This may launch a scheduled maintenance task prematurely.

The Time Zone tab lets you select your time zone from a pull-down menu or by clicking a graphical representation of the world. If the check box at the bottom of the

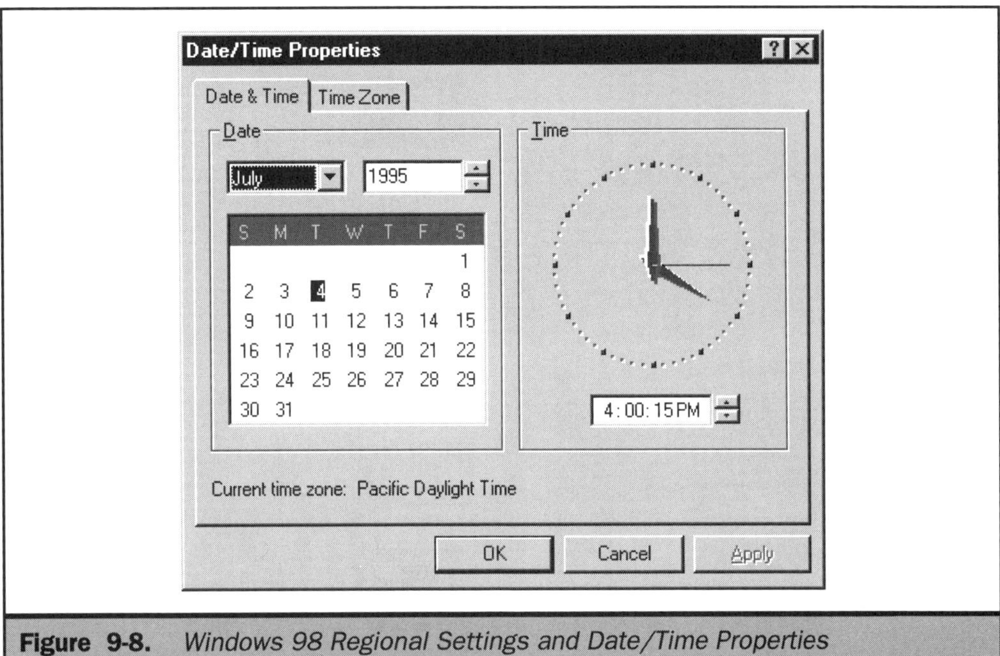

Figure 9-8. *Windows 98 Regional Settings and Date/Time Properties*

screen is selected, Windows 98 will automatically adjust the system time and date for Standard and Daylight Savings Times (notifying you at the next login).

You can right-click the digital time readout on the taskbar and select Adjust Date/Time for faster access to Date/Time properties.

Happy Easter Egg!

Traditionally, Microsoft includes a special multimedia screen in every one of its applications and operating systems to acknowledge all of the people who worked on the production team. In Windows 98, this screen (called an Easter Egg) is activated through the TimeZone map in the Date/Time properties applet.

To see the Easter Egg, you need to click a path from Memphis (Egypt) to Memphis (Tennessee) to Redmond (Washington). To do this, open the Date/Time applet to the Time Zone tab and hold down the CTRL key. With the CTRL key depressed, click in the vicinity of Memphis, Egypt, on the map and drag the mouse pointer to the vicinity of Memphis, TN. Keep the CTRL key depressed, but release the mouse at Memphis, TN. Then click and drag again from Memphis, TN to Redmond, WA. Release the mouse and the Easter Egg credits will roll, as shown in Figure 9-9.

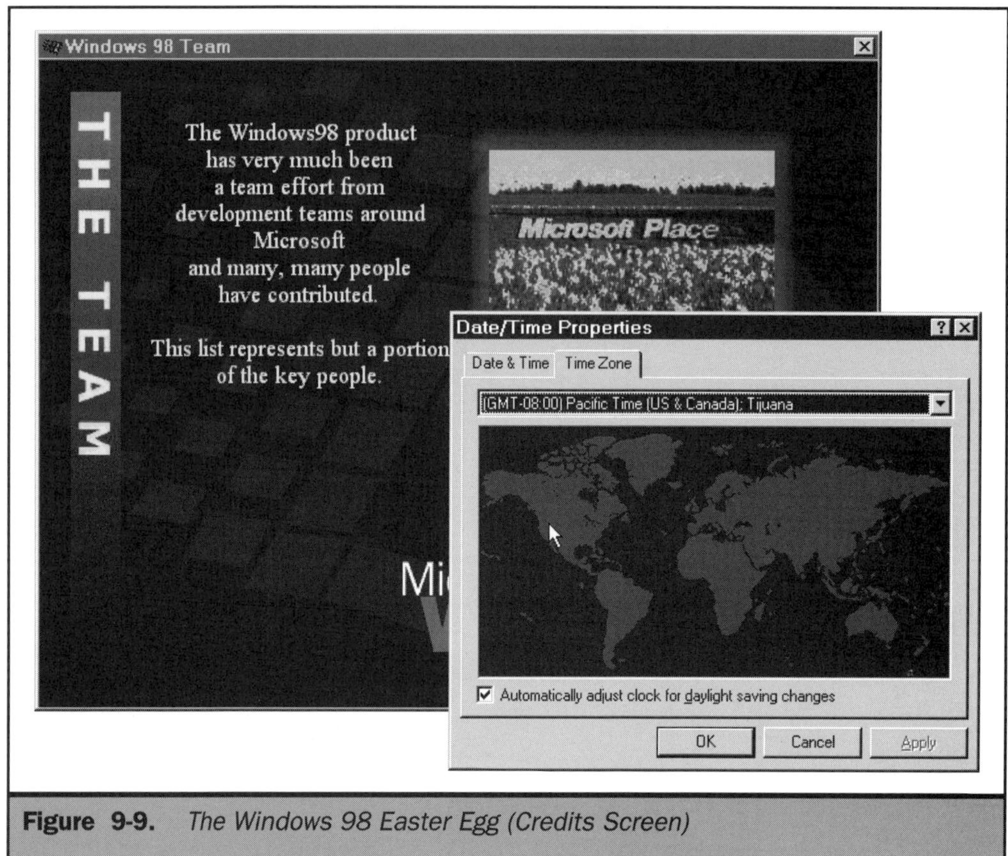

Figure 9-9. *The Windows 98 Easter Egg (Credits Screen)*

Regional Settings Applet

Regional Settings make Windows 98 an international operating system. You can choose a language—from Afrikaans to Swedish. Currency symbols and date styles can also be modified; for instance, you can change settings to accommodate the British day-month format.

Tip *When you select a language on the Regional Settings tab, the settings on the currency, time, and date tabs are automatically changed as well to match the language or geographic location you've selected. The Number, Currency, Time, and Date tabs allow you to edit the formats for individual display components. You can also change individual regional items (date, currency, and so on) to other formats without changing the overall Regional Settings scheme.*

Add/Remove Programs Applet

A new or upgrade Windows 98 installation typically does not implement every available system option. Add/Remove Programs allows you to activate or deactivate a wide variety of Windows 98 accessories and support features. Open this Control Panel applet to add or remove programs from the Start menu and to turn on hidden Win98 system features. Add/Remove Programs provides three functions:

- Add/Remove Programs can be used to install, track, and uninstall third-party applications written for Windows 95 or Windows 98.
- Add/Remove Programs lets you quickly install or remove internal Microsoft applications and system support features bundled with Windows 98.
- Add/Remove Programs allows you to create a Windows 98 Startup disk, so that you can boot the system to DOS for diagnostic purposes.

You can access each of these functions by choosing one of the three tabs in the Add/Remove Programs Properties window.

Install/Uninstall Tab

The Install/Uninstall tab adds and removes *third-party* applications. It helps you avoid the installation and removal pitfalls that could occur under Windows 3.x.

Clicking the Install button at the top of this screen causes Windows 98 to search floppy and CD-ROM drives in your computer for a new SETUP or INSTALL program. If you've inserted an appropriate application disk, Windows 98 opens a Wizard that walks you through the steps necessary to install a program, as shown in Figure 9-10. For Windows 95– and Windows 98–aware applications, this procedure also logs the files copied to your hard disk and modifications made to the system registry. After installation, logged applications are listed on this tab in the Add/Remove field under the trash can icon.

You can still install programs in Windows 98 by manually searching for and opening a SETUP.EXE file or by entering *d*:\SETUP in the Run box on the Start menu. (This is the way new programs were added under DOS and Windows 3.x.) If the application vendor has followed Microsoft's specifications, your installed program will be tracked and added to the Add/Remove list no matter which method you choose. (DOS and Windows 3.x applications are generally not logged during installation.)

Applications distributed on newer CDs often launch an automatic setup program as soon as the CD is inserted into the drive. If a setup program appears on the screen after you insert a new CD, you can follow its instructions. There's no need to open Add/Remove Programs or click the Install button to add these smart applications.

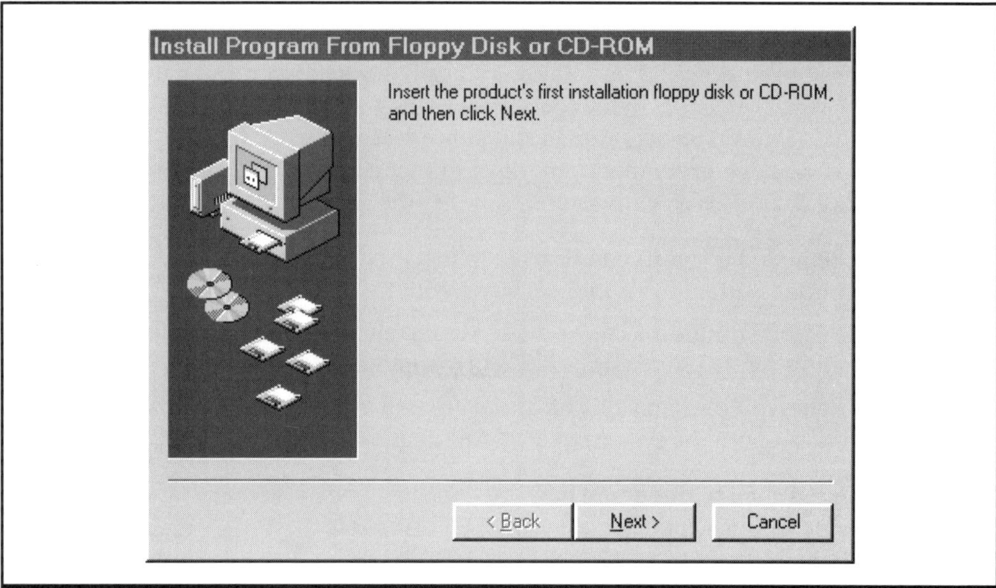

Figure 9-10. *If you click the Install button on the Add/Remove Programs screen, a built-in Win98 installation Wizard appears*

REMOVING APPLICATIONS In Windows 3.x there was no clearly defined, automatic way to get rid of a program. Most people removed applications by nuking file directories with File Manager and then deleting Program Manager icons.

This procedure was far from thorough. Many Windows programs deposit files in the WINDOWS or WINDOWS\SYSTEM directory. In Windows 3.x, these files were untracked and unrecorded. They could remain in the \WINDOWS directory and cause problems long after deletion of their source program. Applications written for Windows 95 and Windows 98 avoid this confusion by taking advantage of the operating system's built-in Install/Uninstall feature.

You can remove most programs that appear in the Add/Remove list by selecting a program and clicking the Add/Remove button at the bottom of the Install/Uninstall tab, shown next.

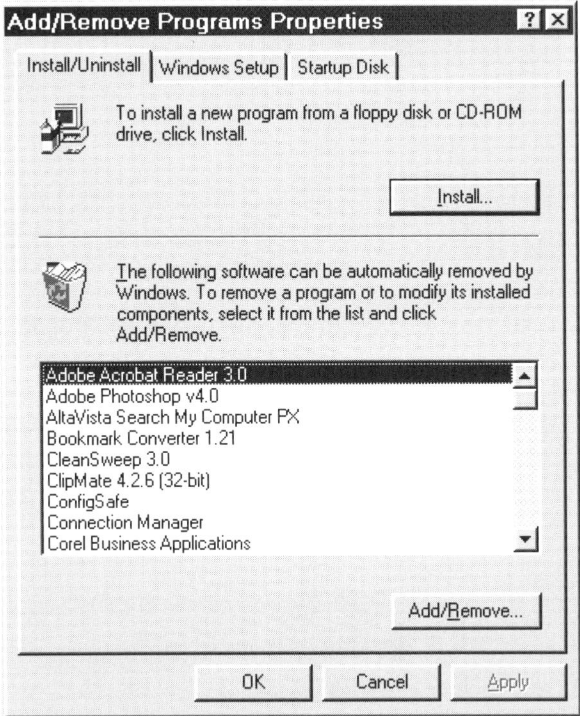

This action should launch a vendor-supplied UNINSTAL utility that removes every trace of the program from your disk. That's the theory, and it works about 75 percent of the time. Unfortunately, some programs try to put their UNINSTAL utilities directly in the \WINDOWS directory, overwriting versions placed by other programs. Users also sometimes inadvertently delete UNINSTAL programs in an attempt to clean up or conserve disk space. Also remember that Windows 3.x programs installed through Add/Remove Programs will probably not appear in the Add/Remove list.

Some vendors offer additional uninstall utilities for their products, which may appear along with the program in an individual Start menu group. If it exists, you should use the vendor-supplied utility to remove the application. In addition, if you need more complete support for application removal, consider one of several third-party solutions designed to track, remove, and transport DOS and Windows applications under Windows 98. Quarterdeck's CleanSweep and Symantec's Norton Uninstaller both handle this task well. They include sophisticated archiving features that can back up and store less frequently used programs or transport them to another computer.

Note *If you selected the option to back up your previous operating system when you installed Windows 98, the Add/Remove list will also allow you to remove the entire Windows 98 system configuration. You probably won't want to do this unless you're pretty unhappy.*

Windows Setup Tab

The Windows Setup tab in the Add/Remove Programs Properties window displays a list of the optional Windows 98 components and accessories bundled with the operating system. The Components list contains 12 general entries. Select a component with the mouse or cursor keys, and a summary of its important features will appear in the Description box below the list. Some components in the list are single items. Others are composites containing multiple applications and support features. The Details button in the Description box becomes active when a component category contains multiple items.

To add any component in the main list to Windows 98, select it and place a check mark in the box to the right of its name. The check mark indicates the status of the component:

- Components with no check mark in the box are currently not installed.
- Components with a dark gray check mark in the box are partially installed.
- Components with a check mark inside a clear white box are completely installed.

You can double-click any composite component or click on the Details button to see the individual applications it contains. For instance, if you select Accessories and click Details, you can add desktop wallpaper, games, mouse pointers, or any other unchecked item. Click OK to return to the main component list. If you install only some of the items listed in a composite component, the check mark next to the component on the main Windows Setup tab will be black against a dark gray background, indicating that the component is only partially installed. Figure 9-11 shows this type of installation.

Startup Disk Tab

To create a Windows 98 startup disk, select the Startup Disk tab in the Add/Remove Programs Properties window and then click the Create Disk button.

Creating a floppy startup disk is roughly equivalent to using Format a:/s, the DOS command for creating a bootable system diskette. If you choose this option, Windows 98 also copies some must-have system files to the diskette (FDISK, a set of universal CD-ROM and SCSI drivers, and so on). In Windows 98, some new options have been added to automate the emergency boot process. When the system boots from a Win98 startup disk, a boot menu appears, providing the option to automatically load an IDE or SCSI CD-ROM drive. (Adaptec SCSI cards are supported.) The boot process goes on

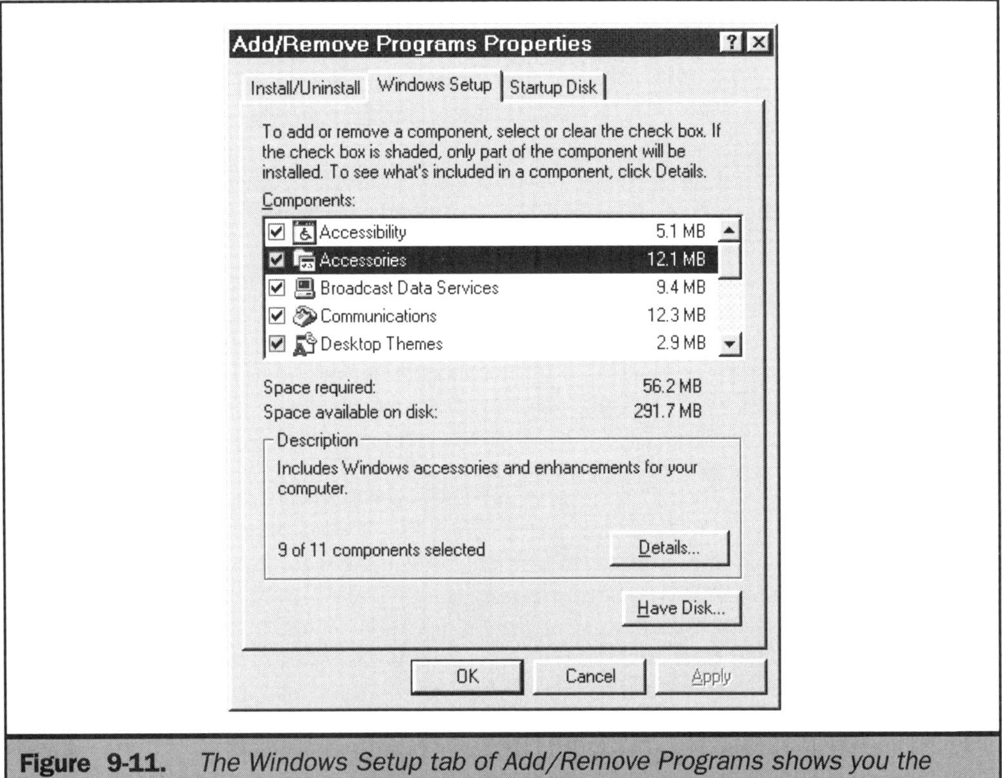

Figure 9-11. *The Windows Setup tab of Add/Remove Programs shows you the features and programs that have and haven't been installed*

to create a RAM disk (a temporary virtual drive) on your computer and copy a set of DOS diagnostic utilities to the RAM drive.

Creating a startup disk is a good idea. If something goes wrong so that your hard disk and Windows 98 won't start, an emergency startup disk can help you to access the system and diagnose the problem.

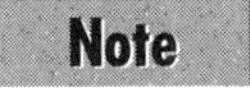

If Windows 98 is installed in a FAT32 disk partition, then the partition will be invisible if you start your computer from boot disks formatted with DOS 3–6, OS/2, Windows NT, Windows 95 Classic, and other non-FAT32 operating systems. If you skipped making a Win98 startup disk during OS installation, I recommend that you make one from the Startup Disk tab A.S.A.P.

The README.TXT file placed on the startup disk contains more complete information about the new emergency boot options built into the disk. To learn how to customize your startup disk and use it when Windows 98 won't start, see Chapter 8.

Win98 Setup May Have Missed These Useful Accessories

If you selected the Typical, Portable, or Compact installation option when you placed Windows 98 on your hard disk, a number of features and accessory applications were probably omitted. Microsoft offers these setup options to save you time and disk space, but you may find that you really want some of the missing features.

For instance, the Accessories group has some handy programs that you may want to add: QuickView is a file viewer with filters that let you inspect documents and bitmap graphics in several formats. Document Templates allows you to quickly create new blank data objects on the desktop for a variety of productivity applications. In the Communications group, Microsoft NetMeeting allows you to participate in online conferencing. If your office has a dedicated local area network, you may want to install virtual private networking for secure remote dial-up through a modem. Infrared support allows wireless data transfer between two computers and also permits digital cameras to download photos to your hard disk. The Web Publishing Wizard in the Internet Tools component can quickly upload HTML elements designed in FrontPage Express to a Web server.

The System Tools component also contains useful items you may want to add. The Windows 98 Clipboard Viewer is not automatically installed on the desktop. Character Map is a utility that lets you identify the upper ASCII characters in any Windows font and paste them into documents. The new Microsoft Backup utility now supports a wide number of tape devices, and System Monitor is a diagnostic tool that allows you to measure the real-time performance of various Windows 98 operating features. (See Chapter 6 for more detailed information on how to use these accessories.)

Another common use for Add/Remove Programs is to add the Microsoft Network (MSN) or another online service to your desktop.

Tip *Unlike Windows 95, Windows 98 does not include Windows Setup tab options to install Microsoft Exchange (Windows Messaging), Microsoft Mail, or Microsoft Fax. These features have been removed from Windows 98. The Outlook Express mail client replaces Windows Messaging. If you installed these features under Windows 95, they are automatically transferred during a Windows 98 upgrade. If your Windows 98 is a new installation, you can add Microsoft Exchange, a Microsoft Mail post office, and Microsoft Fax from a supplementary directory on the Win98 installation CD. See Chapter 5 and the sections "Mail and Fax Applet" and "Microsoft Mail Postoffice Applet" in this chapter for more information.*

If Windows 98 detects a CD-ROM drive or sound card during installation, then the appropriate multimedia applications are placed in the Accessories Entertainment group. Windows 98 also has an assortment of sound schemes for system events. These are not installed unless you select them manually.

For a complete list of Windows 98 components added by each of the clean installation setup options, see Chapter 3.

Add New Hardware Applet

Add New Hardware is the twin sibling of Add/Remove Programs. It's used to make the operating system aware of new hardware components installed on your computer. In Windows 98, the Add New Hardware feature has been upgraded to be more sensitive to plug-and-play devices.

To add a new hardware device, first turn off the computer and plug the new device into an appropriate slot or port. Then turn the computer on again. (For many plug-and-play devices, the procedure is that simple. Windows 98 will automatically detect that something new has been added and automatically install appropriate drivers.)

If your new hardware is not found automatically on startup, use Add New Hardware to detect it. Choose Control Panel | Add New Hardware and click Next on the first screen of the Add New Hardware Wizard.

In Windows 98, the Add New Hardware applet now divides the search for new devices into two phases: The first phase checks the computer for plug-and-play devices that have escaped automatic detection and for devices that have been found but disabled or misconfigured.

Add/Remove Hardware first duplicates the plug-and-play autodetect feature that Windows 98 runs at startup. If any plug-and-play devices have been overlooked, a message indicating that a new device has been found will appear on the screen, and Windows 98 will attempt to install drivers. You may be prompted to insert an OEM driver disk to complete the installation.

Add New Hardware next displays a list of any previously recognized, but currently disabled or misconfigured plug-and-play devices. Select any devices that you want to re-enable from the Devices list. Select Yes, The Device Is In The List, as shown here:

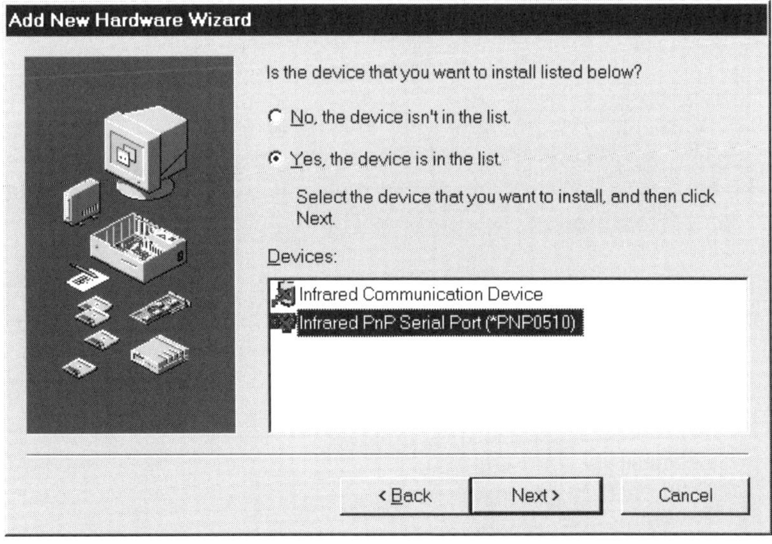

Then click Next. If the component has been disabled, the Win98 Device Manager may appear, allowing you to click the Enable button to turn the device back on. If the component has been misconfigured, Windows 98 may repair the problem automatically, or it may bring up a System Troubleshooter to help you resolve the problem.

After plug-and-play components have been handled, Add New Hardware enters its second phase, offering to search your computer for non-plug-and-play devices.

In phase 2 of the Add New Hardware installation, you can tell Windows 98 to search for non-plug-and-play components, or you can select No, I Want To Select The Hardware From A List. Generally, the best strategy is to let Windows 98 perform the hardware search. (See the following section, "When to Install Hardware Manually," for exceptions to this rule.)

If Windows 98 finds any additional devices, the next Add New Hardware Wizard screen offers to install them. You can click the Details button on this screen to see exactly what Windows 98 has found.

Click Finish to complete the hardware installation. If Windows 98 didn't find the device that you wanted to install, you can click the Back button and select No, I Want To Select The Hardware From A List.

When to Install Hardware Manually

You should choose the No, I Want To Select The Hardware From A List option on the Add New Hardware Wizard screen under the following conditions:

- You have an OEM disk and are following the manufacturer's instructions.
- Windows 98 did not find your device automatically.
- You want to install multiple configurations for the same peripheral. (For example, you can install an ISDN modem to do triple duty as an ISDN device, fax, and analog modem.)

If you choose the No, I Want To Select The Hardware From A List option, the Add New Hardware Wizard displays a screen that lists a variety of hardware categories. If you know the hardware type for your device, select it and click Next to bring up a list of manufacturers. If you don't know the hardware type, select the Other Devices category.

Select the manufacturer and model of your device from the lists in the left and right panes of the next screen, as shown in Figure 9-12, and click Next. Alternatively, if you have an OEM disk for your device, click the Have Disk button, insert your disk in the appropriate drive, and click OK. (You can use the Browse button on this screen to search your hard disk or a CD for the driver directory.)

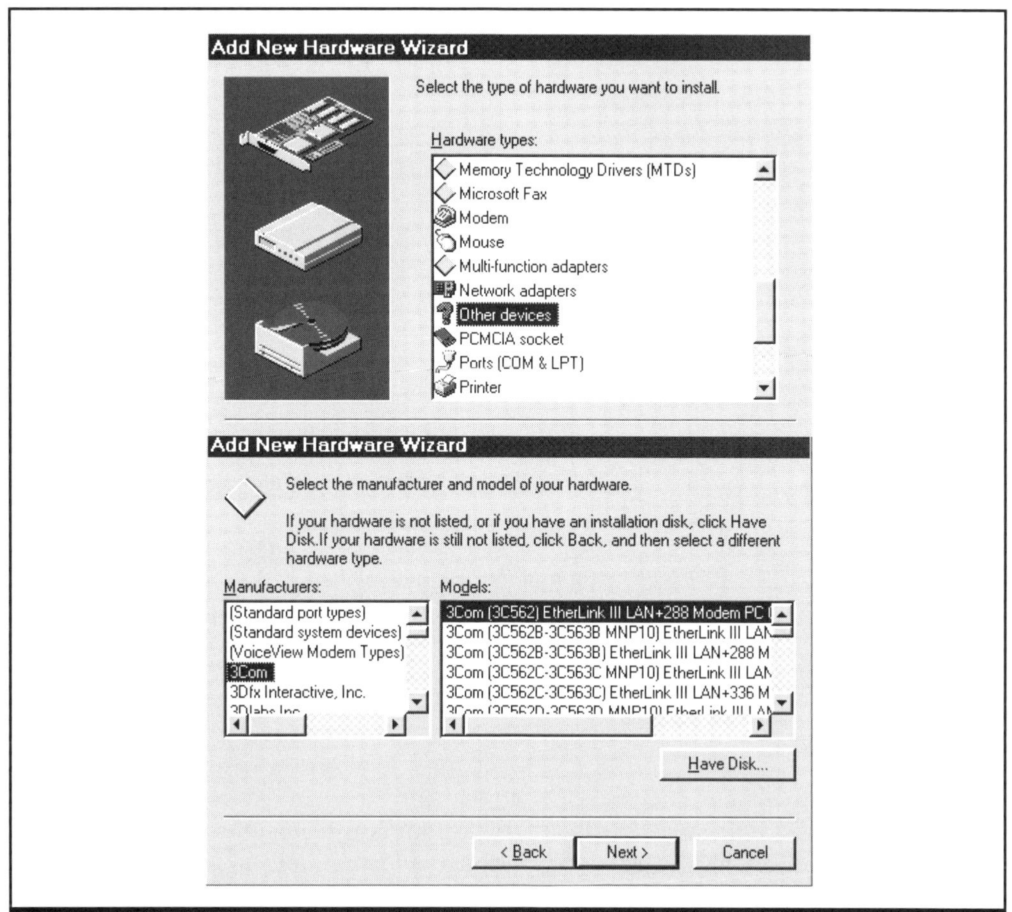

Figure 9-12. *You can add new hardware manually by selecting a hardware type (top screen) and then selecting the manufacturer/model (bottom screen)*

The protracted Windows 98 development process has resulted in plug-and-play detection that actually works in the majority of cases. Your chances are good that Win98's Add New Hardware Wizard magic will be potent enough to recognize many hardware devices automatically and install the proper drivers. (See Chapters 13, 14, and 15 for information about recognizing stubborn SCSI cards, sound cards, and PCMCIA devices.)

Gain Performance Efficiency by Replacing the "Real" with the "Virtual"

If you had a PCMCIA device, Power Management, Sound Card, CD-ROM, or SCSI device attached to your system before you installed Windows 98, it may be slowing down system performance through a series of real-mode DOS device drivers loaded in CONFIG.SYS and AUTOEXEC.BAT. Windows 98 is smart enough to comment out some lines in AUTOEXEC.BAT (MSCDEX.EXE, SMARTDRV.EXE, and real-mode network loaders), but not all of them. Hardware-related multimedia and I/O drivers in CONFIG.SYS usually remain untouched. These drivers occupy DOS conventional or upper memory and can be eliminated if Windows 98 has internal VXD equivalents. For instance, if CONFIG.SYS and AUTOEXEC.BAT still contain drivers for a Creative Labs Sound Blaster or an Adaptec SCSI card, select Add New Hardware and see if Windows 98 can automatically find these devices. If it can't, choose No, I Want To Select The Hardware From A List and select these devices in the appropriate hardware type categories. Windows 98 will install its own drivers, allowing you to remove the real-mode drivers left by DOS in the CONFIG.SYS and AUTOEXEC.BAT files. The same procedure can be used to recognize a PC Card (PCMCIA) controller or to install Win98's internal power management support.

System Applet

The System applet works in conjunction with the Add New Hardware component to list and edit drivers for installed hardware. It has four tabs that let you delve into the guts of your computer's hardware configuration and inspect built-in performance settings. You can use these tabs to do the following:

- Confirm that all of your computer's peripherals are recognized and working properly
- Display or print diagnostic information about low-level operating system settings
- Edit and troubleshoot system settings
- Adjust Win98 performance features such as file system access, hard disk caching, graphics acceleration, and virtual memory (the Win98 swap file)

General Tab

The General tab displays the version of Windows 98 you are running, as well as any incremental beta or revision number. It also displays your registration information, your computer's CPU type, and the amount of RAM installed in the system.

Device Manager Tab

The Device Manager tab lists and manages your computer's installed hardware components. In Windows 98, Device Manager has been upgraded to provide some new configuration options: You can display file details for installed drivers and switch between multiple, dated software versions. Automated IRQ steering now attempts to manage system resources intelligently, allowing multiple peripherals to share the computer's limited supply of hardware interrupts. These enhancements first appeared in Windows 95 Service Release 2 and have been extended for Windows 98. Device Manager can now also reserve specific system resources (IRQs, I/O, memory, and port addresses).

Device Manager doesn't install new hardware components. Instead, you use it to verify that previously installed components are properly configured and operational.

The Device Manager list is displayed in a convenient outline structure, similar to the Windows Explorer's view of files and folders. For instance, you can double-click Ports for a tree display of all the printer and communications ports installed in Windows 98.

Here's a typical use for Device Manager: You can open it immediately after Win98 installation to verify that all of your modems, network connections, and multimedia hardware have been set up correctly. You can then double-click any component in the display list to see what's installed on your system. For instance, if you double-click the Modem component in the display list, as shown here, you'll see a list of all the modems that Windows 98 currently recognizes. (You can also open this list by single-clicking the + box in front of any component to expand the tree.)

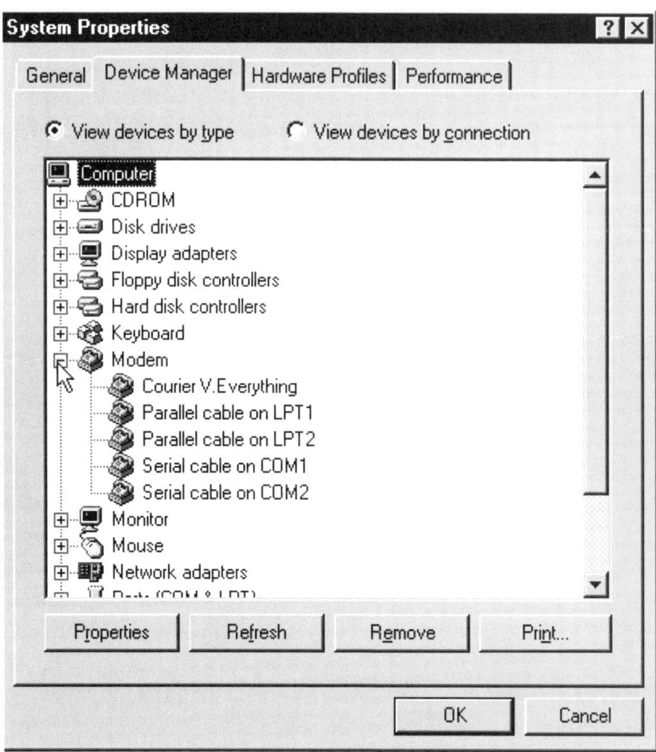

You can then select an installed modem and click the Properties button to open a three-tabbed presentation of modem details. (You can also display this information screen by choosing Control Panel | Modems.)

The tree-based Device Manager list lets you examine nearly every aspect of the system's hardware configuration. For instance, you can view the input/output range of the system speaker by selecting System Devices followed by System Speaker and then clicking Properties., Or you can check your video driver by selecting Display Adapters followed by the name of your adapter, and then clicking Properties. After the Properties screen opens, select Driver and click Driver File Details.

To get a more complete diagnostic dump of your system's configuration than you've probably ever seen before, select the computer icon at the top of the tree and click the Properties button. Once in the Computer Properties box (shown here), you can display a system interrupt list, examine all of the port addresses assigned in conventional memory, view a list of DMA channels used by peripherals, or browse a segment-by-segment list of all reserved memory addresses.

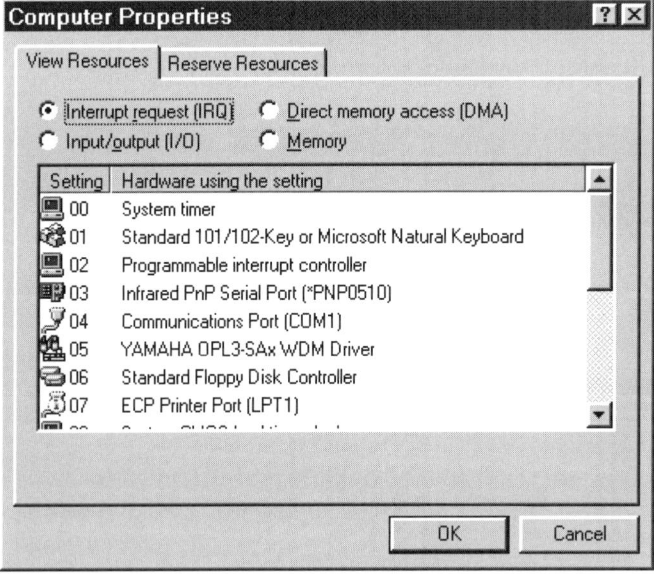

You can also print this diagnostic information by selecting the Computer icon and clicking the Print button. It's a good idea to print all of this information shortly after installing Windows 98. Some of it may look pretty weird and useless to you, but if you discover that something on your system doesn't work, the list will be useful to the consultant or support technician who has to figure out what's wrong.

FINE-TUNING PERFORMANCE Some hardware components allow you to adjust their performance settings. If user options are available, you'll find them on a Settings tab on the component's Properties screen. To find out more about any setting, click the ? icon at the upper-right of the window, drag it over the option in the Properties screen, and click again.

Here are some common settings that may be of use to you:

- The CD-ROM settings allow you to reserve drive letters, enable or disable auto-insert notification, and select synchronous data transfer and DMA options for faster performance.
- The Disk Drives settings for newer drives allow you to increase performance by selecting the DMA option.
- The Hard Disk Controllers settings for newer adapters allow you to activate or deactivate specific IDE channels.

The following System Devices options can be adjusted if you're experiencing hardware difficulty:

- If installed, Advanced Power Management settings allow you to force Microsoft's APM 1.0 mode for compatibility purposes.
- If installed, the Direct Memory Access Controller settings allow you to adjust DMA transfer.
- If installed, the PCI Bus settings allow you to toggle IRQ steering off and on. (IRQ steering permits multiple peripherals to share a single system interrupt.)
- If installed, the Plug-and-Play BIOS settings allow you to disable automatic NVRAM/ESCD (system BIOS) updates.

The Device Manager Properties dialog boxes can also help you perform diagnostic tests on hardware components, and they let you change low-level system resource assignments. For instance, if you select a serial port and open its Properties screen, you'll see that the Port Settings tab sets the default data transfer rate for the port (see Figure 9-13). This accomplishes what you used to have to do in DOS with the MODE command. The Advanced button on the Port Settings tab lets you regulate the Receive and Transmit buffers for a high-speed 16550 serial port (also shown in Figure 9-13).

RESOLVING SYSTEM CONFLICTS If a hardware device has a system resource conflict, it generally appears in the Device Manager list prefixed by a yellow exclamation point (!). When you select the device, you'll see the conflict described in the Device Status box on the General tab. The Driver and Resources tabs in the component's Properties screen allow you to edit the Windows 98 system configuration, when appropriate. For some components, you can change the software device driver and reassign a port address, IRQ, or DMA resource to resolve problems.

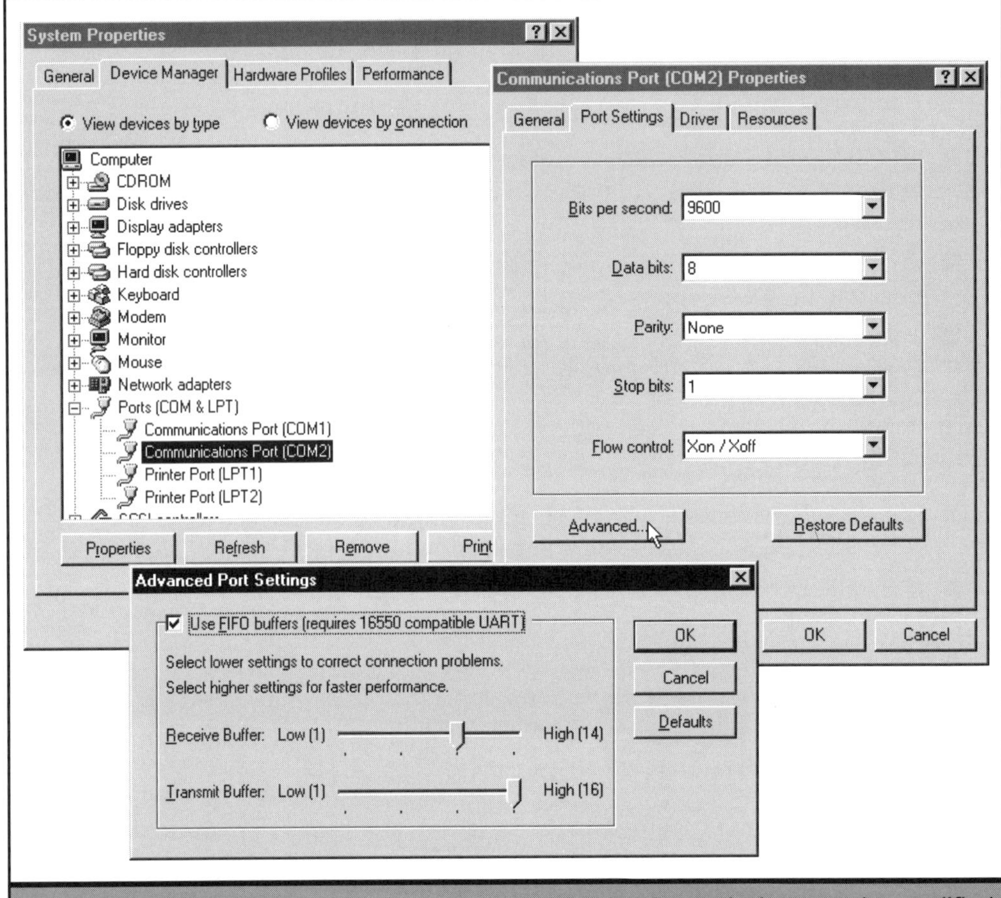

Figure 9-13. *The configuration of some installed hardware devices can be modified by selecting the component in the Device Manager listing and clicking the Properties button*

Tip *If you're using Device Manager to modify a system resource for the first time, you might want to back up your current system registry before proceeding. You can do this by choosing Run from the Start menu and running the SCANREGW utility.*

For example: an internal or PC Card modem might conflict with a physical serial port, both claiming the use of IRQ 4 or Port 3F8. This situation is illustrated in Figure 9-14. Here's how you would resolve the problem:

1. Select the device prefixed by the yellow exclamation point. Open its Properties screen and click the Resources tab. Read the report in the Conflicting Device List box at the bottom of the screen.

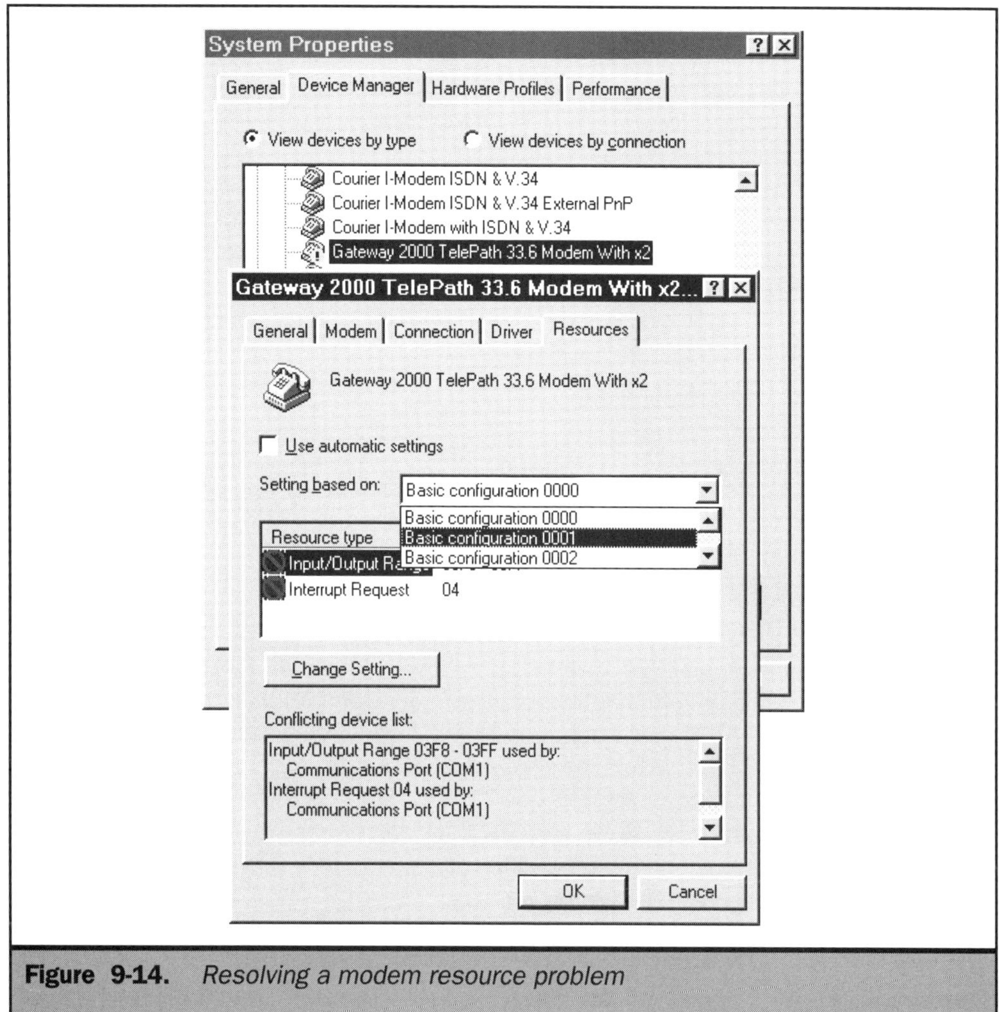

Figure 9-14. *Resolving a modem resource problem*

2. If the problem is a conflict over a shared resource, deselect the check mark next to Use Automatic Settings on the Resources tab.
3. Either select another Basic configuration on the drop-down list or double-click the resource you want to change in the Resource Type field and then modify it.
4. Click OK to enter the change in the system registry. You may see a warning that you are about to override Win98's default settings. Click OK to continue and create a Forced configuration.

After you've modified a Device Manager setting, you can refresh the device list by selecting the Computer icon and clicking the Refresh button. This option is sometimes useful to nudge Device Manager into activating a peripheral that you know is installed but has temporarily become dormant for an unknown reason.

CHANGING AN ASSIGNED SOFTWARE DRIVER You might have a high-speed serial port in your computer running with a low-speed driver, or a high-speed ECP/EPP printer port assigned to a standard parallel port driver. To change the driver assigned to the port, follow these steps:

1. Select the port in the Device Manager listing and open its Properties screen.
2. Click the Driver tab on the Port Properties screen and then click the Update Driver button.
3. In the Update Device Driver Wizard that appears, click Next to continue. On the next screen, Windows 98 offers to search for a better device driver or allow you to select one from a list. Click Next, and Windows 98 will autosearch specified disks for a better driver.
4. If Win98 doesn't find a better driver, click the Back button and select Display A List.
5. The drivers in the list that appears are followed by file dates (see Figure 9-15). You can select any item displayed in the Show Compatible Hardware list or click the Show All Hardware button to display a wider selection. In this example, select Show All Hardware, select Standard Port Types in the Manufacturer's pane, and select ECP Printer Port in the Models pane. (The best strategy is to select the listing with the latest file date.)
6. Click Next on the subsequent screens to locate the Windows 98 installation files and then upgrade the driver. Click Finish on the last screen to complete the new driver installation.

If you discover a resource conflict with a component that's no longer being used on your system, select the component in the main Device Manager window and click the Remove button. With newer plug-and-play hardware, Windows 98 will clear resources automatically.

Hardware Profiles Tab

The System Properties Hardware Profiles tab allows you to create multiple system configurations to choose from when you start Windows 98. For instance, you may use a portable computer with several different monitors or in both stand-alone and docked productivity situations, and the docking station may contain an additional CD-ROM, hard disk, or peripheral controller card.

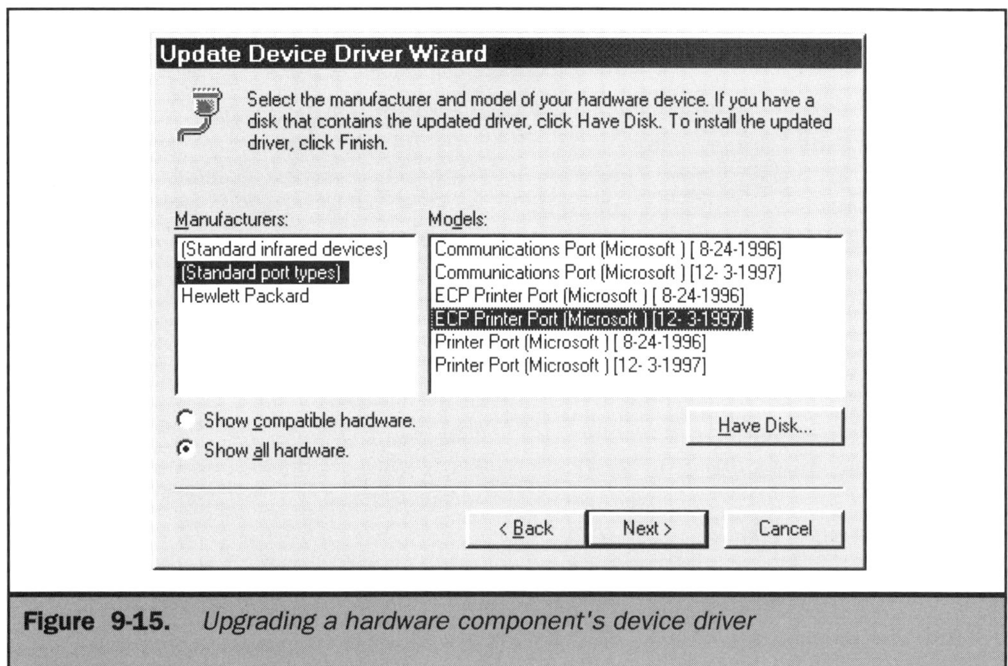

Figure 9-15. *Upgrading a hardware component's device driver*

To create an additional hardware profile, select a current profile and click the Copy button. Enter a name for the new profile in the Copy Profile dialog box.

When you start a Windows 98 computer with multiple profiles, you are prompted to select the hardware profile to use for the current session. Windows loads only the device drivers for components enabled in the profile you select.

If you give a hardware profile the same name as a labeled configuration on the MS-DOS multiple boot menu, the corresponding MS-DOS menu item will be automatically selected and loaded when you choose the hardware profile.

ENABLING AND DISABLING INDIVIDUAL DEVICES IN A PROFILE You can use Device Manager to enable or disable individual elements of a hardware profile on the fly. This feature can be useful for a computer equipped with an infrared serial port. You might want to insert a PC Card or internal modem and assign it to COM2 instead of letting the infrared port grab that mapping.

Here's how to disable just a particular element of a hardware profile:

1. Click the + sign next to the appropriate component type in Device Manager (for the infrared port, choose Network Adapters) to open the device list.

2. Select the device and open its Properties screen. Place a check mark next to Disable in This Hardware Profile in the Device Usage field.

This action disables the selected device in the current hardware profile. The next time you boot the computer with that hardware profile, the specified device—in this case, the infrared serial port—will be disabled. (It will be marked with a red X in the Device Manager listing.) The resources, such as a PC Card or internal modem, formerly claimed by the disabled peripheral will become available to other devices.

If you boot a portable computer with a docking station that includes a CD-ROM or SCSI drive, these peripherals will be detected and added to the current hardware configuration. You might subsequently decide to create both Docked and Undocked hardware profiles for this computer. The next time you boot to the Undocked configuration, you'll want to disable the inactive CD-ROM or SCSI peripherals to stop the system from wasting time searching for them in that profile.

Performance Tab

The System Properties Performance tab displays information about installed memory, used system resources, disk compression, 32-bit versus 16-bit (compatibility mode) file systems, virtual memory, and PC Card management.

The System Resources percentage is analogous to the About Program Manager report in Windows 3.1. Basically, a number between 75 and 100 percent is good and indicates that you have plenty of resources to spare. If you're working with multiple applications, the System Resources value may sometimes drop below 50 percent, in which case you should proceed with caution. If the System Resources percentage drops below 30 percent, you should immediately close all unnecessary windows and applications and be sure to save your work.

You don't have to open the System applet and waste keystrokes to check available Win98 system resources. Instead, install the Win98 Resource Meter and open it from the System Tools group on the Accessories menu. The Resource Meter creates a floating status display in the System Tray on the taskbar.

The File System indicator tells you whether Windows 98 is providing 32-bit (the fast default) access to your files. The 32-bit file system of Windows 98 is similar to the 32-bit file system first provided in Windows for Workgroups version 3.1. It makes a significant improvement in the speed with which programs are launched, files are loaded and saved, and other disk-related operations are executed.

However, certain configurations may bump this setting down to 16-bit (MS-DOS compatibility mode). Your system may provide only 16-bit access if you use any of the following configurations:

- Your CONFIG.SYS file contains real-mode device drivers that conflict with 32-bit file access. Examples are drivers for certain IDE and SCSI controllers, and some drivers for CD-ROM devices, scanners, and other legacy technology (old hardware) peripherals.
- Your system includes third-party .VXD drivers designed for Windows 3.1 that migrated to your Win98 SYSTEM.INI file.

In some cases, removing these drivers from your CONFIG.SYS or SYSTEM.INI file may restore 32-bit file access to your system. In the case of real-mode compression drivers, you'll need to uncompress the drive or upgrade to a version of DriveSpace specifically written for Windows 98.

In the case of real-mode drivers for disk controllers and CD-ROM devices, the first thing you should do is attempt to run the Add New Hardware applet (discussed in its own section earlier in this chapter). Windows 98 may be able to install a 32-bit driver for your peripheral. In some instances, Windows 98 can be told to recognize specific real-mode drivers as safe to restore 32-bit file access. This involves adding an entry in the IOS.INI file located in your \WINDOWS directory. (If you want to experiment, use a text editor to place the name of the device in the [Safelist] section. If this results in boot failure, you may need to boot to an MS-DOS command prompt and use a DOS text editor to remove the IOS.INI entry you just added.)

If your computer has a PC Card controller and Windows 98 includes drivers for it, this item should also be listed as 32-bit. If it isn't, inspect your CONFIG.SYS and AUTOEXEC.BAT files and remove any real-mode PCMCIA drivers. (For example, remove DEVICE=CS.EXE, DEVICE=CSALLOC.EXE, DEVICE=CARDID.EXE, and DEVICE=ENABLE.EXE from CONFIG.SYS.)

Three buttons at the bottom of the Performance tab allow you to fine-tune some of Win98's performance settings. The File System button lets you adjust caching for your hard drives and CD-ROM drive. The Graphics button controls the relationship between Windows 98 and your video adapter, and the Virtual Memory button lets you control the size and location of the Win98 swap file.

VIRTUAL MEMORY BUTTON You can use the Virtual Memory dialog box, shown next, to establish a minimum and maximum size for the swap file, which you might want to do if you have disk storage limitations.

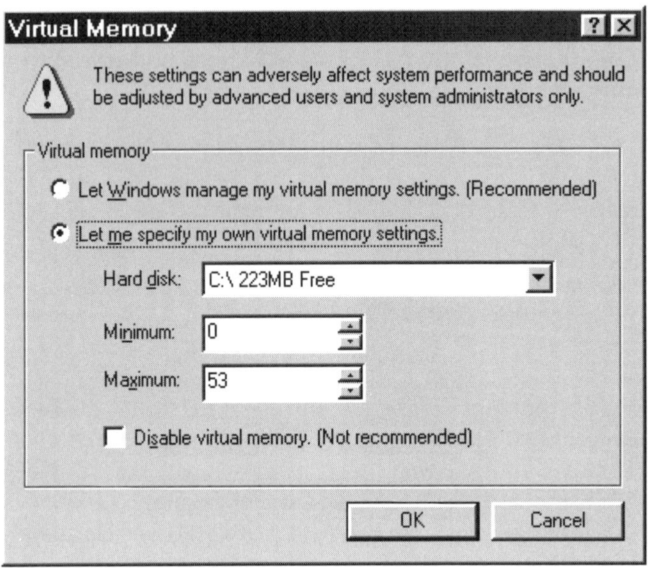

Generally, it's best to allow Windows 98 to regulate the swap file, since it can dynamically expand or shrink it according to the need for additional virtual memory. However, it does no harm to change the physical partition where the swap file resides. This is a useful option when you run out of disk space on the original Windows 98 host drive. If Win98 is installed on drive C and you have 100MB of free space on drive D, then relocating the swap file to the freer drive is a good, logical move.

FILE SYSTEM BUTTON Clicking the File System button displays a dialog box with five tabs. The Hard Disk tab, shown next, regulates the minimum and maximum size of the Windows 98 disk cache. In the Typical Role Of This Computer field, the Mobile Or Docking System option installs the most modest cache parameters, and the Network Server option installs the most liberal parameters. Read-Ahead Optimization speeds up the way programs are loaded from disk by prereading adjacent file sectors before they are actually requested. Generally, you should first try setting this option to Full. Reduce it only if you experience system problems.

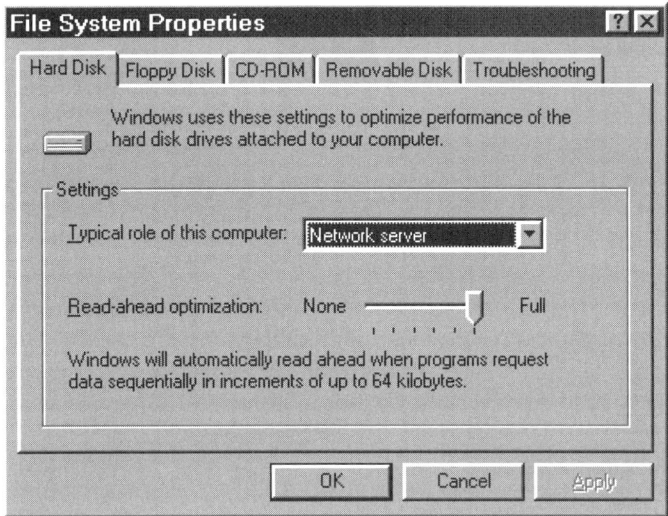

The Floppy Disk tab tells Windows 98 to reinitialize the floppy disk driver each time you restart the system (including after a soft reboot and after you return from MS-DOS mode). If you disable this option, Windows 98 may restart a bit faster by not automatically refreshing the status of floppy disk drives.

The CD-ROM tab optimizes the performance of CD-ROM drives installed on the system if they use Win98's internal 32-bit drivers.

Be sure to check the File System settings for CD-ROM drives after installing Windows 98. On many systems, Windows 98 is configured by default with a small cache for single-speed drives, even if a higher-speed drive is installed on your computer. Older drives will often deliver better performance when the CD-ROM cache is set to Large and the type of drive selected is Quad-Speed Or Higher.

The Enable Write-Behind Caching option on the Removable Disk tab speeds up the performance of removable drives, such as Iomega Zip or Jaz drives.

The Troubleshooting tab disables a series of advanced Win98 options that may cause problems on older computers. You can disable the locking of individual disk partitions, write-behind operations for the disk cache, and protected-mode 32-bit handling of the hard drive. The time to use these options is when your system is not performing properly. Disabling various features on this tab may clear up performance problems and allow you to isolate hardware conflicts.

Shortcuts to System Properties

If you go to the System applet through the Control Panel, it may take three to six mouse clicks to get to the feature you want. You can save time by right-clicking My Computer and choosing Properties to open the System applet. For even faster access, you can create a desktop shortcut that will open directly to any specified System Properties tab. Here's how to create a shortcut for Device Manager:

1. Right-click the desktop and create a file shortcut by choosing New | Shortcut.
2. Enter the following in the command-line field on the Create Shortcut screen:

   CONTROL.EXE sysdm.cpl, system,1

   Be sure not to put any space after the comma in system,1.
3. Click Next and choose a name for the shortcut (such as Device Manager). Then click the Finish button.
4. If you like, you can create a custom icon for the shortcut. Right-click the icon on the desktop, choose Properties | Change Icon, click OK, and then select an icon from the available list. (See Chapter 4 for more information on working with icon properties.)

When you open this new shortcut, it will take you directly to the Device Manager tab of the System Properties screen. You can also create shortcuts to open directly to other System Properties screen tabs.

- Enter **CONTROL.EXE sysdm.cpl, system,0** to go directly to the General tab.
- Enter **CONTROL.EXE sysdm.cpl, system,2** to go directly to the Hardware Profiles tab.
- Enter **CONTROL.EXE sysdm.cpl, system,3** to go directly to the Performance tab.

GRAPHICS BUTTON The Graphics button allows you to minimize or maximize the extent to which Windows 98 uses the accelerator functions built into your graphics card.

Input/Output-Related Components

Other input/output-related Control Panel applets include Game Controllers, Infrared, Keyboard, and Mouse.

Game Controllers Applet

Microsoft wants to be your game company. The Game Controllers feature is an important part of that strategy. On some systems, if you don't have a joystick attached to the game port during installation, the Game Controllers applet won't appear in the Control Panel. To add Game Controllers after Windows 98 has been installed, follow these steps:

1. Open the Add New Hardware Wizard and choose the No, I Want To Select The Hardware From A List option.
2. On the next screen, select Sound, Video and Game Controllers in the Hardware Types list. Below, select Microsoft from the Manufacturer's pane on the left and Gameport Joystick in the Models pane.
3. Click the Next and Finish buttons, and the Game Controllers applet will be added to the Control Panel.

Hardware permitting, you can install up to 16 different joysticks in 17 different modes.

Infrared Applet

The Infrared applet controls the operation of any installed infrared (IR) communication ports. Typical uses for these ports include wireless data transfer between two computers and wireless uploading and downloading of files from multimedia devices such as digital cameras.

The Status tab, shown next, reports whether infrared communication on your computer is enabled or disabled. If another IR device is within range, the Status tab also shows whether a connection has been established.

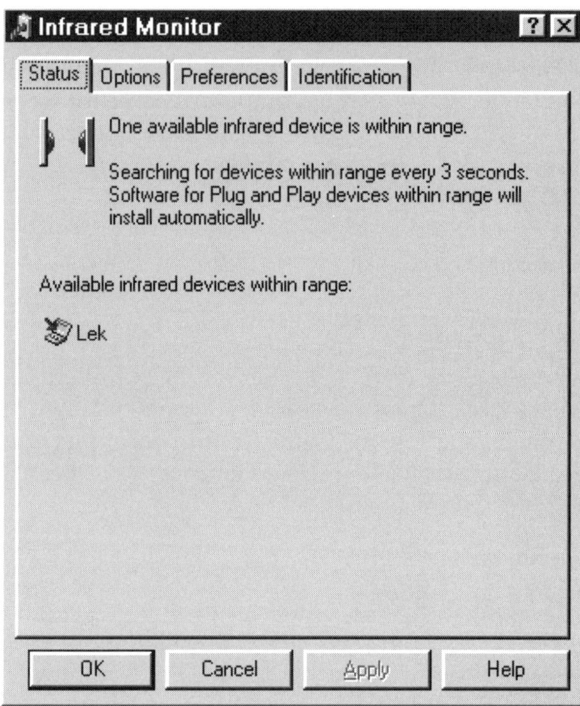

If this screen reports that IR communication is disabled, or if it displays an error message, then your computer's infrared serial port may be disabled or improperly configured. First check the Enable Infrared Communication box on the Options tab and click the Apply button. If the Status tab still reports disabled IR communication, you should check the status of the computer's hardware infrared port: Choose System | Device Manager and examine the device listing for Network Adapters.

- If your computer has a hardware infrared port and the Infrared Serial Port device is missing, try installing it with Add New Hardware.
- If the Infrared Serial Port device is listed with a red X, open its Properties screen and click the Enable Device button. (If you disabled the IR port to install a modem, you may have to remove the modem or reassign its resources to get the IR port to work properly. Another solution is to create both an infrared and a modem hardware profile, allowing you to choose the device you want when you start Windows 98.)

The Options tab enables or disables IR communication and allows you to turn on an autosearch feature that will automatically detect another IR device when it comes within your computer's line of sight. The Limit Connections box (deselected by default) allows you to limit the top data transfer speed for slower IR connections. If the Install Software For Plug And Play Devices option is checked, your computer will automatically install Win98 drivers to communicate with any other IR devices that come within its detection range.

The Preferences tab lets you add or remove the Infrared applet from the System Tray on the taskbar and toggle system sounds on and off to signal a connection.

The Identification tab lets you set your computer's name for recognition by remote and network devices.

Keyboard Applet

The Keyboard applet controls the character repeat rate, delay interval, and cursor blink rate for your keyboard. It also allows you to select different languages and install alternative keyboards. If you have a Microsoft Natural Keyboard, a separate Control Panel applet will be installed that overrides the generic control. (See Chapter 4 for a detailed list of keyboard shortcuts that allow you to control the desktop without a mouse.)

To choose languages other than English on the Language tab, you need to install multilanguage support with the Add/Remove Programs object. For each choice on the Language tab, you can also select an individual keyboard layout.

Mouse Applet

The Mouse applet lets you (1) configure your mouse buttons for right- or left-handed use, as shown here, (2) adjust click and pointer speed, and (3) add or remove trails. (Trails are helpful in finding the cursor.)

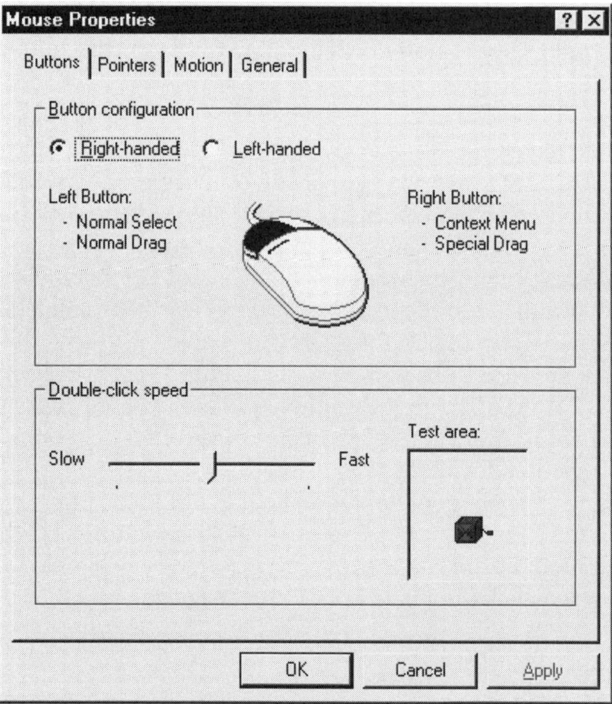

You can also select different pointer shapes and styles. These are similar to the custom mouse cursors you can choose through the Desktop Themes applet, and they become available when you install Mouse Pointers by choosing Add/Remove Programs | Windows Setup | Accessories.

If you have an enhanced pointing device such as a Microsoft Intellimouse or Synaptics Touchpad, additional control tabs may appear in the Mouse applet. Some pointing devices allow you to set special options to scroll within application windows, continue moving the cursor with "edge momentum," or set third-button defaults.

Communications and Connectivity

One of the greatest advantages Windows 98 offers over its predecessors and competitors is well-integrated connectivity. A series of communications-related applets in the Control Panel—Internet, Modems, Mail and Fax, Microsoft Mail Postoffice, Network, and Telephony—let you manage this connectivity.

Internet Applet

The Internet applet controls the default settings for Microsoft's Internet Explorer Web browser. For information on how to customize these options, see Chapter 12 .

The settings on the Internet applet's Connection tab can affect the way programs other than Internet Explorer establish an Internet connection. If you connect through a modem, clicking the Settings button allows you to choose which Dial-Up Networking profile will be opened to establish an Internet connection, as shown in Figure 9-16. The profile you choose may be automatically launched when Outlook Express or a third-party Internet utility is started (depending on the individual program's startup options).

Modems Applet

The Modems applet detects and configures one or more modems attached to your computer—providing one of the more impressive Win98 plug-and-play features. Newer modems may be detected and installed automatically as soon as you add them to the computer. When you open Modems, the General tab displays a list of currently installed serial communication devices. If a modem was not detected automatically at startup, you can install it by clicking the Add button.

When you click the Add button, the Modem Setup Wizard polls your computer's PC Card slots or I/O ports. The first Install New Modem screen asks which modem type you want to install. After you select PCMCIA modem card or Other, the Wizard interrogates any attached devices.

Windows 98 does a fairly good job of detecting and identifying individual brands and modem types automatically, but you can adjust the settings by choosing the manufacturer and model from the Install New Modem list. (If you don't see your modem there, you can click the Have Disk button to install an OEM driver.)

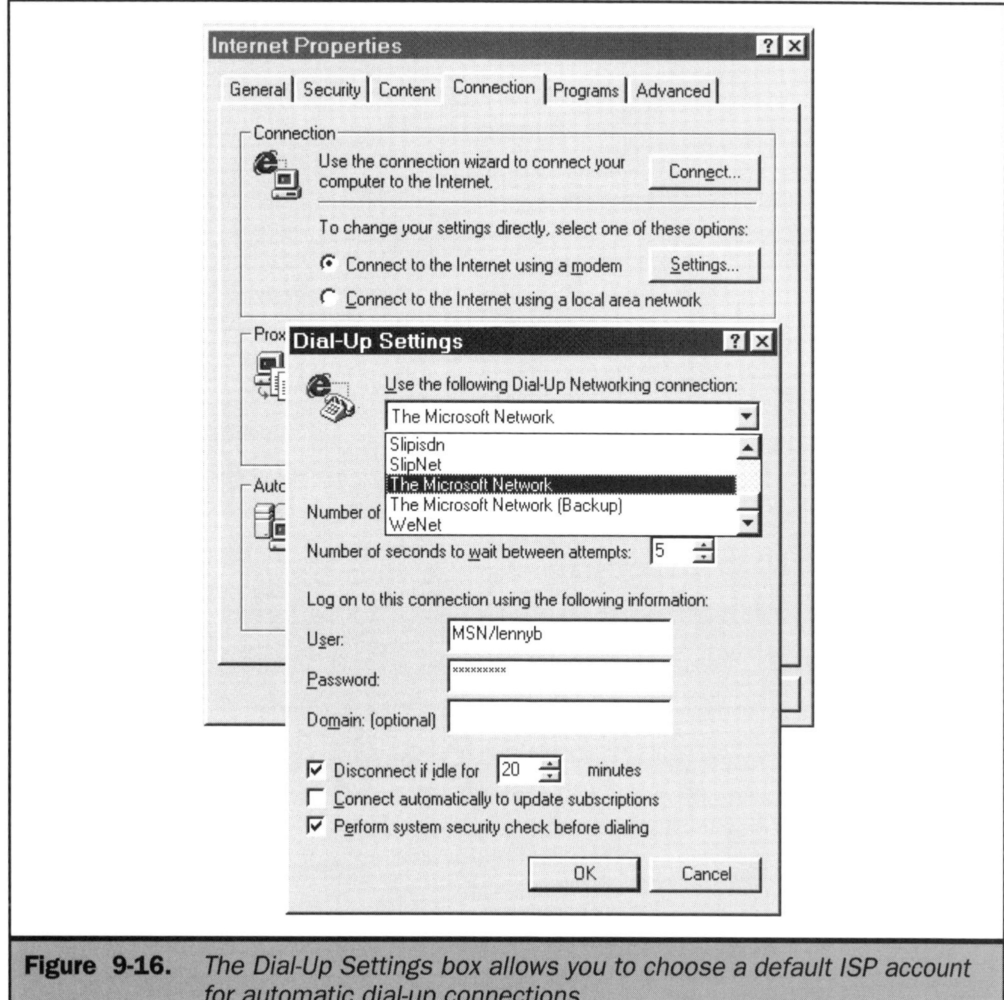

Figure 9-16. *The Dial-Up Settings box allows you to choose a default ISP account for automatic dial-up connections*

The Dialing Properties button on the General tab contains options that let you select tone or pulse, use a calling card, disable call waiting, or dial any other special access codes on the My Locations screen. In Windows 98 these options can also be accessed by opening the Control Panel's Telephony applet. (See Chapter 11 for more information.)

The Diagnostics tab displays port and configuration information for each installed modem. To test connectivity, you can select a port and modem combination and click the More Info button to run a set of diagnostic tests. Windows 98 will attempt to initialize your modem and then report the results in a modem status window as shown next.

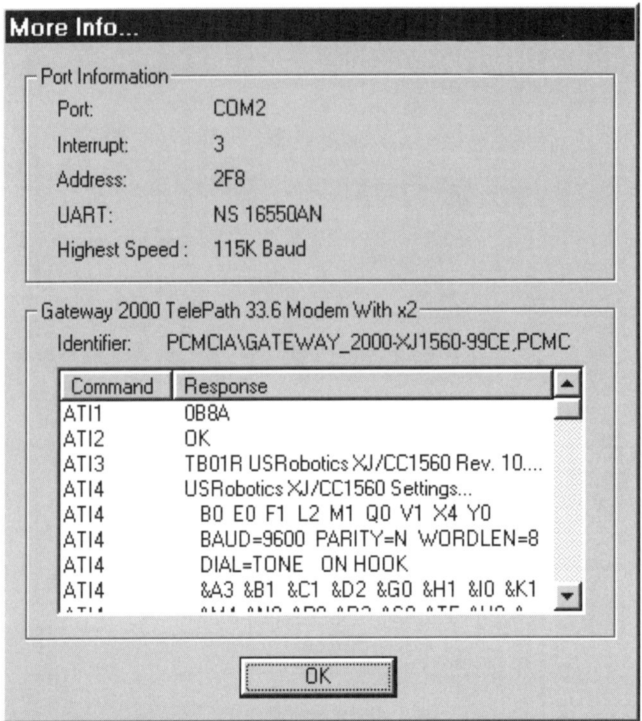

WORKING WITH MODEM PROPERTIES When a particular modem is installed, Windows 98 writes a preconfigured set of initialization strings and protocol settings in the system registry. You can modify or add to these settings by accessing the Properties configuration options for each modem. (Select the modem in the list on the General tab and click the Properties button.)

The Properties screen for an individual modem contains a General and a Connection tab. The General tab displays the port assigned to the modem, a speaker volume slider, and the maximum data transfer speed of the assigned port. If you transfer an external modem to a different serial port, you can change the assigned port on this tab. If the modem is an internal or PC Card model, the port assignment is fixed by the Windows 98 Device Manager. For most modems rated at 14.4Kbps or higher, the maximum speed should be set to 115200. (See Chapter 11 for more information on modems and optimizing data transfer speeds.)

The Connection tab lets you set communication defaults for the modem: data bits, stop bits, parity, and Call preferences. You can wait for a tone before dialing, cancel the call if not connected in 60 seconds, and disconnect a call if the line is idle for a specified time. Waiting for a tone is handy for a PBX line to prevent premature dialing.

If you click the Advanced button, you can toggle settings that govern flow control, error control, and modulation type, as shown next. These menu options correspond to Hayes AT strings delivered to the modem when it is initialized. The Extra Settings field allows you to enter additional, custom command strings. This feature is very useful for modems that don't respond properly to the defaults written by a Microsoft driver. (Your modem's manual should provide information on the Hayes commands that you can enter.)

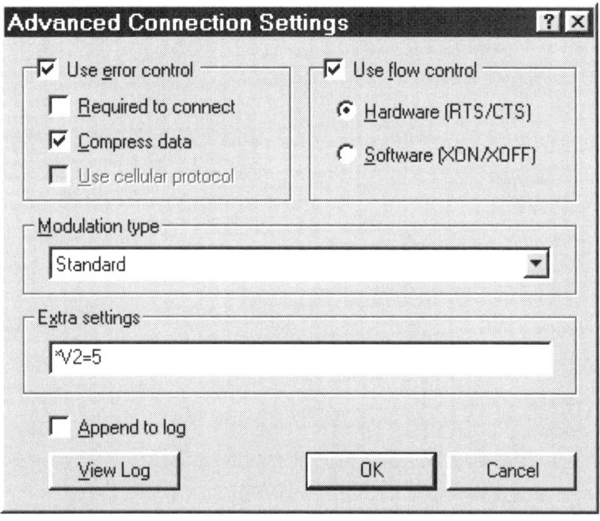

Tip

If an installed modem isn't working properly, first look for an OEM driver from the vendor. In a pinch, if you can't find one, try uninstalling the modem and instead install a generic modem driver (one of the standard modem types). You can also scroll through the list of manufacturers and try selecting a different modem type from the same vendor. If the modem fails to respond, you can add a custom initialization string for it: Open the modem's Properties screen, go to the Connections tab, and click the Advanced button. You can enter additional Hayes modem strings in the Extra Settings box; enter &C2 to enable carrier detection and &F or &F1 to reset the modem to its factory defaults. Consult your modem manual for the specific Hayes commands that apply to your modem.

You can also troubleshoot modem problems by placing a check mark in the Append To Log box on the Advanced Connection Settings screen. This creates a log file in the \WINDOWS directory that bears the modem's name and records all commands sent from and received by that device.

Mail and Fax Applet

The Mail and Fax applet provides configuration information for Windows 95's Microsoft Exchange (or Windows Messaging) feature. Microsoft Exchange was the default e-mail client in Windows 95, before the appearance of Outlook 97/98 (in Microsoft Office) and Win98's Outlook Express mail client. (It was renamed Windows

Messaging in Windows 95 Service Release 2.) The only advantage that Windows Messaging offers over Outlook Express is its ability to interact with a Win95 Workgroup post office or to dispatch faxes in conjunction with the Win95 Microsoft Fax applet.

The Mail and Fax control applet appears in Windows 98 if you've upgraded from a Win95 system where Microsoft Exchange or Windows Messaging was installed. New Windows 98 users who want this feature can add it from the Windows 98 CD.

To install Windows Messaging (and the Mail and Fax applet) on a new Windows 98 computer, follow these steps:

Browse the Windows 98 CD and open the \TOOLS\OLDWIN95\MESSAGE\US folder. (For the International version, open the INTL folder.) Launch WMS.EXE .

The Windows Messaging Inbox is designed to transmit and receive mail from a Workgroup post office, a fax/modem, the Microsoft Network online service, or the Internet through a third-party Internet service provider. The Mail and Fax applet lets you to inspect or edit service profiles for all of the Windows Messaging information services supported by the Microsoft Exchange Inbox. The Microsoft Mail protocol is supported over a dial-up connection, direct connection, or local area network.

The Personal Address Book (listed on the Services tab of the Windows Messaging Settings Properties screen) contains not only e-mail addresses, but names, phone and fax numbers, mailing addresses, and other personal contact information. Through the open MAPI interfaces, the Personal Address Book is accessible from a wide variety of applications, and through the use of MAPI drivers it is also the user interface for corporate e-mail and information services directories. The Personal Address Book can store addresses for multiple e-mail systems at the same time. The Personal Address Book and Personal Information Store are kept in two files, MAILBOX.PAB and MAILBOX.PST, stored in the Microsoft Exchange directory on your Win98 host drive. You have the option of configuring alternative .PAB and .PST files for Windows Messaging with different sets of addresses and e-mail logs. You might want to do this if there are multiple Win95 users on a single computer.

Note *If you want to make Win98's Outlook Express your default mail client, you can import a Personal Address Book or a Personal Information Store (saved messages) into Outlook Express. However, Outlook Express cannot import a Microsoft Mail post office list. (See Chapters 11 and 13 for details.)*

The Mail and Fax applet can configure several different information services in the same service profile. If you decide to do this, each of the installed services can be contacted in succession to transmit and receive e-mail when you open Inbox. Each of the individual service profiles can be edited by selecting it on the Services tab and clicking the Properties button. Services can be added or deleted from an individual profile with the Add and Remove buttons.

To set the delivery order for the services configured in a service profile, open Mail and Fax and click the Show Profiles button. Select the profile you want to adjust and click the Properties button. This will open a three-tabbed menu of settings properties, shown here. Select the Delivery tab. The bottom portion of the window displays the configured services in the order that they will be accessed when Inbox is active. The up and down arrow boxes to the right of the list can be used to rearrange the delivery order.

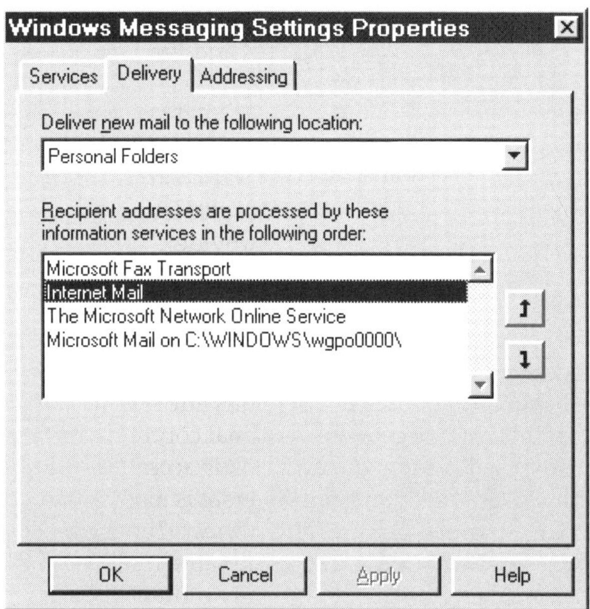

After you click the Show Profiles button on the Windows Messaging Settings Services tab, the Mail and Fax Profiles screen appears. The option at the bottom of this screen lets you select a default service profile. This service profile will be loaded automatically when you open Inbox. You can also configure Inbox to prompt you for the correct service profile each time you open it. Unfortunately, the "prompt on opening" option can't be selected with the Mail and Fax Control Panel applet. To make Windows Messaging prompt you for a service profile, open Inbox with the default profile. Then select Options from the Inbox Tools menu. You'll find a set of radio buttons on the Options screen to toggle Prompt For A Profile on or off.

Note that if Microsoft Fax is installed in a service profile, a variety of fax options are buried on the Message and Modem tabs on the Fax Properties screen. (For more information about configuring and working with Inbox and Microsoft Exchange, refer to Chapter 11.)

Microsoft Mail Postoffice Applet

The Microsoft Mail Postoffice applet configures and manages a Workgroup Microsoft Mail post office on your local computer. This is a Windows 95 feature that appears in

Windows 98 if you've upgraded from a Win95 system where Microsoft Mail was previously installed. New Windows 98 users (a clean installation) can add this feature from the Windows 98 CD.

To install a Microsoft Mail post office on a new Windows 98 computer, browse the Windows 98 CD, locate and run the WMS.EXE program as described earlier in the "Mail and Fax Applet" section of this chapter. This will add the Microsoft Mail Postoffice applet to Control Panel. When you open the Microsoft Mail Postoffice applet, it will prompt you to administer an existing Workgroup post office or create a new one. You can locate an existing post office on a network server by clicking the Browse button. If you have administrator rights, you can enter your mailbox name and password to log into the post office. From there you can add and remove users or modify an existing account. The mailboxes in the post office address list appear in a Windows Messaging or Outlook 97/98 address book. They are not available within Win98's Outlook Express mail client.

Network Applet

The Network applet allows you to install, remove, or verify any of four basic networking components: Client, Adapter, Protocol, or Service. The Network applet's Configuration tab displays all of the network components currently installed under Windows 98. You can add one of the four basic component types by clicking the Add button, or select an installed component and click Properties to adjust its configuration.

The most common uses you'll have for the Network applet are to enable File and Print Sharing, the TCP/IP protocol for Dial-Up Networking over the Internet, or the new Microsoft Family Login feature. Windows 98 does not install these features during setup unless you choose them specifically.

- To install File and Print Sharing, open the Network applet and click the File and Print Sharing button on the Configuration tab. This enables the sharing of local resources (folders, drives, printers, and fax devices) over a Microsoft or Novell network. You must also install this option if you want this computer to share files over a direct cable connection. (See Chapters 5 and 14 for more details.)
- To install the TCP/IP protocol (if it doesn't already appear in the Network Components list), open the Network applet and select the Configuration tab. Then click Add, select Protocol, and select Microsoft and TCP/IP as shown in Figure 9-17. For more information on using these features, see "Direct Cable Connection" and "Dial-Up Networking" in Chapter 5.
- To install the Microsoft Family Login feature, open the Network applet and select the Configuration tab. Then click Add, select Client, and select Microsoft and Microsoft Family Login.

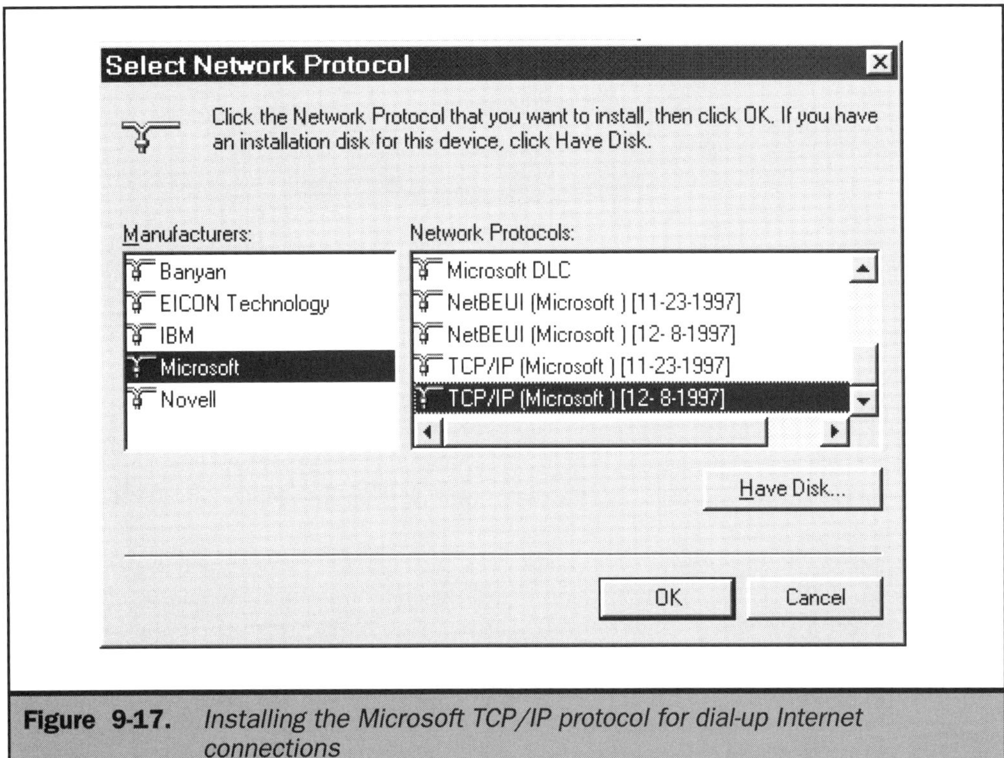

Figure 9-17. *Installing the Microsoft TCP/IP protocol for dial-up Internet connections*

SETTING LOGIN OPTIONS The Primary Network Logon field in the middle of the Configuration tab establishes which network login will be attempted first upon startup. If you don't want to log onto any network, you can select Windows Login or a new Windows 98 feature called Microsoft Family Login.

If you select Windows Login, after the first time you start the computer, you'll be prompted to enter a password to access Windows 98. If you leave the password field blank, you'll go directly to the desktop after startup, bypassing any username or password screen. If you enter a password, you'll be prompted to enter it with your username each time you start Windows 98.

If you select Microsoft Family Login, you can select from a series of users authorized to log into this computer after startup (but you can't log onto a Microsoft or Novell network). A local username and password screen, like the one shown next, appears at Win98 startup.

See "Users Applet" later in this chapter for more information on creating multiple user accounts.

If you select Client For Microsoft Networks, you can log onto a peer-to-peer Microsoft (NETBEUI/IPX) network or a Windows NT domain. A username and password screen for Microsoft networking appears at Win98 startup. To log into a Windows NT server, you'll need to turn this option on in the Client For Microsoft Networks properties. See "Log onto a Windows NT Domain" in Chapter 14 for details.

If you select Client For Novell Networks, you can log onto a Novell 3.x or 4.x user account. A username and password screen for Novell networking appears at Win98 startup. See "Log onto a Netware Server" in Chapter 14 for details.

Tip *If different passwords are assigned to a user for local, Microsoft client, and Novell client logins, up to three separate username and password screens may appear at Win98 startup. To simplify login to multiple networks, you can assign a single password to a user for all three accounts. This will permit the user to log onto a local machine, peer-to-peer network or Windows NT domain, and Novell server simultaneously from a single username and password screen.*

IDENTIFICATION TAB The Network applet's Identification tab displays the computer name and workgroup for this individual computer. To establish a network or direct cable connection, each workstation must be assigned a distinct, individual computer name.

ACCESS CONTROL TAB The Access Control tab allows you to control individual user access to shared resources. Each drive, directory, printer, and so on can be password protected. On Windows NT and Novell networks, access can be restricted to individual users or workgroups. (For details, see Chapter 14.)

Windows 98 provides several different routes to reach these same configuration features. If Windows 98 detects a network card or installs the Dial-Up Networking service, all of the network components you need may be added automatically. Once some network components have been installed, the Network Neighborhood icon appears on the desktop.

You can display the configuration options for installed network components more quickly by right-clicking the Network Neighborhood icon on the desktop and selecting Properties.

Telephony Applet

Experienced Windows 95 users will recognize the Telephony applet as the set of options that also appear when you open the Dialing Properties screen for a modem or Dial-Up Networking profile. The Dialing Properties options allow you to specify default telephone prefixes and connection options for a series of geographic locations. This option is designed for road warriors who telecommute with a portable computer from a variety of area codes in the United States or from other countries.

To create a set of defaults for a new dialing location, click the New button on the My Locations tab. You can then enable or disable the dialing of an area code or outside line numerical prefix, enable or disable call waiting, or set defaults for a special long-distance calling card. For more information on using these options, refer to Chapter 11.

The Telephony Drivers tab allows you to set dialing defaults for alternative telephony devices supplied by third-party vendors.

Passwords Applet

Windows 98 provides both local and network password protection. The local password can't lock others out of the operating system, but it can guard individual user settings such as those for Dial-Up Networking and specific desktop configurations. This feature is designed as a convenience to allow multiple users to work on a single machine. It's not really intended as a stringent security safeguard. (It's easy enough to bypass the Windows login at startup and get to a generic desktop.)

The first time Windows 98 starts, the user is prompted to enter a username and password. If the password is left blank and then confirmed, this login screen does not appear again until you change the password or the machine is configured for a multiuser environment or for network access.

Change Passwords Tab

The Change Passwords tab, shown in Figure 9-18 , allows you to modify your Windows 98 login password after it has been set on the first bootup. The Other Passwords option on the bottom half of the tab allows you to change a password

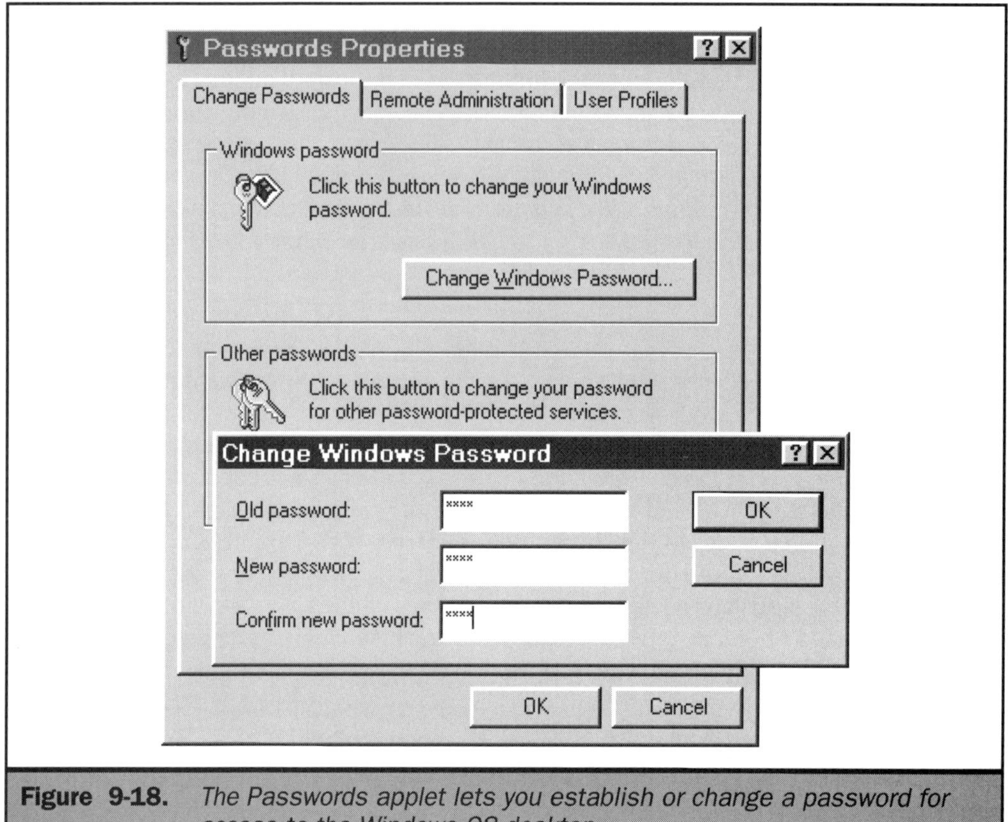

Figure 9-18. *The Passwords applet lets you establish or change a password for access to the Windows 98 desktop*

you've previously entered for a shared resource on another computer (it won't change a password for a Novell Netware account). You'll find more information on Windows 98 networking in Chapter 14.

User Profiles Tab

Win98's support for separate users, which enables the creation of multiple environments on the same PC, can also be used by a single user to create a series of productivity desktops. The User Profiles tab allows you to select a single password configuration for the machine or to customize preferences and desktop settings for each user. This level of customization can extend to desktop icons, fonts, colors, network connections (including Dial-Up Networking), Start menu program groups, and Internet Explorer favorites and subscriptions.

Although the level of security isn't high, these settings can allow several people in the same family to share a computer with a moderate level of privacy.

Note *In Windows 95, the quickest way to enable multiple user profiles was to select the Passwords applet's User Profiles tab and place check marks next to the settings that varied from user to user. These settings would then become active when a new username and password were entered at boot time on the Windows login screen. Windows 98 has automated the process of creating multiple user accounts. While you can still split the desktop for multiple users with the Passwords applet, Microsoft has added a new Users applet that makes it easier to assign constant and variable operating defaults to each new user account.*

Users Applet

The Users applet lets you quickly create and manage new accounts for a single workstation, eliminating the need to reboot and log in each time you want to add a new user. For example, you may want to create multiple accounts to let other people work at a single computer, preserving a custom configuration for each user, or to let a single user log onto a machine for multiple work scenarios, creating a different desktop with different program groups for each productivity project.

To create a new user account, open the Users applet. What you see will depend upon whether you've already enabled the Passwords applet's User Profiles option to let users customize their desktop profiles. If you have enabled this option, you'll see a user list that allows you to add or modify existing user accounts. If you haven't modified the default User Profiles options, you'll see an Enable Multi-User Settings Wizard.

Enabling New User Accounts for the First Time

To enable new user accounts for the first time, follow these steps:

1. On the first Enable Multi-User Settings Wizard screen, click Next and enter an account name in the Add User screen that follows.
2. The next screen asks you to enter and confirm a password. Either type a password or leave these fields blank and click Next to disable password protection for this account.
3. The Personalized Items Settings screen, shown next, allows you to choose the Windows 98 elements that the new user can customize. Place check marks next to any or all of the five listed options. You can also copy all the default settings (Internet subscriptions, URL favorites, and so on) for the current user account or create a new, empty set.

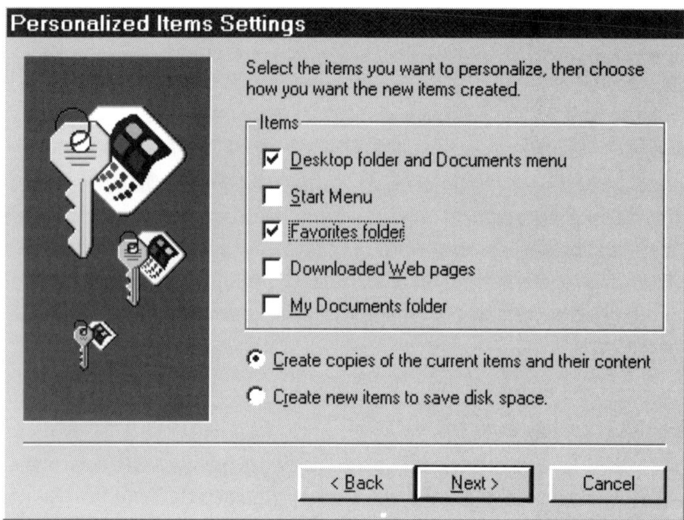

4. Click Finish on the next screen to complete the settings for the new user account. (If Outlook Express is installed, Windows 98 will automatically create a new profile so the new user can maintain separate e-mail records.)

Creating and Editing New Accounts from the User List Tab

If the Passwords option was previously enabled to let users customize desktop preferences (or if you've already created one user account), the Users applet will open to the User List tab. Here's how to create a new user account from this tab:

1. Click the New User button. The Add User Wizard opens.
2. Click Next on the first Add User screen and enter a username on the next screen. Click Next to continue.
3. Enter a password for this account (or leave the fields blank) and click Next to display the Personalized Item Settings screen, shown in Figure 9-19. As with the first user you created, you can select any or all of the five check boxes to enable customization of various Windows 98 system defaults.
4. Click Finish on the last screen to finalize the settings for the new user account.

To edit an existing account on the User List tab, select the account name and click the Change Settings button. This displays the Personalized Item Settings screen, where you can add or remove customization settings for any of the five check box items.

If you delete an account, its separate, itemized defaults will also be deleted from the hard disk.

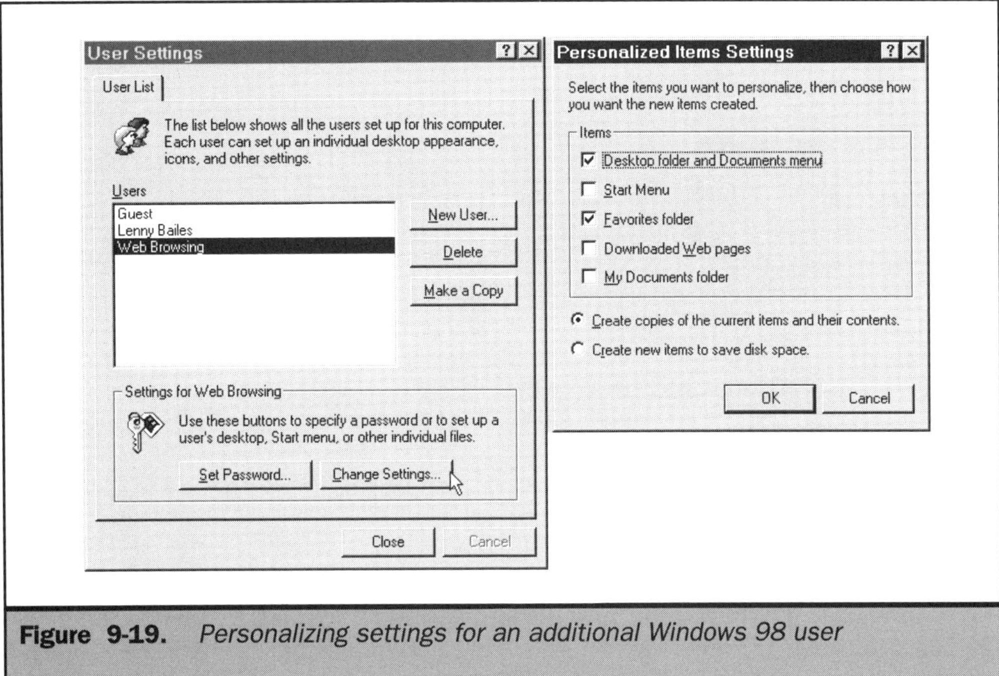

Figure 9-19. *Personalizing settings for an additional Windows 98 user*

Multiple Desktops for Individuals or Workgroups

One of the user accounts shown in the preceding figure is named Web Browsing. In addition to setting up accounts for multiple users, Windows 98 permits you to set up a series of project-oriented desktops that a single user can choose from. For example, you might have one "Username" account configured to show a classic Windows 98 desktop with standard icons and program groups. The second Web Browsing account might be configured to show an ActiveX desktop with embedded HTML resources and the Internet Explorer channel bar. See Chapters 4 and 12 for more information on how to exploit this feature.

Microsoft Family Login

Windows 98 offers a new option that displays all existing user accounts for a computer at startup. You can select any account from the list, enter its password, and log on with that account's customized desktop and user preferences.

To enable Microsoft Family Login, right-click the Network Neighborhood icon (or open the Network applet in the Control Panel). Then select Microsoft Family Login from the Primary Network Logon drop-down list on the Configuration tab. (If this option does not appear in the drop-down list, you can install it by clicking Add, selecting Client, and then selecting Microsoft and Microsoft Family Login.)

Multimedia Options

Windows 98 furthers the development and display of multimedia on Intel PC hardware. In addition to its support for digital video disk (DVD) playback, Win98 incorporates a new, integrated API for sound and video playback. With new WDM audio drivers, the richer MIDI wavetable feature can be emulated in the operating system. Older sound cards that lack wavetable hardware can now produce rich, polyphonic tones. Win98's WDM drivers also coordinate sound and video, making it possible for digital cameras to interface seamlessly with video-conferencing applications. (Microsoft NetMeeting is a free sample application that's bundled with the operating system.)

The Win98 Control Panel includes two multimedia applets: Sounds and Multimedia.

Sounds Applet

On a simpler level, Windows 98 provides sound cues for system events: little buzzes and beeps that keep you in touch with the execution of background processes. The Sounds applet on the Control Panel ties these noises to about 40 different system events: operating system startup, open or close a program, critical stop, menu popup, menu command, minimize window, new mail notification, program or system errors, select text, and so on.

Some people prefer a minimal number of audio interruptions when they're working, and others enjoy making the PC buzz like a music box. The capacity to punctuate program and system events with sounds may have a practical application for visually challenged users. It can also provide alerts for timed processes so you can go to sleep during a long file download, backup, or defragment operation.

The system events listed in the Events window on the Sounds tab, shown next, can be associated with any wavesound (.WAV file) listed in the Name field. For instance, to change the Windows startup sound, scroll down to the Start Windows event, select it, and choose a new sound from the drop-down Name box. (You can also click the Browse button to locate .WAV files stored in separate hard disk directories.) To disable the startup sound, select None at the top of the list.

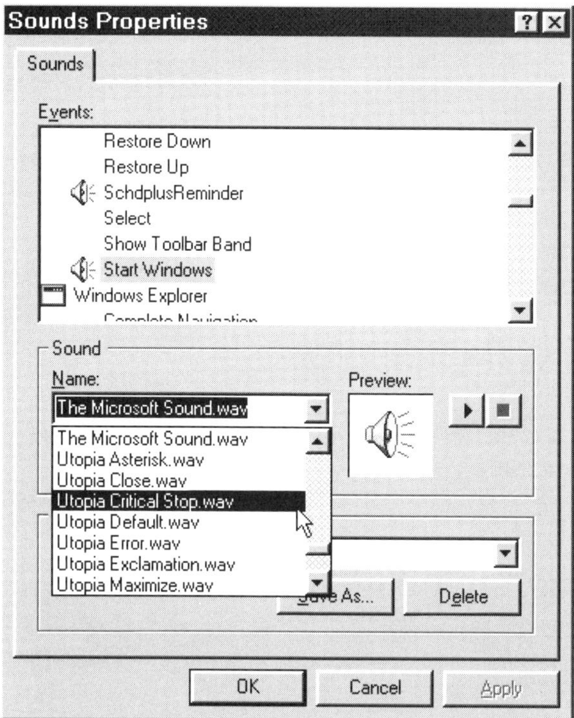

If a small speaker icon appears to the left of an event, then the event has been associated with a specific sound file. You can test the sound by clicking the Play arrow to the right of the Preview speaker icon.

The default events defined by Windows 98 cover operating system functions and several program and operating system interactions. When you install third-party applications, they may add their own events. For instance, Norton Navigator can "speak up" when you create a new folder, delete a file, compress an archive, and so on. Microsoft NetMeeting notifies you when a person requests a conference, leaves a conference, and so on. You can customize the event list by adding your own programs, playing a different set of sounds for each application. See the section "Productivity Tips and Tricks" in Chapter 16 to find a shareware program that accomplishes this by modifying the system registry.

SOUND SCHEMES Windows 98 includes a series of custom sound schemes. You can activate a scheme by choosing it in the drop-down Schemes list at the bottom of the

Sounds Properties screen. Before experimenting, you may want to save your current settings. Saving these settings works the same way as saving a desktop color scheme in the Display applet. Click the Save As button and enter a name for the current sound scheme.

If you don't see any supplemental sound schemes in the drop-down list, you can install them by opening Add/Remove Programs, selecting the Windows Setup tab, and selecting Multimedia and Multimedia Sound Schemes.

Multimedia Applet

The Multimedia applet, shown here, lets you fine-tune sound and video effects through five tabbed Properties screens: Audio, Video, MIDI, CD Music, and Devices.

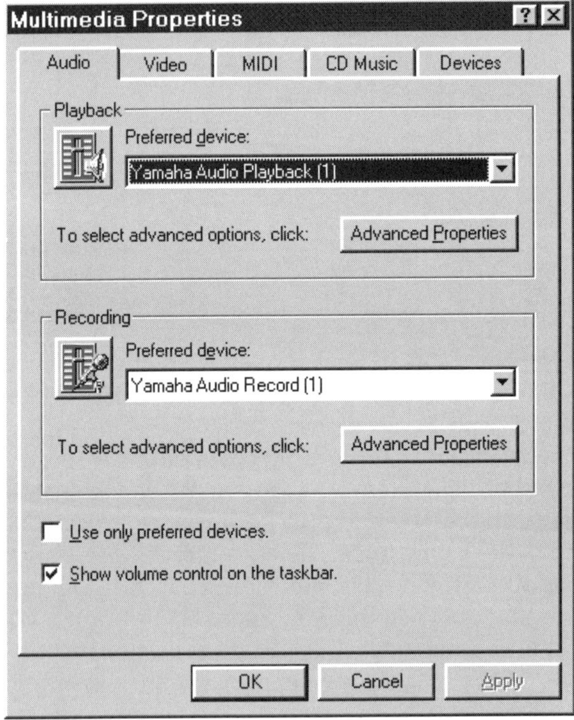

AUDIO TAB The Audio tab lets you choose playback and recording devices. (If you have more than one sound card installed in your computer, this tab lets you switch between the two devices.) The Advanced Properties buttons in the Playback and Recording sections of this tab present options appropriate to the devices listed in the Preferred Device fields. You may be able to configure the sound card for a variety of attached speaker types, adjust hardware acceleration, or change the sample rate conversion for digital audio files. (Higher sample rates yield better sound quality but are also require more processing by the CPU.) See Chapters 5 and 15 for more information about how these options work.

VIDEO TAB The Video tab lets you select between full screen and windowed video playback. These settings affect Microsoft's Active Movie Player and Media Player applets. The Show Video In Window Display option lets you set the screen to the original size, double its original size, or reduce it to one-half, one-fourth, or one-sixteenth of the screen size. You can also select the Full Screen option to maximize playback on the entire screen.

MIDI TAB The MIDI tab allows you to switch between installed drivers for synthesizer playback. Newer sound cards with onboard wavetable chips may offer two or three MIDI profiles. You may want to sample all of them. (To switch profiles, select one in the MIDI Output box and click the Apply button.)

The Custom Configuration button allows you to create new MIDI schemes if you've added third-party instrument voices to a MIDI profile. It corresponds to the Windows 3.x MIDIMAP utility. (New OEM instruments are added by clicking the Add New Instrument button.)

CD MUSIC TAB The CD Music tab shows the letter of the drive that plays music if there are multiple CD-ROM drives in the computer. The volume slider corresponds to the CD output control in the standard Windows 98 Volume Control. A new feature in Windows 98 lets you improve the quality of CD output for USB audio speakers. Selecting this option disables standard CD output through the speaker-out jack on the back of the sound card.

DEVICES TAB New in Windows 98, the Devices tab lets you inspect and adjust settings for installed multimedia devices. If you have multiple sound cards in a computer, you can specify which one is used for primary I/O. The Multimedia Devices tab works in the same way as the System Device Manager tab: You can open the listings for a category by double-clicking it or by toggling the + or - indicator to the left of the category name. To enable, disable, or configure a device, select it and click the Properties button.

32-Bit ODBC Applet

The 32-Bit ODBC applet appears on the Control Panel if you've installed Microsoft Office or another productivity suite that supports Structured Query Language (SQL). SQL provides a method for accessing local or network databases. The ODBC applet allows you to add, modify, or delete ODBC drivers and data sources. ODBC drivers are specific .DLL files that applications such as Excel, Access, and Quattro Pro can use to gain access to a particular data source.

Open Database Connectivity (ODBC) is an open, programmable gateway development tool that continuously brokers requests between client applications and a variety of back-end data sources—including relational and nonrelational databases, real-time data feeds, and electronic mail and scheduling. To plug in here, applications need to be speaking the same language, which is controlled by the Control Panel's ODBC object.

The object's default types—dBase, FoxPro, Access, and MS Excel—provide a compatibility spectrum that most database applications on the market can read or write to.

When developers of other database types want to interface directly with ODBC, they install appropriate drivers. The three DSN tabs allow you to easily set up, delete, or add all ODBC drivers on the system. The Tracing tab allows you to select a log file to trace ODBC calls.

Printer and Font Options

Printers and fonts are discussed in detail elsewhere in this book (see Chapter 10), but the road to typographical bliss begins within the Control Panel. Both printers and fonts are represented here, with applets that manage installation, removal, and performance settings.

Fonts Applet

Under Windows 3.*x* it was easy to inadvertently fill your disk with extra fonts until you finally noticed you were out of disk space and Windows ran 50 percent slower. The Windows 98 Fonts applet lets you catalog exactly which fonts are active. You can add and delete entries as you need them.

The Fonts applet displays icons for active bitmap fonts, Microsoft vector fonts, and TrueType fonts under Windows 98. To manage Adobe Type I Postscript fonts you need to use the third-party Adobe Type Manager utility. (Postscript fonts are not displayed in the Fonts applet.)

You can display the list of supported fonts alphabetically or sort them by typeface similarity. Select the appropriate option from Fonts | View, as shown in Figure 9-20.

By default, Windows 95– and 98–aware applications install fonts in the WINDOWS\FONTS directory. Active fonts also appear in the Font selection menu of Windows applications. Each font in the Fonts folder is a separate file. You can right-click any font file and delete it from the pop-up menu or double-click the file to display a sample of the font itself, in several sizes and styles, as shown in Figure 9-21 . In this way, you can inspect various installed fonts before deciding to delete them from the system. The font samples can also be dumped to a printer: Right-click the font and select Print from the pop-up menu.

In the Fonts folder, font icons are marked with "TT," for TrueType fonts, or "A," for internal Windows system fonts. You can group similar fonts or show the details for each font file by clicking the Similarity or Details button on the standard toolbar (or select these options from the pull-down View menu). The Hide Variations option on

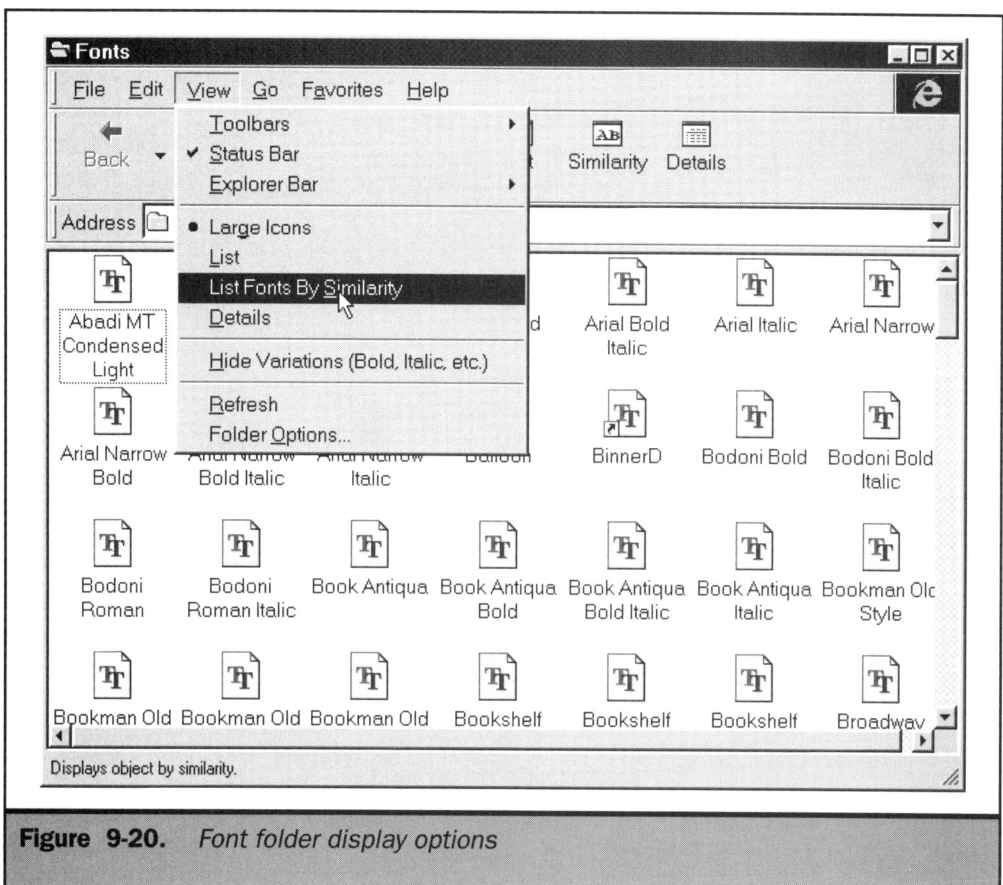

Figure 9-20. *Font folder display options*

the View menu simplifies the font list, weeding out stylistic variations of the same font (Bold, Italic, Bold Italic, and so on). You can further streamline the list by checking the Show Only TrueType box on the TrueType tab of the View | Options menu. This hides the display of non-TrueType font icons in the Fonts folder (although it does not remove these fonts from the disk).

Tip *If you have PostScript fonts installed on your system in the Adobe Type I format, these will not be displayed in the Win98 Fonts folder. The best way to view and manipulate PostScript fonts is through Adobe Type Manager. (See Chapter 10 for more information.)*

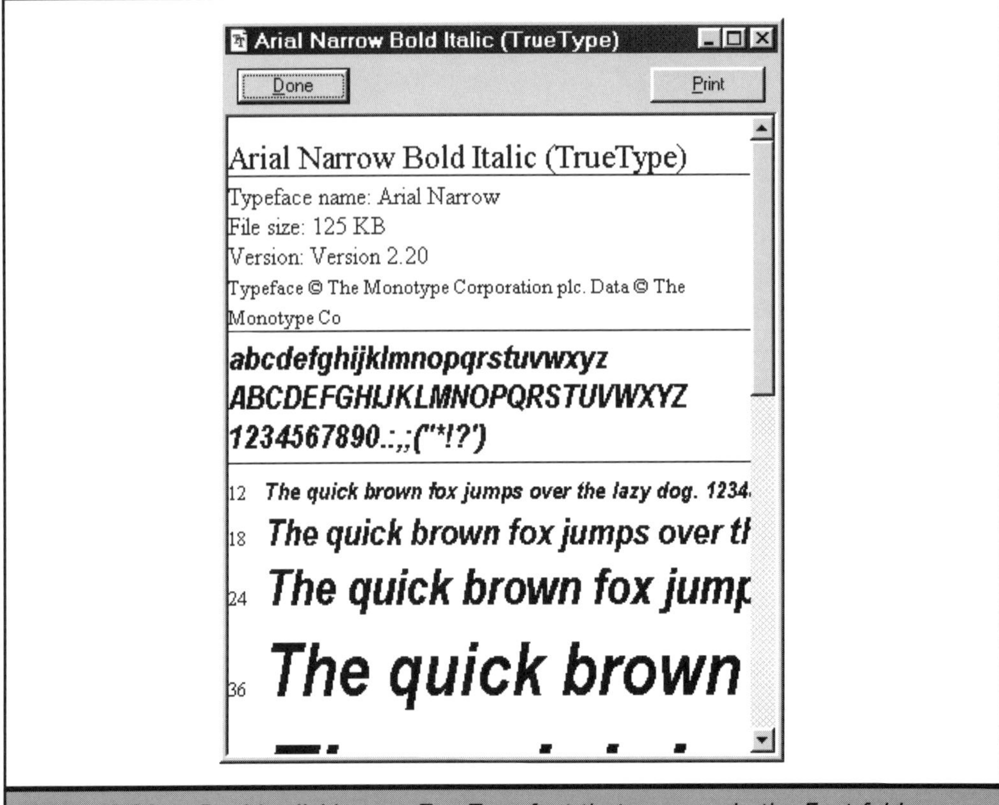

Figure 9-21. *Double-clicking any TrueType font that appears in the Font folder displays a sample of that font*

Printers Applet

The Printers applet lets you add or remove printing devices, view the status of print jobs, and edit performance settings for printers installed under Windows 98. When you open Printers, you'll see an icon for each currently installed device and an Add Printer icon for adding new printers. Windows 98 provides quick access to this Printers folder through several paths. You can open Printers by double-clicking its icon in the Control Panel, by choosing Start | Settings | Printers, or by clicking the Printers icon on the first level of My Computer or Windows Explorer.

ADDING NEW PRINTERS By default, Windows 98 asks you to choose a printer during setup. Many newer, plug-and-play printers can also be detected and installed automatically if they're cabled and switched on when you start the operating system.

To add a new printer manually, double-click the Add Printer icon. This opens the Add Printer Wizard, which leads you through the process of installing a local or network device, selecting the manufacturer and model and output port, and assigning the printer a user-friendly name.

Tip *At the end of a new printer installation, you can choose an option to immediately print a test page. You can also do this at any time by right-clicking an installed printer in the Printers folder, selecting Properties, and clicking the Print Test Page button on the General tab.*

POP-UP OPTIONS Each installed printer has an individual icon in the Printer folder. (For instance, if Microsoft Fax is active on your computer you'll find a Microsoft Fax printer icon.) When you right-click a printer, a set of controls pop up on its context menu. In addition to the standard Create Shortcut, Delete, and Rename options, you can choose the following options:

- **Open** View the print queue for the selected printer.
- **Pause Printing** Suspends printing of the current jobs. This option also permits offline printing to a temporarily disconnected local output device.
- **Set As Default** Makes this printer the default Windows 98 output device.
- **Use Printer Offline** Allows offline printing for network devices.
- **Purge Print Documents** Removes all current jobs from the print queue.

Tip *To cancel an individual print job quickly, double-click the active printer, right-click the document in the print queue, and choose Cancel Printing.*

If you right-click a printer and choose Open (or just double-click the printer icon), a print queue box pops up, as shown next, listing all the current and pending print jobs. This is similar to the display in the bygone Windows 3.1 Print Manager. The print queue information window lists the document name, current status, owner (originating application), progress of all print jobs, and start time. The pull-down menus contain the same set of options as the right-click context menu.

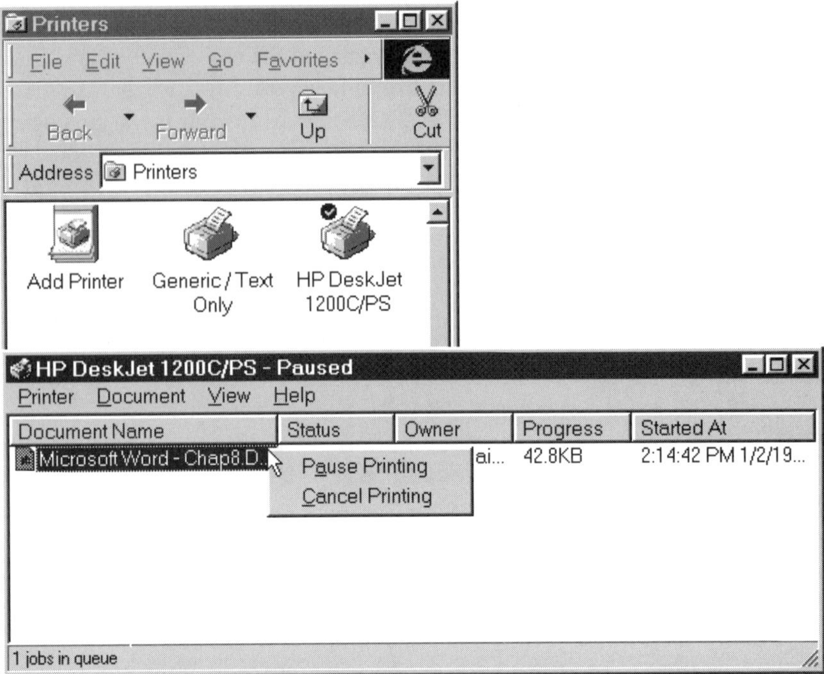

The Properties dialog box for a printer can be opened either from the Print Queue | Printer menu or by selecting Properties from the Printer icon's right-click context menu. The Properties dialog box contains information and performance options in at least five categories:

General	For printing a test page
Details	For specifying port, driver, and spool settings
Paper	For setting the size and orientation
Fonts	For displaying the typefaces available for a specific printer and controlling the use of TrueType and Postscript fonts
Device Options	For displaying or configuring available printer memory and print quality

Additional options, such as the following, may appear for more sophisticated printers (and when Win98's File and Print Sharing feature is installed).

Graphics	For setting the resolution, intensity, and color
PostScript	For configuring Postscript printing options
Color Management	For activating a Windows 98 Color Management profile
Sharing	For managing network printer sharing

Figure 9-22 shows you how to get to the Properties dialog box for a specific printer.

CREATING AN EASY-ACCESS PRINTERS SHORTCUT If you need to access printer control options frequently, you may get tired of burrowing into the recesses of the Control Panel each time you want to adjust a setting. Instead, you can create a shortcut to any printer by dragging its icon to the desktop. (Right-click, drag, and choose Create Shortcut Here to avoid the annoying system message about copying Control Panel components to the desktop.) With a printer shortcut on the desktop, you can right-click directly to place all of the printer control features at your fingertips.

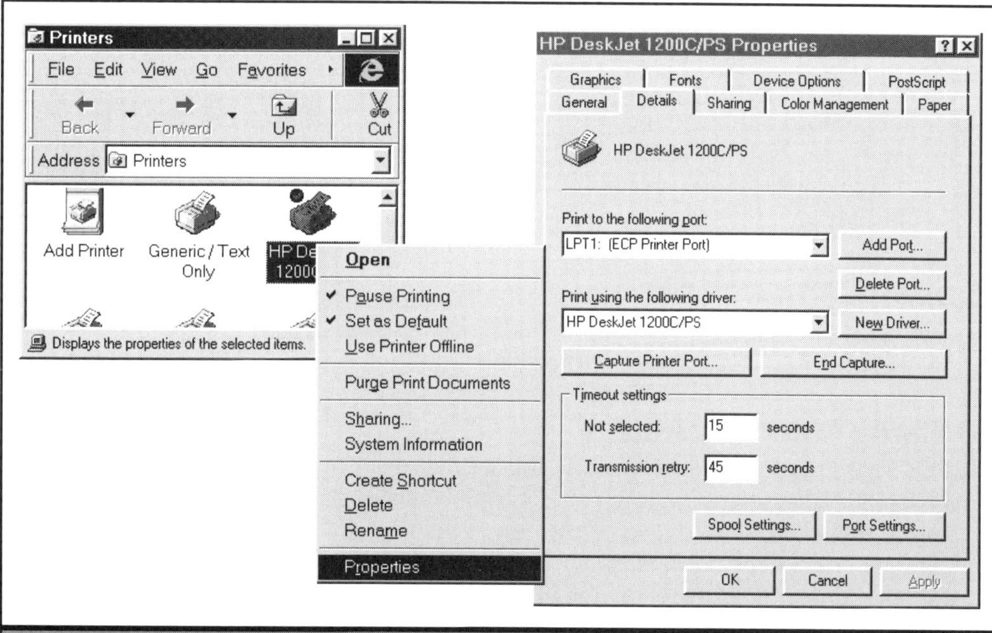

Figure 9-22. *The Properties dialog box for each printer allows you to configure and control device-specific performance settings*

Some Handy Points about Printer Options

Here are a few important points to keep in mind when working with printers:

- In Windows 3.1, font mapping associations between Adobe Type I and TrueType fonts were set in the printer driver's Setup options. In Windows 98, you'll find these options on the Fonts tab in the Properties dialog box for each printer.
- The scaling and resolution options for PostScript printers are found on the Graphics tab in the Properties dialog box. For color printers, a series of color calibration options is also located on this tab.
- Print quality options are found on the Device Options tab of the Properties dialog box.
- If you want to print to a file, you'll find this option on the Details tab of the Properties dialog box. Print spooler controls are also on the Details tab.
- To share a printer across a network or a Direct Cable Connection, go to the Sharing tab of the Properties dialog box.

For more information about controlling and working with printers, see Chapter 10. In Chapter 4, you'll find a trick that lets you create a popout Printers shortcut (similar to the Control Panel class ID discussed at the beginning of this chapter) on the first level of the Start menu.

Additional Components

If you have a computer with Advanced Power Management or PC Card (PCMCIA) sockets installed, some additional options will appear in the Control Panel.

PC Card (PCMCIA) Applet

The PC Card component allows you to display the status of peripherals added to PC Card sockets. (This plug-in feature was formerly referred to as PCMCIA.) Options on the Socket Status tab, shown next, allow you to display or disable the PC Card status icon on the System Tray on the taskbar. If Win98's automatic PC Card configuration causes memory conflicts, the Global Settings tab allows you to specify a specific range in upper memory (640K to 1MB) to be used as a shared memory resource.

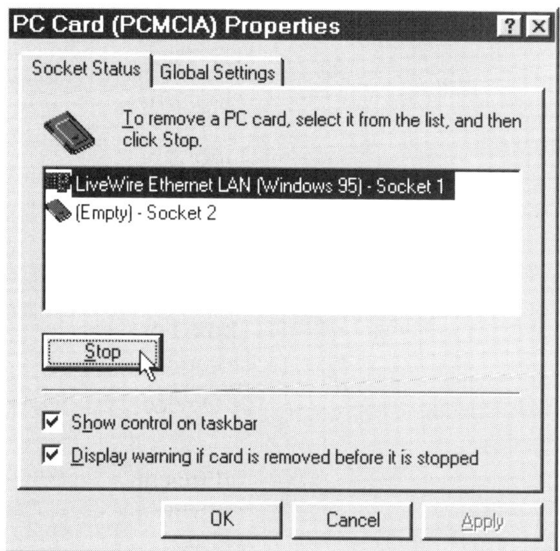

The most common use you may have for the PC Card applet is to temporarily stop (or shut down) a PC Card peripheral such as a network adapter, SCSI controller, or modem so you can remove it and substitute another PC Card without rebooting the computer. The computer should beep whenever a peripheral is inserted or removed. (This option can be disabled by placing a check mark in the Disable PC Card Sound Effects box on the Global Settings tab.)

The PC Card Socket Status display may also be useful in determining whether your PC Card peripherals were recognized when they were inserted and are currently working properly. Sometimes Win98 experiences problems with PC Cards, failing to recognize or initialize a peripheral. If this happens on your computer, the best procedure is to try a cold reboot and reinsert the peripheral. If the PC Card applet fails to show an inserted peripheral or reports an extraneous device, your PC Card services may be improperly configured. You may want to inspect the Device Manager listing for PCMCIA Socket. See "Device Manager Tab: Resolving System Conflicts" earlier in this chapter and "Resolving Startup Error Messages" in Chapter 14 for some PC Card troubleshooting tips.

Tip *To restart a stopped PC Card peripheral without physically removing and reinserting the card, choose Control Panel | System | Device Manager, select the computer icon, and click the Refresh button.*

Power Management Applet

The Power Management component allows you to toggle advanced and standard power management features. Advanced Power Management 1.2 is a new feature in Windows 98. As shown here, it allows you to specify system standby (suspended state) thresholds for both plugged-in and battery configurations. You can also set individual standby options for the monitor and hard disk.

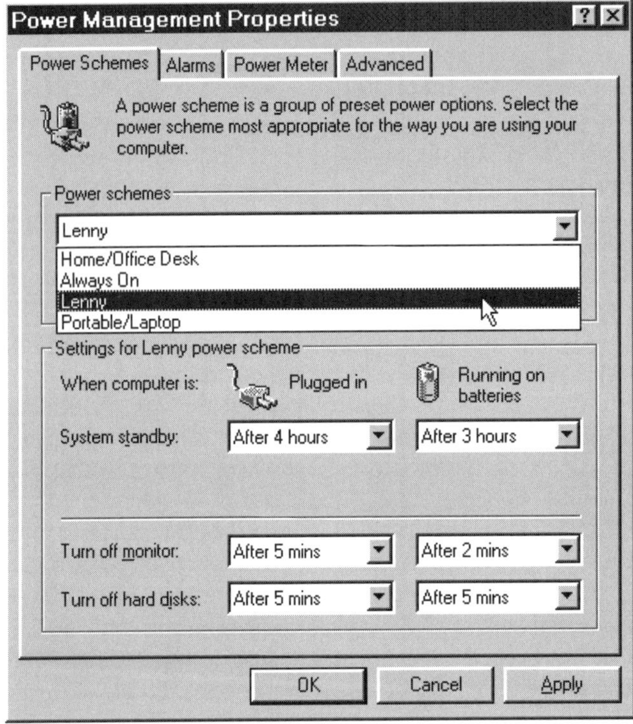

For most newer computers that support APM 1.2, Windows 98 takes over the chore of power management from the hardware BIOS. One of the tradeoffs of this feature is that some hardware power management features may be disabled. Under APM 1.2, the System Standby option is equivalent to a deep suspended state. Once the system enters the standby state, some computers can't be brought back to life with a simple mouse-click or keystroke. You may need to press the power switch. On Notebook computers that offer both Standby and Suspend function keys, both may invoke the suspended state operation unless you disable APM 1.2.

Note *The Hibernate (suspend-to-disk) feature offered on some computers is not generally supported in Windows 98 when the operating system resides on a FAT32 disk partition.*

Users who wish to take advantage of Windows 98 Power Management but retain the "come alert on a keystroke" feature can set the System Standby option in the Power Management applet to Never (or choose a very long interval, such as After 3 Hours). The Turn Off Monitor and Turn Off Hard Disks options can be assigned shorter activity thresholds (for example, 5 to 10 minutes). These settings have the effect of emulating the hardware standby option that some notebook computers offer. As soon as you move the mouse or touch a key, the computer will spring back to life.

You can create your own Power Management schemes in addition to the three Windows 98 defaults. Select any currently available scheme, modify the time settings to your liking, and click the Save As button. Assign a new name to the scheme and click OK.

For computers that can run on battery power, the Power Meter tab displays the amount of battery time you have left, as shown here:

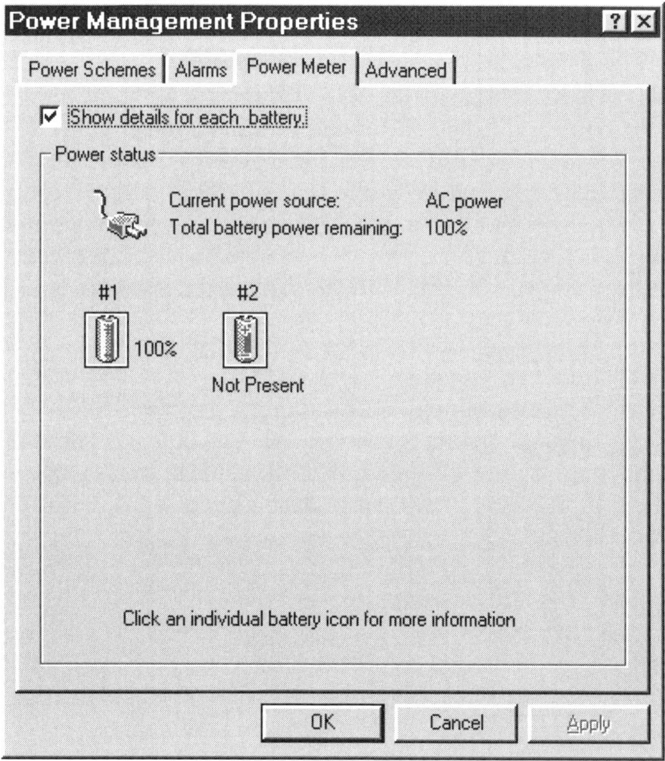

The Power Meter tab also lets you see the status of multiple batteries, which can be in any of the following three states.

Plugged in
(charged)

Plugged in
(charging)

Unplugged
(using battery)

The Alarms tab of the Power Management applet allows you to set thresholds for visual or audio alerts when battery power is low.

To place the Power Status display on the System Tray in the taskbar, go to the Advanced tab and check mark the Show Power Meter On Taskbar option. The icon will toggle from a picture of a plug (running on DC power) to a battery (running on AC power). When you're plugged in and the battery is charging, the plug icon will also show a blue lightning bolt.

POWER MANAGEMENT ON LEGACY SYSTEMS Older computers may be incompatible with Win98's internal Advanced Power Management 1.2 standard. In most cases, if the computer supports Power Management through its BIOS and hardwired function keys, this feature can remain operable under Windows 98. If Advanced Power Management is behaving erratically on your computer (the Standby command on the Shutdown menu doesn't work or your computer locks up when you try to go to Standby), you can disable Win98's software Advanced Power Management. Here's how:

1. Choose Control Panel | System | Device Manager, open the System Devices object, select Advanced Power Management, and click the Properties button. Go to the Settings tab on the Advanced Power Management Support Properties screen (shown next) and first place a check mark in the Disable Power Status Polling box. If problems persist, also place a check mark in the Force APM 1.0 Mode box.

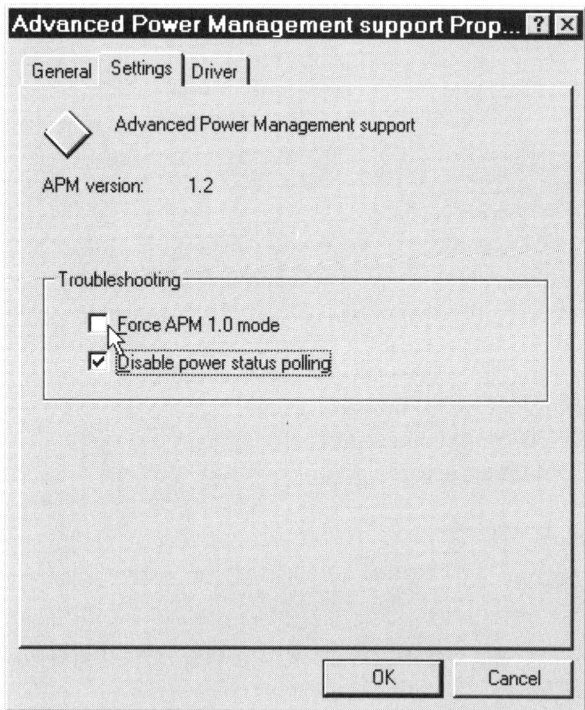

2. If problems still persist, disable software Advanced Power Management entirely by placing a check mark in the Disable In This Hardware Profile box on the APM General properties tab.

Tweak UI Applet

Tweak User Interface (Tweak UI) is a power user's configuration tool. You can use it to customize a number of Windows 98 display and performance settings. Formerly included in a downloadable suite called the Windows 95 PowerToys, Tweak UI has been promoted to a stand-alone Control Panel extension in Windows 98. This upgraded version of Tweak UI includes Paranoia and Repair tabs that let you clear document lists; control CD options; rebuild damaged font folders; and restore default desktop icons, system files, and Win98 file associations.

Older useful Tweak UI features include capabilities for automatically creating new desktop templates; hiding unwanted desktop objects; setting mouse, menu display, and system boot options; and regulating the behavior of desktop shortcuts and the appearance of shortcut icons.

Some users will find that the various tweaks offered in this applet can provide relief from Windows annoyances, eliminating unwanted desktop icons and animation effects. Power users will find ways to fine-tune performance options that would otherwise require serious hacking of the system registry. You might wonder why this Swiss Army Knife utility isn't placed in the Control Panel automatically. The answer is probably that Microsoft wants to discourage new users from experimenting and forgetting how to restore basic system defaults. (Some, but not all, of the Tweak UI configuration tabs contain a Restore Factory Settings button.)

Installing Tweak UI

Tweak UI can be added to the Control Panel from the \TOOLS\RESKIT\POWERTOY directory on the Windows 98 installation CD.

1. Open Explorer to the \TOOLS\RESKIT\POWERTOY directory on the Win98 CD.
2. Right-click the TWEAKUI.INF file and select Install from the pop-up menu. (Note that if your Win98 display defaults are set to hide three-letter file extensions, there will be three files in the PowerToy folder labeled Tweak UI. The file with the picture of a gear superimposed over a text icon is the one you want. (This icon will display an Install option when you right-click it.)

To display tweak Help and view a series of tips and tricks, click the Tips button on Tweak UI's Mouse tab.

Tweak UI Overview

The Tweak UI applet contains 13 configuration tabs for controlling Windows 98 performance options. Six tabs are visible at a time. The forward and back arrows in the upper-right corner of the Tweak UI screen allow you to scroll through and select the following options tabs.

MOUSE TAB The Mouse tab, shown next, allows you to control the pop-up speed of the Start menu and the click, double-click, and drag sensitivity of the mouse.

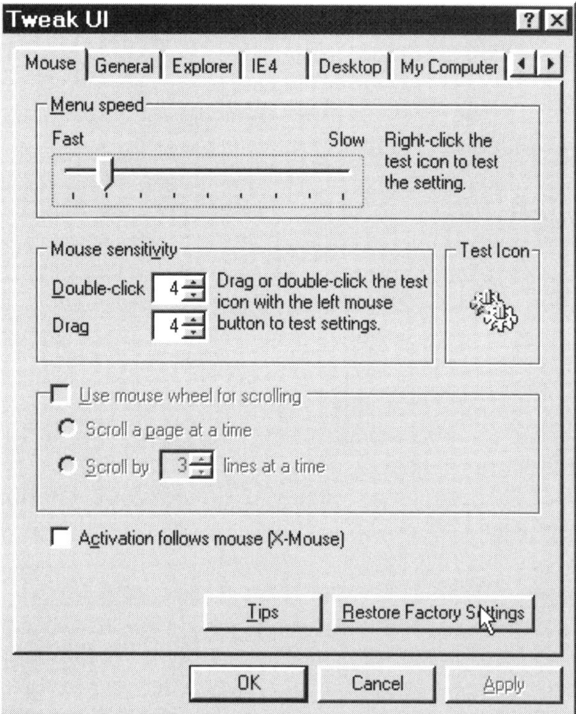

GENERAL TAB The General tab lets you toggle desktop display options on and off: menu, list box, and combo box animation; smooth scrolling; and the location of special Windows 98 system folders. It also allows you to set a default search engine for the Internet Explorer Address bar. (See Chapter 12 for more information on working with Internet Explorer.)

EXPLORER TAB The Explorer tab allows you to change the display format for desktop shortcuts.

INTERNET EXPLORER TAB The Internet Explorer tab contains performance and display settings for the Active Desktop and Internet Explorer browser. Some, but not all, of these tweaks overlap the settings available through the standard Explorer | View | Folder Options menu.

DESKTOP TAB The Desktop tab allows you to hide the display of special desktop icons (My Computer, Network Neighborhood, Internet Explorer, and others). You can also use it to enable the display of Windows 98 system objects that are not normally visible (Infrared Recipient, Scheduled Tasks, URL History folder, and so on).

MY COMPUTER TAB The My Computer tab lets you hide or display selected drive letters in the My Computer or Windows Explorer file browser.

CONTROL PANEL TAB The Control Panel tab toggles the display of applets in the Windows 98 Control Panel.

If your computer serves as a workstation for multiple users, you may find it helpful to use the My Computer and Control Panel tabs to simplify the Windows interface for beginners or hide access to internal system controls.

NETWORK TAB The Network tab allows you to bypass the startup Windows 98 login box and enter custom username and password values. The Clear Last User setting on the Tweak UI Paranoia tab must be disabled for this option to work, and it is available only for logins to a Microsoft network.

NEW TAB The New tab provides some of the most useful Tweak UI options. It allows you to set up a project-oriented desktop, creating a series of work folders and document templates that will automatically open into appropriate applications. By default, Windows 98–aware suites and applications such as Microsoft Office and Corel WordPerfect automatically add a new document template to the template list (available when you right-click an empty part of the desktop and select New). The Tweak UI New tab extends this functionality to let you create document templates for any Windows 3.x, Win95, Win98, or DOS productivity application.

To add a template to the New list, select a document with any file extension in My Computer or Windows Explorer and drag its icon into the tweak's New Document list. (For instance, you can create a template for DOS WordPerfect 5.1 by dragging and dropping a WordPerfect for DOS document into the list.)

For more information on creating and working with document templates, see Chapter 4.

ADD/REMOVE TAB The Add/Remove tab in Tweak UI corresponds to the list of applications you can uninstall through Add/Remove Programs. However, in Tweak UI you can customize the list, reassociating a specific program with a specific uninstall utility. (This feature may be useful when an application in the default Add/Remove list refuses to uninstall.)

If you have Windows 3.x or DOS applications that include uninstall utilities, you can customize the Add/Remove list by adding these utilities with the New button on this tab, as shown next. Advanced users can design their own uninstall procedures for DOS or Windows 3.x programs by using batch files and then adding them to the list.

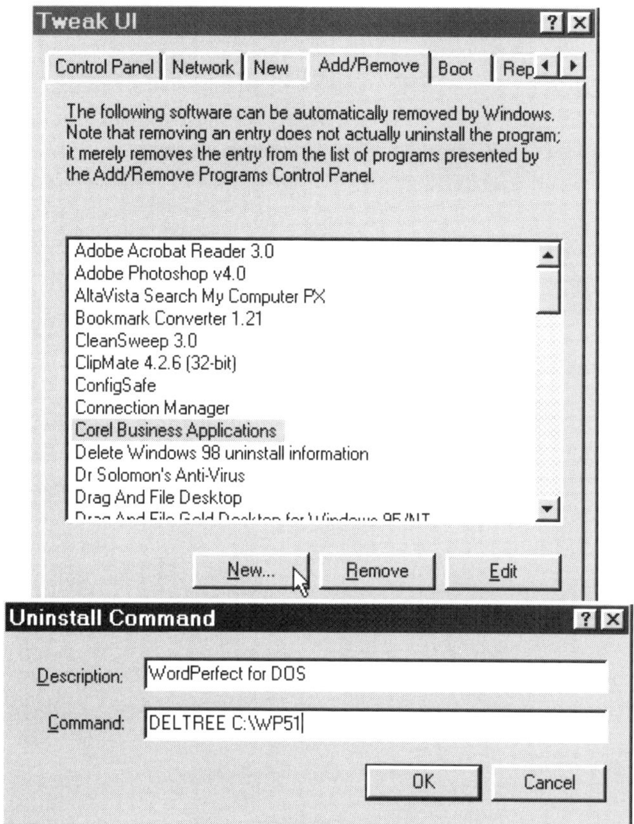

BOOT TAB The Boot tab allows you to customize Windows 98 startup options. You can disable display of the Windows 98 boot menu or boot directly to a DOS prompt instead of the Windows 98 interface. Before Tweak UI, these changes had to be implemented by manually editing the hidden MSDOS.SYS system file on your boot drive. See Chapter 6 for more information on enabling and disabling Windows 98 boot options.

REPAIR TAB The Repair tab lets you attempt a correction of damaged Windows 98 display and file system features. You can select Rebuild Icons, Repair File Associations, Repair Font Folder, and other options from the drop-down list. For details and examples of how to use these features, see Chapter 8.

PARANOIA TAB The Paranoia tab can clear the various Windows 98 lists created for your convenience when you open documents, perform searches, browse Web sites, and so on. In the case of computers with multiple users, some people find it embarrassing to leave a trail of the documents and URLs they've visited. You can clear the Documents, Favorites, Run, and other history lists by selecting them on this tab and clicking the Clear Selected Items Now button.

This tab also provides a shortcut to Win98's auto-insert notification and autoplay features for CD-ROMs. If you'd rather not have these processes run automatically, you can disable them by placing check marks in the Things That Happen Behind Your Back boxes.

Stay in Control

Have we missed anything? Here's a review of things you may want to do in the Control Panel after installing Windows 98:

- Add useful programs not included in a Typical installation with Add/Remove Programs (choose Add/Remove Programs | Windows Setup).
- Make a startup disk if you didn't make one during installation (choose Add/Remove Programs | Startup Disk).
- Adjust video resolution above 640 by 480 pixels, change or remove wallpaper, and adjust the background color of the desktop (choose Display).
- Install or configure Microsoft Exchange if you need it to manage faxes or e-mail (go to the EXCHANGE directory on the Win98 CD and choose the Mail and Fax applet).
- Install your modem if it wasn't detected during initial installation (choose Modems).
- Install network protocols you intend to connect to another computer via Direct Cable Connection or Dial-Up Networking connection. Also set up TCP/IP for Internet and File Sharing (choose Network | Configuration | Add).
- Install your printer if it was missed in the initial Win98 installation (choose Printers).
- Change CD-ROM speed settings if Win95 has configured a default of Single-speed CD ROM (choose System | Performance | File System | CD-ROM). You may also want to adjust cache size and hard disk settings.
- Check the Device Manager list to verify that your computer's peripheral components have been properly recognized and installed (choose System | Device Manager).
- Configure or choose a default Dial-Up Networking profile to connect to the Internet (choose Internet).
- Set custom Advanced Power Management options (choose Power Management).
- Create a shortcut to the Control Panel on the Start menu (see the section "Customizing Control Panel Access" in this chapter).

Chapter 10

Fonts and Printing

Chapter Highlights

New printing and font-management features

Extended drag-and-drop printing support

Plug-and-play printers

Deferred printing

Windows 98 font management

Working with PostScript and Adobe Type Manager

Third-party font utilities

Working with printer options

Network printing issues

Optimizing printer performance

This chapter tells you what you need to know about font management and printing under Windows 98. Thanks to changes made to the Win95 printing subsystem and carried over to Windows 98, your documents will print faster. Also, TrueType fonts are easier to install, and the operating system bundles many new printer drivers with sophisticated features. About the only downside to printing with Windows 98 is the necessity of replacing obsolete font-management utilities. This is an issue primarily for users upgrading from Windows 3.x. Windows 95 print utilities work transparently under Windows 98.

What's New

The Windows 98 printing subsystem carries over an array of important features first implemented in Windows 95:

- Easy access to multiple printers through the desktop
- Faster printing through the 32-bit multithreading subsystem

- Enhanced Metafile (EMF) print spooling replaces Windows 3.x Print Manager and returns control more quickly to the source application
- Drag-and-drop printing (by dragging a document over a Printer shortcut or using right-click menu options)
- Better printer drivers built into the operating system, supporting printing at higher dot-per-inch (dpi) resolutions and Image Color Matching (ICM) that synchronizes the on-screen colors of images with printer output
- Network printer management that supports deferred printing and the use of a Windows 98 computer as a network print management station; multiple printer drivers don't need to be stored on a local workstation

Windows 98 also introduces a few wrinkles that weren't available under Windows 95:

- OpenType font technology extends the older Windows TrueType specification. OpenType fonts contain tables that allow precise baseline positioning and alternative character forms for multilingual typesetting. These fonts are backward compatible with older versions of Windows and the basic TrueType font format.
- Image Color Management 2.0 extends the 1.0 Windows 95 version. Previously, images required links to special color profiles to match screen and printer output. ICM 2.0 supports accurate rendering of red-green-blue (RGB) images from screen to printer without separate profiles or tagged image information. ICM 2.0 also supports output synchronization for images coded with cyan-magenta-yellow-black (CMYK) color information.
- New printer drivers support a wide range of output devices and include support for Adobe's PostScript II printer description language. Windows 98 also includes network print management software: the new JetAdmin 2.5 provides remote configuration and control of Hewlett-Packard printers. It can also manage third-party output devices connected to an HP JetDirect hub.

Win98's Desktop Printing Options

Printer settings are accessed through individual icons for each output device in the Printers folder (located under Settings on the Start menu). You can also create a shortcut for any printer directly on the desktop for more convenient access. Just open the Printers folder, right-click, and drag the printer you want to the desktop. (Select Create Shortcut Here from the pop-up menu.)

When you click a printer icon, other options appear that replace the old Windows 3.x Print Manager and Printer Control Panel settings. You can pause printing, purge print jobs, or fine-tune the printer's performance by selecting Properties from the pop-up menu. If you double-click a printer icon, a document queue appears. The queue lists the current print jobs waiting to be sent to the printer, as shown in Figure 10-1.

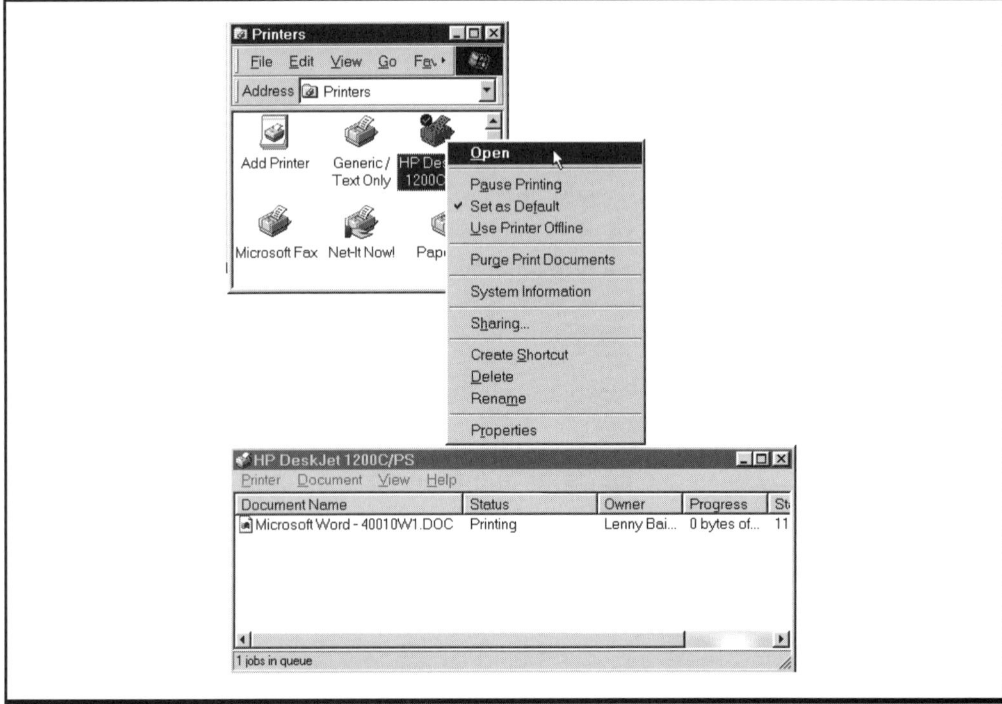

Figure 10-1. *Double-click any printer icon under Windows 98 to open a list of documents waiting in the queue for that printer*

Drag-and-Drop Printing

Drag-and-drop printing allows you to print documents conveniently from the Win98 desktop. Many applications and accessories written for Windows 3.x through Windows 98 have this feature. Individual file support for drag-and-drop printing is usually added to the system registry when a new application is installed: Microsoft Excel adds printing support for .XLS documents, Word adds support for .DOC documents, Corel WordPerfect adds support for .WPD files, and so on.

Documents created with programs that support drag-and-drop printing can be dragged out of a folder and dropped onto your printer icon. The associated application opens and automatically prints the file. (You can drag files onto a printer icon located in the Printers folder or use a desktop shortcut.)

If you have a Windows or DOS program that supports pass-through print commands, you can add drag-and-drop print support for custom file associations. Drag-and-drop print support is enabled by editing the file type properties: you need to modify or create a Print command in the file type's Actions list. This procedure is similar to that for adding an Open command to a file type's right-click menu options, a trick described in the "Using File Associations" section of Chapter 4.)

Adding Pass-Through Print Options to a File Type

For a good example of how to create a Print command, try associating a custom three-letter file extension (.NOT) with the Notepad text editor. Many people find it convenient to supplement the default text (.TXT) file extension with additional descriptive file extensions: Phone numbers can be stored with a .# extension, notes and memoranda with a .NOT extension, addresses as .ADR, and so on.

You can create a Note file type by pressing the SHIFT key while you right-click a file that bears the .NOT extension. Choose Open With from the pop-up menu, select Notepad in the application list that appears, select Always Use This Program to Open This Type of File, and click OK. You can also enter a description for the file type, such as "Note File" in the Description field, as shown here. (For more information, see Chapter 4.)

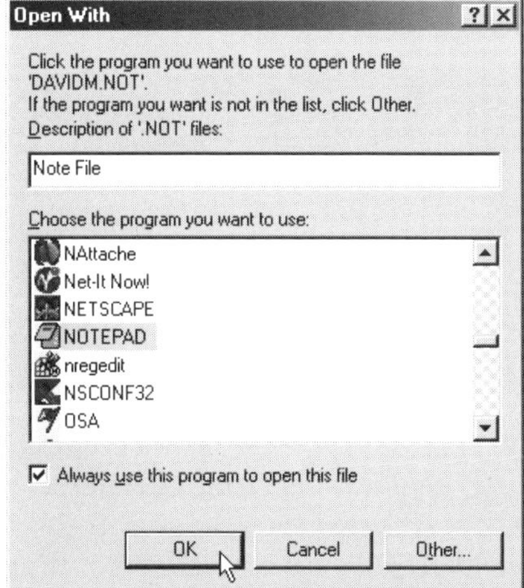

If you try dragging your Note file and dropping it on a printer icon right now, you'll see the message "This file does not have a program associated with it for performing this action." Here's how to add drag-and-drop print support:

1. Choose View | Folder Options | File Types from My Computer or Windows Explorer.
2. Select your Note file type in the Registered File Types list and click the Edit button.
3. Click the New button under the Actions list. When the New Action window appears, enter **Print** in the Action field, as shown in Figure 10-2.

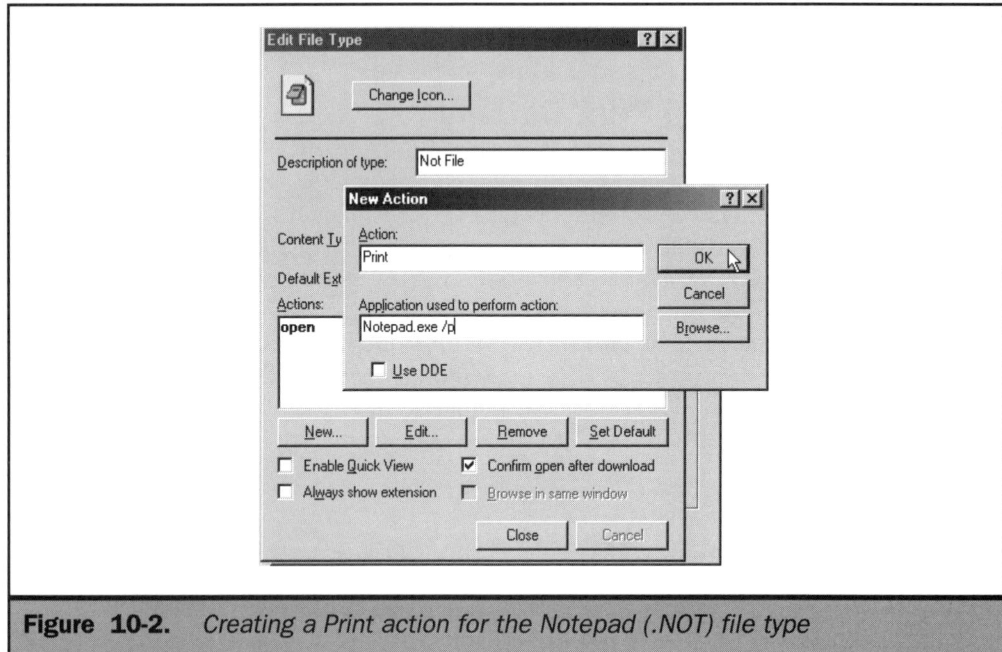

Figure 10-2. *Creating a Print action for the Notepad (.NOT) file type*

4. Enter **NOTEPAD.EXE /P** in the Application Used To Perform Action field and click OK. A new Print command appears in the Edit File Type Actions list.
5. Click OK twice to close the File Types Folder options.

For Microsoft applications, the pass-through Print command is usually enabled by appending a /P switch to the command line: for example, NOTEPAD.EXE /P, or WORDPAD.EXE /P. (More sophisticated programs in the Microsoft Office suite use Print commands that involve DDE links to dynamic link libraries, although the /P option does work with PowerPoint.)

Now when you drag and drop a Note file on the icon for your default printer, Notepad will open and start printing automatically. The default printer in Windows 98 is the one that appears first when you select File | Print in an application.

Tip

You can switch the Win98 default printer on the fly by dragging and dropping a file on another output device icon in the Printers folder (or onto a desktop printer shortcut). If the device is not the default printer, a dialog box will pop up. You can click Yes to make the device the default printer and print the file or No to cancel the operation. Another way to set any output device as the default printer is to right-click it and choose the Set As Default option on the pop-up menu.

Extending Drag-and-Drop Printing with the Send To Option

If you tried the procedure in the preceding section, you saw that dragging a file of an unsupported type over a printer icon produces a complaint that no application is available to print it. If you right-click an unsupported file type, you will not see a Print command on the pop-up menu. Chapter 4 discussed a similar issue concerning Win98's QuickView file filters. In that case, there was no View option on the pop-up menu. In Chapter 4, the problem was solved by dragging a copy of QUIKVIEW.EXE to the \SENDTO folder, thus creating viewing access for unregistered file types.

A similar trick lets you configure right-click print options for some additional file types. Here's what to do:

1. Open Notepad or another ASCII text editor and create the following batch file (make sure to enclose %1 in quotation marks):

```
PADPRNT.BAT
WORDPAD.EXE /P "%1"
```

2. Save the file in the \WINDOWS\SENDTO folder.
3. Open the \SENDTO folder by choosing Run from the Start menu, typing **SENDTO,** and pressing ENTER.
4. Right-click the PADPRNT.BAT file you just created, open its Properties window, and select the Program tab. Select the Close On Exit box.

You now have a quick way to click and print files of any type supported by Win98 WordPad (.DOC, .WRI, .RTF, and .TXT files). Right-click the file, choose the Send To option on the pop-up menu, and select PADPRNT (which is displayed to the left of the Send To option in Figure 10-3).

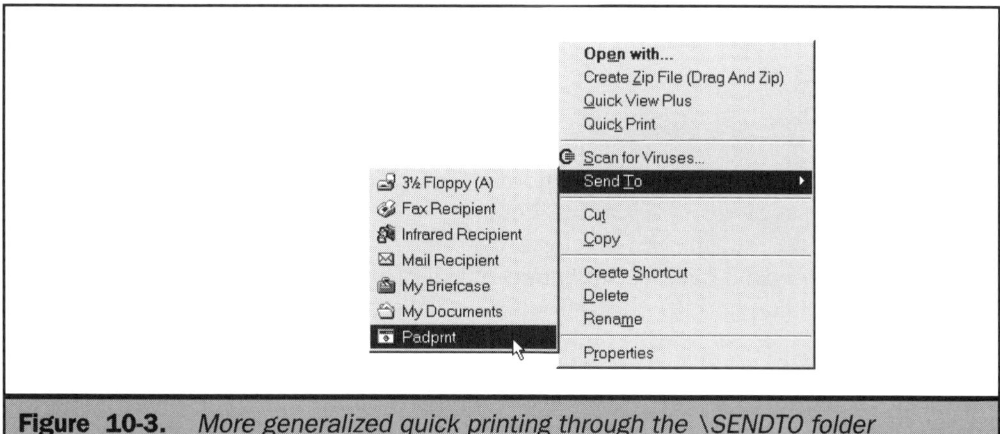

Figure 10-3. *More generalized quick printing through the \SENDTO folder*

You might notice that when you right-click files with the .DOC, .WRI, .RTF, and .TXT file extensions that they already have a preconfigured Print command on their pop-up menus. The Send To shortcut described above allows you to print files in these formats when they don't bear the characteristic file extensions. For instance, you can right-click to quick-print a file called READ.ME or README.NOW. These files show up in Explorer with the generic, "Windows banner" icon that represents an unregistered file type. They have no print command, but the Send To shortcut works to send them to the printer.

You may want to extend this technique by creating Send To shortcuts to other applications that support the /P switch for pass-through printing. For instance, you can create a Send To shortcut for graphic printing with the Imaging for Windows application:

```
GRAPHPRN.BAT
C:\WINDOWS\KODAKPRV.EXE /P "%1"
```

Drag-and-Drop Limitations

You may be tempted to use Win98's desktop printing features to select a whole folder full of files with the mouse and drag them to the printer. The operating system permits you to do this, but be advised: If you drag and drop a large number of files onto a printer icon, you may exceed your computer's memory capacity. Windows 98 opens a new instance of the parent application for every file you drop to print.

If you want to select a large group of files and bulk-print them, you can avoid memory problems by using a smart file manager with built-in queue support. Pacific Gold Coast's TurboBrowser 98 (available at http://www.TurboBrowser.com) allows you to bulk-select files and drop them into a smart print queue.

Faster Printing

Windows 98 has a 32-bit print spooler that supports DOS as well as Windows applications. The spooler provides smoother background printing by using multithreaded background processing. Data is passed to the printer only when the printer is ready to receive more information.

Under the Windows 3.x Print Manager, the operating system did a lot of processing through the printer driver before returning control of an application to you. This meant that you would often wind up staring at an hourglass, unable to continue your work until the print spooler relinquished control. Under Windows 98, the Enhanced Metafile (EMF) spooler works more quickly. The spooler generates an intermediate data file, processing data faster than the printer driver alone. The EMF data file is generated by the Win98 graphical device interface (GDI). Control is returned quickly to the source application while the print processing continues in the background, allowing you to get back to work quickly—a real asset, assuming that working is what you really want to be doing.

DOS applications can now print directly to the 32-bit Windows spooler. However, they don't benefit from EMF spooling. (For more details on EMF spooling see "Working with Printer Options" later in this chapter.)

IEEE-1284 Parallel Port Standard Support

Another important print speed optimization feature in Windows 98 is the operating system's built-in support for the IEEE-1284 parallel port standard. IEEE-1284 is actually a combination of two separate standards for the PC parallel port: Enhanced Parallel Port (EPP) and Enhanced Capabilities Port (ECP). The original goal was to increase the basic data transmission speed of the parallel port and enable true bi-directional data communication.

The original (Centronics) parallel port specification is generally adequate for simple printing processes. However, parallel ports are now used by diverse peripherals such as external disk drives, tape drives, and scanners. Higher data throughput is a necessity for these devices.

The EPP standard was developed by Xircom, Inc., a manufacturer of Ethernet adapters. Using Intel's 82360 chip, Xircom increased the speed of the parallel port from about 150 kilobytes per second to about 2 megabytes per second! Additionally, the EPP chip supports asymmetrical, bidirectional data transfer—so EPP provides fast two-way data transfer between the computer and any EPP-compliant peripherals.

At about the same time, Hewlett-Packard was developing an improved parallel port nicknamed Zippy. Zippy was designed to increase the performance of Hewlett-Packard's line of laser printers. The two technologies were eventually combined into the IEEE-1284 parallel port standard.

If your computer supports the IEEE-1284 parallel port standard, Windows 98 can auto-detect and configure any new output device that you plug into your parallel port.

The following components are necessary for Windows 98 to auto-detect your printer:

- A built-in chipset or I/O card that supports the new, faster parallel ports
- An Intel/Microsoft plug-and-play BIOS
- A printer cable that supports the IEEE-1284 standard
- Plug-and-play support built into your printer

If your computer doesn't have all these features, don't worry. You can still install your printers the old-fashioned way by double-clicking the Add Printer icon in the Printers folder. (For details about enabling and using enhanced printer port features, see "Working with Printer Options" later in this chapter.)

Deferred Printing

If you have both desktop and portable computers, you may want to save time by printing documents that you compose while you're on the road—but there's no printer in your hotel room. With Windows 98, you can use your applications to print any files you want even when your computer isn't connected to a printer. If you're working on a number of projects, this feature spares you from opening them all up again when you get home and then printing them one at a time.

Here's how the Windows 98 deferred printing feature works: If you normally plug your portable computer into a network printer, right-click the icon in the Printers folder and choose the Use Printer Offline option. If you normally plug your computer into a local printer through a parallel cable, right-click the printer icon and select the Pause Printing option. When you print from any application in Windows 98, the output will be stored in a queue for the selected output device. When you reconnect to your network or plug in your local printer, a dialog box will pop up asking whether to print the files waiting in the queue. Simply click Yes to print.

Device Independence

The Win98 printing subsystem is very powerful and flexible. It allows you to set printer properties for each individual printer rather than requiring global properties as Windows 3.x did. For example, each printer can have a different separator page, and printers can be individually set to print jobs directly or to place them in a deferred queue.

Windows Fonts

Windows 98 is bundled with three different categories of fonts: raster, vector, and TrueType. A popular additional format, PostScript, is supported through Adobe Systems' third-party Type Manager.

- *Raster fonts*, also known as bitmapped fonts, are a carryover from Windows 3.x. MS Sans Serif, Serif, Courier, and Symbol are examples of raster fonts. These fonts generate simple bitmapped images of a character set on the screen. A separate file is required for each individual point size. Raster fonts are displayed correctly only in the specific sizes available on disk; they can't be scaled or rotated, and they may not print on a laser or an inkjet printer.
- *Vector fonts*, also called stick, stroke, or plotter fonts, are simple outlines drawn on the screen by mathematical algorithms in the same way you would generate a circle in algebra by graphing the equation X2 + Y2 = R2. With vector fonts, only one physical file is needed for all point sizes. These fonts can be scaled or rotated, but they don't look very nice as body text for documents. Vector fonts are intended primarily for use with pen plotters to produce schematics and engineering diagrams. Modern and Roman are examples of vector fonts.

- *TrueType* is the font technology built into Windows 98. (It includes the newer, OpenType specification.) TrueType fonts are scaleable typefaces for both the screen and printer. One outline file supplies any requested point size. TrueType fonts can be printed on any output device, from dot matrix to PostScript printers. The Windows printer driver for the output device controls the manner in which the TrueType font outlines are converted for output. On dot matrix printers, a bitmapped image of each page is created at the specified printer resolution (which may vary from 75 to 300 or more dots per inch). On Hewlett-Packard PCL printers, a translator called a font rasterizer downloads bitmapped representations of the TrueType fonts for output in the specified point sizes. With PostScript printers, the user has a choice between sending bitmapped representations of the font characters to the printer for output, downloading an outline version of the TrueType font to the printer, or substituting an Adobe PostScript Type 1 font, which prints instead of the TrueType version.
- *Adobe PostScript* is a fourth font format that's commonly used by Windows applications. PostScript fonts may be resident (built into the ROM of your printer) or downloadable (soft font files that reside on your hard disk). Like TrueType fonts, each individual PostScript font outline can supply type in any requested point size. Windows 98 has marginal built-in support for PostScript fonts. By itself, Windows can recognize resident fonts in a PostScript printer or download soft PostScript outlines to a compatible printer, but working with these fonts is cumbersome unless you use Adobe Type Manager (ATM). Without ATM, you don't see what PostScript fonts look like on the screen, you may need to edit your WIN.INI file to install them, and they don't print on Hewlett-Packard PCL or ordinary dot-matrix printers.

  Adobe's third-party utility, Adobe Type Manager, lets you install and remove PostScript soft fonts with a couple of mouse clicks. More important, ATM rasterizes PostScript fonts so you can see them on the screen and print them on Hewlett-Packard laser and inkjet printers and on older dot-matrix models. With Adobe Type Manager installed, Windows is equally versatile in handling TrueType and PostScript font outlines.

Changes in Windows 98 Font Handling

In Windows 3.x, if you wanted to have a large number of fonts at your disposal, you had to load them when you started Windows. This caused several problems. First, it used a lot of memory. Second, it could make starting Windows a pretty tedious experience since all of the fonts had to be loaded before you could start doing anything. Third, having a lot of fonts could affect the overall performance of your computer.

Windows 98 has a different approach to font handling. Instead of loading all fonts into memory on startup, Windows 98 loads only a list of font names (so your programs know they're there). The physical data for screen display and printing is paged from the hard disk as needed. More physical fonts can be installed in the operating system, and more than 1,000 fonts can be used in one document. (This may be a somewhat sobering thought for serious desktop publishers to contemplate.)

Windows 98 specifications indicate that you can use as many as 1,000 different fonts in a single document. You should probably exercise some restraint rather than testing this feature. Not only would a document with that many fonts look pretty ugly, it would also impose a heavy memory and performance tax on your system.

Windows 98 also includes an enhanced rasterizer for more accurate rendering and generation of TrueType fonts.

How Fonts Are Stored

The bitmap, vector, and TrueType fonts bundled with Windows 95 or Windows 98 are not listed in the WIN.INI file as they were under Windows 3.x. Instead, Windows stores the names and characteristics of these fonts in the Windows registry. The registry now holds a wide variety of information that was formerly stored in WIN.INI and SYSTEM.INI. (You'll find detailed information on how the Windows registry works in Chapter 8.)

If you perform an upgrade installation of Windows 98 over a previous version of Windows, the font list that used to be maintained in WIN.INI is automatically transferred to the registry. Physical font files are now stored in the \WINDOWS\FONTS directory. To maintain compatibility with Windows 3.x applications and utilities, fonts stored in the \WINDOWS\SYSTEM directory are still recognized.

Every time Windows 98 starts, the system checks the Fonts section of WIN.INI. Any font information written there by Windows 3.x programs is transferred to the Windows registry. TrueType fonts installed in the \WINDOWS\SYSTEM directory are automatically migrated to the \WINDOWS\FONTS directory the next time you boot Windows 98. The bottom line is that you don't have to worry about the avalanche of TrueType fonts installed by Win 3.x packages such as CorelDraw version 5 or WordPerfect for Windows. Migration to the Windows 98 environment is handled automatically.

Installing and Managing TrueType Fonts

When you upgrade from an older version of Windows to Windows 98, all of your previously installed TrueType fonts are automatically migrated. Additionally, Adobe PostScript fonts that were installed before the upgrade will still be available.

The Fonts folder holds Microsoft bitmap, vector, and TrueType fonts. You can see a list of all active fonts in these formats by double-clicking the Fonts icon on the Control Panel. You can also see this list by opening \WINDOWS\FONTS in My Computer or Windows Explorer. The Fonts folder does not display, store, or manage PostScript fonts of the Type 1, 2, or 3 variety. (For more information, see "Working with PostScript Fonts" later in this chapter.)

The Fonts folder is more than just another window on your desktop. It's actually a mini-application that allows you to inspect and manage your fonts. To use the Fonts folder, click the Start button, choose Settings | Control Panel, and open the Fonts applet, as shown here:

To add a TrueType font to your system, all you have to do is drag the font into the Fonts folder from another hard disk directory, floppy diskette, or CD-ROM. To delete a font, right-click its icon in the Fonts folder and select Delete from the pop-up context menu. Simple? You bet!

Tip *Although you can effectively remove a font by dragging its icon out of the Fonts folder, this isn't the best approach. Windows 98 won't update your application font menus until you restart the system. If you want to remove one or more fonts, the best way is to select them in the Fonts folder and then choose the Delete option from the folder's pull-down File menu.*

You can install a group of new fonts in Windows 98 by choosing the Install New Fonts option on the Fonts folder's File menu. The next dialog box lets you point to a specific folder on your local computer or browse network resources. A list of available fonts in the selected folder will appear. You can choose all of the fonts or select the ones you want to make active. To select multiple fonts individually, hold down the CTRL key as you click the font names in the list.

DISPLAYING AND PRINTING FONT SAMPLES If you want to see what one of the fonts in the Fonts folder looks like, double-click the font's icon. Windows 98 opens a window that contains samples of the font in various point sizes. To print the font sample, double-click the Print button in the upper-right portion of the window, as shown in Figure 10-4.

Some older programs can interfere with some Fonts folder functions. For example, older versions of Corel's Gallery redirect the font display function to Gallery 2's Font Master program. While this program can also display the fonts, they won't appear as in the regular Windows 98 font window.

NOTE FOR TECHIES In Windows 98, the information in the Windows registry points to a single .TTF file for each TrueType font. The .FOT description files that were used in Windows 3.x are no longer needed and are deleted from your hard disk.

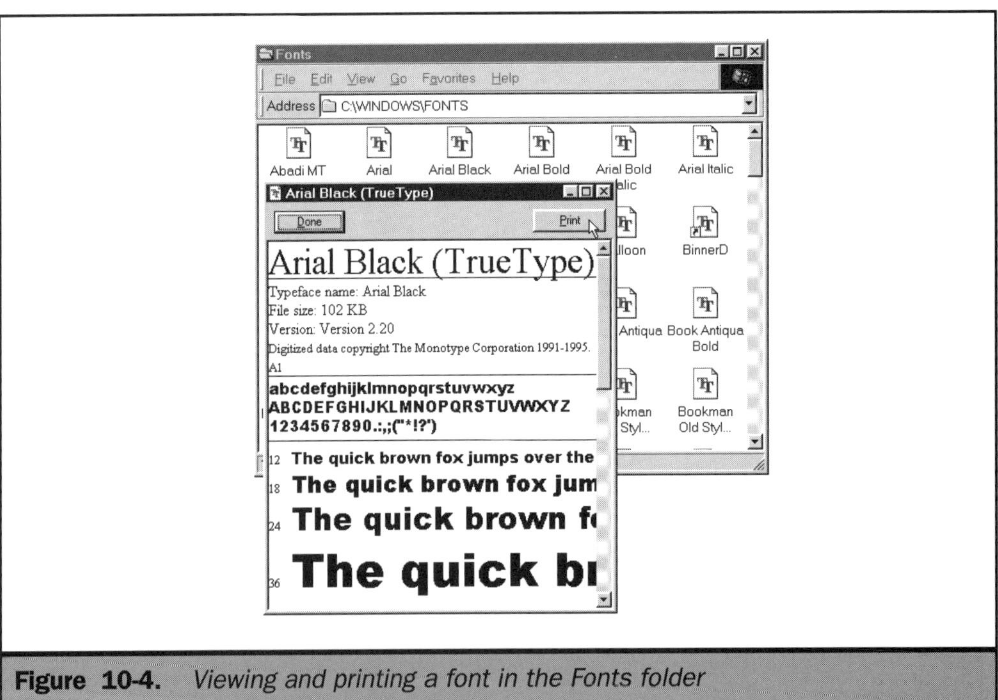

Figure 10-4. *Viewing and printing a font in the Fonts folder*

Working with PostScript Fonts

PostScript fonts are considered a de facto requirement for any enterprise that engages in high-end printing. Although Windows 98 doesn't provide internal support for PostScript fonts, adding Adobe Type Manager (ATM) makes managing PostScript fonts as easy as using the \FONTS folder for TrueType.

To make ATM work properly with Windows 98, you'll need to upgrade to version 3.02 or higher. This isn't hard to do since Adobe includes ATM with quite a few of its products, including many of its font packages. Registered users of ATM 3.0x can also receive the upgrade on floppy disk for $9.95 by calling 1-800-833-6687. Upgrades from earlier versions of ATM are slightly more expensive. Adobe's Web address is http://www.adobe.com/software.htm.

To determine which version of ATM you have, look at the ATM Control Panel's version box.

Using Adobe Type Manager 3.02

To install a new font using ATM 3.02, double-click the ATM icon (usually located in the Main or Adobe Type Manager program group) to open the ATM window, as shown here:

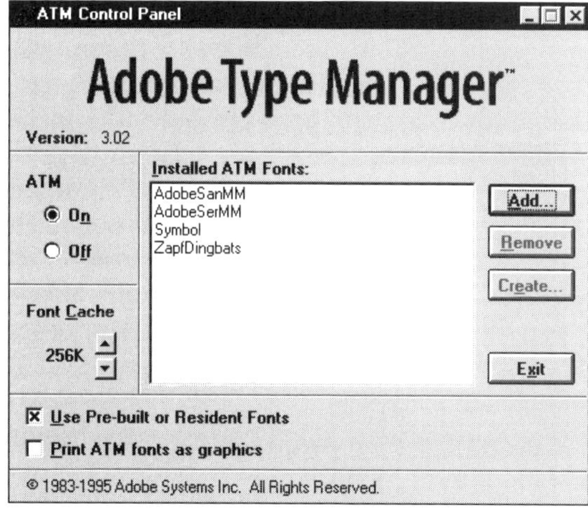

This window lists the currently installed PostScript fonts in the center box and displays the status of some ATM options along the left side. To add a font, click the Add button to open the Add ATM Fonts window, shown next.

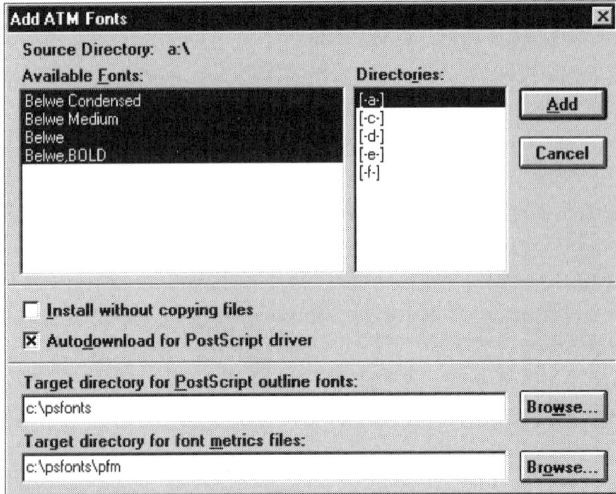

Using Adobe Type Manager 4 and ATM 4 Deluxe

In addition to the support for PostScript fonts found in previous versions, ATM 4.0 offers additional features. It includes an improved Adobe PostScript driver and supports installation and management of both TrueType and PostScript typefaces.

Adobe Type Manager Deluxe allows users to create custom font sets that contain both TrueType and PostScript typefaces. This valuable feature can prevent the font glut that occurs when desktop publishing and productivity suites install thousands of typefaces on your hard disk. (See "Too Many Fonts!" later in this chapter for details.)

Features carried over from the previous version of ATM include capabilities to view and print font samples, control the resident and download status of fonts in your printer, switch between graphic and prebuilt outline versions of a typeface, and create custom variations of fonts in Adobe's Multiple Master format. ATM 4 Deluxe also includes a superior screen font smoothing algorithm that improves the screen display of Adobe Type I typefaces and their printed output on non-PostScript printers.

ATM 4's font-substitution feature searches a 5MB database whenever a document uses a font not installed on your system. ATM finds the closest possible font match for style and width, preserving line and page breaks in your document.

INSTALLING FONTS WITH ATM 4 When you install ATM 4.0, a default font set is created that contains all currently installed TrueType fonts and the PostScript sample fonts included in the ATM package. To display a list of currently active fonts, select the Font List tab. If you double-click a font in the list, a display window opens up similar to the one in Win98's built-in Fonts folder.

To add new fonts in ATM 4, choose the Add Fonts tab and select the currently active font set. The following illustration shows the default font set, called Starter Set.

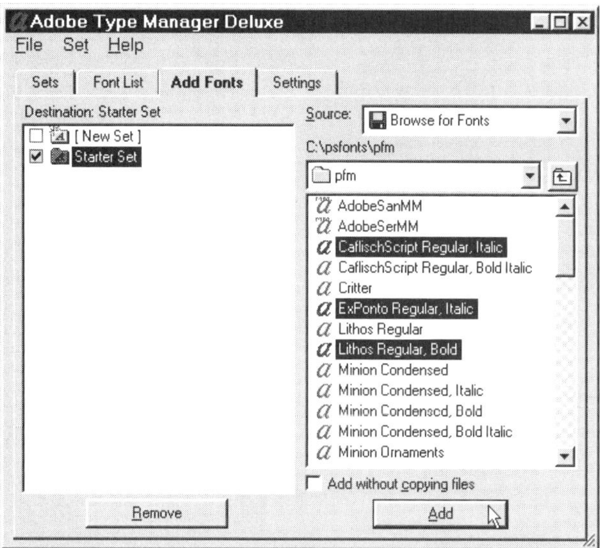

To install new TrueType or PostScript fonts, select Browse for Fonts in the Source box and then select a folder location in the File list box. Note that to install PostScript fonts, you must select a location that contains PostScript Font Metrics (PFM) descriptor files for the font. The default folder location is \PSFONTS\PFM.

Once you've selected the right drive and directory, the names of the available fonts will appear in the file list. To select a font, click it with the mouse. If you want to select multiple fonts, hold down the CTRL key while you click the names of the fonts you want to select. To select a whole block of fonts, click the top font in the list, hold down the SHIFT key, and then click the name of the font at the bottom of the list. This will select all of the fonts between your two selections as well.

To deselect one or more fonts, hold down the CTRL key and click the selected fonts to remove the highlight.

If you are installing your fonts from a floppy diskette or CD-ROM drive, make sure the box marked Add Without Copying Files is not checked since you do want to copy the font files to your hard disk.

ATM 4 CONTROL OPTIONS Adobe Type Manager can be toggled on or off by selecting the On or Off button on the Settings tab. When ATM is disabled, the PostScript fonts it controls will not appear on your application font menus.

The Font Cache setting on the Settings tab sets aside a portion of RAM as a buffer to speed up printing and screen display. A setting of 384K is usually sufficient for managing up to 25 typefaces. If you regularly work with a larger number of PostScript fonts, you may want to increase the cache setting.

If you click the Advanced button on the Settings tab, another set of controls appears, as shown next.

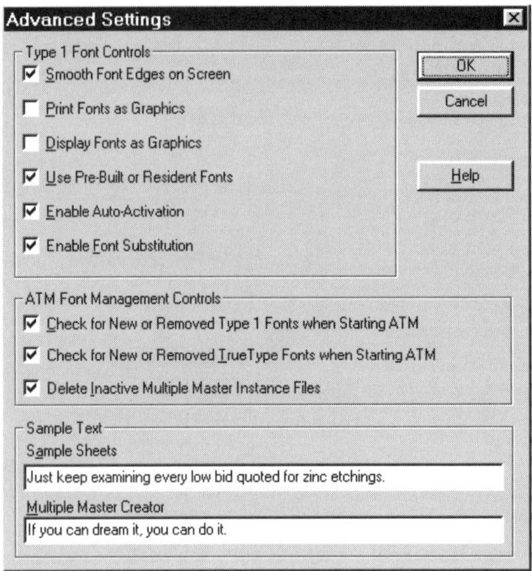

The Use Pre-built Or Resident Fonts check box tells Windows 98 to use fonts that are resident in your printer rather than downloading soft fonts from the hard disk. Most Apple-compatible PostScript printers contain built-in versions of common typefaces such as Helvetica, Times, Bookman, and so on. If this box is checked, the printer-resident versions of those fonts are used rather than the ones installed by Adobe Type Manager. This generally speeds up the printing process.

The Print Fonts As Graphics box forces ATM to send font information to your printer in the form of bitmap graphics rather than downloading soft fonts or using the built-in font rasterizer. If a document that contains mixed type and graphics does not print correctly, you may want to enable this option. It must also be enabled for certain PCL printers that do not support ATM's font rasterizer.

ADOBE POSTSCRIPT DRIVER The Adobe PostScript driver included in the ATM package provides a watermark feature not found in the regular Microsoft PostScript driver: users can create and edit their own simulated paper watermarks. The ATM installation CD also includes the Adobe Acrobat Reader and demonstration versions of a number of Adobe applications: Persuasion, PhotoShop, PageMaker, and Illustrator. Thirty original Adobe typefaces are shipped with the package, including Minion Condensed, Myriad, Utopia, Caflisch Script, Lithos, Nueva, and the TekTon Multiple Master family.

The \PSFONTS Directory

The default path for PostScript fonts in Windows 98 is the \PSFONTS directory. Using this path, you can install up to 900 PostScript fonts. You should be aware, however, that a few limitations make installing that many PostScript fonts unwise. First, Windows 98 imposes a 64K limit on the size of the .INI files. To be properly loaded, all PostScript fonts need to be installed in the ATM or WIN.INI files. Additionally, many applications can display a maximum of 200 fonts, including PostScript and TrueType fonts, in their font lists.

PostScript fonts generally have two parts: the outline of the font and a small file called the font metrics. The Type 1 font outline file always has the three-letter suffix .PFB. The outline files are stored in a directory called \PSFONTS, which contains the actual shape of each character in the font. The font metrics file bears the .PFM extension. This file contains information about how the font should be spaced when it is printed, and how it should be scaled when it is made larger and smaller.

Adobe also includes another kind of PostScript font with Adobe Type Manager, called the multiple master font. While Type 1 PostScript fonts have fixed outlines, multiple master fonts can be modified to make them bolder, wider, thinner, or whatever you want. The names of multiple master font outline files end with the .PFB extension just as standard PostScript fonts do. The metrics files for these fonts, however, have an .MMM extension. To use a multiple master font, you need to create instances of the font. This is accomplished by choosing ATM's Add Fonts tab, selecting Create Multiple Masters in the Source box, and choosing a font from the Multiple Master Base Font list, as shown in Figure 10-5. The drop-down list shows all of the multiple master

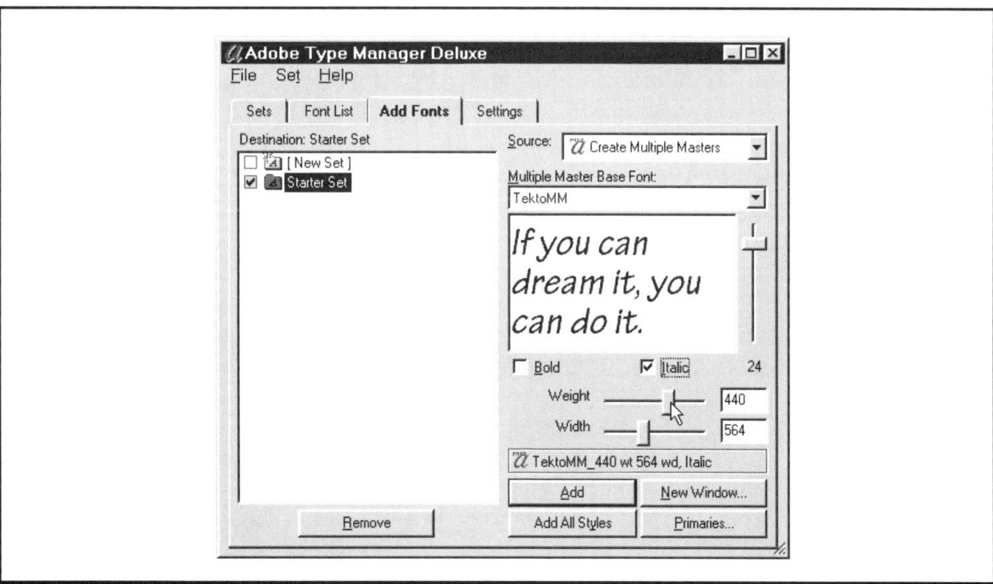

Figure 10-5. *Adobe Type Manager Deluxe 4 multiple master style configuration dialog box*

outlines currently installed, allowing you to vary the weight, width, and typeface style to generate new individual fonts.

Once you've created them, instances of multiple master fonts work just like standard PostScript fonts. ATM creates two additional files for each font instance. The stub file (using the .PSS file extension) contains all of the user-configured data for this instance of the multiple master font. The PostScript Font Metrics (PFM) file contains kerning and width table information for the new font instance.

Too Many Fonts!

Even with built-in support for TrueType fonts, Windows 98 is less flexible than many users might like in its management and handling of fonts. Literally thousands of TrueType and PostScript fonts can be installed in Windows by zealous application vendors. Between WordPerfect for Windows and Corel Systems' CorelDraw and Microsoft's own TrueType font packs, users may become lost in a maze of duplicated typefaces. Arial, Helvetica, Helvetica Narrow, Swiss, Times, Times Roman, New Times Roman—in both TrueType and PostScript versions—may all be present on the system at the same time. Font menus bulge at the seams, applications take longer to load, and system resources are decreased. Take a look at Figure 10-6. Who can remember which font is which?

Under Windows 3.x, commercial and shareware font-management packages made life considerably easier for active desktop publishers. These third-party packages allowed users to deal with font glut by assigning different names to similar typefaces or by changing font IDs on application font menus. Unfortunately, most of these Windows 3.x utilities don't work properly under Windows 95 or Windows 98. Notable in the "incompatible" list are Microsoft's own Font Assistant and Ares FontMinder, versions 1.0 to 2.51.

The good news is that Adobe Systems purchased the rights to the Ares products and now includes some of the old FontMinder functionality in Adobe Type Manager Deluxe. Users can create custom font sets that contain both TrueType and PostScript Type 1 faces. ATM's custom font sets can be activated or switched on the fly, automatically updating the available fonts that appear in application font menus. With a custom font pack, you can banish the 500 display fonts installed by CorelDraw when you work in Microsoft Word; or when you switch to PageMaker, you can call in a different font platoon.

To create a custom font pack with ATM 4 Deluxe, follow these steps:

1. Choose the Add Fonts tab, double-click the New Set icon, and provide a name for your new font set (for instance, "Word Only" for a Microsoft Word working font group).
2. Select Browse for Fonts in the Source drop-down box and locate the folders that contain your fonts in the file list window. (You'll probably want to choose \WINDOWS\FONTS followed by \PSFONTS to see the currently installed

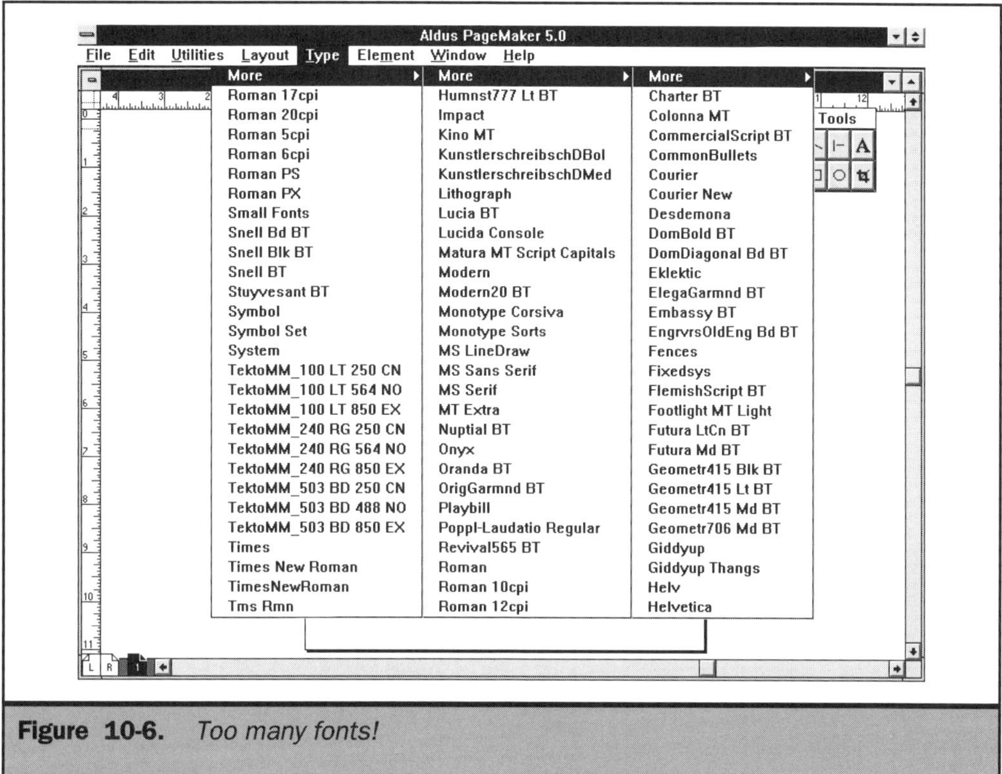

Figure 10-6. *Too many fonts!*

TrueType and PostScript fonts on your hard disk.) Select the fonts you want to include in the new font set and click the Add button.

3. If you've selected fonts that are already installed in another font pack, choose Keep Old Files to avoid creating duplicates. Choose Use New if you want to maintain multiple font storage locations.

Figure 10-7 shows the screen for creating a custom font pack.

Tip *By configuring only 25 to 50 typefaces as the Windows default, you avoid the slow loading time and resource drain that results from trying to handle 500-plus fonts every time you start a Windows session.*

ATM also offers some on-the-fly options for managing fonts. Its automatic font activation feature, accessed by clicking the Advanced button on the Settings tab, allows you to turn off a particular group of typefaces but still print them. To deactivate specific fonts, select them on the Sets tab and click the Deactivate button. The

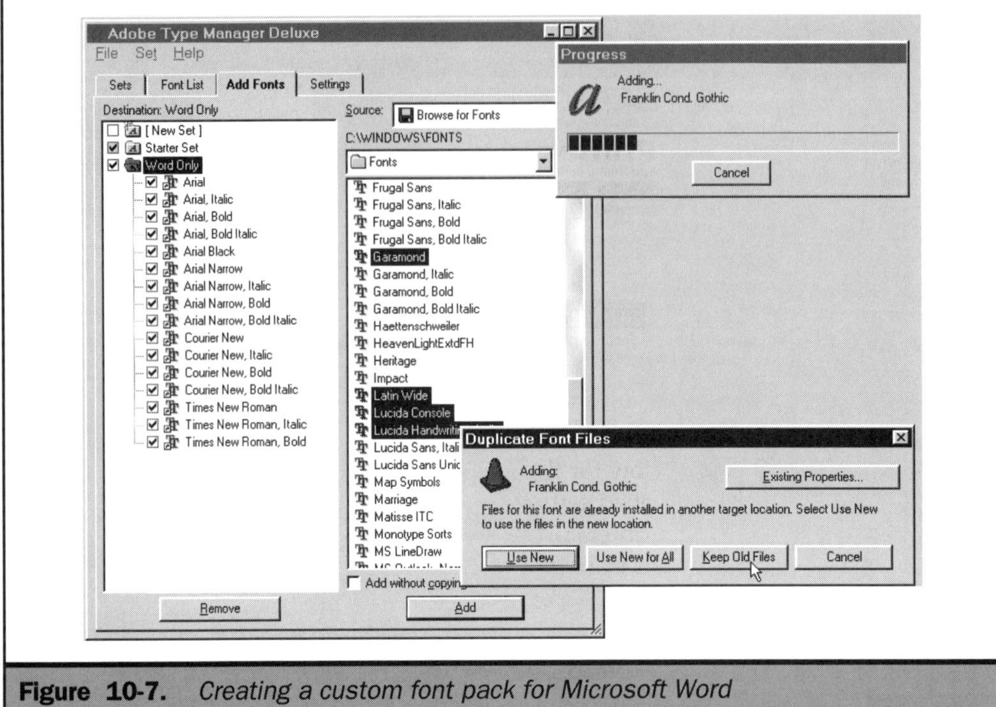

Figure 10-7. *Creating a custom font pack for Microsoft Word*

deactivated fonts don't show up in application font lists, but they are displayed on the screen and printed correctly whenever you open a document that contains them.

ATM 4 Deluxe doesn't offer quite as much flexibility in its on-the-fly options as the former Ares products, which allowed users to associate font sets with individual applications and also included more sophisticated font-sorting options.

If you're on an economy budget, check out an application called My Fonts (http://www.mytools.com). It contains font pack features similar to the ones offered in Adobe Type Manager.

Working with Printer Options

Depending upon which printers you have, Windows 98 lets you adjust various performance settings. Although these options vary from printer to printer, many of features described here should be available to you.

To begin examining or changing printer settings, you need to open your printer's property window. To do this, first choose Settings | Printers from the Start menu. Then right-click the icon for the printer you want to examine. From here, choose Properties from the pull-down context menu:

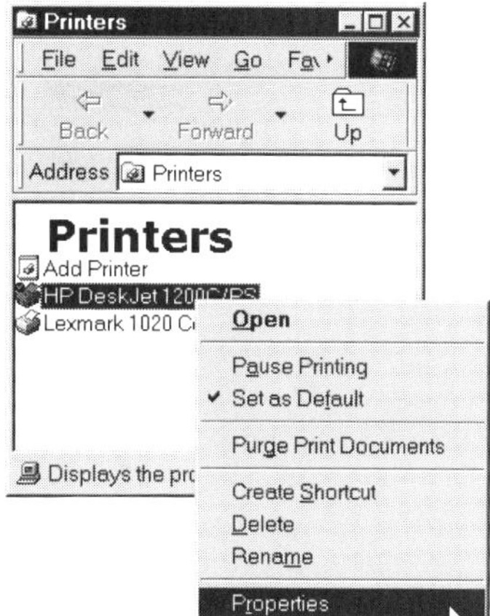

This opens the Properties window for the printer, as shown in Figure 10-8.

The number and type of tabbed settings that appear on the Properties menu vary from printer to printer. Most printers provide tabs marked General and Details. Most printer drivers directly installed from the Windows 98 CD also provide Paper and

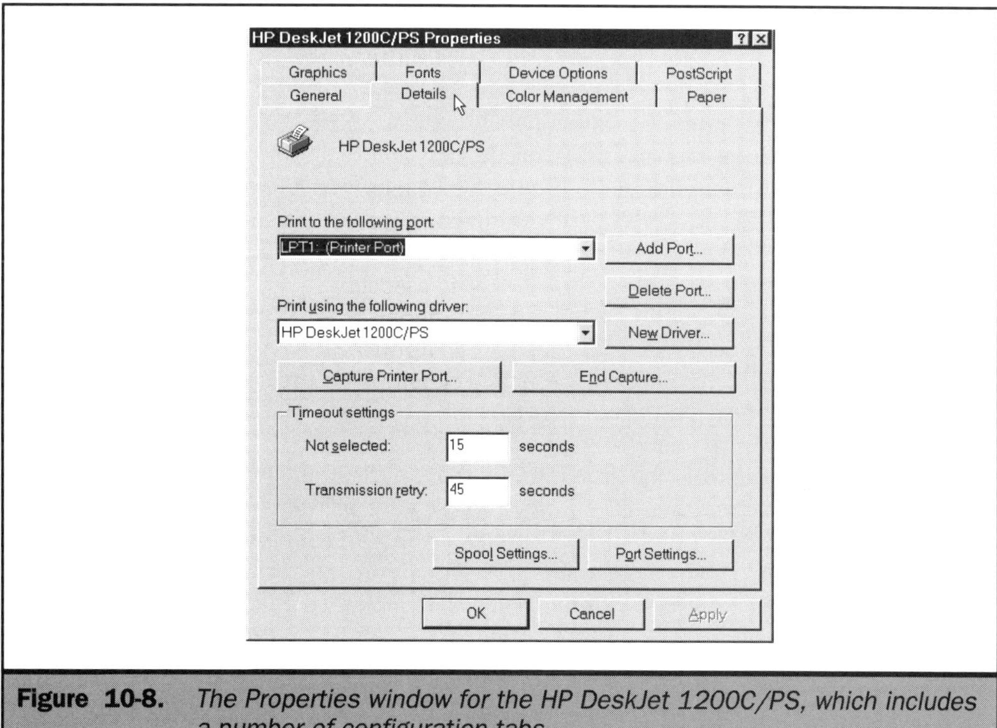

Figure 10-8. *The Properties window for the HP DeskJet 1200C/PS, which includes a number of configuration tabs*

Graphics tabs. More sophisticated printers provide Fonts, Device Options, and (if applicable) PostScript tabs.

General Tab

The General tab under Printer Properties allows you to enter a specific comment about the printer and to choose a separator page. The separator page option allows you divide your print jobs by inserting a special page between each finished document. Separator pages may consist of text, graphics, or a combination of the two. The built-in options allow you to choose a simple (text) page or a full (graphics) page. You can also define your own custom separator page by clicking the Browse button and selecting an appropriate one-page document in the Windows Metafile (.WMF) format.

Details Tab

The Details tab under Printer Properties contains most of the primary configuration options that under Windows 3.x were set through the Control Panel.

The Print To The Following Port option allows you to select a physical I/O port on your local computer, select a network connection, use the Microsoft fax driver, or print to a disk file. You can add network paths and additional ports to the option list by clicking the Add Port button on the right side of the dialog box. The Delete button lets you delete a port from the option list.

The Print Using The Following Driver option should generally be left alone. The setting in this option list usually corresponds to the printer model and manufacturer you selected on installation. For printers not directly supported by Windows 98, this dialog box is used to integrate an OEM-specific driver into a more general Win98 printer control shell. This option may also be used to update an existing Win98 printer driver with a later OEM version. If you want to configure an existing printer control icon with a new OEM driver, you can do so by clicking the New Driver button at the right of the dialog box.

The Capture Printer Port and End Capture buttons are for use with DOS applications and network devices that don't support Microsoft's Universal Naming Convention (UNC) printer protocol. For instance, you can route access to a non-UNC network printer by defining a virtual port that the driver will use to capture output and transmit print data over the network.

Timeout Settings controls the time interval that applications will wait before reporting a time-out error when they cannot access your printer. The Not Selected option specifies the number of seconds Windows will wait for a printer to be online before reporting an error. The Transmission Retry option specifies the number of seconds Windows will wait for a printer to generate a ready signal before reporting an error.

Tip *For PostScript devices, increase the transmission retry interval if you frequently receive time-out errors while printing large jobs.*

Spool Settings controls the printer's use of Win98's EMF spool files and allows you to enable or disable bidirectional printing support.

Disabling EMF Spool Options

Some applications are not compatible with Enhanced Metafile spooling. If you run into a program that has some trouble printing with EMF, you can disable EMF by following these steps:

1. Choose Settings | Printers from the Start menu.
2. Right-click the icon for the printer you are using and choose Properties from the context menu.
3. Click the Details tab and then click the Spool Settings button, shown in Figure 10-9.
4. Choose RAW in the Spool Data Format window to disable EMF (see Figure 10-9).

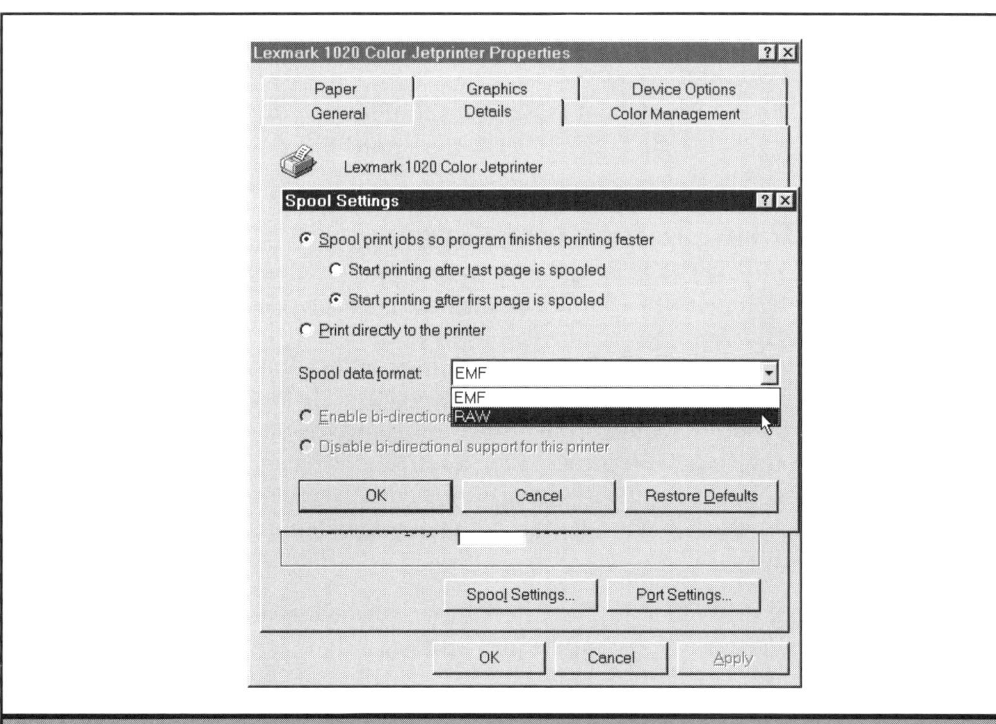

Figure 10-9. *Win98's print spooler format can be changed for compatibility with older applications*

You can also choose Print Directly To The Printer to disable print spooling entirely. (This sometimes improves performance with network printers, which may be configured with other spooling options on the server.)

5. Close all of the windows, and you're done.

Enhanced Port Options

If you own a computer manufactured within the last three years, the chances are good that its printer port supports bidirectional communication. If Windows 98 detects this capacity, it will be enabled automatically for printers that can use it. You can open the Properties window for a printer, choose the Details tab, and click the Spool Settings button to confirm whether bidirectional communication is enabled (see Figure 10-9, shown previously).

Your printer port may support the ECP or EPP specifications discussed at the beginning of this chapter. However, Windows 98 won't install drivers that recognize enhanced port capabilities unless you have toggled these options on in your computer's CMOS settings. To make sure you're getting the most out of your printer port, reboot your computer and inspect the CMOS configuration. (This can usually be accomplished by pressing ESC, F2, DEL, or another indicated key before the operating system begins to load. Consult your computer's documentation for details.) If you see a CMOS setting for Standard Printer Port or Output Only Port, change it to Bidirectional, ECP, or ECP +EPP. The next time you start Windows 98, the change will be detected and the port driver will be upgraded. If you change the CMOS setting to EPP, Windows 98 will not install a new driver. The EPP specification is supported through the standard Windows 98 printer port driver.

Printing to a Disk File for Portability

The trick of printing to a disk file is well-known to desktop publishers, who often send heavily formatted documents to service bureaus that boast superior printers but have incompatible software. Printing a file to disk from an application is like creating a quick-frozen dinner. All of the special formatting instructions in the original document are embedded in the printer file. The file can be dumped directly to a printer (or "thawed") at a remote location without loading it into the original program.

Some desktop publishing and presentation applications (such as Adobe PageMaker and CorelDraw) have special print-to-disk features built into their command menus, but you can print to disk with Windows 98 even with applications that don't include special features. Here's how:

1. Open the Printers folder. Right-click the icon for the target printer and open its Properties window. (Note that the printer itself doesn't have to be physically

attached to the computer. If you want to send your file to a service bureau that has a 2400 dpi Linotronic printer, use Add Printer to configure an icon for that printer on your local computer and then open its Properties window.)

2. Select the Details tab. Change the device in the Print To The Following Port drop-down box to File: (Creates A File On Disk).
3. Load your document into its application and print to the output device you've just modified. (Generally, you'll need to choose File | Print from the application's pull-down menu and select the printer in the Printer Name drop-down list.)
4. When the document is spooled to the specified printer, you'll be prompted to specify a filename and directory location. Specify a name for the output file, such as **MYFILE.PRN**.
5. Copy the output file you've produced to a floppy disk or e-mail it directly to the location where you want to print it.
6. If your original document contains special fonts, make sure that the printer at the target location also has access to these fonts. If not, you may want to prepare another disk or transmit physical copies of the font files in your document to the target location. (Some examples of physical typeface files are BD_____.TTF for Bodoni DTS TruType, and : MOC_____.PFM + MOC_____.PFB for Minion Condensed PostScript. The PostScript typeface requires both the .PFM and .PFB files to print properly.)
7. To reproduce the document at the remote location or service bureau, make sure that the fonts used in the document are resident in the target printer. This can be accomplished with Adobe Type Manager or other printer-specific software. The output file you prepared can be dumped to the printer from a DOS command prompt:

   C:\>**COPY** ***FILENAME.PRN*** **LPT[X]:**

   Here, FILENAME.PRN is the name of your file, and LPT[X]: is the port used by the printer.

Other Tabs

If your printer has been configured with a special OEM driver that has been migrated to Windows 98, some of the options for paper, graphics, fonts, and output quality may be hidden away on submenus accessible from a Setup button on the Details tab as shown next.

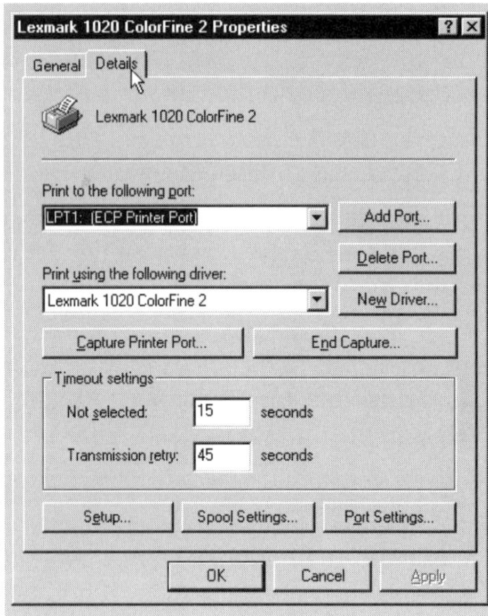

Paper Settings Tab

The options you'll find on the Paper tab for the Lexmark 1020 Color Jetprinter are shown in Figure 10-10. This tab lets you optimize the printer for the size and kind of paper being used for this printout. Paper size for this printer can range from 8 1/2 × 14 inches (legal size) to 3 7/8 × 7 1/2 inches (envelope size). This printer also has options for a variety of other sizes and kinds of envelopes and a custom setting that allows you to define your own page length and width, as also shown in Figure 10-10.

The Lexmark 1020 also lets you choose either portrait mode (vertical page orientation) or landscape mode (horizontal page orientation).

Graphics Tab

The Graphics tab lets you control the resolution of the printed page, the ink intensity, and the method used for color dithering. (Dithering is a technique that simulates a wider range of colors than is directly supported by the printer.) To see more color control options, as shown next, click the Color button.

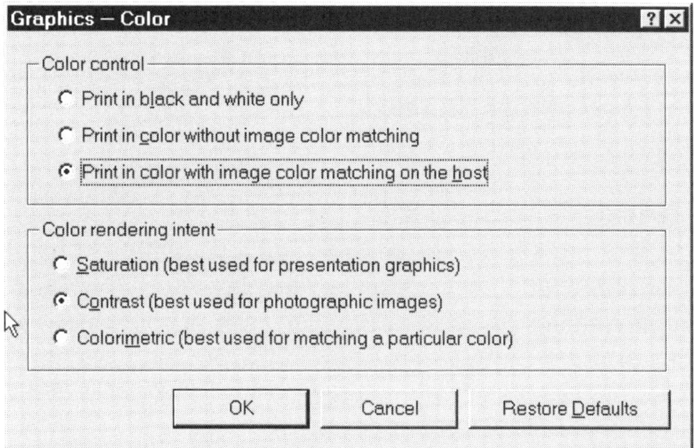

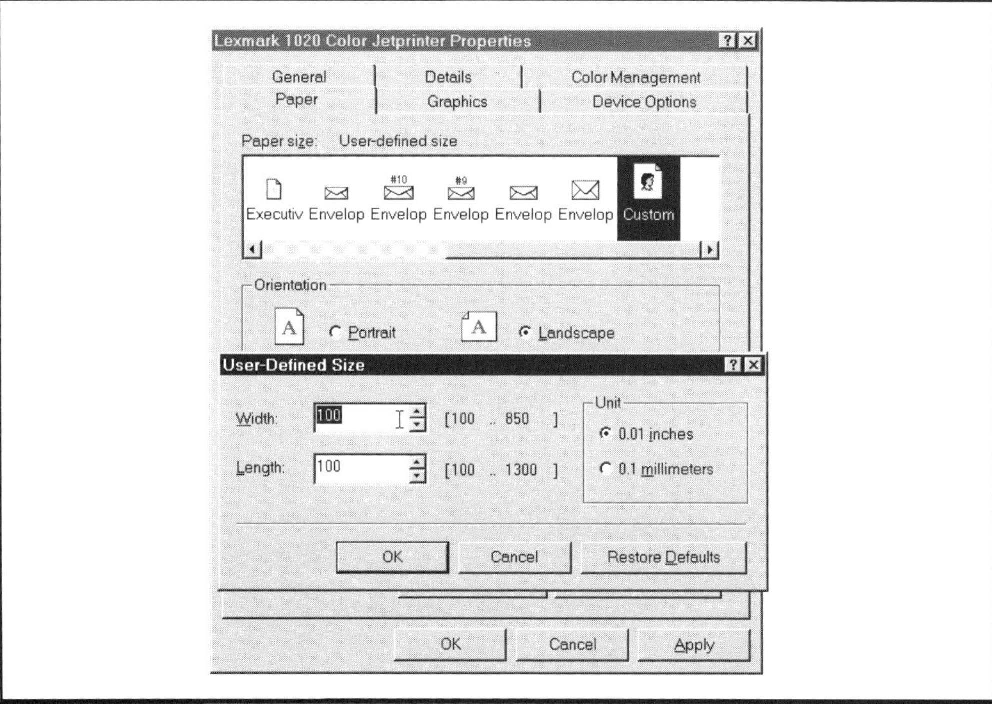

Figure 10-10. *The Lexmark 1020 printer properties include a custom paper size option on the Paper tab that can define a custom page length and page width*

Device Options Tab

The Device Options tab lets you set the output quality for your documents. Fast Mode will turn out pages more rapidly with slightly less precision and clarity. Presentation Mode generally uses more ink and creates the best possible output.

Color Management Tab

The Color Management tab allows you to associate a Windows 98 color-management profile with your printer to synchronize screen display and paper output. Windows 98 includes a few sample monitor and printer color management profiles. More are expected to be available later from individual monitor and printer manufacturers. (For more information on color management profiles, see "Color Management Tab" in Chapter 9.)

Fonts Tab

The Fonts tab allows you to manage the way your printer handles duplication issues with resident hardware fonts and soft fonts on your hard disk in both TrueType and PostScript formats. By default, your printer uses a substitution table configured to choose which version of a font to use in a document. Generally, if a TrueType or PostScript soft font on your hard disk duplicates a font resident in the printer's firmware, the substitution table indicates that the printer-resident font should be used, which results in faster printing. You can, however, override the default settings in the substitution table. If you want to use a specific version of a font stored on your hard disk, click the Edit the Table button on the Fonts tab to display the Font Substitutions Table window shown here:

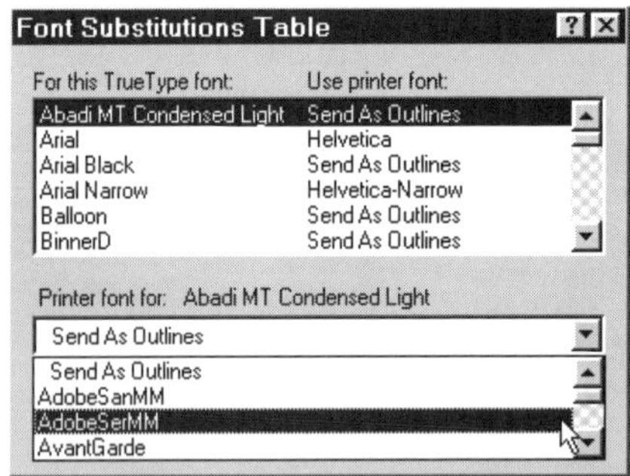

In addition to specifying whether a printer-resident or soft-font version of a typeface will be used, you can also substitute "real" Adobe Type I PostScript fonts for TrueType fonts contained in your document. Why should you want to do this? Many professional designers feel that the PostScript fonts produce a slightly better final printout. In addition, you may want to standardize the appearance of your documents. The substitution table can do more than substitute a PostScript font with the same name for a TrueType font. It can also be used to substitute any PostScript font installed under Windows for any TrueType font used in your document. To make a substitution, select Send TrueType Fonts To Printer According To The Font Substitution Table and click Edit The Table. (This option appears only for printers that include built-in PostScript support.)

Select any TrueType font on the left side of the table and use the drop-down Printer Font For box to make a substitution.

You can always return the substitution table to its default configuration by clicking the Restore Defaults button in the lower-right corner of the Fonts tab.

Additional options on the Fonts tab allow you to send any font to the printer as a set of rasterized bitmaps rather than as font outline characters or to disable the use of either TrueType or PostScript soft fonts. Generally, the only reason to use rasterized bitmaps is if you've created special font characters in your application that have no corresponding character outlines.

To disable the use of TrueType entirely, select Always Use Built-in Printer Fonts Instead Of TrueType Fonts. This will make jobs print faster, but document printouts may look different on different printers.

To disable the use of built-in printer fonts, entirely, select Always Use TrueType Fonts. This option will give your documents a uniform appearance, provided they're printed on computers that have the same TrueType fonts installed.

To favor the use of TrueType fonts over built-in printer fonts that have the same name, click the Send Fonts As button on the Fonts tab and select this option on the Send Fonts As screen that appears.

To send only PostScript soft fonts to the printer, click the Send Fonts As button on the Fonts tab and then select Don't Send in the Send TrueType Fonts As drop-down list on the next screen, as shown here:

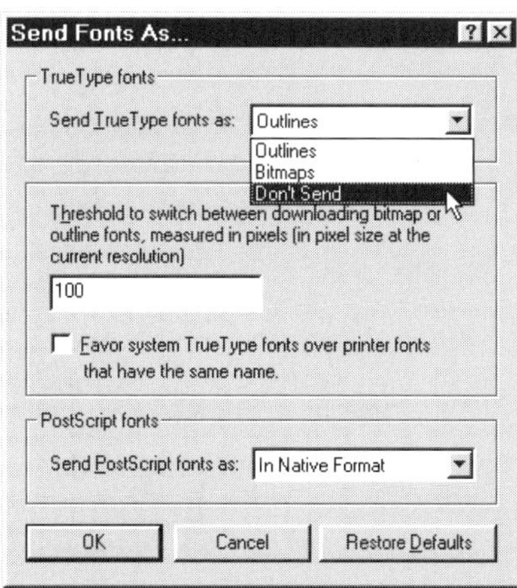

To disable the use of PostScript fonts entirely, click the Send Fonts As button on the Fonts tab. In the drop-down PostScript fonts box on the next screen, select Don't Send in the Send PostScript Fonts As list.

To send TrueType fonts to the printer as rasterized bitmaps instead of outline characters, click the Send Fonts As button on the Fonts tab and select Bitmaps in the Send TrueType Fonts As drop-down list on the next screen.

Network Printing Issues

When Windows 98 computers are attached to a properly configured network, they can share printers over that network. Additionally, computers running Windows 98 can act as print servers for any printers connected through a local I/O port.

To access a network printer, you must create a network printer icon on your local machine. Here's how:

1. Open the Printers folder and select Add Printer. Double-clicking the Add Printer icon starts the Add Printer Wizard, which takes you through the process step by step. When you're asked whether you want to install a local or a network printer, select the Network Printer option, as shown here:

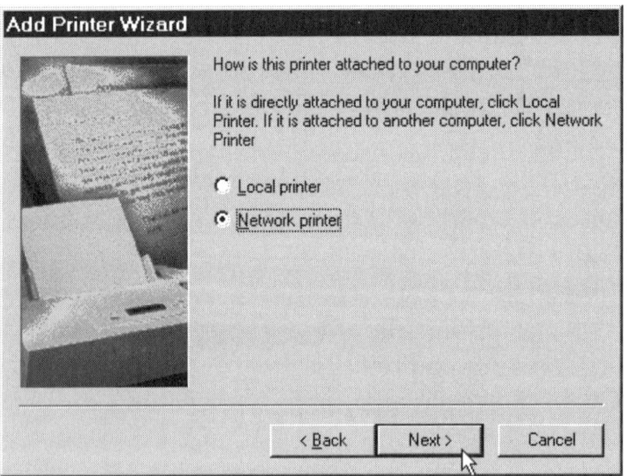

2. In the next dialog box, enter the path to your network printer and its name on the network (for example, **\\LENNY3\BIGIRON**). In some cases, when you are already logged on, this information appears automatically. You can also click the Browse button to search your network for available printers, as shown here:

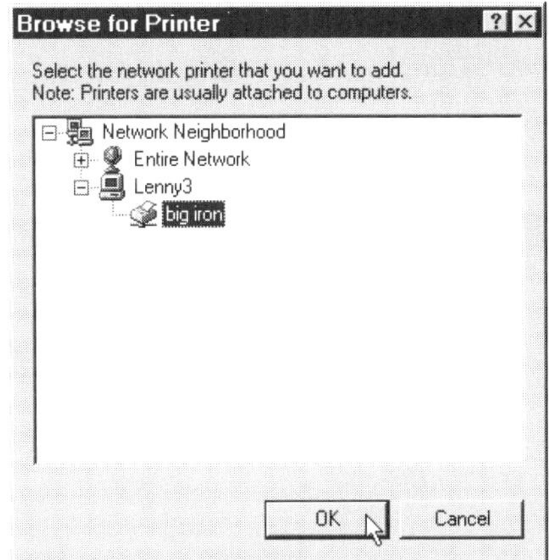

3. If you intend to print from DOS applications, select the appropriate button near the bottom of the dialog box.
4. If you are not currently connected to the printer you specified, you'll see a message informing you that you can work offline until you establish your network connection. Click Next.
5. The next dialog box asks you to select the printer type. Specify the manufacturer and model number of the printer you'll be sharing. In general, when the system prompts you for the printer driver diskette, you will find the driver software on the host computer's drive.
6. The final dialog box gives you the opportunity to change the default name for your printer and asks whether you want to make it the default printer for Windows applications. Make any changes. Then click the Finish button to complete the installation.

From now on when your applications print to this printer, the output will be spooled over the network when you're connected and stored in the offline queue for this printer when the printer is unavailable.

Resolving UNC Naming Problems

If your applications don't support Microsoft's UNC naming convention, the network printer you've just created may not appear as an output option when you issue a Print command. You may experience this problem, for example, when you try to print with older Windows 3.x programs. You can still print over the network with these problem applications. Here's how:

1. Use the Add Printer dialog box to set up a local printer with a driver type that matches the network printer.
2. Configure this new local printer to use a specific local port address. (If LPT1 is already in use, choose LPT2 or LPT3.)
3. Enter the following commands either in the Run box on the Start menu or at a DOS command prompt:

   NET USE LPT2: *SERVERPRINTER***
   CAPTURE LPT2:

   (Replace SERVER and PRINTER with your server and printer names; for example, \\\\LENNY3\\BIGIRON.)

The first command maps LPT2 to the network printer you designate for Windows applications. The second command captures output to LPT2 for DOS applications. You can now print from problem applications to the local printer for LPT2; Windows 98 will intercept the output and route it to the network printer.

Using Point and Print

Point and print is a Windows 98 feature that allows you to quickly install a printer over a network. Simply point to a print server by opening a shared resource in the \\NETWORK NEIGHBORHOOD folder or open a print server's queue by typing its path name in the Run dialog box on the Start menu.

Using JetAdmin

Hewlett-Packard's JetAdmin utility is a network and printer administration program. It allows you to install, remove, and configure any Hewlett-Packard printers connected to a JetDirect print hub on the network. (See Figure 10-11).

Note *Although JetAdmin is a Windows utility, it works in Novell NetWare environments as well.*

To use the JetAdmin management package, first attach the JetDirect hub to your network, cable your printer to the parallel port interface on the hub, and turn on the printer. Uninstall any previous versions of JetAdmin that were installed under previous versions of Windows. (You can do this with the HP JetUninstall utility for versions 2.3 and above. For older versions, choose Add/Remove Programs | Uninstall from the Windows Control Panel.) The version of JetAdmin on the Windows 98 CD requires either the Microsoft TCP/IP or IPX/SPX network protocol. Before proceeding further, you should right-click the Network Neighborhood icon on the desktop, choose Properties, and examine the component list on the Configuration tab to verify that one of these

Figure 10-11. *HP JetDirect EX Plus 3 port with a BNC Ethernet connection and one attached printer*

protocols is installed. (If neither protocol is installed, click the Add button and select Protocol | Microsoft to add IPX/SPX or TCP/IP to the component list.)

To install the Windows 98 version of JetAdmin, open My Computer or Windows Explorer to the \DRIVERS|PRINTERS\JETADMIN\DISK1 folder on your Windows 98 installation CD and run the Setup program. After you click past the Welcome and License screens, you can choose three modules to install:

- The HPJetAdmin Files module allows you to administer and configure the printer from your Windows 98 workstation.
- The HPJetDirect Port Files module installs the client software that makes the JetDirect hub (and attached printers) visible and accessible through Network Neighborhood.
- The HP Desktop Status Files module allows you to view printer performance statistics in real time.

After the JetAdmin files are installed on your hard disk, you'll be prompted to restart the computer. Now when you open Network Neighborhood, you should see an HP Network icon that represents the JetDirect port.

To configure a network printer for use on a Windows 98 workstation, follow the same general procedure described above for installing a network printer:

1. Click the Add Printer icon in the \PRINTERS folder. Click Next on the first screen of the wizard and select Network Printer on the second screen. Click Next to continue.
2. On the screen that prompts you for a network path or queue name, click the Browse button.
3. In the Browse for Printer window, click the + sign next to the HP_Network_Printers icon to display the available printers cabled to the JetDirect port. Select the printer you want and click OK.
4. Continue installing the printer by choosing a name and installing software drivers, as described in the first part of the "Network Printing Issues" section.

Note *The Windows 98 version of JetAdmin does not support the bundled Microsoft Service for Netware Directory Services or the Novell NetWare Workstation Shell. You can find more information about configuring and using the JetAdmin software in the JAREADME.TXT file in the \DRIVERS\PRINTERS\JETADMIN\DISK1 directory on the Win98 CD.*

Optimizing Printer Performance

The speed of printing to a shared network printer depends on the server's operating system. If you print to a server running Windows 98, the rendering from the EMF format to the printer-specific language takes place on the server. This means that less work is performed on the client computer, giving the user better performance.

When you print through NetWare or Windows NT servers, the rendering from EMF to the printer-specific format takes place on the client computer. Although this occurs in the background, it still means more work is performed on the client computer. When you print to a printer attached locally, EMF rendering and device-specific rendering both take place on the computer. To optimize network print performance you need to decide on the trade-off between disk use and return-to-application time when configuring printing in Windows 98.

To define spool settings for print performance, follow these steps:

1. Open the Printers folder, select a printer, right-click, and choose Properties.
2. Select the Details tab and then click Spool Settings to display the dialog box shown next.

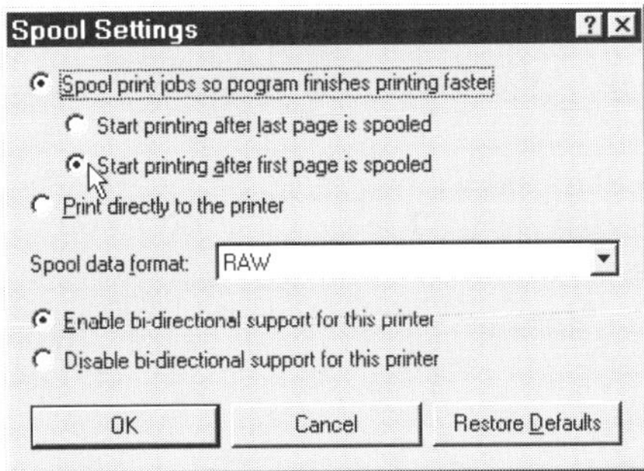

3. Select Spool Print Jobs So Program Finishes Printing Faster and then click one of the following options:

- Select Start Printing after Last Page Is Spooled if you want the return-to-application time to be faster. This option requires more disk space and increases the total print time. The second rendering does not start until the entire file is written to the EMF file, which decreases the amount of work performed on the computer as you print but increases the disk space because the entire file has to be written before the second rendering starts.
- Select Start Printing After First Page Is Spooled if you want the second rendering to take place simultaneously with the writing of the EMF file. This option reduces the total print time and disk space required, but it increases the return-to-application time.

Chapter 11

Communications Nuts and Bolts

Chapter Highlights

What's new in Windows 98

Modem setup

Dial-Up Networking

Faster connections

HyperTerminal

Windows Messaging

Direct Cable Connection

Briefcase

Dial-Up Server

Ten or fifteen years ago, most people bought their first personal computers to run word processors, spreadsheets, and maybe a few games on a stand-alone machine. When they wanted to share files with another computer they probably made a copy on a floppy disk. Modems were expensive, slow, and complicated luxuries.

Today, much has changed. The personal computer has become a sophisticated communications device. The single most common reason that people buy their first computer is for access to the Internet. Modems cost less than half as much as they did in the early 1980s and run more than a hundred times faster. A modem and an Internet connection changes a computer from an isolated word- and data-processing device to an access point for worldwide data exchange systems.

This chapter provides you with the technical information you'll need to install and configure your modem to use Windows 98's principal telecommunications applications: Dial-Up Networking and HyperTerminal. You'll also find information on setting up and working with Windows Messaging, a useful Windows 95 feature that is no longer officially part of Windows 98 but that can be included as an add-in. Since many beta testers raised an outcry at losing the Microsoft Mail Post Office, local network e-mail client, and fax support bundled with Windows 95, these modules have been included as "extras" on the Windows 98 CD.

This chapter starts with a quick look at Windows 98's approach to telecommunications. Later in this chapter you'll find step-by-step instructions for setting up and using these programs. You can skim the topic headings to find basic information about Win98's communications features, or you can delve into each section as deeply as you wish to find more detailed technical information.

Unlike earlier versions of Windows, in which modem support and telecommunications services appeared to have been tacked on as an afterthought, Windows 95 and now Windows 98 closely integrate online communications features into the basic operating system.

What's New in Windows 98

Windows 98 carries forward the underlying design of the communications services in Windows 95. Rather than making any radical changes, Windows 98 brings telecommunications services and technology up to date, reflecting developments since 1995.

Most of the changes incorporated into Windows 98's communications features and functions are internal additions and improvements to the services introduced in Windows 95. You'll find more and better modem drivers, support for many kinds of telephone connections (including traditional analog telephone lines, digital PBX, and ISDN service) and generally improved performance. The multilink feature integrated into Dial-Up Networking allows several modems to combine bandwidth on simultaneous connections to a single host.

The following sections describe the new communication features built into Windows 98.

More Device Support

In theory, the standard set of Hayes command codes should work on any Hayes-compatible modem—but, of course, the world doesn't really work that way. Just about every make and model of modem requires a slightly different command set. Windows 98 includes specific support for hundreds of different modems. For each modem type, Windows uses the particular initialization codes and commands specified by the manufacturer.

Even if a modem does not include plug-and-play features, Windows is often able to identify it, so installing a new modem is usually pretty simple. Of course, new modems will continue to appear, so it's entirely possible that you'll have to obtain a new driver from the manufacturer.

If the Windows 98 package does not include a specific driver for your modem, you can probably find one on the disks supplied by the vendor. If you can't, try the online directory at http://www.winfiles.com/drivers/modems.html or at the modem maker's own Web site.

Direct Modem Control by the Operating System

Microsoft's Telephony Applications Programming Interface (TAPI) is a universal modem driver that controls modem operation within Windows 98. This offers several benefits:

- You can configure your modem once and expect the same settings to work in all applications.
- You don't have to shut down a program (such as a fax client) that monitors incoming calls before you place an outgoing call. You can also easily switch modems in all of your installed programs.

Windows 98 communications programs, including HyperTerminal and Dial-Up Networking, are fine-tuned and controlled through a series of options available in the Control Panel. The Modem Properties sheet, shown in Figure 11-1, lets you set connect rates, port buffers, error control, and other configuration options individually for any modem attached to your computer.

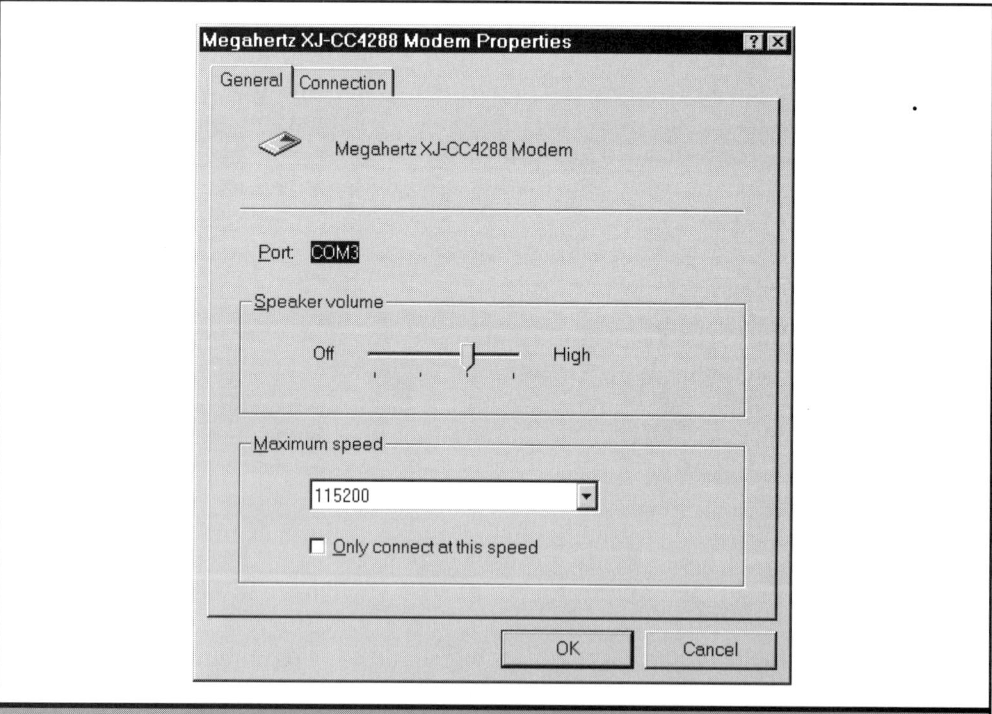

Figure 11-1. *The Modem Properties sheet manages the operation of your modem*

Windows 98 uses a separate strategy for managing older DOS and Windows 3.x communication programs. These applications use their own internal command settings to operate the modem, so you still need to set the modem controls in each of these programs separately.

Multiple–Modem Link Support

Multilink channel aggregation is a new feature of Windows 98 that permits you to combine links to the same host through two or more physical connections running simultaneously. In other words, you can use two or more modems (each on a separate telephone line), ISDN channels, or a combination of both, to increase the data transfer speed between your computer and a dial-up server. This feature requires Internet service providers (ISPs) that explicitly support the multilink protocol.

For example, if you have enough phone lines and data ports (or internal expansion slots) and if your ISP supports multilink aggregation, you can install four 33.6 Kbps modems in your computer and transfer uncompressed data from the Internet at up to 134,400 bps.

In addition to supporting multilink modem pooling to a single server, Windows 98 also permits you to establish simultaneous dial-up connections to independent sources. Thus, if the need arises, you can actually connect to two servers simultaneously to gain access to nonintersecting sets of restricted resources.

Improved Dial-Up Networking

Dial-Up Networking (DUN) was introduced in Windows 95 as a fast and easy way to connect to the Internet and other networks through a modem and telephone line.

The Dial-Up Networking utility frees you from the need to use third-party Transmission Control Protocol/Internet Protocol (TCP/IP) dialers to connect to the Internet. Dial-Up Networking also allows you to connect to a dedicated cable network by dialing into the server or any workstation on the network through a modem.

In Windows 98, the Dial-Up Networking setup interface has been simplified. In addition to clicking the Make New Connection button in the DUN folder, you can open the Connect to the Internet icon on the desktop, and the wizard will help you configure all aspects of an Internet account. (For more information about changes and additions to Dial-Up Networking, see the Dial-Up Networking sections later in this chapter and in Chapter 5 and "Virtual Private Networking" in Chapter 14.)

Updated HyperTerminal

HyperTerminal is the telecommunications and terminal-emulation program supplied with both Windows 95 and Windows 98. HyperTerminal 1.2, the version included with Windows 98, has several new features: a Telnet client for connection to a host computer through the Internet, Zmodem crash recovery, a redial-on-busy option, and improved font handling and display.

HyperTerminal is a simplified version of a more powerful communications program called HyperAccess, both made by Hilgraeve. As you might expect, the commercial HyperAccess has many additional features that are not included in HyperTerminal.

Outlook Express: Internet Mail and News Client

Outlook Express is a new client program for handling Internet e-mail and news. It replaces the old Exchange client that was supplied with Windows 95. Outlook Express is described in detail in Chapter 13.

Infrared Connectivity

Along with traditional hard-wired telephone and network connections, Windows 98 supports the Infrared Data Association (IrDA) standard for wireless connections between computers and peripheral devices, and between two individual computers.

A Few Things That Are Missing

Two important communications programs that were part of Windows 95 are not part of the core Windows 98 operating system: the Microsoft Exchange client for Windows Messaging and the Microsoft Fax program. The new Outlook Express effectively replaces the Exchange client as an e-mail program, but there's no replacement for the Windows 95 fax program.

If Windows Messaging or Windows Fax (or both) were already active on your computer when you installed Windows 98, these programs will remain in place and be fully functional after you upgrade. Both programs are included on the Windows 98 CD-ROM as add-on extra features, but you have to go out of your way to install them. (You'll find full details for installing and working with the Win95 Microsoft Fax program in "Fax" in Chapter 5. For information on working with other Windows Messaging components, see "Using Windows Messaging" later in this chapter.)

How Windows 98 Handles Communications

Although the individual programs have been updated and improved, the basic design of Windows 98's communications services is the same as in Windows 95. The most important elements of this design are the communications application program interface (API) and the communications kernel. The communications API moves control information and content between individual Windows programs. The communications kernel includes the universal modem driver (Unimodem) that sends and receives modem commands through vendor-supplied mini-drivers. Windows 98 also uses a set of 32-bit port drivers to communicate with your computer's serial, parallel, and other I/O ports.

Setting up telecommunications software through Windows 98 is considerably easier than it was in earlier versions of Windows. If you're using standard modems with Windows 95 or 98 programs, the process is generally an automated no-brainer. However, if you're trying to install an older DOS or Windows 3.x program, you may want to pack a lunch before you start. You may have to hunt through particular modem drivers and configuration screens to get these applications to work. Fortunately, if a communications program worked properly under DOS or Windows 3.x, you should be able to use the same settings under Windows 98. The only element that Windows 98 supplies to older DOS and 16-bit Windows terminal programs is access to the modem through the serial port.

Serial Port Management

Windows 98's VCOMM is a protected-mode communications driver that takes advantage of the new plug-and-play services in Windows 98. The VCOMM communications driver supports the high-speed serial ports necessary for smooth data transfer with high-speed modems. Windows 98 allows you to regulate both the receive and transmit data buffers built into ports that use the NS16550 Universal Asynchronous Receiver/Transmitter (UART). VCOMM also improves upon the way Windows 3.x arbitrated serial port access. If two open applications both try to use the same serial port, the system won't crash, as often occurred in Windows 3.1. Instead, Windows 98 reliably awards the port to one program and suspends the other program's access until the port is free. (If you attempt to send a fax while another program is open on the same port, the fax is placed in a queue. When the port becomes available, the fax is sent.)

Modem Setup

To detect or install a new modem under Windows 98, open the Modems component in the Control Panel, select the General tab, and click the Add button. If the modem is external, don't forget to turn on its power switch. On the next screen, you can specify either a Personal Computer Memory Card International Association (PCMCIA) modem or Other. PCMCIA modems—now referred to by Microsoft as PC cards—are plug-in modules that slide in and out of special slots on a portable computer. (Some desktop units may also include PCMCIA slots, but this isn't typical.) After you specify whether your modem is a plug-in PCMCIA modem card or some other variety, the Install New Modem Wizard will try to automatically detect and install your modem. If the wizard can't identify your modem, or if it identifies it incorrectly, you will need to select the modem from a list of known modem types, as shown next:

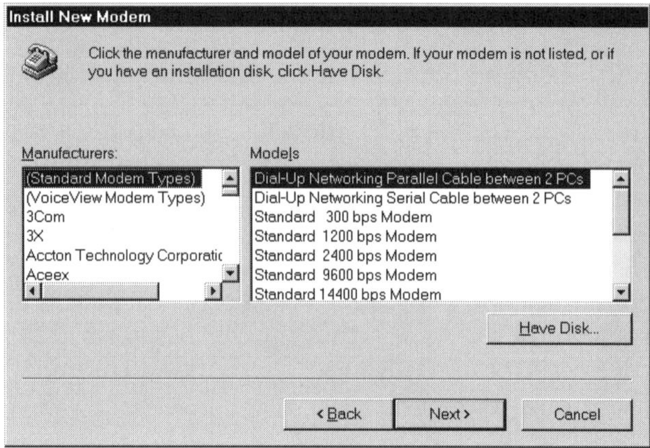

If your modem came with a setup diskette, put it in your computer's floppy drive and click the Have Disk button. If your modem is not on the default list and you don't have a setup disk, try using one of the Standard Modem Types selections. After you get the modem working with the generic settings, use your Web browser to find a specific driver; there are links to most modem makers' Web sites at http://www.winfiles.com/drivers/ modems.html or http://www.microsoft.com/hwtest/hcl/. If you can't find an up-to-date driver for your modem, you can "roll your own" by modifying an existing driver for a similar model. See the sidebar "Constructing a Custom Modem Profile" later in this chapter for details.

When you first install your modem, you will have a chance to specify the area code for your calling region and whether your telephone line uses pulse or tone dialing. You can change these options later by clicking the Dialing Properties button on the General tab in the Modem Properties dialog box to display the dialog box shown here:

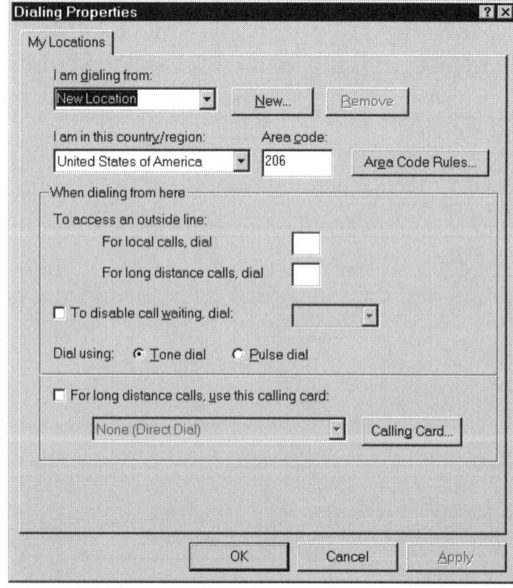

Working with Dialing Properties

The Dialing Properties dialog box contains the specific information your modem needs to place calls from one or more specific locations. For each location, the property sheet identifies your local calling area and supplies all the special codes that you must dial to place local and long-distance calls. If you're using a desktop computer, you will probably need just one location profile, but on a portable system you can create separate profiles for your office, your home, and any other location you expect to visit.

For each location, you must specify the country and area code from which you are placing your calls. When you place calls within your own area code, Windows will omit the area code unless you use the Area Code Rules option to include it.

If you are located in one of the metropolitan centers where the local calling zone has been split into more than one area code (such as Seattle, where area codes 206, 425, and 253 are all local calls), or if you must dial a 1 for certain numbers within your own area code, click the Area Code Rules button to display the screen shown here. Specific dialing rules are different in different locations, so you'll want to consult the first few pages of your local telephone directory for the particular rule you need to use.

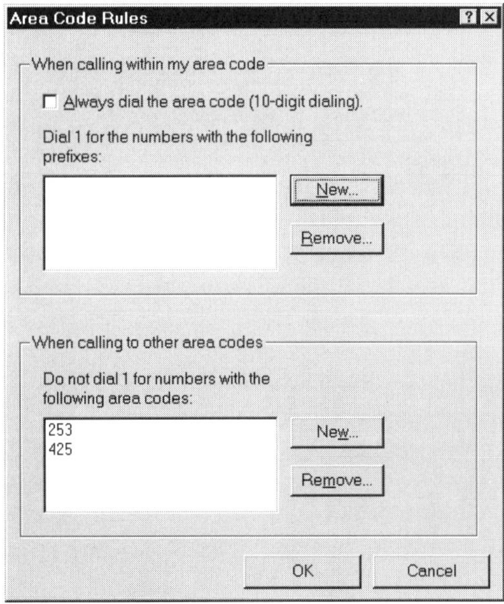

If you are dialing through a switchboard or some other device that requires special dialing code prefixes (such as a 9 for an outside line), you can enter these in the When Dialing from Here section.

Many modems drop a connection when they receive an incoming call-waiting signal, so it's always a good idea to disable this feature if you're using your modem on a telephone line that provides call waiting. Place a check mark next to To Disable Call Waiting, Dial and use the drop-down menu to choose the correct disable code (look in your local telephone book to find the code).

When you place a call through your usual long-distance carrier, Windows will automatically use the correct access codes. However, if you want to use a credit card or an alternative long-distance carrier to pay for toll calls, place a check mark next to the For Long Distance Calls, Use This Calling Card option and select your long-distance service from the drop-down menu. You can create a customized calling card profile or edit an existing one by clicking the Calling Card button. Choose the calling card or other service you want to use from the drop-down menu in the Calling Card dialog box, or click New to specify a calling card or carrier not on the menu. Type the details in the remaining fields of the Calling Card dialog box. You can further customize the dialing defaults by clicking the Long Distance Calls and International Calls buttons, as shown in Figure 11-2.

Modem Diagnostics

After you have completed the basic modem setup, you can perform a simple test to see whether Windows 98 recognizes your modem. Open the Modem Properties screen and selecting the Diagnostics tab. Select the port connected to your modem and click the

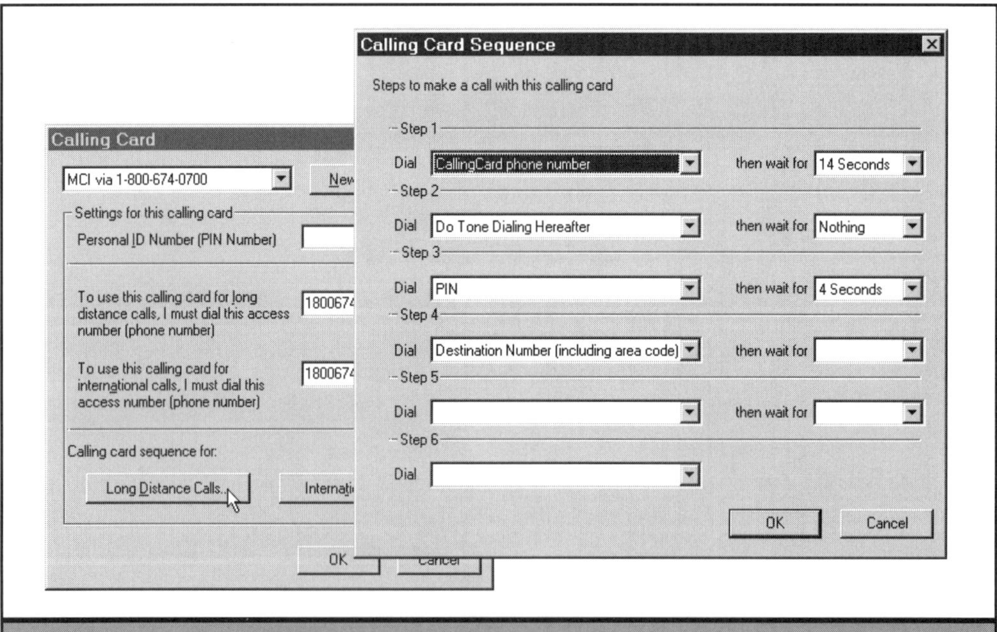

Figure 11-2. *Customizing calling card dialing defaults*

More Information button. Windows will interrogate the modem and deliver a diagnostic information dump, as shown here:

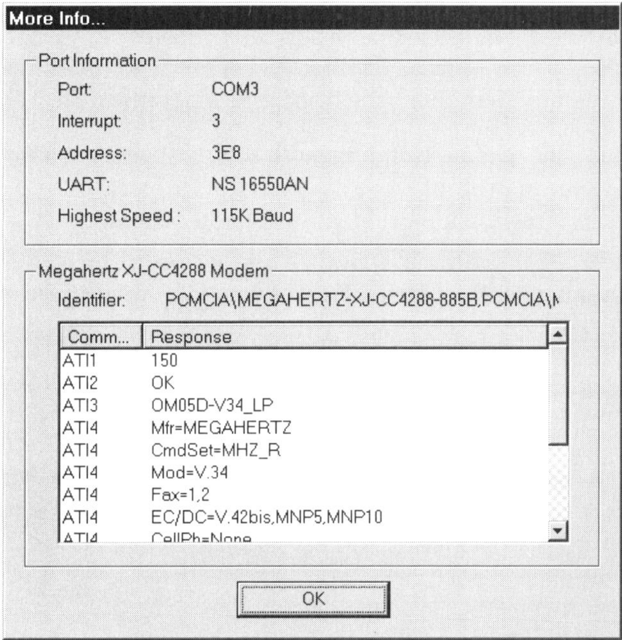

Working with Modem Properties

You can customize the performance settings for any installed modem by opening the Modems object in the Control Panel, selecting the General tab, and clicking the Properties button. The Modem Properties screen appears.

GENERAL TAB The General tab of the Modems Properties screen identifies the communications port connected to this modem and controls the speaker volume and the maximum data transfer rate between the computer and the modem. For PCMCIA and internal modems, the communications port generally can't be changed, but an external modem can be switched to an alternative serial port if one is available.

The settings on the General tabs are used by Windows 95 and Windows 98 applications and utilities that access the operating system through TAPI. Older DOS and Windows 3.x programs set these parameters through their individual setup menus.

Maximum connect speed for a serial port is sometimes referred to as data terminal equipment (DTE) speed or internal connect speed. This value (in bytes per second) indicates the rate at which your modem passes received data through the serial port to the CPU. This setting does not necessarily represent the maximum modem-to-modem data transfer rate over the phone line (it's usually considerably slower). The best strategy for setting the maximum DTE connect speed is to specify as high a value as your serial port and modem will permit without file transmission errors:

- For older, low-speed serial ports with 8250 or 16450 UARTs, the setting should be no greater than 38,400. You may have to drop down to 19,200 if you experience transmission problems at a higher speed.
- For newer, high-speed serial ports equipped with 16550 UARTs or better (this includes most Pentium-based PCs), the maximum connect speed should be set to 115,200 or 57,600.

Generally, the Only Connect at This Speed option should not be active. This option prohibits your modem from accepting connections at speeds slower than the specified maximum.

Tip *If you don't know what kind of UART is in your computer, open the Modems Properties sheet from the Control Panel. Select the port you want to check and click the More Info button.*

Some proprietary serial I/O devices such as the Hayes ESP board and the Turbo Express I/O card (discussed later in this chapter) are capable of higher DTE rates than 115,200 bps. To obtain the high-speed data transfers that these cards promise, you must install the drivers supplied by the hardware manufacturers.

Some newer internal modems and PC Card modems have improved data interfaces that can handle serial port connect rates greater than 115,200 bps. If you have one of these modems, the automatic configuration will set the Win98 speed to 115,200, and the modem's ROM will handle the higher rate.

CONNECTION TAB The Connection tab on the Modem Properties sheet, shown next, sets the initial connection preferences. These settings, as well as the Call Preferences in the bottom part of this dialog box, can be overridden by individual Dial-Up Networking connection profiles. The most common settings are 8 data bits, no parity, and 1 stop bit. The most important exception is a connection to CompuServe through a terminal emulator program (but not through CompuServe's Windows-based graphic interface program). A straight terminal connection to Compuserve expects initial settings of 7 data bits, even parity, and 1 stop bit.

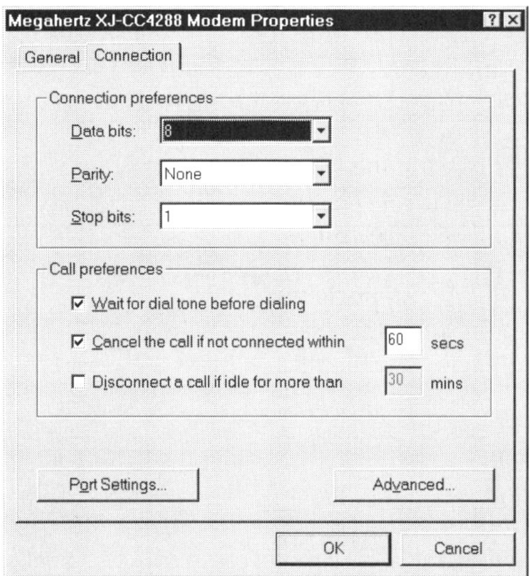

The Call Preferences options let you instruct your modem to wait for a dial tone before it begins to dial out. Outside of the United States, this option should be deselected. This section also lets you specify the amount of time the modem should wait for a connection and the amount of idle time before an automatic disconnection.

The two buttons at the bottom of the Connection tab set advanced options that apply globally to all connection profiles configured to use this modem. Port Settings opens a dialog box that controls the first-in, first-out (FIFO) data buffer used by high-speed ports with 16550 UARTs. The Advanced Connection Settings dialog box specifies error-correction, data compression, and flow control options for your modem. In most cases, you can leave these options at their default settings, but you may want to change them if you experience connection or data-transfer problems.

The check box options in the upper portion of this dialog box send appropriate command strings to your modem when a Windows 95 or Windows 98 communications program opens. If the Append to Log option is active, Windows stores copies of commands and status messages in the existing log file. If this option is not checked, Windows overwrites old call records with a new log for the current call session. The View Log button opens the log. (See "Troubleshooting with the Modem Log" later in this chapter.)

The Modulation Type option allows you to choose between the standard modulation used by most modems and the nonstandard HST modulation used by some U.S. Robotics (now 3Com) modems.

The Extra Settings option allows you to fine-tune your modem's performance by sending additional commands to your modem when you start a Windows 95 or Windows 98 communications program. This field is particularly useful if Windows 98 does not properly initialize your modem. The command string in this field is passed to the modem after the preconfigured commands and before the telephone number. For example, one simple, common entry in this field is **&F**. This command restores your modem's factory defaults before the modem starts to dial, no matter what commands Windows 98 may have sent to it.

Constructing a Custom Modem Profile

Typically, the Win98 Modem Installation Wizard detects at least the manufacturer of your modem (this information is built into the modem's ROM and is usually available via a Hayes dialing command), but the wizard may not always detect the specific model number.

For instance, you may have a USR HST Dual Standard modem that Windows 98 sees as a Courier, v. Everything model. In the case of popular manufacturers, it's easy to fine-tune the modem selection by scrolling up or down the list of units to select the correct model number. However, sometimes a particular model number will not appear in the list. (This can happen with newer 56K modems that Windows 98 sees as older 33.6K versions).

If you don't have the proper modem driver supplied by the vendor, you can try selecting one that is close to it in the Windows 98 list, or you can scroll up the list to Standard Modem Types and select a modem with the appropriate connect speed. You can add custom performance parameters to the profile later by clicking the Advanced button on the Modem Properties Connections tab. Consult the manual supplied by your modem vendor for the appropriate Hayes commands to set the defaults you want. For instance, you may want to add an &F1 command to invoke factory settings followed by the specific command that turns on the modem's high-speed connection features, as shown here:

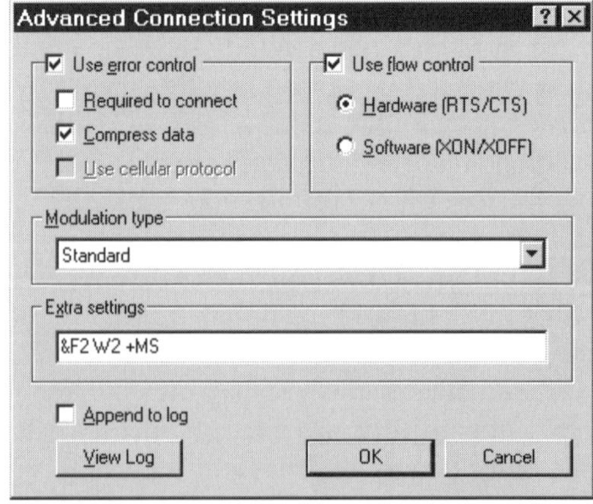

Troubleshooting with the Modem Log

As mentioned earlier, if you're having problems connecting to a particular host through a particular modem or serial port, you can monitor your modem's activity by reading the MODEM.LOG file for that modem in your \WINDOWS directory. To read the modem log, click the View Log button. As Figure 11-3 shows, the log contains a description of all the commands and responses that Windows 98 sent to your modem and the responses that the modem returned to your computer, along with the commands and responses exchanged between your modem and the modem at the other end of the telephone line.

This log can help you track the progress of a call through your modem and isolate the exact point at which a connection failure occurred. For example, a problem may occur when your modem tries to set up a data compression or error-correction protocol

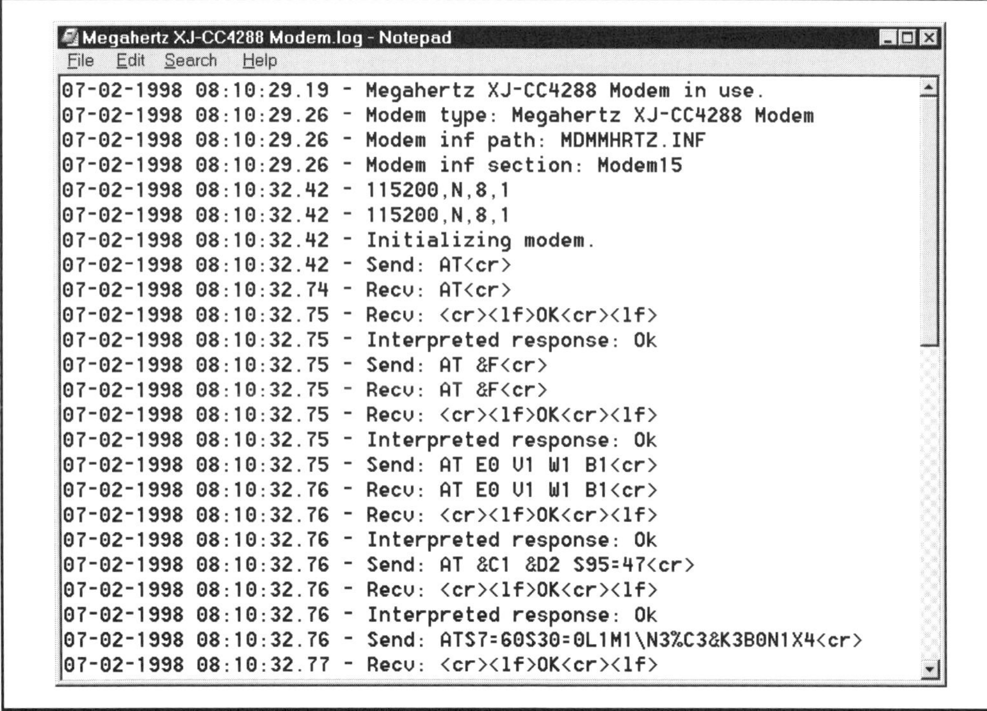

Figure 11-3. *The modem log shows the commands and responses exchanged between the modem and the computer*

that the remote host does not support. If the log file reports this problem, you can use the Extra Settings option to specify a command string to enable or disable V.42 bis or MNP protocols or enter specific S-register commands that change the handshaking signals that pass between the computer and the modem. Your modem manual should include a full list of the commands that the modem supports and suggestions for troubleshooting.

Third-Party Support for High-Speed Communications

Despite the improvements that have been made in the Windows 98 telecommunications features, there are still some limitations that may cramp the style of users with state-of-the-art hardware.

One limitation is Windows 98's lack of built-in support for DTE speeds above 115,200 bps. Some modem manufacturers now include special DTE-doubling firmware that supports a DTE rate of 230,000 bps. One of several competing Integrated Services Digital Network (ISDN) standards, for instance, features Hayes-compatible modems capable of supporting modem-to-modem connect rates higher than 115,200 bps and serial port speeds of 500,000 bps or more. High-speed I/O ports to accommodate these devices now use newer 16650 and 16750 UARTs that are not directly supported by Windows 98's communication drivers.

One company, Pacific Commware of Portland, Oregon, is already well known for its Windows port management packages. At this writing, Pacific Commware offers the Turbo-Express I/O card and Turbo Commander modem management program for Windows 95 and Windows 98. The Turbo-Express card, designed for ISDN modems like the IBM Windsurfer and Motorola Bitsurfer, uses a 16750 UART with twin-64 byte FIFO buffers. It can support DTE rates of 1,121,600 bps with Turbo Commander's Win98 communications drivers. Turbo Commander includes a module that replaces the standard Win98 serial port options, allowing you to fine-tune the performance of I/O ports with all standard UART types. A desktop display panel, shown in Figure 11-4, is used to control your modem and serial port settings and show the status of a current online connection. For more information about these products, visit the Pacific Commware Web site at http://www.turbocom.com.

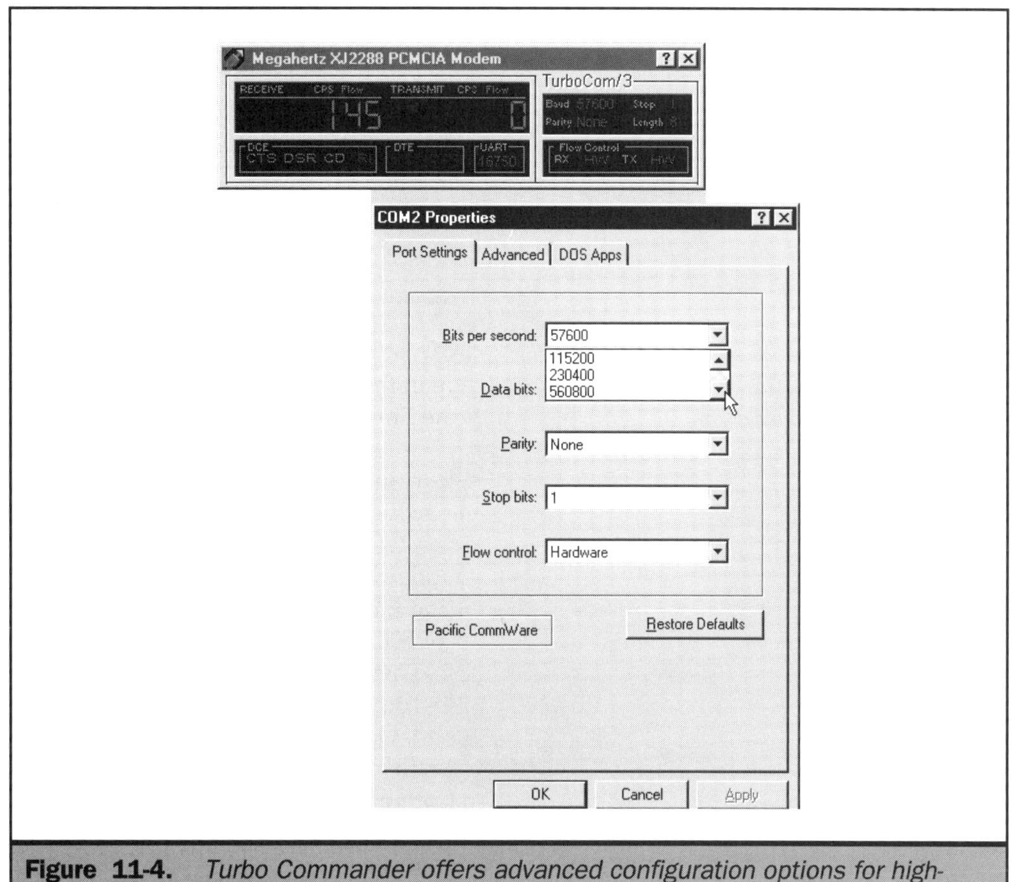

Figure 11-4. *Turbo Commander offers advanced configuration options for high-speed I/O ports*

Modem Troubleshooting Tips

If you're experiencing difficulty dialing out with a DOS or Windows communication program, you may want to try the following troubleshooting procedures:

- Open your communications package to a terminal screen. Type **AT** and press ENTER. If you don't see an OK prompt, check whether the serial port selected in the program corresponds to a port listed in the Modems applet with an attached modem. If the selected port does not show a modem connected, choose one that does, or try reinstalling the modem. If you have an external modem, make sure the cable connection is correct and the power is turned on.

- Type **ATDT** in the terminal screen and press ENTER. You should briefly hear a dial tone. (If you have a pulse-dial telephone system, type **ATDP** instead.) If you don't hear a dial tone, try locating and turning up the volume on your modem's speaker. If you still don't hear a dial tone, check to make sure the cable from the telephone jack is properly plugged into the modem. If you have a switchboard device attached to the line, try removing it and connecting the modem directly to the wall socket. If problems persist, your serial port or modem may not be configured correctly, or there may be a conflict with another peripheral on your system.
- Open the System component in the Control Panel and select the Device Manager tab. If you have a PCMCIA or internal modem, expand the modem listing (click the + sign on the folder) and select the modem you want to test. If you have an external modem, expand the Ports listing instead and select the port to which the modem is connected.
- Click the Properties button near the bottom of the dialog box. The General tab should display a device status message that reports whether the modem (or port) is working properly, as shown here. Select the Resources tab to display information on the port address and IRQ used by the modem.

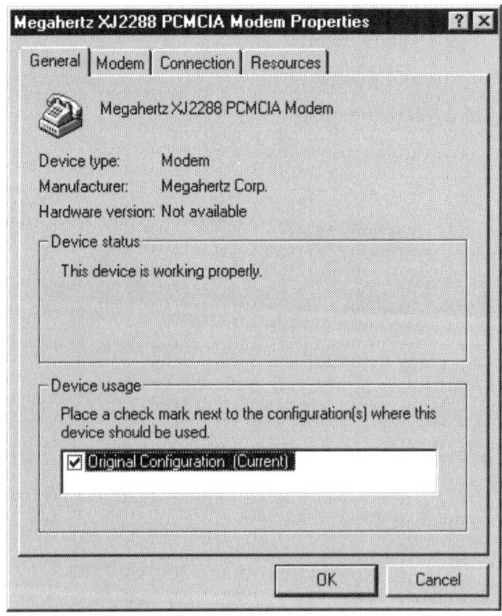

If the modem (or port) has been assigned a conflicting address or IRQ, you can change it. A typical problem with modems configured for COM3 or COM4 is that the port may be using an exotic system interrupt (such as IRQ 10 or IRQ 12). Windows 98 TAPI applications may work with this nonstandard IRQ, but your DOS and Windows 3.x programs will refuse to dial. If this is the case, you can try changing the interrupt used by the modem to a more common configuration, such as IRQ 3 or IRQ 5, that your older programs can recognize. Here's how:

1. On the Resources tab, deselect Use Automatic Settings.
2. Select the Interrupt Request resource type and click the Change Settings button.
3. If a message appears stating that the resource setting can't be modified, try selecting a different basic configuration in the Setting Based On scroll list and clicking the Change Settings button again.
4. Select an appropriate interrupt value in the Edit Interrupt Request dialog box. The Conflicting Device list on that screen will tell you whether the interrupt is available.
5. Click OK to close that screen and click OK again on the Resources tab to save the configuration.

If you want to change the port address instead of the IRQ, follow the procedure just outlined, but select Input/Output Range in the Resource Settings area of the Resources tab instead of Interrupt Request. To get an internal modem or serial I/O card to cooperate, you may also need to open your computer and physically change the jumper settings on the card.

If a DOS telecommunications application slows down or freezes when you run it in the background, open its Properties settings (right-click the icon and select Properties from the context menu) and select the Misc tab, as shown here. Make sure that the Background option Always Suspend is not selected and move the Idle Sensitivity slider on this screen all the way to Low. Click OK to save the new settings.

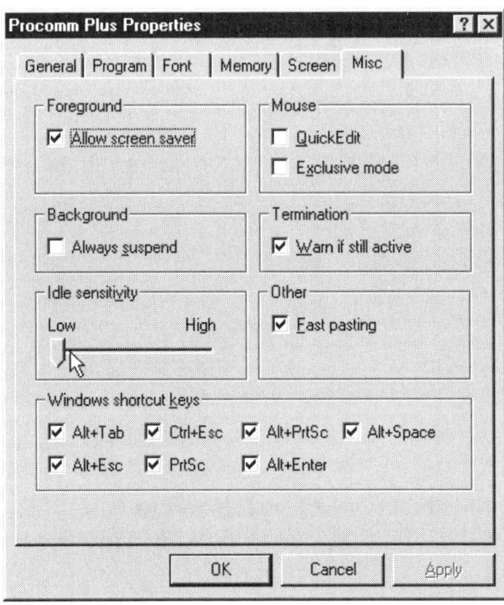

You'll find additional modem troubleshooting tips in the section "Modems and Dial-Up Networking" in Chapter 16.

Dial-Up Networking: Connecting Your Computer to the Internet

To connect to the Internet or a local area network with a modem and telephone line, Windows adds one more software layer called Dial-Up Networking (DUN). DUN is a type of utility called a Windows sockets interface (often shortened to Winsock) that sets up a TCP/IP link between Windows and a network host. Winsock presents a common set of hooks to different kinds of Internet applications, including Web browsers, e-mail clients, and Telnet clients. By connecting to the Internet through a Winsock interface, you can run many separate applications without the need to establish a separate connection for each one. If you expect to connect your computer to the Internet, you're going to need a Winsock program, and for a telephone connection, Dial-Up Networking is as good as any because it's built directly into Windows 98.

The Dial-Up Networking folder in Windows 98 contains a Make New Connection object that opens a wizard you can use to create a new connection profile. If you have access to the Internet through more than one service provider or through network hosts in several locations, you can create individual profiles for each service or location. Each connection profile that you establish can contain individual modem and port settings, network protocol information, Internet Protocol (IP) addresses, and login and password information. By specifying IP information in each profile, you can avoid conflicts with TCP/IP settings for a dedicated network.

To automate connections to Internet service providers and other network hosts that require nonstandard login procedures, each Dial-Up Networking profile includes a Scripting Properties sheet where you can specify a special login script for that connection. Microsoft supplies several sample scripts, with .SCP extensions, in the \PROGRAM FILES\ACCESSORIES folder. If your own ISP requires a special script, your provider will probably give you a copy on request.

There are two ways to use Dial-Up Networking to connect your computer to the Internet:

- Place a call to an ISP first and then start the Web browser or other Internet application you want to use.
- Start the application program and let it set up the link through your default DUN connection profile.

In practice, you can use either one of these methods on any given call. If you make the connection first, any Internet application you start will use the current connection, but if the computer is offline when an application looks for a connection, Dial-Up Networking will make the call through your default profile.

If you have just one DUN connection profile on your system, that profile will obviously be the default. If you have accounts with more than one ISP, or different connection profiles for the same ISP (for example, if you have different dial-in numbers for home and office on your laptop computer), you can set the default by following these steps:

1. From the desktop, right-click the Internet Explorer icon or choose Internet on the Control Panel.
2. Select the Connection tab. For a dial-up connection, select Connect To The Internet Using A Modem option. Click the Settings button to open the dialog box shown in Figure 11-5.
3. In the Use The Following Dial-Up Connection field, choose the DUN profile that you want to set as the default. Your username and password for this profile should appear automatically.
4. If you want, you can customize the number of dialing attempts that DUN makes to establish your connection and the number of seconds between each attempt by modifying the specified defaults on this screen.
5. If you want Internet Explorer to dial your ISP automatically for Web subscription updates, place a check mark in the Connect Automatically to Update Subscriptions box near the bottom of the Properties screen.

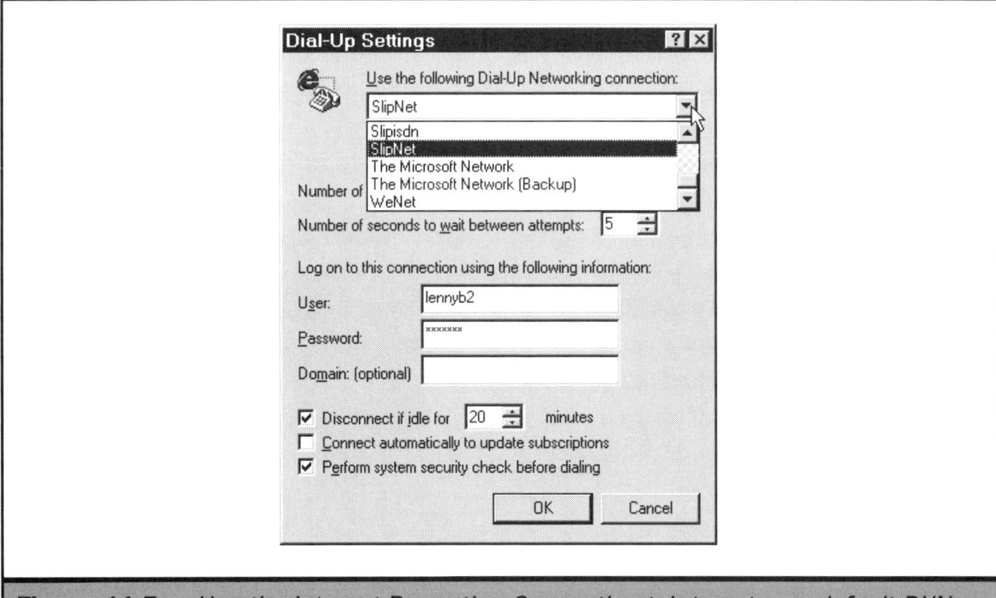

Figure 11-5. *Use the Internet Properties Connection tab to set your default DUN connection profile*

Setting Up SLIP and PPP Dialing Profiles

Once the Dial-Up Networking folder is installed in your Accessories group, you can open it and create connection profiles that will allow you to dial into the Internet or connect to a dedicated LAN through your modem. You can also use Dial-Up Networking to connect to the shared drives, printers, or other resources of a remote computer over the Internet. For information on how to do this, see "Remote Network Connections" in Chapter 14.

Creating a Connection Profile Using the DUN Folder

In addition to using the Internet Connection Wizard to configure a dial-up Internet account, you can create a new dial-up profile by clicking the Make New Connection icon in the DUN folder.

1. Open Dial-Up Networking by selecting it from the Accessories folder on the Start menu.
2. After the Dial-Up Networking folder opens, double-click the Make New Connection icon or select Make New Connection from the Connections pull-down menu.
3. Choose a modem to use, type a name for the connection, and click the Next button. If no modem is currently installed, the Modem Installation Wizard will start automatically and allow you to configure one.
4. On the next screen, enter the area code and telephone number for your Internet service provider. If you're setting up a dial-in connection to a network server, enter the appropriate telephone number to connect to that computer. Click Next.
5. Click the Finish button. A new connection profile icon will appear in the Dial-Up Networking folder.
6. Right-click the connection profile and select Properties to open the profile's connection option.
7. Select the Server Types tab and choose PPP or SLIP UNIX Connection, as appropriate for your Internet account. Toward the bottom of the dialog box, under Allowed Network Protocols, make sure that TCP/IP is checked.
8. Click the TCP/IP Settings button toward the bottom of the Server Types dialog box. This opens the TCP/IP Settings box. Fill in the information in this box with the appropriate information supplied by your Internet service provider. Typically, you'll want to select Server Assigned IP Address and Specify Name Server Address. In the Specify Name Server section, enter at least the IP address for the name server supplied by your Internet provider. Note that you can configure more than one connection profile, specifying different domain naming system (DNS) and Windows Internet Naming Service (WINS) addresses in each. You'll find more information about WINS in the section "Remote Network Connections" in Chapter 14.

9. Click OK twice to close the dialog box and once more to close the configuration window.

Now you're ready to double-click the connection profile and dial into the Internet.

Setting Network Options

If you plan to connect to the Internet through a modem, you should probably not tamper with the TCP/IP options set on the Network object on the Control Panel. Some ISPs make the mistake of advising you to enter ISP information in this series of dialog boxes. Although entering ISP information through the Network applet does allow an Internet connection, this feature was not intended to contain dial-up ISP data; it was designed to contain TCP/IP information for a dedicated TCP/IP network.

Entering ISP information directly through the Network applet can interfere with a connection to a dedicated local area network (LAN). It also slows up the performance of some Internet mail clients, causing them to pause on opening for as much as three minutes while they search for a nonexistent TCP/IP cable connection. The bottom line is that you should enter TCP/IP information for a network adapter through the Network TCP/IP Properties screen, and you should enter information for your dial-up Internet connections in the individual Dial-Up Networking service profiles, as just described.

Making the Connection

To make the connection to the Internet, double-click the connection profile you just created (in the Dial-Up Networking folder). Make sure your Internet username, password, and telephone number are correct (in the Connect To dialog box). Click the Connect button, sit back, and listen to your modem.

At this point, the Dial-Up Networking Adapter will call your service provider. If login succeeds, you'll see a small dialog box showing the speed of your connection. You can then run any third-party Internet tool, such as Netscape, Eudora, or WS_FTP. For more information on setting up and using third-party Windows Internet tools, see Chapter 13.

To reduce the amount of time needed to make a Dial-Up Networking connection, you can change some universal DUN settings:

1. Open the Dial-Up Networking window from the Start menu, My Computer, or Windows Explorer.
2. On the Connections menu, select Settings to open the Dial-Up Networking Properties sheet.
3. In the When Establishing a Dial-Up Connection box at the top of the dialog box, remove the check marks from the Prompt for Information before Dialing and Show a Confirmation Dialog options.
4. Place a check mark in the Redial option box and set the Retry field to five times with no waiting time between tries.

Setting Up Multiple Service Profiles

You can set up connection profiles for more than one service. For example, you may want one for a Windows NT network, one for an Internet account, one for Windows for Workgroups, and so forth. To make multiple connection profiles work, add the IP addresses and required protocol information to each individual profile

Logging into Special Internet Accounts

Some Internet service providers do not support the standard password authentication protocol (PAP) that provides automatic connection through Dial-Up Networking. The CompuServe information service is one example. Accounts with these providers may require special login commands before a connection can be established.

Windows 98 allows you to display a terminal window to enter custom login commands. You also have the option of entering these commands through a simple dial-up scripting tool described in the next section.

To allow manual entry of login commands, do the following:

1. After choosing your modem (step 3 in "Creating a Connection Profile Using the DUN Folder" earlier in this chapter), click the Configure button next to the modem list. If you've already created your connection profile, right-click it and select Properties to access the Configure button.
2. Select the Options tab in the Properties dialog box.
3. Place a check mark in the Bring Up Terminal Window After Dialing box, as shown here:

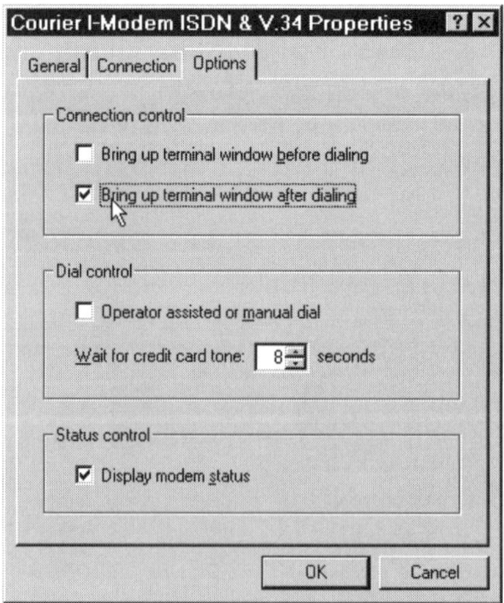

Now, after Dial-Up Networking connects you to your service provider, a terminal window pops up, allowing you to type in your username, password, and any additional necessary information. After entering all necessary login information, click the Continue button in the Terminal window to let the connection procedure continue.

Dial-Up Scripting

The Dial-Up Scripting package can automate login procedures for third-party service providers. Dial-Up Scripting contains a number of sample login scripts, including one for PPP access to CompuServe. To associate a login script with a Dial-Up Networking connection profile, open the profile's properties and select the Scripting tab. Click the Browse button to load an existing script (.SCP file), or enter a filename and click the Edit button to create a new script in Notepad.

Working with the Script Language

To see a complete list of the commands in the script language, refer to SCRIPT.DOC, located in the \WINDOWS directory.

The following is an example of a simple script that will automatically log you onto an Internet account. It requires the use of TIA emulation software to establish a SLIP connection.

```
proc main
 transmit "^M"
 delay 2
 waitfor "login:"
 transmit $USERID
 transmit "^M"
 waitfor "Password:"
 transmit $PASSWORD
 transmit "^M"
 waitfor ">"
 transmit "tia^m"
endproc
```

Other Dial-Up Networking Tricks

Dial-Up Networking can be used to dial into a Novell NetWare or Windows NT server. (Keep in mind that if you use Dial-Up Networking to access NetWare resources, you can access data remotely, but you cannot control another computer remotely. For that, you need Novell's NetWare Connect client software.)

To access the Microsoft client for NetWare, file and printer services for NetWare, or IPX-SPX-compatible protocols, you'll have to install these through the Network applet in the Control Panel folder (see Chapter 5 for details). To specify the appropriate server type, right-click the dialing profile, open its property sheet, click the Server Type tab, and choose the correct server from the Dial-Up Server Type drop-down list.

If you use the Dial-Up Networking utility to access remote network drives, you can automatically reestablish a connection whenever you click a network drive: Choose Settings from the Connections menu in the Dial-Up Networking folder and select Don't Prompt to Use Dial-Up Networking.

Faster Connections

Somebody once said, "You can't ever be too rich or too thin." For those of us who use the Internet and other online communication, this saying could be changed to "You can't ever have too much bandwidth." Moving digital computer data across a telephone line that was designed a hundred years ago to handle analog speech is, at best, a compromise. While it's true that today's 33.6 or 56 Kbps modems are a great deal faster and more reliable than the 300 and 1200 bps modems that were common just a few years ago, the size of the data files that most people want to move around has grown even faster. Full-color pictures, animations, audio clips, and full-motion video are all quite common today, and they all require huge data files. As a result, when you connect to the Internet through a modem and telephone line, you're still likely to spend a lot of your time waiting for Web pages and files to download.

The solution to this problem is simple: pump your data through a faster connection to the Internet. If you have unlimited money to spend, you can simply call your local telephone company and order a dedicated high-speed network connection to your ISP, but that's not practical for most individuals and small businesses. The alternative is to use one of the new technologies that have appeared in the last couple of years: ISDN, DSL, cable modems, satellites, or wireless spread-spectrum links.

It's far from clear which of these alphabet soup solutions will ultimately emerge as the information utility that comes into your house or office alongside today's electricity, natural gas, telephone, and cable TV services. Many large corporations and investors are betting vast fortunes on one or another of these services—but you can be pretty certain that at least one will be available in most urban and suburban locations in North America within the next year or two. Fortunately, Windows 98 includes support for all of them.

ISDN

Integrated Services Digital Network (ISDN) is the oldest and most widely available digital data service. It comes in two forms: BRI and PRI.

Basic Rate Interface (BRI) includes two 64-Kbps data channels (called B channels) and one 16-Kbps D channel (used for administrative purposes).

Primary Rate Interface (PRI) includes twenty-three 64-Kbps channels and one 16-Kbps channel. (In Europe, PRI service has thirty 64-Kbps channels.) Each B channel can carry a separate voice or data signal; or multiple channels can be combined for a single faster connection. For most home and small office users looking for fast Internet

About Bits, Bytes, Baud, Throughput, and Data Compression

The terms bits, bytes, baud, throughput, and data compression are thrown around casually when people attempt to rate modem performance. What do they mean?

Kbps (note the lowercase "b") means kilobits per second, and KBps (note the capital "B") means kilobytes per second. A byte transferred through a modem contains eight bits of data, plus two control bits, which equals 10 bits, or 1 byte (1,000 kilobits = 1 kilobyte).

Modems are generally rated by their top external connection speed (the rate at which they connect to another modem over a telephone line) in kilobits per second: 14.4 Kbps, 28.8 Kbps, 33.6 Kbps, and so on. However, the connection speed reported by your communication programs is often provided in bits per second: 14,400 bps, 28,000 bps, 33,600 bps, and so on. If the connection rate reported by your software is higher than these values (for instance, 57,600 or 115,200 bps), the modem has been configured to report its internal transfer speed to the serial port rather than the connection rate to the other modem through the phone line.

Data file transfer rates (such as the performance of an Internet FTP program) are sometimes reported in kilobytes per second: 2.1 KBps, 4.0 KBps, and so on. This rate is referred to as throughput.

The term baud is used to measure a modem's signaling rate: the number of symbols per second it can send or receive. In the ancient days of personal computing, one symbol could contain only one bit of data, so baud rate was equivalent to Kbps. Now, however, one transmitted symbol may contain multiple bits of information. The term baud now is less useful in measuring a modem's performance, but here is a more useful equivalent: One ASCII character usually occupies one byte of data space. Thus, data flow measured in characters per second (cps) is about the same as data flow measured in kilobytes per second (KBps).

Modems that comply with the international v.34 design specification all have a built-in capability to compress data before transmitting it (much like the PKZIP archive program compresses files on your hard disk). Compression speeds up reception of files by the modem on the other end of a connection. The compression standard used by v.34 modems is referred to as v.42BIS.

service, BRI is the only kind of ISDN that makes any sense; other types of digital data service can supply connections comparable to PRI for less money.

To use ISDN, you need these resources:

- **Internet service from your ISP** A growing number of ISPs and online information services offer ISDN service at a somewhat higher cost than their standard dial-in Internet access. Your ISP, especially if it's a local or regional service rather than a national organization, will know if reliable ISDN service is available at your location. Your ISP may also have some suggestions about ISDN adapters and NT-1 interface units that work reliably with the local telephone company's ISDN lines.

- **An ISDN connection from the telephone company** The regional Bell operating companies, GTE, and many other telephone companies offer ISDN service, but many of them have trouble delivering everything they promise on time and without technical difficulties. That's why it's important to talk to your ISP's technical people before you call the telephone company.
- **An internal or external ISDN adapter** Although an ISDN adapter does different things than a conventional modem, you may find it convenient to think of your ISDN adapter as an ISDN modem. ISDN adapters are sold both with and without the compatible Hayes AT interface that permits them to double as ordinary modems, and they are available as either internal plug-in expansion cards or external devices that connect to your computer through a serial or parallel port. In most cases, an internal device will deliver faster data transfer. However, it may be a bit trickier to install and configure.
- **A Network Termination 1 (NT-1) interface device** The telephone company delivers ISDN service to your house or office on a single pair of copper wires, but the ISDN adapter and any other ISDN equipment (such as a telephone set) requires two pairs of wires. The interface that converts the signal between two-wire and four-wire is called NT-1. Many ISDN adapters include a built-in NT-1 interface.

Although an ISDN BRI connection can replace your existing "plain old telephone service" (POTS) line and at the same time provide a faster Internet connection, it requires a source of local AC power. Therefore, substituting an ISDN line for your regular telephone connection may not be a good idea. In the event of a power failure, an ISDN telephone will go dead, preventing you from calling the electric company or any other emergency service. You should always have at least one old-fashioned POTS line in addition to any ISDN connections.

Configuring Windows 98 for ISDN

Windows 98 supports ISDN network connections through the Dial-Up Networking feature. If you've selected an external ISDN modem, such as the 3COM/USR Courier I-Modem, its installation is very similar to the installation for a conventional modem. Connect the cable interface between the external ISDN device and your serial or parallel port. Then open the Control Panel | Modems applet and click the Add button. Windows 98 will detect the ISDN device automatically or present you with a list of drivers to choose from. If you have a vendor-supplied disk, you can click the Have Disk button on the Install New Modem screen and point Windows 98 to your third-party drivers.

You may also need to initialize your ISDN modem with vendor-supplied software to enter the service profile identifier (SPID) that identifies your account and to select the correct switch interface for your local telephone company. For information on how to specify these options, you should consult both your Internet service provider and your local telephone company.

To install an internal ISDN adapter, follow these steps:

1. Install the ISDN adapter in an expansion slot on your computer.
2. Turn on your computer. When the Windows 98 desktop appears, open the Network object in the Control Panel.
3. If you're installing a plug-and-play adapter, Windows will automatically install it for you. Otherwise, open the ISDN Configuration Wizard in the Accessories | Communications group. To answer the questions on the wizard screens, you will need to obtain the name of the switch protocol from the telephone company, and you will need to obtain the telephone numbers and SPID from your ISP.

You'll find more information about using the ISDN Configuration Wizard in Chapter 5. For more information about ISDN under Windows 98, see the Microsoft Web site at http://www.microsoft.com/windows/getisdn/.

Tricks with ISDN Modems

If your modem is connecting at 56K or less instead of using the full 64K per channel ISDN bandwidth, check the phone number in your dial-up settings. Be sure to dial the full telephone number: area code + seven-digit local number, even if the number is in your local calling area. This routes the connection through your long-distance carrier and ensures that you get the maximum possible connection speed.

USING YOUR ISDN MODEM TO MAKE ANALOG CALLS If you have an ISDN terminal adapter that supports the traditional Hayes command set, you can use it to dial ordinary analog ISP or bulletin board numbers. However, if you try this with the default configuration, it probably won't work. The reason is that the ISDN device uses one initialization string to make a digital call and another to make an analog call.

You could go into the dial-up settings for the modem and change the Hayes initialization string each time you want to switch from digital to analog, but there's a better way to solve the problem. Windows 98 allows you to create multiple modem profiles for the same physical device. For example, suppose you have a U.S. Robotics Courier I-Modem configured to make digital ISDN calls. You can add a second profile for the device to make analog calls, as follows:

1. Open the Modems Applet on the Control Panel and click the Add button. Select Other in response to the question "What type of modem do you want to install?"

2. Click Next and place a check mark next to Don't Detect My Modem, I Will Select It from a List on the next screen.
3. Click Next and select your modem manufacturer and model in the Manufacturers list. (Select Have Disk if you have a custom OEM driver.)
4. On the next screen, select the same communication port that the first copy of the modem profile uses. Then click the Finish button.
5. The new modem profile will appear in the modem list with the same name as the old profile, followed by a number: for example, Courier I-Modem with ISDN & V.34, #2. Select this profile and click the Properties button. Select the Connections tab in the Properties window and click the Advanced button.
6. In the Extra Settings field, enter the correct Hayes command string to convert your ISDN terminal adapter into an analog device. (Consult your documentation to find the string. For the Courier I-Modem, the string is *V2=3.)
7. Close the dialog box.

To make analog calls with your ISDN device, you can now select the #2 modem profile you've just created make it the default modem in your Dial-Up Networking or HyperTerminal connection profile. Use the #2 profile to call analog numbers and continue to use the original profile to make digital and ISDN connections.

Note that this same trick lets a fax-enabled ISDN terminal adapter use Microsoft Fax without interfering with the digital configuration: Open Inbox properties, select Microsoft Fax, display its Properties screen, select the Modems tab, and select the #2 profile in the Available Fax Modems list.

DSL and ADSL

Digital Subscriber Line (DSL) service is another network connection method that uses standard copper wires to provide high-speed network connection. Various forms of DSL connection can deliver data transfer speeds from 500 Kbps to several megabytes per second. In other words, a huge file transfer that might take many hours through a 28,800 bps modem could be completed with DSL in just a few minutes—or less.

Asymmetric Digital Subscriber Line (ADSL) service uses the same kind of circuit as DSL, but it handles the inbound and outbound signals differently. On the assumption that many users need more speed to download files and Web pages than they need to upload commands, an ADSL connection can deliver downstream data at 1.5 to as much as 8 megabytes per second. However, it may send upstream data at only 32 or 64 kbps.

Another variation on DSL is Rate Adaptive Asymmetric Digital Subscriber Line (RADSL) service. With RADSL, your telephone company and ISP can reduce the bandwidth of your downstream connection, charging accordingly. RADSL can also be used to extend the viable distance between your home or office and the telephone company's central office.

A DSL connection requires a special DSL (or ADSL or RADSL) modem connected to your computer and a second modem in the telephone company's central office. The telephone company's modem shifts the data signal away from the public voice telephone network to a separate digital network. An ADSL circuit includes a high-speed downstream channel, a high- or medium-speed upstream channel, and a voice channel for conventional telephone calls. Several telephone companies are just beginning to offer ADSL and RADSL service to customers located within a mile or two of selected central offices. Complementary Internet access service with DSL, ADSL, or RADSL is available from the telephone companies' own ISPs and other local ISPs.

Windows 98 handles ADSL modems just like other modems, but at higher bandwidth. Most ADSL modems will probably be plug-and-play devices. If yours is not, open the Control Panel and use the Add New Hardware Wizard to load the driver.

Cable Modems

The telephone companies aren't the only ones who smell big money in the demand for high-speed access to the Internet. Several major cable TV systems are also in the marketplace. Services such as @Home offer connections in the 1.5 to 3 megabyte per second range. As cable modem service becomes available in your neighborhood, you can expect the cable TV companies to let you know about it.

When you subscribe to cable modem service, the service provider supplies the special modem you need along with the connection to your house or office. If the driver required for your modem is not included in Windows 98, your cable company will provide it. To install the modem and connection, run Add New Hardware. When that process is complete, choose Dial-Up Networking and run the Make New Connection Wizard. On the first screen of the wizard, use the drop-down Select a Device menu to specify your cable modem.

Wireless and Satellite Internet Access

Several other Internet access technologies are on the horizon (or, in the case of satellite service, beyond it). Within the next five years you can expect to see several new Internet services that involve low-orbit earth satellites and wireless spread-spectrum radio links. These connections are not yet available except on a very limited basis. They use external radio transceivers that connect to a network interface card in the computer. In most cases, these wireless services look to Windows 98 just like connections to a local area network.

Using HyperTerminal

HyperTerminal is a terminal emulator program for connection to a remote computer through either a dial-up telephone connection or a TCP/IP Telnet connection. HyperTerminal can also be used to establish a local computer-to-computer connection through a serial cable that links the two machines. HyperTerminal is useful for communicating with bulletin board services, library catalogs, and other host computers that accept input from remote terminals. It can also be used as a file transfer utility between two computers or as a direct link to a minicomputer or mainframe system.

HyperTerminal is automatically installed during a typical Windows 98 installation or standard upgrade from Windows 95. If you don't find it on the Accessories | Communications menu, you can add it through the Control Panel | Add/Remove Programs applet. (Choose the Communications group on the Windows Setup tab.)

Setting Up a Connection

HyperTerminal uses a separate connection file for each host that you call. As a result, it's easy to create a direct shortcut to each host on your desktop or Start menu. To create a new connection file, follow these steps:

1. Open the HyperTerminal folder from the Start | Programs menu by choosing Accessories | Communications | HyperTerminal.
2. Double-click the HYPERTRM.EXE icon to start the program.
3. When the Connection Description window, shown in Figure 11-6, opens, type the name of the host you want to call and choose an icon. Then click OK.
4. In the Connect To dialog box, shown in Figure 11-7, type the telephone number of the host you want to call. If the host's telephone number has a different area code from yours, type the area code in the Area Code field.

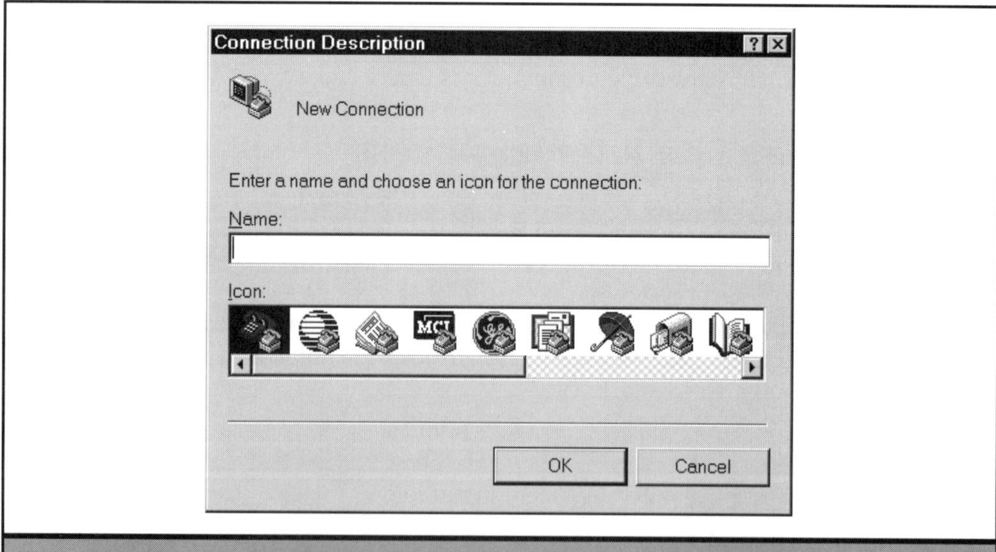

Figure 11-6. *Use the Connection Description window to identify a connection profile*

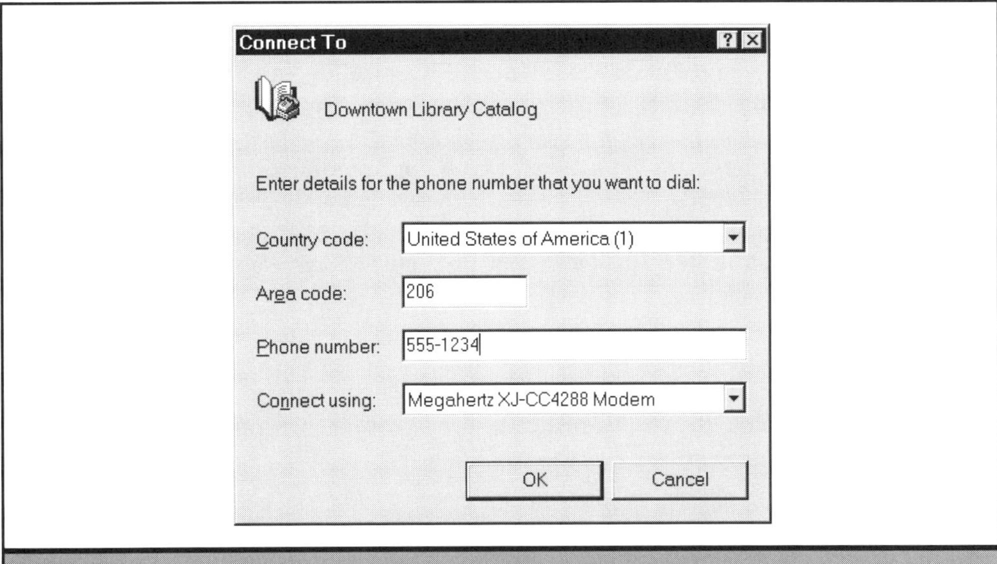

Figure 11-7. *Use the Connect To dialog box to specify the host's telephone number*

5. If you're setting up a Telnet link rather than a connection through a dial-out telephone call, open the drop-down Connect Using menu and select TCP/IP (Winsock). Type the host's Telnet address (such as **library.university.edu** or **well.com**) in the Host Address field. Don't change the port number unless the host's owner has instructed you to use a special port number.
6. If you're using HyperTerminal to connect directly to another computer through a cable, choose the option in the Connect Using menu that identifies the serial port you're using on this computer. Remember to use a null modem cable to connect the two computers.
7. Click OK. HyperTerminal will either display the Connect dialog box (where you can confirm or change the dialing information), or it will set up the Telnet connection.
8. At the end of your data exchange, when you shut down HyperTerminal, the program will ask, "Do You Want to Save Session *Name*?" Answer Yes to store a new connection file in the HyperTerminal folder or No to discard this connection profile.
9. If you expect to call this host frequently, right-click the new icon in the HyperTerminal folder and select Create Shortcut. Drag the shortcut to your desktop or Start menu.

Communicating with a Host

After you have created a connection file for a host computer, you can place a call to that host by double-clicking the file in the HyperTerminal folder or using a shortcut you create to the file.

When the connection is made, either through your modem or through the Internet, the remote computer will send you a welcome message like the one in Figure 11-8. At this point, you're connected directly to the host, which treats your computer as a data-entry terminal. Any characters you type on your keyboard go directly to the host, which echoes them back to your screen. The fact that you see text as you type it tells you that the connection is in place and working properly.

In most cases, you will have to type your login name and password before the host will accept any other commands. Some public systems don't require a password or will tell you how to log on in the welcome message. Many others assume that if you don't know how to log on, you have no business using this computer, which seems like a perfectly reasonable attitude.

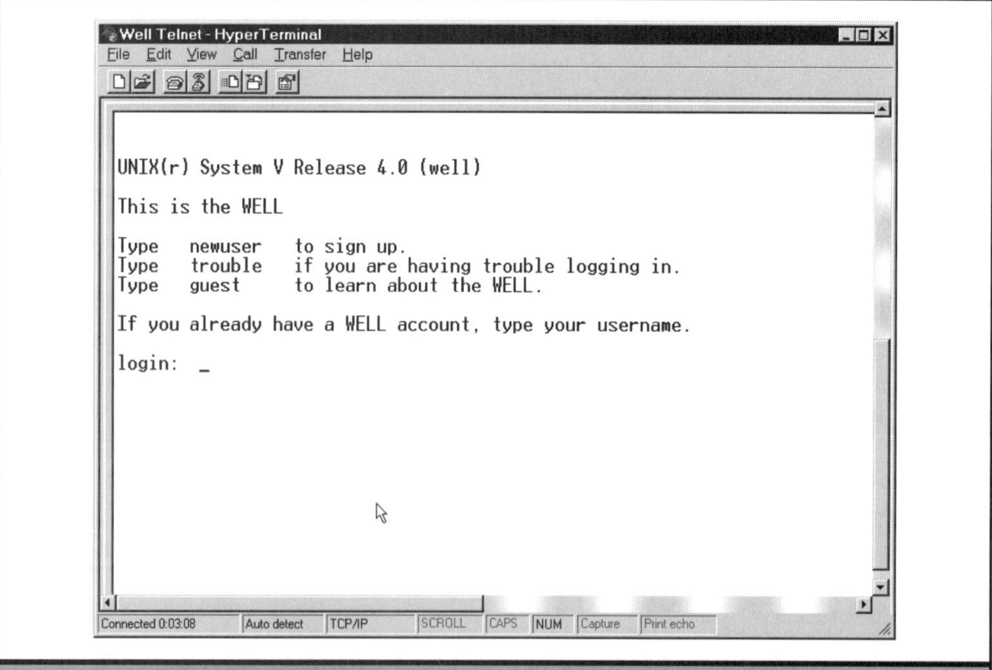

Figure 11-8. *HyperTerminal can be used as a Client terminal for Telnet or modem-to-modem connections*

The HyperTerminal Toolbar

The HyperTerminal toolbar contains most of the commands you're likely to use during a connection session:

- **New** The New command starts the process of creating a new connection file.
- **Open** The Open command opens the specified connection file and connects you to the host specified by that file.
- **Call** The Call command places a call to the host specified in the current connection file.
- **Disconnect** The Disconnect command closes the currently open connection.
- **Send** The Send command opens the Send File dialog box, where you can specify a file for transfer to the host computer using the protocol named in the Protocol field. Both your computer and the host must support the protocol you use for a file transfer. If the host can handle it, your best choice is usually Zmodem with crash recovery, since this protocol can pick up where it left off if a connection fails part way through a file transfer. Zmodem (with or without crash recovery) is also the only option that doesn't require the operator of the receiving computer to enter a receive command. When the distant machine receives the Zmodem handshake signal, it usually will start receiving the file automatically. If the host can't accept a Zmodem transfer, you can try Kermit, which is often more tolerant of noisy lines than any of the other protocols.
- **Receive** The Receive command instructs HyperTerminal to accept an inbound file transfer from the host. The Receive File dialog box specifies the folder where HyperTerminal will store this file and the protocol it will use to accept the file. As with the Send command, Zmodem with crash recovery is your best protocol choice if the host computer supports it.
- **Properties** The Properties command opens a properties sheet for the current connection file. The Connect To tab displays the address or telephone number of the host. The Settings tab controls the way HyperTerminal sends and receives certain keystrokes. It also identifies the type of terminal emulation HyperTerminal will use with this host. Most hosts accept either ANSI emulation or VT100 emulation. If the host uses something else, you should see that information in the welcome message that appears when you connect to the host.

Configuration Options

The View | Font command on the HyperTerminal pull-down menu controls the typeface that HyperTerminal uses to display text received from the host. As the size of the typeface changes, the size of the terminal window expands and contracts to accommodate it. You may want to spend some time experimenting with different fonts, styles, and sizes until you find the combination that you find easiest to read.

The Font setting controls the screen font but not the font that HyperTerminal uses when you print text. To change the print font, select File | Page Setup and click the Font button at the bottom of the window.

While you have the Page Setup window open, you should change the margins. For some reason, by default HyperTerminal prints with no margins at all, resulting in printouts that look terrible. In fact, if you use the default HyperTerminal settings, the half-inch margin forced by many laser printers will cause some of your text to completely disappear off the printed page. Therefore, you should set each of the four margins on HyperTerminal's Page Setup screen to at least 0.5 inch.

Storing Text and Data from the Host

HyperTerminal offers several ways to store copies of the text you see on your screen. The Transfer | Capture Text command sends a copy of everything that comes into HyperTerminal to a text file as it is received. If you want to save text from the host to a file after it has already been received, move your cursor to the beginning of the text you want to save and then drag to the end of the text you want to select (or use the Edit | Select All command). Use Edit | Copy (or choose Copy from the right-click context menu) to move the selected text to the Windows clipboard. From the clipboard, you can transfer the text to Notepad, WordPad, or any other Windows application program.

The Transfer | Capture to Printer command sends copies of everything to your printer as HyperTerminal receives it. If you have an impact printer, each line will print as it arrives at the printer, but if you're using an inkjet or laser printer, the printer will hold text in a buffer until it has a full page and then print the whole page.

Using Windows Messaging

Windows Messaging was the e-mail, fax, and miscellaneous messaging client program in Windows 95. (In the "classic" version of Windows 95, it was referred to as Microsoft Exchange; in fact, this name is still used in some dialog boxes to refer to the program.) Windows Messaging is replaced in Windows 98 by Outlook Express. Outlook Express is a much better Internet e-mail client than Windows Messaging, but it lacks one very important feature: support for Microsoft's Messaging Applications Program Interface (MAPI) standard. Compliance with MAPI permits other Windows 95 and 98 applications to use Windows Messaging as a front end. For instance, as mentioned earlier, Windows Messaging supports both Microsoft Fax and Intranet mail sent from a dedicated Microsoft Mail Post Office. It can also cooperate with the mail transport facility built into Netscape Navigator.

Microsoft includes both Windows Messaging and Microsoft Fax on the Windows 98 CD-ROM as add-in modules. If you're upgrading from Windows 95, the Messaging and Fax programs will remain in place; if you want to install them on a new system, you can find them on the CD-ROM in the \TOOLS\OLDWIN95\MESSAGE\US folder. To install Windows Messaging, run the WMS.EXE program and follow the prompts to install the client and Microsoft Mail Post Office.

Unfortunately, the version of Windows Messaging bundled on the Windows 98 CD does not include the same support as earlier versions that allowed users to send and receive Internet mail through a standard SMTP/POP3 Internet service provider. If you had Windows Messaging installed under Windows 95 before upgrading to Windows 98, this support continues to be available. If you perform a fresh installation of Windows Messaging under Windows 98, it does not appear.

Microsoft has decided that Windows 98 users don't really need the Internet mail transport formerly built into Windows Messaging because they can use Outlook Express instead. However, if you feel this service is important, you can include the full functionality of Windows Messaging Services in a new Windows 98 installation as follows:

1. Run WMS.EXE from the Windows 98 CD, as described earlier, to install Windows Messaging with Microsoft Mail support.
2. If you want to add Microsoft Fax support, run the AWFAX program in the same folder.
3. Go to the Microsoft Web site and download a copy of the Windows Messaging Update for Windows 95. Currently, you'll find this at http://www.microsoft.com/windows/downloads/bin/w95exupdusa.exe. If you enter this download area from another area of the Web site, you can ignore the warning that this file is intended only for Windows 95 users.
4. Run the W95EXUPDUSA.EXE file that you've downloaded and select Reinstall from the menu. This will overwrite the files that have eliminated Internet Mail support, while retaining the Microsoft Mail and Fax features.

Note that Microsoft did not intend the W95EXUPDUSA.EXE upgrade to be installed in this way under Windows 98, but to this date, I've found no problems in using it to restore Internet Mail functionality to Windows Messaging.

Windows Messaging Profiles

Windows Messaging (the Inbox icon on your desktop) can support Internet mail, Microsoft Fax, The Microsoft Network online service, Microsoft Mail Post Office services, and other mail features added by third-party vendors.

When you first install Windows Messaging, the Setup Wizard steps you through the creation of a default profile. You can also start this process by opening the Inbox icon on the desktop. To create your initial profile, select the services you want to install on the Inbox Setup Wizard screen, as shown here:

A good selection strategy is to check the services you'll use most commonly for your default profile and then create additional profiles for the services you'll access less frequently. Your default profile should probably include Microsoft Mail and Microsoft Fax. You may want to create a separate profile exclusively for Internet Mail if you plan to use Windows Messaging rather than Outlook Express as your ISP mail client. Windows Messaging can be configured to select this profile when you open the Inbox or send and receive Fax mail.

You can also include all of the information services in one profile, but this will cause Windows Messaging to consume more memory and possibly run a bit more slowly.

After you choose the information services to include in your new Windows Messaging profile, you'll be prompted to enter a profile name. You may want to specify a name that describes the profile contents, such as "Network Mail and Fax," or "Internet Mail."

The Setup Wizard will now ask you to enter configuration information for each of the services you decided to install.

FAX To install the Fax service, choose a modem. If no modem is installed, you can add one at this point by clicking the Add button. Next, decide whether you want the fax/modem to answer all incoming calls while Inbox is open on the desktop. On the next screen, shown next, enter your name, calling area information, and telephone number. The final screen prompts you to choose a path to the Personal Information Store (.PST file) that will store your fax messages.

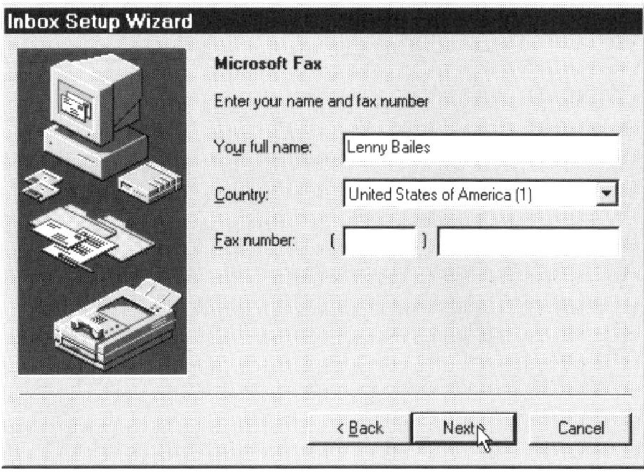

MICROSOFT MAIL If you select Microsoft Mail, the first screen asks you for the location of your Microsoft Mail Post Office. If you don't know, or if you haven't installed one, you must still enter something in this box. If you don't have a post office, enter the path to your \WINDOWS directory and click Next. The next screen will tell you there's no post office in that directory; you can ignore this and click Next again to continue. To create a new Microsoft Mail Post Office on your local computer, you'll need to take time out from the Windows Messaging configuration to run the Microsoft Mail Post Office application that WMS.EXE installs in the Windows 98 Control Panel. Once the Post Office has been created, you can point the Microsoft Mail setup in Windows Messaging to the proper location.

The next screen requests the name of your mailbox and your password. This information should be available from your network administrator. If you don't know the mailbox name and password or are just testing this feature, enter your own name and the word **password**. You can change this information later. If you are connecting to an existing Microsoft Mail Post Office, you can choose a username from the accounts that have already been set up, as shown here:

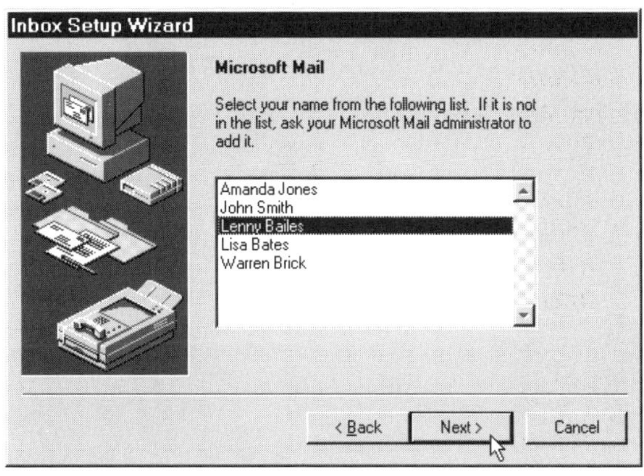

INTERNET MAIL If you migrated from Windows 95 or followed the procedure outlined earlier in this section, the Internet Mail service will be available. The first screen asks whether you want to connect to the Internet through a modem or via a direct TCP/IP network connection. For dial-up Internet access, choose the Modem option. For connection through a dedicated network, choose the Network option.

If you choose the Modem option, you'll be asked to specify a dial-up connection for your Internet service provider. Select a Dial-Up Networking connection profile that you've previously created. If you are using the Microsoft Network as your Internet service provider, choose that connection. (If you haven't already configured an Internet connection profile under Dial-Up Networking, you can do so now by clicking the New button. See the Dial-Up Networking sections in this chapter and in Chapter 5 for information on how to do this.)

The next screen asks you for the name of your Internet mail server. You can enter a site and domain name, or you can enter an IP address, as shown here. Consult your Internet service provider to obtain this information. Some examples of entries on this screen are mail.slip.net and 149.174.211.5.

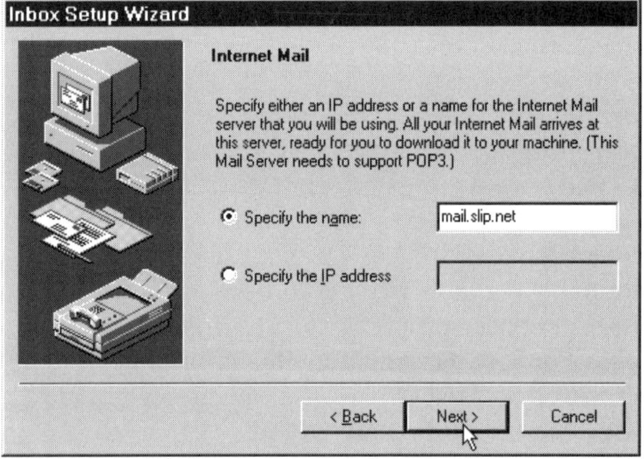

Next, decide whether you want to preview your Internet mail offline before downloading it or automatically download all of your Internet mail to the Inbox. Click Next again and enter your name and e-mail address on the next screen, as shown here:

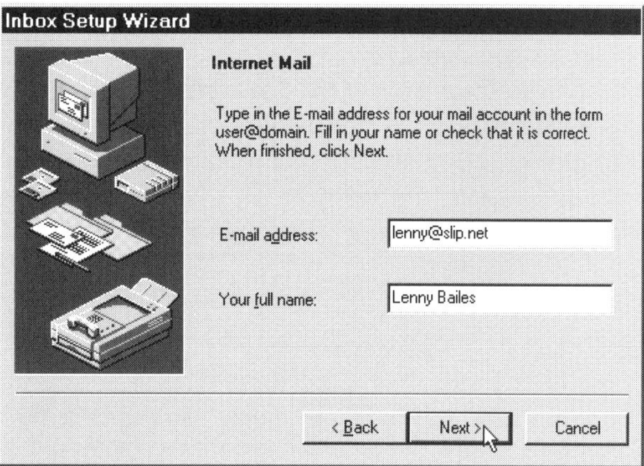

Finally, enter your mailbox name and mail password. (With many service providers, this information duplicates your login ID and password.)

PERSONAL ADDRESS BOOK The Personal Address Book screen allows you to specify the name of the file for your Personal Address Book (MAILBOX.PAB is the shared default). You can use another address book already present on your hard disk or create a new one with a different name. Click Next to continue.

PERSONAL FOLDER The Personal Folder screen allows you to specify the name of the file for your Personal Information Store (MAILBOX.PST is the shared default). You can use another Personal Information Store already present on your hard disk or create a new one with a different name. Click Next to continue.

Finishing the Configuration

After you've configured all the services you want to use, you'll see a summary screen showing the information services that have been installed in the new Windows Messaging profile. Click the Finish button to close the Inbox Setup Wizard and return to the Microsoft Windows Messaging Profiles screen.

Choosing a Startup Profile

By default, double-clicking the Inbox opens the Windows Messaging Settings profile that you created during installation. If you have created other Windows Messaging profiles, any of them can be set as the default, or you can configure the Inbox to prompt you for a profile every time you open it.

To set Inbox to prompt you for a profile, you must first let it open with the default settings you've created. From the open Inbox, select Tools | Options.

The section of the Options screen labeled When Starting Microsoft Exchange, shown here, lets you choose whether you want to be prompted for a profile on startup or to automatically load the profile selected in the Always Use This Profile drop-down list.

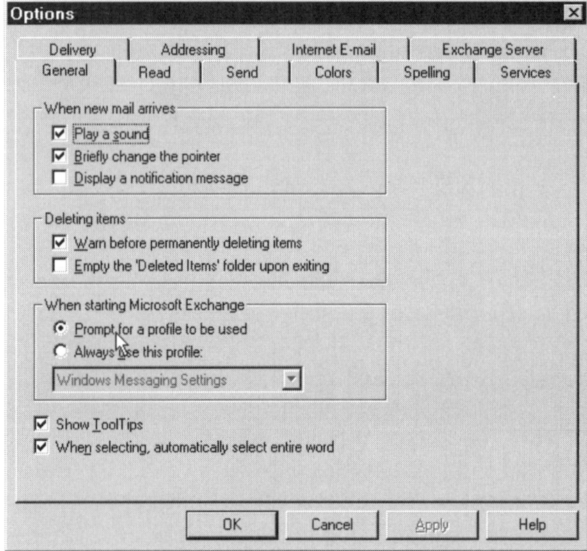

You can change the default startup profile for Windows Messaging without opening the Inbox. Right-click the Inbox icon on the desktop and select Properties from the context menu. The first part of the General screen that appears displays the current list of Windows Messaging profiles. (You can create a new one by clicking the Add button.) The bottom part of the screen allows you to change the default startup profile by selecting a different profile from the drop-down list, as shown here:

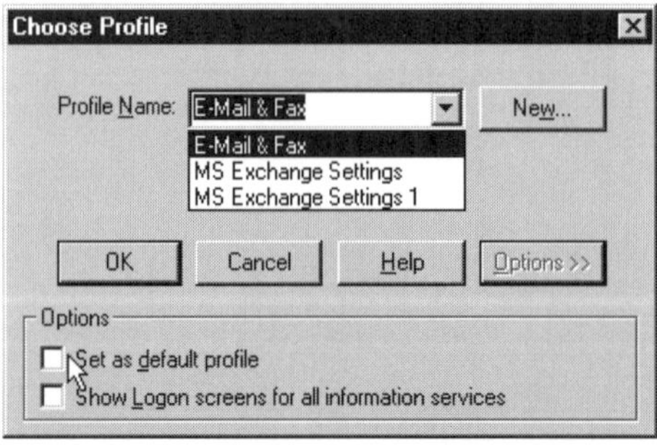

Creating New Windows Messaging Profiles

To create a new Windows Messaging Profile, right-click the Inbox icon and choose Properties from the context menu. Click the Show Profiles button toward the bottom of the screen to display the existing Windows Messaging profiles. Click the Add button to create a new profile.

Modifying Existing Windows Messaging Profiles

Instead of creating new Windows Messaging profiles, you can also modify existing profiles to add, remove, or edit information services.

1. Right-click the Inbox icon and select Properties from the context menu.
2. The General tab shows the information services installed in the default Windows Messaging profile. If you want to edit a different profile, click the Show Profiles button, select the Windows Messaging profile you want, and click the Properties button.
3. To delete an information service, select it and click the Remove button. To add an information service, click the Add button and follow the steps outlined in the previous section for the service you've selected. (Instead of having to click Next after filling in each field, you may be able to enter all of the information for the service using a series of tabbed screens.) Some of the services shown in the following illustration were added to Windows Messaging by third-party applications.

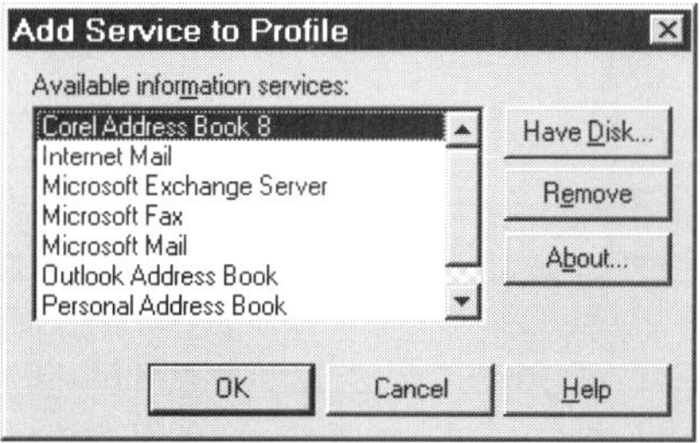

4. To change the connection information for an information service, select it, and click the Properties button.

Other Windows Messaging Profile Properties

In addition to the information services properties in a profile, you can modify some general defaults for the profile. To select a Windows Messaging profile, right-click Inbox on the desktop, choose Properties, and click the Show Profiles button. Select the Profile you want to edit and click the Properties button on the Mail and Fax General tab.

You'll see three tabs on the Windows Messaging Settings Properties screen: Services, Delivery, and Addressing. If you access profile properties through the Inbox pull-down menus, three additional tabs appear: General, Read, and Send.

- The Services tab simply lists the information services installed in the profile.
- The Delivery tab allows you to set some e-mail delivery options. The first section of this tab allows you to switch mail delivery to a second message store configured for the information profile. (Windows Messaging profiles can include as many message stores as you like. See the sidebar "Transferring Personal Address Books and Message Stores Between Workstations" later in this chapter for more details.) The second part of the Delivery tab specifies the order in which the Inbox checks the information services in the profile for new mail and posts new messages that you've composed. For instance, in the following illustration, if you want to change the delivery options to log onto Microsoft Mail before calling the Internet service provider, select Microsoft Mail and click the up arrow to move it to the top of the list.

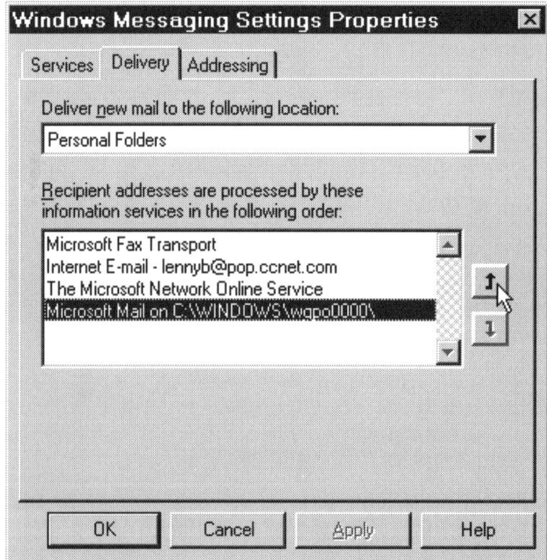

- The Addressing tab, shown next, allows you to specify the Personal Address Book that will be checked first when you want to look up an e-mail recipient. On the second part of the screen, you can change the order in which Windows Messaging checks the address books in the same way that you changed the service delivery options, described in the previous paragraph.

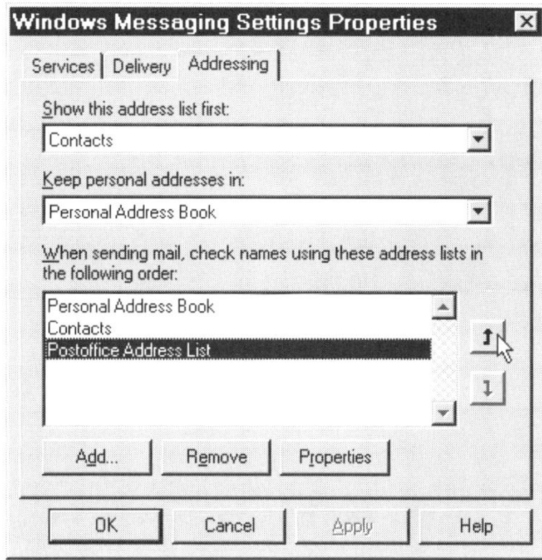

- The General, Read, and Send tabs that appear when profile properties are accessed through the Inbox control the display of mail messages in the Inbox folder windows.

Transferring Personal Address Books and Message Stores Between Workstations

If you are using Windows 98 on several different computers, you may want to transfer an address book or e-mail message database from one machine to another. The name of the default address book that Windows Messaging configures is MAILBOX.PAB. The name of the e-mail message store is MAILBOX.PST. These files are located in the \EXCHANGE directory on your Windows 98 host drive. To transfer the contents to another machine running Windows 95 or Windows 98, use the following procedure:

1. Copy the MAILBOX.PAB and MAILBOX.PST files located in the \EXCHANGE or other directory on the original computer and paste them into new files called MAIL1.PAB and MAIL1.PST.

2. Transfer MAIL1.PAB and MAIL1.PST to the \EXCHANGE directory on the destination machine. You can do this over a network, by establishing a direct cable connection between the two machines, or by copying the files first to a floppy diskette and then transferring them to the destination machine.

3. On the destination machine, right-click the Inbox, select Properties, and select Personal Address Book. (If you want to change the address book in a nondefault Windows Messaging profile, then click the Show Profiles button on the first screen, select the Windows Messaging profile you want to modify, click Properties, and then select the Personal Address Book for that profile.)

4. Click Properties for the Personal Address Book. On the next screen, change the filename for the address book to *d:*\EXCHANGE\MAIL1.PAB, as shown here. Don't worry; your old address book file won't be deleted, and you can always switch back to it later. Click Open to return to the Profile Properties screen.

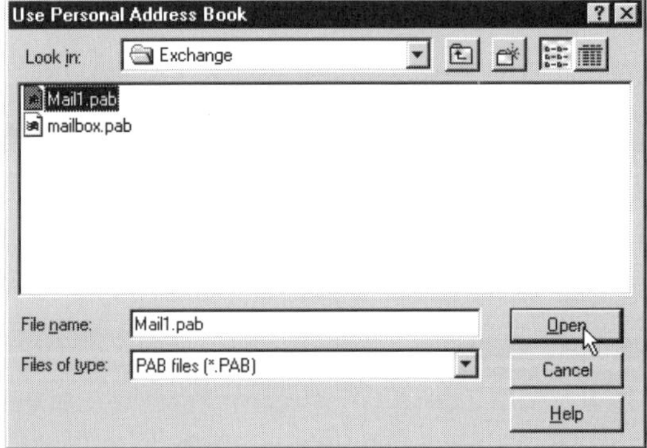

5. Click the Add Button, select Personal Folders from the list of available information services, and click OK.

6. In the next Create/Open Personal Folders file list, locate the \EXCHANGE directory and select the MAIL1.PST file that you copied from the original machine. Assign a new name to this message store (for instance, **New**

Store) in the Name field. Click OK to return to the Profile Properties screen. You should see the new Personal Information Store listed with the name you've entered. Click OK and close the Windows Messaging profile setup screens.

7. Double-click Inbox and open it with the Windows Messaging profile you've just modified. (If you modified the default profile, this profile appears automatically.) Select Tools | Options and click the Delivery tab.
8. Open the Deliver New Mail to the Following Location drop-down list and select New Message Store. You can always change this setting later if you want to return to the original Personal Information Store. Click OK to close the dialog box.

If you select the Inbox View Folders option, you'll see that Inbox has two message stores, as shown here. The New Store folder you've just configured contains all of the message transactions stored on your other Windows 95 or Windows 98 workstation.

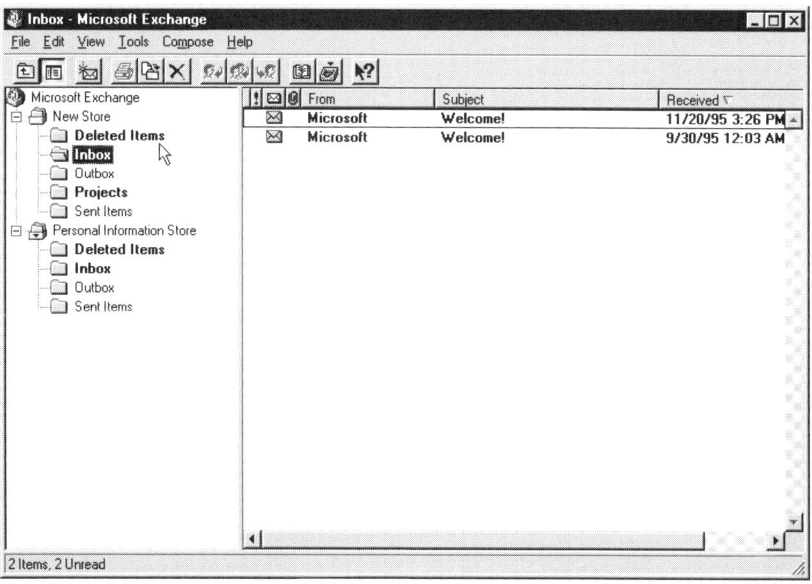

To display the messages in any of the folders in either information store, expand the folder and click the folders pane. Any mail you retrieve and compose from now on will be recorded in the information store you've just made the default.

To switch the Inbox so it again uses the original information store, select Tools | Options, click the Delivery tab, and select the information store you want the mail to be stored in, as shown here. To restore the original Personal Address Book, click the Services tab (also under on the Tools | Options menu), select Personal Address Book, and use the Properties dialog box to return to the original MAILBOX.PAB file.

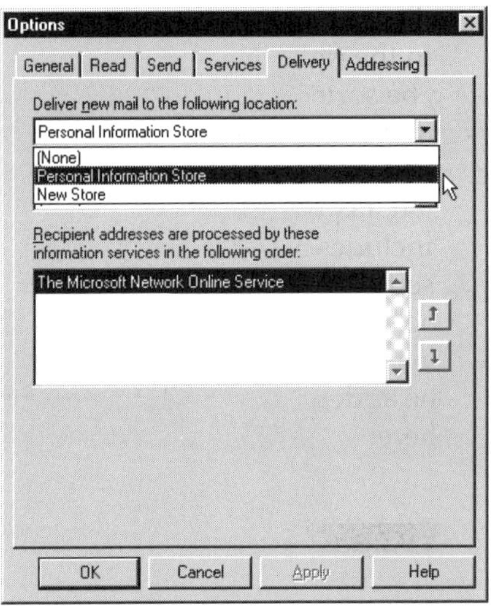

Migrating Mail from Windows for Workgroups

When you upgrade a Windows for Workgroups installation to Windows 98, the Workgroups Mail or Microsoft Mail 3.2 message file (.MMF) is automatically converted into a Windows 98 Personal Information Store if the file is located in the \WINDOWS or \MSMAIL directory. After Windows 98 is installed, you can manually upgrade .MMF mail files to the new format by using the Import option located on the File menu in the Inbox. This option can also be used to upgrade a Windows for Workgroups Personal Address Book.

The Inbox Interface

Initially, when you double-click the Inbox, Windows Messaging opens in a single display window showing all of the messages and faxes stored in the Inbox subfolder of your Personal Information Store. To see the rest of the folders in the Personal Information Store, select the Folders option on the Inbox View menu. By default, the Personal Information Store contains four subfolders: Inbox, Outbox, Sent Items, and Deleted Items. The Outbox contains the messages or faxes you've composed that have not yet been delivered. These messages are transferred to the Sent folder after you go online and Windows Messaging transmits them. The Deleted Items folder serves as an interim recycle bin for messages deleted from the other folders. You can transfer a message from one folder to another by dragging it. To select multiple messages, hold down the SHIFT or CTRL key while you click, as in My Computer or Windows Explorer.

The message queue shown in the right Inbox pane—or the only pane, if the View Folders option is disabled—can be sorted based on a number of criteria. There are 37 column fields that can be used to differentiate messages. Six of them are configured by default. The exclamation point (!) indicates priority messages. The envelope icon indicates the message type: e-mail, fax transmission, or other file type. The paperclip indicates that a message or fax includes a binary attachment. The From, Subject, Received, and Size options are self-explanatory.

Messages in the queue can be sorted by any of the selected criteria. To configure the sort, select Sort from the View menu or right-click the column header for any of the fields. More column fields can be added to the display queue through the View Sort option on the menu, as shown here:

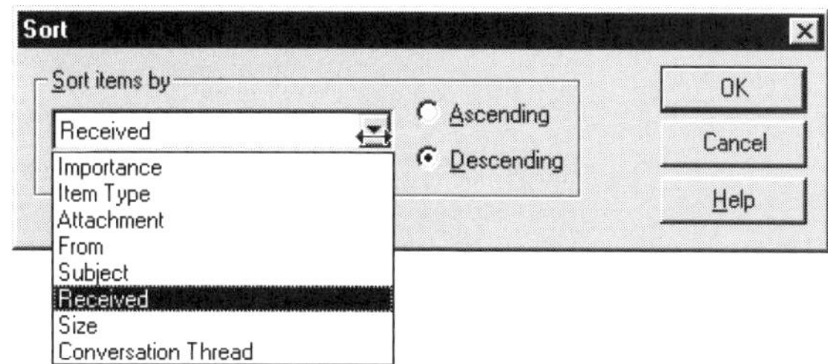

Note that the Inbox display is not limited to your e-mail and fax messages. You can drag and drop any file or document you like into an Inbox folder from the desktop or from My Computer or Windows Explorer. The additional column options can be used to build a file directory database that you can sort by application name, author, edit time, or a number of other column fields, as shown in Figure 11-9.

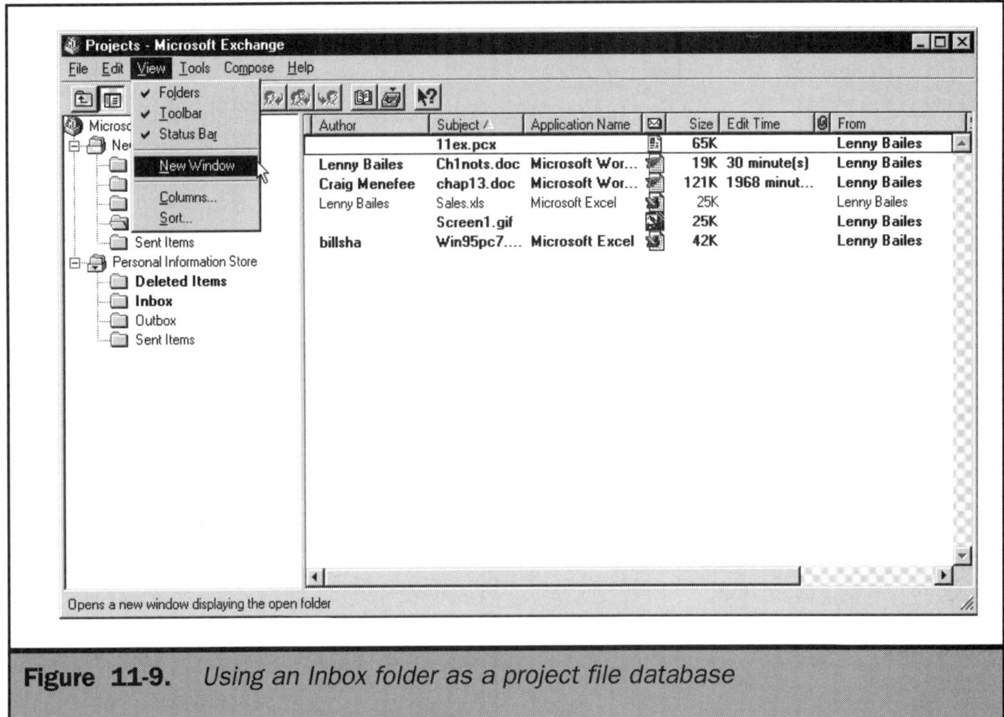

Figure 11-9. *Using an Inbox folder as a project file database*

You can create multiple windows for the same information store by selecting View | New Window from the Inbox menus, and you can then sort each window using different display criteria.

If you right-click any message or document in the display queue, a pop-up context menu appears, allowing you to conveniently view, edit, or forward the message or document via any of the configured Windows Messaging information services. To compose new mail, select the appropriate Compose option on the pull-down File menu. Messages can be sent using either the File Send command on the message window's pull-down menus or the Deliver Now option on the Inbox Tools menu.

Tip *If a lot of message traffic passes through Inbox, you may find that the .PST message file on your hard disk grows to occupy an excessive amount of hard disk space. You can reduce the size of the message store in two ways. You can open the Deleted Items folder, select all of the messages in it (using CTRL-A), right-click, and delete the messages permanently from the message store. Alternatively, you can compact the message store: Select it from the list of services in your Windows Messaging profile (right-click Inbox on the desktop and open the Properties sheet or select Options | Services from the Tools menu in the open Inbox). Open the Properties sheet for the Personal Information Store and click the Compact Now button.*

Using Remote Mail

By default, Inbox does not automatically log onto your Internet service when you launch it. Instead, to collect mail from an ISP, you need to select Deliver Now or the Remote Mail option on the Tools menu. Remote Mail opens a temporary mail queue for the information service you've selected. To log on and collect your mail, choose Tools | Connect on the Remote Mail pull-down menus. You can also log on by selecting Deliver Now from the Inbox Tools menu. Any messages in the Outbox waiting to be sent will be delivered.

Infrared Connections to Another Computer

Up until now, everything in this chapter has assumed that you will use a modem and telephone line, or possibly a local area network, to communicate through your computer. These are the most common approaches to data communications, but they're not the only ones. Windows 98 also supports direct cable connections between your computer and a second computer using a cable or a wireless infrared light link. A direct connection can be useful for sharing printers, sharing network connections and files between two computers, and synchronizing files. When you do some of your work on a desktop computer and other work on a laptop or other computer, the file synchronization feature can be particularly valuable.

For example, if you have copies of the same document on both computers and you (or an associate) make changes to both copies, each document will have content that is missing from the other. To bring the two versions back together, you need to synchronize the two files. The Briefcase program included in Windows 98 can provide basic file synchronization; for more features, you can install a third-party program such as LapLink.

Setting Up a Direct Cable Connection

Note *It's important to remember that you must use a special serial data cable called a null modem cable to connect two computers. Here's why: Each of the wires in a serial data cable moves data in one direction: either out of your computer or into your computer. You can't move data in both directions on the same wire. A modem or other communications device expects to receive data on the wires that the computer uses to send, and it sends signals back to the computer on the wires that the computer uses to receive. When you connect two computers together directly, both serial ports send data on the same wire, which doesn't work because neither computer expects to receive data on that wire. Thus, you need a special cable (or an adapter) that swaps the incoming and outgoing connections at one end. The alternative is to use your computers' parallel ports with a standard or basic 4-bit parallel cable or a special LapLink or InterLink cable. If your computers have Extended Capabilities Port (ECP) parallel ports, you'll get better performance with an ECP cable.*

Follow these steps to install a direct cable connection:

1. Plug the cable into the serial or parallel port you want to use for your direct connection. Don't try to use a serial port on one computer and a parallel port on the other computer.
2. From the Control Panel, open Add/Remove Programs and click the Windows Setup tab.
3. Select the Communications option and click the Details button.
4. Place a check mark next to the Direct Cable Connection option and click OK in both the Communications dialog box and the Add/Remove Programs dialog box.
5. From the Start menu, select Programs | Accessories | Communications | Direct Cable Connection.
6. Follow the instructions on the Direct Cable Connection Wizard screens to complete the installation.

Setting Up an Infrared Connection

If both of your computers support the Infrared Data Association's standard for serial infrared devices, you can transfer or synchronize files between the two computers through a wireless link.

To set up an infrared link, follow these steps:

1. From the Control Panel, use Add New Hardware to install the infrared device on each computer. When the installation is complete, you will see an infrared device icon in the System Tray at the right side of the taskbar.
2. Right-click the infrared device icon on the taskbar.
3. Place a check mark next to the Enable Infrared Communication option.

Synchronizing Files with Briefcase

Briefcase is a Microsoft utility that can update documents on one computer to include changes that were made to a copy of the document on a second computer. In other words, if the master copy of a document is on your desktop system, you can edit a copy on your laptop computer while you are away from the office at the same time that your assistant is working on the same document back at the office. When you return, you can use Briefcase to combine both sets of revisions.

When the Briefcase program is installed on your computer, a Briefcase icon appears on your desktop. If you don't see this icon, use Add/Remove Programs on the Control Panel to install it. You'll find Briefcase in the Accessories list.

To use Briefcase to synchronize a file (or group of files), drag the file to the Briefcase icon on the desktop of each computer. You can open and edit the files you want to synchronize from either their original locations or from the Briefcase folder. When you're ready to update the files, connect the two computers using direct cable connection or an infrared link. When the connection is in place, open the Briefcase folder and select the files you want to synchronize. Then select the Update Selection command on the Briefcase menu or the toolbar. To synchronize all the files in the Briefcase folder, use the Update All command.

If a direct cable or wireless connection isn't practical, you can also use Briefcase with a floppy disk. Follow these steps to synchronize files with a floppy disk:

1. Add the files you want to edit to the Briefcase folder.
2. Place a floppy disk in the disk drive on the machine that contains the files.
3. Open My Computer and drag the Briefcase icon from your desktop to the icon for the floppy disk. This will copy the Briefcase contents to the floppy disk.
4. Remove the floppy disk. When you're ready to edit the files, insert the disk in the other computer.
5. When the edits are complete, move the floppy back to the first computer and open the My Briefcase folder.

6. Either select the files you want to synchronize and click the Update Selection command on the Briefcase menu or toolbar, or choose Update All to synchronize everything in the folder.

If the files on only one of the two machines have changed, Briefcase will make those changes in the other version. If both versions have changed, Briefcase will open the application associated with the file type and merge the two files.

Using Dial-Up Server

Windows 98's Dial-Up Server feature allows other people to set up a Dial-Up Networking connection to your computer through a modem and telephone line. When the connection is in place, callers can run programs and read or copy files on your computer. If you're running one or more Internet server application programs, the caller can use those programs to exchange data with your computer. If your computer is part of a network, a Dial-Up Server connection will provide access to the rest of the network as well as to your own computer, but only through the NETBEUI or IPX/SPX protocol. TCP/IP intranets aren't supported. (See "Remote Network Connections" in Chapter 14 for information about how to set up a dial-up gateway to a TCP/IP network.).

To turn on the Dial-Up Server feature and accept incoming calls, follow these steps:

1. Open the Dial-Up Networking folder from My Computer.
2. On the Connections menu, select Dial-Up Server. If there's no Dial-Up Server command on the menu, choose Add/Remove Programs on the Control Panel and select Dial-Up Server from the list of communications components.
3. The Dial-Up Server dialog box (shown in Figure 11-10) has a tab for each modem connected to your computer. Select the Allow Caller Access option.
4. Click the Change Password button to set the password that callers have to enter before they can get access to your computer.
5. Type a description of your computer in the Comment field. This text will appear in the caller's Network Neighborhood folder when a connection is in place.
6. Click the Server Type button to specify the type of network connection you want to create. The options are as follows:

   - **Default** Use the Default option to accept NETBIOS connections from another Windows 98 or Windows 95 computer.

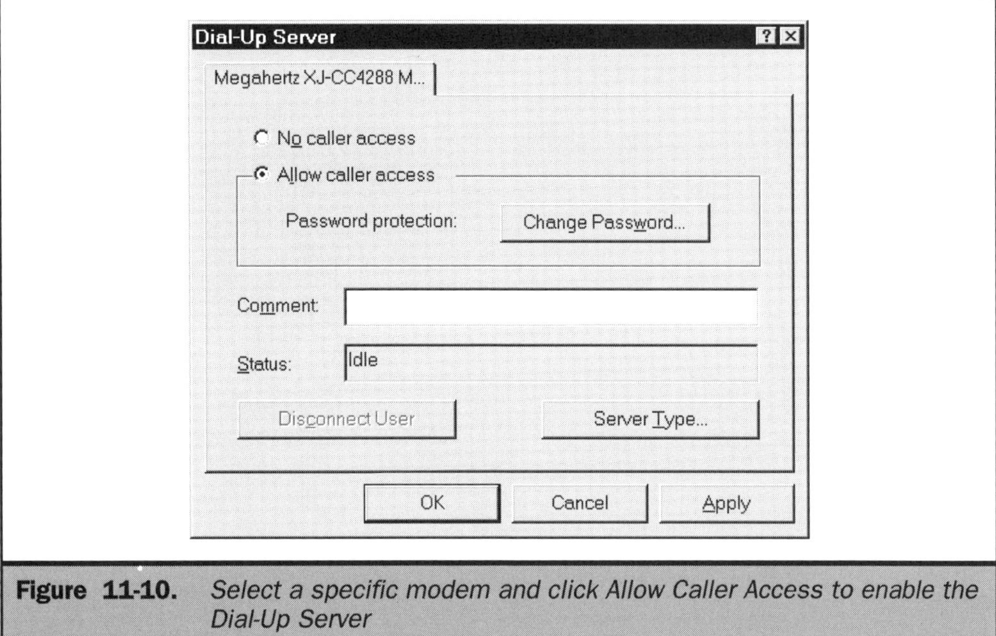

Figure 11-10. *Select a specific modem and click Allow Caller Access to enable the Dial-Up Server*

- **PPP** Use the PPP option to accept TCP/IP connections from a Windows 95, Windows 98, Windows NT, or UNIX system (you are limited to a binary, two-computer connection).
- **Windows for Workgroups and Windows NT 3.1** Use this option to accept connections from computers running older versions of Windows.

It's a good idea to keep the Dial-Up Server dialog box open when an incoming call is in progress because this dialog box includes fields that show the current status of a call and a Disconnect User button that you can use to end the call. You can also use the Net Watcher program (described in Chapter 14) to see what the caller is doing on your system.

Putting the Tools to Work

This chapter has given you a basic grounding in the setup and use of Windows 98's telecommunication tools. In the next chapter, you'll see how to apply some of these tools to the great cultural wonder of the late 1990s: the Internet.

Chapter 12

Internet Tools I: The World Wide Web for Fun and Profit

Chapter Highlights

How the Internet works

Setting up your Internet connection

Web browsers—Internet Explorer versus Netscape Communicator:

Browser commands, bells and whistles, and performance optimization

The World Wide Web as a way of life:

Search engines, news resources, and financial information

Supporting Windows 98 and other programs:

Solving problems and finding driver updates

What Active Desktop means to you

Active channels, subscriptions, and push technology

Win98's Web publishing tools

This chapter and the one that follows are your user's guide to Windows 98 and the Internet. This chapter shows you how to set up an Internet account and take advantage of all the resources available on the World Wide Web. You'll learn how to set up an Internet account, and you'll find browser techniques and tips for Microsoft's Internet Explorer and Netscape Navigator. This chapter also gives you the lowdown on Windows 98's Active Desktop and Subscription features. The "World Wide Web as a Way of Life" section contains tips on using Web search engines and an extensive list of World Wide Web resources: new sites, financial sites, and hardware and software technical support.

The next chapter, "Internet Tools II: Waxing Your Surfboard," shows you how to use Windows 98 to exploit non-WWW Internet services. It shows you how to set up and use the Outlook Express e-mail client and introduces you to other bread-and-butter Internet functions, such as Usenet news, Telnet, and FTP. Chapter 13 also covers more exotic Internet features, online communities, Internet Relay Chat, and Internet conferencing with Windows 98's bundled applications.

Why the Internet?

The Internet has radically changed the way people use personal computers. In addition to the word processors, spreadsheets, games, personal assistants, and other programs that they run on their own computers, people can use the Internet to connect their computers to millions of others around the world. With an Internet connection in place, you can send and receive messages (and attached files), browse and save pages on the World Wide Web, download new programs and information, or chat with people all over the world in real time. You can also update Windows 98 and its applications or operate distant computers without leaving your own chair. Access to information, entertainment, and other people through the Internet has become a major reason for many people to buy and use computers.

Microsoft's intention with Windows 98 is to give you the choice of seamlessly integrating the Internet into your desktop, but you don't have to do this if you don't want to. In fact, by default, these options are turned off. Even if you don't choose an Active Desktop, Windows 98 includes a pretty complete set of Internet tools—the Internet Explorer Web browser, the Outlook Express mail and news program, and the other bundled programs are enough to let you exploit most of the online resources you're likely to find.

This chapter gives you a general idea of how Windows 98 exchanges data and programs with other computers through the Internet, and it explains how to use the Internet tools included in the Windows 98 package.

How Your Computer Works with the Internet

The Internet is a very large and complex network, but you don't have to understand all of the internal routing, switching, and traffic management that takes place behind the curtains to use it. In an ideal world, viewing a Web site or downloading a program from an online archive should be about as easy as selecting a TV channel. The process isn't quite that simple yet, but it's a lot closer than it was just a few years ago.

Almost everything that you can do through the Internet is based on a standard model: A program on your computer (a *client* program) connects through the Internet to a program on another computer (a *server* program), and then the client sends a series of instructions to the server. For example, when you use the World Wide Web, your Web browser is a client program that instructs a Web server on a distant machine to transfer a copy of a Web page or other file back to the client.

The client always starts the transaction by sending a set of instructions to the server. In many cases, the client sends a command to the server that says, "Perform an action and send me the product of that action." The action in question might be retrieving a file from storage, running a program on the computer that contains the server program, or running a program on a third computer connected to the server through the Internet or a local network. But sometimes the client tells the server, "Get ready to receive and process the data I'm about to send you. " For example, when you send an e-mail message, your mail client tells the mail server to read the address of the recipient and forward it through the Internet to another server that will deliver the message to the recipient's mail client.

There are many kinds of servers and clients on the Internet, but they all follow this model. The exchange of commands and data between a client and a server usually runs something like this:

1. The client connects to a server whose address has been specified by the user.
2. The server acknowledges that the connection is in place.
3. The client sends one or more instructions to the server.
4. The server performs the actions requested by the client.
5. When the server completes the action requested, it sends some kind of confirmation back to the client. The client either sends another instruction or closes the connection.

As a general rule, server programs run on computers that have permanent connections to the Internet so they're always available when a client comes looking for them. On the other hand, a client can run on a computer with a dial-in or other on-demand Internet connection because it's only active when it's interacting with a server.

Most of the Internet application programs in Windows 98 are clients:

- Internet Explorer is a Web browser client program that instructs Web servers to send back HTML files.
- Outlook Express is a mail and news client program that exchanges messages with mail and news servers.
- NetShow Player is an audio and video client program that receives and plays Active Streaming Format (ASF) files.
- Microsoft Chat is an Internet Relay Chat (IRC) client program.
- RealAudio Player is an audio client program.
- Microsoft Telnet is a Telnet client program.

The two major exceptions are both related to creating and distributing your own Web pages: Front Page Express is an HTML editor program that supports the uploading of a completed Web site to an Internet server. Personal Web Server allows you to take a Web site created and stored on your hard disk and publish it over the Internet or on a local area intranet.

Setting Up Your Internet Connection

To use the services and information available through the Internet, you must first set up an Internet connection for your Windows 98 computer. Win98 provides several options for establishing a new Internet account: You can connect through an online information service such as America Online (AOL), CompuServe, Prodigy, or the Microsoft Network (MSN), or you can connect through a local, regional, or national Internet service provider (ISP) such as Panix, Slip Net, AT&T, IBM, or NetCom. You can also connect to the Internet through an existing local area network that has direct cable access.

Online Services

The Windows 98 Online Services folder includes built-in support for Internet access through America Online, AT&T WorldNet, CompuServe, Prodigy, and MSN. You can access this folder by choosing Programs | Online Services from the Start menu. If you don't see the Online Services folder, you can install it by opening the Control Panel | Add/Remove Programs applet, choosing the Windows Setup tab, and placing a check mark next to Online Services in the Components list. Click OK to complete the installation. Similarly, if you already have an Internet account and don't need additional online services, you can remove the Online Services folder using the Add/Remove Programs applet. If you deselect Online Services in the Components list on the Windows tab and click OK, this folder will vanish from your hard disk, freeing up some storage space. (You can get Online Services back later, if you want it, by using Add/Remove Programs again.)

About the Big Online Services

America Online, MSN, and the other online services are among the most visible businesses offering access to the Internet. You've probably seen their advertisements in print or on television and received free sign-up diskettes and CD-ROMs in the mail, bound into magazines, or with those packets of peanuts on a recent airline trip. They're difficult to avoid. Each of these services offers a package of proprietary added-value content along with all the conventional Internet services available through other ISPs.

For many users, an online service is an excellent way to connect to the Internet. The online services are easy to install and use because they've been designed for nontechnical consumers rather than hard-core computer geeks. In addition, much of the members-only content is first-rate, especially if you're looking for news, sports, consumer information, or information about popular music, movies, TV, and other forms of popular culture. Similar information may be available from other Web sites, but the online services make them easy to find and use. The CompuServe Forums, AOL conferences and chat rooms, and MSN news groups are among the most active communities anywhere. Because all of these services have dial-in access in hundreds of locations, they can be extremely convenient for people who want to use the Internet while they travel. Figure 12-1 shows the opening screens for the AOL and Prodigy services.

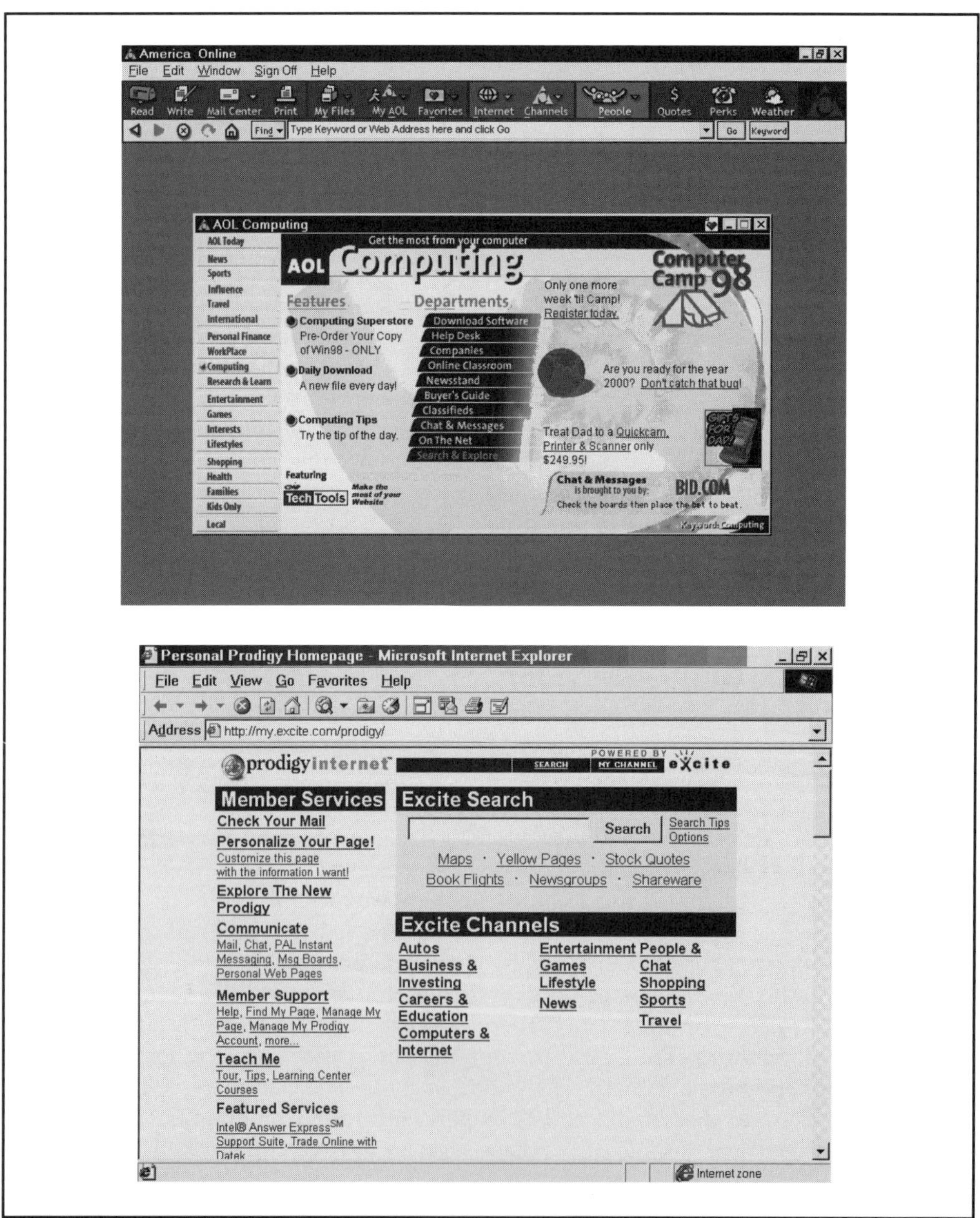

Figure 12-1. *Two popular online services*

Millions of people happily use these online services every day, but before you join one of them, you may want to consider a few drawbacks to connecting to the Internet through an online service:

- **Cost** AOL and CompuServe both charge a few dollars more per month for unlimited connect time than many other ISPs. If you use their members-only services, the extra cost may be acceptable, but if you expect to use your account exclusively for e-mail and access to the World Wide Web, you should probably look for a less expensive account.
- **Overload** Some of these services have *millions* of subscribers. Sometimes it seems as if every one of them is trying to dial in at exactly the same time (especially at peak evening and weekend hours). This can happen on a small local ISP as well as on a big national service, but either way it's an aggravating problem. If you're getting frequent busy signals when you try to connect to your ISP, it's time to look for a different service provider.

Tip *If you can get the marketing department to cooperate, try to find out the number of subscribers on the service compared with the physical number of modems the ISP has available. If this ratio is higher than 10 to 1, consider looking for an alternative provider.*

- **Support** Online services used to be notorious for terrible technical support; if you didn't get a busy signal, you'd wait forever before you could talk to a support person. There was a good reason for the jokes about "America on Hold." Things are not as bad as they were a few years ago, but you may still get faster answers and more hand holding from a good local ISP who understands the quirks of your neighborhood telephone company.
- **Status** If you plan to use your Internet account for business e-mail, to participate in newsgroups and online mailing lists, or as a home for your own Web site, you might discover that an aol.com or msn.com address is not taken as seriously as a less familiar address. Because the online services are homes for many less-experienced Internet users, some self-defined hard-core users assume that all messages from online service accounts are from beginners. They're wrong, of course, but the perception is still out there.
- **Advanced User Options** Many savvy users like to work with an Internet account that supports shell access through a Telnet application. This feature allows you to work with your files on the ISP's server, access Usenet newsgroups, Internet Relay Chat, and other facets of the Internet even when you're not connected through your default account. (More details on this kind of Internet use are provided later in this chapter.) If you're planning to create a Web site, find out about the Web support offered by the ISP: Does the ISP allow you to host your own domain name? How much storage space will you get? Does the ISP support Microsoft Front Page extensions or sophisticated scripting through Web programming languages such as PERL and CGI?

Loading the Interface Access Software

All four online services (AT&T, described later, is a national ISP rather than an online service) offer free trial accounts for new users so it's easy enough to sample some of the proprietary content and subjective "feel" of each one. If you don't like what you find, or if you have trouble with busy signals or tech support, you can cancel the account and try a different service. Don't order business cards with your new e-mail address until you're convinced that you've found a permanent online home.

When the Online Services folder is installed (see the beginning of this section), it contains links to five different national Internet service providers: America Online, CompuServe, Prodigy, the Microsoft Network, and AT&T WorldNet. To open an account with one of the services, double-click the icon for that service. A wizard or a series of local Web pages will step you through the process of finding a nearby telephone number and creating an account. You'll probably need to have a credit card handy if you want to gain immediate access through the online registration process.

If you already have an account with one of these services, click the icon for that service and look for the I Have an Account button to load information about the existing account and the Windows 98 software.

Using Internet Applications with Online Services

AOL, MSN, and CompuServe all provide their own client interfaces that act as gateways to both their own proprietary content and to the public Internet. If you want to use a different Web browser, Telnet program, or other Internet application, you can minimize the proprietary interface to the taskbar and open the third-party program that you really want to use.

AUTOMATIC LOGIN If your online service account is the only Internet connection profile on your computer, or if it's the default, Windows will automatically place a call when you start an Internet client program.

With MSN and CompuServe, a connection profile is created in the Win98 Dial-Up Networking folder when you activate your account. You can connect directly to the Internet (bypassing the MSN or CompuServe interface) by opening the Dial-Up Networking folder (choose Programs | Accessories | Communications | Dial-Up Networking) and launching the appropriate connection profile. If you expect to use this connection frequently, you may want to place a shortcut on your desktop or in the Start menu.

AT&T WorldNet

The Online Services folder also includes access to AT&T's Internet access product, AT&T WorldNet. Unlike the other services in the Online Services folder, WorldNet is a plain vanilla ISP without the additional content available from AOL, MSN, or Prodigy. Like the others, AT&T offers a free one-month trial, but after that there's an extra charge after your first 150 hours (which may or may not be a problem for you—that's about five hours per day). AT&T is an entirely adequate ISP, but the only thing that sets AT&T's Internet service apart from its competitors is that your monthly Internet charge is placed on your telephone bill if you're an AT&T long-distance phone service customer.

To set up an AT&T WorldNet account, click the icon in the Online Services folder.

Using a Third-Party ISP Diskette

The online services included on the Windows 98 CD-ROM are not your only choices. Many other local, regional, national, and international ISPs also offer Internet connections that might come closer to meeting your own particular requirements. If you do a lot of traveling, and you want to send and receive e-mail when you're away from your home base, a large ISP with dial-in telephone numbers in all the places you expect to visit could be your best choice.

Here are some of the most prominent national ISPs:

InternetMCI	(800) 955-6505 (business users) (800) 550-0927 (home users)
SPRYnet	(800) SPRYNET
IBM Global Network	(800) 821-4612
Sprint Internet Passport	(800) 359-3900
GTE Internet Solutions	(800) 363-8483
Earthlink	(800) 395-8425

Bell Atlantic, U.S. West, and all of the other regional Bell telephone companies as well as most other local telephone companies also offer Internet access in major metropolitan centers within their own coverage areas. For information, call the company that serves your area:

Bell Atlantic	(800) NET-2026 or (800) NET-6289
BellSouth	(800) 4DOTNET
Ameritech	(800) NET-8775
Southwestern Bell	(800) SWB-INET
U.S. West	(800) 244-1111
PacBell	(800) 708-4638

If widespread dial-in access is not an issue for you, consider one of the smaller local service providers that seem to have sprouted just about everywhere. A good local ISP can often provide more personal service and tech support than a company located on the other side of the country. However, there are also plenty of bad ISPs out there without enough incoming telephone lines to handle the demand for access and inept technical staff who are not able to keep the equipment operating properly. The cheapest service provider in town is probably not your best choice. The best way to find a good local ISP is to ask friends and colleagues with more online experience for their suggestions. There may also be a local computer user group in your town. Computer tabloids such as *Microtimes* and *Computer Currents*, published in some metropolitan areas, also occasionally contain reviews and ratings of Internet service providers.

It's always a good idea to ask for a free trial to make sure your new ISP is reliable. If you get frequent busy signals when you try to connect, if downloads are consistently slow, or if you lose your connection without warning, you should cancel the account and look for a different supplier.

Most large ISPs, both local and national, will send you a diskette or CD-ROM that contains software that can set up a new account, install a Dial-Up Networking profile, and specify the ISP's home page as the first thing you see when you start your Web browser. If you are a Windows beginner, using this diskette may be the most convenient way to configure your account.

Using the Internet Connection Wizard

If you are a more sophisticated user who wants to bypass your ISP's software, or if no software is provided, you can use Windows 98's Internet Connection Wizard, shown here, to set up your connection profile. The Internet Connection Wizard offers two options: you can use the Microsoft Referral Service to sign up for a new account with AT&T WorldNet or some other participating ISP, or you can configure Windows to work with an existing ISP account. This second option is the easiest way to set up a new Dial-Up Networking connection profile when your ISP doesn't send you a disk or when you're connecting to the Internet through a LAN.

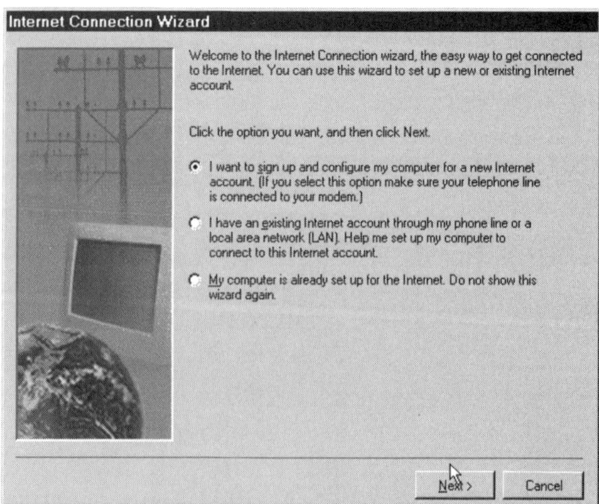

Preparing Information

If you're setting up a connection through a LAN that uses a proxy server to talk to the Internet, you'll have to get the name and port number of the proxy server from your network administrator or help desk.

If you're using a connection through a modem and telephone line, you'll need some information from your ISP. Most ISPs can give you a data sheet that contains all of their telephone numbers, addresses, and login names when you order a new account.

For most accounts, you'll need these items:

- The telephone number you must dial to connect to your ISP
- The login name and password you will use to make a connection
- The type of connection (PPP or SLIP)
- The Internet Protocol (IP) address, if any, that your ISP assigns to your connection
- The address of your domain name server (DNS)
- The addresses of your ISP's incoming and outgoing mail servers (the POP3 or IMAP server and the SMTP server)
- Your mail password
- The address of your ISP's news server

If you are a more sophisticated Windows user, you can probably "roll your own" connection profile by opening the Dial-Up Networking folder directly and clicking the Make New Connection button. This approach, described under "Setting Up SLIP and PPP Dialing Profiles" in Chapter 11, will work if your ISP supports standard Internet logins and connection options.

Some larger ISPs and online services may prefer you to set up your account through their proprietary software. If this is the case, it's probably best to go with the flow, use their software, and complain to their tech support personnel if it doesn't work.

Once You're Connected

Once you've established a connection to the Internet, a small Internet connection icon will appear in the System Tray portion of the taskbar. You can test your connection by opening Microsoft Internet Explorer to see if you're online. Try entering the universal resource locator (URL) http://home.microsoft.com in the Address box at the top of the Internet Explorer window. The Microsoft Internet Start page, shown in Figure 12-2, should appear in the browser. Later in this chapter, you'll learn how to customize this page to add your own features.

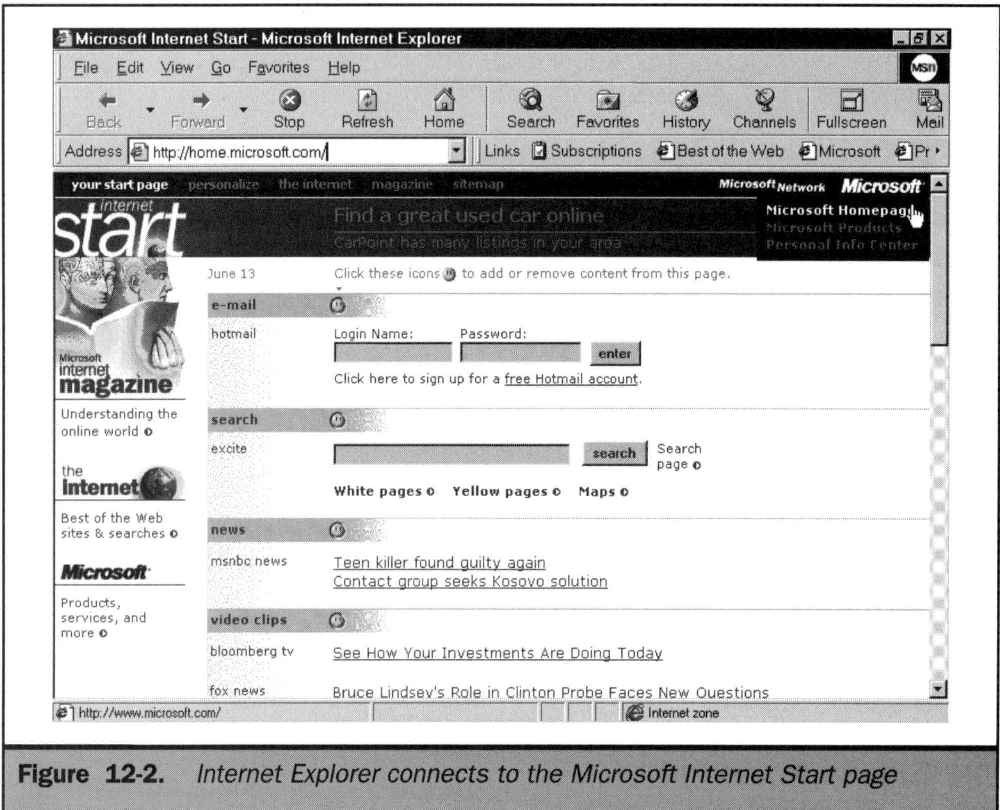

Figure 12-2. *Internet Explorer connects to the Microsoft Internet Start page*

Internet Properties: The Connection Tab

The Internet applet controls important default settings that specify the way Windows 98 logs into the Internet and how Microsoft's Web browser (Internet Explorer) and e-mail client (Outlook Express) work. This applet can be opened in three ways: by double-clicking the Internet icon on the Control Panel, by choosing the Internet Options command in the Internet Explorer View menu, or by right-clicking the Internet Explorer icon on the desktop and choosing Properties from its pop-up menu.

Most of the Internet Properties options apply only to the Internet Explorer browser, but one of the tabs controls your Internet connection—regardless of the application you use after you're connected.

The Connection tab (shown in Figure 12-3) includes these options:

- **Connection** The Connect button in this section is yet another way to start the Internet Connection Wizard described earlier in this chapter. Another button in this section, the Settings button, is dimmed if you are connecting to the Internet through a local area network. If you connect to the Internet through a modem, you can configure your system to automatically dial out to your ISP whenever you start an Internet application (such as your Web browser or e-mail client). Simply choose the Connect to the Internet Using a Modem option. Then, if you have more than one ISP account, or if you have separate Dial-Up Networking connection profiles for different locations, you can click the Settings button to change the default connection profile. If you connect to the Internet through a

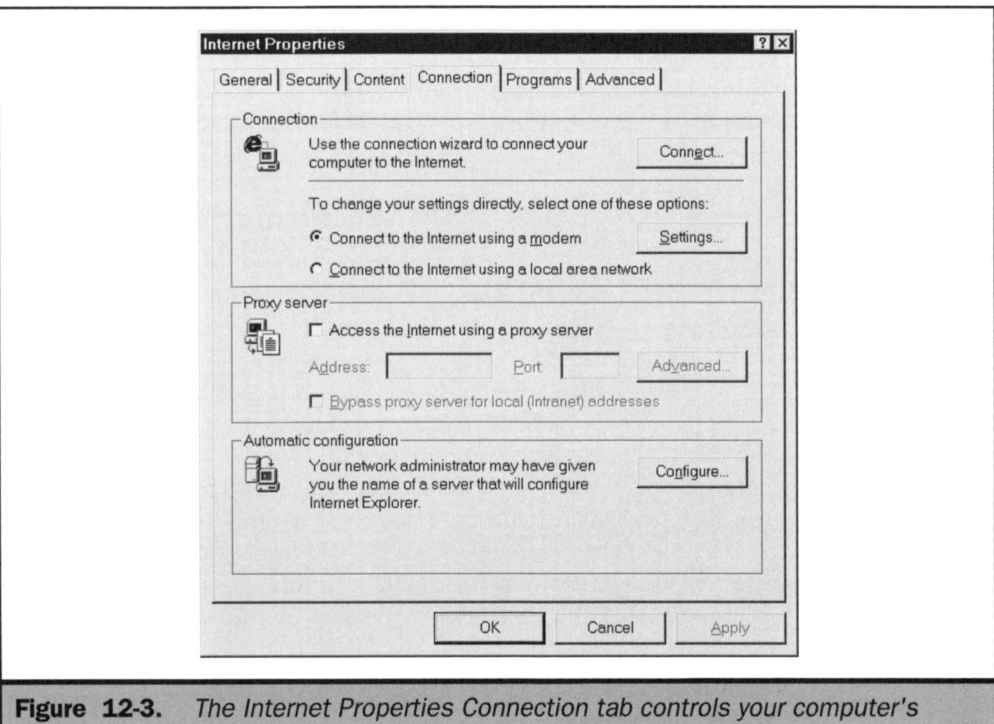

Figure 12-3. *The Internet Properties Connection tab controls your computer's Internet connection*

LAN or a high-speed connection such as an ADSL line, choose the Connect to the Internet Using a Local Area Network option in this section.

- **Proxy Server** As a security precaution, many businesses and other large local networks connect to the Internet through a proxy server that allows users on the local network to make an outbound connection but does not permit outside users to establish a direct connection to the local computers. If you're connecting through a proxy server, the Access The Internet Using A Proxy Server option should be active. The only time you're ever likely to want to change this setting is if you disconnect a laptop computer from a LAN and set up a modem connection.

Note *Some third-party Internet programs change the Proxy Server option automatically when you install them, annexing themselves to the Internet Explorer interface. The documentation for such applications should notify you if this occurs.*

- **Automatic Configuration** If your network administrator has created a standard configuration for all of your company's Internet connections, you can load the configuration from a remote location by using the Automatic Configuration option. (Click the Configure button in this section of the Connection tab.)

You'll find information about the options on the other tabs of the Internet applet in the "Web Browsers: Internet Explorer Versus Netscape Communicator" section of this chapter.

Internet Connectivity Clinic

Although it's certainly fun to stay up-to-date with the latest and greatest 32-bit Windows 98 applications, some people have made a substantial investment in Internet tools written for the Windows 3.x environment. Users with Internet accounts from third-party service providers who have installed dial-up utilities and browsers under Windows 3.x may be reluctant to abandon tried-and-true software that they've already mastered.

The following are a few known problems with using Windows 3.x Internet applications under Windows 98, along with some suggested solutions.

Windows 98 Disables Third-Party Internet Dialers

Users of Netscape's Personal Navigator, Eudora, and other browsing utilities were accustomed, under Windows 3.x, to having a third-party TCP/IP dialer load whenever these programs were opened to access the Internet. Windows 98 replaces an important third-party file called a WINSOCK driver with its own version. The Windows 98 version, WINSOCK.DLL, disables older third-party Internet dialers distributed by CompuServe, NetCom, and Spry. The popular Windows 3.x Trumpet Winsock dialer can also be affected. (Old AOL software usually continues to work.)

CompuServe and AOL users can upgrade to the software provided by Windows 98, discussed earlier in this section. The best solution for users of other third-party dialing utilities such as NetCom's NetCruiser or Trumpet Winsock is to transfer account settings to Windows 98's Dial-Up Networking using the Internet Connection Wizard.

In a pinch, older third-party dialers can be made to work with Windows 98 by making sure that older versions of the WINSOCK.DLL drivers are transferred from the \WINDOWS or \WINDOWS\SYSTEM directory to the individual folders and paths that contain the older software. When Windows 98 is installed, instances of these files in the \WINDOWS directory are usually renamed to WINSOCK.001 or WINSOCK.002. Trumpet users should note that a 32-bit Win98 upgrade for Trumpet Winsock is now available and can be downloaded from the Trumpet FTP site at ftp.trumpet.com.au.

32-Bit Internet Applications Don't Work

The main problem with older Internet dialers is that they don't support any of the newer 32-bit Internet utilities included with Windows 98, such as Internet Explorer and Outlook Express, nor do they support newer, 32-bit versions of Netscape Navigator or Netscape Communicator. These older dialers work only with the original 16-bit Internet utilities that were bundled with them several years ago.

Some people attempt to use new Windows 95 or Windows 98 Internet utilities in good faith, only to find that when they connect to the Internet in the old way, these new applications don't work. The problem here is that the Internet connection is probably being established by an older 16-bit Windows 3.x dialing utility. These older dialers do not support 32-bit Windows applications.

To resolve this problem, either obtain a third-party Internet dialer that supports 32-bit applications or use Windows 98 Dial-Up Networking to establish your Internet connections. (See Chapter 11 for more detailed instructions on setting up Dial-Up Networking Internet connection profiles.)

Web Browsers: Internet Explorer Versus Netscape Communicator

Microsoft has closely integrated its Internet Explorer Web browser into the Windows 98 desktop, but more than half of the Web browser market (if you can call a competition between two free products a market) is still in the hands of Netscape Navigator. Which is the better browser for you? For most users, most of the time, either one will probably provide everything you need. However, there are a few Web sites that have been optimized for just one browser. For example, using Netscape Navigator to download files from Microsoft doesn't always work. Thus, it's a good idea to install both browsers. Since Internet Explorer is included in the Windows 98 package and Netscape Navigator is available for free at http://www.netscape.com/download, there's not much reason to limit yourself to just one of them.

That's not to say that there aren't differences between the two browsers. One of the most important is Internet Explorer's optional Explorer bars, which can display your Favorites list, the results of a search, or your History list in a separate pane within the browser window, as shown in Figure 12-4. The separate window permits you to move quickly from one item on the list to the next without the need to use the Back button after visiting each site.

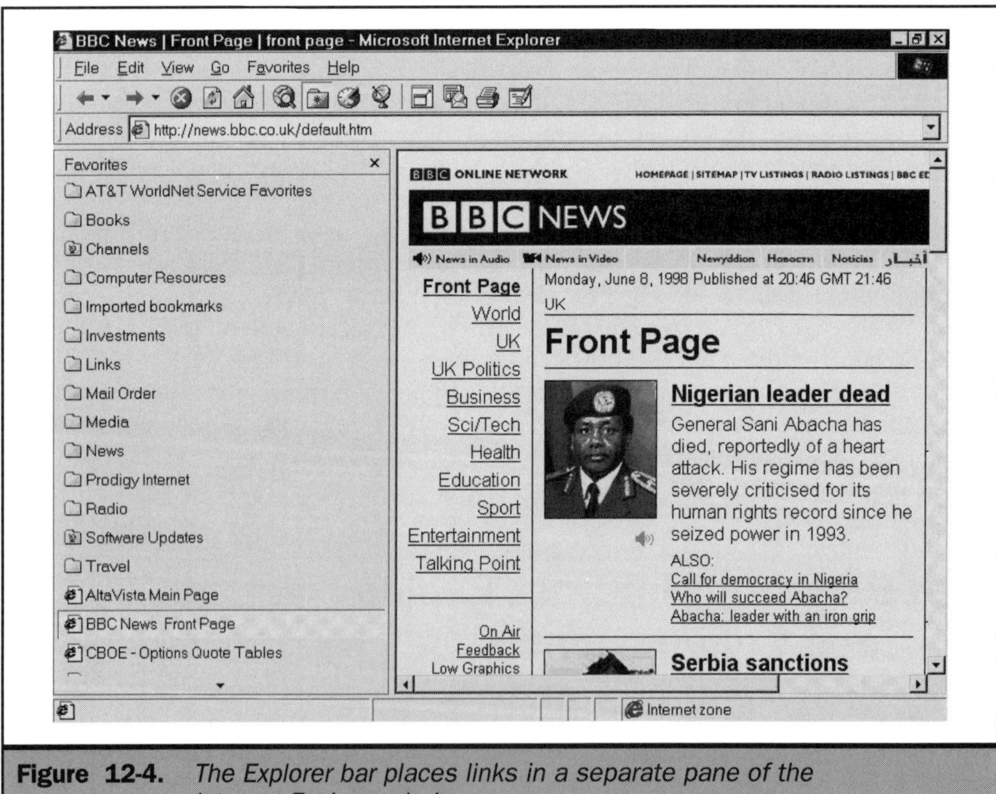

Figure 12-4. *The Explorer bar places links in a separate pane of the Internet Explorer window*

Browser Commands

Both browsers provide many of the same commands and functions even if they don't always use the same names. The most important include these toolbar buttons, dialog boxes, and menu commands:

- **Address (IE) or Location/Go To (Netscape)** To move to a new Web page or other Internet location, type the URL you want to go to in the text entry field and press the ENTER key.
- **Back** Click the Back button to return to the page you viewed immediately before the current page.
- **Forward** Click the Forward button to return to the page you viewed before you used the Back button.
- **Refresh (IE) or Reload (Netscape)** Use this command to load a new copy of the currently visible page or other file from the server.
- **Stop** Click the Stop button to interrupt the downloading of a Web page or other file before it is finished.
- **Home** Click the Home button to return to your start page.
- **Search** Click the Search button to open a link to one or more online Internet search services.
- **Favorites (IE) or Bookmarks (Netscape)** Use this command to open a menu of shortcuts to Web sites that you have previously saved.

Optimizing the Browser Display

You will probably spend a lot of your time looking at your browser so it's worth the time and trouble to make the display window as easy on the eyes as possible. This section describes some things you can do to improve the default display that loads when you install Internet Explorer or Netscape.

Changing the Default Fonts

Some Web site designers specify the typeface that they want used on their pages, but many others allow the browser to specify the font. As a general rule, sans serif typefaces (fonts without the little extensions at the top and bottom of each character, like this) are easier to read on a computer screen. However, the IE and Netscape browsers both use serif fonts by default. You can change the default proportional font to Arial or Trebuchet and the default fixed-width font to Lucida Console or Monotype, if you have these fonts. They all produce Web pages with a clean, easy-to-read appearance.

To change the defaults in Internet Explorer, follow these steps:

1. Select View | Internet Options and click the General tab.
2. Click the Fonts button at the bottom of the window.
3. In the Fonts dialog box (shown in Figure 12-5), open the drop-down Proportional Font menu and select the font you want you want to use.
4. Use the drop-down Fixed-Width Font menu to select a font.
5. Click the Set as Default button and click the OK button.

To change the default fonts in Netscape Navigator, follow these steps:

1. Select Edit | Preferences and click Fonts in the Category list.
2. When the dialog box shown in Figure 12-6 appears, use the drop-down Variable Width Font and Fixed Width Font menus to select the new typeface you want to use.

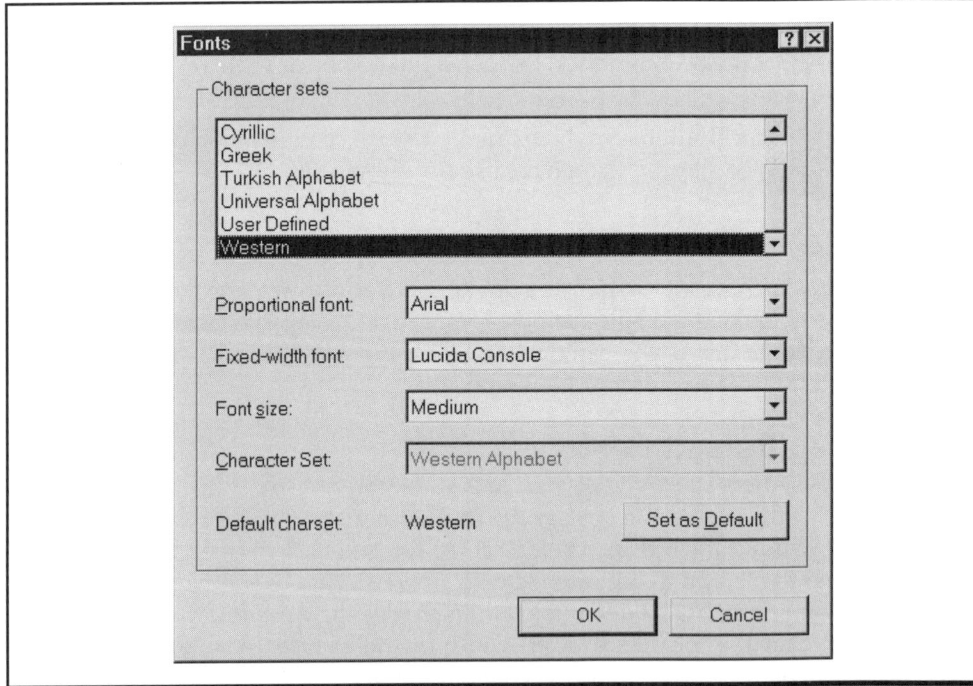

Figure 12-5. *Use the Fonts dialog box to change the Internet Explorer defaults*

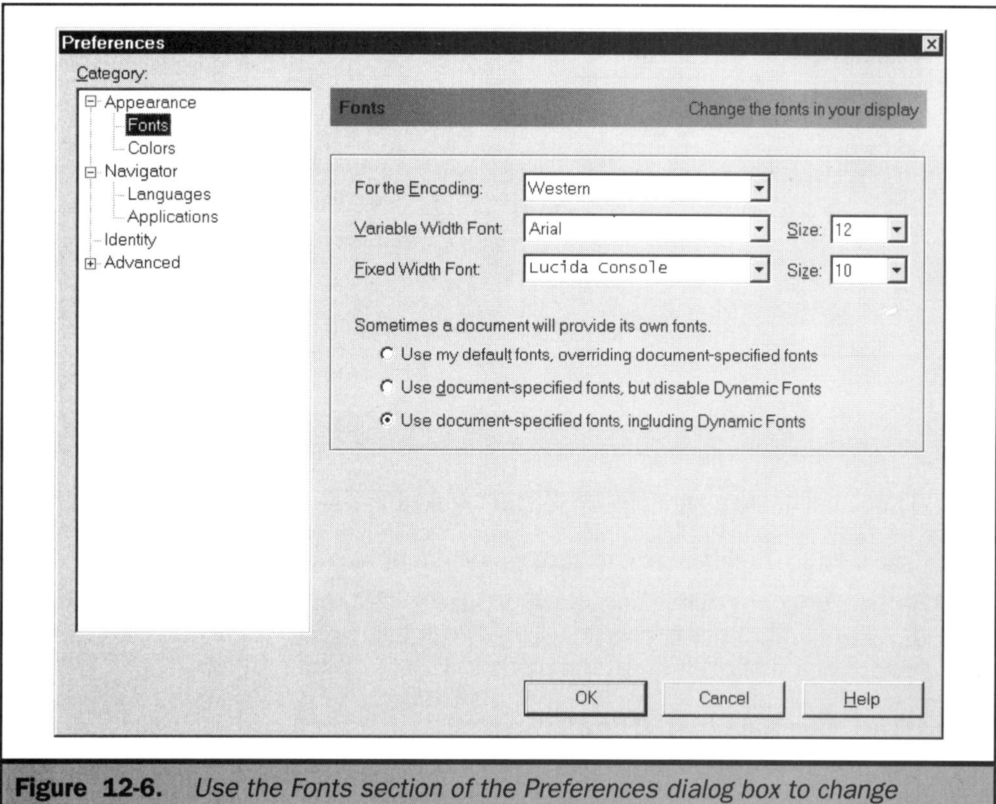

Figure 12-6. *Use the Fonts section of the Preferences dialog box to change Netscape Navigator defaults*

3. If it is not already selected, select the Use Document-Specified Fonts, Including Dynamic Fonts option.
4. Click the OK button to save your choices and close the dialog box.

Changing the Default Colors

The easiest Web pages to read have dark text over a light-colored background. It's probably best to use the colors specified by the designers of the sites you visit, but for sites that permit the browser to set the colors, black letters against a white background is always a good choice as a default. If you prefer, you can use the same foreground and background colors that you use in other Windows applications.

To change the default colors in Internet Explorer, follow these steps:

1. Select View | Internet Options.

2. Click the Colors button at the bottom of the General tab. Then select the colors you want in the Colors dialog box, shown here:

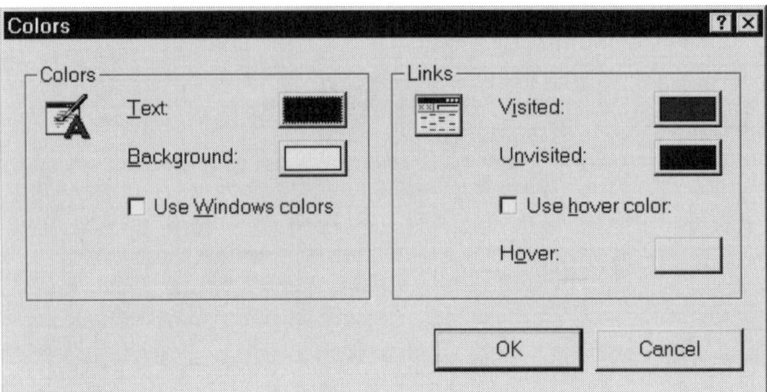

To change the default colors in Netscape Navigator, follow these steps:

1. Select Edit | Preferences and click Colors in the Category list.
2. When the Colors dialog box shown in Figure 12-7 appears, click the Text and Background buttons to choose colors. If you want to use the same colors that you use for other Windows screens, select Use Windows Colors.

Adjusting the Screen Resolution

Many Web pages are designed to look best on video displays with a screen resolution of at least 800 by 600 pixels, which means that the image will extend beyond the right side of your monitor if your display is set to 640 by 480. If your monitor and video controller support finer resolutions, you will save yourself a lot of back-and-forth scrolling if you increase your system's screen resolution.

Opening the Browser in a Full-Screen Window

You can always use the Maximize icon in the upper-right corner of the browser window to make the browser fill your entire screen, but if you want to set full-screen operation as a permanent default in Internet Explorer, select View | Internet Options, click the Advanced tab, and make the Browsing/Launch Browser in Full Screen Window option active.

Internet Explorer also includes a Full Screen button on the toolbar. This opens the browsing window in a special view that minimizes the toolbar icons. To switch back from this view to the normal view, click the Full Screen icon again.

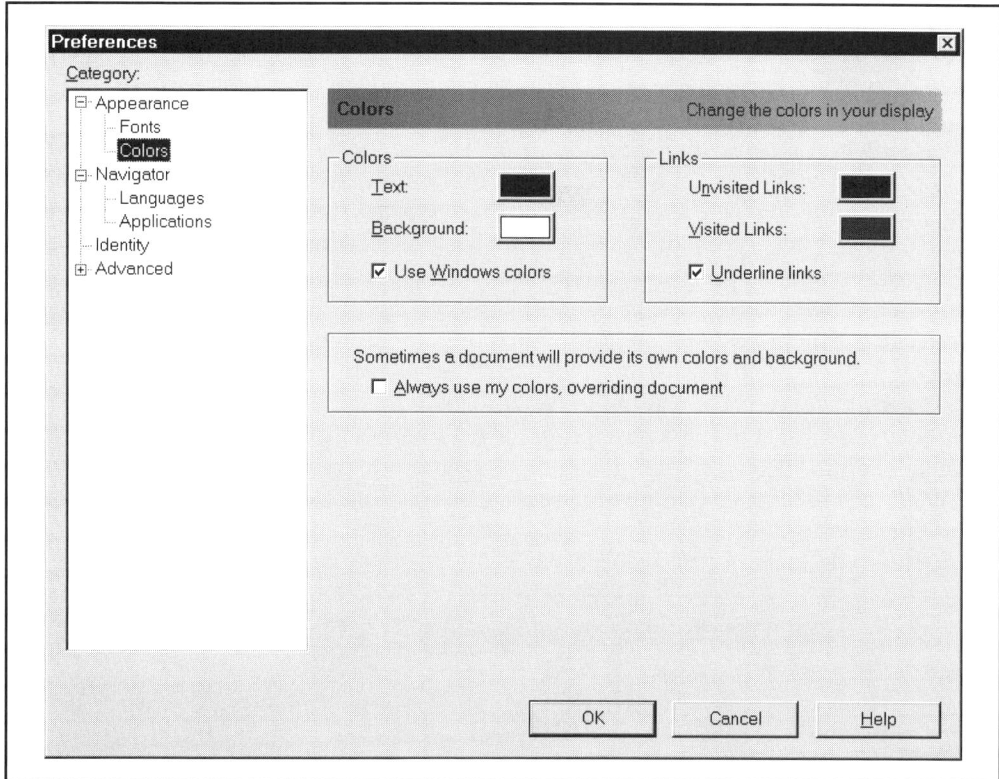

Figure 12-7. *Use the Colors option in the Preferences dialog box to change text and background colors in Netscape Navigator*

Optimizing Download Time

One of the signs of a well-designed Web page is that it loads quickly, even through a relatively slow communications link. However, there is no shortage of bad pages on the Web. The worst can take several minutes or longer to download. When you instruct your browser to get a Web page from a server, the browser normally takes everything that the designer included in the page: text, sound and video clips, still pictures, and even embedded Java and ActiveX programs. If you simply want to read the first paragraph of a complex Web page, the wait can seem like forever.

The worst offenders are Web pages that include audio and video clips and those that contain embedded programs. Embedded audio can be especially irritating because it has a habit of starting without any warning. For example, the Hotel Gasperoni in the Republic of San Marino (http://inthenet.sm/hg/hg.htm) has a Web site that plays a synthesized version of Vivaldi's "Spring" from *The Four Seasons* for no apparent reason.

If your computer does not have a sound card or a video controller that supports movies and animations, there's no good reason to waste time loading them; and if you want to read text only, you don't need to wait for all the pictures on a page to load.

One solution to this problem is to instruct your browser not to automatically download certain types of files. In Internet Explorer, choose View | Internet Options and select the Advanced tab. The Multimedia options, shown in Figure 12-8, allow you to turn off pictures, animations, and video and audio clips.

To filter out ActiveX controls and Java applets in Internet Explorer, click the Security tab and select the Custom option for the Internet Zone. Click the Settings button to open the Security Settings dialog box, where you can enable or disable downloads or specify that you want to evaluate every download when a Web server offers it to you.

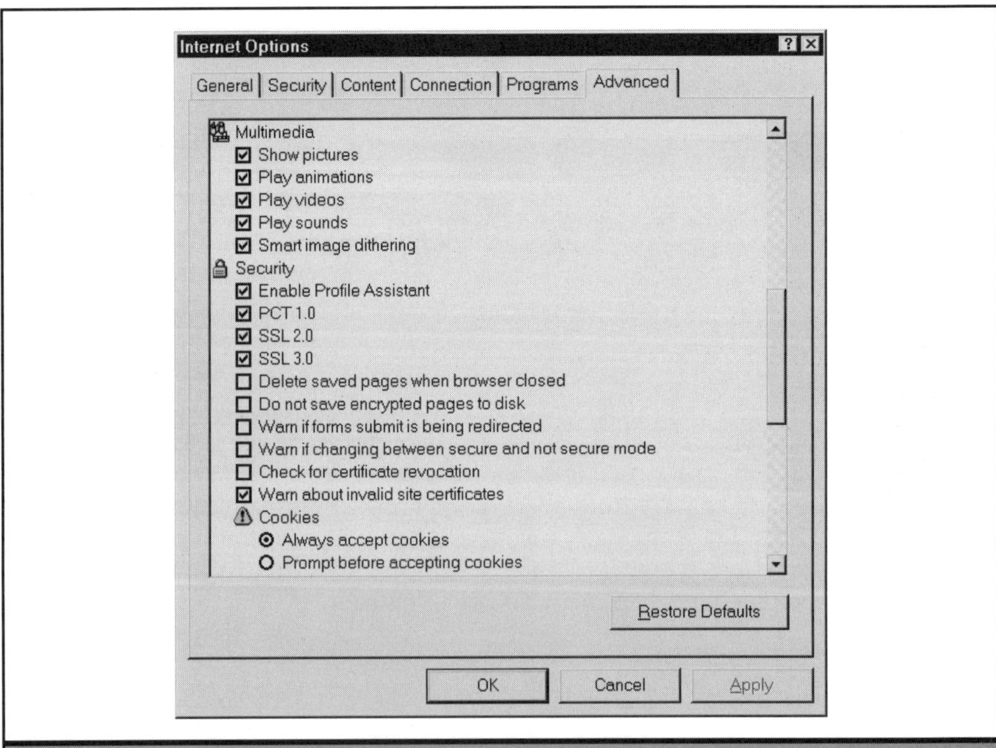

Figure 12-8. *The Advanced Multimedia options control Internet Explorer downloads of images, videos, and sounds*

In Netscape Navigator, choose Edit | Preferences | Advanced. The Advanced dialog box shown in Figure 12-9 includes options for loading images (both still and moving) and enabling Java applets. To reject these file types, turn off the options.

Internet Explorer Toolbars

In addition to the navigation buttons discussed earlier in this section, other useful options are provided on Internet Explorer's toolbar and Links bar.

The Search, Favorites, History, and Channels buttons perform the same function as the Explorer bar menu, opening interchangeable panes on the left side of the screen that provide quick access to URL resources in each category. You'll find more information on working with History lists, search sites, and subscription channels later in this chapter.

You can resize any of the Internet Explorer toolbars by pointing to the raised bar at the far left. When the mouse cursor becomes a bidirectional arrow, click and drag to the left or right. You can also rearrange the locations of the Address and Links toolbars by clicking in an unused area and dragging to the desired position.

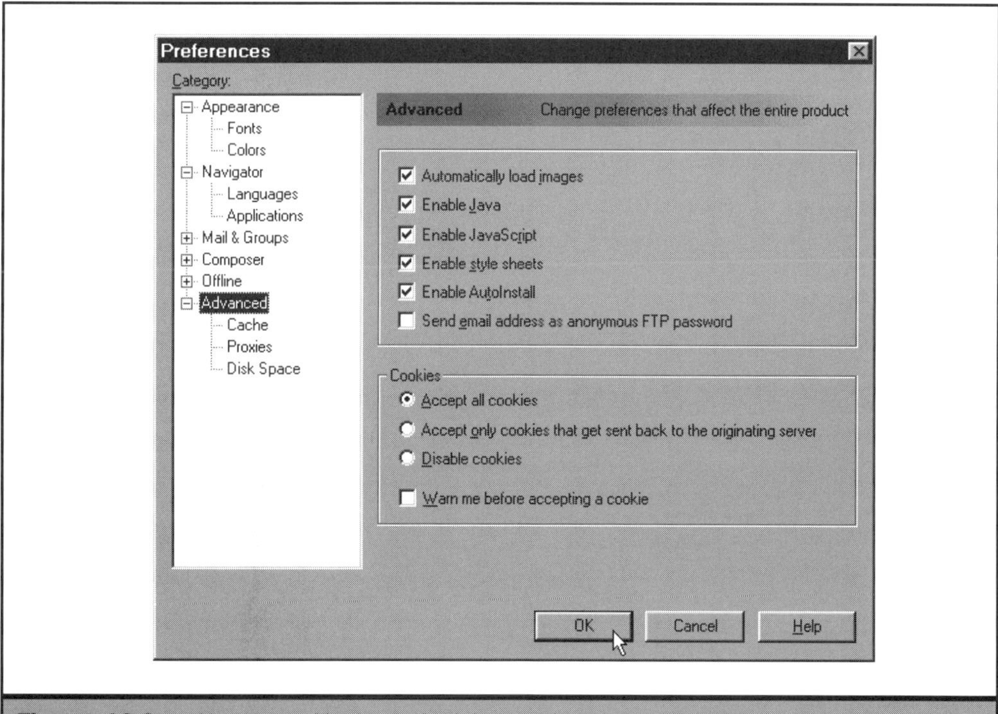

Figure 12-9. *Netscape Navigator's Advanced options allow you to control image loading and Java/JavaScript support*

The Links bar, by default, stores shortcuts to Web sites that Microsoft considers important, plus shortcuts to the My Documents folder and Manage Subscriptions feature. You can also use the Links bar to store shortcuts to any other folder or application on your hard disk. For instance, to create a shortcut to Microsoft Excel, choose Start | Programs | Office (95 or 97) and drag a copy of the Excel icon from the Start menu over the Links bar.

Quick URL Entry

Both browsers try to make it as easy as possible to type a new URL in the Location or Address field. If you omit the http:// prefix, the browser will automatically try to add that information to the address you type. If you omit http://www. from an address that begins that way, the browser will first try to find addresses without the www; if it doesn't find one, it will try an address that includes www. If you type an address with no domain suffix, Netscape Navigator will try adding the .com suffix; Internet Explorer will try addresses that end in .com, .org, and .edu.

When you start to type an address, both browsers will try to complete the address based on addresses you have visited before. If you want to go to the suggested address, press the ENTER key. To see other options, press the DOWN ARROW key.

The Forward and Back commands can help you retrace your recent steps one link at a time, but you can also display a list of the sites you've recently visited by right-clicking the Forward or Back button in the toolbar.

Changing Your Browser's Home Page

The pages that automatically load when you start your browser are some of the most valuable real estate on the World Wide Web. Because millions of people see those pages every day, both Microsoft and Netscape use these pages to promote their other products and services along with links to other sites that may or may not be particularly useful to you.

Both of these default home pages are reasonably benign—they can include news headlines, links to search engines, and other online tools—but you can probably find another page (or a blank screen) that better meets your specific needs. For example, if you're an investor, you could use one of the personalized market quotation services, such as StockPoint at http://www.irnet.com/scripts/setup.asp, as your home page. If you usually start your Web sessions by checking news headlines, a site like CNN Interactive or MSNBC might be a good choice. On the other hand, if you go to a different site each time you connect, you can save a few seconds when you start the browser by configuring the browser to start with a blank screen or a simple HTML document stored on your own computer.

Changing the Home Page in Internet Explorer

To change the home page in Internet Explorer, open the Internet Options dialog box and click the General tab. At the top of the window, either type the full URL in the Address field or click one of the buttons to set the home page to the currently visible Web page, the Windows default, or a blank window.

When you install Windows, the Internet Explorer default page is a Microsoft page, but some ISPs and online services change the default to their own home page. In some cases, the initial default page contains some kind of "welcome to our service" information or possibly an interactive page that forces you to register before you can move past it. The next time you start Internet Explorer, the default page will have changed to the service provider's regular home page. You can avoid all of this rigmarole by setting your home page to a blank window or a site of your own choosing, or you can change the default address instead. Internet Explorer's default page is controlled by the registry setting at HKEY_LOCAL_MACHINE\Software\Microsoft\Internet Explorer\Mail\Default_Page_URL.

Changing the Home Page in Netscape

To change the home page in Netscape Navigator, choose Edit | Preferences and select the Navigator item in the Category list. In the dialog box that appears (shown in Figure 12-10), use the Navigator Starts With option to set the opening page to a blank window, the specified home page, or the page that was open when you last shut down the browser. To specify a different home page, either type the full URL in the Location field or click the Use Current Page button to select the currently visible page.

Changing the IE Default Search Page

Internet Explorer allows you to search for information on the World Wide Web by clicking the Search button on its toolbar. The default search page for Internet Explorer is usually set to http://home.microsoft.com/search/search.asp or http://home.microsoft.com/access/allinone.asp.

You can edit the Windows registry to change the default search page invoked by this button to a different site, such as AltaVista or Infoseek. (For a discussion of Internet search engines and how to use them, see "Specialized Search Engines" later in this chapter.) Do the following:

1. Make sure you have a backup of your Windows registry, for safety's sake. (See Chapter 8 for information on confirming and creating registry backups.)
2. Launch RegEdit (choose Start | Run, enter **RegEdit**, and click OK). Then go to this registry key:

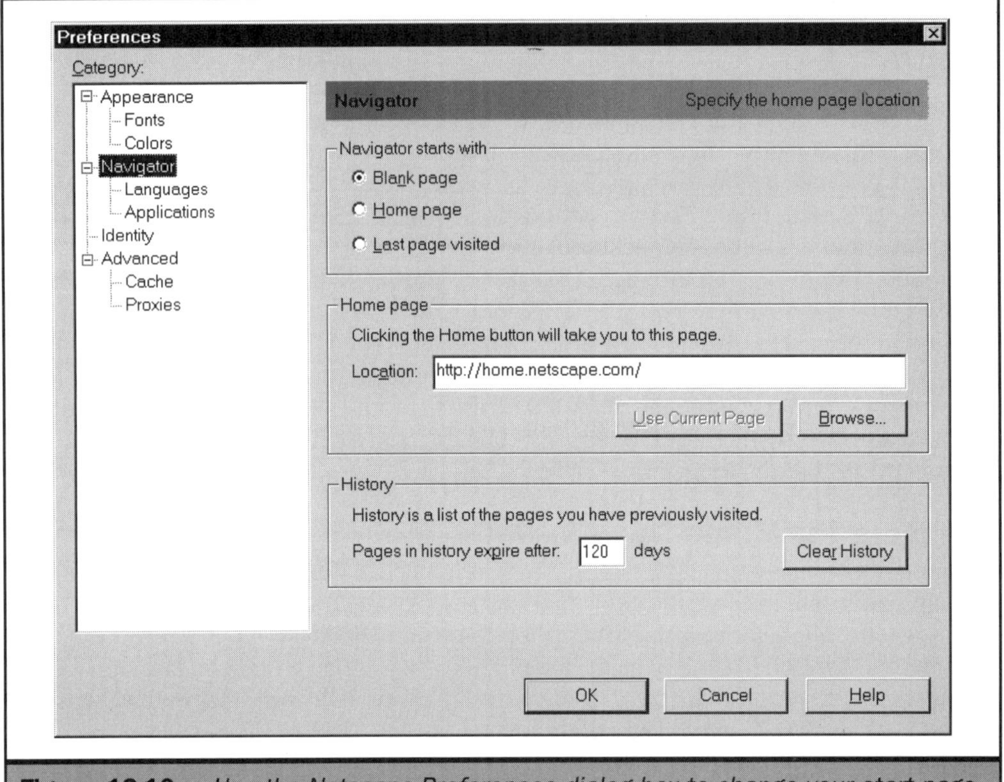

Figure 12-10. *Use the Netscape Preferences dialog box to change your start page*

HKEY_LOCAL_MACHINE\Software\Microsoft\Internet Explorer\Main

3. Double-click the Search Bar value (not Search Page) and enter the URL you want Internet Explorer to go to when you click its Search button (as shown here).

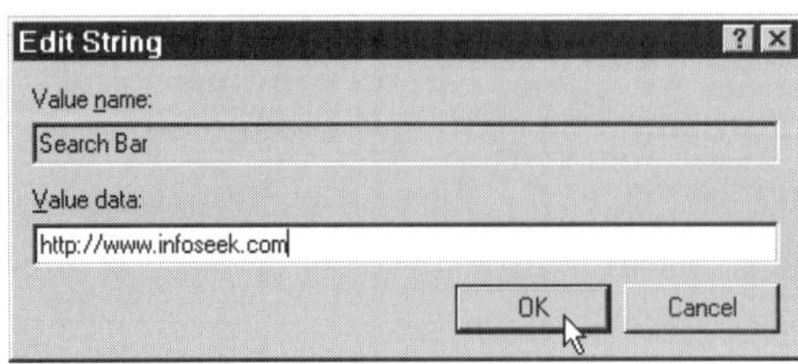

4. Close RegEdit.

Changing the Find | On The Internet Option on the Start Menu

The Search Page that your Web browser goes to when you select Start | Find | On The Internet is independent of the one that opens through the Internet Explorer toolbar. You can change this default to any search site you prefer. The technique is the same as described earlier but uses a different registry key:

1. Make sure you have a backup of your Windows registry, for safety's sake.
2. Launch RegEdit (choose Start | Run, enter **RegEdit**, and click OK). Then go to this registry key:

   HKEY_CURRENT_USER\Software\Microsoft\Internet Explorer\Main

   (Note that this is a different main key than the one used for changing the Search button.)
3. Double-click the Search Page value (not Search Bar) and enter the URL you want Internet Explorer to go to when you choose the Find | On the Internet option.
4. Close RegEdit.

Using History Lists

Both Internet Explorer and Netscape Navigator include History lists that contain links to all of the Web pages that you have visited in the recent past. These lists can be tremendously valuable tools when you want to return to a page that you did not add to your Favorites or Bookmarks list.

On the other hand, if you are sensitive about other people using your computer and seeing your personal History list, you may want to learn how to use your browser's Clear History command.

Using the History List in Internet Explorer

To open the History list in Internet Explorer, click the History button on the toolbar or select View | Explorer Bar | History, as shown in Figure 12-11. By default, every time you visit a Web page in Internet Explorer, a copy of the page (with embedded graphics) is downloaded and stored in the \WINDOWS\TEMPORARY INTERNET FILES folder. The pages you visit are listed in the History pane, organized by week and URL site. When you click to open a URL site, listings are displayed for the individual pages at that site. You can expand and contract the Week, Site, and Page listings by clicking an individual item again to open or close it. When the History list is large, up and down elevator buttons appear to let you scroll through it.

When Internet Explorer is in its default configuration, clicking a URL in the History list logs you onto the Internet to connect to the site (or it connects you directly, if you're already online). If the automatic Internet login feature is turned off, clicking a URL in the History list produces an error message.

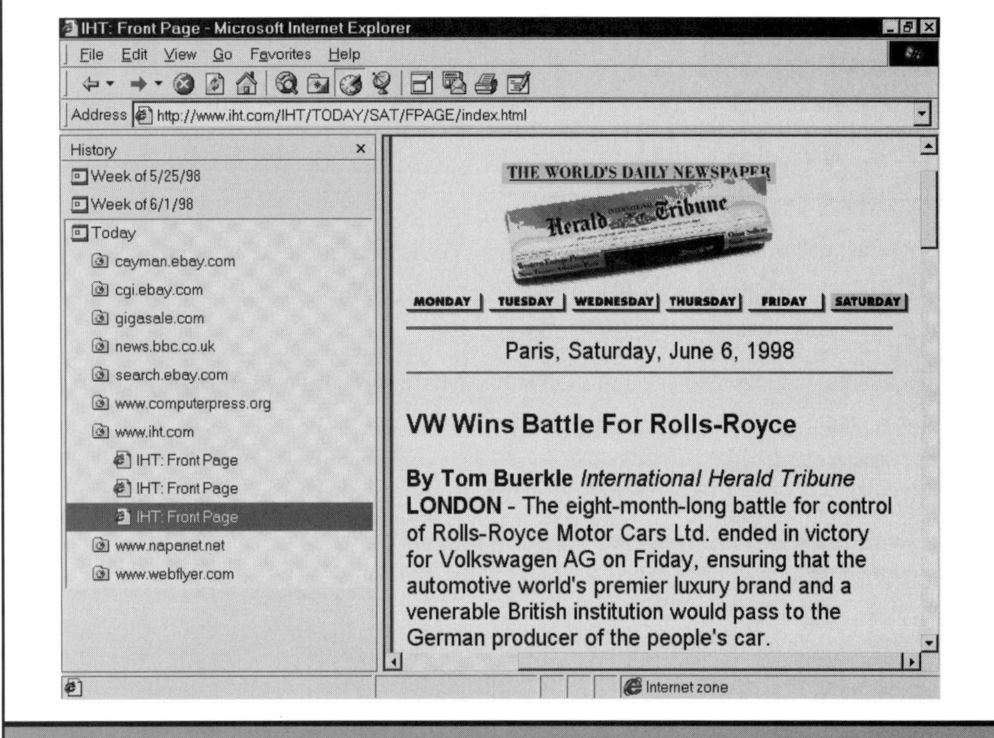

Figure 12-11. *Use the Internet Explorer History list to return to a Web page you've previously visited*

To remain offline and view sites that you've previously visited, choose File | Work Offline from Internet Explorer's pull-down menu. Listed pages that are still in the cache will then load automatically (with graphics intact) when you click them. The page and URL will be displayed just as if you were logged onto the Internet, but the resources are actually loaded from the IE cache in the \WINDOWS\TEMPORARY INTERNET FILES folder.

If you enter a URL that hasn't been cached while the Work Offline option is active, Internet Explorer will display the message "URL not found in offline mode." You can choose either to connect to the Internet to find the site or to remain offline.

When the Work Offline option is active, the History list will indicate that a URL resource isn't in the cache by displaying a crossed circle symbol next to the index finger mouse pointer.

The default History list duration in Internet Explorer is about three weeks. You can make the History list more valuable if you increase the duration of the list to, for instance, 120 or 180 days. To change the duration, follow these steps:

1. Select View | Internet Options and click the General tab.
2. In the History box near the bottom of the dialog box, use the arrow buttons to increase the number in the Days to Keep Pages in History field.

QUICK ACCESS TO HISTORY Normally with Internet Explorer, several mouse clicks are needed to access the History folder from within the browser. Here's how to add a cascading History folder to the Start menu.

1. Open Windows Explorer, right-click the \WINDOWS\HISTORY folder and select Copy from the pop-up menu.
2. Right-click the Start button and select Open or Explore.
3. Paste the History folder onto the top level of the Start menu by right-clicking and selecting Paste from the pop-up menu.

Replicating the Internet Explorer History List

The Internet Explorer History list can be a mission-critical feature for users who depend on the World Wide Web for their livelihood. Chapter 8, in the section "Preserving System Settings with RegEdit," describes a technique for backing up the History list and downloaded Web pages to guard against accidental loss. Although Microsoft doesn't support it, there's also a way for you to transfer a History list and downloaded Web pages from one Windows 98 computer to another.

This is a power-user trick for people who are familiar with the DOS command line, experienced at backing up and transferring files between two computers, and comfortable with using Win98's RegEdit.

1. Create a backup directory for your URL history from a DOS window under Windows 98, as described in "Preserving System Settings with RegEdit" in Chapter 8. Use XCOPY to duplicate the directory (still in a DOS window) to a shared network folder, zip drive, or floppy diskette.
2. Open RegEdit and export the following registry key to a file:

   HKEY_USERS*USERNAME*\Software\Microsoft\Windows\Current-Version\Internet Settings

   (where *USERNAME* is the current user; select the .Default key if there is only one user on the machine).
3. To preserve the downloaded pages, archive the contents of the \WINDOWS\TEMPORARY INTERNET FILES directory with a 32-bit utility such as Drag and Zip, WinZip, or PKZip for Windows. Transfer the archive file to a shared network folder, zip drive, or series of floppy disks.

To transfer your Internet history to another copy of Windows (replacing its current History list), follow these steps:

1. Under the Windows 98 interface, rename the \WINDOWS\HISTORY folder on the new machine to \WINDOWS\OLDHIST.
2. Create a new, empty \WINDOWS\HISTORY directory.
3. Use XCOPY in a DOS window to copy the contents of the backed-up URL History directory to the new \WINDOWS\HISTORY directory. (For example, type **XCOPY A:\HISTBAK*.* C:\WINDOWS\HISTORY /E /H /V**.)
4. After backing up the Windows registry on the second machine, merge the exported .REG file you created from the first machine into the Windows registry on the new machine. (See Chapter 8 for information on how to do this.)
5. If you decided to archive the physical Web pages as well as the History list pointers, unpack the contents of the first \WINDOW\TEMPORARY INTERNET FILES directory into the \WINDOWS\TEMPORARY INTERNET FILES directory on the second machine.
6. Reboot the computer.

After the machine restarts, open the \WINDOWS\HISTORY folder and inspect the History list. If you can't open pages by clicking the week and site name listings, use Tweak UI to repair the \URL HISTORY and \TEMPORARY INTERNET FILES directories, as described in Chapter 8.

The foregoing procedure is totally unsupported by Microsoft, but it has worked successfully for me on repeated occasions. (If you don't like the results, you can restore the registry on the second machine, delete the new \WINDOWS\HISTORY folder, and change the name of the OLDHIST folder back to HISTORY to return the History list to its previous state.

Note *To perform the trick above on a machine with multiple user profiles enabled, you'll have to duplicate the user account on the second machine and then duplicate and copy the \PROFILES\USERNAME\HISTORY folder instead of the \WINDOWS\HISTORY folder. To restore access to the stored Web pages as well as the History list, you'll also have to copy the USER.DAT file in the \WINDOWS directory of the second machine to the machine's \WINDOWS\PROFILES\USERNAME directory after you merge the .REG file.*

Using the History List in Netscape Navigator

In Netscape Navigator, you can open the History list by selecting Window | History or pressing CTRL-H. The History list is a separate window with an entry for each page you have visited, as shown in Figure 12-12. By clicking a header button, you can sort the list by page title, address, date and time of your first or most recent visit, or the number of times you have viewed the page.

Like the list in Internet Explorer, the History list in Netscape Navigator will be more valuable if you increase the number of days for which it saves listings. To change the duration of the Netscape History list, follow these steps:

1. Select Edit | Preferences.
2. In the Category list in the Preferences dialog box, select Navigator.
3. Near the bottom of the dialog box, change the number of days in the Pages in History Expire After field.

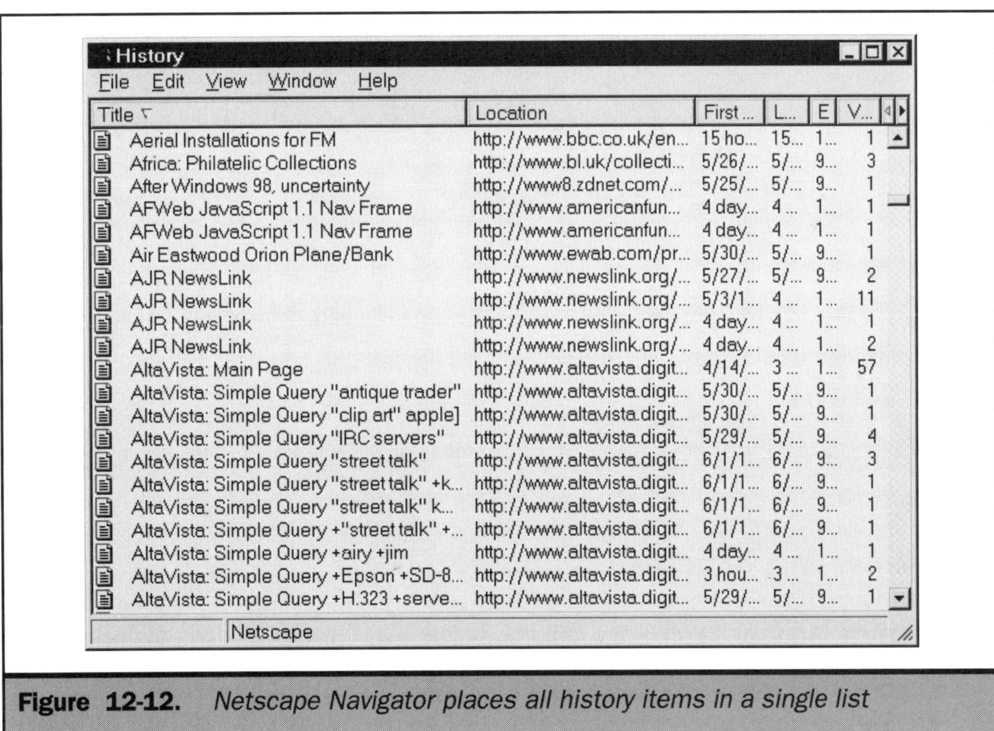

Figure 12-12. *Netscape Navigator places all history items in a single list*

You're probably aware that Microsoft's Internet Explorer 4 allows you to perform file management and Web site browsing from a single application window. Netscape Navigator is not as sophisticated, but you can still use it to explore the contents of your hard disk and view selected documents. To explore a particular folder in Netscape, enter its path in the URL Location box. For example, if you enter **C:\WINDOWS***, a hierarchical view of the Windows folder will be displayed. You can select and open any document format supported by the browser to view its contents in the browser window.*

If you want to view Microsoft Word or Excel documents with Netscape Navigator, you can download special helper applications that do the trick from Microsoft's Web site at http://www.microsoft.com/msdownload/default.asp#viewers.

Changing the Default Browser

File associations to the .HTM file type are usually transferred to the last Web browser you installed. To restore an association from Internet Explorer to Netscape Navigator or vice versa, open the browser you want and answer Yes when prompted to make it your default browser, as shown here:

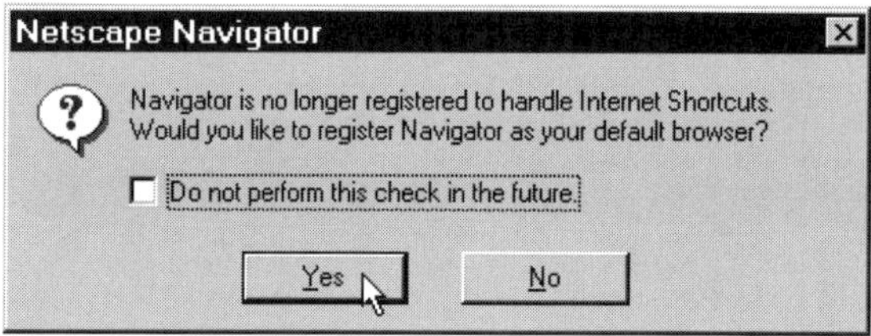

Leave the Do Not Perform This Check in the Future box unchecked if you expect to switch default browsers more than once or twice.

Browsing from the Desktop

It's not necessary to open your Web browser before you jump to a Web page. You can also launch URLs from several other places within Windows 98.

Web Browsing from My Computer

The Address bar is an optional toolbar in all of My Computer's directory windows. If you type the address of a Web page in the Address bar, Windows will switch the My Computer window to an Internet Explorer window, loading the page you request. You can use the Back and Forward buttons or commands to move between Web pages and local folders.

Web Browsing from Windows Explorer

The Address bar in Windows Explorer works just like the Address bar in My Computer. Type an address and press ENTER to open a Web page in the right pane of the Explorer window, as shown here:

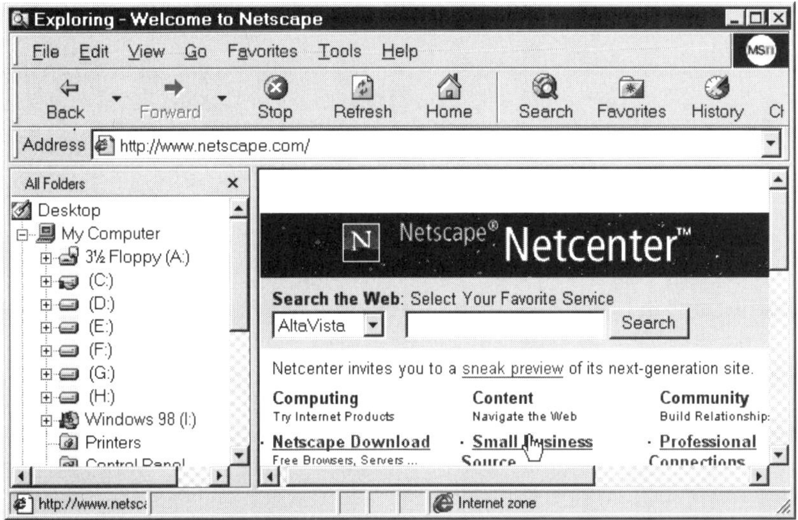

To save a local copy of an image file in a Web page, click the image and drag it to the name of the folder where you want to store it. To save a shortcut to the current page, drag the icon in the Address bar to the name of the folder where you want to store it. To save a shortcut to a page linked to the current page, drag the link to the folder where you want to store the shortcut.

Browsing from the Start Menu

You can open Web pages from several places in the Start menu:

- The Favorites command opens a submenu with links to the pages in your Internet Explorer Favorites list.
- The Run command accepts Web addresses as well as local program commands and file paths.
- The Find submenu includes an On The Internet command that opens the same page by choosing Go | Search The Web in Internet Explorer.
- The optional History menu (see "Using the History Lists" earlier in this chapter) contains submenus for each day of the current week and each previous week in

your Internet Explorer History list. These entries open cascading links to Web pages you have recently visited.

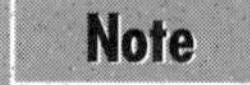

All of these URL launch techniques open your current default Web browser even if it's not Microsoft Internet Explorer. If Netscape is your current default browser, the page you request will load in Netscape. However, the Favorites and History menus still grab their lists from Internet Explorer even when they open pages in another browser.

More Browser Bells and Whistles

Microsoft offers several free add-on utilities and supplementary components that are not part of the standard Internet Explorer installation in Windows 98. Some of these are "official" Microsoft products, while others are unsupported enhancements written by Microsoft developers.

The best place to start looking for these Microsoft enhancements is the Internet Explorer home page at http://www.microsoft.com/ie/. When patches and service packs become available, you will find pointers to download sources on that page.

To find a list of currently available official Internet Explorer add-ons, start at http://www.microsoft.com/ie/download/ and follow the links to the Windows 98 pages. Among the more interesting components that are not on the Windows 98 CD but are available for download are Supplemental Web Fonts and the somewhat irritating Internet Explorer Sound Pack.

The Internet Explorer PowerToys are a set of add-on features and functions that were created by members of the Internet Explorer development team. You can download them from http://www.microsoft.com/ie/ie40/powertoys/. The PowerToys include these functions:

- **Zoom In/Zoom Out** When you right-click an image in a Web page, the Zoom In and Zoom Out commands change the size of the image without affecting the rest of the page.
- **Quick Search** The Address field accepts search requests. To use your default search engine, type **go *keyword*, find *keyword***, or **? *keyword*.** To run an AltaVista search, type **av *keyword***.
- **Toggle Images** The Toggle Images command on the Links toolbar instructs the browser to ignore or display images when you download new Web pages. For the fastest download speed, set Toggle Images to hide the images. Then use the command again to display the images on pages you want to see in all their graphic glory.
- **Highlight Text** The text highlighter places a yellow background behind text. To use this function, select the text with your mouse, right-click, and choose the Highlight command.

- **Open Frame in New Window** Some Web sites force the browser to display a frame around pages that you reach through embedded links. This generally obnoxious practice reduces the amount of space available for the framed site, while keeping the framing site's advertising visible on your screen. To get rid of a frame, move your cursor to the portion of the page you want to view and select the Open Frame in New Window command.
- **Web Search** To use a word or phrase from the currently visible Web page as a keyword for a new search, select the text, right-click, and use the Web Search command.
- **Links List** A Links list is a list of all the links in a Web page, as shown in Figure 12-13. To display a Links list for the current page, right-click anywhere in the page and select the Links List command.

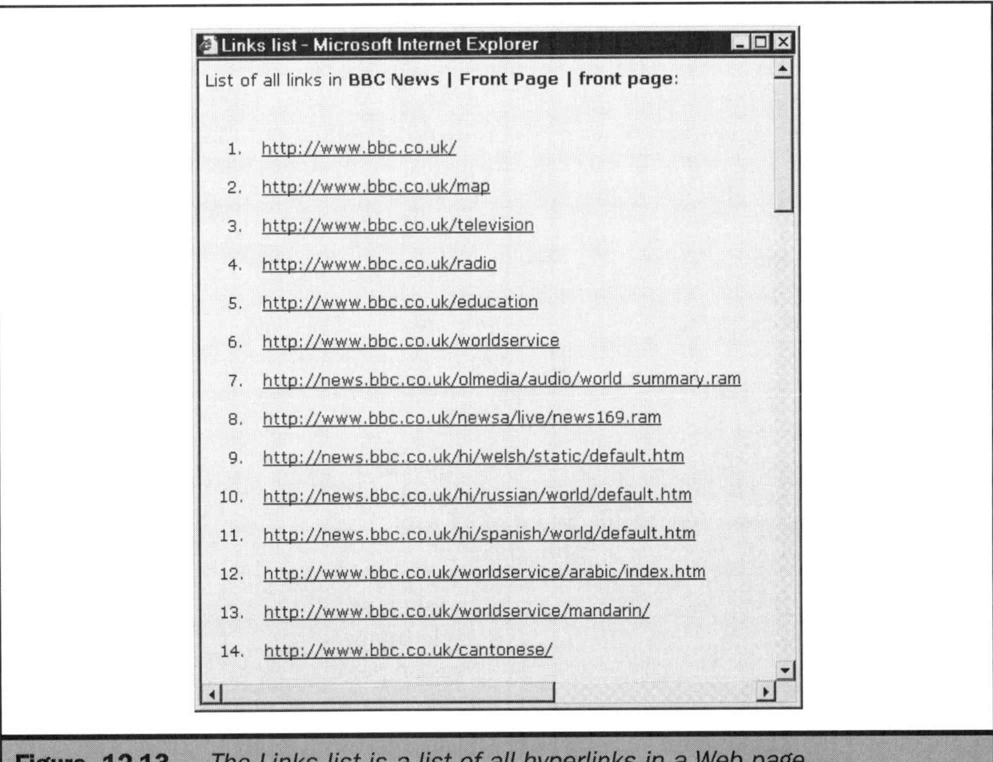

Figure 12-13. *The Links list is a list of all hyperlinks in a Web page*

The World Wide Web as a Way of Life

Whether you settle on Internet Explorer or Netscape Navigator as your browser, the real point of your choice is the information and entertainment resources you can find on the World Wide Web. There's a mind-boggling amount of stuff out there just a few mouse-clicks away from your computer screen. You can easily spend hours (if not months!) wandering aimlessly through the Web, following links and stopping when you find something that strikes your fancy—but if you limit yourself to that approach, you're likely to miss a lot. Fortunately, there are plenty of helpful road signs to help you find your way.

Search Tools

Internet search tools (also called search engines) are Web sites that contain links to other sites. When you send a key word or phrase to the search site, the site returns a list of links related to the search terms. Each search tool uses a different technique for finding matching sites; some simply tell you about every site that contains the keywords, while others apply various subjective criteria to try to give you the closest possible match. Still others limit their searches to sites that are related to a high-level topic, such as gardening or health care.

All of these search services maintain their own Web sites, and many are also accessible through interactive links from other sites. Because many of the major search services make their money by selling targeted advertising (for example, if you run a search for "mutual funds," you might see a banner advertisement for a specific fund on the page that lists the search results), they encourage other sites to link to them.

Limiting Your Search

There are so many sites on the Web, related to so many different topics that the most common problem in working with a search engine is finding too many links. It's not uncommon to discover that your search has located 10,000 or 20,000 matches. If you run a search on the word "colt," you'll find a lot of information about both pistols and young horses. To make the search more productive, include a second keyword in your search. You will, in short, generally obtain more useful results if you learn some techniques for making your search more specific.

The syntax required to perform a search varies from search site to search site. For example, at Digital's AltaVista site, you distinguish a phrase from a series of words by enclosing the phrase in quotation marks. Other search engines provide a separate field to distinguish a phrase from a series of words. Some search engines accept the use of + and – (or AND and NOT) Boolean operators to refine a search. Usually, the search site's initial page provides a place to click to learn about the engine's advanced options.

Following are some ways to refine your search.

USE MULTIPLE KEYWORDS When you enter more than one keyword, most search engines return links that contain one or more of the words you request. The sites that include the largest number of matching terms are usually at the top of the list. The Boolean operators can assist you with a search. If you're looking for paintings by the artist Picasso and are not interested in computer programming languages, you might enter the sequence **+Picasso +painting** or **Picasso AND Painting**, depending upon the requirements of the engine.

USE PHRASES INSTEAD OF SINGLE WORDS Most search engines treat words contained within quotation marks as a single search term. One way to see if this feature works is to examine the statistics reported when the phrase is retrieved. If you enter **"William Butler Yeats"** and see a message that reports 100,000 instances of William, 200,000 instances of Butler, and 1000 instances of Yeats, you'll know that the quotation marks had no effect. You can browse the search engine for advanced fields that permit you to specify "search as a phrase," or you can try concatenating with + signs: **+William +Butler + Yeats**. However, this second method may turn up a page that contains a sentence like "Alas, the 500th Yeats quotation caused the butler to do away with poor William."

Some search engines, such as Infoseek, permit you to refine a search by hunting for a second set of keywords only on the pages retrieved by the first search.

USE WILDCARDS Use an asterisk (*) to replace one or more letters in a keyword to search for more than one form of the word.

LIMIT THE SEARCH BY EXCLUDING IRRELEVANT WORDS Many search engines use a minus sign (–) to exclude keywords. For example, if you're looking for information about the chemical element Krypton, you might run a search on **Krypton –Superman**. Be sure to include a space before the minus sign.

Common Search Engines

It's not uncommon to get completely different results when you enter the same keywords into more than one search engine. Because each service uses different rules and criteria to perform its search, it's often productive to try the same search through several search engines. Some of the most widely used search engines are listed here:

- *Excite* (http://www.excite.com) uses something called "Intelligent Concept Extraction" to find sites related to your keywords even if the actual words are not used at the site. For example, a search for "apples" could produce links to a "tree fruit" Web site.
- *AltaVista* (http://www.altavista.digital.com) is a full-text Web index. Unlike subject-based search engines that point to Web pages that are specifically

related to the keyword, AltaVista maintains a database that includes the full text of more than 35 million pages and identifies every page that includes the keyword. AltaVista's site also includes a "Browse by Subject" search with more than 16,500 topic headings and a translation function that can provide an English (or French, Italian, German, Spanish, or Portuguese) version of text from a foreign-language site. Because AltaVista is intended to be a showcase for Digital's high-end Alpha processors, it usually returns huge lists of matching sites within just a few seconds after you submit a request.

If you get too many results from an AltaVista search, you can click the AltaVista advanced search options on the main page to open a second page that lets you conduct more refined searches.

- *Infoseek* (http://www.infoseek.com) is another subject-based service with a very good range of features, including plain-text searches. Infoseek also offers a Netscape Navigator add-on that places a live search field, shown here, in the Windows, Internet Explorer, and Navigator toolbars.

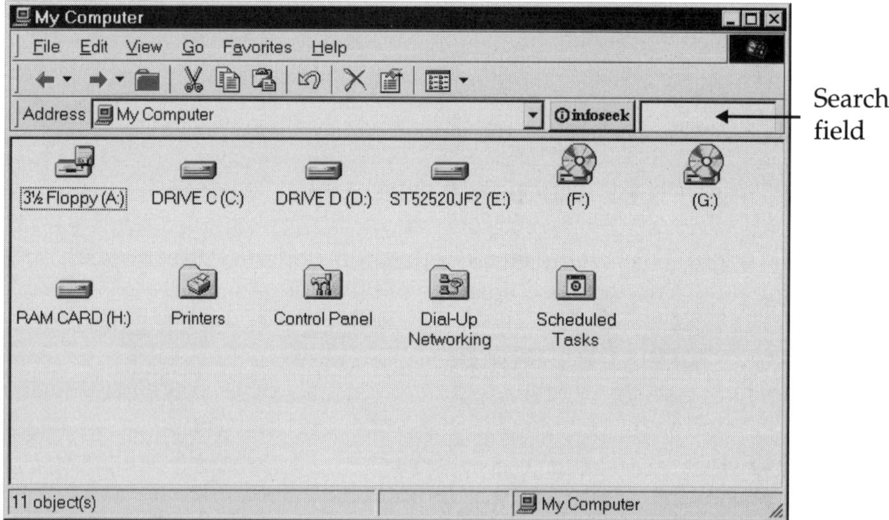

- *HotBot* (http://www.hotbot.com) is a full-text search engine with an even larger database than the one used by AltaVista. Searches through HotBot frequently produce more hits than those through any other search engine, but because its database is constantly updated, it seems to include fewer dead-end links to irrelevant, duplicate, or nonexistent Web sites.

- *Yahoo* (http://www.yahoo.com) is a directory rather than a search engine. It lists Web sites in thousands of individual categories, but when you search for a keyword, it takes you to lists of matching topics rather than individual Web pages. Therefore, it's a good place to look for additional sites related to the same topic. You can also use Yahoo to drill down from a general topic such as "Literature" through "Authors" and "Victorian" to "Charles Dickens."
- *Snap*! (http://home.snap.com) is another directory of Web sites with an easy-to-use format and a well thought-out arrangement of categories.
- *Ask Jeeves* (http://www.askjeeves.com) accepts questions in natural English and links you to sites that contain answers to your question.

Metasearch Tools

If each search engine produces a somewhat different list of matching pages, why not combine several engines in a single search? That's the concept behind the metasearch services that automatically send the same request to several search engines. You can run a multiple-engine search from these Web sites:

Dogpile	http://www.dogpile.com
Mamma	http://www.mamma.com
Metacrawler	http://www.metacrawler.com
MetaFind	http://ww.metafind.com
Savvy Search	http://guaraldi.cs.colostate.edu:2000/form

Search Tools Integrated into the Browser

Both Internet Explorer and Netscape Navigator have direct links from the toolbar to several Internet search engines. In Internet Explorer, the Search button opens a Search bar on the left side of the browser window. The Search bar is particularly convenient because you don't have to constantly move back and forth to the search screen as you investigate the links that the search engine returned.

To run a search, first click the Choose a Search Engine button to open a list of available search sites. Click the link to the site you want to use, and it will open in the Search bar. Enter your keywords, and the search engine will display links in a separate pane, as shown in Figure 12-14.

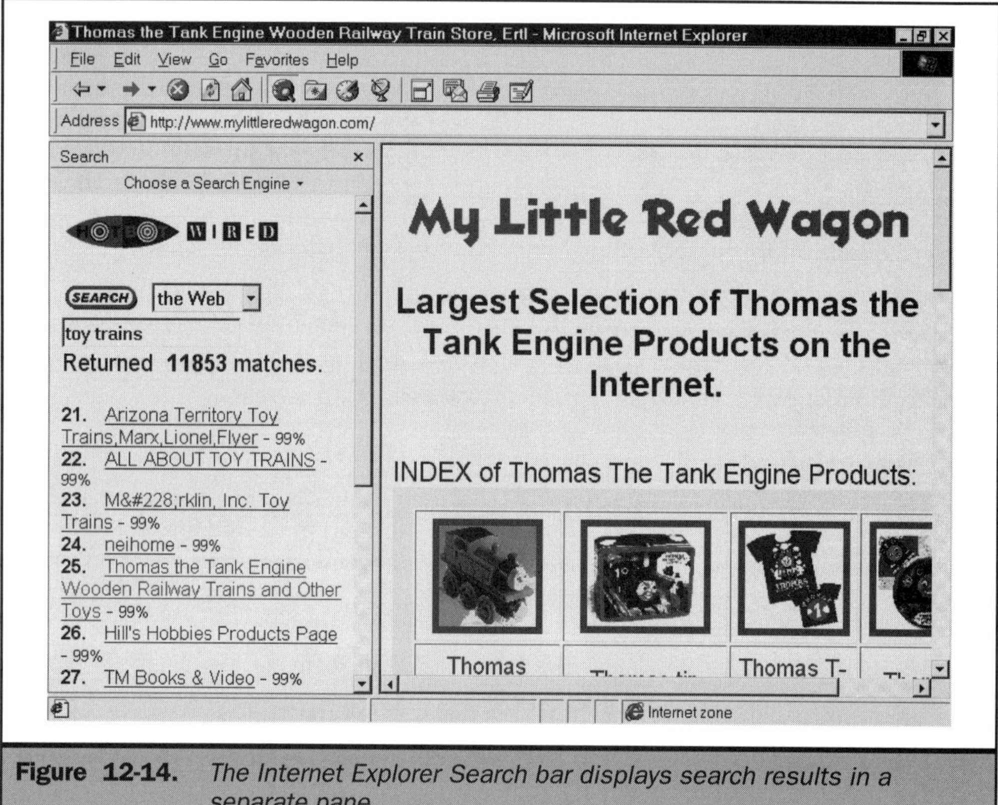

Figure 12-14. *The Internet Explorer Search bar displays search results in a separate pane*

Internet Explorer also has a Search the Web command on the Go menu that opens a Microsoft page with links to several dozen general and specialized search services, as shown in Figure 12-15.

In Netscape Navigator, the Search button on the toolbar and the Edit | Search Internet command both take you to Netscape's Netcenter Net Search page, shown in Figure 12-16, with links to a good selection of other search sites.

Other Online Guides to Search Services

The Microsoft and Netscape search pages are not the only Web sites that contain direct links to several different search tools. Each of the sites in the following list are one-stop search pages that allow you to send a keyword search to any of half a dozen or more

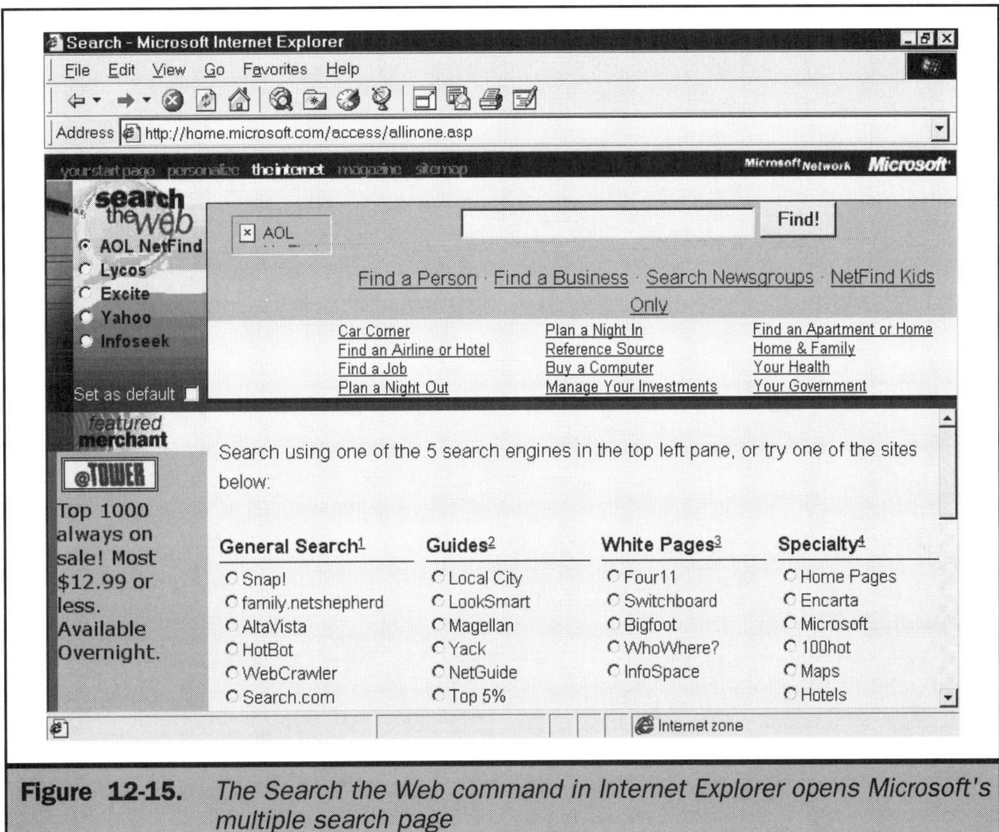

Figure 12-15. *The Search the Web command in Internet Explorer opens Microsoft's multiple search page*

search engines. These are not metasearch services like the ones described earlier in this section because you send your request to just one search engine at a time. If you normally run Web searches whenever you connect to the Web and open your browser, one of these sites might be a good choice as a Start page.

All-in-One	http://www.albany.net/allinone
Search.com	http://www.search.com
Find-It	http://www.itools.com/find-it/
Find It	http://www.sary.com/findit.html

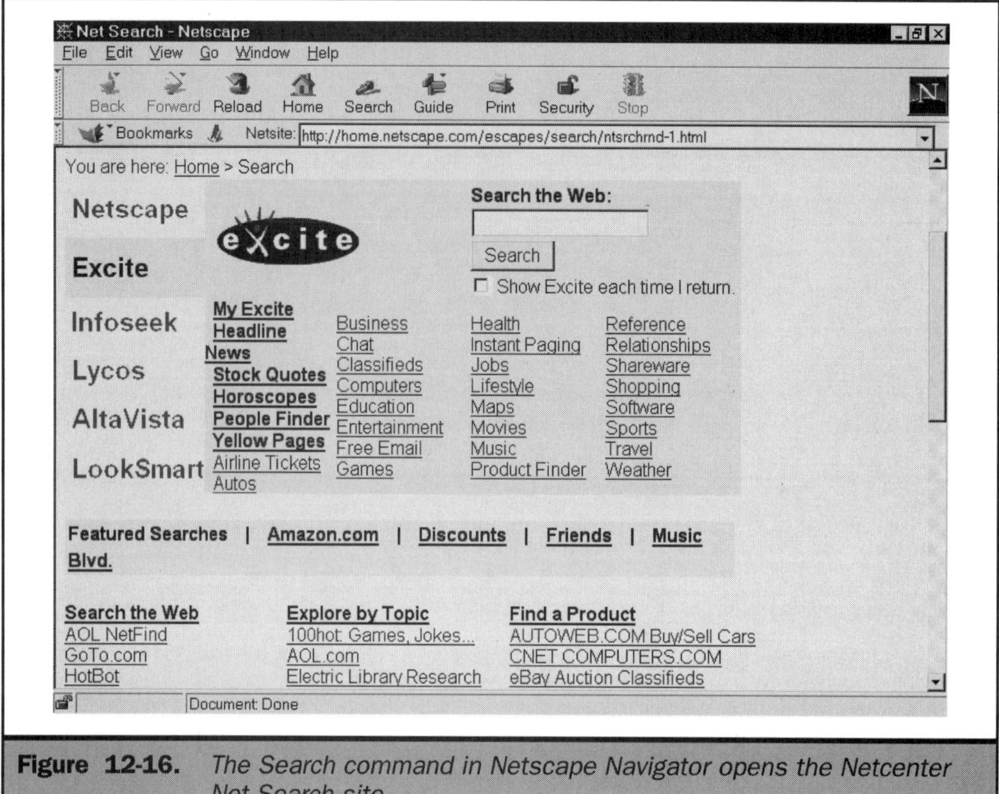

Figure 12-16. *The Search command in Netscape Navigator opens the Netcenter Net Search site*

Specialized Search Engines

If you're looking for a particular type of information, such as medical information or a recipe, it might be more efficient to use a specialized search service that limits itself to information related to the topic rather than one of the general-purpose sites that searches through the entire Internet. For example, the Health A to Z site (http://www.HealthAtoZ.com) is a search engine for medical topics.

If you're looking for information from a specific geographic region, a localized search engine will probably give you more hits than a Web-wide search. So if you're looking for Web sites in Australia, you might do better with the Web Wombat search engine (http://www.webwombat.com.au), with its database of more than 2.7 million Australian pages, than with one of the U.S.-based services.

It should not surprise you to learn that the best places to find specialized Web search engines are other Web sites. One of the best is Beaucoup! (located at http://www.beaucoup.com), which has links to more than a thousand different search engines, directories, and indexes, including everything from CheeseNet and the Scottish Tartan Finder to the Dictionary of Acronyms and Abbreviations. For country-based searches, the Search Engines Worldwide site (http://www.twics.com/~takakuwa/search/) has links to search engines in more than a hundred countries and regions.

News and Other Information Sources

Hundreds of newspapers, radio stations, and other news agencies operate Web sites. In addition, the major news services operate separate 24-hour news sites on the Web. If you're looking for news about a breaking story or news that your local media doesn't cover, the Web is a superb resource.

WEB-BASED NEWS SITES Web sites that contain news stories written specifically for online readers (rather than recycled material from print and broadcast) use are good places to look when you want up-to-the-minute reports.

CNN INTERACTIVE CNN interactive (http://www.cnn.com) is operated by the Cable News Network. Like the CNN broadcast services, the Web site puts new stories online as soon as they arrive in the newsroom. CNN's audioselect service includes live audio feeds from five different CNN channels.

USA TODAY USA Today's Web site (http://www.usatoday.com) is organized into sections like those in the print version of the paper: News, Sports, Money, Life, and Weather. The top-level page contains the latest headlines and links to stories on other pages.

MSNBC MSNBC is a joint venture of Microsoft and NBC News. It has links to reports from NBC's broadcast and cable news programs along with a full budget of news written for the Web.

ABCNEWS.COM As the name suggests, ABCNEWS.com (http://www.abcnews.com) contains text, audio, and video reports from the ABC radio and TV networks.

BBC NEWS The British Broadcasting Corporation operates one of the most extensive news-gathering organizations in the world to support its domestic and international radio and television services. The BBC Web site (http://news.bbc.co.uk) often offers a different perspective on the news from news sites based in the United States.

WIRE SERVICES Most news media outlets depend on the Associated Press, Reuters, or one of the other major news agencies to provide coverage of events that their own reporters are not able to reach. Almost all of the world's news wire services supply their output to Web sites, but in a few cases, you might have to use a back door to get in.

ASSOCIATED PRESS AP operates a very extensive Web service called The Wire, but you have to go through the site of an AP member newspaper to reach it. If you want to bypass the news from the *Reading* (Pennsylvania) *Eagle* or the *Grand Island* (Nebraska) *Independent* and go directly to The Wire, go to http://wire.ap.org and select a gateway. It really doesn't make any difference which gateway you choose because they all take you to the same place, but each shows a different newspaper's logo across the top of the screen.

For much of the same information in another layout, take a look at the AP Update page at http://www.newsday.com/ap/topnewsx.htm.

UNITED PRESS INTERNATIONAL UPI is not as big as AP and it has been in financial trouble for many years, but it still supplies a full budget of news to its remaining subscribers. The direct Internet version of UPI's news feed comes through Clari.net, but access is limited to ISPs that subscribe to the Clari.net service. To learn whether your ISP offers Clari.net, look at the ISP listings at http://www.clari.net/iap.

REUTERS Reuters has been supplying news and financial data since 1851. The reports on their News Room Web site are frequently longer and more detailed than the stories supplied by AP or UPI. Reuters News Room (http://www.reuters.com/reutersnews) includes five different news summaries (International News, U.S. News, U.S. Politics, Business, and Sports).

Several other Web sites, including Yahoo! (http://www.yahoo.com/headlines) also carry news from Reuters.

AGENCE FRANCE-PRESS AFP has correspondents in 165 countries with regional centers in Paris, Washington, Hong Kong, and Cyprus. Its World News Roundup is updated several times every day at http://www.afp.com/english/news/summary/light/.

ITAR-TASS ITAR-TASS is the Russian News Agency. Before the fall of the old Soviet Union, TASS was primarily a source of Soviet propaganda, but today it's a respected international news agency with unmatched coverage of eastern Europe and central Asia. Its English-language News Online Web site at http://www.itar-tass.com/newsdir.htm includes full-text news reports and a photo and information service that almost always includes pictures of dignitaries opening exhibits and conferences, striking miners, and other routine stuff, along with other, more newsworthy items.

THE PRESS ASSOCIATION PA NewsCentre (http://www.pa.press.net) is the British Press Association's online news service. It's almost entirely limited to news from Britain and Ireland.

KYODO NEWS For news from Japan and the Asia-Pacific region, the reports from Japan's Kyodo News may be the best you can find. The first page you will see when you jump to http://www.kyodo.co.jp/ is in Japanese (which may appear on your screen as gibberish characters if you don't have a Japanese character set loaded), but you can click the English button to move to English-language pages.

Newspapers

Newspapers on the Web have become so common that the handful of papers whose daily contents are *not* online are more remarkable than the ones that do have Web sites. From giants like the *New York Times* and the *Washington Post* to tiny weeklies in Humboldt, Iowa, and West Dover, Vermont, the number of newspapers available on the Web is huge and growing bigger every month.

A newspaper on your computer screen will never be as convenient as ink on paper, but there are a lot of good reasons to use the online versions: You can read the news almost as soon as it is published, you can find more than one description of the same event, and you can select and read news stories that your local paper does not choose to cover. A newspaper close to a big story usually devotes more space and resources to that story than another newspaper or broadcaster several thousand miles away.

The American Journalism Review (AJR) maintains a very complete directory of newspapers on the Web at its NewsLink Web site (http://newslink.org/news.html), shown in Figure 12-17. If you can't find the newspaper you want in the NewsLink list, try the Newspaper Association of America list (http://www.naa.org/hotlinks/index.asp) or Editor & Publisher's MediaINFO Links site (http://www.mediainfo.com/emedia/).

Radio Stations

It's entirely possible that the Internet is the future of radio broadcasting. Instead of (or in addition to) sending their programs to a large, expensive AM or FM transmitter that might distribute them to an area of a few hundred square miles, broadcasters can use an Internet audio server that can send the same signals around the world. As a listener, your options are no longer limited to a handful of local stations; you can use your computer to tune in to radio stations and audio services from around the world. For example, if there are no local stations playing classical music, or if the only local classical music station seems to play nothing but screeching sopranos, you can choose KING-FM from Seattle, WQXR from New York, WFMT from Chicago, or CBC Radio 2 from Canada. Still more classical music is available from several Internet-only audio services.

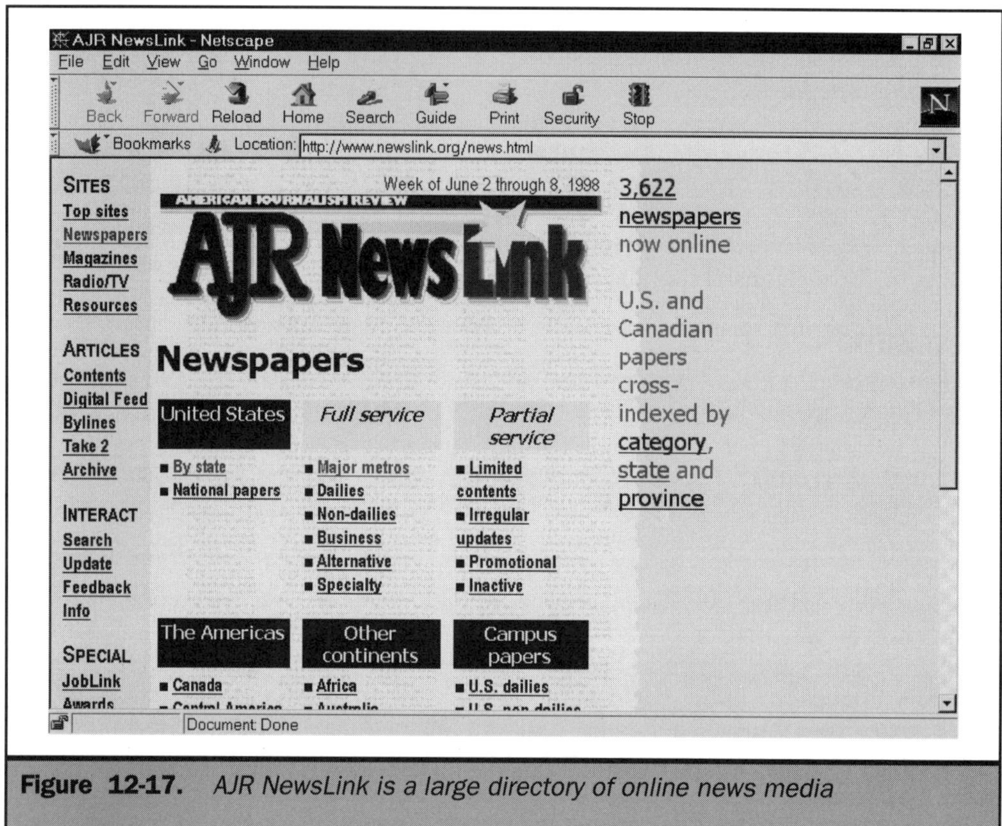

Figure 12-17. *AJR NewsLink is a large directory of online news media*

To listen to audio through the Internet, you must have a sound card in your computer with either a pair of speakers or a headset and one or more audio client programs. The most widely used format for continuous audio (also called streaming audio) is RealAudio, but a few stations use other systems. Windows 98 includes RealPlayer client software for RealAudio and a separate client for Microsoft's own NetShow format, but you may discover that the radio station or audio service you want to hear is using a newer, incompatible version. This is not a serious problem because just about every audio Web site includes a link to a site where you can download the latest and greatest release, usually at no cost (the audio format developers make their money selling servers, so they give away their client software). Both RealPlayer and NetShow also support streaming video.

Windows 98 bundles RealPlayer 4.0, and at least one subsequent version is available. You can install the newer version by connecting to the Internet, opening your existing version of Real Player, and choosing Check for Upgrade on the Help menu; or you can log directly onto the RealNetworks Web site at http://www.real.com.

The following illustration shows the most recent RealPlayer controls. When you link to a RealAudio server, the audio stream automatically launches RealPlayer and starts to play through your sound card.

Note that Microsoft has recently published its own enhanced Windows Media Player that also handles RealAudio and Netshow content. This is a free download (available at http://www.microsoft.com/windows/mediaplayer/default.asp) which replaces the RealPlayer bundled in Windows 98.

To find an online radio station, start with one of these directories:

- *On The Air* (http://www.ontheair.com) lists more than 600 stations in all parts of the world along with some audio oddities, such as live pickups of the Dallas–Ft. Worth air traffic control center and the Los Angeles police radio dispatcher.
- *Internet Radio* at http://goan.com/radio is based in Australia, but it also includes broadcasters in North America and Europe as well as the Pacific region.
- *Radio Tower* (http://www.radiotower.com) lists more than 500 stations arranged by name, type of music, or location.
- *BRS Web Radio* at http://www.web-radio.com/ has links to more than 1,300 stations. It's a little slower to load than some of the other directories, but it seems to include many stations that the other guides have missed.
- *Yahoo* lists several dozen audio services, including some that aren't on most of the other directories, in its Real Time category under Business and Economy | Companies | News and Media | Internet Broadcasting.
- *Broadcast.com* (http://www.broadcast.com) has links to about 300 live radio and TV stations, 200 sports teams, and several other audio services.
- *NetRadio* (http://www.netradio.net) is an audio service with more than 150 music channels. Many of these programs are quite specialized, including reggae, Gregorian chants, and "Classic Crooners" selections.

- *TimeCast* (http://www.timecast.com) is a directory of RealAudio sites that includes a real-time guide to live events and special programs that are currently available and links to several thousand audio archives.

Financial Information

The Internet has had a huge effect on the way investors gather information and manage their portfolios. There are Web sites that offer objective information and subjective advice about every imaginable type of investment. All of the major stock exchanges (and most of the minor ones) operate their own Web sites, but the real action is in the third-party sites that contain stock, bond, option, and mutual fund quotations and information from analysts and investment advisors of every style.

As a start, if you're a light stock market investor, you can customize a home page at Microsoft's Web site to present daily quotations every time you open Internet Explorer, as shown in Figure 12-18. Here's how:

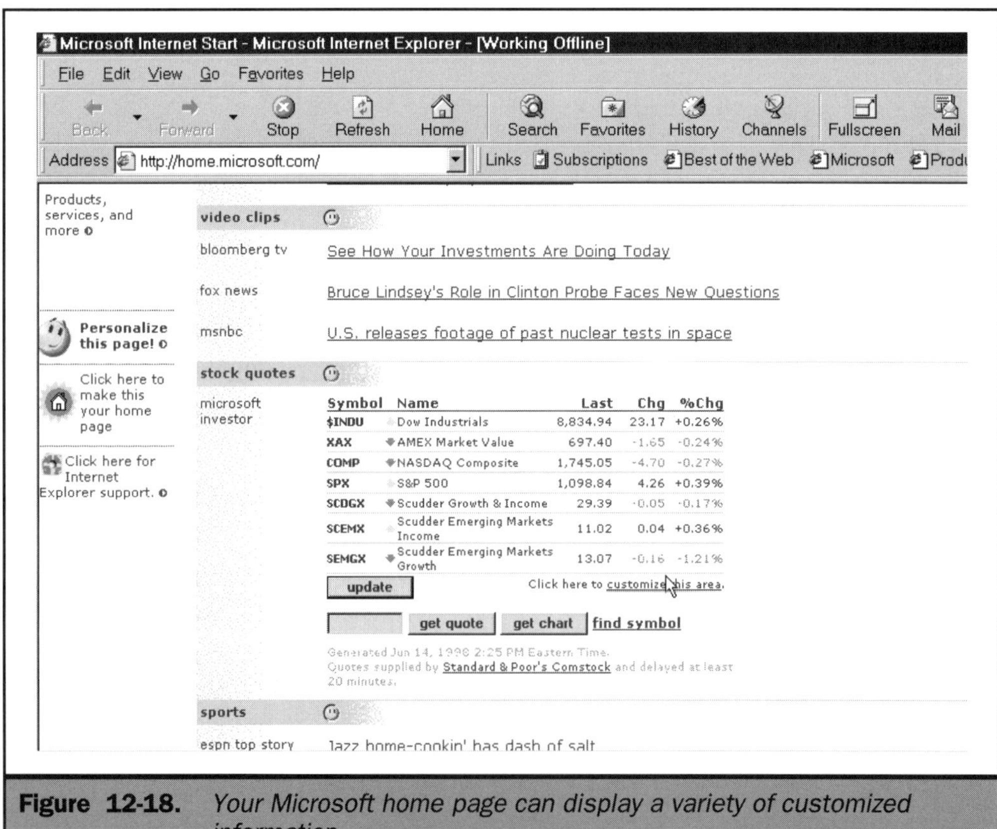

Figure 12-18. *Your Microsoft home page can display a variety of customized information*

1. Log onto http://home.microsoft.com.
2. Scroll down to the Stock Quotes section and click Customize This Area.
3. Enter the abbreviations for the stocks you want listed on the home page, or look them up by searching for company names.

Here are some of the best general-purpose financial Web sites:

- **Thomson Real Time Quotes** Most free financial Web sites supply stock quotes on a 15-minute delayed basis. Thomson Investors Network's RTQ site (http://rtq.thomsoninvest.net/) provides up to 50 real-time quotes for securities traded on major American exchanges. Users are required to register, but there's no charge for this service.
- **Stockpoint** The Stockpoint site (http://www.stockpoint.com) offers stock and mutual fund quotes on a 15-minute delay basis, along with extensive statistical data about each company, including charts and analyst ratings.
- **Morningstar.Net** Morningstar is best known for its mutual fund ratings, and its Web site (http://www.morningstar.net) is invaluable for selecting funds. Morningstar also offers articles and columns from stock analysts, current business news, and much else that can help you become an informed investor.
- **BigCharts** BigCharts (http://www.bigcharts.com) supplies much of the same information as other sites, but as the name suggests, it offers statistical information and history in, um ... big charts.
- **Wall Street Research Net** Wall Street Research Net (http://www.wsrn.com) has more than half a million links to other Web sites that you can use to perform fundamental investment research. When you request information about a stock, WSRN returns a page with links to that company's SEC filings, current stock and option quotes, recent news about the company, earnings estimates, and dozens of other sources of information.

For additional information about a potential or current investment, it's usually productive to run an AltaVista or HotBot search on the company's name or on the type of investment (such as "closed end funds" or "covered calls"). However, remember that anybody can post information on the Web, regardless of how accurate that information may be. Don't believe everything you read, especially if you don't know whether the source of advice and analysis might make a profit on your investments.

Supporting Windows 98 and Other Programs

Before the Internet became a consumer commodity, Microsoft and other software developers distributed updates and patches to their products just once or twice a year on floppy disks or CD-ROMs. The process was both expensive and inconvenient for everybody involved.

Today, a minor product update can be placed at a Web site or in a file archive as soon as the developer lets it loose—and if there's a new and better version tomorrow, it's no big deal to get that one out to the users, too.

Windows Update

Microsoft provides product updates and add-ons to Windows through an interactive Web site that can identify the version currently installed on your computer and automatically replace obsolete pieces that have been updated.

To run the Update Wizard, select the Windows Update command from the Start menu, where it appears in the top-level and Settings menus. The Update Wizard will step you through to the Device Drivers and System Files screen shown in Figure 12-19. Then choose the items you want to load and click Install.

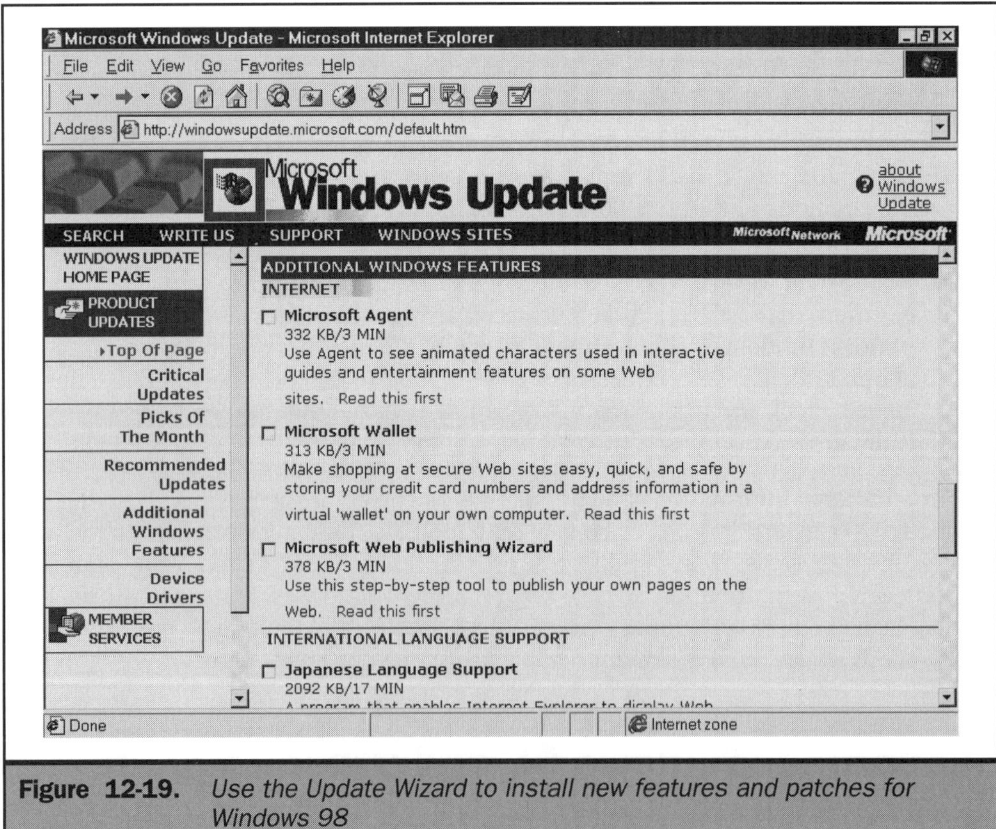

Figure 12-19. *Use the Update Wizard to install new features and patches for Windows 98*

Finding Hardware Drivers

The Windows 98 CD-ROM contains hundreds of hardware drivers for disk drives, modems, controller boards, scanners, printers, video adapters, and other devices. In theory, Windows will automatically recognize all the components in your computer and load the appropriate drivers. In the real world, however, where you're probably using at least one antique controller board salvaged from an old 386 computer or maybe a brand-new network card that was released after Microsoft started shipping Windows 98, the Windows 98 CD-ROM isn't much help, nor is it any help if you're trying to install a sound card you found in a garage sale.

Unless you're using some kind of no-name widget that you bought for $3.75 (marked down from $200) at a swap meet, you can probably download a Windows 98 driver file for that mystery component through the Internet. One of the best places to start looking for driver files is the WinFiles.com 32-bit Hardware Driver Updates Web site (http://www.winfiles.com/drivers/) shown in Figure 12-20.

Figure 12-20. *WinFiles.com provides links to sources hundreds of (sometimes obscure) hardware drivers*

Online Technical Support

You know the routine: Something on your computer doesn't work the way you want it to work, or one of your applications or utilities turns flaky. There's nothing in the 12-page user's manual about green smoke coming out of the floppy disk drive, so you call the company for help. It's probably a long distance call, but you have a report due this afternoon so you make the call. If the line isn't busy, you get one of those automated answering systems. After 17 minutes on hold, an actual person answers and just possibly tells you how to solve the problem. Even worse, some companies now charge for telephone support.

If you can find answers to your questions through the Web, you can probably save yourself a lot of time, money, and aggravation. Most hardware and software companies have online technical support centers at their Web sites where you can find answers to Frequently Asked Questions (FAQs) and send questions to the tech support people by e-mail.

If the user's manual for the product in question was produced after about 1995, it probably contains the address of the company's Web site and possibly an e-mail address for technical support. If you can't find any other address, try http://www.*company_name*.com. If that doesn't work, use AltaVista to search for the company's name or the product name and model number.

Microsoft has placed its entire "Knowledge Base" for all its products at its Web site (see Figure 12-21). This is the reference information that Microsoft's support people use to answer questions from callers. To reach the Microsoft Support Online pages, select Help | Online Support from the Internet Explorer menu. You can also access the Knowledge Base directly by entering http://support.microsoft.com/default.asp in your browser's URL window. You can search here for diagnostic solutions to software or hardware problems with any Microsoft product.

What Does the Active Desktop Mean to You?

The Active Desktop is one of the most visible new features in Windows 98. By integrating the Internet Explorer Web browser into Windows Explorer and the Windows desktop, the goal is to hide the boundary between programs and files that are physically located on your own computer or LAN and other files that the computer downloads through the Internet.

The Active Desktop adds these items to Windows:

- Use of a Web page as Windows wallpaper
- Direct links to Web pages from the Windows Start menu and the taskbar
- Live Web windows on the desktop

It's not immediately obvious that these changes are improvements over the old approach, which treats local operations and Internet services as two quite separate

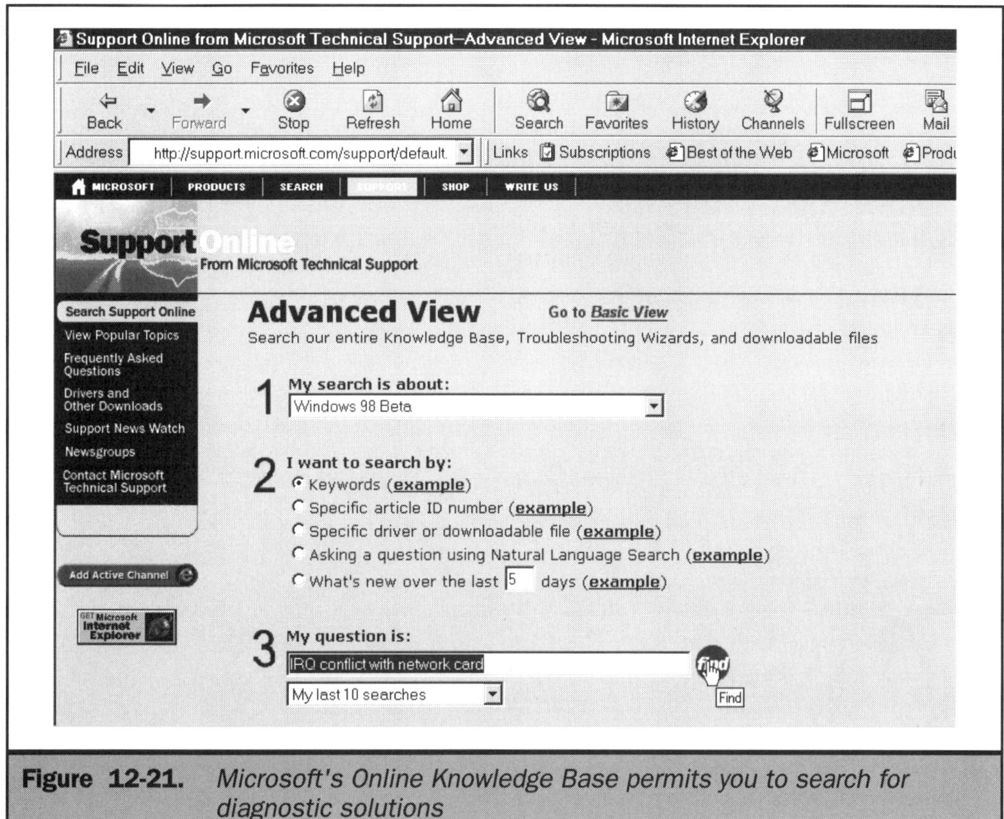

Figure 12-21. *Microsoft's Online Knowledge Base permits you to search for diagnostic solutions*

activities. When Microsoft distributed early prerelease versions of Windows 98 to beta testers, the Active Desktop loaded automatically during Windows installation. However, it was so unpopular that the final release version treats the Active Desktop as an option.

If you use your computer primarily as an Internet appliance, you may discover that the Active Desktop makes your computer a lot easier to use because you can open Web pages without the need to start your browser. (This is similar to opening your word processor by clicking a document icon.) However, if you spend most of your computing time working with local documents, spreadsheets, databases, and other files, or if you want a chance to shift mental gears between "my computer" and "out there on the Internet," you may see the Active Desktop as a lot of clutter that you really don't need. It's purely a matter of your own personal taste.

If you want to keep your desktop as simple as possible, skip this section and ignore the Active Desktop, but to be fair, you may want to try using it before you reject it completely.

Turning On the Active Desktop

For Active Desktop controls to become visible on the Windows 98 desktop, you must turn on the View as Web Page feature by right-clicking an empty desktop area and choosing Active Desktop | View as Web Page. By default when you do this, Windows 98 will load a special wallpaper background called WINDOWS98.HTM located in the \WINDOWS\WEB\WALLPAPER folder. As shown in Figure 12-22, the default Active Desktop includes two embedded links to the Internet: the Microsoft Windows 98 logo (at the top right of the screen) and the IE Channel bar, a floating icon palette. (You must be connected to the Internet through a dial-up or cable connection for the links to be hot.)

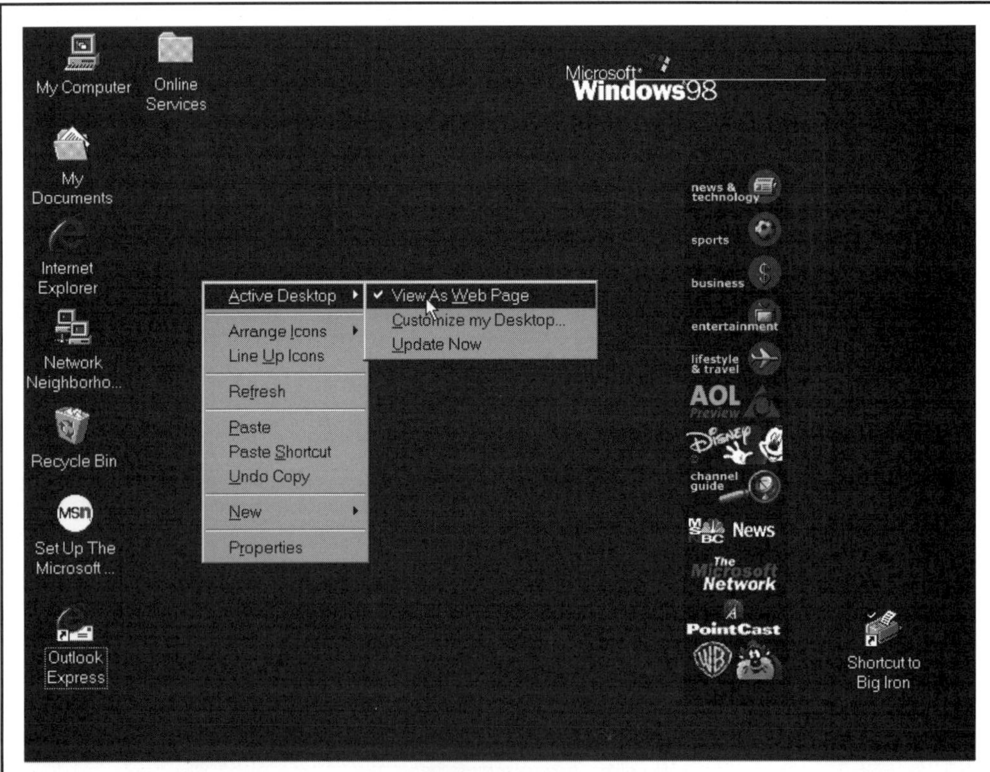

Figure 12-22. *Turning on the Active Desktop*

If you click the Windows 98 logo, your default browser opens and logs you onto the Microsoft Windows 98 Update Web page. (See "Windows Update" earlier in this chapter and "Updating Windows" in Chapter 8 for information about how to use this feature.)

If you click a URL entry in the Channel bar, your default Web browser opens a window for the corresponding Web site.

The IE Channel Bar

The IE Channel bar is a floating icon palette that actually appears by default under both the Windows 98 classic desktop and Active Desktop, but most users prefer to remove it from the classic desktop. (You can do this by clicking the X in the Channel bar's upper-right corner.) If the Channel bar is removed from the classic desktop, it will still reappear when the Active Desktop is turned on. (For more information about using the Channel bar, see "Active Channels, Subscriptions, and Other Push Techniques" later in this chapter.)

Using a Web Page or Image as Wallpaper

When you use a Web page as your Windows desktop, you can click a link in that page to jump to another page just as you can from within Internet Explorer. A page used as wallpaper must be an HTML file located on your own computer or your local network. Therefore, if you don't create the HTML document yourself, you will have to save it when you view it in your browser. To save a Web Page in Internet Explorer or Netscape Navigator, jump to the page you want to save and select File | Save As. Note that if you want the page to retain graphic images, you'll have to save them individually as well.

Once you have stored the Web page you want to use as wallpaper, move your cursor to an empty place on your desktop and right-click. Select Properties and choose the Background tab in the Display Properties window. In the dialog box shown in Figure 12-23, click the Browse button to open a browser window where you can select the file you want to use.

When you use a Web page as wallpaper, you will probably want to rearrange your desktop icons or move them to the taskbar so they don't obstruct live text or artwork on the Web page. To hide your desktop icons, open Display Properties (right-click the desktop and choose Properties), select the Effects tab, and check the Hide Options When the Desktop Is Viewed as a Web Page option. To transfer your desktop icons to the taskbar, right-click the taskbar and choose Toolbars | Desktop. If you check the Desktop toolbar, you can regain quick access to all of your desktop icons and keep a clear view of embedded Active Desktop objects (see Figure 12-24).

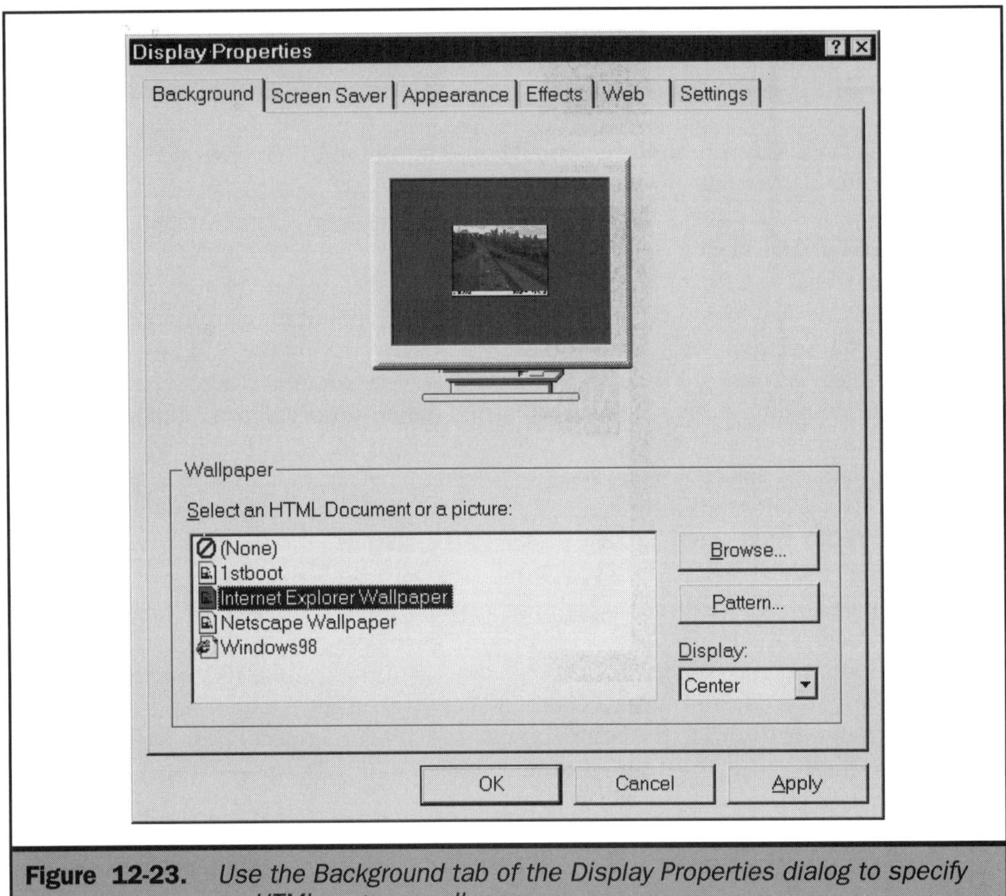

Figure 12-23. *Use the Background tab of the Display Properties dialog to specify an HTML page as wallpaper*

If you prefer, you can use a single picture or graphic image (such as the output of a Web camera) as wallpaper. In either Internet Explorer or Netscape Navigator, move your cursor over the image you want to use and right-click. Select Set as Wallpaper from the right-click menu. If you do this, the wallpaper won't contain any intrinsic live Internet links, but you can embed some Web windows as described in the next section.

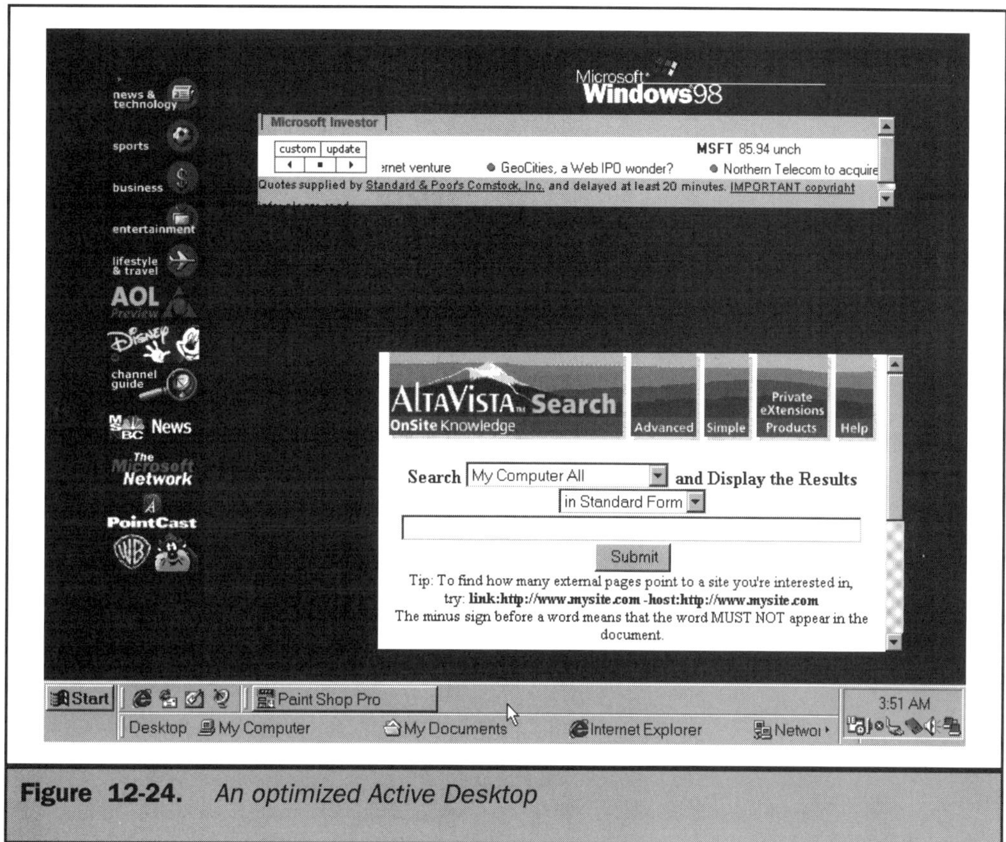

Figure 12-24. *An optimized Active Desktop*

Adding a Web Window to Your Desktop

If you have a live connection to the Internet, you can display active content such as a stock ticker or a scrolling news headline service on your desktop. For example, Figure 12-25 shows a desktop that includes a scrolling news and stock quote service from Microsoft and an image from a traffic observation camera on a Seattle freeway.

Many Web content providers have created special Active Desktop services, but you don't need to limit yourself to those sites; if you discover content on another Web page that you'd like to place on your desktop, go ahead and use it.

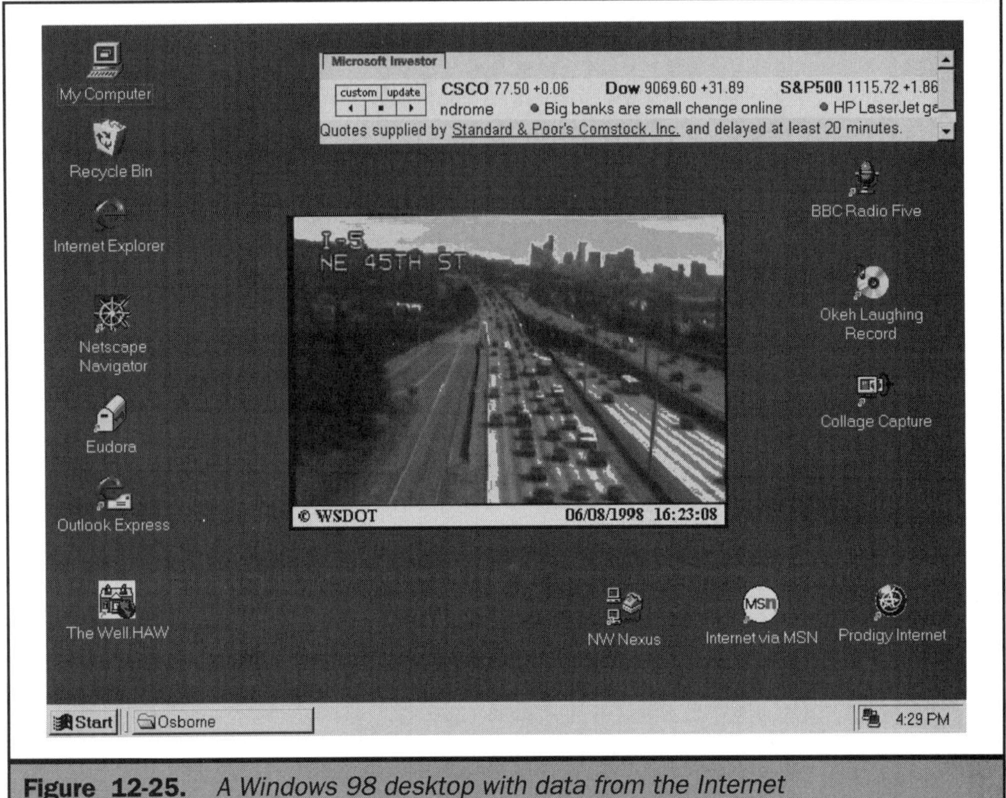

Figure 12-25. *A Windows 98 desktop with data from the Internet*

If you see an Add to Active Desktop button on a Web page like the one shown here, you can import an Active Desktop window to your desktop by clicking the button.

If there is no Add to Desktop button on the Web page or image you want to view on your desktop, follow these steps to add an active window to your desktop:

1. Open the Display Properties dialog box from the desktop right-click menu.
2. Choose the Web tab.

3. Place a check mark in the View My Active Desktop and a Web Page option box.
4. Click the New button.
5. To choose an item from Microsoft's Active Desktop gallery, click the Yes button in the New Active Desktop Item dialog box. To import an image from another site, click the No button.
6. Either choose a site from the gallery list or type the URL of the Web page or image you want to place on your desktop.

If you click the Browse button in the New Active Desktop Item dialog box, the file list will not include CGI scripts (with .CGI extensions) or JavaScript files (with .SHTML extensions). However, you can place one of these items on your desktop by typing the path and filename or URL in the Location field.

Active Channels, Subscriptions, and Other Push Techniques

Push technology has been the Next Big Thing for several years. In theory, it's a great method for receiving Web content without having to specifically request it. The up side of this feature is that you can subscribe to a site that's important to you, such as a news or technology page, and get regularly scheduled updates automatically—but if this sounds like an invitation for advertisers to invade your privacy and bombard you and your computer with unwanted commercial matter, you may begin to understand why many Internet users have avoided it.

Windows 98 and Internet Explorer include support for two kinds of push services: Active Channels and Web site subscriptions. Several other push services from other software developers are also available. For a combined directory of push media services, take a look at the Web site at http://www.phlip.net.

Active Channels

Active Channels are Internet services that deliver information from a content provider directly to your desktop on a regular schedule. You can add a hot link to an Active Channel to the Channel bar that you can access from within Internet Explorer or from a window on your desktop, or you can configure the channel to automatically check for updates at the site and download the new pages for offline viewing.

Channels are available that offer general and regional news, entertainment, travel and lifestyle information, sports, and business and financial news. Microsoft's English-language Active Channel Guide lists more than 370 news and technology channels, 120 sports channels, 550 entertainment channels, 770 business channels, and 300 lifestyle and travel channels.

Many of these channels are provided by familiar national and international media, such as NBC, the *New York Times*, the BBC, and ESPN SportsZone. However, hundreds more offer information from more specialized sources, including newspapers and broadcasters from India and Ireland and sites devoted to single sports (ranging from SoccerNet to In the Loft—The On-line Journal for Pigeon People).

Active Channels are a feature of Microsoft Internet Explorer, so they are not accessible from other browsers. Microsoft maintains a list of Web content providers in its Active Channel Guide as both a conventional Web site and an Active Channel. To view the list in Internet Explorer, either open the Channels Explorer bar and click the Microsoft Active Channel Guide button or jump to http://www.iechannelguide.com.

The lists of channels you see when you choose an Active Channel Guide category are limited to those in your own language and targeted to users in your country (for example, English channels aimed at the United States). To see pointers to more channels, click the Options button in a category list (visible when your cursor is not over a channel link) and choose a different language or country, or scroll to the top of the drop-down menus to choose All Languages and All Countries (see Figure 12-26). Click the Find button with nothing in the search field to see a complete list of channels that fit the language, country, and category criteria you specify.

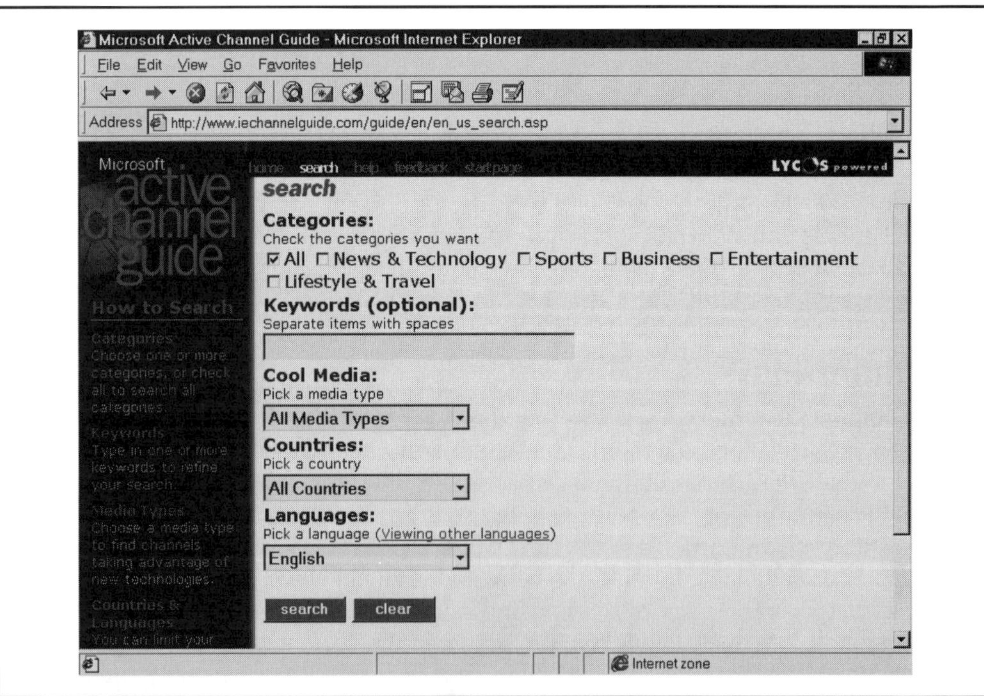

Figure 12-26. *Use the Active Channel Guide's Options page to specify the language and target country for your search*

To subscribe to a channel and add a link to that channel to your Channel bar, click the link to that channel in the Active Channel Guide and look for the Add Active Channel button, shown here. When the Add Active Channel Content dialog box appears, choose the type of service you want from this channel. If you choose to download the channel for offline viewing, click the Customize button to specify the pages you want to download and the download schedule.

If the Channel bar does not appear on the Active Desktop, you can restore it by following these steps:

1. Select the Customize My Desktop command from either the Start | Settings | Active Desktop menu or the menu that appears when you right-click with your cursor over a blank space on your desktop.
2. On the Web tab of the Display Properties dialog box, activate the View My Active Desktop as a Web Page option.
3. Double-click the box next to Internet Explorer Channel Bar to make this option active.

To remove a channel from your Channel bar, right-click the link to that channel and choose the Delete command.

To view a channel, click the link to that channel on the Channel bar.

You'll find more information about working with Active Channels in the "Configuring the Active Desktop and Active Channels" section of the *Windows 98 Resource Kit* book.

Subscribing to a Web Site

Even if a content provider has not set up an Active Channel, you can still instruct Internet Explorer to check a Web site for new content on a regular schedule. It can either notify you when new pages are available or download and store the pages that have changed since the previous download.

If you connect to the Internet through a modem, you can read downloaded pages without the need to make a new connection. This can be a useful feature for travelers who load the latest updates of a news site onto their portable computers and read them from a train or airplane where a live connection is not available.

When Internet Explorer detects that a Web page has changed, it adds a red gleam to the listing for that page in your Favorites list, as shown next.

To subscribe to a Web page, open that page in Internet Explorer and select Favorites | Add to Favorites. In the Add Favorite dialog box, choose one of the Yes options: either Tell Me When This Page Is Updated, or Notify Me and Download the Page for Offline Viewing.

To subscribe to a Web site that's already in your Favorites list, open the Favorites menu or the Favorites Explorer bar and right-click the name of the item you want to subscribe to. Choose the Subscribe command from the right-click menu.

To change the configuration of an existing subscription, choose Favorites | Manage Subscriptions. Select the icon for the subscription you want to change and choose the Properties command from the File menu or the right-click menu.

To cancel a subscription, select the Subscription tab and click the Unsubscribe button. You can also unsubscribe by right-clicking an item in the Favorites menu and choosing the Unsubscribe command.

To turn automatic downloads on or off, select the Receiving tab and choose the subscription type you want to use. If you want Internet Explorer to send you an e-mail message when it detects a change in the subscribed site, make that option active.

To set the schedule that Internet Explorer uses to check for changes in this Web site, select the Schedule tab and click the Edit button to open the Custom Schedule dialog box shown in Figure 12-27. For a daily, weekly, or monthly update, choose an option from the drop-down Schedule Name menu. To check for updates more often than once a day, choose the Repeat Every xx Hour(s) option. The date and time in the Next Update field near the bottom of the dialog box will change as you change the update schedule.

It's also possible to check for new pages between scheduled updates. To obtain the latest versions of all your subscribed pages, use the Favorites | Update All Subscriptions command. To update an individual subscription site, open the Favorites menu, right-click the item you want to update, and choose the Update Now command.

Other Push Services

Microsoft is not the only company that has developed services that use push technology. At least half a dozen other systems can also deliver content and services directly to your desktop. However, because none of these systems are compatible with any of the others, you will have to download separate client programs for each type of push server that you want to use. Many push content providers offer similar or identical services using more than one system, so you probably won't want to download and install more than one or two push clients. The best approach is to wait

Figure 12-27. *Use the Custom Schedule dialog box to change a subscription's update schedule*

until you find a description of a push service that you want to use and then install the client program required to receive it.

When you find a Web site promoting a push service, it will include a link to a download site for the appropriate client program with one of these logos:

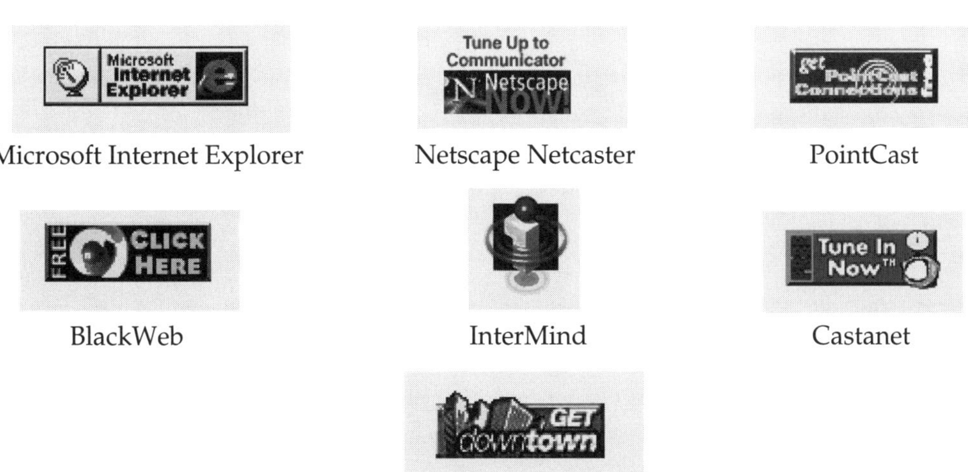

Microsoft Internet Explorer

Netscape Netcaster

PointCast

BlackWeb

InterMind

Castanet

Downtown

One of the most complete online directories of push channels is at the Phlip.Net Web site (http://www.phlip.net), but several push technology developers also maintain separate channel directories, as shown in Table 12-1.

A few content providers also offer push content using their own proprietary software. For example, the British Broadcasting Corporation operates two push services: the BBC Online Companion in a small window, as shown here, and a Windows application called BBC Online Ticker that contains a scrolling headline service. You can install the BBC Companion and download the Online Ticker software from http://www.bbc.co.uk/cdf/1/.

Software	Client Download	Channel Directory
Netscape Netcaster	http://home.netscape.com/downloads/su1.html	http://home.netscape.com/netcenter/cf/index1.html
PointCast	http://www.pointcast.com	http://www.pointcast.com/content
BackWeb	http://www.backweb.com	http://www.backweb.com/html/channels.html
InterMind	http://www.intermind.com/prod_demo/download.html	http://www.intermind.com/globaldir/index.html
Castanet	http://www.marimba.com/products/	http://www.marimba.com/channels
Downtown	http://www.incommon.com/download	http://www.incommon.com/library

Table 12-1. *Directory of Push Channel Providers*

Desktop News provides a scrolling news headline window similar to the BBC Online Ticker, but it supplies information from many content providers, including Bloomberg Business News, CNN, the *Boston Globe*, FOX, ESPN, and a large handful of business publications. For more information and a free download, go to http://www.desktopnews.com.

MSNBC, the Internet and cable TV news service from NBC and Microsoft, offers a Personal News Alert service that places a flashing icon in your taskbar system tray when it receives new stories. When you click the icon, a window opens that contains the latest headlines and links to more complete stories. Personal News Alert software is available for free from http://www.msnbc.com/tools/alert/alermain.asp.

Personalized E-Mail Subscriptions

Not quite the same as mailing lists, in which every recipient receives the same messages, a personalized e-mail subscription is a service that sends you information about specific topics that you have requested. For example, you might instruct an investment news service to send you copies of news releases and analysts' reports for particular stocks and mutual funds, or you might ask a news service to send you news stories related to a specific region or industry.

One such service is Netscape's In-Box Direct, which delivers a choice of news reports in HTML format via e-mail from ABC News, CNN, United Press International (via Clari.net), the *New York Times*, *USA Today*, and other sources. In-Box Direct also delivers sports from CBS SportsLine, Fox Sports, GolfWeb, and the Sporting News; technology news from more than 20 major publications; and news grouped into about a dozen other report categories. To set up an In-Box Direct subscription, use Netscape Navigator 4 to jump to http://form.netscape.com/ibd/.

MSNBC also offers a daily headline summary via e-mail with links to complete MSNBC coverage. To subscribe, go to http://www.msnbc.com/pfp/pd/email_list_tools.asp.

Limitations of Internet Explorer as an Offline Web Browser

The addition of subscription and offline browsing capabilities to Internet Explorer in Windows 98 is a substantial improvement over Microsoft's previous versions of IE. However, if you are a serious computer professional who conducts daily research on the Internet, you should be aware of IE4's limitations as a data-gathering tool.

- The Internet Explorer cache is not 100 percent reliable. There are known complaints of random deletion of pages from the cache and failure to update cached material with the most current version of a page.
- There is a limit of three link levels in downloading and receiving Web sites for offline viewing, with only one link level for links to external sites.

- There are no indexing and search functions for retrieved Web materials. (Users are limited to the Weekly | Site Name | Page Name display of the History list, with no way to organize information by topic or conduct string searches.)
- IE4 does not offer sophisticated features that can compare different versions of the same Web site and highlight updated information.

If you need expanded Web retrieval and indexing capabilities, you may want to investigate the third-party applications discussed next.

Cache Sentry and Cache Monitor

The CacheSentry and Cache Monitor utilities, available at http://www.mindspring.com/~dpoch/enigmatic, complement Internet Explorer. CacheSentry corrects some minor IE caching problems and slightly speeds up performance. CacheMonitor provides more thorough control and access to pages that have already been cached and alerts you when pages are deleted accidentally. (CacheSentry stops this random deletion from occurring.)

Net Attache Pro

In its current version (2.5), Net Attache Pro supports Netscape Navigator and Communicator (up to version 4.04) and older versions of Internet Explorer (versions 2 and 3), but it is *the* page-retriever and offline cataloger of choice for serious professionals. Net Attache Pro, available at http://www.tympani.com, can download up to 100 onsite and offsite link levels, allowing you to set independent options for pages on a server, within a directory hierarchy, and at another site. Downloaded pages are archived into binary collections that save space, and they are subject to Boolean string searches. Difference filters allow you to configure subscriptions that check sites, download only changed pages, and highlight the changes in your Web browser. Net Attache Pro can also retrieve the results of keyword searches on most popular Internet search engines. A companion product, Net Attache Server, runs under Windows NT, allowing network users to access and share retrieved page archives, individual HTML pages, and other text and binary documents.

WebCompass

WebCompass, from Quarterdeck Office Systems (www.quarterdeck.com), is a browser-independent tool that can perform multiple queries on more than 35 Internet search engines simultaneously, downloading and organizing results by relevance. Its sophisticated Boolean search options and retrieval filters allow you to widen or narrow a search to meet individual research requirements.

Even though Internet Explorer has no implicit search function for its cached History list, you can perform simple offline searches on the downloaded pages. Choose Start | Find | Files or Folders. Then enter ****.HTM*** *in the Named field and type the text you want to look for in Containing Text field. Specify* d:***WINDOWS\\TEMPORARY INTERNET FILES*** *in the Look In field (where* d: *is your Windows host drive). Click the Find Now button, and all the cached Web pages that contain your search term will appear. To inspect a page, open it in Internet Explorer from the Search Results window. To conduct a more refined search of the Internet cache, you can specify date and size filters on the other two Find tabs. (See Chapter 4 for more information on file searches with Find.)*

WaveTop: Surfing the Web via TV

WaveTop seems to be one of those interesting ideas that might be really useful if you have exactly the right combination of hardware and interests. It uses the vertical blanking interval (VBI) of many TV stations affiliated with PBS to distribute selected Web pages. The VBI is the black bar you see between the top of one screen and the bottom of the next when your TV's vertical hold is out of whack.

The WaveTop browser is a specially modified version of Microsoft Internet Explorer that receives Web pages through a TV tuner card in your computer and stores them in a cache. Depending on the timeliness of the content, WaveTop updates the pages as new information becomes available. When you open a WaveTop Web page, it appears on your screen almost instantaneously because it's not necessary to wait for a download from the content provider's Web server. WaveTop Content Partners include many popular sites, including USA Today, Time, CBS SportsLine, the Wall Street Journal, and Yahoo. If you try to open a Web page that is not in your WaveTop cache, the program uses your modem or LAN to download it through the Internet (and, of course, it will take a lot longer to appear). Figure 12-28 shows the WaveTop browser.

WaveTop might be worth the price of a TV tuner card to add the service to your computer if

- You're within range of a WaveTop signal (it's in about 50 major markets today, and it will be available to most TV households by the end of 1998).
- You're interested in viewing information from the content providers who distribute their Web pages through WaveTop. You can find a list of compatible hardware at http://www.wavetop.net.

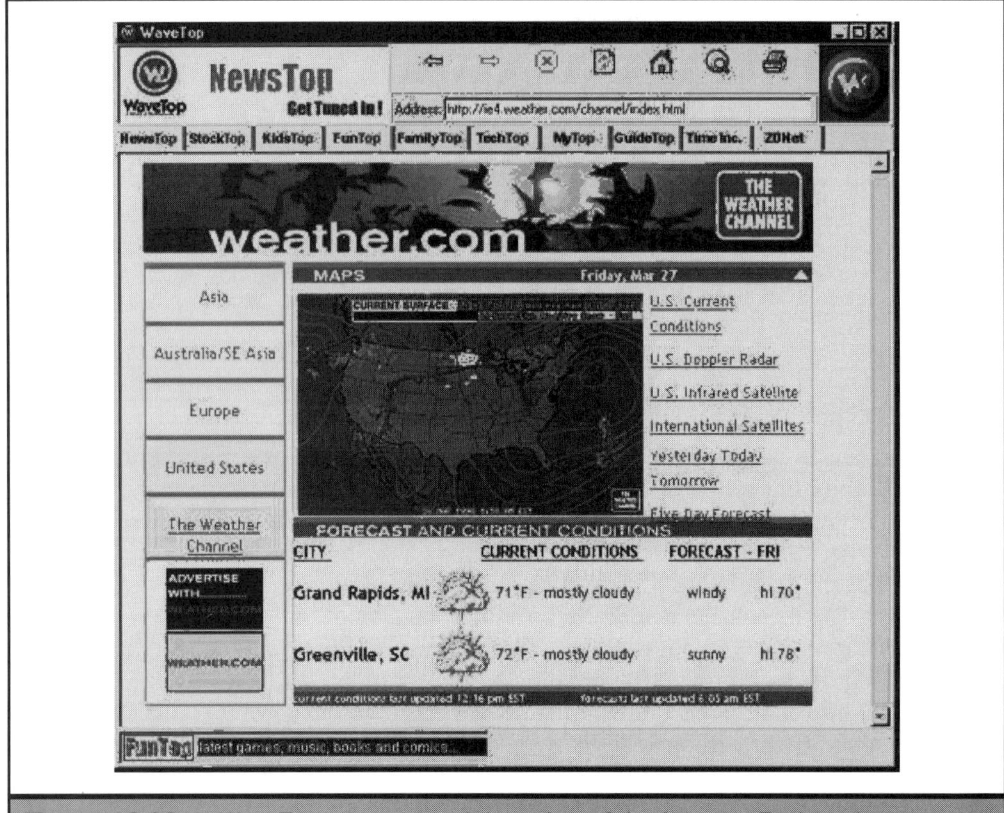

Figure 12-28. *WaveTop uses a special version of the Internet Explorer browser*

The WaveTop service is free (it's supported by advertising), so there's no ongoing cost after you install the hardware.

On the other hand, if you prefer to get your news from the BBC or the Straits Times of Singapore, WaveTop isn't likely to do you much good. For about the same cost as a tuner card, you can buy a faster modem that will increase the speed of all of your Web browsing and other Internet downloads.

WaveTop software is included on the Windows 98 CD-ROM. To install the program, open the Control Panel, select Add/Remove Programs, and click the Windows Setup tab. Scroll down the components list to Web TV for Windows and check the option box.

Web Publishing Tools

The scaled-down versions of Microsoft's Web publishing tools offered in Windows 98 are best suited to small-site composition. They allow you to create and test the integrity of a modest Web site without being physically connected to an Internet server. They also permit you to upload a finished set of pages to the Internet in one step instead of piece by piece.

FrontPage Express

At the current rate of growth, everybody in your neighborhood will have his or her own personal Web site by a week from next Tuesday. FrontPage Express is an HTML authoring tool you can use to create your own Web pages and to modify pages that you download from other Web sites without the need to enter confusing HTML code. FrontPage Express is a What You See Is What You Get (WYSIWYG) program that displays the layout of your Web pages as you work on them. FrontPage Express doesn't have all of the features of Microsoft FrontPage 98 or other programs, such as Adobe's Page Mill for creating and managing complex Web sites, but it does include all the tools that you need to produce individual pages and simple sites.

How HTML Works

The Web pages that you see displayed in Internet Explorer or Netscape Navigator travel through the Internet as a coded text file like the one in Figure 12-29. The browser uses the embedded codes to format the text and add pictures, graphic elements, audio, and animations to the page. Figure 12-30 shows the formatted page specified by the code.

FrontPage Express can automate the process of inserting all the necessary document structure codes and entering codes for text, artwork, hyperlinks, tables, and other elements into a Web page. If you're familiar with Microsoft Word, the basic organization of FrontPage Express will be familiar. The toolbars contain familiar icon buttons that control fonts, type styles, and paragraph styles (called tags in HTML), formatting commands, file management commands, and commands that add special elements such as hypertext links, graphic images, and tables. To assign an HTML tag to a word, phrase, paragraph, or block of text, select that text and click the style or format button in the toolbar. To insert a picture or graphic element in your page, place the cursor in the location where you want the image to appear and choose an Insert command from the toolbar or the Insert menu.

Web page design is an art like any other kind of graphic design. The tools in FrontPage Express (or any other HTML authoring tool) can help you make sure the formatting codes are all in the right places, but they won't do much for your actual

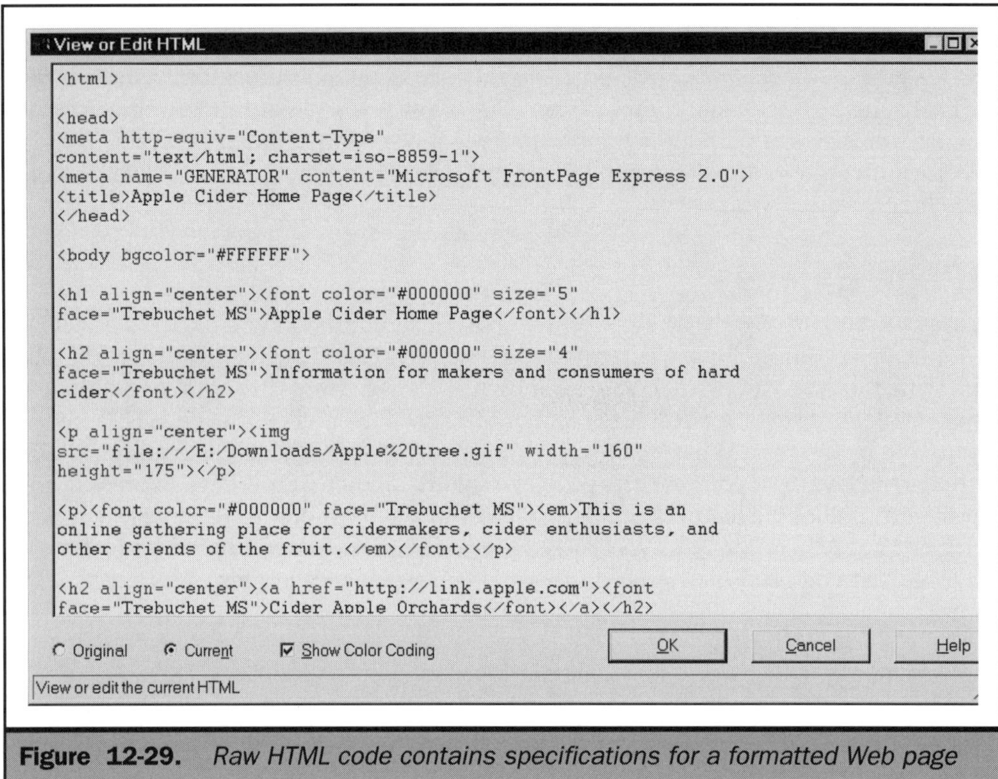

Figure 12-29. *Raw HTML code contains specifications for a formatted Web page*

page design. It's just as easy to lay out a complicated, hard-to-read page as a simple one unless you apply some kind of design sense.

For lots of information about constructing your own Web pages, visit Yahoo at http://www.yahoo.com/Computers_and_Internet/Internet/World_Wide_Web/Page_Creation/ and http://www.yahoo.com/Computers_and_Internet/Information_and_Documentation/Data_Formats/HTML/.

Personal Web Server

After you have created one or more Web pages, you must place them on a Web server before anybody else can view them through the Internet. If your own computer connects to the Internet through a modem and telephone line, you will want to transfer

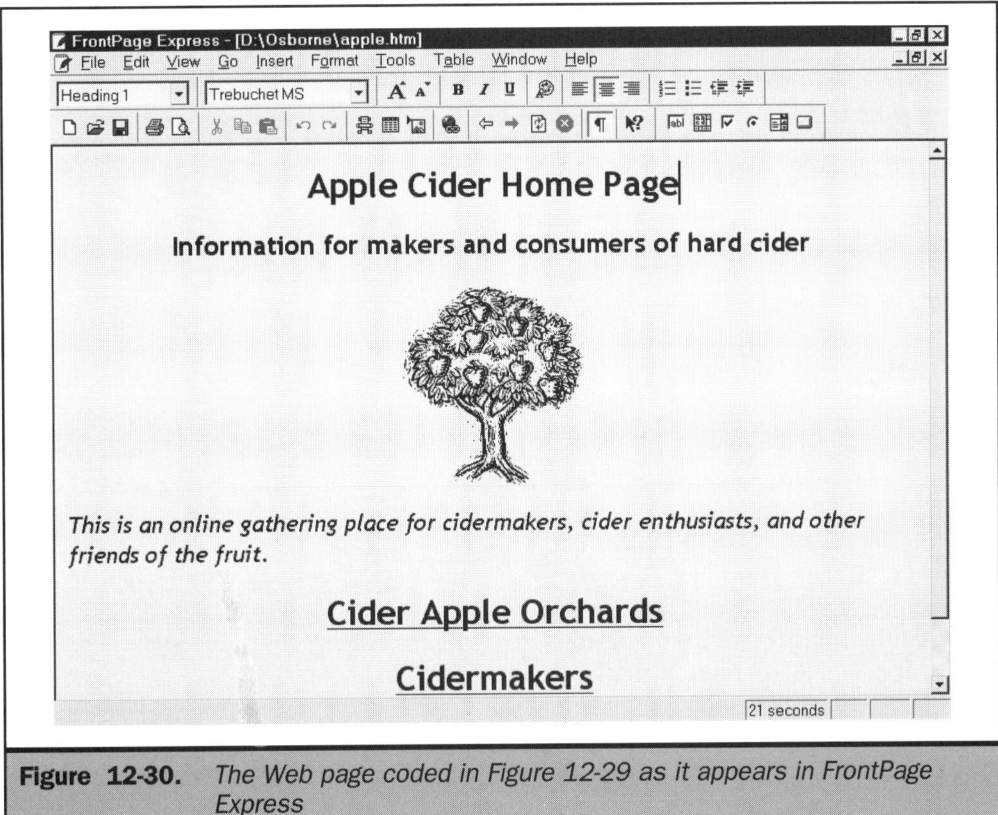

Figure 12-30. *The Web page coded in Figure 12-29 as it appears in FrontPage Express*

your Web pages to a separate server with a permanent connection (see the next section for more details). However, if your Internet connection is always active (for example, if your business or school is on a LAN or you have a permanent high-speed connection between your PC and your ISP), you can use the Personal Web Server included with Windows 98. The program is also ideal for making Web pages and other files on your own computer accessible to internal intranets.

The Personal Web Server software is located on the Windows 98 CD-ROM, but the screen that appears when you choose Start | Programs | Internet Explorer | Personal Web Server is really nothing more than a Web page that gives you instructions for installing the actual program. (If you include all the options, it will take up more than 100 megabytes.) To install the actual program, select Start | Run and enter *d:***add-ons\pws\setup.exe**, where *d:* is the letter for the CD-ROM drive that contains the Windows 98 CD.

After you install the Personal Web Server software, you must also set the address that other computers will use to reach your Web pages. Your network administrator or ISP will tell you what address to use (it's almost always different from the name you entered when you installed Windows). Follow these steps to change the address:

1. Open the Control Panel and select the Network icon.
2. In the Network dialog box, click the Identification tab.
3. Type your Web server's address in the Computer Name field.
4. Click the OK button.

Web Publishing Wizard

In most cases, it's a lot more practical to place your Web pages on an existing Web server than using your own PC as a server. The Web Publishing Wizard makes it easy to transfer HTML documents and all of the related files from your PC to a server.

The Web Publishing Wizard asks you to identify the folder or individual file that contains the page (or pages) that you want to move to the server. When you are through with the wizard, it will set up a connection to the server and upload all the necessary files to the proper locations on the server.

After the uploads are complete, it's a good idea to fire up your browser and confirm that your new site has been properly loaded to the server.

The Rest of the Internet Story

Now that you've finished this chapter on Windows 98 and the World Wide Web, you'll want to read the next chapter, which covers other important Internet communication skills: sending and receiving e-mail, participating in Internet discussion groups, accessing text-based resources with Telnet and Gopher, and retrieving files via FTP.

Chapter 13

Internet Tools II: Waxing Your Surfboard

Chapter Highlights

Some Internet history

E-mail and Outlook Express

Online communities:

> **Mailing lists, Usenet news, Outlook Express as a newsreader, and Internet Relay Chat**

More things to do on the Internet:

> **FTP, Telnet, and Gopher**

> **Win98's conferencing tools**

Internet diagnostics: troubleshooting

Chapter 12 focused on online services and the World Wide Web. This chapter gives you the nuts-and-bolts tutorials you need to use the rest of the Internet. There is life on the Internet beyond the World Wide Web, and there was life before it.

Some Internet History

Electronic mail and news are two of the oldest and still among the most widely used Internet services. The same Internet account that gives you access to the World Wide Web also provides a way for you to send and receive private messages through e-mail and public messages through mailing lists and newsgroups.

You can send electronic messages to users in almost any part of the world through the Internet's array of networked computers. When you send e-mail over the Internet, you are dispatching messages to users who connect to servers in different *domains*. Domains are the Internet equivalent of the post office's ZIP codes to identify different computer hosts all over the world.

A standard Internet e-mail address consists of a username followed by a domain name. For instance: lennyb@hooked.net. The domain name may be divided into several parts, and the username may refer to a group mailbox rather than an individual, as in this example: teachers@spacemet.phast.umass.edu. As you may know or have guessed, this second example is an address located on a server at the University of Massachusetts.

The first part of an Internet domain name may be entirely arbitrary, and Internet users being what they are, you're likely to encounter some pretty bizarre and arcane hostnames. The last part of the domain name obeys a convention; it is a three-letter extension identifying the organization type:

.EDU	An educational institution
.COM	A commercial organization
.GOV	A government organization
.MIL	A military organization
.NET	A large network provider
.ORG	A nonprofit organization

In the days before the Internet became popular, e-mail messages were mostly limited to ASCII text transmissions, but in the last several years, a number of protocols have become popular that allow the addition of binary attachments to text messages. There are several protocols for decoding these attachments when a message shows up in your mailbox. The principal ones are MIME and UUENCODE. Fortunately, Windows 98's Outlook Express mail client supports both of these protocols, so that messages you receive are automatically decoded and displayed, with icons for attached files. To add an attachment to an e-mail message, all you have to do is drag the icon out of Windows Explorer and drop it into the message window. Similarly, to detach a binary attachment from a received message, all you have to do is drag it out of the message window to the desktop or into a folder.

E-Mail and News in Windows 98

Windows 98 includes Microsoft's Outlook Express mail and news client, which is good enough to meet most users' needs. If you deal with heavy volumes of electronic mail or regularly browse Internet newsgroups, you may want more and better message filtering, more flexible screen layout, or other features that Outlook Express doesn't offer. Several free and inexpensive third-party programs, including Qualcomm's Eudora Lite and Eudora Pro mail programs, Ken Ng's News Xpress, and Forte's Free Agent and Agent newsreaders, may provide the features you need.

You'll find some brief reviews of these programs and pointers to where you can download them in the sections "Mail Client Alternatives to Outlook Express" and "Other Ways to Read the News" later in this chapter.

Outlook Express

Outlook Express is the e-mail and news client included in the Windows 98 package. It uses a standard display interface, folder structure, and message editor for both e-mail messages and news articles. This section discusses the Outlook Express interface and e-mail features. For information on using Outlook Express as a Usenet (or private group) newsreader, see "Online Communities" later in the chapter.

The first time you open Outlook Express, a dialog box will appear prompting you to select a folder where Outlook Express should keep your messages. For example, you can choose the Mail folder under your username in the \PROGRAM FILES\OUTLOOK EXPRESS directory.

If you haven't already used the Internet Connection Wizard to set up an e-mail or news account, you can do so now by clicking the Connect to the Internet icon and following the onscreen prompts. You can also set up an optional Internet Directory Service account, which will register your e-mail address on an Internet Lightweight Directory Access Protocol (LDAP) white pages server. If you prefer to remain unregistered on the Internet for now, you can select No at the Do You Want To Set Up Your Internet Directory Service Account prompt. The wizard screens are shown here:

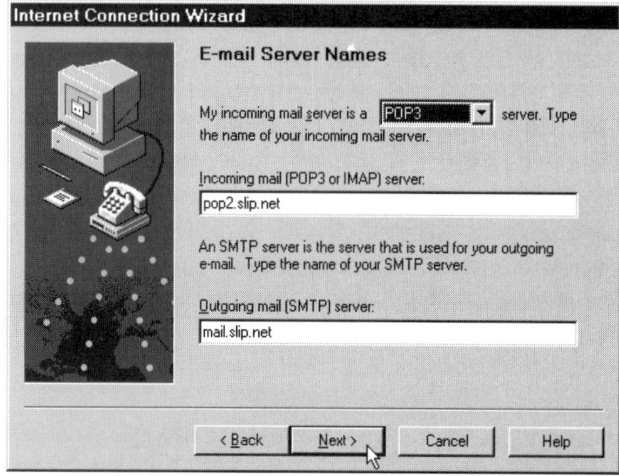

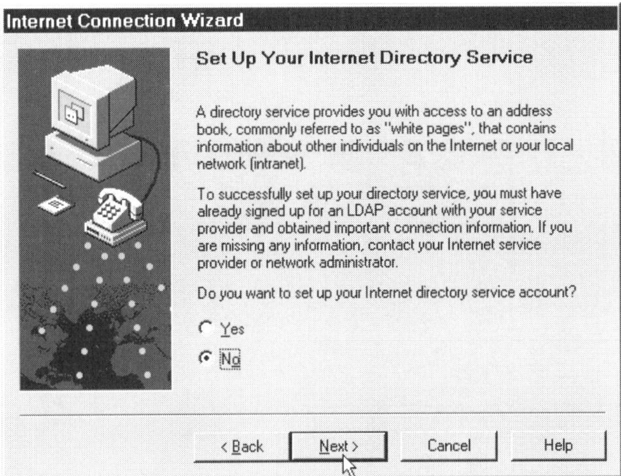

If you've configured an e-mail account with the Internet Connection Wizard, but you're not currently online, Outlook Express will prompt you to dial into the Internet upon startup. You can choose a previously configured Dial-Up Networking connection or select Don't Dial A Connection to remain offline. Place a check mark in the Set As The Default Startup Connection box if you want Outlook Express to use this connection every time you open it. (This option can be changed or disabled from the Dial-Up tab on the Outlook Express Tools | Options menu.)

The Main Screen

When Outlook Express opens for the first time, you'll see two components: the tree-based folder and file pane on the left and the icon menu window on the right, as shown in Figure 13-1. You can access any of the six Outlook Express options by clicking its icon. You can also launch Internet Explorer by clicking the black bar at the top of the menu window. Alternatively, you can go directly to your Inbox folder (where new e-mail arrives) by selecting the When Starting, Go Directly To My "Inbox" Folder option. To return to the icon menu window, click the Outlook Express icon at the top of left folder pane.

Tip *By default Outlook Express displays a user tip at the bottom of the icon menu window. You can turn this off and get a little more screen space for messages by choosing View | Layout from the pull-down menu and removing the check mark next to Tip of the Day.*

Messaging Formats

As you'll notice if you click open the Inbox to read Microsoft's sample messages, Outlook Express is capable of displaying sophisticated HTML graphics that can make a simple message look like a Web page advertisement. Some people enjoy these enhancements, but people who conduct business on the Internet every day tend to see them as more trouble than they're worth.

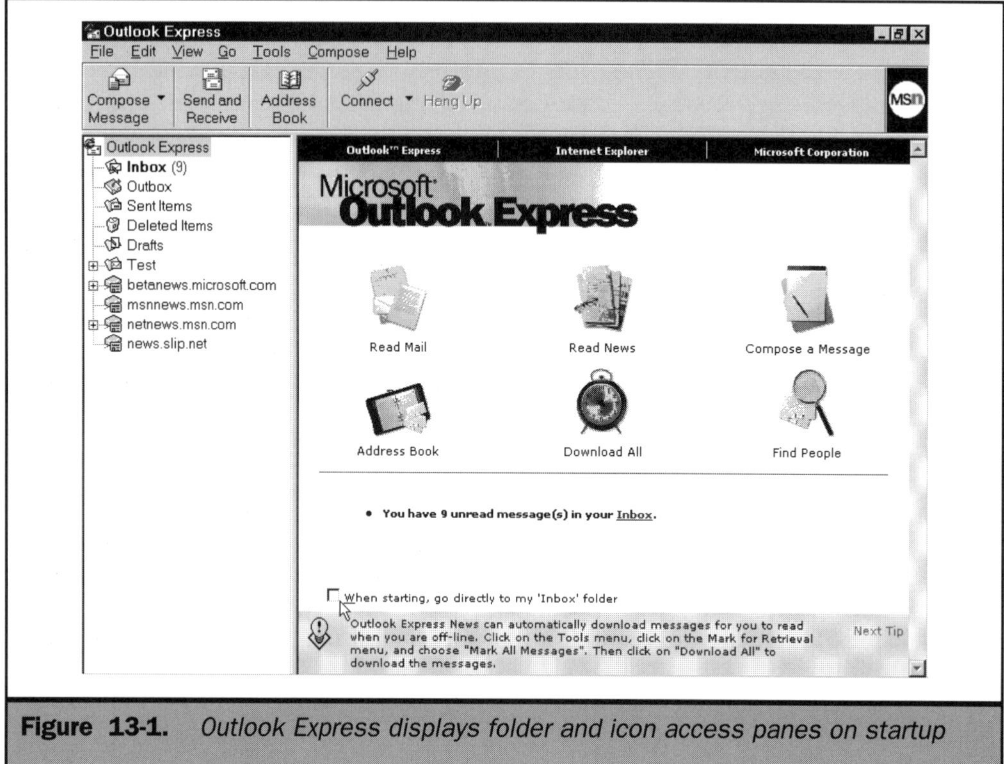

Figure 13-1. *Outlook Express displays folder and icon access panes on startup*

If the recipients of your messages also use Outlook Express or another recent e-mail client program (such as Eudora Pro 4 or Outlook 97 or 98) that recognizes all that formatting, they'll see the messages in their full multicolor glory. However, many people receiving e-mail are using older, less sophisticated software that may look at your fancy message and turn it into something that resembles chicken noodle soup. Therefore, the rule for creating e-mail in Outlook Express is to use plain text for your own messages. (This is the default setting.) Formatted, multicolor text and splash graphics may have their charm for small circles of correspondents who want to "live in the future." but generally, if you want to send a picture, a Web page, or a formatted document in an e-mail message, it's better to send it as an attached file. (See "Sending and Receiving E-Mail" later in this chapter for details.)

Folder and File Structure

Outlook Express organizes messages and news articles into folders in a structure similar to the one used by Windows Explorer to organize data and text files. By default, Outlook Express places folders in one of the standard folders: Inbox for received e-mail, Outbox for e-mail awaiting transmission, Sent Items for messages that have been dispatched, and individual news server folders for newsgroup messages. However, it's a lot easier to manage your messages if you store them in folders dedicated to messages related to a specific topic, received during a specific time period, or sent to and from a specific person or group.

To create a new folder or subfolder, open the File menu and select Folder | New Folder. When the Create Folder dialog box appears, type a name for the new folder and select the location within the file structure where you want this folder to appear. To move a message or article to a different folder, drag and drop the entry for that item from the message list to the name of the new location in the Folder List. (For convenience and compatibility, Outlook Express also has a vertical icon toolbar like the one found in Microsoft's full-featured Outlook products. You can turn on the Outlook bar by choosing View | Layout and checking Outlook Bar.)

Screen Layout

Outlook Express offers several screen layout options. The Outlook bar, the Folder list, and the Folder bar provide three different ways to display your Outlook Express files and to jump directly to a different folder. From any of these listings, choosing a folder displays its contents. However, the Folder bar, shown in Figure 13-2, which displays the list of folders in a drop-down menu, has one important advantage: it doesn't take up space on your screen when you're not using it. If you turn on the Folder bar, you should deselect the Folder list to make the drop-down menu work. However, if you want, you can turn on the Folder bar and Outlook bar simultaneously.

Toolbar

Like most other Windows programs, Outlook Express has an optional toolbar with shortcuts to frequently used commands. However, unlike most other toolbars, the Outlook Express toolbar does not allow you to drag and drop it to a new position. Normally, the toolbar is located at the top of the Outlook Express window just below the menu bar. To move it to any of the other edges of the window, you need to select View | Layout and choose a different position in the Toolbar section of the dialog box.

You can add or remove icon buttons on the Outlook Express toolbar or change the order in which they appear. Choose View | Layout and click the Customize Toolbar button. The Customize Toolbar button opens the dialog box shown in Figure 13-3.

If your screen display is set to 640 by 480 pixels, the Outlook Express toolbar may extend beyond the right side of the visible screen. There are three steps you can take to solve this problem:

- Increase the screen resolution to 800 by 600.
- Reduce the number of icon buttons and separators in the toolbar.
- Turn off the Show Text on Toolbar Buttons option in the Layout dialog box.

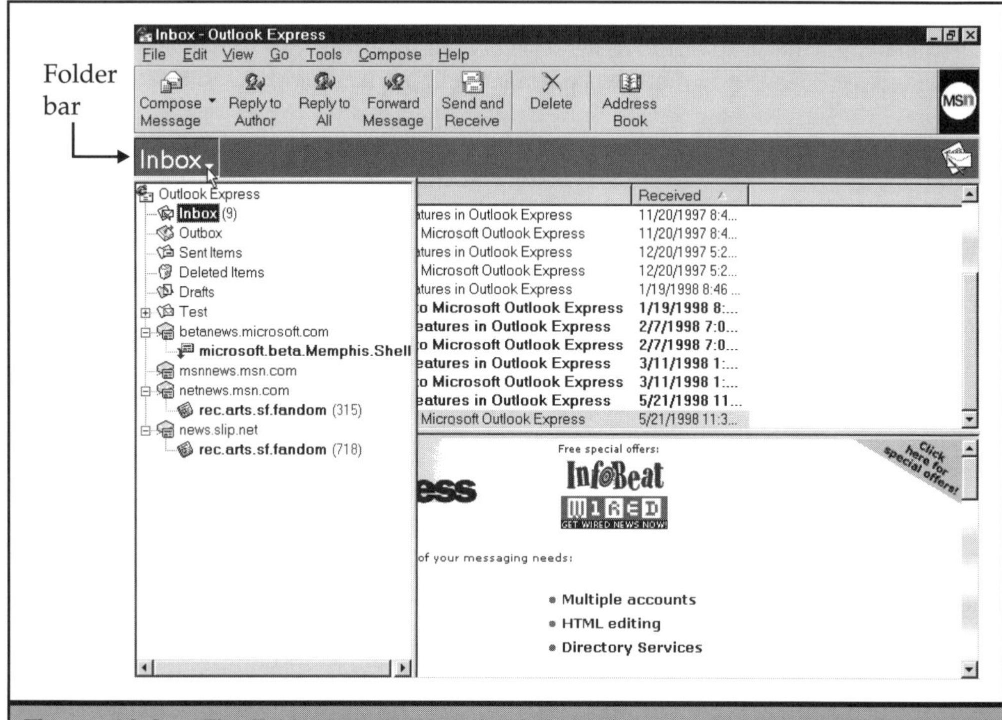

Figure 13-2. *The Folder bar displays the Outlook Express file structure in a drop-down menu*

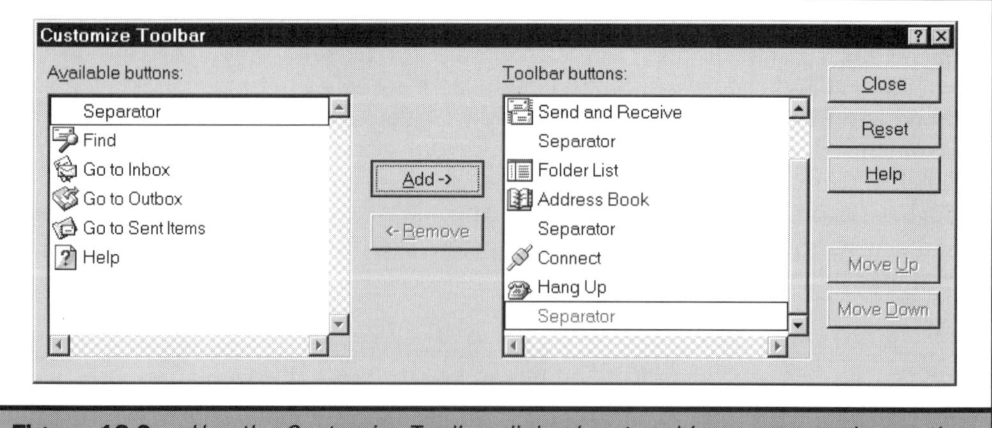

Figure 13-3. *Use the Customize Toolbar dialog box to add, remove, or change the position of icons in the Outlook Express toolbar*

Preview Pane

The Preview pane is yet another Outlook Express option (if you turn on every possible option in Outlook Express there won't be much space left in the window for the current message list). When the Preview pane is active, the program displays the currently selected message or news article in a separate pane within the Outlook Express window. If the Preview pane is not visible, you must double-click an item in a message list to open it in a separate window. You can place the Preview pane either directly below the message list or in the right half of the window and drag the bar between the two panes to change their relative sizes.

To display or hide the Preview pane and to specify its position, choose the same View | Layout Properties dialog box you used to control the toolbar.

Sending and Receiving E-Mail

Outlook Express can act as a central in-box for most of your e-mail accounts. Unfortunately, the major exceptions are America Online and CompuServe, two of the most widely used Internet access providers. If you receive your mail through one of those services, you'll have to use the mail programs supplied by those companies, at least for the moment. Most ISP's use Internet messaging standards called Simple Mail Transport Protocol (SMTP) and Post Office Protocol 3 (POP3). A few use a more exotic standard called Internet Message Access Protocol (IMAP). Assuming your ISP uses the conventional SMTP, POP3, and IMAP4 mail-handling protocols (and just about everybody except AOL does), Outlook Express is an entirely adequate e-mail client program.

Creating messages in Outlook Express is pretty simple: Use the Compose Message button in the toolbar or the Compose | New Message command to open the message editor. Either choose a recipient from your address book by double-clicking the icon to the right of To or type an address in the To field. Next, add a subject line and type your message. The Bcc field permits optional blind carbon copies. (For information on configuring your address book, see "Address Books and Directories" later in this chapter.)

ATTACHMENTS AND ENHANCED TEXT If you want to include a document or other binary file in a message as an attachment, you can do so by choosing Insert | File Attachment from the pull-down menu in the message composition window or by clicking the paper clip icon in the toolbar. When other people receive your message, the attachment will appear as an icon in the Attachment pane. You can also insert ASCII text directly into a message by choosing Insert | Text from File.

If you've enabled HTML as your message sending format (after considering the information offered earlier in this section), the Insert menu offers the additional options of embedding a personal signature, formatted business card, horizontal dividing line, picture, or Web hyperlink directly in your message. You can enable these menu options by choosing Tools | Options from the main Outlook Express pull-down menu, selecting the Send tab, and clicking the HTML button under Mail Sending Format.

REVIEWING A MESSAGE Note that Outlook Express offers a spelling checker. You can access it by choosing Tools | Spelling or pressing F7. The toolbar at the top of the message composition window offers several additional options: you can check the names in address fields against names in your address book, digitally sign a message, or encrypt a message. A digital signature allows you to assign a unique code to the message so the recipient can verify the actual sender. For more information about Outlook Express's support for digital signatures and encryption, choose Help | Contents and Index and refer to the section "What Are Secure Messages?" under Creating and Sending E-Mail Messages.

When you're ready to send your message, click the Send button.

COMPOSING MESSAGES OFFLINE If you're one of those hyper-efficient people who uses every minute productively, you may want to compose new e-mail messages when you're sitting on a train or airplane or are otherwise unable to connect your computer to the Internet. Or you may just want to keep your phone line free by remaining offline until you're ready to conduct your Internet transactions. When a message is ready to send, you can select File | Send Later to place it in a queue for later delivery. To transmit messages queued in your Outbox folder, click the Send and Receive button on the toolbar or use the Send command in the Tools menu.

OPENING THE MAIL EDITOR FROM YOUR DESKTOP Normally, you must start Outlook Express and then select the Compose Message command to open the message editor window. However, if you frequently send messages to the same recipients, it's easy to create shortcuts from your desktop directly to the message editor. Here's the way to do it:

1. From the desktop, right-click in an empty area.
2. Select New | Shortcut. In the Create Shortcut Wizard, type this command: **mailto:name@address**.
3. Click the Next button.
4. Type a name for this shortcut, such as **New Mail to *Name***, and click the Finish button.

A shortcut will appear on your desktop. When you select the shortcut, your default e-mail client program (which may be Outlook Express, Outlook 98, Eudora, or any other mail program) will open its new message editor window with the address of the recipient already filled in. To change your default e-mail program, open the Internet Properties dialog box (from the Control Panel, from Internet Explorer, or from the Internet Explorer right-click menu on the desktop), click the Programs tab, and open the drop-down Mail menu.

READING YOUR MAIL If you have e-mail accounts on more than one server (for example, an online service and a local ISP or a LAN), you can configure Outlook Express to receive and display all your messages. When you run the Internet Connection Wizard, it will automatically load your e-mail account into Outlook Express. To manually add new accounts to Outlook Express, select Tools | Accounts and click the Add button. Choose the Mail option to start the mail section of the Internet Connection Wizard.

To read your mail, select a message from the list in a mailbox folder. If the Preview pane is active, the text of the selected message will be visible; if it is not, double-click the message listing to load the message in a separate window.

Message Filters

Automatic message filters can make your management of e-mail a lot easier. The filters in Outlook Express can do the following:

- Select incoming messages based on the name of the sender or recipient, the subject line, the e-mail account that received the message, the message size, or any combination of these elements
- Automatically store selected messages in a specific message folder
- Automatically place a copy of the selected message in a second folder
- Forward the message to another e-mail address
- Automatically send a standard reply message to the person who sent the original message
- Discard the selected messages
- Keep selected messages on the server so you can download them later to a different location

To configure your message filter, select Tools | Inbox Assistant and click the Add button in the dialog box.

The Outlook Express message filtering feature can be put to good use for channeling unwanted advertisements (referred to as SPAM by Internet veterans) or sorting messages that you receive from a dedicated mailing list.

For example, suppose you've received more messages about obtaining your FBI files, buying a cable descrambler, or raising giant mushrooms in your basement than you care to deal with. You can create your first filter by specifying that all messages addressed to you with "$$$," "Personal/Important," "Don't Delete This Message!," "Great News!," "Buy Now," and so on in the subject line be automatically routed to the Deleted Items folder, as shown in the following illustration. (You'll have to create a separate filter for each header.) If you want to be more aggressive, you can specify that these messages be deleted directly from your ISP's server without downloading them.

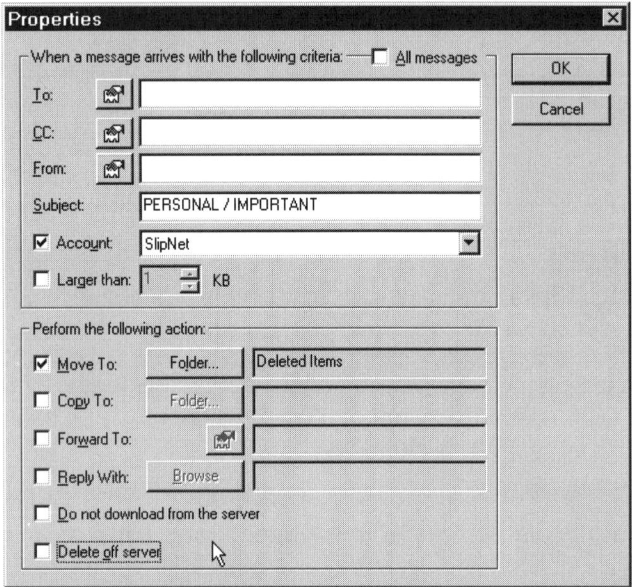

If you subscribe to an Internet mailing list, such as musiclovers@folk.com, you can specify that all messages with this address in the From field be routed on receipt to a special folder called Folk Messages.

Address Books and Directories

Outlook Express uses a local address book to store names, e-mail addresses, and other information about the people with whom you exchange e-mail messages. If a name is in your address book, the program can automatically complete that person's address when you start typing it in the To field of a new message (select Tools | Options | Send to turn on this option). Your address book can also automatically store names and address of people to whom you send messages.

To copy an address from your local address book to a new message, click the file card icon next to the field where you want to use that address. When the Select Recipients dialog box opens, select the name you want from the list and click one of the Message Recipients buttons.

To add a name to the address book, open it by choosing Tools | Address Book or click the Address Book icon on the toolbar. In the Address Book window, click the New Contact button and fill in the fields on the Personal tab with appropriate information, as shown next.

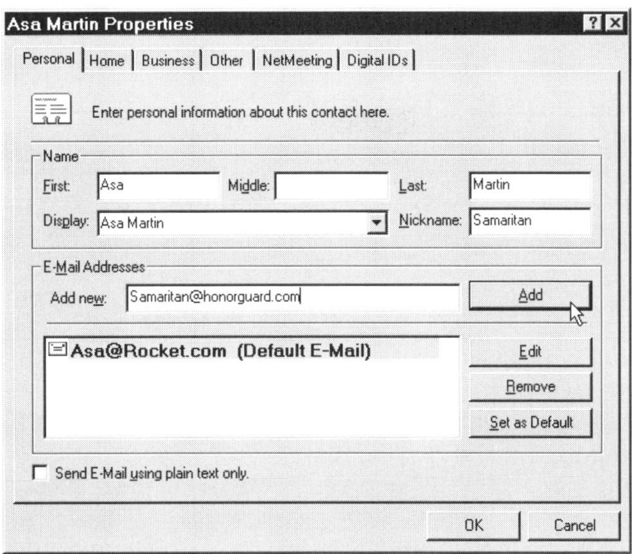

You can enter personal and business contact information for each entry, such as a street address, fax number, or Web page, on the Home and Business tabs. The NetMeeting tab can be used to store information for Internet conferencing via Microsoft's NetMeeting application. (See the "NetMeeting" section later in this chapter for more information.) The Digital ID tab is used to store a secure personal code for this contact to verify messages that you send and receive.

The local address book is not your only option. You can search for a name and e-mail address over the Internet on one of the LDAP directory servers supported by Outlook Express. Click the Find button on the Address Book toolbar and open the drop-down Look In menu in the Find People dialog box. You can search any of the available servers by name or e-mail address.

To access a directory server's Web site directly in Internet Explorer, click the Web Site button. You may find some additional search options that way.

If you get a timeout error message when you try to run an LDAP directory search, you can change the search timeout threshold by selecting Tools | Accounts | Directory Service in the main Outlook Express window and then selecting the name of the directory service, clicking the Properties button, and selecting the Advanced tab.

LDAP is a standard format for online directories, which means that many businesses, organizations, and public directory services may make their lists available as LDAP directories. To add an LDAP directory to Outlook Express, select Tools |

Accounts and click the Add button. The Internet Connection Wizard will step you through the process.

More Outlook Express Tips and Tricks

Outlook Express has a great many features and useful configuration options that are worth exploring. For more information about exploiting Outlook Express, check out the user tips at these sites on the World Wide Web: http://www.okinfoweb.com/moe/ and http://www.windows-help.net/windows95/oetips-idx-nf.shtml.

Mail Client Alternatives to Outlook Express

Outlook Express is a good basic e-mail client, but it's not your only choice. If you connect to the Internet through an online service such as AOL or CompuServe, you can use the proprietary applications built into their interfaces (although these programs may be more limiting than Outlook Express).

Among the most popular third-party alternatives are the full Microsoft Outlook program, and Qualcomm's Eudora. Some people also use Netscape's Navigator or Communicator packages, which both include basic e-mail support in addition to their Web browsers.

Microsoft Outlook 98

Microsoft Outlook 98, the latest full-featured version of Outlook, includes many features not offered in Outlook Express. In addition to more sophisticated message filters, it includes a Personal Information Manager, built-in support for Microsoft Fax, and the ability to interface with Microsoft's corporate Exchange Server. Outlook 98 is also versatile in its folder and message-content display options. It lets you sort messages by any column (Priority, Date, Subject, Attachment Type, and so on). Outlook 98 also includes a series of preset folder views: by sender or receiver, subject thread, messages during the last seven days, messages read or unread, and so on. The Message Timeline view lets you display a graphic timeline of e-mail events by day, week, or month. Advanced search features let you search messages, journal entries, and the contact database for strings in any message field (sender, receiver, subject, date, content, and so on). You can also construct customized search filters for multiple fields and conditions.

Outlook 98's complex interface, shown in Figure 13-4, will be appreciated by power users, but it may be a bit daunting for beginners.

Eudora

Named after women's rights activist Eudora Welty, Eudora is an e-mail program developed and sold by Qualcomm. It is available in both a free "light" version and a commercial "pro" edition. Eudora Pro sends and receives e-mail messages about as well as Outlook Express, but it offers a few more message handling tools, including more and better filtering features, mail sorting functions, and additional securty support. The most important user-benefits are the screen layout and Eudora's support for plug-in

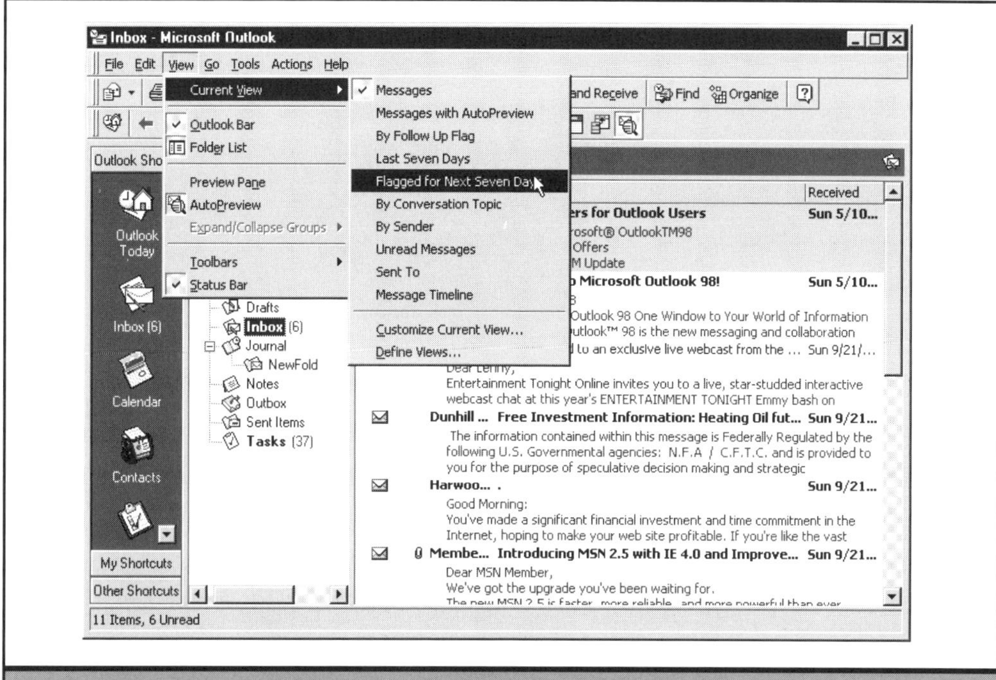

Figure 13-4. *Outlook 98 contains sophisticated folder display options*

programs. Eudora plug-ins can modify the text of messages (a language translation plug-in is currently available), add filtering functions, and support additional types of messages, such as fax and voice mail.

Eudora 4.0 CommCenter, the latest version, includes some additional Internet services: Fax Anywhere allows you to send and receive fax documents as e-mail attachments through a special subscription server. (The package includes a three-month free trial subscription and is $12.50 per month thereafter.)

Qualcomm's Internet Pager permits you to contact and conference with other Eudora users over the Internet. Internet Pager is an extremely simple, text-only utility, unsophisticated in comparison with Microsoft's NetMeeting or Mirabilis ICQ. Another bundled component of CommCenter is a set of trial subscriptions to Internet news and information services (NewsBeat, Inquisit, Infobeat, and Clari.net). All of the other 3.0 upgrade features (including the sample plug-ins) are included in the Eudora Pro 4.0 basic e-mail package.

As you might expect, the $39 Eudora Pro and $59 CommCenter packages both include features that are not available in the free Eudora Light version. Both Eudora Light and a trial version of Eudora Pro are available through the Internet at http://www. eudora.com/.

Figure 13-5 shows a typical Eudora screen.

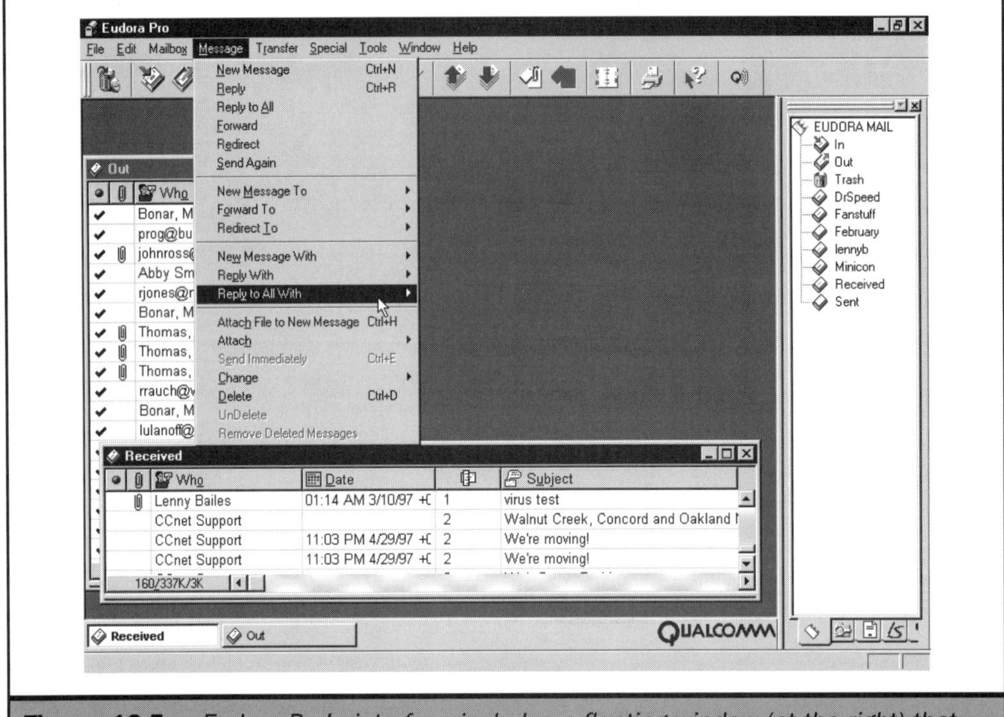

Figure 13-5. *Eudora Pro's interface includes a floating window (at the right) that toggles among a tree list of folders, e-mail personalities, signatures, and filter reports*

Netscape Navigator and Communicator

The e-mail client built into Netscape Communicator 4 is not as full-featured as other stand-alone programs (the one in Navigator 3 is even more limited), but both of these clients may be useful as quick-and-dirty e-mail tools. They load quickly, allow you to view Web pages from embedded URL links, and support Usenet newsgroup browsing, all in one interface.

Changing Win98's Default Mail Client or News Program

Whichever newsreader and e-mail client you decide to use, you will want to set them as the default Win98 programs—with internal links to your Web browser and other applications. To change the defaults, open the Internet Properties dialog box (from the Control Panel, by choosing Internet Explorer's View | Internet Options command, or by right-clicking the Internet Explorer icon on the desktop and choosing Properties) and then click the Programs tab, as shown next. The drop-down menus will list all of the mail and news clients currently installed on your computer.

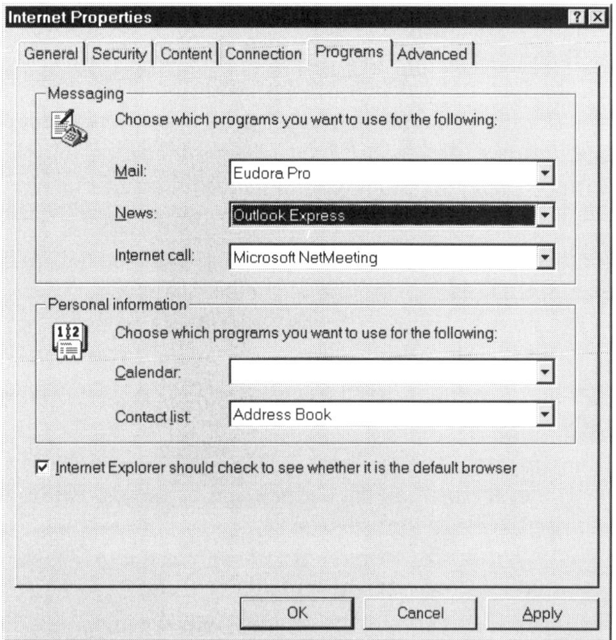

Online Communities

Much of the material on the World Wide Web resembles books and magazines—media that distribute information from a single source to a large number of potential consumers. However, the Web and other Internet services can also enable many-to-many communication. Newsgroups, mailing lists, live chat sessions, and online conferences all encourage "communities of interest" in which people exchange shared messages. The members of these informal communities may be anyone from model railroad enthusiasts to mothers of four-year-olds to particle physicists (or, just possibly, particle physicists who are also mothers of four-year-old model railroad enthusiasts).

Online communities use several different methods for distributing their messages:

- **Newsgroups** Thousands of newsgroups devoted to almost every imaginable subject move around the Internet every day. As you learned earlier in this chapter, Outlook Express can be used as a news client to receive and participate in newsgroups.
- **Mailing lists** An Internet mailing list is a system that automatically distributes e-mail messages to a large number of people simultaneously. When you send a message to the list server, the server automatically resends it to everybody on the list. Some list servers relay each message as soon as it is received; others collect incoming messages into a daily digest that will include all the messages received since the last outbound mailing.

- **Chat groups** Internet Relay Chat (IRC) is a set of tools for conducting live discussions through the Internet. Much of the conversation in IRC channels can best be described as "recreational typing," but there are some congenial IRC communities out there. To participate in IRC chats, you must use an IRC client program, such as the Microsoft Chat program included with Windows 98 (described in the "Internet Relay Chat" section later in this chapter) or mIRC, which you can download from http://www.mirc.com.
- **Web conferences and forums** Many online conferences are based at Web sites. The structure varies from one to the next, but most of the good ones provide instructions for new participants on their home pages. A few of these sites charge a subscription fee, but many others are free. Electric Minds, at http://www.minds.com, is an interesting free forum created by long-time digital communitarian Howard Rheingold.
- **Subscription conferencing systems** These systems, accessible over the Internet via Telnet or through dedicated dial-up access numbers, contain some of the most articulate and knowledgeable participants to be found in the online world. The most famous example (still going after 13 years) is the Well, which has recently added a World Wide Web–based interface. You can find information about the Well at http://www.well.com/index.html.

Two good places to search for online communities are Liszt (http://www.liszt.com), a directory of more than 84,000 Internet mailing lists, with links to about 30,000 newsgroups and almost 6,000 IRC chat channels; and Forum One (http://www.forumone.com), which provides links to several hundred Web-based discussion servers with something like 180,000 separate discussions.

Usenet Newsgroups

Newsgroups are the chief joy of the Internet for people who love electronic correspondence and online debates. These groups are forums for messages and replies posted by computer users all over the world. Most Internet newsgroups are distributed to servers through a subsidiary network called Usenet. Usenet contains literally thousands of newsgroups, and they change from day to day. Any message posted in a newsgroup is available for all members to read and post replies. Not all Internet access providers carry all newsgroups, but many of them will add a newsgroup if you ask.

There's a Usenet newsgroup available on just about any subject you can think of—and on hundreds you wouldn't have thought of in years. Usenet is a welter of fact and opinion, and anyone who wants to join in is welcome.

So just what is a newsgroup? It's really just a bulletin board on which anyone is invited to post messages. People trade facts, opinions, and occasionally *flames*—angry tirades—about everything imaginable. There are some consensual rules, which you can learn by reading a newsgroup's associated FAQs (or Frequently Asked Questions). Break the rules and someone is likely to issue you a friendly reminder or (if you get unlucky) a flame against your ancestors, progeny, and rightful place in the universe.

Newsgroups can be great places to practice vituperation, and many do, but if that bores or upsets you, you're always free to sign off a given newsgroup and join another.

Usenet is not always about politics and raging hormones. If you pick your newsgroups thoughtfully, the possibilities for broadening your knowledge are enormous.

Types of Newsgroups

Usenet newsgroups are divided into a number of categories and subcategories. Table 13-1 shows the basic divisions, along with some examples of newsgroups in each category.

To read Usenet news and post messages to newsgroups, you need a newsreader. Outlook Express, bundled with Windows 98, can do double duty as a newsreader as well as an e-mail client. Details on using it are provided in the following section.

Prefix	Subjects in This Category	Examples of Newsgroups
Alt	Alternative lifestyles	ALT.CALIFORNIA ALT.FAN.TOLKIEN ALT.FOLKLORE ALT.SEX ALT.SOC.ETHICS
Biz	Business	BIZ.COMP.SERVICES BIZ.JOBS.OFFERED BIZ.MISC
Comp	Computers	COMP.GRAPHICS COMP.HOME.MISC COMP.OS.MS-WINDOWS.APPS
Misc.	Miscellaneous subjects	MISC.HEALTH.DIABETES
News	Current events and USENET information	NEWS.ADMIN.POLICY NEWS.ANNOUNCE.IMPORTANT
Rec	Recreation	REC.ARTS.CINEMA REC.GARDEN.ROSES REC.HUMOR
Sci	Science	SCI.MED SCI.PHYSICS SCI.SPACE.NEWS
Soc	Society	SOC.ORG.NONPROFIT SOC.POLITICS SOC.NET-PEOPLE

Table 13-1. *Categories of USENET Newsgroups*

Usenet News through Outlook Express

Outlook Express uses a common structure for both e-mail and news, but you should notice that the commands in the menu bar change when you move between the two types of message folders.

If you didn't configure a news reading account when you ran Microsoft's Internet Connection Wizard, you can do so now by opening Outlook Express, choosing Tools | Accounts, and clicking the News tab. Choose Add | News on this tab to run the Internet Connection Wizard and configure an account.

1. On the first two screens, enter the name you want displayed in your messages and your e-mail address.
2. On the Internet News Server Name screen, enter the name of the news server provided by your ISP (for example, publicnews.msn.com or news.compuserve .com). If you use a service such as MSN, you'll also need to place a check mark in the My News Server Requires Me To Log On box. If you check this box, a supplementary screen appears, prompting you to enter a news account name and password or select Secure Password Authentication. For MSN, you can enter the same username and password that you use to log onto your main account. (Most other ISPs don't require this option. If you have difficulty logging onto a news server, consult your ISP's technical support for additional steps to make Outlook Express recognize it.)
3. On the Friendly Name screen, you can enter any name that you want to identify the account.
4. The Choose Connection screen prompts you to select an Internet connection type, as you did when configuring your e-mail account.
5. Click Finish on the Congratulations screen to complete the configuration.

The news account appears in the Account listing on the News tab.

You can modify the settings for an existing news account by selecting it and clicking the Properties button. You'll see all the properties for this account in four tabbed windows.

The first time you log onto a news server, Outlook Express will automatically retrieve all of the available newsgroups, as shown here:

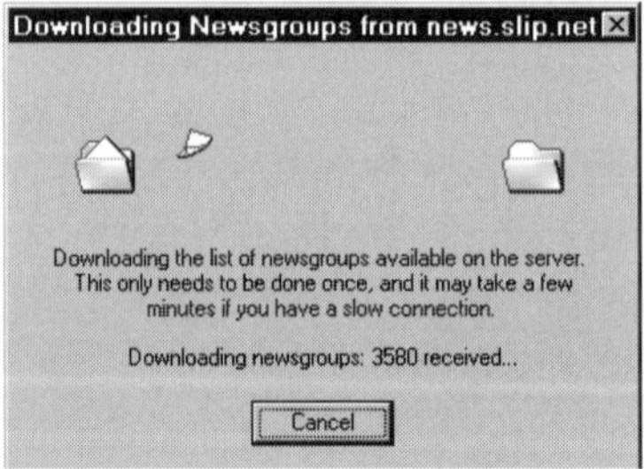

Once you obtain the list of newsgroups, you can log onto the one you want by selecting it from the Newsgroups list. To narrow the search, you can enter keywords in the group's title in the Display Newsgroups Which Contain box, as shown here:

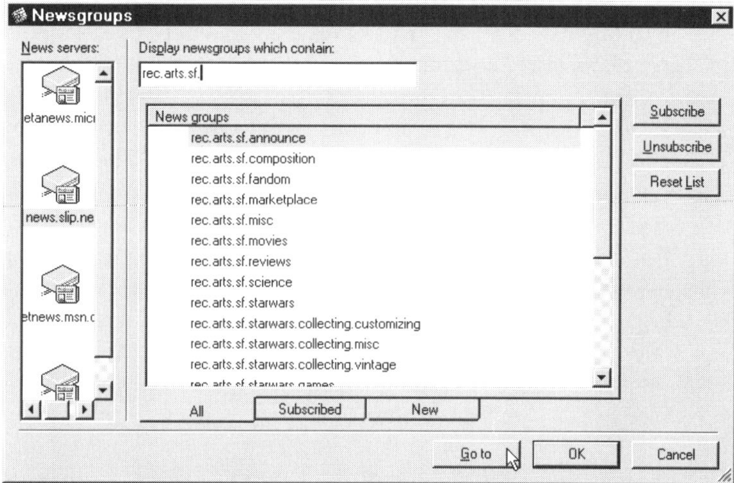

To start reading newsgroup postings immediately, click the Go To button in the Newsgroups window. To subscribe permanently to the newsgroup, click the Subscribe button. If you subscribe to a group, it will be listed when you open the news server in the Outlook Express folder pane. You can click the newsgroup name to open the group quickly and read new messages, as shown here:

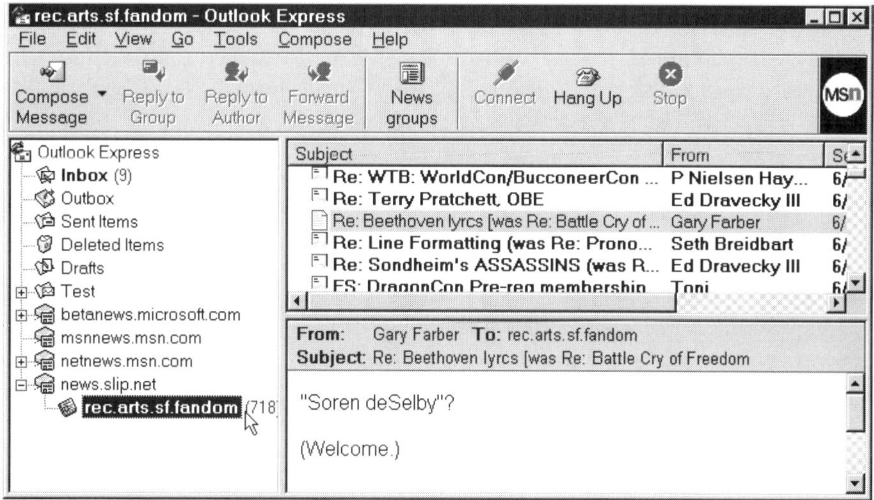

Just as it does for e-mail messages, Outlook Express allows you to add all kinds of formatting and graphic images to the articles you create for posting to newsgroups. However, many of the people trying to read your articles may not have newsreaders that can handle formatted articles. Therefore, you should seldom use anything but plain text when you compose new articles. One exception to this rule is when you're sending an article to one of the alt.binaries newsgroups where embedded images and program files are expected and accepted.

Many newsgroups generate huge numbers of articles every day. You may find the article list easier to use if you limit it to the messages you haven't already seen or even to just the articles that are replies to your own earlier postings. The View | Current View menu offers several ways to limit the number of messages visible in the article list.

Internet News is a very democratic medium; anybody with access to a newsgroup can participate. This is one of the Internet's strengths, but it's also a weakness because many of the people who post articles in newsgroups are people who have nothing to say or, worse, who are more interested in starting online fights than contributing to a conversation. One or two of these bozos can come close to destroying a newsgroup. If you come up against this kind of problem, Outlook Express allows you to ignore disruptive people or topics by filtering them.

Got a bozo on your back? Filter 'em out! To apply a filter to one or more newsgroups, select Tools | Newsgroup Filters and click the Add button.

Other Ways to Read the News

Most Internet service providers also include simple text-based newsreaders that can be read from a UNIX command prompt, but you don't have to struggle with these if you don't want to. Usually, your service provider will have a collection of downloadable shareware and freeware that includes a Windows newsreader or two. In a pinch, you can also access newsgroups through your World Wide Web browser. Web browsers vary in the degree of support they offer for Usenet. Internet Explorer without Outlook Express is very limited. Netscape Navigator and Communicator have built-in newsgroup support, which may be adequate for your needs.

You'll find pointers to a wide variety of freeware and shareware newsreaders at www.winfiles.com/.

Agent and Free Agent

If the newsreader in Outlook Express doesn't have enough bells, whistles, and klaxons to keep you entertained, you should take a look at Free Agent from Forte (http://www.forteinc.com/agent/ freeagent.html). There's also a version with even more features, called Agent, that you can order from Forte for $29.

Both Agent and Free Agent have most of the same features and functions as the newsreader in Outlook Express, but they also offer a much more flexible multipane window layout. Using the Options | Window Layout command, you can arrange the list of available newsgroups, the list of messages in the currently selected group, and the text of the currently selected message in just about any way you want: in vertical columns, horizontal rows, or a combination of both. Figure 13-6 shows the Window Layout dialog box with a typical arrangement selected. You can also expand any of the panes to fill the entire Agent window by clicking the Maximize button in that pane.

If anything, Agent and Free Agent have more features than most people need, but if you don't like the less flexible layout of the Outlook Express newsreader, Agent will almost certainly do what you want it to do. However, if you have accounts with more than one news server—perhaps one server that gives you access to public newsgroups and another that contains private newsgroups—Outlook Express is probably the better choice. To use Agent or Free Agent with multiple servers, you have to load a separate copy of the program for each server. This is a real nuisance compared with the easy mouse clicks that Outlook Express uses to move from one server to another.

Internet Relay Chat

Internet Relay Chat (or IRC) is the citizen's band radio and traveling street circus of the Internet. It consists of a series of text-based discussion channels that can be accessed

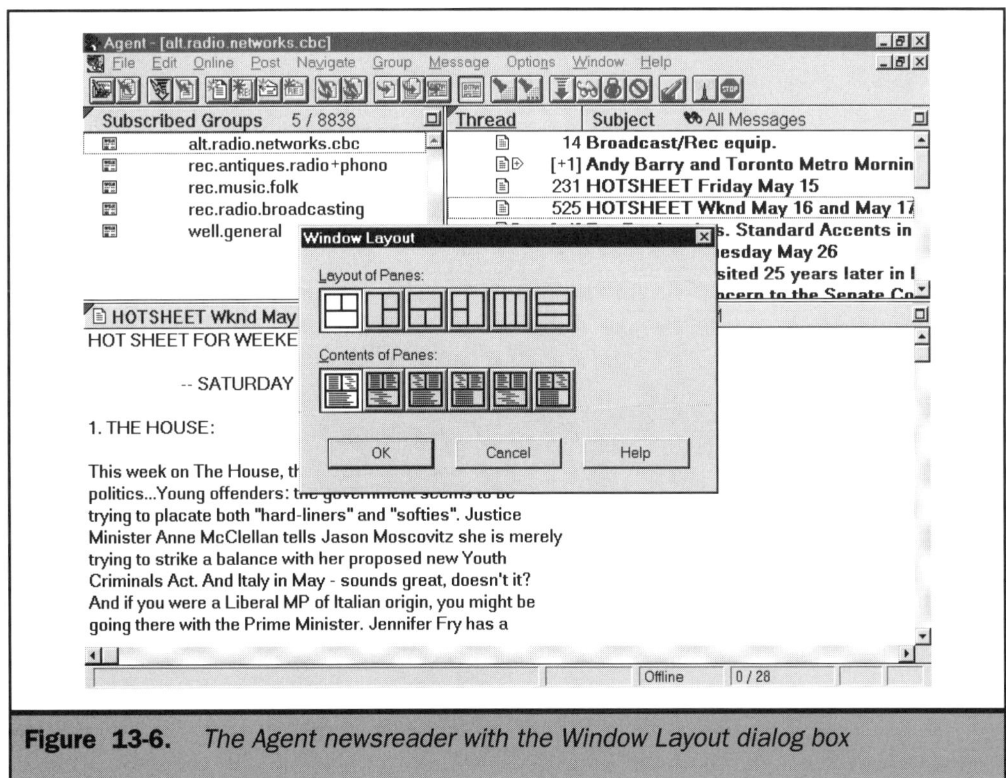

Figure 13-6. *The Agent newsreader with the Window Layout dialog box*

by anyone who is logged onto an Internet IRC server. Typically, IRC is a late-night pastime for college students all over the world cooped up in dormitories with their free Internet access accounts. (Although, in national emergencies, such as earthquakes and armed coups in third-world countries, IRC has also proved to be a surprisingly useful resource for getting information out of troubled areas and into the hands of people who can help.) IRC has an intricate set of customs and byways, with a truly science fictional argot. You may never know whether the people you're talking to are postmodern poets, pizza delivery workers, or *'bots*—computer programs that participate in IRC discussion channels as though they were live human beings.

To join IRC, you need a well-designed Telnet utility or a dedicated IRC client program. Windows 98 includes Microsoft Chat, which can do double duty as a public IRC client and as a tightwave instrument for conversing with users of MSN.

The Microsoft Chat program offers a choice of plain text and a comic strip display that shows each participant as a cartoon character (with each message placed in a speech balloon). The cartoon characters may be entertaining for about 10 or 15 minutes, but if you become an active IRC user, you will almost certainly want to use the commands in the View menu to switch to the Plain Text option.

To participate in an Internet chat, open the Microsoft Chat application (choose Start | Programs | Internet Explorer and select Chat). The Chat Connection dialog box will ask you to specify a server and a specific chat room to log onto, as shown next. (The title of the chat room is preceded by the # character.) If you don't know where you want to go yet, click the Show All Available Chat Rooms button.

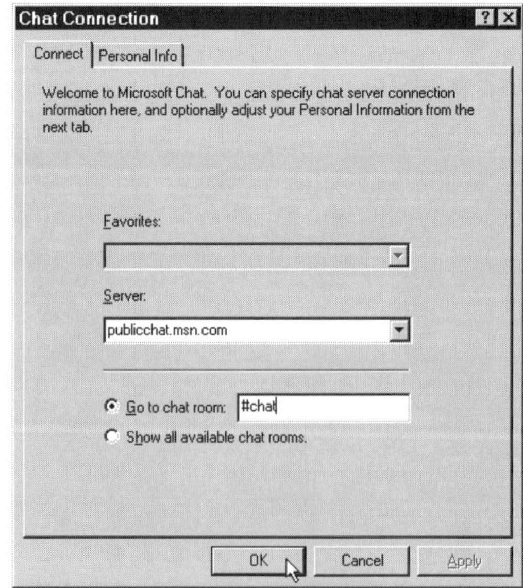

The Personal Info tab in the Chat Connection dialog box lets you specify information to identify yourself to other chat participants. If you're connecting to a public IRC server, bear in mind that you may be socializing with a wide variety of eccentric characters, so you may want to specify a nickname and leave some of the personal profile fields blank

Finding IRC Servers

The drop-down Server list in the Chat Connection dialog box includes two Microsoft IRC networks. There are at least two dozen other IRC networks that establish worldwide computer links with hundreds of separate channels. In addition to the ones run by MSN, the largest and most active networks are EFFnet, UnderNet, DALnet, and GALAXYnet. Currently, you can find good IRC server lists at http://www.what-sup.com/en/irchelp.htm#server and http://www.cet.com/~gizmo/irc/index.html. You can also go to one of the search engines and search by the names of the large IRC networks.

Don't expect a particularly high level of discourse on most IRC channels. The conversations in most chat rooms often seem to be limited to the topics of popular music, pirated software, and adolescent gossip. However, in spite of that, you may find a channel with a lively discussion or a friendly group of participants.

Still More Things You Can Do Through the Internet

Your Web browser, news, and e-mail client programs will probably handle the majority of the services you use on the Internet, but many other kinds of client programs are also available—including general-purpose programs, such as Telnet for remote login to distant computers and File Transfer Protocol (FTP) for file transfers. Some of these client programs are included in the Windows 98 package, and many more are available from online sources.

FTP

FTP, the standard Internet file transfer protocol, is a method for moving files from one computer to another. Millions of files in thousands of file archives are available via FTP to anybody with an Internet connection. Many semi-private FTP servers are accessible to people who have established accounts on those servers.

Both Internet Explorer and Netscape Navigator can connect to FTP servers and download files from them. You will often see hyperlinks in Web pages directly to FTP sites and to individual files. To set up a connection to an FTP server from the browser's address field, type a URL in this form:

ftp://*ftp-server.com*

Your Web browser will establish a connection to the server you name and automatically log you on for anonymous file transfers. Usually when you log onto an FTP site, you'll see a series of buttons or folder icons representing various file directories. To download files, just click open the directory you want to browse and select a file. Your Web browser will probably then pop open a dialog box asking you for a directory to store the file in. (Some browsers simply grab and stash files in a default directory.)

Tip *Some anonymous FTP sites also have pages set up on the World Wide Web. If you know the FTP address for a site, you can see if it also has a Web page. Go to the URL Address field and enter* **http://** *followed by the domain name of the server. Browsing and selecting files from a Web page tend to be easier and more fun than scrolling through descriptionless directory listings.*

Dedicated FTP Utilities

For occasional FTP downloads, your browser will do an entirely adequate job, but a separate FTP client program does offer several benefits: file transfer can be faster, especially for large files; you'll be able to move around the server more easily; and you'll have a lot more control over the way you can handle a file after you receive it.

Using Win98's Command-Line FTP Utility

Readers who are secretly UNIX and DOS command-line junkies may actually like the relatively simple command set of Win98's text-based FTP. You can enter FTP commands at the DOS command line and type a question mark at the ftp> prompt to see the complete list of available commands. For more command information, you can type **help** followed by the command. Here's a typical example:

```
ftp> help open connect to remote ftp
```

To open a remote FTP site while you're connected to the Internet, enter the word **FTP** followed by the site name at the DOS command prompt. If you have the AutoDial feature of Microsoft's Internet Explorer turned on, then entering this command when offline automatically brings up a Dial-Up Networking connection profile to establish your Internet connection.

After you connect to an anonymous FTP server, you must go through a login procedure. Traditionally, you enter **anonymous** as your user ID and use your real e-mail address as a password. (The inclusion of your e-mail address is a courtesy so the administrator of the FTP site has some idea of who has been using it.)

Windows 98 includes a DOS-based FTP client, but unless you're already familiar with FTP commands, it's a bit awkward to use. If you have no other FTP utility, probably the only thing you'll want to use this for is to go online to a server and download a better FTP utility (or better yet, do this through your Web browser, as described earlier in this chapter). See the previous sidebar, "Using Win98's Command-Line FTP Utility" for instructions on using the DOS-based program in a pinch.

Several other much better free or inexpensive FTP programs are available for download through the Internet. One of the best is WS-FTP from Ipswitch (http://www.ipswitch.com). The free (for individuals and educational institutions) Limited Edition version is shown in Figure 13-7. A more sophisticated Professional Edition with an FTP extension to the Windows Explorer is available for sale.

For descriptions and download information for other FTP clients, look in the FTP section of either TUCOWS or Stroud's list of Internet applications, described later in this chapter.

Telnet

A Telnet terminal package lets you log onto a remote Internet site and act as if you were dialing into it directly. Telnet allows you to access all the commands available on the remote server as though you were running them on your local computer. If you

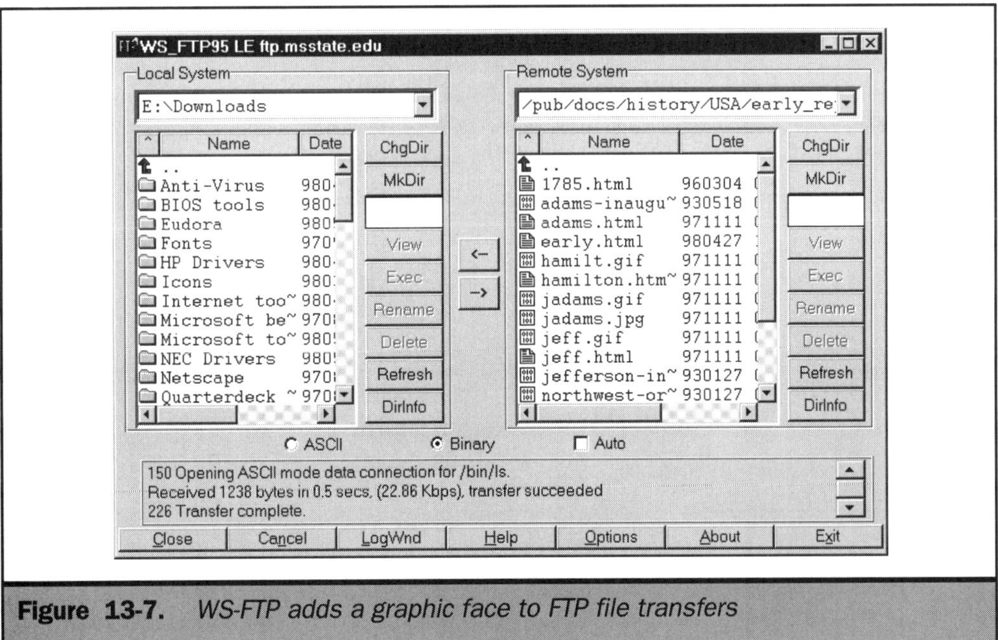

Figure 13-7. *WS-FTP adds a graphic face to FTP file transfers*

have an account on the Telnet host (or if the host accepts public logins), you can open files on that computer, run programs, and do anything else that the owner of the computer permits you to do. For example, many libraries use Telnet to permit direct public access to their catalogs through the Internet (see Figure 13-8).

If you have an advanced Telnet terminal program, you can also use it to upload and download server files and run server-based programs. One common use of Telnet is to access a bulletin board system (BBS) in a distant city via the Internet instead of long-distance phone lines, thus avoiding long-distance charges.

Windows 98 includes a basic Telnet utility that runs on the desktop and is capable of several different terminal emulations. Microsoft says nothing about this application in its documentation, and Win95 Telnet is not installed in a program group unless you do it yourself. (You'll find TELNET.EXE in your main Windows 98 directory. You can open it from the Start | Run menu or create a shortcut to it on the Start menu or the desktop. See Chapter 4 for information on how to create desktop shortcuts.)

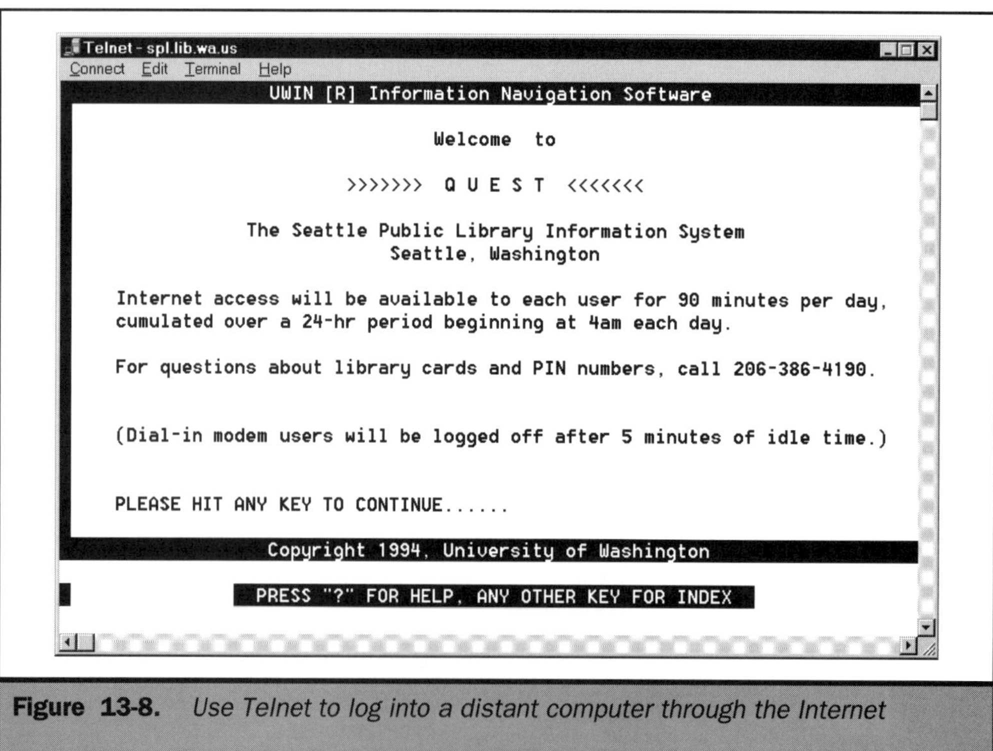

Figure 13-8. *Use Telnet to log into a distant computer through the Internet*

To make a quick Telnet connection, choose Start | Run, enter the Telnet address in the Run box, and click the OK button.

Windows 98 actually includes far superior Telnet support in the HyperTerminal application, licensed from Hilgraeve Commmunications.

To use HyperTerminal as a Telnet application, open the HyperTerminal folder in the Start | Programs | Accessories | Communications group and launch the Hypertrm icon. Then do the following:

1. In the Connection Description dialog box, enter a name and choose an icon for your new Telnet connection profile, just as you would for a terminal dial-up connection. (See "Using Hyperterminal" in Chapter 11 for details.)
2. In the Connect To dialog box, select TCP/IP Winsock from the Connect Using pull-down list. The options will change to allow you to enter a host address, as shown next. This address can be either a host name or an IP address (for instance, Well.com or 206.15.64.10).

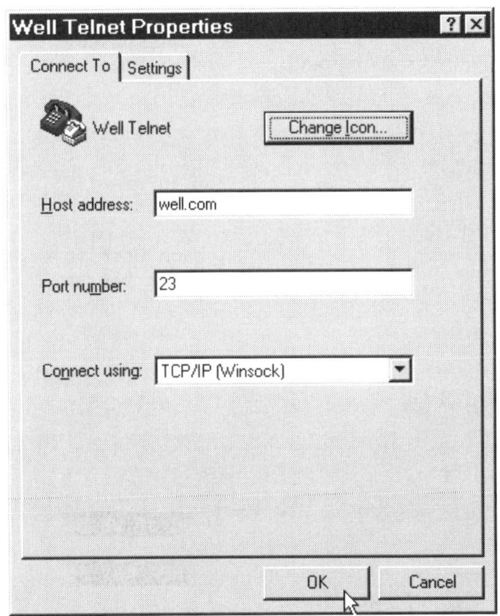

3. Click OK to connect.

You can customize the terminal settings and scrollback buffer for the connection by choosing File | Properties from the Hyperterminal pull-down menu and then clicking the Settings tab. (You'll find more information about terminal emulations in Chapter 11.) When you exit your Telnet session, HyperTerminal prompts you to save the connection profile. The next time you want to use this connection, you can launch the icon in the HyperTerminal folder, and you'll be connected automatically.

Digging Around in Gopherspace

Gopher is the typically cute and indirect Internet name for a menu-driven system developed at the University of Minnesota. Gopher utilities are tools for browsing the contents menus of Internet sites throughout the world, burrowing through systems in search of interesting information.

Millions of subjects included in Internet-connected bodies of information can be found simply by starting at the top-level gopher item—typically, a menu entry reading "all the gophers in the world"—and burrowing ever deeper in the direction of the information you want. The entire system of interconnected menus is known as *gopherspace.*

You can use gopher client software to search for news, research databases, get software files, read electronic books, participate in discussion groups, view directories, and access just about any other text-based Internet resource. The results show up in a hierarchical display window like the folder/file view in My Computer (except, that the names of things can be much longer than 256 characters.

Windows 98 does not include a gopher browsing utility, but you can use the Telnet client to log into a server that does offer a gopher browser. Usually, such a browser can be activated on the remote server by entering the command "**gopher**" (or "**!gopher**") at a UNIX command prompt.

Internet Explorer makes it possible to browse some gopher resources directly through the World Wide Web. If you're familiar with browsing the Web, gopherspace will not feel mysterious at all. It's character-based instead of graphical in nature, but the interconnected hierarchy of subject listings is similar to nested URL links. To log into a Gopher site through your web browser enter **Gopher://gopher.sitename.com** in the URL address field.

Unless you're seeking something very specific (in which case, you'll want to use archie or veronica, described at the end of this section), the best place to start is anyplace that provides general listings of gophers devoted to more specific information for links to specific servers. The following illustration shows one of my favorite gopher starting places, the Gopher Jewels World Wide Web page at http://doradus.tradewave.com/GJ/.

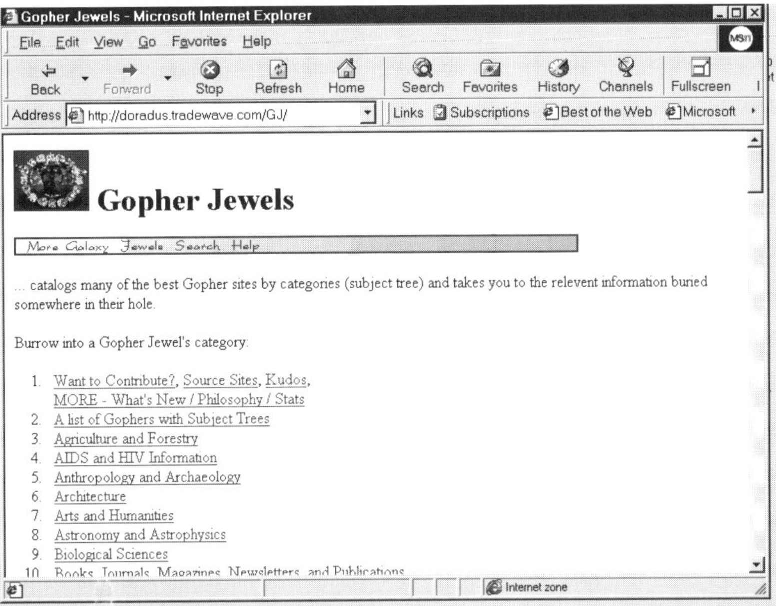

If you start your gopher dig at either the Well Gopher or Gopher Jewels, you should be able eventually to find just about anything you might look for. When you find a site you expect to visit often, you can save the gopher address in your Internet Explorer personal favorites folder just as you would a World Wide Web page.

Other Useful Search Tools

The tools described below complement the World Wide Web search engines discussed in Chapter 12. They are useful for retrieving text-based information from the Internet.

Archie

Archie helps find publicly available files by searching through file databases. Archie servers regularly scan thousands of Internet systems and build a database of files that are available to the public. When you do an archie search for a subject, you get back a list of sites that have files available that fit your search criteria. All files in an archie search are available to anyone, which means you can sign on with FTP using the user ID "anonymous" and automatically have access to the files; no special passwords are required.

Finger

Finger is a tool for getting information about users of systems connected to the Internet. If you simply finger a particular system, you'll get a list of all users of that system. Or you can finger a specific user and get back user-specific information, usually including the target user's e-mail address—a handy feature. Or you can use finger to find information about a specific server's contents. Finally, you can use finger to request the status of a given resource followed on the Internet, such as a hurricane, papal election, political campaign, rock tour, or other natural or unnatural event.

Note *Not all systems support finger because of its potential to give unauthorized users access to private information about authorized users. You may want to check with your service provider to see if it supports finger or, if so, whether it maintains a member directory that finger can search, and then take steps to control the information it contains about you accordingly.*

Veronica

Veronica is a tool to make gopher searches faster and more efficient. Using veronica, you can automate your gopher search for resources that contain the keywords you specify. Instead of browsing through gopherspace, veronica looks for your keyword through all the gopher menus and reports back with a temporary, customized gopher menu that contains all the items that matched your query. This lets you directly select appropriate items instead of branching around in a haphazard search.

Whois

Whois (pronounced "who is") is a tool that finds information about users of a specific network. Whois information is stored in a specific system database that is sometimes called the "white pages" because it resembles a phone book's alphabetical listing. The whois database is limited to people who have something to do with the workings of the Internet in some way and so is less useful than finger to most Internet users.

Additional Internet Tools in Windows 98

E-mail and the Web are the most prominent Internet services, but they're not the only ones that Windows 98 supports. You probably won't use these other tools as often as your Web browser and mail client, but you should know that they're available when you need them.

NetShow

NetShow is Microsoft's protocol for streaming audio and video through the Internet and other networks. As an add-on to Microsoft Internet Explorer, the NetShow client can play live and prerecorded audio, illustrated audio, and video from Web sites, network broadcasters, and other content providers.

Because the NetShow client is integrated into Internet Explorer, the NetShow Player program runs automatically when you receive a file in NetShow format. In practice, NetShow is not used as widely as Real Networks' RealPlayer, but it provides comparable performance. Since clients for both formats are included with Windows 98 and free updates are available online, you will probably want to install both programs. (See the section "Multimedia Advantages" in Chapter 15 for more information about Netshow and RealPlayer upgrades.)

NetMeeting

NetMeeting is Microsoft's client for live audio, video, and multipoint data conferencing through the Internet or a direct modem link to another computer. If your computer has a sound card and a video camera, you can use NetMeeting to conduct "face-to-face" conversations with other people through the Internet or a local network. Even if you don't have audio or video capability, you can exchange text messages, data files, and shared whiteboard drawings.

As Internet conferencing technology improves, it's possible that it will replace (or at least provide serious competition for) the existing worldwide telephone system as the most common method for one-to-one long-distance communication—but don't throw away that telephone on your desk quite yet. Today, arranging an online conference takes careful advance planning and organization because it's still more of a novelty than a common business or social tool.

NetMeeting supports the H.323 audio and video conferencing standard and the T.120 data conferencing standard so you can use it to communicate with other people who use other conferencing client programs, including Intel's Internet Video Phone.

A NetMeeting conference connects all of the participants to a conference server called an Internet locator server (ILS). When all the would-be participants in the conference are connected to the same server, any user can place a call to anybody else with a live connection to that server. If the called party accepts the call, the server sets up a conference link between the two clients. Additional users can join a conference and exchange text and application data, but only two people at a time can exchange voice and video through a NetMeeting conference.

To get started with NetMeeting, open the NetMeeting application in the Start | Programs | Internet Explorer group. (If you don't see NetMeeting there, you can install it through Control Panel | Add/Remove Programs. Select Microsoft NetMeeting in the Communications group on the Windows Setup tab.) Then do the following:

1. When the NetMeeting Configuration Wizard appears, click Next on the introductory screen.
2. The second screen specifies the Microsoft ILS server that NetMeeting will log onto. Make a selection. It doesn't matter which server you select; you can change it later. Click Next to continue.
3. On the third screen, you can enter information about yourself: first name, last name, e-mail address, and so on. If you want to avoid revealing personal information, you can leave any of the first three fields blank by filling them in with hyphens (-). Click Next to continue.

4. The fourth screen asks you to select the category in which your personal information will be displayed to other NetMeeting users. Choose a category and click Next to continue.
5. On the fifth screen, specify the type of Internet connection that you will use. Choosing the higher bandwidth ISDN or Local Area Network option adjusts the way audio and video will be sent and received on your computer. Click Next to continue.
6. If you have a sound card, the next screen brings up an Audio Tuning Wizard. Click Next and you'll see a volume slider and Test button. You can leave the slider at the default setting in the middle or click the Test button to adjust your sound card's playback level. Click Next to continue, and the same dialog appears for the microphone record level. Click Next when you're done and then click Finish on the final Audio Tuning Wizard screen.

NetMeeting now prompts your computer to log onto the Internet (or opens directly, if you're already logged on). If Microsoft's servers are up and running, you'll see a list of participants who you can conference with on the NetMeeting directory screen, as shown here:

To connect to someone in the list, double-click the name entry. NetMeeting notifies that user that you want to initiate a conference.

Note *If you don't see a list of names in the Directory window after a minute or two, you can try shifting to a different server in the drop-down server list.*

Tip

The drop-down Server menu in the NetMeeting Directory window contains a short list of Microsoft's core ILS servers, but the list is far from complete. Also, because so many people are using this limited number of servers, they're frequently slow and overcrowded. If you don't want to use one of Microsoft's servers, you can find a directory that lists more than a hundred additional ILS servers around the world at http://www.netmeet.net. The same site offers a free download of NM Super Enhancer, an add-on program that allows you to add and remove servers in NetMeeting's server list.

When you are connected to someone through NetMeeting, that person's information will appear on the Current Call screen. If you both have sound cards in your computers, you can have a live audio chat in addition to sharing files or participating in a text-based chat. If you or your correspondent have video cameras installed, you can send or receive video. The speaker and camera icons next to a name in the Directory listing indicate whether NetMeeting recognizes audio and video conferencing capabilities for that person.

To talk to someone in your conference who has audio support, just speak into your microphone. If you have a full-duplex sound card, you can listen and speak at the same time. If your computer has a half-duplex sound card, you must wait until the other person has finished speaking to reply. (See Chapter 15 for more information on sound card configuration and how to upgrade some half-duplex cards to full-duplex support.)

To activate transmission of video from your end of the connection, choose Tools | Video | Send from the pull-down menu. The My Video window on the Current Call screen will display a preview image, as shown here:

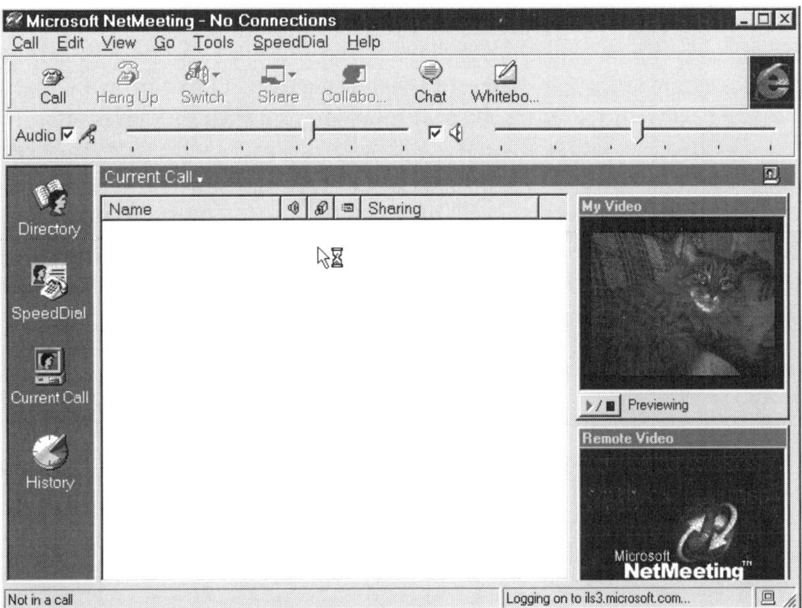

To initiate a text-based chat, select Tools | Chat or press CTRL-T. This is a useful option if you're conferencing with more than one person, since NetMeeting sends audio and video signals to only one recipient at a time. The Tools | Switch Audio and Video option allows you to toggle audiovisual transmission on and off between other conference participants.

NetMeeting permits you to share an application on your local hard disk over the Internet with other conference participants. For instance, you might open a drawing program and allow another participant to draw a picture. To share an application, choose Tools | Share Application and browse your hard disk for the appropriate program. Once you do this, the application will open in a window for both you and the other participants in your conference. To permit the other participants to manipulate your mouse and control the application, select Tools | Start Collaborating.

You'll find more information about sound cards, video cameras, and Internet conferencing with NetMeeting and other applications in the section "Video Conferencing" of Chapter 15.

Chat

For a description of this "talk to people on the Internet" application, see "Online Communities" earlier in this chapter.

Internet Diagnostics

If everything always worked properly, you'd never need to worry about tracing the connections through the Internet between your computer and a server. Every time you clicked a link or typed an address, your browser would load and display it in just a few seconds (and if my grandmother had had wheels, she could have been a streetcar). However, in the real world, and on the real Internet, things are much more complicated. Connections don't always go through, and when they do, they're sometimes agonizingly slow.

Windows 98 includes several simple network diagnostic tools. Most of them are DOS programs, so you should start by selecting Programs | MS-DOS Prompt from the Start menu.

Ping

Packet Internet Groper, or Ping, sends a short message to another computer requesting that acknowledgment be returned. The Ping client measures and displays the amount of time used for the whole transaction. The Windows 98 Ping program sends four consecutive test packets, displays the duration for each one, and then calculates an average. This information can tell you if the distant host is currently alive and connected to the Internet and if there are any serious delays along the way between the host and your computer.

To run a Ping test, type **ping *address*** at the C:> (or C:\WINDOWS>) prompt, using the address of the host. This may be either a host name or an IP address (for example, ping well.com or ping 206.15.64.10).

Ping Responds Promptly

If Ping delivers a status report that shows responses within 50 to 200 milliseconds, your basic TCP/IP connection to the Internet is probably working properly. To confirm this, you can try Telneting to a well-known host (for example, choose Start | Run Telnet and enter **compuserve.com**.) or logging onto your Microsoft home page with Internet Explorer. If you get responses, you can assume that all is well and that any browser problems are related to your ISP or the Internet, itself rather than your local computer.

If you get a response with Ping but no response with Telnet or Internet Explorer, there may be something wrong with your modem or serial port configuration. You may want to try reinstalling these components.

Ping Hangs Up, Times Out, or Reports "Unknown Host"

If Ping just hangs up at the command prompt or reports "Host timed out," "Host unreachable," or "Unknown host," the chances are good that something is wrong with your TCP/IP Internet connection. You should try running a Ping test on several well-known hosts to confirm that the problem is not related to one server at the other end of your connection (for example, specify **ping compuserve.com** or **ping msn.com**).

If you don't get a response when you run Ping for well-known servers, there may be a problem with your Dial-Up Networking connection. Verify that your ISP configuration information is correct and that the TCP/IP networking protocol is bound to the Dial-Up adapter in the Network Neighborhood properties. (See the "Dial-Up Networking" sections in Chapter 5 and in Chapter 11 for more troubleshooting information.)

Ping Is Very Slow

If Ping tells you that a connection is very slow (it takes longer than about 500 milliseconds, unless you're trying to reach an overseas server), there are a couple of things you can do:

- Run a traceroute (described in the next section) to try to isolate the exact location of the problem.
- If you can, try a different server. For example, if you're trying to run an FTP download, look for a mirror server in a different part of the world where local

users are probably asleep. (When it's 5 p.m. in California, it's after midnight in Europe.)

- If you have accounts with more than one ISP or online information service, try connecting through a different local host. The difference can be quite astonishing, especially if the two ISPs use different backbones.

Traceroute

Traceroute carries Ping testing a step further: it shows you the addresses of all the intermediate steps between you and the destination of your test. If a Ping test doesn't get an answer from the host, Traceroute can tell you where the connection is breaking down; if Ping is consistently slow, Traceroute will show you the location of the bottleneck.

Even if you're not having a problem connecting, Traceroute can be fascinating if you're curious about how the Internet operates because it shows you exactly where your data is going; it's not at all uncommon to discover that an apparently short run (say, from Boston to New York or from London to Madrid) may go several thousand miles out of the way to pass through one or more network interface centers.

To run Traceroute, type **tracert *address*** at the C:> prompt (for example, enter **tracert msn.com** or **tracert panix.com**).

Netstat

Netstat displays a list of currently active TCP/IP connections to your system along with statistics. If you have duplicated an IP address between your ISP and local area network, this command will reveal it. Netstat also tests connectivity to PPTP servers, which generally don't respond to Ping requests.

Winipcfg

Winipcfg is a Windows interface utility that reveals information about all of the IP addresses currently assigned to your computer. You can use it to reveal conflicts between the Dial-Up adapter and a dedicated cable connection. Click the More Info button on the IP Configuration screen to display complete information about all the TCP/IP addresses assigned to your computer.

Winipcfg, shown next, allows you to release and renew all the bindings of individual applications to the TCP/IP protocol stack. This may occasionally resolve timeout problems caused by one application's attempting to monopolize the connection. Choose Release All to sever all the application bindings. You'll then need to close and restart the applications to reestablish them. Choose Renew All to refresh application bindings to TCP/IP without closing and restarting.

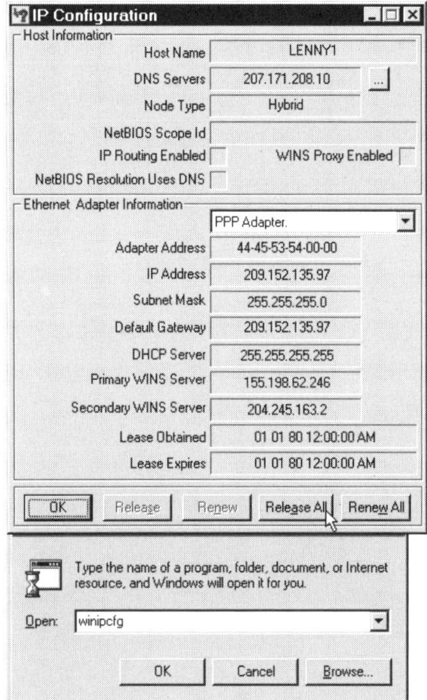

For more information about all of these diagnostic utilities, see the "Microsoft TCP/IP Protocol" section in the "Network Adapters and Protocols" chapter of the *Windows 98 Resource Kit* book on the Windows 98 CD.

Sources for Other Internet Tools: Stroud and TUCOWS

A Web browser, an e-mail and news client, and maybe an FTP client and Telnet program are all you really to need to take advantage of most of the wonders that the Internet has to offer, but there are plenty of other tools available. The Internet was created with a tradition of freely shared programs and protocols, and that tradition continues to this day, with hundreds of free and inexpensive Internet applications and utilities available to you.

Several Web sites provide very large lists of Internet client programs and other tools. The Ultimate Collection of Winsock Software (TUCOWS), at http://www.tucows.com, and Stroud's Consummate Winsock Applications list, at http://cws.internet.com, both contain reviews and links to hundreds of useful programs, organized by topic. You'll also find a good Internet tools list at http://www.winfiles.com.

Chapter 14

Networking with Windows 98

Chapter Highlights

Network topologies

Setting up network support hardware and software

Logging onto peer-to-peer, Windows NT, and Novell networks

Configuring and fine-tuning network client, adapter, and protocol settings

Sharing network resources: drives, folders, printers, modems, and fonts

Using remote access services

Using virtual private networks

Peer-to-peer connections over the Internet

Windows 98 is an operating platform well suited to small business networks. Improving on the peer-to-peer network services of Windows for Workgroups and Windows 95, Windows 98 also permits automatic connections to a Windows NT or Novell NetWare server. Connections to a dedicated network server can be made side by side with links to other Windows 98 computers on a peer-to-peer LAN.

With Windows 98, you can send and receive network e-mail and share your computer's resources—folders, drives, applications, printers, fonts, or a fax modem—and you can do it all without additional third-party software.

Windows 98 also includes a Remote Access Services (RAS) module. RAS allows you to connect to a dedicated network through a modem, parallel cable, or serial cable. Portable computers that lack network cards can still get full or partial access to shared drives, programs, and printers through a dial-up or direct cable connection.

Virtual private networking, new in Windows 98, permits you to establish a reasonably secure link to a local area network through the Internet.

If your Windows 98 network software and hardware are installed and configured properly, you'll see a Network Neighborhood icon on the desktop. When you open Network Neighborhood (double- or single-click, depending on your desktop settings), you should see a list of all the network computer resources available to you.

The first few sections of this chapter cover installing and verifying the integrity of a Windows 98 Network. If your network is already up and running (you can see shared resources in the Network Neighborhood window and can open them), you may want to skip ahead. You'll find information on working with remote resources and sharing local computer resources in the "Working with Shared Resources" section of this chapter.

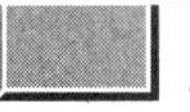

About Network Topologies

Windows 98 workstations can be integrated into a network through several different network topologies (that is, layouts or architectures).

Client-Server Topology

The client-server topology, shown in Figure 14-1, is commonly employed in large businesses. One computer, called the server, is the center of the network. The server houses all the management software, data storage areas, and printer connections that people on the network will use. The server can also contain shared programs that other computers (called clients) run remotely. Client workstations are usually cabled to the

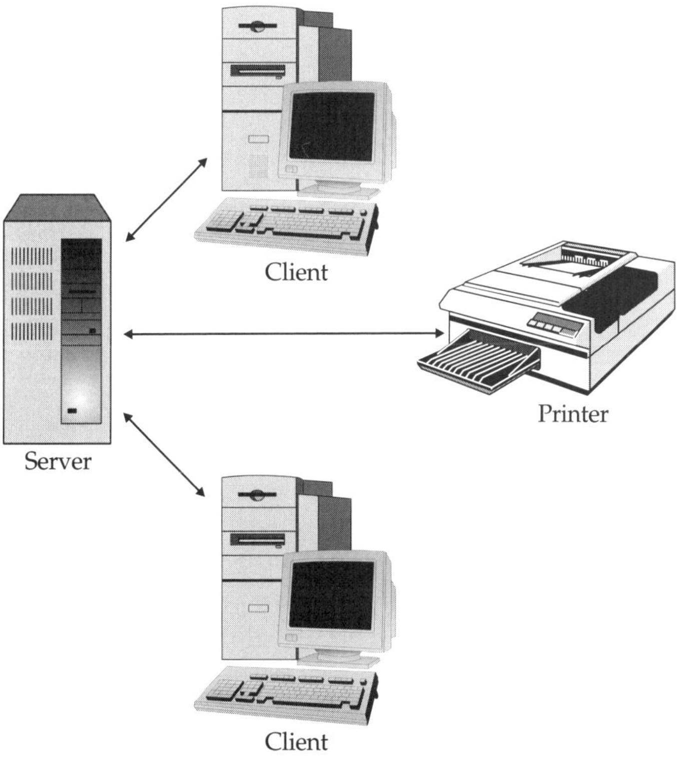

Figure 14-1. *Client-server network topology*

server in radial spokes or through a network hub. Printers may be cabled directly to the server through a serial, parallel, or USB port or integrated into the network through a hub.

Windows 98 computers on a client-server network are often cabled to a Windows NT or Novell NetWare server that manages connections, messaging, and user access rights to shared resources. It is possible to use a Windows for Workgroups 3.x, Windows 95, or Windows 98 computer as a central server. These versions of Windows offer File and Print Sharing and e-mail support through a messaging post office. However, they are limited in their ability to manage access rights and security for a large number of users.

Peer-to-Peer Topology

With peer-to-peer network architecture, shown in Figure 14-2, many computers share the chores of running the network and offering shared resources. One computer may house an e-mail post office, another may be cabled to a printer, and a third may be

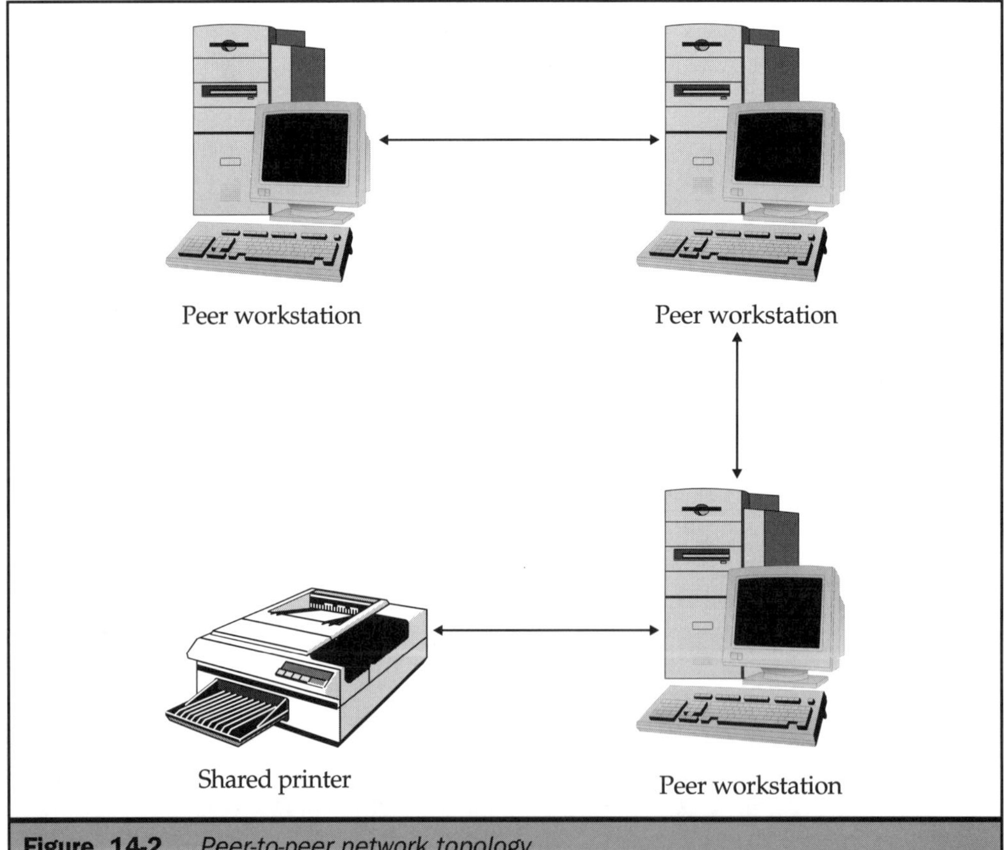

Figure 14-2. *Peer-to-peer network topology*

configured as a file or program server. In contrast to a client-server network, computers on a peer-to-peer network often establish permanent or temporary connections to one another.

Computers on a peer-to-peer network are usually cabled to one another end-to-end or are all cabled to a shared network hub. This topology, supported completely in Windows 98, is well-suited to a small business or home office.

The network hardware interface used most commonly with Windows 98 workstations is Ethernet. Ethernet network cards are sold with two common data transmission bandwidths: 10Base and a faster 100Base. Windows 98 also supports the IBM Token Ring hardware interface, in which workstations and servers are cabled in a circle instead of in a wheel-spoke or end-to-end geometry.

Client-server and peer-to-peer architectures can be (and in corporate settings often are) combined into an integrated network managed by dedicated Windows NT or Novell servers. Users on these networks can share Windows 98 resources with one another as well as connect to a central file or printer server.

This chapter focuses primarily on setting up and using a Windows 98 peer-to-peer network. It also contains information about connecting to Windows NT and Novell NetWare servers and exploiting the Windows 98 access features available through these servers.

Tools and Materials for a Win98 Peer-to-Peer Network

To set up a peer-to-peer network using Windows 98 you need the following:

- Two or more personal computers with 486DX2/66 or higher processors. Each computer should be Windows 98 compatible and have at least 16MB of RAM. One ISA or PCI slot on each computer should be available for a network card. (Some desktop models may include a built-in network port. Notebook computers may include a network port or support network adapters through PC Card sockets)
- Microsoft Windows 98 operating system for at least one machine
- Network hardware: network interface cards (NICs) for each machine, plus appropriate cables. A network hub is generally required for a twisted-pair 10BaseT network configuration. Computers can also be chained directly to one another in a coax 10Base2 configuration with T-shaped BNC connectors

A Windows 98 computer can network with DOS, Windows for Workgroups, Windows 95, Windows NT 3.x or 4.x computers, and other Win98 machines through Microsoft's peer-to-peer networking services. Windows 98 computers can also network with workstations running other operating systems, such as UNIX, Novell NetWare, Macintosh OS, and OS/2 Warp through other common networking protocols built into the operating system.

Setting Up Network Support

If you're installing your network hardware for the first time, follow these steps:

1. Shut down the Windows 98 computers you want to upgrade. For computers without a built-in network port, open the case for each machine and insert a network adapter into an available motherboard slot. (For notebook computers, insert the network adapter into a PC Card slot.)
2. Close the machines and set up your network cabling. This may involve connecting Ethernet cables from the computers to a shared network hub or connecting the machines in an end-to-end or ring configuration. In BNC network topology, the T-connectors at the remote ends of the network must be capped with terminators. (See Figure 14-3.)

Caution *Novice users should be aware that different network architectures can't be mixed casually. You can't connect a computer with an ARCnet or Token Ring adapter to computers that use Ethernet adapters. 10BaseT and BNC/10Base2 machines must be integrated through special hubs or routers. If you try to set up your system without special routers and expert help, the most likely outcome is burned out hardware!*

BNC T-connector (thin coax)

RJ-45 connector (10BaseT)

Figure 14-3. *Ethernet connector types*

Ethernet Cabling

The most common network topology for Windows 98 computers is called Ethernet. The cables that link an Ethernet network plug into the network adapter through one of two common cable interfaces.

The first type, BNC/10Base2, resembles the coax cables that link a television set to a VCR. The second type, 10BaseT/twisted-pair (shown in Figure 14-4), resembles the cable that connects a telephone receiver to a wall-socket jack. The modular plugs on twisted-pair cables link the indented socket on the back of each network card to a network hub.

Note *Although twisted-pair ports look like the ports that your telephone line uses, don't plug a telephone line into a hub or network port. These devices have different voltage requirements.*

Some newer Ethernet adapters support a faster 100BaseT network standard. As you might expect, traffic flow over a 100BaseT network is about 10 times as efficient as over a 10BaseT network. Connectors for 100BaseT ports resemble 10BaseT connectors, but the two topologies should not be mixed casually unless your network adapters specifically support an integrated 10BaseT/100BaseT topology.

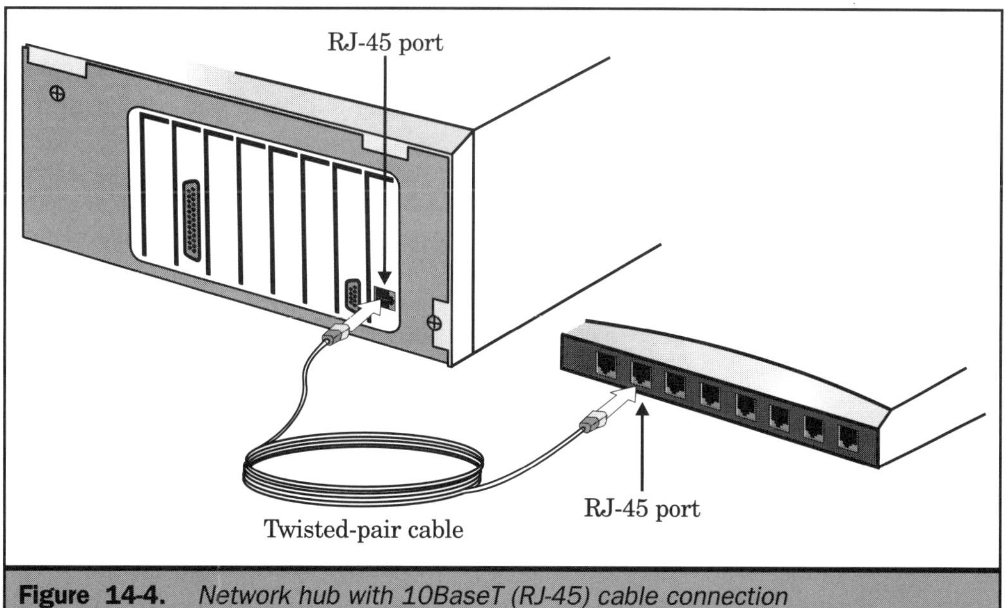

Figure 14-4. *Network hub with 10BaseT (RJ-45) cable connection*

BNC Connections

If your network cards and cables use the BNC topology, you can simply string the cables between two or more computers in a straight line. The network card interface on each computer has a T-shaped BNC connector. The extra BNC jacks on the computers at each end of the network are capped with a metal terminator. No hub is required for this network architecture. Network peripherals, such as Ethernet-enabled printers and print hubs, should be added to the chain sequentially. The thin BNC cables are inserted into each end of the T-connector. If the peripheral is at either end of the chain, place a metal terminator cap on the second T-connector port, as shown earlier in Figure 14-3.

Twisted-Pair Connections

If your network cards and cables use the twisted-pair topology, each computer on the network is cabled directly to a network hub instead of to another computer. Ethernet-ready peripherals are also networked through ports on the hub. The hub is usually powered through a bundled AC power adapter, as shown in Figure 14-5.

Figure 14-5. *3COM Ethernet hub and AC power adapter*

Verifying Network Integrity

Once the cables are in place and you switch on the computers, the network cards will automatically attempt to negotiate a hardware connection. Status LEDs on the network adapters (or on the hub) will generally flash green to indicate a functional network connection. To verify network integrity:

1. Switch the machines back on. The plug-and-play features of Windows 98 should detect and configure most network cards for you automatically.
2. Reboot each computer after its network card has been detected. Examine the status LEDs on the network card or hub. Check to see that they light up to indicate a functional physical connection.

After the first reboot with the network card installed, your computer may request a network logon or it may display network error messages. If the logon prompt appears, you can enter a username and password (see "Primary Network Logon" later in this chapter for more information), or you can press the ESC key to bypass the network logon.

If Windows 98 reports that your network adapter is not working properly, you can acknowledge the message by clicking OK. You may need to adjust the network configuration to complete the setup. See the next section for details.

Setting Up Network Support

If Windows 98 recognizes your network adapter, a Network Neighborhood icon should be installed on the desktop. You can view the current network resources available to any Windows 98 machine by opening the Network Neighborhood icon. If Network Neighborhood displays the shared resources on your network, then your workstation is properly configured. (You may want to skip the remainder of this section and proceed to "Working with Shared Resources.")

Note *Your local computer won't appear in the Network Neighborhood listing unless you've installed Microsoft File and Print Sharing services. (See "Sharing Local Resources" later in this chapter for more information.)*

If the Network Neighborhood Icon Is Missing

If there is no Network Neighborhood icon on your desktop, your network adapter card and connection protocols have not yet been configured by Windows 98. To confirm this, open the Control Panel | Network applet and examine the Configuration tab. When a network card is detected automatically, Windows 98 generally also installs the Client for Microsoft Networks and NetBEUI transport protocols. If no network adapter or protocols are listed on the Network Configuration tab, you must install them.

To install the network adapter, first confirm that it is physically in place in your computer. Before starting Windows 98, you may need to configure jumpers or run DOS-based setup software to set the port address and IRQ that the card will use (see Figure 14-6). This is generally the case if you have older, non-plug-and-play network hardware. (You can boot to a DOS command prompt by pressing the CTRL key at boot time and selecting the Boot To Command Prompt option from the Windows 98 startup menu.)

Start Windows 98. If all is well, you should see a message indicating that the network card has been detected and set up automatically. Otherwise, after the desktop appears, open Network Neighborhood properties and inspect the Network Configuration tab as described earlier. If you don't see a listing for your network adapter, try installing it by running the Control Panel | Add New Hardware applet. (See the section "Add New Hardware Applet" in Chapter 9 for information on working with this utility.)

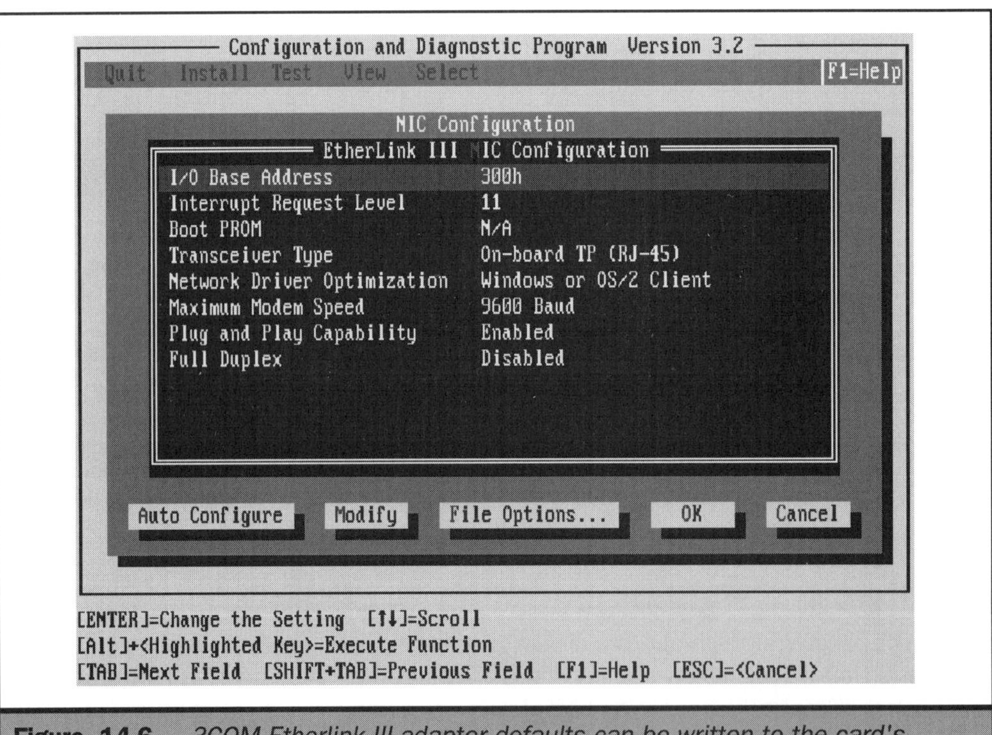

Figure 14-6. *3COM Etherlink III adapter defaults can be written to the card's firmware through the 3COM configuration program*

Note

If you install the network adapter through the Add New Hardware applet, Windows 98 will attempt to assign a currently available port address and interrupt. This may not correspond to the jumper settings or flash ROM configuration for the adapter. You can also install the network adapter by clicking the Add button on the Network Configuration tab. If you add the adapter this way, the default port address and IRQ suggested by the manufacturer will be used. In either case, you may need to change these settings, as described in this section.

After your network adapter appears in the component list on the Network Configuration tab, confirm that the Client for Microsoft or Novell Networks and the NetBEUI or IPX/SPX-compatible protocols also appear. For an Internet-compatible connection, the TCP/IP protocol is also required. (If you don't see these components listed, you can install them by clicking the Add button and selecting them from the options that appear on the Configuration tab. See "Network Applet" in Chapter 9 for more detailed information.) The Configuration tab is shown in Figure 14-7.

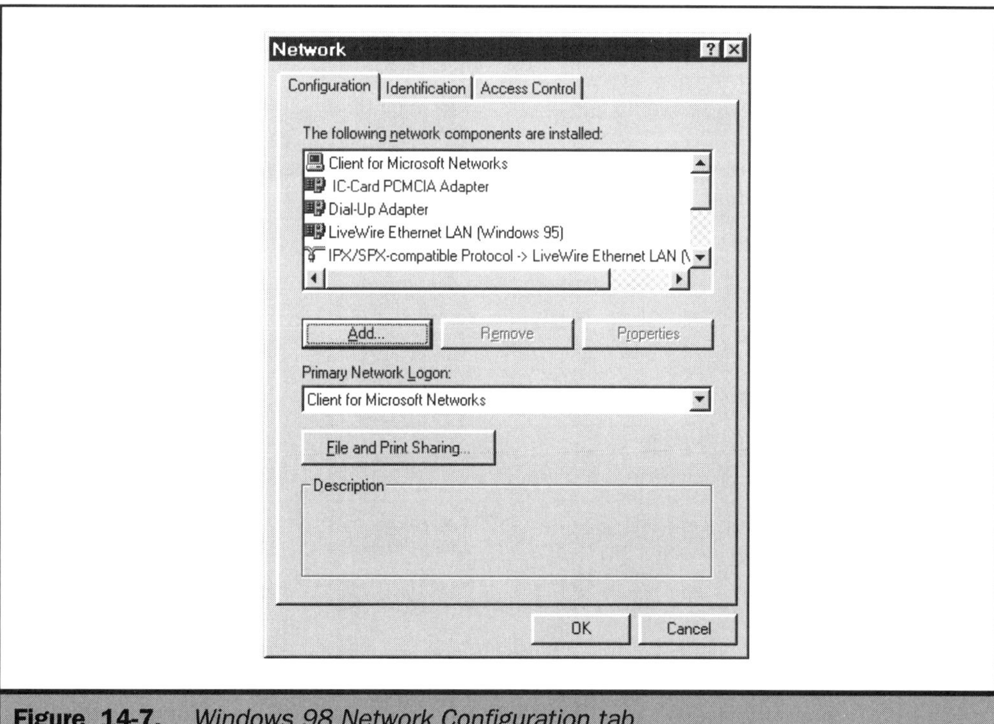

Figure 14-7. *Windows 98 Network Configuration tab*

Resolving Startup Error Messages

If you see an error message about your network adapter when the Windows 98 desktop appears, the card's settings may conflict with a previously installed device driver, port, or interrupt. You can troubleshoot the card's configuration through the Windows 98 Device Manager, as follows:

1. Open the Device Manager by opening the Control Panel | System applet and choosing the Device Manager tab.
2. Display the Network Adapters list on the Device Manager tab. If you see a red X or yellow exclamation point next to your network card, the configuration is incomplete or conflicts with other system devices.
3. Select your network card in the list and click the Properties button. Consult the Device Status message box on the General tab for diagnostic information.

If the diagnostic information for your network card indicates that the adapter is currently disabled (a red flag appears in the device list and code 22 is listed), you can activate it by clicking the Enable Device button on the General tab, as shown in Figure 14-8.

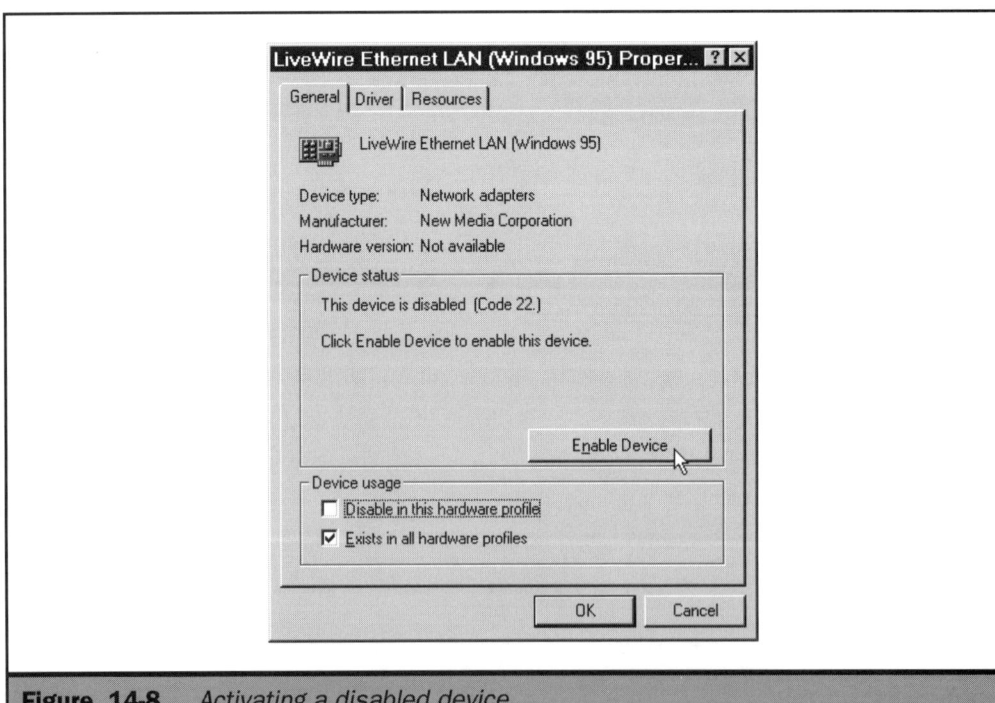

Figure 14-8. *Activating a disabled device*

If the diagnostic information for your network card says that the device is not present, not working properly, or lacks appropriate software drivers, a yellow exclamation point appears in the device list and code 10 or 28 is listed. You may be able to activate the adapter by reinstalling the appropriate software drivers. Click the Update Driver button on the General tab, as shown in Figure 14-9. This will open the Update Device Driver Wizard, which allows you to install software for your network card. The procedure is the same as when you use the Add New Hardware applet. You can tell Windows 98 to search for device drivers in specified locations (on disk or at the Microsoft Update site on the Internet). If this procedure isn't successful, you can display a complete list of currently available drivers and choose one manually. (See "Add New Hardware Applet" in Chapter 9 for more details.)

If a yellow exclamation point next to your network card still appears after you reinstall drivers, there may be an interrupt request or an input/output range conflict. Select the network card in the Device Manager list, click the Properties button, and choose the Resources tab. Check the input/output range and interrupt request (IRQ) in the current configuration to make sure that they match the hardware settings of your adapter. Check the status message in the Conflicting Device List box, shown in Figure 14-10, for information about system conflicts.

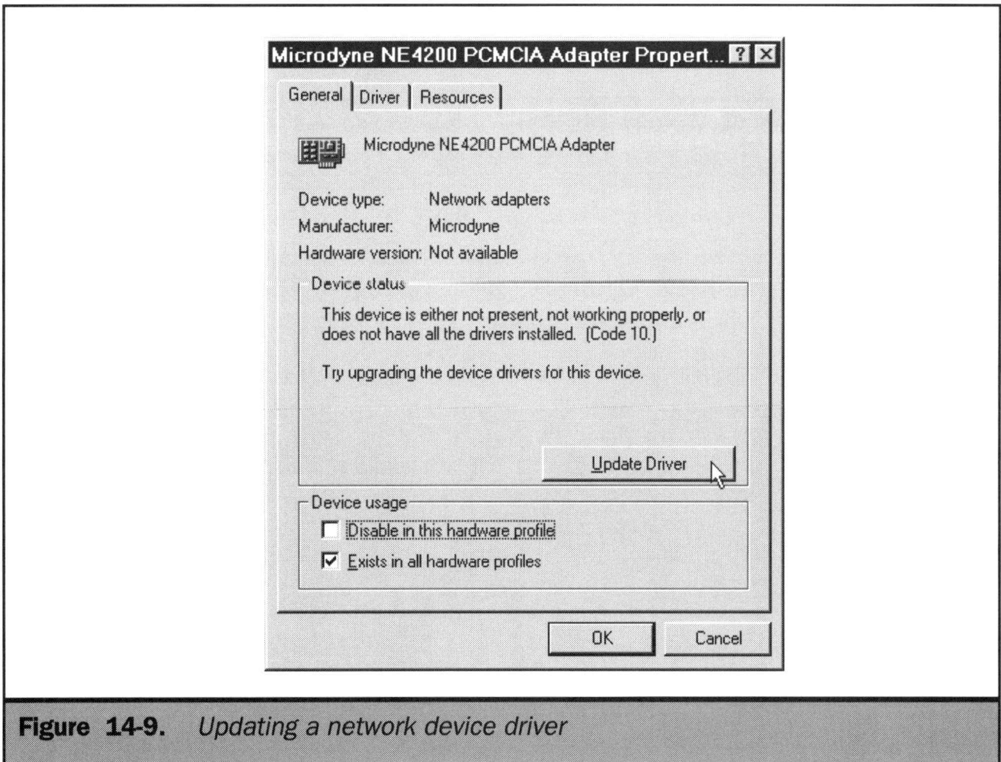

Figure 14-9. *Updating a network device driver*

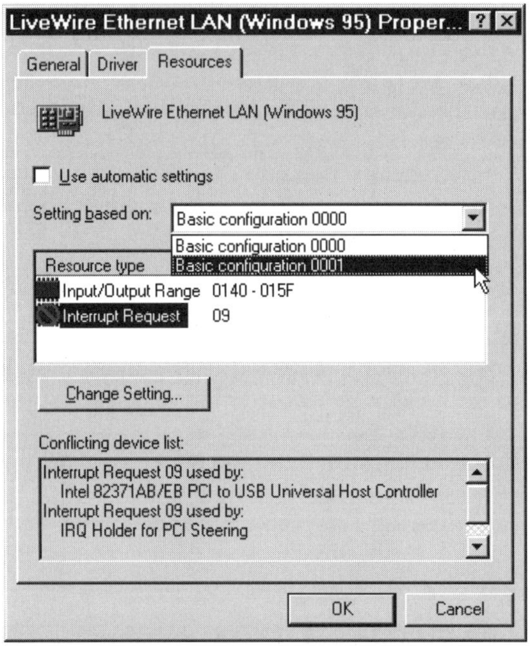

Figure 14-10. *Resolving a network interrupt conflict*

If the settings shown on the Resources tab don't match the physical configuration of your network card (set through jumpers or an OEM setup program), or if a system conflict is reported, you can adjust the Windows 98 resource settings:

1. Try clicking the Settings Based On drop-down list on the Resources tab and choosing another configuration. The Edit Interrupt Request dialog box will appear. Check the status message in the Conflicting Information field (shown next). If no conflicts are reported, click OK and restart Windows 98. When

you've selected an available port and IRQ configuration that conforms to the adapter's physical settings, the error message should disappear.

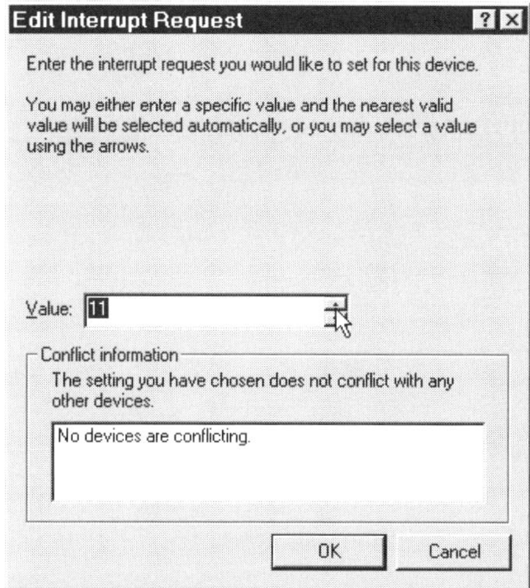

2. If none of the preset configurations resolve the problem with your network card, you can sometimes force configure the interrupt or port address within a specific configuration. On the Resources tab, remove the check mark next to Use Automatic Settings. Then select Input/Output Range or Interrupt Request in the Resource Type field and click the Change Setting button. If the resource can be reassigned, a new window appears that lets you adjust the numerical setting by clicking the up or down arrow in the Value field.

If you manually override (force configure) the settings for a device, a warning box, shown next, appears informing you that Windows 98 will not automatically readjust this setting. You can click Yes to continue. If worst comes to worst and this configuration doesn't work either, you can always recheck the Use Automatic Settings box on the Resources tab to let Windows 98 reset a default value.

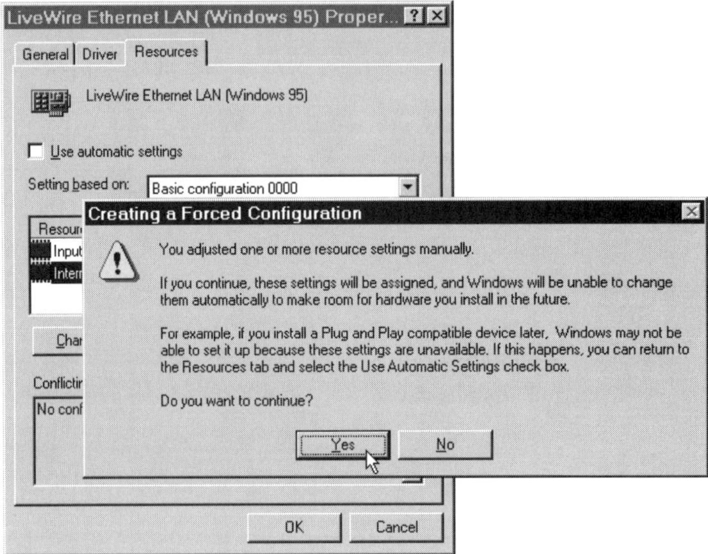

When you get Windows 98 to boot without a startup network error message, you can proceed to the next step in verifying network integrity. (See the section "Identifying Yourself on the Network.")

The "This Resource Setting Cannot Be Modified" Message (!?#)

Sometimes Windows 98 will not permit you to manually override the input/output range or interrupt request for a particular device. If you see the message "This Resource setting cannot be modified" when you click the Change Setting button, you have several recourses for properly configuring a network card:

- Reconfigure the physical settings for the network adapter. Older cards may have jumpers that you can set. Newer cards can be physically configured through OEM software. (See Figure 14-6)
- Try disabling CMOS and Windows 98 autoconfiguration options to allow more freedom within the Device Manager. To disable the computer's autodetect routines, boot to the System CMOS at startup. Look for options such as Use Plug and Play Operating System or AutoDetect and toggle them off.
- To disable Win98's software autoconfiguration, open the Device Manager and expand the System Devices listing. Select PCI Bus and click Properties. Choose the IRQ Steering tab and remove the check mark in the Use IRQ Steering box, as shown in Figure 14-11. Be aware that if you do this, the Device Manager will be more flexible in manually overriding settings. However, you may have to manually readjust settings for other installed peripherals.

It may appear to be impossible to adjust the input/output range for a PC Card network adapter in a notebook computer. Some older cards prefer port addresses that initialize in hexadecimal ranges from 0100 to 0400h, yet the Device Manager stubbornly assigns an input/output range that begins above 1000. You can get around this problem by manually adjusting the input/output range for the PC Card Manager instead of for the network adapter. Here's how:

1. Temporarily remove any PC Cards other than the network card from their slots. (You can ensure safe removal by opening the Control Panel | PC Card applet, selecting the device on the Socket Status tab, and clicking OK to disable it.)
2. With the network adapter present in the PC Card slot, choose it in the Device Manager list (not in the PC Card applet). Open the network card's properties and select Disable In This Hardware Profile. Click OK to continue.
3. Without restarting the machine, expand the PCMCIA socket listing in the Device Manager. Examine the Resource properties for each of the PC Card Services entries. One of the entries will show an Input/Output Range listing on the Resources tab. When you find this listing, click the Change Setting button and reset the input/output address range. (Settings of 120, 140, 300, or 340 usually work, if they don't conflict with other peripherals.) Click OK and then Yes to force configure this setting.

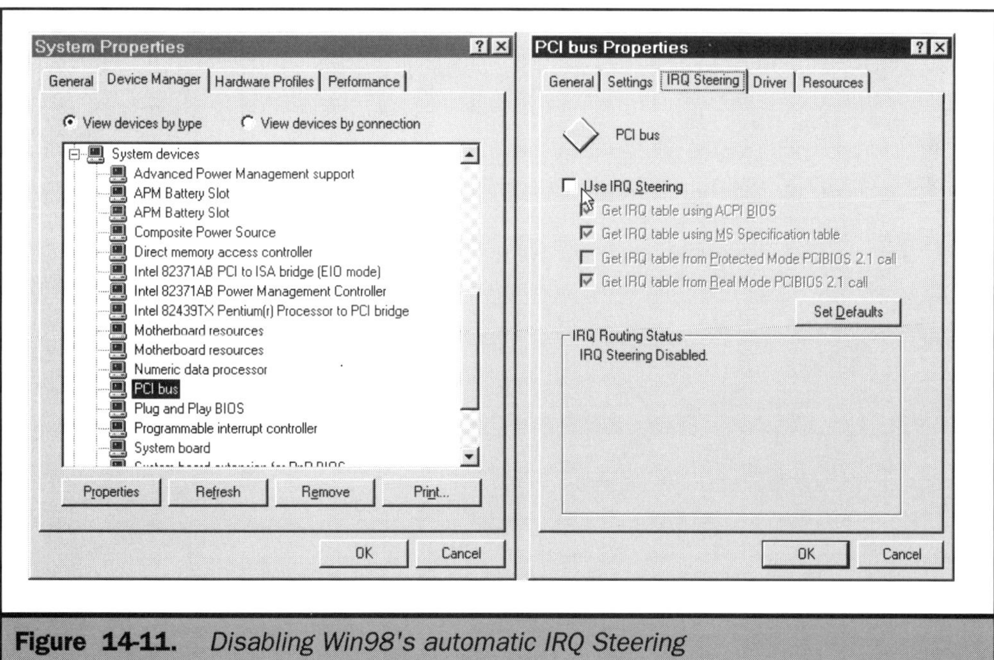

Figure 14-11. *Disabling Win98's automatic IRQ Steering*

4. Reselect the network adapter (which should now have a red flag) in the Device Manager list. Open its properties and click the Enable Device button.

Once you are able to start Windows 98 without network error messages, double-click the Network Neighborhood icon, which should now appear on your desktop. (Refer to the previous section of this chapter if you don't see a Network Neighborhood icon.) If your Microsoft peer-to-peer network has been configured to share any resources, they should be visible in the Network Neighborhood status window.

Identifying Yourself on the Network

After you install Windows 98 networking support, you'll need to give your computer a unique network name and assign it to a network workgroup.

1. Right-click the Network Neighborhood icon on the desktop and select Properties.
2. Select the Identification tab in the Network Configuration window. In the Computer Name field, enter the name this workstation will use to identify itself on the network. You can have more than one user account on each computer but only one unique name for the machine itself. You can also optionally enter a description of the workstation in the Computer Description field.
3. Assign your computer to a network workgroup. For a Windows 98 peer-to-peer network, you can keep the default Workgroup designation, as shown next. To log onto a Windows NT workgroup, use the workgroup name entered on the NT server. (See "Logging onto a Windows NT Domain" later in this chapter for information about logging into a Windows NT domain.) Computers that will connect frequently to one another should all be placed in a common workgroup. If you are planning a large network with several divisions, you may want to establish multiple workgroups (for example, Payroll, Billing, Administration, and so on).

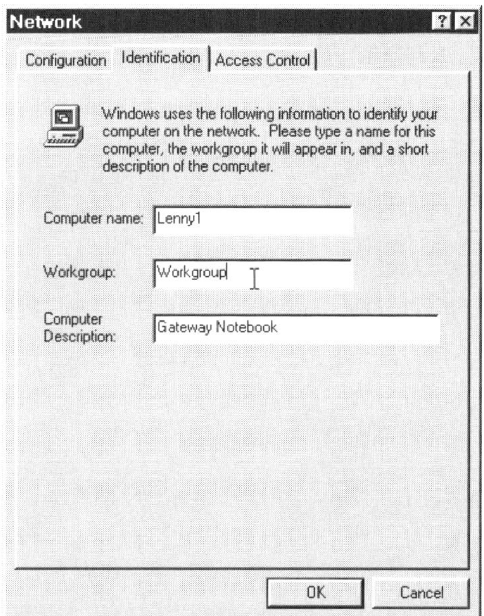

Testing Your Network Connection

You should now have created a network ID for each of your Windows 98 workstations and assigned them to an appropriate workgroup. To verify that your network is up and running, at least one computer must be configured as a file or print server.

Win98 Peer-to-Peer Network

If your computers are on a peer-to-peer network (no Windows NT or Novell server), pick one of the Windows 98 workstations to use as a test server.

1. On that machine, right-click Network Neighborhood, select the Configuration tab on its Properties screen, and click the File And Print Sharing button.

2. Confirm that the I Want To Give Others Access To My Files box is checked and click OK. (It's not necessary to share any specific resources at this time. Installing File and Print Sharing services will cause this workstation to appear in the Network Neighborhood list for all the other computers in the workgroup.)
3. Click OK to close the Configuration dialog box. Windows 98 will prompt you to reboot the machine.
4. Open the Network Neighborhood icon on the desktop of each Windows 98 workstation in the workgroup. After a minute or so, an icon for the test file server should appear in the window next to the Entire Network icon, as shown here. (The Lenny1 icon appears in this screen because it also has File and Print Sharing enabled.)

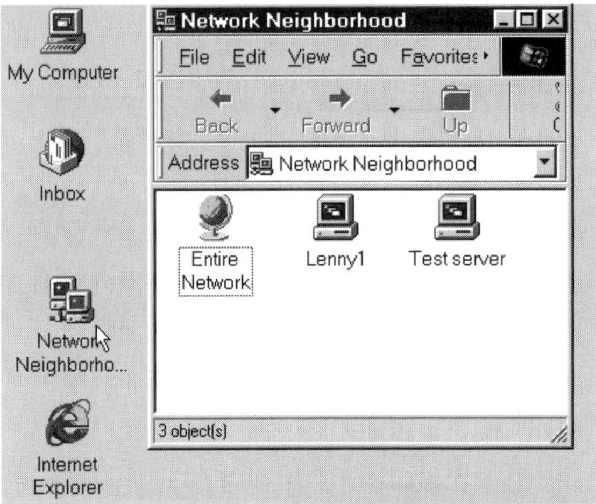

If you don't see a listing for the test server, try opening the Entire Network icon. A child window should appear that lists the names of the workgroups on the network. Open the workgroup that contains your test server, and you should see your test server listed. Each computer in the workgroup with File and Print Sharing enabled should appear in the Network Neighborhood list, even if no specific resources have been shared.

If you don't see the test server icon in the Network Neighborhood window, wait a few minutes and try again. If you still don't see it, there is a problem with your network configuration. Review the previous entries in this section or refer to "Troubleshooting and Additional Resources" toward the end of this chapter for additional assistance.

Client-Server Network

If your computer was connected to a Windows NT or Novell NetWare server before it was upgraded to Windows 98, a logon box should appear at startup so you can log onto the network with a username and password. If Win98 networking support is properly configured, the Windows NT or Novell resources available for this user account will appear when you open Network Neighborhood.

For information on configuring a new Win98 computer to log onto a Windows NT domain or Novell NetWare server at boot time, see "The Network Control Tabs" later in this chapter.

Primary Network Logon

Windows 98 offers several logon options. You can change the settings for your computer by right-clicking the Network Neighborhood icon, choosing Properties, and opening the drop-down list under Primary Network Logon on the Configuration tab, as shown in Figure 14-12.

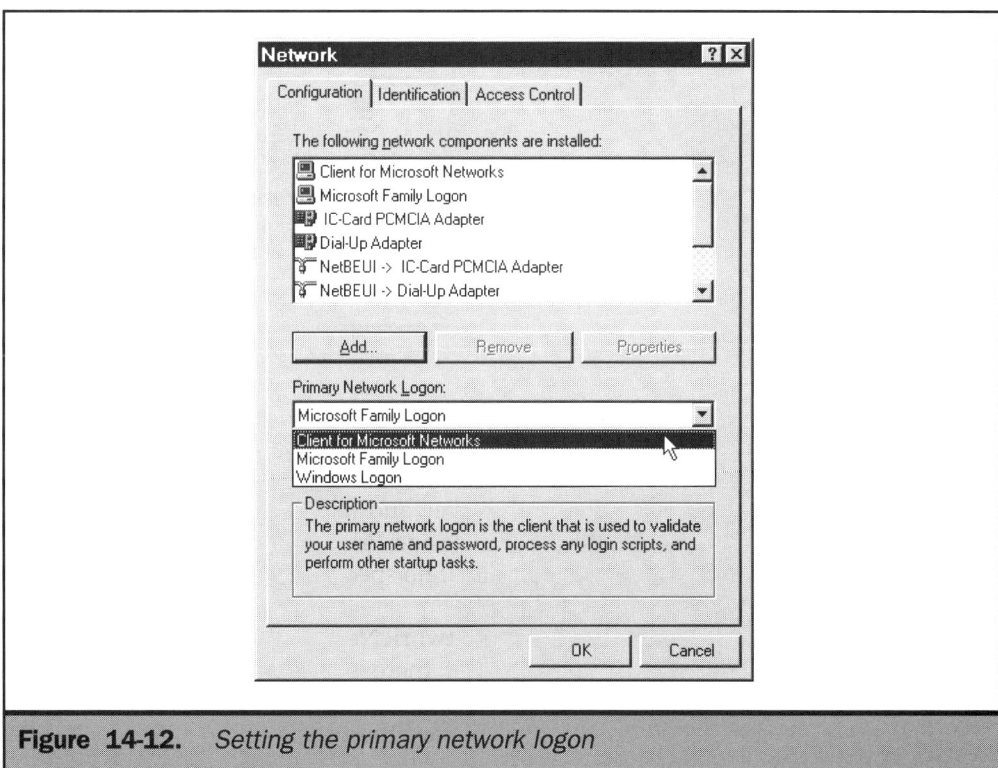

Figure 14-12. *Setting the primary network logon*

By default, Windows 98 uses Windows Logon or Microsoft Family Logon if the multiple users feature has been enabled. The Windows Logon screen, shown here, appears the first time that you boot Windows 98 on the computer. If you enter a username and no password on this screen, this screen will not be displayed again on subsequent startups with a Windows Logon.

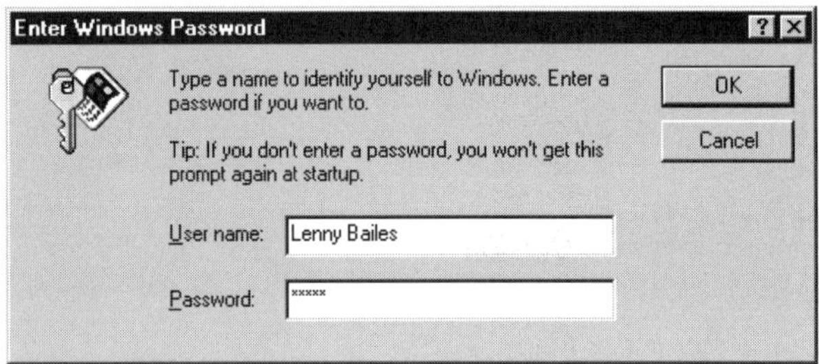

You can access peer-to-peer resources through Network Neighborhood after a Windows Logon or Microsoft Family Logon, but you may need to log on again to use specific shared resources. No message will be shown if your computer fails to connect to the network (which may happen if a server is down or if you enter an incorrect password).

The Microsoft Family Logon option is designed for workstations that will be used by more than one person. (See the "Network Applet" section of Chapter 9 for more information.) As far as the network is concerned, a Microsoft Family Logon is the same as a Windows Logon. The opening logon screen is shown here:

Client for Microsoft Networks must be selected to log onto a Windows NT or Microsoft LAN Manager domain. You can also use this option to reconnect automatically to resources shared over a Windows for Workgroups, Win95, or Win98 peer-to-peer network. If your computer has not been configured to search for a Windows NT domain, the logon box for this option is identical to the Windows Logon box, requesting a username and local computer password. If the computer is configured to log onto a Windows NT domain, then a three-field logon box appears, as shown here. The third field specifies the NT domain that will verify the user account and password entered in the first two fields.

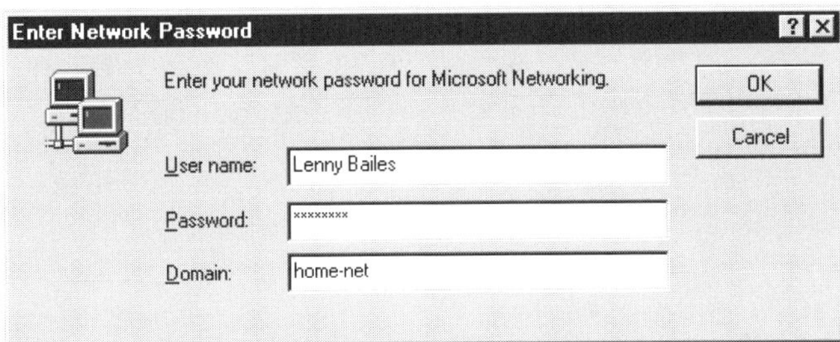

If Windows 98 is configured to log onto a Novell Network using NetWare Directory Services, the computer will display a two-field logon box like the one shown here:

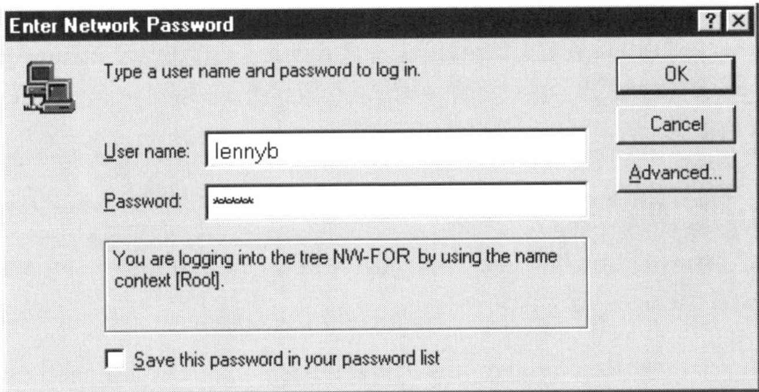

If Windows 98 is configured to log onto a Novell NetWare server without NetWare Directory Services, a three-field logon box will appear, as shown here. The third field allows you to specify the server that will verify the user account and password entered in the first two fields.

Enter Network Password
Type your password to log in to the server.
OK
Cancel
User name: lennyb
Password: ************
Login Server: netware_server

Tip *If there is a Windows NT or Novell NetWare server on your network, you can log onto the peer-to-peer network and the servers simultaneously through a single logon box. To do this, you must have the same username and password for both networks. For instance, to synchronize your Windows 98 or Microsoft peer-to-peer logon with a Windows NT server, open the Control Panel | Passwords applet and click the Change Windows Password button on the General tab. Enter the same password that you use for your Windows NT user account and log onto Windows 98 with the same username. If the same username and password are assigned to accounts on a Windows NT domain and a NetWare server, you can log onto Windows 98 and both networks simultaneously through a single logon box.*

The Network Control Tabs

When you right-click Network Neighborhood and open its Properties window, a three-tabbed configuration screen appears. You can also access this screen by opening the Control Panel | Network applet. As discussed earlier, if Win 98 networking support is incompletely installed, you may have to use this second route since the Network Neighborhood icon may not appear on the desktop.

The three control tabs on the Network Properties screen let you adjust defaults for installed network components, assign a network name and workgroup to your computer, and configure user access rights.

Network Configuration Tab

The Network Configuration tab lists the network components that are currently installed under Windows 98.

Logging onto a Windows NT Domain

The Client for Microsoft Networks component allows you to log onto a Windows NT domain and control the persistence of network connections. To configure a Windows 98 workstation to log onto a Windows NT 3.5x or 4.x domain, do the following:

1. Select Client for Microsoft Networks in the network component list in the top half of the screen and click the Properties button.
2. Check the Log On To Windows NT Domain box on the General tab.
3. You can specify a specific NT domain or workgroup to log onto in the Windows NT Domain field, as shown in Figure 14-13. If you do, it will appear automatically in the Windows NT logon box. (Otherwise, the Domain field will be left blank.)

You'll find more information about using Windows 98 on a Windows NT network in the *Windows 98 Resource Kit* online book, which is bundled on the Win98 installation

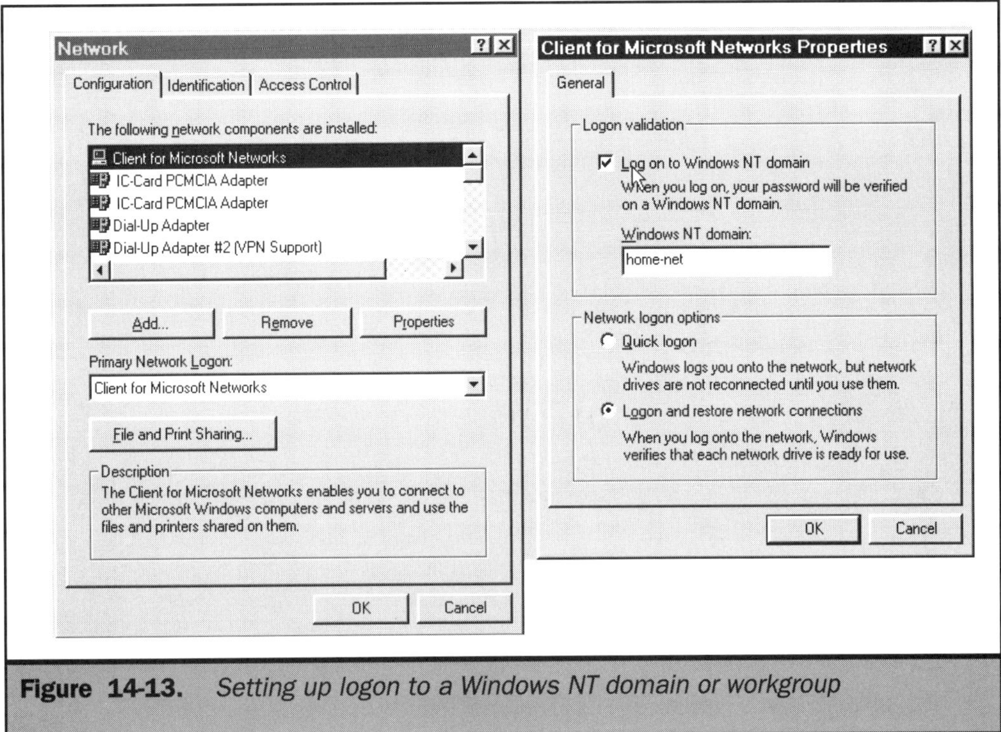

Figure 14-13. *Setting up logon to a Windows NT domain or workgroup*

CD. Open the *Windows 98 Resource Kit* online book from the Start | Run menu (browse to *d:*\tools\reskit\help\rk98book.chm), and see "Windows 98 on Microsoft Networks" in the section "Running Windows 98 in a Mixed Microsoft Environment."

Logging onto a NetWare Server

To log onto a NetWare server from a Windows 98 workstation, one of the clients for NetWare networks must appear in the network component list. The easiest way to connect to a NetWare server is to install the Microsoft Client for NetWare Networks.

1. Click the Add button on the Network Properties Configuration tab.
2. Choose Client on the Select Network Component Type screen and click Add.
3. Choose Microsoft on the Select Network Client screen. Select Client For NetWare Networks in the Network Clients pane at the right and click OK.
4. Select Client For NetWare Networks on the main Configuration tab and click Properties.

5. Enter the name of your preferred NetWare server on the Client For NetWare Networks Properties screen, as shown here. Then click OK.

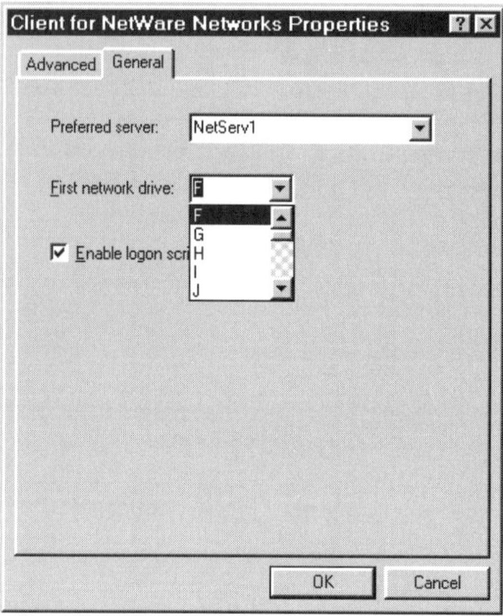

6. Click OK on the Network Configuration screen to close the network components list. You'll be prompted to reboot the computer. The next time you start Windows, the three-field NetWare logon box will appear with your preferred server preselected.

As an alternative to the Microsoft Client for NetWare Networks, you can install the Microsoft Service for NetWare Directory Services. This module allows Windows 98 users to access NetWare Directory Services, a tree-based interface that simplifies access to many network services. Users also have the option of connecting to a Novell network by installing Novell's third-party network shell (NetX for NetWare 3.x and VLM for NetWare 4.0 and above). These shells, not bundled with Windows 98, allow network users to run some NetWare-specific utilities not supported by the Microsoft Client for NetWare Networks. Novell's Windows 98 NetWare client can be downloaded from its Web site at http://www.novell.com/download/#Clients.

You'll find more information about using Windows 98 on a Novell network in the *Windows 98 Resource Kit* online book. Open the *Windows 98 Resource Kit* online book as described earlier and see the section "Windows 98 on Third-Party Networks."

Unbinding TCP/IP from a Network Adapter

If you plan to connect to the Internet and to a small LAN through a Windows 98 computer, you may want to bind the TCP/IP Internet protocol to your modem but unbind it from your network adapter. This security precaution can prevent intruders from gaining access to your private LAN while you surf the World Wide Web.

Select your network adapter on the Network Configuration tab and click the Properties button. Choose the Bindings tab in the Network Card Properties window, and you'll see a list of the protocols currently bound to the card. If your LAN supports connections through either the NetBEUI or IPX/SPX-compatible protocol, you can remove the check mark next to TCP/IP, as shown in Figure 14-14. This will not affect your ability to connect to the Internet through Dial-Up Networking (the Dial-Up adapter), but it will deter clever hackers on the Internet from using your computer as a gateway to your corporate intranet. Note that the TCP/IP protocol must remain bound to the network card if you plan to access the Internet or a corporate Web site through a cable connection instead of a modem.

If you have a Megahertz CC10BT/2 PC Card network adapter installed in a notebook computer, you may be unable to connect to your network until you set the Connector Type option on the Advanced tab for this card. Open the CC10BT/2 Properties screen, choose the Advanced tab, and set the Connector Type value to either Twisted Pair (10Base-T) or Thin Coax (10Base2), depending upon your network topology.

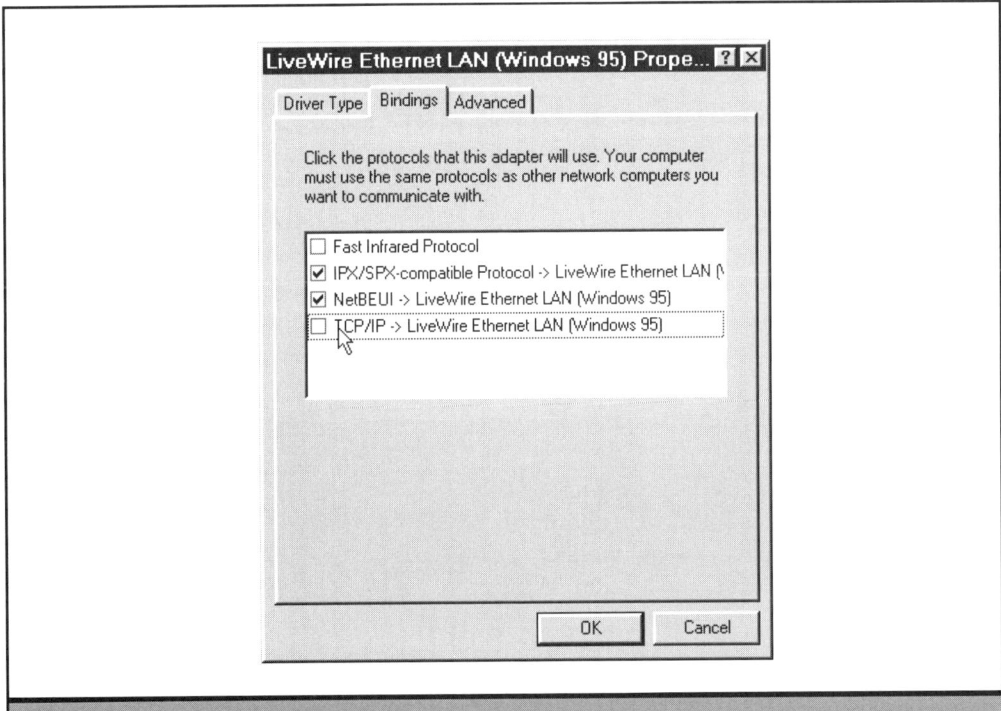

Figure 14-14. *Unbinding TCP/IP from your network adapter*

Configuring Network Protocols

Each of Microsoft's common network transport protocols has a set of customizable performance options, accessed by selecting the protocol on the Network Configuration screen and opening its Properties screen. Just as you can use network adapter properties to toggle the binding of individual protocols to the network card, you can use protocol properties to toggle the binding of individual protocols to network services such as the Client for Microsoft or NetWare Networks or File and Print Sharing.

An administrator may be able to improve the throughput over a network by enabling specific protocols only when they are required. For instance, NETBEUI can be unbound from the Client for Microsoft Networks or File and Print Sharing for Microsoft Networks if no specific applications require it. (IPX-SPX and TCP/IP are generally considered to be more economical, bandwidth-saving transport protocols.)

Similarly, as shown in Figure 14-15, TCP/IP may be unbound from File and Print Sharing for Microsoft Networks. This safety precaution permits the computer to access the Internet and browse the World Wide Web while deterring intruders from accessing private LAN resources.

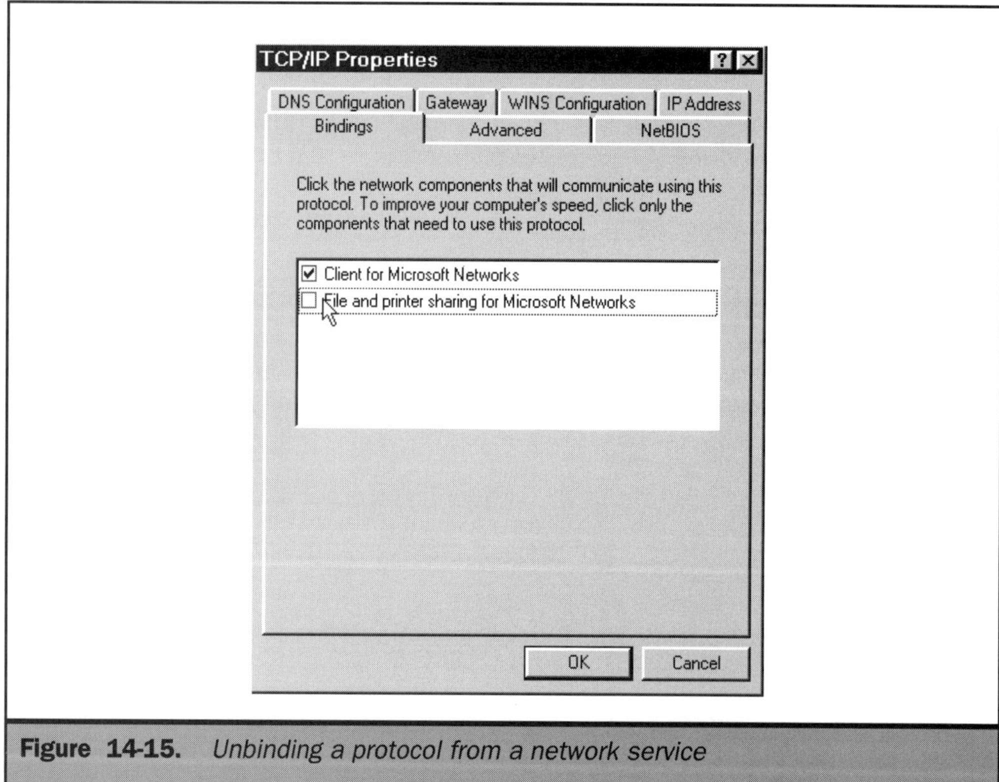

Figure 14-15. *Unbinding a protocol from a network service*

NETBEUI PROTOCOL The Microsoft NETBEUI transport protocol is necessary to generate status reports through the Windows 98 NET command and for network applications that require it. Generally, if NETBEUI is installed, you won't need to modify its default configuration except to unbind NETBEUI when it is a superfluous backup protocol (as described earlier).

You'll find more information about the Microsoft NETBEUI protocol in the *Windows 98 Resource Kit* online book; see "Network Adapters and Protocols" in the section "Microsoft NETBEUI Protocol."

NETBIOS SERVICES Both the IPX/SPX-compatible and TCP/IP transport protocols include a NETBIOS Properties tab. NETBIOS is an interface used by some applications to provide specific network services. (For instance, Innovation Software's Ghost can use NETBIOS to copy and archive disk partitions.) Microsoft's NETBEUI protocol, if active, includes built-in NETBIOS support.

A Windows 98 computer that uses IPX-SPX without NETBIOS can connect to a Windows NT server that uses IPX without NETBIOS. However, a Windows NT computer can't access shared resources on a Windows 98 machine through IPX-SPX unless NETBIOS support is enabled.

NETBIOS under TCP/IP can be used to set up local broadcast name resolution. (This means that if you enter an IP address for a computer in a Web browser or Telnet application, Windows 98 will automatically look up its English hostname.) By default, if TCP/IP is installed, Windows 98 automatically adds NETBIOS support.

To enable NETBIOS support under the IPX/SPX-compatible protocol, select the protocol on the Network Configuration screen, open its Properties screen, and choose the NETBIOS tab. Place a check mark in the I Want To Enable NETBIOS box and click OK to close this screen. When you click OK to close the Network Configuration screen, you'll be prompted to restart your computer.

OTHER IPX-SPX PROPERTIES If you have an account on a Novell NetWare server and the Novell logon screen does not appear, you may need to change the frame buffer setting for your IPX/SPX connection protocol. Choose the IPX/SPX-compatible protocol on the Network Configuration tab, click the Properties button, and select the Advanced tab on the next screen. Select Frame Type in the Property list on the left side of the screen and select a value other than Auto on the right side of the screen. Older Novell 3.11 networks are often configured to use an Ethernet 802.3 frame type, whereas Novell 3.12 and later versions use the 802.2 frame type for small local networks, as shown in Figure 14-16. (For TCP/IP configurations, Novell networks require the Ethernet II or Token Ring frame types.)

You'll find more information about the IPX/SPX-compatible protocol in the *Windows 98 Resource Kit* online book; see "Network Adapters and Protocols" in the section "IPX/SPX-Compatible Protocol."

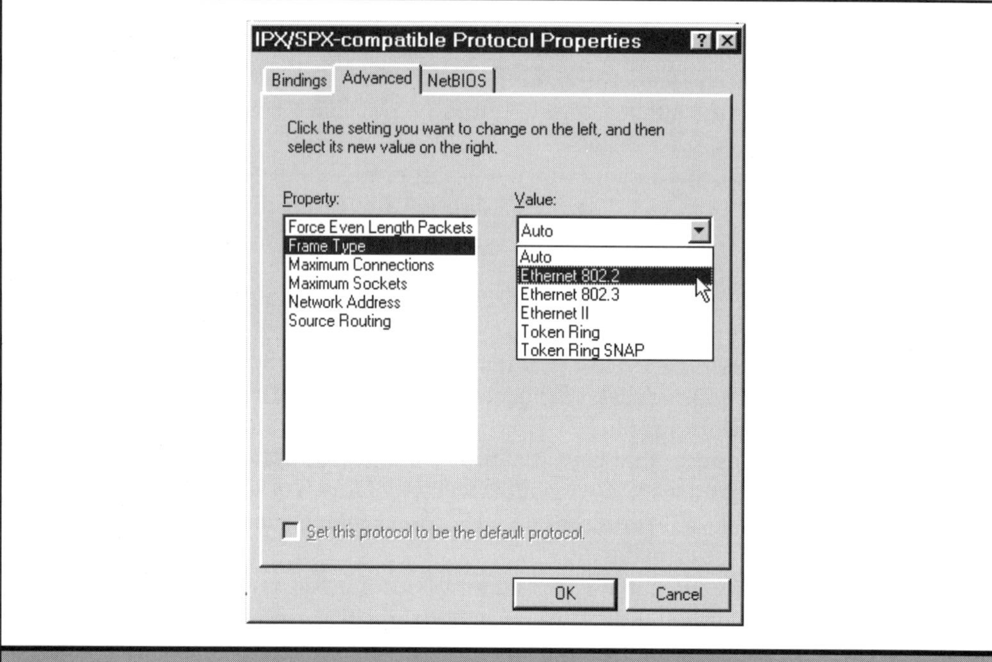

Figure 14-16. *Setting the Novell-compatible (IPX-SPX) frame type*

OTHER TCP/IP PROPERTIES The good news about Microsoft's TCP/IP protocol in Windows 98 is that it supports automated services that weren't available under Windows 95. You won't see annoying messages telling you that a DHCP server (a Windows NT feature that identifies computers over the network) can't be found. This was a common problem under Windows 95.

Under TCP/IP networks (including the Internet), every computer is identified by a unique 32-bit IP address. This address tells the network how to deliver data intended for each computer. On a simple LAN, Windows 98 automatically assigns an IP address to a TCP/IP-enabled computer without the need for manual configuration (or DHCP or WINS services on a Windows NT server). This means you may never have to open the TCP/IP protocol properties and manually change the default settings.

In Windows 95, to configure a TCP/IP network without a Windows NT server, the administrator had to manually assign a four-segment IP address to each computer. Windows 98 includes a feature called Automatic Private IP Addressing; so Win98 machines running the TCP/IP protocol are automatically assigned a class B IP address without the help of a Windows NT server.

To verify the automatically assigned IP address for your computer, open a DOS prompt and issue the command **ping *computername,*** where *computername* is the identity assigned to your computer on the Network Identification tab. (See the next section for more information on network identification.) Windows 98 will display the IP address currently assigned to the computer through your network adapter, as shown here:

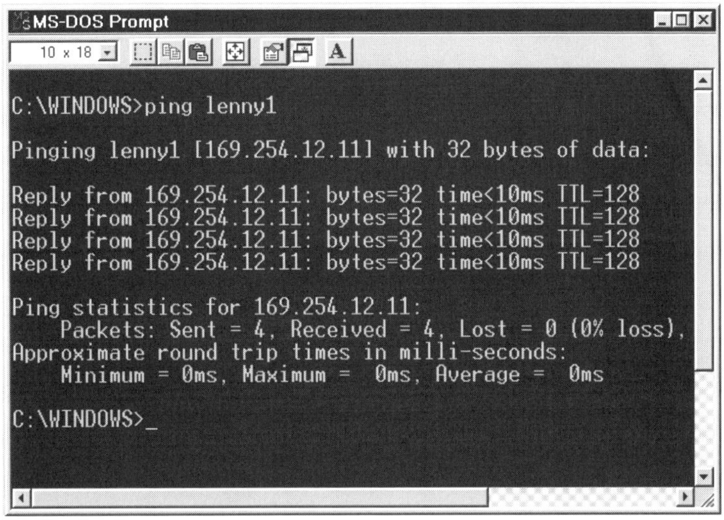

```
MS-DOS Prompt

C:\WINDOWS>ping lenny1

Pinging lenny1 [169.254.12.11] with 32 bytes of data:

Reply from 169.254.12.11: bytes=32 time<10ms TTL=128
Reply from 169.254.12.11: bytes=32 time<10ms TTL=128
Reply from 169.254.12.11: bytes=32 time<10ms TTL=128
Reply from 169.254.12.11: bytes=32 time<10ms TTL=128

Ping statistics for 169.254.12.11:
    Packets: Sent = 4, Received = 4, Lost = 0 (0% loss),
Approximate round trip times in milli-seconds:
    Minimum = 0ms, Maximum =  0ms, Average =  0ms

C:\WINDOWS>_
```

Note *If you are connected to a TCP/IP LAN through a network card, Windows 98 uses a separate instance of the TCP/IP protocol. This instance assigns an IP address to the computer that's independent of ISP-assigned addresses obtained through a modem/Dial-Up Networking connection.*

If you are running the TCP/IP protocol on a more complicated intranet, you may need to edit individual defaults on the TCP/IP Advanced, DNS Configuration, Gateway, WINS Configuration, and IP Address tabs. You'll find extensive information on setting TCP/IP options in the *Windows 98 Resource Kit* online book; see "Network Adapters and Protocols" in the section "Microsoft TCP/IP Protocol."

Network Identification Tab

The Identification tab on the Network Properties screen, shown in Figure 14-17, lists the name of your computer, its assigned workgroup, and an optional description.

The computer name you assign to your workstation is used to identify it to other network users. If you install File and Print Sharing services, this is the name for your

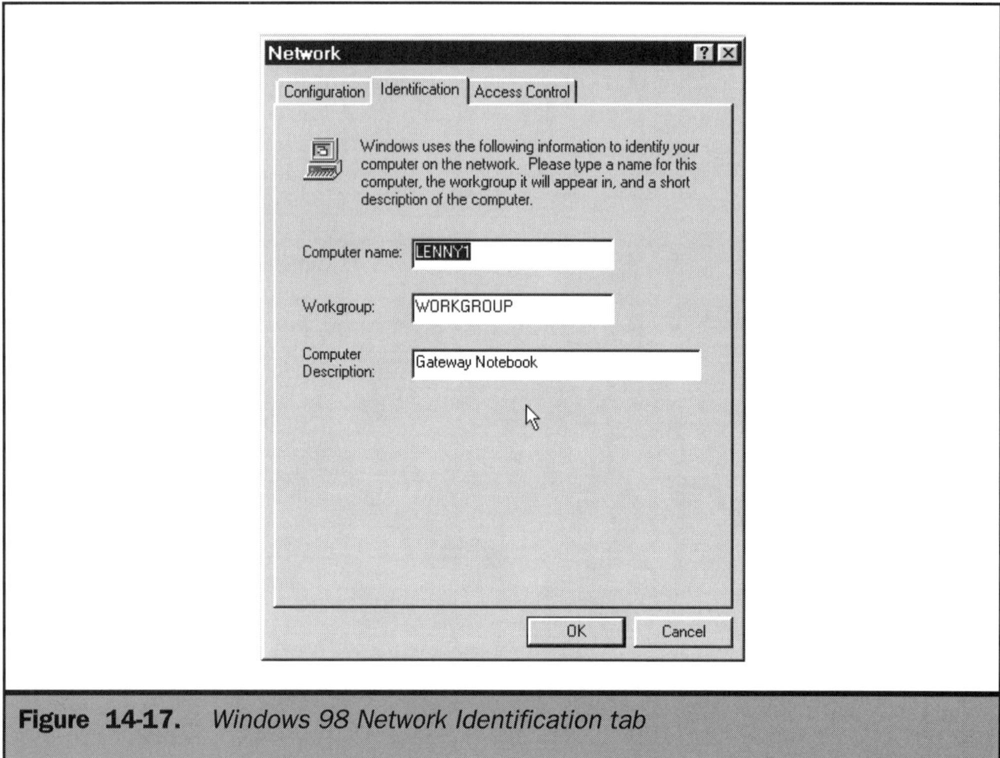

Figure 14-17. *Windows 98 Network Identification tab*

computer that will appear in Network Neighborhood. The same computer name will appear no matter which user is currently logged onto the machine. The computer name that you enter in this field is synonymous with the NETBIOS name used to identify your computer over the Internet and to NETBIOS-aware applications.

To avoid logon problems, assign a different computer name to every workstation on your network.

The workgroup name you assign to your computer determines which peer-to-peer network resources are listed as immediately available on the first Network Neighborhood screen. Note that you won't see resource listings for computers assigned to different workgroups on the first Network Neighborhood screen. To display all the workgroups on the network, you can open the Entire Network icon.

The Computer Description field lets you enter an optional comment that will be visible to other people in your workgroup when they browse your computer on the network.

Network Access Control Tab

The Access Control tab sets the security level for resources on your computer that you make available as shared resources. Windows 98 supports two kinds of access control: Share-level and User-level control.

- **Share-level Access Control** This type of control is available for resources shared on a Win98 peer-to-peer network. In this model, global passwords can be assigned to shared resources, but they remain the same for all users. You can assign separate passwords for read-only and read-write access to resources such as a folder or printer. However, the only way to control access to a shared resource is to request that the global passwords be kept secret by everyone who uses them. You can make a resource open to everyone on the network by not assigning a password to it.
- **User-level Access Control** This type of control is available only when your Windows 98 computers are connected to a security provider such as a Windows NT or Novell NetWare server. In this model, individuals or groups can be assigned separate passwords and access rights to the same shared resource. You can grant read-only access, full access, or customized access rights on a case-by-case basis to individuals or groups of individuals. Customized access rights can include separate permissions to read, write, create new files, list files, delete files, change file attributes, or change access rights of other users. You can also grant a particular user or group of users blanket access to all shared resources on your computer.

If you choose User-level access, your Windows 98 resources can be shared only among other people who are logged onto Windows NT or Novell server accounts.

You'll find more information on setting access rights to shared resources in the section "Sharing Drives, Folders, and Printers" later in this chapter.

Working with Shared Resources

To see the shared resources available on other computers on your network, open the Network Neighborhood icon. You can open any computer listed in the Network Neighborhood window to display a list of its shared drives, folders, and printers, as shown here. To connect to a listed resource, you may be required to enter a password before the resource opens on the desktop.

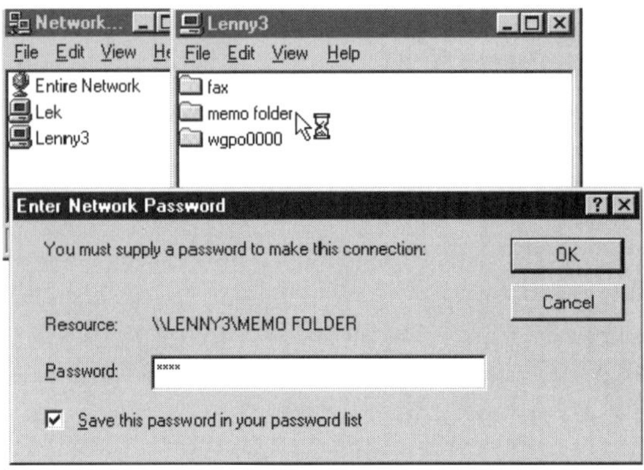

Depending on your access rights, opening a remote network resource lets you browse folders, open data files in associated applications, or run remote programs as if these files were located on your local computer. If you have write access to a folder, you can edit data files and resave them in their source location. If you have read-only access to a folder, you can open its files in an application, but you must save any changes you make to a new file on your local hard disk rather than overwriting the original on the server.

If you have access rights to a shared printer in Network Neighborhood, you can install the printer on your local computer and print to it over the network from any application. Right-click the printer icon and select Install from the pop-up menu, as shown here. (For more information on configuring and using a network printer, see "Network Printing Issues" in Chapter 10.)

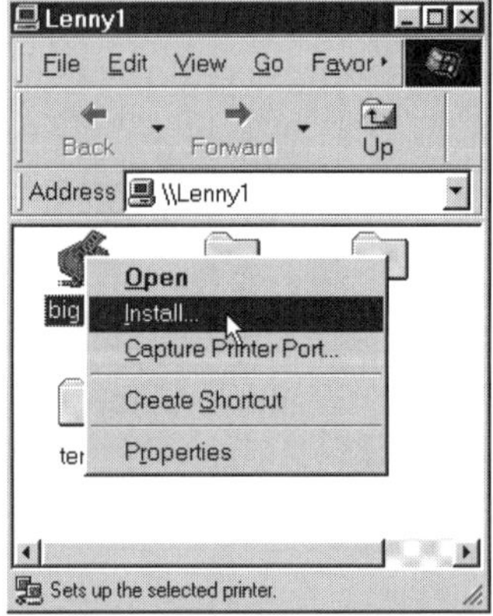

Getting Quick Access to Network Resources

In addition to viewing shared resources through Network Neighborhood on the desktop, you can browse the network in Windows Explorer or in the File Open and File Save As dialog boxes in Windows 95 and Windows 98 applications.

To browse the network through Windows Explorer, expand the Network Neighborhood listing in the All Folders list in the left pane.

To browse the network in a 32-bit application's File Open or File Save As dialog box, click the Up One Level icon on the toolbar until you get to the Desktop listing; then open the Network Neighborhood icon to browse through computers and shared folders, as shown here:

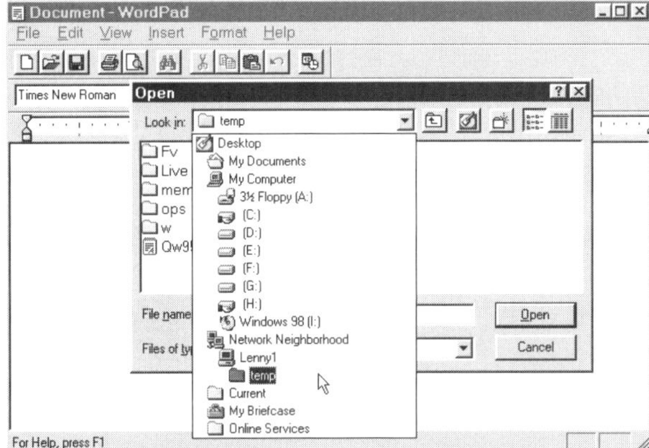

Direct Access to Any Network Resource

If you know the Universal Naming Convention (UNC) path to any resource on the network, you can log onto it directly through Win98's Start | Run box. This is a convenient way to connect to shared resources in other workgroups that are hidden from Network Neighborhood. For instance, if a computer called Pan35 in another workgroup has shared a folder called Billing, you won't see it on the first Network Neighborhood screen, but you can access the folder quickly by opening the Start | Run box: enter **\\pan35\bulletin**, as shown in Figure 14-18, and click OK.

Mapping a Network Drive

Older DOS and Windows 3.x applications lack the ability to open and save files through Win98's Network Neighborhood. For these applications, you can map a remote network drive or folder to a drive letter on your local computer. Once a network resource has been mapped in this way, it becomes accessible to applications with no built-in network support. Here's how to map a network drive:

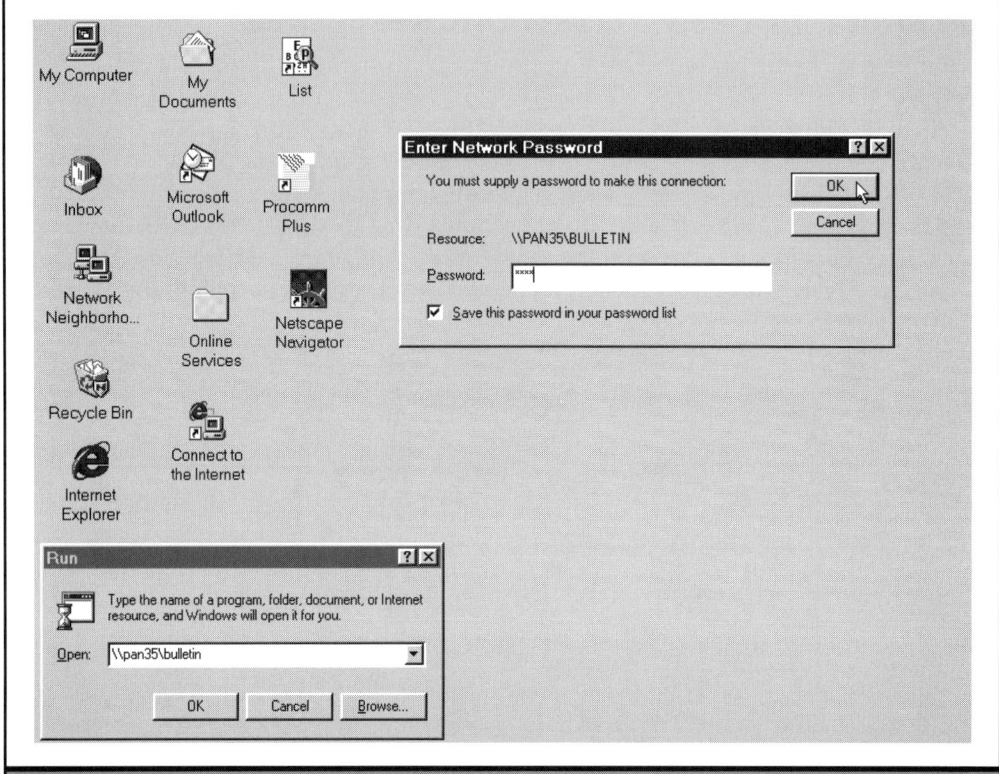

Figure 14-18. *Logging onto a network resource directly through the Start | Run box*

1. Browse Network Neighborhood and right-click the remote drive or folder you want to access.
2. Choose Map Network Drive from the pop-up menu, shown next. (If you don't see Map Network Drive on the pop-up menu, back up to the previous level in the folder list until the option appears. You should always find the Map Network Drive option if you right-click a shared folder in the first level after opening a computer icon.)

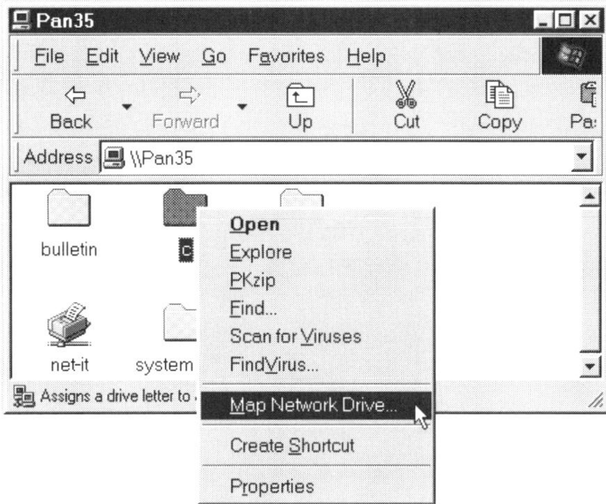

When you choose Map Network Drive, a dialog box appears on the desktop, displaying available local drive letters and the UNC path to the network resource, as shown next. Select a drive letter and click OK. Check the Reconnect At Logon box toward the bottom of the dialog box if you want the mapping to persist the next time you start the computer. You may be required to enter a password.

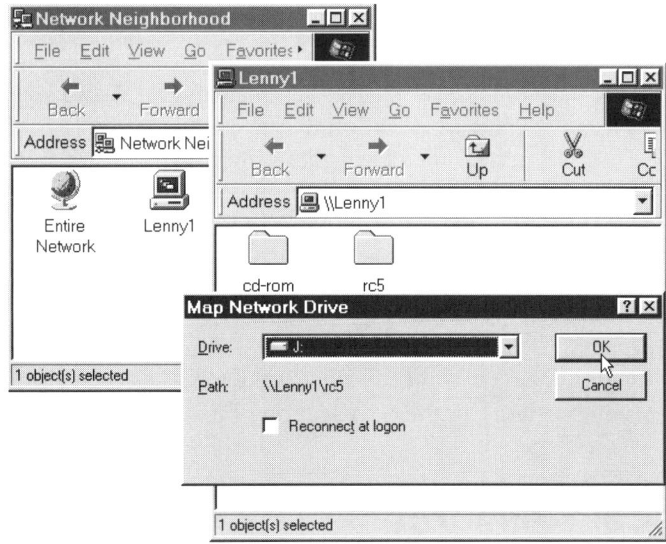

After a network folder has been mapped, it will appear in My Computer (shown here), in Windows Explorer, and under DOS bearing a local drive letter. You can browse and open files with DOS and Windows 3.x applications on a mapped drive as though they were on your local hard disk. If you've been granted full access or write access to the shared folder, you can save file changes to the mapped drive letter. (Under User-level access, you must have "full" or "create" rights to save new files on the mapped drive. See "User-level Access Rights" later in this chapter for a discussion of the customized privileges that can be assigned.)

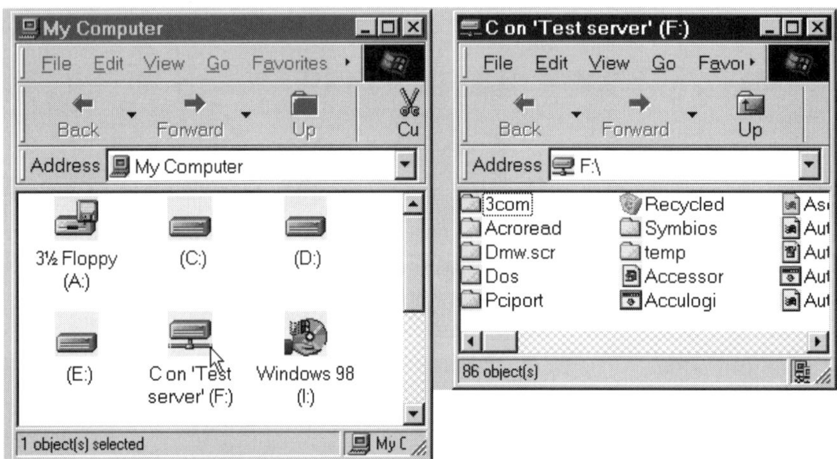

One common use for mapped network drives is to permit DOS and Windows 3.x database applications to use a common location to serve information to multiple users. Typically, each workstation can include a local client interface for the database and save new entries to the shared folder. If an application has limited multiuser support, but doesn't understand UNC network paths, you can enter a mapped drive letter such as **E:** or **F:** in the configuration dialog that asks where common files should be stored.

Another good use for mapped network drives is to publish a CD-ROM drive over the network for use by workstations that don't have one. Some multimedia applications are blind to UNC pathnames but may request a CD-ROM drive letter to access clipart or run supplementary modules. You'll learn how to share and map a CD-ROM drive over your network in the next section of this chapter.

Sharing Local Resources

To share resources on your local computer over a peer-to-peer network or through the Internet, you must first install File and Print Sharing services. Here's how:

1. Open Network Neighborhood properties (or the Network applet in the Control Panel).
2. Click the File And Print Sharing button, place check marks next to the resource types you want to publish, as shown here. Then click OK.

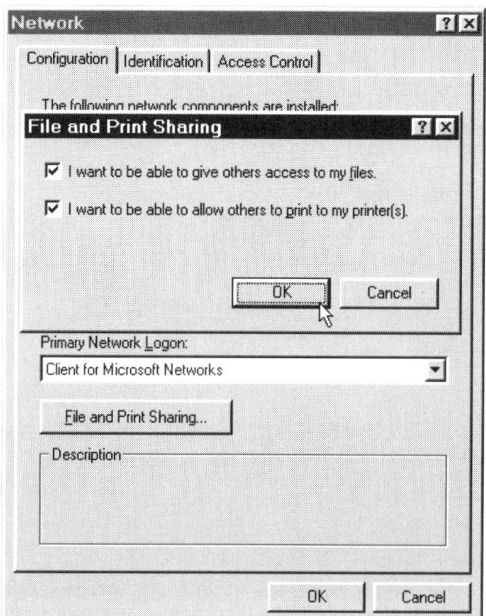

3. Click OK to close the Network Properties screen. You'll be prompted to restart the computer.

If your Primary Network Logon destination is Windows or the Client for Microsoft Networks, then File and Print Sharing for Microsoft Networks will be installed. (A Windows NT logon is not required but, if present, can provide additional user-access controls.)

If your Primary Network Logon destination is the Client for NetWare Networks, then File and Print Sharing for NetWare Networks will be installed. You must log onto a Novell server to assign access rights to shared resources.

File and Print Sharing can be installed for only one network client at a time; you can't run both services simultaneously.

Note *When you install File and Print Sharing, file and printer services are bound to all currently installed network transport protocols. To conserve network resources and avoid performance slowdown, you may want to examine the binding properties for each protocol and deselect the file and printer bindings that are superfluous.*

Once File and Print Sharing is installed, you can share your computer's local drives, folders, printers, and fax modem.

Sharing Drives, Folders, and Printers

To share a drive or folder, select it in My Computer or Windows Explorer, right-click, and choose the Sharing option on the pop-up menu, as shown here. (To share a printer, right-click the device in the Printers folder and choose Sharing.)

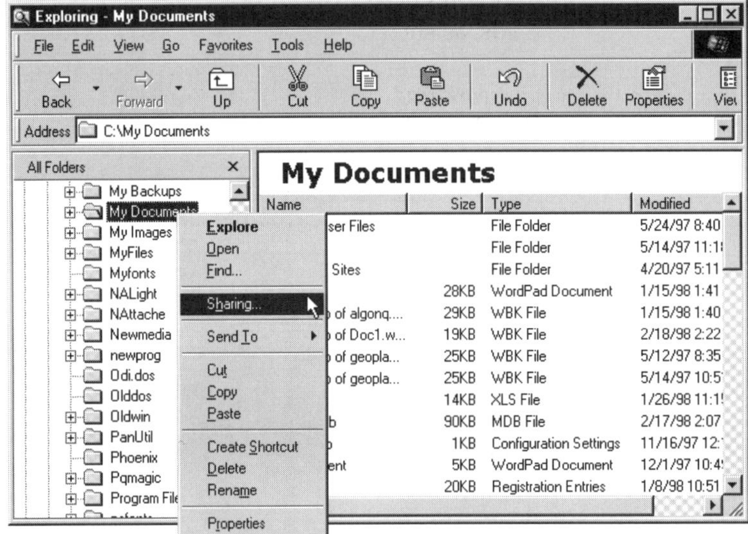

Depending on the type of access control that is enabled, one of two menu screens will appear: for Share-level access rights or for User-level access rights.

Share-level Access Rights

To set Share-level access rights, click the Shared As button. By default, Windows 98 will use the name of the drive, folder, or printer as the share name (accepting up to 12 characters). You can edit the share name by clicking the Share Name field and assigning the name you want.

The Comment field allows you to add a note about this shared resource (using up to 48 characters) that will be visible to users who browse your computer with the Win98 NET command.

The Access Type field allows you to choose three different options for users who will connect to this folder:

- **Read-Only** This access type permits files in a shared folder to be opened over the network. Some applications can also be run remotely. Users can't save changes to files in the source location, modify file attributes, delete files, or create new files in the folder. Read-only resources can be openly shared or password protected.

- **Full** This access type permits users to modify files in the shared folder, change file attributes, delete files, and create new files. Full-access resources can also be openly shared or password protected.
- **Depends On Password** This option allows you to create two access levels for a shared resource by assigning two passwords: one for read-only access and another for full access. If you select this option, the Passwords field on this screen displays two fields, as shown in Figure 14-19.

Tip *To give everyone on the network read-only access to a folder and grant full control to just a small group, leave the Read-Only Password field blank and assign a separate full-access password.*

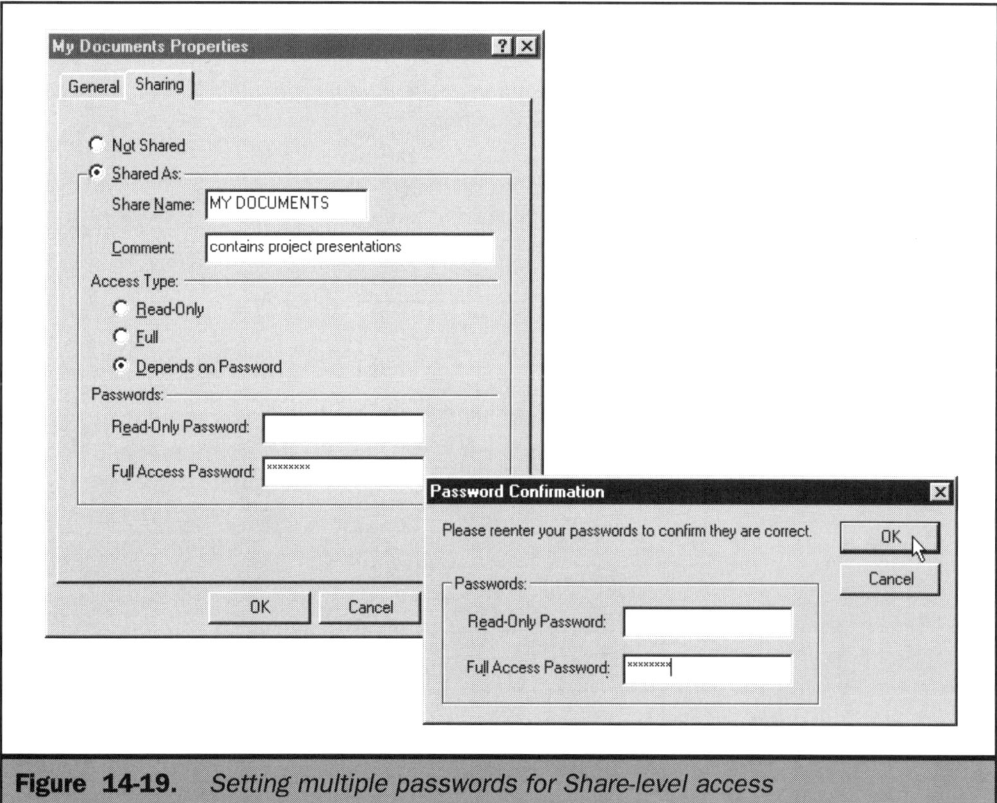

Figure 14-19. *Setting multiple passwords for Share-level access*

User-level Access Rights

If you have an account on a Windows NT or Novell NetWare server and you are logged on, you can provide User-level access to Win98 resources. This option allows you to set a variety of access rights for other individuals or project groups that have server-based network accounts.

To enable User-level access, open the Network Neighborhood Properties screen, choose the Access Control tab, and click the User-level Access Control button, as shown in Figure 14-20.

You must also enter the name of a Windows NT or NetWare server that will provide the access list of groups and individual users.

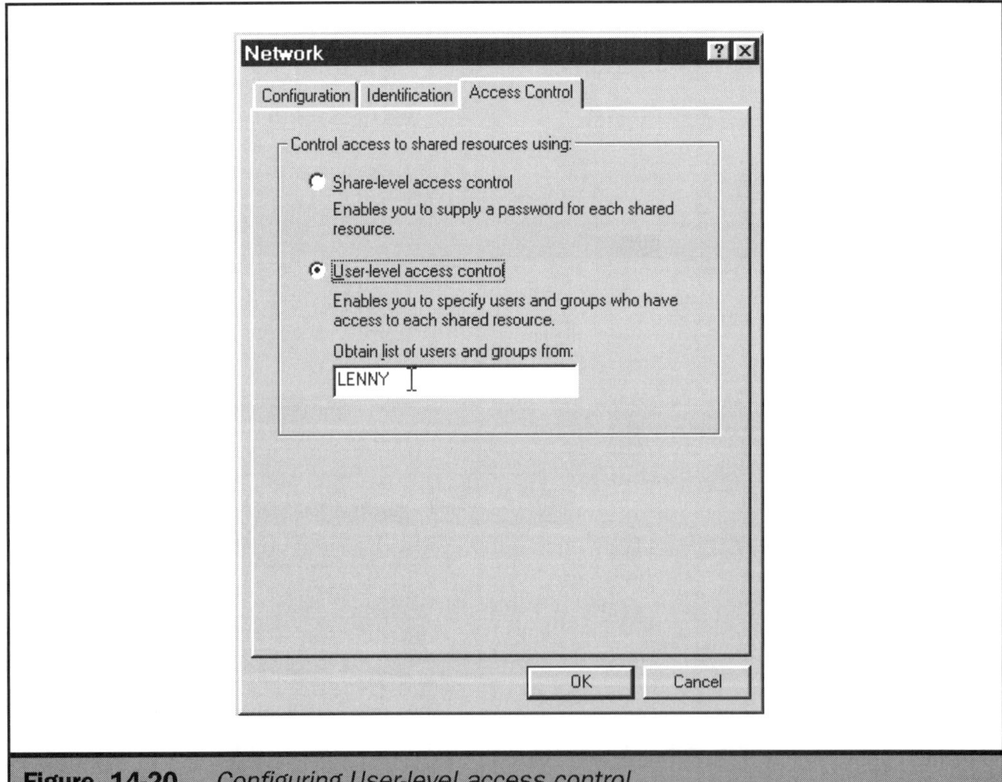

Figure 14-20. *Configuring User-level access control*

To share a drive or folder under User-level access, right-click the drive or folder in My Computer or Windows Explorer and choose the Sharing option on the pop-up menu. (To share a printer, right-click it in the Printers folder and choose Sharing.)

Click the Shared As button. By default, Windows 98 will use the name of the drive, folder, or printer as the share name (accepting up to 12 characters). You can edit the share name by clicking the Share Name field and assigning the name you want.

The Comment field allows you to add a note about this shared resource (accepting up to 48 characters) that will be visible to users who browse your computer with the Win98 NET command.

The Name And Access Rights field allows you to select individuals or groups who will connect to this resource when you click the Add button.

If you are sharing a drive or folder, you can also assign specific access rights: Read Only, Full Access, or Custom. To grant specfic access rights, select an account in the Name field and click the appropriate button, as shown here:

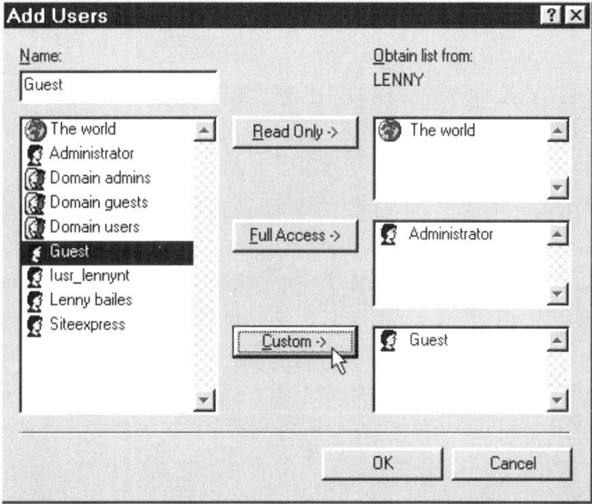

- **Read Only** This access type write-protects the folder, as under Share-level access control. Files can be opened but not modified or deleted.
- **Full Access** This access type allows the user to create new files and subdirectories and to open, modify, and delete existing files, as under Share-level access control.
- **Custom** This access type allows you to assign a variety of specific rights to a user, as shown next.

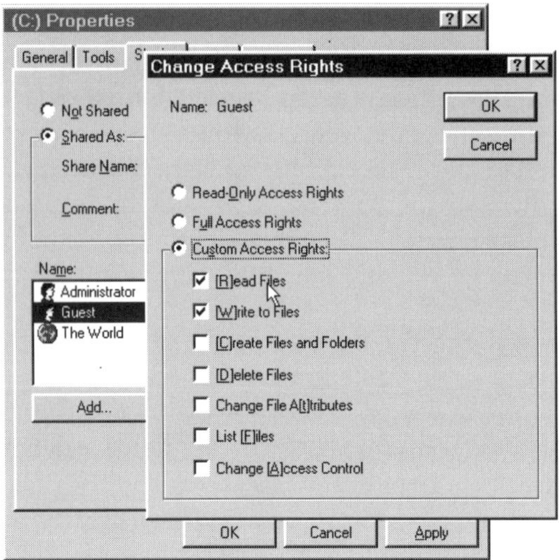

To change the access rights for an individual or group of users, select the account in the Name field and click the Edit button.

For shared printers, there is only one default access configuration: users can print to the device over the network. Thus, the Add Users screen contains no separate access fields.

Sharing a CD-ROM Drive over a Network

Sharing one computer's CD-ROM drive among the other workstations in your office is a useful network trick. A CD-ROM drive is not only valuable for its ability to run multimedia applications and browse clipart libraries; workstations without a CD-ROM unit can use the shared drive to install new applications.

To share a CD-ROM drive, right-click the drive in My Computer or Windows Explorer and choose Sharing. Click the Shared As button and assign any necessary passwords or access rights, as shown in Figure 14-21.

Accessing a Network CD-ROM Drive

To access a network CD-ROM drive, insert a CD (such as the Microsoft Office 97 installation CD) in the shared CD-ROM drive. To access this CD from another computer, do the following:

1. Open Network Neighborhood on the client workstation. Locate the icon for the computer that is sharing its CD-ROM drive and open it.

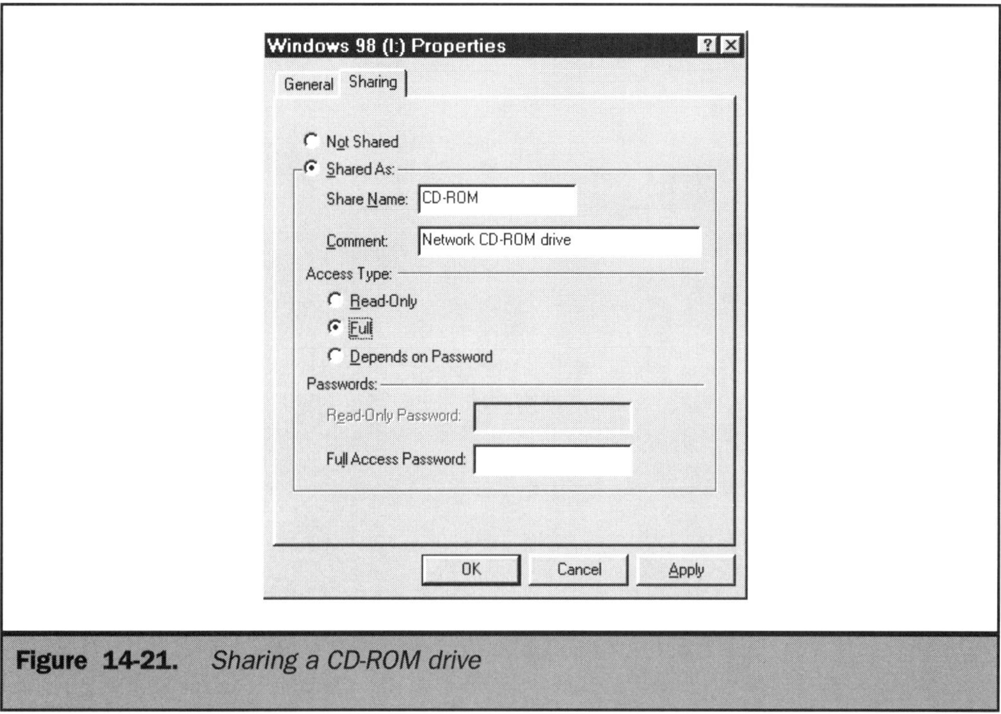

Figure 14-21. *Sharing a CD-ROM drive*

2. Locate and open the CD-ROM drive in the shared resource list for the computer you've just opened.
3. When the file list window for the CD-ROM drive opens, you can run the Setup program to install Office 97 on your local computer from the CD in the remote drive, as shown in Figure 14-22.

Sharing Public Message Folders

The Windows Messaging Service, available on the Windows 98 CD, supports the sharing of public e-mail folders through a Microsoft Mail post office over a peer-to-peer network. (No additional mail server or Windows NT computers are required.) You can use a Microsoft Mail shared folder to post public bulletins, received faxes, e-mail messages (with attachments), or direct pointers to documents on your local hard disk. You'll find instructions for installing and configuring Windows Messaging Services and a Microsoft Mail post office in the section "Using Windows Messaging" in Chapter 11.

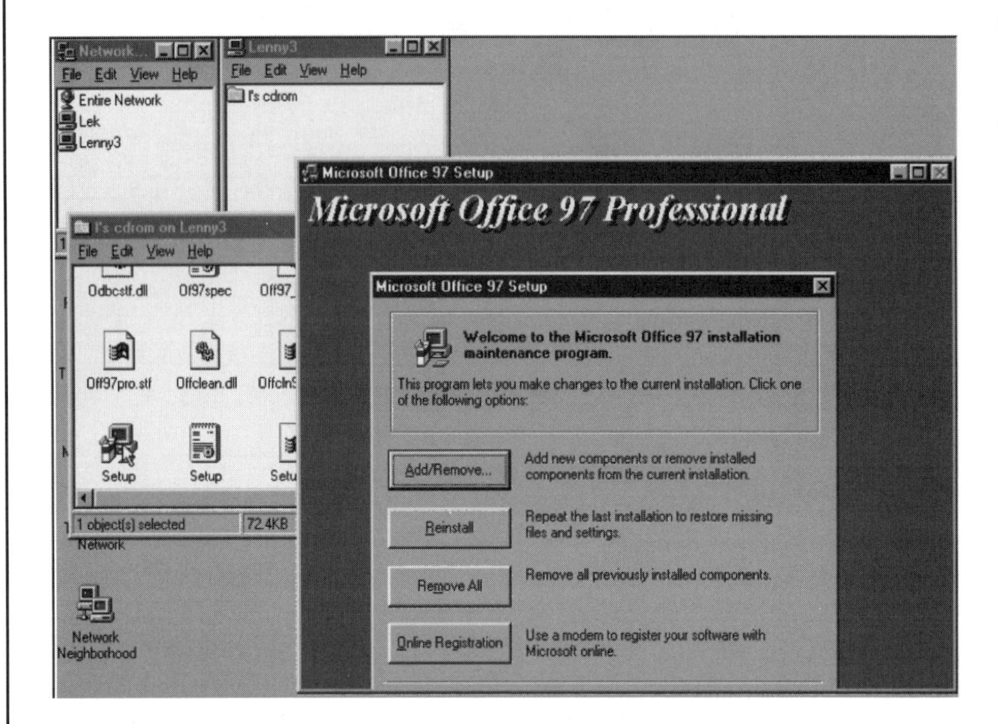

Figure 14-22. *Installing Microsoft Office 97 from a network CD-ROM drive*

To share public folders under Windows Messaging, follow these steps:

1. Make sure the users you want to reach are connected to a common Microsoft Mail post office. (See Chapter 11 for details.)
2. Open the Inbox and make sure the View | Folders option is selected.
3. Select Microsoft Mail Shared Folders in the left pane of the Microsoft Exchange (or Windows Messaging) window. Then choose File | New folder and assign a name, as shown next.

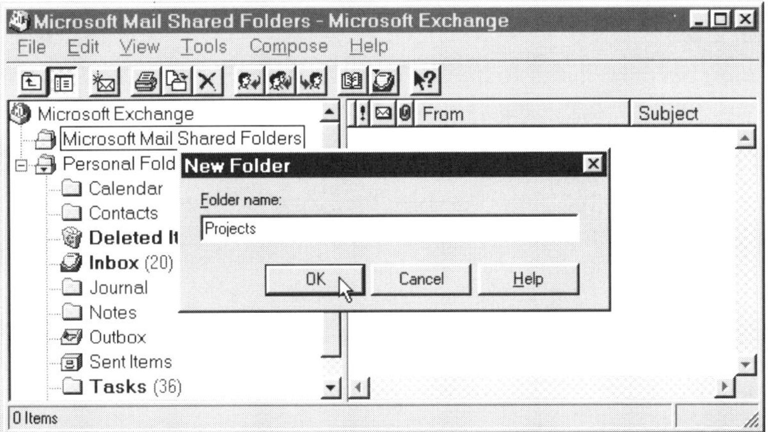

This folder will now appear under the Microsoft Mail Shared Folders group for all network users logged onto a common Microsoft Mail post office. Users of Microsoft Outlook 97 or 98 can also access the folder, provided that Windows Messaging is installed on their computers.

To set access rights for the folder, right-click it and choose the Permissions tab.

To move or copy received or sent messages into a shared folder, right-click and choose Move or Copy from the pop-up menu. You can also drag and drop files into a shared folder directly from the Windows 98 desktop, as shown here, or from My Computer or Windows Explorer.

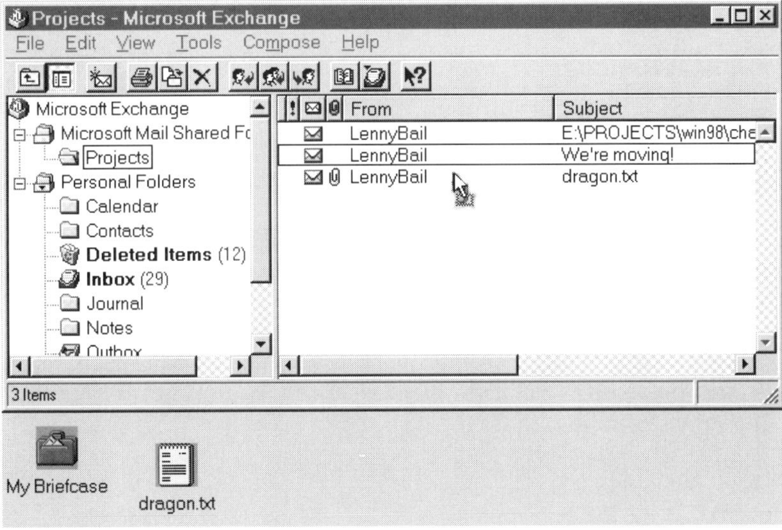

"Rapid-Express" File Sharing Through the Send To Folder

You can use the Send To folder to immediately dispatch documents from your desktop (or Windows Explorer) to anyone in your project group. Users on small, informal LANs may find this trick particularly useful. Each person in the project group creates a new shared files folder on their Windows 98 desktop. Then each member of the project group browses Network Neighborhood for the other members, locates their desktop folders, and drags appropriate shortcuts into the Windows 98 Send To folder. Here's how to set up this "rapid express" file sharing:

1. Create your own shared files folder on the desktop. Right-click the folder, select the Sharing tab, and then assign a sharename and appropriate access rights.
2. Open your Windows 98 Send To folder. (Choose Start | Run, enter **SendTo**, and click OK.)
3. Open Network Neighborhood and browse for the other computers in your project group. Open them and locate the shared files folder for each group member. Drag and drop a shortcut from the Network Neighborhood window into the SendTo folder, as shown in Figure 14-23. After each shortcut appears, you can rename it for your own convenience.

From now on, you can immediately dispatch documents from the desktop or Windows Explorer to anyone in your project group. Just right-click the document, choose SendTo, and point to the recipient. To see what other project members have sent to you, open the Shared Files folder on your own desktop. Both of these operations are shown in Figure 14-24.

Sharing a Fax Modem

If you have installed fax support through Windows Messaging, a fax/modem cabled to one Windows 98 computer can be shared with other computers on the network. Network users can use this resource to send faxes but not to dial into the Internet.

Making a Fax/Modem Available to Others

To make a fax/modem on a local computer available to other computers on the network, follow these steps:

1. Make sure the fax/modem, Windows Messaging, and Microsoft Fax support have been previously installed. (See "Modems Applet" in Chapter 9 and "Fax" in Chapter 5 to learn how to do this.)

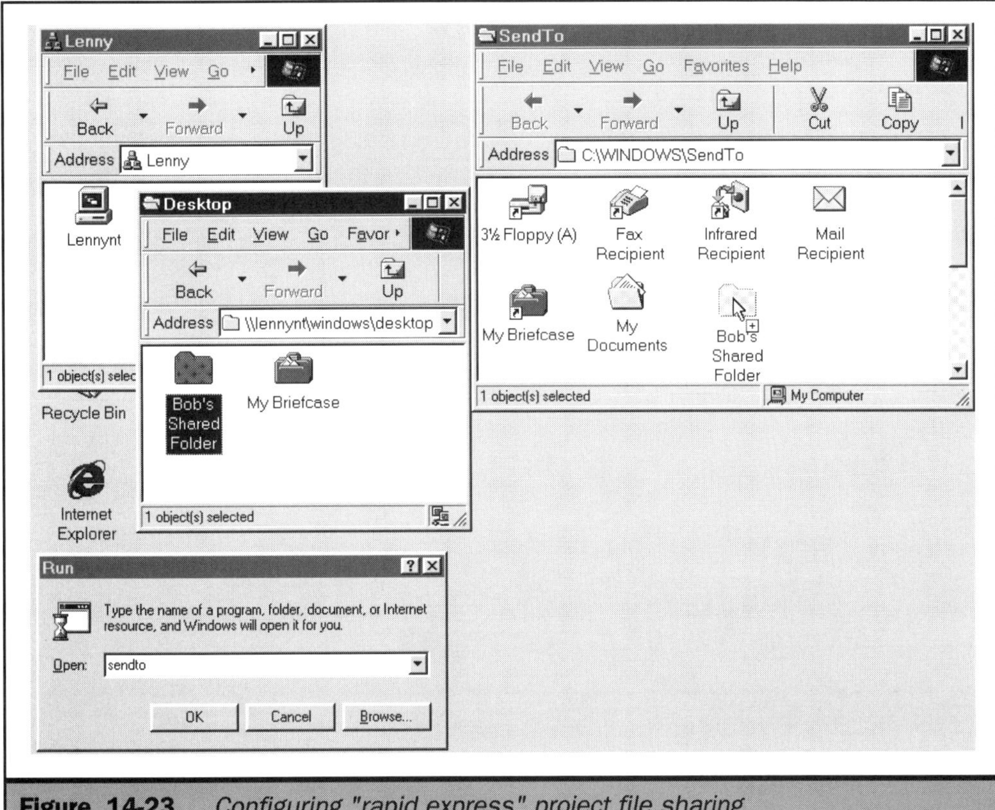

Figure 14-23. *Configuring "rapid express" project file sharing*

2. Open the Inbox with a Windows Messaging profile that includes the Microsoft Fax service. (See "Using Windows Messaging" in Chapter 11 for details.)
3. Choose Tools | Microsoft Fax Tools | Options from the pull-down menu. Then select the Modem tab on the Microsoft Fax Properties screen.
4. Select the modem that you want to share in the Available Fax Modems list. Click the Set As Active Fax Modem button and check the Let Other People On The Network Use My Modem To Send Faxes box toward the bottom of the screen, as shown next. If you have multiple disk partitions, a dialog box will

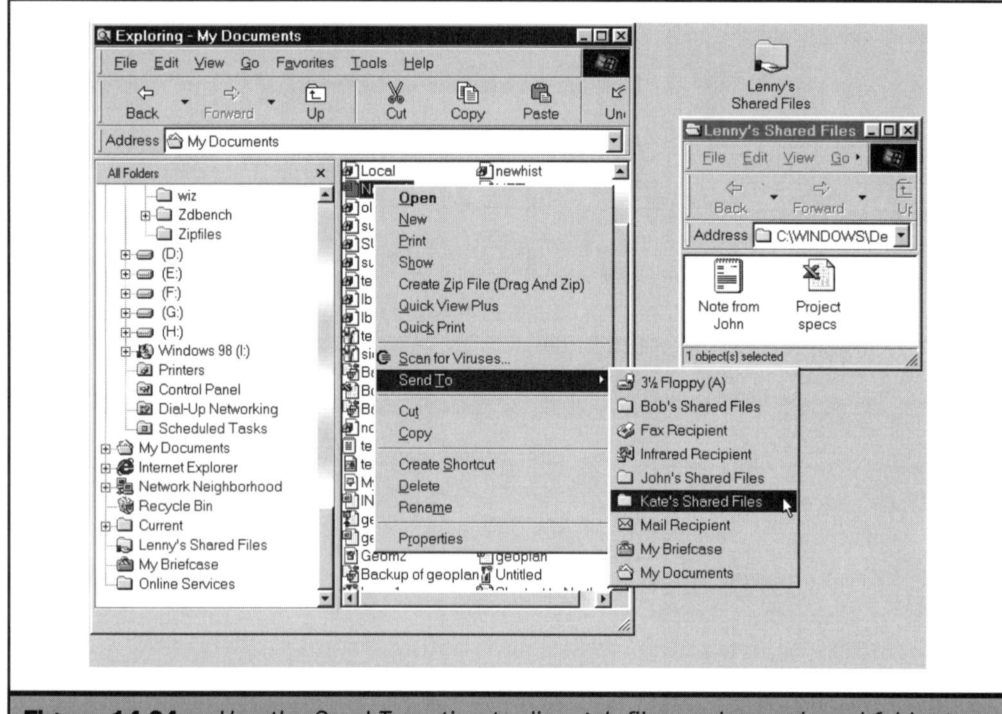

Figure 14-24. *Use the Send To option to dispatch files and your shared folder to access incoming files*

appear requesting you to designate the drive that the network fax service will use. Select your Windows host drive.

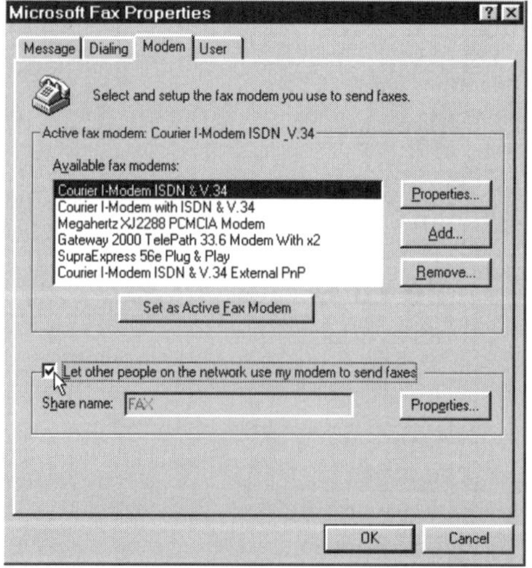

5. Click the Properties button (to the right of the check box you enabled in the last step). Assign user access rights and passwords, as appropriate.
6. Click OK and close the Microsoft Fax Tools setup screen.

Using a Shared Fax/Modem

To use to the shared fax/modem on another computer, make sure that computer is logged onto the network.

1. Verify that Windows Messaging and Microsoft Fax support are installed on the computer.
2. Open Network Neighborhood and find the path to a shared fax modem on the network. (Open computers in your workgroup, inspect the shared resources, and open Fax when you see it. The network path will appear in the Network Neighborhood address window: for example, \\Lenny1\Fax.)
3. Open Inbox on the client computer and select Microsoft Fax Tools | Options from the Inbox Tools menu.
4. Select the Modem tab on the Microsoft Fax Properties screen and click the Add button under Available Fax Modems.
5. Choose Network Fax Server from the Add A Fax Modem list.
6. In the next dialog box, enter the network path to the fax modem that you found in step 2 (for example, **\\Lenny1\Fax**).
7. Click OK to close this setup dialog box.
8. Select this shared fax modem in the Available Fax Modems list and click the Set As Active Fax Modem button.
9. Click OK to exit to the Inbox.

You can now send faxes over the network just as with a local modem (see "Fax" in Chapter 5 for details).

Sharing Fonts over a Network

If you have a large number of fonts installed on one computer on the network, and if your licensing agreement permits, you can share those fonts with other computers.

Making Fonts Available to Others

Follow these steps to make fonts available to others on the network:

1. Create a network directory for shared fonts on the host computer: for example, C:\NETFONT. Copy all of the font files for the fonts you wish to share into that directory. For TrueType fonts, copy the files with the .TTF extension found in your \WINDOWS\FONTS or \WINDOWS\SYSTEM directory. For PostScript fonts, copy the contents of both the \PSFONTS and \PSFONTS\PFM directories into the C:\NETFONT directory.

2. Open the Windows 98 Fonts folder on the host computer. If any of the TrueType fonts you copied to the \NETFONT directory are currently installed, remove them. (See "Installing and Managing TrueType Fonts" in Chapter 10 for information on how to do this.)
3. Reinstall TrueType fonts on the host computer from the instances you copied to the \NETFONT directory. Open the Fonts folder, choose Install New Fonts from the File menu, and open the C:\NETFONT directory. Select the fonts you want to install and make sure the Copy Fonts To Fonts Folder option is not selected.
4. Click OK and close the font installation dialog box.
5. Share the \NETFONT folder over the network as read-only, assigning an appropriate password.

Using Shared Fonts

To use the fonts in the \NETFONT folder on another computer, follow these steps:

1. Select the font server in the remote computer's Network Neighborhood. Right-click the \NETFONT folder and map it to a local drive letter. (Choose Map Network Drive from the pop-up menu as described earlier in this chapter.) Check the Reconnect At Login option toward the bottom of the Map Network Drive dialog box.
2. Open the Control Panel | Fonts folder on this client computer. Choose Install New Fonts from the File menu and browse to the mapped drive that you've just created. Select the fonts you want and deselect the Copy Fonts To Fonts Folder check box.
3. Click OK to install the shared fonts on the client computer.

Note that if you know the path to the shared font directory on the server, you can skip step 1. Map the shared fonts folder to a local drive letter by opening the client computer's Fonts folder, choosing Install New Font, and clicking the Network button on the Add Fonts screen. (For example, enter **\\SERVER\NETFONT** in the Path field.)

Sharing Postscript Fonts

To share PostScript fonts over a network, share the \PSFONTS folder on the server. Map this folder to a local drive letter on the client computer and then open Adobe Type Manager. Click the Add button and browse to the mapped drive for a list of the available shared fonts. If you plan to access the fonts only while connected to the network, select the Install Without Copying check box.

You'll find more detailed information about font installation procedures for TrueType and PostScript fonts in the "Windows Fonts" section of Chapter 10.

Remote Network Connections

Windows 98 offers several ways to connect to a small business or corporate network at a distance:

- Direct modem connections through Remote Access Services
- Virtual private networking over the Internet
- Share-level access over the Internet with the aid of a public Windows NT Internet server

Direct Connections Through Remote Access Services

You can dial into your network from Windows 98 directly through a modem. For you to do this, the network must include a Windows NT, Slip/UNIX, or NetWare workstation configured as a Remote Access Services (RAS) server. Although Windows 95 and 98 and Windows for Workgroups computers can function as RAS servers, they offer only limited network gateway support.

You'll find information on configuring a Windows 98 machine as a RAS (dial-up) server later in this chapter.

Dialing into a Network RAS Server from Windows 98

To dial into a private network through your modem, Windows 98 uses the same Dial-Up Networking feature that connects you to the Internet.

To create a RAS connection profile, you must first confirm that Dial-Up Networking has been installed on your computer and has been bound to the TCP/IP transport protocol. (To install Dial-Up Networking, choose Control Panel | Add/Remove Programs and select the Windows Setup tab. Open the Communications component, check Dial-Up Networking, and click OK. Click OK again to close the first screen. You'll be prompted to reboot the computer.)

After Dial-Up Networking has been installed, you can create a RAS connection profile, as follows:

1. Open the Make New Connection icon in the Dial-Up Networking folder, enter a connection name, and choose a modem on the first Make New Connection screen. (If no modem is currently available, Windows 98 will prompt you to install one. You'll find more details on modem installation and configuration in "Modem Setup" in Chapter 11.)
2. Enter the area code and telephone number for your network's RAS server on the second screen. Click Next and Finish to add the profile to the Dial-Up Networking folder.
3. Right-click the profile you just created and open its Properties screen. Choose the Server Types tab and select the network protocols you want to use for the

connection. (If you plan to surf the Internet remotely from your LAN, make sure TCP/IP is checked.)

4. If you are dialing into a Windows for Workgroups 3.x, Windows NT 3.1, Slip/UNIX, or NetWare Connect RAS server, display the Type Of Dial-Up Server drop-down list and choose the appropriate server type, as shown here:

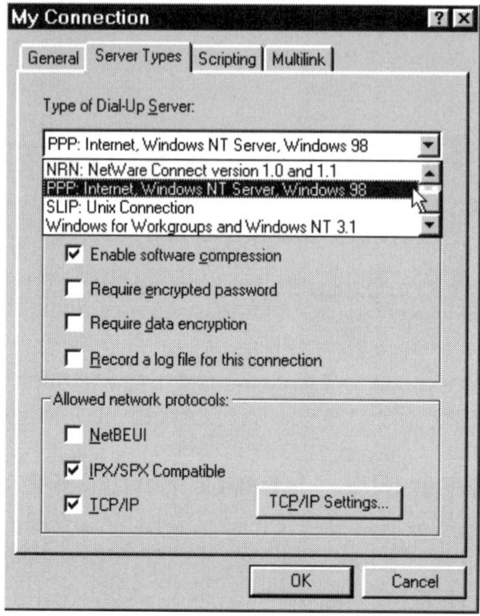

5. If you selected the TCP/IP protocol, click the TCP/IP button on the Server Types screen and enter the IP address(es) for the RAS server on the TCP/IP Settings screen. (See "Setting Up SLIP and PPP Dialing Profiles" in Chapter 11 for more information on configuring TCP/IP for Internet connections.)
6. Click OK to close the connection configuration settings screen.

To connect to your LAN, open the Dial-Up Networking Connection profile, enter the username and password for your network account, and click the Connect button.

Setting Up RAS on a Windows 98 Workstation

As a dial-up server, Windows 98 provides fewer administrative and security features than Windows NT or Novell NetWare. Windows 98 RAS is suitable for establishing a dual-computer remote connection, but the operating system can handle only one remote user at a time. Windows 98 can act as a RAS gateway to an IPX or NetBEUI network, but it lacks built-in gateway support for a TCP/IP intranet.

To install Dial-Up Server support, choose Control Panel | Add/Remove Programs, choose the Windows Setup tab, open the Communications component, and place a check mark next to Dial-Up Server. Click OK twice to close the Add/Remove Programs applet.

To share resources located on the dial-up server computer, you must also enable the File and Print Sharing services for either Microsoft or Novell NetWare networks. (See "Sharing Local Resources" earlier in this chapter for details.)

Once Dial-Up Server has been installed, you can activate it on a Windows 98 machine by opening the Dial-Up Networking folder and choosing Dial-Up Server on the Connection tab. The Dial-Up Server configuration screen appears with an individual tab for each modem installed on the computer. Although you can set up multiple configurations, Dial-Up Server can use only one modem at a time. To turn it on, click the Allow Caller Access button, as shown in Figure 14-25.

If the Dial-Up Server is configured for Share-level access, you can assign an optional password for users to log onto the server. Once the user is connected, shared resources on the Dial-Up Server are available according to the individual passwords that have been set for them.

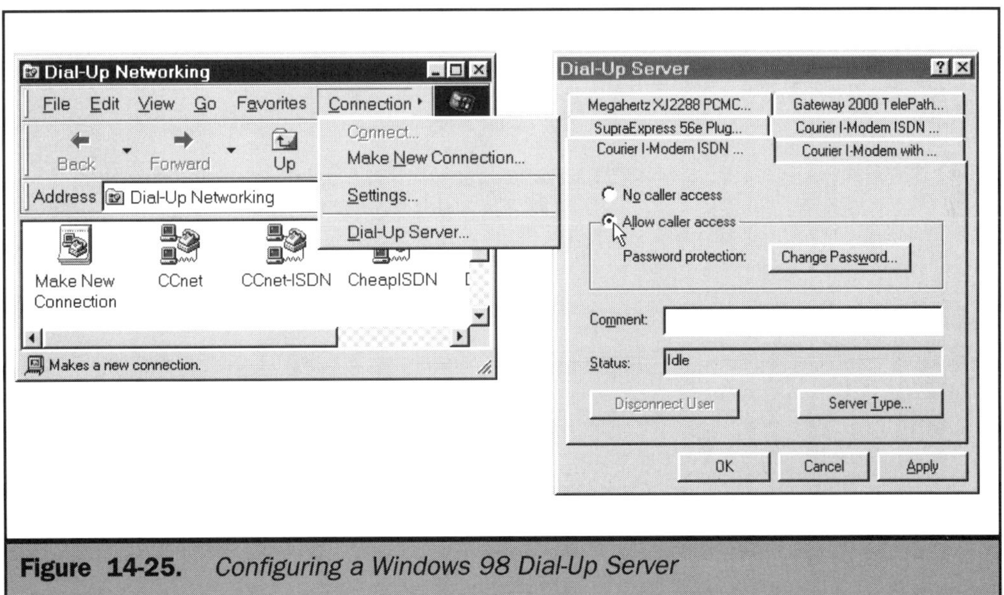

Figure 14-25. *Configuring a Windows 98 Dial-Up Server*

If the Dial-Up Server is configured for User-level access, you can assign separate access rights to shared resources for each user by selecting the account from the Security Server access list and clicking the Add button, as shown here:

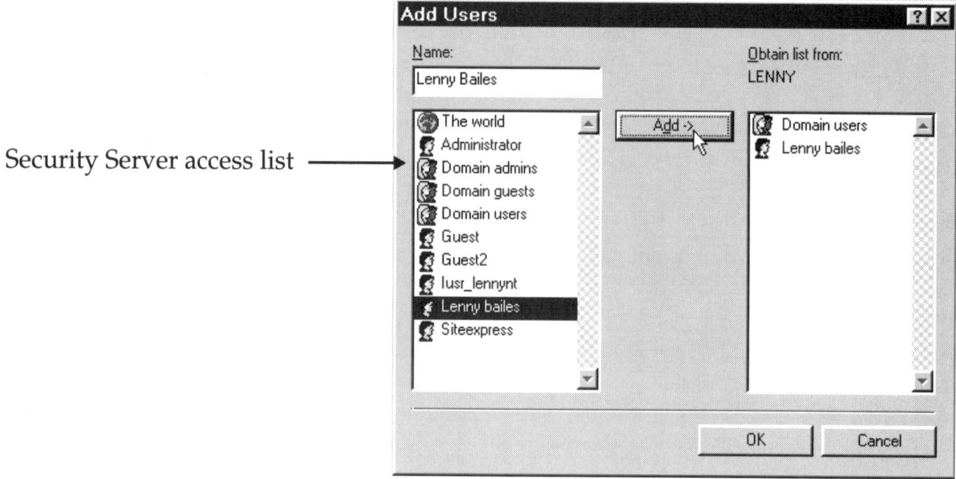

Windows 98 Dial-Up Server can serve as a NetBIOS gateway to other computers on the network through the NetBEUI or IPX/SPX transport protocol. It does not provide TCP/IP gateway services, which means that you can't dial into a network to access the Internet or an HTML-based intranet through a Windows 98 Dial-Up Server.

Some third-party vendors offer complementary TCP/IP gateway services for Windows 98. Generally, however, if you want to dial into a large LAN, you'll get better results by using a Windows NT or Novell NetWare computer as the Remote Access Services host.

Virtual Private Networking

Windows 98's "LAN-through-Internet" features are particularly useful for computer road warriors. You can bring a notebook with you to a hotel room in a distant city, and if your Internet service provider offers national access numbers, you can access a home or corporate network for the price of a local phone call.

For secure Internet connections to corporate resources, Windows 98 includes a new feature called virtual private networking (VPN). To use VPN, your local area network must support logon through Microsoft's point-to-point tunneling protocol. Windows 98 includes a VPN client, but to make the connection you also need a virtual private networking server on the network. Currently, VPN servers run under operating systems such as Windows NT 4.0 or Novell NetWare. (At this writing, there are no third-party VPN servers for Windows 98, but by the time you read this, there may be.)

Setting Up Access to Your LAN

To create a VPN connection profile to access your LAN over the Internet, do the following:

1. Install Windows 98 VPN support on your mobile (or home) computer. Choose Control Panel | Add/Remove Programs and select the Windows Setup tab. Open the Communications component, check Virtual Private Networking, and click OK. Click OK again to close the first screen. You'll be prompted to reboot the computer.
2. Create or verify a standard Dial-Up Networking connection profile to the Internet through your Internet service provider. (See Chapters 11 and 12 for details.)
3. Open the Dial-Up Networking folder (choose Start | Programs | Accessories | Communications | Dial-Up Networking) and open the Make New Connection icon to create your VPN connection profile.
4. Enter a name for the profile on the Make New Connection screen. Choose Microsoft VPN Adapter in the Select A Device drop-down list and click Next.
5. On the Make New Connection screen, enter the hostname or IP address for your LAN account, as shown here. (For example, enter a name such as **Server@Bigbiz.com** or **170.10.1.1**.) You can obtain this information from your system administrator.

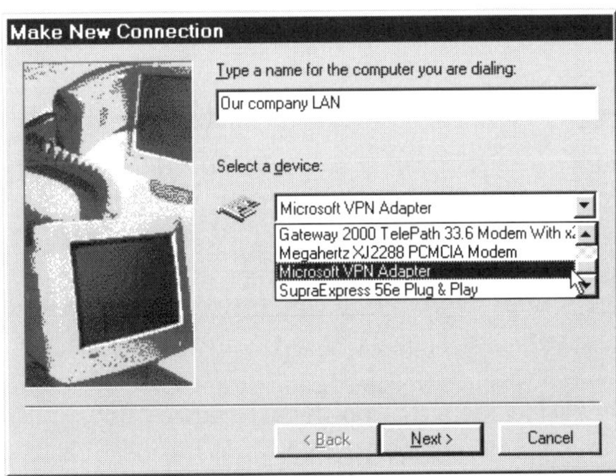

6. Click Next and Finish to add the VPN profile to the Dial-Up Networking folder.

Connecting to Your LAN over the Internet

To connect to your LAN over the Internet:

1. Log onto the Internet through your ISP with your regular Win98 Dial-Up Networking profile. (If you're calling from a different city, you may need to look up the phone number for a local ISP access node. You can adjust the calling location information with the Control Panel | Telephony applet. See "Working with Dialing Properties" in Chapter 11 for details.)
2. Open the VPN profile that you created in the Dial-Up Networking folder. Enter the username and password for your account on the local area network and click the Connect button. The VPN connection is established.

After the LAN connection over the Internet is established, your ISP routes information from your computer over the Internet to your LAN's VPN server. The VPN server then routes information to the other workstations on your network. All of the commands and data you transmit are encrypted. You can access resources through Network Neighborhood just as if you were connected locally. Access to Internet functions outside of your network (such as World Wide Web browsing and Telnet) are suspended until you terminate the VPN connection. However, if your company LAN is connected to the Internet, you can browse Internet resources through its connection rather than through your ISP.

Note *When you are connected to your LAN through VPN, you may not be able to see hosts and servers outside the local subnet of the LAN that houses the VPN server. For more information on implementing and working with virtual private networking, see "Remote Networking and Computing" under "Implementing" in the "Virtual Private Networking" section of the* Windows 98 Resource Kit *online book in the \TOOLS\RESKIT\HELP folder on the Win98 installation CD.*

Establishing a Peer-to-Peer Connection over the Internet

Windows 98 also allows you to make economical "back-door" connections to a single workstation or a private network over the Internet. Virtual private networking provides an encrypted, secure connection to a local area network, but it also requires a VPN server application running on an expensive network operating system such as Windows NT 4.0. Users who have modest security requirements can access a single workstation or private network over the Internet through a public peer-to-peer connection.

This little-known trick depends upon the assistance of Internet-based Windows NT servers that offer public access to a feature called Windows Internet Name Services (WINS). To make this procedure work, you need to locate a public Windows NT server on the Internet that offers the WINS lookup service. Several large universities, including Carnegie Mellon University (www.cmu.edu), the University of Illinois at Urbana-Champagne (www.uiuc.edu), and Imperial College in the United Kingdom (www.cc.ic.ac.uk) permit the use of public WINS servers. At the time of this writing, you'll also find a public WINS server at www.localnet.org. You can also look for a

WINS server through one of the World Wide Web search pages. (Infoseek at http://www.infoseek.com and Yahoo at http://www.yahoo.com are good places to begin.)

For peer-to-peer networking over the Internet, you must use a standard ISP point-to-point protocol (PPP) connection. Unfortunately, WINS doesn't work with Serial Line Internet Protocol (SLIP) connections.

What you'll need to obtain from the publishers of a Windows NT WINS server is the name of a public workgroup that you can use and the server's IP address. Once you locate a public WINS server, familiarize yourself with the terms under which access is granted.

Configuring the Connection

To add the WINS service to a Windows 98 workstation, open the Network Neighborhood Properties screen. Then choose the TCP/IP Dial-Up Adapter protocol and open its Properties screen. Click OK to bypass the TCP/IP Properties warning message. (If this makes you nervous, run ScanReg and make a backup of the Windows 98 registry before proceeding further. See "Registry Checker" in Chapter 6 for details.) Then do the following:

1. Choose the WINS Configuration tab on the TCP/IP Properties screen.
2. Click the Enable WINS Resolution button.
3. Enter the IP address you obtained for the public WINS server, as shown here, and click the Add button.

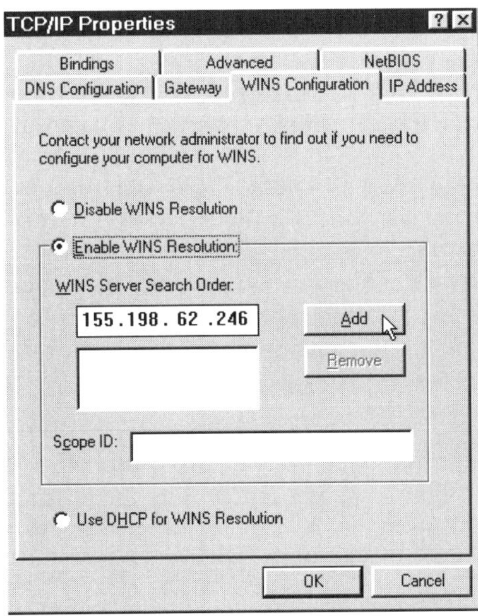

4. Verify that File and Print Sharing for Microsoft Networks is installed. If it isn't, add it to the network components list as described in the "Sharing Local Resources" section of this chapter.
5. Choose the Identification tab on the Network Configuration screen. Enter the name of the public workgroup that you got from the site that's sharing the WINS server. (This last step is not essential. If you don't have this information, you can keep your old workgroup name.)
6. Choose the Access Control tab on the Network Configuration screen. Select Share-Level Access.
7. Click OK to close the Network Configuration screen. You'll be prompted to restart the computer.
8. After the computer reboots, you'll need to make a small adjustment to the Dial-Up Networking profile that you use to connect to your ISP. Open the Dial-Up Networking folder. Then right-click your ISP connection profile and open its Properties screen.
9. Choose the Server Types tab and place a check mark in the Log On To Network box. Click OK to close the connection settings.

File and Print Sharing

The setup of File and Print Sharing services is important if you intend to establish a peer-to-peer networking connection over the Internet.

To share the resources of other computers but prohibit access to your own computer, the safest procedure is to remove the File and Print Sharing option on the machine that will be the client. This choice is not always practical, however, since you may want to make resources available to other computers on a local network. To allow file sharing with other locally networked machines but prohibit anyone on the Internet from zeroing in on you, here are a few strategies you can use:

- Password protect all the files and resources that you share on your local machine. You can use the Netwatcher utility in the Programs | Accessories | System Tools group to do this. Open Netwatcher and select the View By Shared Folders option on the View menu. A list of all public resources on your local computer will appear in the shared folder window. To check for password protection, highlight each resource in turn and press ALT-ENTER or select Shared Folder Properties from the Administer menu.
- To enable file sharing on a local Microsoft peer-to-peer or Novell network but not over the Internet, open the TCP/IP protocol for the Dial-Up Adapter or network card on the machine that will be the client. Click the Bindings tab and disable the binding to File and Print Sharing, as described earlier in this chapter.

Tip *You can make shared drives or folders invisible in the Network Neighborhood window. To do this, open the Sharing properties for the resource and append a dollar sign ($) to the Share Name under the Share As button. For example, assign drive C on USER1 the share name C$. When a network user opens the Network Neighborhood and accesses the USER1 computer, drive C will not be visible. However, if a user has been told that the drive is available, that user can log onto it directly by entering* **\USER1\C$** *in the Run box on the Start menu.*

Establishing a Peer-to-Peer Connection

To establish a peer-to-peer connection, dial into the Internet. If you log on through the Microsoft Network icon on the desktop, Windows 98 is thoughtful enough to perform a security check and warn you when File and Print Sharing is bound to the TCP/IP protocol. If you log on through a third-party ISP, this security check is not performed.

Once you connect to the Internet, your peer-to-peer networking services will be enabled. To test them, open the Network Neighborhood. If you have logged onto the workgroup provided by the WINS server, you should see an awe-inspiring sight: open the Entire Neighborhood icon, and you may see the screen filled with hundreds of workgroups, as shown in Figure 14-26.

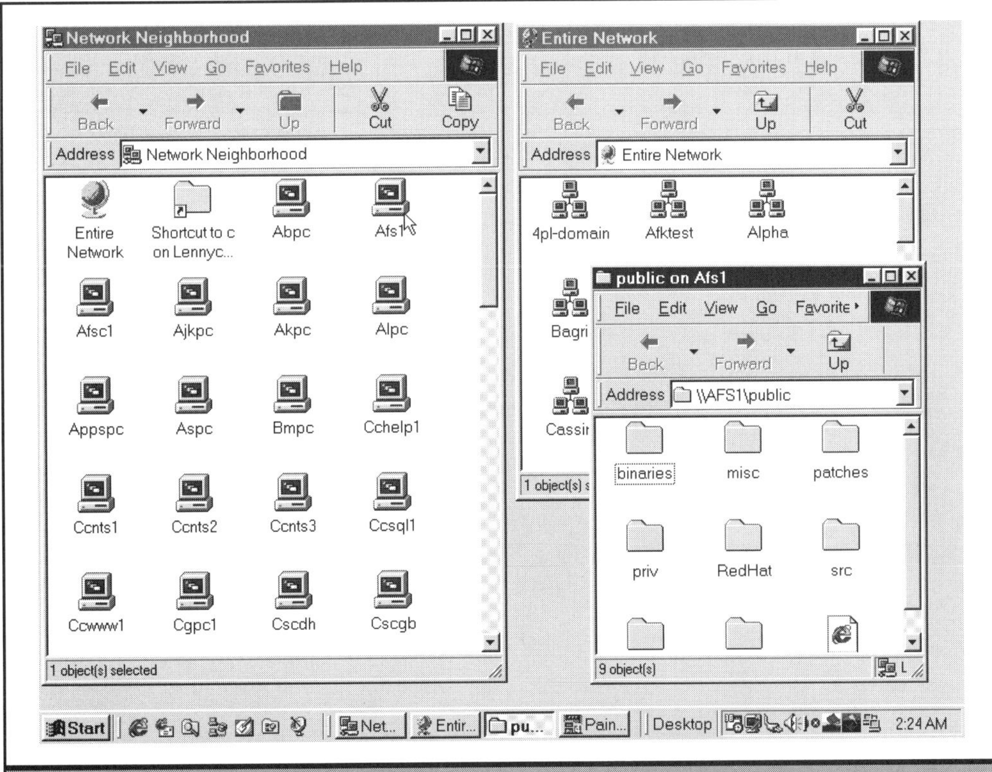

Figure 14-26. *With public WINS services installed, multiple workgroups and computers may appear in Network Neighborhood*

To see the shared resources available for any of the computers in your workgroup, open it in Network Neighborhood or enter a network path in the Start | Run box. If the site administrator is on the job, you'll have to enter a password before the resource window opens on your desktop.

If you open Network Neighborhood and don't see any computers or workgroups listed, e-mail the administrator of your WINS server. You may have to change the name of the workgroup for your local computer. If you know that a computer in a specific workgroup is logged onto the Internet and is using the WINS server, try logging onto that workgroup by entering its name in the Address field of the Network Neighborhood window. For example, enter **UIUC** (if you are using the University of Indiana Urbana-Champagne WINS server) or **LocalNet** (if you are logged onto the LocalNet.Org WINS server).

When WINS is up and running, you can log onto a computer through Network Neighborhood over the Internet and map its resources to local drive letters, as shown in Figure 14-27. The computer will work the same way as if it were cabled to the workgroup locally through a network card. (Bear in mind that connections will be slower over the Internet than through a dedicated network card. Performance depends upon the bandwidth of your modem.)

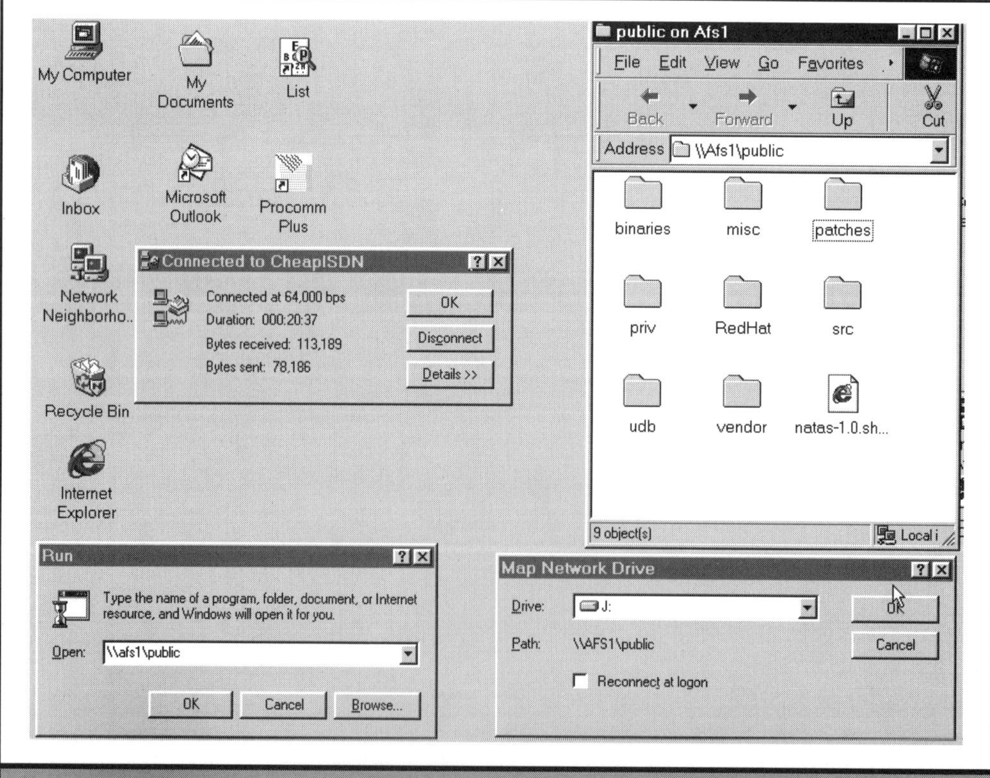

Figure 14-27. *A peer-to-peer connection through the Internet*

If you are logged onto the Internet with WINS services enabled, you can connect directly to any computer registered with the WINS server by entering its NetBIOS name in the Start | Run box (see Figure 14-27). For example, enter **\\Ted** *or* **\\AFS1\Public**. *In Windows 98, the NetBIOS name is the name of the computer on the Identification tab of the Network Properties screen.*

Sharing Resources with a Friend (or Yourself) Through Public WINS

Now that you know how this peer-to-peer connection trick works, you can do something useful with it:

1. Set up your client and server computers to share the same public WINS server and Windows 98 workgroup. Enable File and Print Sharing for Microsoft Networks on the server(s) and set access control to shared-level access.
2. Share the resources that you want to publish, using appropriate password protection. If security is an important concern, hide the resources from Network Neighborhood by appending a dollar sign ($) as the last character of each share name.
3. Log the server computer(s) onto the Internet through Dial-Up Networking or a dedicated LAN connection.
4. Travel to the location where the client computer is located or take a notebook computer with you on the road. Log onto the Internet through Dial-Up Networking or a dedicated LAN connection with the client computer.

You can now use Network Neighborhood on the client computer to access shared resources on the servers. (If you decided to hide the resources from Network Neighborhood, connect to them by entering the pathname in the Start | Run box.)

Tip

For quick access to a computer or shared folder in Network Neighborhood, you can drag and drop a shortcut into the first-level Network Neighborhood window, as shown here, or onto the desktop.

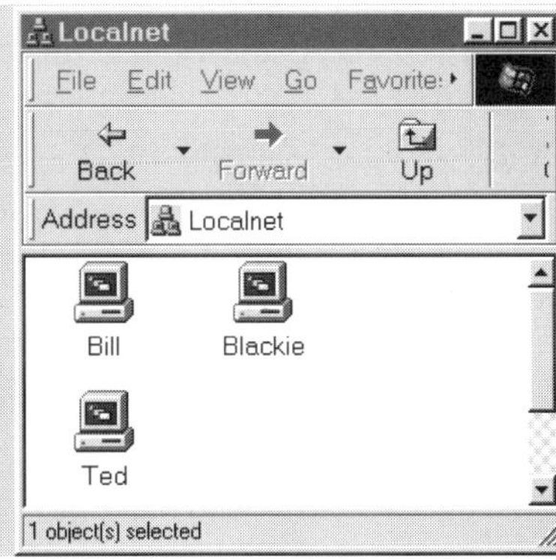

Mapping Network Resources to a Local Drive

The procedure for mapping a folder shared over the Internet to a local drive letter is the same as for any other network connection.

1. Log onto the server through the Run box or open it in Network Neighborhood.
2. Right-click the resource you want to add to your local computer and select the Map Network Drive option from the context menu.
3. Enter the password for the resource, if one is required, and click OK.
4. In the Map Network Drive dialog box (see Figure 14-27), choose an available drive letter and click OK. If you want to reassign this resource to the same drive letter whenever you log onto the network, check the Reconnect At Logon option at the bottom of the dialog box.

The drive or folder you've mapped will now be accessible in My Computer and Windows Explorer and in the File | Open and File | Save windows of your Windows and DOS applications.

Direct Cable Connections

For information on setting up and using the Microsoft Direct Cable Connection option, refer to "Direct Cable Connection" in Chapter 5.

Converting Direct Cable Connection into a Peer-to-Peer Network

Normally, when you use Win98's Direct Cable Connection option, one machine is designated the guest and the other machine is designated the host. The host user does not have access to shared resources on the guest computer although local work continues while the guest uses shared resources in the background.

An undocumented feature (or bug) in Direct Cable Connection allows the host machine to access resources on the guest anyway, establishing a true peer-to-peer network connection. Here's how to exploit this quirk:

1. Set up a Direct Cable Connection with one machine as the guest and the other as the host.
2. Share appropriate folders and other resources on the host computer (as described earlier in this chapter). Then log onto this machine through the guest computer. (Open Direct Cable Connection in the Accessories group and click the Connect button.)
3. After the connection is established, click View Host in the guest computer's Direct Cable Connection window. This will display all of that computer's shared resources in a desktop window.

4. Log the guest computer off the direct cable connection without closing the shared resources on the desktop.
5. On the guest machine, share the resources or folders that you want to make available to the other computer.
6. Here's the trick: Now reconfigure Direct Cable Connection to reverse the Host and Guest settings. Turn the guest machine into the host. Then, close Direct Cable Connection on the old host machine and reconfigure it as the guest.
7. Log onto the new host from the new guest machine. The folders and resources you've shared on the new host will appear when you click the View Host button.

Additionally, the new host machine retains the shared resources on its desktop from when it was the guest. If you open one of these left-over resources, you'll get a message telling you that it is no longer available on the network. Windows 98 will offer to connect through Dial-Up Networking. Answer No in this dialog box, and you'll find that the old shared resource becomes available again through the Direct Cable Connection. Thus, either machine on the cable connection can access resources on the other.

Direct Connections via EZ-link USB Instant Network

Windows 98's Direct Cable Connection can be a useful feature for quick-and-dirty file transfers, but the top speed of a parallel cable link is too slow for convenient sharing of applications or the extended synchronization of file directories on two computers. AnchorChips' EZ-link USB Instant Network is a convenient way to set up a higher-bandwidth peer-to-peer connection between two computers equipped with Universal Serial Bus (USB) ports. Although EZ-link throughput is not as fast as a 10 Mbps Ethernet connection, its USB connection is considerably more efficient than linking two computers through parallel ports.

The EZ-link kit includes a smart USB cable and all the necessary software required to establish a peer-to-peer connection between two USB-enabled computers. Once you plug the cable into both computers, the connection is established automatically, permitting you to use the EZ-link manager, or Win98's Network Neighborhood to share drives, folders, printers, and so on, just as with a standard network adapter.

To give you an idea of relative throughput speeds, a Direct Cable Connection through an IEEE-1284 compliant parallel cable averages from 15 to 20 KBps per second through the NETBEUI transport protocol. A dedicated 10 BaseT Ethernet connection averages from 500 to 1000 KBps per second. An EZ-link USB connection transfers from 150 to 350 KBps per second, at least 10 times faster than a direct cable parallel link.

You can find product details and ordering information about EZ-link USB at http://www.ezlinkusb.com/.

Network Neighborhood Behavior

You may be puzzled at times by the behavior of Network Neighborhood. Sometimes when you connect to other computers through a network card, by modem-to-modem connection, over the Internet, or through a Direct Cable Connection, nothing appears in the Network Neighborhood window. The rules are basically as follows:

- Your local computer appears in a Network Neighborhood window only if you have enabled File and Print Sharing services.
- Sometimes it may take several minutes for the available computers on a network to appear in the Network Neighborhood window.
- For a Direct Cable Connection to show up in the Network Neighborhood window, your local computer must be a guest dialing into a dedicated network or, as the host, it must also have a dedicated network adapter card.
- If your computer has a network card and File and Print Sharing is enabled and it still doesn't appear in its own Network Neighborhood window, you can configure the machine as a backup Browse Master for the network. (Open the Network Properties screen, choose File and Print Sharing services in the component list, open the Properties screen, and change the Browse Master value on the Advanced tab to Enabled.)

Troubleshooting and Additional Resources

If you have difficulty with any aspect of your Windows 98 network, the first step you should take is to review the procedures for installing the network hardware and configuring the software outlined earlier in this chapter. Here are a few common problems you might encounter along with suggested solutions.

THERE IS NO NETWORK NEIGHBORHOOD ICON ON MY DESKTOP Try right-clicking the desktop and selecting Line Up Icons to make sure Network Neighborhood isn't concealed behind another icon. If the icon is still missing, open the Control Panel, open the Network settings, and make sure that the Configuration tab contains listings for a network interface card, the Client for Microsoft Networks, and the NetBEUI or IPX/SPX transport protocol.

NO COMPUTER LISTINGS APPEAR WHEN I OPEN NETWORK NEIGHBORHOOD If you can't see shared resources in Network Neighborhood, review "Setting Up Network Support" at the beginning of this chapter. Also check the following elements of your network setup:

- Make sure all computers on the network have installed network cards and proper cabling. (Make sure a BNC network is terminated at both ends or that a 10-BaseT network has all nodes properly plugged into the hub with the hub's power switched on.)
- Make sure all workstations attached to the network have been assigned unique computer names.
- Make sure the network card in each computer is working properly. If you suspect that a machine has problems, turn off its power, restart it, and watch the system startup process for error messages that may help you identify the problem. Inspect the network card listing in the Windows 98 Device Manager to see whether the system reports it to be functioning properly. Review "Resolving Startup Error Messages" earlier in this chapter.
- Make sure that at least one computer on the network has been configured as a file or print server (File and Print Sharing for Microsoft Networks will appear on the Network Properties Configuration tab in the Network components list.)

If you've followed these steps and still continue to receive logon error messages, you may need to adjust the internal settings of your network interface card. If the Device Manager shows the hardware to be working properly and Network Neighborhood continues to remain empty, recheck the integrity of your network cables connections. If computers are configured in a BNC chain, try truncating the chain and terminating the network at strategic points to see if the cabling on a particular link is defective.

Command-Line Network Utilities

Windows 98 includes a set of command-line diagnostic utilities that can be used to list network resources, display information about a connection, and test the integrity of a connection. These programs are installed in the \WINDOWS directory when you enable networking support.

Listing Network Resources from a DOS Command Prompt

The Net command in Windows 98 is similar to previous versions included in the DOS and Windows for Workgroups operating systems. You can use NET from a DOS session under the Windows 98 interface to list all available resources on the network or perform a diagnostic test.

To display all of the computers and resources available in your workgroup, enter **net view** at a DOS command prompt within Windows 98.

To display all of the computers and resources available in a different workgroup, enter **net view /workgroup:***groupname* at a DOS command prompt, as shown next.

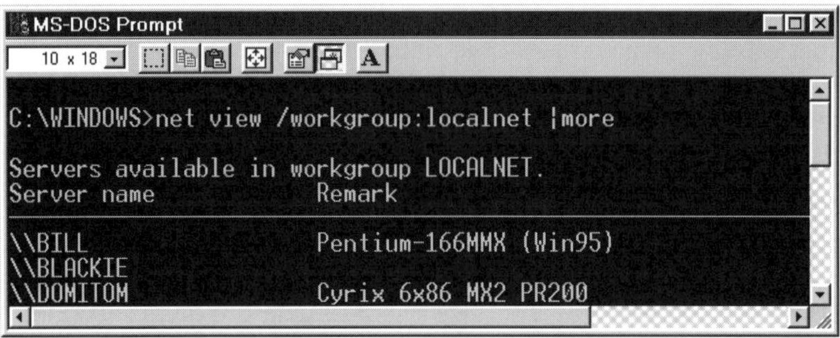

To perform diagnostic tests on your network, enter **net diag** at a DOS command prompt. You'll be prompted to convert this local machine into a diagnostic server or enter the path to another diagnostic server on the network.

For an overview of all the browsing options for the Net command, enter ***Net/? | More*** *at a DOS command prompt.*

Other Command-Line Network Utilities

IPCONFIG can display all of the IP addresses assigned to your local computer through TCP/IP connections established with Dial-Up Networking or a dedicated network card.

NBTSTAT can display protocol statistics and the NetBIOS names of computers recognized over a TCP/IP network.

ARP and *ROUTE* can be used to manipulate a local TCP/IP routing table.

WINIPCFG can display detailed information about the properties of a dial-up or dedicated TCP/IP network connection.

For more information about all of these command-line utilities, see "Network Adapters and Protocols" in the "Microsoft TCP/IP Protocol" section of the *Windows 98 Resource Kit* online book on your Windows 98 CD.

Measuring Network Performance

The Windows 98 System Monitor tool can be used to clock the performance of your network. This tool can be useful to confirm that your hardware is performing according to its specifications. An Ethernet 10BaseT network adapter is capable of file transfer speeds up to 10 megabits (approximately 1,250 kilobytes) per second. Over a hubless, BNC architecture, the average speed is often 50 percent of that figure.

To monitor file transfer speeds on your network, open the System Monitor applet (located in the Accessories | System Tools folder). Choose Edit | Add Item and select Microsoft Network Client or Microsoft Network Server and add sensors for Bytes Read/Second and Bytes Written/Second. For Novell or other IPX/SPX networks, choose the IPX/SPX-compatible protocol and add IPX Packets Received and Sent/Second.

Select some files on a network server in Network Neighborhood and drag them to a local folder (or open an application that loads a remote data directory). System Monitor will benchmark network performance as shown here:

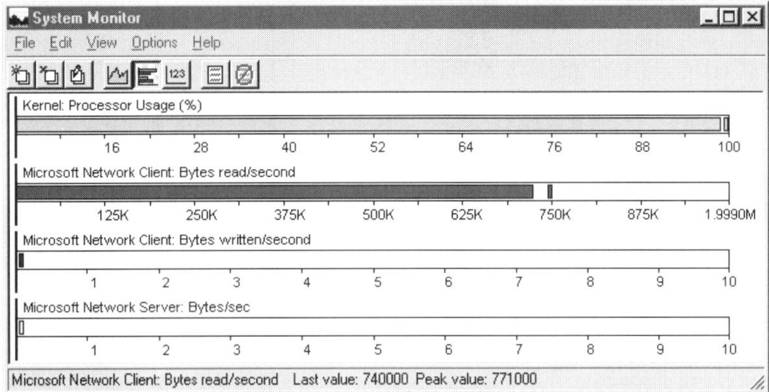

Chapter 15

Multimedia under Windows 98

Chapter Highlights

Multimedia advantages

What's New in Windows 98

Shopping for a multimedia PC

Installing multimedia peripherals

Using Windows 98's multimedia utilities:

- Working with DVD
- WebTV and WaveTop

Video conferencing

Working with USB peripherals

Using multiple display monitors

Speech recognition

Multimedia troubleshooting

Hot multimedia titles

Multimedia refers to the use of text, graphics, animation, audio, and video in a single, integrated computer environment. Windows 98 was specifically designed to make multimedia applications more accessible than in previous PC operating systems. The use of multimedia greatly expands the personal element of computing, giving you new ways to assimilate and distribute information.

Behaviorists tell us that we are more likely to remember things that are spelled out and demonstrated. The multimedia capabilities of Windows 98 allow us to watch movies, listen to accompanying narrative, and link our eyes and ears to the learning process. Multimedia discs are likely to change how we assimilate information. They won't replace books, but they can make the contained information come alive. At the same time, multimedia provides the opportunity for people to create compound documents that contain sound, video, and animation, all embedded between the text—enhancing the message a document conveys.

For many multimedia features, Windows 98 builds upon the multimedia support offered in Windows 95, including enhanced support for digital video, sound, and CD-ROM/DVD controls. Microsoft tends to ballyhoo Windows 98 as the platform that premiers support for digital video disks (usually referred to simply as DVDs), desktop TV reception, and Universal Serial Bus (USB) scanners, and cameras. In reality, these features were around for users of Windows 95.

Windows 98 does a superior job of integrating these technologies into the operating system. DVD movies, desktop TV reception, and USB peripherals work better under Windows 98 than under Windows 95. Windows 98's new file systems and driver support allow you to run multimedia events on the desktop with less of a performance hit to other applications and system features. Windows 98 provides wavetable synthesis (built-in voices for MIDI playback) in software for older sound cards that lack this hardware feature. The new streaming device driver model also enables CD-ROM audio and video to play back with more fidelity, even on older computers.

One fact of life about living with Microsoft as an operating system provider is that the company does try to nudge consumers into the future by incorporating features that require new and more powerful hardware. It can't be argued that to enjoy 3-D thriller games, full-length motion pictures, instant TV reception, and video, you'll be more comfortable with a Pentium II class machine, 64MB of RAM, a large monitor, and a powerful video card with 8MB of video RAM.

But it is possible to use some of these features on an older, more modest Pentium 133 or 166 MHz MMX machine with an inexpensive TV tuner-card add-in. (You'll find details on hardware requirements for various multimedia features later in this chapter.)

And Windows 98 supports a second tier of useful multimedia features that have even lighter hardware requirements. These features can be valuable to business users as well as home users who want to build a computer entertainment center.

Multimedia Advantages

Picture this scenario: Your boss has sent you to a conference to give a sales presentation with all the trimmings. Your boss wants you to take some snapshots of conference participants and scan artwork for an on-the-spot update to the company Web page. You've had your fill of tiny notebook keyboards, funky displays, and touchpads. You want a scanner, a digital camera, a full-sized monitor, and a real mouse and keyboard, but you don't want to hire a truck just to tote your luggage around.

Or here's another scenario: You've been sent to a music conference, and you want to demonstrate a multimedia CD through a good pair of speakers. Is there some way to just point at the computer from across the room and make it take photos, launch applications, or adjust multimedia volume settings? How about a decent sound system that you can control by clicking a remote control device?

Windows 98's support for USB peripherals makes it possible for you to connect inexpensive, lightweight accessories and use them on a moment's notice. Storm Technology's trim PageScan scanner weighs only two pounds and will fit into a shoulder bag. PageScan comes with a CD full of software, but you can just plug it in and Win98's Imaging for Windows application is transformed into a full-fledged scanning interface. Add a small PC Card modem, and your notebook becomes a full-service fax machine.

E-Tek's KwikKey PC remote controller can be installed in about ten seconds, turning a Windows 98 computer into a pushbutton multimedia appliance. This USB infrared device has four mouse-cursor keys and six programmable function buttons. Business types can use it to run a PowerPoint slide show from across a room—but you can also use the KwikKey controller to kick back and play CD tracks or watch a full-motion DVD movie.

Multiple-monitor support is another new Windows 98 feature. (Microsoft has finally added this Macintosh staple.) Users can now extend the Windows 98 desktop over up to nine individual monitors. The virtual desktop can be configured so that icons or windows can be dragged left, right, up, or down to transfer them to another display screen. Applications can be moved seamlessly from one monitor to another, or the second display can be used to duplicate data on the first display, enabling you to simultaneously edit and proof a presentation.

If your appetite is whetted, read on; you'll find detailed information on how to use all of these features later in this chapter.

Why It Works: New Multimedia Technologies

Windows 98 integrates a number of new technologies to deliver smoother, more full-featured multimedia performance.

Direct X

The Direct X 5.0 video application program interface (API) is the technology that puts the zing into game playing under Windows 98.

In Windows 3.x, game programmers were limited by the necessity of routing all video functions through a 16-bit graphics device interface (GDI). Under DOS, programmers have long been able to write directly to video hardware, squeezing better performance and more impressive effects out of their products. In Windows 98, Direct X technology provides similar fast access to video hardware. The latest version of Direct X allows faster screen rendering of 2-D and 3-D graphics than was possible under Windows 95.

The Direct Draw and Direct 3D APIs allow games and digital video to write 2-D and 3-D display information directly to a video card's frame buffer. They allow applications to manipulate video memory easily, taking full advantage of the page flipping, blitting, transparency, and color and space-conversion capabilities of display hardware. (*Blitting* is the act of transferring bitmap data from one device context to another to create smooth animation.)

Direct X also lets digital-video playback take advantage of hardware features included on advanced graphics adapters. Most notably, AVI animation playback can be scaled and enlarged on the screen without image degradation.

For an application to bypass the traditional Windows GDI layer and use Direct X, your video card must use a display driver that supports the Direct X API. Most PC video adapters manufactured since 1996 include this feature.

Additionally, your application or game must be programmed to make program calls supported by the Direct X API. Figure 15-1 shows Activision's Direct X–enabled Heavy Gear.

Late-breaking news: Microsoft has recently released a Direct X 6.0 update for Windows 98 that you can download and install through the Windows Update utility on the Start menu. See Appendix B for more details.

Figure 15-1. *Activision's Heavy Gear illustrates the new Direct Draw 3D API*

Media Control Interface

Microsoft's media control interface enables more intelligent integration of multimedia in Windows 98. Applications written to MCI programming specifications can exploit device-independent capabilities to directly control audio and video hardware peripherals. MCI devices can share a common command set for the playback and display of different kinds of audio and video media.

The Windows 98 media control interface allows all Windows applications to manipulate multimedia devices (including DVD and CD-ROM drives, sound cards, and streaming multimedia players such as Microsoft NetShow and Enhanced Media Player, Shockwave, and Real Media's Real Player). These devices can be run in concert or independently. Windows 98 makes it easy to embed or link video clips to documents or attach them to system events. Portions of full-length movies can also be captured and saved to disk. With the addition of appropriate video hardware, input can be directly captured from or recorded on an ordinary VCR.

Enhanced Support for Digital Video

In the past, Microsoft's Video for Windows was a separate technology from the Windows operating system. The Microsoft Media Player under Windows 3.x was also limited in its playback functionality. In Windows 95, this changed so that full-length audiovisual interleave (AVI) and Motion Pictures Expert Group (MPEG) videos could be played without using third-party players and drivers. In earlier versions of Windows, digital video display depended on 16-bit drivers to read, decompress, and display data on the screen.

The currently shipping version of Windows 98 includes Microsoft's ActiveMovie applet (in the Accessories | Entertainment group) to complement the older Media Player. ActiveMovie can take advantage of both software and hardware acceleration features to enable smooth full-screen playback of MPEG videos.

Since the initial release of Windows 98, Microsoft has posted an additional Enhanced Windows Media Player application on its Web site (at http://www.microsoft.com/windows/mediaplayer/default.asp), which you can download for free. The Enhanced Windows Media Player has all the features of the ActiveMovie applet and adds support for streaming video playback over the Internet, a feature formerly included in the NetShow Player.

In effect, the Enhanced Windows Media Player is Microsoft's answer to RealNetworks' Real Player, supporting playback of all of the Real Player 5.0 streaming audio and video formats in addition to Microsoft's ActiveMovie and NetShow files. At this writing, RealNetworks is about as happy about this development as Netscape Communications was when Microsoft invented Internet Explorer. The two Player applications can coexist and function independently, so long as you use an official release of RealNetworks' products and not a beta version. (Some users have reported success in getting a beta version of Real Player to work by reinstalling it after installing the Microsoft Enhanced Media Player.)

Enhanced Support for Sound and MIDI

Windows 98 incorporates a number of audio compression and decompression schemes (referred to as *codecs*) to pack more waveform sound information into smaller files on your hard disk. Enhanced support is also included for the musical instrumental digital interface (MIDI) used to record, encode, and play back poly-voiced instrumental music. Windows 98 includes a number of recorded MIDI compositions as part of its desktop sound schemes feature. In addition to supporting the general MIDI standard, which is an industry standard, Windows 98 includes a new technology called *MIDI streams*. This technology allows a MIDI-compatible sound card to play complex MIDI sequences with minimal CPU use.

New in Windows 98, as discussed in Chapter 7, the Win32 Driver Model (WDM) provides software emulation for the hardware wavetable synthesis built into newer and more expensive sound cards. In Windows 98, users can often select two or three individual configurations for a sound card that lend slightly different harmonics and voices to recorded MIDI compositions.

Enhanced CD-ROM and DVD Support

Windows 98 includes a built-in CD-ROM file system (CDFS) with internal caching to improve the read/playback speed for CD data. CDFS is a 32-bit file system designed to read files from CD-ROM drives as quickly and efficiently as possible. The dedicated CD Player, installed in the \ACCESSORIES\MULTIMEDIA folder, has a sophisticated feature set that includes random play, programmable playback order, and the ability to save program lists that you define. Windows 98 also supports the Sony/Phillips enhanced CD format. This format can be played on standard stereo CD units as well as on computer CD-ROM drives. This format also supports CDs that mix data, audio, and video. Windows 98 also includes extended support for CD-ROM drives that read Kodak PhotoCDs and video CDs.

New in Windows 98, CD playback quality can be enhanced with USB speakers by selecting the Enable Digital CD Audio option on the CD tab of the Control Panel | Multimedia applet. (Selecting this feature disables conventional analog CD output through headphones and speakers connected to standard sound card ports.)

Windows 98 maintains dual file system support for DVDs. The older ISO 9660 file format is used on many disks, and Win98 is backwardly compatible with this format through the CDFS file system. The new universal disk format (UDF) file system permits faster multimedia playback through VCACHE, the main Windows 98 disk cache. Unlike CDFS, it optimizes itself automatically, with no performance settings for users to adjust. (For information on adjusting the CDFS file cache, see "Performance Tab" in the "System Applet" section of Chapter 9.)

Most current DVD discs encoded with multimedia contain both ISO 9660 and UDF file system structures. UDF takes precedence in mounting such discs. If UDF is unavailable, the disc is mounted through the less-efficient CDFS file system. The DVD player bundled with Windows 98 requires the UDF file system, but third-party DVD players (included on most computers with DVD support) are usually backwardly compatible.

Movies and other multimedia encoded for DVD format contain a great many features not available on ordinary CDs. Users can often choose between alternative sound tracks, display simultaneous text commentary, skip between different sections, and choose alternative camera angles for video presentations. See the section "Working with DVD" later in this chapter for more details.

AutoPlay

The AutoPlay feature automatically runs a specified program or starts playing music when the user inserts a Win98-aware CD or DVD in an appropriate drive. When a disk is inserted in a CD-ROM drive, Windows 98 searches it for a file called AUTORUN.INF. If this file exists, Windows 98 opens it and follows the configuration instructions. This improvement makes the setup of multimedia applications and games much easier. CD vendors can set up an automatic installation routine that eliminates the need to locate specific directories or manually launch programs (see Figure 15-2).

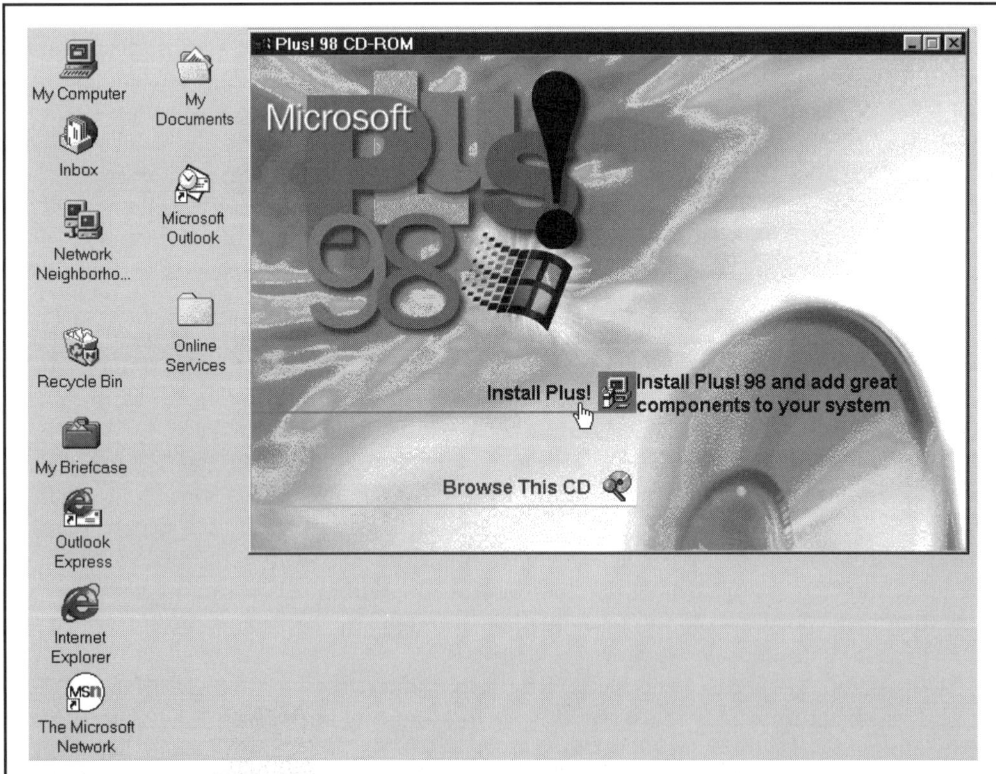

Figure 15-2. *Windows 95– and 98–aware CDs automatically play a vendor-specified menu or startup program when they are inserted into a CD-ROM drive*

Plug-and-Play Hardware Support

Plug-and-play hardware support in Windows 98 lets you install and upgrade audio, video, CD-ROM and DVD components simply by putting cards into slots and connecting cables. USB peripherals are installed simply by plugging them into a port. For most supported devices it's no longer necessary to set jumpers, worry about address conflicts, or install third-party device management software; Windows 98 automatically detects and configures your hardware.

The magic of Win98's plug-and-play support extends not only to newer machines with plug-and-play BIOS and PCI peripherals, but also to older motherboards running ordinary 8-bit and 16-bit ISA peripherals. The Device Manager included in the Windows 98 Control Panel presents a birds-eye view of the configurations for all your peripheral devices, allowing you to troubleshoot and reconfigure hardware that escape autodetection.

Shopping for a Multimedia PC

Microsoft has, since the introduction of Windows 95, defined a number of PC hardware standards for vendors who want their products to be "ready for multimedia." The most recent of these is the Entertainment PC 98 System standard. This set of requirements calls for a PC optimized for the following uses:

- Games, including the best titles, with the most complex, realistic graphics and audio.
- Education, using the most engaging titles, with full-screen video, interactive animation, and so on.
- Active Internet, providing enhanced Web communications capabilities, with personalized and animated Web sites, chat rooms, and so on.
- Personal communications through multimedia e-mail, Internet audio phone, video phone, and so on.
- Interactive, high-resolution television and movie viewing through higher video quality, real-time links to content producers, and so on.
- Connection with traditional consumer-electronics devices, providing home theater surround audio such as Dolby Digital (AC-3) for games and DVD movies, and fast and easy capture, editing, and playback of personal video.

If you're shopping for a multimedia PC that's Windows 98–ready, the following minimum hardware guidelines may be helpful.

- 200-MHz Pentium processor with Intel MMX technology or equivalent. The CPU should have a minimum 256K Level 2 (L2) cache or equivalent.
- 32MB minimum system memory; 64MB recommended. Memory should be 66-MHz dynamic random-access memory (DRAM) or better.

- 2GB or larger IDE or SCSI hard disk.
- 10X or faster IDE or SCSI CD-ROM drive (a 2X or higher DVD-ROM drive can substitute).
- Graphics adapter using PCI, AGP, or other high-speed bus. The graphics adapter should have at least 4MB of onboard memory.
- 15-inch or larger monitor, with dot pitch of 0.28 or better, capable of displaying a screen resolution of 1,024 by 768 pixels with a vertical refresh rate of 80 Hz or higher.
- Two USB ports to support connection of auxiliary input devices, such as cameras, scanners, game pads, and joysticks.
- One enhanced parallel port and two serial ports (or one serial port plus an internal or PCMCIA modem).
- 33.6 Kbps or higher data/fax/voice modem.
- A sound card (at least 16-bit quality) that supports line-in as well as line-out (speakers or headphones) and microphone capabilities. The card should support internal connections to CD-ROM or DVD drive, with full-duplex support to record and play sounds at the same time. (Ideally, the card should be capable of capturing audio at one sample rate while playing audio at another sample rate.)

Microsoft recommends that you balance your multimedia PC, even at the expense of horsepower. Multimedia playback places heavy demands on many parts of the computer, from the CD-ROM or DVD drive (for reading data), to the hard disk (for writing data), to the CPU (for decompressing data), and to the video and audio subsystems (for playing data). A fast CPU does not guarantee a great playback system. A chain (or computer system) is only as good as its weakest link. For computers that require hardware decoding and playback of DVD or MPEG-2 video, the CPU should be at least a Pentium 133 MHz MMX.

Some faster PCs include video adapters that allow DVD and MPEG-2 playback without the use of a separate DVD encoder/decoder card. For direct software decoding and playback of DVD video, a Pentium II 266 MHz CPU or better is recommended along with a supporting video adapter.

A 10X CD-ROM drive is the minimum you want to use for multimedia playback. Your drive should be capable of a data transfer rate of no less than 300 Kbps per second. Your CD-ROM drive should also support the multisession Kodak PhotoCD format, which means that it will read disks with photos added cumulatively.

The 16-bit audio and MIDI capabilities should be features of any sound card that you consider. Choose a sound card with a 16-bit digital-to-analog converter (DAC) for playback and, for developers, a 16-bit analog-to-digital converter (ADC) for recording.

Microsoft also recommends a system that supports stereo sound and 8, 11, 22, and 44 KHz waveforms. CD-quality sound uses 44 KHz. The 11 and 22 KHz waveforms are sampled less frequently. The low sample rate is often used for compressed waveforms that save CPU processing time and hard-disk space. The 8 KHz waveform is used for a Windows 98 capability called Truespeech compression. The Truespeech format is designed primarily to reproduce voice messages attached to system events or documents.

The video and disk I/O performance of a computer with a PCI bus is about ten times better than one without a PCI bus, assuming everything else on the computers is equal. A video card with 1MB of RAM can support a color depth of 64,000 colors (16-bit display) at a screen resolution of 800 by 600 pixels. At this color depth, photographs and paintings are displayed with a much higher degree of realism than when using the standard 256-color palette supported by an ordinary VGA card. There are many games and CDs programmed to display themselves in 32,000 and 64,000 color modes. However, for compatibility with the high-end industry standard called TrueColor, you must use a video card capable of a 24-bit (16 million colors) display. Also make sure that your video card is capable of rendering high-resolution screen displays in a noninterlaced format. Noninterlaced display modes avoid the annoying screen flicker common in older EGA and VGA monitors.

A 24-bit display monitor is necessary for TrueColor support and will offer far better video reproduction than a simple VGA monitor. Your monitor should accommodate a screen resolution of 800 by 600 pixels or higher and be capable of a noninterlaced

Features to Look for in Sound Cards

Look for the following features when choosing a sound card:

- **Support for the General MIDI format** This means that the MIDI files you play and record will be universally compatible with other systems.
- **Inclusion of sample sounds** Sound cards imitate musical instruments either by simple 16-bit emulation programmed into a chip, by a 32-bit process known as wavetable synthesis, or by including actual sample sounds from real musical instruments. This last method is the best way to obtain real musical fidelity.
- **A standard MIDI port** This 15-pin connector allows you to plug in a keyboard or other MIDI recording device.
- **Support for MIDI streams** This Windows 95 and Windows 98 feature allows your card to play back without consuming large quantities of CPU time. The result is better multimedia performance.
- **Wavetable synthesis** This feature, found in newer sound cards, allows more faithful simulation of the true sound of musical instruments. Windows 98's WDM support can emulate wavetable synthesis for some, but not all, common sound cards.

screen display. The display font should also be crisp and readable in high-resolution modes. Generally, these monitor capabilities are tied to three performance specifications: horizontal scan rate, vertical scan rate, and dot pitch. Minimal specifications for Windows 98 are a horizontal scan rate of 30 to 35 KHz; a vertical scan rate of 60 Hz; and a dot pitch of 0.28 mm. (You can do much better than this with a newer computer.)

You need speakers to use multimedia effectively unless you don't mind wearing headphones while using the computer. (This tends to preclude using the telephone or carrying on conversations during the multimedia experience.) Many people go out and purchase tinny-sounding plastic speakers with built-in preamplifiers. We recommend avoiding the low-end on this item. If you want to economize, you can probably find a pair of wooden 15- to 25-watt stereo speakers in a thrift shop that give you better sound than the cut-rate multimedia specials you find at swap meets. The rated, unamplified capacity of a Creative Labs Sound Blaster 16 is only 4 watts, but in the authors' experience this sound card satisfactorily drives a pair of 20-watt, 4-ohm speakers. For larger speakers, you'll need units that include their own plug-in power supply.

The popularization of the Universal Serial Bus in Windows 98 adds a new wrinkle to speaker technology. Currently, manufacturers such as Altec Lansing sell USB speakers that can process multimedia sounds without the presence of a sound card in the computer. Altec Lansing also manufactures complex six-piece systems that take advantage of DVD Dolby six-channel separation.

Installing Multimedia Peripherals

To add multimedia peripherals such as a CD-ROM drive, CD-ROM controller, sound card, or video capture board before installing Windows 98, simply place the peripherals in the appropriate slots and drive bays in your computer and connect the appropriate cables.

For a CD-ROM drive and/or controller card, if Windows 98 has not yet been installed, boot your current version of DOS and run the appropriate configuration software supplied by the vendor.

For other peripherals, you may not need to run third-party software intended for Windows 3.x. Simply install the physical hardware in the computer and proceed to the installation of Windows 98. If your peripherals are not recognized and supported automatically, then you may need to run the Add New Hardware applet or special third-party installation software. (See Chapter 9 for details.)

Sometimes the drivers included on the Windows 98 CD are the best fit for your multimedia hardware; other times, drivers bundled by the manufacturer deliver better, more reliable performance. In general, you should start out by using the drivers (whether Microsoft or third party) with the most recent chronological date. If you have difficulty with individual features, or if your system behaves erratically, you may want to experiment with alternative driver versions. (This is particularly true with drivers for video adapters and sound cards.) The Windows Device Manager (accessed by right-clicking My Computer, selecting Properties, and clicking the Device Manager tab) allows you to view the dates of the software drivers for all of your installed peripherals and switch to alternative versions. (See "Changing an Assigned Software Driver" in Chapter 9 for details.)

To use a DVD drive in conjunction with a hardware encoder/decoder card and sound card, you'll need to configure cables properly to interconnect these hardware pieces. Generally, wiring a DVD drive to a sound card is similar to wiring a CD-ROM drive. A tiny, thin cable goes from a jack on the drive to a connector on the sound card. In the case of Creative Labs' add-on Encore DVD kit, you must run an external video cable between the standard D-Sub (video-out) connector on the video card and a video-in jack on the Creative encoder card. The display monitor is then attached directly to a D-Sub connector on the back of the encoder/decoder card. See the instructions that come with your computer or DVD kit for more detailed information.

Using Your Headphones and Speakers

If you decide to use headphones, make sure to plug them into the sound card itself and not the front of the CD-ROM drive if you want to get the sound from a multimedia program. The front jack on the CD-ROM drive is fine for listening to audio CDs but won't reproduce MIDI or WAV files.

If you don't get any sound from an audio CD-ROM when the headphones or speakers are plugged into your sound card, a tiny patch cable used to route output from the CD-ROM drive to the sound card may be missing. This problem is confirmed if adjusting the CD slider in the Windows 98 Volume Control applet doesn't work. Internal CD-ROM units can use a variety of proprietary cables and plugs to channel their output to a sound card. Sometimes this cable connection is omitted during installation. External CD-ROM players are sometimes configured to route audio CD sound through the line-in channel slider instead of the CD slider. A stereo cable is run from the line-out jacks on the CD-ROM unit to the line-in jack on the sound card. If adjusting the CD slider on the Win98 Volume Control produces no output from an audio CD, try adjusting the line-in slider. (See the section "Volume Control" later in this chapter for detailed information on using the Win98 Volume Control.)

Other Connections

Some notebook computers are shipped with an accompanying docking station that contains a CD-ROM drive. Plugging the computer into the docking station usually activates a series of ports and other I/O devices mounted on the rear of the docking station. With these systems, CD-ROM audio through the docking station output jack may not be enabled. The following procedure may allow you to control or mix CD audio on such a system:

1. Purchase a stereo male-to-male 1/8-inch (tiny plug) cable at an electronics supply store.

2. Plug your notebook computer into its docking station. Connect one end of the male-to-male tiny-plug cable to the external headphone jack on your CD-ROM drive. Connect the other end of the male-to-male tiny-plug cable to the line-in jack that is physically located on your notebook computer.
3. Connect your speakers or headphones to the output jack mounted on the back or side of the docking station.
4. Play an audio CD and experiment with the settings of the external volume control located on your CD-ROM drive. Use the line-in slider on the Windows 98 Volume Control to mix output to your speakers or headphone.

This same procedure can be used to connect the output of an internal CD-ROM drive on a desktop computer to the line-in jack of its sound card, but you'll need a longer cable. You can use this procedure on a desktop machine if it's inconvenient to open the case and install the proprietary CD cable.

Working with Sound

Windows 98 reproduces sound for several supported formats: MIDI sequencer (.MID and .RMI), waveform (.WAV), and CD audio. In addition, you can still play third-party sound formats that were developed for DOS PCs and for other computing platforms. Third-party utilities let you work with sounds in DOS formats such as .CMF and .VOC, Macintosh .SND and .MOV files, and Amiga .MOD files.

CD Audio

The audio CD Player application is part of Windows 98 and can serve as a replacement playback unit, along with your CD-ROM drive, when your regular CD player or stereo system is in the shop.

To use the audio CD Player, follow these steps:

1. Place a CD in the CD-ROM drive.
2. From the Start menu, open CD Player, located in the Programs | Accessories | Entertainment group.
3. To start playing the first track, click the right-arrow Play button in the top row of the CD Player controls.

Note that if the Win98 Autoplay feature is enabled, CD Player will start automatically when a music CD is inserted into the drive. The CD Player status window shows an LED display of elapsed play time. The two rows of buttons to the right are a standard series of CD controls, as shown in Figure 15-3.

The Artist and Title areas allow you to enter information for a program of tracks that you create. Other options, available on the Options menu, include Continuous

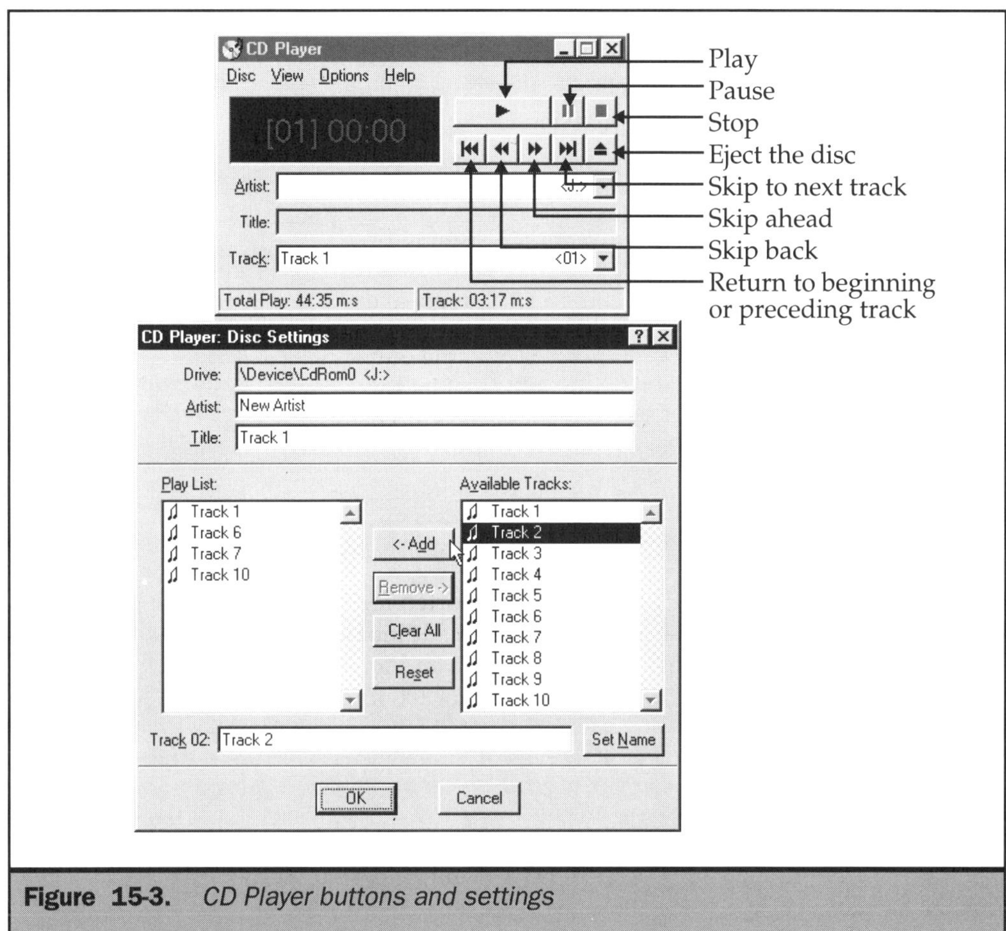

Figure 15-3. *CD Player buttons and settings*

Play, Random Play, and an Intro Play preview feature. If you select Intro Play, the CD cycles through the first few bars of each song. When you hear something you want to play all the way through, simply deselect the Intro Play button. The Preferences dialog box, on the Options menu, allows you to adjust the length of an intro clip from 1 to 15 seconds and also controls the CD Player display font.

Here's how to define a play list for your CD:

1. From the Disc menu, select Edit Play List.
2. Use the Add and Remove buttons to specify the play list.

The volume of CD playback can be adjusted by selecting Volume Control from the View menu. Your CD output can be controlled through either the CD slider or the line-in slider. (Refer to the section "Using Your Headphones and Speakers" earlier in this chapter for a discussion of how to determine which slider to use.)

CD Player can be set to terminate play when you close the program or to continue to play tracks sequentially. This option is toggled from the Options | Preferences menu.

You can essentially multitask with CD Player, using different applications as you listen to music. You can format a disk, print a document, or perform any other task that doesn't require a CD-ROM drive. If you have tied system functions to sounds, these can play concurrently with the CD.

Microsoft Plus Deluxe CD Player

If you have purchased and installed Microsoft Plus for Windows 98, the standard CD Player application in the Entertainment group is replaced by Deluxe CD Player, shown here:

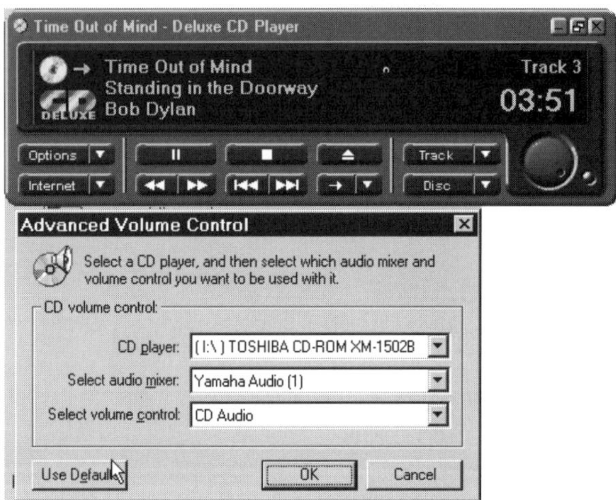

Deluxe CD Player has more sophisticated control options than the basic application. It allows you to collect supplementary information about albums from the Internet, construct more sophisticated play lists, and switch among discs in multiple CD-ROM drives on the same computer.

Media Player

Media Player is located in the Programs | Accessories | Entertainment group on the Start menu. It is a simple playback device with a simple, rectangular interface, shown next. Media Player is outfitted with VCR-like controls: Start/Pause, Stop, Eject, Skip to Previous Mark, Skip to Next Mark, Rewind, and Fast Forward. The two buttons to the right of these controls let you mark the beginning and end of a selection to be played or copied to another program. The sliding timer shows where you are in the tracks (for a CD), frames (for a video), or time.

By default, if you have a sound card, Windows 98 configures Media Player to handle four file types: waveform (.WAV), Microsoft audio-video interleave (.AVI), ActiveMovie (MPEG), and MIDI sequencer (.MID and .RMI). If you have a CD-ROM drive, CD audio is added as a fifth type.

Media Player can control most of the multimedia devices on your system used to play sound or video recordings. (Exceptions and instructions for working with third-party formats are described later in this chapter.) To play a multimedia file or activate a device (such as a videodisc player), choose the appropriate entry from Media Player's Device menu. To install new devices, use the Add New Hardware option on the Control Panel to add appropriate drivers.

Multiple copies of Media Player can be opened to play back more than one file at a time. Two sound files in the MIDI format can't be played concurrently, but you can play CD audio, a MIDI selection, and a .WAV file simultaneously. If you have a full-duplex sound card, you can play two .WAV files simultaneously. Multiple video files can be opened and played concurrently, but playback quality will suffer.

MIDI Support

MIDI is a widely recognized hardware and software interface standard that allows music synthesizers and musical instruments to be connected to your computer. It condenses input into a special digitized file that contains an encoded description of music and other sounds. MIDI, as a musician's tool, is widely supported by all advanced musical equipment, from pianos to piccolos.

To play a MIDI sound file, follow these steps:

1. Open Media Player, ActiveMovie, or Enhanced Windows Media Player.
2. Choose File | Open and load the MIDI Sequencer file into the playback application you've selected. (In Media Player and Enhanced Media Player, you can select the MIDI file type in the Open dialog box to filter out extraneous files. In ActiveMovie, you must select All Files to display MIDI selections on the file list.)
3. Click the Play button.

In Windows 3.x, the mapping of MIDI instruments to particular recording channels was accomplished through a Control Panel applet called Midimap. In Windows 98, this feature is accessed by loading a particular MIDI file into Media Player and selecting Properties from the Device menu. (You can also access this screen by opening the Multimedia applet on the Control Panel and selecting the MIDI tab.) The MIDI Properties screen allows you to select an existing map of MIDI instruments and channels or to design your own custom map. To do this, you may need updated third-party MIDI software containing instrument profiles written in the new Windows 98 format. The default drivers Microsoft includes for standard sound card devices are not as flexible as the Midimap configurations that were supplied in Windows 3.x.

Tip

If you plan to create a custom MIDI instrument configuration, first back up the default map configured for your sound card. On the MIDI Properties screen, select Custom Configuration and click the Configure button. On the next screen, click the Save As button and type a new name for this copy of your default MIDI profile.

Videotape Support

Windows 98 includes support for some third-party multimedia authoring devices such as laser discs and video-capture devices. This makes it easy to set up a computer for single-frame or frame-by-frame capture, a process in which the author captures digital video data one frame at a time, usually to be compressed later. This is a slow process, but it is absolutely the best way to get the best possible quality of digital video. Frame-accurate control of the VCR is also important for recording broadcast-quality special effects to use in commercials, movies, television programs, music videos, and so on.

Windows 98 provides VCR control services through the MCI VISCA device driver, which is based on the MCI command set for VCRs. This device driver is used with a video-capture or overlay card to control SONY VISCA-compatible videotape recorders, such as the CVD-1000 VDECK. The VISCA-compatible driver controls the parts of the VCR, including the tape transport, channel tuners, and VCR input and output channels.

Note

The VDECK specifications show it to be accurate to about plus-or-minus one frame. In reality, I have found it to be accurate, at best, to plus-or-minus three frames. With cheap tape, the accuracy may even drop to plus-or-minus half a second.

To play a videotape on your computer, you must connect the video and audio output from your VCR to the video capture or overlay card of your computer and to the audio input of your computer. You may also need to install an MCI digital-video device driver. The Advanced tab on the Multimedia Properties screen selected from the Control Panel shows a number of devices. Double-click the Media Control Devices icon, select a listed device, and click Properties to enable Win98's built-in support for a listed MCI peripheral (see Figure 15-4).

Inserting and Linking Multimedia to Documents

Media Player allows you to use OLE to insert multimedia files in a document. To do this, load a file or mark a selection in Media Player and then select Copy Object from the Edit menu. To insert the file in another application, choose Paste or Paste Special from the application's Edit menu. Microsoft's media control interface (MCI) pops up a control bar to play back the file when you double-click it in the target application. This feature can be toggled on and off by selecting Edit | Options in Media Player and selecting Control Bar on Placement. If this option is checked when you copy the selection to the clipboard, the control bar will appear in the target application. This option can also be used to assign a caption to the multimedia file inserted in the target document.

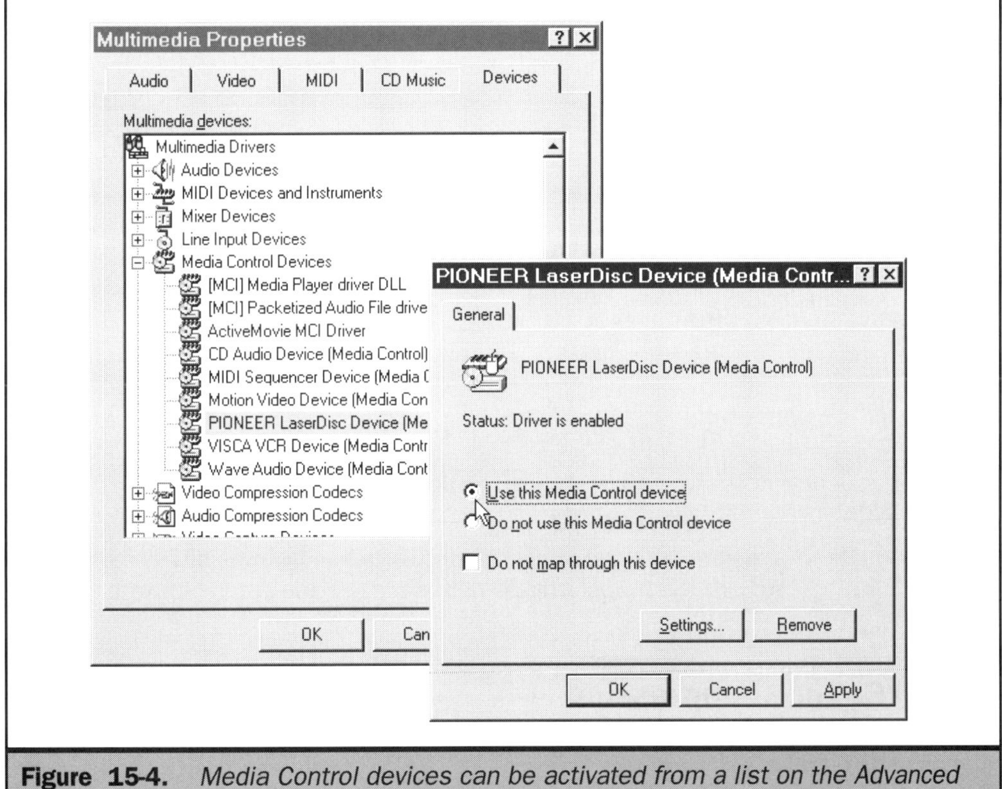

Figure 15-4. *Media Control devices can be activated from a list on the Advanced tab of the Control Panel's Multimedia Properties screen*

Sound Recorder

The Sound Recorder is used to record, play, and embed sound files in the wave (.WAV) format. It has five buttons—Go to the Beginning of the Clip, Go to the End, Play, Stop, and Record, from left to right, as shown here:

You can use the Sound Recorder to open, create, and save .WAV files. You can also create a compound sound effect by inserting one file within another. To do this, use the Insert File option on Sound Recorder's Edit menu or open the Media Player and use the clipboard to cut and paste captured sound information into the Sound Recorder. A series of special effects are available on Sound Recorder's Effects menu. You can add an echo or make the file play in reverse. You can also increase or decrease the volume of a sound in 25 percent increments and double or halve the playback speed.

Here's another handy tip: Use the Sound Recorder to increase or decrease the default playback volume of Windows 98 system events. This procedure is useful, for example, if you want music and multimedia to play back at one level and system messages to announce themselves at a different level. For instance, to change the volume of the Critical Stop error message, do this:

1. Open the Sound component of the Control Panel and determine which .WAV file is attached to the Critical Stop event. The default file is CHORD.WAV.
2. Start Sound Recorder and open the CHORD.WAV file, located in the \WINDOWS\MEDIA directory.
3. From Sound Recorder's Effects menu, select Increase Volume or Decrease Volume. Play back the file as often as necessary to adjust the volume as desired.
4. Save the file and close Sound Recorder.

Win98 Sound Compression

You can use compression to condense an existing sound or record a new one at a variety of different quality levels.

Uncompressed stereo audio contains a lot of data—about 150K for every second of sound—which is why an audio CD holds only a bit more than one hour of music. Win98 includes both music- and voice-oriented sound compression codecs. Music-oriented codecs (such as IMA ADPCM or Microsoft ADPCM) allow not-quite-CD-quality sound at about one-quarter of its uncompressed size. Voice-oriented codecs (such as Truespeech or GSM) allow even more efficient sound compression. Table 15-1 shows the Win98 sound codecs and descriptions. (Other codecs may be added by the drivers for your sound card.)

Sound Recorder's Audio Properties option (located on the Edit menu) lets you customize playback options and switch among multiple sound devices. You no longer need to open the Control Panel to specify an output device, and the Audio Properties menu also lets you set the volume and preferred quality for new recorded sounds.

To expand or compress an existing .WAV file using another compression algorithm, open the file in Sound Recorder and then select Properties from the File menu. The Format Conversion scrollbox lets you choose among the compression formats listed in Table 15-1.

Windows 98 Sound Codec	Description
DSP Group, Inc., Truespeech	Offers good compression for voice-oriented sound but is not a good option for sound other than voice. Truespeech offers a better data rate than GSM, the other voice-oriented codec provided with Windows 98. This makes Truespeech a good option for users who want to record notes in their documents or spreadsheets, store voice mail on their computers, and so on. Truespeech does not offer real-time compression rates but does offer real-time decompression rates, making this codec a good alternative for use with modems and networks.
Microsoft GSM 6.10 Audio	Offers real-time compression (so long as the hardware is fast enough to support it), making this codec a good option for recording voice with the Sound Recorder. GSM conforms to the European Telecommunications Standards Institute Groupe Spécial Mobile recommendation 6.10. GSM also allows you to select from among a range of sampling rates.

Table 15-1. *Windows 95/98 Sound Compression Codecs*

Windows 98 Sound Codec	Description
Microsoft CCITT G.711 A-Law and u-Law	Provided for compatibility with telephony standards for Europe and North America. This codec is supported by many hardware configurations and offers a 2-to-1 compression ratio (from 16 to 8 bits per sample).
IMA ADPCM	Defined by the Interactive Multimedia Association for multiple hardware platforms; similar to Microsoft ADPCM. This codec offers real-time compression.
Microsoft ADPCM	Offers both real-time and non-real-time compression. When authors choose the latter option, the compression process takes longer, but authors can create better-sounding audio files. Microsoft ADPCM is the codec used for Microsoft Encarta multimedia encyclopedia and other CD-based publications.
Microsoft PCM converter	Included for use with Sound Blaster and other 8-bit sound cards. With this codec, 8-bit cards can play 16-bit samples by reducing the quality of the audio produced to match the card's capabilities. Similarly, you can use this converter to play a sample at a 1 KHz rate on a card that supports another rate.

Table 15-1. *Windows 95/98 Sound Compression Codecs (continued)*

Recording and Capturing New Sounds or Spoken Messages

You can use Sound Recorder to capture sound from an internal source, such as a CD-ROM drive or an existing .WAV file. You can also create your own sound for manipulation, although this requires that a microphone be plugged into the sound card.

Here's how to record sound from a microphone:

1. From the Start menu, choose Programs | Accessories | Entertainment and then click Sound Recorder.
2. Click the Microphone button in Sound Recorder and record.
3. Click the Stop button to end recording.
4. From the File menu, select Save As and type a filename for this .WAV file.

You can also record sound from a CD player or other component that you connect to your sound card's line-in input. Use the Volume Control tool to turn on CD or line-in input and turn off the microphone input. (See the following section for information on how to do this.) From Sound Recorder, click the Microphone button and record.

Volume Control

The Volume Control governs the input and output audio levels for all of your multimedia devices. When Windows 98 installs drivers for a particular device, a sliding control for that device may be placed in the Volume Control panel. You can control the speaker or headphone output level, left-right channel balance, and mute (which cuts off the channel when selected).

When you first open the Volume Control, you should see a series of mixing sliders. These adjust playback volume and channel balance for each multimedia source. If your system can support sound sources not shown in the mixer, you can activate them by selecting Properties from the Options menu and placing a check mark next to each additional sound source.

The Volume Control's mixing sliders can be toggled back and forth between playback and recording settings by selecting either Playback or Recording on the Options | Properties screen. When the Volume Control is set to Playback, a series of Mute boxes appears underneath each slider. A check mark placed in a Mute box turns off the playback for that source. When the Volume Control is set to Recording, the box under each input source becomes a Select box—a check mark in a Select box turns the control for that source on, and removing the check mark turns that recording source off.

You can record a new waveform sound (.WAV file) from multiple input sources by setting both the output playback level and the record input level for each source. Here's how to do it:

1. From the Start menu, choose Programs | Accessories | Entertainment and then click Volume Control.
2. If only the master control (Vol) is displayed, right-click the icon in the upper-left corner of the Volume Control window and select Expand. (Or choose Options | Properties.)

3. On the Properties screen, check the check boxes for the audio input lines from which you want to receive sound; clear the others.
4. Adjust the volume and balance for each input line that you have checked.

In recording sounds from multiple input sources, you can monitor playback and recording levels simultaneously by opening two copies of the Volume Control, as shown in Figure 15-5. Just double-click the Speaker icon at the right side of the taskbar to bring up another instance.

Capturing a CD or VCR Audio Sample in a .WAV File

Windows 98 offers a number of sound schemes and sample MIDI pieces that you can play back if your computer has a sound card. If you have a CD-ROM drive or VCR, you can also create your own custom Windows 98 sound events.

CD Player and Sound Recorder can work in conjunction to let you capture a selection from an audio CD, TV set, or VCR and save it as a waveform (.WAV) file.

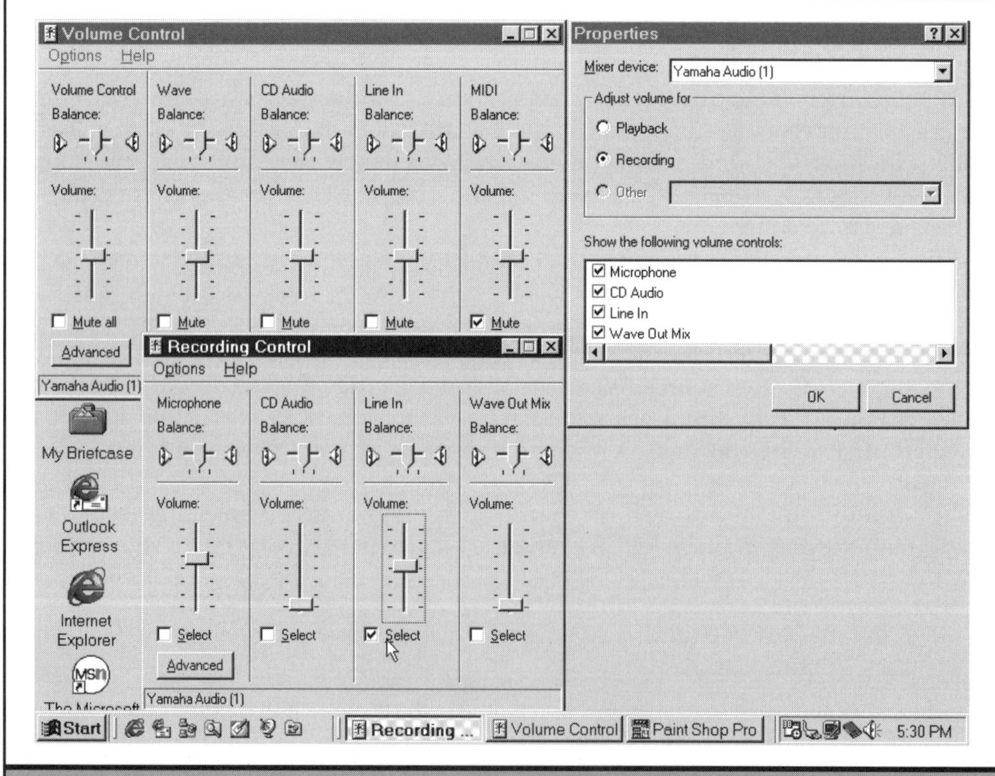

Figure 15-5. *Monitor playback and recording levels simultaneously by opening two copies of the Volume Control*

Once you've extracted a sample, it can be played in Media Player, dropped into an OLE-compliant application, or used as a sound for a system event.

Capturing a Sound from a CD

Follow these steps to capture a selection from a CD:

1. Open CD Player and the Volume Control. Confirm that CD audio is recognized by either the CD or line-in slider of the Volume Control. (See the section "Using Your Headphones and Speakers" for details.)
2. Open a second copy of the Volume Control. Set one copy to monitor playback levels and the other to monitor recording levels, as described in the previous section. Set an appropriate playback level for the CD audio selection. Duplicate the setting for this slider on the Recording Control slider. (After you perform this process several times, you may want to customize the input level for this slider.)
3. Insert the source CD into the CD-ROM drive and find the selection to be captured. Stop audio playback immediately before the selection is due to play.
4. Open the Sound Recorder. Choose a recording format by selecting File | Properties. The Details menu shows you the default audio format for your recording. To customize this format, choose Recording Formats from the Format Conversion menu and click the Convert Now button.
5. The Sound Selection dialog box allows you to choose the recording quality, compression format, and sampling rate for the selection you are about to capture. To record a stereo selection from the CD, you will probably want to change the default from monaural to stereo. Set the quality (radio, CD, and so on), bandwidth (8, 16, or 32 bits), and sampling rate (22 KHz, 44 KHz, and so on) to accommodate your CPU type and available disk storage space. The suggested settings are as follows: For a slow computer, choose 22,000 Hz 8-bit. For a faster computer, choose 44,100 Hz 16-bit.)
6. Click the round Record button on the right end of the Sound Recorder controls to begin recording. Now quickly click the Play button on the CD Player to resume CD audio output. When the passage you want is through, click the square Stop button to the left of the Record button (as shown in Figure 15-6).
7. To listen to the selection before saving, click the Seek to Start button in Sound Recorder followed by the Play button.
8. If you're satisfied with the way the sample sounds, select File | Save in the Sound Recorder and enter a descriptive name for the clip.

If you want to edit the file, open Media Player and load the clip you've created. You can cut unwanted material from the beginning or end of the file by marking a position with the slider control and using the Start Selection and End Selection buttons to mark

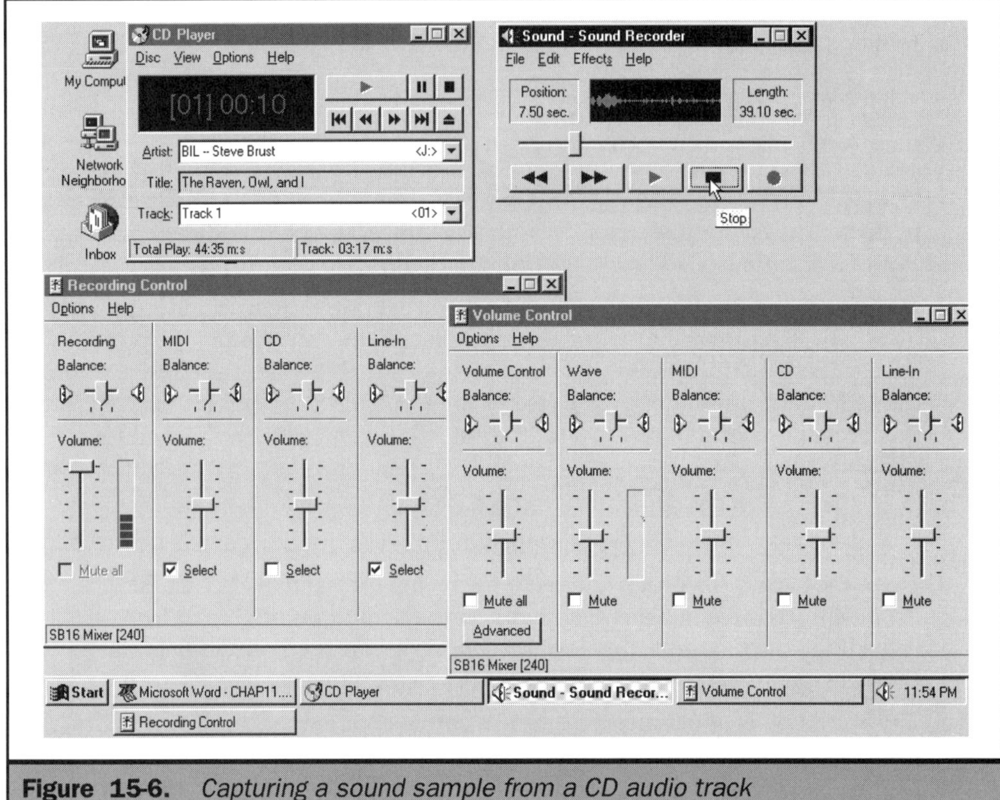

Figure 15-6. *Capturing a sound sample from a CD audio track*

the portion you want to save. Press CTRL-C to copy the marked portion of the file to the clipboard and then paste it back into Sound Recorder and save it again.

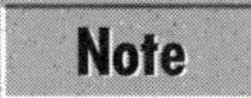

A similar procedure can be used to capture a selection of a MIDI file by substituting the Media Player for the CD Player. Portions of CD-Audio, .WAV files, and MIDI files can also be played concurrently and captured to build a collage, or layered effect.

The .WAV files you create with this procedure can be embedded into a word processor, spreadsheet, database, presentation, or any other application.

Capturing a Sound from a TV or VCR

Follow these steps to capture a sound sample from a TV or VCR:

1. For movie or TV capture, connect the line-out plug on your TV or VCR to the line-in jack of your sound card at the back of the computer. (You'll find

appropriate cables for this connection at Radio Shack or your favorite local electronics store if they didn't come with your sound card.)

2. Open the Windows 98 Sound Recorder and Volume Control as described in steps 1 through 5 in the section "Capturing a Sound from a CD."
3. Queue the cassette in the VCR to the spot you want to record and use the VCR's Pause or Stop control. Click the Sound button in the Sound Recorder window to begin recording and press the Play button on your VCR. (If you're recording from a TV, just click the Record button in Sound Recorder to capture a real-time sample.)
4. Click Stop when you want the selection to end.

You may want to take a couple of trial runs and adjust the line-in slider in the Recording Volume Control window to achieve an optimum playback level.

Associating a Saved Sound with a Windows 98 Event

To associate your saved sound with a Windows 98 event, do the following:

1. Open the Win98 Sound applet (from the Start menu, choose Settings | Control Panel | Sounds).
2. Choose an event in the Sounds Properties events window. For instance, select Start Windows.
3. Click the Browse button under the Name field and find the sound you just recorded.
4. To test this startup sound, click the Play button in the Sounds Properties window.

MPEG, QuickTime, and Other Third-Party Multimedia Formats

Windows 98 can be used to display multimedia presentations in formats developed for other computing platforms.

MPEG Video

Support for the Motion Pictures Expert Group (MPEG) video format is built into Windows 98's ActiveMovie application as well as Media Player.

MPEG videos opened in either application can be scaled to any screen size, but the results and rendering may be somewhat less than ideal. Media Player also limits the file size for the MPEG format; very large MPEG video clips may refuse to load.

The MPEG specification actually supports a multiplicity of formats, generally lumped into the categories MPEG-1 and MPEG-2. The MPEG-1 flavor (with file extensions .MPG, .MPE, .M1V, and .MPEG) is the type supported by ActiveMovie. You can view these videos in full-screen windows, but the playback quality tends to degrade unless your computer has a newer graphic adapter with MPEG acceleration features.

Working with DVD

MPEG-2 is the specification used to encode movies for DVD discs. This format is not supported by ActiveMovie, but some flavors can be played in Microsoft's new Enhanced Windows Media Player. If you have a computer with a DVD drive, you can play these files with Microsoft's DVD Player or the DVD player software supplied by the vendor. With most DVD setups, you'll have to use the vendor-supplied player.

Some users may be a bit puzzled by the fact that the Microsoft DVD Player bundled with Windows 98 is not generally available for installation. Even on computers with DVD drives, the option to install DVD Player is often missing from the Add/Remove Programs list under Multimedia. The reason for this is that Microsoft's DVD Player is designed to work with only a limited set of supported DVD decoder/encoder cards. The presence of a DVD drive *without* a PCI hardware decoder card is insufficient to permit Microsoft's player to operate. At present, the hardware cards supported directly in Windows 98 must use one of the following chipsets:

- Toshiba, Toshiba Infinia
- Quadrant, Dell XPS series
- Luxsonor, Creative PC (not the Dxr2 card found in the Creative Encore DVD kit)

Because of the density and complexity of MPEG-2 movies, many computers equipped with DVD drives use a hardware decoder card to assist the video adapter in rendering and synchronizing DVD video images. Generally, such a decoder card is required for accurate DVD playback on computers with CPUs below the Pentium II class. Although Windows 98 directly recognizes only a small number of decoder cards, it is compatible with a much larger range of decoder hardware with vendor-supplied software. The Creative Labs Encore DVD kit is an example of an older package that works fine with Windows 98 on computers with a Pentium I 125- to 200-MHz CPU—but you must use the Creative Labs DVD player since the Microsoft version is unavailable.

The good news for people with newer Pentium II computers is that separate hardware decoder cards are no longer necessary to faithfully render DVD MPEG-2 full-motion video. A computer with a Pentium II 266-MHz or better CPU can feed the output from a DVD drive directly to the video card with the signal decoding performed by software drivers.

Users of the Rage Pro and All-in-Wonder models of ATI video adapters can currently download a flexible and useful DVD video player at http://www.atitech.ca/showcase/dvd. Shown in Figure 15-7, this player works directly with the ATI Rage family of PCI and AGP video cards, eliminating the need for a separate PCI decoder card. For best results, this player should be run on computers with Pentium II CPUs. The ATI DVD player can run DVD and other MPEG-2 videos, as well as MPEG-1 and Dolby six-channel audio (.AC3) files.

One of the advantages of the ATI DVD player is that it can load and display DVD MPEG-2 video on a file-by-file basis, regardless of whether the files reside on a DVD, CD, or local hard disk. Some DVD players don't have File Open functions. Instead, they automatically search your computer for a DVD drive and then read the drive to see if a correctly formatted disc has been inserted. If you have CDs that contain MPEG-2 presentations, or if you've copied these files to your hard disk, some DVD players will be unable to open and display them.

To get either Microsoft's or ATI's DVD player to display MPEG-2 video, the files must reside in a folder called VIDEO_TS. (This is the automatic default on DVDs.) If you want to play MPEG-2 files from other media, such as a local hard disk, they must be copied into a folder that bears that name. This tells the software player to open the video streaming process.

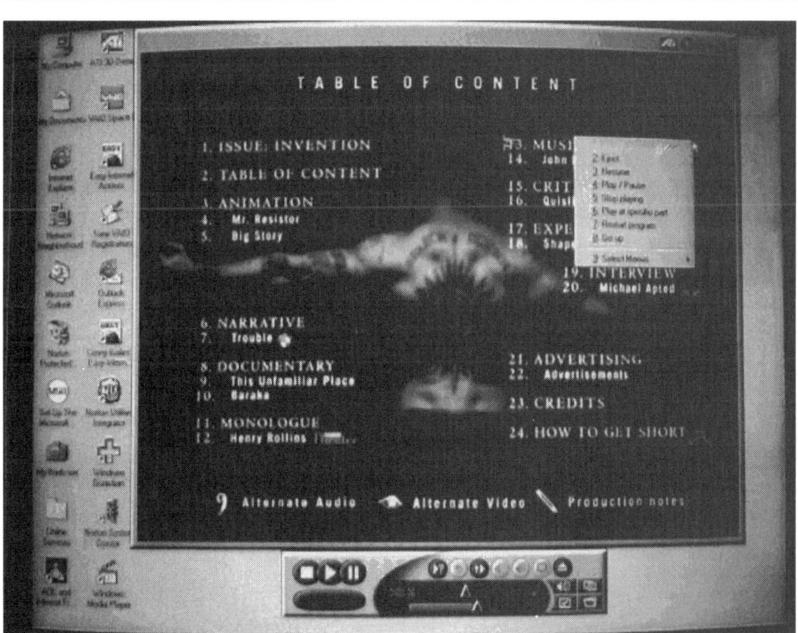

Figure 15-7. *ATI's DVD Player supports MPEG-2 display on computers with ATI Rage video adapters*

QuickTime: .MOV and .PIC Files

QuickTime support is added automatically to Windows 98 when you install a multimedia CD that is programmed to be compatible with both the PC and Macintosh operating environments. However, some of these programs use older versions of Apple's QuickTime extensions, which may cause general protection faults (GPFs) under Windows 98.

If you have access to the Internet, one easy solution to this problem is to download the current Apple QuickTime for Windows package from Apple's World Wide Web site at http:\\www.apple.com. Click the Apple QuickTime subheading and download the file called QTINSTAL.EXE. The QuickTime extensions are also available on CompuServe, but the most recent versions are always posted at the Apple site first.

The self-extracting QTINSTAL.EXE file can be run from a DOS command prompt or through the Run command on the Windows 95 Start menu. When you run the program, it offers to search for and replace previous versions of QuickTime on your hard disk. An Apple QuickTime folder is created that contains a Movie Player and Picture Viewer. The Movie Player (see Figure 15-8) shows QuickTime movies (sound

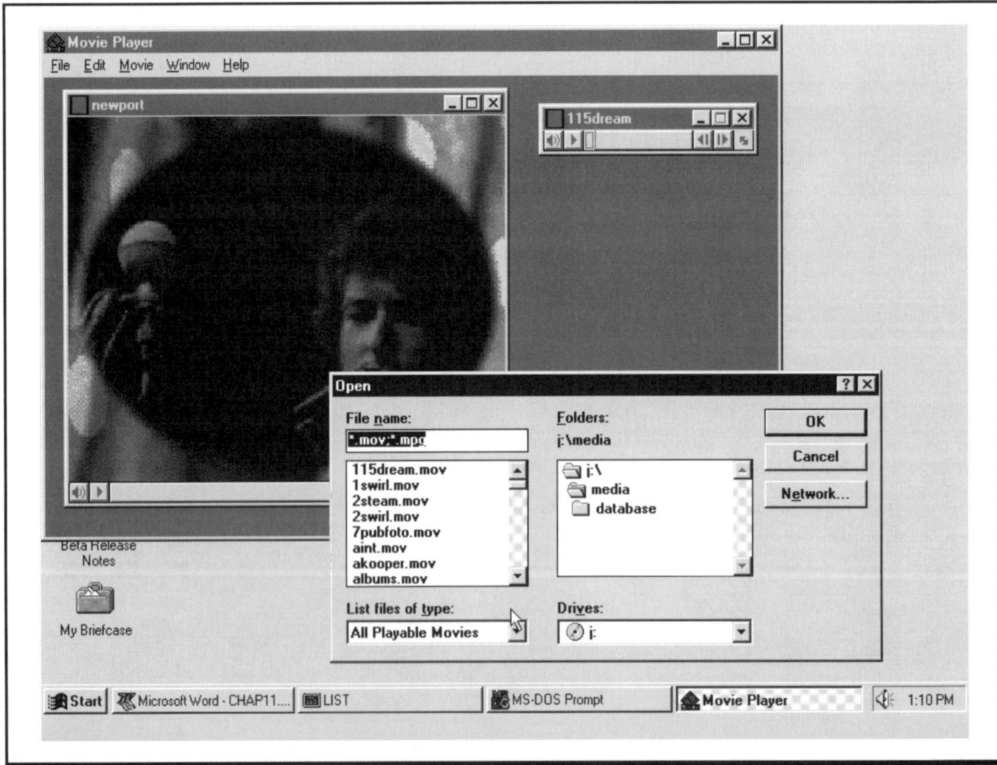

Figure 15-8. *The Apple Movie Player for Windows plays QuickTime video and sound clips*

and video clips bearing the .MOV file extension). The Picture Viewer displays bitmap images in the Macintosh (.PIC) and compressed JPEG (.JPG) formats.

AutoDesk FLI/FLC and Other Formats

To play AutoDesk FLI/FLC animations, you should be aware of a Windows 3.x shareware package called VIDVUE. In addition to running AutoDesk animations, VIDVUE also runs Microsoft .AVI videos, Apple QuickTime movies, and Microsoft .WAV and MIDI files. (For VIDVUE to handle QuickTime files, Apple's QuickTime for Windows support must be installed separately. See the previous section for details.)

A large number of display and editing options are available in this program. It's easy to resize display windows on the fly and adjust various playback options, such as the display rate for video frames and the brightness, contrast, and gamma-color settings for your monitor.

VIDVUE, shown in Figure 15-9, is also a dedicated picture viewer, supporting .EPS, .TIF, AutoCad DCX, Kodak PhotoCD, and several other bitmap formats.

Figure 15-9. *The VIDVUE Multimedia Player supports a number of movie and sound formats (Betty Boop cartoon shown here from the Chestnut Classic series, courtesy CDRP, Inc.)*

WebTV and WaveTop

Windows 98 has great undocumented potential as an electronic babysitter. Add an inexpensive TV tuner card to your computer, and the new WebTV application lets your kids surf and watch VHF, UHF, and cable television broadcasts directly on the Windows desktop. With an ATI video adapter, such as the ATI All-in-Wonder Pro, you can also pipe TV to and from a VCR or dedicated television set. (Microsoft specifically designed Windows 98 to work with the All-in-Wonder Pro, a combination video card, tuner, and capture device, which can also record TV, CD, and DVD output directly to files on your hard disk.) If you use WebTV, you don't need to buy *TV Guide* anymore. WebTV can automatically download new program listings over the Internet from GemStar's Web site. If you have a tuner card but no Internet account, program listings are retrieved over the air directly from local TV stations, as shown in Figure 15-10.

Figure 15-10. *WebTV downloads television listings from the Internet or directly from local TV stations*

Tip

If you have an ATI Technologies All-in-Wonder or All-in-Wonder Pro video adapter, you'll need to install version 5.20 or later of the ATI driver set in order to use both Microsoft's WebTV and the ATI Video Player and capture utility. These drivers can be downloaded from the ATI Web site at http://support.atitech.ca/drivers/drivers.html. For PCI models, you must also make sure that the physical interrupt jumper on the card is enabled. (See http://support.atitech.ca/Win98/index.html.)

WaveTop, another Win98 application, provides a glimpse of the future marriage of TV broadcasting and the Internet. Currently available in major cities nationwide, WaveTop automatically receives World Wide Web content through the carrier signal of your local PBS TV station, organizing it into a cache on your hard disk. (To find out whether WaveTop broadcasts in your area, you can check the availability listing at http://www.wavetop.net/aboutwt/availindex.html.)

The WaveTop browser, shown in Figure 15-11, is a scaled-down version of Internet Explorer. It can display enough free pictures, text, quiz games, and advertising

Figure 15-11. *The WaveTop browser retrieves Internet pages directly from local PBS television stations*

soundbytes to keep children occupied for hours. Currently, WaveTop is organized into 10 browsing categories: NewsTop; StockTop; KidsTop; FunTop; FamilyTop; TechTop; MyTop; GuideTop; Time, Inc.; and ZDNet. Users can choose the content they want to receive from providers including USA Today, CBS Sportsline, People Magazine, Fortune Magazine, ZDNet, Women's Wire, Universal Comics, Warner Bros. Online, Kelloggs Cereal City, Sports Illustrated, and PBS Backstage for Kids.

WebTV and WaveTop Support for Hauppauge Tuner Cards

Although WebTV and WaveTop do not support the Hauppauge series of tuner cards on the Win98 CD, Microsoft is currently beta testing a Windows 98 service Update that will add support for these cards. By the time you read this, driver patches for the inexpensive Hauppauge tuner cards should be available at the Microsoft Web site or at http://www.hauppauge.com.

Video Conferencing

The Internet has already established itself as an inexpensive universal vehicle for long-distance transmission of text and data. During the past two years, clever programmers have also developed software that transforms the Internet into a cheap long-distance telephone system. Cumbersome algorithms that provide scratchy voice simulation have been replaced by software that allows cellular-quality, full-duplex voice conferencing over the Internet. Traditional text-based chat on the Internet imposes limitations on communication that have been overcome by the newest generation of conferencing software.

The arrival of small, inexpensive USB cameras (such as Kodak's DVC 300/320 and Xirlink's C-It) has paved the way for more sophisticated conferencing applications. Video kits that bundle cameras, video capture cards, modems, and conferencing software have appeared at both the high and low ends of the market spectrum. These kits permit the transmission of synchronous live video and audio for conferencing through ISDN lines, modem-to-modem telephone connections, and the Internet.

Microsoft's NetMeeting application, bundled with Windows 98, combines all of the features required for video conferencing: text-based chat, voice and video support, and a whiteboard for sharing drawings. NetMeeting also has built-in features for sharing files and applications.

Whiteboard conferencing applications permit geographically scattered participants to exchange files and share ideas through a common interface that appears on the desktop of each participant. The good news is that this kind of conferencing doesn't require a lot of additional hardware or Internet bandwidth. Packages such as Microsoft's NetMeeting, Mirabilis ICQ, and Xirlink's C-It Conference Center run comfortably through a standard 28.8K Internet PPP connection. The shared conferencing interface usually contains a text-based chat window or audio link plus a drawing screen (the whiteboard). The whiteboard can display common text and graphic elements on each participant's desktop. It typically contains a palette of drawing tools, a text tool, and a clipboard to capture text or images from each participant's local applications. Group members can take turns drawing or modifying simple diagrams, sharing bitmapped images, or entering text commentary. Additionally, the conferencing interface supports binary file transfers among group members as well as application sharing. Whiteboard conferencing, file-transfer capability, and application sharing, when added to text-based chat, greatly enhance the possibilities for productivity in a remote-group conference. Whiteboard/document-sharing applications are also convincing some companies to upgrade their hardware for full-blown video conferencing as they discover the power of collaborative software.

If you purchase and install a USB camera, the ability to transmit video images is automatically added to Microsoft NetMeeting. A successful video conference may also require good audio. Many sound cards currently installed in older PCs operate only in half-duplex mode. When you speak into the microphone with a half-duplex card, reception on speakers or headphones goes dead until you stop talking. To conduct a conversation that permits simultaneous microphone access by multiple users, you need a full-duplex sound card and corresponding drivers. Although most newer Sound Blaster cards manufactured by Creative Labs can run in full-duplex mode, this feature is not supported by the drivers included in Windows 98. Fortunately, you can convert Sound Blaster 16 to support full-duplex communications by downloading a driver fix from the Creative Labs BBS or the company's Web site (http://www.creaf.com).

How Does Internet Conferencing Work?

To originate or participate in an Internet-based conference, you must either log onto an established Internet Conferencing Server or contact a participant directly through an assigned IP address.

Both Microsoft NetMeeting and Mirabilis ICQ use the server-based approach. In the case of NetMeeting, you have a choice between using the public Internet or running an intranet of your own. The server interface for NetMeeting is a separate product that runs under Windows NT 4.0. The client interface for Mirabilis ICQ ("I seek you") can be downloaded for evaluation from the Mirabilis Web site: http://www.mirabilis.com/.

Once you're connected to the appropriate Internet Conference Server, the client interface displays a list of potential meeting participants. You can start your own meeting, inviting people on the list, or ask to join an existing meeting. When you establish a meeting connection, a text-based chat window and a shared window become available.

NetMeeting's options for voice-to-voice and video connections are currently limited to two participants. Additional participants joining a NetMeeting group are limited to text- and whiteboard-based functions, but you can switch the audio and video among all participants through the Tools | Switch Audio and Video option on the pull-down menu. By default, Xirlink C-It uses the Microsoft conferencing servers, but many additional conferencing servers are available on the World Wide Web. (For more information, see "NetMeeting" in Chapter 13.)

Working with USB Peripherals

The Universal Serial Bus (USB) is designed to put an end to the Laurel and Hardy follies of installing and configuring new PC peripherals. It combines the best features of SCSI architecture with an advanced plug-and-play standard. No more worry about bus slots, IRQs, or fishing around the back of the computer to find an empty port. New external devices (keyboards, monitors, digital telephones, scanners, modems, video cameras, and so on), can be daisy-chained to one another or plugged into a multiport hub controller. When a new device is plugged in, your operating system recognizes and installs it on the fly without even rebooting the computer. USB was originally invented by a seven-member consortium that intended it to provide support for computer telephony. The consortium consisted of Compaq, Digital Equipment Corporation, IBM PC Company, Intel, Microsoft, NEC, and Northern Telecom. Since that time, as USB applications have expanded, the bus standard has won support from a wide number of computer manufacturers and peripheral vendors.

USB provides higher bandwidth for up to 127 peripherals on a single bus. Peripherals can be daisy-chained to one another through simple rectangular cable connectors or plugged into a multiport hub controller. Hub controllers can be mounted on a large peripheral, such as a monitor, or plugged into the bus as separate units. All USB devices are managed by a USB host controller mounted on the motherboard or installed through an add-in card on the PCI bus. The host controller is, in turn, managed by USB system software installed in the operating system. Data on the USB bus flows through a bidirectional pipe regulated by the host controller and by subsidiary hub controllers. The USB standard allows for both low- and high-speed data paths (1.5 Mbps or 12 Mbps). An improved version of bus mastering allows portions of the total bus bandwidth to be permanently reserved for specific peripherals (isochronous data transfer).

USB is not designed to offer the high-bandwidth data transfer required by digital cameras and camcorders, high-speed printers, network cards, and mass storage devices. (The IEEE 1394 firewire interface was created for that purpose.) USB's function is to support a large number of external low-bandwidth peripherals: keyboards, pointing devices, joysticks, modems, scanners, telephony devices, light workload printers, and low-bandwidth cameras used in video conferencing.

Bandwidth and Controller Issues

USB has some flaws that are best resolved by purchasing a current computer with a fully Win98-compatible USB controller chip. Unfortunately, some early implementers of USB jumped the gun a bit, selling desktop and notebook systems with USB controllers that were not quite up to specs. Originally, two competing standards were developed for USB host controllers: Compaq sponsored the Open Host Controller Interface (OHCI), and Intel lent its support to the Universal Host Controller Interface (UHCI). Computers with an early implementation of OHCI are the ones most likely to encounter USB bandwidth problems.

USB peripherals are supposed to follow one of several methods for claiming bandwidth on the USB bus. Peripherals not dependent on a constant reserved share of the bus (such as pointing devices and scanners) are supposed to relinquish bandwidth when a higher priority device (such as a printer or scanner) is active. Some devices, such as digital cameras and modems, require a certain guaranteed percentage of the USB bandwidth at all times. These peripherals, called isochronous devices, are programmed to reserve a portion of the USB bus for permanent use whenever they are plugged in.

Poorly designed USB host controllers fail to manage bandwidth traffic properly. Specific devices may be allocated too great or too small a portion of the bus. The result is that a digital camera may present a clipped, low-frame-rate video display, or a scanner may steal bandwidth from a USB file-transfer cable. USB power management creates an additional problem. The host controller is supposed to meet the electronic voltage requirements of all peripherals on the bus, but some USB hubs function erratically, causing power-hungry devices to fail.

If you suspect that your computer's USB implementation is not up to specifications, you can check it with Phoenix Technologies' PlugWorks. PlugWorks, shown in Figure 15-12, is a TSR application that monitors both the bandwidth and power consumption of all active peripherals on a USB bus.

For more information about PlugWorks, see the Phoenix Technologies Web page at http://www.phoenix.com.

Tip *Microsoft includes the USBview diagnostic application in the \TOOLS\RESKIT\DIAGNOSE folder on the Win98 installation CD. Although this utility is less full-featured than Phoenix PlugWorks, you can run it to display basic information about the USB peripherals attached to your computer.*

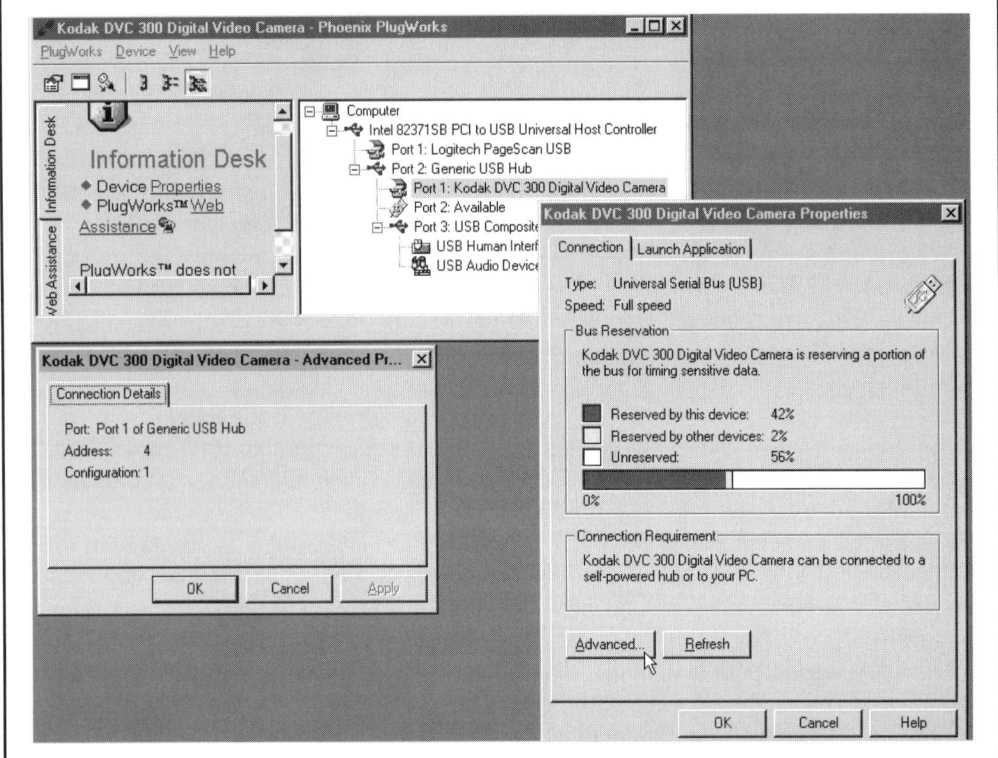

Figure 15-12. *Phoenix PlugWorks is a diagnostic application that can be used to troubleshoot USB configuration problems*

Using Multiple Displays

Multiple display support is a feature that can come in handy when working with multimedia presentations or running a number of applications simultaneously on Windows 98's extended "virtual" desktop (see Figure 15-13).

To use multiple monitors under Windows 98, you must have at least two PCI video adapters (or one AGP and one PCI video adapter) for the primary and secondary display. Almost any PCI or AGP video adapter can be used for the primary display. However, the video adapter used for the secondary display must use a specified, compatible chipset. The general rule is that the adapter must be able to run in GUI mode without using specific VGA resources.

In the *Windows 98 Resource Kit* online book, Microsoft includes a table listing the common video adapters that can be used for secondary displays. To find it, open the *Windows 98 Resource Kit* book (see Chapter 4 for information on installing and accessing this feature from the Win98 CD) and search for an entry titled "Technical Notes on

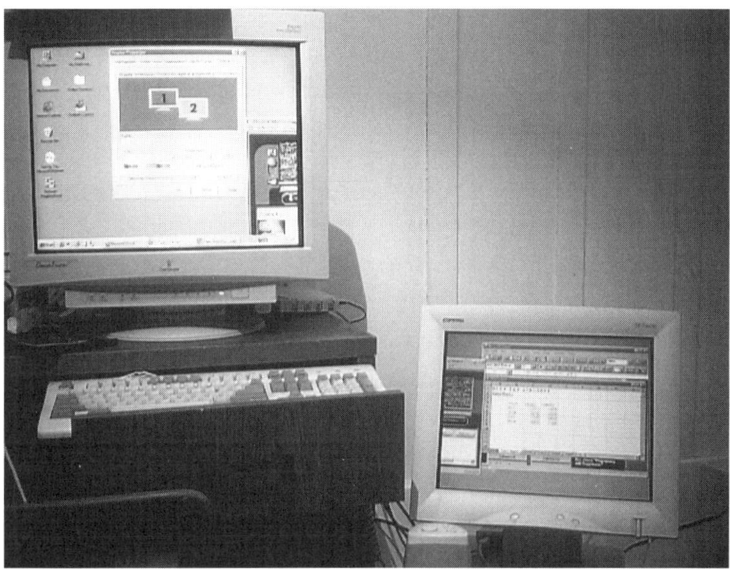

Figure 15-13. *Here, Windows 98 splits the desktop between two monitors: a 21-inch DecaView PA 630 CRT and a Compaq TFT 500 flat panel display*

Multiple Display." Choose the "Configuring Device Settings" topic that appears in the Select Topic window and scroll down to the Technical Notes section.

Tip *If you want to add an inexpensive video adapter to support a second monitor, try visiting a computer swap meet in your local area and searching for a used card such as the S3 Virge or STB Nitro. These video cards are reliable and can usually be purchased for less than $50. Note that other S3 chipsets (such as S3 928, 964, and 968 chipsets) are unsuitable.*

Installing a Second Video Display

Once you've determined that you have a supported PCI video adapter for the secondary monitor, you can install it in your computer as follows:

1. Open the computer and insert the second video card into a spare PCI slot. Attach the cables to the second monitor and power up the machine without closing the case. Inspect both the original and secondary monitors to see which one lights up when you turn on the computer.
2. If the monitor attached to the original video card lights up, you can close the case and let Windows 98 complete the installation of the second display.

3. If the monitor attached to the second video card lights up, your computer is using its video card as the primary adapter. To make this card the secondary adapter, switch the PCI slots used by the two video cards. (Some computers will also let you reverse the priority of two PCI slots through settings in the system CMOS.) After you've reversed the slots used by the two adapters or changed the CMOS settings, start the computer again. Confirm that the card you want for the primary adapter is attached to the monitor that lights up at boot time.
4. Allow the computer to boot to Windows 98. The operating system will now detect the secondary card and install appropriate software drivers. You'll be prompted to restart the computer one more time.

If the secondary adapter has been properly configured, an ASCII text message will appear on the second display when the regular Windows 98 interface appears on the first display. You can now activate the secondary display by opening the Control Panel | Display applet to the Settings tab. Right-click the icon for the secondary monitor and choose Enabled, as shown in Figure 15-14.

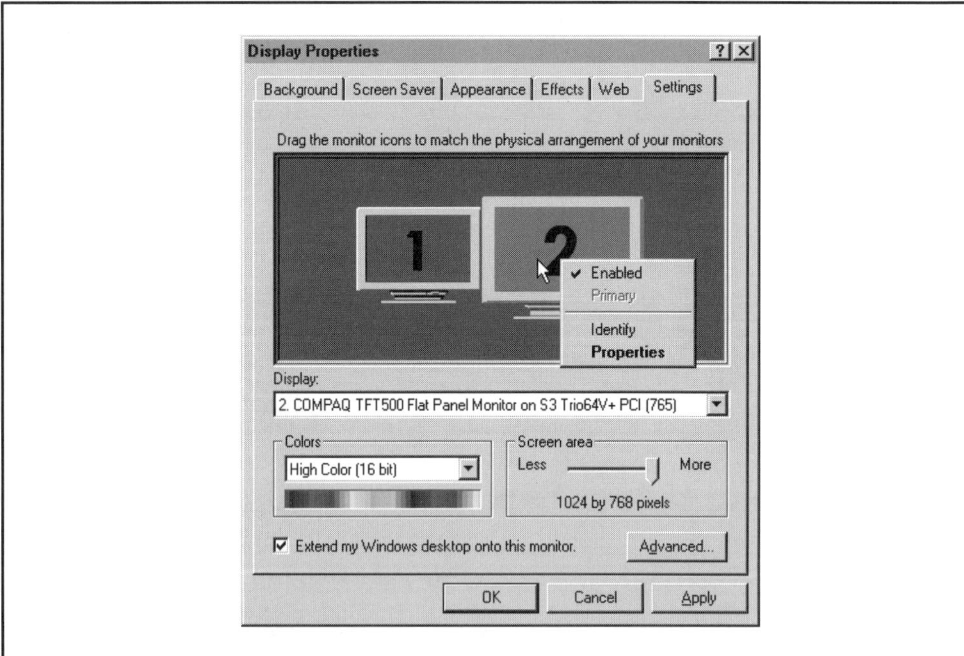

Figure 15-14. *The Settings tab in Display Properties allows you to control the properties of a multi-monitor desktop*

Note that you can reposition the icons for your active displays to determine which direction the mouse will move to jump from one monitor to the other. If monitor 2 is positioned to the right of monitor 1, then the mouse pointer will jump to the second monitor when you move it past the right edge of the screen on the first monitor.

Speech-Recognition Software

Vendors of dictation and speech-recognition software have made remarkable progress during the past year in developing products that permit users to easily dictate spoken text into a word processor or operate a Windows computer through voice-actuated commands. Dragon Systems' package, Naturally Speaking (Preferred Edition), requires a computer with at least 32MB of RAM and a Pentium 166-MHz MMX CPU or better. Optional features, such as the Best Match system, which reduces the need for manual corrections, require a 200-MHz Pentium CPU.

Naturally Speaking allows users to dictate text into a word processor, speaking in a natural, continuous voice without pausing between words. The Natural Word module is specifically designed to record text in Corel Systems WordPerfect 8.0 and Microsoft Word for Office 97. The Natural Text module allows Naturally Speaking to translate voice into text for most other Windows applications. Hands-free mouse and keyboard support allow you to dictate commands that open and close programs and navigate the desktop. Users can construct voice macros to handle more complex multiple-facet tasks, such as logging onto an Internet service provider and collecting e-mail. For more information on Naturally Speaking, see the Dragon Systems Web site at http://www.dragonsys.com.

You can check out Naturally Speaking's principal competitors, IBM Via Voice and Kurzweil Voice Command for Microsoft Word, at http://www.ibm.com and http://www.lhs.com, respectively.

Multimedia Troubleshooting

Reliable multimedia performance can be one of the most problematic areas in personal computing. The multimedia display process is hardware intensive. Individual pieces of software may use independent standards and techniques to display animation and sound. If you're having difficulty playing a particular multimedia file, you may want to check the following basic points:

- Make sure your multimedia peripherals have been installed, the power is turned on, and the appropriate cables have been connected.
- Make sure that microphones, speakers, and line-in devices are plugged into the proper jacks on your sound card.

- If you don't hear any sound, check the volume controls on your hardware and software, including the software mixing controls.
- Use the Add/Remove Programs utility on the Control Panel to make sure that all relevant Windows 98 multimedia components have been installed.
- Open the System utility from the Control Panel and select the Device Manager tab. Expand the entry for sound, video, and game controllers. Examine the settings for your sound card and determine whether Windows 98 reports any device conflicts. If a device conflict is reported, refer to the "Troubleshooting" section of Windows 98's online Help. Open the entry titled "Hardware Conflict." The Win98 Hardware Troubleshooter Wizard may help you resolve the problem.

Troubleshooting WaveTop with ATI All-in-Wonder Cards

If you're having difficulty getting WaveTop to detect a PBS broadcast channel with an ATI All-in-Wonder card, first make sure that you've enabled the interrupt jumper on the card and installed the latest ATI drivers, as described in the tip in the section "WebTV and WaveTop" earlier in this chapter. Due to a weakness in the Microsoft VIDSRVR module that controls WaveTop reception, the PBS channel detection routine sometimes fails before it has a chance to scan the entire VHF bandwidth. If you know that a particular TV station in your viewing area supports WaveTop, you can force the detection routine to use it by running a utility called SETCHAN.EXE, available from the WaveTop Web site at http://www.wavetop.net/wtusers/techsupport.html. You'll also find step-by-step configuration instructions and additional troubleshooting details at this location.

Hot Multimedia Titles

PC-based multimedia technology is about nine years old. During this time, there have been some inspiring and some downright terrible examples of multimedia applications—sometimes on the same disc! There are certain must-have discs of long standing, however. Many of them, unsurprisingly, are from Microsoft. Both Microsoft Bookshelf and Beethoven were early multimedia applications that still have value today. Bookshelf, after several upgrades, is now the must-have reference tool that belongs on every, well, bookshelf.

Encarta 98 (Microsoft)

Previous editions of Encarta have won dozens of industry awards. The newest version of this multimedia encyclopedia contains more articles, animations, and online features than previous versions. It also provides a direct connection to the Microsoft Network so you can access late-breaking information on a variety of subjects (see Figure 15-15).

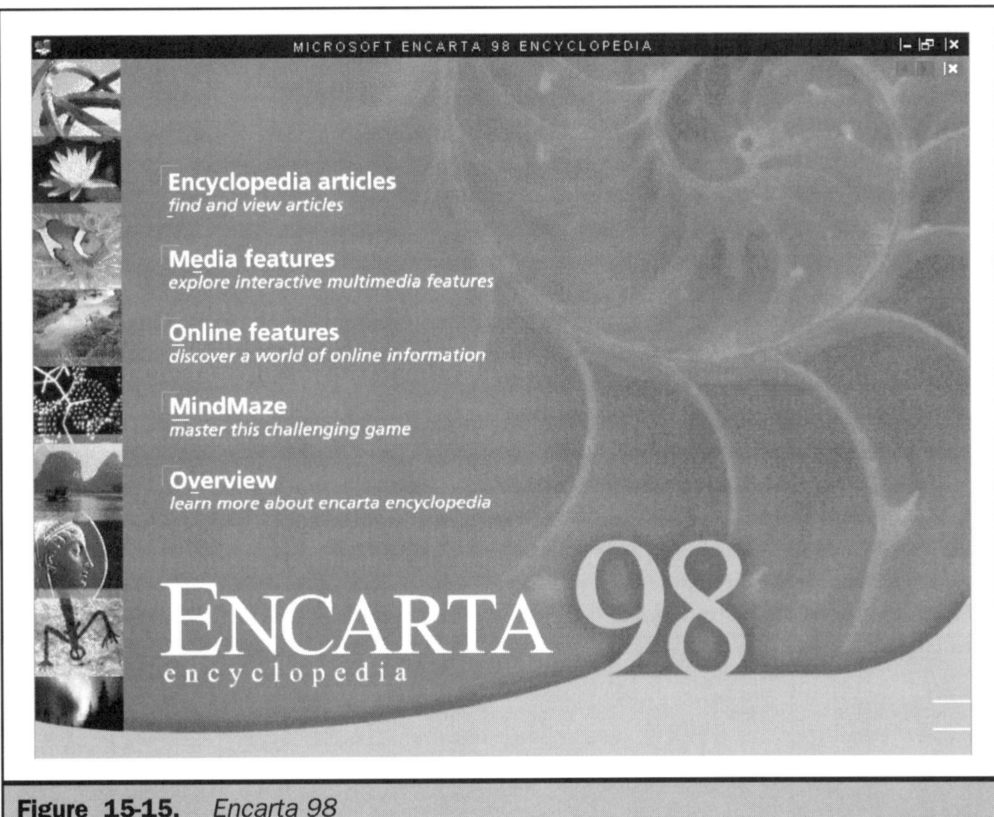

Figure 15-15. *Encarta 98*

Short Cinema Journal (DVD-Express)

The Short Cinema Journal is a novel filmmaker's magazine-on-a-DVD. The short films contained in the sample first issue are definitely a cut above the ubiquitous boilerplate Hollywood flicks that are currently finding their way into the DVD format. Short Cinema Journal number 1 contains Mark Gustafson's award-winning "Mr. Resistor" animation as well as "Big Story," another Animation Festival favorite that bears repeat viewing. "Big Story" includes an alternative camera angle viewing option that lets you toggle the display between full-blown 3-D animation and the artist's storyboard sketches. The first issue also contains 20 other film excerpts and short-subject documentaries, including an excellent one on blues guitarist John Lee Hooker, plus interviews with cinematographers and some experimental films. (Figure 15-7 earlier in this chapter shows the DVD magazine's contents page.) Issue number 2 contains a sequel to "Mr. Resistor" and a short film by Jane Campion.

Short Cinema Journal is distributed monthly by DVDMAGS, a media publishing house. Individual issues are $10 plus postage, or you can subscribe for six months for $68.14, postage included. For details, go to http://www.dvdmags.com, where you can preview the movies over the Internet, as shown in Figure 15-16 (and maybe win a free sample DVD issue).

TechNet CD (Microsoft)

One of the most useful discs manufactured by Microsoft has nothing to do with multimedia and contains no sound or video. TechNet, a monthly compendium of technical documents, questions and answers, and miscellaneous information, is designed as a technical support tool for anyone who needs answers to specific

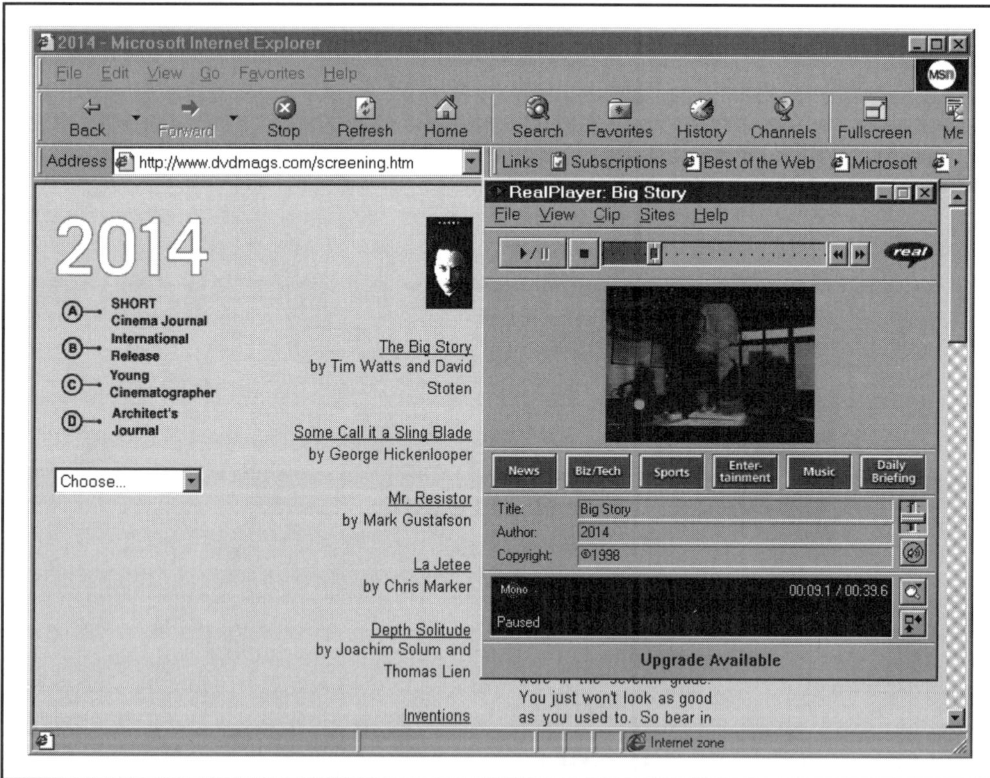

Figure 15-16. *You can sample the contents of the Short Cinema Journal at the DVDMAGS Web site*

questions about Microsoft products. In fact, it will fascinate anyone who takes any flavor of Windows really seriously by providing a searchable database of the most arcane technical information.

TechNet also represents a greater initial investment than your average multimedia disc. A subscription service, TechNet costs about $300 a year to keep the discs coming. The temptation, as with any "overpriced" CD-ROM subscription service, is to make a group purchase—but alternating months and sharing discs among friends will soon fall by the wayside when you see how useful these discs can be. TechNet is something that you'll want to use every month, and you'll want to keep back issues on hand for reference.

Haight Ashbury in the Sixties (Rockument)

Another disc that deserves a special mention is Haight-Ashbury in the Sixties (Rockument). Here's a sample to help you remember that groovy scene:

You can put this disc on autoplay and get eight hours of sound, video, and light shows from one of the century's most potent cultural periods, or you can "grow your own" and select the clips, text (the complete San Francisco *Oracle*), and music to provide a kinetic portrait of the period. This disk was assembled by DTP maven Tony Bove and *Oracle* editor Allen Cohen. Among other highlights, you'll find Janis Joplin and Big Brother and the Holding Company singing "I Know You Rider," and the famous Grateful Dead concert from the back of a pickup truck on Haight Street.

Songs from The Gypsy (Boiled in Lead/ Steven Brust—Omnium Recordings)

From the music of the '60s, you can go straight to the '90s if you're interested in reading a great story of magic and music with soundtrack by America's most famous underground Celtic punk rock 'n roll band, as headlined here:

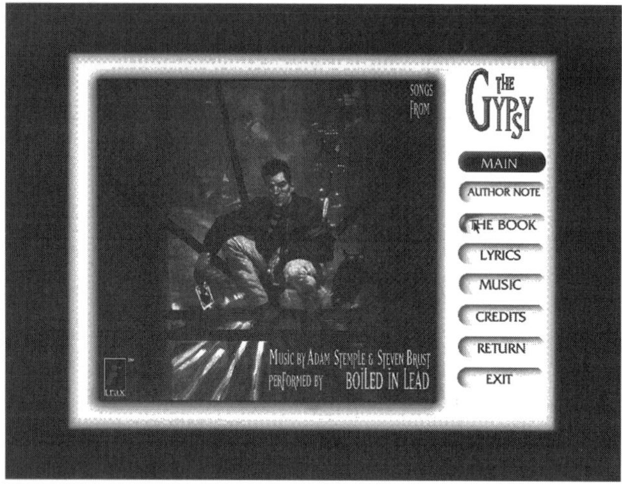

This CD includes the complete text of The Gypsy, a psychological fantasy adventure by Steven Brust and Megan Lindholm. It also includes the "Songs from The Gypsy" album, with words by Steven Brust and music by Boiled in Lead. The album can be played as an ordinary music CD, or you can browse through the story and click the lyrics to play the songs.

Highway 61 Interactive (Graphix Zone)

For the majority of the public, watching Bob Dylan has often been like one of his most famous lyrics, here taken out of context: "There's something going on here, but you don't know what it is." The Dylan CD-ROM, called "Highway 61 Interactive," provides a reasonable explanation. Its potpourri of collected sounds, images, and clips show what Dylan has done and, ultimately, why you should care. The Highway 61 Revisited Collage, shown here, allows you to explore Bob Dylan's career by clicking strategically placed objects.

This is the antithesis of the CD-ROM products that feel it is their function to immediately startle your senses as they stretch technological limits. The technology in this CD-ROM is certainly up to snuff, but it is the content that makes it outstanding. In this respect, Highway 61 Interactive strikes a balance between the interests of a fan and a Dylan newbie. Someone who knows there's something going on but doesn't know what it is can take digestible bites of the legend, and enthusiasts can find a variety of minutiae and collectibles.

Stephen Hawking's "A Brief History of Time" (Blasterware)

Stephen Hawking's book *A Brief History of Time* managed to explain complicated scientific concepts to ordinary people. The CD-ROM goes a few steps farther: The CD makes you feel as if you were attending a lecture or presentation. Hawking's computer-generated voice is either spooky or compelling, depending on your point of view. If you like, you can also skip from one topic to another, exploring areas of specific interest (simulating the act of asking questions at the lecture). Trained physicists might look askance at some of the simplified explanations this CD provides, but the disc offers a pleasant means for the rest of us to gain some basic knowledge of the nature of time and the universe. Hawking has proven that such concepts can be explained, and the disc version serves to further democratize this knowledge.

A Hard Day's Night (Voyager)

This frame-by-frame dissection of the first Beatles movie offers some cool tricks. You can jump from scene to scene or follow along with the script (this is especially helpful, as some of us Yanks still find the accents incomprehensible). Since this film is a documentary (of sorts), it doesn't really follow a linear plot line and so lends itself well to this format; you can jump in at any point and not really lose anything. The video window is too small, but in fact this complements the unpolished, spontaneous character of the film itself.

The Flexibility of Multimedia

With a sound card and a CD-ROM or DVD drive, you can expand the horizons of your PC. It can be one byte at a time: For instance, with an older CD-ROM and no sound card at all, you can enjoy all of the benefits of the aforementioned TechNet CD. If you translate "multi" to mean "more than one," the concept can shrink to fit your system.

At the same time, remember that multimedia will suck up as much power as you can throw at it. The clips on the Short Cinema Journal DVD will look better as you add hardware power to your system. With a 266 MHz Pentium II and 8MB of video RAM, everything will look better. It may remind you of an old dialog, about money:

"How much do you need?"

"Well, how much do you *have*?"

Chapter 16

Tips, Tricks, and Troubleshooting

Chapter Highlights

Productivity tips and tricks:

- Add a Subscriptions or My Documents button to Internet Explorer
- Create bookmarks for Word and Excel documents
- Quickly delete Win98 files
- Quickly restart Windows 98
- Use long filenames with DOS and Windows 3.x programs
- Open Explorer views from DOS

Windows registry tips and tricks:

- Guard against accidental merge of REG files
- Safely compact the Windows registry
- Customize the position of Windows wallpaper
- Quickly back up any folder

Troubleshooting tips and tricks:

- Resolve modem and DUN connection problems
- Connect 56K modems at their highest bandwidth
- Resolve Windows 98 shutdown problems
- Recover from login and screensaver password lockout

This chapter provides a number of useful tips, tricks, and troubleshooting strategies that will help you make the most of Windows 98.

This chapter is divided into three sections. In the Productivity section you'll find better ways to use programs and networking features, cut and paste data, create desktop shortcuts, and maximize productivity with DOS applications. The Windows Registry section contains useful techniques and scripts for customizing the desktop and adding new interface features through RegEdit. In the Troubleshooting section you'll find tips for resolving modem, Internet connection, printer, and Windows shutdown problems and for restoring improperly configured hardware devices.

Productivity Tips and Tricks

This section contains tips for exploiting program features, creating and using desktop shortcuts, working with DOS applications, and increasing network productivity. Tips and tricks are divided into four categories: applications, desktop, DOS, and dedicated networks and Dial-Up Networking.

Applications

With a little ingenuity you can modify programs included in the Windows 98 package and popular third-party software to save time and keystrokes.

Add a Subscriptions or My Documents Link to the Internet Explorer Toolbar

By default the Internet Explorer toolbar has icon buttons for Search, Favorites, History, and Channels, but no button to open a Manage Subscriptions or My Documents window. You can correct this deficiency by dragging shortcuts to these folders onto the Internet Explorer 4 Links toolbar.

Follow these steps to add a Manage Subscriptions link:

1. Open Windows Explorer, select the \WINDOWS\SUBSCRIPTIONS folder, and drag a shortcut to it onto the desktop. You can press F2 to rename the shortcut and eliminate the words "Shortcut to" in the title.
2. Open Internet Explorer and drag the desktop shortcut you've just created onto the Links toolbar.

Once the Subscription shortcut appears on the IE Links toolbar, you can delete the copy you created on the Windows desktop. This technique can also be used to add a My Documents shortcut to the Links toolbar.

Open Netscape News or Netscape Mail Directly (Navigator 3.x or Communicator 4.x)

If you use Netscape Navigator as a multipurpose Internet tool, you may be interested in the following tip, which shows you how to create a desktop shortcut that will directly open Netscape Mail or Netscape News. This trick works with both the 3.x and 4.x versions of Netscape.

Here's how to create a direct shortcut to Netscape News:

1. Right-click the desktop and select New | Shortcut from the pop-up menu.

2. Click the Browse button for the Create Shortcut file list and locate the path to your Netscape Web browser: for example, C:\PROGRAM FILES\NETSCAPE\NAVIGATOR\PROGRAM\.
3. Select NETSCAPE.EXE as the program to run and append the string **NEWS://*NEWSSERVER*** to the shortcut's command line, replacing *NEWSSERVER* with the name of your own news server after the quotation marks that enclose the program path to Netscape. For example, the command line might look like this:

   "C:\PROGRAM FILES\NETSCAPE\NAVIGATOR\PROGRAM\NETSCAPE.EXE" NEWS://NEWS.COMPUSERVE.COM

4. Click Next, assign a name for your shortcut, and click the Finish button to place the shortcut on the desktop.

Follow the same procedure to create a desktop shortcut that directly opens Netscape Mail, except in step 3 select NETSCAPE.EXE as the program to run and append the string **POP3://*MAILSERVER*** to the shortcut's command line, replacing *MAILSERVER* with the name of your own mail server after the quotation marks that close the program path to Netscape. For example, the command line might look like this:

"C:\PROGRAM FILES\NETSCAPE\NAVIGATOR\PROGRAM\NETSCAPE.EXE" POP3://MAIL.COMPUSERVE.COM.

From now on, double-clicking the Netscape News shortcut will connect you to your news server and open the Netscape Newsreader. Double-clicking the Netscape Mail shortcut will connect you to your mail server and open the Netscape Mail window.

Quickly Copy and Paste with a Word Processor or E-mail Client

Have you ever wanted to copy and paste a lot of text quickly in a word processor document or e-mail message?

In Microsoft Word, WordPad, and many e-mail clients (including Microsoft Outlook, Outlook Express, Windows Messaging, Netscape Mail, and Eudora), you can select all the text from the current cursor position to the end of the document by pressing CTRL-SHIFT-END. This moves the cursor to the bottom of the document and selects all text and attachments from the original cursor position. You can then copy and paste the selection into another e-mail message or word processor document. To select everything from the current cursor position to the top of the message, press CTRL-SHIFT-HOME.

Note in some e-mail packages, this trick works only in message composition windows, not in message receipt windows.

Create Bookmarks for Microsoft Word and Excel Documents

Microsoft Word and Excel have no built-in bookmarking feature. If they did, you would be able to immediately open a long document or spreadsheet to a specific page, paragraph, or worksheet cell. However, the OLE features of these applications combined with the Windows 98 desktop will let you improvise.

To create a bookmark to a specific place in a Microsoft Word document (Office 95 and above), highlight a word or sentence on the page you want to bookmark. Right-click and drag the selection to the desktop and then choose Create Document Shortcut Here from the pop-up menu. Resave the document in Word.

To open the document automatically to the bookmarked location, double-click the desktop shortcut you've created (or single-click, if you've selected Web style desktop options to open files).

To create a bookmark to a specific cell in an Excel spreadsheet, select the cell, right-click, and drag the cell to the desktop.

Save, Cut, and Paste Information in Microsoft Office and WordPad Through Desktop Scraps

Microsoft Word and Excel (and Win98's WordPad) have a useful feature that allows you to select any part of a document and drag it to the desktop to create a desktop scrap. (See "WordPad" in Chapter 5 for details.) In the illustration below, a section of text was highlighted in Microsoft Word before right-clicking the mouse and dragging the selection to the desktop. When the mouse button is released, the pop-up menu appears, as shown. Select "Create Scrap Here" to complete the operation.

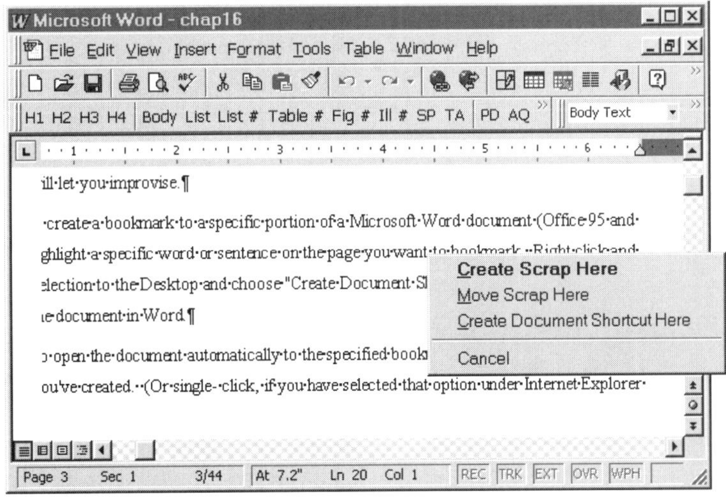

Once a selection has been saved on the desktop as a scrap, you can double-click it to open the selection in Microsoft Word or WordPad. You can also paste the scrap into an open document. For instance, you might select an address list in a Word document and drag it to the desktop to create a quick-access address list or drag it into another open document window.

An even better use for desktop scraps is to transfer information between WordPad, Microsoft Word, Excel, and PowerPoint. For instance:

- You can drag a sentence scrap to the desktop from Word and then drop it into an Excel spreadsheet to create a text cell.
- You can create an Excel scrap on the desktop from a selection of spreadsheet cells and then drop it into a Word document to transfer the spreadsheet data to a report. You can also drag the scrap into a PowerPoint slide to create a new spreadsheet element.
- You can create desktop scraps out of elements in a PowerPoint slide and then drop them into open Word or Excel documents.
- You can drag spreadsheet data directly from Excel to Microsoft Access (instead of using the Access 95 File | Get External Data command). With the Tables tab selected in an Access database, switch to Excel, select a series of cells, position the cursor on the edge of the cells, and drag the Excel data into the Access Tables list.

Insert ASCII Text into Microsoft Word

If you work in Microsoft Word and want to incorporate ASCII text into a current document, don't use Word's Insert | File option. If you use that approach, the text will come into the document as a collection of single-line paragraphs. You can turn these into real paragraphs with Word's Replace feature (searching for ^p and replacing each instance with a single space), but there's a better way. Simply open the text file you want to import as a new Word document. Word is much more likely to format the file to your liking, with multiple-line paragraphs that you can easily copy and paste into the main document.

If you open an ASCII file in Word, you can also reformat it in a number of ways by saving it in a different format and reloading it. The Save As Text, MS-DOS Text, Text With Layout, MS-DOS Text With Layout, and similar options all produce slightly different variations.

Gain Full Management of ZIP and Other Archive Formats with a Freeware Archive Manager

Are you looking for a Windows archive manager? If you're still compressing and unpacking file archives with a DOS utility, you may eventually run into trouble with files that have long filenames of more than 32 characters. Installation programs may fail, and other problems may arise simply because archives handled by DOS utilities don't retain the proper names for bundled files.

If you're on a low budget or just looking for a bargain, you'll want to check out PowerZip, a full-featured freeware Win95/Win98 archive manager that includes the bells and whistles of many commercial products. PowerZip works directly with the

Windows shell, allowing you to manage, pack, unpack, and convert ZIP archives to .EXE format and drag and drop files into and out of archives. It also includes support for a variety of archive formats besides ZIP through external programs.

You can find this freeware gem at http://www.powerzip.lco.net/.

Desktop

The Windows desktop can be as flexible as you want to make it. This section describes some tips and tricks that you can try in addition to the techniques presented in Chapter 4.

Quickly Close a Series of Windows in My Computer or Network Neighborhood

If you've opened a series of desktop windows in My Computer or Network Neighborhood, you can close them all quickly by holding down the SHIFT key while clicking the Close box in the upper-right corner of the screen.

Quickly Delete Win98 Files

You can quickly delete files from folders or the Win98 desktop with a single, continuous right-click motion. This is accomplished by placing a shortcut to the Recycle Bin in the Windows 98 SendTo folder.

Open the SendTo folder by entering **SENDTO** in the Run box on the Start menu. Then right-click the Recycle Bin on the desktop and drag it into the SendTo folder (select the Create Shortcut Here option on the pop-up menu).

From now on, to delete a file or group of files, just right-click the selected object(s), move the mouse pointer to the Send To option on the pop-up context menu, and click the Recycle Bin, as shown here. This removes the files with one quick, continuous motion.

Create Your Own Start Menu Editor

Normally, opening the Start Menu folder to add or remove programs and groups takes several keystrokes no matter what method you use. Here's how to create a more convenient Start Menu Editor shortcut:

1. Create a new program shortcut on the desktop. (Right-click a blank part of the desktop and select New | Shortcut from the pop-up menu.)
2. Enter the following in the command-line field for the shortcut:

   ***D:\WINDOWS*\EXPLORER.EXE /E, /ROOT, C:\WINDOWS\START MENU**

   where *D:\WINDOWS* is your Windows 98 directory.
3. Name the shortcut **Edit Start Menu** (or enter another name if you prefer).

A new icon appears on your desktop. From now on, you can double-click this icon to open the Start Menu folder and add or remove programs.

Quickly Restart the Win98 Desktop

Normally it takes four keystrokes to shut down and restart the Windows 98 desktop. To avoid a cold reboot, you need to press the SHIFT key when you select Restart The Computer from the Start | Shut Down menu.

Here's how to create a shortcut on the desktop that will restart Windows with a quick double-click of the mouse:

1. Open Notepad and create a batch file with a single command: **@exit.**
2. Save this file in your \WINDOWS directory with a .BAT extension (for example, **REBOOT.BAT**).
3. Right-click the Win98 desktop and select New | Shortcut from the pop-up menu. Enter **REBOOT.BAT** in the command-line field on the next screen. Click Next, enter a name for the shortcut, choose an icon on the next screen, and click the Finish button.
4. Right-click the icon shortcut after it appears on the desktop and select Properties. Go to the Program tab on the Properties screen.
5. On the Program tab, place a check mark in the Close On Exit box. Then click the Advanced button, place a check mark in the MS-DOS Mode box, and select Use Current MS-DOS Configuration. Click OK twice to exit the Properties screens for this shortcut.

From now on, you can force Windows 98 to shut down and restart by double-clicking the REBOOT desktop shortcut you've just created.

Run TASKMAN.EXE to Access Additional Program Management Options

If you remember the Task Manager from Windows 3.1 and wonder where it disappeared to in Windows 98, you'll be happy to know that it's still there. If you display the Run box on the Start menu and enter **TASKMAN**, you'll see the Windows 98 version of this useful program switcher. Taskman allows you to jump to any open application by selecting it from the icon-based list. The Taskman Windows menu contains a number of useful options: Switch To, End Task, Cascade, Tile Horizontally and Vertically, Arrange, and Minimize. The Options menu allows the Taskman window to float always on top and allows you to set display options for the program list.

Once Taskman is open, you can minimize it to the regular Windows 98 taskbar to retain quick access to its Switch To, End Task, and Minimize options. You can also create a desktop shortcut to the Task Manager: Right-click the desktop, select New | Shortcut, enter **TASKMAN.EXE** in the command-line field, and enter a name for the shortcut.

Use Long Filenames with DOS and Windows 3.1 Applications

Like Windows 95, Windows 98 frees you from the tyranny of 8.3 DOS filenames. However, if you open a file in a DOS or Windows 3.x program, its long filename may be lost when you save it.

Here are a few workarounds for assigning long filenames to documents that you edit in older applications that are unaware of Windows 98:

- You can load any existing document with a long filename into a DOS or Windows 3.x application (such as WordPerfect 5.1 or Microsoft Word 6). Make changes and keep saving the document with the Save option so that you don't change the document's name. Windows 98 long filename information will be preserved so long as you don't use the Save As option (which prompts you to enter a new filename).
- You can create a blank document with a long filename on the desktop (right-click the desktop, choose New, and select a document template from the pop-up list). Or at the DOS prompt create the document: issue the command **copy con "This long document.txt"**. Press ENTER, type in a few dummy characters, and then press F6 (or CTRL-Z) to create the document before filling it with content. Once you've created it, you can open the document in several ways: (1) from within a DOS or Windows 3.1 program, (2) by dragging the document icon into your application, or (3) by double-clicking it (if the file extension has been associated with a program). Edit the document and make any changes you like. The long filename will be preserved so long as you use your program's Save option rather than Save As.

Back Up File Directories to Multiple Floppy Disks

The Copy command built into My Computer and Windows Explorer has an enhancement that isn't present under DOS. When the first disk in your A drive is full, you'll be prompted automatically to insert a new disk. You can create a backup of a group of files without having to use a third-party disk-spanning program. (This trick works only when no individual file exceeds the storage limit of a single floppy disk, which is usually 1.44MB.)

1. Select a folder or group of files to copy. (To select a group of files, open My Computer or Windows Explorer, point to the first file in the group, and then hold down the SHIFT key and point to the last file in the group.)
2. Choose Edit | Copy from the pull-down menu.
3. Select the floppy drive (A or B) and then select Edit | Paste from the pull-down menu.

When there's no room to copy the next complete file to the floppy disk, Windows 98 prompts you to insert another disk in the drive.

What if you want to back up a file or files that are individually larger than 1.44MB? In that case, you'll need to use the Microsoft Backup application or a third-party archiving utility that allows you to split files.

Make Windows 98 Recognize Your SCSI Drives After the Desktop Is Loaded

This tip may come in handy if you have Iomega JAZ or other portable SCSI drives that you frequently transfer from one computer to another. Normally, a SCSI drive must be powered up and connected to the computer at boot time. If you plug it in later, no icon for it will appear in My Computer. Here's a clever trick that will make Windows 98 recognize a SCSI drive after the boot process has been completed:

1. Plug your drive into the SCSI port and then turn on its power.
2. Open Device Manager (choose Start | Settings | Control Panel | System | Device Manager). Select the SCSI Device listing and then click the Refresh button at the bottom of the Device Manager screen.

This causes your SCSI card to reinitialize and refresh the My Computer display (which also recognizes your portable drive).

DOS

The connection between the Windows 98 interface and the DOS command prompt is deeper and more flexible than it might appear at first glance. Try the following tips and tricks in addition to the techniques described in the section "Running DOS Applications Under Windows 98" in Chapter 4.

Customize the DOS DIR Command

When you run the plain-vanilla DIR command from a Windows 98 DOS prompt, you generally see a list of directories and files in capital letters. The files are displayed in the order in which they were written to the hard disk.

The DIR command has many additional display and file sort options that can be invoked by adding command-line switches. (For a complete list of all DIR command-line options, enter **DIR/?** at the C prompt.) If you prefer an alphabetical file list or one of the other sort options, you can make this the default behavior for the DIR command instead of appending command-line switches.

To customize the DIR command, enter a **SET DIRCMD=** statement in your AUTOEXEC.BAT file. The parameters you enter on this line will automatically be appended whenever you enter the DIR command under Windows 98.

For example, to make DIR display the file list one screen at a time in alphabetical order, enter **SET DIRCMD= /P /O:N** in the AUTOEXEC.BAT file. To make DIR display all subdirectories one screen at a time in wide format, enter **SET DIRCMD= /S /W /P** in the AUTOEXEC.BAT file.

Close "Dead" DOS Windows

If you're annoyed by "dead" windows that remain on the screen after you close a DOS application, you can get rid of them. Right-click the shortcut icon for the DOS program, select Properties from the pop-up menu, and click the Program tab. Place a check mark in the Close On Exit box near the bottom of the window.

You can also configure DOS programs to terminate when you click the close control in the upper-left corner of their display windows. (Normally if you try this, you'll see the message "Windows cannot shut down this program automatically.") Right-click the shortcut icon, select Properties and click the Misc tab, then remove the check mark next to Warn If Still Active.

Open an Explorer View of Any Folder from DOS

In the "Windows Registry Tips and Tricks" section of this chapter, you'll find out how to modify the Windows registry to open a DOS command prompt quickly in any directory from an Explorer view of the folder.

To reverse this trick, you can easily open a My Computer window on the desktop to any folder from the DOS command prompt.

- To open a folder from the DOS command line, enter **START** ***D:\Path***.
- To open the current folder from the DOS command line, enter **START .** (period).
- To open the parent directory from the current folder, enter **START . .** (two periods) on the DOS command line.
- To open the root directory of the current drive, enter **START ** on the DOS command line.

Dedicated Networks and Dial-Up Networking

Here are some tips for working with dedicated networks and Dial-Up Networking. For additional techniques, see Chapters 11, 12, and 14.

Turn Off the Windows 98 Login and Password Prompt

If your default Windows Logon is Client for Microsoft Networks, you'll be prompted to log on and enter a password each time you start Windows 98. If you don't log onto a Windows NT or Novell Netware server, you can bypass the Microsoft Networking login box and go directly to the Windows 98 desktop. Here's how:

1. Right-click Network Neighborhood and select Properties from the pop-up menu.
2. Select Windows Logon in the Primary Network Logon box and click OK. You'll be prompted to restart your computer. Click No.
3. Open the Passwords applet located in the Control Panel (choose Start | Settings | Control Panel | Passwords). Click Change Windows Password on the Change Passwords tab and enter a blank password.

The next time you start Windows 98, your computer will bypass the logon box and go directly to the desktop. This will not affect your ability to browse and connect to Microsoft Networking resources in Network Neighborhood.

The Tweak UI applet on the Win98 Control Panel can also configure the operating system to enter your username and password at startup for automatic logon to the Client for Microsoft Networks.

Increase FTP Performance

To increase the speed of file downloads from FTP sites, try using a dedicated FTP utility such as WS_FTP or CuteFTP instead of a Web browser such as Microsoft's Internet Explorer or Netscape Navigator. These shareware programs can be downloaded from http://www.tucows.com. In addition to being more flexible for multiple downloads, a dedicated FTP utility can improve transfer speed by 5 to 15 percent.

If you're interested in timing the efficiency of your Internet connection, download a test file and check your browser or FTP utility to see if it reports data throughput statistics. (Both Netscape Navigator and WSFTP will do this.) Comspeed (available at http://ourworld.compuserve.com/homepages/cordes/homepag0.htm) is a shareware utility that provides detailed information about the current, average, and cumulative data transfer rates of an Internet connection.

Turn On High-Speed Fax Settings

If you have a modem with 14.4 Kbps fax capability and get fax connections of only 9,600 bps, the high-speed transmission feature is probably turned off. To enable it, right-click Inbox, select Properties, and choose Microsoft Fax on the Services tab. Click Properties again, go to the Modem tab, select your fax/modem, open its Properties window, and click the Advanced button. Remove the check mark next to Disable High-Speed Transmissions and click OK four times to back out of the settings windows.

Windows Registry Tips and Tricks

This section focuses on RegEdit as a tool for customizing the display and tweaking the performance of Windows 98. The following tips and tricks are registry hacks that allow you to take control of Windows 98 and shape some of its performance options to your liking. You'll need to know a few basic things about working with the RegEdit application to implement them.

You can locate any key in the registry through the Edit | Find pull-down menu option. Enter a key name, value name, or data string and click Find Next to locate the specified item. If you know you are looking for a key rather than a value name or data object, you can deselect inappropriate items in the Look At dialog box to speed up the search.

You can create new keys and values and their data content through the Edit | New option. The values in a key can be any of three types: string value, binary value, or DWORD value.

You can change the content of a value in any existing key by double-clicking the value in the right RegEdit pane or selecting the value and choosing Edit | Modify from the pull-down menu. This will open an Edit window that allows you to enter modified content for the value.

Detailed RegEdit instructions are provided for the first few tips in this section to help you get the hang of the procedure.

Guard Against Accidental Merging of .REG Files

When you export a registry key to disk or create a special RegEdit script, double-clicking the file will automatically add changes to the Windows registry, which can be difficult to undo. For safety, you can change the default action that Windows 98 associates with files that have the .REG file extension. Instead of letting Windows 98 automatically merge those files into the registry when they are opened, you can set the default action to display their contents in a text editor.

1. Open My Computer and select View | Folder Options | File Types.
2. Select Registration Entries in the Registered File Type list and click the Edit button. You'll see three actions in the Actions field at the bottom of the Edit File Type window. Choose the Edit action and click the Set Default button.

From now on, double-clicking a .REG file that you've saved will open the file in Notepad instead of directly adding it to the registry. To merge a .REG file into the registry, you can right-click it and select Merge from the pop-up menu.

Customize the Registered Name and Organization for Your Copy of Windows 98

During Windows 98 installation, you're prompted to enter a user name and organization. This information is displayed whenever you open System Properties (right-click My Computer and select Properties).

You can use RegEdit to change this information if it was originally entered incorrectly:

1. Open RegEdit (choose Start | Run and enter **REGEDIT** in the Run box).
2. Scroll down to and open the following key (or press CTRL-F, type the key name in the Find box, and click Find Next):

   HKEY_LOCAL_MACHINE\Software\Microsoft\Windows\CurrentVersion\

3. Select the Registered Owner value in the right RegEdit pane. Double-click it to change the information it contains in the Edit String window. You can also double-click the Registered Organization entry to change that information.

Safely Compact the Windows 98 Registry to Improve Performance and Save Disk Space

A number of third-party applications are available that offer to compact the Windows 98 registry—with varying degrees of success and safety. Here is a technique that can reduce the size of the registry by up to 10 percent:

1. Go to a true DOS prompt, not a DOS window, by choosing Start | Shut Down | Restart in MS-DOS Mode or by rebooting the computer, pressing CTRL at boot time, and selecting Command Prompt from the Windows 98 Startup menu.
2. Enter **SMARTDRV** at the C prompt to load the DOS disk cache. You're about to run RegEdit to export the Windows 98 registry to an ASCII file. With a large registry, this process can be time-consuming, but the presence of the SMARTDRV cache will speed things up.
3. Run RegEdit from the C prompt with parameters entered as follows: **REGEDIT /E MYREG.REG**.
4. For safety's sake, make a backup of the existing binary Win98 registry with the ScanReg utility. (See "Maintaining the Windows Registry" in Chapter 8 for details.) You can delete this backup as soon as the registry has been successfully re-created.
5. After the MYREG.REG export file has been successfully created, run RegEdit once more from the C prompt by entering **REGEDIT /C MYREG.REG**.

This will re-create the Windows 98 registry in the \WINDOWS directory. The new version will be up to 10 percent more compact than the original.

Now reboot the computer and confirm that it properly boots to Windows 98. After you've verified that the system operates properly, you can delete the backup registry file that you created.

Change the Default Location for Windows 98 System Cabinet Files

Some users install Windows 98 from a CD and later copy the installation files to a hard disk directory. If you've done this, you should find this tip useful.

After installation, whenever you want to modify settings or add or remove programs, Windows 98 will always prompt you to insert a disk at the original location of your installation files. If you've changed that location, you can modify the registry so you won't have to retype a new path to the cabinet (.CAB) files every time you make a system change.

1. Open RegEdit. Scroll down to or find the following key:

   HKEY_LOCAL_MACHINE\SOFTWARE\Microsoft\Windows\
   CurrentVersion\Setup

2. Double-click the SourcePath value in the right RegEdit pane and enter the correct path to the location where your Win98 installation files are located. For example, you might change the original CD file location D:\WIN98\ to the hard disk location **C:\WIN98**, or you might change the hard disk location C:\WINDOWS\OPTIONS\CABS to the CD file location **D:\WIN98**.

Edit MS-DOS Batch File Association Properties

Every registered Windows 98 file type has a user option that specifies the default action to be taken when you double-click files with that extension. You can create, edit, or switch actions associated with registered file types by choosing View | Options | File Types from a My Computer or Windows Explorer window. Scroll through the file types and select the one you want and then click the Edit button.

Suppose you want to switch the default double-click action for MS-DOS batch files from Open to Edit. By default, this file type is an exception to the general rule: Windows 98 has disabled the ability to edit Action properties for DOS batch files. So if you select MS-DOS Batch File in the Registered File Types list, the Open action cannot be deselected, and the Print and Edit options are inaccessible. If you want to change this default setting, perhaps to avoid running MS-DOS batch files by accident, you can open batch files in a text editor when you double-click. Here's how:

1. Open RegEdit, the Windows 98 registry editor, (click the Start button, choose Run, and enter **REGEDIT.EXE**).
2. Scroll down to the HKEY_CLASSES_ROOT\batfile\shell\open key. (You can get to this key more quickly by pressing CTRL-F, entering **batfile** in the Find window, and clicking Find Next. When the batfile key appears, select the Open subkey.)

3. Change the name of this key from open to **r&un**. (Right-click the Open subkey in the left RegEdit pane and choose Rename from the pop-up menu.)
4. Double-click the EditFlags value for this subkey in the right RegEdit pane. Change its value to **00 00 00 00**. (Type exactly four pairs of zeros.)
5. Reboot the computer. You will now be able to select MS-DOS Batch File in the View | Folder Options | File Types list in My Computer and modify the default double-click action. For example, to switch the default action to open batch files in Notepad, select the Edit action and click the Set Default button.

Open Windows Explorer to Any Designated Folder

Sometimes you may be browsing a nested series of folders in My Computer or Windows Explorer and want to open up an Explorer view with the selected folder at the top of the hierarchy. (The regular Explore option on the right-click pop-up menu opens the entire desktop hierarchy in the left pane.)

You can create a right-click Explore From Here option by making a small modification in the Windows registry. (As with all RegEdit hacks, you may want to make a backup of the registry before trying this.)

1. Open RegEdit and scroll down to the HKEY_CLASSES_ROOT\Folder\Shell key (or select HKEY_CLASSES_ROOT, press CTRL-F, type **Folder** in the Find box, make sure Keys and Match Whole String Only are selected, and click the Find Next button.)
2. Right-click the shell subkey under Folder, choose New | Key, and name the new key **View From Here**.
3. Right-click the View From Here key you've just created, choose New | Key, and name the new subkey key **Command**.
4. Select the Command subkey that you've just created (under View From Here) in the left RegEdit pane. Then double-click the default value for Command in the right RegEdit pane. Enter the following value in the Edit String dialog box:

   Explorer.exe /e,/root,/idlist,%I

   (Make sure to reproduce the commas exactly, with no spaces before or after.)

From now on, you can right-click a folder in My Computer or Windows Explorer and select the "View From Here" option to open a new Explorer view with the selected folder at the top of the hierarchy.

Adjust the Position of Your Windows 98 Wallpaper

By default, Windows 98 provides two ways to position your wallpaper on the desktop: you can select Tile or Center on the Appearance tab of the Windows 98 Display applet.

Here's a registry trick that will let you place desktop wallpaper on the screen in any location you want:

1. Select a wallpaper image on the Background tab of the Display applet and center it. (You can also create wallpaper by dragging your own custom .BMP file from Windows Explorer into the Wallpaper list.)
2. Open RegEdit to this key: HKEY_CURRENT_USER\Control Panel\desktop.
3. With this desktop key selected in the left RegEdit pane, create a new string value in the right pane (choose Edit | New | String Value from RegEdit's pull-down menus). Name this new entry **WallpaperX**.
4. Repeat this operation to create a second new string value named **WallpaperY**.

You can now move your "centered" wallpaper to any location on the desktop by entering numerical X and Y offsets for the string values you've just created. For instance, you can double-click the WallpaperX value and enter **200**, and then click the WallpaperY value and enter **400**. After you reboot your machine, the wallpaper will appear at an offset of 200 horizontal and 400 vertical pixels (0,0 is the centered default). You may need to experiment with different horizontal and vertical pixel coordinates to position the wallpaper where you want it.

Transfer Windows Color Schemes from One Computer to Another

If you take pride in the color customization of your Windows desktop and want to use the same scheme on other computers (or if you just want to transfer a familiar scheme from your home to your office), you can do so. Your color schemes are stored in the Windows registry.

First make sure you've saved your current desktop settings as a custom scheme. (Open the Control Panel | Display applet to the Appearance tab, click the Save As button under Schemes and assign a name.) Next you'll use RegEdit to export the key that contains all of the available Windows 98 color schemes to a file. Then you'll take that file to the second Win98 computer and import the color schemes key into the registry. Here are the details:

1. Open RegEdit to the HKEY_CURRENT_USER\Control Panel\Appearance\Schemes key. You'll see all of your color schemes displayed in the right RegEdit pane.
2. With this key highlighted in the left RegEdit pane, choose Registry | Export Registry File from RegEdit's pull-down menus. Set the export range to Selected Branch and enter a name (such as **SCHEMES.REG**) for the file. You can save the file directly to a floppy disk or network drive to save time.

3. Bring the disk that contains SCHEMES.REG to the second computer. Double-click the file in a My Computer or Windows Explorer window to merge it into the registry on the second machine.

This procedure will transfer all the Windows 98 color schemes from the first computer to the second computer for the user who is currently logged on. However, it will also overwrite any custom schemes that were previously present on the second machine. To retain the color schemes on the second machine, read the next tip.

Preserve Existing Color Schemes When Importing Color Schemes from Another Computer

If you use the preceding tip to transfer Windows 98 color schemes from one computer to another, the imported schemes will overwrite any custom schemes present on the second computer. Suppose you have a color scheme on the second machine that you really want to preserve in addition to the imported schemes. You can save existing schemes on the second computer as described here. (This is a good exercise for learning your way around RegEdit.)

1. Before merging the Schemes key from the first computer, open RegEdit on the second computer to the HKEY_CURRENT_USER\Control Panel\Appearance\Schemes key. The color schemes appear as hexadecimal value entries in the right pane.
2. If you have a scheme you want to save, double-click its value in the right pane, select the entire hexadecimal listing with the mouse, and press CTRL-C to copy it to the Windows clipboard.
3. Go back to the left RegEdit pane and move up one level. With the Appearance key selected, choose Edit | New | Key from the pull-down menus. Create a new key under Appearance called **Temp**.
4. With the Temp key selected in the left pane, choose Edit | New | Binary | Value from the pull-down menus to create a new binary value in the right pane. Give it the same name as the color scheme you want to preserve.
5. Double-click the new value in the right pane and press CTRL-C to paste the binary value of your color scheme from the clipboard into the key.
6. You can now merge the imported color scheme key from the first computer into the second. To reintroduce the scheme you saved, create a dummy value for your "leftover" scheme in the HKEY_CURRENT_USER\Control Panel\Appearances\Schemes subkey. (Select Edit | New | Binary Value.)
7. After you've created the New Value dummy key, go back to the Temp key you created in step 4, copy its binary value contents to the clipboard, and then paste this value into the New Value dummy key. (Double-click the New Value key

and press CTRL-V.) You can rename this New Value key to any name you want (right-click it and choose Rename). This key will retain the color and font settings of the Temp key scheme. When you're done, you can delete the \Appearance\Temp key from the registry.

Reset the Window Defaults for Windows 98 Telnet

The Windows 98 Telnet application automatically remembers the window size and desktop location of the last open session by writing these parameters to the system registry. Occasionally, though, Telnet gets stuck. You open the application, but you don't see it on the desktop. When this happens (typically after you change the Win98 screen resolution), the Telnet application is remembering some off-screen coordinates from the previous display.

To reset Telnet display coordinates, follow these steps:

1. Open RegEdit and scroll to this key:

   HKEY_CURRENT_USER\Software\Microsoft\Telnet

2. In the right RegEdit pane, delete the WinPosLeft and WinPosTop values.

Enable Double-Clicking with the Middle Button of a Logitech Mouse

By default, the middle button of a three-button Logitech mouse is inactive in Windows 98. You can enable the double-click feature of the middle button as follows:

1. Open RegEdit to this key:

   HKEY_CURRENT_USER/software/logitech/version*xxx*/

2. Open the "Doubleclick" value in the right RegEdit pane and change its value from 000 to **001**.

Incorporate Registry Changes on the Fly and Restart Windows Explorer Without Rebooting

You can refresh the Windows 98 desktop and registry settings without rebooting your computer. This is useful when you've changed a registry entry and want to see the effect without restarting the machine. Here's what to do:

1. Press CTRL-ALT-DEL. Select Explorer in the Task list and click the End Task button.
2. When the Shut Down dialog appears, choose No. Then click End Task in the Explorer End Task dialog box that appears. Explorer restarts, and the desktop and taskbar are refreshed.

Open a DOS Prompt Quickly in Any Selected Directory or Drive

The ability to add pop-up menu options through the Shell key of any registered Windows 98 object has a number of useful applications. Here's one:

1. Open RegEdit and go to the HKEY_CLASSES_ROOT\Directory\shell\ key.
2. Create a new subkey under Shell called **DOS Prompt**.
3. Create a new subkey under DOS Prompt and name it **Command**.
4. Double-click the default value for the Command subkey and enter this string:

   COMMAND.COM /K CD %1

You can now right-click any folder in a My Computer or Windows Explorer window and select the new DOS Prompt option from its pop-up menu. This will open a command-line session in the selected directory.

To extend this option to drive icons as well as folders, follow the same procedure, except in step 1, open the HKEY_CLASSES_ROOT\Drive\shell\ subkey. In step 4, enter this string:

COMMAND.COM /K %1"

Quickly Back Up Any Selected Folder

You can use a variation of the preceding tip to quickly perform a DOS file backup of any folder.

1. Open RegEdit to the HKEY_CLASSES_ROOT\Directory\shell\ key.
2. Create a key under Shell called **Backup**.
3. Create a subkey under Backup called **Command**.
4. Modify the default value for the Command key to read as follows:

   COMMAND.COM /C XCOPY /S %1 C:\BACKUPS

   or

   COMMAND.COM /C XCOPY /S %1 A:

You can append any XCOPY parameters you want on this line to customize a backup by date, reset file attributes, and so on. If you have a backup program that accepts command-line parameters, you can enter the path to it instead of running the XCOPY command.

Troubleshooting Tips and Tricks

This section contains some of the tricks of the trade that I've learned in my other career as a Windows computer consultant. You'll find diagnostic procedures and fixes for some common problems that crop up from time to time in the various subsystems of Windows 98.

Modems and Dial-Up Networking

Few aspects of personal computing are more aggravating than modems and Internet connections that don't work the way they're supposed to. The following tips and tricks may help you to pinpoint and remove some prickly telecommunication problems.

If you don't find the solution to your problem in this section, consult the following sites for possible solutions:

- http://www.nb.rockwell.com
- http://www.hayes.com/support/index.htm
- http://www.diamondmm.com/product-support/
- http://www.teleport.com/~curt/modems.html
- http://www.winfiles.com
- http://www.usr.com/home/online/files_f.htm

Check Your Modem's Hardware and Software Configuration for Better Performance

Make sure your modem is properly connected to both the computer and the telephone line. If you are using a telephone cord other than the one supplied with your modem to connect to the modular phone jack, replace it with the cord that was supplied with your modem. (Using extra-long telephone cords or serial cables can degrade a modem's performance.) If you are replacing an older modem with a new, faster one, be sure to use all of the cables, cords, and power supplies that were shipped with the new modem. The new modem may require this hardware to maintain the highest level of performance. If your modem appears to be underperforming, you may want to inspect your telephone connection and remove additional telephone headsets or other devices that may be tapping power on the line.

Also, keep your modem's firmware up to date. (This is especially important for newer V.90, K56Flex, and X2 modems.) Many newer, high-speed modems can have their internal firmware updated via flash-ROM software. To ensure optimal performance of your modem, check the manufacturer's Web site or dial-in bulletin board system for downloadable flash upgrade software.

Most modems can be made to display version information for their firmware with a Hayes AT command entered through a terminal program. For example, for many modems, the commands **ATI3**, **ATI4**, **ATI7**, and **ATI10** will report configuration information.

Eliminate Time Out and CRC File Transfer Errors

If your communication software constantly reports time-out or CRC errors when you're uploading and downloading files, you may be using an older, inadequate serial card, or your high-speed port may not be properly configured. If your serial port (used with an external modem) is built into the motherboard, you may need to turn on the high-speed 16550 UART buffer in the system's CMOS settings and/or in the Windows 98 Control Panel. To activate the UART buffer in the Control Panel, open the Modems applet, choose the modem on the General tab and open its Properties window, select the Connection tab, and click the Port Settings button, as shown in Figure 16-1.

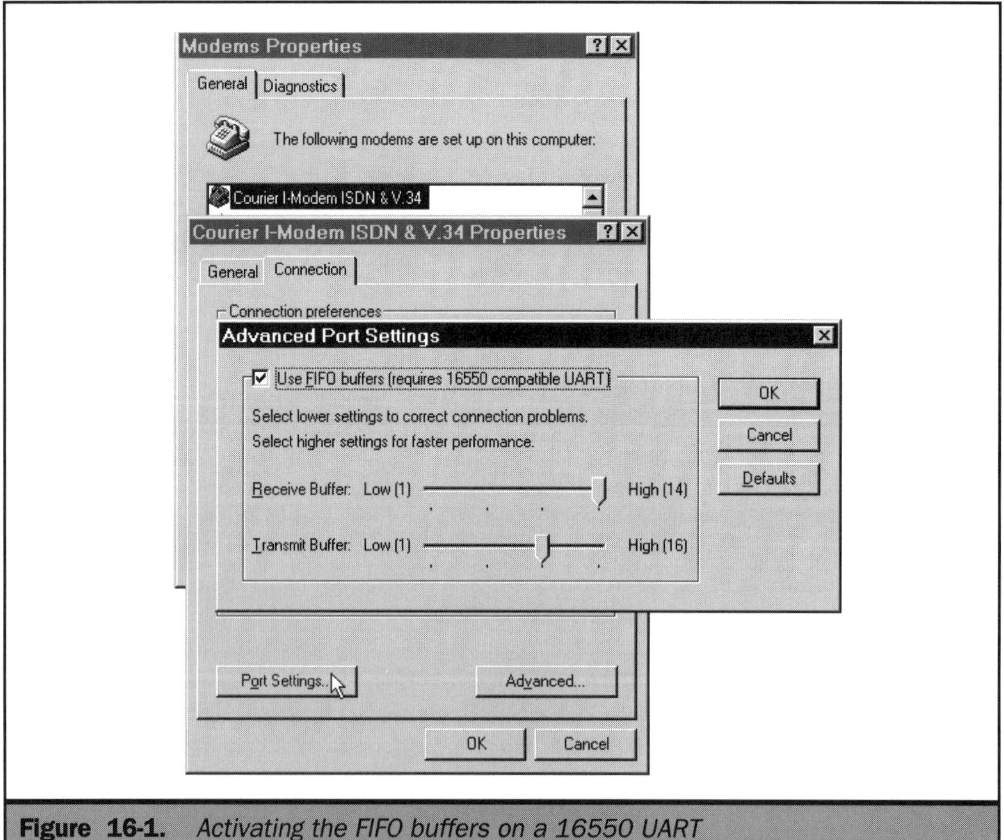

Figure 16-1. *Activating the FIFO buffers on a 16550 UART*

Set Up Dial-Up Networking Correctly

Whenever possible, use Win98's built-in Dial-Up Networking connections rather than older Windows 3.1 dialers (which allow only 16-bit Internet connections).

- If your ISP has more than one DNS server, be sure to enter *both* addresses in the Dial-Up Networking profile. (Right-click the connection profile properties in the Dial-Up Networking folder, select Server Type, and click the TCP/IP Settings button.)
- Most ISPs support (and some require) software compression to speed up file transmission. Enable this option in the Dial-Up Network Server Type settings.
- Find out whether your ISP supports IP packet compression and enable or disable this check box in the TCP/IP settings.

Avoid Sudden ISP Disconnection

Have you been disconnected from the Internet in the middle of a long file transfer? Here's what you can do to avoid this problem:

- If you have an external modem, check your cable connections (serial and/or telephone line) to make sure they're tight. If you experience frequent sudden disconnection from the Internet, you may also want to try a new serial cable. If you have an internal modem, open the case and make sure that the modem is properly seated in its slot.
- Check your modem configuration (open the Modems applet, display the Properties window, and select the Connection tab). Make sure there's no check mark next to the Disconnect Call If Idle For More Than XX Minutes option.
- Check your modem's documentation for information about two Hayes command settings: one that disconnects the modem if signal deterioration persists for a timed interval, and one that disconnects automatically if no modem activity occurs within a specified interval. Adjust these settings to increase the permissible interval of signal fluctuation and disable the no-activity disconnect feature. (On some Rockwell modems, these settings are controlled with the commands ATS25=?? and ATS30=??.)
- Many modems can also dynamically shift their connection speed up or down during a file transfer to adjust for line noise conditions. This feature is called rate renegotiation. It's designed to optimize your connection, but it may sometimes cause your server to time out during the renegotiation process. Therefore, if you experience disconnection problems, you may want to turn off your modem's rate renegotiation feature. Consult your modem's documentation for the appropriate Hayes command string. The command to do this with Diamond's Supra modems is AT %E0 %G0.

Get Accurate Modem Status Information

Many modems have diagnostic commands that can display a status report of the last connection, including the speed, protocols invoked, and amount of data that was transferred. However, under Windows 98 it's difficult to bring up a terminal program after you've connected to the Internet for the purpose of displaying the statistics of your last PPP Internet session. This is because Windows 98's default modem profiles will generally reinitialize your modem with an ATZ command as soon as the Internet connection is closed.

To troubleshoot modem performance, you can disable this feature in the Windows 98 registry. Here's how:

1. Open RegEdit to the following key:

   HKEY_LOCAL_MACHINE\System\CurrentControlSet\Services\Class\Modem

2. Find your modem in one of the subkeys numbered 00 to xx. Select that subkey and double-click the Reset value in the left RegEdit window. Change the value from ATZ to **AT**.

This change will allow you to open a terminal program such as HyperTerminal or Procomm Plus after you log off the Internet. You can then send AT commands to your modem to display diagnostic information about your last connection.

Troubleshoot 56K Modems That Habitually Connect at Less Than 33.6 Kbps

The following troubleshooting drill may help you pinpoint problems that prevent a 56-Kbps modem from establishing connection speeds above 33.6 Kbps:

- Confirm that you've selected an ISP that matches the 56K connection standard built into your modem.
- Your ISP may have more than one dial-in number. Make sure your connection profile uses the right telephone number to support the K56Flex, X2, or V.90 protocol built into your modem.
- If your dialer's status window consistently reports connections of 33.6 Kbps or less, try dialing the same telephone number through a terminal communications program (such as HyperTerminal or Procomm Plus). Watch the connection status message that the terminal program reports. After you disconnect, you can get additional information through your modem's internal diagnostic commands. (On a K56Flex modem, enter the command **AT&V1**. For a USR X2 modem, enter **ATI11**.) This will allow you to confirm the highest connect rate your modem achieved on the last call.

- Confirm that you've installed the proper Windows driver for your modem. If your modem vendor has a Web site, check it out, and download and install the most recent drivers.
- See if you can upgrade your modem's internal BIOS. Many 56K modems (both client and ISP models) are still being tweaked and upgraded by manufacturers. Call the vendor and ask whether internal BIOS revisions for the modem are available. Some modems support software flash upgrades. Other modems require a chip upgrade or must be replaced. If a BIOS revision is available for your modem (either a chip or flash upgrade), get it and install it.

Note that the actual limit of K56Flex, X2, and V.90 modems is really 53 Kbps. An FCC regulation prohibits faster connections on an analog line. In reality, modems using these technologies generally achieve connect speeds between 42 Kbps and 50 Kbps. The quality of the telephone line and the distance to the phone company's analog/digital switchbox can affect the connect speed.

If you've taken care of all the prerequisites for a 56K connection described here and still can't get the proper rate, the most probable culprit is the quality of your local telephone line. In some parts of the country, telephone cabling must pass through one or more analog switch nodes before reaching a digital switch in the telephone company's central office. If the distance between your modem and the digital switch is too great, line noise may prevent the modem from negotiating the analog-to-digital 56K connection. Currently, K56Flex can be particularly finicky in this regard. (USR's X2 modems are slightly more forgiving of line noise.) You may find that if you take the computer to a different location or dial a different telephone exchange, the problem disappears.

Printing and Printers

Here are a few tips and tricks for troubleshooting printers.

Print from DOS WordPerfect

If you have trouble printing from a DOS version of WordPerfect, try the following:

- Make sure you've selected an appropriate printer driver in WordPerfect to match the Windows 98 driver for the printer. (Apple Laserwriter II NT is a good generic WordPerfect Postscript driver for any Postscript printer.)
- Look at the settings for the printer you've chosen in WordPerfect (press SHIFT-F7, Select, and Edit). If the Print To Hardware option is set to No and your computer has a bidirectional printer port, you might try setting this option to Yes. (Check the printer cable and confirm that it supports bidirectional printing.) Check the CMOS settings for your computer and confirm that the printer port is configured optimally. (Choose EPP, ECP, or Bidirectional Printing instead of a generic setting.)

- Check the fonts you're using to print. Make sure you're using a font that's resident in your printer rather than a downloadable font. If your WordPerfect documents contain special characters, printing may be delayed by the generation of bitmapped symbols.
- At the Windows 98 level, right-click the Printer icon in the Printers folder, select Properties, and examine the various configuration options. On the Details tab, select Spool Settings and try experimenting with print spooling enabled and disabled. (If your output port supports bidirectional printing and this option is dimmed, try switching the setting in the CMOS from ECP to EPP or Bidirectional.)
- On the Device Options tab of the Windows 98 Printer settings, make sure you've entered the correct amount of available printer memory. You may also want to experiment with the Print Quality settings.

Eliminate Annoying Printer Warnings

When you're printing large documents or multiple jobs, do warning messages frequently appear on the desktop telling you that your printer has timed out?

You can avoid these messages by opening the Properties window for your printer (choose Start | Settings | Printer, right-click the printer icon, and select Properties). Go to the Details tab and increase the Not Selected and Transmission Retry values under Timeout Settings. Instead of the default values of 15 seconds and 45 seconds, try 30 seconds and 90 seconds.

System

The following tips and tricks may help you resolve some Windows 98 configuration issues that occasionally materialize on some systems.

Troubleshoot Windows 98 Shutdown Problems

Are you having problems with Windows 98's automatic shutdown procedure? Many users find that running Windows 98 for a long period of time with multiple configuration changes can cause the system to hang at shutdown instead of exiting gracefully. This can create registry problems and prevent configuration changes from taking effect.

The first step you can take to cure this problem is to turn off the fast shutdown feature of Windows 98:

1. Open the System Information applet (choose Start | Programs | Accessories | System Tools | System Information).
2. Open the System Configuration utility from the System Information Tools menu and click the Advanced button on the General tab.

3. Place a check mark next to Disable Fast Shutdown on the Advanced Troubleshooting screen.
4. Close the System Information utility and restart the computer.

If the shutdown problem isn't resolved the next time you power down the computer, you may want to access Microsoft's Startup and Shutdown Troubleshooting Wizard located at http://support.microsoft.com/support/tshoot/default.asp. You can also look up Knowledge Base article q145926 at http://support.microsoft.com/support/kb/articles/q/145/9/26.asp.

Resolve Out-of-Memory Problems

Generally, a low amount of DOS conventional memory under Windows 98 does not produce out-of-memory messages in Windows applications. However, these messages do occur when you haven't allocated enough space on the hard disk for the Windows 98 swap file. You can check how much swap file space is available by right-clicking My Computer and selecting Properties.

Go to the Performance tab of the System Properties screen and click the Virtual Memory button. For a machine with 16MB of RAM, there should be at least 35 to 40MB of disk space available for the swap file. In general, disk space equal to at least 2.5 times the amount of physical memory in the machine should be reserved for the swap file. If the Virtual Memory screen shows less disk space available, you may want to remove unnecessary files or programs to free up space.

You may also be able to increase the amount of memory available for DOS sessions under Windows 98 by inspecting the contents of the CONFIG.SYS and AUTOEXEC.BAT files for redundant or unnecessary driver statements.

- Remove any DEVICE=DBLSPACE.SYS or DRVSPACE.SYS statements in CONFIG.SYS.
- If there is a statement that loads MSCDEX.EXE in AUTOEXEC.BAT, you may also be able to remove that.
- Remove any BUFFERS= statements in CONFIG.SYS if the setting is higher than BUFFERS=5.

(Make backups of your AUTOEXEC.BAT and CONFIG.SYS files before modifying them.)

Locate Any Windows System File in Its Cabinet Archive

Have you ever discovered that a Windows 98 system file is missing from your hard disk, or have you ever wanted to search the installation CD for particular filenames? Most Windows 98 installation and system files are stored in a set of compressed cabinets (.CAB files) on the Windows 98 CD. (On notebook computers, these files are often copied to the hard disk in a C:\WINDOWS\OPTIONS\CABS directory.)

The Extract tool (EXTRACT.EXE in the \WINDOWS\COMMAND directory) allows you to search cabinet files individually or globally to retrieve or extract specific files. In Chapter 2, you saw how to use Extract to precopy all the readme files with the .TXT extension to your hard disk before Windows 98 places them in the \WINDOWS directory.

Here's how to generate a complete CAB-by-CAB list of *every* system file in the \WIN98 directory on the Windows 98 CD:

1. Place the Win98 CD in your CD-ROM drive. Open a DOS command prompt and log into the \WIN98 directory. (If the CAB files are stored on your hard disk, log into the \WINDOWS\OPTIONS\CABS directory.)
2. Issue the command

   EXTRACT /A /D BASE4.CAB *.* >>*D:\PATH\FILELIST.TXT*

   where *D:\PATH* is the target location for the file list, and *FILELIST.TXT* is the name of the file. This command will create an ASCII text file that you can search in Notepad or WordPad to locate any driver stored in the Win98 cabinet files.

Once you know the file's name and location, you can use the System File Checker option of the System Information tool to automatically unpack and install it. (See Chapter 6 for more information on working with System File Checker.)

Recover from Screen Saver Password Lockout

Have you ever assigned a Windows 98 screen saver password and then forgotten it? For all intents and purposes, it might seem that you've locked yourself out of your own desktop. However, there's an easy way to get around this problem. (Just don't use this technique on someone else's computer.)

Follow these steps to regain access after a screen saver lockout:

1. Reboot the computer by switching the power off and on. This may result in partial data loss in unsaved documents, but Windows ScanDisk should repair any file system errors, and sooner or later you'd have to do this anyway.
2. Open the Control Panel Display applet before the screen saver kicks in again, choose the Screen Saver tab, and remove the check mark next to Password or reset the Screen Saver option to None.

Recover from Login Password Lockout

If you forget your login password, follow these steps to regain access after a Startup login prompt lockout:

1. Reboot the computer, hold down the CTRL key, and select DOS Command Prompt from the Windows 98 Startup menu.

2. Go to the \WINDOWS directory on your hard disk and search for a filename that begins with your username and has the extension .PWL (for example, DIR LENNY*.PWL).
3. When you find this file, rename it with another extension, such as **PW**.
4. Restart Windows 98. The next time you log in, enter your username without a password or select it from the Microsoft Family Login screen.
5. After you gain access to the desktop, open the Control Panel Passwords applet and choose Change Password on the Change Passwords tab. Then assign a new password to your current login ID.

Restoring Improperly Configured Hardware Devices

Chapters 3, 9, 14, and 15 of this book described procedures for using Windows 98's Device Manager list to restore the functionality of improperly configured hardware devices. Here are a few more general tips and hardware recovery strategies:

- To access a list of all the Windows 98 troubleshooters, open Windows 98 Help to the Index tab and enter the word **Troubleshooting**.
- The best general strategy for fixing a device that appears in the Device Manager listing with an exclamation point and error message is to remove the device, reboot the computer, and try redetecting the device through Add New Hardware.

Restore Advanced Power Management

If you are experiencing difficulties with Windows 98 Advanced Power Management, try opening the Device Manager, expanding the System devices list, and removing the entry for Advanced Power Management support. Then reboot the machine, open Add New Hardware, and let Advanced Power Management be redetected and reinstalled. Advanced users note: The registry settings for Advanced Power Management are located in HKEY_LOCAL_MACHINE\System\CurrentControlSet\Services\Class\System among other settings in a group of numbered subkeys.

Revive a Modem

If you repeatedly experience modem connection difficulties, particularly with "Port Is Open" error messages, no matter how many times you remove and reinstall the device through the Modems applet, you may want to remove the listing for the modem directly from the Windows registry.

Open RegEdit to HKEY_LOCAL_MACHINE\System\CurrentControlSet\Services\Class\Modem. Examine the numbered subkeys under the Modem key. You may find one or more listings for a particular modem even after you've removed it through the Modems applet. If you discover these entries, delete them from the registry, restart the computer, and reinstall the modem in the standard way.

If "Port Is Open" messages persist with an external modem, you can try removing the Device Manager listing under the Ports group for the serial port the modem is using. The port will generally be redetected when you restart the computer. If it isn't, you can redetect the port with the Add New Hardware applet.

Revive 'Invisible' Disabled Devices

If a plug-and-play device is not recognized no matter how many times you use the Add New Hardware Wizard, open the System Information utility in the System Tools folder and choose the Automatic Skip Driver (ASD) agent from the Tools menu. Sometimes if Windows 98 has had trouble with a device, the ASD agent will permanently disable it. If you find the device in this list, you can try reactivating it.

Resolve PC Steering IRQ Problems

If yellow exclamation points appear next to components in the Device Manager list and an error message says that no system interrupts are available to assign to the device, try manipulating the settings for Win98's IRQ Steering feature. IRQ Steering is a Microsoft technology for reserving and sharing system interrupts among a number of devices, but sometimes it doesn't work. The settings for IRQ Steering can be accessed by opening the System Devices group in the Device Manager list, selecting the entry for the PCI bus, and clicking the Properties button. Then choose the IRQ Steering tab, as shown here:

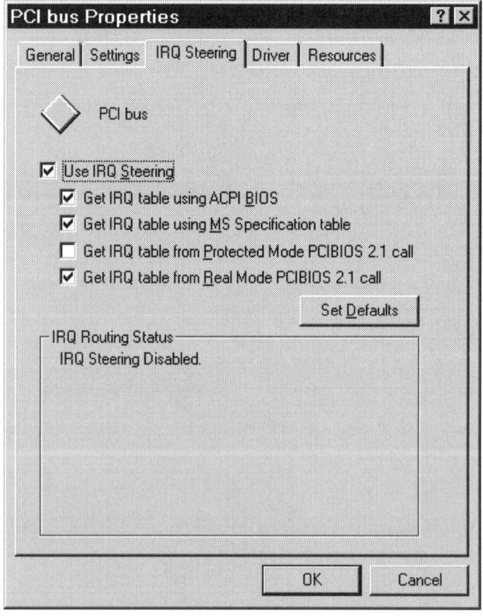

For some notebook computers, such as Gateway's Solo 9100, detection of PCMCIA devices works best if Use IRQ Steering is deselected. (This allows interrupts to be assigned directly through the PCI bus.)

For other notebook computers, such as the Panasonic CF-35, detection of PCMCIA devices works best when IRQ Steering is enabled by placing check marks next to Get IRQ From MS Specification Table and Get IRQ from Real Mode PCBIOS 2.1 Call.

You may want to experiment with various IRQ Steering configurations on your own computer or consult the manufacturer to see which configuration works best.

If there is a shortage of IRQ settings available on your computer, sometimes you can free up an interrupt by assigning your sound card to a single IRQ instead of a double IRQ. Open the Device Manager Properties window for the sound card, select the Resources tab, remove the check mark next to Use Automatic Settings, and examine other basic configurations.

Sometimes you can free up a system interrupt on a notebook computer by disabling an unused infrared serial port in your current configuration. If you aren't using the Infrared Connect feature, open the Network Adapters group in the Device Manager list and look for an infrared serial port listing. If you find one, open its Properties window and place a check mark next to Disable in This Hardware Profile.

For information about force configuring a port address or IRQ for a recalcitrant PCMCIA device (such as the New Media Livewire Ethernet adapter), see "The 'This Resource Setting Cannot Be Modified' Message" in Chapter 14.

Appendix A

Installation and Migration Tips

This appendix provides tips to help you install Windows 98 with dual boot options so you can use multiple operating systems, use Windows 98 for mobile computing, and migrate your entire personal Windows 98 configuration from one computer to another.

Preserving Dual Boot Options During Windows 98 Installation

Windows 98 is flexible. It can coexist with previous versions of DOS, Warp OS/2, Windows NT, or all of these operating systems on the same hard disk. If you want to set up multiple operating systems easily, the order in which you install the programs can dramatically affect the time and effort you spend on the process. This section outlines the general sequence you should follow when you install multiple operating systems.

Dual Boot with OS/2

If OS/2 is to be one of the operating systems on the hard disk, install it before Windows 98 or Windows NT, so it won't wipe out the dual boot features built into these operating systems. If you must install OS/2 after Windows 98 or Windows NT has been set up, then make sure that you place it on a separate disk partition and select the option to create an OS/2 Boot Manager partition. Do not install OS/2 to share a partition with Windows 98 or Windows NT. You can install OS/2 on either a FAT or an HPFS disk partition. If you choose the HPFS partition, then files stored on this partition will be visible under Windows NT, but not under MS-DOS or Windows 98.

Windows 98 should generally be installed on a computer after any installation of OS/2, but before any installation of Windows NT. If you have installed OS/2 on an HPFS partition, you will need to make sure that one FAT partition containing a previous version of MS-DOS is also ready and available through OS/2's Boot Manager menu. Simply choose that partition when the computer starts, boot to MS-DOS, and proceed with the Windows 98 installation as outlined in Chapters 2 and 3. (You can ignore the warning messages displayed by the Windows 98 Setup Wizard that say that OS/2 will become inoperable—provided you install Windows 98 and OS/2 on separate partitions.)

When Windows 98 has been successfully installed on your hard disk, the OS/2 Boot Manager will be temporarily disabled. The system will boot directly to Windows 98. You can restore the OS/2 Boot Manager simply by opening a DOS command prompt under Windows 98 and running the FDISK utility. On the FDISK screen, choose option 2, Set Active Partition. On the next FDISK screen, you'll see a listing for a small non-DOS partition, 1 to 2MB in size. Enter the number in front of this partition to make it the active boot partition and then exit FDISK. The next time your computer starts, the OS/2 Boot Manager will reappear, allowing you to select either OS/2 or the partition that formerly launched MS-DOS but now launches Windows 98. When you are running the OS/2 operating system, you can use the OS/2 version of FDISK to modify the Boot Manager menu if you want, changing the name of the MS-DOS partition to **Windows 98**.

Dual Boot with Windows NT

If Windows NT is to be one of the operating systems on the hard disk, it should generally be installed last. Start Windows 98 and press the CTRL key to bring up the Windows 98 Startup menu. Select the option to boot to a DOS command prompt, not the Windows 98 desktop.

Next, run the Windows NT Setup program, making sure to choose a different directory from the one that contains Windows 98. You can install both Windows 98 and Windows NT on the same disk partition, if it is a FAT16 partition. Note that if you are installing the CD-ROM version of Windows NT, you will have to make sure that your Windows 98 CONFIG.SYS and AUTOEXEC.BAT files contain the necessary real-mode drivers for your CD-ROM drive to be recognized under MS-DOS.

When you install Windows NT, make sure to select the option that allows Windows NT to dual boot back to the previous operating system. After installation is completed, you can set the Windows NT default to start either Windows NT or the previous operating system, which in this case is Windows 98.

If you are the rare, must-have-everything user who has also installed OS/2, then the boot order that results from the procedure just outlined is as follows: Open the OS/2 Boot Manager, where you can select between OS/2 and another operating system. When you choose the other operating system from the OS/2 Boot Manager, the Windows NT dual boot menu will appear, giving you the option to go straight to Windows NT or to use NT's dual-boot option, which will start Windows 98.

Special Dual Boot Setup for Windows NT and Windows 98

What if Windows NT is already installed on your hard disk and you want to install Windows 98 over it, retaining access to both operating systems?

If Windows NT has been installed first on a FAT16 partition, use the following procedure to add Windows 98 to your computer:

1. Ensure that the computer is configured to dual boot between Windows NT and MS-DOS.
2. Start the computer using the MS-DOS operating system.
3. Remove the read-only attribute from the BOOTSECT.DOS and BOOT.INI files in the root directory of drive C by typing the following:

   ATTRIB -R BOOTSECT.DOS
   ATTRIB -R BOOT.INI

4. Back up the BOOTSECT.DOS file by copying it to another name, such as **BOOTSECT.SAV**.
5. Run Windows 98 Setup, installing the operating system in an existing Windows 3.x directory or in a new directory, but *not* in a directory that already contains Windows NT.
6. After Windows 98 has been installed, remove the read-only attribute from the BOOTSECT.DOS file in the root directory.
7. Rename the BOOTSECT.DOS and BOOTSECT.SAV files by typing the following:

   REN BOOTSECT.DOS BOOTSECT.W40
   REN BOOTSECT.SAV BOOTSECT.DOS

8. Use a text editor to modify the BOOT.INI file to add Windows 98. For example:

```
[BOOT LOADER]
TIMEOUT=30
DEFAULT=C:\WINNT

[OPERATING SYSTEMS]
C:\WINNT="WINDOWS NT"
C:\BOOTSECT.DOS="MS-DOS V6.22" /WIN98DOS
C:\BOOTSECT.W40="WINDOWS 98" /WIN98
```

At system startup, the Windows NT Dual Boot menu will appear, allowing you to select Windows 98 as a startup option.

Remember: If you want to install Windows 98 in a FAT32 partition and preserve dual booting with Windows NT, the C drive must be a FAT16 partition. If you like, you can configure a small FAT16 C drive, place the main Windows NT operating system files on an NTFS D drive, and install Windows 98 on a FAT16 E drive. Later, you can use the Windows 98 Drive Converter to switch the E drive to FAT32. If you do so, this drive will not be visible under Windows NT. If your computer has any NTFS partitions, they will not be available from within Windows 98.

Mobile Computing with Windows 98

This section addresses the concerns of Windows 98 road warriors. With the right notebook computer, an upgrade to Windows 98 is eminently desirable. The added features and ease of use of the new operating system can simplify your day-to-day computing tasks. However, if you must make do with an older, less powerful notebook computer with a small hard disk, you're better off sticking with Windows 95 or Windows for Workgroups. Gateway 2000's Solo 9100 series is an excellent notebook line for Windows 98.

For newer, more powerful systems, Windows 98 really makes life easier. Advanced power management, automatic installation of PC Cards, hot docking to a workstation, automatic network connections, and convenient e-mail and fax management are all present in the operating system, waiting to be exploited. Windows 98 mostly eliminates the need to fidget with third-party software for CD-ROMs, SCSI devices, and PC Card socket services. Just pop a PC Card modem, SCSI adapter, video capture card, or added memory into a socket, and Windows 98 magically detects it. Plug a notebook into a docking station, and the system configuration is automatically swapped to recognize new ports, peripherals, and network connections

In addition to the autoconfiguration advantage for PC Card hardware, Windows 98 offers a number of software benefits for computing on the road.

DIAL-UP NETWORKING AND DIRECT CABLE CONNECTION Dial into the Internet on the road or connect via modem to a network server through TCP/IP, Novell IPX/SPX-compatible, or Microsoft NetBEUI protocols. Direct cable connection lets you set up a two-computer LAN with your desktop machine, sharing files and printers through a simple parallel cable.

BRIEFCASE The Briefcase feature lets you quickly synchronize local and remote directories. You can edit files copied from your desktop machine and have the changes copied automatically back to the host machine the next time you connect.

DEFERRED PRINTING You can work offline with a network printer. When you're not connected, you can still print as many jobs as you like. The output is stored in a spool directory on the notebook system. The next time you connect to your network machine, the jobs are automatically queued and spooled to the printer.

HOT DOCKING Hot docking requires a plug-and-play BIOS. If your notebook computer has the current Microsoft/Intel plug-and-play BIOS, it will automatically reconfigure itself whenever you plug it into or remove it from a docking station. Older notebooks can *cold-dock*. (This means you must power down the system and reboot each time you connect or disconnect from a docking station.)

Hardware Requirements for Win98 Mobile Computing

A top-range "road warrior" notebook computer suited to Windows 98 will have 32 to 64MB of onboard RAM, a Pentium 166 MMX or faster processor, PC Card (PCMCIA) Type II and III slots, a 2GB hard disk, and a CD-ROM drive option. The CD-ROM drive can be built into the computer, or it can be a module that's swappable with a floppy drive. Newer notebooks will soon include DVD-ROM and extended options such as support for an Iomega Zip drive. A good, new notebook system should also include at least one Universal Serial Bus port.

In addition, a notebook system may include an internal modem, sound card, and built-in SCSI support. Most contemporary notebooks include a 64-bit PCI video bus with at least 2MB of video RAM. (Multimedia models support 128-bit video adapters with 4MB of video RAM.)

Notebooks unsuitable for Windows 98 includes older machines with 486 CPUs, DX50 and below, non-VGA displays and configurations with less than 16MB of RAM, or small hard disks (less than 350MB).

This leaves a large number of computers in between the desirable top-range and the incompatible bottom-range configurations. A 486 DX2-75 or Pentium 100 notebook with 16MB of RAM will be functional for basic computing tasks under Windows 98, but it may have difficulty taking advantages of some of the operating system's bells and whistles. Without a PCI bus for the hard disk and video display, application performance may also be unacceptably sluggish. The absence of a sound card or built-in CD-ROM drive can be remedied, in some instances, by the addition of PC Card peripherals.

Making Room on a Small Hard Disk

If your notebook computer's hard disk has a storage capacity of 350 to 850MB, DriveSpace disk compression can make Windows 98 a more viable option. Using disk compression slows down performance, but if you want to take Windows 98 on the road, you can probably live with this.

Note *You should probably not use disk compression software on any partition intended to store and play back .AVI video files.*

Installation Issues and CD-ROM Support

If your notebook system does not include implicit CD-ROM support, you have other alternatives for installing Windows 98:

- You can install from floppy disks.
- If you have access to another computer with a CD-ROM drive and to a portable file transfer utility, you can connect your notebook to the machine with the CD-ROM via a serial or parallel cable. Create a Win98 installation directory on the notebook's hard disk, and use your file transfer utility to copy the Win98 directory from the CD-ROM to the notebook. (See Chapter 2 for details.) This installation directory will occupy about 105MB of hard disk space on the notebook, with another 120MB required as temporary file space.

If you plan to use a notebook computer as a multimedia machine, it will probably be worth your while to spend a little extra money and buy one with an active-matrix color display and stereo sound card. The dual-scan display panels on cheaper models are adequate for business applications but do a mediocre job of rendering video for Windows. You can, of course, simply plug a standard SVGA monitor into the notebook for movie watching. Most notebooks can handle at least a 1,024-by-768 pixel external noninterlaced display with 256 colors or 800-by-600 display with 65,000 colors, although they may be restricted to a resolution as low as 640 by 480 and 256 colors on the internal display panel.

Note *If you are upgrading an older notebook system from Windows 95 to Windows 98, you may need special driver updates from the manufacturer. Notebook vendors often issue OEM versions of Windows system files to meet the requirements of individual hardware configurations. Before attempting to upgrade an older notebook to Windows 98, consult the manufacturer's Web site or contact the company's technical support personnel to learn about specific configuration issues.*

The Bottom Line

The bottom line on Windows 98 and mobile computing is that it's probably worth your time and trouble to install the operating system on a current machine that meets the minimum hardware requirements. You don't have to wait for next year's models with ACPI power management and DVD-ROM. Windows 98's built-in plug-and-play support, Internet features, network support, and pleasant interface all combine to ease the burdens of a traveling road warrior.

Transferring Your Personal Windows 98 Software from One System to Another

If you're an active Windows 98 user, you may find yourself pondering the question of how to "change horses in midstream." You've been running Windows 95 or Windows 98 on one computer for some time, installing new applications and developing a customized, personal configuration. Eventually, the time comes to upgrade to a larger hard disk or to buy a new computer. You'd prefer to transfer your working configuration from one place to another without starting all over again from scratch.

Hard Disk Upgrades

For a simple hard disk upgrade (without switching computers), you will usually be faced with the task of installing a new, blank drive. For desktop machines, the simplest way to transfer an existing Windows 98 configuration is to install the new drive, initially, as a slave or secondary unit. When you start Windows 98, your original drive will continue to be the C drive. The second drive will, at first, contain no partitions. Then do the following:

1. From within Windows 98, define a primary partition on the second drive that's large enough to contain all the files on your current C drive. Optionally, you can also create extended partitions.

2. After you restart the computer, format the partitions on the new drive. (Right-click the drive letter in My Computer and choose Format from the pop-up menu.) The primary partition on the new drive should be recognized as drive D or E.
3. Determine the location of the Windows 98 swap file on your original drive. By default, this file (WIN386.SWP) will reside in your \WINDOWS directory, unless you've edited the Windows swap file settings.
4. In My Computer or Windows Explorer, select all of the files and folders on the original C drive, *except* the folder that contains the swap file (generally C:\WINDOWS). Right-click, choose Copy from the pop-up menu, and paste all of the selected files and folders into the primary partition on the new drive.
5. Now open Windows Explorer to the folder that contains the swap file. Click the right pane and press CTRL-A to select all of this folder's files and subfolders.
6. Before copying and pasting to the new drive, deselect the swap file. (Hold down the CTRL key and click WIN386.SWP in the list of highlighted files.) With all the other files in this directory (probably C:\WINDOWS) highlighted, right-click and choose Copy from the pop-up menu. Then select the primary partition on the new drive, right-click, and choose Paste.

This procedure should successfully clone the contents of your original Windows 98 host drive to the primary partition you've created on your new drive. To begin using the second drive as your new Windows 98 host drive, power down the computer and reconfigure the cables and CMOS settings. The new drive should become the first IDE master drive or the first drive in your SCSI chain. You can now remove the original drive from the computer or, optionally, cable it as a new slave or secondary drive.

Notebook Drive Upgrades

Preserving your Windows 98 configuration on a new notebook computer disk drive is a bit trickier than on a desktop machine. Since most notebook systems can't support two physical drives simultaneously, you must use another computer or a large removable drive to migrate a personal Win98 configuration.

1. Use an Ethernet network or direct cable connection to transfer the contents of your original notebook drive to a temporary storage location on another computer. (Use the procedure described in the preceding section.) You'll need enough storage space to accommodate this transfer.
2. If you have a second desktop machine and are comfortable with manipulating PC hardware, you can purchase a 3.5-to-2.5-inch IDE adapter kit for around $15, and temporarily plug a blank IDE notebook drive into the desktop machine. (Take care, if you do this, to plug in the cables correctly and to

insulate the drive. It's easy to inadvertently reverse the power connection to a notebook drive and short it out unless you watch what you're doing.)

3. After copying the contents of the original notebook drive to the desktop computer through a network connection, power down and attach the blank notebook drive to the desktop machine as a slave or secondary drive. Use the copy-and-paste procedure described previously to transfer the notebook files again.
4. Power down. Remove the new notebook drive from the desktop computer and insert this drive in the notebook computer (replacing the old disk).

Upgrading a Notebook Through a Network Connection

If you're not up to the task of cabling a notebook drive to a desktop computer, an alternative way to complete the file transfer is to insert the blank drive directly into the notebook. Then use the support diskettes that come with the machine to install a fresh copy of Windows 98 or make the computer network-ready under DOS. When the notebook is network-ready and running with the new drive, use an Ethernet or direct cable connection to transfer the original configuration from its temporary storage location on the desktop machine. Follow these steps:

1. Create a \TEMP directory on the new notebook drive.
2. Establish the network or cable connection to the desktop machine. (See Chapters 5 and 14 for information on how to do this.)
3. Copy your original notebook files from the desktop machine to the \TEMP directory.
4. Boot the notebook to a real-mode DOS prompt. Rename the directories you installed on the new drive to establish the network connection (including any new \WINDOWS and \PROGRAM FILES directories). Then use the DOS Move command to restore the original \WINDOWS, \PROGRAM FILES, and other transferred folders from the \TEMP directory.
5. Once you confirm that the notebook starts successfully with your original configuration on the new drive, you can delete any extraneous files and directories that you installed to establish the network connection.

Real Brain Transplants: Installing the Same Win98 Configuration on Multiple Computers

Although Microsoft doesn't advertise it, you can often transfer a personal Windows 98 configuration between two completely different computers. If you buy a new notebook system, you can transfer the personalized setup you have on your desktop machine, and vice versa. If the new computer lacks hardware peripherals present on the old one (such as a DVD drive, video capture card, and so on), naturally you won't be able to use software specific to those peripherals. *However*, the odds are good that you can successfully migrate a customized desktop and your basic program configuration. Your old Windows 98 can adjust itself to equivalent hardware in the new machine (a new motherboard, video adapter, hard disk controller, modem, and so on).

This trick is not guaranteed to work automatically 100 percent of the time, but it can be useful for purposes such as these:

- Upgrading a desktop machine to a new motherboard (while you retain the original hard disk)
- Transferring a working configuration from a desktop machine to a notebook (or vice versa)
- Maintaining near-identical Windows 98 configurations on multiple computers

Here's how to transfer a Windows 98 hard disk to a new computer (or computer with new motherboard), with good chances for a successful hardware update:

1. Boot Windows 98 on the old computer. Back up the System registry with Scanregw. Then open the System applet and create a new hardware profile, copying settings from the current profile. (Choose Control Panel | System, select the Hardware Profiles tab, and click Copy.)
2. Restart the computer, hold down the CTRL key, and boot into Safe mode. You'll be prompted to select a hardware profile. Choose the copy that you just created.
3. Open the System applet to the Device Manager tab and remove the listings for all of the peripherals in the device list. (Systematically select each peripheral and click the Remove button.) After you make the Device Manager listing blank, close Windows 98 completely by choosing Shut Down the Computer from the Start | Shut Down menu.
4. Now install your new motherboard and transfer the hard disk (or move the hard disk to your new computer).
5. Power up the system, stand back, and watch the electrodes crackle. You've transferred the brain into a new body! When the Windows 98 interface is loaded, its plug-and-play module will redetect the hardware configuration of the new motherboard and its new installed peripherals. You may be prompted to insert OEM driver disks to activate new hardware peripherals or motherboard features. These disks should be supplied by the vendor of the new system.
6. After plug-and-play detection, odds are good that the machine will reboot to the Normal mode Windows 98 desktop. If it does, go to Device Manager tab and inspect the device list for yellow exclamation marks. If you find any, update the driver or disable the device in the current hardware profile until you have the correct driver. (If the computer won't start in Normal mode, you may have to boot into Safe mode to do this.)

7. When the computer boots successfully to the Normal mode Win98 desktop, use the Add New Hardware applet to autodetect the rest of the configuration on the new computer.

The foregoing procedure is often successful with no further intervention required. If, however, you notice problems or irregular performance on the new system, you can perform a refresh installation. Boot to a real-mode DOS prompt, make sure the DOS CD-ROM drivers are installed in CONFIG.SYS and AUTOEXEC.BAT, and run SETUP from the Windows 98 CD. Reinstall Windows 98 into the current \WINDOWS directory on your hard disk.

Carrying on When Your Notebook Computer Fails

This doesn't mean indulging in histrionics when your notebook computer must be repaired. (Although I've occasionally been tempted to do just that!) Rather, if your notebook's problem isn't related to the hard disk and you have another computer, then you can continue working with that hard disk while the notebook system is away at the shop.

The techniques described in the preceding section and in this section can be combined to temporarily transplant your notebook's hard disk to another computer.

1. Create a copy of your current hardware profile on your notebook system while it is still in good working order.
2. If the notebook develops a motherboard or display problem that requires it to go into the shop, remove the hard disk and mount it as the primary drive in another computer. (As stated earlier, most notebook hard disks can be become IDE drives in a desktop machine through a 3.5-to-2.5-inch interface adapter. Often, a notebook hard disk can also be transferred to a second notebook machine if the form factors of the two units are compatible. If you're not a hardware-savvy user, you may need to consult a techie friend or technical support person to smoothly perform this operation.)
3. Boot the second computer with your notebook hard disk as the primary drive. Choose Safe mode and select the Copy hardware configuration when prompted.
4. Open the Device Manager and remove all the components in the device list, as previously described. (Make sure you do this in the *Copy* configuration unless you have a good, reliable registry backup to use when the first computer comes back from the shop.)

Reboot the computer and let Windows 98 detect the hardware components of the new system. In most cases, this procedure should allow you to continue using your applications and personal operating system settings until you get back your notebook computer. (If it doesn't, then store the hard disk, reinsert it in the repaired notebook computer. Then boot Windows 98 on the repaired machine using the original hardware configuration, which should be left undisturbed.)

Desktop-to-Desktop, Desktop-to-Notebook, and Notebook-to-Notebook Migrations of Windows 98

Most new computers are shipped with Windows 95 or Windows 98 preinstalled on the hard disk. However, you can still migrate a personal Windows 98 configuration to such a computer if it has sufficient unused disk space. Many new computers ship with anywhere from 1.5 to 7GB of free disk space in addition to their basic Windows 98 system configurations.

The easiest way to migrate your personal Windows 98 configuration to such a computer is to use a third-party partitioning utility such as PowerQuest's Partition Magic, Quarterdeck's Partition-It, or V-Communications' System Commander to divide the new computer's large hard disk into two or more separate, primary partitions. Here's what to do:

1. After creating and formatting an additional primary partition on the new computer, make the original partition active and boot to the already installed OEM version of Windows 95 or Windows 98.
2. Use a direct cable or Ethernet network connection to link the new machine to your old Win98 computer.
3. Copy the contents of your old computer's hard disk to the new, empty partition on the second computer. (Use the copy-and-paste techniques described in the section "Hard Disk Upgrades" earlier in this chapter.)
4. Use your partitioning utility or DOS FDISK to make the additional partition on your new computer the active boot partition.
5. Reboot the new computer into Safe mode using the migrated version of Windows 98 that you've just copied. Open Device Manager and remove all of the components in the device list, as described previously.
6. Reboot the new computer and let your old, transferred Windows 98 detect the new hardware configuration.

The new computer may contain motherboard features and hardware peripherals that weren't present on your original machine. Most notebook machines include custom drivers supplied by the manufacturer for PC Card chipsets, disk controllers, video adapters, sound cards, USB controllers, and so on. The \WINDOWS directory of your old, migrated configuration may not include all of the appropriate software for the new computer. Here's how to resolve that problem:

If Windows 98's plug-and-play wizards can't find an appropriate driver for a device on the new computer, then point them to search the OEM Windows directories shipped with the computer on the original (now secondary) partition.

In particular, if the migrated partition is now drive C and the OEM partition is drive D, then point the Windows 98 driver wizards to search D:\WINDOWS\INF and/or D:\WINDOWS\SYSTEM, if no files are found in C:\WINDOWS\INF or C:\WINDOWS\SYSTEM. Check the OEM partition for special folders titled \DRIVERS or \UTIL that may contain files for video adapters, sound cards, and other peripherals. Additionally, you can check for driver files on diskettes supplied by the vendor.

Incorporating Information from the OEM Installation

Once you've confirmed that your migrated Windows 98 works satisfactorily on the new computer, you can consolidate important information from the original OEM partition as follows:

1. Back up the original OEM partition to a tape device or other storage media.
2. Copy all the contents of the \WINDOWS\INF folder and its subdirectories from the original OEM partition to C:\WINDOWS\INF in your migrated partition.
3. Copy all the contents of the \WINDOWS\OPTIONS folder and its subdirectories from the original OEM partition to C:\WINDOWS\OPTIONS in your migrated partition.
4. Copy the contents of any \DRIVERS or \UTIL folders from the original OEM partition to your migrated partition.

Once you've performed these operations, you can delete the contents of the OEM partition from the drive, keeping it as a data storage location or using your third-party partition utility to recombine it with the migrated partition. To access useful application software originally installed on the OEM partition, use the application disks and CDs supplied with the computer to reinstall these applications on your migrated partition.

Retaining Both Your Personal and the OEM Win98 Configurations

If you can spare the disk space, you can keep the OEM partition instead of deleting it. You can then set up a dual boot configuration between your personal Windows 98 and the OEM version that shipped with the computer. This is accomplished by using FDISK or your partitioning utility to toggle the active boot partition back and forth. You may want to do this if the vendor has installed useful software applications on the original partition.

This last tip is a professional reviewer's trick. It allows you to switch back and forth between a manufacturer's original configuration for a computer and your customized, personal version of Windows 98. You can also use this trick to dual boot between Windows 95 and Windows 98. Just make sure that each operating system is contained on its own primary disk partition.

Appendix B

Internet Support Resources

This appendix contains pointers to Internet resources for Windows 98—official Microsoft pages that contain operating system updates, and home-grown user sites with tips, tricks, technical support information, and freeware and shareware applications.

Windows 98 Update Patches and Utilities

To download and install the latest patches for Windows 98, open the Windows Update shortcut on the Start menu or log onto Microsoft's Windows 98 home page at http://www.microsoft.com/windows98/default.asp.

Multimedia Updates

Microsoft's Multimedia Updates for Windows 98 are primarily aimed at multimedia users. The following modules are currently available:

- Enhanced Windows Media Player
- DirectX Video, version 6
- Microsoft Chat, version 2.5
- Internet Explorer Sound Pack
- Supplemental Web fonts

The Enhanced Windows Media Player combines the ability to play back multiple audio formats, AVI, MPEG, and QuickTime video with the Internet streaming features formerly incorporated in the Microsoft NetShow Player.

Direct X 6 improves the native video APIs of Windows 98, allowing faster rendering of 3-D graphics in software for video adapters that lack explicit 3-D hardware support. In addition, new Direct X features permit finer display of multiple 3-D textures and improved management of accompanying DirectSound. (A subsequent Windows 98 patch is expected to include a new API called DirectMusic that will make further improvements in the real-time features of multimedia games.)

Microsoft Chat 2.5 updates the 2.0 version shipped with Windows 98. Microsoft Chat permits you to have real-time conversations in Internet chat rooms or on private Microsoft servers.

The Internet Explorer Sound Pack adds additional sounds to signal various IE 4 Web browsing events.

Supplemental Web Fonts allow you to display Web pages the way they were meant to be seen by installing a collection of TrueType fonts created especially for use on the Web. This new updated version includes symbols for the new European currency, the Euro.

Other Windows 98 Patches

In addition to multimedia enhancements, Microsoft has issued a number of other patches for Windows 98 since the release of the operating system.

Microsoft Active Accessibility Update

This update of Active Accessibility fixes several compatibility issues with programs and clients that use Microsoft Active Accessibility. When you install this upgrade, your accessibility aids, such as screen readers, voice-input utilities, and the Microsoft Magnifier will perform better with a wider range of programs. You need this update only if you are experiencing difficulties with an accessibility aid or the Microsoft Magnifier. No additional functionality is provided with this update.

Fix for Outlook Express File Attachment Issue

This is a fix for an issue that can cause Outlook Express to terminate unexpectedly when you open a message that contains an attachment with an extremely long filename. It is difficult but possible for an individual to cause malicious code to run on your computer as a result of this problem.

For more information on this issue—including how it affects Microsoft Outlook 98—see the Microsoft Security Advisor bulletin at http://www.microsoft.com/security/bulletins/ms98-008.htm.

Fix for 'Window.External' JScript Vulnerability Issue

This is a fix for a security issue that may affect Microsoft Internet Explorer 4. When Internet Explorer encounters a Web page that uses a JScript script, Internet Explorer could close unexpectedly.

This problem does not occur accidentally on Web pages, but rather must be intentionally created by a Web site administrator with malicious intent. A skilled hacker could use such a script message to run arbitrary code on your computer.

In order to be affected by this problem, you must visit a Web site that was intentionally designed to include a malicious script. For more technical details on this issue, see Microsoft Security Bulletin MS98-011 at http://www.microsoft.com/security/bulletins/ms98-011.htm.

World Wide Web Support Resources

One benefit of being a Windows 98 user is that you have lots of company in the freeware/shareware hacker community. The following list of Windows 98 resources on the World Wide Web includes pointers to sites that feature freeware and shareware software, Windows 98 customization tips, and technical information.

Freeware and Shareware Windows 98 File Resources

Some of the best software written for Windows 98 can be found in the following freeware and shareware listings. If you're looking for additional ways to customize the desktop or improve the efficiency of built-in Win98 features, these sites are well worth checking out.

Microsoft Downloads: http://www.microsoft.com/msdownload/default.htm

This page contains listings for patches, enhancements, and bug fixes for Windows 98 and all of Microsoft's application products.

WinFiles.com: http://www.winfiles.com

Formerly known as Windows 95 HQ, this site is the number-one place to look for the latest and greatest home-grown software for Windows 98. It contains a number of specialized file categories, with reviews, recommendations, and search indexes to let you find exactly what you're looking for. WinFiles.com also features a wide variety of user tips and tricks (organized into accessible categories) plus technical tutorials on Windows 95/98 networking.

Download.com for the PC: http://www.download.com/

Formerly known as Shareware.com, this site includes a large number of files you can download, with a searchable index and weekly picks list.

DaveCentral: http://www.davecentral.com/

This site contains a wide selection of Internet utilities.

Freeware32.com: http://www.freeware32.com/

This site contains a wide selection of freeware applications and utilities in a well-organized tree display of file categories.

Tucows (The Ultimate Collection of WINSOCK Software): http://www.tucows.com/

This site has a large collection of Internet-related software.

WinSite: http://www.winsite.com/

This site also has a large collection of freeware and shareware.

WindowsWare.com: http://www.windowsware.com/

This site contains a number of useful Windows performance benchmark applications.

Windows 98 Tips, Drivers, and Home Pages

As this book goes to press, all of the World Wide Web links listed in this section are up and running. By the time you read this, some of these home-grown resources may shift URL locations, while others go on to become commercial Web-based enterprises.

Windows 98 Guide: http://www.microsoft.com/magazine/guides/windows98/win98page.htm

This site contains Microsoft's guide to using Windows 98 and obtaining updates and add-ons.

Windows Help Net: http://www.windows-help.net/

This site contains a wide variety of Windows 95 and Windows 98 system tips, including a series devoted to fine-tuning Internet Explorer version 4.

Windows 98 Annoyances: http://www.annoyances.org/win98/

Originally created as an information resource for tips on eliminating nuisances in Windows 95, this site has been expanded to include a large collection of tips and tricks applicable to both Windows 95 and Windows 98.

Frank Condron's World O'Windows: http://www.conitech.com/windows/win98.asp

In addition to containing a tips section, this site includes useful pointers to sites where you can download Windows device drivers for a wide range of peripherals.

Global Computing: http://www.globalcomputing.com/win95.html

This site contains a huge listing of links to other Windows 95 and Windows 98 resources.

Delwin Lee's IE Resources: http://www.darkstorm.com/ie/

This site contains a variety of tips for using and customizing Internet Explorer.

Eric Miller's User Tips: http://www.okinfoweb.com/moe/

This is the site to visit for information and tips on working with Microsoft's Outlook Express mail client.

WUGNET (Windows Users Group Network): http://www.wugnet.com

WugNet features a Windows Tips Center with a new tip every day. This site also contains an archive of popular Windows shareware.

Windows 95-98/NT Links: http://www.refdesk.com/win95.html

This site contains pointers to many additional Windows 98 information and file resources.

Other Technical Support Resources

These sites are technical resources for Wintel computers. They contain information about the inner workings of your computer that you probably won't find in most reference books or OEM manuals.

Tom's Hardware Guide: http://www.tomshardware.com/

This site contains more information than you can digest in one lifetime about every aspect of Intel PC hardware. You'll find reviews and hardware specs for motherboards, CPUs, BIOS and controller chipsets, memory chips, hard disks, and video adapters, along with user-friendly tutorials that explain these PC devices.

Wim's BIOS Page: http://www.ping.be/bios/

This site contains an alphabetical index of links to a wide variety of BIOS manufacturers, including pointers to Flash BIOS upgrades.

Index

B

C

D

E

F

G

H

I

J

K

L

M

N

P

T

U

X

Y

Z